fic 2~

BUSINESS
for
HIGHER AWARDS

Dave Needham • Rob Dransfield

Rod Harris • Martin Coles

Heinemann

Heinemann Educational
a division of Heinemann Educational Books Ltd,
Halley Court Jordan Hill Oxford OX2 8EJ

OXFORD LONDON EDINBURGH
MADRID ATHENS BOLOGNA PARIS
MELBOURNE SYDNEY AUCKLAND SINGAPORE TOKYO
IBADAN NAIROBI HARARE GABORONE
PORTSMOUTH NH (USA)

© Dave Needham, Rob Dransfield, Rod Harris, Martin Coles
1995

First published 1995
99 98 97 96   11 10 9 8 7 6 5 4 3 2
A catalogue record for this book is available from the British
Library on request

ISBN 0 435 28534 3
Designed by Roger Denning
Typeset by Wyvern Typesetting Ltd, Bristol
Printed by Bath Press Ltd, Bath

Acknowledgements

Many people have been associated with the development of this
text. It has not been an easy project, and we are grateful for
their help and support in enabling us to meet deadlines – well,
nearly all of them! The authors would particularly like to thank
the following individuals for their support, encouragement and
contributions.

Margaret Berriman
Jan Nikolic
Roger Parker
Judith Nelson
Aubrey Nokes
Alan Field
Laura Schuster
Bryan Oakes
Stephanie Howkins
Brian Yeomans

The authors and publishers would also like to thank the
following for permission to reproduce photographs and other
material, and for providing advice and information:

Accountancy Age magazine
Action Images Sports Photography
The Body Shop International plc
British Motor Industry Heritage Trust
Dixons Group plc
East Midlands Electricity
Ebury Press Limited
The Economist magazine
Ford Motor Company Ltd
Investors in People UK
Marketing magazine
Marks and Spencer plc
Shell Education Service
The Thatcher Foundation

Finally, we would like to thank wives and families for their
patience, understanding, help and tolerance. Martin would
particularly like to thank Judith Nelson, and Rob would like to
thank Ken and Jean Dransfield, who have helped to make
everything possible.

Contents

Preface

Business for Higher Awards is a single-volume text intended for all students of business and finance undertaking Higher National awards, as well as undergraduate students in business, management and related studies. It has been structured around the HNC/D core modules but also includes a broad overview related to the first option module in each of the finance, marketing and personnel pathways. The core module on planning and decision-making has been placed at the end of the book so that students can apply all their earlier learning.

Our primary aim in writing this text has been to develop a comprehensive, student-centred resource which helps to reinforce many learning activities. Throughout the book, the teaching material emphasises the dynamic nature of the world of business and the importance of relating current events to the acquisition of knowledge and the development of understanding. For this reason it is extensively supported by case studies which pose questions for discussion, by tasks, and by frequent references to theorists within each field, as well as suggestions for further reading.

Finally, in writing this book we hope that we have translated some of our enthusiasm, experience and beliefs into a practical and enjoyable text which enables students to focus upon their areas of learning while also encouraging them to pursue their own specialisms and interests.

Dave Needham, Rob Dransfield, Rod Harris and
Martin Coles
May 1995

Market relations

On completion of this chapter students should be able to:

■ evaluate the effectiveness of a production and marketing orientation as the basis for business operations under different conditions

■ identify and analyse relationships within the marketing system

■ identify and evaluate how business environmental forces affect marketing.

Marketing orientation

Case Study
Using technology for your religious needs!

Do you think that technology could be used to deal with personal or sensitive issues? For example, would you feel happy about proposing marriage to someone over an electronic mail system or faxing someone details of a death? Does this mean that it would be inappropriate for technology to help us in our dealings with God, or would this depend upon the sort of product developed for our needs?

Though technology has not exactly taken churchgoers by storm, it is beginning to encroach upon the lives of some. For example, some churches use recorded bells and some mosques use tapes to call the faithful to prayer. Religious programmes appear on television and Franklin's electronic bible has been around for a decade. So, how far can this process of using technology to serve religious needs go?

It can be argued that rosary beads are a technological aid to worship, albeit with old technology. Father Pasquele Silla today owns the patent for electronic rosaries which are sold at Italian places of pilgrimage. The rosary resembles a Nintendo Gameboy and is considered a good buy at around £35. Synthesised music accompanies texts for Hail Mary observances and silent reflections. The machine has no graphics and is tastefully decorated with a picture of the Madonna.

Though the electronic rosary system has not ruffled too many feathers, Greg Garvey, a professor of art at Concordia University at Montreal, has found that his confessional system has been resisted. His software system prescribes penances for any sins the user confesses through keyboard entry. For example, a user clicks on and confesses one or more sins from an electronic list and then the computer chooses the appropriate response.

These two short examples help us to understand marketing as a process. Both Father Silla and Greg Garvey – whether rightly or wrongly – **identified a need** and, for a variety of **reasons or objectives**, decided to commit themselves to **fulfilling that need**. In the early stages of development they would probably have undertaken some form of **research** which involved talking to a lot of people to find out what their reaction would be to their ideas. They would both have been aware of other products on the market and may have felt that the unique nature of their ideas would be more appropriate than **competing products**. Finally, given the nature of the products they wished to launch, they would also have been sensitive to the **reaction of the church and other churchgoers** – the last thing they would have wished to do would be to ruffle too many feathers. Marketing enabled Silla and Garvey to match outer needs and opportunities with inward product development and, at the same time, be aware of and sensitive to the reactions which others may have to their ideas (see Figure 1.1).

What is marketing?

If you go out into the street and ask a number of people what marketing is, they will probably come up with a variety of answers which might include selling, advertising, branding or researching. Yes, they are right, but though marketing does concern itself with these activities, as a process it goes further.

Runyon defines marketing as:

> The performance of business activities that direct the flow of goods and services from producers to consumers.

Figure 1.1 Matching opportunities with the development of products

This clearly recognises that marketing is a **process** which matches the operational activities of an organisation with the goods and services required by customers.

The **Chartered Institute of Marketing** uses the following definition:

> Marketing is the management process responsible for identifying, anticipating and satisfying consumer requirements profitably.

The key feature of this definition is that it places the consumer at the centre of an organisation's activities.

Identifying consumer requirements
+
Anticipating consumer requirements
+
Satisfying consumer requirements
=
PROFITABILITY

- **Identifying** – This will involve answering questions such as 'How do we find out what the consumer's requirements are?' and 'How do we keep in touch with their thoughts, feelings and perceptions of our good or service?'
- **Anticipating** – Consumer requirements change all the time. For example, as people become richer they may seek a greater variety of goods and services. Anticipating involves looking to the future as well as the present. What will be the Next Best Thing that consumers will require tomorrow?
- **Satisfying** – If you do not satisfy consumers they will look to alternatives. Consumers want their requirements to be met. They will seek particular benefits. They will want the right goods or services, available at the right price, at the right time and in the right place.

■ **Profitability** – Profitability is one of a range of organisational objectives. Whereas in the private sector profitability may be an overriding business objective, for public sector organisations this may not be the case. Profitability, therefore, for the purpose of this definition is best interpreted as **achieving a series of marketing objectives** which may or may not include profits. For an organisation to achieve these objectives it must find out in good time what its customers want to buy and then satisfy these requirements.

Kotler emphasises this broad interpretation of marketing. He defines marketing as:

> human activity directed at satisfying needs and wants through exchange processes.

So *how* is marketing activity used to satisfy customer needs and wants? The **American Marketing Association** (AMA) identifies the importance of planning in the marketing process. It defines marketing as:

> the process of planning and executing the conception, pricing, promotion, and distribution of ideas, goods and services to create exchanges that satisfy individual and organisational goals.

It is important that we appreciate that marketing is a process of planning. Every organisation needs to have clear **goals**, and the major route to achieving organisational goals will depend on **strategy**. It is, therefore, important to be clear about the difference between strategy and **tactics**.

These terms originate from military use (military strategy before and during a battle is the general policy overview of how to defeat the enemy). *Developing a strategy* involves establishing clear aims and objectives around which the framework for a policy for the whole organisation is created. Having developed a strategy, an organisation can then work out its day-to-day tools and tactics to meet objectives.

Marketing can thus be seen as the process of developing and implementing a strategy to plan and coordinate ways of identifying, anticipating and satisfying consumer demands, in such a way as to make profits or satisfy a range of other marketing objectives. It is this strategic planning process that lies at the heart of marketing.

So do companies believe that marketing is the key element in their strategy? In its 1993 Annual Report, IBM's chairman and chief executive, Louis V. Gerstner Jr, stated:

> *'The fact is, no company is going to succeed without a clear set of tough-minded strategies grounded in a clear understanding of what's happening in the marketplace. Some call it a mission. Some call it vision. I call it strategy. And strategy is particularly important for IBM because our industry is going through a period of fundamental change at breakneck speed. So are our customers.'*

This statement helps to show that there is a direct relationship between satisfying the needs of customers and the ability of an organisation to survive. It is therefore essential to match the production and development of goods and services with the identification and anticipation of consumer desires. The ability to meet customer needs and requirements may be identified in almost all areas of organisational activity from the original idea, through to design, including operational activities as well as in providing the product, through the sale and exchange right up to the post-sale support.

The evolution of the marketing concept

Very few organisations operate in a static situation. Today we live in a global marketplace for many goods and services, in which technology, purchasing power, tastes, as well as many other factors, are all changing at the same time. In adapting to many of these changes, good marketing is a key factor. Good marketing involves:

■ looking *outwards* in order to respond to changes in markets, business conditions and competition
■ looking *inwards* in order to develop the organisation so that it can meet all of those consumer needs which have been identified by the marketing process (see Figure 1.2).

Figure 1.2 Ensuring a good fit between the external environment and the resources of the organisation

Satisfying customer needs has not, however, always been a priority of organisations. In fact, we can map the development of marketing orientation into the three distinct stages shown in Figure 1.3.

Production orientation

Where goods are scarce and in markets where very little competition exists – where there is an unsatisfied thirst for products – organisations do not really have to pay close attention to customer needs. The production era

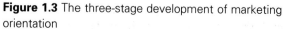

Figure 1.3 The three-stage development of marketing orientation

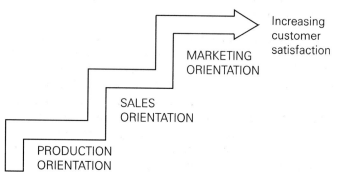

was characterised by post-industrial revolution, massive changes in technology and strong consumer demand. At this time the emphasis was on scientific management and structured work based on output. In terms of customer satisfaction this whole era can best be understood by the statement made by Henry Ford that 'customers can have any colour they want as long as it is black'.

For many organisations a commitment towards production orientation lasted too long. The classic example comes from the motorcycle industry. At the beginning of the 1950s British roads were seldom graced with the sound of a foreign motorcycle. The heavy, slow-revving, large-capacity machines with the names of BSA, Triumph, Ariel and Norton predominated. Imports from Italy in the form of lightweight, high-revving machines, particularly from Ducatti, were hardly given a second glance by British manufacturers – they didn't make them so customers couldn't have them! And, in any case, research and development costs to meet any demand for the new-style machines would mean reduced profits.

Someone *had* noticed the new machines, though, and thousands of miles away research and development programmes were under way. Factories were being built, work forces trained – Japan was about to enter the market. Today that transformation is part of industrial history. The motorcycles on British roads rejoice in names like Kawasaki, Honda and Suzuki and, as for the profits of British manufacturers – they are mainly non-existent. By listening to the marketing missionaries and, in effect, the consumers, the position might have been very different today.

Production orientation was predominant in the UK in the 1930s and 40s when goods were in short supply. If an organisation operates in a stable environment where it is possible to sell all that it produces, then why should it become market orientated? Lack of competition simply created a **sellers' market**. However, the signs were there

that change was on the way. The world depression did mean that in some cases suppliers had to be increasingly sensitive to the wishes of consumers.

An important feature of production orientation is **monopoly power**. Where monopolies exist there is less of a need to improve products. The big pre-privatised nationalised industries were frequently associated with production orientation. For example, little choice of telephone design or service existed in the UK in the 1960s and 70s. Production orientation may also return during a period of shortage.

Figure 1.4 Lack of competition creates a production orientation

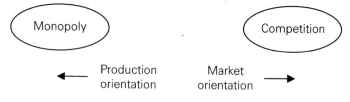

Sales orientation

The beginning of the 'age of the consumer' is particularly associated with the period just after the Second World War. During the 1950s incomes began to increase faster than the cost of basic necessities of life and the standard of living began to rise. The shift of power from the seller to the buyer really began to bite during the 1950s as the hardships of the recent war and its immediate aftermath – for example, rationing – faded into memory.

The population's desire for a higher standard of living, and therefore an increased level of consumption, was transformed into reality. However, the age of the consumer was still in its infancy. In the face of these changes the first reaction of many organisations was to become more sales orientated. This sales orientation led to increased spending on advertising, selling and other promotional elements rather than on satisfying customer needs. Organisations thought that simply by increasing sales increased profitability would follow. They believed that all marketing activities involved advertising and personal selling. Sales orientation increased competitiveness but rarely helped to improve consumer satisfaction. According to one expert, '*Selling focuses on the needs of the seller; marketing on the needs of the buyer.*'

Although marketing departments emerged during the sales era, they assumed only tactical responsibilities and were frequently subordinate to financial and production activities. Sales orientation was a move forward from production orientation but was still not focused on consumer needs.

Figure 1.5 From production orientation to marketing orientation

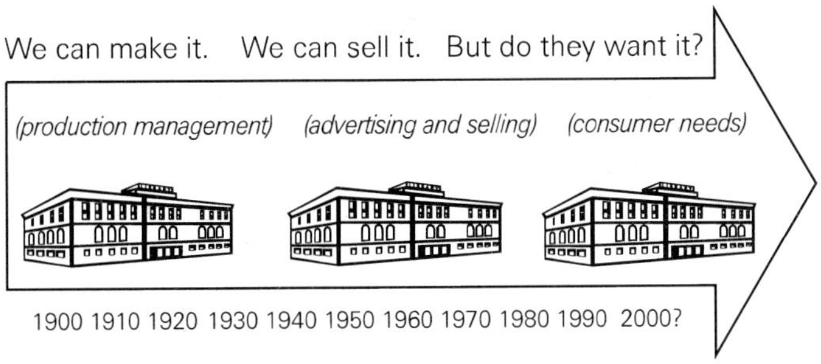

We can make it.   We can sell it.   But do they want it?

(production management)   *(advertising and selling)*   *(consumer needs)*

1900 1910 1920 1930 1940 1950 1960 1970 1980 1990 2000?

Marketing orientation

During the 1970s marketing came to be recognised as an essential function within a successful organisation. However, marketing usually took place within a separate department or it was a discrete function with only a tactical responsibility. Increasing competition and developing consumer awareness during the 1980s and 90s led marketing to be viewed as a strategic discipline *which puts the customer at the centre of an organisation's activities.*

At the heart of marketing lies the degree to which an organisation becomes marketing orientated. The more committed an organisation is to its marketing activities, the more able it will be to pursue its **corporate objectives** and develop and retain customers. The basic premise is that organisations rely on customers for survival and those who best meet customer needs will be more successful and always survive a period of change.

The great benefit of marketing orientation is that the needs of the customer are taken into account ahead of the production process. This approach has three major benefits:

■ It identifies the difference between customer needs and the ability to satisfy such needs.
■ It uses marketing to coordinate, organise and link production decisions with market needs and requirements.
■ It places an onus on businesses to meet customer needs successfully if they wish to remain competitive.

Marketing is now well accepted in most well-run businesses as a strategic discipline or general management function, and in this respect it must care for the health of the business – especially against competitive influences. This is because it is increasingly realised that, although making a profit is important, an organisation should also develop its **market share** and search for **brand leadership** as well. Successful marketers must therefore be concerned with every aspect of their business, including future projects and other areas of their industry.

Successful companies plan five, ten years and more in advance and often know as much about the competition as they know about themselves.

So, how many companies in the UK are truly marketing orientated? A study in 1987 concluded that, though chief executives frequently recognise the need to become marketing orientated, 'boards of directors are frequently dominated by a financial outlook'. This study showed the degree of acceptance of marketing orientation within UK industries (see Figure 1.6). Financially orientated businesses were organisations which measured success by their ability to use resources to optimise profits and return on capital.

Figure 1.6 Corporate philosophies identified in one study in 1987

Corporate philosophies (%)	
Production orientated	10
Sales orientated	21
Marketing orientated	50
Financially orientated	19

Remember that marketing orientation as a business philosophy puts the customer at the centre of an organisation's activities. It is a business philosophy designed to develop an attitude of mind which should be shared by everyone in an organisation and is often enhanced by both frequent and open communication. A personnel manager recruits staff on the basis of how well individuals can satisfy *customer needs*, and in the mind of the production manager would be the need to monitor and improve *customer satisfaction*. Developing these attitudes throughout the organisation will help it to move forward, reduce the likelihood of crises and use strategies and tactics to adapt to change.

Case Study
'McPloughman's!'

McDonald's disclosed recently that it had considered plans to introduce a 'McPloughman's' in Britain to combat opposition to its American brashness. The McDonald's move came after it was hit hard by the British economic recession of the 1990s – when it realised that the service formula which had sustained it since opening the first fast-food hamburger restaurant in 1974 was simply not working. Exhaustive research by the chain revealed that British customers found them loud, brash and insincere.

The company's proposal for a McPloughman's was based on a version of the traditional British Ploughman's lunch of bread, cheese and pickle. However, McDonald's found that this idea was insufficiently researched and did not go down well with either its customers or its staff – who were too embarrassed to mention or serve it. According to the UK company president, Paul Preston, 'If we had done our homework we would have found that our customers didn't want the product and our staff were embarrassed even to have to say McPloughman's let alone to have to sell it to our customers.'

As a result of customer research, McDonald's has disclosed that its UK staff will no longer have to say 'have a nice day!' to every customer. McDonald's is bringing about a radical change in approach to doing business in the UK by listening more closely to what customers want.

Questions for discussion

1 *What criteria would you use to determine whether an organisation was, in your opinion as a customer, production orientated, sales orientated or marketing orientated?*

2 *Why was it unlikely that the McPloughman's would achieve any degree of success?*

3 *What suggestions would you recommend for McDonald's to overcome many of the perceptions which UK customers have of their business? To what extent are your suggestions market orientated?*

Degrees of marketing orientation

Marketing is, therefore, concerned with being close to customers. But how close can an organisation get to its customers and what strategies can it use to serve this need to become market orientated? Over recent years organisations have used a number of approaches to help them sharpen their focus upon the consumer. These include 'sur/petition', customer relationships, sensitivity to consumer issues, and mass customisation.

Sur/petition

Edward de Bono coined the term 'sur/petition' to signify a situation in which business organisations concentrate on providing a range of *integrated values* for consumers.

The word 'competition' comes from Latin and means 'seeking together' or 'choosing to run in the same race'. Sur/petition means 'seeking above'. Sur/petition would take place even if there were no competition. The business seeks to beat its own previous results.

Edward de Bono argued that there have been three phases of business:

- *Phase 1* – Product driven, in which a firm simply provided a good or service.
- *Phase 2* – Competition, in which the firm sought to beat rivals.
- *Phase 3* – Sur/petition based on *integrated values*. In this phase business creatively seeks to provide a range of integrated goods or services for consumers. For example, when a man or woman purchases a car, they will need to drive the car, to park the car, to insure the car and so on. De Bono talks about creating value monopolies resulting from **valufacture**, which is the creation and formation of values. Company strategies should therefore be directed at valufacture. Businesses that take sur/petition to heart will create value monopolies focused on the consumer that will be successful simply because they are the best.

Customer relationships

Don Peppers and Martha Rogers, in their book *The One Future: Building One Customer at a Time*, urge businesses to form impregnable relationships with individual customers. They argue that even the mass marketer can strike up these relationships. This involves gathering as much information as possible about individual customers and then developing the organisation to meet their individual needs. They refer to this as **customer segmentation**.

Peppers and Rogers illustrate this point by reference to gift order catalogues.

- The customer may order gifts for friends and relatives many months in advance.
- The company would then schedule delivery of the gifts on the right days.
- The customer would be charged for each gift two days before delivery.
- The customer would receive a reminder postcard 10 days before each gift is sent.
- When the annual catalogue is sent out the customer would receive a reminder form of last year's gifts and addresses.

The main selling point is the *high-quality relationship* with the customer. The same logic can be applied to a variety of other products so that the business can develop individual relationships with customers for their lifetime purchasing requirements. **Customer loyalty** would be the key to the success of this proposal.

Sensitivity to consumer issues

Greater equality, freedom of speech, improved educational standards and vastly improved communications in a more rapidly changing and more technological world have increased consumer awareness of issues and expectations. Consumers are concerned about the wider issues which relate to the products they purchase.

Increasingly, modern organisations are trying to balance internal and external expectations. *Internally* they have to make profits for shareholders and monitor how the organisation is run. *Externally* they have to contend with having to sell products in the face of competition, respond to regulatory influences exerted upon them by governments, and also respond to other interdependent consumer influences. Failing to take heed of organised pressure groups such as Friends of the Earth, the National Anti-Vivisection Society and Greenpeace may lead to the worst possible outcome – a consumer boycott, perhaps on an international scale. In order to satisfy consumer needs and show consumers that they are matching their activities with their expectations, organisations have to broach these wider issues.

Mass customisation

Mass customisation is probably the ultimate in marketing orientation. It involves meeting the needs of each customer *personally*. Ron Westbrook and Peter Williamson, writing in the *European Management Journal*, identified this as the latest stage of an industrial revolution emerging from Japan.

The period between the mid-70s and the mid-80s was known as 'market in' in Japan. While introducing cost savings through component and process design over this period, Japanese manufacturers added additional features to standard products in order to stimulate increased demand. However, by the late 1980s Japanese customers were again reaching saturation. They not only had most types of products, they now had a range of each. Worse still, the gadgets, bells and whistles were losing their novelty.

A new strategy was therefore required for the 1990s – to personalise the products for each customer. This has involved responsive marketing to find out what customers need and coupling it with highly responsive and flexible production methods. Westbrook and Williamson quote an example of the Melbo company which makes and supplies customised suits within just three days:

> 'What you will not find are the usual acres of racks, crammed with stock or occupying lots of phenomenally expensive Tokyo real-estate. Instead the entire store carries less than a hundred suits, with a floor space requirement only a fraction of that needed by competitors. Melbo's customers do not come to fit themselves into a suit on the rack because the company's Ready-Made-Order-System will guarantee that a suit

> individually cut and sewn to fit them, from a choice of over a hundred fabrics, will arrive at their home or office within the week!'

And so, what of marketing orientation in the future? Marketing orientation will help to provide market-led flexible factories with shorter delivery times, catering for higher levels of demand change and optimised to provide maximum product variety and choice.

Criticisms of marketing orientation

Though marketing orientation clearly matches an understanding of customer needs with an organisation's ability to satisfy them, in order to secure the health of the business, critics of this concept would say that marketing orientation is just a more sophisticated way of persuading customers to buy products.

In fact there is a feeling that, where marketing orientation takes place, technical developments tend to suffer. This bias towards marketing, therefore, may lead to the development of inferior products which offer *less* customer satisfaction. Another argument is that satisfying perceived customer needs now fails to take into account what their needs might be in the future, *and this stifles innovation.*

It is important, no matter how strong the case for marketing orientation, that these downside arguments are understood so that organisations can cater for the influence which marketing may have on the technical areas of the business.

Marketing relationships

As a process, marketing involves a series of relationships and these are important elements for us to understand when looking at the marketing concept. These 'core concepts' can be identified as:

■ needs, wants and demand
■ products
■ value and satisfaction
■ exchange and transactions
■ markets.

Needs, wants and demand

A **need** is considered to be a state of deprivation of some basic satisfaction. For example, we all have a need for food, shelter and clothing. **Wants** are used to satisfy needs. For example, we need to eat but may want a particular type of food. Our wants are shaped by many of the social influences within society such as peer group pressure, media, culture or the family. **Demand** takes this process of wants one stage further. We cannot always afford everything that we want. Demand is simply the willingness to buy a product combined with the ability to pay for it.

Products

Products are anything offered to satisfy a need or a want. A product may come in the form of a tangible physical item, or it may be an intangible service. For example, if you buy a pint of beer, the drink itself is the physical product which satisfies a want. You may buy the pint of beer in a pub which provides a friendly service and a hospitable environment. Whereas the tangible product is clearly an item, the service may be provided by people, places, organisations and ideas.

Value and satisfaction

Buyers will seek 'something of **value**' from a transaction which provides them with **satisfaction**. Satisfaction is dependent on the excess of return over the investment. So, how do consumers weigh up alternatives to make decisions? The seller needs to understand the needs, desires and wants of the target buyer. The various issues involved in understanding the behaviour of buyers are discussed in detail in Chapter 19.

Exchange and transactions

Understanding needs, wants, demand, products and something of value is not enough. **Exchange** is a process of acquiring a product from one party by offering something in return. It is generally accepted that there are four elements to this (see Figure 1.7):

- Two or more groups participate.
- Each party must possess something of value that the other party desires.
- Each party must give up something of value for something of value. The satisfaction of both parties is dependent on the excess of return over their investment. For a business this may mean a healthy return from the price charged, and for the individual this would be satisfaction greater than he or she would otherwise have had if the exchange had not taken place.
- The parties must communicate so that they generally know about the product of value becoming available.

The long-term nature of marketing relationships is vital in the exchange process. This depends on an organisation's success in matching customer satisfaction with the achievement of corporate goals. The early days of a

Figure 1.7 The exchange process

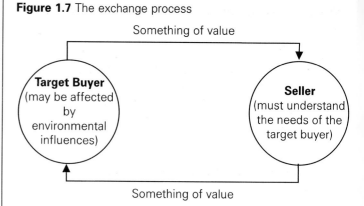

relationship with a customer may depend on **supplier push**, whereby a producer persuades a customer to participate in the exchange process. Over a period of time the exchange process may create a more interactive relationship between the buyer and the seller which takes into account the views of the customer in the exchange (see Figure 1.8).

For example, the seller may engage in research to find out the views of the buyer, or provide intangible benefits attached to the product. The aim of this would be to maintain the exchange relationship and make sure that the customer continues to buy and come back for repeat purchases. This developing relationship between buyer and seller may provide each with opportunities to improve their levels of satisfaction and their excess of return over investment.

Figure 1.8 From supplier push to an interactive relationship over time

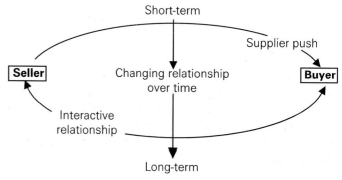

Markets

A market exists when buyers and sellers come into contact. In some markets buyers and sellers meet, whereas in others they may do business by some other form of communication such as letter, phone or fax. Markets simply provide the opportunity for exchange to take place, by bringing together consumers who share a

Figure 1.9 The marketplace brings together consumers and producers

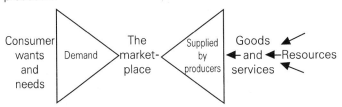

common need or want and who are in a position to engage in a transaction.

The way in which an organisation responds to market signals (such as rising demand) will reflect its corporate objectives, and this will in turn influence the strategies and techniques it employs. These objectives give an organisation a unifying purpose and create a yardstick against which to assess achievements.

The **marketplace** has a number of ingredients. The key players are buyers and sellers. A transaction will involve:

- communication
- an offer for sale
- acceptance of the offer
- an exchange (normally goods or services for money or credit).

Figure 1.10 The marketplace

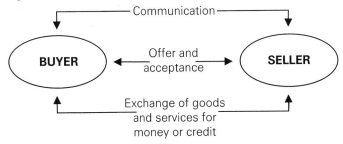

A failure of any of the above could affect the success of the exchange. For example, if the information from the seller to the buyer is not communicated effectively, the buyer may not have sufficient information to assess whether there would be an acceptable excess of return for an investment.

Forces influencing marketing

Marketing is responsible for creating desirable exchanges between buyers and sellers. Thus it is the *energy* which drives the economy, by helping producers to make desirable returns while, at the same time, providing consumers with what they want.

The marketing mix

The role of the marketing function is to develop a strategy which enables the organisation to achieve its marketing objectives. Decisions are then made which turn ideas and proposals into reality. A **marketing strategy** involves identifying the customers which an organisation wishes to reach and then creating an appropriate **marketing mix** – product, price, place and promotion – directed at those customers in the target market.

The marketing mix is made up of the four Ps. To meet the needs of customers an organisation must:

- develop PRODUCTS to satisfy them
- charge them the right PRICE
- get the goods to the right PLACE
- make customers aware of the goods through PROMOTION.

Figure 1.11 The ingredients of the marketing mix

The marketing environment

Marketing strategies must take into account not only internal functions which involve decisions affecting the marketing mix, but also factors outside the organisation which make up the **marketing environment** (see Figure 1.12).

The marketing environment is made up of many distinct factors: social, legal, economic, political, historical, competitive, technical, cultural and environmental. Whereas factors *within* the marketing mix can be controlled directly by an organisation, those within the marketing environment are subject to less control. However, environmental changes may influence consumer decisions in the same way as changes made to the marketing mix. For example, they might influence a consumer's lifestyle and standard of living, and consequently the choice of products. It is, therefore, important that we look at these factors and understand what they involve early in the marketing process.

Though the forces in the marketing environment may be generally viewed as uncontrollable, it may be possible for an organisation to control one or more of them – such as competitive influences designed to foster loyalty, or the development of new technologies. These forces may be highly interrelated and, though they provide some uncertainty, they can also create opportunities.

Figure 1.12 Developing a marketing mix within a marketing environment

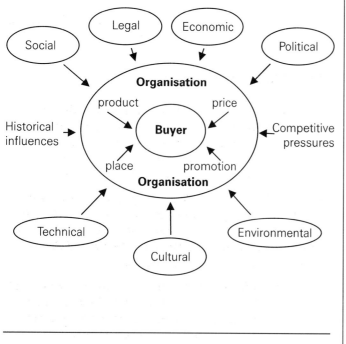

Garden retailing has weathered the recession better than many other sectors. Though fewer people have been moving house, the slump in property prices has not stopped the rest from improving the houses and gardens they cannot sell. In fact over the past five years the garden products market is estimated to have grown by 25–30 per cent in real terms.

The industry is characterised by single-site centres, often family-owned, that have developed from long-established nurseries which have moved from wholesaling into retailing to take advantage of better profit margins. Further development for a lot of centres is hampered by their fierce commitment to independence as well as the daunting cost of expansion. It costs around £1 million to build a garden centre, and with planning authorities now taking a much tougher line on this type of development, for many garden centres expansion means improving operations on existing sites.

Changes in the DIY sector have affected the retail garden market. Since 1980 the number of DIY superstores, most of which include a garden centre, has increased to 1050, carving out a quarter to a third of the market. Competition from superstores has encouraged many garden centres to form buying and marketing groups, to give independent retailers collective muscle.

In the long term, the pace of change in the garden centre market is set to accelerate once a stronger house market develops. Analysts expect many centres to be acquired into bigger groups so that the strong will get stronger and the weak may come under pressure.

Case Study
The development of garden centres

Gardening has grown into big business. Gardeners today do not just buy bulbs, seeds and compost – they want conservatories, barbeques, garden furniture, strimmers and pet products. Today they spend around £2.6 billion per year on their hobby.

Despite this expansion the highly profitable world of the garden centre is under threat from the large DIY chains. The chains have spotted the hefty margins on garden products and are entering an industry which was once the preserve of the smaller family business.

With Sunday trading restrictions now relaxed, when previously they had left garden centres untouched, other shops in the High Street are also competing for the same business. Adding insult to injury, the new regulation means that garden centres with floor space of more than 3000 square feet will in fact have to reduce their Sunday opening hours to six.

Questions for discussion

1 *Identify and then discuss the likely effect of a range of external influences, such as those highlighted by the study, upon small independent garden centres.*

2 *How might these relatively small independent garden centres counter some of the changes in their external environment?*

The social environment

The **social environment** consists of the ideas, attitudes and behaviour patterns involved in human activities. For example, older people may have more conservative ideas about clothes and fashions than teenagers; these attitudes will affect the buying patterns of the two groups.

Social systems can be viewed:

- at a *macro* level (which studies the features of large-scale systems such as national groupings – for example the buying behaviour of different age groups in Britain)
- at a *micro* level (which studies small-scale groupings – such as the buying behaviour of a small number of female members of the royal family).

Larger markets can be seen as being made up of various sub-groups. For example the market for clothes is divided into the market for fashion clothes, the market for skirts made out of specific materials, the market for clothes bought by people in a particular income range, and so on.

The legal environment

Every society is governed by a set of laws and codes established by the **legal and political framework**. Local, national and international laws may affect the running of organisations in a variety of different ways.

- Laws may affect the relationship an organisation has with its customers – for example in the fields of credit regulations, rights of buyers, etc.
- Laws may influence the relationship an organisation has with the general public. For example, one law restrains a pub from selling alcohol to those under 18, and another bans advertisements that may be racially prejudiced.
- The legal environment may also influence the ways in which an organisation competes against others in areas such as *anti-competitive practices*.

The economic environment

The **economic environment** has a major influence on business activity, particularly in the field of consumer spending. For example, in a boom period unemployment starts to fall, more businesses start up, sales of goods expand, output increases and prices start to rise. This may continue for four or five years. Then sales of goods start to fall, output of goods is reduced, employees are laid off, wages rise but only at a decreasing rate, price

rises start to tail off, and the economy experiences a period of 'recession' (see Figure 1.13).

Figure 1.13 The changing economic environment

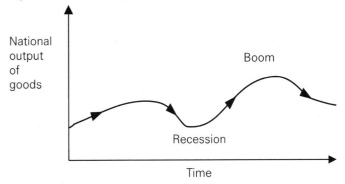

The political environment

The political environment is linked closely to the legal environment in that legal restrictions are imposed by governments to regulate business practices. The political environment, too, is cyclical because governments have to seek re-election within five years of taking office.

Ideologies differ between the main political parties and also change over a period of time. For example, the 1980s saw a movement away from state ownership and control of major organisations like British Telecom and British Gas, which were sold to new shareholders.

It is important for an organisation to monitor the political environment because the government of the day may pass legislation which markedly affects its activities (e.g. credit controls, pollution controls, design standards).

The technical environment

Throughout history, society has experienced change. The industrial revolution, for example, changed people's lives radically. It brought great wealth to the mill owners, but it also brought social upheaval by throwing thousands out of work from their traditional occupations. Today the pace and scope of change are as fast as ever.

Technology affects the ways in which we work, live, shop and pursue leisure activities. Over recent years major technological revolutions in industries such as information technology and food processing have transformed our lives and organisations. If organisations fail to adapt to new technologies they find that they lose their market share and eventually have to close down.

The cultural environment

Culture describes the traditions, beliefs and values of the community in which we live. It includes our religious beliefs, our attitudes towards alcohol, the food we eat and the importance we attach to family life. Cultural values can be strong and impose important constraints on business activity.

At the same time it is important for organisations to understand cultural influences on consumer behaviour, particularly with regard to consumption. For example, it would be unwise to sell products that are seen to insult religious sensitivities in particular countries. If businesses are to make the best use of opportunities, then decision makers need to understand the cultural framework in which they are operating.

The natural environment

Ecology is the study of the relationship between living things and their surroundings. Over the years, a balance is created in the natural environment. However, rapid changes created by human developments can upset this balance.

For example, human activity involves the use of *resources*. Some resources are replaceable – i.e. they are *renewable* resources. Other resources can only be used once – they are *non-renewable*. Some raw materials such as coal and oil may take millions of years to form, yet they can be used up in seconds. Other recent major environmental concerns have been the problems created by acid rain and the destruction of the earth's protective ozone layer.

The survival and growth of an industrial society requires a careful balance between industrial and biological systems. Decisions concerning the natural environment require careful collaboration between individuals, businesses, consumers and governments on an international scale. Organisations need to show clear concern about the wider effects of their activities – they must be responsible 'corporate citizens' in this respect and communicate their concern to their customers.

Competitive pressures

Competition is one of the basic facts of business life and is widely covered in this book. One bus company may compete directly with another bus company, and then indirectly with other means of transport. Potential passengers may buy their own cars or decide to walk. Competition is always present in business and should be viewed as a threat. To be competitive means to get ahead of the competition.

Historical influences

Time is another basic fact of business life. Things change and marketers need to be aware of these changes. The company that was market leader 10 years ago with very little competition may today be faced with many types of direct and indirect competition. With the passage of time, social and cultural attitudes change, political and legal structures change, technologies evolve, the economy goes through periods of boom and recession, and the environment is affected by and affects business in a variety of different ways.

Further reading

- *The Business and Marketing Environment* by Adrian Palmer and Ian Worthington. McGraw-Hill, 1992.
- *Marketing Concepts and Strategies*, 2nd European edition, by Dibb, Simkin, Pride and Ferrell. Houghton Mifflin, 1994.
- *Meeting Customer Needs* by Ian Smith. Butterworth-Heinemann, 1994.
- *Marketing*, 6th edition, by Joel R. Evans and Barry Berman. Prentice Hall, 1994.
- *Principles of Marketing*, 10th edition, by William Stanton, Michael Etzel and Bruce Walker. McGraw-Hill, 1993.
- *Elements of Marketing*, 3rd edition, by A. R. Morden. DPP, 1993.
- *Marketing* by Steven J. Skinner. Houghton Mifflin, 1990.
- *The Marketing Casebook: Cases and Concepts* by Sally Dibb and Lyndon Simkin. Routledge, 1994.
- *Improving Marketing Performance* by W. J. Parsons. Gower, 1987.
- *Gower Handbook of Marketing*, edited by Michael Thomas. Gower, 1995.

2 Stakeholders and social responsibilities

On completion of this chapter students should be able to:

■ identify and assess the aspirations of stakeholders

■ review the effectiveness of approaches by the organisation to satisfy stakeholders

■ identify the social responsibilities of marketing and evaluate organisational responses.

Stakeholders

Case Study
Healthy profits for MFI

The following details appeared in the financial press in 1994:

'Strong sales growth is expected to fuel a healthy first-half profits advance when MFI, Britain's biggest kitchen and bedroom furniture retailer, presents its report. At Morgan Stanley, the securities house, they expect MFI's interim pre-tax profits to advance to £39 million from £24.5 million over the previous half-year.

'Morgan Stanley say that the group, which is chaired by Derek Hunt, has been increasing its market share in a flat market and they expect sales growth of about 10.5 per cent. However, higher raw material costs may put pressure on margins, which are expected to dip by around 0.2 per cent. MFI manufactures more than 50 per cent of the furniture it sells.

'Analysts remain optimistic about the group's long-term prospects, but are wary about current trading after last week's interest rate rise, which has revived worries about consumer spending and a struggling housing market.

'Attention will focus on what Mr Hunt has to say about current trading and prospects ahead of the key two-month period after Boxing Day, when MFI does much of its business.'

Questions for discussion

1 *What groups of people would be particularly interested in reading about MFI's results?*
2 *Discuss why they would be interested in the results.*
3 *How important is it for MFI to satisfy the needs and aspirations of these groups?*

What are stakeholders?

Organisations have a prime responsibility to serve their **stakeholders**. These are individuals and groups who have a stake in the running of the organisation and in the consequences of organisational activities. As in the MFI case study, frequently they will have shared expectations based on the well-being of the organisation. These individuals and groups may include shareholders, managers, employees, suppliers, customers, creditors, society and the public at large.

Figure 2.1 Examples of stakeholders

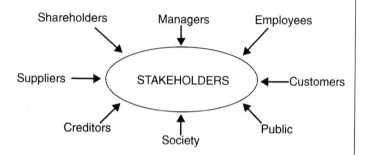

Stakeholders appear both within an organisation (managers and employees) as well as outside the organisation (customers and shareholders).

The expectations of stakeholders may influence how an organisation seeks to achieve its objectives. While most stakeholders will share common expectations, there may well be other areas over which disputes arise. Furthermore, expectations may change with time.

Power is the key to how stakeholders may exercise influence over an organisation's strategies. Few stakeholders are likely to hold sufficient power to influence the actions of an organisation on their own. Influence is more likely to come from stakeholders sharing expectations with other stakeholder groups. Coalitions may develop between groups of stakeholders (e.g. between managers and shareholders). Most people associated with an organisation will be a member of more than one coalition. For example, there may be a coalition between departments in an organisation, between individuals in the management structure, etc. In a large organisation or one which operates in international markets these coalitions will be extremely complex.

There may be direct conflict between the expectations of groups of stakeholders. In some, but not all, conflicts a compromise will be reached between the various expectations which cannot all be achieved at the same time. The following are examples of situations where conflicts may arise:

- Improved technology and efficiency may be at the expense of jobs.
- A management may choose short-term profits instead of awarding employees a pay rise.

- In the public sector, increased funding to education may be at the expense of decreases in funding to hospitals, or vice versa.
- Opening up a new business may create jobs and provide much-needed income for a local community, but at the same time it may create unacceptable noise levels and increased traffic to inconvenience local residents.

There is an almost endless range of issues where conflicts can occur between stakeholders because of differing expectations. It is important, therefore, that we look in turn at each of these stakeholder groups so that we can understand and weigh up the power they exercise.

Shareholders and owners

The traditional view from classical economists such as **Adam Smith** is that an organisation exists solely for the benefit of its owners, that the sole objective of owners is to maximise their wealth, and that this is achieved with the single objective of *profit maximisation*. It is assumed that profit maximisation is possible because the owner has total control over the business, makes all decisions and has perfect knowledge of all organisational activities.

Though this is probably true of many small to medium-sized businesses today, it is unlikely to be the case with much larger organisations. There, few shareholders will either work for the organisation or be in a strong position to influence its activities. Also, though profitability may be an overriding objective for many shareholders, they will also be concerned with other objectives which seek to develop the overall health of the business.

Managers

Research by **William Baumol** in the 1950s revealed that, in many organisations, top managers rather than owners have most control over activities and wealth generation. In the many organisations, particularly larger ones, ownership and control are divorced and do not go hand-in-hand. Many shareholders do not attend Annual General Meetings or take part in decision-making processes.

Where there is a clear division between ownership and control, managers will have much more freedom to develop activities which meet their own aspirations – for example, developing brand or market leadership, the positions they hold within the organisation and the salaries they receive.

Though managers may reduce the influence of the owner/shareholders, it is still necessary to pursue objectives which seek also to satisfy the interests of shareholders. Baumol saw top managers pursuing aspirations through the maximisation of sales revenue rather than profitability. Growing sales meant more prestige and better bargaining power for managers.

Employees

Managers and workers at different levels are all employees, but within an organisation managers may have objectives which are quite different from other groups of workers.

Senior managers have the role of satisfying different groups of stakeholders. This can be difficult, particularly where conflict exists between groups. According to one view, decision makers have neither the time and resources, nor information and cognitive ability, to make maximising decisions. They simply try to provide acceptable levels of satisfaction to everybody. Stakeholders amend their expectations according to how the business is performing, how they see environmental conditions affecting economic performance, and how well other stakeholders are being treated.

Henry Mintzberg considers managers and the workforce as 'the internal coalition' within an organisation. Mintzberg then categorises them into six groups of influencers:

- top or general management (top strategist and aides)
- operators (involved in producing goods or providing services)
- line managers (these appear in the hierarchy between the chief executive and supervisors)
- analysts of the technostructure (staff specialists)
- support staff (those who provide indirect support for the operations such as accounting and legal staff)
- the ideology of the organisation.

The last item in the list may seem curious, but Mintzberg suggests that though technically an organisation is inanimate, the beliefs shared by people who work for the organisation help to create a business culture which develops an identity of its own.

Suppliers

In providing goods and services for an organisation, suppliers hope that by winning contracts they are securing income and profitability for their businesses. There will, however, be many other concerns.

The supplier will be concerned about discounts and payment periods. The organisation receiving the supplies may be concerned about other issues, such as the consistency of the quality of supplies and the supplier's ability to keep to delivery dates – both could impact on its operations and ultimately affect its competitive advantage.

Customers

In the first chapter we saw that marketing orientation involves 'identifying, anticipating and satisfying customer requirements profitably'. It is for this reason that customers are high-priority stakeholders for the organisation. Customers will want something of value from their transaction which provides them with an excess of return over their investment. If organisations are not marketing orientated or do not provide customers with desired levels of satisfaction, the needs, wishes and aspirations of customers will have been ignored and this could affect the success of the organisation.

Creditors

Anybody owed money by the organisation, whether a bank or a supplier, is called a creditor. Creditors may be particularly interested in the success of the organisation, if this might affect its ability to make payments to creditors.

Society and the public

It is unacceptable for a modern organisation to ignore the impact of its activities on the wider community. People living in the society in which a business operates should be seen as an additional stakeholder. At the same time the business should be seen as a key stakeholder in the wider community.

Today many people recognise that development can only be beneficial if it takes into account community losses as well as profits. Organisations, therefore, have to work out how to strike a balance in order to become 'a responsible corporate citizen'.

Satisfying the aspirations of stakeholders

People running an organisation need to understand the various expectations of stakeholder groups and assess them in terms of the power they exercise. This is particularly important when implementing strategies which involve change.

The power of stakeholders

According to Johnson and Scholes (see *Further reading*), power is 'the extent (to which) individuals or groups are able to persuade, induce or coerce others into following courses of action'.

At any one time, stakeholders have three basic options:

■ to stay and contribute
■ to leave
■ to stay and try to change the system.

Stakeholders who try to influence planning will endeavour to make the organisation respond more closely to their demands. This will ultimately depend on the power of the stakeholder, their own personal objectives, and how well they present their case to the decision-makers.

Perhaps the most useful power a stakeholder can have is **exchange dependency**. If a stakeholder has control over a *resource*, a *body of technical knowledge*, or a *skill*, particularly if it is fundamental to the running of the organisation, then this power has to be considered by managers involved in the decision-making process.

Another power, based on exchange dependency, is **social power**. Two authors, French and Raven, developed a social power model in which they referred to the degree to which the position of an owner or manager enables them to reward or dismiss those lower down in the hierarchy. They referred to five powers:

■ *Legitimate or position power* is determined by the job held.
■ *Reward power* encourages people to obey if they feel that they are likely to receive something, financially or psychologically.
■ *Coercive power* arises from the ability to punish or reward.
■ *Expert power* arises from using knowledge to influence others.
■ *Referrant or charismatic power* derives from the initiator's status, prestige or charisma.

Another power which may be available to a stakeholder *comes from simply being present*. For example, an individual may have little exchange power, but the same person sitting on a committee is presented with a wonderful opportunity to influence others. People with persuasive skills can use them in such a way.

Do you ever consider the influence of ordinary individuals who have access to power? The spouse of a chief executive or prime minister has access to power, and many of their beliefs will filter through in a way which influences policies or decisions.

A decision maker may also be influenced by a stakeholder if he or she believes, rightly or wrongly, that the stakeholder has power. Thus this **perceived power** may encourage the decision-maker to take into account the demands of the stakeholder. It is possible, for example, for people to convince others of their importance in the decision-making process, even though their role in the organisation is a minor one!

Stakeholder mapping

It is possible to assess the likely effect of various strategies by mapping out the expectations of stakeholders (particularly where they conflict), together with an assessment of the power structure. Johnson and Scholes use two methods to do this: the power/dynamism matrix, and the power/interest matrix.

The power/dynamism matrix

This is a useful way of assessing, in the early stages of developing a new strategy, where 'political effort' might be needed to influence stakeholders (see Figure 2.2).

Figure 2.2 The power/dynamism matrix

PREDICTABILITY

	High	Low
Low	A: Few problems	B: Unpredictable but manageable
High	C: Powerful but predictable	D: Greatest danger or greatest opportunities

(POWER labels the vertical axis)

■ Stakeholders in the A and B groups have low power. However, this does not mean that they are unimportant, because their views may be used to influence other stakeholders.
■ Stakeholders in the C group have high power but their views are predictable. There should be no surprises.
■ Stakeholders in the D group are the most difficult to influence or persuade and their views may also be the most difficult to predict.

Power/interest matrix

This matrix classifies stakeholders in relation to the power they hold and the degree of interest they show in the organisation (see Figure 2.3).

Figure 2.3 The power/interest matrix

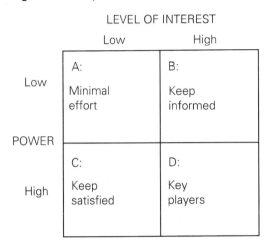

- Stakeholders in the A group have low power and low interest. Only minimal effort is required to satisfy their aspirations.
- Though stakeholders in the B group have low power they have high interest. Their interest needs to be satisfied with plenty of information.
- Stakeholders in the C group have low interest but high power. These must be considered as they might respond to specific events.
- Stakeholders in the D group are the most difficult to satisfy and should be a key ingredient in strategy formulation.

Bargaining strategies

By assessing the aspirations of a stakeholder, understanding the sources of power and mapping the levels of predictability and interest, a strategy can be developed to bargain with or try to influence that stakeholder. In the early stages the strategy will depend on how good or strong at bargaining an influencer is.

I. I. Mitroff offers nine bargaining options:

- *Change or convert the stakeholder.* This may take place by means of:
  - exercising power and authority in a way which makes demands of the stakeholder
  - persuading the stakeholder in a way which appeals to reason, values and emotions
  - using economic exchange in the bargaining process
  - negotiating and reaching a compromise

  - problem-solving by sharing and debating to arrive at agreed perceptions.
- *Fight the stakeholder.* This might involve using the organisation's resources, forming coalitions with other stakeholders and ultimately overpowering the stakeholder.
- *Agree to and absorb the stakeholder's demands.*
- *Form a coalition with the stakeholder.*
- *Ignore the stakeholder altogether.*
- *Appease the stakeholder.*
- *Surrender to the stakeholder.*
- *Form a special relationship with the stakeholder.*
- *Transform the organisation into the stakeholder through merger, imitation or role modelling.*

The appropriate bargaining process will depend on the particular stakeholder group concerned, and their reactions to particular bargaining strategies directed at them. Given the number of options, strategies are not always guaranteed to work and may simply depend on historical relationships between various stakeholder groups.

Stakeholder satisfaction/dissatisfaction cycles

An important objective for decision makers is the development of a **stakeholder satisfaction cycle**. By developing activities which satisfy external stakeholders – for example, prompt payments to creditors, satisfied customers, non-intervention by consumer groups, environmental pressure groups and government agencies – an organisation will improve its ability to carry out activities which earn rewards for internal stakeholders such as employees, many of whom will have contributed to this planning process. Thus the organisation will have created **mutual benefits** in a cycle which has involved both internal and external stakeholders (see Figure 2.4).

Figure 2.4 The stakeholder satisfaction cycle

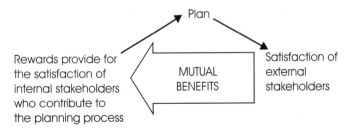

On the other hand, if the plans an organisation makes seriously disturb external stakeholders, a stakeholder *dissatisfaction* cycle may occur. For example, if the organisation provides environmentally unfriendly goods which are considered by consumers to be sub-standard, and at the same time has a bad reputation for late payments and other business practices, it will reduce its ability to be profitable. Internal stakeholders will then not reap the rewards they might otherwise like.

Summary

Stakeholder analysis helps us to appreciate, particularly when developing marketing objectives, the need to understand the power positions and expectations of various stakeholder groups. Stakeholders influence an organisation through their power and this power may be gained in a variety of ways, not least through a coalition. Bargaining is important, though sometimes it is hard to quantify the aspirations and expectations of different stakeholder groups. Therefore it is useful for organisations to adopt a broad approach to strategies which takes into account their understanding of stakeholders – for example, how their activities may influence the wider community and society as a whole.

Social responsibilities

By looking at stakeholder satisfaction cycles we can understand the need for organisations to make sure that developments take into consideration community losses as well as profits. Organisations must consider carefully how they can strike a balance between different stakeholder aspirations, taking account of areas such as consumerism, business ethics and environmental issues.

Consumerism

Before the 1960s, consumers had few rights and very little say in the bargaining process. They often had to rely on their own vigilance and common sense. The Latin expression *caveat emptor* – 'Let the buyer beware' – summed up the position. As large and well-developed organisations often dealt with individual consumers, **consumerism** developed to break down this vast inequality in bargaining power and so provide consumers with more rights.

The need for consumers to be better protected against the actions of the organisations they bought from arose because of problems such as:

- poor-quality services or damaged goods
- goods or services which failed to match the descriptions applied to them
- manufacturer's or supplier's negligence affecting the safety of products or services

- breach of contract
- misleading offers, information, advertising and labelling
- unfair terms in contracts
- artificially high prices resulting from a lack of competition.

Factors that have contributed to increased consumer power include greater equality, freedom of speech, improved educational standards, were governmental regulation, and vastly improved communications. Consumers today *expect* a product to be safe and to perform and function well. They also feel that it is important to be *protected* against questionable products or unfair practices. Producers are expected to behave in a socially responsible manner. Newspapers, television, radio and consumer organisations are poised to bring wrongdoers to the public attention, and the law courts are there to punish offenders when necessary.

Case Study
An international organisation and consumer responsibility

In the early 1990s, Body Shop had over 600 shops trading in 38 countries and in 18 languages producing over 5 million kilos of products. Body Shop had a bigger presence overseas than any other British retailer, and was the fastest-growing company in the UK personal care market.

Anita Roddick who founded Body Shop argues that businesses and consumers working together can help to create social change. Consumers have the power to create change, by asking questions about sources and manufacture, by demanding information, and ultimately by the use of their feet and their wallets to shop elsewhere.

Over 30 million people pass by Body Shop stores around the world each month. Anita Roddick believes that the shop window can be used to educate people about consumer issues. Body Shop sets out to inform consumers clearly about what they are buying, where the ingredients come from and how products are produced. Ms Roddick argues that consumers need to have information so that they can make informed choices. All too often, she asserts, other producers hide the true nature of their products through glossy advertising.

Questions for discussion

1 *Should producers inform and educate consumers, or leave them to find out about products for themselves?*
2 *Is it possible to identify examples of advertising and sales promotion which mask the true nature of products? Cite examples.*

3 *How can (a) consumers and (b) producers benefit from businesses and consumers working together more closely?*

Consumer protection

Laws provide a framework within which transactions can take place and also serve to provide a means of settling disputes. The legal basis of the contract which exists between a buyer and a seller sets out the obligations that individuals and organisations have to each other every time they enter into an agreement.

Over the years, governments have responded to consumerism with successive Acts of Parliament designed to protect and increase the powers of buyers in relation to sellers. Such laws cover unfair business activities, poor quality of goods and services and the provision of credit. For example, the *Sale of Goods Act 1979* states that sellers must provide goods which are of merchantable quality, match the description applied to them and are fit for the purpose for which they are sold. Other important Acts include the *Trade Descriptions Act of 1968 and 1972*, the *Fair Trading Act 1973*, the *Consumer Protection Act 1987*, the *Consumer Credit Act 1974*, as well as Acts referring to 'food and drugs' and 'weights and measures'. Laws relating to marketing cover areas such as agency, use of trademarks, infringement of copyrights, insurance, and company law.

The Office of Fair Trading (OFT)

The OFT was set up by the government to investigate monopolies and mergers, collect information on unfair consumer practices, and play a key role in developing consumer legislation. The Director General of Fair Trading:

- analyses information affecting the well-being of consumers
- refers matters where consumers' rights may be violated to the Consumer Protection Advisory Committee
- encourages the publication of 'codes of practice' for dealing with consumers
- takes action against organisations which persist in conduct which is against the interests of consumers
- produces consumer protection literature.

The Advertising Standards Authority (ASA)

The ASA is an independent body which exercises control over all advertising except that on radio and television. The ASA draws up its own codes of practice which it uses to ensure that advertisements are 'legal, decent, honest and truthful'. Advertisements should be prepared with a sense of responsibility to both consumers and society and should conform to the principles of fair competition.

For example, a number of complaints were made to the ASA over a campaign by Rover cars to extol the virtues of wood-panelling on their model 820Se; suspended by the main body of the text appeared a box with the words 'A woman, a dog and a walnut tree – the more you beat them, the better they'll be'. At Rover they insisted that the words were only put there to inject humour! The ASA was also unconvinced of the cholesterol-reducing properties of Common Sense Oat Bran Flakes, and brought in a team of top nutritional scientists amidst fears that the product and the advert might create needless worry for consumers.

The Independent Television Commission (ITC)

The ITC has a stong voluntary code of practice which covers all terrestrial television broadcasting (i.e. not including satellite broadcasts). As a statutory body the ITC has a remit to develop such a code for advertisers and, like the ASA code, this constantly changes to meet changing attitudes and expectations.

The British Standards Institution (BSI)

The BSI was incorporated by Royal Charter as a voluntary non-profit-making organisation to prepare and publish standards for safety, performance, size and testing. The BSI is identified by the now-famous **kitemark** displayed on packaging to denote that a product meets BSI requirements.

The Monopolies and Mergers Commission (MMC)

The MMC investigates possible monopolies and proposed company mergers referred to it by the Director General of Fair Trading. The Commission's role is to assess whether such monopolies and mergers are likely to be against the public interest (see Figure 2.5).

For example, in early 1994 the Central and Granada TV companies were told that they could not engage in mergers that would give them more than 25 per cent of ITV's net advertising revenue. This was to prevent any one concern from developing a dominant position in television advertising.

Trading standards and consumer protection departments

These are departments of local authorities which work with the Office of Fair Trading and help to enforce laws,

Figure 2.5 Assessing whether monopolies or mergers are in the public interest

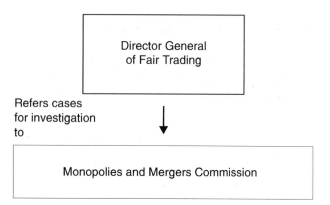

offer advice for shoppers and traders and watch for unfair trade practices. There is also an extensive network of *Citizens' Advice Bureaux* (CABs) in the UK which provide advice on consumer complaints and queries.

The National Consumer Council (NCC)

The NCC is another body established by the government. It was set up in 1975 to provide independent advice to government and business organisations. It also seeks to further consumer interests by representation on public and other bodies, as well as oversee the development of voluntary codes of practice.

Consumer and Consultative Councils

Nationalised industries have Consumer and Consultative Councils to influence their policies and ensure that they do not abuse their powers. Privatised industries (i.e. those that have formerly been in the public sector) also have consumer councils which are set up to serve consumers' interests. For example, the Office of Water Services (Ofwat) has a director-general who is responsible for the economic regulation of water and sewage services; its Birmingham-based office has over 130 staff, many of them employed on ten Regional Customer Services Committees. The Office of the Railway Regulator (ORR), as well as issuing licences to new railway operators, is charged with investigating rail-users' complaints which are taken up from Consumer Consultative Councils.

Pressure groups

Consumerism has also led to the formation of a number of influential pressure groups and movements. The *Consumers Association* has over 800 000 members and is the largest consumer organisation in the country. *Which?*, its magazine, carries the results of extensive product tests

and scrutinises services. The *National Federation of Consumer Groups* comprises a large number of local consumer groups which concentrate upon local issues, such as retail facilities and prices. Other pressure groups which might aim to influence businesses and the government include ecological lobby groups, sports organisations, women's groups, the RSPCA, the Campaign for Real Ale, etc.

There is no doubt that when consumers' rights or obligations are abused, or when dangerous goods are brought into the marketplace, feelings tend to run high. Television and radio have increasingly become a focus for consumer campaigns, through programmes like 'Watchdog'.

Trade associations

In response to consumer pressures and increasing concern about the quality of goods and services, organisations in a number of industries have formed **trade associations** which have established codes of practice to go beyond the basic legal requirements and to provide the highest possible level of consumer satisfaction.

For example, the Association of British Travel Agents (ABTA) set up a fund to protect holidaymakers if a company fails to deliver. Other codes of practice apply to products such as cars and car repairs, shoes and shoe repairs, electrical goods and servicing and mail-order trading. Many of these codes have been produced after consulting with the Office of Fair Trading.

The *Chartered Institute of Marketing* has its own code of practice which members are required to adhere to as a condition of their membership. The code refers to professional standards of behaviour in securing and developing business and demands honesty and integrity of conduct. The *British Code of Advertising Practice* is supported by advertisers, agencies and the media whose representatives make up the Code of Advertising Practice Committee. The code sets out the rules which those in the advertising industry agree to follow, and also indicates to those outside advertising the regulations designed to ensure that advertisements can be trusted.

The European dimension of consumer protection

Consumer protection takes place today within a local, national and European framework (see Figure 2.6).

Over the years the European Commission has set out to create a climate of competition between organisations in the European Union. Agreements between organisations are forbidden if they set out to prevent or distort

Figure 2.6 Regulations and laws to protect consumers

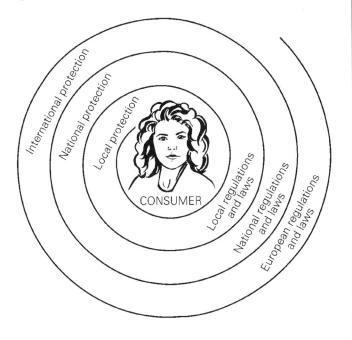

competition within the common market. In particular, agreements fixing prices, sharing markets, discriminating against third parties, or imposing territorial restrictions which split up the common market are all outlawed. Of course, today this competition policy must cover the whole of the European Economic Area (EEA) as well as the fifteen members of the European Union.

The European Commission, supported by the *European Court of Justice*, is responsible for safeguarding competition rules in the EU. In addition, a new body – the *EFTA Surveillance Authority* (ESA) – has been set up to maintain these rules in the EFTA area supported by the EFTA court. The two bodies will work closely together and it seems inevitable that these bodies will merge together at some stage in the future.

- *Restrictive agreements and monopoly abuse.* The Commission will handle cases where trade between EU member states is affected and where more than two-thirds of the EEA turnover of the undertakings concerned is within the EU. However, responsibility will pass to the ESA if the effect on trade within the EU is not great.
- *Mergers and takeovers.* The Commission will handle all cases where the combined worldwide turnover of the organisation is greater than 5 billion ecus, and where the EU turnover of at least two of them is in excess of 250 million ecus.
- *Pricing and exclusive distribution.* As a general rule, firms are free under EU competition law to charge different prices for the supply of their goods in different parts of the Union or to different categories of consumer. The

exception to this rule is where prices are fixed by agreement with other firms.

Some aspects of EU consumer law

In addition to measures between organisations, the EU has introduced many **directives** aimed at protecting consumers. The following are some examples since 1984:

- The *Misleading Advertising* directive aims to protect businesses and the general public against the effects of misleading advertisements.
- The *Product Liability* directive makes manufacturers and importers strictly liable for injuries caused by defective products.
- The *Doorstep Selling* directive brought in a seven-day cooling-off period for certain sales contracts concluded at the consumer's home or place of work.
- The *Consumer Credit* directive protects consumers entering into credit agreements.
- The *Toy Safety* directive harmonises toy safety standards.
- The *Price Indication* directive requires the selling prices (and in some cases unit prices) of goods and non-food products to be displayed.
- The *Package Travel* directive establishes minimum standards of consumer protection for packaged travel and package holidays and tours.

Business ethics

Ethics are *moral principles* or *rules of conduct* which are generally accepted by most members of a society. They involve what individuals and groups believe to be right and what is considered to be wrong. An 'ethic' is therefore a guide as to what should be done or what should not be done.

From an early age, parents, schools, religious teaching and society in general provide us with moral guidelines to help us to learn and form our ethical beliefs. Many ethics are reinforced in our legal system and thus provide a constraint to business activities, while others are not. In areas covered by law, there may well be social pressure to conform to a particular standard. Pressure groups often set out to force individuals or organisations to operate in an 'acceptable' way.

Through the media we hear about questionable business activities – issues such as insider dealing, animal rights protesters involved in disputes with organisations producing cosmetic and pharmaceutical products, protests about tobacco sponsorships, and trading links with unfriendly or hostile nations. As a result, consumers have become more aware of the ethical and moral values underlying business decisions.

Today's consumer is more concerned than ever before about what an organisation stands for, who it trades with, what is does, whether it supports any political party, whether it is an equal opportunities employer and how it behaves in the community as a whole. When *Which?* carried out a survey, 63 per cent of those who responded were concerned about the activities of companies they might invest in.

Case Study
Responsibility for what?

The philosopher Robert Frederick poses some important questions about the responsibility of businesses to the community. He puts forward his arguments in the following manner.

■   A number of people seem to think that it is obviously true that businesses have a responsibility to protect the environment. These responsibilities go beyond what is required by law and regulation. Businesses frequently have the knowledge and the resources to limit environmental damage from their activities. To refuse to take responsibility for these actions can be seen as irresponsible and a neglect of moral duty.

■   A business person may reply that businesses have only a limited power to serve the economic needs of society and must operate within the bounds of law and regulations. However, a business has no moral obligation to try to solve other social problems which may be partly caused by its activities. Businesses have no moral duty to do more than meet the requirements imposed on them by law and regulation.

■   A basic ethical principle is that you should 'do no harm', because creating harm violates the rights of another person not to be harmed. However, perhaps this should be limited to a statement that you should do no *'unwarranted'* harm. For example, in a football game if one person is accidentally hurt in a tackle, then this is acceptable because the injured party must have been aware that going into a fair tackle sometimes causes hurt. If a knowledgeable and competent investor loses money on the stock market, his or her rights have not been violated. The harm in both examples is an acknowledged risk of participating in the activity.
If, on the other hand, the footballer were to have his watch stolen while he was on the floor, or if the investor were to be trampled underfoot in a rush by floor traders to sell on the announcement of bad news, then their rights would have been violated.

■   The same principle can be applied to business life. If individuals or groups are harmed by business activity, and the harm is *unrewarded* in that it is not offset by a balancing benefit, or if the harm is *unnecessary* in that it is

a preventable rather than an inevitable peril of ordinary life, then there has been a violation of the right not to be harmed.

Questions for discussion

1 *What is your view on the nature of harm outlined by Robert Frederick?*
2 *How important is it to develop into a strategy a series of business principles related to the notion of harm?*
3 *Discuss a series of examples where 'harm' may have been caused by business activity.*

The idea of organisations working in and for the community is not new. Many of the great entrepreneurs of the past such as William Hesketh Lever took action to support their ethical beliefs. Marks & Spencer today contributes to a programme which it claims touches all areas of the community; it includes contributions to 'health and care', with involvement in projects for the elderly, the mentally ill and handicapped, the abused, to hospitals and Childline. It also includes contributions to 'arts and heritage' as well as 'community services, education and training'.

Health and safety is an area that has come to the forefront of company policies over recent years. Accidents at a chemical plant or in the North Sea can permanently tarnish an organisation's image. There is always the example of the American corporation which discovered that it was more cost efficient to pay compensation to ill, injured and dying employees than to invest in research to improve safety.

At the same time organisations have become increasingly aware of the adverse effects their products can have on the health and safety of consumers. A recent report attacked standards in the food industry and called for the government to fund better research and better training for environmental health officers, and to legislate against farmers who produce infected stock. Food scares such as the salmonella egg scandal, listeria and 'mad cow disease' (BSE) shocked consumers and led to sudden short-term changes in demand. Cancer links with the use of chlorine bleach rocked the paper industry.

Buying cheap imports from 'sweat-labour' overseas, Sunday trading, dumping of goods on overseas markets, the need to invest in areas of high unemployment, contributions to political parties, encouragement of trade unions and restrictive practices, treatment of employees, investment policies and insurance schemes, social clubs etc. – the list of issues facing organisations is endless.

No organisation is ever going to be able to give the sort of response to these pressures that will please all parties all the time. However, by becoming good corporate citizens and being socially responsible for their actions, organisations can generate considerable goodwill and develop a useful marketing advantage whilst, at the same time, pursuing their other business objectives. However, many environmentalists would argue that being 'green' is not an optional extra but a vital – and tardy – step to preserve the future of mankind.

Ethical and environmental perspectives need to be built into corporate strategy. In his book *The Age of Eco-Strategy*, Matthew Kieran has argued that, in order to manage a global shift to environmentally sound practice, organisations will need at a strategic level to provide three key elements of competitive weaponry:

■ the capacity to manage organisational learning, innovation and change
■ powerful new tools for environmental management
■ new, 'greener' sources of investment capital.

The new tools of environmental management will include (see Figure 2.7):

■ *Environmental impact assessment* (EIA) – carrying out an assessment of the likely impact of major capital projects.
■ *Environmental audits* (or eco-audits) – carrying out an audit of current activities to create a snapshot of the environmental impact of these activities.
■ *Product life-cycle analysis* – looking at the environmental impact of a product throughout its life-cycle. Such an analysis would examine what happens to a product from the sourcing of raw materials to the ultimate disposal of waste (an analysis that led McDonald's to discontinue its styrofoam 'clamshell' hamburger box).
■ *Environmental accounting* – accurately recording the value of environmental assets and their depreciations, as well as the true size of environmental liabilities and pollution costs.

Figure 2.7 Tools of environmental management

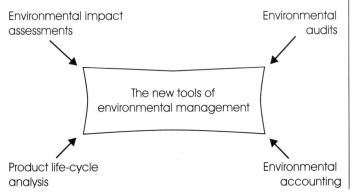

Environmental impact assessments

Environmental audits

The new tools of environmental management

Product life-cycle analysis

Environmental accounting

There is no doubt that in the future, in the world of the articulate consumer, we will see more 'social' marketing. Organisations will have to respond with increasing sensitivity by constantly analysing their activities and revising their strategies to match the wishes of their consumers.

Environmental issues

Today a company's environmental performance is increasingly central to its competitiveness and survival. The following illustrations give a very stark warning to businesses that fail to take environmental action:

■ One of the world's largest paper-producing companies committed a minor, technical environmental violation in the American state of Maine. In May 1992 the US government imposed a three-year ban on government paper purchases from the company.
■ The German government's privatisation programme in the Bitterfield region of the former East Germany ground to a halt when western investors concerned about environmental clean-up costs were unwilling to buy shares in a single business.
■ An American bank foreclosed on a $1 million building mortgage, thereby becoming the legal owner of the property. However, it also inherited an environmental clean-up bill of $2 million.

Case Study
Why develop an environmental strategy?

Sir John Collins, the Chairman of Shell UK, recently made the following comments on this subject:

'We recently carried out a survey of 100 British companies active in the environmental area – doing such things as environmental audits, waste recycling, energy management, emission control and site improvement. We asked why they took these initiatives.

'Some two-thirds believed there was a direct financial benefit – in saved costs or increased profitability. Another important set of reasons involved "reputation" and the resulting better relations with regulators, local communities and staff. A quarter mentioned "competitive advantage" and a substantial number "survival" – by meeting customer requirements or making essential financial savings. Better management of energy and other resources, waste control and recycling are obvious routes to profitable environmental improvement.

'The question of environmental "image" is important. Hard-pressed business people may feel that it is less so than the financial bottom line. But we all depend on a "licence to operate" from the community. If our reputation is poor – business in general, a particular industry, or a company – profits will certainly suffer in the long run. Regulators will treat us with suspicion, we will lose customer and employee loyalty and legislators will no longer accept our views. And, by "image" I don't mean just a cosmetic one. Good communication is always important but reputation, in the environmental field as in all others, depends on being seen to be taking concrete measures to improve performance.

'Competitive advantage is something business people must always pursue – our competitors surely do. I am convinced that environmental improvement offers many opportunities. We all know businesses that have harnessed the power of green consumerism. Again, it is an area where developing opportunities may require ingenuity.

'Finally, the question of "survival". The survey mentioned the growing tendency for companies to require their suppliers to match certain environmental standards. This obviously creates great problems for those ill-prepared – but offers the opportunity for those in advance to push their higher standards.'

Questions for discussion

1 *Do organisations really benefit if they build environmental concerns into business strategies?*
2 *What is competitive advantage? How can this be aided through the responsible marketing of products?*
3 *What do you think Sir John Collins meant by 'a licence to operate'? What are the implications in terms of pleasing stakeholders in an organisation?*

Seven environmental sins

In July 1993, the UK government identified seven major environmental 'sins' leading to the unsustainable use of resources. These are:

- emission of carbon dioxide from burning coal, oil and gas
- worsening local air-pollution, caused mainly by increasing emissions from road transport
- the rising demand for water, threatening to dry out streams
- water pollution caused by farming, sewage, industry and acid rain
- loss of countryside to roads, homes and other developments
- damage to habitats and loss of wildlife
- rising demand for sand, gravel and rock quarries and pits which harm wildlife, landscapes and communities.

A national strategy for sustainable development clearly involves taking action in each of these areas.

A survey of the annual reports of the UK's 100 largest companies was carried out by Dr Shailendra Vyakarnam to find out what they were doing to protect the environment. Dr Vyakarnam breaks down their actions into two main categories.

- *Socially responsible actions* have a direct bearing on the nature of the business carried out by a company (e.g. investment in the reduction of toxic emissions by a heavy industrial company).
- *Charitable donations and sponsorship* bear no direct relation to the company's business, and fulfil a useful public relations function for the company concerned as well as benefiting the recipients.

As an example of the second category, Tate & Lyle match employees' contributions to a rain-forest conservation programme. Dr Vyakarnam concludes by saying:

> *'The charitable donations being made by the companies are clearly based on the principle that charity begins at home, rather than one where it needs to be targeted at the most needy. It seems that the companies are doing things which are right for them, in terms of strategic fit, whether it is donations, links with education and training, recycling of materials or the use of unleaded (and cheaper) fuel for a large fleet of cars.'*

Case Study
Accepting environmental and social responsibility at Cadbury Schweppes

The following text is adapted from a policy statement made public by Cadbury Schweppes, a major company in the food and drinks industry:

'Environmental issues have a high priority on our business agenda. We have now completed a worldwide review of our operations to assess our environmental performance more systematically. The results of this review helped to finalise our corporate environmental policy which the Board formally adopted in September 1993. In summary the policy embraces eight key commitments:

- To comply with applicable environmental laws and regulations and reflect industry best practice.
- To undertake performance evaluation and compliance reviews.
- To aim for efficient use of energy, raw materials and the minimisation of waste and pollution.
- To promote efficiency in solid waste management.
- To provide a healthy and safe environment, training and communication for employees.

■ To communicate our environmental policies.
■ To institute procedures to implement our policies successfully.
■ To have regular policy reviews and updates.

A copy of this policy is available on request.

'An Environmental Management Programme is now being developed which will translate the policy into clearly understood responsibilities, requirements and procedures.

'Cadbury Schweppes contributes actively to the communities in which it operates around the world and is committed to improving the environment in which people live and work.

'Corporate giving is managed in the UK through the Cadbury Schweppes Charitable Trust. In addition, operating companies around the world support community activity through locally targeted programmes, the provision of facilities and management resources or by financial support, often as a by-product of commercial sponsorship.'

Questions for discussion

1 How well do Cadbury Schweppes' eight key commitments match the government's key environmental concerns?
2 Suggest and then discuss the sort of community projects that a large company like Cadbury Schweppes ought to be involved in.
3 How do external stakeholders benefit from Cadbury Schweppes' approach to environmental and community issues?

Social costs and externalities

The **environmental lobby** works hand-in-hand with the consumer movement to provide protection against some of the excesses of the industrial and commercial world. Many environmental groups (such as Greenpeace) are organised at an international level and have strategies based on integrated worldwide action. These organisations serve to remind firms that they create external costs which go beyond their balance sheets. These costs are sometimes known as **spillover costs** or **externalities**:

Externalities = social costs – private costs

At the end of the day, organisations will probably be more interested in weighing up decision-making using their private costs, but will be forced to assess the fuller implications in order to use resources in a more socially acceptable way.

Pollution

The most obvious social cost of business activity is **pollution**. Many heavy industrial plants choose locations near canals, rivers and the sea so that they can use water in the manufacturing process and pour effluent into the rivers and the sea. In some countries firms are charged heavily for causing water pollution.

Air pollution was highlighted by several horrifying events of the 1980s. In December 1984, the leak of poisonous gas from the Union Carbide plant in Bhopal, India, killed more than 2000 people and at least ten times that number suffered from severe respiratory damage and eye complaints. Even more dramatic – and potentially catastrophic – were the events at the Chernobyl nuclear reactor in the former Soviet Union in 1986 where wide tracts of land were made uninhabitable and a cloud of nuclear waste was carried airborne across Europe by the release of nuclear material. Emissions from UK power plants are said by some to contribute to the acid rain that has devastated forests in Scandinavia and Germany – half of the Black Forest has been designated a 'total damage area'. (However, it is important to point out that a number of scientists argue that the destruction of forest lands may also be a result of natural processes.)

The industrial response to environmental issues

Dereliction, traffic congestion, long-term waste and noise are other external effects of business activities which influence the wider environment and determine how organisations are perceived by external stakeholders.

At the same time organisations have to be careful about what they produce. For example, what types of additives should go into food and drink? How should the products be tested? Should animals be used in tests? What use should be made of wood and plastics? The more an organisation analyses environmental issues, the more it is likely to be faced by competing interests.

Balancing internal and external expectations

Internally, a business usually needs to make a profit for shareholders, managers and other stakeholders. *Externally*, the business has to contend with selling products in the face of competition and the regulatory influences exerted by governments. It also has to take into consideration the interests of external stakeholders and the pressures from a variety of other independent factors. Failing to take heed of organised pressure groups such as Friends of the Earth, the National Anti-Vivisection Society and Greenpeace may lead to the worst possible outcome – a consumer boycott, perhaps on an international scale.

Governments have given international undertakings to work towards **sustainable patterns of growth**. The Rio summit of world governments in 1992 committed countries to developing sustainable patterns of economic growth with widespread implications for everything from trade policy to electricity generation, from shopping to motoring. In late January 1994, the UK government published its response in setting out ways of creating sustainable growth – reconciling economic growth with protection of the environment and natural resources for future generations; controlling rising emissions of man-made climate-changing gases; protecting the richness and diversity of wild plant and animal species; and conserving and expanding the nation's forests (see Figure 2.8).

Figure 2.8 A global policy for sustainability

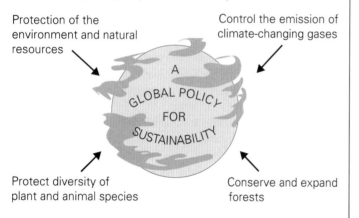

Protection of the environment and natural resources

Control the emission of climate-changing gases

Protect diversity of plant and animal species

Conserve and expand forests

Case Study
Environmental rules and industrial relations attract German investment

German companies, led by Hoechst, Bayer and BASF, account for around 7 per cent of the UK chemical industry's £32 billion annual turnover, and their share is rising. The German–British Chamber of Commerce expects more German *investment* to enter the UK once German companies have accomplished their task of building their presence in Eastern Germany, following the removal of the Berlin wall.

A key factor attracting German chemical companies to the UK seems to be the more flexible and less prescriptive approach to environmental control. David Culpin of the UK Chemical Industries' Association comments:

'We're no less rigorous than the Germans, but where legislation lays down maximum quantities of an effluent that may be emitted, the British approach is more qualitative and goal-orientated.'

He believes that this leaves companies with more scope for innovation and that the Germans find this a more

sensible regime to work in. Arno Balzer, chairman of Hoechst (UK), agrees with this and feels that, though Britain's environmental standards are similar to Germany's, applications for new chemical plants are handled more pragmatically and with less bureaucracy.

BASF's profile in the UK rose dramatically during the 1980s, its latest move being to acquire ICI's polypropylene production facilities at Wilton on Teesside. BASF is well entrenched around Middlesbrough, which contributes strongly to the company's £700 million annual turnover in the UK.

All three companies report encouraging results from their UK operations. But what are the pluses and minuses of working in Britain? As well as environmental rules, they cite *industrial relations* as a real plus. However, on the downside they refer to high energy costs, lack of a coordinated infrastructure – particularly in contrast to the extensive German railway network linking industrial plants – and poor training facilities.

Questions for discussion

1 *The way in which the UK has developed and interprets environmental standards clearly has the capability of attracting inward investment. Discuss the pros and cons of this type of investment for the UK.*
2 *How good is industry in the UK at satisfying the aspirations of external stakeholders? Identify particular instances of public relations and other activities designed to communicate with and inform various sectors of the public.*
3 *Discuss briefly the importance of the critical points made about the UK as a place for investment.*

Further reading

- *Exploring Corporate Strategy*, 3rd edition, by Gerry Johnson and Kevin Scholes. Prentice Hall, 1993.
- *Strategic Marketing Management – Planning Implementation and Control* by R. M. S. Wilson and Colin Gilligan, with D. Pearson, Butterworth–Heinemann, 1992.
- *Management*, 4th edition, by Stephen P. Robbins. Prentice Hall, 1993.
- *Business Strategy and Planning – Text and Cases* by Tony Morden. McGraw-Hill, 1993.
- *Environmental Management Handbook*, edited by B. Taylor, C. Hutchinson, S. Pollack and R. Tapper. Pitman, 1994.

■ *The Green Manager's Handbook* by Kit Sadgrove. Gower, 1992.
■ *The Greening of Business*, edited by Rhys A. David. Gower, 1991.
■ *Handbook of Good Business Practice: Corporate Codes of Conduct* by Walter W. Manley II. Routledge, 1992.

■ *The Foundations of Business Organisation* by Tony Shafto. Stanley Thornes, 1990.
■ *Business*, 4th edition, by William Pride, Robert Hughes and Jock Kupoor. Houghton Mifflin, 1993.

3 Analysing the market

O n completion of this chapter students should be able to:

■ investigate and report on an organisation's position in its market

■ select and use appropriate data collection methods

■ identify, evaluate and apply analytical techniques.

The need for market analysis

It is unlikely that any business today operates in a complete vacuum unaffected by market forces. Business activities, by their very nature, are competitive. Within a dynamic environment producers may constantly be entering and leaving the market and, at the same time, changing customer preferences may provide signals for them to develop new strategies with different products and services. Some businesses will inevitably succeed and achieve or even surpass their marketing objectives, while others may not perform quite so well.

How can marketing analysis help? Organisations require information on which to base their decisions and develop their strategies. Market analysis helps them to:

■ identify the competition
■ improve their knowledge of consumers and competitors so that changes and trends can be identified
■ use trends to forecast future activities
■ monitor their market position and develop plans and strategies which provide them with a competitive advantage.

Case Study
Who are the victors of the 'supermarket war'?

The supermarket war has made the headlines for some time. The war has been marked by intense price competition, with the price of a can of baked beans falling to 7p and of a loaf of bread to less than 20p. While the margins of the retailing giants have suffered, consumers have reaped the benefits.

Somerfield, the former Gateway chain, is widely credited with starting the war with its Price Check campaign. Its rivals could not ignore this competitive action. Tesco quickly followed with the introduction of its economy Value Lines range. Others were forced to respond. Sainsbury launched its Essential for Essentials campaign which cut the price on 300 own-label products, and Argyll pitched in with selective price cuts and multi-save promotions.

Probably the biggest factor influencing the ongoing development of the supermarket war has been the rapid expansion of *discount stores*. The aggressive pricing of many commodity items has appealed to recession-weary consumers and has lowered prices across the industry. Kwik-Save plans to open more than 160 new superstores over three years. Netto and Aldi are believed to be opening about 30 stores a year and, with the opening of the first warehouse club in Britain – Costco in Thurrock in December 1993 – retailers have a lot to be worried about. A recent survey by Verdict, the retail research firm, showed that the price of an average basket of shopping has dropped by 5.5 per cent in a year, saving the average family £150.

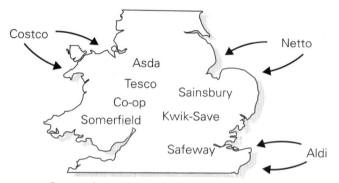

Some of the players in the supermarket war

The actions of the discount stores and continued new store development by the major chains have led to *overcapacity* in the market – supply growth has begun to exceed demand growth in many areas. At the same time the revivals of Asda and Somerfield mean that many large and capable players are competing for market share. Sir Ian MacLaurin, chairman of Tesco (Britain's second biggest supermarket chain) claimed that Tesco was emerging as one of the victors of the supermarket war by reporting a 4 per cent rise in like-for-like sales.

However, price competition has put operating margins and profits under pressure, and many believe that the next step in the war will see improved services as retailers try to differentiate their facilities in order to gain competitive advantage.

Questions for discussion

1 *What were the probable objectives of the retail chains during the supermarket war? How would these objectives influence their strategies?*
2 *If a major retailer had ignored the actions of competitors, how might it have been affected by all these activities in the market? How important was market analysis?*
3 *Who are the winners and who are the losers from all of these competitive activities?*
4 *Speculate on what might happen next in the supermarket war.*

By understanding the market environment, organisations can develop strategies which take into account market conditions. This market environment is sometimes described as the **micro environment**. It refers to all the factors which influence an organisation's activities in a market. This includes changes in the needs and expectations of customers as well as patterns of competition. A useful definition of a market is 'a collection of individuals and organisations who are actual or potential buyers of a product or service'.

The importance of the market should never be underestimated as it can have a major influence on the operational achievements of nearly all organisations. By their very nature, particular markets rarely remain static as they change and evolve over time. At the same time, the market is one aspect of an organisation's environment in which individual suppliers may be able to control partially the nature of change.

An organisation needs to identify and monitor the key elements of a market in order to understand its overall size, shape and development. Questions may include:

- *How do we define the market?* What are its key features, such as size and character, and what is the nature of the competition?
- *What do customers require?* At the heart of all marketing should be the ongoing activity of satisfying the needs and aspirations of customers.
- *Who are the target groups and how do we reach them?* The market may be made up of many groups or segments. Different distribution channels may be used to reach different groups of customers.
- *What strategies are used by competitors?* It is important to know and understand how the actions of competitors might influence the market.
- *How do we measure our performance?* Market performance may be measured according to a number of different criteria, such as the value or volume of sales as well as brand or market share.
- *Where is our competitive position?* An important feature of marketing analysis is an ongoing review of where the organisation is within the market, its competitive advantage and how changes in actions might influence the market shape and market share.

The marketplace

Whereas marketers tend to limit their definition of the market down to buyers of a product or service, economists argue that a marketplace exists whenever buyers and sellers come into contact to make an exchange. The marketplace communicates the wishes of buyers and sellers most effectively when these two groups are well-informed and there is no interference from outside forces. In some markets the buyer and seller may meet face to face every day. In some markets they may rarely meet and simply contact each other by letter, fax or messenger.

The key players in the marketplace are the buyers and sellers. When a buyer and a seller decide to undertake a transaction, the sale will involve:

- communication
- an offer for sale
- an exchange (usually goods or services for money or credit).

Figure 3.1 The marketplace transaction

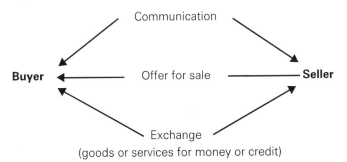

Buyer

Seller

Communication

Offer for sale

Exchange
(goods or services for money or credit)

All organisations, whether in the public sector or the private sector, have **customers** (who may also be called *users* or *clients*). A customer may be either a person or another organisation. A customer in a newsagent's shop is clearly a person buying goods on offer. In the public sector it might be an organisation asking for advice from a government department. You yourself, in your capacity as a student, may be a customer of a college, university or other type of institution. So, customers may be roughly divided into two distinct types: consumers and organisations.

Consumer markets

These markets are made up of individuals who purchase items for personal or domestic consumption, typically from *retailers*. Purchases within these markets can be categorised thus:

- *Tangible non-durable goods* have a short shelf-life for immediate consumption. Examples are food and confectionery.
- *Durable goods* have a longer life and are expected to last a long time. Examples are cars, washing machines and video recorders.
- *Services* are intangible benefits such as education, a haircut and a bus ride. Though these cannot be saved or stored, the benefits from a service may last a long time.

Organisational markets

These markets consist largely of buyers who purchase goods or services to use towards the production of *other* goods or services. Purchases within these markets can be categorised thus:

- *Tangible non-durable goods* have a pattern of frequent purchase but limited life. Examples are chemicals and stationery.
- *Durable goods* last longer. Examples are machinery and equipment.
- *Services* include intangible activities, such as those provided by an accountant or a banker.

Some organisations provide goods and/or services for both consumer and organisational markets. A motor retailer, for example, may sell cars to private customers as well as commercial vehicles to businesses.

Market growth

Market analysis is used by an organisation to identify the *size* of its potential market. Market size may be expressed in sales value or sales volume. If the total size of the market is known, an organisation can thus work out what *percentage* of the market it has (its **market share**) and then develop a strategy which enables it to increase that share.

The market analysis should also be able to predict *changes* in the potential market in both the short term and the long term. Few markets are static and, as changes take place, it is important to understand about potential buyers as well as existing buyers. For example, for the marketers of BSkyB it is as important to know how many households do *not* have their satellite dishes as those who have them.

If the market has potential new buyers, how long will it take to reach these buyers or to increase market share? In high-growth markets it is usually easier to meet growth objectives and these markets are often considered to be more profitable. Low-growth markets, by their nature, are more nearly static and might even be declining. As the market size approaches the market potential, growth slows and competition usually intensifies.

Figure 3.2 Market growth

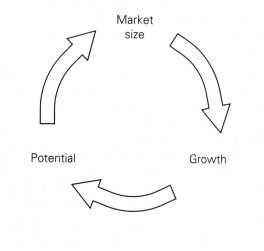

Case Study
Grocery shopping habits

The figures below, produced from a survey conducted by the British Market Research Bureau, show the percentage market shares of major grocery outlets between April 1992 and March 1993. The figures, in fact, sum to more than 100 per cent because people taking part in the survey were allowed to mention more than one outlet.

Sainsburys	27.8	Somerfield	2.4
Tesco	20.8	Leo's	2.4
Asda	13.3	Lo-Cost	2.2
Safeway	13.0	Aldi	1.7
Kwik Save	12.8	Wm. Low	1.4
Co-op	10.3	Food Giant	1.3
Marks & Spencer	7.8	Presto	1.3
Milk delivery roundsman	7.7	Spar/Vivo	1.0
Gateway	6.4	Cash and	0.9
Morrisons	5.1	carry	
Waitrose	3.0	Netto	0.8

Questions for discussion

1 *How, if at all, might this information be used by major grocery chains?*
2 *What other information would help to provide a more accurate picture of this market?*
3 *Do all of the above outlets compete directly with each other?*

4 *Discuss any changes currently taking place in this market.*

Looking at the competition

An organisation must at all times be aware of its competitors and the nature of what they are doing. Competitors are those who sell similar products or services in the marketplace, or who could sell similar products or services. In some markets there may be a lot of competition, signified by an abundance of products and services, so that consumers have a massive choice. In other markets competition may be limited and customers may only be able to choose from a limited range of products and services on offer.

Types of competition

Direct competition exists when organisations produce similar products which appeal to the same group of customers. *The Daily Star* is in direct competition with *The Sun*; and if you want to have a wall built, all of the builders in your area looking for that type of work are in direct competition.

Even when an organisation provides a unique end-product with no direct competition, it still has to consider **indirect competition**. Potential customers *might examine slightly different ways of meeting the same need*. Instead of buying a car they might buy a moped; instead of buying a bag of sweets they might buy a box of chocolates from a different supplier.

A third type of competition is known as **need competition**. We do not all satisfy our needs as and when they arise. For example, you may need to change your car but instead you might decide to pay to have your house decorated. Competition has therefore occurred between completely different types of needs and, for the moment, your need to change your car may remain unsatisfied.

Is competition a good thing?

It is frequently argued that competition is good for consumers and organisations alike. It forces organisations to act reasonably, stimulates the marketplace and increases choice. Organisations have to become more efficient and offer better products at prices acceptable to the market. Customers thus have a wider selection of goods and services and better value for money. Without competition customers may have only a limited range of goods and services at higher prices.

On the other hand, others argue that a lot of money spent on competitive activities such as advertising and brand building is wasteful, and that too much competition is harmful to industries which might otherwise be able to flourish. Another argument is that sometimes competition is not fair – cheap imports based on 'sweated labour' may be extremely competitive on price but for the wrong reasons.

Competition, however, thrives on *change* and provides consumers with greater benefits through better products. As new competitors and products come into the marketplace, market shares may constantly alter. For example, Spain used to be the most popular tourist destination but over recent years its popularity has been affected by other holiday destinations such as Greece and Miami.

Task

On a sheet of paper draw a grid like the one below. Identify and enter in the grid three *direct* and three *indirect* competitors of the educational institution you attend.

Complete the grid by writing in the strengths and weaknesses of the competitors.

COMPETITOR PROFILE	Strengths	Weaknesses
Direct competitors		
1.		
2.		
3.		
Indirect competitors		
1.		
2.		
3.		

Living with competition

Competition and market share may also be affected by changes in an organisation's *external environment*. Many of these changes may be beyond the organisation's control. The threat of a takeover, technological discoveries and high interest rates may all have dramatic effects on how an organisation behaves. Organisations have to be able to respond to changes within the business environment with appropriate measures.

If the competitive forces within a market lead to a trade war between rivals, then sometimes participants call for a 'ceasefire'. The competition can be so fierce as to make their trading unprofitable. To cite a famous example, the cigarette card war was ended by mutual consent of the tobacco companies in the late 1930s. Competition may also be overcome by taking over a rival – Iceland took over Bejam. It may also be reduced by engaging in joint ventures with rivals, such as Courage with Carlsberg.

When looking at an organisation's competitive position it is important to understand the opportunities which exist within the market as well as the other competitive threats. The ideal situation, which rarely exists, would be a large market with growth potential and little competition. In the business environment, however, where a market has growth potential competition is more likely to be fierce.

Some organisations view themselves as innovators within a market. They are prepared to take the risk of being first in the market in the hope that, if successful, rewards will be high (for example Sony with the Video Walkman). Other organisations may allow their competitors to 'test the water' first before following them into the market in a way which builds upon the success of the competition.

Five competitive forces

Michael Porter, a Harvard academic, has argued that 'the key aspect of (an organisation's) environment is the industry or industries in which it competes'. He refers to five basic forces which he calls 'the structural determinants of the intensity of competition'. These, he feels, determine the profit potential of the industry. The five forces are:

- rivalry amongst existing competitors (competition)
- the bargaining power of buyers
- the bargaining power of suppliers
- the threat of new competitors entering the industry
- the threat of substitute products.

Porter argues that the strength of these five forces will determine not only the sort of competition a business has to face but also the profitability of the whole industry. Existing competition between competitors can be shown to be influenced by the other four factors (see Figure 3.3).

Figure 3.3 Competitive forces

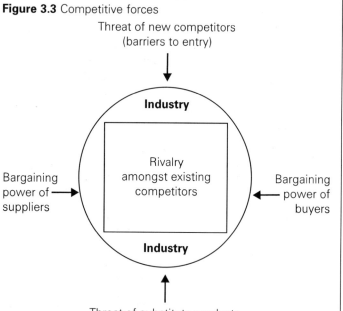

Porter's model may be used to improve an organisation's analysis of the nature of competition by weighing up the relative strengths of the other four forces. We shall briefly go through each of these forces in turn.

The threat of new competitors

A new entrant to an industry poses a threat which influences the market share and profitability of others already in the marketplace. In some industries businesses may constantly enter or leave the marketplace, particularly in areas like retailing. In other markets it may be difficult for newcomers to enter the market because of **barriers to entry**. These represent a series of influences which make it difficult for businesses to enter. Porter lists seven major barriers to entry:

- *Economies of scale*. If a newcomer is small and does not come into an industry with large-scale production, it will not benefit from economies of scale (see page 122). It will therefore suffer from significant cost disadvantages. This fact alone may deter new entrants to the market who have not got the investment potential to use technologies and processes which enable them to compete on level terms with existing competitors.
- *Product differentiation*. Existing organisations in a marketplace may develop a brand heritage and loyalty with which customers can readily identify. This 'product differentiation' may have taken many years to build up. Newcomers have to overcome such loyalties to get their brand accepted.

- *Capital requirements*. Start-up costs and investment in research and production facilities to set up in some markets may be extremely large. These may provide a huge disincentive to newcomers.
- *Switching costs*. These are the one-off costs incurred when changing the use of resources to develop products for a different market. They may include the retraining of staff, use of a different computer system, product redesign or changing the uses of machinery.
- *Access to distribution channels*. This is a market barrier frequently overlooked. Where channels are long-established it may be difficult to get products through to dealer networks.
- *Cost disadvantages*. Newcomers to a marketplace, irrespective of their size, may incur some further cost disadvantages, such as locational costs and the higher cost of supplies.
- *Government policy*. Certain regulations may limit the numbers of competitors in an industry.

Task

Identify the barriers to entry in the markets for (a) beer manufacture and (b) electrical retailing.

The bargaining power of buyers

Buyers will try to obtain the best possible deal for themselves. They will want better quality products at low prices and, if they succeed, they may force down the profitability of their suppliers. An organisation's profitability is therefore likely to be dependent on the bargaining strength of its customers.

For example, imagine the differences between supplying a market where there are a few customers and a market where there are many. Whereas in the market with few buyers each buyer may dictate product quality, terms and price, in the market with many buyers this is unlikely to happen as individual buyers will exert less influence.

The bargaining power of suppliers

Suppliers may also influence profitability by exerting pressure for higher prices for their products. Their ability to do this depends on the number of suppliers to the industry, the relative importance of the supplier's product for the business, the nature of the product, and the contractual nature of the relationship between the supplier and the buyer.

The threat of substitute products

Products and services produced by one industry may have **substitutes** that are produced by another industry. For example, coffee is a substitute for tea and vegetarian products may substitute for meat products.

According to Porter, where there are substitutes the returns of an industry may be limited by placing a ceiling on the prices an industry can charge: 'The more attractive the price–performance alternative offered by substitutes, the firmer the lid on industry profits.' According to this analysis, industries with fewer substitutes are more likely to be stable, and thus profitable, than those where products may be substituted readily.

Task

This exercise is to help you to develop your understanding of an organisation's competitive position. On a sheet of paper draw a grid like the one below, which refers to Porter's five forces. On the grid, make comments which analyse the competitive position of a large retail chain *of your choice*. Then, having developed your analysis, discuss other issues of which managers ought to be aware if they wish to improve their competitive advantage.

COMPETITIVE FORCES	Strength of forces		
	Low	*Medium*	*High*
Rivalry			
New competitors			
Substitutes			
Power of buyers			
Power of suppliers			

The PIMS study

A programme of research in the USA came up with another theory concerning factors that influence organisational competitiveness. The study was called 'Profit Impact of Marketing Strategies', more usually referred to as **PIMS**. This attempted to analyse the marketing factors which had the biggest influence on profits. Though a number of conclusions were drawn, the study highlighted the close relationship between *market share* and *profitability* (see Figure 3.4).

Figure 3.4 Linking market share and profit (PIMS)

Market share	Profitability
Under 7%	9.6%
7–14%	12.0%
14–22%	13.5%
22–36%	17.9%
+36%	30.2%

The PIMS research showed clearly that organisations with a large market share were more likely to be profitable. This concept was taken further by the research to show that a high market share and increased performance were the results of moving along a 'learning curve', so that the more an organisation learnt about its market through market research, the better it would perform.

Why are firms with a large market share likely to be more profitable? One reason is that with high market share and larger levels of output, firms benefit from larger production runs and, when unit costs are reduced, firms benefit from increased margins. Though the PIMS study showed that the best competitive strategy for a business was to develop policies which would increase market share, this theory has been criticised for making only weak links between the variables.

Summary

This brief analysis of competition has emphasised the dynamic nature of the marketing environment. If organisations fail to define and measure their markets in areas such as size, composition and consumption patterns, they may fail to spot changes as and when they occur. In order to analyse and measure new markets, so that problems can be dealt with and strategies developed, organisations need to invest in market research.

Case Study
UK targeted for attack

A wave of cheap and brash shopping is poised to arrive in the UK from America. It may have a dramatic impact on

British retailers and consumers. A recent survey identified 50 US retailers planning to use Britain as a springboard for their attack on northern and western Europe. Some, including Blockbuster Video, Toys 'R' Us and The Gap clothing stores, are already here and others are set to follow.

According to one survey, the American market is near to saturation and there is a realisation that post-recession UK is ripe for 'price-led, value-for-money power retailing'. The survey indicates that American retailers will bring with them new styles of shopping such as warehouse clubs, factory outlet malls and speciality stores. These organisations have transformed virtually every country's market they have entered.

This expansion may be fuelled by what the survey identifies as 'the international appeal of American culture'. Based on globally known US brands, this is promising new opportunities for western Europe.

This should mean lower prices for British consumers. One result may be to move the attitudes of British shoppers, many of whom still like to be seen to pay a full price for a good, towards cut-price products. There could, however, be casualties. Many US firms are hostile to unions. They have also been known to use 'predatory pricing' – selling at prices below cost to kill off competitors.

Questions for discussion

1 *Why might American shopping chains be seeking to enter the UK market?*
2 *Using Porter's 'barriers to entry', explain the sort of problems such retailers might meet when trying to enter the UK market.*
3 *Outline how British retailers should prepare for such an attack.*

Market research

In his statement to shareholders in the IBM Annual Report of 1993, Louis Gerstner wrote that 'no company is going to succeed without a clear set of tough-minded strategies grounded in a clear understanding of what's happening in the marketplace'. This simple statement about the need to understand the activities of the marketplace emphasises the importance of market intelligence. When planning ahead, though market research may not eliminate the risks associated with being in business, it will help to reduce them. As a tool of management, the purpose of market research is therefore to provide information which cuts out unsubstantiated guesswork and hunches.

Information requirements vary from organisation to organisation. Some view market research simply as an *ad hoc* data gathering and analysis function, but others see the market research function as an information centre for decision-making, providing meaningful information for planning and control. The information reduces errors in decision-making and increases the areas over which planning developments may take place. Market research therefore provides the information which pulls together the activities of the organisation and focuses them on the needs of customers in the marketplace.

Defining market research

Perhaps the most widely used definition of market research is that of the American Marketing Association:

> Market research is the systematic gathering, recording and analysing of data about problems relating to the marketing of goods and services.

We can break this definition down into its various ingredients.

- *systematic* – in other words, using an organised and clear method
- *gathering* – collecting appropriate information
- *recording* – keeping clear and organised records of what you find out
- *analysing* – making sense of what you find out
- *problems relating to marketing* – questions about potential customers and other details of the marketplace.

Another similar definition of market research is provided by the Chartered Institute of Marketing:

> Market research is the 'objective gathering, recording and analysing of all facts about problems relating to the transfer and sale of goods and services from producer to consumer or user.'

Market research should not be a 'one-off' activity which takes place only as part of a new product development. It should be ongoing. Marketers are constantly collecting and analysing information and feeding it through for planning, control and decision-making purposes.

What information is needed?

This will depend on the objectives of the organisation. Market research aims should be agreed with decision-makers so that specific information requirements can be identified. The more specific and accurate the information, the more successful decision-making is likely to be. Unhelpful decision-making may result from poor market research efforts.

A market research programme can have five stages, as shown in Figure 3.5.

Figure 3.5 Five stages of a market research programme

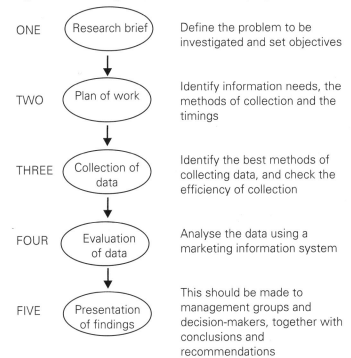

ONE — Research brief — Define the problem to be investigated and set objectives

TWO — Plan of work — Identify information needs, the methods of collection and the timings

THREE — Collection of data — Identify the best methods of collecting data, and check the efficiency of collection

FOUR — Evaluation of data — Analyse the data using a marketing information system

FIVE — Presentation of findings — This should be made to management groups and decision-makers, together with conclusions and recommendations

Research is not cheap, so it is important to ensure that what is undertaken is relevant to an organisation's information requirements. Specific uses of market research can include the following:

- Identification of new markets
- Monitoring of changes in customer needs and preferences
- Identification of new product opportunities
- Improvement of the quality of information available for tactical and strategic decision-making
- Increasing the organisation's understanding of changes in the marketplace, particularly of competitors' strategies
- Monitoring of the effects of political, economic, social and technological trends (PEST – see Chapter 7).

Market research may be either *basic* or *applied*. Basic research attempts to develop some aspect of the process of marketing goods or services. The information obtained may have limited influence on the management process. In direct contrast, applied research is specifically directed at obtaining information to assist managers in making key business decisions.

Market research may also be *proactive* or *reactive*. Proactive research deals with the new ideas of tomorrow,

while reactive research looks at what has happened in the past.

Information obtained from market research may be either *quantitative* or *qualitative*.

- Quantitative information involves amounts, such as the average number of customers who come into a shop at various times in a day. This information is **objective**.
- Qualitative data involves descriptions, which may be made by respondents in surveys, such as attitudes, opinions, reactions and suggestions. This sort of information is more difficult to categorise and measure, and because it is based on thoughts it is **subjective**.

Case Study
'Gramma's Concentrated Pepper Sauces'

Dounne Alexander-Moore's herbal pepper sauces sell at department stores and in supermarkets, yet until a year ago she was running her business from a kitchen in her flat in East London, and supporting herself and two teenage daughters on family credit.

Ms Alexander-Moore was determined to go into a business of her own when her marriage broke down. She started with a £3000 bank loan, guaranteed by her former boss.

Her idea was to market the hot pepper sauces with which, she swears, her herbalist grandmother saved her life as a premature infant in Trinidad. She made the sauces on her home cooker, and bottled them as 'Gramma's Concentrated Pepper Sauces', designing the labels and packaging herself. She won orders from Harrods and six prestigious department stores.

As a black single parent living in a rented flat with no collateral to offer, she still found it difficult to persuade any bank to back her.

It took two years before she found a branch of NatWest Bank bold enough to finance her for expansion into the supermarkets.

'I went for department stores first, because they had prestige but would not order more than I could supply.'

From her London flat she could prepare just 500 jars a month.

Last January, production of Gramma's moved out to larger premises. One of Ms Alexander-Moore's daughters works for her full-time, the other part-time. Her mother, who had sacrificed her income to help the business start, is on the payroll too, and a brother-in-law is financial director.

Production capacity is now 100 000 jars a month, and Gramma's are on trial at a chain of major supermarket branches. The sauces come in four strengths, priced from £1.90 to £2.50.

(*Source*: adapted from *The Times*)

Questions for discussion

1 *What sort of information do you think Dounne would have required before setting up this type of business? In your analysis, indicate whether each piece of information you mention would have been (a) basic or applied, (b) quantitative or qualitative, and (c) proactive or reactive.*
2 *The business having been set up and developed, how would Dounne's information needs have changed? For example, what sort of information would she now require to move the business forward?*

Sources of market research information

There are three broad areas in which market research can take place (see Figure 3.6). Existing organisations will have **internal information** kept within their own record systems. Secondly, a lot of information will already be published and available as **external** (or **secondary**) **information**. The third category of information will not already exist in any identifiable form and will have to be collected first-hand – this is **primary information**.

Figure 3.6 Sources of information

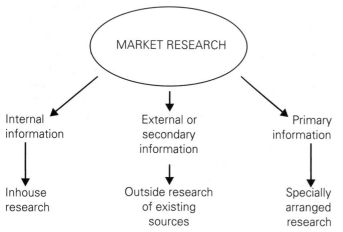

Internal information

Much of the information an organisation requires will already be held within its various departments, although at least some of this is likely to be out-of-date. The secret is to know where to find it.

Most organisations accumulate vast quantities of data which may be of use in the market research process. Its usefulness will depend on how well it has been organised and whether it is accessible to the researcher. For example, in the past it was often difficult to get regular and reliable *feedback* from sales representatives, because their paperwork was kept in their vehicles, was haphazard, bulky and rarely filed. This information was potentially enormously valuable because it represented feedback from first-hand experience with customers – it is often said that a sales force is an organisation's 'eyes and ears'.

Today's information technology, and databases in particular, have revolutionised the way information is stored, retrieved and analysed, and so dealing with internal information is much easier. Computers provide the means whereby information can be recorded in a simple manner, and contacts with each customer can be 'processed' so that information can be retrieved very quickly and then displayed in a way that is easy to understand. Techniques like this improve the quality of the market research process.

The internal data to be found within an organisation might include information about the following:

- *purchasing* – stock levels, unit costs, usage rates
- *production* – output, materials, labour inventory, physical distribution, overheads, machine use
- *personnel* – wage costs, efficiency levels, staff turnover, absenteeism, production details
- *marketing* – promotional and administration expenditure, brand and market data
- *sales* – customer details, product volumes and value, order size and market data, bids and quotations, reports from sales representatives
- *finance* – cost and accounting data, payment records, correspondence.

Example: Inhouse research by a bank

Each bank customer has a unique account number with a branch which has a code number, and these clearly provide a way of identifying and sorting information about the customers. The information, when sorted, can be held internally and used for marketing purposes.

The bank's information will undoubtedly cover the following points:

- date when account opened
- age, marital status and occupation
- address/area of habitation and (possibly) the type of property
- size of mortgage (if this is with the bank)
- pattern of use of banking services
- spending and consumption patterns as shown by bank statements
- credit rating.

This information can be used to place customers into different categories in order to target services. From such information it may also be possible to obtain answers to questions such as:

- What type of customers use different banking services?
- Who are the best, and possibly the most profitable, customers for the bank?
- How do customers use banking services?
- To what extent do customer requirements vary according to age and occupation?
- What type of customer is most likely to require services currently promoted by the bank?
- When do customers like to use the bank?

Internal information may also have a valuable second purpose, and that is to know as much as possible about an organisation's capability of fulfilling the demands within its main market as well as its potential outside that market. However, the scope of new projects may require other methods of research.

External sources of information

Internal information must be put into context, since on its own it simply provides a snapshot of an organisation and its customers. In particular it tells an organisation nothing about how effective its performance is relative to that of its competitors, nor how the organisation could be threatened by its competitors.

External information is more commonly called 'secondary data' because it is often to be found in published materials such as reports, periodicals and books and has been collected by somebody else. It can provide a broader dimension to data previously collected and can be used in two main ways.

Firstly, external information can enhance an organisation's existing knowledge. For example, postcodes help to group customers geographically. By identifying and labelling the characteristics of its customers, an organisation may be able to make assumptions about their needs. Two examples of useful external sources are:

- *Domestic socio-economic data* – Certain assumptions can be made about lifestyles.
- *Industrial classification* – Organisational customers may be classified according to the nature of their activities. Certain organisations can then be expected to have predictable demands for certain services.

Secondly, external information may complement an organisation's own information by providing useful comparisons with competitors. It may also help to identify markets offering potential and put performances into context by relating them to the economy/industry as a whole.

The main advantages of using secondary data are the savings in time and money in comparison with having to collect data first-hand. Compare the cost of buying a report or visiting a library with that of having to spend weeks planning a market research activity, preparing a questionnaire, training researchers and then analysing the results. Though secondary data rarely fulfils all of the information requirements of a project, it does provide a useful source of comparative information.

The main drawbacks of secondary data are that it may not be sufficiently accurate or specific for the project being undertaken.

Figure 3.7 Sources of external data

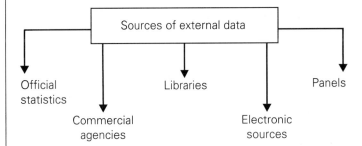

Official statistics

A wide variety of UK government statistics are available to marketers. The government's statistical service is coordinated by the Central Statistical Office (CSO) which publishes a booklet called *Government Statistics: A Brief Guide to Sources*. Government departments prepare statistics and the CSO publishes both a monthly and an annual analysis (*Annual Abstract of Statistics*). In addition, *Business Monitors*, published quarterly, provide detailed information about specific markets. Other information comes in the following publications:

Financial Statistics (monthly)
Economic Trends (monthly)
Department of Employment Gazette (monthly)
British Business (weekly)
Housing and Construction Statistics (quarterly)

Government information on particular groups of industries is identified by a code which relates to a **Standard Industrial Classification** (SIC). SIC codes run from division 0 to division 9 and within each division there are subdivisions into more specialised industries. The codes are frequently used in market research as they are the government's official way of classifying organisations and markets. The following two examples will convey the idea:

DIVISION 0: AGRICULTURE, FORESTRY AND FISHING

01000 Agriculture and horticulture (general)

01001 Arable farming and livestock production

01002 Horticulture

01003 Agricultural and horticultural services

02000 Forestry

03000 Fishing (general)

03001 Commercial see fishing

03002 Commercial fishing in inland waters

DIVISION 1: ENERGY AND WATER SUPPLY INDUSTRIES

11100 Coal extraction and manufacture of solid fuels (general)

11130 Deep coal mines

11140 Opencast coal working

11150 Manufacture of solid fuels

12001 Colliery coke ovens

12002 Iron and steel industry coke ovens

12003 Other coke ovens

12004 Low-temperature carbonisation plants

13000 Extraction of mineral oil and natural gas

14010 Mineral oil refining

14020 Other treatment of petroleum products (excluding petrochemical manufacture)

Another useful source of government information, particularly for organisations working in consumer markets, is **census data** published by the Office of Population, Censuses and Surveys. A full census is carried out every ten years, the last one being in 1991. This office also carries out two ongoing surveys which are published as *Family Expenditure* and *General Households*.

Case Study
UK economic indicators, 1987–93

Questions for discussion

1 *Study the chart of economic indicators on the next page. Comment upon the usefulness of this type of information for marketers.*

2 *How might this information affect the decision-making in an organisation?*

In addition to the UK government, many international organisations provide useful statistics and publications. Information comes from the United Nations (UN), the International Monetary Fund (IMF), the statistical offices of members of the European Union, and the Organisation for Economic Cooperation and Development (OECD).

For example, the UN publishes *Directory of International Statistics*; *Demographic Yearbook*; *Yearbook of National Accounts Statistics*; and the monthly *Bulletin of Statistics*.

The IMF publishes *Balance of Payments Yearbook* and the annual *Directory of Trade*. The European Union publishes various bulletins and publications, including *General Statistical Bulletin* and *Economic Survey of Europe*. The OECD publishes various surveys and forecasts, including *Main Economic Indicators*.

Commercial agencies

The supply of information is itself a very important business. There exist various types of agencies which collect information, compile it into reports and then sell these reports to anyone who needs them.

Figure 3.8 Nielsen regions and ITV areas

Estimated Population 1993

	(000s)	(%)
London	12357	21.8
Anglia	3629	6.4
Southern	4519	8.0
Wales, West & Westward	5797	10.2
Midlands	8565	15.1
Lancashire	7607	13.5
Yorkshire	6106	10.8
Tyne-Tees	2858	5.1
Scotland	5120	9.1
Totals	56559	100.0

Source: Calculated from OPCS figures

UK Economic Indicators		1987	1988	1989	1990	1991	1992	1993
Gross domestic product								
at current prices	£billion	423.4	471.4	516.0	551.0	575.3	597.1	630.0
	% change	+10.0	+11.3	+9.4	+6.8	+4.4	+3.8	+5.5
at 1990 prices	£billion	511.6	537.2	548.9	551.1	540.3	537.6	548.6
	% change	+4.8	+5.0	+2.2	+0.4	−2.0	−0.5	+2.0
Gross domestic product per capita								
at current prices	£	7437	8261	9015	9600	9953	10296	10826
	% change	+9.7	+11.1	+9.1	+6.5	+3.7	3.4	+5.1
at 1990 prices	£	8987	9414	9591	9600	9348	9268	9426
	% change	+4.5	+4.8	+1.9	+1.0	−2.6	−0.8	+1.7
Consumers' expenditure								
at current prices	£billion	265.3	299.4	327.4	347.5	365.0	382.2	405.6
	% change	+9.8	+12.9	+9.3	+6.2	+5.0	+4.7	+6.1
at 1990 prices	£billion	311.2	334.6	345.4	347.5	339.9	339.9	348.7
	% change	+5.3	+7.5	+3.2	+0.6	−2.2	—	+2.6
Retail sales	index	92.0	97.3	99.2	100.0	98.8	99.6	102.9
	% change	+5.2	+5.8	+2.0	+0.8	−1.2	+0.8	+3.3
Retail prices	index	80.8	84.7	91.3	100.0	105.9	109.8	111.5
	% change	+4.1	+4.9	+7.8	+9.5	+5.9	+3.7	+1.6
Population (mid-year est.)	million	56.9	57.1	57.2	57.4	57.8	58.0	58.2
Average earnings	index	76.9	83.6	91.2	100.0	108.0	114.6	118.5
	% change	+7.8	+8.7	+9.1	+9.7	+8.0	+6.1	+3.4
Industrial production (total)	index	93.7	98.2	100.3	100.0	96.1	95.9	97.9
	% change	+4.0	+4.8	+2.1	−0.3	−3.9	−0.2	+2.1
Unemployment (% of labour force)		10.0	8.0	6.3	5.8	8.1	9.8	10.3
Vacancies at jobcentres	thousands	235.4	248.6	219.5	173.6	117.9	117.2	127.9
	% change	+24.7	+5.6	−11.7	−20.9	−32.1	−0.6	+9.1
Interest rate (bank base rate)	%	9.74	10.09	13.85	14.77	11.70	9.56	6.01

Mintel is a commercial research organisation which, in return for a fee, provides a monthly journal containing reports on a variety of consumer markets – for example, bread, alcoholic drinks and insurance. The Mintel reports are up to about 20 pages long with information on market size, main competitors, projected growth, market share of main producers, advertising spend of main brands, trends, etc. Mintel also produces in-depth reports on certain markets. Another similar research outfit is **Euromonitor** which provides monthly compilations and special reports. **Key Note Reports** differ slightly as they produce detailed reports for business markets.

Research establishments may also provide useful information for specific sectors. For the food industry there are the Food Research Association and the Food Policy Research Unit.

A. C. Nielsen and **Retail Audits** are research organisations which collect data about retail sales through supermarkets and large chains and sell figures to organisations wishing to buy them. These figures enable suppliers to work out their share of the market, the sales of different products, and the effects of any recent strategy such as a price change or a promotion campaign. These *audits*, therefore, offer a window directly onto the marketplace. Regions for these audits usually approximate to ITV areas or combinations of these (see Figure 3.8).

Specific data may often be obtained through **trade associations**. These relate to specific industries and can be contacted using *Directory of British Associations*. Information is available from the Advertising Association, the Incorporated Society of British Advertisers, the Market Research Society, the Industrial Market Research Society and the Chartered Institute of Marketing.

Research of overseas markets usually involves contacting either the same or similar types of agencies. The British Overseas Trade Board (BOTB) helps UK organisations by supplying an Export Intelligence Service.

Case Study
Own-label *versus* superbrands

Backed by huge advertising budgets, 'superbrands' such as Coca-Cola, Persil, Nescafé, Pedigree Chum and Kellogg's Cornflakes have hardly been affected by supermarkets' own-label equivalents. Until recently they have been totally unassailable. Though own-labels have triumphed in fresh and tinned vegetables, and in other areas such as fruit juice and wine, in key areas where the big brands exist the efforts of the large grocery chains to capture a good market share have failed. In the superbrand product areas shoppers seem to be willing to pay between 20 and 40 per cent more for their favourite foods. The following list shows the top ten UK brands in 1993 (according to total value of annual sales – the figures are from A. C. Nielsen):

1 *Coca-Cola, £242m*
2 *Persil detergents, £236m*
3 *Ariel detergents, £231m*
4 *Nescafé instant coffee, £228m*
5 *Andrex toilet roll, £183m*
6 *Silver Spoon sugar, £152m*
7 *Whiskas cat food, £142m*
8 *Flora margarine, £133m*
9 *PG Tips tea, £130m*
10 *Walkers crisps, £127m*

However, with increasing competition in the grocery trade and reduced margins, many supermarkets have tried to attack the blue-chip superbrands with their own-label competitors. For example, Sainsbury launched Novon in 1992, their own-label washing powder. Since then it has captured 8 per cent of the £900 million detergent market in the UK.

Given that the grocery market is today dominated by a few large organisations, own-brand labels now account for an increasing proportion of sales – 55 per cent in the case of Sainsbury (see the chart). Industry consultants McKinsey, who carried out a study of this in 1993, predicted that the proportion of own-label products would continue to grow.

Questions for discussion

1 *Knowing the actions of the supermarket chains, what sort of information would the manufacturers of the top ten UK brands require in order to keep their market shares?*
2 *How might they use this information?*

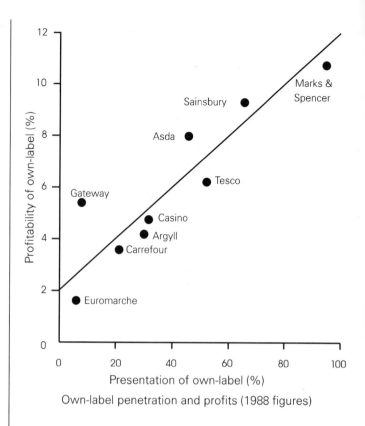

Own-label penetration and profits (1988 figures)

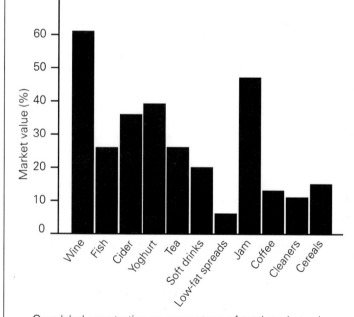

Own-label penetration as percentage of total market value (1987–90)

Libraries

Libraries are a rich source of information. College, university, town and city central libraries often have a wide range of reference materials such as those below which may be of use.

Libraries frequently have major data sources and subscribe to many business and trade journals. They usually also have a variety of sources providing information about the media. These are useful for organisations wishing to look at how to get their promotional messages across to prospective customers. *Benn's Media Directory* provides details of TV and radio companies, newspapers and magazines. *British Rate and Data* (BRAD) provides coverage of virtually all the media that sells advertising space, together with rates. *Advertisers Annual* makes detailed comparisions of advertising agencies.

Information about companies is available from many sources. **Kompass** publishes two volumes of products and services listed under the SIC codes mentioned earlier. **Extel** provides details extracted from the published accounts of all the public companies and from many of the larger private companies. The annual publication *Who Owns Whom* gives details of the ownership of subsidiary companies.

Electronic sources

Changes in the electronic transmission of information are in the process of transforming traditional reference sources and the ways in which information is handled. The two basic forms are **Teletext** which transmits information through the broadcast media and **Viewdata** which sends information via the telephone network. With further developments in the use of ISDN lines and the new era of remote databases, some traditional reference sources are likely to become obsolete or available only in electronic form.

Panels

Another way of finding out what is happening in the marketplace is to buy information from **panels**. A panel is a group of consumers who record their purchases and/or media habits, usually in a diary. The purpose of this diary is not just to record purchases but also to provide research information which relates purchasing habits to social status, occupation, income, demographic details and neighbourhood. Audits of Great Britain Ltd (AGB) produces panel data across a variety of areas. Some panels, such as those set up by the Broadcasters' Audience Research Board (BARB), are designed simply to see how many people are watching the various television programmes at different times of the day.

Case Study
Using panels to capture data

It was crisis time. A malicious product tamperer was at work. The crisis management plan was in full swing, and the client wanted to see how the public was responding. Thanks to new technology he was able to get an update on sales, by the hour. Across the country, 300 in-store PCs were tapping into scanning data as it was coming off the grocery store tills. Immediately the data was downloaded to Nielsen in Chicago, where the client could sit at a desk and watch how the situation was developing.

Such 'real time' monitoring is out of the question in the UK, where most companies are still struggling with a shift from monthly to weekly reporting. It is still extremely rare in the US. But it underlines the point: scanning is now a very old 'new' market research technology, but there's still a lot more mileage yet to be gained from its full exploitation. Likewise with other old–new technologies such as in-home barcode scanning and Computer Assisted Personal Interview.

The use of hand-held barcode scanners, for example, has revolutionised home consumer panels like Nielsen's *Homescan* and AGB's *Superpanel*. And increasingly these companies are realising that as well as increased speed and accuracy, there is further, enormous potential to tap. Opinion poll-type questions can be downloaded to the device and barcodes used for answers, with 24-hour turnaround. And, as barcoding spreads from packaged goods to areas such as magazine and newspaper readership, consumer durables and so on, so can in-home research.
Source: *Marketing*

Questions for discussion

1 *How might panels help to resolve market research issues?*
2 *To what extent is the use of information technology making panel data more valuable?*

Primary research

Internal and external data may not answer all the questions an organisation wants to ask. It may be out-of-date or it may not cover the right market sector. Then, to meet an organisation's specific needs **primary** or **field research** has to take place.

Primary data is first-hand knowledge, 'straight from the horse's mouth'. Information an organisation compiles from its own research is called primary. This type of research involves the collection of new data which is to be used for a specific purpose. For example, before a supermarket chain opens a new supermarket it will commission a local shopping survey.

Surveys are the most common method used to collect primary data. They involve contacting **respondents** to find out how they react to a range of issues contained in a **questionnaire**.

There are two types of survey, a **census** and a **sample**. A census involves questioning everybody in a particular market – but, unless the market is very small, this is unlikely to be practicable. Taking a sample involves questioning a selection of respondents from the target market. In order to ensure that the results of a sample survey are accurate, the market research process must identify a representative cross-section of customers. If the selection of the sample is fair and accurate, then information should be *statistically reliable*. If the sample is incomplete and does not accurately represent a group of consumers, misleading data is obtained – the sample is said to be *biased*.

Choosing a sample

Samples fall into either of two categories.

- **Probability samples** are so constructed that every customer or element has a known *probability* or *chance* of selection and the limits of possible error are known in advance. Included in this category are simple random sampling, systematic sampling, stratified random sampling, cluster sampling and multistage sampling.
- **Non-probability samples** are based simply on the choice of the selector and may be subject to error in sample selection. These include quota sampling, convenience sampling and judgement sampling.

Simple random sampling

With this method the researcher chooses the size of the sample required and then picks the sample on a random basis. The sample must be selected in such a way that every item in the 'sampling frame' has an equal chance of being selected. One way of doing this is to use a computer to draw names or numbers from the list at random.

Systematic sampling

Another way is to use systematic sampling, which involves selecting items from the list at regular intervals after choosing a random starting point. For example, if it is decided to select a sample of 20 names from 1000, then every 50th name (1000 divided by 20) should be selected, after a random start anywhere in the first 50. If 18 is

chosen as the starting point (possibly using a table of random numbers), then the sample series would start:
18 . . . 68 . . . 118 . . . 168 . . . etc.

Stratified random sampling

If some customers are more important than others, then simple random sampling can distort the results. Stratified random sampling therefore weights the sample on the basis of the importance of each group of customers in the market.

For example, if an organisation has 5000 small users of products accounting for sales of £1 million, 4000 medium users accounting for £1 million, and 1000 big users accounting for £2 million, a random sample of 200 would not be representative of the market. To make the sample more representative would involve allocating the big users half the sample because they make up half the total sales, with one-quarter of the sample to medium users and one-quarter to small users. The stratified random sample would then include 100 big users, 50 medium users and 50 small users, all randomly chosen from their respective categories.

Cluster sampling

With cluster sampling the population/customers are divided up into small areas, but instead of sampling from a random selection of these areas, sampling is carried out in a few areas which are considered to be typical of the market in question. For example, you might divide Newcastle into 200 segments and then, because of the nature of your survey, decide that you will sample only from a segment which contains at least one school, one church and one shopping centre, and any segments without these facilities are avoided.

Multistage sampling

Multistage sampling cuts the field to be sampled down into small units or segments in much the same way as with cluster sampling. The purpose of a multistage sample is simply to cut down sampling and research costs.

Quota sampling

Although random sampling, if properly conducted, produces the best results, it can be expensive and time-consuming, and in some situations it is not possible to identify a random sample. In these situations quota sampling is more commonly used. Interviewers are given instructions as to the number of people to interview along with certain characteristics – such as sex, age, socio-economic group or other demographic detail.

For example, if the interviewers are asked to investigate housewives aged 36–50, they will quiz every housewife 'fitting the bill' (possibly in interviews in the high street) up to their maximum quota. The problem is that there is no assurance that the housewives interviewed are typical of housewives in that band, and the statistical accuracy of such sampling is questionable.

Convenience and judgement sampling

Convenience sampling involves gathering information from anybody available for the interviewer to survey, no matter what their background. Judgement sampling involves selection of the respondents by the interviewer based on his or her judgement that they seemed to be representative of the group of consumers in the market being researched.

Preparing a questionnaire

When the sampling issues have been settled, a questionnaire must be designed. This is a systematic list of questions designed to obtain information from people about:

- specific events
- their attitudes
- their values
- their beliefs.

Questionnaire design is probably the most crucial part of the survey. Although it is easy to make up questions, it is very difficult to produce a good questionnaire – and a badly designed questionnaire may lead to biased results. For example, if people completing the questionnaire are unaware of its purpose they may place the wrong emphasis on the questions.

Another problem may arise if very few completed forms are returned, or if those returned are only partially completed. In addition, if the questionnaire is being administered by an interviewer, there is always the danger that the interviewer may misinterpret the questions and introduce his or her own personal bias in a way which prompts certain answers from respondents.

A good questionnaire will:

- ask questions which relate directly to information needs
- not ask too many questions
- not ask leading or intimate questions
- fit questions into a logical sequence
- use the language of the target group
- not use questions which are ambiguous
- avoid questions on sexuality, politics and religion unless these are highly relevant.

Sequencing the questions logically is very important. It may be useful to start with a few factual questions which are easy to respond to. These may be followed up by some form of multiple-choice questions before introducing questions which require the respondent to think about the issues being researched. The

questionnaire may be closed with 'filter questions' which help to locate the respondent in the sampling frame.

It is useful to test or **pilot** the questionnaire before the full research process is undertaken. As well as identifying any errors in the questionnaire, a pilot study will help to determine whether it will meet the research objectives.

Case Study
Customer survey

Read through the four-page questionnaire reproduced on pages 48–51.

Questions for discussion

1 *What are the likely objectives of this piece of research?*
2 *How has the questionnaire been structured? Refer to question types (open/closed etc.) and whether answers are likely to be quantitative or qualitative in nature.*
3 *How easy would it be to analyse information from this questionnaire?*

Administering a questionnaire

There are three main ways of using a questionnaire:

- with face-to-face interviews
- by telephone
- through the post.

Face-to-face tends to be the best form of contact. It allows two-way communication between the researcher and the respondent and may allow an experienced researcher to glean more detailed and sensitive information. It is also flexible, and so gestures, facial expressions and other signs may be noted. A questionnaire put to a person in the street is likely to be less friendly and detailed than a group discussion in a home. A street interview is brief, impersonal and uses a broadly defined sample group, whereas a home discussion can be exactly the opposite – detailed, personal and with a tightly defined sample group. One problem with face-to-face interviews is that, because of the nature of the interaction between the interviewer and the respondent, there is the risk that some of the responses become biased.

Telephone interviewing is usually more appropriate for business surveys as the respondents are often busy people and unavailable for discussion. However, this method is often regarded as intrusive since it catches people unawares, especially in the home. This means that the respondent can start the interview with a negative

1994
CUSTOMER SURVEY

Please take a few moments to complete this customer survey – we will be using the results to help us develop our products in response to your needs.

As you'll see there are some general topics concerning your computer but also some specific sections about the way you use our software.

If there are issues we haven't covered or if you would like to go into greater detail on any particular area please include a separate sheet with your comments.

Lastly, I should like to emphasise that the information you provide is being used solely for our own product development and WILL NOT be sold or passed on to any third parties.

Thanking you in advance for taking the time to complete the questionnaire.

Customer Services Manager

① Your hardware specifications
Thinking of the PC which you use to run your software programs, please confirm your machine specifications.

PROCESSOR TYPE
☐ 286   ☐ 386   ☐ 486   ☐ sx   ☐ dx
☐ 25Mhz   ☐ 33Mhz   ☐ 50Mhz   ☐ 66Mhz

HARD DISK DRIVE CAPACITY
☐ 40MB   ☐ 80MB   ☐ 100MB   ☐ 120MB   ☐ 170MB
☐ 200MB   ☐ OTHER

RAM CAPACITY
☐ 2MB   ☐ 4MB   ☐ 8MB   ☐ 16MB   ☐ OTHER ____ MB

OPERATING ENVIRONMENT
Which environment do you use to run most of your software programs?
☐ Windows   ☐ DOS/GEM   ☐ Both

PERIPHERALS
Please tell us which peripherals you use with your PC:
☐ Colour Screen   ☐ CD-ROM Drive
☐ Colour Printer   ☐ Fax Card or Modem
☐ Black & White Scanner   ☐ Sound Card
☐ Colour Scanner

Which, if any, of the following are you planning to buy this year?
☐ Colour Screen   ☐ CD-ROM Drive
☐ Colour Printer   ☐ Fax Card or Modem
☐ Black & White Scanner   ☐ Sound Card
☐ Colour Scanner

Where is your machine located?
☐ At work   ☐ At school/college
☐ At home – working from home   ☐ At home – for personal use

Please tick below, if you also have access to another PC
☐ At home   ☐ At school/college   ☐ At Work

② Your programs
Which of our software programs are you currently using?

DESKTOP PUBLISHING
☐ Pressoft for Windows   ☐ Timesoft Publisher for Windows
☐ Pressoft for DOS   ☐ Timesoft Publisher DOS/GEM

ILLUSTRATION/GRAPHICS
☐ Designsoft ver. 1   ☐ Designsoft ver. 2

③ Computer experience
How much experience of computing have you had?
☐ Just starting   ☐ 2 to 3 years
☐ Less than 6 months   ☐ 4 to 5 years
☐ 6 to 12 months   ☐ Over 5 years

④ **How you use your computer**

How often do you use your computer?

DESKTOP PUBLISHING

☐ Every day ☐ Once a week

☐ Several times a week

Please tick which types of software you have loaded on your machine and how often you use them.

☐ **Desktop Publishing**
 ☐ All the time ☐ Regularly ☐ Occasionally ☐ Never

☐ **Graphics**
 ☐ All the time ☐ Regularly ☐ Occasionally ☐ Never

☐ **Presentation Graphics (Charting etc.)**
 ☐ All the time ☐ Regularly ☐ Occasionally ☐ Never

☐ **Photo/Image Editing**
 ☐ All the time ☐ Regularly ☐ Occasionally ☐ Never

☐ **Word Processing**
 ☐ All the time ☐ Regularly ☐ Occasionally ☐ Never

☐ **Spreadsheet**
 ☐ All the time ☐ Regularly ☐ Occasionally ☐ Never

☐ **Database**
 ☐ All the time ☐ Regularly ☐ Occasionally ☐ Never

☐ **Games/Entertainment**
 ☐ All the time ☐ Regularly ☐ Occasionally ☐ Never

☐ **Specific task programs**
 ☐ All the time ☐ Regularly ☐ Occasionally ☐ Never

Have you bought any upgrades to your programs in the last 12 months?

☐ Yes – if so please name them below ☐ No

Have you bought any brand new (i.e. not upgrade) software programs in the last 12 months?

☐ Yes – if so please name them below ☐ No

⑤ **Learning to use your software**

Which was the first software program that you learnt to use?

Name of the Program:

Please tell us why you chose to learn this program first:

Have any programs proved difficult to learn?

Please name them:

Have you found any programs particularly easy to learn?

Please name them:

When learning new programs which of the following would you tend to do (please tick more than one option if you prefer).

☐ Just start the program and have a go at using it.

☐ Work through the 'getting started' tutorials.

☐ Read the manual before starting.

☐ Read the manual if you come up against specific problems.

☐ Read the manual as a last resort.

⑥ **If you own both a Desktop Publishing and a Graphics program please answer the following section:**

Did you buy both programs at the same time?

☐ Yes ☐ No

If you did not buy the programs together which did you buy first?

☐ Desktop Publishing ☐ Graphics

When you are creating documents how often do you use the desktop publishing and graphics programs together?

☐ All the time

☐ Regularly

☐ Occasionally

☐ Never **(please go to section 7)**

Please indicate which types of document you have created using both programs together:

☐ Advertisements

☐ Brochures (multiple sheets of paper)

☐ Forms

☐ Invitations

☐ Leaflets (single sheets of paper)

☐ Newsletters

☐ Posters

☐ Reports and Presentations

☐ Stationery

☐ Other – please make a note of these below

⑦ If you own a copy of Timesoft Publisher or Pressoft please answer the following section

Did you buy your DTP program to produce a particular type of document?

☐ Yes – please note the type of document you wanted to create below:

```
[                                                    ]
```

☐ No – I wanted to use the program to create a wide variety of document styles.

☐ No – The program was supplied free with the computer I bought.

THE TYPES OF DOCUMENT YOU CREATE

Please tick which types of document you have created using your DTP program and how often you create each type.

☐ **Advertisements**
  ☐ All the time ☐ Regularly ☐ Occasionally ☐ Never

☐ **Brochures** (multiple sheets of paper)
  ☐ All the time ☐ Regularly ☐ Occasionally ☐ Never

☐ **Certificates**
  ☐ All the time ☐ Regularly ☐ Occasionally ☐ Never

☐ **Fax Cover Sheets**
  ☐ All the time ☐ Regularly ☐ Occasionally ☐ Never

☐ **Forms**
  ☐ All the time ☐ Regularly ☐ Occasionally ☐ Never

☐ **Invitations**
  ☐ All the time ☐ Regularly ☐ Occasionally ☐ Never

☐ **Letters**
  ☐ All the time ☐ Regularly ☐ Occasionally ☐ Never

☐ **Leaflets** (single sheets of paper)
  ☐ All the time ☐ Regularly ☐ Occasionally ☐ Never

☐ **Memorandum**
  ☐ All the time ☐ Regularly ☐ Occasionally ☐ Never

☐ **Menus or Price Lists**
  ☐ All the time ☐ Regularly ☐ Occasionally ☐ Never

☐ **Newsletters**
  ☐ All the time ☐ Regularly ☐ Occasionally ☐ Never

☐ **Posters**
  ☐ All the time ☐ Regularly ☐ Occasionally ☐ Never

☐ **Presentations** – E.g. OHP slides
  ☐ All the time ☐ Regularly ☐ Occasionally ☐ Never

☐ **Reports and Long Documents**
  ☐ All the time ☐ Regularly ☐ Occasionally ☐ Never

☐ **Stationery** – E.g. letterheads or compliments slips
  ☐ All the time ☐ Regularly ☐ Occasionally ☐ Never

☐ **Other** – please make a note of these below
  ☐ All the time ☐ Regularly ☐ Occasionally ☐ Never

```
[                                                    ]
```

Have you found it difficult to produce any particular type of document?

☐ Yes   ☐ No

If so please make a note of the type of document. Is there a new or improved feature which we could offer to help?

```
[                                                    ]
```

THE PROGRAM FEATURES YOU USE

Which of the following features do you normally use when working with your DTP program?

Please tick those you use.

☐ Clipart   ☐ Different Fonts
☐ Drawing Tools   ☐ Text Runaround
☐ Spell Checker   ☐ Define Borders
☐ Autoflow Text   ☐ Thesaurus
☐ Tabs   ☐ Importing Text
☐ Templates   ☐ Send Frames to Front or Back
☐ Frame Alignment   ☐ Frame Tints
☐ Keypad   ☐ Search & Replace Words
☐ Text Font & Size   ☐ Automatic Back-up
☐ DTP File Compression   ☐ Kerning
☐ Crop Picture   ☐ Text Expansion/Compression
☐ Frame Borders   ☐ Help
☐ Name Text   ☐ Column Guides
☐ Headers & Footers   ☐ Page Insert or Delete

Would you like to see specific improvements to any of the features listed above? If so please list up to 3 features which you feel we should improve.

```
1.

2.

3.
```

Looking to the future which brand new features do you feel would be most useful to you? Please rank the features you would like to have – using number 1 for the most useful new feature, then number 2 and so on – *ignoring* any that do not appeal to you.

☐ **Instant Newsletters**
offering a range of designs
you simply 'fill in'

☐ **Table Editor** – an easy way
to create tabulated charts.

☐ **Mail Merge Facility** – so
you can personalise any
document you plan to mail.

☐ **Instant Chart Utility** – to create
instant charts and graphs.

☐ **Word Processor** – for fast text entry.

☐ **Dynamic On-screen Help** – to offer advice and explanations. on screen as you work.

☐ **Headline Designer** – will run through a variety of font and style options while you watch

☐ **Proactive Spell Checker** – works as you type rather than as an option when you finish.

If you have any suggestions for other new features you would like to see please include them on a separate sheet.

⑧ If you own a copy of Designsoft please answer the following section

Did you buy your Graphics program to produce a particular type of document?

☐ Yes – please note the type of document you wanted to create below:

☐ No – I wanted to use the program to create a wide variety of document styles.

☐ No – The program was supplied free with the computer I bought.

THE TYPES OF DOCUMENT YOU CREATE

Please tick which types of document you have created using your Graphics program and how often you create each type.

☐ **Advertisements**
  ☐ All the time ☐ Regularly ☐ Occasionally ☐ Never

☐ **Certificates**
  ☐ All the time ☐ Regularly ☐ Occasionally ☐ Never

☐ **Cover Pages** – E.g. the front cover of a report
  ☐ All the time ☐ Regularly ☐ Occasionally ☐ Never

☐ **Customising Clipart Images**
  ☐ All the time ☐ Regularly ☐ Occasionally ☐ Never

☐ **Drawings or Illustrations**
  ☐ All the time ☐ Regularly ☐ Occasionally ☐ Never

☐ **Forms** – E.g. Order Forms
  ☐ All the time ☐ Regularly ☐ Occasionally ☐ Never

☐ **Invitations**
  ☐ All the time ☐ Regularly ☐ Occasionally ☐ Never

☐ **Leaflets** (single sheets of paper)
  ☐ All the time ☐ Regularly ☐ Occasionally ☐ Never

☐ **Logos**
  ☐ All the time ☐ Regularly ☐ Occasionally ☐ Never

☐ **Menus or Price Lists**
  ☐ All the time ☐ Regularly ☐ Occasionally ☐ Never

☐ **Newsletters**
  ☐ All the time ☐ Regularly ☐ Occasionally ☐ Never

☐ **Posters**
  ☐ All the time ☐ Regularly ☐ Occasionally ☐ Never

☐ **Presentations** – E.g. OHP slides
  ☐ All the time ☐ Regularly ☐ Occasionally ☐ Never

☐ **Stationery** – E.g. letterheads or compliments slips
  ☐ All the time ☐ Regularly ☐ Occasionally ☐ Never

☐ **Other** – please make a note of these below
  ☐ All the time ☐ Regularly ☐ Occasionally ☐ Never

Have you found it difficult to produce any particular type of document?

☐ Yes   ☐ No

If so please make a note of the type of document. Is there a new or improved feature which we could offer to help?

THE PROGRAM FEATURES YOU USE

Which of the following features have you used when working on your own documents/images?

Please tick those you use.

☐ Text on a curve
☐ Skew Text on a curve
☐ Layers
☐ Colour Separations
☐ Custom Fill Styles
☐ Blending Images
☐ Sample Files
☐ Align
☐ Predefined Fill Styles
☐ Template Files

☐ Clipart Browser
☐ Mirror Tool
☐ Rotate
☐ Paste Inside
☐ Pantone
☐ Undo/Redo
☐ Custom Line Styles
☐ Pattern Fills
☐ Predefined Line Styles
☐ Text Tool

Would you like to see specific improvements to any of the features listed above? If so please list up to 3 features which you feel we should improve.

1.

2.

3.

Thank you for taking the time to complete our questionnaire

viewpoint, which questioning will not necessarily help to overcome. However, it is a cost-effective way of reaching people, and the replies received are likely to be truthful.

The level of response to a **postal questionnaire** will vary enormously, depending on its relevance to the reader and his or her interest. Response rates are often as low as 10 per cent, so answers are unlikely to be representative. The way to try to avoid this outcome is to ensure that the questionnaire is brief, succinct and sent only to those for whom it is directly relevant.

Other primary research methods

Another way of obtaining primary information is through **direct observation** – for example, looking at how consumers behave when shopping. Information obtained like this can help to make decisions about packaging, or influence the choice of materials designed to attract the attention of shoppers. This is important in the retail trade. Sophisticated recording devices can also be used to monitor individual responses:

- A psycho-galvanometer measures perspiration and this may be used in a variety of forms of testing.
- An eye camera may record reactions to visual stimulation.
- A tachistoscope exposes material for a short period and measures the response.

Opinion polls are often used to find out about consumer awareness, opinions and attitudes. Perhaps the most famous in this field is Gallup, but there are many others. Questions are short and are designed to find out how respondents feel about issues.

Discussion groups are an inexpensive method of obtaining useful qualitative information from consumers. For example, under the guidance of a chairperson, a group of users of the same product may be invited to provide opinions on its use. This method is often used in the motor industry. Car manufacturer Vauxhall states that:

'Like other manufacturers, Vauxhall has to cope with a rapidly changing world and to keep pace it begins planning the next model even as the wraps are coming off a new launch.

'This begins with the first of a series of 'clinics' where the reaction to a new shape is tested out on a number of pre-selected motorists. These motorists are recruited by an outside agency from owners of cars in the target group together with a small number positioned above the group (who may be persuaded to trade down) and below the group (who may be persuaded to trade up). They will be people who have no connection with the motor or advertising industries.

'Confidentiality is very important at this stage, so the cars are not badged and the respondents are not told which manufacturer is conducting the clinic. This also avoids any personal prejudices against a particular marque coming into play.'

Electronic interviewing is a market research technique based on an interactive system with a telecommunications network. A respondent need only be a television subscriber and will be able to respond instantly with a range of answers while a television campaign is being carried out.

Experimentation involves setting up a monitored marketing environment and then introducing variables, the effects of which can be measured. For example, it may be possible to assess the reaction of consumers to promotions within a controlled environment. In fact marketing often goes beyond this form of experimentation to test market products within a part of a market.

Psychodrama involves an element of role play in the research process. Respondents imagine that they *are* the product being researched and express their feelings about how it may be used in a series of dramatic exercises. The aim of this technique is to uncover subconscious needs which might not be identified through any other form of research.

Qualitative and quantitative data

One important thing to remember is that what comes out of market research is only as good as what goes in. The structure of the questions, the sample size and type, and the nature of the questioning should all be carefully considered before any project proceeds.

Qualitative information often provides the context within which the *quantitative* facts operate. The 'What do you think about . . .?' approach gives people the opportunity to offer a variety of opinions, reasons, motivations and influencing factors. A group discussion allows different opinions to be offered which will frequently lead to a consensus, giving an idea of the popular view. People enjoy offering their opinions on subjects as diverse as the current political climate and the taste of a particular margarine, and what this gives the researcher is an overall view of that particular audience's reaction to a proposition. As with all research, it is vital that the audience be carefully selected to provide relevant replies. For instance, if you are sounding out large cereal-farmers' opinions of their advisory body with particular reference to grain-drying techniques, the sample chosen for the research should reflect that and be composed of cereal-farmers with the appropriate acreage.

A useful perspective is provided by a **control group** – a second, non-target group added to the sample for comparison. This will often provide direction for the more precise quantitative research which will give depth to any particular aspect of qualitative work.

The process of market research helps an organisation to develop a clear picture of the effectiveness of its strategies, and gives it an opportunity to assess the size and shape of its markets. Quantitative information should provide a clear indication of:

- the relative success of different products and brands
- the influence and timings of strategies
- quarterly and annual sales and trends
- market potential
- current and potential market share.

This can be supported by qualitative information which provides:

- data to enable the organisation to establish the reasons for such trends
- opportunities for further market development
- first-hand ideas that might influence the development of products and strategies
- an opportunity to assess and evaluate the effectiveness of strategies.

In summary, quantitative data helps to produce an idea of the size and overall shape of markets and the effects of strategies on the demand for goods and services. Qualitative data helps to take this process further to show how goods or services have met the needs of current and potential customers.

Analysing market research data

Having collected data, the market researcher must decide on the analysis technique(s) to be used. The technique(s) will depend on the aims of the research. Statistical analysis of the data will allow decisions to be taken with greater precision and probability of success.

Central tendency

One way of analysing a collection of values is to use measures of **central tendency** – middle values. When we talk about middle values in everyday speech we normally think of an 'average'. This average is more correctly called the *arithmetic mean*. Two other measures of average or central tendency are the *median* and the *mode*.

The mean

This is quite simply the sum of a set of numbers divided by the number of items. For example, if sales figures (in pounds) over a six-day week were 165, 190, 185, 190, 180 and 170, the mean would be:

$$\frac{165 + 190 + 185 + 190 + 180 + 170}{6} = \frac{1080}{6} = £180.$$

Therefore we can say that:

$$\text{Arithmetic mean} = \frac{\text{Sum of observations}}{\text{Number of observations}}$$

If data, such as daily sales figures, is collected over a long period, adding up all the levels and dividing by the number of days may be time-consuming and prone to error. In these circumstances it could be useful to derive a **frequency distribution table**. For example, assume that a business's sales figures (in units) over 50 days are as follows:

5	6	2	6	5	2	6	4	6	5
5	6	4	5	3	5	6	5	6	5
6	5	3	3	2	4	3	2	3	5
4	3	5	2	1	4	2	5	1	4
5	4	4	4	5	3	5	2	4	5

These can be put into a frequency table as shown below (Σ, which is Greek sigma, stands for 'sum of'):

Daily sales levels in units (x)	Frequency of occurrence (f)	Level × frequency (fx)
1	2	2
2	7	14
3	7	21
4	10	40
5	16	80
6	8	48
	$\Sigma f = 50$	$\Sigma(fx) = 205$

On multiplying each value or daily sales figure (x) by the frequency with which it occurs (f), a total is achieved – $\Sigma(fx)$. This can then be divided by the number of days to derive the arithmetic mean. The arithmetic mean is usually shown as $\bar{x}$ and the formula by which it is calculated is:

$$\bar{x} = \frac{\Sigma(fx)}{\Sigma f}$$

In our example the arithmetic mean is 205/50, or 4.1 units per day.

The mode

This is simply the value that occurs more frequently than any other value. If sales levels over four days were 15, 12, 15 and 17, the mode would be 15 because that number had occurred more than any other in this period. If two or more frequencies occur the same number of times there is clearly more than one mode, and the distribution is *multimodal*. When there is only one mode the distribution is *unimodal*.

Finding the mode is more complicated when the values are not known precisely but have been found to be in definite ranges. In the example below there are five ranges:

Range		Frequency
At least:	Less than:	
10	20	5
20	30	12
30	40	18
40	50	10
50	60	4

The mode is now calculated approximately from the formula:

$$\text{Mode} = L + \left[\frac{(F - F_{m-1}) \times c}{2F - F_{m-1} - F_{m+1}} \right]$$

where L is the lower limit of the modal class (30), F_{m-1} is the frequency of the class below the modal class (12), F is the frequency of the modal class itself (18), F_{m+1} is the frequency of class above the modal class (10), and c is the class interval (10). Our estimate of the mode in this case would therefore be:

$$\text{Mode} = 30 + \left[\frac{(18 - 12) \times 10}{(2 \times 18) - 12 - 10} \right]$$
$$\text{Mode} = 34.28$$

The mode, calculated in this way from a frequency distribution, is only an estimated figure.

The median

When figures are arranged into numerical order, the median is the one in the middle. For example, data ordered into the array 2, 7, 9, 12 and 15 would have the number 9 in the middle, so 9 would be the median value.

In our earlier example of daily sales figures, there was an even number of figures (50). When calculating the median for a frequency distribution it is usual to say that the middle value is:

- $(n + 1)/2$ if the total frequency (n) is an odd number
- $n/2$ if the total frequency (n) is an even number.

In this example, the 25th number reflects a daily sales figure of four units.

Task

The chart on the next page shows how the government's Actuaries Department sees the UK population growing up to the year 2020. Comment on the population figures given for the whole period, using: (a) the arithmetic mean, (b) the median, and (c) the mode to support your analysis.

Questions for discussion

1 *Discuss how the information might be used by a manufacturer of white goods (washing machines, etc.).*
2 *Comment on other ways (if any) of breaking this information down into a useful form for a manufacturer.*

Time series

A **time series** is the name given to a set of figures recorded as they occur through time. The series may be plotted daily, weekly or monthly, and it is usual for the horizontal axis to be used to denote the time dimension.

Figure 3.9 A time series showing monthly sales

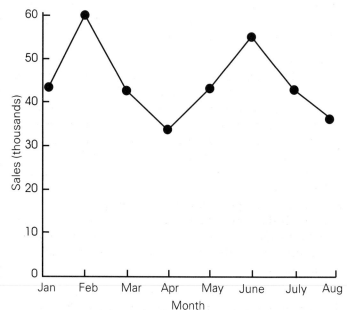

Population Projections for the UK		*1992*	*1995 base*	*2000*	*2010*	*2020*
Home population	millions	58.0	58.6	59.6	61.1	62.1
	index	100.0	101.0	102.8	105.4	107.0
Sex distribution	males %	48.9	49.0	49.3	49.6	49.7
	females %	51.1	51.0	50.7	50.4	50.3
Age distribution	0–14%	19.3	19.5	19.5	18.1	17.2
	15–29%	22.0	20.6	18.9	19.1	18.5
	30–44%	21.1	21.6	22.6	19.9	18.1
	45–59%	16.9	17.8	18.5	20.2	20.9
	60–74%	13.7	13.5	13.0	14.9	16.6
	75+%	7.0	7.0	7.5	7.8	8.7

If there is a clear trend, these historical figures can be used to predict what will happen in the near future.

Figure 3.9 is an example of a graph showing a time series. Here, the sales figures vary month by month, with troughs and peaks. The movement from trough to trough and from peak to peak is called a **cycle**. However, what we need to know is whether the sales, while fluctuating, are steadily increasing in the longer term. Somehow, we need to decide how to distinguish the *trend* from the short-term fluctuations.

To separate out a trend from a cycle we can use a statistical technique known as a **moving average**. Imagine that a business which sells financial services wants to keep a weekly moving average of sales in order to identify a trend. Its sales tend to peak every four weeks. The moving average smoothes out the peaks so that the underlying trend can be followed. The table opposite shows how this is done, and Figure 3.10 shows the data plotted as a graph. The moving average is calculated in three stages.

- *Stage 1* – Calculate the four-week moving totals using the sales figures from the second column. For example, 25 + 28 + 33 + 38 = 124. The total then moves by deleting the first week and adding the following (fifth) week. The second total is 28 + 33 + 38 + 34 = 133.
- *Stage 2* – Calculate the four-week moving averages by dividing the four-week moving totals by 4. For example, 124 divided by 4 is 31, 133 divided by 4 is 33.25, etc.
- *Stage 3* – The four-week moving averages show the trend. If the trend line in Figure 3.9 is extended to the right, this is known as a process of *extrapolation* which will help to provide a *forecast* of sales activity in the coming weeks.

One criticism of the moving average is that it tends to disguise the most recent changes to figures, as these are

Week	Sales (thousands)	Four-week moving totals	Four-week moving averages
1	25		
2	28		
3	33		
4	38	124	31.00
5	34	133	33.25
6	37	142	35.50
7	42	151	37.75
8	43	156	39.00
9	39	161	40.25
10	42	166	41.50
11	45	169	42.25
12	48	174	43.50
13	43	178	44.50
14	47	183	45.75
15	50	188	47.00
16	52	192	48.00

counterbalanced by figures from earlier weeks. The moving average, therefore, may not adequately identify any *sudden* changes in trends. To cater for this, *exponential smoothing* can be used. This uses a weighting technique to emphasise the importance of the most recent figures. The weighting is chosen at the discretion of a manager, depending on how much emphasis he or she wishes to place on the later figures.

For example, imagine a business in a typical high street. When a new shopping centre opens, they would expect to see more shoppers in the town and the later figures would then take on more importance. The new table shows that the weighting was increased from 1.0 to 1.1 when the new store was opened. As a result the exponential smoothing provides a more optimistic forecast than the

Figure 3.10 Weekly sales of financial services, showing a moving average

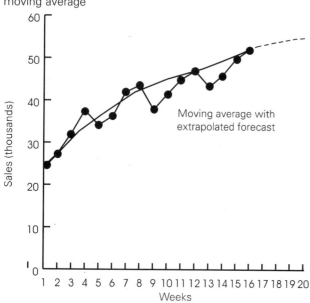

A **scattergraph** may be used to illustrate the relationship between two variables. It shows the independent variable on the horizontal axis and the dependent variable on the vertical axis (see Figure 3.11).

Figure 3.11 A scattergraph

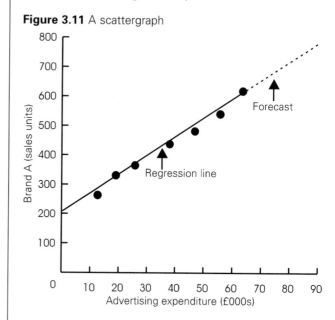

moving average. The new figures could be plotted on a graph similar to Figure 3.10, when a new trend line would show this.

Correlation and regression

Correlation analysis is concerned with the relationship (the correlation) between two sets of variables. For example, it might be used to assess the relationship between the use of a variable in the marketing mix such as advertising, and its influence on the sales of a particular brand.

Where the relationship or correlation between two variables is high, the better and more accurate predictions are likely to be. For example, look at the table opposite which shows the relationship between advertising expenditure and the sales of brand A.

If both variables rise, as in this case, then this is known as a *positive correlation*. The straight line or 'line of best fit' is called the **regression line** (the closer the points lie to the line the stronger the linear correlation). Beyond the end

Advertising Expenditure (£000s)	Brand A (sales units)
12	284
18	325
27	376
39	447
47	499
55	530
64	602

Week	Sales (thousands)	Four-week moving totals	Four-week moving averages	Weighting	After exponential smoothing
10	42	166	41.50	1.0	41.50
		NEW SHOPPING CENTRE OPENS			
11	45	169	42.25	1.1	46.48
12	48	174	43.50	1.1	47.85
13	43	178	44.50	1.1	48.95
14 etc...	47	183	45.75	1.1	50.33

Figure 3.12 Scattergraph showing negative correlation

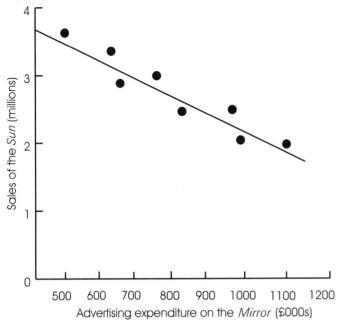

of the regression line it is possible to use extrapolation to forecast future sales.

In other circumstances it is possible to come across a situation which is described as *negative correlation*. Then, as one variable gets bigger the other gets smaller. This produces a scattergraph in which, though the points may again be close to a straight line, this line slopes downhill from the top left to the bottom right. As an example, Figure 3.12 shows what might happen to the sales of *The Sun* if advertising expenditure on *The Daily Mirror* was substantially increased.

Figure 3.13 Zero correlation

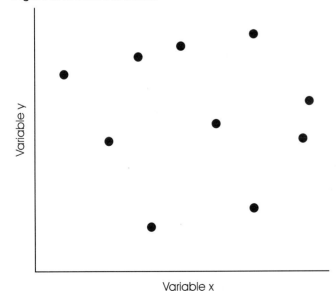

There are some situations where virtually no relationship can be identified between two variables. In such a case there is said to be *zero correlation*.

The marketing information system

Market research undertaken properly creates a considerable flow of information throughout an organisation. In order to coordinate this information and ensure that data is collected and used properly, it is important to set up some form of **marketing information system**.

A well-constructed marketing information system should ideally be able to identify sales levels, together with stock and output figures, and then analyse these together with market share details, trend data and information on profitability. The system should regularly generate:

- *internal* weekly or monthly operating data, such as sales trends, price information, production targets and budgets
- *external* data such as sales performances in the market, information on consumer behaviour lifestyles and attitudes, and needs of consumers for products.

The marketing information system helps an organisation to develop in response to its research objectives, and provides information in a usable form for a range of management purposes. This **database** of knowledge and supporting statistical analysis will then help managers to ensure that they supply goods and services effectively for their customers.

Further reading

- *The Effective Use of Market Research – A Guide for Management*, 2nd edition, by Robin Birn. Kogan Page, 1992.
- *Marketing Everybody's Business*, 2nd edition, by Dave Needham and Rob Dransfield. Heinemann Educational, 1995.
- *Quantitative Approaches in Business Studies*, 3rd edition, by Clare Morris. Pitman, 1993.
- *Business Fluctuations – Forecasting Techniques and Applications*, 2nd edition, by Dale Bails and Larry Peppers. Prentice-Hall, 1993.
- *Statistics for Business*, 4th edition, by D. Gregory, H. Ward and A. Bradshaw. McGraw-Hill, 1993.
- *Market Research – An Applied Approach*, 4th edition, by Thomas Kinnear and James Taylor. McGraw-Hill, 1991.

- *Basic Marketing Principles and Practice*, 3rd edition, by Tom Cannon. Cassell, 1992.
- *Marketing Research in Action* by Raymond Kent. Routledge, 1993.
- *Information Management for Marketing* by T. Kendrick. Routledge, 1994.
- *Qualitative Market Research* by Wendy Gordon and Roy Langmaid. Gower, 1994.

4 The competitive process

On completion of this chapter students should be able to:

- identify and analyse the interactions of market forces

- analyse features of consumer, industrial and service markets

- identify and describe key features of alternative marketing and other competitive strategies.

Market forces

The word **economics** originates from the Greek meaning 'household management'. As a discipline it broadly involves looking at the allocation of resources of all types. By studying economics we can understand more closely the things that happen in the world.

Economists assume that human behaviour is rational – that people always have reasons for making their choices.

- **Macroeconomics** ('macro' meaning large) is the study of collective or global decisions by households or producers. If we look at unemployment figures or income and expenditure totals for the country as a whole, we are looking at information useful for macroeconomic analysis.
- **Microeconomics** ('micro' meaning small) is the study of individual parts of the economy – for example, how people spend their money, what products organisations produce and how they price their products.

Macroeconomic theory is dealt with later in this book (see Chapter 5). In the early parts of the present chapter we look at an economist's view of market forces based on economic theory; in doing so we are looking at microeconomic theory.

Chapter 3, dealing with market analysis, distinguished between (a) the marketer's concept of the market which is focused on customers (the demand side), and (b) the economist's interpretation of the market which involves the interaction of two groups, both purchasers (the demand side) and suppliers (the supply side). Students of economics learn that both the supply side and the demand side of the market are important in determining the production, allocation and consumption of resources in a market economy. When we look at the interaction of these two elements in markets we are looking at the interaction of **market forces**.

Figure 4.1 demonstrates that where individuals demand goods and services, suppliers will respond to this market force by trying to provide them. **Demand**, in economics, is the quantity of a good or service that purchasers will buy at a given price, while **supply** is the quantity that

Figure 4.1 Market forces

producers will provide for a price. An equilibrium or balance will be successfully achieved when the quantity customers are willing to buy at a certain price matches the quantity that producers are willing to sell at the same price.

The link between a producer and a customer, through market forces, is the **price**. The price helps to express what consumers want and are willing to pay for as well as what suppliers are willing to provide. For marketers, price is a key element in the marketing mix and an important influence on the generation of sales revenue. For this reason the study of market forces is important, as it provides the marketer with an understanding of the operation of markets. Though in the real world the setting of prices is much more complicated than this, it does provide a series of principles which the marketer will find useful.

Power relations in the marketplace

The distinguishing feature of a **market economy** is that consumers are free to spend their money as they think fit. Consumers are free to choose one pair of jeans rather than another, Coke or Pepsi, margarine or butter. This freedom of choice is supposed by many people to support the argument that 'the consumer is king' in a market economy. The consumer effectively 'votes' (with his or her income) for resources to be channelled into certain goods or services rather than others. The clothes shop that fails to keep up with fashion trends will rapidly find out that sales fall off. But how much power does the consumer really have? Inevitably, there are a number of important restrictions to consumer power.

Firstly, individual consumers have only limited incomes. With the development of new market-based economies in eastern Europe in the early 1990s, it did not take consumers long to find out that without incomes they had very little power in the marketplace. This is true of any market economy – the possession of a sizeable income gives an individual far greater power to claim scarce resources for his or her own use.

Secondly, the power of consumers depends in part on the intensity of competition in the marketplace. If there are three petrol stations at the end of your street they are far more likely to respond to your wishes than if there is only one petrol station within 20 miles.

Thirdly, consumers have more power the greater the proportion of a commodity they purchase. For example, a wholesaler who buys half the output of a potato farm may be able to influence the size, type and quality of potatoes grown on the farm. The wholesaler may also be able to negotiate a bulk discount. A person who turns up at the farm gate to buy one bag of potatoes will have far less influence.

Fourthly, consumers have greater influence if they can organise themselves into buying groups. For example, if several retailers join together to purchase items they may be able to gain better discounts and other terms.

Fifthly, consumers have greater influence the more they know about a product. The greater the knowledge the better the opportunity to make an informed purchase from a position of strength. An experienced buyer is unlikely to be taken in by 'woolly sales talk'.

Finally, consumers are in a stronger position if they are supported by consumer-rights organisations and government legislation. Consumer and government bodies can help to spread information, and to insist on minimum standards in production and selling.

To summarise these points, we can say that consumers have more power in markets in which:

- they have considerable buying power
- competition exists
- individual consumers are responsible for significant proportions of all purchases
- they are organised into buying groups
- they are informed
- they are protected.

It follows that *producers* have more power when all or some of these considerations do *not* apply. For example, producers have considerable powers when consumers have little information about what is available, there are few suppliers, or there are many consumers. At the end of the day, one of the key factors determining power relations is the urgency with which a purchase or a sale needs to be made.

Demand

Demand is the quantity of a product that consumers will be prepared to buy at a given price over a period of time. There are three important features in this definition:

■ Individuals must be willing and *able* to purchase a product. For example, we may all want a better car, but only few of us may have the ability to buy one.

■ There is a direct link between demand and price.

■ A time period is involved. Over a longer period of time, if prices change, demand will also change.

The best way to demonstrate the dynamics of demand is to use an example. If the price of a printer for a computer is £500, John will be prepared to buy one printer. If it is more than £500 he will not be willing to buy one. If the price, however, fell to £300 he might be prepared to buy two – one for his home and one for his office. We can set out John's demand for computer printers:

Price	Quantity
More than £500	0
£500	1
£300	2

Quite clearly, as the price of printers falls they become more affordable, and consumers may be prepared to purchase them instead of spending their money on alternatives. In this example, therefore, there is an *inverse relationship* between the quantity demanded and the price – i.e. as price goes down, quantity demanded goes up. (Note that this is not the case in all situations, as there are some examples such as luxury items or shares where demand may increase as price increases.) Equally, one printer will be very useful to John, as will two. However, if the price continues to fall there will come a point at which John has enough printers, *and then further price falls will not entice fresh purchases at the same rate.*

In the example we concentrated on one individual's demand for a product. Some markets *are* made up of just a few consumers, but some are made up of a few hundred, whilst others are made up of thousands or even millions of consumers. We talk of a **global market** where demand for a product is worldwide.

Demand schedules can be set out by adding together the individual demands of all consumers in a particular market. For example, the demand schedule below shows the possible national market for a particular type of printer in a six-month period – the figures could have arisen from market research.

Price of printer (£)	Quantity demanded (p.a.)
1000	500
800	1000
600	10 000
400	12 000
200	14 000

The information in the demand schedule can be illustrated in the form of a **demand curve** (see Figure 4.2). For the moment it is convenient for us to think of

demand as fitting a nicely drawn curve, but of course in the real world demand patterns are not so simple. The demand for products varies considerably with fresh price changes. Some price rises will have little effect on quantities bought, while other quite small price rises may be critical.

By taking a single point on the curve – for example, £400 – it is possible to calculate total expenditure on the product at that price. (£400 with a demand of 12 000 product units would yield a total market expenditure of £4.8 million.) This is an important concept for the organisation and is shown by the shaded rectangle.

Figure 4.2 A demand curve for a printer

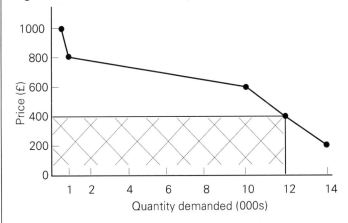

Elasticity of demand

As and when prices change, this could affect consumers, suppliers as well as other competitors within the marketplace. It is important for all concerned to understand *what will happen* if prices change. The degree to which these parties may be affected by a price change is shown by the concept of 'elasticity'.

Elasticity of demand is a measure of how much the quantity demanded of a good responds to a price change.

■ Demand is said to be **elastic** if the proportional change in quantity is greater than the proportional change in price. For example, if the price increases by 5 per cent and the quantity demanded falls by 6 per cent, demand is elastic.

■ There is **unitary elasticity** of demand when the proportional change in quantity is equal to the proportional change in price – for example, if the price falls by 5 per cent and demand rises by 5 per cent.

■ Demand is said to be **inelastic** if the proportional change in quantity is less than the proportional change in price – for example, if the price falls by 5 per cent and demand increases by only 2 per cent.

For all normal goods, a rise in price will lead to a fall in demand and a fall in price will lead to a rise in demand.

The responsiveness of consumers to price changes is critical for producers. We can safely conclude that producers may consider price reductions if demand is *elastic* and they may consider price rises if demand is *inelastic*.

However, as we have seen, elasticity varies considerably as we alter the price. We can use Figure 4.3 to describe the implications for a soft drinks manufacturer of increasing price. If it does this, at first sales will not fall off by much because consumers will remain loyal to this cheaper brand which is better than slightly higher priced (but inferior) substitutes. At first, then, demand will be *inelastic* as the price rises. However, as price rises into the bracket of prices charged by comparable and superior products, then demand for this brand will become increasingly *elastic*. Sellers need to carry out extensive market research to find out what will be the likely effects of raising or lowering prices.

Figure 4.3 Prices of soft drinks in the marketplace

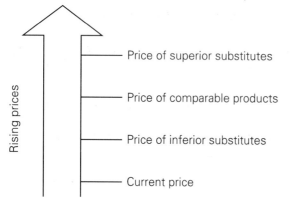

Case Study
Falling circulation revenues

1994 was the year of the broadsheet circulation war. *The Daily Telegraph* warned shareholders that it might take up to five years for profits to recover to levels achieved before the price cuts. The cut in cover price may have restored the daily newspaper's readership to above the one million mark – but at the expense of falling revenues from circulation.

The news from the group revealed the first indications of the damage caused by the broadsheet circulation battle. Profits were lower than expected and shares fell by 14p. City analysts were disappointed by the results from the *Telegraph*. Dividends had been held, and this was the first time they had not been raised since the company was floated. According to Stephen Grabiner, managing director of the *Telegraph*, 'Things are going to get rough for the rest

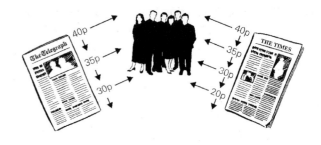

of 1994 and 1995.' But he added that he thought the *Telegraph* would be successful in seeing off competition from *The Times*. To assist the *Telegraph* in the circulation war, there was a surprise additional promotional spend of £8 million in the first six months, but this added to operating costs.

Although the cut in its cover price helped to restore much of the *Telegraph*'s circulation, this was at the expense of falling revenues. The severe effects of cover price reductions affected the group's results, which meant that the group had to engage in cost-cutting which involved some job losses. The only engine for growth was a strong recovery in classifed advertising revenues.

Questions for discussion

1 *Given the clear relationship between lowering its cover price and falling circulation revenues, how important was it for* The Daily Telegraph *managers to understand the influence of price elasticity in this market?*
2 *What other action did the* Telegraph*'s management take to improve it's circulation?*
3 *Using newspaper articles as a guide, look at another market where price seems to be a key issue. Comment on the nature of price elasticity in this market.*

Measuring elasticity of demand

Elasticity of demand can be calculated in the following way:

$$\text{Elasticity of demand} = \frac{\text{Change in quantity demanded (\%)}}{\text{Change in price (\%)}}$$

Demand is said to be elastic when demand is highly responsive to a small price change and inelastic where demand is relatively unresponsive to a price change.

The most important aspect of price elasticity is its general effect on revenues. As we have seen, total revenue is price multiplied by quantity demanded (sales). As price changes, sales also change, and therefore so does total revenue. The crucial question is: 'To what extent will total revenue change as a result of a change in price?'

In the example of *The Daily Telegraph*, even though as a result of the price change daily circulation went again above one million, the price change actually resulted in *reduced* revenue. The reduction in the cover price of the newspaper, despite this increase in sales, was not sufficient to recoup the lost income – and so total revenue declined. This would indicate that, over the price range where the lowering of price took place, demand was price inelastic because the increase in sales and the revenue it earned was not sufficient to make up for lost revenue caused by the price reduction. It is possible to use elasticity to show the effect of price variations and their influence on total revenue (see Figure 4.4).

Figure 4.4 Relationship between elasticity and total revenue

Type of elasticity	Change in price	Effects on total revenue
Inelastic	increase	increase
	decrease	decrease
Elastic	increase	decrease
	decrease	increase

Factors influencing elasticity of demand

Correct pricing is critical. If prices are judged by consumers to be too high then the lack of sales may ruin a business. If prices are too low it may not be possible to recover costs. A number of factors influence price elasticity:

- *The price of competitive products.* In competitive markets sellers have little choice over what prices they charge. When competitors alter prices firms may have to alter their prices too, particularly when prices fall.
- *The proportion of income that households spend on a particular commodity.* Most households spend a lot on housing, clothes, fuel and food. When the prices of items in these categories rise, households may be forced to cut back spending. However, there are items that are bought rarely and cost relatively little – for example, salt, food seasoning, shoe laces and so on. When these items rise in price, quantities bought will not be greatly affected.
- *The price of a good or service.* We have already seen that the current price is critical. If it is already considered to be high, then a price rise may lead to a greater fall in demand than if the initial price is considered low.
- *The necessity of making a fresh purchase.* When your watch is old you can still use it provided it works well – you do not have to purchase a new one. This is not the case with soup – when you have finished one tin you

will want to buy another one if you like soup. The demand for **consumer durables** may therefore be more elastic as a result of a price increase than the demand for **consumer disposables** such as foodstuffs.

- *Whether a good is a basic necessity or not.* Goods which are 'essentials' will have inelastic demands. We cannot easily do without items such as bread and milk, but we can do without many exotic and fancy foods that we only buy on special occasions. The same applies to many other commodities such as clothes and luxury models of cars.

Another very important factor influencing elasticity of demand is the time period in question. In the short term, consumers may feel that it is necessary to buy a particular good or service. Given more time, however, they may better appreciate the benefits of looking around and switching to alternatives. A product which at one time seemed indispensable may lose its sales as time moves on and new substitutes replace it.

Movements along the demand curve

For convenience we will now redraw the demand curve as a straight line in order to simplify the text (see Figure 4.5).

- If the price of a good rises we can refer to 'a move up the demand curve'.
- If the price of a good falls we can refer to 'a move down the demand curve'.

Figure 4.5 A simplified demand curve drawn as a straight line

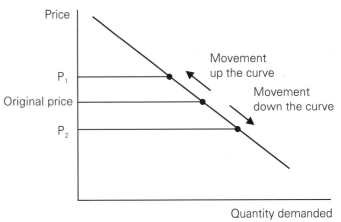

The marketplace is a dynamic concept, and price is not the only factor that alters demand. The behaviour of both producers and consumers may be affected by a number of other influences, including:

- the price of complementary products
- the price of substitute products
- changes in tastes

- changes in incomes
- changes in population
- promotional activities and publicity
- the weather.

Imagine the effects of good weather or bad weather on ice-cream sales. Good weather might encourage consumers to spend more time outside and visiting places, thus increasing the likelihood of their consuming ice-cream. Conversely, cold and windy weather might encourage consumers to stay indoors and not be in the market for ice-cream. These changes in demand are capable of shifting the demand curve bodily either to the right from DD to D_1D_1 in the case of an increase in demand for ice-creams *or* to the left from DD to D_2D_2 with a decrease in demand for ice-creams (see Figure 4.6).

Figure 4.6 Changes in demand for ice-creams

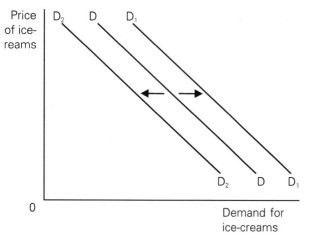

When we draw a demand curve we are assuming that only one influence comes into play at a time. Of course, in the real world many of these factors are changing at the same time. Some may work in the same direction, or at times against each other. However, it will be clearer if we look at them in isolation before looking at a combination of their influences.

Complementary products are those you use together. For example, a computer keyboard complements a monitor and printer, and a car radio is complemented by a car. If the price of a PC falls you may be more inclined to buy a printer as well, or if the price of ham rises you may buy fewer eggs.

Substitute products compete with each other. When one brand of soap powder becomes more expensive you may switch to a cheaper rival. The same is true for canned drinks such as Coca-Cola and Pepsi-Cola, for brands of petrol such as Shell and BP, and for newspapers such as *The Sun* and *The Daily Mirror*. In Figure 4.7 we can see the effect of a rise in the price of

Coke on the demand for Pepsi, whose price remains unaltered.

Figure 4.7 Changes in demand for Pepsi when the price of Coke increases

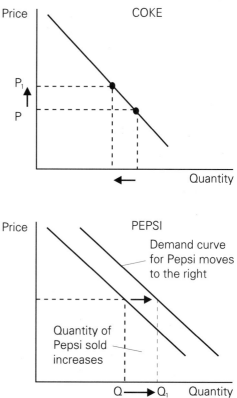

Tastes obviously affect demand. Clothing fashions change not only with the seasons but from year to year. Many of this year's garments will end up as cast-offs. This year's car registration will drop in popularity once next year's appears. The **life-cycle** of a product depends very much on whether it is in a fashionable sector of the market or in a sector that lasts for a long period of time. When tastes move in favour of a good its sales will boom, and when tastes move against a good its sales will fall. If it is quite difficult to think of products and brand names that are in decline, this is because many of them slip gradually from memory.

Income is an important determinant of expenditure. In a period of recession, high street sales will slump and expenditure on most goods will fall. This is particularly true of luxury items and incidental extras. In the boom years of the late 1980s, *niche marketing* developed. We saw the growth of firms such as Tie Rack, Knicker-box and Sock Shop. In the early 1990s, with a period of recession, the profits of these concerns slumped as consumers had to hold back their expenditure for more essential items.

Population affects the demand for goods. For example, population increases will increase demand for goods.

However, population tends not to increase uniformly, and marketers are more likely to be interested in the *demographics* and *distribution* of population. For example, they will be interested to note the current trend is towards an ageing population. As we move towards the twenty-first century we have a far higher percentage of people past official retirement age – so that products can be developed towards this group geared towards the channels that reach them.

Promotional activities involved with the marketing mix, such as advertising, and adverse **publicity**, for example, health fears about the product, may clearly influence the number of consumers wishing to purchase a brand.

For some products the **weather** is another factor influencing demand. Not many people will be bothered to buy antifreeze for their car in warm seasons.

We can see from the foregoing examples that there are many factors influencing demand and that these frequently work against each other. Demand in the marketplace is in a constant state of change. Businesses are concerned about how strategies, such as price changes, will affect the choices which customers make. By looking at elasticity it is possible to deduce the likely response of buyers to a change in price, and this is an essential factor to consider before the price change is made. Pricing decisions may then be linked to marketing objectives such as market share and a series of sales targets.

Supply

Supply is the quantity of a product producers are willing to make available and provide for a market at a given price over a period of time. There are two important features in this definition:

- It underlines the role of price in determining the quantity which suppliers are willing to provide for the market.
- As with demand, a time period is involved.

To simplify our supply analysis we will assume that companies seek to make profits. The profit from selling a good is the difference between the price at which it is sold and the total cost of producing and selling it. The quantities of the good that the company offers will therefore depend on the price it receives for each unit sold relative to the cost of producing each unit.

As price rises (other things remaining the same), the company will at first make a larger profit on each item it sells. This will encourage it to make and sell more. However, the company may face rising costs as it expands

production beyond the limit that it had originally planned (for example, the cost of paying employees at overtime rates will increase). For these reasons we should expect that companies will offer more for sale at higher prices, and as they increase their output they will ask for higher prices.

This can be shown by developing a **supply schedule** which shows the supply side of a market, for example for printers. Assuming that price is the only variable and that other supply factors remain constant, as price falls the quantity supplied falls and as price rises the quantity supplied rises (see Figure 4.8).

Price of printer (£)	Quantity supplied (p.a.)
1000	16 000
800	12 000
600	10 000
400	8 000
200	2 000

The information in the supply schedule can now be used to construct a **supply curve** (see Figure 4.8).

Figure 4.8 Supply curve for a printer at various prices

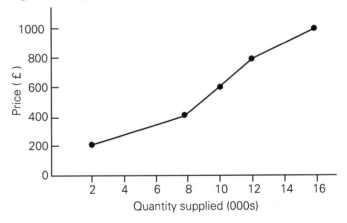

Elasticity of supply

Elasticity of supply measures the responsiveness of supply to changes in price. If producers can increase production substantially as price increases, their supply is said to be **elastic**. Conversely, if producers fail to respond to an increase in price, their product may be described as being **inelastic** in supply. Elasticity of supply can be calculated in the following way:

$$\text{Elasticity of supply} = \frac{\text{Change in quantity supplied (\%)}}{\text{Change in price (\%)}}$$

Supply is said to be elastic when the quantity changes by a greater proportion than the price change. Inelastic supply is when the quantity changes by a smaller proportion than the price change.

Factors influencing elasticity of supply

Time has a great influence on elasticity of supply. We can identify three time periods:

■ *The momentary period.* At a moment in time it is impossible to alter supply. In a shoe shop at 3.30 pm on a Saturday afternoon there may be only three pairs of size 7 trainers in stock. In business we define the momentary period as that in which it is impossible to alter both our fixed factors of production (such as the machinery or buildings in a processing plant) and our variable factors (such as labour and energy).
■ *The short period.* Between 3.30 pm and 4.00 pm on a Saturday afternoon it may be possible to rush extra training shoes to the shop from a local warehouse. In business we define the short period as the period in which fixed factors remain fixed, but variable factors can vary.
■ *The long period.* Because of a general increase in the demand for trainers, a factory producing trainers may expand its plant and equipment. In business we define the long period as the period in which all the factors of production can become variable.

We can illustrate elasticity of supply in different time periods. Momentary supply is represented by a vertical line, short-period supply by a relatively inelastic supply line, and long-period supply by a relatively elastic supply line (see Figure 4.9).

Figure 4.9 Influence of the time factor on elasticity of supply

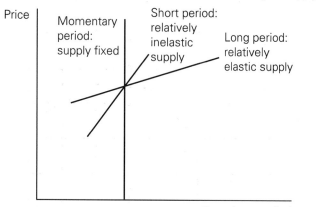

What constitutes a short or long period varies from company to company and from industry to industry. For example, it takes a lot longer to increase fresh flower production than it does to expand artificial flower production. Some products have an extended long term (e.g. coffee and rubber production), while others have a shorter long term. If you have ever grown cress on your window sill you will know that it can be grown within days.

Elasticity of supply also varies according to how close to **capacity** a company or an industry is running. If a factory is using only half its machines, it would be relatively easy to expand production. However, if the factory is already working at full capacity, then the company would have to invest in new plant in order to expand its supply.

Another factor influencing elasticity of supply is the availability of **components and raw materials**. In order to expand production it is necessary to increase inputs. If inputs are readily available, then supply will be far more elastic than if inputs are scarce. Another factor is the **cost** of producing additional outputs. If the extra cost of producing additional units is rising sharply, then producers will be reluctant to expand output in response to higher prices.

Changes in supply

In addition to price, there are a number of factors that influence the supply of a product. These include:

■ prices of factors of production
■ prices of other commodities
■ changes in the level of technology
■ producers' objectives
■ the weather
■ government policies.

If one of these factors alters, the conditions of supply are said to have changed. Changes in one or a combination of these factors may cause bodily shifts in the supply curve. The supply curve can shift in either a leftward or a rightward direction. A shift to the left from SS to S_1S_1 indicates that smaller quantities will be supplied than before at a given price, while a shift to the right from SS to S_2S_2 indicates that larger quantities will be supplied than before at given prices (see Figure 4.10).

Figure 4.10 Shifts in the supply curve

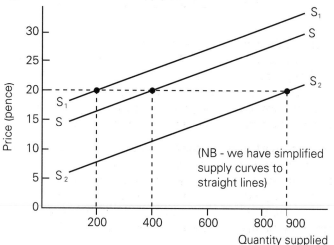

Prices of factors of production are important because production is based on the combination of factor inputs in order to produce outputs. If the cost of a factor rises then it will be more expensive to produce outputs. As factor prices rise, fewer factors will be used in production, and hence the supply of a product will fall.

For example, let us assume that an agricultural crop requires three main inputs: land, labour and chemical fertiliser. If the cost of one or more of these inputs were to rise, then farmers might cut back on the acreage committed to this particular crop. Conversely, if the price of one or more factors of production were to fall, then supply conditions would move in favour of increased production and supply is likely to shift to the right.

By looking at the **prices of other commodities** in areas of production, it may be possible to switch from production of less profitable products to more profitable lines. For example, many arable farmers have a certain degree of flexibility over which crops to grow. A shipyard can choose to build tugs, oil rigs or bulk carriers. If a particular line becomes more profitable, then scarce resources such as equipment, time and materials can be switched into producing it and away from producing other products.

Changing levels of technology means that more output can be produced with fewer resources. This means that the supply curve for a product may shift to the right. Modern technology based on use of computers and robotics has enabled a number of producers to produce larger outputs at lower unit costs – for example, in car production, newspapers and the processing of cheques by banks.

Organisations have a range of both **business and marketing objectives** and, to a large extent, supply will be seen to follow such objectives. For example, expansion may be a goal in itself, so the firm might produce more to gain market share or to increase its profile.

The **weather** may be a major factor in the supply of many goods and services. A number of products respond to changes in the weather, not least the appearance of umbrella-sellers at the entrances to underground stations in rainy weather! The supply of agricultural products depends very much on changing weather conditions.

Government policies may include further regulation of a market, or deregulation, or perhaps subsidies or taxation. Such policies may either encourage or discourage producers to provide products for the market and, at the time of introduction, may have a marked effect on the marketplace for a particular type of product.

Formation of a market price

In the marketplace the forces of demand and supply will interact to create a **market price**. In economics this is more usually called the 'equilibrium price' and is the price at which the quantity demanded equals the quantity supplied.

To illustrate this point, consider a fictional daily demand and supply schedule for fish at a small fishing village. When the price of fish is high, the owner of the only fishing boat will (we assume) spend more time fishing than when it is low. Conversely, consumers will want to purchase more fish at low than at high prices:

Price of fish (p)	Quantity demanded	Quantity supplied
60	300	600
55	400	550
50	500	500
45	600	450
40	700	400
35	800	350

This information can then be plotted on a graph (see Figure 4.11). If you study this graph, you can see that there is only one price – the equilibrium price – at which the wishes of consumers and the supplier coincide, i.e. 50p. At this price the quantity that will be bought and sold is 500.

Figure 4.11 Demand and supply of fish in a daily fish market

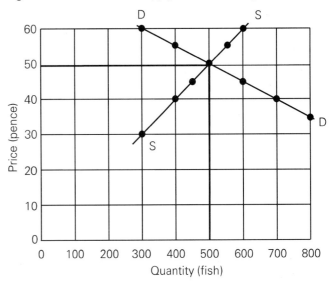

We can see that the market provides a mechanism for bringing the decisions of consumers and producers into line automatically, even though the two groups have different motives (the producer will want to sell at the highest possible price, and the consumer will want to purchase at the lowest possible price).

We can appreciate the process of forming an equilibrium price by considering two *disequilibrium* situations (see Figure 4.12). If, for example, we consider the price of 60p, we will see that the owner of the fishing vessel would be prepared to work longer to supply 600 fish. However, at 60p consumers would only be prepared to buy 300 fish – thus leaving a surplus stock of 300 fish which would go unsold. In this situation the owner of the fishing boat would lower prices and resort to working fewer hours.

Figure 4.12 Movements towards equilibrium

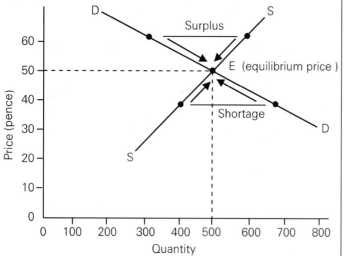

Alternatively, if the price of fish was pitched at 40p, consumers would be prepared to buy 700 fish. However, the owner of the fishing vessel would only be prepared to work long enough to catch 400. There would now be a shortage of fish – stocks would rapidly sell out and customers would try to bid up the price. This would make it worthwhile for the owner of the fishing boat to work longer hours.

This example illustrates the workings of market forces. At prices above 50p too much will be produced and so forces will interact to pull prices down to 50p. At prices below 50p too little will be produced, and so forces will interact to pull prices up to 50p. At 50p prices are just right and so there is no tendency to change.

This analysis is, of course, a simplification. In the real world markets rarely move in such a way towards equilibrium as consumers and producers frequently lack important market information which would help them to respond promptly to market changes.

Markets in motion

So far we have analysed the formation of an equilibrium price solely in terms of the relationship between price and demand and supply. This has been like taking a snapshot under the assumption that factors other than price do not alter but has provided us with an important insight into how markets operate.

Producers and consumers respond to price signals, and in this way their wishes and plans are coordinated by the market mechanism. These wishes and plans change regularly since, as we saw earlier, there are a number of factors influencing demand, and a number of factors influencing supply so that markets are constantly in motion.

Changes in the marketplace lead to adjustments by consumers and producers. *Demand and supply curves change shape and position*, and very quickly a new equilibrium position is established. However, this will only be a temporary equilibrium point because markets are characterised by change. Indeed one beauty of the marketplace is that it can accommodate changes.

Whenever a factor changes which affects demand or supply there are four basic changes which may take place (see Figure 4.13). These illustrate:

A – a shift in the demand curve to the right resulting in more being bought at a higher price.

B – a shift in the demand curve to the left resulting in a smaller quantity being bought at a lower price.

C – a shift in the supply curve to the right resulting in more being supplied at a lower price.

D – a shift in the supply curve to the left resulting in less being supplied at a higher price.

Figure 4.13 Changes to the equilibrium price

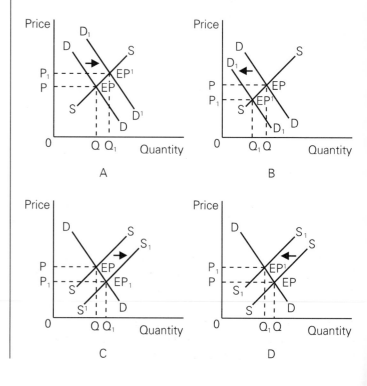

The best way to show how the market dynamics work in this process is through an example. Imagine that, for a variety of reasons, fish suddenly becomes a more popular dish for consumers to have – tastes have changed in favour of fish. At present OQ is produced at an equilibrium price of OP. Following this change in tastes the demand curve shifts to the right causing a new equilibrium of EP^1 where the new demand curve intersects the original supply curve. Equilibrium price, therefore, rises to OP_1 and the equilibrium quantity to OQ_1.

Now that this new market equilibrium has been formed, bad weather may affect the ability to put the fishing fleet to work. This is clearly a factor affecting supply which shifts the supply curve to the left. As we would expect, at the new equilibrium position of EP^1, the price of fish rises to OP_1 and the quantity of fish on the market falls to OQ_1.

Case Study
Hot chocolate

Coffee first, then cocoa: the list of new commodity agreements reads like a breakfast menu. Last year coffee-producing governments agreed on a scheme to withdraw supplies from the market if prices should fall too far. It has not yet been put to the test. Instead falling stocks and worries about this year's harvest have pushed up the price of coffee to $1.17/lb, almost double the average for 1993. Cocoa too has been rising of its own accord – to $1400 a tonne, or 50% more than it was two years ago. Now the cococrats are trying to come up with a feisty new agreement of their own. They too are wasting their time.

The producing and consuming governments who are members of the International Cocoa Organisation (or the ICCO as it is known, so as not to be confused with the ICO – the International Coffee Organisation) already have an innocuous five-year pact, signed in February. It contains vague resolutions to promote demand and stabilise the price – about as convincing as a promise to eat no more than one chocolate truffle. At a meeting in London this week the ICCO is struggling to give its agreement some teeth by drafting clauses that oblige producers to match their supply with expected demand.

What emerges from this and future meetings is unlikely to be worth the paper it is written on – for two reasons. First, the ICCO has only limited control over supply. Indonesia, the world's fastest-growing producer – and by next year probably the second-largest after the Côte D'Ivoire – has refused to join the ICCO. It is unlikely to join any cartel because production targets will be based on historic

figures – which is fine for countries such as Brazil, where output is falling anyway, but would penalise an expanding producer, such as Indonesia.

As for demand, the ICCO's exhortations look like a waste of breath. Nestlé, Mars, Cadbury Schweppes and other multinationals are quite capable of marketing chocolate on their own. One reason why cocoa prices are rising is recovering demand from Russian and East European chocolate-fiends. Russia now imports 100 000 tonnes of cocoa – four times the amount in 1991, according to ED&F Man, a trading house. With demand there still growing rapidly, world production should fall short of consumption for the third year in a row.

If governments are determined to help the cocoa industry is there anything that they could usefully do? Actually there is. Chocolate also needs milk and sugar. When they buy chocolate, European consumers pay more in subsidies to dairy farmers and sugar-beet growers than they do for cocoa. One more reason to wind down farm subsidies.
(Source: *The Economist*)

Questions for discussion

1 *Identify the factors affecting the demand and supply for coffee and cocoa.*
2 *Explain briefly how each factor identified might affect prices.*
3 *How might winding down subsidies to dairy farmers and sugar-beet producers affect cocoa sales? Explain why.*
4 *How typical are the dynamics of these types of markets?*

Other elasticities

Another important measure is **income elasticity**. This simply expresses how demand responds to changes in income. Income is an important influence on both individual and whole-market demand. For many people the size of increase in income over a time period will affect their ability to buy products. The relationship between increases in income and the sale of luxury products tends to be significant, particularly when contrasted with the sale of inferior goods.

In most years the total income of the country rises (i.e. the national income increases). As incomes rise so does the ability of consumers to buy new goods; people move into bigger houses, acquire bigger cars, buy a range of new gadgets, clothes and food. More expensive goods can replace inferior products.

Income elasticity can be measured by:

$$\text{Income elasticity} = \frac{\text{Change in quantity demanded (\%)}}{\text{Change in income (\%)}}$$

Normal goods are those for which demand increases as income goes up. Inferior goods are those for which demand falls as income goes up.

Another important influence on the price of a good is the price of other products, particularly if these products are either substitutes or complementary. **Cross-price elasticity of demand** refers to the relationship between the change in demand for one product against a change in the price of *another* product. It is measured by:

$$\frac{\text{Cross-price}}{\text{elasticity}} \quad = \quad \frac{\text{Change in demand for product X (\%)}}{\text{Change in price of product Y (\%)}}$$

For example, Pepsi-Cola is viewed as a substitute for Coca-Cola (or vice versa). If the price of Pepsi were reduced we would expect to see a fall in demand for Coke. In contrast, with complementary products such as bricks and mortar, if the prices of cement and sand – the ingredients of mortar – go up, then sales of bricks would go down as consumers buy less because of the change in price of the complement.

Market structures

Competition is a major influence on business behaviour. A firm's prices and many other policies may be determined by the level and type of competition it faces, and the degree of competition will constantly change. This competition will depend to a great extent on the willingness and ability of consumers to transfer their spending to substitute products. This in turn will depend on the answers to a cluster of interrelated questions, including:

■ Are substitutes available?
■ Can consumers obtain them?
■ Do consumers shop around?
■ Do consumers know what is available?
■ Can buyers switch to alternative sources of supply?
■ Are the benefits of changing greater than the costs?

The functioning of market forces will relate to the structure of the market and the type of competitive environment in which an organisation is operating. In some markets there are many suppliers competing for business, while in others there may be only a single supplier. Clearly the single supplier will have more influence and greater strength in determining supply-side factors, particularly in price determination, than where

there are many suppliers. In contrast, where there are many suppliers competing for business and the strength of each individual supplier is weak, prices are more likely to be determined by demand-side factors.

The key features of a market environment are:

■ the number of buyers and sellers operating within the market
■ how easy it is for firms to enter that market
■ the influence which individual firms operating in the market have over prices
■ whether there are substitutes for products being sold
■ any collusion between buyers and/or sellers.

These factors have wide-ranging implications for both the market and the behaviour of organisations and individuals – whether buyers or sellers – operating within it.

Each marketplace has its own character. Some consist of a few old-established businesses, while in others there may be many buyers and sellers, many of which are constantly changing. Businesses and markets differ in character, competitive climate, age and traditions. In order to classify the behaviour of organisations in markets, economists use a series of factors that are principally concerned with the degree of *price competition* (see Figure 4.14).

Figure 4.14 Classifications of market structures

Market structures are classified as monopoly, oligopoly, monopolistic competition and perfect competition. At one extreme the monopoly has a single supplier controlling the market and setting prices, while at the other extreme is the perfectly competitive market in which there are many firms, virtually no barriers to entry of new firms, and with such a high degree of price competition that firms accept a price determined by market forces – supply and demand. Between these extremes are oligopoly, where there are just a few sellers, and monopolistic competition where businesses are constantly differentiating their products from each other to emphasise their monopolistic characteristics.

Perfect competition

For **perfect competition** to exist within a market there are a number of conditions.

- There have to be a large number of buyers and sellers so that no one person or organisation alone can affect the market.
- Freedom of entry to and exit from the market must exist for buyers and sellers.
- There must be homogeneity of products (i.e. all products must be identical).
- Buyers and sellers must have perfect knowledge of the market.

Given these assumptions we can see clearly that a perfect market exists more in theory than in practice, though there are in fact some close approximations which are near-perfect, particularly in commodity markets or local markets for fruit and vegetables. Despite this there are some important lessons to be learnt from this type of model. In perfect competition, organisations are 'price takers' as each has no influence over the price. Given the intensity of competition in the marketplace, consumers benefit from the efficient, low-cost nature of the good or service being provided as well as the plentiful choice of suppliers. As firms are free to enter or leave the market, any large profits disappear in the long-run. This type of market would certainly be good news for consumers. On the other hand, for producers it will not provide the prospect of long-term sustained profitability.

Perfect competition, being not really typical of any market in practice, can be used as a theoretical model against which other markets are compared.

Monopoly

An organisation that does not have to face competition is said to have a **monopoly** market. It does not have outside pressure put on it to be competitive. We must be careful, however, not to assume that monopolies are necessarily inefficient or all bad. Monopolies can put a lot of money into product development and research in order to keep ahead of potential competitors.

In practice, single control over the supply of a product rarely exists and we tend to talk about degrees of monopoly. In the UK the Monopolies and Mergers Commission regards a monopoly as a situation where either one or a group of producers control at least 25 per cent of a market. In the UK there are state monopolies such as the BBC and the Post Office as well as private monopolies such as British Gas and Tate & Lyle, the sugar producer.

Monopolies are often in a position to erect barriers to stop others from entering the market. Given its strength and dominant position in the market, a monopoly can dictate market price and is a 'price maker'. Since the market for monopolistic products may have few substitutes, a monopoly may enjoy inelastic demand, and

have the power and ability to charge high prices which lead to very large profits. This may mean that consumers are faced with restricted output at much higher prices than if more competition existed. For this reason, monopolies frequently have the power to abuse their position and make decisions which are against the public interest. From a government's point of view it is important to monitor the actions of monopolies to make sure that practices do not work unfairly against the interests of consumers.

A monopoly may wish to increase revenue and profit by means of price discrimination. This is a situation where different prices are charged to consumers in different parts of the market for the same product. For example, British Rail has an APEX ticket, a Supersaver, a Saver, etc. To do this it must be possible to divide the market and the price elasticity of demand must be different for each market segment.

Oligopoly

There are many possibilities between perfect competition and monopoly, one of which is **oligopoly** where just a few firms dominate a market. Examples of products in markets with a few supplier firms are:

- national newspapers
- breakfast cereals
- banking services
- washing powder
- pet foods
- petrol
- disposable nappies
- contraceptives.

A common feature of oligopolistic competition is product differentiation, often through products with a strong brand identity. There are no set rules as to the degree of competition that exists in oligopoly. Each producer will spend money on actions designed to foster brand loyalty – such as advertising and promotion – and will attempt to differentiate its product from others that are available.

However, there is always the danger that open warfare with regard to pricing and other elements of competition will be to the disadvantage of all producers and sellers. The ability to make profits, and to plough profits into promotion, research and product development, is viewed as being of crucial importance. Though such markets are typified by lulls and surges in the extent of competitive practices, prices are often stable for long periods, except for occasional price wars. Prices tend to follow the price of the leading brand, though there is the danger of collusion.

Monopolistic competition

Oligopoly is in fact a concentrated form of **monopolistic competition**. Monopolistic competition exists where products or services are in some way differentiated from others. In other words, firms create monopolies in the short term by developing products which are different from those of the competition; however, this differentiation may be eroded in the course of time because new firms have the freedom to enter the industry. Levels of profit in monopolistic markets will vary with the level of competition. The ability of firms to survive and prosper depends on whether they can keep innovating by researching and developing new product lines.

Over recent years the view of monopolistic competition has changed. Originally the theory was based on large-group competition with many small suppliers, but today it tends to refer to more oligopolistic markets where a smaller number of firms compete using extremely differentiated products.

Case Study
Mower returns to the stock market

The following details appeared in the financial press:

'In what will effectively amount to a seven-year round trip out of the stock market and back again, AQ Holdings – the Qualcast lawnmower manufacturer – is heading back to the stock market as a fully quoted company. The Suffolk company was bought 18 months ago by its management from the cement-maker Blue Circle and is planning a stock market flotation. The move is expected to value the company at about £40 million.

'AQ Holdings also owns the Atco and Suffolk brands and was formerly part of Birmid Qualcast, the building supplies group, which was taken over by Blue Circle in 1988. Four years later, AQ was sold to its management with backing from Candover Investments, the venture capital company and the Bank of Scotland. Since then AQ has restructured production and management to create a more team-based environment which has reduced tiers of middle management, cut costs and improved quality.

'The company boasts a 30 per cent stake in the UK lawnmower market, which is about the same as each of its two nearest rivals – Flymo owned by Electrolux, the Swedish Group, and Black & Decker. AQ has a 40-strong product range priced from £50 to £2500.'

Questions for discussion

1 *How would you describe the structure of the lawnmower market?*
2 *What sort of competitive activities would you (a) expect, and (b) not expect, to take place in this type of market?*

Market features

Organisations can be classified according to the goods and services they produce. In Chapter 3 we divided markets into consumer markets and organisational (sometimes known as industrial) markets.

Consumer markets are made up largely of individuals and families who buy things for personal and home use. Consumers do not buy products to make other goods while engaging in profit-making activities. Consumers typically buy from **retailers** and the purchases tend to involve low money values. We all belong to numerous consumer markets for things such as food, clothes, magazines and so on.

Industrial or organisational markets are made up of buyers who purchase goods and services to use in the making or providing of other goods and services. We shall see later that there are four generally accepted types of organisational market, these being producers, resellers, government departments, and institutions.

The division between consumer and organisational markets is not sacrosanct and some organisations sell products in both.

A market's **size** must be large enough – i.e. have sufficient purchasing power – to generate profits for the organisations operating within it. Market size figures are usually expressed in *volume* or *value* and may be available in some published form (see Chapter 3). These figures are important because if the size of the market is known, and a business feels that it is capable of gaining a certain market share, then production and sales can be forecast.

Markets may have potential buyers as well as existing buyers. For example, there have been many buyers of satellite dishes but the potential sales of such dishes are much larger. If, as with satellite dishes, potential size is larger than market size, there is often uncertainty in **growth industries** about how the market will develop, particularly with regard to changes in technology and consumer behaviour. High-growth markets are usually the more profitable; but, as market size nears market potential, competition intensifies, growth slows and profitability tends to decline.

Some markets are attractive to producers because of low **barriers to entry** such as capital costs and regulations. For example, in fragmented industries with many small units there are few economies of scale, so it is possible to 'start small' and expand later.

Economic influences in consumer markets

In Chapter 19 we look closely at **segmentation** and **behavioural factors** which influence customers. In particular we refer to how, when and where they buy, and how much they spend. For common consumer goods markets, published figures are readily available. As well as this, it is usually possible to obtain information on areas such as:

- population size, distribution and growth
- age distribution
- changing family patterns
- social trends and fashions
- trends in income and expenditure.

We all have a certain **buying power**, determined by our income or wealth. This buying power is affected by a number of factors. For example, a student's buying power is usually determined by his or her level of grant. Another person's buying power may be affected by a recession. In a recession unemployment increases and total consumer buying power declines. There may be high interest rates which commit more spending to the repayment of mortgages and other loans.

The main sources of buying power in consumer markets are (a) **income**, which is the amount of money received from wages, salaries, grants, pensions and investments over a given period, and (b) **wealth**, which is an accumulation of past income and financial resources. The distributions of income and wealth are not evenly spread (see Figures 4.15 and 4.16). In Figure 4.15, marketable wealth includes cash, liquid assets, houses, land, shares and personal chattels, but excludes occupational and state pension rights.

What do people do with their income and wealth? Income used for spending or saving is called **disposable income**. Any income left over after one has bought basic necessities such as food and shelter is called **discretionary income**, because this is income that one is free to spend on entertainment, cars, holidays, etc. Any unexpected changes in income will affect these types of purchase in particular.

Marketers analyse how consumers spend their disposable income by looking at consumer and household spending patterns (see Figures 4.17 and 4.18). Clearly a lot can be gained by studying these. For example, after income tax, *housing* is the largest item of weekly household expenditure, and more is spent on meat and poultry than on any other food item.

The **willingness to spend** of each individual consumer is influenced by a number of key factors. Firstly, the amount of satisfaction that a consumer expects to receive from such spending will clearly influence his or her behaviour. Price, too, is a key factor, particularly a product's price in relation to substitutes. Other wider expectations are influential: politicians and the media frequently cite the lack of a 'feel-good factor' affecting the confidence of consumers in the High Street. There is no doubt that tenure of employment, income levels, family size, the prospect of inflation, interest rates and economic conditions in general have an important role to play in the willingness of consumers to spend.

Economic influences in organisational markets

It is often the case that figures for organisational markets are more difficult to obtain. However, if a company knows the size of its market and knows it can achieve a certain share, it can make much more accurate decisions about stock levels, production and sales forecasts.

Every day in towns and cities across the UK, car dealers hand the keys of new cars to customers. A complex manufactured product such as this is made up of numerous parts and materials from many suppliers. Whereas it might be easy to think about the single sale of a car from a showroom, we tend not to think of the vast number of sales transactions that have taken place beforehand to bring together the components to manufacture the car.

Consider some of the transactions required to manufacture a car. Iron ore is mined and transported to a plant to be made into steel. The steel is bought by the car manufacturer and formed into a chassis and body. In order to construct a car with about 12 000 different parts, a manufacturer will probably produce about 6000 parts and then buy the other 6000 from other companies. Many of these companies will only supply one part, so the car manufacturer may have to buy from several thousand companies. The companies supplying these parts will also have suppliers.

When a company is selling to other organisations it still needs to understand the behaviour of its customers. But whereas a consumer product might have a potential market of 56 million users, there are fewer than 3 million organisations in the UK and the likelihood is that the

Figure 4.15 Distribution of marketable wealth of individuals in the UK in 1992

(i) Range of net wealth in £:	Number of owners over 18		Marketable wealth	
	(000s)	(%)	(£000m)	(%)
Nil – 4 999	11 644	26.0	22	1.2
5 000 – 14 999	7 443	16.6	56	3.1
15 000 – 24 999	6 904	15.4	130	7.2
25 000 – 49 999	8 823	19.7	350	19.3
50 000 – 99 999	6 878	15.4	489	27.0
100 000 +	3 073	6.9	764	42.2
Totals	**44 765**	**100.0**	**1811**	**100.0**

(ii) Percentage of wealth owned by:	Marketable wealth		Marketable wealth plus occupational and state pension rights	
	1977	1992	1977	1992
Most wealthy 1% of population	22	18	14	11
" " 10% " "	50	49	36	35
" " 25% " "	71	72	57	57
" " 50% " "	92	92	80	83

Figure 4.16 Distribution of total income of individuals before and after tax in the UK in 1991/92

Range of total income (lower limit) (£)	Number				Value after tax (%)
	Before tax		After tax		
	(000s)	(%)	(000s)	(%)	
3 295	3 980	14.1	4 780	17.0	6.2
5 000	4 890	17.4	5 880	20.9	11.4
7 500	4 310	15.3	4 920	17.5	13.3
10 000	6 570	23.3	6 650	23.6	25.3
15 000	3 920	13.9	3 160	11.2	16.9
20 000	2 900	10.3	1 980	7.1	14.7
30 000	1 140	4.1	561	2.0	6.4
50 000	327	1.2	164	0.6	3.4
100 000	104	0.4	41	0.1	2.4
All ranges	**28 100**	**100.0**	**28 100**	**100.0**	**100.0**

product on offer will appeal to only a very small number of them.

Types of organisational markets

The four types of organisational market are:

- **Producer markets**. These are organisations which purchase products for the purpose of using them in their own manufacturing processes or operations to make other products. Products bought may include raw materials, partly completed goods or finished goods.
- **Reseller or intermediate markets**. These are wholesalers and retailers who buy finished goods and then sell them on to customers in order to make their profit. Most products bought by consumers have first come through reseller markets.
- **Government markets**. Both national and local government departments make up these markets. Examples are education and defence.
- **Institutional markets**. These include institutions such as charities, clubs, museums and other organisations which provide a wide range of public goods and services.

Demand and oyoloo

The demand for organisational products and services is sometimes called **derived demand** because the quantity

Figure 4.17 UK household expenditure in 1993

Commodity or service		Average weekly expenditure	
		(£)	(%)
Housing (mortgage interest, rent, rates) (net)		44.85	11.9
Purchase and alteration of dwellings		14.40	3.8
Food		49.96	13.2
Alcoholic drinks		11.95	3.2
Tobacco/cigarettes/cigars		5.59	1.5
Clothing and footwear		17.40	4.6
Household goods		23.05	6.1
Household services		15.44	4.1
Personal goods and services		11.04	2.9
Leisure goods		13.26	3.5
Motoring expenditure and other travel costs		43.23	11.4
Fares (railway, bus and coach)	2.52		
Purchase, maintenance, running of motor vehicles	36.28		
Other	4.43		
Fuel, light and power		13.24	3.5
Gas	5.20		
Electricity	6.68		
Coal, coke, etc.	0.62		
Fuel, oil and other	0.72		
Entertainments, including TV licences		6.54	1.7
Educational and training expenses		4.05	1.1
Hotel and holiday expenses		10.75	2.8
Cash gifts, donations etc.		4.23	1.1
Income tax payments less refunds		47.92	12.7
National Insurance contributions		12.83	3.4
Insurances, pensions and subscriptions		19.29	5.1
Savings		5.44	1.4
Betting payments less winnings		0.74	0.2
Miscellaneous		2.96	0.8
Totals		**378.16**	**100.0**

purchased is determined by (i.e. derived from) the demand for *related* goods and services. For example, the number of tyres purchased by a motor manufacturer depends on the demand for vehicles. The industrial supplier is therefore aware that goods are being supplied to help produce someone else's product so that the demands of the final customer can be met.

Goods in industrial markets may also be in **joint demand** as they may be used in combination with other products to produce a finished product.

Depending solely on derived demand can have serious limitations. Organisational markets are subject to **business cycles** and the demand for industrial products and services fluctuates when the pace of business activity changes. Recessionary economic conditions can therefore lead to severe cutbacks in derived demand and cause a business to close down some production facilities and lay off workers.

Reciprocal buying

Reciprocal buying is simply a situation in which two organisations agree to buy from one another. This sort of agreement may occur between both small and large businesses. For example, a component business may supply parts to a motor manufacturer and, in return, buy vehicles for its own fleet. These types of agreement can be a problem because they limit competition and can lead to coercion to support contracts.

Contingency factors

Companies supplying products in organisational markets face constantly changing circumstances which are often called **contingency factors**. Marketers need to be alert to information relating to such specific conditions. For example:

Figure 4.18 UK household expenditure on food in 1993

Commodity or service	Average weekly expenditure		
	(£)	(%)	(Index 1980 = 100)
Bread	1.87	3.7	151
Flour	0.10	0.2	91
Biscuits/cakes	2.48	5.0	203
Breakfast and other cereals	1.10	2.2	306
Meat/poultry	8.23	16.5	143
Fish/fish and chips	1.82	3.6	182
Butter	0.34	0.7	71
Margarine	0.39	0.8	170
Lard/fat	0.18	0.4	106
Milk/cream	3.64	7.3	169
Cheese	1.17	2.3	202
Eggs	0.47	0.9	96
Potatoes	1.55	3.1	221
Vegetables	2.73	5.5	204
Fruit	2.69	5.4	234
Sugar	0.29	0.6	94
Jam/syrup, etc.	0.23	0.5	164
Sweets/chocolate	1.58	3.2	219
Tea	0.55	1.1	157
Coffee	0.53	1.1	166
Cocoa/drinking chocolate, etc.	0.13	0.3	325
Soft drinks	1.33	2.7	277
Ice cream	0.37	0.7	218
Other foods	5.78	11.6	431
All food consumed at home	39.53	79.1	190
Meals out	10.43	20.9	242
Totals	**49.96**	**100.0**	**199**

- The value of an order may follow a lengthy negotiation period and credit facilities will be very important.
- Buyers often exercise buying power to influence the conditions of supply, such as terms and prices.
- Large companies often seek out small companies so that they can exercise buying power more easily.
- Large buyers may pursue a deliberate policy of delaying payment for goods and services received. This can have serious implications for the cashflow of suppliers.
- There is a risk of supplier dependence on the customer.
- There may be the risk of takeover by the customer.

Vertical and horizontal markets

Organisational markets are often described as either vertical or horizontal (see Figure 4.19).

Where a product or service is used by only a small number of buyers, it has a **vertical market**. For example, there are few buyers of passenger aircraft or

Figure 4.19 Vertical and horizontal organisational markets

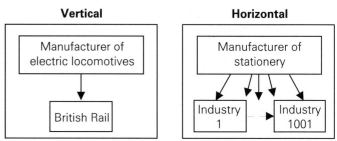

electric railway locomotives. A product has a **horizontal market** if it is purchased by many different kinds of organisations in many different industries. For example, the supply of stationery and lubricants is widespread.

The process of selling

The process of selling in an organisational market differs greatly from selling in consumer markets. Selling can often require technical knowledge, particularly if products are complex or specifications need to be altered or 'customised'.

Decisions may also involve numerous people across a range of departments. For example, the purchase of a computerised management information system should involve discussions with representatives from a range of departments likely to be using the technology.

Whereas consumers are likely to be influenced by a variety of behavioural factors, these are less evident in organisational markets where the main concern of customers is obtaining the best possible products at the lowest cost.

Marketing strategies

The first question an organisation must answer is 'Where are we going?' Rather than seeking maximum profits, an organisation may seek to be the *brand leader* or otherwise to dominate a particular market. This could give it a strong long-term position. *Corporate growth* is another common objective. Taking over companies, diversifying and introducing new products may not help profitability, but it may provide managers with control over a larger corporate unit. Other organisations take great pride in the way they are seen by the public, and may be prepared to sacrifice profit but never reputation.

At the heart of corporate planning lies the need to match marketing objectives with corporate objectives (see Figure 4.20). Doing so directs an organisation's activities towards satisfying the wishes of the consumer and enables it to achieve its goals.

Figure 4.20 Matching objectives

As we have seen, customers in a market must have the willingness and ability to purchase products as well as the authority to make a purchase. In Chapter 1 we saw that for an organisation to reach a market there are two major components in a marketing strategy:

Figure 4.21 Undifferentiated marketing – using the same mix to the whole market

- identifying and targeting customers in a market which an organisation wishes to reach
- the creation and maintenance of a marketing mix (product/price/place/promotion) for customers in that market.

In using the marketing mix to target customers, an organisation has to decide whether to use an **undifferentiated** or **total market** strategy based on providing a single marketing mix to the whole market (see Figure 4.21), or to use a more **differentiated** approach based on market **segmentation** (Figure 4.22). In the latter case the organisation might decide to target just one segment (Figure 4.23).

Figure 4.22 Differentiated marketing – using a different mix for each segment

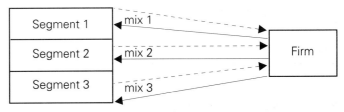

Most markets consist of customers with different types of needs and wants and these vary quite widely. Though customers are not all the same, *groups* of customers may be divided into discrete 'segments', in the same way that we divide an orange up into separate segments. For example, Levi sell jeans, but the jeans market is split into a number of segments all catered for by Levi. One way of segmenting the market is by gender, another is by the

Figure 4.23 Concentrated marketing – developing a mix for one segment

type of jeans – e.g. loose-fit, regular-fit, stone-washed, pre-wash (see Figure 4.24).

Figure 4.24 Two ways of dividing up (segmenting) the jeans market

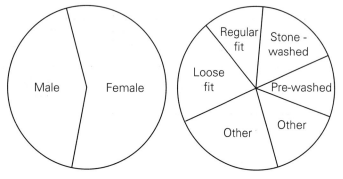

Segmentation can be defined as the strategy whereby a firm partitions the market into sub-markets (segments) which will respond in similar ways to marketing inputs.

When you walk into a large superstore and look at the sheer number of product lines geared towards our slightly different preferences, you can appreciate that producers use market segmentation as a way of meeting our various needs. For example, in the past an OXO cube meant only one thing; look at the many different types of OXO on the supermarket shelves today. Market segmentation helps producers to provide products geared to customers who share the same characteristics and needs and which improve customer satisfaction. In contrast, using a mass marketing or market aggregation approach which treats the market as an undifferentiated whole fails to recognise these different wants or needs. That is not to say that mass marketing is wrong; if the needs of all customers are similar and can be satisfied with a single product, then that approach is appropriate.

The market-share/market-growth matrix

A method organisations commonly use when developing a marketing strategy is based on the **market-share/market-growth matrix**. This was devised by the Boston Consultancy Group (BCG). The technique is based on the 'experience curve' which shows that the unit costs of adding value fall as cumulative production increases (see Figure 4.25).

Gains in efficiency stem from greater experience. The Boston Consultancy Group argues that the principle has general currency, and that, as a rough rule, average cost per unit falls by 20–30 per cent with each doubling of experience. Greater experience leads to:

■ economies of scale
■ the elimination of less efficient factors of production

■ increased productivity, stemming from technical changes and learning effects
■ improvements in product design.

The key lesson to be learned is that the benefits of experience do not just arise – they need to be *engineered*. Companies must act to ensure that these benefits are reaped. They will result from active strategies.

Figure 4.25 An 'experience' curve

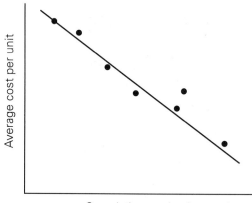

An important implication of the work of the Boston Consultancy Group is that 'experience' is a key asset. Companies that have a high market share should be able to accumulate more experience. Therefore companies should strive for a high market share.

The best indicator of market share is relative – that is, the ratio of a company's market share to that of its largest competitor:

$$\text{Relative market share of A} = \frac{\text{Market share of company A}}{\text{Market share of nearest competitor}}$$

This indicator gives a clear measure of comparative strength. The Boston Consultancy Group used statistical evidence to argue that a ratio of 2:1 is likely to give a 20 per cent cost advantage.

With regard to market growth, the Boston Consultancy Group argues that the faster the growth of a particular market the greater the costs necessary to maintain market share. In a rapidly growing market, considerable expenditure is required on investment in product lines. and to combat the threat posed by new firms and brands.

To summarise, the Boston Consultancy Group identified two key elements in the analysis of a product portfolio:

■ The greater the cumulative experience, the greater the cost advantage.
■ The faster the growth of a market the greater the cost of maintaining market position.

On the basis of these two general rules, BCG devised a portfolio matrix which is illustrated in Figure 4.26. The matrix identifies four main types of product:

Figure 4.26 Growth/share matrix

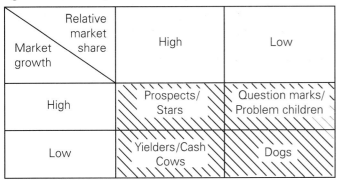

- *Prospects/Stars*. These products compete in rapidly expanding markets. They take up large sums for investment purposes. However, they also yield high cash returns. On balance they provide a neutral cash flow – but generally, they will go on to be the yielders/cash cows of the future.
- *Yielders/Cash cows*. These have a high market share in markets that are no longer rapidly expanding. Because the market is relatively static they require few fresh injections of capital. Advertising and promotional activities may be required to inject fresh life from time to time. However, the net effect is positive cash flow. Cash cows often provide the bread and butter of a business in the form of profits.
- *Question marks/Problem children*. These have a low market share in fast-growing markets. The question is, can they be turned into market leaders? Though a business knows that these may go on to be powerful earners, they might be a drain on resources.
- *Dogs*. These products have a low market share in low-growth markets. Because of the importance of experience these products are relatively poor competitors. As such they will generate negative cash flows.

In terms of cash flow the matrix can be redrawn as in Figure 4.27. Cash generated by the yielders is used to help with the development of question marks. The purpose of this is to increase the market share of the question marks in order to move them into the prospect category, with the expectation that eventually they will become yielders.

In order to manage the development of products effectively, it is important to have a balanced portfolio. For example, a company may require a number of yielders, as well as prospects, at any one time.

Figure 4.27 Cash flow and product flow

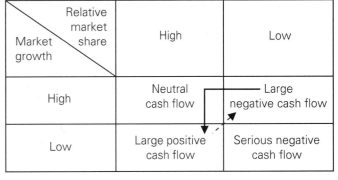

Product flow ⟶
Cash flow - - - -➤

What happens when a question mark fails to become a star or when a cash cow goes into decline? These are questions which have to be constantly reviewed by marketers. It is necessary to review the performance of products. This may be done in a number of ways:

- *Expected sales and profits*. A product's performance can be evaluated against its previous performance. Once these indicators start to dip, then it is clear that remedial action needs to be taken.
- *Relative market share*: This is always important because once it starts to fall the product may lose its competitive edge.
- *Threats*. The development of threats in the marketplace needs to be carefully monitored. Threats include the emergence of new technology, the arrival of competition, changes in consumer expenditure patterns and so on.

The product/market matrix

Another way of analysing a marketing strategy is to look at a **product/market matrix**. This theory was developed by H. Igor Ansoff. It looks not just at the management of the product portfolio but also more widely at market developments and opportunities. Ansoff's matrix matches existing and new product strategies with existing and new markets (see Figure 4.28). The matrix suggests five alternative marketing strategies which hinge on whether the product is new or existing or whether the market is new or existing.

- *Consolidation* implies a positive and active defence of existing products in existing markets.
- *Market penetration* suggests a further penetration of existing markets with existing products. This will involve a strategy of increasing market share within existing segments and markets.
- *Product development* involves developing new products for existing markets.

Figure 4.28 Ansoff's product/market matrix

	Existing products	New products
Existing markets	Consolidation Market penetration	Product development
New markets	Product development	Diversification

- *Market development* will use existing products and find new markets for them. These new markets will be identified by better customer targeting, market research and further segmentation.
- *Diversification* will lead to a movement away from core activities. This might involve some form of integration or diversification into related activities.

Further reading

- *Marketing*, 3rd edition, by B. H. Elvey. Butterworth–Heinemann, 1991.
- *Discovering Marketing* by D. Stokes. DPP, 1994.
- *Introduction to Marketing*, 3rd edition, by John Frain. Pitman, 1993.
- *Economics: A Student's Guide*, 3rd edition, by John Beardshaw. Pitman, 1992.
- *Economics*, 4th edition, by D. Begg, S. Fischer and R. Dornbusch. McGraw-Hill, 1994.
- *Marketing Strategy in Action* by Alfred Tock. Gower, 1986.
- *Economics* by William Boyes and Michael Melvin. Houghton Mifflin, 1991.
- *Economics Now* by Colin Isaac. Stanley Thornes, 1986.
- *Principles of Marketing* by Geoffrey Randall. Routledge, 1993.
- *A Foundation in Economics* by Graham Donnelly. Stanley Thornes, 1991.

2

Operating environment

5 The national economic context

On completion of this chapter students should be able to:

■ recognise the structure of the national economy and assess the significance for businesses of the operation of mixed economic systems

■ analyse the role of government economic management and its impact through participation in, and regulation of, the business environment

■ identify the key components of the UK financial system and its role and functions within the business environment

■ assess the significance of the world economy to UK businesses.

Introduction

The UK economy in late 1994 experienced a surge in economic activity that caught many commentators by surprise. During the November of that year the government estimated that the growth rate had exceeded 4 per cent, a figure that few had expected at the time of the budget in 1993. With good news on low inflation (the underlying rate was 2 per cent), and unemployment falling to below 9 per cent, the prospects for the future were looking good. However, there had been an increase in interest rates which the Bank of England and the Treasury had raised to counter any inflationary pressure in the system. Despite this move there were many commentators who were arguing that rates should be put up again by as much as 1 per cent. Business leaders, the CBI and others reacted in alarm to this suggestion, realising that there were still tax increases to come and that such a move in interest rates would have a detrimental effect on both spending and investment.

The main point to appreciate is that these economic events have a significant impact on government policy and on the environment faced by firms. An appreciation of the importance of the **economic environment** for business is the starting point for the review of the **macroeconomic issues** which will be explored in depth throughout this chapter. To return to the example, certain points are of great interest, and for speed of appreciation the main ones can be listed as follows:

■ Why had the economy expanded so quickly and what factors were driving it forward at such a pace?
■ Would firms be able to maintain the level of output to meet the demand? How many were in fact working at near, or close to, full capacity?
■ Despite the rapid growth, inflation was subdued. What pressures on costs and prices were being exerted to keep inflation low?
■ Unemployment had fallen from nearly 3 million in 1992 to just over 2.5 million, but what had prompted firms to recruit staff? Had people left the labour market altogether, thereby adding to the dramatic reduction? What sort of jobs had been created: were they

part-time or full-time permanent? Who had taken the jobs?

These questions have to be answered if an understanding of the economic context is to be gained. The structure of the economy, and the macroeconomic influences affecting business activity in the economic system found in the UK, will all be reviewed in this chapter. From this starting point the developments throughout Europe and beyond can also be incorporated to provide an international perspective to business activities and the chances of successful strategies being incorporated into the corporate plans of organisations.

The need for an international perspective can again be made using the example of the performance of the UK economy in 1994. Growth had been spurred by the **export opportunities** that had opened up to UK firms, as European markets recovered from the recession and with the fall in the value of the pound after it had left the exchange rate mechanism (ERM) in 1992. Moving further afield, the Pacific countries, with China and India, were developing apace with growth rates of 10 per cent (or more), providing a clear opportunity for the astute and well-managed firm to move into these emerging markets.

If a partial explanation of the success of the economy can be found in these trends, then the same problems can be identified for the future welfare of the country. A fall in the value of the currency can only provide a short-term stimulus; countries coming out of recession will eventually experience a slowing down of growth, emerging markets will be seen as opportunities by other companies from many other countries. Future **export-led growth** would not be an easy way for the country to generate expansion in the future. Firms would find that the factors that have led to the globalisation of trade would be a mixed blessing, posing many questions for UK-based firms to answer.

The **world economy**, and the trends within it, have to be part of the overall picture, as a focus on one country would produce too limited a level of analysis to be worthwhile. So while the main structure and processes of the home economy will form the bulk of this chapter, there is a small but significant section on the trends in the European Union, eastern Europe and the Pacific Rim, that can develop an understanding as to the forces shaping the opportunities that organisations will face.

In reviewing the economic environment, it would be impossible to leave out the political and regulatory aspects of economic management. This is often most visible when the European Commission is held up to ridicule because of its efforts to create a single market, or when a government quango provides an example of

inadequate administrative acumen. Despite the public's annoyance, all economies have to be managed; the way this is undertaken has to be understood if a business is to be successful, either in cooperation with the regulatory bodies or in lobbying to control their power or to influence their actions.

Economic systems

Since 1989 the success of **market economies** has led some to assume that a certain type of free-market economic structure has become the basis for economic activity across the globe. However, it is relevant to ask whether the type of economic system we see in the UK or the USA is to be found in other economies in the European Union, Japan, China, Burma and the remainder of the world's nation states. The organisation of economic activity differs remarkably across these countries; so, despite the retreat of communist (planned) economies, there are important differences that will be of significance for companies and managers trading abroad.

In essence, all economies are trying to solve the same problems. A society has needs and wants which will have to be satisfied by the organisations who are given the opportunity to organise production and distribution. Clearly there are more needs and wants than any society can deal with, however rich it appears to be. The problem of the use of scarce resources presents itself wherever we turn our attention, so all societies have to decide how to ration out production amongst competing demands, bringing to the fore the problem that a use of scarce resources for one activity inevitably deprives another activity of access to them.

Choices and sacrifices have to be made. The challenge for each country is how this should be done. Should it be left to individuals and organisations to bid for resources, on the basis that they can produce what people need as long as it is profitable for them? If they fail to produce what is required, then they cease to trade, and the resources that they were using can be purchased and used by others to produce profitable items. We know this as the **free-market solution**, but this approach is trying to solve the problem of scarcity by providing a rationing mechanism based on price and profit.

A major challenge for the free-market approach is whether it could build a long-term future, with the requirement to undertake investment that may not be profitable for some considerable time. Would the market, for example, be able to provide for skills in the work force that may be needed for the future? In an article in November 1994, Lloyds Bank outlined the factors that could limit improvements to Britain's manufacturing performance. Amongst these were the **skills gap** that exists between the UK and its competitors. Not only did the gap appear in the compulsory schooling stages, but also between workers at whatever level in organisations. Is it possible to provide a market-led solution to this problem or to see a key role for government?

What is true for education and training can also be the case for health, social security, police and defence, which would then introduce a defined and high-profile role for government. This **mixed-economy** regime could also incorporate anti-competitive measures to deal with the rise of monopolies and monopolistic practices that free markets have a tendency to create. Likewise, the problem of **externalities** – such as air and land pollution – can create a role for government. It can try to measure the pollution costs borne by the general community, and reach a decision as to the most effective way to deal with this.

The **planned economies** of eastern Europe and the old USSR took the role of government to be of paramount importance. Under the name of 'democratic socialism', the state owned the **means of production** in the name of the people, arguing that a market system exploited the masses, by building up profits that benefited the minority at the expense of the majority. A market solution was divisive and degrading for the population, so the state had to organise production and distribution, in order to resolve the problem of scarcity without the exploitation normally associated with **capitalism**.

These three broad-based classifications of the free market, mixed and planned, are useful devices for seeing the basic differences that exist between them in trying to resolve the problem of scarcity. A degree of caution is required when using this approach. It is clear that many countries do not conform to the classification allotted to them, so even under the old Soviet-style planned economies immense differences could be found between Hungary, East Germany and the USSR. Likewise, the mixed economies of France, Germany and the UK show clear preferences in respect to government intervention that goes some way to explaining their problems over European integration. Moving further afield, where would the Islamic countries of Iran, Iraq and Syria be placed? And Japan and South Korea could be just as difficult to categorise as the Islamic countries.

Many approaches to international business focus on the degree of **risk** associated with business opportunities in overseas countries. One aspect that has not been mentioned so far is the degree of **political and legal control** exerted by government and the regulatory agencies. From the brief description of the three economic systems, it is clear that legal and regulatory control in a planned economy would be high, with

individuals given few opportunities to own property or to have ownership rights when it comes to natural resources or the assets of an enterprise. Free- and mixed-market approaches would create opportunities for individuals and groups to have ownership rights, as private companies provide a high proportion of the output that a society requires. Figure 5.1 is a method of rating the economic and political–legal systems based on the opportunities created or devised to set up private enterprises, own projects and promote individual freedom.

Figure 5.1 The politico-economic field

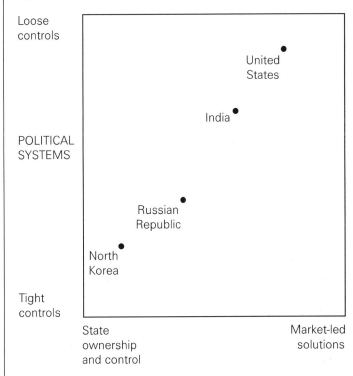

The new Russian Republic is in the early stages of moving from a centrally planned economy with tight political and legal controls over activity, so in a few years' time a very different picture may emerge, with the Russian government having privatised many enterprises and introduced democratic reforms.

A number of issues emerge from the review of economic and political–legal systems:

■ Many companies and organisations in the UK trade overseas, so in order to be successful an awareness of the mechanics of the political and economic regime is essential.
■ To be successful in the home territory of the company, an appreciation of the values that underpin the mixed economy of the UK can produce a more informed insight into the way it operates.

- If a country is rated as having a high preference for economic and political control, it is not to be assumed that its chances for economic success might be low. China (ranked as having a high preference) is experiencing large increases in economic growth. A current rating needs to be treated with caution as it can only provide a static picture of a country – extra attention needs to be given to movements and changes in a country's activities. For example, China has been granting more economic freedom, creating enterprise zones where largely uncontrolled economic activities are permitted. This is at the same time as maintaining the role and importance of the communist party, so showing a pragmatic approach to the challenge of economic development.

The UK's mixed economy

Moving from the foregoing general approach, we now need to focus more clearly on the mixed system found in the UK. The 1980s saw a promotion of **private sector** activity, with the disintegration of state industries, promotion of the **enterprise culture** and the constant review of public sector services and activities – which could be subject either to a more competitive environment, such as the internal market in the NHS; the putting out for tender of services, such as the compulsory competitive tendering of many local authorities; or the request to drive down costs and raise the quality of services, as can be seen in the further- and higher-education sectors.

These changes have continued into the 1990s, with many now supported by the main opposition parties. Alongside the promotion of the private sector and the introduction of business-style management in the public sector, the government has also set up regulatory agencies, often referred to as **quangos** (quasi-autonomous non-governmental agencies) to monitor the work of the new privatised companies such as British Gas and BT. It has also promoted self-regulation in the financial services sector and introduced new guidelines and laws concerning pollution, health and safety and other factors relating to the management of production, distribution and retailing.

All these initiatives and changes can be difficult to appraise. A formal approach to this can be to look firstly at government **macroeconomic objectives**, and secondly at the **microeconomic approach** concerned with regulatory bodies, law and regulations.

Macroeconomic objectives

All governments have five broad objectives that they wish to see achieved. These are:

- sustainable growth
- low inflation
- falling unemployment or full employment
- balance of payments equilibrium
- controlled public borrowing.

Sustainable growth

Total **demand** in the economy comprises consumer spending, government spending and exports, minus the amount spent on imports. This **aggregate demand**, and the changes that either increase or decrease it, are of vital importance to the economy and the government.

The largest part of aggregate demand is made up of consumer expenditure, and whilst the other aspects of demand are important in their own ways, it is still the confidence of consumers that can provide strong growth prospects for the economy. At the time of writing the economy was experiencing strong growth, at 4 per cent with a forecast of 3 per cent for the next few years, with consumer expenditure showing a slight improvement. This was being helped by a much larger improvement in investment and exports, a feature of the UK economy that has not been seen for many years.

Government approaches to spending and taxation can significantly influence the direction of each element. To these **fiscal** influences can be added the **monetary policy** of central government that can, through the movement of **interest rates**, alter the balance one way or another. While it can be easy to blame the government for mistiming changes in their monetary and fiscal policies, it is by no means easy to judge when these should take place. Figure 5.2 shows the traditional business cycle that economies can be seen to move through. The obvious conclusion to draw would be to use forecasting methods to predict when a downturn was due to occur and adjust policy accordingly. Likewise a boom with its associated problem of inflation and production bottlenecks could be headed off with appropriate changes.

Despite the common criticism of government policy errors, a number of problems have to be faced by any administration. These can be seen as a series of **lags** when information is uncertain or unclear. For convenience these may be grouped under three headings: recognition, administration, and operation.

Figure 5.2 Stages in the business cycle

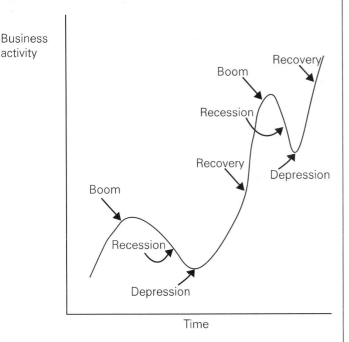

Recognition lag

This is the time it takes to collect enough information so that a reasonable analysis can take place. As already mentioned, governments rely on **indicators** to provide them with a comprehensive analysis of the economy, and studies of the UK business cycle suggest that economic indicators fall into four broad groups:

- *longer leading indicators*, which point to turns in activity about a year in advance (e.g. CBI quarterly survey: change in optimism)
- *shorter leading indicators*, which indicate turning points six months in advance (e.g. new car registrations)
- *coincident indicators*, which mark current turning points (e.g. retail sales)
- *lagging indicators*, which confirm turning points about a year after they happen (e.g. unemployment and investment in plant and machinery).

In theory these indicators should show at what point in the business cycle the economy is heading for or has arrived at.

Four stages can be seen to repeat themselves in the **business cycle**, as shown in Figure 5.2. In simple terms the four stages have the following characteristics:

Boom
- Consumer spending rising quickly.
- Output capacity reached; labour shortages occur.
- Output can only be increased by new labour-saving investment.
- Investment spending high.
- Increase in demand stimulates price rises.
- Business profits high.

Recession
- Consumption falls off.
- Many investments suddenly become unprofitable and new investment falls.
- Production falls.
- Employment falls.
- Profits fall; business failures increase.
- Recession can turn into severe depression.

Depression
- Heavy unemployment.
- Low consumer demand.
- Over-capacity (unused capacity) in production.
- Prices stabilise or even fall.
- Business profits low (confidence low).

Recovery
- Investment picks up.
- Employment rises.
- Consumer spending rises.
- Profits recover.
- Business confidence rises.
- Prices stable or rise slowly.

Whilst the workings of the business cycle are complex and there are various schools of thought on what causes recession – and what are the most appropriate policies to stimulate a recovery – *most economists accept the cycle as a useful model which can identify the main dynamics of the economy.*

What appears to be possible from the use of indicators and the business-cycle model is that a government can use **monetary and fiscal policies** to 'fine-tune' the economy. Examples are moving interest rates higher to head off inflation and to cool the economy down, or using extra government expenditure to spur the economy forward when growth threatens to slow. However, the recognition lag means that time has to elapse before a meaningful set of statistics can show that a problem has occurred. For example, an indicator showing one month's inflation up on the previous month would not be a justifiable foundation for action. Two, three, or even up to six months of rising inflation should spur the government to action.

Administration lag

Once a trend has been identified the choice over what to do to control a problem is potentially large, but most administrations have clear economic preferences that determine the choice of control **instrument** that they wish to use. In the 1970s and throughout a large part of the 80s, the Labour and Conservative parties differed markedly in their economic philosophies. The Labour Party preferred a more **interventionist policy** based on Keynesian **demand management**, while the Conservative Party favoured a **monetary policy** and **supply-side improvements**. In the late 80s and throughout the 90s, both parties have seen their ideas converge, with a more pragmatic combination of supply-side and demand-management initiatives.

Whatever the constraints on choice, there is still an issue in choosing the most appropriate course to take.

Operation lag

Once a course of action has been chosen – say, increasing interest rates – it will take some time to impact on the economy, with perhaps a period of three to six months elapsing before the full impact of the change can be seen.

These three lags or delays may mean that it can be six months to a year before a turning point in the cycle has been identified, action taken and some effect is seen. Also, the influences of the international markets may force changes through that no government could ever envisage. A government's ability to choose its own policy direction may be severely curtailed.

Economic growth levels

Economic growth is a goal for all governments. However, it is not just that growth of any level is desirable, but that growth should be such that it generates enough demand to maintain existing jobs, create new jobs and increase the wealth of the nation. This normally means that growth of less than 2 per cent will cause problems for the economy, leading as it will to a loss in jobs as productivity gains will be greater than the change in demand. What, then, will be acceptable levels of growth, and how will this be measured?

Growth is measured as the change in the 'gross domestic product' (GDP) of the country over the year, after subtracting an amount due to the level of inflation to produce a figure for **real growth**. The long-term growth pattern of the UK economy is considered to be $2\frac{1}{2}$ per cent a year, although the business cycle often means that this figure can fluctuate from year to year.

Growth, though, can produce its own problems, and this requires a closer look at its underlying factors. If growth is fuelled mainly by changes in consumer demand (the main component of aggregate demand), then this could cause problems with the balance of payments by sucking in imports. If growth is generated by changes in

investment and more exports, then a so-called 'golden scenario' may be produced, which seems to provide for more **sustainable growth**. But even here there is a downside, with investment being paid for at the expense of consumption, leading to a loss of the important 'feel-good factor'.

The contrast between the mid-1980 growth patterns and those of the mid-1990s show the difference. In the 1980s, credit and loans were easy to obtain, house prices were rising quickly (providing a base against which lending could take place), and consumption was encouraged. The problems came when the housing market collapsed as inflation and interest rates peaked, imports soared and the economy experienced **negative growth** – that is, a period over which the economy actually shrank. Compare that with economic growth a decade later and notable differences emerge. In the 1990s the housing market remains sluggish, with lenders (banks and building societies) and borrowers cautious over taking on more financial burdens. Industry, however, turned its attention to export markets and invested to compete overseas. The annual economic growth rate moved from negative growth to a more healthy 3 per cent plus, but a noticeable feeling in the work force was that they were not seeing the benefits of growth as wage levels were held down.

The make-up of growth is of great importance to business. As we have seen, it is possible for governments to play a role in setting the conditions for growth, either through lowering interest rates and/or increasing the amount of spending on capital projects or job-creation programmes. The first approach may be justified on the grounds that inflation is low, but may be set at a level that encourages extra consumption based on credit creation (an issue we shall explore later in the section on inflation), thereby producing a consumer-led boom. The second approach has to be judged very carefully to take out the party political aspect. All parties use public spending to pursue economic and social objectives (we will ignore the political aims that may also be a part of government expenditure), so what is at issue here is how these are paid for. If extra **government borrowing** is undertaken, it *may* **crowd out** private sector borrowing, thereby leading to an increase in interest rates, putting pressure on private sector investment. If this happens then the growth phase will be short-lived.

Businesses prefer a stable economic environment. The influence of the business cycle suggests that this is unlikely, creating a difficult set of decisions for government to be able to encourage conditions for growth, whilst at the same time having enough scope to invest in the nation's **infrastructure** and to provide social benefits to those who need them.

Inflation

Inflation has been given a high priority by governments throughout the last 20 years, particularly as international comparisons have shown that the UK's level of inflation is too high compared with that of Japan, Germany and other advanced industrial countries.

The measurement of inflation can be undertaken in a number of ways. The most common method is by the **retail price index** (RPI) which measures, on a monthly basis, the changes in the price of goods and services purchased by the average family. The RPI is now more often referred to as the **headline measure of inflation**. The preferred measure used by the government, excluding mortgage payments to make comparisons easier with other countries, is known as the **underlying rate of inflation** (or RPIX). It is this figure that is currently targeted, with the aim to keep it under 4 per cent a year.

Both the headline and the underlying figures produce a picture of inflation as consumers experience it in the shops. However, there is a need to look at inflation as experienced by industry, particularly as this will provide – it is hoped – ample warning of **inflationary pressures** building up in the economy. Changes in the prices of imports and changes in factory-gate prices are monitored to see what trends are emerging in raw-material and wage costs that could feed through into retail prices, and hence to the RPI. The difficulty here is that factory-gate prices may not have a large impact on retail prices because pressure in the distribution chain may be to keep prices down in the face of consumer resistance.

The problems of inflation

Measuring inflation can provide the 'moving picture', but there is still the need to predict the problems that are likely to come with it.

- Any economy experiencing inflation higher than its international competitors loses out on **competitiveness**.
- When there is inflation, companies and trade unions have to try to set prices and wages in an unpredictable situation, causing problems for both sides of industry.
- Groups of people on fixed and low incomes which are not index-linked experience a loss in buying power, and these groups do not have the protection of a trade union or staff association to argue their case.

Causes of inflation

Inflation is a problem, so what are the factors that cause it? There are numerous theories concerning its causes and likely cure, and these can be summarised under two general headings: supply-side and demand-led pressures.

Supply-side theories of inflation

The emphasis here is on the pressure put on firms to raise their own prices by influences such as higher raw-material costs, wage increases, and other members of the supply chain who have power to raise their prices. The government can monitor and to a certain extent control the wage and other supply-side pressures, so it is not always the case that inflation will rise because of them. Demand may be weak in the economy, keeping profits down rather than allowing prices to rise. If this happens, firms will still wish to rebuild their profit margins by price rises when the conditions are favourable – a factor monitored by the CBI quarterly survey of companies' price intentions.

Demand conditions

Demand here relates to government spending (and borrowing), credit availability and real disposable incomes. Here again, it is not a straightforward issue to look at changes in wages and disposable income (income measured after tax and other commitments have been deducted). Households may well experience an increase in both of these but, because the future is uncertain, they feel the need to rebuild their financial position by saving, and so do not come forward to spend their money. If, though, this situation is experienced for any length of time, the so-called 'feel-good' factor can come into operation and feed into the marketplace.

In practice a multitude of factors feed through into inflation, building up pressures that are difficult to resist. Through most of the 1980s the UK government took the view that monetary conditions – the level of the supply of money – were the main indicators and cause of inflation. Policy was aimed at adjusting interest rates to keep both inflation and monetary growth in check. In the late 80s and into the next decade a more comprehensive view was taken – a view shared across the political divide. This approach takes account of both demand- and supply-side pressures, adjusting the policy according to the interpretation of the data available. This process is now made public by means of publicising of the relevant discussions between the Chancellor of the Exchequer and the Governor of the Bank of England – showing the conclusions they arrive at on the current situation and on the likely future course of inflation. These discussions can then feed through into action to tighten or relax monetary and/or fiscal policy.

Unemployment

The state of the labour market is a more emotive issue than inflation because it directly affects individuals' current and future prospects. **Unemployment** should be considered in the same way as inflation – namely that it needs to be measured, trends should be noted and cures sought.

With inflation, governments can set targets (e.g. up to 4 per cent) and decide policy accordingly. Until recently the employment target was to maintain almost full employment, with no more than 3 per cent unemployment. From the Second World War until the late 70s, both Conservative and Labour governments strove to keep unemployment down to this level. From 1979, starting with the first of Mrs Thatcher's three Conservative administrations, the government tried to adhere to supply-side solutions and monetarist economic theory. The unemployment policy target was abandoned on the premise that it was not a government's role to create jobs, but to establish the right conditions for the private sector to expand and thereby create job *opportunities*. The current situation is that there is no agreed target for unemployment, but there is an aim to reduce it to the lowest possible level compatible with low inflation, which may be some way removed from the 'full employment' figure of 3 per cent. The Conservative government will adjust policy to keep inflation low, even if this means that unemployment rises.

While there is little agreement on the target that should be set for unemployment, there is general agreement on the causes. These can be grouped together under the following headings.

Structural unemployment

When there are changes in the industrial structure of a nation or region, decline of the traditional industries will increase unemployment among those whose skills are no longer needed. In the north of England, for example, the decline of shipbuilding, steel production and coal-mining produced a major problem for some communities, which saw unemployment rise to 20 per cent or more. Individuals were unable to compete for jobs in the 'hi-tech' industries that came into the region. This resulted in **long-term unemployment** for many people.

Frictional unemployment

A situation can easily occur whereby the labour market is unable to operate smoothly to match people to available jobs. Those with the skills in one region may be unwilling, or unable, to move to a new region where the jobs are available, either because of social pressures or because they could not afford to buy or rent a home in the area where the job is. The policy challenge here is to create conditions whereby workers find moving home easier, or to encourage organisations to relocate to where the skilled workers reside.

Cyclical unemployment

As its name suggests, this is caused by the business cycle – there is an increase in unemployment as the economy slows down. Unlike the types of unemployment discussed above, this type can be reduced by demand measures such as the relaxation of monetary and fiscal policy. For frictional and structural issues, generating more demand will not help solve the problem, so supply-side approaches would have to be considered.

Seasonal unemployment

The employment level in certain industries varies according to the seaon. Seasonal factors affect in particular the building industry, tourism and farming, so these variations have to be taken into account when assessing the significance of the overall unemployment figure. All monthly figures are subject to **seasonal adjustment**, a device that can produce a truer picture of the rise and fall of underlying unemployment.

Other factors leading to unemployment

Technology is often blamed for job losses. While this may be true in the short term, history suggests that technological developments create new job opportunities. However, the new jobs demand new skills and ways of working, an issue that involves training and alternative ways of organising work.

Restructuring – sometimes referred to as re-engineering, de-layering or rationalisation – leads to unemployment. Although the terms relate to different strategies, they share this common outcome. This unemployment is created by competition that forces organisations to become leaner and fitter.

Cures for unemployment

Unemployment in the UK at the end of 1994 was described officially as 2.5 million out of work and claiming state benefits. This figure included those who had lost their jobs through the economically difficult years and those who had been made redundant through structural and rationalisation changes. No single cure or aspect of government policy could cope with all the causes, so as with inflation it is convenient to group the initiatives together, under supply-side and demand headings.

Supply-side solutions

Here the emphasis is on improving the *quality* of the nation's work force, by training as well as by encouraging people to think about setting up their own businesses. In addition, the unemployed can be given help in looking for work and improving their communication skills, so that they appeal to prospective employers. There are numerous organisations involved in this process, from the Training and Enterprise Councils (TECs) through to local authorities, who can all provide a valuable contribution.

Demand-led initiatives

This is a more contentious area than the supply-side initiatives outlined above. Keynesian economic theory focuses on aggregate demand (total demand) which can be affected by withdrawal or injections of money. One solution to a lack of demand in the economy is to inject extra public expenditure into the system, thereby boosting activity, which can lead to job creation. The difficulty with this is that the government has to borrow the funds, which may ultimately lead to higher interest rates and the crowding out of private sector investment, as noted earlier. A further criticism is that the boost to expenditure could, over time, lead to higher inflation, an effect that could set back economic progress.

Demand management is a difficult policy to implement, but despite the possible side-effects the policy should not be discarded as it offers a viable way forward.

The cures for unemployment can only be summarised here. All political parties will seek to combine these approaches to gain the maximum possible benefit. In recent years the economy has not been able to deliver full employment – the fall to 6 per cent unemployment in the 1980s was a short-lived success that soon petered out as inflation and then recession took their toll. The problem for the UK and many of the European Union countries is how to achieve an effective record of job creation whilst maintaining a grip on inflation. High rates of growth, low inflation and a successful record of helping the long-term unemployed would be required to approach the goal of 'full employment'.

The balance of payments

All countries trade internationally, with the UK being heavily dependent on this for about 30 per cent of its gross domestic product (GDP). While smaller economies, such as Switzerland and Norway, are heavily dependent on trade, it is unusual to find a large economy, such as the UK, with so much of its prosperity resting on this activity. Any difficulties experienced in the international trading position of the UK will have a severe impact on the well-being of the whole economy.

The balance of payments is a record of transactions between residents and non-residents of the UK. The difference between credits (exports) earned by residents and debits (imports) earned by non-residents produces either a favourable balance (or surplus) or an unfavourable balance (deficit). The balance of payments account provides information on flows of goods, services and capital, but it is the movement of goods and services, summarised in the **current account**, that provides a useful guide to the health of the economy.

Although the accounts always balance, as they would do for a business organisation, it is the deficits or surpluses on the current account that act as a guide. So, for example, a surplus on this account would suggest that the economy was experiencing favourable trading conditions. However, this line of reasoning should not be taken too far because a surplus is not the same as profit, a thing that is seen as a measure of success. One country's surplus is another country's deficit, so a large surplus is frowned on by international bodies such as the International Monetary Fund. This raises a question as to the acceptable size of a surplus – when is it acceptable or unacceptable to the international community?

A deficit is a situation that a country would clearly wish to amend. But here the same problem emerges – a large deficit builds up debts for the economy and should be dealt with, whilst a small deficit is easy to finance and may be tolerated if the reason for it is to bring in capital goods and raw materials from abroad.

In March 1995 the Treasury estimate for that year showed a current account deficit of £186 million, a very small proportion of GDP. In this case the deficit can be financed, but a deficit that showed an increase to 4 per cent of GDP, as happened in the 1980s, was unsustainable. If this reasoning is transferred to surpluses, then the same conclusions can be drawn.

With *large deficits* the problems are related to the incapacity of the economy to meet demand, either because demand is rising too quickly or because there are structural problems with declining and uncompetitive industries. In addition, the exchange rate, if it is fixed, may be forcing exports out of the marketplace – an accusation levelled at the Exchange Rate Mechanism (ERM) of which the UK was a member until 1992. Possible solutions would be to let the exchange rate find its right market level, and put the brakes on the economy by fiscal and monetary measures.

Large surpluses appear to be a mixed blessing, apart from attracting the criticism of other countries that such prosperity is at their expense. Here the problem will be increased pressure on the exchange rate, either allowing it to float upwards to new levels, or (if it is fixed) pressure to see it revalued – an outcome that exporters would not welcome. A long period of surpluses could even result in the threat of punitive action by countries or trading blocs, a threat that the UK would have to take very seriously. The solution could be a combination of relaxing fiscal and monetary policy, or seeing the currency move higher, a shift which would only be possible if other economic factors permitted such a move.

The aim is to see the balance of payments *in balance* or, more practically, to see small deficits or surpluses that can be sustained over time.

Public borrowing

Figure 5.3 reveals the extent of public borrowing, or in some years debt repayment ('public sector debt repayment' – PSDR).

Governments always need to borrow money to finance their activities, particularly on a day-to-day basis when income is low. The demands of delivering public services require financing. The short-term financing arrangements are not particularly contentious, but long-term borrowing leading to a high **public sector borrowing requirement** (PSBR) has an impact on the economy that is seen as negative. It may crowd out private sector investment by causing an increase in interest rate, and by the fact that the government is a better credit risk than companies.

Figure 5.3 Public borrowing

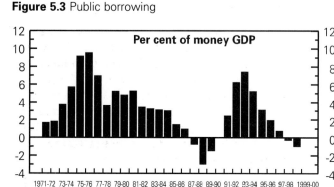

Negative values indicate a public sector debt repayment   **Projections**

The pressure on the government to borrow money becomes greater in times of slow growth and recession, particularly as revenue goes down in these periods. To restrain the PSBR would require a cut in public spending, and possibly an increase in taxation, a tactic used from 1993 to 1995 as the PSBR of £50 billion was gradually reduced.

Macroeconomic policy objectives determine the environment within which businesses operate. What is apparent is that to achieve a balance between them is a difficult task for any government. Inevitably the pressure to tilt the balance one way or another is affected by

political conditions as well as economic, and these should be understood when reviewing a particular government's policy achievements.

Government policy: monetary, fiscal and industrial

To achieve macroeconomic goals, both monetary and fiscal policies will be used to move the economy towards the desired outcome. Further reflection might also reveal the fact that fiscal and monetary measures may contain within them other attributes that the government of the day wishes to exploit.

For example, increasing taxation to cope with a high PSBR might well achieve its goal, but deciding which taxes will be raised is a major policy issue that has other implications. Pursuing the tax example a little further would show that Conservative governments since 1979 have wished to shift the tax burden away from **direct taxation** (such as income tax) towards **indirect taxation** (like VAT). Although the overall **tax burden** has not been reduced in line with their wishes, the shift was made to allow taxpayers to keep more of their earned income and then make choices on what they spend it on. Increasing the VAT rate and bringing more items into the VAT framework pushes prices up, but the hope is that the switch allows market forces to operate as freely as possible. Whether this is ever likely to happen or has in any way been achieved is not for discussion here; what is clear is that fiscal and monetary policies are not a neutral armoury for the politicians to use – they contain additional benefits for the politician to consider in pursuit of other goals.

These factors show the importance of having a government that can look both at the macroeconomic issues and the effect of their policies on the behaviour of industries or on individual organisations and companies. Additionally, provision of government services involves consuming **resources** in order to supply them, and seeking to regulate business activity via health and safety legislation, employment law and so on.

The importance of government – whatever the political rhetoric – is clear for all to see. The Conservative Party may wish to reduce the role of government, but the role that remains is still very large. Likewise the Labour Party may call for an increased role, but it is difficult to see how much more a government could do without moving away from the concept of a mixed economy. Both parties are fully aware that, from the provision of goods and services through to the regulation of the economy, the party of government has a key role to play in helping the country maintain its success. It is necessary to look at policy instruments a little more closely.

Monetary policy

The essence of monetary policy is to control interest rates and/or the supply of money. The government's targets for money supply growth are contained within the **medium-term financial strategy** (MTFS), a statement that sets out targets for public spending and money supply growth over the following three years.

Interest rates are set in line with the prevailing economic conditions, and particularly with respect to forecasts for inflation. The point of focus here is not the economic rationale for the changes in rates, but the impact that increasing or falling rates will have on business activity.

A falling interest rate should encourage investment, an action that will further inject demand into the economy and boost future production. Similarly the benefit to the consumer is felt by reducing the mortgage burden, thereby boosting disposable income and leading to a higher rate of consumption. The effect of a falling interest rate may take time to come through, as mitigating circumstances play their part. For example, because of **negative equity** (the situation houseowners find themselves in where the current values of their properties are less than their mortgage loans), a fall in interest rate may not bring forward extra demand until such time as house prices rise.

Increasing interest rates produces the opposite effect, hitting consumption and investment, although here again there may be a time-lag. Using the mortgage market example again, mortgage repayments may only be adjusted on a yearly basis, so an immediate interest rate increase may not raise monthly payments until some months have elapsed.

Money supply changes are monitored carefully by the government for signs of inflationary pressures. Changes in M0 (mainly notes and coins in circulation) and M4 (M0 plus retail deposits in banks and building societies) can cause the Bank of England to put further pressure on monetary growth by various interventions in the financial markets, as well as by interest rate changes. This can result in restricting credit, with all that it implies for consumption.

Fiscal policy

Fiscal policy is made up of two elements: taxation and government expenditure. In 1995–96 the public expenditure plans were for £300 billion divided as follows:

	£bn
Social security	87.1
Health services	33.0
Defence	21.7
Local government	73.4
Other spending	60.7
Debt/interest	24.5

These categories of expenditure were balanced by tax and other receipts of the following:

	£bn
Income tax	70.1
National insurance contributions	44.5
Corporation tax	26.4
Value added tax	49.0
Excise duties	28.0
Other receipts	60.8
Borrowing	21.5

As already noted, the government plays a large role in the economy. A planned total of £300 billion represents 44 per cent of GDP, so any decisions to cut public expenditure have a sizeable impact on economic prosperity. This emphasises that the scope of action enjoyed by the government is not as great as first imagined. A further limiting factor is that a large part of the expenditure plans are covered by legally binding commitments, such as those on social benefits and education that account for large areas of expenditure.

Taxation is not simply a means to gain revenue, it also allows the pursuit of further political objectives. We have already referred to a shifting of the burden to indirect tax such as VAT, but published figures reveal how large a dependence is still placed on income tax. A government can pursue other goals; for example, the tax on cigarettes can be increased to help to deter smoking, and unleaded petrol can be taxed less heavily for environmental reasons, to provide a price advantage over leaded fuel.

If policy objectives can be pursued using taxation, then it is equally clear that expenditure can be used for the same purpose. Student recruitment has been encouraged, first in higher education and then in further education, by providing extra funding, export guarantee cover has been made cheaper, and so on. What this means for business is that opportunities to supply goods and services in the new spending areas can be created, or taken away as funds dry up.

Industrial policy

Despite the large share of GDP that is still accounted for by public expenditure, the privatisation of nationalised industries has reduced direct state intervention in industry. The main policy initiatives can be summarised as follows:

- *Enterprise culture* – There have been initiatives to help create small businesses and reduce the tax burden on them. Additionally the enterprise culture has been used to introduce an internal market into the National Health Service, to bring in compulsory competitive tendering for local authority services, and to introduce students to the world of business early in their studies.
- *Reduction of subsidies* – The aim has been, where possible, to reduce subsidies or phase them out altogether. Whether it be in steel production or shipbuilding, or the running of a railway, the market will be asked to work without the distortion of subsidies. This also applies to regional grants and assistance.
- *Privatisation* – Many things, from council houses through to public utilities, have been sold off. Privatisation does not on its own create competition, so regulations and the gradual introduction of competition have been seen as the way to reduce the monopoly power of water, electricity, gas and other utilities.
- *Deregulation* – Sometimes referred to as 'reducing red tape', the purpose of deregulation is to eradicate as many restrictions as possible. This has meant the abolition of nearly all the wage councils that formerly set pay for the lowest paid workers, and looking for ways to make it easier to set up in business.
- *Incorporation* – From trust hospitals to further education colleges, incorporation allows the organisation to make more decisions on its own, and crucially to be free of local authority control. Funding becomes more centrally controlled and the organisation is rewarded (or not) on its success in meeting nationally determined performance criteria.
- *Mergers and business practice* – There are various regulating agencies that review mergers, monopoly power and practice and unfair trading.

The overall aim is to promote the **enterprise economy** and to introduce **market forces** into as much of the public sector as possible. Although the political parties do have markedly different views on this, the point still has to be made that the difference often lies in how the government organises and delivers the service, rather than in the question of whether it ought to be involved in the first place.

International influences

Many of the policies and initiatives reviewed above are not unique to the UK. The influence of the European Union is felt in the issue of subsidies, as they try to produce a **single market** that can work with as few distortions as possible. Likewise GATT, and subsequently the World Trade Organisation that took over from it (see later), promotes free-market policies, supported by the International Monetary Fund. The Maastricht agreement has its effect on the amount of public borrowing that countries can undertake, a condition that seeks to create the foundation for monetary convergence between the EU members.

Lastly, it is not the case that in a borderless world the UK is completely free to raise and lower interest rates at will. The financial markets are too big to control, so governments, like businesses, have to understand how they operate and what they can do to work *with* them. It is important, therefore, to appreciate how this can influence both policy and its implementation.

The UK financial system

Advanced market economies function with the help of financial intermediaries, whose main role is to channel funds from those individuals and organisations who wish to lend money to those who wish to borrow it. It is such a common part of everyday life that a review of why we require financial intermediaries would appear unnecessary. However, there are good reasons why a closer look is required.

The benefits of financial intermediaries can be outlined using two diagrams. In Figure 5.4 the flow of funds is not interrupted, so in theory the economy will work in a simple and straightforward way. On further reflection it will become apparent that the units that have surplus funds would have to search out those who wished to borrow and then vet them to ascertain their creditworthiness. As this increases the risk to the lender, the interest charged would have to increase, particularly as the liquidity (the ability to turn the investment back into money at short notice) would also be compromised. Looking at the situation from the borrower's point of view, they would also have the problem of searching out those who would be willing to lend money and to satisfy themselves that they were dealing with a reputable organisation or individual.

The second diagram, in Figure 5.5, introduces financial intermediaries. This complicates the flow of funds, but endeavours to overcome the problems already outlined. It does not stop 'disintermediation' (i.e. a situation where the intermediaries are bypassed), but it helps to promote an efficient movement of funds between borrowers and lenders.

Figure 5.4 Uninterrupted flow of funds

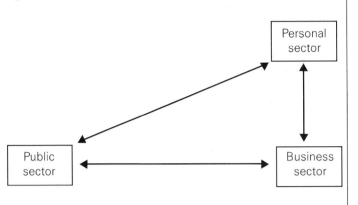

Figure 5.5 Financial intermediaries

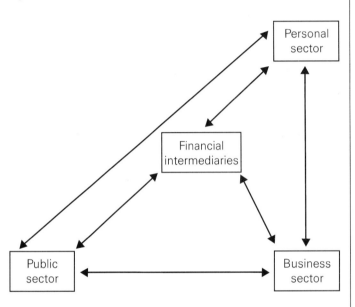

The advantages can be listed as follows:

- There are convenient ways to save money, with a choice of intermediaries (banks, building societies etc.) and financial instruments (national savings, deposit accounts etc).
- The money lent by savers is packaged. For example, by pooling the deposits of many small savers, a bank is able to package up the amount and lend to borrowers in the form of mortgages and business loans.
- By lending to a large number of individuals and organisations, it is possible to spread the risk of any losses suffered by the default of borrowers (bad debts). The risk is effectively pooled. As long as the intermediary is in sound financial health, the bank does not run the risk of losing the investment.
- There is a ready source of funds for borrowers. Ignoring the cost of borrowing, and assuming that borrowers are creditworthy, they will be able to obtain some money from an intermediary. In addition, there is provision for 'maturity transformation', which is the

ability of the intermediary to solve the problem of the borrowers requiring long-term loans and the lenders requiring liquidity.

- The benefits help businesses to operate more effectively as they use the funds and services of the banks and other intermediaries.

Financial institutions and markets

The variety of financial institutions reveals the complex requirements of both borrowers and lenders. Banks, building societies, investment trusts and pension funds are just a few of the organisations whose job it is to channel funds to those who require them. These institutions operate in the short-term (money) market and the long-term (capital) market. These rather arbitrary distinctions serve to differentiate the basic needs of those who make use of their services.

In the money market, the main activity centres around funds which are lent for periods from as short as overnight up to about one year. The capital market focuses on money borrowed and lent for periods of five years or more. There is a grey area, of one to five years, that is not incorporated into the two definitions, and hardly surprisingly this is called the medium-term market. For simplicity, the terms 'money market' and 'capital market' will be used here to cover all the operations of the financial markets.

Institutions and markets develop along with the needs of the business community, which can be summarised as the need to manage risk and to supply corporate finance.

Risk management

Organisations may have exposure to the risk of foreign exchange movements that could mean that they make a loss on a transaction overseas. In addition, all firms, whether exporters or not, face the problem of changes in interest rates, which could severely reduce profitability. One response to risk, of which these are two examples, is to find a way to reduce it (i.e. manage it). A second response is to seek to avoid risk if at all possible, so firms may seek to avoid exchange risks by invoicing and receiving payment in sterling.

For any particular risk there is usually an organisation or individual who will be prepared to accept that risk, and as markets become more complex and international the solutions offered by those helping businesses to reduce their risks become more sophisticated. Banks and other financial institutions have developed solutions that, at a cost to the customer, will provide a way of overcoming the problem.

Corporate finance

Organisations need to borrow in the short term to provide themselves with working capital, so that they can meet their commitments to their suppliers before income is received from customers. Likewise, there may be a need to purchase equipment, which will eventually be financed by selling existing assets, but bridging finance is required to fund the purchase. The role of banks in both these examples is clear, but the range of solutions on offer will not be.

For longer-term financial needs the provision of funds can be achieved in many ways, from the use of bank loans, through debentures and equity to Eurobonds. Each of these provides various options to the company that the bank can advise upon and organise.

The role of financial intermediaries is to facilitate the smooth flow of funds throughout the economy. Financial institutions and markets develop in such a way that trends in business that produce new risks and needs for corporate finance can be met in the most suitable way. This part of the business environment is as important to monitor and understand as any other. The solutions offered to managers become ever more complex and sophisticated.

Challenges to banks

Banks in all countries are facing formidable challenges, particularly with the loss of the monopoly status that had bolstered their position in the financial system. Institutions other than banks will in the future be providing traditional banking services, so that banks will need to keep their costs down, go for profitable business and move into new markets. According to financial and banking experts, the traditional role of intermediation will become less important for banks, as they seek to diversify into other services such as insurance.

Examples of new entrants into the banking markets are:

- the use of in-house banks in Volvo (Sweden) and BP (UK)
- Marks & Spencer offering a range of financial services to its customers
- major shops offering short-term money market investment.

Developments in technology and delivery systems have also had an effect on the provision of financial services, with branch banking becoming less important and direct banking by post or by phone increasing in popularity.

Banks are not, therefore, the sole suppliers of banking services. Many traditional activities of banks can now be undertaken equally well by markets, non-bank financial intermediaries and ordinary (non-financial) companies.

Supervision of the banking system

An important institution, used both for economic management and for supervision of the banking system, is the **central bank**. In the UK this role is taken by the Bank of England, a nationalised corporation that has to work closely with the government of the day.

Over the years the Bank of England has developed a number of functions, the most important of which are summarised below.

- It is banker to central government, holding the public deposits (the government's bank accounts).
- It is banker to the commercial banks, with each bank keeping its own account at the Bank.
- It is lender to the banking system, a function which provides liquidity to the banks at a suitable interest rate, when the system is short of cash, or takes in any surplus cash.
- It manages the national debt, which means it looks after the short- and long-term borrowing needs of government and manages the repayment of debt when it falls due.
- It issues money in the form of bank notes.
- It manages the Exchange Equalisation Account, which is the account where the nation's gold and foreign currency reserves are held.
- It advises the government on monetary policy.
- It acts as agent for the government in carrying out its monetary policies.
- It supervises the national banking system, where it seeks to ensure that individual banks retain sufficient liquidity and do not undertake ventures that carry a high risk.

Many of these activities do not have to be carried out by the central bank, they have simply developed over many years as areas the Bank has come to dominate.

Many commentators and business leaders are critical of the closeness of the Bank of England to government. They point to countries where the central bank is independent of government – such as the Bundesbank in Germany. This bank sets interest rates according to its view of the likely trend in inflation, with obvious impact on exchange rates and economic activity.

Whether the Bank of England remains independent of the government or not, its freedom to act is circumscribed not only by the role of the politicians; it must also take account of the fact that world financial markets have emerged in which, because of their size and significance, the Bank's room for manoeuvre is reduced. With regard to interest rates, for example, movements in other countries' rates have to be recognised as exerting pressure to change UK rates. If the pressure builds up it could result in the pound coming under attack, a change which could badly affect economic policy objectives.

The money markets are so powerful that extreme pressure on one currency cannot be relieved by using the foreign exchange resources of the affected nation's central bank. A key group of banks in America, Japan, Germany and France, as well as the UK, would have to coordinate their activities to defend a currency against such pressure. Clearly, this could not be done unless action were being taken to remove the problem, such as the need to reduce inflation.

Knowing that the Bank of England, along with the government, is not free to determine interest rates without reference to the financial markets and other central banks, is important for business organisations. Calls to reduce interest rates to help stimulate business activity may fall on sympathetic ears, but the Bank of England may not oblige when rates in other countries are rising to head off inflation. It may be more important for a trading nation like the UK to see stability in the exchange rate, rather than short-lived reductions in interest rates.

Internationalisation of business

One of the most significant developments over the past 50 years has been the internationalisation and globalisation of business. **Internationalisation** refers to the process of increasing involvement in international operations, whereas **globalisation** is an approach that actively seeks homogeneity in products, markets, promotion and image, based on the belief that the world is becoming more homogeneous and differences in material markets are disappearing.

The implications of this development are that it has altered the nature of competition as well as the balance of economic power on a global scale. This has been reflected in the rapid growth of world trade and investment and the growing co-operation and number of joint ventures between companies of different countries to gain both competitive and technological advantages.

Both in macroeconomic policy-making and from the point of view of strategic decision-making in companies, external economic factors have to be incorporated in any appraisal. In Chapter 7 the role of the European Union

and its regulatory activities are reviewed, but other significant international bodies that have helped to promote trade development and encourage internationalisation need to be considered here.

General Agreement on Tariffs and Trade/World Trade Organisation

GATT was organised in 1948 and was originally planned to be a temporary agreement to complement the international commercial agreement, known as the International Trade Organisation, but this failed on the refusal of the USA to endorse it. However, the membership of GATT gradually increased over the years, reaching 100 in 1986, as members perceived the benefits to be gained by working together to reduce barriers to trade. The organisation is independent of the United Nations, but has a loose affiliation to it.

The main objectives of GATT were to reduce, or if possible eliminate, trade restrictions and to create an international forum in which trading nations could discuss trade issues, resolve trade conflicts and plan trading policies. As a multilateral agreement, GATT had no binding authority over its members, but acted to persuade members to adopt the following policies:

- eliminate tariffs and quotas among the members of GATT
- improve the trading environment through negotiations on trade matters
- follow the most-favoured-nation rule, in which all members treat each other equally and without discrimination
- treat exports from developing countries preferentially.

The members of GATT met in annual sessions to discuss and resolve trade issues and to hold conferences which lasted over a number of years and focused on specific restrictions. The last round of conferences, known as the **Uruguay Round**, lasted from 1986 to 1994 and included issues related to food and drink, intellectual property rights, textiles, services and farm subsidies. The complexity of these issues and the threat to some groups' incomes (e.g. farmers) caused many stumbling blocks along the way, but the trading groups of the EU, Japan and the USA finally passed the Uruguay Round proposals in December 1994, providing a huge potential boost to world demand and trade prospects.

In addition to the agreement to reduce protective measures, a new organisation was created. It came into existence on January 1995. Replacing GATT, it is known as the **World Trade Organisation**. This will produce a more formal response to trading issues and will look at the implementation of the 1994 agreement and focus on those areas – mainly services – that were not the subject of previous rounds.

The success of GATT is important for business organisations as it has created opportunities that companies should recognise and be prepared to exploit. Although the advanced economies are expected to be the main beneficiaries, there will be losers as adjustments and structural changes take place.

International Monetary Fund (IMF)

The main purposes of the **International Monetary Fund**, established in 1944, were to produce stability in international exchange markets, to promote monetary cooperation, and to produce short-term financial help (liquidity) to member countries.

The role of the IMF has developed over the years as it has attracted more and more nations. The main advantage of membership is in obtaining bank loans, as a country that does not belong will be viewed as a credit risk.

In recent years the IMF has helped the former communist countries to introduce financial reforms, and has helped developing countries improve their prospects and growth by bringing in a more market-orientated approach.

For the advanced economies the role of the IMF has been reduced, particularly as a global financial market has emerged. The richest countries – known as the Group of 7 or G7, and made up of the USA, Japan, Germany, France, Italy, UK and Canada – have set up meetings, or summits, to review items of interest to these important economies. However, the long-term importance of the G7 is uncertain as economic development in Far Eastern countries has shifted the balance of economic power towards that region.

International Bank for Reconstruction and Development (IBRD)

More commonly referred to as the **World Bank**, this was set up at about the same time as the IMF, to provide loans to developing countries for long-term economic projects. The World Bank is the major provider of long-term loans at low rates to these countries and is in effect the largest provider of aid assistance.

Funds are provided mainly by the subscriptions of member states, and as poorer countries have often found it difficult to meet the IBRD conditions, the Bank set up the International Development Association and the

International Finance Corporation to provide longer-term loans at very low rates to those countries with severe difficulties.

The IMF and World Bank started out with a clear demarcation, with the former concentrating on short-term loans and the latter providing long-term assistance. But as a consequence of the involvement of the IMF in resolving the Third World debt crisis and the reforms and restructuring of eastern Europe, it has been increasingly involved in providing long-term loans to debt-ridden nations. Likewise the World Bank has provided loans against promises of macroeconomic reform, providing a focus not dissimilar to the IMF. The convergence between the two organisations points to the possibility of a merger at some time in the future. However, owing to the volume of work that each of them has, this is not likely to happen very quickly.

Organisation for Economic Cooperation and Development (OECD)

The **OECD** is made up of 24 members drawn from the richest industrialised countries, which explains the term 'the rich man's club' that is often used. Although gradually expanding as more countries reach higher levels of economic stability and income, it will still focus on the interests of a minority of the world's population.

The OECD conducts numerous research projects dealing with economic and industrial development of both advanced and developing countries, international trade, foreign investment, and other areas. Its main influence is to persuade governments of the wisdom of a certain course of action, and to help this process it provides periodic economic forecasts and surveys both of its members and of other countries. A forecast is an event that is awaited with interest by governments and by the financial community, as a favourable report can act as a valuable endorsement of macroeconomic policy.

Conclusion

This chapter has set out the broad framework for understanding the national economy. From a review of the objectives that governments wish to pursue, through the area of fiscal and monetary policy to the international economic relations that influence the UK, an overview has been provided that has one main underlying lesson. If business is to perform well, there is a need to understand both the framework, the thrust of economic policy and the room for flexibility that is available to a government, so as to plan a company's strategies and to see them through to successful implementation. Organisations must be prepared to understand the new competitive environment, and to identify the threats and opportunities that inevitably accompany them.

Case Study
The 'feel-good factor'

Business cycles are closely connected to political cycles, which are the periods between each general election. In theory the general election is held every five years (the maximum life of a parliament), but in practice governments seek re-election after four years. The shortened life of a parliament is due to governments seeking to choose the best time to go to the country, and obviously the right time to do this is when the economy is recovering, unemployment is falling and consumers feel that it is possible to increase their expenditure – the so-called 'feel-good factor'.

The recovery from recession in the UK which started in 1992, however, was not accompanied by the feel-good factor, and looking at the economic statistics it is at first difficult to see why. The economy was growing at well over 3 per cent, inflation was low, unemployment was falling, as was the balance of payments deficit, and PSBR had shown a noticeable fall. Despite this, the Conservative government was lagging badly in public opinion polls and was defeated in the European elections and at some key by-elections. The problem was to find out why this recovery was so different from the others. Political and economic commentators pointed to the following:

- Tax increases had been phased in, starting in 1993, denting consumer confidence.
- The recovery was mainly export-led, with signs of investment picking up to help maintain growth.
- Restructuring in many industries was still going on, and many middle management posts were being shed – causing job losses among a key group of government supporters throughout the previous decade.

Questions for discussion

1 *What additional items could be cited that would explain the lack of the feel-good factor?*
2 *Taking the complete list, look more closely at each item, filling in more detail that might explain the problem; or look at the impact it would have on government policy.*

Further reading

- *Understanding the UK Economy*, edited by P. Curwen. Macmillan, 1990.
- *International Business Competing in the Global Market Place* by C. W. L. Hill. Irwin, 1994.
- *International Business Economies – A European Perspective*, edited by J. Piggott and M. Cook. Pitman, 1993.
- *European Economies – A Comparative Study*, edited by F. Somes. Pitman, 1991.
- *Economic Theory and Marketing Practice* by Angela Hatton and Mike Oldroyd. Butterworth-Heinemann, 1992.
- *Economics* by Stephen Ison. Pitman, 1993.

6 Environmental factors and business activities

On completion of this chapter students should be able to:

■ assess the impact of technological change on businesses

■ assess the role of social and community processes in business activity, including social protection and social safety nets

■ examine the significance of the environment, and its protection, for business decisions

■ evaluate the impact of political issues and democracy on business relations.

Technological developments

Technological change is rapid, and business organisations need to find ways to adapt themselves to it. Some of the main technological advances have been reviewed in Chapter 13, and in examples used throughout the book the impact of technology can be seen through the way firms have to respond by adapting their strategies.

Change of this nature can be seen in the impact technology has on markets and products. The following are examples of such changes:

■ *The type of products or services that are produced* – Both consumer and industrial markets have seen major innovations, ranging from microchips to CD–I's and local area networks for office information systems.
■ *Production methods* – There is a continuing trend towards the use of labour-saving production equipment, new manufacturing technology and automation.
■ *Provision of services* – This is most noticeable in the financial services sector, with telephone banking. All services are looking towards the 'information superhighway' to review the delivery of their product.
■ *Market identification* – Database systems can be exploited to seek out opportunities with either existing customers or potential clients.
■ *Employee flexibility* – This is a contentious area. Automation and computerisation can provide opportunities for organisations to dispense with staff, often at the middle-management level. These functions still have to be performed by someone, so those that remain may need to improve their skills and knowledge. In addition, the way employees are organised may also be influenced by the use of technology.

The effects of these changes are radical, helping organisations to cut their costs, both on the production and delivery side, make their products more competitive and pass on these savings to the customer. The quality of existing products and services can be improved, and new ones produced. On the human resource side, the use of technology can create new work and produce a more varied type of work that has the potential to motivate staff.

Many industries have found that what was previously a cosy club, with known competition and products, can almost overnight be thrown into confusion by the lowering of the **barriers to entry** that technology brings with it.

Case Study
Book publishers and the threat of CD–ROMs

With advances in multimedia publishing, many of today's traditional book publishers may soon find themselves out of business. Some multimedia experts expect that within a few years CD and online multimedia will hit about half of all the categories of books being published today. From 1971 to 1994 the number of encyclopaedias sold halved, but the launching of encyclopaedias on CD–ROM bucked the trend.

Many book publishers will be able to make money by moving their titles into the multimedia mode, but they have a much smaller share of the CD–ROM market than the software companies who are becoming their competitors. Firms such as Microsoft, WordPerfect and others are learning the book publishers' art faster than the publishers are coming to terms with the new technology.

Microsoft, for example, understands the importance of copyright and has been investing in intellectual property assets. Microsoft owns a significant stake in Dorling Kindersley in Britain, and more than 800 people in America are employed in producing multimedia products. The firm is also able to spend far more than any book publisher can afford, with $100 million being spent on consumer multimedia in 1990.

Television and film companies are also big players in this market and are well-placed to capture a slice of the CD–ROM market. Such companies can provide inexpensively for multimedia applications.

A further factor for publishers with existing brands, such as the copyright character Paddington Bear, is that the publishing rights position is less than clear, and many will find that they do not own the multimedia rights for existing characters.

For authors these developments provide opportunities to experiment, particularly as creativity can be encouraged with this new approach.

Many traditional publishers are unsure how to respond to these challenges, but one thing is certain – the industry is never going to be the same again as new players enter and reorganisation takes place.

Questions for discussion

1 *Is it likely that all books will be affected by multimedia?*
2 *Despite the suggestion that 'multimedia is the future', how would a publishing company convince itself that this was a valid position to take, in order to consider its strategy?*
3 *How will authors benefit from these changes?*
4 *Suggest why authors might feel threatened.*

Developments in production

As we will see later, the influence of technology is normally linked to the use of new and improved machinery. Flawed and limited though this definition of technology is, there is a need to keep in mind the reasons why new machines are seen as important areas for consideration by business. There are significant pressures pushing managers into a review of their technological and human resource requirements.

One term sums up the move towards further automation, and that is **world-class manufacturing**. The term was first used in the mid 1980s and covers certain key factors.

- *Production quality* – The traditional approach to controlling product quality had been limited to the identification of defective products. The new approach is aimed at looking at the original causes of poor product quality and trying to eliminate them. This is summed up in the phrase '**right first time**', meaning that there should be zero defective items.
- *Just-in-time (JIT) production* – This is a process that has different names in different industries, but is taken to mean the elimination of waste which occurs when resources are left idle and fail to add value to the product. Examples of waste would be stocks of material and components that are unused for some time, or the inefficient movement of materials.
- *Managing the human resource* – To obtain benefits to go alongside JIT production and quality control, the skills and knowledge of employees should be such that flexibility is encouraged, team approaches are used, and more responsibility is taken by each worker.
- *Responding to the customer* – Often described by marketers as 'relationship marketing', understanding the needs and wants of customers and building a long-term relationship with them is the key challenge for firms in the 1990s, particularly as consumers and industrial buyers constantly change their demands and require the supplier to follow suit.

World-class manufacturing (WCM) puts into perspective the fact that a whole range of changes are required if UK and European companies are to maintain their present markets. WCM appears to be an issue that faces manufacturers, but its influence can be seen in the services sector, from transport through to food retailing, so all firms and organisations have to find a suitable response.

How are UK companies faring compared with the best in the world? There are some companies that match the best that Japan, America or Germany can offer, but these are the exception and not the rule. Studies in much of the manufacturing sector, for instance, have shown that most companies currently lag far behind, and appear to be falling yet further behind, the best. Studies in 1993 and 1994 on UK car-component companies show that they are far less efficient, with much poorer quality levels, than any in western Europe, Japan and the USA – an issue that is worrying given the much improved performance of the UK car manufacturers. A government study of competitiveness showed that this was an issue right across the manufacturing sector of the economy.

A closer look at technology

If technology is examined in the wider context of change, then it will be easier to understand the motivation behind its use. However, the term is imprecise and can cover various meanings and interpretations. Buchanan and Huczynski in their book, *Organisational Behaviour*, identify three ways in which the word can be used:

- *apparatus*, meaning machines and associated tools
- *technique*, meaning skills and procedures
- *organisation*, meaning the way in which social organisation is manipulated to foster production.

This broad definition suggests that we must always regard technology as encompassing both tangible (machines) and intangible (social relations) elements, with new machines requiring new skills and even new work patterns for workers. This might appear to be a fairly banal observation, but far too often investment in machinery is wasted if the organisation is not altered to accommodate the change. To explain this further we can look more closely at two examples, computer integrated manufacturing (CIM) and just-in-time (JIT) production.

Computer integrated manufacturing

This approach covers the computer-aided design of products, the use of computers to assist in the production process by, for example, giving instructions to machines, and the (partial) automation of administration by (amongst other things) computerising the customer order process. This allows the company to produce customised products in whatever numbers the customer requires.

WCM firms, or those aspiring to that status, also want to invest in CIM, but the organisational impact must be considered – many firms overlook this fact at their peril.

For example, this type of manufacturing requires flexibility on the part of the work force, a reduction in the levels of hierarchy, and multi-skilling. These changes are not easy to introduce and may be resisted by those whose traditional role and status are threatened. It is asking a lot to keep the old ways of working running alongside the new system and expect to be successful.

Just-in-time production

This approach has already been mentioned as part of WCM, but more needs to be said about it because it is a popular way for firms to adapt to a competitive environment.

JIT is a technique that focuses on the organisation of work flows to provide a quick, high-quality, flexible production approach that leads to minimum waste and stock levels. The Japanese car industry is often cited as an example, where the car is not built until the customer orders it, so that the suppliers and the car manufacturer are linked into a **demand-led** system. This is a radical departure from the traditional mass-production techniques that looked for economies in long production runs and capacity utilisation. JIT requires that production is as smooth and effortless as possible, because the customer will be unable to purchase from stock and is not going to be impressed if told that there has been some malfunction in production. If production is to be maintained, then the maintenance and production team will have to be able to deal with a machinery problem immediately it occurs, an approach that would have been impossible when strict divisions existed between the work of production and maintenance staff.

The links between firms and their suppliers become critical under JIT, and any disruption due, for example, to industrial action would be catastrophic.

Figure 6.1 summarises the types of production process seen in firms. For each approach it can be appreciated that the key elements to look for are the machines, skills and work organisation to be found in firms using it.

Likewise, the choice of approach would itself be related to the type of industry under consideration. The impact of JIT, for example, has been a popular focus for the media in the UK, and many industries have adapted it to their own requirements.

What is certain, though, is that the use of JIT is not as widespread as many suppose, especially where the type of product or the demand for it is such that this method is, at the moment, inappropriate.

Service industries

The use of technology has been a key focus of interest in services as competition has increased and standards of service have been expected to improve.

Figure 6.1 A summary of types of production

Job production. This is the production of items in separate jobs, often used when a product is being made to order. In job production, work will not commence until an order has been received, and it is difficult to keep stocks in advance of the order. Workers are often highly skilled, with each job requiring individual planning and preparation.

Batch production. This occurs when a batch of items is produced in one go, where the items are not for any one specific customer, or when being made at regular intervals in specific quantities. This means that batch production requires work to be passed from one stage to another, with each group of workers carrying out a specific function, so that planning and the design of the system are given a high priority.

Flow production. This happens when a product is made on a continuous basis. Examples of this are paper and oil, where treatment of the item is undertaken via a continuous process (process production). Another example would be mass production of white goods. Here the standardisation of the method and equipment is high, with very specialised equipment being required to facilitate the process.

Although these three types of production are distinguishable, many manufacturers adopt more than one type. In car production, for example, the final assembly may be undertaken using the flow production approach, while certain components may have been produced using batch production. Whichever approach is used, the same issues apply – with tools, techniques and organisation being adapted to provide the best possible use of resources.

As outlined in other sections of this book, services and goods are usually distinguished by the intangible elements of services compared with the tangible aspect of goods. In practice, however, services often have tangible elements. Technology is used to support the service, rather than to interfere with the important interaction that takes place between the service provider and the customer.

Many financial services, such as insurance and banking, now use telephone ordering to keep costs down and to provide an efficient service. Although this is popular with many customers, banks have been accused of reducing the all-important direct human link that traditional sales outlets provide – a fact noted by the banks as they seek to maintain a branch network alongside telephone banking.

Technology and work

New technologies require new skills and have the potential to reduce the amount of time spent on boring and repetitive tasks. They can also *reduce* skill and *produce* boring and repetitive jobs. Both trends can be seen throughout industry, and management faces the task of responding to this challenge.

For example, improved information systems allow senior managers to centralise decision-making based on the regular collection, interpretation and dissemination of information – a development that bypasses middle management and makes it redundant. The problem is to reorganise with a smaller middle-management group, with more responsibility passed down to teams and individuals. However, this is not an easy process, with redundancy costs, morale and motivation issues all contributing to a situation that can weaken the reorganisation effort.

Technology can also involve sub-contracting work to other organisations, over which the manager has no direct control. A further development is that, with the push to the creation of a communication highway, people can work from home without the need to meet together in offices – a move that can mean that some staff seek to become self-employed and work for several companies.

Charles Handy in his book, *The Age of Unreason*, suggests that a new form of organisation will emerge, which he describes as a 'shamrock', based around a core of essential executives and workers supported by outside contractors and part-time help. Although this form has been seen before, it has been confined to small companies and professional partnerships. What is new is that it is now being seen in large organisations and in the public sector. The implication of this for the work force will be outlined in the next section, but Handy suggests that by the end of the century only 50 per cent of all jobs will be traditional full-time ones, with a fairly clear career structure. The remainder will be self-employed and part-time.

Technology and changes in manufacturing processes and the way services are delivered will continue to influence work organisation. What is unclear is how the benefits will be exploited and the challenges met. In 1995, the director general of the Confederation of British Industry spoke about the problem of uncertainty, as the 'job for life' became a thing of the past. Workers who were self-employed and part-time would need to provide for themselves if they were to gain adequate pensions and insurance coverage. This will be discussed later in the chapter.

Technology and innovation

It is important to remind ourselves that innovation in business has become a strategic issue. Innovation can involve the creation of new products, improvements to existing ones, enhancing the quality of the production process to contribute to cost reduction, or simply responding more flexibly to customer requirements. Whatever the mixture, innovation along these lines can be found in firms and organisations throughout the private and public sectors, and the competitive drive to improve products, systems and procedures will mean a constant review of organisational structures.

Labour market trends

The work force of the UK is about 28 million adults, who are either in work or actively seeking it (see Figure 6.2). This total is expected to rise steadily over a decade, reaching nearly 30 million people. Hidden in these totals are some changes to the structure of the UK working population.

Figure 6.2 Features of the UK work force

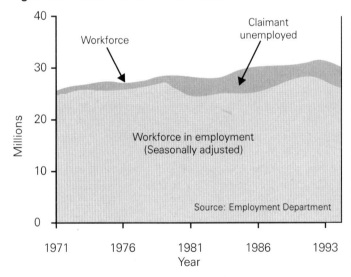

Source: Employment Department

For example, the country has both an ageing population and an ageing work force. In 1986 nearly a quarter of the work force was under 25, but by 2001 this will have changed to being one sixth. Figure 6.3 shows that there has been a general trend towards women becoming increasingly economically active, with more than a half of women aged over 16 participating in the work force.

To a certain extent the rise in female activity rates can be explained by the increasing availability of part-time work, but other factors need to be given consideration when looking at this change – the rise in female participation in

further and higher education, alongside a rise in the average age at which they have children, helps to encourage women to seek work.

The changing age and sex structure of the work force presents challenges for employers. Traditionally, employers could rely on a ready supply of young workers they could employ relatively cheaply, train in the skills required for the job and hope to keep for a reasonable time. Although some might leave to seek alternative careers, there were always those willing to replace them. This is no longer the case. It has been estimated that if the National Health Service wanted to maintain its traditional recruitment pattern for nurses, it would have to employ *all* the 16-year-old female school-leavers in any one year! Employers in general are looking at alternative sources of workers – such as married women returning to the work force after raising a family, and older workers who have been made redundant. This approach presents its own problems because the management and motivation of these groups will be significantly different.

Figure 6.4 shows the number of employees in paid employment as well as those who were self-employed. Various trends can be identified. One trend is the switch from employment in manufacturing to employment in services, with nearly three-quarters of employees working in services in 1993.

Figure 6.5 shows that people from Pakistani or Bangladeshi ethnic groups are three to four times more likely to be self-employed than those from the black ethnic groups.

Explaining the differences between the participating roles of ethnic groups, of men and women, and of various age categories, requires careful analysis, because social, historical and economic factors combine to produce the patterns we see here. Whatever the causes of the lack of participation of one group or the over-representation of another, *the main challenge is to overcome the waste in skills and knowledge of those who are in some way excluded from making a valuable contribution.*

One obvious way in which problems associated with the working population are often encountered is in the area of unemployment. In Chapter 5, government policy to assist with this issue was reviewed, but it will be useful to examine a little further the ways in which unemployment is calculated. There are two basic methods of doing this.

The first method, known as the **claimant count**, uses administrative systems to count the people recorded as unemployed at government offices. Rules for unemployment benefit and other benefits change from time to time, and this obviously affects the claimant count. In order to remove distortions of this nature, the Department of Employment publishes a seasonally

Figure 6.3 Work force economic activity rates (percentages)

	16–19	20–24	25–34	35–44	45–54	55–59	60–64
				AGE RANGES			
Males							
1984	73.5	85.0	93.7	95.4	93.0	82.5	57.3
1986	73.2	86.2	93.7	94.8	91.8	81.1	53.8
1990	75.6	86.8	94.3	94.7	91.5	81.0	54.4
1991	73.4	85.6	93.9	94.7	91.0	80.3	54.1
1992	70.6	84.4	93.2	94.0	91.0	78.0	52.9
Projections:							
1996	67.5	80.5	92.9	93.9	90.2	77.6	48.6
2001	67.9	77.0	92.9	94.0	89.8	77.7	46.6
2006	69.5	77.0	92.8	94.0	89.5	77.7	45.9
Females							
1984	69.4	70.2	61.1	70.9	69.5	51.8	21.8
1986	70.3	70.7	63.5	72.1	70.5	51.8	19.1
1990	71.5	75.1	70.0	76.5	72.8	54.9	22.7
1991	70.7	72.7	69.7	76.7	72.7	54.5	24.1
1992	67.3	71.8	69.4	77.0	74.5	54.7	23.4
Projections:							
1996	64.4	71.4	72.3	79.0	75.4	55.2	22.6
2001	65.4	72.0	76.0	82.0	76.2	55.9	24.0
2006	67.4	74.2	79.5	85.0	76.5	56.6	25.9

Source: Employment Department

Figure 6.4 Workers in manufacturing, services and other industries

	Employees			**Self-employed**		
	1986	1991	1993	1986	1991	1993
All industries (thousands)	20 886	21 719	20 795	2 566	3 066	2 902
of which (percentages)						
Males	55	52	51	75	76	75
Females	45	48	49	25	24	25
Manufacturing	25	21	20	8	9	10
Services	67	71	73	63	61	62
Other	9	8	7	29	29	28

Source: Employment Department

adjusted series which is consistent with the current coverage of the count. This is recalculated back to 1971 each time there is a change, and is the series given most coverage in the national press.

The second method used to measure unemployment is a survey. Individuals are asked whether they have a job and, if not, whether they would like a job and what steps they have taken to find one. The **Labour Force Survey**

(which is supported by the International Labour Organisation) has the advantage of not being affected to the same extent by benefits rule changes, but it has the drawback of taking time to complete and is not, therefore, so readily available as the claimant count method. Both methods are used by the Employment Department and, although the two methods are obviously different, they do show a similar pattern of unemployment trends.

Figure 6.5 The self-employed as a percentage of all in employment, by ethnic origin (spring 1993)

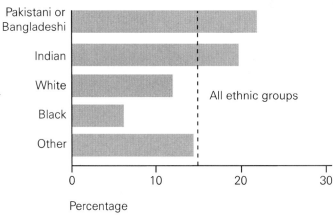

Source: Employment Department

The methods outlined above seek to produce a total figure for unemployment, but they are not easy to use to compare performances between countries. A more useful way to do this is to express unemployment *as a rate*. Unemployment is measured differently in different countries and so the OECD uses a standard set of concepts to compare rates. These rates are estimated by the OECD to conform, as far as possible, to the guidelines and are calculated as percentages of the total work force.

Figure 6.6 shows, for member countries of the OECD, the movement of unemployment rates. What is noticeable is that EU countries have a poorer record on unemployment than Japan, the USA and some Scandinavian countries, a feature that produced the review of supply-side and demand policies by governments to see how a reduction in unemployment could be encouraged.

Skill trends

Figure 6.7 shows the projected changes in types of jobs until the year 2000. Modest overall employment growth is forecast, with a continuous trend towards growth in services and a further decline in primary and manufacturing industry. Clearly, this change will require further investment in new skills for the work force, but demand from businesses for new skills to accommodate new production methods is likely to continue to increase. This will be driven by the growing need for workers to have a sound basis of core skills, a move towards more highly skilled white-collar jobs, and the professionalisation of the work force (whether part-time or full-time).

Figure 6.7 Projected change in jobs, 1991–2000

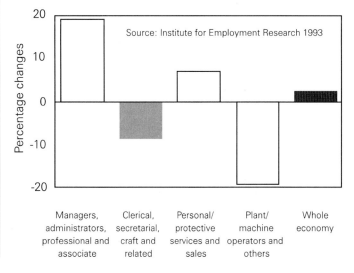

Figure 6.6 Unemployment rates percentages adjusted to OECD concepts

	1976	1981	1983	1984	1985	1986	1987	1988	1989	1990	1991	1992
United Kingdom	5.6	9.8	12.4	11.7	11.2	11.2	10.2	8.5	7.1	6.8	8.7	9.9
Belgium	6.4	10.8	12.1	12.1	11.3	11.2	11.0	9.7	8.0	7.2	7.2	7.9
France	4.4	7.4	8.3	9.7	10.2	10.4	10.5	10.0	9.4	8.9	9.4	10.3
Germany	3.7	4.4	8.0	7.1	7.2	6.4	6.2	6.2	5.6	4.8	4.2	4.6
Italy	6.6	7.8	8.8	9.4	9.6	10.5	10.9	11.0	10.9	10.3	9.9	10.5
Netherlands	5.5	8.5	12.0	11.8	10.6	9.9	9.6	9.2	8.3	7.5	7.0	6.8
Portugal	..	..	7.9	8.4	8.5	8.4	7.0	5.7	5.0	4.6	4.1	4.1
Spain	4.6	13.9	17.2	20.0	21.4	21.0	20.1	19.1	16.9	15.9	16.0	18.1
Australia	4.7	5.7	9.9	8.9	8.2	8.0	8.1	7.2	6.1	6.9	9.5	10.7
Canada	7.1	7.5	11.8	11.2	10.4	9.5	8.8	7.7	7.5	8.1	10.2	11.2
Finland	3.8	4.8	5.4	5.2	5.0	5.3	5.0	4.5	3.4	3.4	7.5	13.0
Japan	2.0	2.2	2.6	2.7	2.6	2.8	2.8	2.5	2.3	2.1	2.1	2.2
Sweden	1.6	2.5	3.5	3.1	2.8	2.7	1.9	1.6	1.4	1.5	2.7	4.8
USA	7.6	7.5	9.5	7.4	7.1	6.9	6.1	5.4	5.2	5.4	6.6	7.3

Projections such as this can chart the need for new skills, but consideration has to be given to the needs of the economy now. For instance, are businesses geared up to take full advantage of the opportunities on offer, or will growth be slowed down by skill shortages? During 1994 and 1995 there were skill shortages reported at a fairly early stage in the business cycle, a feature that would be further complicated by 'hidden' skill shortages which are not identified as recruitment problems, but which would erode competitiveness in home and overseas markets. The lack of skills in the existing work force could compel firms to leave markets if they believed that they did not have the skills to compete.

Figure 6.8 provides an analysis of where the jobs will be created or lost. New jobs will occur in white-collar occupations, covering highly skilled as well as less skilled roles. Overall the new jobs will occur in knowledge-based industries in services and manufacturing, showing that higher-level qualifications will be needed to cope with such changes. Looking at the changes another way, highly skilled occupations will require increased numbers, but also increased skills. The biggest impact of increasing skill requirements will be felt where numbers *and* skills are on the increase, which is group 1 in Figure 6.8. Most of these are jobs where knowledge is very important, but additional competencies are required to carry out the job.

Figure 6.8 Jobs affected by changes in numbers and skill levels

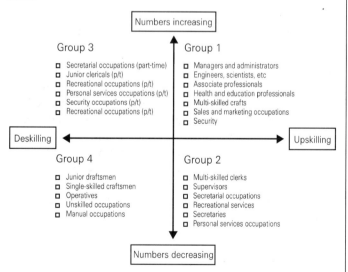

At the other end, group 4 jobs will see a fall in numbers and the skills required, mainly as a consequence of automation but also influenced by the drive towards WCM. Group 2, on the other hand, will be given more responsibility but will see a fall in numbers; whilst employees in group 3 occupations will increase by making

more jobs attractive to part-timers through task simplification and reduced responsibilities.

This analysis has a clear conclusion – greater skills will be required to carry out most jobs, with various surveys of employers confirming that this is the case. The increase in technical skills, though, is linked to the demand for general skills based on the ability to work in teams, work independently when required, and generally to be competent at the job. Employers now demand that school, college and university students be provided with opportunities to develop both technical and work-related skills and that these be assessed by the educational establishment. This is a challenge that has caused major changes in the way education and training is delivered.

Changes in the working population, occupations and skill levels are such that business organisations, if they are to produce an effective human resource strategy, must understand these trends and incorporate them into their planning. If they do not, achievement of corporate objectives will become ever more difficult.

The environment and social responsibility

To generate wealth, firms and other organisations engage in production and the consumption of resources. One of the main macroeconomic objectives is to see that economic growth (i.e. extra production) is facilitated and encouraged. Needless to say an expanding economy is one that consumes more, and is likely to pollute more. If this is true for the UK it must also be true for all the countries of the world, with Brazil, India, Vietnam and others all aspiring to the living standards of the west.

Growth, though, comes with associated costs. Extra cars that bring freedom to travel have resulted in congested cities and health problems. In Europe more than a fifth of households have two or more cars, whilst in the USA the average number of cars per household is two. Other examples of pollution sources are the CFCs in aerosols which have caused a depletion of the ozone layer, leading to problems with skin cancer; the increased use of energy that has added to the so-called greenhouse effect of global warming; and chemical and sewage contamination of streams and rivers, logged by the National Rivers Authority. This all adds to the picture of industry pursuing growth at any cost.

The responsibility of organisations towards the environment is a major issue. If polluters take little or no account of their actions, but they have an effect on the rest of society with money and time being needed to clear up the problem, the conclusion must be that the output of these industries is less than optimal for society as a whole. Economists call the costs of pollution **externalities** because although *private* costs and benefits determine that goods are made and purchased, these may come at a social or *external* cost to the community.

Does the solution lie in allowing the marketplace to solve the problem, so that well-informed consumers choose the products that do least harm to the environment? Or is there a need to take a more **interventionist** line that brings organisations face to face with the consequences of their actions?

If polluters were forced to pay for any pollution they caused, they would be encouraged to change their production techniques to minimise pollution. This could be done by levying a tax that would be equal to the cost of removing the problem. However, this approach is not so simple to put into effect. Producers would argue that a tax would eat into their profits, and as a consequence of this prices would have to rise, something many consumers would not wish to see. It would be necessary for consumers to support such moves, and it is not altogether clear that they would, particularly as a large amount of atmospheric pollution affects mainland Europe more than it does the UK. Also, there is often little agreement on what *causes* pollution, with scientists being uncertain on the causes and the effects.

Amid this confusion, there is one main issue to focus upon. What is the responsibility of the producer towards the community in which it is located? Or to extend this a little further: what are the attitudes of those who have a stake in the business likely to be towards environmental issues?

Stakeholders are a very diverse group, but the main ones can be identified as trading partners, customers, employees, investors, the community and pressure groups (including the media). It is not necessary to go through each of these in turn, but two examples will show the types of environmental concern these groups have (see the extracts from the *Financial Times* of 16 November 1994, reproduced on the following pages as Figures 6.9 and 6.10).

Both examples show that the push towards a concerted effort on environmental issues is moving along at different speeds. The example from the USA shows how companies can respond to pressure from the state government, while the UK example demonstrates the problem of monitoring activity in order to comply with regulations, or to be seen to be putting things in order before laws or regulations or taxation are imposed.

The moves in the EU and North America to bring in more legislation to help in controlling pollution are likely to continue. Recent surveys reveal that more consumers are demanding information on the composition and manufacture of products – to help them make suitable choices between, for example, furniture made of wood from sustainable forest programmes and that which is using up timber without a thought to its replacement. If legislation and regulation continue to grow, this poses a threat to many organisations who are unable to see the opportunities, and the problems, that may overtake them.

The major groups of environmental laws cover the following areas of operation:

- development control
- control of emissions
- disposal of waste
- protection of species, habitats, landscapes and heritage
- impact of the environment on people's health and safety.

The environmental challenge should also be linked to social responsibility (see Figure 6.11, which is an extract from the *Independent* of 24 December 1994) and consumer legislation. The former covers working conditions, health and safety, employment practices, social security and pension provision, whilst the latter covers the performance of products, product safety, food hygiene and labelling of goods.

Environmental policy: making a start

All aspects of an organisation's operations, from accounting to production and distribution, have an impact on the environment, and the policy should recognise this fact.

In practice, companies and organisations are being encouraged to take a long hard look at all their activities. Government departments are producing information for distribution to companies, colleges and universities. This provides a framework to review current operations and to set objectives to review waste. The approach covers all aspects of the organisation and ranges from the mission statement through to the use of resources, and the following headings are a guide to the comprehensive nature of this approach.

The mission statement
A commitment to the environment and other corporate responsibility issues implies a fresh look at the mission statement and a re-evaluation of corporate objectives and the needs of the stakeholders. Creating a greener mission and objectives might include sustainable growth, obligations towards staff, and even promoting a larger timeframe over which the company plans its activities.

Figure 6.9 Extract from the *Financial Times*

US staff biking to work

US workers who commute by bicycle are becoming pampered employees at many companies. Nike, the Oregon-based sports shoe manufacturer, gives workers a cash credit at the company's cafeteria, fitness centre or store if they pedal to work.

At Fleetwood, a maker of motor homes in Southern California, biking employees enjoy mini-garages for storage, a free repair facility, showers and changing rooms, the free loan of a bicycle, and a safety kit. USAA, an insurance group in San Antonio, Texas, encourages workers to form bicycling clubs to articulate needs to management and to help riders devise the best routes to the office.

The bike-to-work movement is being pushed along by government initiatives. Next year, Oregon will enforce a law that requires all businesses in the state to provide covered storage spaces for customers and workers. Massachusetts plans to spend $6m (£3.6m) over the next few years to adapt roads to bicycle use.

Under Clean Air legislation passed during the Bush administration, every state must present a plan to encourage bicycle use by the end of 1995.

"San Antonio has launched a big bicycle-mobility plan because they are on the edge of non-attainment of the Clean Air Act standards," says Andrew Clarke, deputy director of the Bicycle Federation of America. "If they do not take the initiative themselves, the federal government will force them to."

Biking is an increasingly popular way to reduce air pollution, say politicians, because it costs relatively little compared with public transport improvements.

Refitting roads to accommodate bicycles does raise the ire of many, though. In densely populated cities, it often means eliminating traffic lanes, slowing the flow for drivers. And by providing shelters for bicycles, businesses may have to cut the parking spaces available for cars.

Structural change

This focuses on the organisational changes required to incorporate the issues raised in the mission and objectives. It can include the identification of responsibility for these issues in the senior management team. Germany leads the way on this, with the majority of companies having a board member with explicit responsibility – perhaps a reaction to that country's stringent environmental legislation.

Supporting the mission on environmental approaches

It is easy to produce statements of the policy of the organisation and then assume that this is enough to satisfy various groups. As with any major initiative, it has to receive the wholehearted support of senior managers. This will be achieved when it is clear to senior managers that an environmentally aware company can achieve reduction in waste at the same time as exploiting new opportunities in the marketplace.

Staff

The work force has been identified as offering support for the reduction in waste and the promotion of greener production processes. This is especially so amongst the younger recruits and women managers, with the implication being that a company that is seen as half-hearted or antagonistic in its approach to environmental issues will find it harder to recruit or retain people of the right calibre.

Systems

To make a success of becoming a greener organisation new approaches will be required. The Department for Education encourages colleges and universities to review their activities. For example, they are dependent on paper to produce handouts for students, to circulate memoranda, to keep minutes of meetings and so on, and the question has been asked: Are there alternative ways to disseminate information of this type that are more environmentally friendly? A further example is that inner-city colleges and universities have problems with car parking facilities for students and staff, with the traditional demand being for more spaces to be created. In Liverpool, the John Moores University has a long-term objective to reduce car parking spaces and cooperate on the development of public transport links, which will contribute to the creation of more opportunities to develop new buildings and reduce pollution in the city.

In essence the green organisation would wish to:

- measure and control overall performance
- provide and process the relevant information

Figure 6.10 Extract from the *Financial Times*

Second push for Green reporting

Environmental reporting is a waste of time and money. This could be the view of the vast majority of companies that steadfastly ignore demands to publish regular voluntary reports on their emissions, waste, and efforts to reduce their impact on the environment.

After a spate of reports in the early 1990s from blue-chip companies in western Europe and North America, environmental reporting appears to be at a cross-roads. Those companies that have reported – about 150 worldwide – are wondering whether it is worth continuing. The non-reporters appear to be hoping that reporting is a dying fashion.

"Reporting by some companies spurs on competition among others. But a diversity of styles and lack of conformity had undermined this competition because because there is no benchmarking. And, of course, those companies which choose not to report are deeply comfortable with this," says John Elkington, a director of SustainAbility, a UK consultancy advising the United Nations Environment Programme on reporting.

UNEP is trying to encourage small and medium-sized companies throughout the world to report. Such companies produce most of the world's pollution, but because of their size and low visibility they are less affected by public pressure. UNEP's underfunded campaign is only beginning, but the chances of success look slim unless there is renewed pressure to report.

The future of voluntary reporting is uncertain, for three reasons. First, those companies that have so far reported have received, at best, a muted response from the audience that was calling for voluntary reporting, mainly campaign groups.

Second, recession and the rapid slide of the environment down the political agenda have reduced the pressure to report. Only businesses in those sectors whose record is constantly under public scrutiny, such as water, chemicals and energy, feel the need to report.

Third, information contained in the vast majority of reports lacks credibility and is of little use to most audiences, such as investors. "Environment reporting is still the product of the public relations industry," says Clive Bates, a campaigner at Greenpeace UK. "Investors, employees and the public need the unexpurgated environmental facts just as much as they need to see the mandatory financial accounts," he adds.

Greenpeace is not alone in its criticism of the value of the information found in environmental reports. Bill Dale, environment analyst at S. G. Warburg, says the City finds it difficult to identify potential environmental risk because of the poor quality of information made available by companies.

"Although more data are now being revealed in annual reports there is a high degree of discretion in what is reported," he said. It seems unlikely that companies will ever be forthcoming with all the facts until they are forced. Although there have been hints that the European Union could legislate on the issue, this now seems unlikely.

The EU's voluntary scheme, called Eco Management and Audit Scheme, is up and running but has yet to fulfil one of its primary goals – to encourage companies to conform to its standards and so gain a competitive advantage. And EMAS is only aimed at very large industrial operations.

The general trend in the EU's attitude towards the environment is away from prescriptive legislation and towards a greater use of voluntary and fiscal measures to encourage improved environmental performance.

This does not mean, however, that environmental reporting is off the agenda. Elkington sits on the EU's consultative forum on the environment, a group of business people and representatives from consumer groups, local government, trades unions and non-governmental groups. "In our discussions, reporting is seen as absolutely fundamental," he said.

And companies that continue to report say they find benefits other than public recognition for their efforts. The process forces them to set up the systems to gather information about their products and processes. This enables them to manage their businesses better.

"Our report gives us the opportunity to provide concise information on our environmental performance to outsiders and employees. We find it a useful communications tool," says Richard Robson, environment communications manager at ICI. Thorn EMI has just produced a highly detailed report on its performance and the Kingfisher retailing group, which includes Comet, B&Q, Superdrug and Woolworths, is expected to publish its first environmental report this year.

"Reporting is a primary strategic communications tool," says Elkington. "A prime example here is the success of Dow Europe. Because it does not have an annual report for the European business its environmental report is a window through which people can view Dow."

But in spite of such advantages, it appears that many companies will not take environmental reporting seriously unless they are put under more pressure. Early indications are that in the absence of any official initiative, the financial community could provide the impetus.

Asbestosis claims, and concerns about possible effects of climate change on catastrophic property casualty exposures, have increased the world insurance industry's interest in the environment. Banks are paying more attention to their exposure to environmental risk and investors are starting to show concern about risks posed by companies with poor environmental records.

But if the financial community is to convert its concerns into action it needs better information. Dale says: "Most of the information, including specific quantitative detail, is arbitrary and self-determined. In very few cases is it possible to draw direct conclusions as to the implications for revenues and profit margins. While investors wait for better standards of reporting they will be more impressed by those companies which publish separate reports on their environmental performance. Particular credit will be given to informa-tion that is independently audited or verified."

Figure 6.11 Extract from *The Independent*

Tetra Pak and international aid

Tetra Pak, the international food processing and packaging company, is actively considering moving into the aid business to deliver essential food and medical supplies to disaster zones such as Rwanda and Bosnia.

Tetra Pak regularly gives supplies of oral rehydration solution to aid agencies, but this is believed to be the first time that a commercial enterprise has considered being directly involved in supplying relief aid.

Sources close to the Swedish company said it has conducted market research to find out how the press and public would react to

a company conducting direct relief and whether it would improve its brand image. It wanted to find out how journalists cover disasters, what they consider good stories and what coverage they give to the distributors of aid.

Aid agency officials have reacted with surprise and caution to the prospect of working alongside a transnational company. One asked what motives Tetra Pak could have in working in a field associated with altruism rather than profit. Another pointed out that the skills and finance Tetra Pak would bring could change the whole approach to aid.

The company is owned by two Swedish brothers, Hans and Gad Rausing, now resident in England and estimated to be the richest men in Britain. They are said to be worth £5.2bn. The company's sales of the milk and fruit juice containers which are its sole product were estimated at $6bn last year. But it avoids publicity and does not advertise.

In August it announced it was giving cartons of oral rehydration solution, a mixture of salts and carbohydrates, to combat the cholera and dysentery epidemics in the refugee camps in Zaire.

- reinforce the strategies through appraisal and rewards
- develop new products and technology
- replace existing systems and activities with more efficient ones.

The move towards environmental excellence will require a step-by-step approach, summarised by John Elkington in his book *The Green Capitalist* as follows:

- Develop and publish an environmental policy.
- Prepare an action programme.
- Arrange the organisation and staffing of the company, including board-level representation.
- Allocate adequate resources.
- Invest in environmental science and technology.
- Educate and train.
- Monitor, audit and report.
- Monitor the evaluation of the green agenda.
- Contribute to environmental programmes.
- Help to build bridges between the various interested groups.

When organisations observe the growing European and UK legislation, the creation of various inspectorates to reinforce compliance, the more active involvement of pressure groups such as Friends of the Earth, and a more litigious approach to penalise companies and organisations who flout the law, they should consider it to be good management practice to start on the adaptive

process before they find themselves the subject of a hefty fine and with the expense of rectifying problems they have created.

Social trends and their impact on business activity

In the previous sections the effects of technology and environmental issues on business activity have been reviewed. Their influences have been noted on the way work is organised and the groups who will gain or lose from the changes. Likewise, the impact on the working population of demand for part-time work and those seeking such employment has also been recognised. Business organisations then seek to influence matters to benefit themselves, but are in their own turn influenced by broad changes in society.

Some of these need to be looked at a little more deeply to understand how they will impact on the way organisations are structured and managed. Reviews of health, housing, social benefits and taxation will provide an overview for further consideration.

Health

For how long can a baby born in 1994 be expected, on average, to live? A boy born in that year could be expected to live for 74 years, while a girl could be expected to live for 79 years. Compare this with the situation 50 years ago, when the respective life spans would be 62 and 67 years. Not only have the chances of survival improved, but they continue to do so – by two years every decade. The improvement can be put down to various factors such as reduced infant mortality, health care, diet, standard of living and family size.

Despite the improvements there are clearly areas of great concern. Respiratory and circulation diseases (heart attacks and strokes), and breast and lung cancers cut life short unnecessarily.

What has this got to do with business activity? Longer life expectancy creates new markets and new consumer needs, so that we see, for example, housebuilding companies switching their attention to houses and flats that suit the needs of the elderly. Many of those who are retired have high disposable income and varied leisure interests, a factor that can influence firms in their product development. Many pensioners, of course, are not included in this development and a high incidence of poverty can be found.

Another more difficult problem to deal with, for both government and industry, is the distribution of the population. Government figures reveal that the population over 65 years old at the last census date was already significant and expected to grow. (The figure for young workers will not increase at the same rate, producing a heavy burden on those in work.) If the social and health benefits currently available are to be maintained, then those currently in work will have to contribute more of their income to support the older population – a factor that could produce a backlash. The gradual increase in the retirement age for women to 65 may have been instituted to bring about a degree of harmonisation in the EU, but it has the advantage of increasing the supply of workers.

Employers are required to make a contribution towards National Insurance. Any increase in the contribution rate raises the cost of employing workers, with the consequence that organisations may reduce their work forces, creating unemployment at least in the short term. To get around this, employees are being encouraged to join private pension schemes – both by deregulating the market and by offering tax advantages. Such schemes are taken up mainly by professional workers, who hope to take care of their future by saving for pensions and health care costs.

Housing

At the end of 1992 there were 24 million dwellings in the UK, with more than twice as many being owner-occupied as there were 30 years ago. New dwellings completed in that year were only half the number completed in 1967. However, the number of dwellings lacking basic amenities (wash basin, hot and cold water, indoor toilet, kitchen sink, bath or shower) had fallen to 1 per cent of the housing stock compared with $2\frac{1}{2}$ per cent in 1986.

These overall figures hide regional variations, and in particular the fact that inner-city and isolated rural areas tend to have more houses with poor facilities. In addition some houses are overcrowded, even if they have decent facilities, and there has been an increase in the numbers of homeless families – up from 118 000 in 1986 to 167 000 in 1992.

The rise in owner-occupation and the gradual improvement in the housing stock may appear to have little impact on the business community. Here again, though, there are significant issues that need to be recognised.

Reduction in completion of new dwellings

The fall in activity for this sector of the construction industry can be accounted for mainly by the reduction of the role of local authorities. Whatever the cause, construction is a major employer and a useful indicator of economic activity.

Rise in homelessness

The bulk of the responsibility for homeless people falls on local authorities who must provide temporary or permanent accommodation. The main reason for homelessness is the breakdown of a relationship with a partner or relatives. However, a significant amount of homelessness has been caused by problems over mortgage repayments or rents, these cases being a hangover from the recession of the early 1990s.

The housing market as a vehicle for economic growth

A healthy housing market, and the buying and selling of properties, is in many ways critical for the success of other markets. When confidence is high, the housing market improves and people are prepared to take on the commitment of a mortgage as they seek to enter the market or move to a bigger house. The fact of moving also stimulates other purchases, with white goods, soft furnishings, furniture and other items seeing an increase in demand. Take the confidence away and this important economic stimulus goes with it.

As the government reduces the tax advantage of having a mortgage, it is unlikely that rising house prices will act to spur the economy forward as they have done in the past. House prices will rise, but many commentators believe that houses will in future be seen as a place to live rather than as a guaranteed capital asset with tax advantages.

Household savings and investment

If households will see less of a benefit from rising house prices, and there is an increasing need to save for the future, then new methods to enable them to do this have to be found. Personal Equity Plans (PEPs) are one way in which tax advantages can be found that can benefit both individuals and industry.

Housing issues provide benefit for the individual and society if improvements can be gained. Likewise, the state of the housing market has a large impact on economic welfare throughout the country.

Social benefits and taxation

In discussing these two issues, and to bring together some of the aspects outlined under the health and housing headings, it will be helpful to look at the bottom 20 per cent of households by income – a segment that comprises 11.2 million people.

The bottom 20 per cent of any income range is subject to distortions and problems. So, for example, the self-employed may show that income is low for tax purposes, but the true picture may be rather more healthy than that reported. Despite this, the main picture remains valid for the bulk of this group and can be summarised as follows:

- The over-60s and the unemployed make up the bulk of this group, along with a significant group of self-employed people.
- Single-parent families are over-represented in this group.
- Two-thirds of children live in families without a full-time worker.
- This group has 7 per cent of total UK household income before housing costs are taken into account.
- Expenditure patterns show that they have a higher proportion of expenditure on necessities, such as food, fuel and housing, and less on so-called non-essentials such as leisure. Food, for example, accounts for 25 per cent of expenditure.
- Most of the income of this group (70 per cent) comes from social security benefits.
- 20 per cent are skilled manual workers, 26 per cent are retired, and 30 per cent are unoccupied.
- Most people in this group had savings of less than £3000 in 1991.

This pen-picture of a significant part of the population is probably not unexpected, but it throws up certain issues on which political parties disagree.

For those in this group who are of working age, to become more prosperous presents difficulties. To take work would be to lose some or all of the social benefits that the state allows. This could then mean that they are worse off taking a job than staying unemployed. This is the so-called **poverty trap**. One solution is to reduce income tax for those on low incomes and to create a situation whereby their take-home pay is equal to or greater than the benefits that they were receiving.

Encouraging people into work by changes in the tax system is one thing, but many would have had temporary work or no work at all for some considerable time, and thereby lack the skills required by employers. In addition, firms may be wary of taking on such workers as they could have a very poor track record. Providing training courses and encouraging employers to look more favourably on these applicants are initiatives that have been introduced.

The large group of retired people in the bottom 20 per cent require a different approach. They will need benefits and access to social and health workers for a long time; the providers have to acknowledge that this is a long-term commitment. The challenge, though, lies in the future. As the population ages it is possible that, unless adequate pensions are provided, the numbers of poor elderly people living on low incomes will rise. An obvious solution is to increase the state pension, but given the numbers involved this will not be easy. Neither will the promotion of private pension plans for those below retirement age be easy – people will see this as additional savings, the benefit of which will not be apparent for some considerable time.

The taxation and benefits system provides protection for those who require it, but it comes at a cost if it works in such a way as to keep people from working and fulfilling their potential. From a business point of view, the burdens of benefits and pension provision may be such that the cost of taking on workers becomes prohibitive – a fact that could provide an incentive towards the introduction of automation.

Striking a balance is not a straightforward issue, as pressure groups seek to influence the government to favour them. Business organisations have to be aware of the effects on them and how they can understand the demands and respond accordingly.

The political process

In both this chapter and the previous one, the role of government in determining policy and in its implementation has been seen as a vital ingredient in the business environment. What has been hinted at, rather than made explicit, is that the political process has to be appreciated and understood as well. Political parties and groups, the structure of local and national government, and the role of lobbying, all have to be incorporated into the analysis.

In the UK the political system is often described as being **pluralist** and/or **liberal democratic**. The support for pluralism is at the heart of liberal democracy and operates in three spheres: economic, social and political. **Economic pluralism** allows different agents to operate freely in the market as entrepreneurs and traders. However, the market produces situations whereby some intervention is required, so monopoly control or market failure mean that governments of the Right and Left have to consider how they will preserve the market, while overcoming the problem. The resulting **mixed economy** is constantly reviewed, especially for the advisability and extent of such intervention.

Social pluralism implies the acceptance of autonomous groups, which are considered as the normal desirable means of organising individuals. **Political pluralism** is identified with certain liberties such as freedom of assembly, freedom to form associations, religious freedom, and the right to property. The affirmation of these liberties entails at least one important consequence – recognition of the freedom of choice and the right to defend this in an appropriate manner.

The political culture of a country is made up of the pattern of beliefs and practices which govern the life of the community, so that beliefs about the nature of political leadership and authority, about the proper and improper way to settle political differences, and about the proper and improper functions of government, are governed by this. If pluralism in all its forms is a fundamental part of the beliefs, then the debate is often about the degree to which government intervention is harmful to the freedom of economic agents (businesses) or helpful to them.

Taking the analysis further, political culture concerns the rules by which politics is conducted, which can be broken down into how decisions are taken and the substance of the policies government can pursue.

Procedure covers the rules of parliament and also covers how decisions should be taken and then put into effect. Going a little further, it can also cover the problem of when it is right to challenge a decision and how this might be done. The substantive part of political culture is concerned with the actual policies of government, and in particular how far it should go in controlling or

influencing what people do. These issues can be seen in the debate that took place in the USA at the mid-sessional elections in 1994, where the Republicans were swept to power in both Congress and the House of Representatives on a policy of cutting back on government intervention.

In the UK the political culture is accepted by both main parties – that is, that a pluralist and liberal-democratic society should be supported. The difference lies in the emphasis placed on market solutions by the Conservative Party and more government intervention to deal with abuse of market and political power by the Labour Party. This is a rather simplistic distinction, as to promote market solutions the Conservative governments of the 1980s actually centralised power, while the Labour Party proposed decentralisation fostered by devolution for Scotland and Wales and regional assemblies in England.

The consensus in British politics is based on agreement – both among the population at large and among the 'professional' politicians and political parties – about the social and economic system which should prevail, and about the proper function of government. Differences there certainly are about how this is to be interpreted; but each of the main political parties would find no difficulty in supporting the mixed economy. This, though, has important consequences for the daily practice of politics. For instance, freedom of association and freedom to voice an opinion mean that in British politics there are many groups (**pressure groups**) who seek to be given the right to be heard in the process of policy-making.

Political lobbying can affect the formation and drafting of legislation, the ways in which regulations are implemented (from the EU for example), and even the structure of government, so that government departments can either be stripped of powers or expand their influence. Lobbyists at the local, national and European levels are an important part of the process.

When lobbying is undertaken by the business community with clear vested interests, it is not without its critics. Members of Parliament have to declare their outside interests – interests that, it is argued, keeps MPs abreast of developments.

Traditional lobbying groups are businesses, trade unions and charities, but Figure 6.12 shows that there has been a surge in membership of environmental groups, many of whom act as pressure groups. In addition, new religious pressure groups have been formed in the Muslim community to seek state funding for Muslim schools similar to that for Catholic and Church of England schools.

While these groups have seen their memberships increase, trade unions have seen their representation fall from just

Figure 6.12 Memberships of environmental organisations in the UK (thousands)

	1971	1991	1992
British Trust for Ornithology	5	9	9
Campaign for the Protection of Rural Wales	–	4	4
Civic Trust*	214	222	222
Council for the Protection of Rural England	21	45	46
Friends of the Earth†	1	111	116
Greenpeace	..	408	411
National Trust	278	2 152	2 186
National Trust for Scotland	37	234	237
Ramblers Association	22	87	94
Royal Society for Nature Conservation	64	250	250
Royal Society for the Protection of Birds	98	852	850
Woodland Trust	..	150	150
World Wide Fund for Nature	12	227	209

*Members of local amenity societies registered with the Civic Trust.
†England, Wales and Northern Ireland only.

over 50 per cent of the work force in the 1970s to 37 per cent (in 1991).

It is through pressure groups that many people participate actively in the political process, other than by voting in an election. The group they support will seek help in collecting signatures, raising money or in an administrative function.

How the business community seeks to influence policy

Since lobbying and pressure groups are vital aspects of democracy, the business community must understand how they can seek to influence decisions. Government has a large influence on all aspects of business activity, so strategic planning can only be undertaken if an appreciation of this influence and the direction of policy can be incorporated.

A pressure group is really an agent of activity representing an interest group. Interest groups would, in the main, like to influence the government, rather than to become the government. Clearly this can change, as with the emergence of Green interest groups who have fought elections on environmental and other issues. However, the majority of interest groups do not make this transition, concentrating instead on putting pressure on government on particular issues, or carrying out other activities. The Confederation of British Industry (CBI)

acts as an interest and pressure group, but also carries out work in research and training.

The existence of these groups is controversial because it is unclear how far they have gone in influencing policy. Many people accuse tobacco companies of influencing policy on advertising; while one accusation levelled against past Labour governments was that they bowed too much to pressure from the trade unions, who were the providers of the majority of funds for the party.

It is possible to sub-divide pressure groups who have economic interests as follows:

- *Businesses* – From the CBI to trade associations, these keep a watch on developments and often lobby the government to institute changes, particularly at the time when the national budget is drafted.
- *Trade unions* – Although fewer in number and with less influence on government than in the past, unions still represent a sizeable and influential group of workers, and sometimes seek legal redress for decisions made by government ministers.
- *Professional associations* – Associations of accountants, marketers, engineers etc. can promote good practice and adopt advisory roles.
- *Consumer groups* – The most prominent of these is the Consumers Association, which is most famous for its publication *Which?* and associated titles. It promotes the needs of consumers for safer products and better labelling and has extended its interest to environmental issues.

A business can be part of more than one group to promote its interests, being a member of the CBI, the relevant industrial trade group, or even linked to a professional group. It can also be on the receiving end of campaigns and activities by consumer groups or environmental pressure groups who wish to curtail its activities. In either case, lobbying will remain an integral part of the political process and, despite criticisms, it needs to be understood by managers if they are to fulfil the mission of their organisation.

Case Study
Using technology to help the marketing effort

Technology is becoming increasingly important in telephone marketing (telemarketing), with more widespread use of applications such as interactive voice response, predictive dialling and computer telephone integration. The advantages of this use of technology are that it improves productivity, helps to reduce costs, and seeks to add value for customers. There are, though, drawbacks – a careless application would call into question a company's claim to being customer focused.

An example is the dilemma in deciding when to automate call handling using interactive voice response (IVR) technology, where customers hear pre-recorded messages and use the phone keypad to select options. As many as 60 per cent of customers hang up when connected to such a system, and there is no real dialogue with the remaining 40 per cent. To use it effectively would require finding out how familiar the customer group is with IVR and how they feel about using it.

The digital telecommunication network provides businesses with the means to unite every office into a single virtual entity. Voice and data and their applications are no longer tied to one geographic location. Data can be made available to any site, with the relevant customer data being transferred on request. There are far-reaching implications for customer-contact strategy. Callers to a company can be directed to a specialist who can access relevant customer data. This improves the service to the customer and reduces the time spent in seeking out the relevant information.

For out-bound calling there is growing interest in predictive dialling systems, which automatically dial telephone numbers on a computerised list. These are systems which pace the dialling according to criteria such as the number of agents, the proportion of calls being answered and the average length of calls. The aim is to provide a constant flow of answered calls to keep agents busy, without their having to dial and wait for an answer.

All of these developments can be exploited by any firm and can obviously be subject to mis-use, so the industry has worked on a code of practice to submit to OFTEL. This can also be linked to the technology of Calling Line Identity which enables the recipient of a call to identify the number of the caller.

Abuse has been a problem, with unlawful database building and unsolicited calls. Although as yet OFTEL only receives a few complaints about unsolicited calls, there are pressures to introduce regulations or to encourage the industry to produce more robust codes of conduct. One thing is certain – the advance in technology will continue to raise new issues concerning consumer protection. Businesses will wish to provide themselves with more efficient and effective market opportunities.

Questions for discussion

1 *What pressures will be placed on business organisations to invest in telephone and computer technology systems?*
2 *Identify the corporate responsibility issues that should be taken seriously by organisations using these approaches.*
3 *What internal reorganisation will be implied in the use of this technology?*

Further reading

- *Green Marketing* by K. Peattie. M & E Handbooks, 1992.
- *Environmental Management and Business Strategy* by R. Welford and A. Gouldson. Pitman, 1993.
- *Politics UK*, 2nd edition, edited by B. Jones. Harvester Wheatsheaf, 1992.
- *Government and Politics in Western Europe*, 2nd edition, by Y. Mény. Oxford University Press, 1993.
- *The Green Capitalists* by J. Elkington and T. Burke. Victor Gollancz, 1994.
- *The Environmental Audit and Business Strategy. A Total Quality Approach* by Grant Ledgerwood. Pitman 1992.
- *Case in Environmental Management and Business Strategy*, edited by Professor Richard Welford. Pitman, 1994.

7 Business firms in markets

On completion of this chapter students should be able to:

■ analyse the competitive environment in which business firms operate, and identify competitive strategies likely to generate successful results

■ examine the role of business in factor markets

■ investigate and interpret the main regulatory controls on the operation of organisations

■ identify the main regulatory bodies within both the UK and the European Union, and investigate how they influence the operation and activities of business organisations.

The competitive environment

The importance of the marketplace in solving the problems of production, distribution and the allocation of resources and products is a major theme throughout this book. This is not to say that the market solution is applicable to the provision of all products or services, and for various reasons the state steps in to provide some. Even here, though, private sector strategies have been introduced to provide for a more efficient and effective provision of services that the public sector is supposed to lack.

In many cases, such as the privatisation of public utilities, short-term competition has been noticeable by its absence. With water companies it is unclear how competition could exist even in the longer term, as viable alternative supplies are not currently possible, without prohibitive costs. On the other hand, the selling off of British Telecom in 1984 did not immediately provide alternatives to the customer, despite the competition by Mercury in the business sector of the market. It was the power of the regulatory body OFTEL that pushed through changes that the customer could see in the prices of local and international calls. Over time competition has increased, particularly from cable companies and with the introduction of mobile communication networks that have finally begun to provide the degree of competition found in many markets.

It is not only from privatisation that examples can be found of less than competitive conditions and practices. In many parts of industry monopoly or monopoly practices exist, and in others oligopolies (dominance by a few major sellers) hold sway, competing against each other by using non-price competition – because a price war would be harmful to each firm's profitability. Although oligopolies can be expected in mature industries, even here fundamental changes, often resulting from the European single market, have introduced new competitors who traditionally have been kept out. The degree of competition in food retailing has changed with the introduction of foreign-based food chains such as Aldi and Netto, who along with the UK-based Kwik Save have exploited the desire for cost reductions on essential food and toiletry items. An added advantage was that the customer in the UK desired a reduction in the price of these items as the recession of the late 1980s took hold, a marketing benefit that these companies exploited to the full.

The desire of the traditional supermarkets to avoid a price war was severely dented by a recession, by the single market, and by the willingness of foreign-based retailers to enter the UK market. So, despite the traditional power of Sainsbury, Tesco and others, they had to respond or see their market share eroded by the aggressive newcomers.

Many industries could be used as examples to try to work out the competitive situation, but one clear conclusion can already be arrived at. Each industry would be different and could take a great deal of research and analysis to identify how it currently operates and the degree to which current trends will either erode or increase competition.

A lot of background has been provided on markets and the competitive process in Chapters 3 and 4. The focus here is to look at the general competitive environment and to link this to the structure provided by Michael Porter ('competitive rivalry'). There are many ways to look at the business environment, but one of the easiest to understand is the **Political, Economic, Social and Technological (PEST) review**. It should be seen as a method of applying knowledge gained through the review of each of these issues to the market in question.

Although the PEST approach is easy to remember it does require careful use. For one thing, it is broad-based and encompasses many issues and trends that may not on further reflection be seen to be that important. Because it is so wide-ranging a review, it requires a lot of information and market intelligence to feed it, a feature that could be difficult for small companies to accommodate. Despite its scope, it provides the basis for a full review that can inform the decision process by focusing on two issues:

- the state of the market now
- the market as it may be in the future.

The *external environment*, which is the focus of this type of review, must be linked to the *internal environment* that is brought together in a **SWOT analysis** (corporate appraisal).

Figure 7.1 shows the typical sequence of events used in **strategic planning**, and although this may be seen as a very basic mechanistic approach it does help to align the use of PEST and SWOT and the competitive strategies that depend on them.

The planning model depicted in Figure 7.1 shows the stages through which an organisation will pass during the process of preparing its strategic response. It is important to understand the significance of each stage or feature of this approach, so the following reviews explain the demands made on the organisation and its managers when they are involved in such a task.

Figure 7.1 Stages in strategic planning

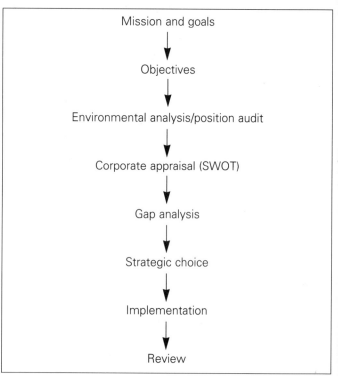

The mission statement

The **mission statement** broadly serves three purposes. Firstly, it shows the long-term approach to business and its reasons for existing. Secondly, it can be used to target key stakeholders, using this as part of its public relations. Lastly, the statement can reveal the values which the organisation wishes to promote.

The majority of firms and organisations in both the public and private sectors have a mission statement that they use for all or a selection of these purposes. An interesting feature of the mission is in the marketing orientation that it reveals, when the firm may look to focus attention on the total needs of the customer. For example, instead of a firm that manufactures pens describing itself as such, it may – if the research shows this to be justified – state that it is in the gift business. This can only be done if a review of the purchasers' intentions has shown that the pens are bought for gifts, and that a refocusing of the firm in this way can provide it with opportunities to exploit.

If values are to be added to the mission statement, then these may include the environment, equality of opportunity or social responsibility.

Objectives

Objectives are usually quantitative ones against which performance can be measured. Objectives can and do change, whereas the mission will not change on such a regular basis (or not at all).

The traditional primary objective for the private sector is profitability, supported by secondary objectives on market share, growth and cash flow. Increasingly, other objectives that are not so easily quantifiable have been added, and these can include customer satisfaction, employee relations and working conditions. In the public sector the objective of profitability is substituted by service level objectives that incorporate efficiency improvements – a particular challenge as public spending is squeezed.

A useful exercise is to look at examples of corporate objectives and to see that not all of them will be achieved and they may even conflict. The two most likely problems concern profitability and increased market share. To increase sales, prices may be reduced, but this could jeopardise profits. At first glance it is not easy to see how they can be reconciled, but it is possible to do so, by increasing market share in the short term and raising profits in the long term.

Environmental review (PEST analysis)

As stated earlier, all organisations have to be aware of the environment in which they operate and the PEST analysis encourages this. To focus on the dynamics of the industry and markets, Porter's 'competitive rivalry' approach helps to structure the task facing managers.

Position audit

This incorporates features of the environmental review, such as markets, but promotes a review of the internal advantages and disadvantages of an organisation. Issues such as financial soundness, skill levels and operating efficiency can show how ready the organisation is to face the challenges of the marketplace.

SWOT analysis

SWOT approaches are often used to brainstorm ideas, but are being used here after a great deal of analysis has already been done. In essence a SWOT analysis used for this purpose is a summary of the position that the company is in or will face after the external and internal appraisals have taken place.

Gap analysis

In summary, a **gap analysis** may cover a profit or sales gap that shows what the firm's objectives are (say for the next three years) and what is the projected outcome if the organisation continues its present activities. If there is a difference between the objectives and the projection of the existing approach, then a gap has appeared that will need to be closed. Closing this would require the adoption of a new strategy.

Strategic choice

This is a critical stage for the firm as the wrong choice could cause problems. The problem is to collect reliable information on the options available, evaluate each and then make a choice. In many companies more than one strategy can be pursued, particularly if this is the only way to reduce the sales gap. Consideration may have to be given to new markets for existing products, becoming more efficient in existing markets, and even the development of new products.

Implementation

Surprisingly, **implementation** is often glossed over – which may account for the fact that this is the stage where things can go wrong. What should happen is that the strategy is put into plans and objectives for the operating units of the organisation. This is a repeat of the entire process whereby unit objectives are set (external and internal), reviews undertaken, choices made and implementation carried out.

One problem is that middle managers often lack the time or skills to undertake such tasks, and might even be unaware of their significance.

Review

The **review** stage looks at the actual performance and compares it with the planned. Adjustments may have to be made to the strategy or to some aspect of implementation.

Although this approach has its critics, it does help to place in context the activities that can lead to a more refined and effective strategy. The advantage of this approach is that it can give a purpose to the company, and also help to decrease the risks involved as it increases in size. The competitive environment is such that it is difficult for a company to remain static, so that the strategic planning process can help to identify those areas where change and adaptation are necessary. The conclusion is that, although time-consuming, this approach is a vital facet of a company's activities.

Competitive strategies

To develop competitive advantages a firm needs to carry out an analysis not only of its external environment and competitors, but also of its internal environment. This assessment will establish whether the firm has distinctive competencies and resources with which to exploit market opportunities.

To identify its competitive advantages, a firm needs to link its unique competencies with the factors required for success. The firm should be aware of factors in the environment which may be central for success. For example, a UK manufacturer of English china exporting to Japan may find that a central factor in that market is networking skills.

A firm's competitive advantages, then, are its unique competencies which are in demand in the market and which competitors are unable to provide at that moment. So, for example, if similar products or services are offered and the quality of the competitors' products is poor or the items are expensive, then these facts constitute the firm's competitive advantages. The advantages can be derived from:

- the firm's products, which are competitively priced
- the firm's markets
- the firm's technological orientation (i.e. technologically superior products)
- product quality
- delivery
- flexibility of service.

From these distinctive competencies, the company can develop its strategies.

There are a number of observations to make about competitive advantages. Firstly, when these advantages are unique to the firm, they tend to be the strongest advantages. Secondly, when a firm does not possess a *unique* competitive advantage on which to build its strategy, it can create **niches** in the market. This is done by examining what the differences are between itself and its competitors, which can then be exploited in various ways:

- It could develop new products.
- It could develop customer segments that have not been exploited yet. For example, Japanese car companies offered American consumers a compact car, which was not previously available, but which fulfilled a clear need. The manufacturers used this advantage to gain a strong presence in the market.
- International firms have the potential to develop competitive advantages which are not available to firms operating only in domestic markets, as the following examples show.

Cost-leadership advantages

These can be derived from many sources. The global company can attain advantages from economies of scale because the demand for its products will be from many international markets. The firm will derive economies from its manufacturing process and thereby gain a low-cost advantage over its competitors. If the firm operates in various countries, it can also take advantage of cost differences in resources and labour to reduce its administrative and manufacturing costs, and this develops a further competitive advantage over its rivals. Furthermore, the firm can spread its research and development costs across many national markets. This would result in lower costs per unit of output, which is then transferred into customer benefits.

Access to global resources and information

The global firm can develop its advantages by having access to global resources and information. An advantage can stem from operating in markets where technological innovation is taking place. The firm will be in a position to acquire this information to improve its technical operation and product offerings. The firm can also gain competitor information when it operates in the domestic markets of its foreign competitors. The global firm will then be in an advantageous position to understand its competitors' strategies and business practices. For example, American and Japanese firms operating in the EU markets will be able to evaluate their European rivals and gain much valuable information.

The global firm has access to other resources which may give it a comparable advantage – such as financial resources obtained from foreign markets where they are abundant and inexpensive. Other resources could include access to experienced international managers, access to valuable market information, etc.

Duplication of effort and resources in the firm's various markets can also be reduced and economies can be gained. For example, when developing and testing products it need not carry out these processes in more than one country.

Portfolio assessment

Portfolio assessment provides an overview of how a firm classifies markets. It therefore has a bearing on strategic decisions, because the way a market is classified indicates its importance to the firm and its role in attaining the company's objectives.

A review of a firm's portfolio of markets will identify which business activities should be maintained, reduced or eliminated. A technique to help a firm evaluate its current business activities is the **Boston Consultancy Group matrix**. (See also page 79.)

A simplified version of the BCG portfolio matrix is shown in Figure 7.2. The aim of the matrix is to assist managers to determine the role of each business unit or product on the basis of:

- its market growth rate and market share relative to its competitors
- its cash flow potential.

Figure 7.2 The BCG growth/share matrix

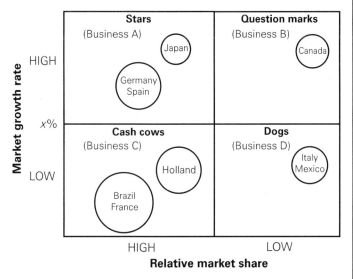

Market share is on the horizontal axis relative to the firm's largest competitor, and market growth of the industry is on the vertical axis with *x* per cent of growth rate arbitrarily used to separate the markets into high and low growth. Each circle represents a product with sales equivalent to the area of the circle. Four basic strategies of the BCG matrix can be adopted with a given product.

The simplest strategy for a firm to follow is to divest its *dogs* and harvest the cash flows from the firm's *cash cows* to assist the growth of the *stars* and help the position of the *question mark* businesses. The implications for strategies in terms of objectives are as follows:

- For *cash cows*, maintain market share while at the same time generating large cash flows.
- For star businesses, build market share and thus improve their competitive position.
- *Question marks* could also be used to increase market share.

- *Dogs* could be divested or harvested; if the latter, it is to generate short-term cash flows.

The strategy selected will depend on:

- the product's present market position
- the company's resources relative to major competitors
- the likely reactions of its competitors
- the product's life-cycle stage
- the information such as social, legal and political pressures, etc.

Although the BCG matrix was designed for the domestic market, it can be used (as shown in Figure 7.2) in the international market but it must be interpreted and used with caution. The growth–share matrix does help managers to formulate international strategy. For example:

- If a UK company had a cash cow in Brazil, but due to government regulations it was not allowed to transfer funds from Brazil to its star businesses in Germany or Japan, then the global strategy would be seriously affected.
- The matrix technique can also assist the firm in establishing where funds should be generated or where they should be reinvested.
- The growth–share matrix can highlight the company's competitive position, in that it may be strategically sensible to retain a business unit in a country with a slow market growth rate in order to defend its position and pre-empt entry by its competitors.

However, there are problems with using the BCG matrix in the international evaluation of markets. For example:

- Government regulations which block the transfer of funds or increase operational costs, etc., may turn a cash cow into a dog. Thus the matrix cannot account for changes in the environmental parameters, and risk dimensions are excluded from the analysis.
- There are other factors which affect the product portfolio, such as profitability, the effects of diversification, etc.
- The model does not incorporate the costs of entering various markets.

Strategic options

After making an assessment of its portfolio, a firm must choose a competitive market strategy to implement its portfolio strategy. There are numerous types of strategy available to a firm, ranging from the cooperative to the confrontational. Two of the better-known are Porter's 'generic strategies' model, introduced in his book

Competitive Advantage: Creating and Sustaining Superior Performance, and the 'product/market expansion' strategy. These are discussed below.

The generic strategies model

In developing a portfolio strategy, the firm can select from Porter's three generic strategies:

■ overall cost-leadership
■ differentiation
■ focus.

Operating in different markets, the firm can select different strategies or a combination of them for each market.

Cost-leadership strategy

A cost-leadership strategy is based on achieving low-cost production. This is normally associated with high-volume output, so that economies of scale, and experience and learning-curve factors, result in cost savings. Experience-curve economies come from the firm's increased expertise in managing its functional activities. The learning-curve economies are the result of workers becoming more efficient and effective as they learn from their mistakes over time, and so productivity increases.

Differentiation strategy

This involves differentiating the firm's products or services so that they will be perceived as being unique in quality, brand or some other feature. The firm is then in a position to market the products at a higher-than-average price, which consumers will be willing to pay. For example, IBM holds a differentiated position in the computer market in terms of quality and research and development.

Focus strategy

This involves concentrating on a small market, product or geographic segment. The firm's efforts and resources are focused on serving a particular customer group and it does not compete on an industry-wide basis. For example, some computer software companies compete for certain customer segments such as the chemical industry or banking sector only.

Porter's model is illustrated in Figure 7.3. Firms in the upper right-hand of the curve are profitable and successful because they have a larger market share resulting from lower prices and lower costs than their competitors, or because they have differentiated their product offerings and still capture a high market share. Firms in the upper left-hand corner of the curve are also successful because their focus strategy entails specialist products or markets which can command high prices.

The firms having difficulties are those situated in the middle portion of the curve, with fairly low market share and profits.

Figure 7.3 Porter's general strategies model

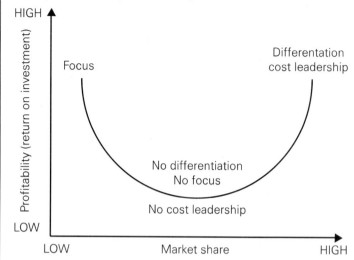

Porter's model also illustrates the trade-off between profits and market share. For example, a focus strategy would give the firm higher profits but at a cost, as it would have a smaller market share.

Product/market expansion strategy

In developing its portfolio strategy, a firm can choose a number of alternatives to generate intensive growth. Figure 7.4 illustrates the possibilities open to the firm – the grid is called **Ansoff's product/market expansion grid**.

Figure 7.4 Ansoff's product/market expansion grid

	Current products	New products
Current markets	Product market penetration	Product market development
New markets	Market development	Diversification

The four strategies open to the firm are as follows.

Product market penetration

The firm tries to increase its product's share in the markets it currently serves. It can achieve this in various ways.

- *Product-line stretching* – The firm would add new items to its existing product line in a market segment which it has already penetrated. The aim is to attract more customers from rivals and current non-users of the firm's products (i.e. to reach a broader market). For example, Coca Cola has added new items to its basic product and now offers Diet Coke and Cherry Coke in some of its world markets. The Japanese car manufacturers first penetrated the European car market with medium-sized cars; this product line then stretched to small cars, and now they have extended their product lines to target the luxury segments of the car market.
- *Product proliferation* – This involves offering many different product types. For example, Seiko offers a variety of watches with different features, functions, etc.
- *Product improvement* – This involves updating and augmenting the existing product. It entails application of the latest technology to improve the product's capabilities, improving customer services, etc.

Market development

This strategy involves developing new markets for the firm's current product lines. Expansion of this type is most suitable:

- where minimal product modification is required
- where profit margins are diminishing because of intense price competition in the firm's existing markets
- if the product's life-cycle is similar in various markets.

Product market development

This strategy involves the firm maintaining its existing overseas markets but developing new product markets within them. For example, a firm selling software to the industrial segment in market X might go after the consumer segment in the same market.

Diversification

Diversification strategies involve the firm entering new product markets outside its present business. The firm may wish to pursue this line of expansion in the following circumstances:

- when opportunities in the new product market are highly attractive
- when the firm wishes to reduce the impact of a negative environmental trend in its existing industry –

for example, to reduce the economic impact of a decline in cigarette smoking or the ageing of the UK population.

To diversify, a firm could engage in *forward or backward integration* whereby the outlets or sources of supplies are joined with the firm. This is prevalent in the semiconductor industries where manufacturers of microprocessors join forces with semiconductor producers to ensure a continuous supply.

Alternatively a firm can engage in a *conglomerate diversification strategy*, which involves the firm expanding into businesses that have no relationship to its current product, markets or technology. For example, Coca Cola purchased a movie company as a strategic move to counter a possible decline in the customer segment for its products, which is presently the youth group.

This overview of strategic systems has to be judged very carefully in order to ensure that the final choice fits best with circumstances found in the market and with the strengths of the company. Choosing an appropriate strategy must be linked into the permissible options provided to the company by the laws and regulations that govern operations. It is therefore necessary to review the regulatory environment in some detail.

The regulatory environment

When companies wish to understand their external environment they can use a structural approach such as the PEST review. With the political elements of this approach should be included legislative and regulatory issues that have to be understood if progress is to be made on the successful implementation of strategy.

Organisations operate within a framework of laws which is very broad in scope. The framework encompasses:

- the way an organisation does business, covered by laws on contract, unfair selling practices, safety of goods, law of agency, and so on
- the way it treats its employees (employment law)
- how it deals with the owners and provides information about its performance (Companies Act)
- criminal law
- how it relates to society (pollution legislation).

UK companies are now affected by laws passed by the European Union, so what was already a complex area has become rather more difficult to deal with as the EU plays its part in drafting legislation.

However, except in extreme circumstances that require legislation to be passed and enacted quickly (a very rare circumstance), there is a period of consultation at both the UK and EU levels. Although not essential, the publication of a Green Paper inviting comments on a proposal is usual. This is then followed by a White Paper which provides a more definitive statement of proposed changes. This leads to the passing of a Bill through parliament, which on passing successfully through both Houses becomes law. Organisations must monitor proposals so that they can make their views known at the appropriate stages.

In business, laws are there to protect citizens against the practices of powerful bodies and individuals. The legal system provides a framework governing, as we have seen, a wide range of activities and the ways in which these activities affect the providers of finance, employees, customers and society. At the same time, this framework allows businesses to achieve their chosen objectives.

Laws relating to the constitution of businesses

When people associate together to engage in a business or profession for profit, they are deemed to be in **partnership** under the Partnership Act 1890. As a result, each partner is separately liable for all of the debts of the business they engage in. If these people **incorporate** and create a separate legal 'person' which owns the business and is responsible for paying debts and fulfilling contracts, they then become members of a corporation that is carrying on business on their behalf. Successive Companies Acts control the establishment, performance and functions of companies.

For example, for a company to be registered, the Registrar of Companies must receive both a Memorandum and Articles of Association. The Memorandum describes factors that affect outsiders of the company – such as features of the company's constitution and the objectives it was incorporated to achieve. The Articles contain rules governing shareholders' relationships with each other and with the company and these do not generally affect outsiders. Companies must have at least three kinds of officer: directors, a company secretary and auditors. Directors of a company must present the annual accounts and a report to members of the company (i.e. shareholders), and members have the right to dismiss directors. The word 'Limited' warns creditors that there is a limitation on the liability of members. It is an offence to use the word 'Limited' if the person(s) in business are not incorporated with limited liability.

Consumer protection

Organisations provide goods and services for consumers in return for payment. The legal system provides a

mechanism for resolving disputes. Laws also attempt to overcome the inequality in bargaining power between large organisations and relatively small consumers. The need for such laws arises because of the possibility of problems with poor-quality or unsafe goods, misleading information, manufacturer's negligence, and breach of contract.

Legislation concerning business activities includes the Fair Trading Act 1973, which set up the **Office of Fair Trading** (OFT) to keep a constant watch over monopolies and restrictive practices. The Restrictive Practices Act 1976 ensures that traders who restrict competition by making agreements with other traders must register their agreements with the OFT, and the Competition Act 1980 allows the Director General of Fair Trading to investigate businesses operating anti-competition policies. Other areas of consumer protection refer to the poor quality of goods and services and to the provision of credit.

Contract law

Contract law consists of legal rules governing the enforcement of obligations between individuals arising from voluntary agreements. By making contracts, companies can buy raw materials and sell finished goods in relative safety as long as each side gives something of value.

The law of torts

The law of torts protects parties from each other's actions, particularly if a party suffers injury as a result of these actions (e.g. negligence).

Employment law

Under the Employment Protection Act 1978, employers are required to provide employees with copies of the terms of their employment within 13 weeks of their employment commencing. These terms relate to holidays, pay, hours of work, job title, periods of notice to terminate the contract and pensions. Of particular importance in recent years has been the Health and Safety at Work Act 1974, designed to maintain and improve standards of health, safety and welfare at work.

The law of agency

When organisations use outside specialists, the relationship of **principal** and **agent** is created. An agent is someone empowered to act on behalf of a principal in contractual relations with third parties. With this strong element of trust, clear legal guidelines are set to ensure the success of the relationship.

The potential list of areas covered by our legal system is almost endless. We could also mention the requirements of the legal system in relation to insurance, negotiable instruments, bankruptcy, data protection, financial services and the topical area of environmental law.

EU and regulations

The Single European Act of 1987 provides a guide to the enormous importance of the EU in the regulation of markets. This Act, which was popularised under the more easily understood term **Single European Market**, was born out of frustration with the continued fragmentation of the European community, which reduced the ability of firms to trade freely across borders and to reap the benefits of the economies of scale that an integrated market of 320 million people (in the then 12 member states) would provide.

The Cecchini Report sought to quantify the benefits of a single market and by implication noted the drawbacks that continued fragmentation brought with it. According to the report, the gains from a single market would be an increase of 4.5 per cent to the GDP of the community; a reduction of inflation, with average consumer prices falling by 6.1 per cent; an improvement in the balance of public finances of 2.2 per cent of GDP; and a reduction in unemployment of up to 1.8 million. Whether these improvements will actually come about is a matter for intense debate, but they do point to the supply-side improvements that would be encouraged by integration.

On comparing the US and European markets it is easy to see the problems. The case study at the end of the chapter reviews the domestic appliance industries in the USA and Europe, and the strategic response of one particular firm to operate across Europe. The problems this firm found were:

- different technical standards applied in each of the 12 national markets, making it expensive and difficult to trade across borders
- different tax regimes existed that created price differentials from market to market
- country-by-country adaptation tended to reduce competition and increased the power of the national suppliers.

Every country followed its own trade policy towards imports, a notable example being in the car industry where each country had a different way of dealing with Japanese car imports. It was against this background that the Single European Act was introduced, which was to have a huge impact on the control and regulation of business activity. The Act set out certain changes which were to be introduced by the end of 1992.

Border controls
These were to be reduced to allow for the speedy passage of goods and people. Businesses would benefit, as they would find a borderless Europe would get rid of the waiting at borders whilst documents were checked.

Mutual recognition of standards
This was a difficult issue that could have derailed the whole process. Each country would wish to jealously guard its own approaches, but some way had to be found to create a system whereby products and services would not be subject to changes in order to accommodate the system in each country. The solution adopted was one of mutual recognition, whereby a standard developed in one country should be accepted by another, provided it met basic requirements on such issues as health and safety. (This approach affected not only product standards, but also the movement of people, as a qualification gained in one country would be recognised in another.)

Public procurement
Put simply this would open up procurement opportunities to non-national suppliers. The aim was to reduce costs by allowing low-cost suppliers into national economies and increasing competition. Public sector organisations would then be able to choose the best supplier irrespective of nationality.

Financial services
Insurance, banking and other financial services could now be offered across Europe.

Freight transport
The restrictions on cabotage were abolished, giving freight delivery companies the right to pick up and deliver goods within another member state's borders. This was estimated to reduce the cost of haulage by up to 15 per cent.

The implications of these changes are enormous. The potential benefits to the member states are in the reduction of costs and thereby in the reduction of price and the greater choice that is offered.

Another aspect of the changes is the shift in power and influence to the European level. The regulations, directives and decisions to create the single market and to implement many of the Maastricht changes (see the section below) are used to promote progress. **Regulations** are directly applicable in all member states and do not have to be ratified by the national parliaments. They have a binding legal effect and prevail over national legislation. On the other hand, **directives** are binding on member states as to the result to be achieved within the period stated. Most of the changes introduced to further the single market were of this sort, and they leave to the individual member states the method of implementation. If a directive is not followed then certain punitive sanctions could be used. Lastly, decisions are binding on those to whom they are directed, whether member states or companies.

The Maastricht Treaty

After the moves towards the creation of a single market, the Maastricht Treaty was drawn up in 1991 to strengthen the community. Its main objectives are to build closer cooperation on foreign policy and justice/home affairs on an intergovernmental basis, and to enshrine the principle of **subsidiarity**, limiting the community's involvement in national affairs.

In areas where both the community and member states have power to act, the community will do so only if the objectives of the proposed action cannot be achieved sufficiently by an individual member state. In addition, an action by the community in any field must not go beyond what is necessary to achieve the Treaty's objectives. If there is a dispute the European Court of Justice will judge whether action is necessary.

The subsidiarity principle should ensure that:

- the community will not stray into areas where it is not needed
- where community action is needed, it will go no further than is required
- the European Court of Justice can clamp down on those that do not implement agreed rules
- the scope for community activities is defined in such areas as education, training and health by setting out the sort of action the community should take
- community action is possible in areas such as the environment, which affect all countries
- the European Commission is made more accountable to the European Parliament
- new rights for citizens are established
- movement is made towards economic and monetary union.

The Maastricht Treaty also established a new framework – the European Union – which is made up of three areas of cooperation.

- the Treaty of Rome (that set up the European community); the Single European Act; the Maastricht Treaty; and community rules

- foreign and security policy
- justice and home affairs.

In summary, the purpose of the Treaty was to gain increased political cooperation under the European Union, which would provide for a closer union in which political decisions would be taken as near to the people as possible. The economic impact was in the area of economic and monetary union, with target dates for the introduction of a single currency. To this end the European Monetary Institute (the forerunner of a Central Bank of Europe) would oversee the move towards the single currency.

The Treaty has not been without its critics, both in the UK and throughout the other member states. It was also a major issue when Austria, Finland and Sweden were negotiating their entry into the EU on 1 January 1995, and goes some way to explaining the rejection of membership by Norway. The political issues are important, but the single market and the Treaty have had a significant impact on the way the regulatory environment operates.

As an example of this, the control over mergers that may bring into being a monopoly can show the problems over the national approach and the need to work on a European level as firms merge to gain extra advantages in the single market. In summary, the regulation on the Control of Concentrations between businesses came into effect in September 1990. This regulation attempts to establish a division between community-scale mergers, for which the Commission is responsible, and those mergers that affect primarily the territory of a single member state, where the national authorities are responsible. The regulation requires prior notification from concentrators with a community dimension. The concentrations come about when two or more previously independent businesses merge or one or more businesses acquire control of the whole or parts of one other business. Control may be obtained by the purchase of shares or assets, by contract, or by any means that permits the possibility of exercising a decisive influence on a business.

The creation or strengthening of a dominant position which impedes effective competition will be declared incompatible with the single market, and the Commission is able to take appropriate action to rectify the situation.

Regulatory agencies

UK practices

Competition policy embraces policy towards monopolies, mergers and restrictive practices, while also recognising that firms constituting an oligopoly can have market power, and that groups of firms acting together through collective agreements can behave like a monopolist. Policy must focus on mergers that create oligopoly or monopoly situations, and look at the conduct of firms in relation to entry barriers and any agreements that try to reduce competition.

UK competition policy is based on legislation that dates from 1948, concerned with monopolies, mergers, restrictive practices, retail price maintenance and consumer protection. Usually a monopoly is defined as one firm (or group of firms acting together), accounting for 25 per cent or more of the relevant regional or national market. This may be referred for investigation to the Monopolies and Mergers Commission (MMC) by the Office of Fair Trading or the government. Mergers can also be investigated when they constitute 25 per cent or more of the market. Additionally, vertical or conglomerate mergers may be subject to review when they exceed a certain limit. This approach is based on two Acts: the Fair Trading Act 1973, which provided the definition of a monopoly, and the Competition Act 1980, which extended monopoly control to public sector bodies.

When a monopoly or proposed merger is investigated, the MMC has to determine whether it is likely to be against the **public interest**. Public interest is defined to include not only the maintenance and promotion of competition and price, quality and choice, but also the promotion of technical progress and international competitiveness. UK policy is *not* based on the assumption that monopoly is undesirable – it recognises that there are potential benefits, from economies of scale to international competitiveness, that need to be set against the reduction of competition. Each case is judged on its merits.

If the MMC finds against the merger or that monopoly practice is against the public interest, it can make recommendations to the relevant Secretary of State. It is up to the minister to enforce remedies against a monopoly or to forbid a merger. So, Sainsbury's proposal in 1995 of a takeover of Texas (the DIY chain), to merge it with its own Homecare DIY stores, was of interest to the Office of Fair Trading and the MMC. Likewise, the insistence that brewers must sell some of their 'tied houses' (pubs) was an attempt to introduce more competition into the retailing of beer and other drinks in public houses.

One of the major criticisms of UK policy is that it is very slow and ineffective. Investigations are inevitably complex and can go on for up to three years, a period which could be prolonged as government ministers are lobbied about accepting or rejecting the findings by various interested groups. Some speeding up of the process has taken place, but the criticism still remains valid.

Restrictive practices are covered by the 1976 Restrictive Practices and Resale Price Acts. The Restrictive Practices Court concerns itself with price agreements and market-sharing agreements. A restrictive practice is considered to be against the public interest unless it can satisfy at least one of eight so-called 'gateways':

- it protects the public against injury
- it provides substantial benefits to the public
- it acts as a counterbalancing power against the anticompetitive practices of third parties
- removal would result in serious and persistent local unemployment
- it helps to maintain exports
- it supports other acceptable restrictions
- it assists the negotiation of fair trading terms for suppliers and buyers
- the agreement neither restricts nor deters competition.

Even if one or more of these conditions can be met, the firm still has to show that the benefits outweigh the drawbacks. Although many practices have been registered with the Court, most of these had been ended by the firms concerned before a court decision. However, the Court is still weakened by the fact that the Office of Fair Trading has few powers of investigation and there are no financial penalties for failing to register a restrictive practice.

The Restrictive Practices Court can grant exemption from the provisions of the Retail Price Act, which prohibits producers from fixing *minimum* retail prices for their goods. With the exception of books and medicines, fixed prices for goods in all shops have virtually disappeared.

Other regulations have been introduced as industries have been privatised. All the utilities, from gas to tele-communications, have been subject to review of the prices they charge or the extent to which they are allowed to compete in certain industries. For example, the Office of the Rail Regulator – acting as a passenger watchdog in the preparation for rail privatisation – can exert considerable influence. In early 1995, the regulator reduced the charges that Railtrack were seeking to charge to the franchise holders, thereby making it profitable for the franchise companies to operate train services over the system.

Self-regulation is a major way in which industries come together to construct a framework that can be applied to companies. Self-regulation can cover areas of activity from takeovers, or the way individual pensions are sold, to advertising standards. The benefit of this approach is that the guidelines often reflect the operational reality of businesses, but they do suffer from a lack of authority and enforcement procedures.

EU practice

The rules of competition are set out in Articles 85 and 86. The former deals with agreements that may restrict competition, while the latter refers to the abuse of a dominant position.

As we have seen, each of the member states has its own laws on these issues, but in the single market national laws would be ineffective in their operations. Wherever there is a conflict of laws then the EU law takes precedence. If, however, there is an overlap, then it would be feasible for there to be parallel actions under both EU and national law. (Some of these issues have already been reviewed when looking at the division of control relating to monopoly in the EU and elsewhere.)

It is important for companies to consider the implication of EU involvement when planning marketing, production and takeover activities. Fines can be levied on companies that are deemed to have violated Articles 85 and 86, and contracts that violate the rules are void. The threat of heavy fines can clearly act as a deterrent, but the same criticism that has been aimed at UK approaches can be used against the EU. Firstly, the procedures are slow and cumbersome, a feature not made any easier by the complexity of a single market made up of 15 countries. Secondly, the budget and powers of the EU in this area are not as great as the two Articles would suggest.

Although it is beyond the scope of this section, note should be taken of Article 92, which covers state aid and subsidies. Its importance lies in the use of state aid to protect national industry from competition, an approach that would fly in the face of the single market. Subsidies have to have the agreement of the EU. They can be offered to industries such as state-controlled airlines, but the intention is to phase them out and to rely on the discipline of the market. Whether this will ever happen is not relevant here; it is the *intention* that should be of concern to the managers of firms who currently receive such subsidies.

UK and EU regulations cover an extensive range of operations, from competition, barriers to entry, and industrial fragmentation to exit from an industry. The comprehensive nature of the regulations should not go unnoticed, as business activity comes under more intense scrutiny by formal bodies such as the MMC and as part of media and wider public interest.

The UK labour market

The labour market is subject to government influence in much the same way as any other market. During the 1980s, various changes in laws relating to trade unions were enacted to reduce the unions' powers and to promote a market that was more flexible and responsive to the changing needs of the economy.

In Chapter 5 the macroeconomic objective of job creation is reviewed, along with the parallel problem of unemployment and the policy issues that go with it.

While the UK government was keen to participate in the move towards a European single market, it has been less prepared to accept a key feature of the Maastricht Treaty, namely the **Social Chapter**. The UK has opted out of this aspect of the agreement on the ground that it would add to the cost of employing people and so go against the labour market reforms introduced throughout the previous decade. This is a stance that supporters say is vindicated by the fact that a major reason for Japanese, American and Korean firms locating in Britain, rather than in the rest of the EU, is the benefit of a flexible labour market. Opponents of the stance point to the low wages and rising poverty in the UK compared with France, which has accepted the Social Chapter.

Main elements of the Social Chapter

Right of freedom of movement
This allows workers to move freely across the EU, and enables any citizen to engage in any occupation in the EU under the same terms as those applied to nationals of the host country. In theory, therefore, firms that experience skill shortages can draw from a larger pool of workers, increasing the amount of **migration**. Clearly, there is a need to develop common qualifications, a development that will take time especially as new member states will have their own approaches to training and qualifications.

Wages and social benefits applied in a host country must be guaranteed to other workers from another member state working in that country. This arrangement has produced problems for UK construction companies working in Berlin, who have employed workers from the UK on lower rates than their German counterparts.

Remuneration
A key principle is to provide **fair remuneration** for all those in employment, but it is not clear what 'fair' should actually mean. For some it would, as in France, be the creation of a minimum wage, but this is not accepted by many in the UK and elsewhere. A further issue is the acceptance by workers of their responsibility for

performance, a feature that would not be unacceptable to many in Britain as it implies some form of performance-related pay.

Living and working conditions

The main focus is on **working conditions**, and the establishment of a maximum duration of working time per week. Further to this, the rights of part-time workers will be improved (an issue that has already been the subject of a ruling by UK courts), and regulations will apply to night work and shift-work. Finally, every worker will have the right to annual paid leave and a weekly rest period.

Freedom of association

This is, broadly, the freedom to belong to a **trade union**. Organisations that ban unions will be forced to reassess their position. The changes in union legislation in the UK have put unions into a much weakened position, so it is not surprising that they would wish to see the Social Chapter applied in the UK – especially as it would also allow procedures to facilitate conciliation and arbitration. In short, the aim is to promote constructive dialogue between trade unions and management, as has been the case in western Germany for many years.

Participation of workers

This is often seen as the right to have worker representation at board level, or to have a parallel supervisory board or '**works council**'. This would promote the idea of dialogue on issues associated with strategy, mergers and other features of the operation of the company – a development that would increase workers' stake in the company.

Although the UK has opted out of the Chapter, many of the country's largest companies have operations scattered throughout the EU. A tactic could have been to promote councils in countries that required it, but to leave the situation as it is in the UK. However, this would have flown in the face of creating a unified base from which to launch a pan-European approach, so many of these companies have decided that all their plants and offices will have improved participation rights.

Protection in the workplace

This covers health and safety, training and so on. The problem is to encourage better practice, but not to impose onerous costs so that small and medium-sized firms are penalised.

To implement the provisions of the Social Chapter, it is up to each member state to take appropriate action either via legislation or collective agreements. The European Commission is of the view that the UK, despite its opt-out, should be encouraged or compelled to join – an approach that would be resisted by many politicians and businesses. Despite this, the Social Chapter – and in fact the whole Treaty – provides only a general statement of principles and each member state will approach it in a way that seems suitable. Nevertheless, its impact is already evident in the UK as companies and the courts respond to its challenges.

Conclusion

This chapter has reviewed a broad range of influences that affect the business environment. Regulations and European influences are key factors that have to be considered. The following case study provides an example of how a company has sought to understand and respond to these changes and to develop a successful strategy that will help to create a successful European operation.

Case Study
White goods manufacturing and marketing in Europe

Whirlpool, the white goods (washing machines, refrigerators, etc.) manufacturer, completed its two-stage purchase of its Philips domestic appliance rival in 1991.

By the spring of 1995, Whirlpool Europe executives had completed detailed discussions with unions and staff on reducing the work force by 15 per cent. Such a cutback often reveals that a company is in trouble and desperately seeking to cut costs, but for this company it is a planned reduction in costs to help transform an inefficient operation into one that can compete effectively with its major competitors.

The aim is to raise the European operation's profitability to levels achieved in North America, and thereby secure its future in the highly competitive European market and advance the company's long-term aim of becoming a global player.

There are, though, striking differences between the US and European markets. In western Europe the industry is fragmented along national lines, which is partly a reflection of traditional differences between national products. Whirlpool estimates that it took an average of 7.7 days of household income in 1992 to buy a dishwasher in Europe, against 3.8 days for a comparable machine in the USA.

It is not just Whirlpool that is taking this line. Electrolux, the Swedish-based producer of consumer goods, is now a pan-European organisation, with a product renewal programme based on brands to suit customers with different income levels.

Whirlpool achieved an improvement in profits and has seen its market share in Europe rise to 12.5 per cent. This has been achieved against a background of an industry-wide decline in retail prices of 3 per cent a year, with restructuring costs and a large expenditure on promoting its name in Europe. (This is particularly important as the Philips name has been dropped from its market, to be replaced with the Whirlpool brand name.)

The company has recognised that, despite its improved market share, it is still too small to compete effectively on a country-by-country basis. Hotpoint (UK), Thomson (France) or Bosch–Siemens (Germany) are much larger in their home markets than is Whirlpool, thereby providing them with a competitive advantage in selling and administration costs.

Creating a European-scale operation would allow the company to work across markets, as regionalisation and centralisation can reduce costs, but provide a response to each region's requirements. This should provide greater control of the products and the channels and provide an effective challenge to a well-entrenched national supplier.

One additional challenge is the problem of brand loyalty, with very few customers repurchasing the same brand when the time comes. Whirlpool has embarked on a customer loyalty programme to try to overcome this, although there may be problems in seeing this working in the short-term.

Various research studies on the European market have shown that the removal of internal tariff barriers in the EU has not made Europe homogeneous. So, although Electrolux and Whirlpool would prefer the creation of such a market, and would argue that not only would they benefit, but so too would customers as prices fell, the problems have not been reduced by the creation of a single tariff-free market.

This provides a challenge. To create a European or indeed a global market would require a large investment, without the possibility of short-term gain. In France, for example, top-loading machines account for 70 per cent of the market. In western Germany the consumers prefer front-loaders with high spinning speeds. In Italy consumers prefer front-loaders with lower spin speeds. The British, on the other hand, prefer the front-loader with a hot and cold water fill, rather than a cold water supply. The extent of the differences is such that machines that sell well in one market sell poorly in others. If these differences are compared with the US market, then that market is much more homogeneous, with regional and climatic differences having less of an impact on purchasing behaviour.

The causes of such differences are not easy to determine, as they seem deeply ingrained in cultural behaviour. Interestingly, since the 1960s – when automatic washing machines were considered a luxury and were owned by only a few households – the differences between markets has increased. In that period most machines had similar spin speeds, but now this is not the case. As if to confuse matters further, the UK's preference for top-loaders was even then the opposite of the French – and both changed their preferences as machines became more popular. If there was the chance for a homogeneous market, then, it was lost in the 1960s when the differences emerged. For Whirlpool and others with an intention to reduce costs, and thereby prices, this presents a major problem. There may be the potential for a more globalised (European) market, but it would seem to require changes on a large scale, with distribution, cost, promotion and consumer preferences all requiring detailed consideration.

Questions for discussion

1 *What competitive strengths is Whirlpool trying to create, and how likely is it to be successful?*
2 *Using a PEST analysis, outline the major influences in the domestic appliances market.*
3 *Summarise the findings of (1) and (2) in a SWOT analysis and identify what you think this would mean for the strategic choices facing the company.*

Further reading

- *Business Studies*, 2nd edition, by D. Needham and R. Dransfield. Stanley Thornes, 1994.
- *Applied Economics – An Introduction Course*, 5th edition, edited by A. Griffiths and S. Wall. Longman, 1993.
- *International Business – Competing in the Global Marketplace* by C. W. L. Hill. Irman, 1994.
- *Marketing – An International Perspective* by H. Chee and R. Harris. Pitman, 1993.
- *The Business Environment* by I. Worthington and C. Britten. Pitman, 1994.
- *Strategic Business Planning* by Clive Reading. Kogan Page, 1995.
- *The Business Plan Workbook* by C. Barrow, R. Brown and P. Barrow. Kogan Page, 1992.

Managing finance and information

8 Managing finance

On completing this chapter students should be able to:

■ identify and analyse organisational financial resources

■ identify and evaluate alternative sources of finance

■ use financial information and procedures to support decision-making

■ evaluate the financial performance of organisations.

For a business to operate it needs resources. Whether these are physical resources, such as property, equipment and materials, or less tangible human resources, money is required to pay for their use. Hence the management of finance is inseparable from the management of the business as a whole. In this chapter we examine how money is generated and consumed in the business, and identify appropriate sources of finance. We consider how business activities can be planned using financial techniques, and how business performance can be measured for control and subsequent decision-making purposes.

Nature of costs

Cost is the term used to describe the consumption of money. Knowledge about the nature of costs is important for many management tasks including:

■ evaluation of alternative courses of action for business planning
■ measuring, analysing and controlling performance against objectives.

We can classify costs in a number of different ways.

Cost elements

Resources used by a business can be categorised into three cost types:

■ **Labour** – payments to the business's employees.
■ **Materials** – the physical goods consumed in making a supply to a customer. This element is not confined to suppliers of goods; service firms also use materials, e.g. decorators use paint, solicitors use paper.
■ **Expenses** – other resources consumed, including rent, power, services of other businesses and depreciation (the loss in value of property and equipment that is used over a number of time periods).

Direct and indirect costs

For some decision-making purposes, such as pricing products and services on a cost plus basis, it is necessary to establish the actual cost of each product and service provided.

- **Direct costs** can be identified and easily assigned to a particular product or service, whether these be individual units, batches or continuous production. Total direct cost of a product is known as **prime cost**.
- **Indirect costs** are not easily identifiable with specific products or services and are commonly called **overheads**. Examples include rent and the consumption of electricity. Indirect costs are generally analysed by the organisation's departments and are added to direct product costs in proportion to some measure of business activity. For example, a product assembly department that is labour intensive may use direct labour hours or direct labour wages as a measure of activity. An automated bottling plant may use machine hours. Once an appropriate base has been identified, indirect costs can be included in product costs by finding an overhead rate for each unit of business activity, e.g. overhead per direct labour hour.

Case Study
Analysis of costs

A multi-product business has the following analysis of sales value for the month of June:

Category		£
Direct costs:	Direct materials	1 500
	Direct labour	1 000
	Direct expenses	500
	Prime cost (total of all direct costs)	3 000
Indirect costs:	Manufacturing overhead	2 000
	Total manufacturing cost (stock valuation)	5 000
	Administration costs	1 000
	Selling and distribution costs	3 000
	Total product cost	9 000
	Profit	1 000
	Sales value	10 000

The business absorbs manufacturing costs into product costs in proportion to product labour cost, so the amount of manufacturing overhead per £1 of labour is £2 (i.e. £2000/£1000). Administration and selling costs are absorbed on the basis of manufacturing costs, so for every £1 of manufacturing cost, £0.80 of administration and selling costs will be added. A margin of 10 per cent of sales value is required from every product. With this information we can work out the total cost of a single product.

Each unit of product alpha requires:

Direct materials	£2
Direct labour	£2
Direct expenses	£2
Prime cost	£6

We can, therefore, work out the indirect costs to be absorbed and then the selling price:

Manufacturing overhead	£4 (Direct labour £2 × 2 = £4)
Total manufacturing cost	£10
Administration and selling	£8 (£10 × 0.80)
Total product cost	£18
Profit	£2
Selling price	£20

Case Study
Direct and indirect costs

A factory manufacturing components and assemblies for the motor industry will have the following direct and indirect costs.

Materials

- Direct material – can be identified with specific products, e.g. steel sheets supplied to a job making wheel caps.
- Indirect material – cannot be easily charged to specific products and is classified as a factory overhead, e.g. rivets, lubricating oil and rag to clean machines.

Labour

- Direct labour relates to those workers whose time and effort can be allocated to making specific components and assemblies, e.g. assembly workers.
- Indirect labour consists of labour costs that cannot be related to specific products and are classified as a factory overhead, e.g. stores personnel and factory supervision.

Expenses

- Direct expenses can be identified with specific products, e.g. patent royalties and work sub-contracted out.
- Indirect expenses cannot be identified with specific products, e.g. rent and machine maintenance.

Questions for discussion

Consider the costs incurred by a bakery and a bus company. In each case:

1 *identify the main cost elements of labour, materials and expenses*

2 *classify direct and indirect costs*

3 *suggest methods in which indirect costs could be included in total product costs.*

Cost behaviour

Costs can be divided into categories according to how they change as business activity changes (see Figure 8.1).

Figure 8.1 Costs by category

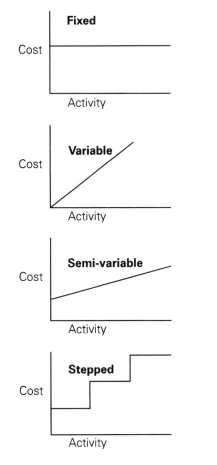

Fixed costs

Costs that remain unchanged with business activity, e.g. property rents and interest payable on loans.

Variable costs

Costs that change in direct proportion to the level of business activity, e.g. materials used in the manufacture of products and sales commissions.

Semi-variable costs

Costs that contain a fixed and variable element, e.g. telephone charges, where the line rental is a fixed cost and charges for calls are a variable cost.

Stepped costs

Costs that are fixed for a range of business activities, but above a certain level of activity they jump to a new level, e.g. supervision wages. Since supervisors become ineffective with wide spans of control, the recruitment of one extra worker may result in the simultaneous need for a further supervisor. Other examples include the use of assets, from equipment to whole factories. There comes a point where the current business set-up is inadequate for greater capacities and investment in new business infrastructure is required.

All costs are variable in the long run

Care must be taken when classifying costs between fixed and variable. In the long run all costs may be considered variable as there is always the possibility of discontinuing business activities, and in extreme cases, the whole business could be closed down. Costs are fixed for as long as there is a contractual agreement to incur them.

Most costs are fixed in the short run

Costs are often too readily classified as variable. For example, direct workers are only variable costs in the short term if they are paid on a piece-work basis. Where there is a contractual obligation to pay wages on a time-period basis (i.e. so much per week), wages are a fixed cost in the very short term. For many businesses it is often impractical and undesirable to change the size of the work force in line with fluctuations in workload, even when considering periods running into several months. They have to take into account the existence of contracts of employment and the time taken to train new workers should activity increase again, so most work forces have to be considered fixed for at least several months. Cost analysis will depend on the circumstances, but in the short run perhaps only material usage can be considered a variable cost.

Basis of cost variation

Another important consideration when analysing whether costs are fixed or variable is to be clear on what basis costs vary. The cost of electricity for a factory will depend on a number of factors, including:

- the power requirement of machines
- the amount of lighting required depending on the time of year.

The power used by machines will vary according to the number of products being produced; the lighting will only vary according to business activity, e.g. if overtime working extends into periods of darkness.

Task

1 Explain the difference between direct costs and variable costs.
2 Consider the following costs to be incurred next month by a computer assembly plant:

- telephone
- piece-work assembly workers
- vehicle running expenses
- sub-contract machine drilling work
- goods-received inspectors
- purchasing costs
- executive's secretary
- gardener
- telephone switchboard operator
- advertising.

  a Classify them into fixed, variable, semi-variable and stepped costs.
  b Analyse the costs into direct and indirect categories.
  c In what time period might those you consider to have a fixed-cost element become variable costs?

Contribution from sales

For a business to make a profit it is necessary that sales revenues exceed total costs. However, provided the value of each individual supply to customers does at least cover the variable costs incurred, then the sale does make a contribution towards fixed costs and profits.

$$\text{Contribution} = \text{Sales value} - \text{Variable cost}$$

Break-even point

One of the most important financial targets that businesses must attain if they are not to fail is the level of sales required to pay for all costs. This is called the **break-even point**.

Total sales value at the break-even point = Total fixed costs + Total variable costs

To calculate the break-even point in sales units =

$$\frac{\text{Fixed costs}}{\text{Contribution per unit}}$$

Case Study
The business plan

John Newell is preparing a business plan to present to his bank manager to raise finance for a new restaurant. He wants to show how many customers he needs to attract each week to break even. Fixed costs are estimated to be £480 a week and a typical three-course meal priced at £12 will incur him variable costs of £4.

$$\text{Contribution per customer} = £12 - £4 = £8$$

$$\text{Break-even point} = \frac{£480}{£8} = 60 \text{ customers per week}$$

Sales value at break even =
Number of customers × Sales price = $60 \times £12 = £720$

A target profit

The level of sales needed to attain a target profit can be calculated using a similar approach.

$$\text{Number of sales units} = \frac{\text{Fixed cost} + \text{Profit}}{\text{Contribution per unit}}$$

John Newell is aiming to make £200 profit each week so using the formula above:

$$\text{Number of sales units} = \frac{£480 + £200}{£8}$$
$$= 85 \text{ customers per week}$$

Case Study
Lotus-eater

'Frazer Nash, Austin Healey, Triumph and MG may have pulled into the pits long ago, but a clutch of small firms still carry the chequered flag for Britain's sports-car makers. Lotus and TVR have led the way. Of the two firms, Lotus looked as if it has the best chance of surviving. Surely its giant parent, General Motors, had the money and expertise to succeed in the sports-car business. But on 15 June 1992 Lotus startled the motor industry by dropping the Elan, its most popular model, barely two years after it went into production, because the car was making heavy losses. Perhaps Lotus's managers should have taken a look at their much smaller, independent rival. TVR continues to make a profit selling a smaller number of cars to the same kinds of customers that Lotus was trying to woo with the Elan.

'Lotus planned to produce 3000 of its £22 000 Elans each year, but ended up making only half that number. The firm's mistake was to apply GM's mass-production techniques to the Elan's tiny production runs. It spent

six years developing the Elan and building a partly automated factory in which to make it. This led to fixed costs of £35m per annum. Lotus stopped making the Elan after losing £13m in each of the previous two years.

'Compare the debacle at Lotus with the success of TVR which sells just 700 cars per year. They made a profit of £700 000 on sales of £15.4m last year. The company's factory looks old fashioned and there are no sophisticated machine tools to make its components. Such machinery can produce cheaper parts, but only at far higher volumes than TVR needs – as Lotus discovered to its cost. All this enables the firm to cut overheads to the bone. However, TVR has to use expensive materials that require little machine tooling – this increases their labour and material costs to £12 000 per car.'

(Source Adapted from *The Economist*, 20 June 1992)

Questions for discussion

1 *Calculate the variable cost per car for Lotus.*
2 *Calculate the fixed cost per year for TVR.*
3 *What is the break-even point for each company?*
4 *How much profit would Lotus have made on the Elan if it had achieved sales of 3000 cars per year?*
5 *Why has TVR been successful compared to Lotus?*
6 *Do you think survival for TVR is easy?*

Relevant costs

A knowledge of how costs behave with changes of activity can aid in decision-making. When approaching a business decision, it is important to consider only those costs and benefits that are relevant to the decision.

Case Study
Bananas at any price?

Jill Parker has come to the end of another day selling fruit and vegetables at the local market. She purchased 100 lb of bananas for £20 and has sold 90 lb of bananas at 3 lb for £1. The remainder will not keep till next market day. What is the minimum price she should charge for the remaining 10 lb of bananas?

The cost of the bananas is not relevant to the decision as it has already been incurred. Hence there is no minimum price Jill requires. She should take whatever she can.

The principle when making decisions is to maximise contribution from sales. Selling prices higher than the relevant cost provide a contribution towards fixed costs and profit. Fixed costs are not relevant to decision-making, although an increase in step costs may be.

Case Study
A furniture manufacturer

The sales director is unhappy with the current selling price of £70 per chair and has forecast sales volume for a range of selling prices.

Selling price (£)	55	60	65	70
Volume (units per month)	5750	5250	4500	3500

Each chair incurs variable costs of £45. Fixed costs are £50 000 per month. On the basis of this information, at what price should chairs be sold?

Answer

	At selling price (£)			
	55	60	65	70
Total sales value (£)	316 250	315 000	292 500	245 000
Variable cost (£)	258 750	236 250	202 500	157 500
Contribution (£)	57 500	78 750	90 000	87 500

The sales price of £65 gives the highest contribution, so is the desired price on this information.

Task

Jack Caroak forecasts increasing sales volume if he lowers the sales price, and there will come a point when he will need to expand his premises if the prices are low enough. Projections of monthly activity:

Selling price (£)	12	11	10	9
Volume (units)	15 000	18 000	22 000	29 000
Factory overheads (£)	30 000	30 000	35 000	35 000

Variable cost is £5 per unit.

1 What is Jack's contribution and net profit at each price level?
2 On the basis of this information, what level of sales should Jack be planning for?

Task

Rhodda's makes a range of products that are not dissimilar to those provided by its competitors. The business has capacity for 500 of each product every month. Unfortunately, resources are dedicated to each type of product.

	Product				
	Red	**Blue**	**White**	**Orange**	**Purple**
Direct materials	5	10	7	20	14
Direct labour	10	15	8	10	6
Prime cost	15	25	15	30	20
Fixed overhead apportioned	5	5	5	10	10
Total unit cost	20	30	20	40	30
Profit on cost	4	6	4	8	6
Selling price	24	36	24	48	36

An increase in the number of competitors has led to changes in market prices and Rhodda's can no longer charge prices calculated on a cost plus basis.

Market price	21	37	24	38	18

1 Calculate Rhodda's profit, assuming 500 units of each product are sold at the new market prices.
2 On what basis could Rhodda's maximise its profit?
3 What is the maximum profit Rhodda's can earn?

Task

A factory extension has been started with £25 000 costs incurred to date. Further costs will amount to £100 000. Total future benefits from having the larger factory are now thought to be £100 000 less than the £200 000 originally forecast. If work is terminated, compensation of £20 000 will have to be paid to the builder. State, with reasons, your recommended course of action.

Task

Troy Engineering Ltd has incurred expenses of £4000 working to secure its first contract with British Aerospace. The contract will require 5000 hours of direct labour. The salaried shop floor workers are paid £19 000 for a 1900-hour working year. The materials for the contract have erroneously already been purchased for £30 000. They can be returned to the suppliers for a 10 per cent handling charge. Due to ferocious competition, the managing director is concerned the contract will not be gained and an important opportunity to gain a large potential customer will be lost. The time has come to quote a price for the contract. Advise the managing director.

Accounting classifications

For accounting purposes, expenditure is classified into two categories:

- capital expenditure
- revenue expenditure.

The correct classification into these categories is important for a meaningful measurement of business performance.

Capital expenditure is incurred to purchase fairly permanent resources that are required to carry on the business. Examples include property, machinery, motor vehicles, furniture and computer equipment. These items are called **fixed assets** and would normally last for more than one year.

Revenue expenditure includes all amounts paid in the day-to-day operations of the business. This includes wages, purchases of stock and payment of expenses such as heat, advertising and repairs. Examples of capital and revenue expenditure are shown in Figure 8.2.

Task

Classify the following items of expenditure into capital or revenue expenditure:

a a computer purchased for use in the business
b a computer purchased by a computer retailer for resale
c a garage purchasing a car for resale
d an office extension
e office redecoration
f insurance for a motor vehicle
g carpet for an office.

The importance of the correct classification of costs for accounting purposes will become clearer later in the chapter. At this stage, it is important only to appreciate that fixed assets are not consumed in a short period of time and so it is necessary to spread the cost of a fixed asset over the periods that are to benefit from its use. The proportion of an asset's cost that is treated as an expense in a particular accounting period is called **depreciation**.

Cost–benefit analysis

So far we have assumed that the income and costs from business decisions and activities are easily quantifiable. This is not always the case. Many decisions that involve the business in costs are made with a subjective judgement as to the benefits that will result. Will a training programme for staff result in improved morale

Figure 8.2 Examples of capital and revenue expenditure

	Capital expenditure	Revenue expenditure
Property Building work	To buy land and buildings To improve the building, e.g. alterations and extensions	Rent and rates To maintain in good order, e.g. redecoration
Equipment, motor vehicles furniture, fixtures and fittings used in the business	Purchase price, delivery and installation	Running costs – power and maintenance
Salaries and wages	Only capitalised if incurred in the making of fixed assets	All other expenditure
Goods bought for resale to customers	No	Yes
Research and development	Only where future benefits are almost certain	All expenditure not classified as capital expenditure
Marketing and selling costs	Only for fixed assets used, e.g. delivery vehicles and office equipment	All other expenditure
Management and administration	Only for fixed assets used, e.g. office equipment	All other expenditure

and efficiency? Will a refurbishment of the firm's social club be covered by a corresponding improvement in staff goodwill, effectiveness and drop in labour turnover? These are typical questions asked and require some basis to allow decisions to be made. The first stage of cost–benefit analysis attempts to state all costs and benefits that appertain to the organisation in monetary terms to allow comparison.

Taking this further, it is possible to consider the costs and benefits to society at large of pursuing a particular course of action. Under the banner of 'social accounting', some businesses attempt to measure the effect of their activities on society as a whole.

The extent that firms espouse community spirit must be set within the context of the business's objectives. The primary objective for most is the maximisation of profit, so it would be expected that social aspects will only be considered in business decisions if they are thought to provide quantifiable, if somewhat uncertain, financial benefits (see Figure 8.3). For example, the reduction of pollution will only be business policy if the goodwill and promotional value afforded outweighs the cost. The commercial success of some businesses is almost entirely attributable to their 'green' credentials. Despite Anita Roddick's undoubted concern for the environment, the Body Shop benefits greatly from its green image.

To manage the social impact of business, it is necessary for government to ensure that social costs and benefits

Figure 8.3 Weighing up the commercial/social aspects of a business decision

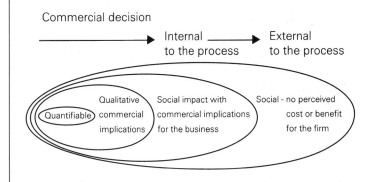

are considered in the commercial decision-making process, i.e. ensure 'externalities' become internal to the commercial decision-making process. This either requires legal restrictions or a system of incentives and taxes to ensure business decisions reflect social concerns. Currently, governments are reviewing methods for passing the social cost of pollution and waste disposal on to business with ideas for carbon taxes and levies for river pollution and the disposal of toxic waste. Regional grants for attracting new businesses to a depressed region reflect the social benefits of increased economic activity and reduced unemployment.

Task

Identify the nature of the costs and benefits for the following business activities and classify them into the four categories of quantifiable; qualitative – commercial only; qualitative – social and commercial; and social implications only:

a an advertising campaign
b new glossy packaging for kitchen utensils
c open a supermarket on Sundays
d support an employee's education even though not relevant to current job responsibilities
e motorway maintenance during the night
f incinerate business waste
g import noxious waste into the UK where it is better contained by the clay soils in the south of England.

For each activity, do you believe government intervention is necessary to ensure social costs and benefits are considered in the commercial decision-making process? Give reasons.

Cash flow

It is important to analyse the way in which cash flows through a business if forecasting for future finance requirements is to be accurate.

The flow (cycle) of money is similar to the water cycle. It is transformed from a liquid (flexible) resource into other assets like property, equipment and stocks, etc. These assets help generate income from customers and result in cash being received back at the bank ready to continue the cycle. Like the life-giving qualities of water, cash is essential for a business to survive and so it is vital that the receipts and payments of cash are properly monitored and controlled.

Cash flow statements

The cash flow statement (see Figure 8.4) is a valuable tool in the financial management of a business. It identifies all sources and applications of cash that are forecast for the future.

The format of the cash flow statement should convey a clear and accurate message to its user.

Guidelines

- Use headings that are appropriate to the business.
- The statement can be for any division of time – weekly, quarterly, and for any number of periods.
- The total period covered by the statement depends on the purpose of the forecast. A forecast that indicates a continuing cash deficit after six months should continue into future periods to identify the duration for which additional finance is required. It is not unusual

Figure 8.4 Example of a cash flow statement

Heading	Month 1	Month 2	Month 3	Month 4	Month 5	Month 6
Capital	5 000					
Loan	3 000					
Sales receipts	____	4 000	5 000	6 000	7 000	7 000
Total receipts	8 000	4 000	5 000	6 000	7 000	7 000
Payments:						
Salaries and wages	2 000	2 000	2 000	2 500	2 500	3 000
Rent and rates	1 000			1 000		
Power				500		
Purchase of materials	2 000	1 000	1 250	1 500	1 750	2 000
Equipment	3 500	500				2 000
Drawings						2 000
Total payments	8 500	3 500	3 250	5 500	4 250	9 000
Receipts minus payments	(500)	500	1 750	500	2 750	(2 000)
Balance brought forward	0	(500)	0	1 750	2 250	5 000
Balance carried forward	(500)	0	1 750	2 250	5 000	3 000

for a new business venture to construct a cash flow statement for its first three years of operations. The first year should be analysed on a monthly basis, with the second and third years perhaps analysed on a quarterly basis.

■ Positive final balances indicate money in the bank. Negative final balances indicate that finance is insufficient to pay for all the forecast commitments. Arrangements have to be made to cover the deficit, perhaps by applying for an overdraft facility if it is seen as a temporary situation.

■ It is important to identify the point when cash is actually received or paid. Hence if customers are allowed up to 30 days credit before they need to pay for supplies, then the revenue from sales for month 1 will not be received until month 2. Likewise it may be possible to delay the payment of suppliers. It is necessary to be prudent and, where there is uncertainty, to tend towards a pessimistic outlook by assuming an extended customer settlement period and restricted credit allowed by suppliers.

Business activity and cash flow

Businesses are continually using resources of various types and so it may be helpful to understand the utilisation and provision of cash by examining three important cycles:

1 operating cycle
2 investment cycle
3 financing cycle.

Operating cycle

The operating cycle describes the processes of normal trading activity. For a manufacturing business it starts with the purchase of materials, through making of the product, and finishes with the receipt of cash from customers (see Figure 8.5).

For any product going through this cycle, cash is being invested to increase its value until the customer finally pays (see Figure 8.6). Finance tied up in this operating cycle is called **working capital**.

It follows that the greater the number of products being produced, the greater the amount of cash that is required. We therefore come across the common, but initially incomprehensible, situation of overtrading! **Overtrading** describes a situation where the financial resources invested in a business are inadequate for the rate at which expansion is occurring. In fact the business is too successful! This occurs when business planning has failed to forecast accurately the level of finance required.

Figure 8.5 The operating cycle of a manufacturing business

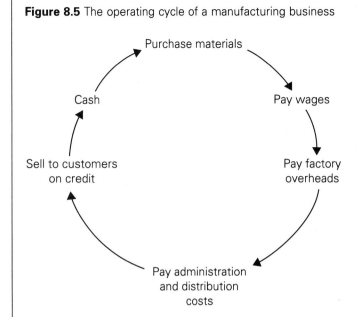

Figure 8.6 Working capital

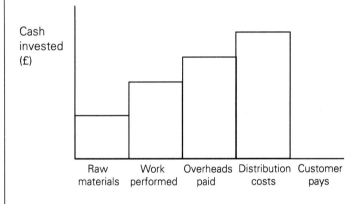

Case Study
Example of overtrading

Joanne Paterson commenced trading in January 1995 with a bank loan of £1000 repayable in full nine months later. She knew that her suppliers had to be paid cash on delivery, despite the fact that her customers would demand one month's credit. She forecast her first month's sales would be £1000, which would represent her costs of £800 plus a 25 per cent markup.

Joanne's business proved highly successful and her sales increased by roughly 50 per cent a month – until the bank finally said she could have no more money. At the end of June 1995 she owed a total of £3340. How could she run out of money when things were going so well?

Joanne's profit and loss account compares her sales values with costs for the six months in business:

Joanne Paterson
Profit and loss account for the six months ended 30 June 1995

Month	Jan.	Feb.	Mar.	April	May	June
Sales	1000	1500	2200	3300	4900	7400
Costs	800	1200	1760	2640	3920	5920
Profit	200	300	440	660	980	1480
Cumulative profit	200	500	940	1600	2580	4060

Joanne does indeed seem to have done very well. In fact, she has made a total of £4060 profit. How could she have failed? A closer look at the business's cash for the period gives the answer.

Joanne Paterson
Cash flow statement for the six months ended 30 June 1995

Month	Jan.	Feb.	Mar.	April	May	June
Sales receipts	0	1000	1500	2200	3300	4900
Payment for stock purchases	−800	−1200	−1760	−2640	−3920	−5920
Receipts less payments	−800	−200	−260	−440	−620	−1020
Balance at the start of the month	1000	200	0	−260	−700	−1320
Balance at the end of the month	200	0	−260	−700	−1320	−2340

From the cash flow statement we can see why Joanne got into difficulty. At the end of each month she is owed money by her customers so that in January she received no money from them. By the end of June, customers owed her £7400. We can reconcile the two financial statements as follows:

	£
Money owed to bank (initial £1000 + overdraft of £2340)	−3340
Add: Customers who owe Joanne	7400
Profit for the six months	4060

Joanne was adding to her problems every month. At 50 per cent sales increase each month, her working capital requirement was growing faster than the business could generate money, even though it was making a profit.

The operating cycle does not always result in a consistent flow of cash and it may be important to recognise two phases that can affect it.

Product life-cycle

The level at which products use up or generate cash will depend on the point reached in the product life-cycle (see Figure 8.7). Joanne Paterson's business is an example of a product still in its growth phase.

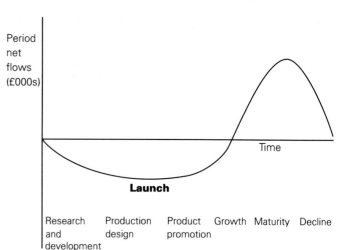

Figure 8.7 Cash flows during the product life-cycle

During product development cash flows out of the business but none flows in. Later in the cycle cash receipts, it is hoped, exceed cash payments. For the financial well-being of a business that is subject to marked product life-cycles, it is important to maintain a balanced portfolio of products, where sufficient funds are being generated for the development of new products.

The size and duration of each phase depends on the product. It may also be found that on-going development and promotional expenditure are incurred at later stages of the product life-cycle to allow a period of further sales growth. Positive cash flows may still be significant during sales decline as little development and promotional expenditure is being incurred. Hence the term 'cash cow' for products that are being 'milked' to generate funds for other uses.

Case Study
Ford

'Financial strategy is affected by product life cycles no more than in the motor industry. In 1993 Ford launched the Mondeo, the European version of its "world car"; this was followed by the Contour, the American version in 1994. In all the project has cost Ford $6 billion for which it has gained refurbished factories in addition to new standard car bodies, engines and gearboxes. The Mondeo and Contour will now be cash cows to pay for new investments to keep Ford near the top just as new markets are emerging in the Far East. Much of the cash generated in the next four years will go into car production facilities in China and India.'

(Source *The Economist*, 23 July 1994)

Questions for discussion

The case study shows that financial planning and business strategy go hand in hand.

Identify three other industries that experience marked product life-cycles and highlight those products that are probably generating cash and suggest possible new products that the cash is being used to develop.

Seasonal sales

Many businesses experience specific times of the year when trading activity is particularly high or low. Examples include building and gardening materials, power generation, travel and leisure industries, clothing, farming and products bought for gifts.

It is usual for more cash to be tied up in the operating cycle at times of increased business activity, as more resources have been purchased, but the business is awaiting payment from its customers.

Task

Trevor Bentley is about to set up in business supplying bags of sand and gravel to garden centres and DIY stores. The industry experiences large variations in demand depending on the season. During summer there is heavy demand – at this time the gardener and the DIY enthusiast are at their most active. Demand is minimal during the winter.

Trevor needs to purchase plant and machinery worth £100 000, but he intends to rent premises, vehicles and other equipment as he requires them.

	Spring	Summer	Autumn	Winter	Spring	Summer
Sales	45 000	110 000	50 000	7 000	45 000	110 000
Costs (excl. finance costs):						
Rent	5 000	5 000	5 000	5 000	5 000	5 000
Wages	12 000	30 000	15 000	1 500	13 000	33 000
Materials	25 000	55 000	20 000	0	20 000	45 000
Other costs	5 000	10 000	5 000	500	5 000	10 000

One aspect of the industry that makes it hard for a small business is the size of the major customers. They tend to be large national retail chains that use their purchasing power to dictate trading terms to their suppliers. One consequence of this is that Trevor will have to accept payment for his sales in the quarter following delivery. All purchases will have to be settled promptly.

Trevor has £40 000, but the majority of finance will have to come from other sources. One possibility is his bank. Also, a number of friends and relatives have said they would like to invest in any venture he may have in mind.

Prepare a cash flow forecast for Trevor to show how much finance he will require to set up and run the business (excluding finance costs).

Where the cycles experienced by a business are particularly marked, it may be necessary to prepare a cash forecast for a longer period than for a business that enjoys stable demand.

Investment cycle

Unlike operating expenditure, investment in fixed assets is usually more uneven. Some periods may experience heavy expenditure, others none at all (see Figure 8.8). For those industries where capital expenditure requirements can be massive, businesses have to forecast cash flows many years in advance, e.g. shipping companies and power-generation plants.

In the normal course of business, capital assets mean an outflow of funds. However, businesses undergoing reorganisation may decide to raise funds from the sale of fixed assets. This may be to:

- pay for past operating losses
- lower overheads and become 'fitter and leaner' for the future
- relinquish funds for more efficient use on other assets, e.g. selling under-used factory space to pay for a new production process.

Figure 8.8 The investment cycle

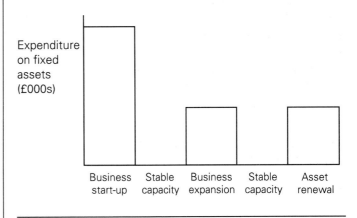

Case Study
Dixons PLC

Dixons continued its business restructuring in the year to 30 April 1994 with the closure of high-street locations and the development of profitable out-of-town Currys Superstores where operating costs are lower. At the same time the business was able to strengthen its cash position with more sale proceeds than purchase costs. The following appeared in the financial review of Dixons' annual report.

> 'Investing activities generated an inflow of £15.6 million. Cash expended on purchases of tangible fixed assets was £52.0 million, of which approximately £41.0 million was in respect of UK Retail, principally on new Superstores and computer systems. The disposal of Dixons US Holdings Inc. generated £37.5 million and termination of UK Property resulted in a cash inflow of £28.6 million.'

Questions for discussion

Identify two other companies that have restructured and identify the actual or anticipated financial benefits.

Finance cycle

The finance cycle is by necessity the flow of cash required to balance with the other cycles and is also, therefore, not a uniform flow of cash. It commences with the business owners and other finance providers injecting cash into the business. Cash provided by the business owners and other long-term investors is referred to as **capital**. Later in the cycle these providers of finance will require a return on their investment, and some may require repayment of the amounts they have contributed. The profits paid out to the business owners are called **dividends** in the case of companies and **drawings** for sole traders and partnerships.

Task

Clare Stanton owns a small building firm, working mainly on house repairs and extensions. She employs four workers, each paid an average £6.00 an hour. They work for a basic 162.5-hour calendar month, equivalent to 7.5 hours a day. When necessary she pays overtime at time and a half. Clare estimates that work measured in worker hours for the next twelve months, together with related material costs, will be:

	July	Aug.	Sept.	Oct.	Nov.	Dec.
Hours	900	850	900	800	600	300
Materials (£)	4000	4000	4000	3500	2500	1000

	Jan.	Feb.	Mar.	Apr.	May	June
Hours	250	300	400	500	600	800
Materials (£)	1000	1500	2000	2500	2500	4000

She has agreed the following total number of holidays each month with her workers, including her own:

	July	Aug.	Sept.	Oct.	Nov.	Dec.
Holidays	10	10	10	15	5	35

	Jan.	Feb.	Mar.	Apr.	May	June
Holidays	12	5	5	8	5	5

Clare takes £2000 out of the business each month and works a basic 37.5 hours a week on productive work. Running costs every month amount to £900 for her yard and £500 for a van and various items of small plant. Hire of specialist equipment incurs about £1 of charges for every productive worker hour.

Building jobs are quoted at £15 per worker hour plus material cost. There are no partly completed jobs at the end of each month and customers pay in the month following work completion. Clare believes in paying for all costs in the month in which they are incurred. On 31 May there was £250 in the business bank account and customers owed £16 000 for work completed in May.

In February Clare plans to purchase a new van for £10 000 and in May a concrete mixer for £1800.

1 Prepare a twelve-month cash flow forecast for Stanton & Co. (round all figures to whole pounds).
2 Comment on the pattern of cash flow for the firm and establish reasons for it.
3 Recommend ways in which the cash deficit could be financed assuming similar trading activity in future years.
4 How could the firm's cash position be improved without resorting to additional finance?

Management of cash

Financial resources should be properly controlled and deployed in ways that maximise the benefit from their utilisation.

Fixed assets

The overriding principle is to retain flexibility to react to unforeseen eventualities. To minimise the risk of tying up funds in resources that may be little used, assets could be rented or hired on a short-term basis. If some assets are to be hired and some to be purchased, risk is reduced and flexibility maintained if business funds are tied up in general-purpose assets rather than specialist assets.

Stocks

Stocks should be minimised within the context of operational needs. Stock-out situations can be ruinously expensive if they affect the ability to satisfy customer needs. The business should aim for high stock turnover with systematic ordering in line with economic batch quantities. This requires good knowledge of supplier and factory lead times, cost structures and accurate forecasting of future requirements. Purchasing parameters for stock should be reviewed with forecast changes in sales.

Debtors (amounts owed by customers)

Debtors should be minimised and tight control maintained of credit allowed to customers. Potential customers should be evaluated for their credit-worthiness before being allowed a credit account. Once a supply has been made the business should invoice its customers promptly and chase hard those customers who persistently extend the credit period afforded them. Methods for ensuring early receipt of cash include the offering of cash discounts, say 2 per cent for payment within 30 days, and the factoring of debts. Although low debt is an ideal attainment, over-strident methods and the early use of legal action can threaten the working relationship between customer and supplier. However, customers who do not pay are worse than no customers at all. A firm but considered approach is best, perhaps involving sales personnel in the credit negotiations before relationships become strained.

Creditors (amounts owed to suppliers)

It is better to have cash in the business's bank account than in that of suppliers, so a relatively high level of creditors is seen as good financial management. It is important to consider industry norms for credit and not to strain the trading relationship between the business and its suppliers. Pushing credit periods to the limit can result in disruptions to supplies and the failure to negotiate best prices.

Cash budgeting

The overriding principle is be conservative and recognise bad news earlier rather than later. Banks and other financial backers are more sympathetic towards businesses that can warn of impending cash problems than those that seem to enter a crisis unprepared.

Sources of finance

Businesses generally use a number of sources of finance, including:

- individuals – founders, employees, venture capitalists, etc.
- organisations that specialise in venture capital for businesses
- banks and other financial institutions
- suppliers
- government
- profits retained in the business.

Investors do not, even within a particular category, make investments with the same expectations. The type of investment they make reflects their interests and priorities. We now examine the different forms that finance for business can take and how they can be used to meet the specific needs of the business.

Owner's capital

The business owners are the ultimate risk-takers, as they provide the business with capital and only expect a return if the business proves profitable. Providers of owners' capital benefit most when the firm is successful, but stand to lose the most if it fails. The form these funds take depends on the legal form of the business.

Unincorporated businesses

This type of business comprises individuals acting as sole traders and groups of individuals who set up in partnership. The business is simple to set up but is not recognised in law as being separate from its owners. The assets and liabilities of the business belong directly to the owner or partners. It means, therefore, that when a partner leaves or joins the business, the inconvenient situation arises of one partnership ceasing and another commencing. In addition, the owners may be forced to transfer more of their personal wealth into the firm if the business cannot generate enough funds to pay its debts. The advantage of a partnership is the opportunity to raise funds from a number of individuals, but there are problems of raising funds outside the working partners. Other investors cannot easily take their funds out of the business because their part of the partnership is not tradable.

Incorporated businesses

Unlike sole traders and partnerships, companies are legal identities quite separate from that of their owners. This enables easier exit for investors who only wish to tie up their money for a finite period of time, as the company's ability to trade is unaffected by changes in its ownership. The capital contributed by the owners of the business is divided into **shares**. Hence an owner is called a **shareholder**.

Shareholders enjoy limited liability as the maximum amount they can lose in the business venture is the amount they paid for the shares they hold. Shareholders receive benefits from profits earned in the form of cash dividends and an increase in the value of their shares.

The distinction between a **private limited company (ltd)** and a **public limited company (plc)** is that the plc can offer its shares to the general public, whereas the methods for issuing shares in a private company are restricted. Plcs that have obtained a listing on the stock exchange gain a number of advantages, including:

- easier access to funds
- enhanced reputation of the company
- more satisfactorily operated employee share schemes, where shares are marketable and an up-to-date price is available to monitor capital gains
- easier buying and selling of shares which increases their value.

Disadvantages of a listing on the stock exchange include more onerous reporting requirements and a greater risk of the founders losing control to corporate predators. Requirements for a stock exchange listing include a minimum £1 million market valuation, and at least 25 per cent of the shares have to be held by the general public.

Types of shares
Shares can be issued with different rights to dividend and capital repayment. The types of shares issued and the rules governing them are decided by the company founders, but typically they fall into two main categories:

1 **Ordinary share capital.** An ordinary shareholder is a part owner of the business and shares in the profits of the business after all other investors have been paid their dues. The shareholder is able to vote at general meetings of the company, including the appointment of the board of directors. Ordinary share capital is often called 'equity capital'.
   a *Cost.* Like other forms of finance, there is a cost associated with the use of shareholders' funds and, as the directors are responsible to the shareholders, they should recognise that to use shareolders' funds implies an opportunity cost, i.e. the return the shareholders could earn on alternative investments. So management should not invest in a new project unless the increased profits are at least what the

shareholders could earn on the money if they invested it in securities of similar risk. For a plc, significant costs are also incurred in the issue of shares – up to 10 per cent of the sum raised. Returns to the shareholder come in two forms: the receipt of cash dividends and the appreciation in value of the shares as the business grows.
   b *Limit.* The maximum amount of funds that can be raised by the issue of shares is only limited by the availability of willing investors. However, the main consideration from the existing shareholder's point of view is that their ownership will be diluted if more shares are issued.

2 **Preference share capital.** Preference shareholders are entitled to receive a dividend out of profits even when there may be insufficient profits to pay ordinary shareholders. However, they have few voting rights and hence less influence on company policy. Methods of issue are the same as for ordinary shares.
   a *Cost.* Usually a fixed rate of return, e.g. 8 per cent £1 preference shares would entitle the holder to 8p per year for each share held. Additionally, there are significant issue costs for a plc.
   b *Limit.* It is not in the interest of preference shareholders or ordinary shareholders for too many preference shares to be issued. There are usually less preference shares than ordinary shares and some companies have none at all.

Methods of issuing shares for a plc
- **Issue by prospectus** invites offers from the general public in the form of a newspaper advertisement giving information about the company and its future prospects.
- **Offers for sale.** The company sells all of the shares to an issuing house, which then publishes a prospectus as above. The success of the issue is more certain by this method, but the issuing house takes a profit.
- **Placing.** Blocks of shares are sold to private investors, pension funds, unit trusts, investment trusts and others via a financial intermediary, such as a stockbroker or issuing house.
- A **rights issue** gives existing shareholders the right to buy new shares in the company in proportion to their existing holding, usually at a favourable price.

The private limited company is unable to issue shares to the general public, so it relies on placings and rights issues.

The share capital of a business is classified into:

- **authorised share capital**, i.e. the maximum number of shares the directors can issue according to the memorandum of association. It can only be increased by the existing shareholders, who may do so as the company expands.

- **issued share capital**, i.e. the number and nominal value of the shares actually issued.

Long-term loans

For unincorporated businesses the opportunity to arrange long-term loans is often limited to the individuals who are actively participating in the business and their families. For a company, long-term loans are usually in the form of **debentures**. Debentures are bonds made under the company's common seal. The debenture document confirms that the holder has made a long-term loan to the company, and hence it has the advantage of being a tradable security that can be bought and sold like shares. Debentures can either be redeemable or irredeemable. The company has to purchase back redeemable debentures on a fixed date, whereas it has no obligation to do so for irredeemable debentures. It is possible for debentures to be 'secured' on the assets of the business. This entitles the debenture-holder to take possession and sell the assets if interest payments or repayment of capital are not made on the agreed dates. If the company is listed on a stock exchange, the debentures can be traded there in a similar fashion to shares.

- **Source** – financial institutions such as pension funds, investment trusts and 3i PLC; as well as individual investors who require a fixed return.
- **Cost** – the debenture carries a fixed rate of interest that must be paid irrespective of the level of profits having been earned.
- **Limit** – neither debenture-holders nor shareholders will favour a very high proportion of business funds being raised by fixed-return capital, because of the volatile effect it may have on profits (see **Gearing** on page 155).

Banks and other financial institutions

Bank loans

Bank loans are taken out for a fixed period, repayment either being in instalments or in full at the end of the term. Banks generally provide funds on a short- to medium-term basis, with relatively few loans over more than ten years' duration.

- **Source** – main clearing banks and merchant banks.
- **Cost** – in addition to interest charges levied at so many percentage points over base rate (LIBOR), e.g. 3 per cent over base, there may be arrangement fees and a security fee (if the loan is secured on personal or business assets).
- **Limit** – banks are unlikely to lend more than the

owners are putting into the business. In particular, the banks need to be convinced of the owner's commitment to the enterprise before they will pledge their own funds.

Bank overdraft

The overdraft is repayable on demand, but has the advantage of greater flexibility as interest is only charged on the balance outstanding.

- **Cost** – the same as for bank loans with the possibility of a periodic renewal fee.
- **Limit** – same as bank loans.

Hire purchase

Hire purchase (HP) allows the business to use an asset without having to find the money immediately. A finance house buys the asset from the supplier and retains ownership of it during the period of the hire-purchase agreement. The business pays a deposit and then further payments to the finance house as stipulated in the agreement. At the end of the HP agreement, ownership of the asset is passed to the business.

- **Source** – finance houses that are often subsidiaries of the clearing banks and equipment suppliers, e.g. Lombard Tricity Finance, RoyScot Trust and Ford Motor Credit Co.
- **Cost** – the payments made by the business under the HP agreement are in excess of the cash price of the asset. The difference is the finance charge required by the finance house.
- **Limit** – the finance house will want to be sure the company's profits will be well in excess of the planned repayments, and that it has a good payment record on existing HP agreements and other debt arrangements.

Leasing

Leasing an asset provides similar benefits to hire purchase, in that a leasing agreement with a finance house (**lessor**) allows the business (**lessee**) to use an asset without having to buy it outright. The real distinction between the two forms of finance is that leasing does not confer an automatic right to eventual ownership of the asset. It is a very popular form of finance for company vehicles, office equipment and factory machinery. There are two types of lease:

1 An **operating lease** is like a rent agreement and is for a period that is shorter than the asset's economic life. For example, two-year agreements for motor cars are fairly typical. The finance house realises a return on the arrangement by charging the business more than the

anticipated reduction in the asset's value during the agreement.

2 A **finance lease** tends to run for longer periods than operating leases. The agreement will run for most of the asset's economic life and so the lessor requires payments under the agreement to be in excess of the cash price of the asset. Because the asset has relatively little value at the end of the lease term, the agreement often allows the lessee to continue leasing on a pepper-corn (minimal) rent or to purchase the asset for a nominal sum.

The different nature of the types of lease is reflected in other terms to the agreements. Under an operating lease, the finance house is concerned that the asset retains a high resale value, so to ensure maintenance is carried out, this cost is often borne by the lessor (although this will, of course, have been considered when setting the lease terms). Under a finance lease, the risk of ownership is largely transferred to the lessee, who usually has to maintain the asset.

- **Source** – finance houses, e.g. Lombard North Central and Anglo Leasing.
- **Cost** – total payments are in excess of the cash price of the asset for a finance lease, and for an operating lease are in excess of the fall in value of the asset.
- **Limit** – similar considerations as HP.

Factoring

Factors provide finance against a business's trade debtors in two main ways:

1 **Invoice factoring** involves the factor undertaking to collect amounts due from the business's debtors and advancing immediately up to 80 per cent of the value of the invoices outstanding. This enables the business to receive quick payment on debts that might otherwise take 30 to 90 days to collect. The other advantage is that the task of debt collection is passed to the factor. As the monies are received from the debtors, the factor pays the business the balance of the debts transferred less their charges. Many factors also provide cover for bad debts under 'non-recourse' agreements.

2 **Invoice discounting** also allows an advance of cash against trade debtors, but responsibility for debt collection remains with the business. The debtors are requested to pay the factor for amounts due and so, as with invoice factoring, the customers do know their debt has been passed to a factor. Another form of this type of financing is called **confidential invoice discounting**. This allows debtors to continue paying their debts to the business, but turnover must be at least £1 million per annum.

Factoring may be particularly appropriate for fast-growing businesses. The amount of finance provided grows automatically in line with the growth in debtors and so satisfies the need for working capital to finance higher sales.

- **Source** – finance houses, e.g. Alex Lawrie Factors, RoyScot Factors, and Lombard NatWest Commercial Services.
- **Cost** – factors will charge interest at typically 1–3 per cent in excess of bank lending rates on amounts advanced, which is similar in cost to bank overdrafts. For invoice factoring, a further fee of up to 3 per cent of the value of debts is charged for sales ledger administration.
- **Limit** – minimum annual turnover of £100 000 is required for factoring and around £1 million for discounting arrangements. Otherwise, this form of finance is only limited by the balance of acceptable debtor balances. Finance houses will not wish to purchase debts that are likely to include substantial bad debts.

Commercial mortgages

A **mortgage** is a loan secured on land and buildings and can either be used to finance the purchase of the property, or to provide security for a loan applied to some other purpose. It is a long-term financing arrangement of typically 10 to 30 years.

- **Source** – financial institutions, such as insurance companies and pension funds, in addition to the banks.
- **Cost** – interest on amount outstanding.
- **Limit** – the value of the property is the basis for determining the maximum mortgage permissible.

Sale and lease-back

The firm sells its freehold property to an investment company and then leases it back over a long period of time. This releases funds for other purposes in the business without incurring further debt. A major disadvantage is the loss of capital appreciation in times of rising property prices.

- **Source** – the same as for commercial mortgages.
- **Cost** – lease payments and potential loss of property appreciation.
- **Limit** – the value of marketable freehold property.

Government

The Department of Employment Loan Guarantee Scheme

The government guarantees the repayment of 70–85 per cent of a medium-term bank loan (2–7 years) in return for a 2.5 per cent per annum premium. The scheme enables banks to lend money to businesses of less than 200 employees for projects that would otherwise be thought too risky.

The European Union

There are a number of institutions of the European Union that can provide finance for business. The European Investment Bank provides loans or loan guarantees for investment projects in industry to improve an area's infrastructure. The European Social Fund can finance schemes that improve employment opportunities such as training. The European Regional Development Fund makes grants for one-off development projects as opposed to on-going subsidies to help redress regional economic imbalance. Grants are available for up to 50 per cent of a project subject to a maximum of 15 million ECUs.

Suppliers

Suppliers are a valuable source of finance for many businesses. Just as the business may give credit to its own customers, the firm may be able to negotiate credit terms with its suppliers. Credit terms are typically 30 days from date of supply or the end of the month following the month of delivery, i.e. 30 to 60 days.

- **Cost** – normally, there is no cost attached to trade credit. However, where the business overextends the agreed credit period, the trading relationship may become strained and so affect the level of service and goodwill between supplier and customer. In addition, where 'prompt payment' discounts are offered, failure to take them usually proves expensive in annual terms.

Retained earnings

A major source of finance for many firms is the retention of profits in the business. Instead of distributing profits to owners, some of the wealth created each year is invested in further assets to increase earnings potential for the future.

- **Source** – from business activity.
- **Cost** – opportunity cost suffered by the owners in having to forgo returns on alternative investment or the chance to consume the profits earned.

Financial planning

Often the financing decision is constrained as circumstances may preclude some options and obviously the interests of some investors are not always the same as those of the business. Financing strategy should consider:

- the duration for which finance is required
- cost of alternative sources of finance
- gearing – the proportion of fixed-return finance to equity capital.

Other considerations include:

- security – assets demanded by the investor in case of problems with failure to meet repayment and finance charge obligations
- government intervention – incentives from government agencies such as grants and loan-guarantee schemes.

It is usual for businesses to utilise a number of sources of finance to ensure finance is appropriate to specific needs.

Duration

As individuals we would not purchase a house on a bank overdraft, nor would we finance a personal CD player with a 25-year mortgage. In business we apply the same principles of matching the purpose of finance with the source of finance (see Figure 8.9). This makes sense:

- for the business, as it ensures finance is guaranteed for as long as the need exists
- for the investor, where necessary it ensures adequate security can be obtained for the duration of the loan, e.g. a 20-year loan is secured against property that will continue to have value in 20 years' time.

We can see from Figure 8.10 that there appears to be a shortage of sources for medium-term finance. This situation is not new, having been identified in the 1960s,

Figure 8.9 Finance duration for different types of expenditure

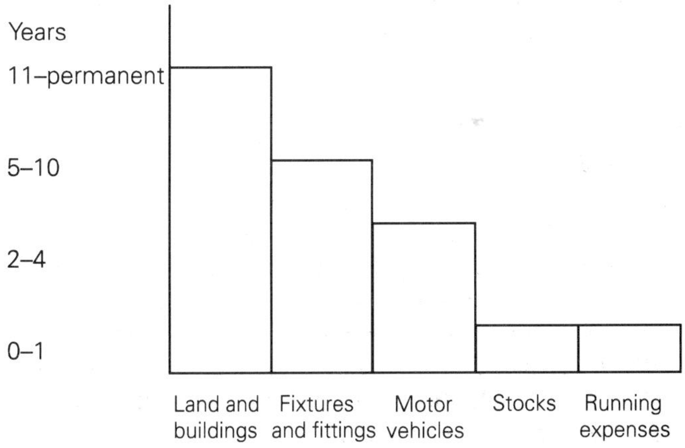

Figure 8.10 Main sources of finance according to duration

Source of finance	Duration
Ordinary share capital	Long term: indefinite
Preference share capital	Long term: specified date of redemption to indefinite
Retained earnings	Long term: indefinite
Debentures	Long term: specified date of redemption to indefinite
Commercial mortgage	Long term: typically 10–30 years
Bank finance – lease, HP and loan	Medium term: typically 1–7 years
Bank overdraft	Short term: repayable on demand
Debt factor	Short term: depending on credit periods
Trade credit	Short term: typically 7–60 days

and is a major issue which successive governments have sought to rectify. The problem is seen as being particularly acute for small private businesses with restricted access to the financial markets, where the issue of medium-term debentures would be possible.

The financing of a business is not a precise science where finance and expenditure can be matched exactly. Generally, the cash flows of a typical business are quite complex and financing requirements can change on a daily basis. It is more important that the general structure of a firm's capital is appropriate to the makeup of its assets.

Some items of expenditure seem quite short term, but it should be remembered that business is a continuous process of similar short-term transactions. There is usually a job to start on just as another is being finished. Hence working capital, for such things as materials, wages and overheads, will continue to be a long-term requirement. We have to identify what minimum level of permanent finance is required and ensure this is properly funded. Short-term fluctuations should then be accommodated as they arise with appropriate sources of short-term finance. Finance has a cost, so it is essential not to pay unnecessarily for more finance than is needed. Taking out a loan that results in a healthy bank balance is not good financial management.

In Figure 8.11 the dotted line MM indicates the forecast minimum level of finance required. It would seem appropriate, therefore, for at least some of the current assets to be financed by long-term finance to ensure continuity of business even when credit facilities become difficult to obtain, say line LL. The difference between the total finance required and MM should, if possible, be financed by a flexible source where finance charges are only incurred when it is required, e.g. a bank overdraft or factoring.

Figure 8.11 Amount of finance required

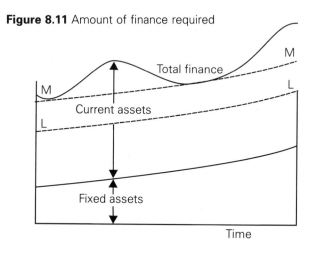

Bank loan versus bank overdraft

Using the logic developed above, we can examine the relative merits of bank loans and bank overdrafts. Even if the bank loan carried the lowest interest rate, would it really be the cheapest option?

We have to consider the particular situation the business is in. If there is a constant requirement with little fluctuation in cash being tied up, then if a lower interest rate applies the loan will be the best alternative. However, if there are significant fluctuations, then we may wonder why we have a loan when the same bank is holding our money in a current account at times when demand for cash is low (see Figure 8.12). A bank overdraft may be cheaper after all.

Of course, before a final decision can be made full consideration should be given to other factors. A loan has a fixed term and hence is less exposed to the vagaries of the bank manager. In addition, bank overdrafts are often subject to other charges including a periodic arrangement fee. If a choice arises, it pays to consider carefully.

Figure 8.12 Fluctuations in finance required compared to value of loan

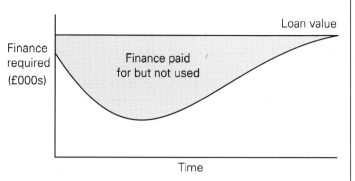

Cost of finance

Raising finance invariably results in a cost and so the financial benefits arising from a particular project should outweigh the cost incurred of using the funds. Unfortunately, it is not always possible to identify specific sources with specific needs and, therefore, it becomes necessary to calculate the average cost of capital for the business as a whole. For example, a company has shareholder funds of £200 000, debentures of £50 000 at 10 per cent and trade credit of £30 000. If the shareholders require a return of 15 per cent, what is the required return from the average business activity?

Weighted average cost of capital =

$$= \frac{\text{Total finance returns}}{\text{Total finance employed}} \times 100\%$$

$$= \frac{(£200\,000 \times 15\%) + (£50\,000 \times 10\%)}{£280\,000} \times 100\%$$

$$= 12.5\%$$

It may be that a number of projects would provide a return in excess of the cost of the funds required to finance them. If funds are limited, the true cost to the business of using finance on a project is the opportunity cost of not being able to fulfil the highest rated alternative.

Gearing

Gearing is the term used to describe the relationship of fixed-return finance to equity (capital that enjoys profit-related returns). Fixed-return finance includes preference shares, debentures and other loans. Equity capital in a company includes ordinary share capital, retained earnings and other reserves.

$$\text{Gearing ratio} = \frac{\text{Fixed-return capital}}{\text{Equity capital}}$$

Ratios in excess of 1 indicate highly geared companies.

Case Study
The effects of gearing

Denton & Co. Ltd employs £100 000 of capital and generates profits in the range £5000 to £20 000 before interest per annum. The composition of the capital structure greatly affects the return that ordinary shareholders receive.

			£
Gearing	**High**	**Medium**	**Low**
Capital structure			
Ordinary shares	10 000	50 000	90 000
Debentures at 10% p.a.	90 000	50 000	10 000
	100 000	100 000	100 000
Returns on profits of £5000			
Shares	–4 000	0	4 000
Debentures 10%	9 000	5 000	1 000
	5 000	5 000	5 000
Returns on profits of £10 000			
Shares	1 000	5 000	9 000
Debentures 10%	9 000	5 000	1 000
	10 000	10 000	10 000
Returns on profits of £20 000			
Shares	11 000	15 000	19 000
Debentures 10%	9 000	5 000	1 000
	20 000	20 000	20 000

Whatever the level of profits, debenture holders will always receive 10 per cent of the value of debentures. However, the percentage return enjoyed by ordinary shareholders varies widely, depending on the level of profits and capital gearing.

From this analysis we can summarise ordinary shareholder returns on their investment:

Gearing	**High**	**Medium**	**Low**
On profits of:			
£5000	–40%	0%	4.4%
£10 000	10%	10%	10.0%
£20 000	110%	30%	21.1%
Range of returns	150%	30%	16.7%

The range of percentage returns to ordinary shareholders increases as gearing increases. We can, therefore, say that as gearing increases, there is a greater risk of not attaining a particular return for ordinary shareholders. In addition, as can be seen from the case study, there is a risk that interest paid on fixed-rate capital may result in losses for ordinary shareholders. Business losses are eventually bad news for everybody, so the level of gearing is of interest to the providers of all types of finance.

It is difficult to generalise about preferred levels of gearing. The main issue is the extent to which financial risk is affected by gearing. The more volatile the level of business profits, the more marked will be the effects of gearing. In the case of Denton & Co. Ltd, which does experience volatile profits, low gearing would appear to be more appropriate. However, if the business could expect a narrower range of profits it could possibly be more highly geared.

Task

Recalculate, for each level of gearing, the returns to the shareholders of Denton & Co. Ltd for profits of £8 000 and £12 000. Evaluate the results.

Businesses that are heavily influenced by economic cycles, such as capital goods suppliers, would not normally wish to be highly geared. On the other hand, stable industries, such as food producers may be able to provide adequate interest cover at all stages of economic cycles (see Figure 8.13 below). They are unlikely to make losses for ordinary shareholders even if highly geared.

Task

Christine Massey is an investment analyst in the Small Business Division of a London merchant bank. She is currently considering an investment proposal for a startup venture in the advertising industry.

Two gifted advertising people, Pete and Fiona, from a well-known agency, have decided to go on their own. They have set up a limited company called Saturn Advertising. Long-term finance of £1 000 000 is required. Towards that total they have £250 000 to put into the business.

Christine has examined their profit forecasts and has confirmed that average annual profits of £120 000 look reasonable. However, she does have some concerns. Although quite a number of potential clients have promised

to give them advertising work, the exact number is not certain. Christine believes profits could range from £80 000 to £140 000, and so she must bear this in mind.

Christine's bank looks for a minimum return of 10 per cent when investing in company debentures. The bank will also invest in ordinary shares if the potential returns are attractive and not too risky. She has prepared three financial structures for evaluation:

	£ Gearing		
	Very High	**High**	**Medium**
Ordinary shares:			
Pete and Fiona	250 000	250 000	250 000
Bank	0	250 000	500 000
Total share capital	250 000	500 000	750 000
Debentures at 10% interest	750 000	500 000	250 000
Total finance	1 000 000	1 000 000	1 000 000

1 Calculate how estimated profits of £80 000, £120 000 and £140 000 would be split between share capital and debentures for each of the three financial structures being considered.
2 From **1** calculate the percentage return on money invested in shares.
3 Write a brief report from Christine to the bank's investments manager evaluating the figures calculated and making a recommendation.

Interest cover

Another valuable measure of financial risk is the relationship of interest payments to the profits generated by the business.

$$\text{Interest cover} = \frac{\text{Profit before interest}}{\text{Interest payments}}$$

A low interest-cover ratio indicates that interest payments are a burden. The larger the profits earned in relation to interest commitments, the less risk there is of interest payments pushing the business into a loss-making situation.

Figure 8.13 Gearing and the level of financial risk

High gearing	Medium financial risk	High financial risk
Low gearing	Low financial risk	Medium financial risk
	Stable operating profits	**Volatile operating profits**

Case Study
Southland Merchant Bank

The following companies from the same industry wish to issue £100 000 of debentures to replace existing debentures that have to be repaid next year. They have approached your bank for the money.

	Prima	Middling	Shaky
Profits before interest	£100 000	£100 000	£100 000
Capital structure:			
Ordinary share capital	£600 000	£400 000	£200 000
Debentures at 10%	£200 000	£400 000	£600 000

Forecasts indicate profits may fall by 20 per cent during the next year.

1 Calculate the current year gearing ratio for each company.
2 Calculate the current year interest cover for each company.
3 Repeat the interest-cover calculations for the forthcoming year, assuming the bank did provide finance.
4 Which proposal would you recommend investing in?

The investor's perspective

Individuals and organisations other than the business founders may be willing to invest in a business opportunity. They include insurance companies, pension funds and others looking for opportunities to invest funds for periods from months to many years. Their willingness to do so will depend on the likely risk and financial return for their investment. In addition, they will be interested in how easy it is to sell when they want to. Some investors may wish to participate in the profits of the business and so join the business founders as partners or shareholders. The ability to buy and sell shares more freely in a company is likely to mean that companies will prove more attractive to investors than sole traders and partnerships.

Return on investment

Other things being equal, investors are looking for the highest returns possible on their investment and will compare the returns of various investment opportunities. It is a measure of how profitable the investment is, just as interest rates at a building society are a guide for many individuals.

Return on investment in shares

$$= \frac{\text{Dividend per share} + \text{Share price movement}}{\text{Market price of share}}$$

Risk

It is not possible to consider the rate of return without considering the risk attached to it. Risk can take two forms:

- the underlying risk of the business operation, i.e. whether it is a commercially viable proposition
- the financial risk, depending on the conditions of the particular security (share or debenture) and the gearing of the company.

There is often a trade-off from the investor's point of view between rate of return and risk. Treasury bills attract a modest rate of return, but are considered risk free. Shares in a new business may promise high returns, but are accompanied by anything up to a 50 per cent chance of failure, when the capital invested may also be lost.

Security

With a risk that the business venture may not be successful, providers of funds will be interested in what assets can be pledged to ensure they can protect their money in the event of business failure. For entrepreneurs that are required to pledge their family homes, this often negates the value of a company's limited liability.

Case Study
Macstablishment

'Why does Scotland have so few entrepreneurs? . . . The biggest problem is their access to finance. Throughout Britain small firms complain that banks neglect their need for long-term credit, leaving them dependent on short-term overdrafts. Many banks require loans secured against assets such as houses. Banks in Germany and France, by contrast, often lend on the strength of prospective cash flow. Reliance on overdrafts is a particularly acute problem in Scotland, where only 53 per cent of householders own their own homes, compared with 69 per cent in England.'

(Source *The Economist*, 3 September 1994)

Questions for discussion

1 Describe the advantages and problems of a financing system based upon 'prospective cash flow'.
2 As entrepreneurs profit from business success, what arguments can be provided for and against protecting them from total loss in the case of failure?

Duration

Different investors have different expectations from their investment. Many business founders have no desire to leave the business they have set up. Other investors, including some founders, will want to leave the business after it has proved successful and take their profits. For many of the larger startups, including management buyouts, the initial backers may want assurances that the company will go public after, say, five years. With a planned exit date, investment fund managers can ensure sufficient liquidity in their investment portfolios to repay obligations and to invest in new opportunities.

Venture capital

Capital provided for new or expanding commercial ventures where the sources participate in the risks and rewards of success is called **venture capital**. It may take the form of both share capital and loan stock in the company.

Case Study
Tech-Board

'Malcolm Graham's search for £40 million to fund a state-of-the-art hard-board mill in Wales demonstrates the difficulty in raising money for a business startup. Tech-Board is rated Britain's biggest-ever industrial startup and is to start operation in 1996 creating 200 new jobs. Graham insisted on thinking big and using his knowledge of the hard-board market is aiming to capture 40 per cent of the home market. Aiming for large market share and utilising the latest technology, he believes he can replace plastics and other materials used in a whole range of products from shoes to cars. The market shows good prospects for growth but obtaining finance took over five years of hard work. Venture capitalists proved reluctant to invest in such a large startup. They prefer management buyouts of firms with a history of trading results. Assistance came from 3i and Peter Learmond, a veteran industrialist who had experienced similar financing difficulties 20 years ago when he required £10 million for a steel mill. In the end a total of 14 separate groups of backers were assembled including suppliers and the management team. Learmond's 'old-boy' network broke the log-jam. Personal contacts who had confidence in Learmond and were impressed by Graham provided the commitment and equity capital to entice other investors on board. This hard core of investors provided £2 million of equity and £13.5

million of subordinated loans. The Welsh Office gave a grant of £3.4 million.'

(Source *Management Today*, November 1994)

Questions for discussion

Malcolm Graham's hard work and perseverance have eventually allowed him to pursue his business ideas. His experience illustrates a possible competitive disadvantage for the UK as it fails to encourage new job-creating businesses. Things might have been different for an entrepreneur with Graham's ideas setting up in Germany. Research the financial markets of Germany and suggest practices that might usefully be used in the UK. What is needed to bring them about?

Financing plan

The capital structure of the business has to be designed to accommodate a range of investors' expectations, perhaps offering debenture-holders fixed redemption dates or the option to convert loans into shares once the business has proved successful. For shareholders, preference shares can provide greater security, but the option to convert into ordinary shares or for redemption at a fixed date will add to the attractiveness of the investment opportunity. Of course, the offer of reassurances and options that reduce the risk for one group of investors correspondingly increase the risk and reduces the potential returns for other groups.

Financing exercises

Task

For each of the following identify the most relevant sources of finance as requested. Where you recommend the issue of share capital, also state the method of issue.

a Roger Inman needs a new computer system costing £5000 for his business. Identify three ways of financing the purchase, and state when each would be most appropriate.

b Harwood & Sons Ltd wants to expand its factory building. The cost will be £500 000. State three ways of financing the expansion, and say when each would be most appropriate.

c Sinclair and Symons Ltd is having temporary problems with its cash flow. Identify two ways of financing the company's working capital shortfall, and state when each would be most appropriate.

d Pantheon International PLC needs to raise £5 million for a new office complex. It currently has a gearing ratio of 2. Identify two ways of raising the finance, and state when each would be most appropriate.

e IBM, the computer industry giant, has recently suffered massive losses. If the company wanted to maintain its gearing ratio at the same level as previous years, what type of finance would it have to raise?

f Carlton Holdings PLC has a long-term strategy to increase the number of companies it owns. Identify three ways of financing this growth and state when each would be most appropriate.

g Connors and Moore Ltd has experienced poor sales in the last few years and this has resulted in substantial losses. The business needs to develop and launch a new product if it is to be saved. It could take up to four years for the new product to add substantially to company profits. The company's gearing ratio is currently just under 1. Identify two ways of financing this project, and state when each would be most appropriate.

Case Study
Lesray Computers Ltd

Lesray Computers Ltd has experienced fast growth since the company was set up three years ago by two ex-IBM engineers, Lesley and Raymond. The firm now needs to move to larger premises if it is to exploit its product's market potential.

The company's financial position is as follows:

Ordinary share capital	£200 000
Debentures	£200 000
Bank loan (repayable in two years' time)	£100 000
Trade creditors	£50 000
Bank overdraft	£50 000
	£600 000

Represented by:

Land and buildings	£150 000
Plant and machinery	£200 000
Stocks	£50 000
Debtors	£200 000
	£600 000

The cost of expansion is estimated to be as follows:

New land and buildings	£500 000
Additional plant and machinery	£300 000

In addition, working capital is likely to increase substantially as a result of a forecast 100 per cent increase in sales over the next year.

Further stocks	£50 000
Increase in debtors	£200 000

Retained profits are unlikely to increase over the coming year because of heavy expenditure on development and marketing. Lesley and Ray have therefore asked you, as the company finance director, to investigate external sources of finance.

Questions for discussion

In a report:

a *recommend the types, amounts and sources of finance you think most appropriate*

b *give reasons for your proposal, including any difficulties you foresee.*

Task

A large UK engineering group is planning to close down a car components factory in the face of fierce Japanese competition and you are a member of its management team.

The factory's senior management is convinced that the parent company is being too hasty. It has often been short-sighted in the past. They have undermined the efforts of both management and work force by not providing the necessary finance to re-equip the factory with state-of-the-art machinery. This is partly as a result of the parent company never fully appreciating the work force's positive attitude towards changes in work practices. The days of union militancy are over. The main shop-floor union has been a driving force in improving workers' training and enhancing job interest through flexible working practices.

You have been asked by your management colleagues to look at ways in which the management team could buy the business. You have ascertained from the parent company that it would be willing to sell the factory building and plant for £4 000 000. (The market value of the buildings alone is thought to be around this figure, but the parent company spots an opportunity to save on redundancy payments.) However, further finance will be required for new plant – £1 000 000 – and also for working capital – £750 000.

As a management team of 30 people you can raise £500 000 from savings and personal loans taken out on the security of your houses. Not much, it seems, towards the £5 750 000 you need.

Write a report to your colleagues stating:

a the types, amounts and sources of finance you think most appropriate to this situation

b reasons for your proposal, including any difficulties you foresee.

Financial performance

Various measures are used to evaluate financial performance, and three main financial statements have been developed to provide this information:

- profit and loss account
- balance sheet
- cash flow statement.

Profit and loss account

The profit and loss account values in money terms the transactions of a business over a specified time period of normally one year. It reports on the sales made to customers and the costs incurred in making those supplies. Hence its basic format is the value of goods or services provided less the costs of resources consumed.

The format of the profit and loss account is similar, although not identical, for a wide range of business organisations (see Figure 8.14).

The precise layout and item descriptions depend on the nature of the business. It is important to grasp that values in the trading and profit and loss account do not just represent cash received and paid out in the period. Preparers of business accounts use accounting conventions that measure the value of goods or services actually provided to customers, together with related cost of resources actually consumed. These are the main issues that the preparer of accounts has to address:

- Customers may not have paid for goods or services provided. The profit and loss account is prepared with a sales figure including the amounts still receivable from customers on credit.
- Similarly, the company may have used resources, such as purchases of stock or consumption of electricity, that it has not yet paid for. These too are recognised and included in the profit and loss cost figures.
- Certain items may be purchased but not consumed at the date the accounts are prepared. In particular, stock held at the period end will be used on sales in a future period. In this case, period-end stock balance should be deducted from the purchases of the current period.
- Fixed assets are purchased for use over a number of years. If the consumption of the business's resources is to be properly reflected, then the cost of these items should be spread over the years in which they will be used. The cost allocated to a particular accounting period is called **depreciation**.

Figure 8.15 explains the terms used in a profit and loss account.

Figure 8.14 Example of a profit and loss account

Pina Mistry – sole trader
Trading and profit and loss account
for the year ended 31 December 199–

	£	£
Sales		25 000
Less cost of sales		
Opening stock	3 000	
Purchases	15 000	
	18 000	
Closing stock	6 000	
		12 000
Gross profit		13 000
Less expenses		
Wages	2 000	
Depreciation of fixed assets	1 500	
Power	1 000	
Motor vehicle expenses	1 500	
Wages		6 000
Net profit		7 000

Figure 8.15 Trading and profit and loss account terminology

Term	Description
Trading account	The top section of the financial statement starting with sales less cost of sales and resulting in gross profit
Profit and loss account	The lower section of the financial statement adds other income and deducts expenses from gross profit to arrive at net profit
Sales	Total amount receivable from customers for goods or services provided during the accounting period. Sales includes sales of goods, provision of services, renting of facilities, commissions, etc.
Purchases	The value of stock purchased for resale (excluding items purchased for consumption by the business)
Cost of sales	Purchases are adjusted by opening stock and closing stock to arrive at the cost of goods actually sold
Gross profit	Sales less cost of sales
Net profit	Gross profit plus other income less expenses

Case Study
A trading account

During September Roger Pinter purchased 100 table lamps for £5 each. He sells 40 of them for £8 each. Calculate his gross profit for the month of September.

Remember the importance of matching costs with revenues. At the end of the sale he will still have 60 table lamps in stock. His profit is calculated by taking the cost of 40 lamps from the revenue of 40 lamps.

	£	£
Sales		320
Purchases	500	
Less closing stock (60 × 5)	300	
Cost of sales		200
Gross profit		120

Task

1 Geraldine Moore had 20 caravans in stock which cost her £5000 each. She sells four at £7000 each and buys three more for a total of £15 000. Calculate her gross profit.
2 Prepare a trading and profit and loss account for Ladds & Simmons for the year ended 31 December 199–. During the year the business achieved sales of £69 000 and incurred the following expenses: rent and rates £5000; wages £19 000; advertising £1500; stationery £2000; and lighting and heating £2000. Purchases of £25 000 were added to an opening stock of £3500. On 31 December 199– stock was valued at £4500.

Earlier in the chapter when considering overtrading (page 145), we identified that a profitable business was not one that necessarily generated a positive inflow of cash. It is important to appreciate the difference between cash flow and profit. It is a mistake to believe that if the bank balance moves up or down that this necessarily indicates the business performance is good or bad.

Case Study
Cash flow and profit compared

Two firms in the same industry have different cash flows, but the better cash position of Lennon & Co. does not necessarily mean the business has made more profit.

Cash flow statement for the month of September 199–	Lennon & Co. £	Kettering Engineering Ltd £
Receipts:		
Cash sales – units at £200 each	10 000	12 000
Payments:		
Stock purchases – units at £100 each	5 000	10 000
Receipts minus payments	5 000	2 000
Balance b/f	5 000	5 000
Balance c/f	10 000	7 000

Calculate gross profit for both companies for September.

Trading accounts for the month of September 199–	Lennon & Co. £	Kettering Engineering Ltd £
Sales:	10 000	12 000
Purchases	5 000	10 000
Less closing stock	0	4 000
Cost of sales	5 000	6 000
Gross profit	5 000	6 000

After matching costs with the revenues earned, the relative trading performance of the two firms is more evident. Despite greater expenditure during the month, Kettering Engineering Ltd actually made a greater profit.

Tasks

1 From the cash flow statement below, prepare a trading and profit and loss account for each firm. All sales and purchases are made on cash terms.
2 Explain the difference between the month's cash flow (receipts – payments) and net profit.
3 How can a profitable business run into cash flow problems?
4 Distinguish between net profit and gross profit.

Cash flow statement for the month of September 199–	D. Stringer £	M. Lloyd £
Receipts:		
Cash sales – units at £150 each	19 500	18 000
Payments:		
Motor expenses	300	200
Wages	3 200	3 000
Stock purchases – units at £80 each	16 000	12 000
Total expenditure	19 500	15 200
Receipts minus expenditure	0	2 800
Balance b/f	5 000	5 000
Balance c/f	5 000	7 800

Balance sheet

The balance sheet shows the financial affairs of the business at a specified point in time. It provides information concerning:

■ the nature and value of assets employed in the business
■ the nature and value of liabilities to others
■ how the business has been funded.

The outline format of a balance sheet is:

	£
Assets	50 000
Less liabilities	20 000
	30 000
Financed by:	
Owner's capital	30 000

This basic format is common to most businesses although it may vary in detail, depending on the nature and legal type of the business. The net assets of the business (total assets less total liabilities) represent the owners' investment in the business. Figure 8.16 on the next page shows an example of a balance sheet for a sole trader.

Assets are presented according to their liquidity (how easily they can be converted to cash) starting with the least liquid items:

■ **Fixed assets** – the least liquid of assets
■ **Current assets** – recognising the operating cycle they have to go through to get to cash, starting with stocks, then debtors, then cash.

Liabilities are likewise presented from those making demands on cash in the near future, through to those liabilities due at a later date:

■ **Current liabilities** – alternatively labelled 'creditors payable within one year'
■ **Long-term liabilities** – alternatively labelled 'creditors payable after more than one year'.

Figure 8.17 on page 164 explains the terms used on a balance sheet.

Task

When analysing a set of accounts comprising a profit and loss account and balance sheet, where would you find the following items?

a Money owed to the business for supplies made
b An item of stock sitting in the warehouse
c An item that has now been sold to a customer
d A piece of equipment used to make the firm's products
e Money owed to a supplier of stock materials
f Rent paid in advance for the next three months
g Electricity consumed to heat the sales office
h Electricity consumed to make an item of stock still sitting in the warehouse
i An item of stock in bad condition
j Cost of an advertisement

Characteristics of published accounts

The format and content of company accounts prepared for external users have to conform to the requirements of the Companies Acts and accounting standards (see Figures 8.18 and 8.19 on pages 165 and 166). In order to provide a general framework that all companies can use, expenditure is categorised under general headings, such as 'administration expenses', as opposed to the usual detailed analysis for management's use and for unincorporated businesses.

Figure 8.16 Sample balance sheet

Pina Mistry Balance sheet as at 31 December 199–	£ Cost	£ Depreciation	£
Tangible fixed assets			
Land and buildings	30 000	5 000	25 000
Furniture, fixtures and fittings	5 000	1 000	4 000
Motor vehicle	5 000	2 000	3 000
	40 000	8 000	32 000
Current assets			
Stock		6 000	
Debtors		1 000	
Cash at bank and on hand		1 500	
		8 500	
Current liabilities			
Trade creditors		1 500	
Net current assets			7 000
Assets less current liabilities			39 000
Long-term liabilities			
Bank loan – repayable 30/6/9–			9 000
Net assets			30 000
Financed by:			
Capital at 1 January 199–			27 000
Profit for the year		7 000	
Drawings		4 000	3 000
Capital at 1 December 199–			30 000

The objectives of accounting regulations

Legal and accounting regulations attempt to ensure that accounts provide information that satisfies the following information needs.

Stewardship
Shareholders are remote from the day-to-day activities of the business and so the reporting framework provides certain safeguards against directors acting against the shareholder's interests. For example, details are required concerning the remuneration of directors and the company's auditors.

Adequate for needs
All businesses should be required to provide similar information that is relevant to the needs of the users of company accounts. Although there is less detail provided on the face of the profit and loss account and balance sheet, some supporting analysis is found in the 'notes to the accounts'. It is also a requirement that figures are

provided for the previous accounting period for comparative purposes.

Financial position
The accounts should facilitate a proper understanding of the nature of assets and liabilities. In addition to a balance sheet, supporting information is required in the notes to the accounts. For example, disclosure is required concerning the nature of loans, interest rates applicable and when they are to be repaid.

Financial performance
To facilitate a better understanding of the main factors that have led to current business performance and how these impinge on future prospects, the directors are required to comment on both issues in a 'directors' report'. In addition, where companies are involved in more than one type of business, or operate in more than one geographical market, the accounts must provide certain information concerning each segment. Where the company has undergone some restructuring that has

Figure 8.17 Balance sheet terminology

Term	Description
Fixed assets	Assets that have an initial life of over one year
Intangible fixed assets	Assets that do not have a physical form, e.g. ■ Goodwill – arising from the purchase of company for a greater value than the amount that can be attributed to the assets less liabilities of the acquired business ■ Research and development expenditure that can give a reasonably certain future commercial benefit
Tangible fixed assets	The tools of the business. Physical assets that are used in the business including land, buildings, plant and equipment, fixtures and fittings and motor vehicles
Investments	Investments, including shares and debentures in other companies, that are intended to be held for more than one year
Current assets	Assets that will be realised into cash within less than one year of the balance sheet date
Stocks	Materials and goods purchased for subsequent resale
Stock – raw materials	Materials to be converted in the business's production processes
Stock – work in progress	Materials that have been partly converted in the business's production processes
Stock – finished goods	Goods ready for resale to customers
Debtors	Amounts owed by customers for goods and services they have received but have not yet paid for
Prepayments	Amounts paid by the business for resources not yet consumed, e.g. rent paid in advance at the balance sheet date
Bank and cash	Cash in bank accounts and on hand
Creditors: amounts due in less than one year	Liabilities due within less than one year of the balance sheet date (alternatively called current liabilities)
Trade creditors	Amounts owed to suppliers for goods and services received but not yet paid for
Accruals	Resources consumed for which the supplier has not yet invoiced the business, e.g. the value of electricity consumption since the last invoice will be a liability at the balance sheet date
Dividends proposed	Dividends 'proposed' by the directors but not paid to the shareholders at the balance sheet date
Taxation	Corporation tax on profits for the current financial year are not paid until up to nine months after the balance sheet date
Net current assets	Current assets less current liabilities
Total assets less current liabilities	Fixed assets plus net current assets (capital employed)

Term	Description
Creditors: amounts due after more than one year	Liabilities due in over one year's time (alternatively called long-term liabilities)
Debentures	Loan stock issued under the company's common seal
Total net assets	Total assets less total liabilities
Financed by: For unincorporated businesses	
Capital brought forward	The value of the owner's investment in the business at the end of the previous period
Profit for the period	The net profit from the current profit and loss account
Drawings	The amount of capital or profit taken out of the business by the owner during the period
For companies	
Ordinary share capital	The issued ordinary share capital at nominal value, e.g. 25p shares
Preference share capital	The issued preference share capital at nominal value
Share premium	Amounts paid by shareholders to the company in excess of the nominal value of shares purchased. This arises because new issues of shares in existing companies are priced at near the market value, not the nominal value of the shares (note that this only arises on issues of shares by the company, buying and selling of shares between shareholders does not affect the company).
Profit and loss account	Profits retained in the business after dividends have been paid to the shareholders. The balance in the balance sheet is the accumulated total over the life of the business, not just the profit for the current period

resulted in businesses being purchased or sold during the year, further analysis of trading results is required. Sales, operating costs and operating profits have to be analysed according to whether the trading units of the company are continuing activities (traditional businesses or newly acquired) or have been discontinued.

Accounting policies

The company's annual report should provide information concerning the company's accounting policies – different policies on the treatment of certain items can affect the profit reported. For example, one company may depreciate motor vehicles over three years and another company over five years. To enable financial analysts to restate profits on a similar basis information concerning base assumptions must be provided.

Figure 8.18 Profit and loss account from the Body Shop's annual report and accounts

Consolidated Profit and Loss Account

For the year ended 28 February 1994

	Note	1994 £m	1993 £m
Turnover	2	**195.4**	168.3
Cost of sales		**89.5**	78.0
Gross profit		**105.9**	90.3
Net operating expenses	3	**75.8**	66.0
Operating profit	2,5	**30.1**	24.3
Profit on disposal of subsidiary undertaking	21c	**1.1**	–
		31.2	24.3
Interest (net)	4	**1.5**	2.8
Profit on ordinary activities before tax		**29.7**	21.5
Tax on profit on ordinary activities	7	**10.1**	7.6
		19.6	13.9
Minority interests		**0.2**	0.1
Profit for the financial year	8	**19.4**	13.8
Dividends paid and proposed	9	**3.8**	3.2
Retained profit	20	**15.6**	10.6
Earnings per ordinary share	10	**10.3p**	7.4p
Adjusted earnings per ordinary share	10	**10.1p**	7.4p

All amounts relate to continuing activities.

A statement of the movement in reserves can be found in note 20.

The notes on pages 31 to 49 form part of these financial statements.

Figure 8.19 Balance sheet from the Body Shop's annual report and accounts

Balance Sheets

As at 28 February 1994

	Note	Group 1994 £m	Group 1993 £m	Company 1994 £m	Company 1993 £m
Fixed assets					
Intangible assets	11	**3.7**	5.2	**3.7**	5.2
Tangible assets	12	**67.9**	64.8	**49.2**	50.0
Investments	13	**–**	–	**12.7**	9.7
		71.6	70.0	**65.6**	64.9
Current assets					
Stocks	14	**34.6**	35.3	**18.0**	20.6
Debtors	15	**37.2**	33.6	**38.8**	28.8
Cash at bank and in hand		**24.9**	14.0	**22.0**	9.2
		96.7	82.9	**78.8**	58.6
Creditors: amounts falling due within one year	16	**35.6**	31.2	**32.0**	26.8
Net current assets		**61.1**	51.7	**46.8**	31.8
Total assets less current liabilities		**132.7**	121.7	**112.4**	96.7
Creditors: amounts falling due after more than one year	17	**(32.4)**	(35.2)	**(1.9)**	(3.4)
Provisions for liabilities and charges					
Deferred tax	18	**(3.4)**	(3.8)	**(4.2)**	(3.5)
Minority interests		**–**	(0.5)	**–**	–
		96.9	82.2	**106.3**	89.8
Capital and reserves					
Called up share capital	19	**9.4**	9.4	**9.4**	9.4
Share premium account	20	**35.7**	33.5	**35.7**	33.5
Profit and loss account	20	**51.8**	39.3	**61.2**	46.9
		96.9	82.2	**106.3**	89.8

These financial statements were approved by the board on 10 May 1994 and signed on its behalf by:

TG Roddick
Director

The notes on pages 31 to 49 form part of these financial statements.

Figure 8.20 Cash flow statement from the Body Shop's annual report and accounts

Consolidated Cash Flow Statement
For the year ended 28 February 1994

	Note	1994 £m	1994 £m	1993 £m	1993 £m
Net cash inflow from operating activities	*21a*		**40.3**		38.6
Returns on investments and servicing of finance					
Interest received		**1.0**		0.7	
Interest paid		**(2.5)**		(3.0)	
Dividends paid		**(3.3)**		(3.0)	
Net cash outflow from returns on investments and servicing of finance			**(4.8)**		(5.3)
Taxation					
UK corporation tax paid		**(6.4)**		(7.3)	
Overseas tax paid		**(0.2)**		(0.2)	
Tax paid			**(6.6)**		(7.5)
Investing activities					
Purchase of tangible fixed assets		**(12.7)**		(13.5)	
Purchase of intangible fixed assets		**–**		(6.0)	
Purchase of subsidiary undertakings (net of cash and cash equivalents)	*21b*	**(0.2)**		–	
Goodwill acquired		**–**		(1.8)	
Sale of tangible fixed assets		**0.1**		0.1	
Disposal of subsidiary undertaking	*21c*	**0.8**		–	
Net cash outflow from investing activities			**(12.0)**		(21.2)
Net cash inflow before financing			**16.9**		4.6
Financing					
Issue of ordinary share capital		**2.2**		–	
Issue of USA loan notes		**–**		31.7	
Other loans		**(1.3)**		4.0	
Loan repayments		**(5.1)**		(1.0)	
Capital element of finance lease rental payments		**–**		(0.1)	
Net cash inflow/(outflow) from financing	*21d*		**(4.2)**		34.6
Increase in cash and cash equivalents	*21e*		**12.7**		39.2

The notes on pages 31 to 49 form part of these financial statements.

The cash flow statement

Unlike the cash flow forecast examined earlier in the chapter (see page 144), the cash flow statement that accompanies the other published financial statements of companies (see Figure 8.20) is concerned with reviewing past cash movements. The cash flow statement shows the ability of the business to generate cash flows and gives users of accounts a fresh insight into the quality of profits earned and the ability of the business to remain solvent.

The basic format of the cash flow statement

Figure 8.21 explains the terms used in a cash flow statement.

The figures in the cash flow statement relate to actual cash movements in the current accounting period, and do not necessarily correspond to figures included in the profit and loss account. For example, dividends paid will almost certainly not be the same as those shown as appropriated from the profit and loss account. Some of the payments may have been in respect of the previous period's proposed dividends and the current period's proposed dividends will not have resulted in a cash flow at all.

The cash flow statement starts with 'the net cash inflow from operating activities', which can be derived from the operating profit on the profit and loss account. The relevant note to the accounts (see Figure 8.22) reconciles operating profit to net cash inflow and provides further insight to the distinction between profit and cash flow.

It is useful to consider why each of these adjustments is made. We need to look at items in the profit and loss account that do not result in a corresponding transaction at the bank:

1 **Depreciation** is a cost in the profit and loss account, but is not an outflow of money, so should be added back to profit.
2 **Amortisation** is similar to depreciation, but is the term used to spread the cost of intangible assets.
3 **Loss on sale of a fixed asset** is a profit and loss account expense representing the difference between sale proceeds of an asset and its net book value (original cost less accumulated depreciation). The cash

Figure 8.21 Cash flow statement terminology

Term	Description
Net cash inflow (outflow) from operating activities	The net cash flow from the operating activities of company. It represents actual cash receipts from customers less cash payments to employees and suppliers of goods and services. It excludes payments for fixed assets
Returns on investment and servicing of finance	The returns on investments and the payments made to those who financed the business are analysed here: ■ Cash coming into the business as a result of making investments that generate receipts of dividends and interest. ■ Cash going out of the business as a result of payments of interest and dividends to those who have financed the business, e.g. the business owners, debenture holders and banks.
Taxation	Payment of taxes on profits to the Inland Revenue are separately disclosed here. Mainstream corporation tax paid will relate to the previous period's tax liability
Investing activities	Cash goes out of the business on the purchase of fixed assets and cash flows in when fixed assets are sold. This section shows the extent to which cash has been invested to maintain and expand the future earnings capacity of the business
Financing	This section shows how the financing needs of the business have been met. Cash flows into the business on new share and loan stock issues. Cash flows out of the business on loan repayments and the redemption of shares
Increase in cash and cash equivalents	The total of all the above cash flows results in a movement on cash holdings or cash equivalents. Cash equivalents are short-term investments that have a maturity date of less than three months from the date they were acquired

Figure 8.22 Example of a 'note to the accounts' from the Body Shop's annual report and accounts

Note 21a Reconciliation of operating profit to net cash inflow from operating activities		
	1994 £m	1993 £m
Operating profit	30.1	24.3
Depreciation of tangible fixed assets	8.0	6.4
Amortisation of intangible fixed assets	1.5	0.8
Loss on sale of tangible fixed assets	0.4	0.4
Exchange differences	0.3	(1.5)
Decrease/(increase) in stocks	(0.5)	3.3
Decrease/(increase) in debtors	(4.6)	3.9
Increase/(decrease) in creditors	5.1	1.0
Net cash inflow	40.3	38.6

flow resulting from this transaction is the sale proceeds which is considered further down the cash flow statement under 'investing activities'. Thus an accounting loss is another book-keeping item that needs to be added back to profit.

4 **Decrease/(increase) in stocks** reverses the adjustment made to purchases in the trading account. If there has been an increase in stocks, then this will not have decreased profit, but it has certainly decreased cash. It, therefore, needs to be deducted from profit to arrive at the cash position.

5 An adjustment for a movement in debtors is necessary because if debtors increase, as in the case of the Body Shop, then the cash received from debtors must have been less than the value of credit sales included in the profit and loss account.

6 An adjustment for a movement in creditors is necessary because if creditors increase, as in the case of the Body Shop, then the cash paid out to creditors must have been less than the value of purchases charged to the profit and loss account.

Interrelationship of financial reports

The three main financial reports come from the same base information (see Figure 8.23). The balance sheet is concerned with balances at a point in time. The profit and loss account and cash flow statements are concerned with describing how two of those balances changed over the accounting period, namely profit and cash.

Budgets

The cash flow forecast examined earlier is only one of many statements that can make up a forecasting system. It is often necessary in all but the simplest of businesses to make a review of the business functions. After all, how can a company forecast how much it will receive from customers if it has not first estimated the level of sales for the same period? Likewise, how can payments to suppliers be forecast without first identifying stock usage, stock levels and changes in creditor levels?

The process of financial forecasting results in **budgets** for each area of business activity (see Figure 8.24). The money values used in the budgets are often underpinned with quantities (units, weights and other measures) to ensure consistency across the various functions. They also provide some relevance to operational activity and so facilitate subsequent monitoring of a function's performance. The exact nature of functional (subsidiary) budgets depends on the organisation structure and the operational processes of the business. It is, however, usual for each budget to be analysed by time period, e.g. by week or by month.

The following case study is for a manufacturing business that for simplicity only uses annual totals.

Figure 8.23

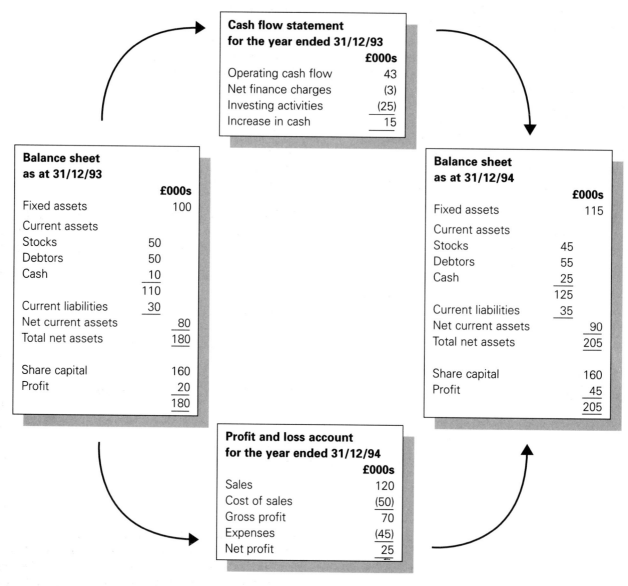

**Cash flow statement
for the year ended 31/12/93**

	£000s
Operating cash flow	43
Net finance charges	(3)
Investing activities	(25)
Increase in cash	15

**Balance sheet
as at 31/12/93**

	£000s	
Fixed assets		100
Current assets		
Stocks	50	
Debtors	50	
Cash	10	
	110	
Current liabilities	30	
Net current assets		80
Total net assets		180
Share capital		160
Profit		20
		180

**Balance sheet
as at 31/12/94**

	£000s	
Fixed assets		115
Current assets		
Stocks	45	
Debtors	55	
Cash	25	
	125	
Current liabilities	35	
Net current assets		90
Total net assets		205
Share capital		160
Profit		45
		205

**Profit and loss account
for the year ended 31/12/94**

	£000s
Sales	120
Cost of sales	(50)
Gross profit	70
Expenses	(45)
Net profit	25

Figure 8.24 Budgets for a manufacturing business

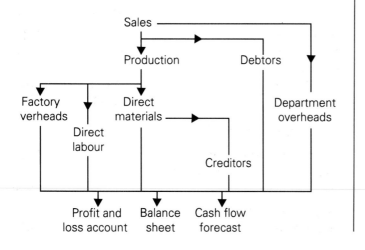

Case Study
Randle & Hopkins

Randle & Hopkins manufactures and sells one design of filing cabinet. It is the start of 1995 and the company wishes to budget for the coming year.

1 The company anticipates selling 8800 cabinets at a price of £50.
2 Each cabinet requires 10 sq. m. of materials that cost £0.75 per sq. m. and 3 hours of direct labour paid at £4 per hour.
3 Other factory costs include variable indirect labour of £0.50 per unit and expenses including power and paint of £1.00 per unit. Fixed overheads comprise £40 000 and depreciation on plant calculated at 10 per cent on cost.

4 Halfway through 1995 the partners intend to purchase additional plant at a cost of £20 000.

5 Stock levels at the end of 1994 were 300 finished cabinets and 7000 sq. m. of raw materials.

6 Stock levels at the end of 1995 are forecast to be 500 finished cabinets and 5000 sq. m. of raw materials. Finished goods stock is valued to include the costs of direct labour and materials and factory overhead.

7 Each cabinet incurs distribution costs of £2 and salesperson's commissions of £3. Selling and distribution fixed costs are forecast at £40 000.

8 Administration costs are forecast at £54 000 for salaries, £8000 for stationery and telephone and £20 000 for other expenses.

9 Trade debtors are currently historically low, so Randle suggests it may be prudent to assume they will increase by £10 000 over the coming year.

10 Trade creditors are forecast to end the year at one month's worth of raw material purchases. Unless otherwise stated, all other transactions are on a cash basis.

11 The balance sheet has just been prepared for the end of 1994.

Randle & Hopkins
Budgeted balance sheet
as at 31 December 1994

	£	£	£
	Cost	**Depreciation**	**Net**
Fixed assets			
Plant	100 000	50 000	50 000
Current assets			
Raw materials stock		5 250	
Finished goods stock		7 380	
Debtors		65 000	
		77 630	
Current liabilities			
Creditors		12 000	
Bank		10 000	
		22 000	
Net current assets			55 630
			105 630
Capital b/f			95 000
Profit			10 630
Capital c/f			105 630

Prepare the following budget statements for 1995:

1 Sales budget
2 Production budget
3 Raw materials usage budget
4 Raw materials purchases budget
5 Direct labour budget
6 Factory overhead budget
7 Selling and distribution budget
8 Administration budget
9 Debtors budget
10 Creditors budget
11 Cash budget
12 Budget profit and loss account
13 Budget balance sheet

Answers

1 Sales budget

Forecast number of units	8 800
Selling price (£)	50
Sales turnover (£)	440 000

2 Production and finished goods budget

Stocks of finished goods are budgeted to increase by 200 units, therefore production has to be in excess of sales.

	Units
Forecast sales units	8 800
Add required closing stock to start the next year	500
Less anticipated opening stock from this year	−300
Production required	9 000

3 Raw materials usage budget

	Sq. m.
Forecast production units	9 000
Material per unit	×10
Total	90 000
Price per sq. m.	£0.75
Total value	£67 500

4 Raw materials purchases budget

Stocks of raw materials are budgeted to fall over the coming year, so purchases will be less than production requirements. We know the opening and closing balances and the production requirement so by deduction we can arrive at purchases.

	Sq. m.	**£**
Opening stock	7 000	5 250
Add: purchases at 75p (balancing item)	88 000	66 000
Less: production usage	90 000	67 500
Closing stock	5 000	3 750

5 Direct labour budget

Forecast production units	9 000
Direct labour hours per cabinet	3
Total direct hours	27 000
Wages rate per hour	£4
Total wages	£108 000

6 Factory overhead budget

For factory overhead, we need to identify expenses that will vary with the level of business activity and those that are fixed costs.

	£
Variable overhead per unit	
Labour	0.50
Expenses – power and paint	1.00
Total variable overhead per unit	1.50
Forecast production units	9 000
Total variable overhead	13 500
Fixed overhead	
Depreciation	11 000
Other	40 000
Total fixed overhead	51 000
Total factory overhead	64 500

7 Selling and distribution budget

As with the production overhead budget, we have to identify both fixed and variable elements of the various indirect expenses charged to the profit and loss account.

	£
Variable costs:	
Distribution per cabinet	2
Commission per cabinet	3
	5
Total variable costs for 8800 cabinets	44 000
Total fixed costs	40 000
Total selling and distribution cost	84 000

8 Administration budget

	£
Salaries	54 000
Stationery and telephone	8 000
Other	20 000
	82 000

9 Debtors budget

Debtors are forecast to increase over the year, so we know that the amounts received from customers will be less than the level of sales included in the profit and loss account.

	£
Opening debtors balance	65 000
Sales	440 000
Cash received (balancing figure)	430 000
Closing debtors balance	75 000

10 Creditors budget

As with debtors, if we know the level of creditors at the beginning and end of the year, together with the purchase figure, we can calculate the amount to be paid to suppliers in the year.

	£
Opening creditors balance	12 000
Purchases	66 000
Cash payments (balancing figure)	72 500
Closing creditors balance (£66 000÷12)	5 500

11 Cash flow forecast (cash budget)

In the subsidiary budgets we have identified all of the cash to be received and paid out, so we are in a position to prepare the cash budget.

Randle & Hopkins
Cash budget
for the year ended 31 December 1995

	£
Receipts	
Sales	430 000
Payments	
Raw material suppliers	72 500
Direct labour	108 000
Factory overhead	53 500
Selling and distribution	84 000
Administration	82 000
New machinery	20 000
Total payments	420 000
Receipts less payments	10 000
Opening cash balance	–10 000
Closing cash balance	0

Remember, when preparing cash flow statements, we are only interested in items that relate to actual cash transactions. The factory overhead budget included a depreciation charge of £11 000 which is not a cash flow so should be excluded from the cash flow forecast (£64 000 – £11 000 = £53 500). The cash flow forecast shows the satisfactory position of the bank overdraft being repaid by the end of the year 1995. However, care should be taken when interpreting annual balances such as these. The annual figures may hide wide fluctuations in the cash balance from one month to the next.

12/13 *Master budget*

We also have all the necessary information to prepare the budgeted profit and loss account and balance sheet.

Randle & Hopkins
Budgeted trading and profit and loss statement
for the year ended 31 December 1995

	Units	£	£
Sales	8 800		440 000
Opening stock	300	7 380	
Raw material usage	9 000	67 500	
Direct wages		108 000	
Factory overheads		64 500	
	9 300	247 380	
Closing stock at £26.60/unit			
(£247 380 ÷ 9300)	500	13 300	
Cost of sales	8 800		234 080
Gross profit			205 920
Less expenses:			
Selling and distribution		84 000	
Administration		82 000	
			166 000
Net profit			39 920

Randle & Hopkins
Budgeted balance sheet
as at 31 December 1995

	£	£	£
	Cost	Depreciation	Net
Fixed assets			
Plant	120 000	61 000	59 000
Current assets			
Raw materials		3 750	
Finished goods stock		13 300	
Debtors		75 000	
Bank		0	
		92 050	
Current liabilities			
Creditors		5 500	
Net current assets			86 550
			145 550
Capital b/f			105 630
Profit			39 920
Capital c/f			145 550

Limiting factors

One of the objectives of the budgeting exercise is to provide a formal framework on which the various functions of the business can coordinate their activities. During budget preparation it is necessary to ensure that the plans for each of the functions in the organisation are consistent with one another on a period-by-period basis. It will be found that one aspect of the business limits the overall volume of business activity. While for most organisations the level of sales is the limiting factor, for an individual period there may be some other function that proves to be a bottleneck for workflow. Where possible, the effects of the limiting factor should be minimised by careful planning. For example, if a manufacturer of non-perishable goods identifies that production cannot keep up with sales during a particular month, it will be necessary to build up stocks during the preceding months.

Case Study
Souvenirs manufacturer

A manufacturer of souvenir mugs has a production capacity of 2000 mugs a month and aims to maintain a minimum stock of 500 mugs at any point in time. Sales of mugs are forecast to be 1000 in both March and April, 1500 in May, 2000 in June, and 3000 in July. Prepare the production budget to cover the five-month period.

It is necessary to work back from July to find the nearest month or months that will have sufficient excess production capacity to build up stocks in readiness for the 1000 excess sales over production.

Production budget

	March	April	May	June	July
Stock b/f	500	500	1000	1500	1500
Production	1000	1500	2000	2000	2000
Sales	1000	1000	1500	2000	3000
Stock c/f	500	1000	1500	1500	500

To maintain a stock level of 500 at the end of July, it is necessary to start the month with 1500 mugs. As budget sales for June match production, it will be necessary to start June with 1500 mugs in stock. In May it will be possible to contribute 500 towards the stock balance of 1500 so the month should start with 1000 mugs in stock. During April it will be possible to produce 500 more mugs than sales to reach the required 1000 mugs needed at the beginning of May. On the basis of this production budget, the subsidiary budgets of direct labour, direct materials and production overhead can be produced.

Task

The Premier Christmas Pudding Company requires you to prepare its budget statements for the seven months to January 1996. You have been given the following forecast information:

1 *Sales forecast:*

	Jul.	Aug.	Sept.	Oct.	Nov.	Dec.	Total
Sales of 1 kg puddings	100	100	500	1 300	10 000	20 000	32 000

2 No sales have been made in the previous six months.

3 Each 1 kg pudding sells for £2.50.

4 Customers are mainly retailers and wholesalers who take one month to pay for puddings received.

5 It is company policy to hold a minimum stock of puddings each month that is equivalent to the next month's forecast sales. Sales are not forecast after December until July of the next year. The requisite minimum stock would be held at the end of June, valued at £1.20 per pudding.

6 Sufficient dry fruits are held in stock to cover the next month's forecast production. Other ingredients are purchased in the month of use.

7 All suppliers are paid on delivery.

8 Production capacity is limited to 10 000 kg a month.

9 Direct labour is employed on a piece-work rate of £0.20 per kilo of pudding.

10 *Costs for a 100 kg batch:*

	kg	£
Dried fruit	50	60
Other	50	30
Packaging		10
Distribution		20

11 The whole period's packaging materials will be received from the printers at the beginning of July. The packaging is of a special design to celebrate the firm's 50 years' existence. In case sales exceed forecast, sufficient packaging for 35 000 puddings has been ordered. Excess packaging is to be disposed of in December.

12 Administration overhead is fixed at £3000 per month and is payable up to the end of January 1996.

13 The bank balance at the end of June 1995 is forecast to be £15 930.

14 No losses are to be assumed in the production process.

Prepare for *each* of the seven months to 31 January:

a Sales budget

b Finished stock and production budget

c Raw materials stock and purchases budget (separate for mixed fruit, packaging and other)

d Direct labour budget

e Distribution costs budget

f Cash budget

g Forecast trading and profit and loss account

Objectives of the budgeting exercise

Budgets are prepared for a number of reasons and for parties both internal and external to the organisation. Where a firm is required to supply a business plan to raise finance, to a bank manager or venture capitalist for instance, then budgeted financial statements will be an integral part of the plan.

Budgets also have an important role to play as part of the strategic and tactical planning process of the business, and once prepared, they provide a valuable benchmark against which to measure and judge actual performance. The investigation of actual results compared with budget provides insight for better planning in the future and also provides a mechanism to control adverse trends.

Budgeting objectives include:

1 An opportunity to examine and state organisational objectives.

2 Long-term direction – a process for focusing management attention on wider horizons.

3 A framework in which specific short-term budgets can be consistently formulated.

4 A framework in which the objectives of departments and individuals are made consistent with those of the organisation as a whole. Each departmental budget is coordinated and interrelated with other budgets. For example, the production department's budget is based on the sales budget with adjustment for planned stock balance increases or reductions.

5 A system of communication whereby employees are aware of objectives and the performance expected of them. It can also facilitate an informed message to outside parties, such as 'it is our intention to raise profits by 15 per cent per annum'.

6 Motivation by setting targets for all to strive towards. Budgets should be set with a view to maximising actual performance. A target that is too difficult or too easy will not have the desired motivating effect.

7 Monitoring and controlling activity by comparing actual performance with budgeted performance and, therefore, providing a catalyst for remedial action if necessary. The reporting process that measures actual performance against budget will save management time by highlighting only significant variances – management by exception.

Methodology

■ The annual and medium-term budget exercise needs to be set in the context of long-term objectives and strategies that have been formulated by the highest level of management.

- Environmental factors need to be identified, including economic, social, technological and regulatory factors. Current and forecast market conditions concerning sales, supplies, labour and finance should be analysed for their implications.

- It is important to recognise any limiting factor on business development. Sales demand is often limited, but other constraints, such as lack of skilled workers or machine capacity, should be identified.

- The budgeting process is prepared over a time-constrained period when specific deadlines have to be met (see Figure 8.25). The administration of the process is often the responsibility of the accounts department, although some organisations set up a budget committee to oversee and review budget submissions.

- Budget models are often constructed with specialist modelling programs or computer spreadsheets, and can provide decision makers with a valuable 'what if?' tool. The effect of decisions can quickly be simulated through a structure of functional interrelationships. For example, the effect on cash flow and profit of reducing the sales price by 5 per cent and increasing volumes by 10 per cent can be viewed in a matter of seconds, despite the need for perhaps thousands of recalculations in the business model.

The accounts department is involved at all stages of the budgeting process. An effective accounts team provides helpful information and advice to line management and directors as the exercise progresses.

There is a danger of stating everything in monetary terms and every interrelationship in a fixed logical manner, but budget models do help managers understand the reasons for the incidence of cost and how different functions interact.

Budgets for control purposes

Once constructed, functional budgets provide a basis for subsequent monitoring of actual performance. An important feature of this process is the highlighting of variances to budget. However, it is important to recognise that while the level of some costs varies according to a particular manager's decisions, others do not. In particular, the ability to control costs depends on the position of the manager in the organisational hierarchy. Some costs may be in the control of one manager, but not his or her subordinate. It would wrong and demotivating for individuals to be held accountable for costs over which they have no control. It is not unusual when presenting reports monitoring past performance to distinguish between those costs that are controllable and those that are not (see Figure 8.26).

Variances are recorded as being either adverse (A) or favourable (F) depending on whether actual expenditure is more or less than budget respectively. In the example shown in Figure 8.26, the departmental manager cannot be held accountable for the overall cost overrun because it has arisen from items over which the manager has no control.

Figure 8.25 An example of a budget timetable

Budget timetable For year 1 April 1996 to 31 March 1997		
Date	**Narrative**	**Responsibility**
1/9/95	Board of directors review long-term objectives and strategies and specify short-term goals for the year	Directors
22/9/95	Budget guidelines and standard forms issued to line managers	Accounts
6/10/95	Actual results to September 1995 are issued to line management with comparisons to current budget and last year's actual results	Accounts
20/10/95	Budget submissions to the management accountant	Line management
27/10/95	First draft of master budget is issued	Accounts
3/11/95	First draft of the budget is reviewed for results and consistency – line managers to justify their submissions	Managing director and individual directors
6/11/95	New assumptions and guidelines issued to line management	Accounts
10/11/95	Budgets revised and resubmitted	Line management
27/11/95	Second draft of master budget issued	Accounts
24/11/95	Final review of the draft budget	Managing director and finance director
30/11/95	Final amendments	Accounts
1/12/95	Submission to the board for approval	Finance director

Figure 8.26 Controllable and uncontrollable costs

Machine Shop Overhead Report For October 1995	Budget (£)	Actual (£)	Variance (£)
Controllable costs			
Indirect wages	8 000	8 200	200A
Machine maintenance	2 250	1 900	350F
Consumable materials	500	550	50A
Total controllable	10 750	10 650	100F
Uncontrollable costs			
Depreciation	5 700	6 000	300A
Property cost apportionment	8 500	9 000	500A
Total uncontrollable costs	14 200	15 000	800A
Total cost centre overheads	24 950	25 650	700A

A: Adverse   F: Favourable

Task

Which of the following costs are controllable by a marketing manager? Qualify your answers where appropriate.

a Depreciation of furniture
b Insurance of the building
c Wages paid to staff
d Advertising
e Stationery
f Office redecorations
g Training costs

Flexible budgeting

For the budgeting process to be of value as a source of reference when assessing business performance, the original budget may need some adjustment in the light of actual business performance. If the sales force failed to achieve prices and volumes outlined in the budget, then the responsible managers would be required to provide senior management with satisfactory explanations. However, there are almost certainly some implications for other departments as well. If there was a sales volume variance to budget, then this might result in other departments under- or over-spending compared to budget. For example, if the factory has to produce 20 per cent more production to satisfy booming demand, other things being equal, production costs will increase. It would not be equitable to expect factory management to produce more without allowing them to use more resources, so there is a need to 'flex' the budget.

We know from our examination of cost behaviour on page 139, that not all costs rise in line with business activity. Each cost item should be examined to discover its behaviour in relation to changed activity. Variable costs move in line with activity; fixed costs should not vary; semi-variable costs include features of both fixed and variable costs; and stepped costs may vary by more or less than the change in the level of activity.

Case Study
Extract from annual budget for a bus company

	Fixed/ variable	Original budget	Flexed budget
Mileage		250 000	300 000
Depreciation of vehicles	Fixed	£50 000	£50 000
Maintenance of vehicles	Semi-variable 50/50	£25 000	£27 500
Petrol	Variable	£50 000	£60 000

Variable costs, such as petrol, move directly in proportion to the number of miles travelled. Other costs will have at least an element of fixed expenditure unrelated to the level of activity, so this part is not flexed. Depreciation is a book-keeping entry that will probably have been calculated on a time-based method, hence the charge is fixed in the accounts irrespective of the number of miles travelled. Of the maintenance costs, £12 500 is fixed and the variable part flexed from £12 500 to £15 000, giving £27 500 in total.

Task

A hotel with a capacity of 150 beds has assembled the following information for an average week:

BUDGET DATA

	Fixed (£)	Variable per guest/ week (£)	Actual (£)
Charges		300.00	30 690
Rent	5 000		5 000
Power	2 000	1.50	2 300
Food	1 000	45.00	5 100
Laundry and cleaning	1 500	15.00	3 050
Drinks	0	7.50	775
Reception	600	200.00 (per 50)	1 150
Management and administration	2 000	0	1 975
Cooks, waiters, etc.	1 800	100.00 (per 30)	2 350
Repairs and renewals	1 000	1.00	2 900
Other	750	0	900
Total cost			25 500
Profit			5 190

1 Prepare the original budget for week 35 based on an average 70 per cent occupancy.

2 In week 35 actual occupancy was 66 per cent. Prepare a profit statement with supporting commentary for the general manager, showing clearly how well the hotel has performed.

Task

The following budget data for April 199– relates to Brampton Tools Ltd, a manufacturer of machine tools.

		Budget		£ Actual
Level of activity	**80%**	**90%**	**100%**	
Direct materials	28 000	31 500	35 000	24 250
Direct labour	39 200	44 100	49 000	35 400
Rent	10 000	10 000	10 000	10 000
Electricity	3 400	3 650	3 900	3 450
Factory supervision	18 000	19 000	20 000	17 500
Administration	37 000	40 000	43 000	35 400
Selling and distribution	23 300	25 000	26 700	21 000
Total cost	158 900	173 250	187 600	147 000

The original budget was constructed on the assumption that business activity would be 90 per cent of factory capacity. This equated to 12 600 standard units of work and would produce a 20 per cent margin. An analysis of costs was undertaken at the time the budget was prepared and this was used to produce indicative amounts if output deviated by 10 per cent of total capacity. Actual production at 70 per cent capacity fell outside the anticipated range but budget selling price was achieved.

1 Produce a profit statement with details of sales and costs and columns for actual performance, original budget, 'flexed' budget and variance from flexed budget.

2 Comment on the results.

Interpretation of accounts

When analysing and evaluating the financial performance of a business it is important to identify trends and be able to differentiate the significant from the unimportant. Accounting ratios are an important set of tools to aid the financial analyst with these objectives.

Accounting ratios

Accounting ratios entail the comparison of one piece of financial data with another to aid the analysis of financial performance. Absolute money values are of little use unless they are set in the context in which they arose. For example, W. H. Smith will incur a far greater cost in money terms for the products it sells compared to a local newsagent, but a comparison of costs in relation to sales revenue would almost certainly indicate the national chain enjoyed a cost advantage.

How ratios can be used

- Comparison of ratios for the same business over different time periods is a useful way of detecting favourable or adverse trends.
- Comparison with comparable businesses indicates whether the business is operating efficiently in terms of profitability and how it uses the capital tied up in the business.

The following case study demonstrates the most commonly used ratios.

Case Study
Mirage PLC

Mirage PLC operates a theme park and sells novelty products from its own outlet at the park and through retailers at other tourist attractions. Half of the sales of novelty products are on a credit basis. The financial statements of the company have been prepared for internal purposes, and are not in a form for publication.

Mirage PLC
Theme parks and novelty products
Trading and profit and loss account
for the year ended 31 December 1995

	1995 £000s		1994 £000s	
Sales		10 294		8 980
Opening stock	468		385	
Purchases	4 256		3 678	
	4 724		4 063	
Closing stock	612		468	
Cost of sales		4 112		3 595
Gross profit		6 182		5 385
Wages and salaries	3 662		2 945	
Rent	150		150	
Power	125		101	
Distribution	90		80	
Maintenance and repairs	365		210	
Marketing	195		160	
Depreciation	525		495	
Other	195	5 307	153	4 294
Operating profit		875		1 091
Interest payable		180		180
Net profit (after interest)		695		911
Taxation		170		221
Net profit after tax		525		690
Dividends		200		300
Retained profit		325		390
Retained profit b/f		719		329
Retained profit c/f		1 044		719

Analysis of gross profit

	1995			1994		
	Sales	Cost of sales	Gross profit	Sales	Cost of sales	Gross profit
Theme park entrance	1 319	0	1 319	1 480	0	1 480
Sale of novelty products	8 250	3 787	4 463	6 800	3 300	3 500
Catering	725	325	400	700	295	405
Total	10 294	4 112	6 182	8 980	3 595	5 385

Mirage PLC
Theme park and novelty products
Balance sheet
as at 31 December 1995

	1995 £000s		1994 £000s	
Fixed assets				
Land and buildings		1 000		1 000
Motor vehicles		425		350
Fixtures and fittings		1 896		1 740
		3 321		3 090
Current assets				
Stocks	612		468	
Debtors	305		200	
Prepayments	42		35	
Bank	0		216	
	959		919	
Current liabilities				
Trade creditors	270		380	
Tax and dividends	200		210	
Bank overdraft	66		0	
	536		590	
Net current assets		423		329
Total net assets (capital employed)		3 744		3 419
Long-term liabilities				
Debentures		1 200		1 200
		2 544		**2 219**
Capital				
Authorised share capital – 2 000 000 shares of £1 each		2 000		2 000
Issued share capital		1 500		1 500
Profit and loss account		1 044		719
		2 544		**2 219**

Note: The market price of ordinary shares in Mirage PLC was £2.50 on 31 December 1995 (£3.40 on 31 December 1994).

Return on capital employed (ROCE)

ROCE indicates how well the business has used the financial resources it has invested in it. The business should return at least the weighted average cost of finance.

$$\text{Return on capital employed} = \frac{\text{Operating profit}}{\text{Total net assets}} \times 100\%$$

ROCE for our case study Mirage:

$$\text{For 1995} = \frac{875}{3744} \times 100\% = 23.4\%$$

$$\text{For 1994} = \frac{1091}{3419} \times 100\% = 31.9\%$$

The ROCE for 1995 looks good, but the 1994 return was 31.9 per cent, so there has been some erosion in the effective use of capital between the two years. This situation will be of concern to Mirage and further analysis is warranted to identify its cause.

Return on equity (ROE)

The ROE indicates how well the business has used the financial resources invested in it by the ordinary shareholders. It differs from ROCE because of the gearing effect of partially financing the business with fixed-return finance. The numerator and denominator are different from those used for the ROCE to reflect this change in perspective.

Return on equity =

$$\frac{\text{Net profit (after tax and pref. dividend)}}{\text{Ordinary shares and reserves}} \times 100\%$$

Return on equity of Mirage:

$$\text{For 1995} = \frac{525}{2544} \times 100\% = 20.6\%$$

$$\text{For 1994} = \frac{690}{2219} \times 100\% = 32.0\%$$

The ROE for Mirage has deteriorated markedly, but is in line with the drop in ROCE, bearing in mind gearing has only fallen slightly during the year. Shareholders will not be happy.

Profit margin

The profit margin measures operating profit as a proportion of sales. The ratio is an indication of how profitable the business is without considering the cost of funds utilised in the business. As some expenses of businesses are fixed costs, we would expect the profit margin to increase as sales increased, provided gross margin percentage is maintained.

$$\text{Profit margin} = \frac{\text{Operating profit}}{\text{Sales}} \times 100\%$$

Profit margin of Mirage:

$$\text{For 1995} = \frac{875}{10\,294} \times 100\% = 8.5\%$$

$$\text{For 1994} = \frac{1091}{8980} \times 100\% = 12.1\%$$

Even though sales increased in 1995, the proportion of operating profit actually fell. The size of the fall is a worrying feature of these accounts for Mirage. Its fall will

be a major reason for the deterioration in ROCE and so reasons for it must be ascertained if Mirage's management is to control the situation. As operating profit is the difference between gross profit and expenses, the next step is to calculate ratios for gross profit and expenses to find reasons for the fall in profit margin.

Gross profit to sales

Gross profit to sales depends on the selling price of goods compared with the cost of buying or manufacturing them. Most businesses should expect to make a gross profit of 40–60 per cent if the business is to make a profit after paying for other expenses.

$$\text{Gross profit to sales} = \frac{\text{Gross profit}}{\text{Sales}} \times 100\%$$

Gross profit to sales for Mirage:

$$\text{For 1995} = \frac{6182}{10\,294} \times 100\% = 60.1\%$$

$$\text{For 1994} = \frac{5385}{8980} \times 100\% = 60.0\%$$

The ratios are similar for both years; the reason for the drop in profit margin would not appear to be found here. However, it would be valuable to know the gross profit to sales for novelty products and catering separately. Make these calculations and evaluate your results.

Expenses to sales

Calculated as:

$$\text{Expenses to sales} = \frac{\text{Expenses}}{\text{Sales}} \times 100\%$$

Expenses to sales for Mirage:

$$\text{For 1995} = \frac{5307}{10\,294} \times 100\% = 51.6\%$$

$$\text{For 1994} = \frac{4294}{8980} \times 100\% = 47.8\%$$

Clearly, expenses have increased by more than the increase in sales and this feature of Mirage's accounts must be the main reason for the company's drop in profit margin. Expenses have consumed 3.8 per cent more of sales revenue in 1995 than they did in 1994. Mirage's expenses must be analysed further if the true reason for its adverse profitability trend is to be monitored and controlled.

Taking the wages and salaries:

$$\text{For } 1995 = \frac{3662}{10\ 294} \times 100\% = 35.6\%$$

$$\text{For } 1994 = \frac{2945}{8980} \times 100\% = 32.8\%$$

Salaries and wages account for 2.8 per cent of the 3.8 per cent adverse variance from 1994 to 1995. If reasons are not known for the variance, then the situation should be investigated. Of course, just because an adverse trend exists does not necessarily indicate an unavoidable or indeed an unwarranted cost. It may be that the business has raised salaries during the year so that employees can share in the success of the business. Or perhaps more personnel have been taken on and trained in readiness for greater sales in the future. In both cases the current adverse trend can be explained in terms of goodwill or greater capacity and this should bode well for the future. The important issue is to find reasons for unexplained trends or differences with comparable businesses.

Task

For each of the other expenses listed in Mirage's profit and loss account, calculate their percentage of sales for both 1995 and 1994. Find which are the main items that have contributed to the other 1 per cent of the expenses variance.

Current ratio

The current ratio is a measure of financial liquidity. It compares cash and assets that should soon be converted into cash, to liabilities that will soon require payment.

$$\text{Current or working capital ratio} = \frac{\text{Current assets}}{\text{Current liabilities}}$$

Current ratio for Mirage:

$$\text{For } 1995 = \frac{959}{536} = 1.79$$

$$\text{For } 1994 = \frac{919}{590} = 1.56$$

It is important that there are sufficient resources to pay short-term liabilities and so a ratio of around 2 is often recommended. However, this is an arbitrary figure and some financially strong businesses have ratios that are significantly less. For example, the current ratio for J. Sainsbury PLC as at 12 March 1994 was only 0.47, from 0.53 in March 1993. Different industries require

different ratios. The food retailers have relatively low stocks and debtors, but enjoy strong and stable cash flows from which to pay current liabilities.

Acid test ratio

The acid or quick test ratio is a more stringent test of liquidity than the current ratio as it excludes stocks from the calculation. Stocks are less liquid than other current assets because they have to be sold before money can be collected (perhaps on credit terms) and so may not provide funds soon enough to pay short-term liabilities.

$$\text{Acid or quick test ratio} = \frac{\text{Current assets} - \text{stock}}{\text{Current liabilities}}$$

Acid test for Mirage:

$$\text{For } 1995 = \frac{(959 - 612)}{536} = 0.65$$

$$\text{For } 1994 = \frac{(919 - 468)}{590} = 0.76$$

Most businesses should be looking for a ratio of around 1, although like the current ratio it does depend upon the type of business. Mirage, like Sainsbury's, does receive a significant part of its sales receipts on cash terms and so these figures do not in themselves indicate liquidity problems. The deterioration in the ratio may be of more of a concern than its actual value.

Debtor days

The measurement of debtor days is an indication of how long the average credit customer took to pay the business. For the external analyst it is not always possible to determine the value of sales on credit, in which case a general measure of credit extended to customers could be calculated based on total sales. Care must also be taken when extracting the debtor figure from the accounts. Trade debtors are those who owe the business for sales items only; a set of published accounts for a company will include an analysis of total debtors in the notes to its accounts.

$$\text{Debtor days} = \frac{\text{Average trade debtors}}{\text{Credit sales}} \times 365$$

In cases where there is limited information concerning debtors it may be necessary to use the period-end debtor balances only to make the calculation. This is the case with Mirage PLC. We could, of course, calculate the average debtors for 1995 which is $(305+200) \div 2 = 252.5$ but we could not do the same for 1994. The most important rule when calculating ratios for comparison purposes is consistency, so for Mirage we will use period-end debtor balances.

Debtor days for Mirage:

$$\text{For 1995} = \frac{305 \times 365}{4125} = 27 \text{ days}$$

$$\text{For 1994} = \frac{200 \times 365}{3400} = 21 \text{ days}$$

Half the novelty products sales were on a credit basis and so it is that figure we use to determine the average time taken for a customer to pay their debts.

Mirage's debtor days are not particularly high – any period less than 30 days would be enviable for most businesses. What may be worrying is the adverse trend. Reasons for customers taking extended credit compared to 1994 should be investigated.

Creditor days

The period taken to pay for credit purchases indicates the extent to which the firm is using suppliers to finance its business. Supplier credit should be maximised where possible because trade credit is free provided no settlement discounts are lost. As with debtor days, care should be taken to ensure the information extracted from the accounts results in correct and consistent calculations for both periods. For Mirage, period-end balances will once again have to suffice.

$$\text{Creditor days} = \frac{\text{Average trade creditors}}{\text{Credit purchases}} \times 365$$

Creditor days for Mirage:

$$\text{For 1995} = \frac{270 \times 365}{4256} = 23 \text{ days}$$

$$\text{For 1994} = \frac{380 \times 365}{3678} = 38 \text{ days}$$

Mirage took less time to pay its suppliers in 1995 than it did in 1994 and reasons for this should be investigated. Shorter payment periods could be justified if it were found the business was taking discounts for prompt payment. However, there are no discounts in the profit and loss account to support this idea.

Stock turn

To ensure efficient use of funds tied up in stocks, the level of stocks should be kept to a minimum. Of course, the greater the level of business activity, the greater the level of stocks to service customer demand. We can measure the efficiency of stock control by relating the stock balance to the level of stock usage.

$$\text{Stock turn} = \frac{\text{Annual cost of sales}}{\text{Average stock}}$$

The resulting ratio indicates how many times a year the average £1 in stock is converted into sales.

Stock turn for Mirage:

$$\text{For 1995} = \frac{4112}{(468 + 612) \div 2} = \frac{4112}{540} = 7.6 \text{ times}$$

$$\text{For 1994} = \frac{3595}{(385 + 468) \div 2} = \frac{3595}{426.5} = 8.4 \text{ times}$$

Mirage turned its stock over fewer times in 1995 than in 1994. If we wanted to know how long the average item of stock remained in the stores, then we could divide the stock turn into 365 days. This gives us 48 days for 1995 and 43 days for 1994.

Gearing ratio

We discussed the gearing ratio on page 155. There are a number of different ways in which the ratio can be calculated, so again it is very important to compare only ratios that have been calculated on the same basis. Fixed-return capital generally refers to preference share capital plus long-term debt including debentures. Some analysts compare fixed-return capital to total capital employed. Another valid method includes short-term loans and overdrafts with fixed-return capital, on the basis that they all represent prior changes before earnings can be attributed to ordinary shareholders.

$$\text{Gearing ratio} = \frac{\text{Fixed-return capital}}{\text{Ordinary shareholder funds}}$$

Gearing ratio for Mirage:

$$\text{For 1995} = \frac{1200}{2544} = 0.47$$

$$\text{For 1994} = \frac{1200}{2219} = 0.54$$

There has been little change in the gearing ratio as Mirage has the same amount of prior charge capital in both years.

Interest cover

By relating profit before interest to interest payments, it is possible to determine the relative burden of interest payments on the earnings capability of the business. The higher the ratio, the less risk there is that payments will push the business into a loss situation if earnings were to fall.

$$\text{Interest cover} = \frac{\text{Profit (before interest and tax)}}{\text{Interest payable for year}}$$

Interest cover for Mirage:

$$\text{For 1995} = \frac{875}{180} = 4.9 \text{ times}$$

$$\text{For 1994} = \frac{1091}{180} = 6.1 \text{ times}$$

Not surprisingly, with the drop in operating profits, the interest cover has fallen in 1995. Despite this, the interest payments are covered nearly five times and the debenture-holders should not feel at risk.

Earnings per share

Earnings per share (EPS) is an important measure for determining the value of a share. In addition to dividend payments, the EPS includes amounts retained by the business for internal investment. It therefore provides a more accurate figure of wealth created for shareholders than the amount of dividend paid out per share.

$$\text{Earnings per share} =$$

$$\frac{\text{Net profit (after tax and preference dividends)}}{\text{Number of ordinary shares}}$$

Earnings per share for Mirage:

$$\text{For 1995} = \frac{525}{2000} = 26.25\text{p}$$

$$\text{For 1994} = \frac{690}{2000} = 34.5\text{p}$$

With the number of shares issued not changing, the fall in earnings per share is directly proportionate to the reduction in after-tax profits.

Price earnings

For listed companies, the price earnings (P/E) ratio shows how many times current earnings the capital market values the company. It is a measure of confidence in the growth potential of the company and its business sector.

$$\text{Price earnings ratio} = \frac{\text{Market price of share}}{\text{Earnings per share}}$$

Price earnings ratio for Mirage:

$$\text{For 1995} = \frac{2.50}{0.2625} = 9.5$$

$$\text{For 1994} = \frac{3.40}{0.345} = 9.9$$

The fall in share price by 90p was slightly more than the corresponding fall in EPS and has resulted in a drop in the P/E ratio. The financial markets obviously believe the fall in profits is a permanent situation and, with a relatively low ratio, do not foresee significant prospects for future growth.

Asset utilisation

The effective use made of assets can be measured by relating sales value to net assets employed. The higher asset utilisation is, assuming stable profit margins, the greater will be the return on capital employed.

$$\text{Utilisation of total net assets} =$$

$$\frac{\text{Sales}}{\text{Average net assets employed}}$$

Asset utilisation for Mirage:

$$\text{For 1995} = \frac{10\,294}{3744} = 2.75$$

$$\text{For 1994} = \frac{8980}{3419} = 2.63$$

Despite signs of weaker control of working capital balances (stock turn, debtor days and creditor days), the utilisation of capital employed has improved in 1995. This is due to better use of fixed assets; each £1 of fixed assets helped generate £3.10 of sales in 1995, from £2.91 in 1994 (check the figures yourself).

The results of Mirage in summary

Despite sales increasing by 14.6 per cent, profits fell in 1995, largely due to a greater proportion of sales being consumed by wages and salaries. If wages and salaries had been 32.8 per cent of sales in 1995 as in 1994, then profits before tax would have been £286 000 higher. This would have given a ROCE of 31 per cent, very similar to 1994. There were other factors both helping and adversely affecting ROCE, such as better utilisation of fixed assets, but the wages bill is the single biggest cause for concern in an otherwise promising situation. Other areas worth further investigation would be the change in mix of business away from theme park entrance fees and the reduced use of working capital.

Summary of accounting ratios

See Figure 8.27 on the next page. The ratios used in the case study are not comprehensive and will not all be appropriate or essential to every situation. While these ratios are commonly accepted as providing meaningful

Figure 8.27 Guide to accounting ratios

Ratio	Calculation	Measure	Better if
Profitability			
Return on capital employed (ROCE)	$\dfrac{\text{Operating profit}}{\text{Average total net assets}} \times 100\%$	%	High
Return on equity	$\dfrac{\text{Net profit (after tax and pref. dividend)}}{\text{Average ordinary shares and reserves}} \times 100\%$	%	High
Profit margin	$\dfrac{\text{Operating profit}}{\text{Sales}} \times 100\%$	%	High
Gross profit to sales	$\dfrac{\text{Gross profit}}{\text{Sales}} \times 100\%$	%	High
Expenses to sales (in total and by expense type)	$\dfrac{\text{Expenses}}{\text{Sales}} \times 100\%$	%	Low
Investment ratios			
Gearing ratio	$\dfrac{\text{Fixed return capital}}{\text{Ordinary shareholder funds}}$	Number	Less than 1
Earnings per share (EPS)	$\dfrac{\text{Net profit (after tax and preference dividend)}}{\text{Number of ordinary shares}}$	Pence	High
Price earnings (P/E) ratio	$\dfrac{\text{Market price of share}}{\text{Earnings per share}}$	Number	High
Dividend cover	$\dfrac{\text{Net profit (after tax and interest, before dividends)}}{\text{Dividends}}$	Number	High
Dividend yield	$\dfrac{\text{Dividend (gross)}}{\text{Market price of share}} \times 100\%$	%	High
Earnings yield	$\dfrac{\text{Earnings per share}}{\text{Share price}} \times 100\%$	%	High
Interest cover	$\dfrac{\text{Profit (before interest and tax)}}{\text{Interest payable for year}}$	Number	High
Financial ratios			
Current or working capital ratio	$\dfrac{\text{Current assets}}{\text{Current liabilities}}$	Number	Usually 2 or more
Acid or quick test ratio	$\dfrac{\text{Current assets} - \text{stock}}{\text{Current liabilities}}$	Number	Usually 1 or more
Debtor days	$\dfrac{\text{Average trade debtors}}{\text{Credit sales}} \times 365$	Days	Low
Creditor days	$\dfrac{\text{Average trade creditors}}{\text{Credit purchases}} \times 365$	Days	High
Stock turn	$\dfrac{\text{Annual cost of sales}}{\text{Average stock}}$	Number	High
Utilisation of resources			
Utilisation of total net assets	$\dfrac{\text{Sales}}{\text{Average net assets employed}}$	Number	High
Utilisation of fixed assets	$\dfrac{\text{Sales}}{\text{Average fixed assets}}$	Number	High
Utilisation of current assets	$\dfrac{\text{Sales}}{\text{Average current assets}}$	Number	High
Utilisation of working capital	$\dfrac{\text{Sales}}{\text{Average net current assets}}$	Number	High

information for many circumstances, it is important to consider the context in which they are to be used.

Ratio framework

To enable ratios to be used in a systematic fashion, it may be useful to view them in a logical framework (see Figure 8.28).

Figure 8.28 Ratio framework

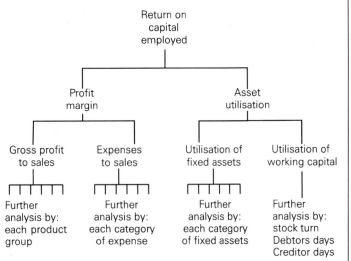

When analysing the accounts of Mirage we knew that ROCE had dropped in 1995, and using the framework we know that this must either have been due to a change in profit margin, asset utilisation or a mixture of the two. (This is so because ROCE is the product of profit margin and asset utilisation.) In the case of Mirage it was because of a deterioration in profit margin; asset utilisation actually improved. We then checked the next level, gross margin and expenses to sales. Expenses to sales were high and with further analysis it was found that one expense item in particular was to blame.

Information is rarely complete, so the important rule is consistency when calculating accounting ratios. It may not be possible to use the precise ratios planned because similar information is not available for all periods or for all businesses being compared – for example, the debtor and creditor calculations for Mirage. The important point being to evaluate the results having regard to any inherent information deficiencies.

Cash operating cycle

Another measure for reviewing the efficient use of working capital is the cash operating cycle, measuring the length of time that funds are tied up in working capital.

Cash operating cycle =
   Stock turnover days + Debtor days – Creditor days

For manufacturing businesses that have stock in the categories raw material, work in progress and finished goods stock, it is necessary to calculate stock turnover days for each category of stock, relating each balance to a relevant throughput value, i.e. raw material used, cost of goods manufactured and cost of sales respectively.

The cash operating cycle for Mirage in 1995 was 52 days (48 + 27 − 23) and in 1994, 26 days (43 + 21 − 38). The cycle has doubled in length and should be a cause for concern.

The cash operating cycle is a rather crude measure. Stock and creditors relate only to materials purchased whereas debtors also contain labour, overhead and profit elements. However, it is a consolidated measure of working capital efficiency that may be appropriate for a summary management report.

Task

Rowland Furniture produces quality furniture using traditional labour-intensive methods. In an economic climate where many consumers are looking for value for money in addition to quality products, sales are forecast to be 20 per cent down in the coming year compared to last year. Rowland's sales director believes the drop in sales units could be made up if sales price was trimmed by 10 per cent. Alex Rowland decides to accept this proposal, but costs need to be cut as the profit margin percentage should not be allowed to fall by more than 5 per cent from last year's 20 per cent. Last year's profit was £200 000 when cost analysis as a percentage of sales was: materials and other production costs 25 per cent; labour costs 25 per cent; and fixed indirect expenses (which will remain stable in money terms) 30 per cent.

Labour costs are considered to be the real target. Work practices are to be reviewed, including the introduction of additional hand machinery and standardisation of some processes. It is agreed the savings will be made by not replacing two workers retiring shortly. Customers' perception of quality is thought not to be afffected. To support the monitoring of the profit margin ratio, the management accountant suggests the following subsidiary ratios should also be monitored:

- production cost to sales
- labour costs to sales
- actual labour hours for each product compared to last year's averages.

1 What net profit would have been earned if no changes were made for the coming year?

2 Calculate this year's planned net profit.

3 For a wardrobe which routinely took twenty worker hours to make, what time is now required to achieve the stated profit margin percentage (assuming no change in wage rates)?

4 Why do you believe the accountant recommended each of the supporting ratios?

Task

As a management consultant in the catering industry you have been asked by Red Ltd to evaluate its financial performance for the two years 1994 and 1995. You have also been provided with information concerning Orange Ltd for comparison purposes, another catering firm in the same town.

Using accounting ratios, analyse and evaluate the performance of the two companies and prepare a report to the management of Red Ltd based on your findings.

Segmental reporting

Difficulty can be experienced when attempting to interpret the accounts of companies involved in more than one type of business and operating in more than one geographical area. From the profit and loss account it is possible to determine the average profit margin on each £1 of sales, but this does not tell us how profitable each type of business is or the company's relative success in different areas of the world. Companies that engage in more than one business segment are required by Statement of Standard Accounting Practice 25 to disclose separately for each class:

- turnover
- profit
- net assets.

Costs and assets that cannot be attributable to a particular part of the business need to be identified separately to ensure that the analysis provided reconciles to the totals disclosed in the profit and loss account and balance sheet.

Profit and loss accounts

	Orange Ltd 1994 £000s	1995 £000s	Red Ltd 1994 £000s	1995 £000s
Sales	2500	2600	1900	1850
Cost of sales	1000	1010	850	860
Gross profit	1500	1590	1050	990
Wages	800	825	600	610
Rent	200	200	150	160
Other	200	220	180	170
Total expenses	1200	1245	930	940
Net profit	300	345	120	50
Dividends	200	220	100	30
Retained profit	100	125	20	20

Balance sheets

	Orange Ltd 1994 £000s	1995 £000s	Red Ltd 1994 £000s	1995 £000s
Fixed assets	1000	900	750	900
Current assets				
Stocks	110	130	90	95
Debtors	50	70	150	300
Cash	40	25	50	0
Total	200	225	290	395
Current liabilities				
Trade creditors	200	200	100	80
Bank overdraft	0	0	0	355
Total	200	200	100	435
Net current assets	0	25	190	−40
Capital employed	1000	925	940	860
Less long-term liabilities	300	100	300	300
Total net assets	700	825	640	560
Capital and reserves:				
Share capital	500	500	500	500
Profit and loss account	200	325	140	160
	700	825	640	560

Task

First Leisure Corporation is a large company in the leisure industry, operating such well-known leisure facilities as Paradox night clubs, Super Bowls and Blackpool Tower. In June 1993 the company acquired its bingo business.

	26 weeks to 1.5.94 £m	26 weeks to 1.5.93 £m	Year to 31.10.93 £m	Year to 31.10.92 £m
Turnover:				
Resorts	13.4	11.9	41.9	40.1
Dancing	25.6	22.8	44.5	38.2
Sports	18.9	17.3	32.1	30.2
Bingo	5.0	0	3.3	0
	62.9	52.0	121.8	108.5
Operating profit:				
Resorts	1.3	1.6	11.7	12.3
Dancing	8.5	7.5	14.5	12.5
Sports	6.6	7.6	13.7	14.1
Bingo	1.5	0	0.9	0
Theatres	0.3	0.1	0.4	0.2
Central administration expenses	−2.9	−2.8	−5.9	−5.8
	15.3	14.0	35.3	33.3
Net assets:				
Resorts			84.9	106.7
Dancing			71.7	100.9
Sports			82.0	89.5
Bingo			13.5	0
Theatres			6.7	6.4
Administration			4.1	3.6
			262.9	307.1

1 Using the information above, calculate the following financial ratios for each part of business: (a) return on capital employed, (b) utilisation of net assets, (c) profit margin.

2 Evaluate the financial performance of First Leisure.

3 What trends do you believe require monitoring for the future?

Using annual reports

Accounts for limited companies are contained in an annual report that also includes a directors' report. It is not unusual for companies to provide other reports, perhaps from the chairman, chief executive, or managing director. They provide a valuable narrative to the accounts by describing the events behind the figures. Significant events may include programmes for buying or selling fixed assets, new financing arrangements or changes in accounting policy.

Case Study
Dixons PLC
Accounts 30 April 1994

Chairman's statement

This has been a year of considerable progress. The restructuring of our business, although necessitating substantial exceptional charges, has strengthened the Group and enhanced its prospects. Profit before exceptional items (£238.5 million) and taxation was £73.3 million, only marginally down on last year, and we are proposing a 6.5 per cent increase in total Ordinary dividends to 6.60 pence per share.

Chief Executive's review

The most significant cause of lower operating profit was a reduction in gross margins in Dixons and Currys.

Dixons
Dixons sales were £520.5 million, a decrease of 1 per cent overall and 3 per cent like for like. Performance was affected by declines in the camcorder and computer games consoles markets, of which Dixons has large shares. Sales of television, video and audio products, and business equipment and related software were ahead. Dixons gained a significant share of the fast-growing retail market for mobile communications products.

Dixons' offering is becoming increasingly focused on carry-home products and related accessories and software. These categories are well suited to High Street trading.

Currys Superstores
A key element of Currys' strategy over recent years has been the restructuring of its property portfolio through investment in out-of-town Superstores and the closure of High Street stores. Superstores are taking an increasing share of electrical sales, reflecting customer preference for this format and continued expansions of selling space. Sales per square foot are now at similar levels to those achieved in Currys High Street stores, but operating cost ratios are considerably lower.

Currys High Street
During 1993/4, 27 Currys High Street stores closed, taking total closures over the past few years to over 200 units . . . and around 61 further closures are planned before the end of the 1994/5 financial year. Store closure costs are estimated to be £20.0 million

Dixons PLC Segmental information	Turnover £m	1993/4 Operating profit/loss £m	Net assets £m	Turnover £m	1992/3 Operating profit/loss £m	Net assets £m
Continuing operations						
UK retail – base	1402.1	72.3	142.7	1274.3	77.0	121.8
– exceptional	0.0	−24.5	−15.9	0.0	0.0	0.0
European property	176.2	9.5	133.0	45.4	11.4	116.3
	1578.3	57.3	259.8	1319.7	88.4	238.1
Discontinued operations						
UK retail	4.9	−0.2		49.6	0.6	−2.2
US retail	308.6	−13.0		611.9	−22.4	93.0
UK property	29.6	−0.3		4.7	−1.7	33.6
Utilisation of provisions	0.0	0.3		0.0	1.7	0.0
	343.1	−13.2		666.2	−21.8	124.4
	1921.4	44.1	259.8	1985.9	66.6	362.5
Net operating assets			259.8			362.5
Net unallocated liabilities			−25.2			−147.2
Net interest bearing current assets			50.0			74.3
Net assets			284.6			289.6

Note: UK retail exceptional charges comprise provisions of £20.0 million for store closure costs and £4.5 million for the rationalisation of the Group's administrative offices.

before taxation, which has been charged as an exceptional item against 1993/4 operating profit.

Questions for discussion

1 *Evaluate Dixons' results for 1993/4.*
2 *What does the information tell you about the company's future prospects?*
3 *Using a recent copy of the* Financial Times, *compare Dixons' P/E ratio with other companies in the retail sector. What can you deduce from the exercise?*

Using computers

For those involved regularly in the interpretation of accounts, the use of computers can be of benefit. Specialist modelling programs can be used but spreadsheets are also effective and flexible. Once a standard proforma sheet has been created, subsequent sets of data need only be keyed in. Advantages include time saving, increased accuracy, improved presentation of output, easy extension for further periods and ensured consistency between company sets.

Task

Create a spreadsheet model to calculate a full range of accounting ratios and demonstrate its use, using the Body Shop accounts on pages 165–7.

Limitations of financial performance indicators

Financial performance indicators in the form of ratios place significant emphasis on short-term results. Shareholder ratios, such as earnings per share and the primary ratio return on capital employed, are subject to accounting conventions that might deter businesses from pursuing policies that are in their long-term interests. For example, most expenditure on research and development and all staff welfare costs, including training, are charged against the current year's profits even though some or all of the benefits might accrue in subsequent years. Listed companies that are subject to the rigours of the stock market have to recognise that financial performance criteria are the main tools used by investors and so aim to produce good short-term results.

Other limitations

■ It must also be recognised that results may be distorted because of non-recurring items. An inefficient factory may have been closed down and the costs of laying off workers have deflated profits in one year. There is a need to either adjust figures in the light of such occurrences or provide a narrative for any variances caused. While accounting regulations in recent years have required greater information concerning exceptional items and different classes of businesses, it is likely analysts will not possess all the information necessary to come to full and accurate conclusions.

- The external analyst has to use information that is a minimum of several months old.
- Comparison of results between businesses is often difficult as rarely are the business activities of one business identical to those of another.
- Some values may have been affected more than others by changes in price levels, distorting the analysis if care is not taken. In particular, the value of property used in a business will very much depend on when it was purchased. Low property valuations will result in artificially high returns on capital employed.
- The valuations used in the balance sheet depend on the vagaries of accounting policies adopted. Where different businesses are being compared, the accounts of each should be restated on a like basis before ratios are calculated. The policies relating to the depreciation of fixed assets, the capitalisation of research and development expenditure and the valuation of stocks are all examples of areas that could make comparison difficult.

Despite these problems, financial performance indicators do have a valuable part to play in the management of a business. Accounting ratios do not provide immediate answers, but they provoke searching questions that should result in tighter control and a better understanding of the business. Where financial indicators are inadequate for helping to direct the business towards its strategic goals, they should be complemented with non-finanical ratios.

The two types of performance indicators, financial and non-financial, can create tensions where the achievement of one type of measure appears to undermine the attainment of the other. This is particularly so in the short term. For example, to develop new products and processes and to upgrade customer care often involves costs that will only be recouped in the long run.

However, with care, businesses should be able to use both types of performance indicators to achieve the organisation's objectives. It requires forethought and a view for the long term.

Task

The new managing director of Chemco Ltd has identified skill shortages not covered by the courses available at the local college. She and the rest of the board decide that an in-house training facility to provide tailor-made courses is essential if the company is to survive in the long term. However, they had to recognise the cost of the training building, trainers and the productive time lost while workers attended the courses. Financial performance indicators such as profit to sales and return on capital employed would deteriorate in the short term.

Recommend performance measurements that would be appropriate to Chemco's situation.

Strategic perspective of costs

In recent years many businesses have experienced ever faster changes in their operating environment, and management accountancy has come under increasing pressure to provide information relevant to strategic issues. Many of the techniques and reporting processes used by management accountants are focused on the internal operations of business, with an emphasis on cost efficiencies. The challenge now is to provide information that helps management more fully to understand changes in market conditions and to identify activities that help achieve corporate objectives.

Case Study
Compaq

'Once the fastest growing firm in American corporate history, Compaq had by 1991 grown fat and lazy, standing aloof while new, nimbler rivals undercut its prices.

'Mr Pfeiffer's recovery strategy was disarmingly simple: cut costs to the bone, then use Compaq's economies of scale and powerful brand to drive out the small "clone makers", which by 1992 commanded 60 per cent of the PC market. And forget the industry tradition of 40 per cent plus profit margins. Mr Pfeiffer reckoned that if he could put Compaq in what he calls "cost leadership mode", the firm could get by on a gross margin of 20–25 per cent – and still clear a decent net profit.

'Compaq has executed its battle plan with remarkable precision. In June 1992 it introduced a new range of

Figure 8.29 Price of PCs in $

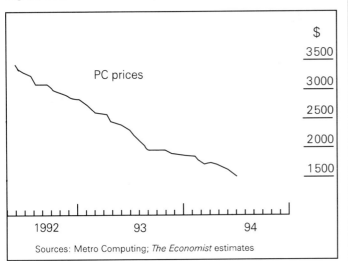

Sources: Metro Computing; *The Economist* estimates

Figure 8.30 Compaq's sales and net profit

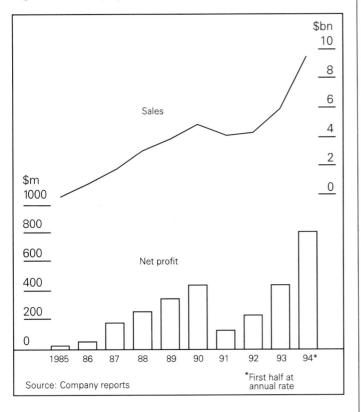

Source: Company reports

*First half at annual rate

PCs that were a third cheaper than their predecessors – and which undercut the price of many rivals. And it has continued to cut its prices by 20–30 per cent a year ever since, forcing many rivals to do likewise. This year Compaq overtook IBM and Apple to become the world's largest PC maker, with a 10 per cent share of the global market by volume.

'As Compaq has cut prices it has vastly improved its efficiency. The firm's combined labour and overhead costs have shrunk by 75 per cent in the past two years. Revenues per manufacturing employee now stand at $1.5m. It is making money – lots of it. Although its gross profit margin has tumbled from 43 per cent in 1990 to 27 per cent in the first half of this year, its net profits have risen sharply. In the first half of 1994, Compaq made a profit of $423m, more than double the level in the same period of 1993. Its sales soared by 47 per cent to $4.8 billion.

'Other firms have done less well . . . in Europe, on which PC companies once relied to recoup their American losses, price cutting has driven out more than 100 small clone makers.'

(Source: *The Economist*, 17 September 1994)

Questions for discussion

1 How has Compaq used its knowledge of cost behaviour to become the number one PC manufacturer?
2 Using rough figures:
   a How many computers is Compaq projected to sell in 1994 compared to 1992?
   b Analyse the results for 1990 and 1994. Prepare profit and loss accounts for 1990 and 1994 to include sales, cost of sales, gross profit, expenses and net profit. What can we learn from the figures?

Case Study
The PC software industry

Compare the situation in the hardware sector with that for software firms.

'The PC industry's troubles have now spread to software companies, for two main reasons. First, cheaper PCs have made applications software look expensive: few buyers are willing to pay $500 for software to use on a $1000 PC. Second, applications software is becoming increasingly commoditised – one spreadsheet is much like another. So sellers are having to compete on price . . . last year, the price of such software fell by a quarter in America and by a third in Europe.

'The price war has come at a time when software industry's costs are rising fast. According to Datamonitor, an industry consultancy, spending on sales and marketing now stands at around 40 per cent of big software firms' annual revenues, and may soon hit 50 per cent. Expenditure on research and development, by contrast, has stuck at around 14 per *cent. Given the rapidly rising costs of developing new software – each generation tends to be more complex and labour intensive than the last – that may be too little to save even some of the software business's best-known names from extinction.'*

(Source: *The Economist,* 17 September 1994)

Questions for discussion

1 *What are the similarities and differences in the circumstances of hardware and software firms?*

2 *What possible strategies could firms in each sector adopt to overcome their current problems?*

3 *In what way will a knowledge of cost structures be important in the future?*

Summary

It is important for managers of all businesses to understand how costs are incurred and how they behave with changes in activity. Comparing levels of costs with competitors could have a significant impact on corporate strategy. Cash flows can be categorised according to operating activities, investing activities and financing arrangements. Net cash flows relating to operating and investing activities need to be coordinated in a financial plan with sources of finance. Sources of finance should be adequate and appropriate to business needs. The business should not rely on short-term finance for long-term needs, and the level of gearing should be appropriate to the operating risk of the business. There should be an appropriate spread of debt maturity dates to match the anticipated cash flows of the business.

The budgeting process makes a valuable contribution towards the effective and efficient management of the business. Budgeting impinges on business planning, coordination, communication, monitoring and control. Financial performance is reported using three main financial statements: the profit and loss account, the balance sheet and the cash flow statement. Interpretation of these financial statements is aided by the use of accounting ratios. The use of financial performance indicators can provide a valuable insight into business performance and provide a starting point for control and continued improvement in performance.

Further reading

- *Management and Cost Accounting,* 3rd edition, by Colin Drury. Chapman and Hall, 1992.
- *Foundations of Business Accounting* by Roy Dodge. Chapman and Hall, 1993.
- *Management Accounting,* published monthly by the Chartered Institute of Management Accountants.
- *Company Accounts – analysis, interpretation and understanding,* 3rd edition, by Maurice Pendlebury and Roger Groves. Routledge, 1994.
- *Fundamentals of Managerial Accounting and Finance,* 2nd edition, by Roger W. Mills and John Robertson. Mars Business Associates, 1991.
- *Financial Management,* 5th edition, by R. Brockington, D.P. Publications, 1990.
- *Financial Times Guide to Using and Interpreting Company Accounts* by Wendy McKenzie. Pitman, 1994.
- *Managerial Finance* by Alan Parkinson. Butterworth-Heinemann, 1994.
- *Accounting for Business,* 2nd edition, by P. Atrill, D. Harvey and E. McLaney. Butterworth-Heinemann, 1994.

9 Managing information

On completion of this chapter students should be able to:

■ evaluate the scope, key areas within and purposes of a management information system

■ use information technology to store, retrieve and analyse information

■ review systems for monitoring and providing management information

■ evaluate the relevance and appropriateness of information generated from a management information system.

Major information needs and flows

Management has to reach decisions if a business is to operate and achieve its objectives. Decisions can only be made on the basis of the information available, so the management of information is of fundamental importance for business success. The smallest of businesses has the advantage that its decision maker has no need for a formal information system. As soon as a business grows, however, the management function is performed by individuals who are removed from the day-to-day activities, and hence a management information system (MIS) is required. A management information system uses data to produce meaningful information to enable its users to make appropriate decisions to achieve business objectives. The MIS may be either formal or informal, but the bigger and more complex the business, the greater the need for a reliable and consistent process for providing information.

The business writer T. Lucy defines a management information system as:

> '*a system using formalised procedures to provide management at all levels in all functions with appropriate information, based on data from both internal and external sources, to enable them to make timely and effective decisions for planning, directing and controlling the activities for which they are responsible.*'
> – Management Information Systems

The continuing trend towards global markets, where firms compete in a particular market segment on a world-wide basis, has been driven by advances in technology. New systems of transportation have facilitated the movement of goods. However, it is the technology of communication that has broken down national boundaries by transmitting images of different cultures and their associated material products. In addition, information flows concerning market conditions and the means to make and finance transactions have made international trade relatively quick and easy. For many businesses, it is essential that they are viewed in their global context to ensure that information systems provide what management needs.

Case Study
Information giving competitive advantage

Benetton

Benetton operates on a global scale with the efficient movement of goods, minimised stock levels and quick response to customer needs. The business employs relatively few people and is concerned with the logistics of work flow from sub-contract factories through to franchised retail outlets. An essential element of this competitive strategy is the handling of information from point of sale through to production, with products dyed at the last minute to the colours currently being purchased by customers.

Dell

Dell manufactures and direct mails personal computers to countries in Europe from its base in Ireland. The business uses sophisticated stock-control programs and advances in telecommunications to take sales orders, customise the product to customer requirements, arrange delivery and provide after-sales support. Information systems allow the business to bypass the retail chain that other manufacturers utilise, and so cut costs in this price-competitive market.

Questions for discussion

Describe how two other businesses use information as part of their competitive strategy.

Information is increasingly being viewed as a strategic resource to achieve corporate objectives. For some businesses, such as Benetton, managing information is their primary function. Another business that is largely concerned with information processes is The Progressive Corporation.

Case Study
The Progressive Corporation

'The ninth largest car insurance company in the United States, Progressive has been extraordinarily successful in its target market of high-risk drivers. Studiously avoided by other insurers, these customers are profitably welcomed by Progressive. For years, Progressive's secret was a re-engineered underwriting process that was much more detailed and precise than those of their competitors and led to very precise pricing. Eventually, however, Progressive's larger competitors began copying it and invading its niche. Progressive's response was more re-engineering, this time of its claims process. By exploiting a technique called "immediate response", Progressive can now despatch an adjuster to examine a claimant's car on the day of the accident – in many cases, going to the accident site itself. Having protected its turf, Progressive then realised that its new processes would allow it to enter new markets (those of standard and low-risk drivers). Progressive's business strategy is now based on first-class processes that provide high degrees of customer service.'

(Source: *The Economist*, 5 November 1994)

Questions for discussion

1 *Describe the nature of Progressive's operating environment and the main factors that ensure success in it.*
2 *What can Progressive's information processes tell management about this environment?*
3 *Which management functions are being aided by Progressive's information systems?*

The primary function of management is to make decisions within the following framework:

- planning – identifying business objectives and the strategies required to achieve specific goals
- organising and coordinating – putting the strategies into practice, assigning responsibilities and procuring the necessary resources
- leadership and motivation – harnessing the effort of all employees
- control – monitoring actual performance against goals and deciding corrective action if necessary.

These functions are performed by a large number of employees at all levels of the organisation structure. To fulfil these functions, individual managers need information that is relevant, available on time, accurate and in appropriate detail for the task.

The nature of a business does have a bearing on what information its MISs should be reporting (see Figure 9.1).

Features of a MIS

Management information systems consist of:

- physical resources – computers, telephone lines, manual records, etc.
- personnel – human resources necessary to operate the system

Figure 9.1 Examples of types of information required by a business

Type of business	External information	Internal information
Car manufacturer	■ Technological innovations ■ State of world and national economies ■ International trade regulations ■ Market share ■ Political and legal changes	■ Production rate ■ Quality tests ■ Waste ■ Product development lead times
Supermarket chain	■ Market share ■ Competitors' prices ■ Competitors' product and service innovations ■ Changes in population distribution ■ Political and legal changes	■ Sales value per sq. ft. ■ Sales per employee ■ Stock levels ■ Delivery times ■ Number of stock-outs

■ methods – how the physical and human resources are brought together to produce a coherent system.

It is important to appreciate that the term MIS is not restricted to the use of computers. Computers are merely tools to be employed in the information process. In a formalised MIS the elements above are documented and the roles of individual staff are defined as part of their job descriptions. Where there is an interaction between the user and a computer system this is called a **user interface**.

The main categories of systems for management purposes are for:

■ control – monitoring, motivating and taking corrective action if required
■ planning and decision-making.

Control systems

Whatever their strategy, cost leadership or product differentiation, businesses need to be efficient in the use of resources. For businesses to be efficient, management needs information to monitor and control performance.

Closed-loop system

Some business activities are performed where the desired outcome is known with a fair degree of precision. Examples include tolerance in standard production processes, and departmental expenses where budgets can be prepared with some degree of accuracy. Where an outcome can be compared with a previous or expected value, then a closed-loop control system can be utilised (see Figure 9.2). The essential feature of the system is a feedback loop to allow the monitoring of output on the basis of expected values. This type of system often operates on the basis of 'management by exception'. The system reports on conditions of output and inputs that do not conform to a predetermined standard, for example where the number of product rejections has exceeded 1 per cent in the last batch of 1000 items. The control of inputs and processes is part of the system.

Figure 9.2 A closed-loop system

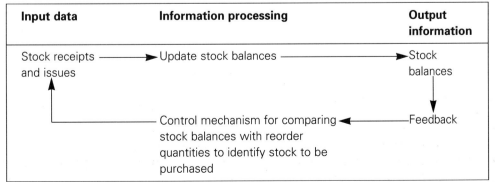

Feedback is also required to give information concerning the effect of decisions, e.g. advertising campaigns, the effect of a new price structure or the methods adopted for handling after-sales complaints. Actual performance should be compared to plan and variances reported and explained promptly. The nature of this type of system means that it uses primarily quantitative information.

Many of the costs incurred by businesses are fixed, so the greater the volume of work, the lower the unit cost. Hence management is concerned with volumes processed, and these should be reported in units of measure that are meaningful to those involved in the operating process, perhaps on a daily basis. For example, car manufacturers may use numbers of vehicles completed, a garage workshop hours of direct labour charged to customers, and a retail outlet money terms. Management knows from past experience and the annual budget that a certain level of performance is required to achieve corporate objectives. Other measures concerning utilisation of resources are used to identify areas for improvement. It is often of particular value to compare the inputs and outputs of the business process. A ratio of this nature is valuable to indicate the operating efficiency of a business. This perspective of efficiency puts an emphasis on the speed of work through the system, and the minimisation of stocks and operating costs.

Automatic closed-loop system

Some business systems provide automatic control without further involvement by management or staff. A prime example is the automatic ordering of stock once the reorder quantity has been passed. The comparison of stock balances with control totals and the automatic printing of purchase orders mean that a time-consuming management function has been largely eliminated.

Open-loop systems

Open systems do not have a feedback loop and so are not control systems at all. In business, many systems at the operational level are best served with a control mechanism; however other systems, including those at higher management levels, require decision-making that cannot easily be pre programmed. In situations that are unstable and subject to unpredictable outside pressures, then management intervention may be required. The important thing is that the management mechanism, and hence the information system required to support it, is appropriate to the circumstances. Many organisations have automated the process of stock ordering, but consider that capital expenditure should be authorised on an item-by-item basis by the managing director or, above a certain limit, by the board of directors. An element of discretion is reserved by management to take into account current environmental issues, together with latest information concerning financial and organisational factors.

Informal information channels, often through personal contacts in the organisation, can make a valuable contribution to the information available to management. Some businesses encourage informal channels of information with an open organisation culture and relatively flat hierarchical structure. Informal systems can also be useful for obtaining external information. Managers may be encouraged to participate in industry associations and local chambers of commerce where informal contacts can be built up.

Information flows

MISs start with the collection of data from data sources, with data flowing through certain processes before it becomes information communicated to managers. To satisfy legal and commercial requirements, particularly for data of a financial nature, it is usual to maintain data stores. These can be accessed for trend analysis in addition to historical reference, and so provide a valuable resource in the provision of management information. As many business transactions are composed of discrete stages, output from one process becomes the input for the

Figure 9.3 Control information needs of a manufacturing business

Stage:	Raw materials	Work in progress	Finished goods	Distribution to customer
Management concern:	Stock turnover	Utilisation of: ■ labour ■ materials ■ machines	Stock turnover	■ Delivery times ■ Load factors ■ Sales per salesperson ■ Average prices

next, but after each process management information may be available (see Chapter 16 for the purchase and sale of stock items).

Data capture

Much of the information that flows through a business emanates from the recording of financial transactions. Other information can be obtained from procedures set up to control business activities, such as machine logs, workers' time sheets and work progress reports. This is often augmented by additional measuring devices such as for the monitoring of external operating conditions.

As business activities use scarce resources, it is inevitable that the recording and processing of business transactions provide much of the raw material for a MIS. Examples include:

- accounting systems – processing financial transactions with customers and suppliers, financial reporting including budgetary control, credit control, payroll and job costing
- personnel systems – databases of employees' details including current skills and training needs
- engineering – computer-aided design and production of bills of materials
- manufacturing – computer-aided manufacturing, production planning, monitoring production efficiency by a variety of methods such as factory throughput volumes, machine utilisation and quality rejection rates
- resource procurement – purchase order systems and stock control
- service functions – allocation of work, e.g. maintenance programmes and measures of productivity
- distribution – sales order processing, planning physical distribution, sales analysis, analysis of response to promotion campaigns and market-research analysis.

Much of the data recorded as a result of these activities can be transformed into useful management information if formalised recording and reporting systems are in place.

The methods adopted for the collection of data depend upon the nature of the transactions and the relative costs of manual procedures and computer systems. They include:

- manual recording on standard forms
- keying in to a computer system
- Electronic Data Interchange (EDI), which enables data to be transferred from one computer system to another – problems of compatibility between systems have so far restricted the use of EDI, although it is widely used in the retail sector where large retailers can pass stock requirement details to suppliers without manual intermediate steps

- electronic input with transactions recorded by scanning equipment, such as reading bar codes on sales at supermarkets (EPOS) and optical character reading by the banks for clearing cheques.

The processing of information

Businesses can accumulate vast volumes of data, largely from the recording of financial transactions. Individually, each piece of data, such as the sale of a vegetable curry in a Marks & Spencer store is a fact which, although important for the accurate monitoring of stock balances, is not sufficient information in itself on which to run a business. If management were presented with every piece of data that the organisation collected, then it would have no time to interpret meaning and make appropriate decisions. Data collected needs to be transformed by the management information system into information that managers can act upon. Data processing involves sorting, analysing and summarising.

Communicating information

Management information systems can communicate information to end-users in a number of different forms:

1 verbal – telephone, meetings, audio tapes and video conferencing
2 written – memoranda, newsletter, printed reports (standard and ad hoc)
3 presentation media – videos, slides, overhead projector, black/white boards.
4 electronic systems – E-mail via computer network, computer disks and tapes, teletext, viewdata, fax
5 other – microfiche (sheet film) or microfilm (roll film).

The choice of medium should reflect the nature of the information, the audience it is to reach and the use to which the information is to be put. Regular performance reporting is perhaps best presented using a standard printed report to allow users to read it at their convenience. The results of the latest market research could be effectively communicated at a formal presentation conducted by the researchers, the overall format allowing managers the opportunity to ask questions, have discussions and perhaps make decisions.

Data storage

Data stores may be manual records or computer files, with most organisations using both. Manual records include:

- documents in filing systems such as filing cabinets or documents recorded on microfiche or microfilm
- written entries in registers, ledgers and diaries
- card indexes.

Where data are stored in a computer file, each data record is structured into fields. A data field stores a certain type of information concerning the data records, such as the ages of employees, their addresses, etc. Data records stored in this highly structured manner are known as **databases** and are a basis for sharing data between different applications.

The Chartered Institute of Management Accountants defines a database as:

'a file of data structured in such a way that it may serve a number of applications without its structure being dictated by any one of those applications, the concept being that programs are written round the database rather than files being structured to meet the needs of particular programs.'

Data processed are typically stored in two types of database:

- Master file – permanent data concerning the data entity, such as a stock part or customer (see Figure 9.4).
- Transaction file – details of individual transactions (typically date, description, quantities and value). The transactions' history required will dictate how often transaction files are erased.

Features of a database

- A record is the term used to describe the details of each data entity.
- Each record comprises a number of fields, e.g. customer address. It is necessary to specify the size and format of the field contents when the database is set up. In Figure 9.4, the account number is alpha-numeric, the customer name field is in alpha format and the credit limit is numerical.
- Depending on the features of the program being used, data may be accessed in many different ways. In general the user specifies the field on which the search is to be based and the search criteria that are to be used. For example, for the database in Figure 9.4 searching the field for 'credit limit' with the search criteria of '>£3000' will output all records satisfying the search criteria, such as JAC003 in the format and on the output medium specified by the user.

The aim when designing a database structure is to allow for long-term flexibility, perhaps for a use not known at the time of design.

Figure 9.5 Business data and information flows

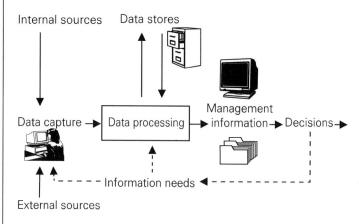

Task

1 For an organisation that you are familiar with:
a identify its specific information needs
b identify its information sources
c identify information stored, on what medium and for what purpose.

Figure 9.4 Example of a database holding master file data on the sales ledger

Account number	Customer Name	Customer Address	Credit limit	Currency	Contact name
JAC002	Jacobs	79 Newman Walk Luton	£2 000	£	M Rowland
JAC003	Jacksons	49 London Road Hemel Hempstead	£6 000	£	J Jackson

2 *Draw a business data and information flow chart from the information you have obtained.*

Design and implementation of a MIS

How information systems are designed and implemented is of crucial significance to their efficiency and effectiveness. It is important to overcome the tendency for individual managers to decide on information systems that only satisfy their department's needs. It must be appreciated by all employees that data stores are a corporate resource. There is a danger that individual managers may attempt to solve departmental problems without the need to justify expenditure, and hence purpose, to a higher authority. System development should be coordinated by a senior figure in the organisation to overcome problems of sharing information, such as uncooperative staff, hardware and software incompatibility and inappropriate data-file structure. Too often the output from one system is manually keyed into another because of a short-sighted approach to systems design. This causes delay, more cost and the possibility of errors.

There are a number of methods used to design and implement MISs and a choice should be made on the basis of the particular situation. However, the basic approach is to start with a general overview of the business and its needs, and as the design project progresses, consider each area of the system in degrees of greater detail. The implementation of a management information system typically has to go through the following stages:

1 feasibility study – whether the system will produce net benefits to the business
2 systems design – the logic of the system
3 physical design – writing the programs, training the user and obtaining the hardware
4 system test
5 implementation.

After implementation, systems have to be maintained and subsequently evaluated to ensure needs continue to be met. System improvements may have to go through the same stages as initial implementation to address problems or new needs.

The first step in the development of a system is the recognition of a need – either a problem with an existing system or a need at present not addressed by any existing system. There is a danger that new systems are developed by trying to improve ways of performing current

procedures. Even where a system currently exists, it is important that systems designers go back to organisational objectives and business strategies, and hence identify management's information needs.

Feasibility study

The objectives of a feasibility study are to:

- assess the realism of a system and find a solution or a number of alternative solutions to the issue
- identify resources needed to develop a system – knowledge, hardware, software
- identify costs and benefits of the new system
- issue a report of recommendations with projected timescale.

Costs and benefits

It is important that the benefits of a new system outweigh costs of developing and operating it. Benefits commonly identified include:

- more accurate and relevant information on which to make decisions
- staff savings
- lower stocks
- better utilisation of resources such as machinery and labour
- improved flow of work resulting in better utilisation of working capital and increased customer satisfaction
- quick reporting for fast response to new threats, e.g. increase in production errors.

Costs may include:

- expenditure to investigate and design a system, including specialists and participation of users in the design stage
- purchase price of software and/or time of programmers to write programs
- equipment purchases
- increased staffing to operate the system
- expenditure on training
- disruption to work flow during system implementation.

Case Study
Costs and benefits

A wine merchant Red and White Ltd, employing twelve staff, decided to replace its manual system for stock recording with a computerised system. The company had lost two large customers because it was unable to deliver orders fast enough as a result of insufficient balances on certain stock lines. The managing director decided a feasibility study should be undertaken to investigate the possibility of a formalised stock-control system that would interface with the purchase and sales accounting programs.

The study identified the main benefits of a system to be greater precision in the timing and size of stock orders, hence reducing the risk of being out of stock and also reducing average stock balances as some lines had experienced low stock turnover. Other advantages included faster picking of orders, the ability to record forward orders to calculate a 'free stock' balance, and easier and more accurate billing of customers for supplies made. The managing director also hoped that the system would provide greater integration of the purchasing and sales sides of the business with the use of more information concerning suppliers and customers.

Immediate costs of the system included the computer hardware and software and staff training. Ongoing running costs included hardware maintenance and insurance, and interest on the bank loan taken out to finance the project. Most of the costs of the project were quantified quite accurately at the time of the feasibility study, although there was some uncertainty over the staff training required and the programming costs for modifying a standard personal computer stock program. Total costs were expected to be in the range £7000–£8000 initially and about £1000 a year thereafter. The list of benefits was more difficult to quantify in money terms, but the gross profit forgone on the customers already lost amounted to £10 000 a year. With total gross profit forecast to be £150 000 in the current year, it was decided to go ahead with the project.

Questions for discussion

Prepare a concise feasibility study report to the managing director, including additional points you consider should be covered in such a report.

System development

If a project is given the go-ahead, the next step is often the appointment of a steering committee to represent senior management and user departments. The steering committee oversees the project through to implementation. The steering committee:

- appoints a team and project manager
- approves the budget for the project
- sets the team's terms of reference
- monitors and controls the project's progress

- reports its recommendations to a higher level, perhaps the board of directors.

To develop a system that addresses business needs it is important that the project team undertakes its work within the context of the firm's objectives and strategy. The exact composition of the project team is dictated by the nature of the information system and the area of the business in which it is to operate. It is possible some team members may change over the project's life as requirements change. The team may include the business's own staff seconded to the project as well as outside specialist consultants. The team may comprise:

- system users
- business analysts
- system designers
- computer programmers and engineers.

Case Study
Red and White Ltd

- **Objectives:** to become a respected and long-term supplier of quality wines to hotels and restaurants in addition to supplying small wine retailers.
- **Strategies:** using numerous personal contacts in wine-growing countries, to offer wines of good quality from some of the smaller vineyards. Regular visits abroad to source new as well as established wines. Wines will often be bought on a speculative basis although usually with specific customers in mind. Mailing lists to customers with information concerning availability and details of current stocks and awaited special consignments.
- **Information needs:** formal and informal information sources in producing countries. Awareness of other wine wholesalers and relative position in the market. Details of individual customers' sales history, forward sales orders and products of particular interest. Details of physical stocks, awaited deliveries and commitments to customers to provide a current free stock balance.

The managing director decided to hire a systems specialist who impressed her when installing the company's accounts system. She liked the way the specialist hadn't tried to computerise the fixed-asset register and cash book but had accepted the advantages of manual procedures in certain areas. Preliminary discussions identified the need to report on three different types of data entity and hence there would be a database for each: a supplier database, a customer database and stock database.

Questions for discussion

1 *Design output reports for Red and White Ltd to satisfy its information needs.*
2 *Design a field structure for each of the three types of database identified.*

A starting point for many systems projects which are to replace existing systems is to understand exactly how things are done currently. Although it is important not to replicate slavishly the methodology of the current system, together with all its faults, the current system can provide valuable information concerning data sources, business operations and, perhaps more importantly, verification that users do use information in the way they claim. Information should be sought concerning:

- the documentation in use and the information it conveys
- who receives and uses the information
- for what purpose the information is used
- the exact flow of information – an analysis of system inputs and outputs to see how they relate to each other may be useful.

Various methods could be adopted to obtain this information. It is good practice to involve the user in affected areas early on in the development process, e.g. by interviewing staff and management about their function and their information needs. Using existing documentation to establish what should be done and finding explanations for divergences is another useful exercise. To ascertain methods of work and volumes of data, investigations could utilise questionnaires in addition to direct observation of tasks. The systems analyst needs to be continually asking questions such as 'What are the information requirements for each task? What information is currently available? How must the system interact with other systems of the business?' This micro-view of the system functions should also be viewed from a 'big picture' perspective (see Figure 9.6).

Constraints

When evaluating possible solutions, all constraints should be assessed. The system may have to utilise existing computer hardware or a particular software package. There may be organisational constraints, having to use particular staff or perhaps having to interact with other systems and existing databases. Rarely can anything be done in business without considering the financial impact, as financial resources are usually limited. Most systems have to be introduced in an environment with at least some constraints and to that extent are always

Figure 9.6 Views of system functions

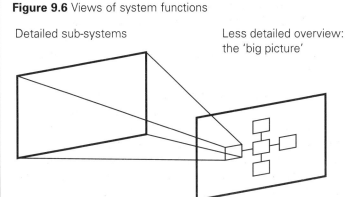

Detailed sub-systems   Less detailed overview: the 'big picture'

suboptimal. The systems designer has to tread a middle way and reach a satisfactory compromise solution to the problem.

Data flow diagrams

Having identified information needs, existing systems and constraints, it may be useful to draft a system overview with the use of data flow diagrams (DFDs) (see Figure 9.7) The DFD's pictorial view of data flows is good for establishing and confirming data needs and information flows without committing the project to specific methods and physical resources (see Figure 9.8). The DFD is concerned with representing the problem in a logical and comprehensible manner. The systems designer should not be afraid to present pictures of everyday office objects on the charts if this facilitates understanding for all those concerned.

The DFD becomes a basis for discussion between the analyst and user, allowing the user to participate in the system's design. During this period of dialogue new ideas may develop and users may become more specific as to their requirements as their understanding of what is possible also develops. This has the advantage of confirming the analyst's understanding of the system and thus minimising errors that may be costly to rectify later.

The DFD is useful in defining the system boundaries. Where a MIS is to utilise computers it is also important to identify at this stage the boundary between manual and computerised activities. Everyone needs to be clear where the system is to operate and what factors are external to it. Information flows are clearly presented and the relationship between functions and data stores is shown.

Once the problem has been defined, specific requirements and constraints can be incorporated so that a more detailed system emerges. In particular, ideas should be forming on how information can be collected and the

Figure 9.7 Data flow diagrams – symbols

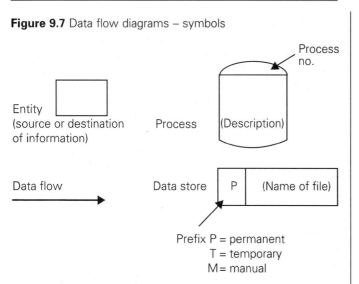

Entity
(source or destination
of information)

Process

Process no.

(Description)

Data flow

Data store

P | (Name of file)

Prefix P = permanent
T = temporary
M = manual

Figure 9.8 Red and White Ltd: wine wholesalers data flow diagram – finding customers for special consignments

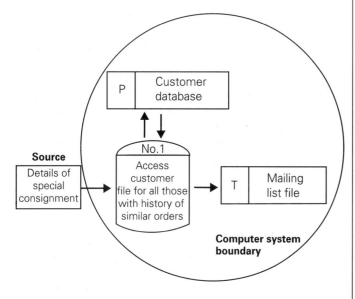

P | Customer database

Source
Details of special consignment

No.1
Access customer file for all those with history of similar orders

T | Mailing list file

Computer system boundary

user interfaces appropriate for inputting data and receiving information.

As the system evolves it may prove useful to break down the overall system into discrete modules with a series of diagrams for each part of the system. Later on this will allow individual programmers to work on a clearly defined area of the system, helping to share workload and also facilitating the testing of parts of the system as they are completed, as opposed to waiting until the whole system is written. It is particularly important at this stage to be very specific as to the structure of common databases and the format of input and output messages so that the modules interact properly when the whole system is put together. The use of common databases to avoid unnecessary duplication of effort throughout the organisation has the added advantage of data consistency

between all parts of the business, but it requires careful thought as to data file structure.

As the system unfolds, system flow charts are a valuable tool for describing in more detail how the system will work (see Figures 9.9 and 9.10). Flow charts show the system's decision logic and describe in greater detail than the DFD how data are stored and the user interfaces for data input and information output.

Figure 9.9 System flow chart symbols (an abbreviated set)

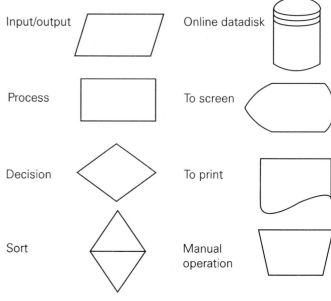

Input/output

Process

Decision

Sort

Online datadisk

To screen

To print

Manual operation

Appropriate media of input and output messages should be specified together with precise designs for databases, documents, screen displays and printed reports. The opportunity may be taken very early on in the development process to produce a system prototype (called prototyping). This concentrates on the user interfaces of inputting and outputting with some working features. It may be quickly written for user evaluation before the full system is written.

Other aspects that need to be considered include the timing and method of data processing. For example, data such as sales invoices may be more efficiently processed in batches within specified time periods, but output such as the current unpaid balance on a customer's account may be by online screen enquiry.

By the end of the design phase, all aspects of the system's logic will have been considered in detail. Specific requirements for hardware, software and other resources such as programming skills will have been reported to the steering committee, together with precise system specifications describing what the system will be like to use and the performance to be expected.

Figure 9.10 Red and White Ltd: extract from the system flow chart

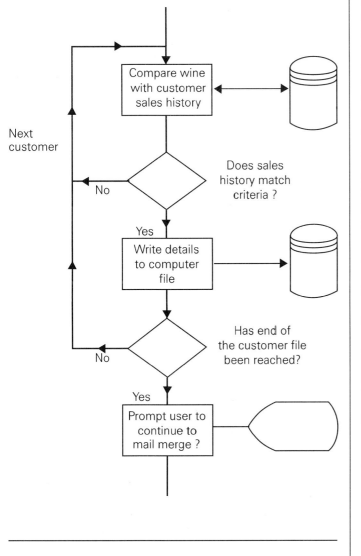

Next customer

Compare wine with customer sales history

Does sales history match criteria ?

No

Yes

Write details to computer file

Has end of the customer file been reached?

No

Yes

Prompt user to continue to mail merge ?

been adjusted. The new system is to be computer-based, using either a database or spreadsheet package, and operate on orders actually delivered to the customer. The system will be linked to the sales order processing system and details of every sales order delivered and invoiced to the customer will be transferred to the computer. The commission program will sort orders by sales representative. To calculate commission earned, it will look up a matrix of commission payments based on volumes sold and the average sales price achieved that month.

The management is, therefore, concerned about a number of issues which it will wish to monitor. It wants to:

- increase sales prices
- maintain sales volume
- continue paying commission
- maintain the high morale and low staff turnover of the sales team.

The processing of sales orders is to remain unchanged:

- The customer's order is input into the sales order processing system.
- A packing note is generated by the system in the stores area.
- The stores personnel confirm the stock has been moved to the despatch section and stock records are updated.
- A delivery note is produced and this accompanies the goods to the customer.
- When the delivery note is returned signed by the customer, a sales invoice is produced.

Questions for discussion

1 *Draw a high-level data flow diagram for the whole system, including for commission payments.*
2 *Draw a more detailed systems flow chart of the new commissions system.*
3 *Advise on the content and format of output reports that management should receive.*
4 *What other issues need to be considered when designing the system?*

Physical design of the system

The system elements of hardware, human input and methods have to be brought together to produce a working whole.

For computerised tasks, software needs to be purchased or specially written for the application. Even where the software is a standard package, usually some work has to be undertaken before it can be used. Sometimes the work is substantial, requiring modifications or additions to the program. As a minimum, the software allows certain data

Case Study
Staybright Cleaning Services

Staybright is a newly acquired subsidiary of Newlook Cleaning Services. The new management team appointed at Staybright is particularly concerned at the low sales prices being charged for industrial vacuum cleaners sold, despite large commission payments made to sales representatives for impressive volumes sold. It decides to modify the sales commission scheme so that commission is only paid on sales over a set threshold price. The aim is not so much to reduce costs that would affect staff morale, but to encourage the attainment of higher sales prices.

Another failure of the current system is that it pays commissions on the basis of orders logged by the sales manager's assistant and some orders have been subsequently cancelled, although commissions have not fields to be formatted in a certain way and for some features to be disabled if preferred. The system parameters need to be set when the software is loaded on to the computer and before actual data can be input.

For programs being written specifically, it is necessary to test that they work and that they satisfy system requirements. Where the software programs have been broken down into discrete working modules, testing can be performed in stages without having to wait till the whole system is written. Each module is tested to ensure output from one module will be in the correct format and form for the next module to accept. System documentation to accompany the software should be appropriate to both system specialists and system users.

Hardware needs to be purchased or leased. The importance of ensuring adequate maintenance backup in case of machine breakdown should be considered, and hardware purchased from a reputable supplier who can be relied upon to give good after-sales service.

Implementation

A new project team may be assembled to implement the system to reflect the change of skills and knowledge required. The original project team has had to talk and work with people in the user departments from the feasibility study onwards, but a different type of problem may arise at this stage. There is a need for user training and the resolution of user problems to ensure that staff have a positive attitude to the system.

The system may be new, but it usually requires some historical data for it to operate. Master file data concerning the data subjects will be essential. For a stock-control system the master file will include numbers, descriptions, units of measure, etc.; for a sales ledger accounting system, customer details and credit limits will be needed. In addition, it may be desirable to start the new system with some historical transaction data. Some historical data may be essential, such as how much customers owe the business or how much of a particular item is in stock. Where the new system replaces an existing computer-based system, it may be possible to transfer data files from one system to the other. Problems will be encountered when the data files have different data structures and a specially written data-file conversion program may be needed to facilitate the transfer. This may be a major piece of work in its own right, especially if the format of existing data has to be changed or the data for one record have to be picked up from a number of different sources. Where the system is replacing a manual system, data will have to be keyed into the databases manually.

Those affected by the introduction of the system should have been kept informed of its objectives and its effect on individuals from very early on in the development process. Progress reports should be issued regularly to ensure an atmosphere of openness even when some individuals may be hostile, perhaps due to job losses. Lack of proper communication may cause unnecessary bitterness and isolation because of perceived underhand action by management. This situation should not be allowed to endanger the successful implementation of the system.

An effective training programme should have been planned at the commencement of the project and an adequate training budget established. Without proper training the confidence of users and the operation of the system will be undermined.

Once the program has been tested and users educated in the use of the new system, the time has come to test the whole system with real data. Testing of computer-based systems should include related manual office procedures and evaluation of output by users of the information generated.

Where the new system is to replace an existing one, various methods can be used to effect the actual transfer from one system to another. These include:

- Direct change over. Installations that are relatively small and limited in range of activities can be made all at one go at a particular time on a certain date. For larger systems this may also be a preferred option if other alternatives are less practical. On a direct change over, the old system may be closed down at close of business one Friday afternoon, with final data transfers, hardware changes, etc. being made that weekend so that the user goes straight on to the new system on Monday morning. This direct change over method, although simple in concept, may not be appropriate in all circumstances. It may be physically impossible to change the computer system of a whole business in one go. It may also be thought desirable to minimise risk and complete the installation in one department before proceeding to the next.
- Phased change over. Where parts of the system can be introduced one at a time a phased introduction may be preferable. For example, if a number of different locations are to use the same system, minimisation of the risk of failure and reducing the demands on limited systems personnel could be achieved by having a pilot scheme in one location, taking in the whole organisation over a specified timescale.
- Parallel running. If it is possible to operate both systems at the same time, parallel running could be

adopted. Assurance in the operation of the new system is achieved before it is relied upon to replace an existing system, although duplication of tasks is time-consuming and costly.

Once up and running, time must be allowed for continued user support and the resolution of operating problems.

Case Study
Red and White Ltd: implementation

The new stock order processing system was to replace the manual stock cards for each type of wine and the manual keying in of sales invoice details (the new system would automatically trigger the production of sales invoices to customers). It was decided:

1 Stores personnel would continue to update the manual stock cards for one week, at which point the cards would be compared with the stock movements and balances on the computerised system. Discrepancies would be resolved and, if the system had performed satisfactorily, the stock cards would be moved to the record store.
2 The continued keying of invoice details would prove impractical if customer records were not to be updated twice, so the old procedures were to be halted on implementation of the new system.

Project management

Throughout the development process, from feasibility study to implementation, there is a need to manage project teams efficiently and to implement the system to the timetable required by the steering committee.

It is usual to analyse the project at distinct stages, such as end of design and end of implementation, and to break these down further into discrete tasks with target milestones. These can be used with critical path analysis (CPA) and Gantt charts to ensure the effective planning of activities. The progress of the project can then be monitored against the plan and corrective action taken to bring the project back on time, or if necessary, to reschedule future activities to ensure all interested parties including the steering committee are kept informed.

Case Study
Red and White Ltd: time required to design and implement new stock order processing system

The firm identified the following major activities at the time of the feasibility study for its new stock order processing system:

Activity	Estimated time required
System design	20 days
Writing the program	15 days
Lead time on ordering hardware	10 days
Training staff	5 days
Software test	3 days
Testing the system	3 days
Printing system documents	10 days
Inputting existing manual records for customers and stock	5 days

Critical path analysis

The various activities of the project are presented in a logical order.

Figure 9.11 highlights the 'critical path' that measures the minimum duration of the project at Red and White Ltd. Change in timescale of any activity on the critical path changes the finish time of the whole project. Other activities not on the critical path can take longer without extending the overall project time. In the case of Red and White, the planned project time is 43 working days and is indicated by the double activity lines.

Figure 9.11 The 'critical path' at Red and White Ltd

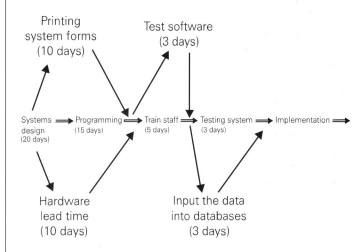

For planning exercises that require the technique of critical path analysis, software packages such as Microsoft Project could be invaluable. They highlight the times certain resources need to be employed, including the specific responsibilities of the project team members. In addition to helping to solve the problem, the software facilitates the effective communication of the plan, making use of aids such as Gantt charts.

Gantt charts

The Gantt chart uses the logical sequence of activities identified by critical path analysis and allows the project team to monitor its performance against plan (see Figure 9.12).

Systems review

The implementation of a system may be as a result of management's perceived need or it may be the result of a more formal review of business systems. Once a system has been introduced it should be periodically evaluated against organisational goals. The flows of information with suppliers and customers could also be considered for those organisations strong enough to harness the whole vertical process for competitive advantage, e.g. the information interface between Marks & Spencer and its suppliers.

When evaluating a system it is not sufficient for the reviewer to follow through the system checking that data flow as required. Information is of no value unless it is being acted upon. As part of the evaluation process the reviewer should ensure that the message from the MIS system is being received and understood correctly. Evidence of this would be appropriate action taken as a result of the information communicated. Managers should be initiating internal change in response to changes in circumstance, whether these be external

influences such as technological change or internal conditions such as plant breakdown. Inaction could be due to:

- problems with the message – not relevant, not timely, not accurate
- interference or distortion of the message – incorrect mode of communication or incorrect format (interfaces such as screen and printout formats should be user friendly to ensure accuracy of data input and proper understanding of information output)
- problems with the receiver of the information – lack of motivation or inability to act, perhaps due to insufficient training and skills (problems outside the MIS system)
- information not being received by the right person.

To establish whether a MIS does provide the right information, it is necessary to identify the key factors for organisational success. In a system of 'management by objectives', individual managers at all levels are set objectives that support corporate objectives. Information needs should be recognised when setting these objectives, as failure to do so may undermine the manager's attainment of his or her target. For example, in targeting how many hours of labour are needed for the average repair job, the responsible manager needs information concerning actual performance with comparison against some other meaningful measure, such as the contents of the business plan or last month's performance. Supporting information should help the manager identify reasons for variances and may include average number of miles travelled per repair, types of repairs undertaken, etc.

Figure 9.12 Red and White Ltd: Gantt chart

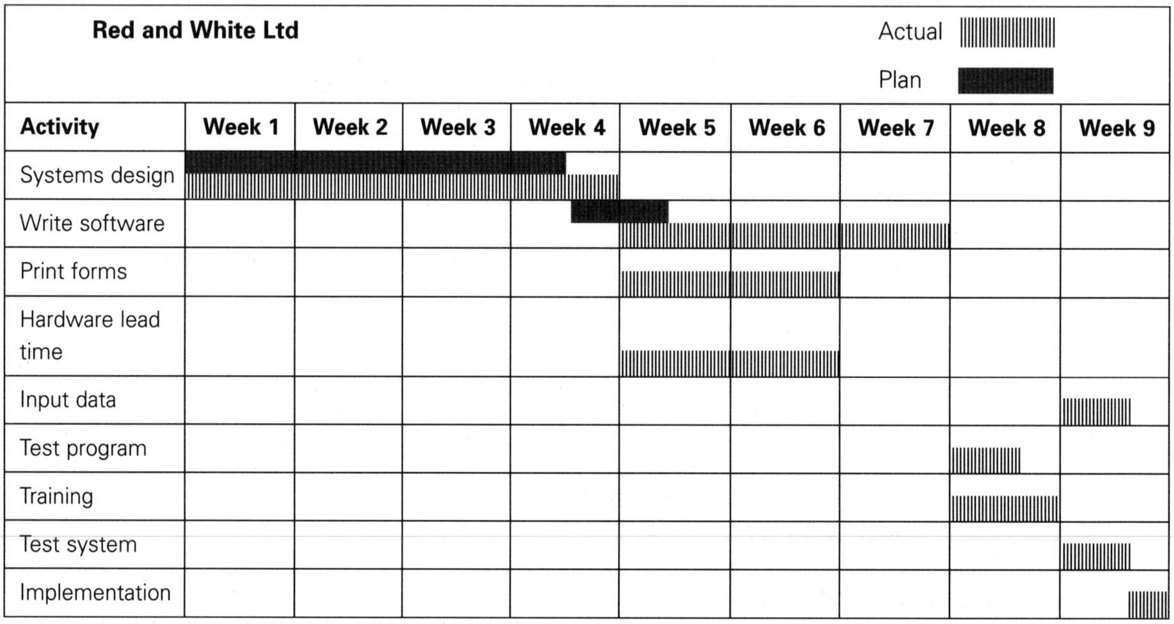

| Red and White Ltd | | | | | | | | Actual ▥▥▥ | |
| | | | | | | | | Plan ▬▬▬ | |
Activity	Week 1	Week 2	Week 3	Week 4	Week 5	Week 6	Week 7	Week 8	Week 9
Systems design	▬▥	▬▥	▬▥	▬▥					
Write software				▬	▥	▥	▥		
Print forms					▥	▥			
Hardware lead time					▥	▥	▥		
Input data									▥
Test program								▥	
Training								▥	
Test system									▥
Implementation									▥

The characteristics of the MIS must suit the organisation's operating environment and if it changes, then the MIS may have to change also. Stable environments can allow formalised, structured systems. However, operating conditions may be different for different departments. In stock control, precise and formal methods are appropriate; but the customer service department must be flexible in its approach to the resolution of customers' problems, so information and decision routines must be capable of change and adaptation.

Changing operating environments may be due to changes in technology, national and international politics, societal values (such as environmental concern), legislation, economic growth and relative competitive advantage.

Figure 9.13 looks at two examples of business environment changes and resulting changes in information requirements.

Task

Identify two businesses that have experienced change that has resulted in an adjustment in their need for information.

Evaluation

The review process may consider whether:

- information is reliable, accurate and without omission
- information is relevant to the user
- information is available when required with acceptable processing and response times
- the system is economical to operate
- the system is user friendly.

Relevance

Relevant information increases knowledge, reduces uncertainty and is usable for its intended purpose. A particular piece of information may be more relevant to one manager than another because of the nature of their work and their relative position in the organisational hierarchy.

Case Study
Food retailer digests information

Here are two pieces of information concerning a large food retailer:

1 A customer wants to return a carton of fresh cream purchased yesterday which he claims is no longer edible.
2 A food retailer from continental Europe has started to open discount stores in Britain.

Each piece of information is important, and while of interest to all managers, is especially relevant to the responsibilities of particular managers. The complaint is important for the dairy products supervisor to investigate; the new discount store is relevant to the board of directors when it reviews corporate strategy.

Figure 9.13 Business environment changes

Business sector	New information needs
British holiday resorts were once alone in satisfying the British custom for a one- or two-week holiday at the seaside. Today, with affordable travel to sunnier destinations, UK facilities have had to provide new holiday products such as weekend breaks, often at traditionally off-peak times of the year.	■ Details of overseas travel – exchange rates relative prices, including airfares, and political developments in foreign countries ■ Innovations in holiday formats offered by other British resorts ■ Evaluation of own-product innovation and promotional campaigns ■ Social and leisure trends
British supermarket chains were until recently enjoying lucrative profit margins of around 7% on sales compared to continental returns of nearer 4%. The 1990s has seen foreign firms such as Netto and Aldi provide fierce price competition for Sainsbury's, Safeway and Tesco.	More knowledge of competitors, home markets and methods of cost saving

Strategic management

Senior managers have long-term planning horizons with a view of the business as a whole within its external environment. They take the major business decisions concerning market strategies and resources procurement, including personnel policy. Issues tend to be unpredictable, difficult to quantify and concern the future. External information is important.

Tactical management

Middle managers tend to hold more functional responsibilities and specialise in marketing, production, finance, etc. They are concerned with medium-term planning and controlling of activities, largely with an emphasis on management by exception. Duties and decision-making are split between the routine and the moderately structured ad hoc. Information sources are largely internal, although some external information is required, depending on functional responsibilities.

Operational management

Junior managers tend to take day-to-day decisions within the constraints imposed by operational budgets. Conditions are relatively stable and in many businesses there is a standard format for information received and reported. Information is almost entirely historical and detailed, is needed quickly and comes mainly from internal sources.

Information flows

Figure 9.14 Management information flows

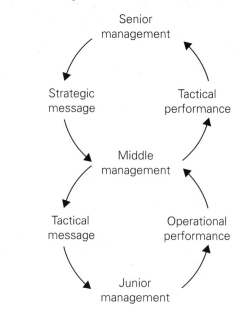

Enterprise Information Systems

Enterprise information systems (EISs) are flexible reporting packages that senior management with little computer knowledge can use. Summarised data from the main business databases are transferred into computer files for the EIS to utilise. The information held on

Figure 9.15 Example of information needs at different levels of the management hierarchy

Position	Management issues	Information needs
Finance director	Corporate and financial strategy	1 Regular information in summarised form to monitor performance of business activities. 2 Information on request from internal and external sources on a wide range of issues, e.g. long-term sales forecast, product development, fixed-asset investment programs, etc.
Management accountant	1 **Routine** – management of the finance department in its processing of routine data and the issue of standard reports. 2 **Ad hoc** – exercises to satisfy management information needs, including cost analysis, project appraisal and forward planning.	1 Formalised reporting systems to produce performance reports in summary form with exception analysis. Regular feedback from the finance department concerning workloads and problems, including staffing, training and cost budgets over the next 12 months. 2 Flexible and easily accessible sources of information to satisfy adhoc requests from management.
Office supervisor	1 Supervision of day-to-day tasks. 2 Resolution of task problems and responding to information requests from the management accountant and other managers.	1 Knowledge of report requirements of senior management to ensure accurate and timely issue of information. 2 Actual and planned workloads of individual office staff. 3 Detailed transaction data.

computer is updated periodically with the latest business transactions and measures of operational activity. The multi-dimensional databases used by many EISs are specifically designed for holding time-series data such as sales by month, by product, by region and customer, etc. The system provides an easy-to-use interface that allows the user to manipulate and analyse the data with the ability to obtain levels of greater analysis if they so wish.

Case Study
Greenalls Inns

'Greenalls Inns, the largest division of the Greenalls Group, which owns and operates a chain of more than 2000 pubs, introduced its new EIS at board level to help directors monitor the performance of their rapidly growing business. So successful has the system been that lower management was willing to pay for the equipment they needed to run the system out of their own budgets.

'In just ten weeks, finance director Tim Kowalski and a consultant had built a system based around IRI's Express EIS product. When the system was ready, Kowalski held a board presentation at which the live system was demonstrated. To their astonishment, directors saw a fully working system that enabled them to report all key performance ratios, compare the performance across similar outlets, drill down to review details of an individual pub and so forth.

'Whilst the meeting was going on, Kowalski had arranged for the EIS to be installed on each executive's desk. Each was then handed a sealed envelope containing that individual's password, so they could go straight back to the office and begin using the system.

'Highly visual in design, the system is so self-explanatory that no manuals or training were needed, even though most of the directors had never used a PC before. Kowalski commented: ''One member was on holiday when we unveiled the system. When I phoned him the morning after his return, to arrange a familiarisation session, he was already happily using the system, having found only his password in the envelope.''

'Kowalski described the manner in which the EIS spread through the organisation as ''not so much a trickle-down as a push up. Within one or two weeks, the area managers, each of whom run about 25 pubs, came clamouring for the system. The directors had all this information about their performance and, in effect, they needed the same information to defend themselves.''

'More junior users of the system are given access to a subset of the total information, since they do not need to know about peer performance outside their own region. All 36 area managers now have portable Toshiba PCs which carry their subsets of the performance information out to the pubs for review with the publicans. And Kowalski foresees a time when individual pub managers will have their own access to the system. ''You could take it right down to the bar staff. It's equally applicable for them to ask the question: 'How am I doing against my fellows?' ''

'A system like this is valuable for everyone because it enables you to base business decisions on comparisons of real benchmarks, rather than on gut feel. If you're running a town bar with a beer garden, you can select other outlets with the same characteristics and in a comparable location, and see how your performance compares with those. And it's fast – you can get immediate access to information that used to take us two overnight reporting runs to produce before.'
(Source: *Accountancy Age*, 8 December 1994)

Questions for discussion

1 Identify why users were so enthusiastic about Greenhalls' EIS.
2 Suggest performance information for Greenhalls that would be relevant to the needs of a director, an area manager and an individual pub manager.
3 Identify positive and negative aspects of the need for managers to 'defend themselves'.

'Decision support systems' are another form of information system allowing managers to evaluate information themselves. The software allows managers to access business databases and to use report generators and statistical analysis programs to manipulate data and present information as a basis for decision-making. These programming tools allow the user to develop solutions to ad hoc problems, including scenario facilities to simulate the effects of decisions with modelling programs.

Value of information

The value of information depends on the benefits that arise from its provision and it is important that the costs of providing it are considered in this light (see Figure 9.16).

Figure 9.16 Costs and benefits of provision of information

Information	Purpose	Benefits	Costs
Rejection rate of manufactured components	1 Provide clear focus on a key corporate objective – quality 2 Monitor production methods	Reduce customer dissatisfaction, hence stemming loss of sales and cut warranty costs	Cost of product inspection, data processing, reporting and investigations
Comparison of department overheads against budget	Identify exceptional levels of expenditure to stem adverse trends	Minimise unnecessary expenditure	Data processing, reporting, investigations and management time

Physical security and control

Managing information includes physical protection against loss or improper use. The major concerns are:

- physical security – against fire, theft, systems breakdown and malicious damage
- confidentiality
- control over illegal use.

The risk of information loss and the consequent effect on the business should be formally reviewed. Computer data that is important for the well being of the business should be copied regularly on to backup storage media with copies stored off site. For example, the irretrievable loss of records relating to debtors could potentially mean the loss of two or three months of sales revenue, too much for many businesses to survive if not insured against. Consideration should be given to security doors to restrict unauthorised personnel entering areas where important and confidential information is processed and stored. Access to sensitive information on computer files should also be restricted with frequently changed user passwords. For audit purposes, the passwords should be logged by the system each time the user interrogates the files.

The effects of hardware breakdown should be minimised by a comprehensive maintenance agreement, and it may be worthwhile to have an agreement with another business operating the same computer system to provide a backup processing facility.

The Data Protection Act of 1984 was passed in the wake of widespread concern about the proliferation of information on individuals and how it was being used. Every person or organisation who stores details of individuals on computer storage devices has to register with the Data Protection Registrar the details of the information held and a description of the purposes for which the information is held. Individuals may scrutinise the register and may also request individual organisations to disclose the precise information held about them.

Task

The company secretary of Red and White Ltd has discovered that the business is not registered under the Data Protection Act for the information it holds on computer files. You have been asked to investigate the requirements of the act and to specify what information Red and White Ltd needs to disclose in its application to the Registrar.

Computerised systems

Computers can be valuable tools in the operation of a management information system. They have made possible the reporting of information that would have been too time-consuming, too expensive and too late if provided manually.

A computerised system has several advantages.

- It is relatively cheap to run.
- It speeds up the process of data capture, editing and analysis.
- It speeds up and improves the presentation of reporting.
- It allows information to be shared throughout the business for multiple use.
- It offers a fast, easy and compact facility for the storage of information.

Historically, computers have been more useful at the operational level than at senior management level, although the advent of EISs and decision support applications, such as spreadsheets, have extended the computer's use up the management hierarchy. Computers are now found on the desks of most executives.

Case Study
Selling books at W. H. Smith

'Selling books at W. H. Smith is about picking fast-moving winners, and they move fastest out of its branches in Terminal One, Heathrow, and Victoria Station. In this era of book buying on the run to plane and train, the company uses its computer records to break down, region by region and shop by shop, exactly who buys Jeffrey Archer or Joanna Trollope. On the basis of this, the buyers of W. H. Smith know whether to sell horror in Chelmsford or humour in Bolton . . .

'Reference to computer data gives evidence of writers' past performance, and the probable sales of their next work, and so influences any decision about a book . . . "What we really aim to do nowadays is to work with publishers, building an author, looking at how we can develop them."

'W. H. Smith is not only "developing" individual authors but is now in the business of developing genres. Genres take the risk out of backing new authors. It means that the all-powerful computer records can be used to predict exactly how certain kinds of book will sell, even if a particular author is unknown.

'The success of Joanna Trollope's rural novels led to a whole wave of Aga Sagas from publishers hoping to cash in, but today's best-selling formulaic products are legal thrillers, featuring powerful lawyers struggling against adversity and conspiracy . . .'

(Adapted from *The Independent on Sunday*, 11 December 1994)

Questions for discussion

1 *What advantages has W. H. Smith derived from using computers in its book purchasing function?*
2 *Do you think there are any disadvantages, commercial or otherwise, of using the computer's power in this way?*
3 *Which data have to be stored to satisfy a W. H. Smith buyer's information needs? How will the data have been collected? With what other systems will the data have been shared?*
4 *Draw a data flow diagram for a comparable system to W. H. Smith's.*

Where computers can be used as an aid in making routine decisions, whole layers of management are currently under threat in a range of industries.

In banking, the role of the professional manager has diminished as more decisions are made automatically by computers. Decisions on loans are made after inputting an applicant's financial details. The computer program now evaluates all the variables according to standard formula, where once the time of an experienced and professionally trained manager was necessary. Small bank branches may now share managers; the current emphasis is on individuals who can sell financial products. After thousands of redundancies, even the current bank structures are only temporary. With the proliferation of home banking, started in the UK by Midland Bank with First Direct, the current branch network must shrink further. Branch outlets may only remain in large towns when visits to the bank need only be minimal. Information technology will allow head office management to control their businesses with just computers between them and their customers. Computers will have flattened the organisation structure and led to the annihilation of a vast bureaucracy.

All computer systems essentially comprise two elements: the equipment or hardware that can be seen and the computer program or software that is not visible but instructs the hardware to do useful things.

Hardware

Computer hardware can be divided into three main categories: mainframes, mini-computers and personal computers (PCs). Mainframes are used by larger businesses to process vast quantities of transaction data, but an increasing proportion of departmental managers and small businesses are satisfying their computer needs with PC-based systems. For those who can afford them, mainframes do offer massive processing power and perhaps just as importantly facilitate a disciplined and more secure method of data processing. However, the proliferation of PC-systems, particularly in their networked mode of operation, offers flexible processing power at very little cost. This section concentrates on PC-based systems.

Networks are classified into two main types:

■ Local area networks (LANs) are used for fast sharing of data within the same site. An example is Novell Netware.

- Wide area networks (WANs) link PCs over long distances, including international communication systems. Where the volume of data does not justify the expense of a direct line, the telephone networks of British Telecom and Mercury can be used. To access the voice communication system it is necessary to convert the binary voltage pulses that computers use into sound for transmission. This is performed by a modem linked to computer and phone line.

Software

The cost-conscious PC owner demands flexible software packages that do not require computer experts to operate. Most of the software used on PC systems is in the form of ready-written packages, although when using sophisticated database programs, such as DBaseIV or FoxPro, it is possible to have systems developed to individual needs. The terms 'programs', 'software packages' and 'applications' are often used interchangeably to mean the same thing.

Transaction processing

Accounts packages, such as those offered by Sage and Pegasus, provide program modules for stock control and job costing in addition to the usual ledger modules. The various modules link with one another to ensure data consistency and so data do not have to be input more than once. Output can be:

- on to the computer's screen for quick enquiries
- printed out in one of the standard formats provided with the system or in a format designed by the user
- in digital format into a computer file for reading by a spreadsheet package.

Popular PC applications software

Database packages
A PC database package allows the user to define the type, content and features of a database. Like a card index, data records can be accessed individually for enquiry purposes, but the computer's power is best applied to finding and sorting records according to specified criteria, e.g. a list of all those patients who receive meals on wheels and are vegetarian. Using the command language on some of the more sophisticated packages, the systems designer can automate procedures so that the user need have very little knowledge of the actual database functions.

Spreadsheets
Spreadsheets can be likened to a sheet of electronic analysis paper, organised into hundreds of columns and thousands of rows. They allow the user to manipulate and analyse both text and numerical data. Recent editions of popular packages, such as Lotus 123 and Microsoft Excel, include sophisticated features that facilitate the construction of multi-dimensional spreadsheets where a value can be analysed into more than two dimensions. For example, an expenses budget may need analysing by type of expense, by department, by location and into twelve monthly periods. When constructing models, such as for budgets or project appraisal, the spreadsheet automatically updates calculated cells each time numerical data is input. Regularly performed procedures can be automated with a simple programming routine called a 'macro'.

Word processing
Word processing has revolutionised the preparation of printed material, allowing many managers to type their own memoranda and reports. Whether this is an effective use of manager's time is debatable, but many managers have become more effective with fewer stages in the communication process, using products such as Microsoft's Word and Novell's WordPerfect. Some managers still wait hours or even days for a typist to produce a typed version of their longhand report, to be followed by checking and resubmission for corrections. It is becoming more commonplace for the manager to type a document in rough form, allowing secretaries to retrieve the file from networked PCs and to complete the message with proper introductions, closing paragraph and date, etc. This arrangement is seen as the best compromise in the use of manager's time and communication effectiveness.

Desktop publishing
Desktop publishing packages like Aldus Pagemaker and Microsoft Publisher enable the user to combine text, pictures and graphics on the same document. It is possible to produce professional-looking newsletters, reports and business forms; and advanced packages, such as CorelDraw, can help with the creation and running of slide presentations.

Computers in the future

Current developments are combining computer and telecommunication technologies to provide voice recognition, video links, access to remote databases and new methods of data capture. Add to this the continuing reductions in cost, with some forecasts predicting computers with the power of today's mainframes eventually costing the same as today's PCs, the computerisation of business information processes is set to continue.

Figure 9.17 Red and White Ltd: a sales journal – a detailed listing of sales transactions

Invoice number	Customer	Type of sale	Product	Value £
10090	Bean & Son	Mail	European red	305
10091	Jones	Counter	White	96
10092	Whiting	Mail	European red	610
10092	Whiting	Mail	Sparkling white	65
	Total			90 000

Using PCs to present information

Analysing data succinctly and presenting it in an unambiguous manner is essential for decision-making. Accuracy should be appropriate to the information's use, and reports should be kept as simple as possible. Too much detail diffuses the message.

It is usual for a computerised system to provide simple arithmetic calculations such as value totals, percentages and variances. However, it may be necessary for users of the MIS to perform statistical calculations themselves because of the ad hoc nature of some exercises. This section concentrates on developing skills in presenting information with a personal computer. Illustrations are based on Microsoft Excel and Microsoft Graph, but functions are similar to other software packages such as Lotus 123. It is important to recognise what a PC can do and to perform the exercises in this section with a software package with which you are familiar.

Summary tables

Simple summary tables can be a very effective method for communicating transaction analysis. Columns can be added for budget figures or for last year's comparable period to aid comprehension by the reader.

The preparation of summarised tables, such as the one shown in Figure 9.18, from hundreds or even thousands of individual sales records (see Figure 9.17) could be achieved in a matter of minutes with Excel's 'Crosstab table' facility. The user specifies the spreadsheet range to be summarised, then selects 'Crosstab' from the 'Data' pull-down menu, and follows the stages as prompted by the spreadsheet. The user is asked to specify the column and row analysis required and the values to be summarised; the spreadsheet does the rest. The Crosstab table is created on a separate worksheet that can be transferred into another worksheet of the user's choice, or alternatively into another application altogether, such as a word-processing document.

Task

Prepare, using a spreadsheet package, a sales journal for Red and White Ltd. Record at least 20 lines of sales details continuing on from invoice number 10092 shown in Figure 9.17. Using 'Crosstab', or a similar function provided by your spreadsheet, create a summarised sales report in the format of the one shown in Figure 9.18.

Graphs and charts using PC software

Presenting information in the form of a chart can be a very effective way of conveying a message.

Pictograms use pictures of everyday objects to represent a certain number of items or transactions. This form of presentation is very visual and an effective way of conveying information about the relative size of items (see Figure 9.19). PC programs often allow the insertion of objects from picture libraries for the creation of pictograms.

Many of the charts used to present information can be produced in very little time using personal computers. The data to be used can be displayed quickly in a variety of formats, allowing the user to choose before printing the favoured chart type, with titles and legends as required (see Figure 9.20).

Figure 9.18 Red and White Ltd: analysis by product and type of sale

Red and White Ltd Sales of wines for April 1995	Mail	Counter	Total	%
	£	£	£	
White	12 000	15 000	27 000	30.0
Sparkling white	6 000	3 000	9 000	10.0
New world red	7 000	11 000	18 000	20.0
European red	21 000	15 000	36 000	40.0
Total	46 000	44 000	90 000	100.0

Figure 9.19 Red and White Ltd: sales in April 1995

Each represents £3000 of sales

Figures 9.20A and C can be prepared using Microsoft Graph and inserted into a Microsoft Word document. The procedure while in Word is to:

1 Choose the 'Insert' command, click the mouse on 'Object', highlight 'Microsoft Graph', click OK.
2 Once in Graph the information to be plotted is keyed into a data grid:

	White	Sparkling white	New world red	European red
Sales	27 000	9000	18 000	36 000

3 An example of the chart is shown immediately in bar chart form. A toolbar for pull-down menu options allows the user to change chart type and format, with the changes viewed as they are made.
4 Select menu option 'Gallery' and the following chart types can be chosen in two or three dimensional views: area, column, bar, line, pie and in two dimensions only, a XY (scatter) chart.

5 Select menu option 'Chart' and the following can be added: chart title, data keys, data labels (names and values) and other format options such as grid lines.
6 On closing 'Graph' the program asks the user to confirm that the designed graph is inserted into the original document.

Many spreadsheet packages have a charting facility built into the program. Microsoft Excel features a quick graph 'wizard' that makes the preparation of graphs from data in the spreadsheet very simple. Figures 9.20 B and D can be prepared using Excel, as follows:

1 Select the range of data to be plotted using the mouse.
2 Select the 'Chart wizard' from the toolbar.
3 The mouse pointer becomes a cross that should be positioned in the top left-hand corner of the area to receive the chart, then hold down the mouse button to paint the area to be used by the chart. Release when a suitable rectangle or square has been selected.
4 The charting routine prompts the user to make choices concerning chart type, format titles, etc. Standard chart types are similar to those available with Microsoft Graph.

Tasks

1 Brampton Tools Ltd manufactures machine tools. The cost accountant has analysed the production costs for the month of January 1996 to be labour £46 000; materials £26 500; depreciation and maintenance of machinery £55 000; management and indirect labour £29 600; and building costs £18 900. Present the information for factory management using a PC charting application.
2 Delaney & Stokes Ltd has been concerned at the increase in labour turnover during 1995. You have been asked to present an analysis of employees to the Personnel Policies Committee, using two charts prepared on a PC charting application.

Figure 9.20 Different presentations of the same data

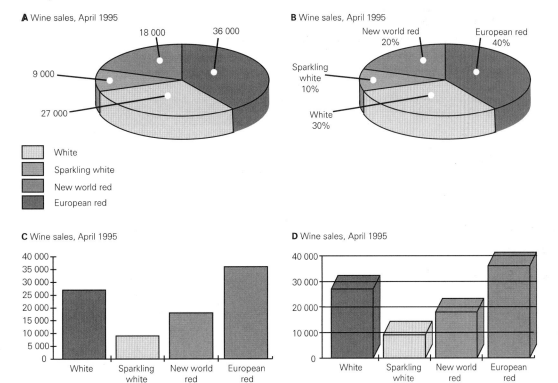

Alpine Office Supplies: sales performance (for Task 3)

Month	1	2	3	4	5	6	7	8	9	10	11	12
Actual (£000s)												
Furniture	25	36	50	36	32	39	54	38	29	42	46	34
Stationery	25	24	19	16	24	27	22	23	26	21	20	18
Computers	60	95	74	78	63	105	104	114	97	80	81	76
Budget (£000)												
Furniture	30	35	40	40	50	40	40	40	45	50	50	30
Stationery	20	20	20	20	20	20	20	20	20	20	20	20
Computers	75	80	80	90	90	90	100	100	100	100	90	70

Delaney & Stokes Ltd: analysis of employee turnover, 1994 and 1995 (for Task 2, page 212)

	1994	1995
Average number of employees	506	569
Numbers of leavers:		
Better pay	25	35
Promotion prospects	31	38
Physical working conditions	8	7
Social working conditions	6	10
Management demands	14	19
Fired	4	2
Redundancy	3	0
Total	91	111

Provide a supporting narrative for each chart.

3 You have been given the task of preparing for the sales director of Alpine Office Supplies a set of charts using a PC charting application. They are to be used to present the sales performance of Alpine Office Supplies for the year ended 31 December 1995 to a meeting of senior managers.

The sales director wants you to explain in the form of a memorandum:

a your choice of charts

b what they show so that they can plan the presentation to the meeting.

Averages

Another method for comparing one set of data with another is to calculate an average for each set. This is then used to represent that data set, e.g. an average of £1500 of European red wine and £1125 of white wine is sold every day. There are three methods of calculating an average from a set of data: **mean, median** and **mode**.

A spreadsheet package can make average calculations particularly easy if there is a large volume of data. The format of the three spreadsheet functions is similar, each allowing numbers to be averaged to be specified by the range of spreadsheet cells they occupy.

Figure 9.21 relates to prices of wine cases sold by Red and White Ltd during a particular week. We shall use it to demonstrate the calculation of various statistical measures.

Mean

The mean is the average of all the values in the table. The average is calculated by summing all of the case prices (which equals £2490), and dividing by the number of cases (giving £41.50). The change in average price over time may indicate to Red and White the extent to which people have changed their spending priorities.

Using the average function in Excel keyed into cell b8: = average (a1:j6)	The cell returns the mean value of the 60 cells specified in the function

Median

The median is the middle value in a set of numbers. To find the median manually, place all the case prices in order and find the middle value. In this example, we have two middle values so we would have to average the

thirtieth and thirty-first prices. The calculation is much quicker using a spreadsheet.

Using the median function in Excel keyed into cell b9: = median (a1:j6)	The cell B9 returns the median value of the 60 cells specified in the function

The median indicates to Red and White Ltd the middle price buyers are willing to pay without the distortion of the highest prices.

Mode

The mode is the value that occurs most frequently in a set of numbers. In this example customers buy cases priced at £46 five times – more often than any other value – so this is the mode. Where there are two values with the same frequency the set of numbers is said to be bimodal.

Using the mode function in Excel keyed into cell b10: = mode (a1:j6)	The cell B10 returns the mode value of the 60 cells specified in the function

By analysing wine sales by country, the mode would indicate to Red and White Ltd the most popular country, and perhaps the one it could justify travelling to in the search for new sources.

Dispersion

While averages are used widely for comparison purposes, it is difficult to know how typical the average is of the data set without some indication as to the dispersion of values.

The set of data in Figure 9.22 entered into a spreadsheet relates to time taken in hours on a sample of repair jobs undertaken by washing-machine service engineers.

Using the spreadsheet functions illustrated above, the following averages have been calculated: mean 2 hours,

Figure 9.21 Red and White Ltd: one week's sales of wine cases in £

	A	B	C	D	E	F	G	H	I	J
1	41	35	36	48	52	41	60	32	33	34
2	37	44	53	46	49	29	28	31	30	46
3	51	42	28	26	27	34	35	26	42	65
4	46	48	37	39	42	31	30	56	29	54
5	46	42	81	31	35	34	39	41	35	68
6	24	90	35	36	43	44	52	46	42	33
7										
8	Mean	£41.50								
9	Median	£40.00								
10	Mode	£46.00								

Figure 9.22 Washing-machine repairs: time taken in hours

	A	B	C	D	E	F
1	2.0	1.5	1.75	1.8	2.25	2.0
2	3.0	1.6	2.3	2.2	2	2.1
3	2.4	1.8	2.6	2.1	1.9	1.8
4	2.0	1.8	2.0	1.5	1.6	1.7
5	1.8	1.9	2.1	2.0	1.9	1.9
6	1.8	1.6	1.7	2.4	3.0	2.2

median 1.95 hours and mode 2 hours. The service manager allocates four jobs to each engineer at the start of every eight-hour day. The exact time required by a job is not known in advance and so some overtime payments have been paid. The service manager wonders whether working on average times of two hours is a practical guide to job allocation.

One measure of variability is the 'range', which is the highest value less the lowest value in any set of data. For this example, the range is 3 hours less 1.5 hours = 1.5 hours. The range is obviously heavily influenced by extreme values and it fails to show how the values are bunched. It may be useful to know whether the values occur evenly across the range or if they bunch around a particular value.

We could break the range down into intervals and analyse the frequency for each of these groups (see Figure 9.23). Again, this exercise is speeded up, especially for large volumes of data, by using spreadsheet functions.

Figure 9.23 Range in intervals

	A	B	C	D	E	F
10	Interval	Cum.	Band no.			
11	1.6	5	5			
12	1.8	14	9			
13	2.0	24	10			
14	2.2	29	5			
15	2.4	33	4			
16	3.0	36	3			

Using the function 'Frequency (data range, data intervals)' the total number of jobs under a certain value is returned in column B. The function entered in cell B11 is: =frequency(a1:f6,a11:a16). This is copied down into cells B12 to B16. Column C is simply the cumulative frequency less the previous cumulative value. The time taken on jobs does indeed bunch around the average values of two hours.

From this information a frequency histogram (see Figure 9.24) can be prepared for presentation purposes using a PC charting package.

Figure 9.24 A frequency histogram

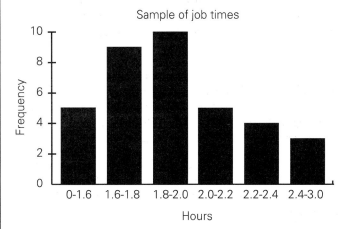

Another technique concerned with the measurement of dispersion in the data set is to use the range of the middle 50 per cent of readings. This is called the interquartile range, and again is simply calculated when using a spreadsheet package. Using the function 'Quartile (data range, quartile number)' we can analyse the data set into 25 per cent segments. Using the example of service times we can input into blank cells on the spreadsheet:

=quartile(a1:f6,1) – this returns the longest job in the first quartile, i.e. in this case the ninth job which took 1.8 hours.

=quartile(a1:f6,3) – this returns the longest job in the third quartile, i.e. in this case the twenty-seventh job which took 2.1 hours.

We can, therefore, deduce that 50 per cent of jobs took between 1.8 and 2.1 hours to complete – an interquartile range of only 0.3 hours compared to the full range of 1.5 hours. The service manager may decide on the basis of this information that the current system of work allocation is generally valid. However, any jobs taking less or more than a certain range of times should be reported immediately so that the remaining days' work can be reallocated.

Task

1 Key the price data in Figure 9.21 into a spreadsheet. Using the spreadsheet functions calculate:
   a the mean, median and mode
   b the interquartile range.
2 Of what value is the interquartile range in this example?

Correlation

Scatter charts

Scatter charts are useful to demonstrate a relationship between two variables. A number of observations are recorded as crosses against the x and y axes. The controllable variable is usually plotted on the x axis, the dependant variable against the y axis. Where a straight line can be drawn that passes through or close to each of the plots, then it is possible a relationship exists between the two variables. A scatter chart can be quickly prepared using a PC graph application (see Figure 9.25).

Figure 9.25 A scatter chart

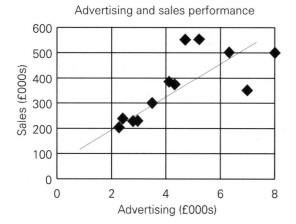

Advertising and sales performance

Correlation coefficient

The correlation coefficient used to establish a possible relationship between two variables can be calculated quickly and accurately using a spreadsheet function. The data in Figure 9.26 relate to advertising spend on twelve advertising campaigns and the sales turnover achieved in the period immediately following each.

The function keyed into cell B5 is =correl(bl:ml,b2:m2) and is in the format =correl(1st data range, 2nd data range).

The correlation coefficient indicates the direction of the relationship and its strength. The coefficient will vary between 0 and 1 for a positive correlation and between –1 and 0 for an inverse correlation. The correlation coefficient of 0.767 in Figure 9.26 shows a fair degree of correlation, confirming that within the range examined, sales performance is dependent to some extent on advertising expenditure.

Task

Cavetron UK Ltd manufacture on a batch production basis to customer orders. The following sales and profit figures relate to jobs completed in June:

- **Sales** 23 82 26 52 36 46 67 97 20 10 5 59 (000s)
- **Profit** 4 22 5 11 7 11 15 29 3 1 0 14 (000s)

In your role of management accountant you have noticed a possible relationship between the size of the job and the percentage profit earned.

1 Using a spreadsheet, calculate the correlation coefficient.
2 What does your work indicate?
3 Write a concise report to appropriate senior executives using a word processor, describing your findings and suggesting possible causes.

Responsibility for management information

Most departments in a business have some responsibility for contributing to the corporate information system. In particular, the data processing department often has the task of processing much of the data. However, as a large volume of the information is of a financial nature, e.g. cost per repair job, then the accounts department is often the central point for coordinating the preparation and the issue of management reports. Some businesses have recognised the importance of management information by

Figure 9.26 Advertising spend and sales turnover

	A	B	C	D	E	F	G	H	I	J	K	L	M
1	Period	1	2	3	4	5	6	7	8	9	10	11	12
2	Advertising	5.0	8.0	7.0	2.5	6.5	5.5	4.1	2.3	2.8	4.2	2.9	3.5
3	Sales	550	500	350	250	500	550	375	200	250	350	250	300
4	£000s												
5	Correlation	0.767											
6													
7													

creating a board position for the head of information services.

Summary

Managing information is an important part of running any business. Information managers should understand business objectives, the strategies and tactics being employed to pursue them, and the resultant information needs. Systems should be regularly reviewed to facilitate effective management by ensuring the provision of relevant and timely information. When implementing a system it is important to establish information needs and systems logic before considering how these might be fulfilled. Where appropriate, MISs should harness the processing potential of computer systems, but it should be realised that computers are only tools. Systems design should not be hampered by preconceived views of hardware and software resources. Providers of management information can use PC presentation tools to improve the quality of the message by highlighting important issues, trends and correlations. Computers make the analysis of information much easier but their advantages do not replace human intuition where interpretation of information is required. As with many other areas of business, the provision of management information should be on a contingency basis, within a corporate perspective of costs and benefits.

Further reading

- *Management Information Systems*, 6th edition, by T. Lucy. DP Publications, 1991.
- *Managing Information* by D. A. Wilson. The Institute of Management Foundation/Butterworth-Heinemann, 1993.
- *Introducing Systems Design* by S. Skidmore and B. Wroe. NCC/Blackwell, 1990.
- *Data Processing: Volume 2 Information Systems and Technology*, 7th edition, by R. G. Anderson. M&E Handbooks/Pitman, 1991.
- *Information Technology* by Roger Canfer. Butterworth-Heinemann, 1991.
- *IT Management Handbook*, edited by Rob Dixon, Butterworth-Heinemann, 1992.

4

Managing people and activities

10 Managing people

On completion of this chapter students should be able to:

- evaluate the effectiveness of alternative styles of and approaches to managing people

- analyse the factors influencing the effectiveness of individuals and teams

- evaluate alternative approaches to motivating people at work, improving performance and dealing with staff work problems

- work within a team and identify techniques for team-building

- analyse and evaluate the effect of their own and others' behaviour on interpersonal relationships at work.

Part 1 Management styles

Management

Management is usually defined as getting things done with or through other people. It involves deciding on *objectives* and ways of meeting those objectives. It is concerned with making *decisions* to ensure that objectives are met. Management involves *planning, organising* and *coordinating* activities. It is particularly concerned with bringing together sets of separate activities and tasks which contribute towards the completion of whole projects. It involves *controlling* – making sure that things are going to plan and that objectives are being met. This may involve setting up information systems to record progress.

Above all, management involves *working with people*. It is necessary, through effective communication, to make sure that people are committed to activities and to the organisation.

Most people who work for an organisation will be concerned with 'management'. Generally speaking as they work up an organisation they will become responsible increasingly for management decisions.

Management style

One definition of style is 'the way something is done'. It will be all too apparent that different organisations have different management styles – for example 'the leave it to someone else style' where things are usually badly organised because nobody is prepared to take responsibility for decisions. In contrast there is the 'highly bureaucratic style' in which there is a clear hierarchy for decision-making. In this type of organisation there are set patterns for taking the decisions. In the bureaucratic organisation decisions will be made; however, they may be made slowly and members of the organisation may become frustrated by the machine-like nature of the organisation which may prevent them from making decisions themselves.

Figure 10.1 Elements of management

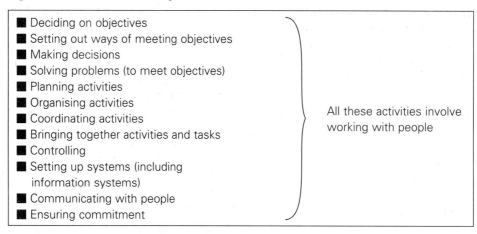

- Deciding on objectives
- Setting out ways of meeting objectives
- Making decisions
- Solving problems (to meet objectives)
- Planning activities
- Organising activities
- Coordinating activities
- Bringing together activities and tasks
- Controlling
- Setting up systems (including information systems)
- Communicating with people
- Ensuring commitment

All these activities involve working with people

On pages 225–30 we shall look at some of the research that has been carried out exploring different types of management style.

Task

Consider some of the organisations that you have worked for. In your own words try to describe their different management styles. What are the strengths and weaknesses of these different styles?

Organisational cultures

It is widely recognised that organisations have distinctive **cultures**. A commonly used definition of organisational culture is 'the way we see and do things around here'. Through tradition, history and structure, organisations build up their own culture.

Culture therefore gives an organisation a sense of identity – 'who we are', 'what we stand for', 'what we do'. It determines, through the organisation's legends, rituals, beliefs, meanings, values, norms and language, the way in which 'things are done around here' (see Figure 10.2).

An organisation's culture codifies what it has been good at and what has worked in the past. These values can often be accepted without question by long-serving members of an organisation.

One of the first things a new employee learns is some of the organisation's legends – perhaps how the founder worked long hours and despised formal educational and training qualifications. Legends can stay with an organisation and become part of the established ways of doing things. Perhaps the founder's views about the importance of education and training will stay current; in the course of time there may be a 'culture shift' as new managers move

Figure 10.2 Factors influencing organisational culture

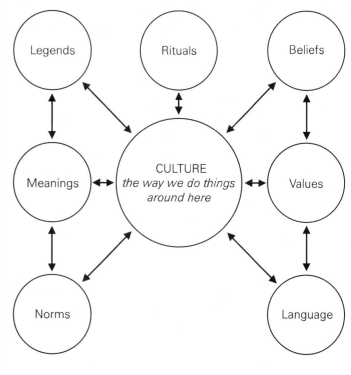

into the organisation and change the old ways. However, a number of legends continue to be important determinants of 'the way we do things around here'.

Task

Can you think of any examples of the way in which legends continue to influence behaviour in organisations of which you have been a member?

Organisations also have rituals. These are things that get repeated time after time and have almost a ceremonial feel about them. These rituals may include the way in which the office is ceremonially opened on a Monday morning and closed on a Friday by whoever has the power over the keys. Rituals may also include annual conferences and management 'away days', or even the ritual the office staff have of sharing cream buns on a Friday afternoon with their coffee.

In the course of time members of an organisation develop shared meanings and beliefs about the way things operate within the organisation and within the wider environment. For example, staff may come to share a belief that if management call an unexpected meeting then something is 'wrong' in the organisation; if the company receives a new order then employees may believe their jobs are more secure; and so on. A general belief may arise among employees that it is important that the rules and procedures of the organisation be followed. Individuals who fail to follow the rules may be informally (or formally) given a dressing down by other employees.

What is viewed as normal behaviour – the **norm** – can vary between organisations, even between those in the same industry. Norms are usual patterns of behaviour within an organisation and there is a great deal of pressure on individuals to conform to these norms.

Organisations also have their own language and jargon – for example, terms they use to describe competitors, or even officials within the organisation such as 'the boss', 'the shrink', 'the number cruncher'. Parts of an organisation may attract particular names such as 'the hot house'. It is surprising how quickly new recruits adapt to the language of an organisation.

In the course of time new members take on the values of the organisation. Without thinking, they begin to adopt the cultural norms of the organisation because they have adopted the predominant values.

Case Study
Democracy at work at Body Shop

Anita Roddick founded the high street retailer Body Shop. The following extract is taken from her book *Body and Soul*.

'Two general themes ran through all our education and communication programmes when we set them up. The first was that information was power. Staff were constantly invited to challenge the rules, to question the status quo and things we took for granted, and never to accept that a manager, simply because he or she was a manager, necessarily knew better. We stressed the importance of the individual and the fact that we wanted to hear from anyone, no matter what their position was in the organisation, if they thought they had a better way of doing things, or if they had a complaint. We were always saying to them: "Tell us how we can make things better, how we can ennoble your lives, how we can make your spirits sing."

'We invited contributions from everyone to something we called DODGI – the Department of Damned Good Ideas. Many of the ideas are put into practice. As a result of DODGI, for example, we now have a company lottery with 50 per cent of the money going in prizes and the remainder to charity; we recycle the backing from sticky labels and use it as shred in gift baskets; and we have a new approach to problem solving: if one department cannot come up with a solution, another department will brainstorm it for them.

'Gordon (Roddick) and I both did our best to get feedback from the grass roots of the company, to find out what was happening on the shop floor without having it watered down or interpreted through the mouths of managers. We made it our business to walk about everywhere and chat to everyone; we poked our noses into every corner, barged into meetings and made sure everyone knew we were around. We tried to break down the barriers that isolated work from family activities by holding meetings and presentations at our house in Sussex and at our holiday home in Scotland. We organised dinners for directors and members of staff selected at random to talk about everything and anything. At one of these dinners a guy from the warehouse filling room asked me why they had to wear stupid hats, since everything was automatic and they never even saw the products. I could see his point, so I told him to go in the next day and hide all the hats. His mouth dropped in amazement. "Look," I said, "if you don't want to wear the hats, don't wear them. But have fun not wearing them."

'Sometimes it was an uphill battle trying to convince staff not only that they had the right to challenge everything but that they also had the power to effect change. All the shop staff wear uniforms which we change about four times a year, usually to coincide with the launch of a new range or a campaign, when we will put the campaign slogan on their T shirts. One day I was having a conversation with a group of management staff and they were complaining about the red culottes that they had been given to wear for their current uniform. I said, "Do you like them?" and they said "Oh no!". So I said, "Then why the fuck are you wearing them?" I told them to parcel all the culottes up and send them to me and I would find someone in the world that did want them, which I eventually did in Romania. Those situations always surprised me. There we were, banging the drum about empowering our staff, encouraging them to speak up whenever they were unhappy about anything, yet they waited until I was around before they said how much they hated the culottes." '

Questions for discussion

1 *What does the extract tell you about the corporate culture at Body Shop? Consider in particular:*
   a *meanings and beliefs; i.e. views about how things should happen within the Body Shop organisation*
   b *the rituals that were developed to encourage employee participation*
   c *the values the Roddicks tried to instill in employees.*
2 *What do you think the impact of the above would have on the norms of behaviour of employees and managers at Body Shop?*

Types of organisational culture

The culture of an organisation is something that develops and changes over a period of time. This culture will exert pressure on individuals working within the organisation and so acts as a constraint on their behaviour.

Organisations are as unique as nations and societies. They have widely differing cultures, and these are reflected in the values, ideals and beliefs. The culture of an organisation influences the way in which it operates, so it is necessary to understand the culture before analysing ways in which people might contribute to the success or failure of the organisation. We need to examine broadly different types of culture before looking in greater depth at styles of management.

Cultures are built up over time by the dominant groups in an organisation. We shall consider four main types: power, role, task, and person.

Figure 10.3 Types of organisational culture

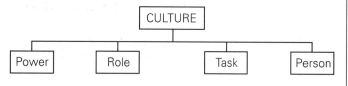

The power culture

Centralisation of power is the key feature of this type of culture. It is frequently found in small entrepreneurial organisations where control rests with a single individual or a small group of individuals.

The structure of power cultures can be illustrated as a web (see Figure 10.4). There is a central power source and rays of influence spread out from the centre.

Figure 10.4 The web structure of the power culture

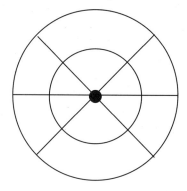

Decisions are made by high-status individuals rather than by the group. Decisions can be made quickly.

The weakness, however, is that people in the organisation may feel demotivated by the lack of challenge and suppressed by the individuals with power. Size is also a problem – the 'web' can break if it has to support too many activities.

The role culture

The **role culture** would be typical of a bureaucratic organisation that is divided into layers of offices and officials. This type of organisation is divided by sets of functions that are determined by rules and procedures (see Figure 10.5). Such an organisation operates by using logic and reason.

The organisation could be arranged according to a set of functions – marketing, human relations, finance etc. The work of the organisation is organised along these functionally distinct spheres of operation which focus on specific areas of competence.

In a role culture, power is hierarchical and is determined by an employee's position in the organisation (e.g. field marshal, general, colonel, major). The relationship between various roles is determined by job descriptions and set communication procedures. The system of

Figure 10.5 Role culture

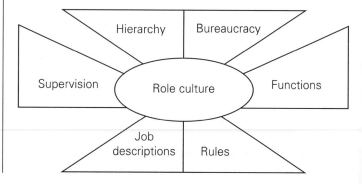

supervision and the role set out in a job description should make sure that job-holders carry out their allocated tasks – performance beyond this role is not required. Position is the main source of power, and rules and procedures are the main source of influence.

A major disadvantage of the role culture is that there is little scope for individual initiative. Job-holders can feel cramped by their position, as there is little scope for individual growth and development.

The task culture

A **task culture** is job- or project-orientated and emphasis is placed on completing a specific task. It is a team culture. The task determines the way in which the work is organised, rather than individuals or the rules of the organisation.

A task culture can be illustrated by a net of which some strands are thicker and stronger than others (see Figure 10.6). Much of the power and influence lies at the interstices of the net.

Figure 10.6 The net-shaped task culture

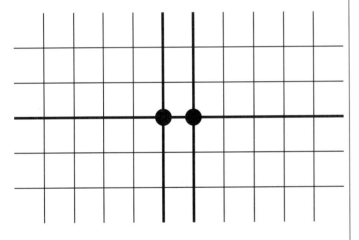

Bringing together a work-team for a particular project provides the basis for a task culture. The success of the team depends on the unifying power of the group to complete a specific task.

In task cultures employees may have considerable freedom, and this flexibility can make such organisations rewarding environments to work in. However, lack of formal authority and the considerable number of 'strands' can make management and control of a task culture difficult.

The person culture

In a **person culture** individuals are central – the organisation exists only to serve the interests of those within it. Not surprisingly, person cultures are more likely to be found in communities such as *kibbutzim* than in profit-motivated enterprises. Other examples may include co-operatives, barristers' chambers and architects' partnerships, where there is a cluster of individuals or a galaxy of stars all operating at the same level (see Figure 10.7).

Figure 10.7 The person culture

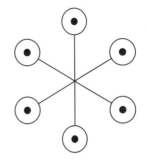

In a person culture, hierarchies are impossible except by mutual consent. Given a choice, many people would opt for this type of culture.

Cultural changes

Most organisations start with power cultures. Then, as they mature and become less dependent upon the founders, they tend to become role cultures. When the role culture needs greater flexibility, there might be a further change towards a task culture to fit the requirements and needs of each part of the organisation.

Broad approaches to managing people

A human resources (supportive) approach

It is fashionable to argue that people are the most important resource of any organisation. Indeed, it may be difficult to argue against this assertion.

The human resources approach to management is concerned with the development and growth of people towards higher levels of skill, competency, creativity and fulfilment. The approach is therefore supportive of the human resource. It sets out to foster individual improvement in the workplace. Work satisfaction is enhanced when employees are able to make fuller use of their abilities. More satisfaction increases commitment to the organisation and to work goals. This contrasts with scientific management which was the traditional management approach in the early 1900s.

The scientific management approach

The aim of the scientific management approach was to increase efficiency by carefully planning workers' movements in efficient ways. The most famous exponent of scientific management was **Frederick W. Taylor** (nicknamed Speedy Taylor), who stated that:

> *'The principal object of management should be to secure the maximum prosperity for the employer coupled with the maximum prosperity for each employee.'*

Taylor set out to find ways of maximising the efficiency of labour using the stopwatch and **'time-and-motion'** studies. He studied the movements made by production line workers in order to reduce the movements and tasks performed to the minimum for maximum efficiency. Labour tasks were thus reduced to machine-like efficiency. He felt that operatives would be prepared to work in this way in order to gain greater rewards in the form of higher pay.

In his book *Scientific Management* (1947), Taylor outlined four principles of management:

- The development of a science of work to replace the old rule-of-thumb methods by which workmen operated. Fulfilling optimum goals would earn higher wages; failure to do so would result in loss of earnings.
- Scientific selection and progressive development of the worker – training each to be 'first class' at some task.
- Bringing together the science of work and the scientifically selected and trained workers for best results.
- Equal division of work and responsibility between workers and management, cooperating together in close interdependence.

Although Taylor's work has been 'discredited' for a number of years, there are still writers who argue that many modern managers continue to practise 'Taylorism' without realising it.

Case Study
A high priced man?

Speedy Taylor illustrated his methods in the following conversation which took place between him and a 'Pennsylvania Dutchman' who worked at the Bethlehem Iron Company where Taylor had been employed to introduce efficient work methods.

'Schmidt, are you a high-priced man?'

'Vell, I don't know vat you mean.'

'Oh come now, you answer my question. What I want to find out is whether you are a high-priced man or one of these cheap fellows here. What I want to find out is whether you want to earn $1.85 a day or whether you are satisfied with $1.15, just the same as those cheap fellows are getting.'

'Did I vant $1.85 a day? Vas dot a high-priced man? Vell yes, I vas a high-priced man.'

'Now come over here. You see that pile of pig iron?'

'Yes.'

'You see that car.'

'Yes.'

'Well, if you are a high-priced man, you will load that pig-iron on that car tomorrow for $1.85. Now do wake up and answer my question. Tell me whether you are a high-priced man or not.'

'Vell – did I got $1.85 for loading dot pig iron on dot car tomorrow?'

'Certainly you do – certainly you do.'

'Vell den, I vas a high-priced man.'

'Now hold on, hold on. You know just as well as I do that a high-priced man has to do exactly as he's told from morning till night. You have seen this man before, haven't you?'

'No, I never saw him.'

'Well, if you are a high-priced man you will do exactly as this man tells you tomorrow, from morning till night. When he tells you to pick up a pig and walk, you pick it up and you walk, and when he tells you to sit down and rest, you sit down. You do that right straight through the day. And what's more no back-talk. Do you understand that? When this man tells you to walk, you walk, and when he tells you to sit down, you sit down, and you don't talk back at him. Now you come on to work here tomorrow and I'll know before night whether you are a high-priced man or not.'

(Source: *Scientific Management* by F. W. Taylor, Harper & Row, New York, 1947)

Questions for discussion

1 *What are the advantages of being a 'high-priced man'?*
2 *What are the drawbacks of being a 'high-priced man'?*
3 *Why were employees in the first decade of the twentieth century prepared, apparently, to accept Taylor's methods?*
4 *Why might employees be less prepared to become 'high-priced men and women' today?*
5 *To what extent does your personal experience tell you that the legacy of Taylorism is still with us?*

The Hawthorne experiments

In 1927 a series of studies were carried at the Hawthorne plant of the Western Electric Company in the USA. The '**Hawthorne experiments**' helped to bring in a new emphasis on human relations.

Initially the studies were concerned with testing scientific management principles. For example, the first experiment was concerned with showing that workers would increase their output if the lighting under which they worked was increased. For this the experimenters worked with a small sample of female employees in a separate room. However, a surprise result was that a reduction in lighting did not lead to a fall in output – in fact output increased up to the point at which it was virtually too dark to see!

What had happened, to the surprise of the researchers, was that showing an interest in what the workers were doing had raised their motivation, interest and efforts. No longer were the girls isolated individuals, working together only in the sense of being near each other. They had become participating members of a working group with all the psychological and social implications peculiar to such a group. Since that time the term **Hawthorne effect** has come to be used to describe a situation in which an experimenter's interest in people being studied induces those people to work harder.

Further experiments and surveys at the Hawthorne plant went on to show that workers were motivated not just by pay and working conditions but also by needs and desires. Employee performance depended to a large extent on the supervisor's leadership style and on employees' beliefs that they were being treated and respected as human beings and as valued members of a working team.

Theory X and Theory Y

Douglas McGregor's development of Theory X and Theory Y is a good example of a human relations approach to people management.

Theory X

McGregor used the term **Theory X** to apply to the types of management assumptions being made by 'scientific' managers. Examples of these assumptions are:

- Most people dislike work and responsibility and prefer to be directed – to be told what to do.
- The primary motive that people have for working is financial rather than a desire to do a good job.
- Most employees need to be closely supervised, controlled and coerced into achieving the objectives of the organisation.

McGregor also argued that, under Theory X, supervisors' behaviour would reflect their attitudes and assumptions about their workers. Supervisors with Theory X attitudes will assume that employees dislike their jobs and thus *require* close supervision.

Theory Y

McGregor proposed that managers should use more of a human-relations approach to management and supervision based on an optimistic view of human nature. This is **Theory Y** and is based on these assumptions:

- If you provide opportunities, people can enjoy their work and will exercise considerable control over their own performance.
- Employees are not just concerned with financial rewards, they also want to mix with their workmates, and want to do a good job.
- Employees may work better and more productively if supervision is kept to a minimum and if they are allowed to make decisions for themselves.

McGregor put forward the proposal to managers: *Expect the best from employees and they will respond in kind.*

Task

Which of the following statements would you associate with Theory X and which with Theory Y managers?

a Basically employees get personal satisfaction from seeing a job done well. Give them the opportunity to do so.
b Employees will react unfavourably to having a supervisor standing over them all the time!
c When this man tells you to walk, you walk, and when he tells you to sit down, you sit down, and you don't talk back at him.
d People might work better if control is kept to a minimum.

e My employees want to be told what to do! They expect me to make all the decisions for them. They are happy if they have a fat pay-packet to take home at the end of the week.

Post-Fordist society

The term **Fordism** came to be associated with mass manufacturing organisations producing high-volume output of standardised products with specialist machinery, and extensive stocks of spare parts, in a 'tall' organisational structure with clearly defined responsibilities and roles. The term originated because the car manufacturer Henry Ford used a management style based on hierarchical decision-making with strict functional specialisation and tightly defined job design and specialised machinery to produce standard models for 'mass markets'. Fordism clearly lent itself to the scientific management approaches of the Theory X type.

A Ford mass-production line in 1953.

In recent years such organisations have suffered from relatively poor productivity. They have had to become 'leaner' and 'flatter' organisations. Japanese companies gained a competitive advantage by using the bare minimum of human and material resources, keeping minimum stocks, reducing trade union influence in the workplace and building work-teams with devolved responsibilities. Japanese organisations fostered the spirit of working together to share ideas and to tackle problems together, coupled with security of employment.

By the late 1980s, Japanese companies had come to dominate many consumer markets because of these effective production techniques. More than 80 per cent of watches, 35mm cameras and video recorders were of Japanese origin, as were more than 70 per cent of microwave ovens and calculators, and more than 50 per cent of motor cycles and colour TVs.

Companies throughout the developed world responded to the Japanese **product re-engineering** phenomenon with a complementary phase of **process re-engineering** (the Ford motor company has itself carried out such process changes). 'Process re-engineering' is a term used to describe ways of fundamentally changing the design of an organisation. Tied in with the idea of the 'flat' organisation, it calls for the overhaul of job descriptions, organisational structures and management systems. By involving people from all areas of an organisation at an early stage, business objectives such as the launch of a new product will be achieved more quickly and at a lower cost by going through things one step at a time – for example, designing, engineering and marketing.

Peters and Waterman, in their book *In Search of Excellence*, argued that:

> *'the effective organisational structure for good management practice is now seen to be one which is loose-knit and flatter than the traditional bureaucratic forms that were preferred in previous decades.'*

However, in a more recent study of 374 men and women employed in very large UK-based corporations, Richard Scase and Robert Goffe (*Reluctant Managers*) found that:

> *'managers are often reluctant to adapt to changing organisational circumstances and prefer, instead, to work in more tightly-controlled and hierarchically arranged systems.'*

One of their findings was that managers become 'reluctantly' committed to their employing organisations. As a result they develop sources of motivation and personal satisfaction outside rather than within work. Many managers were seeking greater personal rewards in their private lives.

The importance of people

In an article in the magazine *Business Studies* in October 1992, Sue Cartwright argued that:

> *'organisations are human creations. They consist of people rather than material assets . . . It is individuals working within an organisational structure who produce the product, make the decisions, conceive the strategies, etc.'*

She then went on to focus on four key issues related to managing people within an organisation. These were:

- *Recruiting the asset* – the selection issue.
- *Utilising the asset and putting it to work* – the motivation issue.

- *Developing the asset* – the training issue.
- *Maintaining the organisation* – the change issue.

Selection

This is a key issue because an organization can only be as effective as the people it employs. People work alongside others in an organisational setting. Individuals therefore need to fit in with the work environment, other employees, the organisational climate, the style of work, and the culture of the organisation. Selection should not be made on quick decisions based, for example, on unstructured interview questions. It is essential that the organisation recruits people who will fit in best with the needs of the organisation, as well as the organisation meeting the needs of the people it recruits.

Utilising the asset

People do not work simply to gain money. Their work also provides:

- activity – an opportunity to use skills and knowledge
- variety – taking people out of the house
- temporal structure – giving a structure to the day
- social contacts – mixing with other people
- status and identity – a sense of worth and importance.

Effective organisations therefore need to improve the quality of work life of employees by making their work interesting. **Human resource management** is about enabling and empowering individuals within the organisation by creating autonomy, involvement and commitment. For example, we can learn a lot from Japanese styles of work organisation involving consensual decision-making and participation. Jobs should be enlarged and enriched, giving more scope to the individual.

Training

Lack of training is wasteful because it leads to mistakes and accidents. Employees should not be forced to 'learn on the job', often through making mistakes. It is essential for organisations to invest in training – after all, this is an investment for the future. Training leads to more capable and more motivated individuals who are constantly stretching out to new horizons.

Maintaining the organisation

Today the pace of industrial and economic change is faster than ever. Recognising and responding to change leads to a multitude of outcomes for the organisation, such as:

- revising and reformulating new corporate philosophies and market strategies
- developing new products
- introducing new technologies, systems and procedures
- restructuring or 'downsizing' (see Chapter 13)
- pooling resources and expertise to expand market position, etc.

All of these and many other changes directly affect the working lives of employees. So the human resource needs to be involved directly in the process of change and the management of change within the organisation. Change can be very stressful, particularly if it is managed poorly.

Clearly, ideas about styles of managing the human resource have changed considerably since Henry Ford's day. It would be inconceivable for his practices to dominate modern industrial structures. However, a number of commentators believe that undercurrents of 'scientific management' still shape management thinking even in this **post-Fordist** era.

Task

Draw on your own experience of management styles in organisations with which you are familiar to decide whether 'scientific management' is still with us. Summarise the advantages to an organisation of adopting a human relations approach.

Modern contingency approaches

The earliest management theorists such as **Henri Fayol** (writing in the 1930s) treated organisations almost as if they were devoid of people. The scientific management school then more or less discounted the human side of an organisation. In contrast, the human relations school placed the emphasis on people.

Each of the above approaches was based on the assumption that there was 'a single best way' to manage an organisation. The modern **contingency approach** stresses that organisations consist of tasks which have to be performed and of people who perform those tasks. The tasks and the people exist within an organisational environment. The people with responsibility for designing organisations should try to create the best 'fit' between people, tasks and environment (see Figure 10.8).

The best fit will depend on prevailing circumstances. Contingency theory therefore argues that there is no one best style of managing people – the most appropriate style

Figure 10.8 The best fit approach

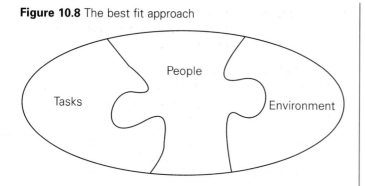

is 'contingent' on existing conditions (the word 'contingency' means 'it depends').

The implication is that even within the same organisation there will be scope for different organisational patterns and structures. For example, there may be scope for some activities to be carried out using a top-down hierarchical approach, while others are done in a far more democratic style.

Andrzej Huczynski and David Buchanan, in their best-selling text *Organisational Behaviour*, distinguish four main classes of activities that are carried out within an organisation. These are:

- *Steady-state activities* – the routine activities carried out in an organisation, comprising about 80 per cent of the tasks carried out by people.
- *Policy-making activities* – identifying goals, setting standards, allocating resources, and getting people to do things.
- *Innovation activities* – concerned with changing what a company does or how it does things (e.g. research and development, introducing new products).
- *Breakdown activities* – concerned with dealing with emergencies and crises.

The ways in which these activities are handled may be quite different, so a number of structures are likely to exist together. Within these structures there may be differences in:

- the types of people best suited for working within the structure
- the appropriate means of motivating people
- the management style.

Case Study
The dangerous folly called Theory Z

The following article, by B. Bruce-Briggs, appeared in *Fortune* magazine in May 1982.

'America should learn from Japanese management, claim a recent spate of books and articles, including even some in *Fortune*. According to this outpouring of facile advice, Japan's economic success is founded on a superior concept of "human resources" management that is directly needed here. One writer, William Ouchi, has called this approach Theory Z and claims that it is already the practice in some highly successful US companies. As the Japanese might say in their understated way, the idea is not quite so good as it seems. In plain American, Theory Z is downright silly. It is also dangerous . . .

'To the westerner, Japan may seem bizarre, even inhuman. But calling the Japanese "robots" is unjust. The system was not adopted as policy by Japanese management nor willingly elected by Japanese workers. It has been imposed on them all . . . Do you think they like to work hard? Do you think they enjoy singing company songs? Do you think the Kamikaze pilots wanted to splatter their guts on the decks of American ships?

'Learned commentaries on Japanese culture emphasise dominant values of *on* (obligation) and *giri* (duty) and so forth – the values promoted from above. From below, however, the most relevant value is *gaman* – patience, endurance, putting up with it . . .

'In short, to imitate the Japanese we would need a labour force disciplined by a social hierarchy controlled by an oligarchy. The danger of Theory Z and allied nostrums is that they may strip us of what little competitive advantage we now have. Americans . . . cannot match the Japanese at corporatism. We can, however, innovate, and invent. We can also move faster than the Japanese, unless hobbled by pseudo-consensus. It is appalling to observe how much time and effort is expended by business cajoling people into doing what obviously must be done. We may have too much Theory Z already . . .'

Questions for discussion

1 *What do you understand by the term Theory Z?*
2 *Compare Theory Z with Theories X and Y.*
3 *Why might western companies be attracted to Theory Z?*
4 *Why does B. Bruce-Briggs feel that Theory Z cannot be transplanted to US corporations? Why is he opposed to it?*
5 *To what extent does this article support the view that there is no one best style of management?*
6 *What factors are likely to affect the best style of management in an organisation? Try to relate your answer to your own experiences of working in organisations.*

Leadership

All organisations depend on **leadership**. In some there is one leader or a small number, while in others there are many leaders. Some organisations are characterised by a top-down management framework, while others have devolved management in which managers are encouraged to see themselves as 'ground-level' decision-makers (see Figure 10.9).

Figure 10.9 Top-down and ground-level management

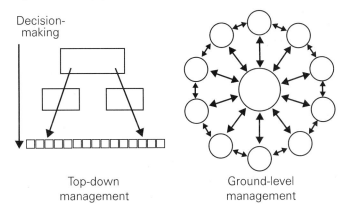

Top-down management   Ground-level management

Leadership occurs when one person influences another to work towards a pre-determined goal. There are two main approaches, the trait approach and the style approach.

The trait approach

The **trait approach** is based on the assumption that certain individuals are born with or acquire outstanding leadership qualities. These *personality traits* might include self-assurance, dominance, intelligence, determination, and/or a desire to work hard and achieve.

It is not too difficult to think of individuals who are intelligent, self-assured and decisive. In addition the successful leader is likely to be a high achiever with a strong need to 'self-actualise' – to use his or her capabilities to the fullest.

Charles Handy, in his book *Understanding Organisations*, pointed out that many studies single out the following traits as being most important for successful leadership:

- *Intelligence* – The leader should be above average but not of genius status. Leaders are particularly good at solving complex and abstract problems.
- *Initiative* – The leader should have independence and inventiveness, the capacity to perceive a need for action and the urge to do it. This appears to correlate quite well with age; i.e. it drops off after 40.

- *Self-assurance* – This implies self-confidence, reasonably high self-ratings on competence and aspiration levels, and on perceived ultimate occupational level in society.

Handy went on to identify the importance of the 'helicopter factor', by which he meant the ability to rise above the particulars of a given situation in order to develop a *clear overview*.

Additionally, most successful leaders appear to enjoy good health, are of above-average height or well below it, and come from the upper socio-economic levels of society.

However, Handy also outlined some key criticisms of trait theories. For example:

- There are many exceptions of good leaders who do not exhibit a number of these traits.
- The traits are poorly defined so there is no real clarity about them.
- Intelligence, initiative and self-assurance are necessary but not *sufficient* qualities for good leadership.

Task

Identify a group of five current leaders. To what extent do your five appear to have the traits of leadership? Perhaps you can focus on leaders whom you work with more closely to consider their traits. To what extent does the leadership trait theory seem to be valid?

Case Study
Heroes defy the mould

In an article in the *Independent on Sunday* on 19 June 1994, Tom Peters discussed twelve of his heroes. He argued that they share, more or less, 13 traits that add up to a fair guide to success in general. The traits were as follows.

'(i) *Self-invented.* "I am an American, Chicago-born," begins Saul Bellow's novel *The Adventures of Augie March*, "and go at things as I have taught myself, free-style, and will make the record in my own way." All my Mount Rushmore nominees have chiselled their masterpieces from the granite of life in a distinct, unusual fashion. Standard career path? Forget it. One company, one job? Not even close.

(ii) *Ever changing.* I don't think any of my dandy dozen has a split personality in the clinical sense of the term; but surely all are chameleons, not bound by consistency they have tried a plethora of outfits while remaining desperately and passionately committed to whatever it is they are pursuing at the moment.

(iii) *Battered and bruised.* My heroes have screwed up things at least as often as they have gotten them right. Their collective motto could be: "A road without potholes is not a road worth travelling". Failure does not seem to faze them. If anything, setbacks amuse them and motivate them.

(iv) *Inquisitive.* No question goes unasked for this squad of achievers. Sometimes I think there is literally nothing that does not interest them. They are determined to get to the bottom of any topic they touch – on or off the job. (Job? They are what they do. Job is not part of their vocabulary.)

(v) *Childlike.* This naive crew – who refuse to grow up – are not afraid to ask dumb (even very dumb) questions if they are not getting the message. Their appetite for knowledge and exploration is far greater than any fear they have of looking idiotic.

(vi) *Free from the past.* Gravity has no meaning for this group. They are not weighed down by history. In a flash they will thumb their noses at what only yesterday they were fervently espousing.

(vii) *Comfortable, even cocky.* My Hall of Famers are at ease with themselves, unperturbed by the idea of life as an elusive moving target – an adventure to be relished, mostly for its detours.

(viii) *Jolly.* These people laugh a lot. They marvel at human intrigues, and their appreciation of the absurd stokes their marvelous sense of humour, All of them have wrinkles – you know the kind . . . those that can only be attributed to smiles and laughter.

(ix) *Audacious and a bit nuts.* They will try anything – from learning a language to starting a new career – with barely a moment's hesitation. Moreover, by the standards of the majority, they view the world through decidedly cockeyed glasses.

(x) *Iconoclastic.* Conventional wisdom, to my pilgrims, is like a red cape to a bull. I sometimes think they're only happy when they're on the 'wrong' side of an issue or truism.

(xi) *Multidimensional.* We're not dealing with saints. All members of this tribe have flaws, often as pronounced as their strengths. But, then, when was the last time you observed an insipid soul accomplishing much of anything?

(xii) *Honest.* It's not that they always tell the truth or are above pettiness. Hey, we're all human. It's just that this set is attuned to reality and especially to their own foibles. They are consummate and often quixotic truth-seekers, with little time for those who aren't as confused as they are.

(xiii) *Larger than life.* Our Gang of Twelve are all heroic. That is they paint the canvasses, large and small, with bold strokes. They are fearless in their own fashion. They embrace the circus of life, rather than shrink from it.'

Questions for discussion

1 *Do you think the traits outlined would 'add up to a fair guide to success'?*
2 *Is there anything you think should be removed from the list?*
3 *Is there anything you would like to add to the list?*
4 *Try to establish your own list of traits that you think would contribute to success.*
5 *Identify your own list of people who have some or all of these traits.*

The style approach

A person's **leadership style** is the pattern of behaviour they exhibit in carrying out a leadership role over a period of time. An assumption can be made that employees will work harder and perhaps better for managers who employ certain styles rather than others.

The most common division of styles is between autocratic (or authoritarian) and democratic. In the highly authoritarian style, power is vested strongly with the leader.

Rensis Likert, in his book *New Patterns of Management*, outlined a model of leadership styles which highlighted four types (see Figure 10.10).

Figure 10.10 Likert's model of leadership styles

AUTHORITARIAN ←————————→ DEMOCRATIC			
System 1	System 2	System 3	System 4
Exploitive authoritarian	Benevolent authoritarian	Consultative	Participating groups

- *System 1* – Under the exploitive authoritative regime, threats and punishments are employed and communication and teamwork are poor.
- *System 2* – The benevolent authoritative regime is paternalistic and allows some opportunities for consultation and delegation.
- *System 3* – The consultative regime moves forwards to greater democracy and teamwork. Rewards are used instead of threats.
- *System 4* – The participative group regime is the ultimate democratic style, leading to commitment to organisational goals.

Tannenbaum and Schmidt outlined a continuum of leadership styles which fall between the authoritarian and the democratic (see Figure 10.11). In the diagram, as we move further to the right (i.e. towards an increasingly democratic model) subordinates within the organisation are given increasingly more freedom to make decisions for themselves.

Figure 10.11 Continuum of leadership styles

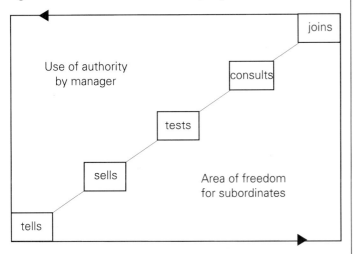

Charles Handy argued in favour of a supportive style of leadership because this is likely to foster:

- subordinate satisfaction
- lower turnover and grievance rates
- fewer inter-group conflicts.

Moreover this is usually the preferred style of subordinates. Handy argues that, although research findings indicate that style alone is not the only answer to effective leadership, a supportive style of management will lead to a higher degree of contentment and greater involvement by the working group.

Another aspect of management style we need to look at is the contrast between **task-orientated** styles and **people-orientated** styles. A leader who is wrapped up in the task will be mainly concerned with output, work results and rigid standards. This may result in the leader trying to closely monitor each and every task that employees carry out. (Task orientation may thus be closely associated with scientific management and autocratic styles.) In contrast, a person-orientated style will show itself in a strong concern for employees. This leader may set out to boost morale and encourage employees to work together to get tasks completed.

The 'management grid' devised by Blake and Mouton is a matrix model of management which, instead of concentrating on autocratic versus democratic styles, looks at 'concern for people' and 'concern for production'. Again, this is easier to understand by looking at a diagram (see Figure 10.12).

Of the five styles of management shown in the grid, only [9:9] is the ideal style because it combines deep concern for people with clear concern for production – getting things done and keeping everyone happy. The compilers of the grid called this style 'Team'. Looking at the others:

- [1:9] is too concerned with people and gets very little done ('Country Club').
- [9:1] is too concerned with production and creates an atmosphere of low morale ('Task').
- [1:1] has no concern for people or output ('Impoverished').
- [5:5] shows some concern for people and some concern for production ('Middle-of-the-road').

The managerial grid enables managers to assess their own management style and compare it with other possibilities.

Another dimension of style is the difference between a **positive** and a **negative** leader. A positive leader will emphasise rewards, which may be in the form of money, benefits, etc. or in the form of better working relationships. Negative leadership in contrast places more emphasis on punishments and sanctions. Negative leaders may stress their superiority and domination over others. These are bosses more than leaders – they use power as a threat.

The nature of power over people

To have **power** is to have the ability to influence people and events. Power is acquired by individuals and groups through their personalities, their activities and the situations in which they operate.

Politics is concerned with the way in which leaders gain and use power and involves them in all sorts of activities such as bargaining, striking deals, forming coalitions with others, etc. Clearly it is important for a leader to have political skills in order to gain and keep power.

The four major types of power which individuals develop or acquire are personal power, legitimate power, expert power and/or political power (see Figure 10.13).

Personal power

Personal power is possessed by certain individuals and is sometimes termed 'charismatic' or 'referent' power. Some individuals have tremendous charisma and are able to build up personality cults. Other people look to these individuals to make decisions for them – they can be very forceful and determined. Charismatic leaders (whether you like them or not) have a personal magnetism which draws other people to accept their right to lead. These

Figure 10.12 The management grid

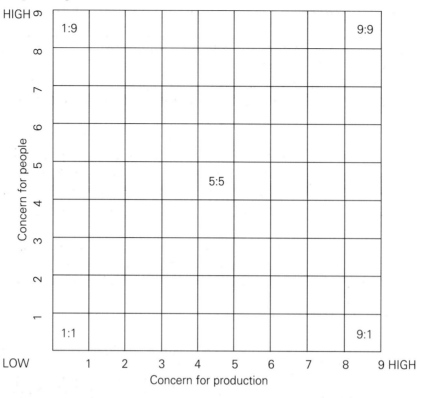

Figure 10.13 Major sources of power

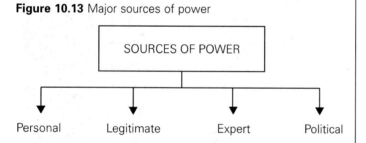

leaders may sense the needs of their followers and provide a focus which meets those needs. Often leaders of new religious cults have this sort of personal magnetism and can persuade others to follow them down many uncharted paths.

Legitimate power

Legitimate power is based on people having positions within a structured framework. In a particular culture, power will be delegated to different offices or positions and this will be accepted by members as being legitimate. People believe that it is desirable and necessary to run and maintain society in this way. For example, in Norman England people accepted that there was a king, with rich landholding barons, who would have their own stewards and officials who would control activities in a particular locality. In large bureaucratic organisations it is accepted that senior officials will make major decisions and pass down commands to junior officials. There is social pressure within the organisation to accept the legitimacy of this decision-making process.

Expert power

Expert power is based on the specialised knowledge possessed by certain individuals. It frequently arises where there is complex knowledge that can be gained only through education and training. For example, when there has been a road accident resulting in casualties, we recognise that doctors and other members of the emergency services are the best people to make decisions. If there are structural defects in your house you might turn to an architect to tell you what to do, and so on. There are many situations in which we turn to the expert and hand over the decision-making.

Political power

Political power stems from being supported by a group. To gain political power the leader will need to be able to work with people and social systems to gain support and allegiance from them. Gaining political power involves having an understanding of those factors most likely to encourage others to support you, as well as understanding how systems can be used in your favour. Politicians have

Figure 10.14 Tactics to ensure political power

Tactic	Example
■ Alliance	A group of department heads join together to exert pressure for improved health and safety standards in an organisation
■ Association with those with more power	An individual has social contacts with someone in a senior position in his or her organisation (e.g. membership of the same club). The power then 'rubs off' on the junior, increasing the latter's power base
■ Trade-offs	One departmental head supports another in return for reciprocal favours
■ Control of information	The market research department has first insights into customer needs and preferences which determines new products that the production department will go on to make
■ Status symbols	Access to certain facilities within an organisation are restricted to certain post-holders
■ Power plays	One manager increases the size of his or her sphere of influence by creating new sub-divisions, departments, etc.
■ Selective service	Favouritism is shown to certain individuals, groups and departments in an organisation (e.g. their work is processed more quickly by another department)
■ Networks	Individuals can develop formal and informal contacts within an organisation which enhance their power base

to set out to appease different groups in order to maintain their power base. Political leadership also involves having access to sanctions and rewards. A number of tactics can be employed to obtain and retain political power (see Figure 10.14).

Political **power-broking** is an aspect of organisational life. Anyone working in an organisation quickly becomes aware of internal politics and power alliances. Gaining political power in an organisation can be an immensely subtle and time-consuming activity.

Case Study
Margaret Thatcher's leadership

Margaret Thatcher led the Conservative Party from 1979 to 1991. She was regarded by many as an inspirational leader who placed the United Kingdom firmly on the modern world stage. She showed tremendous charisma, giving other people a focus to follow.

Mrs (now Baroness) Thatcher has also been described as a transformational leader – a person who seeks and brings about radical change. Such leaders are capable of being ruthless in pursuit of what they believe to be right and can be willing to take many risks. Margaret Thatcher's strong sense of direction (characterised by her famous saying 'This lady's not for turning') and her ruthless determination earned her the label Iron Lady. Huge risks – such as those taken in the Falklands War – as well as her personal charisma generated strong feelings amongst colleagues and the electorate.

Some of the Thatcher qualities were her high energy level (long hours and little sleep), her mental power (ability to absorb, digest, retain and recall information, to keep in touch with details and to focus on major issues), her courage (the Brighton bombing) and the conviction that she was right. This conviction has, however, been described as her Achilles' heel. If you are completely convinced of the correctness of your own views this often stirs up challenges.

Another of her weaknesses, it has been said, was her inability to build a cohesive and stable team. She frequently changed her cabinet when ministers did not see things in the same way she did.

Theorists tend to believe that transformational leaders should transform and then move on to look for fresh challenges – and that Margaret Thatcher's mistake was to stay too long as leader. It is often argued that 'nothing is so dangerous as yesterday's success'.

Questions for discussion

1 *What do you think were the major sources of Margaret Thatcher's power – individual, legitimate, expert, or political? How would these different sources of power be important in different situations?*
2 *Contrast Margaret Thatcher's sources of power with a more recent political or business leader.*
3 *List five other charismatic leaders. What do these leaders have in common?*
4 *What tactics might a political leader employ to maintain their power base?*
5 *Do you agree that transformational leaders need to move on?*

Power and style

Davis and Newstrom, in their book *Human Behaviour at Work*, argue that the way in which leaders use power establishes a type of style. They identify three major styles, autocratic, participative, and free-rein. Leaders will tend to use all three of these styles over a period of time, but one of them tends to dominate.

- *Autocratic leaders* centralise power and decision-making in themselves. They establish what subordinates will do, when and how. Power tends to be based on threats and punishments, although the benevolent autocrat may also dish out rewards.
- *Participative leaders* delegate authority. Decisions are made after consultation and participation of a number of individuals, with the leader and the group working as a social unit. Participative management is becoming increasingly popular as a leadership style.
- *Free-rein leaders* avoid power and responsibility. They expect groups to establish their own objectives and to sort out their own problems.

Participative leadership

It is worth looking at participative leadership in more depth because it is a style that has gained importance in recent years. Participative leaders encourage their subordinates to take part in decision-making and to solve problems for themselves. This type of practice has been commonplace in Japan. Decisions are based on team inputs of ideas, and the emphasis is on **consensus management**.

As we saw earlier, 'Theory Z' is used to describe this philosophy of participation. Theory Z will work only if leaders are prepared to share responsibilities and if employees are prepared to take on responsibilities. Participation at job level involves the team leader and the working group interacting at an informal level. For example, a quality circle is a small group of volunteers who meet regularly to discuss work methods and arrangements under a trained leader.

Contingency leadership

In addition to trait and style theories of leadership, increasing emphasis is now placed on **contingency theories** of leadership. Contingency theorists take account of the many different variables involved in the leadership situation – the task, and/or the work-group and the position of the leader within the work-group.

Perhaps the most important early contribution to contingency theory was made by **Fred Fiedler**. He looked at the position of the leader in terms of 'favourableness' to lead. Fiedler studied leadership situations in a variety of organisations before coming up with the conclusions that the effectiveness of a leader depends on:

- the leaders' position (in terms of power)
- the type of relationship between leader and followers
- the extent to which the task is structured.

The task is structured if goals are clear, there are clear criteria for success, there are only a small number of successful outcomes to the task, and a limited number of ways of completing the task.

The leader will operate in three main types of conditions:

Condition 1:
Highly structured task.
Leader has a high position of power.
Good relationships between leader and followers.

Condition 2:
Unstructured task.
Leader has a low position of power.
Moderate relationships between leader and followers.

Condition 3:
Unstructured task.
Leader has a low position of power.
Poor relationships between leader and followers.

Where *Condition 1* exists then a leader who concentrates on getting tasks carried out will be most likely to be

Figure 10.15 Fitting leadership to the situation

Situational control

Employee-centred leader	**Performance** POOR	**Performance** GOOD	**Performance** POOR
	High control	Moderate control	Low control
Task-oriented leader	**Performance** GOOD	**Performance** POOR	**Performance** RELATIVELY GOOD

successful. There is a clear focus on the task, there are clear objectives, work performance can be monitored and progress made quickly. There is no real need in this situation for a leader oriented towards human relationships, because working relationships are already good.

Where *Condition 2* exists, however, the leader oriented towards human relationships will be more successful. Good relationships are required to ensure that tasks are performed. Because the tasks lack structure it is necessary for relationships to be good to hold things together.

In *Condition 3* there is a lot of uncertainty. Fiedler argued that what is required is a task-orientated leader because pressure needs to be exerted on followers to get things done. A leader oriented towards human relationships may be seen as being too weak in these circumstances. There is a necessity to reduce ambiguity when these conditions apply.

The most effective type of leadership will be contingent on the situation, and Fiedler developed the grid in Figure 10.15 to outline the relationship between the style of leadership and the situation. Situational leadership therefore involves analysing the situation before deciding on the best way to lead. A situational analysis involves looking at the powers vested in leaders, the type of task to be completed and the relationship between leaders and followers.

A best-fit approach

A best-fit approach explores the idea that there should be a good fit between the main ingredients of a leadership situation. The four main ingredients are:

■ the leader – his or her preferred style of operating and personal characteristics
■ the subordinates – their preferred style of leadership in a given context
■ the task – the job to be performed and the technology involved

■ the environment – the organisational setting of the leader, group and task.

There will be no one best-fit because it is all contingent on the situation. However, leadership will be most effective when the requirements of the task, the leader, and the followers do not conflict. We can present 'fit' on a scale running from 'tight' to 'flexible'. Figure 10.16 shows an example of a situation in which the task is relatively unstructured, the leader likes to operate in an unstructured way, and yet employees are looking for structure and organisation. This is likely to lead to poor performance. However, there will be a tendency for the three factors to move closer together during the course of time. If this does not happen the effectiveness of the group will be poor and tasks will be handled badly.

Figure 10.16 Diagrammatic representation of 'fit'

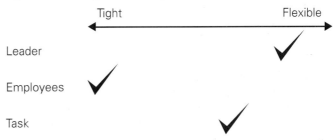

Charles Handy argued that, confronted with lack of fit, leaders need to adjust factors towards a fit. In the short term it may be easiest to adjust managerial style. However, in the longer term the most benefit may be achieved by redesigning tasks.

Case Study
Qualities of leadership

In his book *Understanding Organisations,* Charles Handy wrote that individuals need to learn to do the following:

a develop and communicate a clear vision of the task, so that a sense of purpose develops in the group

b allow others to influence the vision, so that they are committed to it

c build up the trust and respect of their group so that they have the essential conditions to allow them to adapt their style to the contingency requirements

d remember that successful performance of their ambassadorial role is essential if they are to have freedom to behave as they think best within their group

e remember that they represent the organisation to their subordinates and should practise all the precepts enjoined on the senior managers.

Individuals and organisations should bear in mind that the individual who meets these requirements will tend to:

a have high tolerance for ambiguity and be good at handling open-ended problems

b be good at differentiating between people and situations

c have a clear self-concept which will tend to go with self-confidence

d have a high reservoir of the 'E factors' – in particular, Energy

e be prepared to set moderately high standards for himself or herself and co-workers and to give and receive feedback on performance.

Questions for discussion

1 *What form of management do you think Handy is advocating, autocratic, participative or free-rein?*
2 *To what extent does Handy advocate a 'contingent' approach to management?*
3 *What do you perceive to be the benefits of the approach outlined by Handy?*

Changes in working patterns

Modern economies are characterised by working patterns that are radically different from the past. These patterns are likely to continue to change. In today's competitive climate businesses throughout the world are increasingly adopting more flexible approaches to working patterns.

Flexible working

In a survey of top Japanese executives conducted by the Kyodo news agency in the summer of 1993, 86 per cent said the lifetime employment system (under which Japanese employees were guaranteed a job for life with a particular company) was set to disappear. An even larger 95 per cent said that companies would increasingly adopt pay scales based on merit, rather than the current system under which employees are rewarded according to seniority.

In the UK, the second annual Survey of Long-term Employment Strategies published in September 1993 reported that the use of more temporary and contract workers and other methods of **flexible working** will permanently change Britain's employment patterns. The prime reasons for these changes are the need for increased productivity, flexibility and cost control. Between 1988 and 1993 more than 90 per cent of the UK's largest organisations restructured, with job losses at all levels. Thirty-nine per cent expected to go through the restructuring process in 1994, with 66 per cent doing so by 1998.

Most British employers already use some form of flexible working. This trend will no doubt increase, coupled with more 'contracting out' of work. Temporary and part-time workers will be used more and more to supplement existing employees. Key changes supporting flexibility include:

■ an increased emphasis on the flexible firm
■ the growth of contracting-out
■ the growing importance of women in the work force
■ more emphasis on skills and training
■ the 'collapse of skills'
■ the spread of teleworking
■ the trend towards 'performance-related pay'.

The flexible firm

The concept of the **flexible firm** has become very popular in management theory and has been put into practice by many large business organisations in the public and private sectors. The notion of the flexible firm distinguishes between various types of workers.

■ *Core workers* are employees who are multi-skilled (i.e. educated and trained to do a variety of job tasks), work full-time and receive good pay, conditions and benefits.
■ *Peripheral workers* are short-term, temporary and part-time, who receive less favourable pay, conditions and benefits.
■ *External workers* are not employees of the firm but are self-employed, agency workers, or working for sub-contractors.

The flexible firm will cut its wages costs to a minimum by limiting core workers relative to peripheral and external workers (see Figure 10.17).

Figure 10.17 The shrinking core of a flexible firm

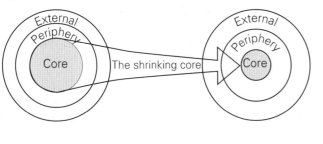

Task

Identify the core, peripheral and external workers associated with one organisation with which you are familiar. Why does the organisation employ or use these three types of workers to carry out different tasks?

Some writers have claimed that the ideal of the flexible firm was a deliberate strategic decision being made by informed organisations in order to create a competitive edge. Other researchers argues that, rather than being a strategic decision, new working patterns have been almost forced on organisations – temporary work, short-term contracts, agency temping, part-time work and self-employment were all developing trends that accentuated from the 1980s into the 90s rather than being elements of a master strategy on the part of an organisation. Perhaps the reality lies between the two viewpoints – some firms may have chosen flexibility while others had it thrust upon time and used management theory to justify the inevitable.

Contracting-out

The flexible firm 'contracts-out' non-core functions wherever possible. There is no need for a large organisation to take responsibility for transporting all of its inputs and outputs, to produce all of its own advertising materials and to undertake many other functions which can be effectively delegated to outside agencies. Contracting-out can thus help to reduce the core workforce of an organisation, reduce central costs and increase operational efficiency.

Marks & Spencer is a company that has long been associated with the contracting out of non-core functions, such as garment and food manufacture, so that it can concentrate on its core retailing role. In recent years the massive oil corporations such as BP and Shell have carried out extensive 'downsizing' operations, particularly of many administrative and office functions which can be contracted-out to agencies.

In the public sector, too, contracting-out is now the order of the day. For example, many civil service jobs are coming under threat as private firms are invited to run government services. 'Efficiency scrutinies' have been used to find areas where cutbacks can be made. When Margaret Thatcher became Prime Minister in 1979 there were nearly three quarters of a million civil servants, but by the mid-1990s that figure was closer to half a million.

Many jobs, including waste disposal, street cleaning and the running of some prisons, are now contracted out to the private sector.

Case Study
Shrinking the civil service

A White Paper published in July 1994 announced the government's intention to further reduce the size of the civil service by 50 000 by 1998, to increase competition and efficiency. Departments and agencies were asked to draw up 'annual efficiency plans' showing how they would keep within a budget for the following three years. This process started in the spring of 1995.

In addition, departments and agencies are now able to decide whether to contract-out services to the private sector. This may lead, for example, to departments contracting-out work to private computer companies, law firms, surveyors, designers and catering companies. Individual departments are given responsibility for deciding on their own pay and grading structures for middle and junior ranks.

Departments have been given the power to review their own management structures and to remove layers of bureaucracy. Increased priority is to be given to leaner, flatter structures with greater scope for talented individuals to make their mark.

Questions for discussion

1 *What benefits would you expect to arise from the civil service contracting out services? Who will reap these benefits?*
2 *What benefits would you expect to arise from civil service departments being given more responsibility for their own management?*
3 *Can you imagine any drawbacks from the civil service operating more like a private sector concern?*

Women in the workplace

In 1985, the number of men in employment (full-time and part-time) far exceeded the number of women – 13.1 million compared with 9.4 million. Figures released by the Income Data Service, a private research company, in May 1993 showed about 10.7 million men in work compared with 10.1 million women. According to this research company, the trend towards female employment is likely to increase (see Figure 10.18).

Figure 10.18 Male and female employment in the UK

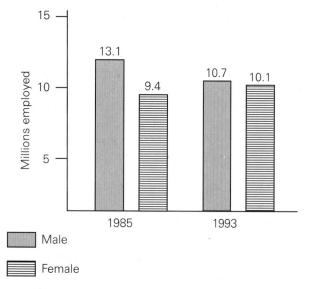

Male

Female

However, some evidence shows that women are less likely to be core workers, more of them being part-time peripheral workers – almost half the women now working are in part-time jobs. Huge numbers of these women, and a large percentage of their female colleagues in full-time work, are 'low paid'.

The trend towards more female employees is likely to be encouraged by the abolition in 1993 of **wages councils**, which fixed statutory minimum wages for two million low-paid workers (80 per cent of whom were women).

In the UK, women now account for just a quarter of all managers and only 1 per cent of 'top' managers. There is a significantly lower proportion of women in managerial jobs in Britain than in Germany, France, the USA, Canada and Australia. One explanation for the lack of women's career progression is that they may be less mobile than men. Also, management may be seen to require certain 'male characteristics' such as aggression and drive. The stereotypical female is sometimes assumed to lack these qualities. It is argued that women are socialised into female attitudes and behaviour which discourages others from perceiving them as ideal managers.

However, there is increasing pressure to change personnel practices by introducing provision for childcare and extended periods of paternity as well as maternity leave. Social stereotypes are beginning to change, but only very slowly.

An emphasis on skills and training

A report on competitiveness by the Department of Trade and Industry in 1993 suggested that the UK was lagging badly behind its international rivals, with a productivity gap of about a quarter compared with France, Japan and Germany. The report cited the UK's inferior skills base and the lower standards of overall educational attainment. Another report in the same year, from the National Institute of Economic and Social Research, showed that the proportion of French and German 16-year-olds gaining the equivalent of GCSE A, B or C grades in maths, their national language and a science subject was more than double the figure for England and Wales. The report's authors pointed out that the most striking disparity between the attainments in Britain and those in other countries was in the lower half of the ability range. Many commentators in the UK feel that if we can improve our education and vocational training then the output of goods and services will increase because employees will be more productive.

Figure 10.19 shows that the UK's biggest skills 'shortfall' is among intermediate-level crafts of the sort that are commonplace on continental and Japanese production lines, where employees are trained to maintain their own machinery and to correct simple faults.

Inferior skills mean that there are more breakdowns and faults take longer to put right. A worker on the production line has to wait for the maintenance specialist rather than tackle the fault personally. Managers have to design production schedules to allow for periodic hold-ups. Highly skilled workers may have to do jobs themselves which in competing countries would be done by those with lesser skills. British manufacturers struggle to produce short and specialised production runs because of the time taken to change the production line. All of these factors lead to lack of competitiveness.

National Vocational Qualifications (NVQs), which are job-related, and **General National Vocational Qualifications** (GNVQs) through which students learn a particular field of knowledge supported by core skills, will help to prepare people for a variety of jobs (see page 266). The creation of the 'Vocational A level' in July 1993 was aimed at giving vocational qualifications parity of esteem with more 'academic' qualifications. Employer-led Training and Enterprise Councils (TECs) are responsible for organising training and educational initiatives in regions.

Figure 10.19 Vocational qualifications compared (percentages of the work force)

	Britain (1989)	France (1988)	Germany (1988)	Netherlands (1989)	Switzerland (1991)
University degrees	11	7	11	8	11
Intermediate vocational qualification of which:	25	40	63	57	66
technician	7	7	7	19	9
craft	18	33	56	38	57
No vocational qualification	64	53	26	35	23

The availability of job-related training varies according to employment status and age. Part-time employees are less likely than full-time employees to be offered training. The older an employee, the less likely it is that he or she will be offered job-related training.

The 'collapse of skills'

Michael Hammer and James Champy popularised the notion of **'re-engineering'** in their influential book *Re-engineering the Corporation – A Manifesto for Business Revolution*. The term applies to massive, fundamental upheaval of the ways in which organisations reorganise themselves as part of a process of continuous change. During a period of recession the concept was associated with 'downsizing' (reducing the size of the organisation) so that fewer, more highly qualified, people did more complex work. Grass-roots employees might take over many aspects of management as the manager moved from a supervisory role to a more strategic one.

This 'collapse in skills' means that managers have to create the operating models that give the company its distinct quality. For example, these could be based on features such as customer satisfaction or innovation. The return to focusing on the business is in contrast to the traditional approach of managers moving steadily away from operations as they are promoted.

The spread of teleworking

Teleworking means that employees work for most or part of their time at a distance from the office, often at home. They use some form of telecommunications equipment, above and beyond the normal domestic telephone or answerphone. Such workers cannot be judged by the traditional checks on attendance but on the results they produce.

Teleworking, with its promise of productivity gains, fits well with other popular current management practices such as the wider use of performance measures, devolution of responsibility and the setting of clear quality standards and targets. The National Economic Development Office estimated the number of people teleworking in 1992 to be 1.5 million, which is about 6 per cent of the workforce. However, a number of human resource specialists have argued that this type of work may be somewhat impoverished because it reduces human contacts from the work situation.

Performance-related pay

It has become popular to introduce **performance-related pay** in both the private and public sectors. Schemes based on performance appraisal techniques have been adopted in a wide range of occupations, including the police force, universities, insurance and banking. Up to three-quarters of all employers are using some form of performance appraisal to set pay levels.

Managerial jobs are the most affected. Performance is increasingly assessed against work objectives. Individuals' objectives can be set by reference to company goals and are known as 'accountabilities'. Short-term goals may be attached to each objective. Scoring systems are then worked out to measure performance against objectives, and these distinguish levels of attainment (e.g. high/ medium/low).

A great deal of thought is required to develop proper assessment systems. Sir Patrick Sheehy who in 1993 developed proposals for performance-related pay in the police force was clearly offended when some national papers suggested that 'accountabilities' could be measured simply by the numbers of arrests a police officer made!

One way of rewarding performance is to give a bonus if certain targets are met. Another method is to give increments when targets are achieved – each year an individual could move up an incremental ladder.

Flexibility in the labour market

Conditions in the employment market change with time, but are linked to the state of the national economy as a whole. In the first quarter of 1993 the UK economy moved out of recession more rapidly than some people had expected, and commentators looked for the reasons why employers were more willing to take on extra staff. One of the popular explanations was that employment legislation made it easier to lay workers off when they were no longer needed. It follows that when order books start to pick up employers will be prepared to take on extra staff knowing that they can be dispensed with if bad times set in again.

The government has been a prime mover in encouraging flexibility in the labour market, both through employment policies in the public sector and by the creation of a legal framework that has successively reduced state interference.

The European Union's Social Chapter

The UK is the only member of the EU to side-step the **Social Chapter**, which guarantees minimum rights for employees. The UK government did not want to be bound by regulations on such things as **minimum wages**.

The Chapter was adopted by the other eleven EU countries in 1989. It led to measures such as the work time directive with a proposal for a 48-hour maximum working week, to which the UK government objected.

The eleven other countries said that their objectives under the Chapter were the promotion of employment, improved living and working conditions, proper social protection, dialogue between management and labour, and the development of human resources with a view to lasting high employment and the combating of social exclusion. The UK government opposed the Chapter on the grounds that it would allow working conditions to be decided at EU level and would add unacceptable costs to business.

One aim of the Chapter was to avoid so-called 'social-dumping' – the move of investment to countries with lower employment standards. There is concern that this is already taking place, with the transfer of jobs by Hoover from France to Scotland.

Case Study
The 'inclusive company'

Within Europe there is a clash of thinking between those such as the free-marketers in the Conservative Party who would like to see a return to nineteenth century free markets, and those such as the Scandinavians and Germans who press the case for social democracy based on setting minimum standards for all citizens.

The free-marketers in this country argue that barriers like minimum wages and powerful trade unions prevent businesses from keeping costs down in a highly competitive global economy. They claim that the route to prosperity is to minimise the part played by the state in creating social justice.

Recently the Royal Society of Arts presented a vision of the 'inclusive company' which rejects the free-market model. The 'inclusive company' recognises its responsibilities to its staff, its suppliers, its customers and the community, as well as satisfying the needs of its investors. This concept is already applied extensively in Japan and in social democracies in Europe.

Social democrats argue that the concept of an 'inclusive company' shares the same principles as the EU Social Chapter – i.e. increasing job opportunities, improving hiring and working conditions, promoting dialogue between management and workers, encouraging investment in training. Companies such as Northern Foods, which has always had a strong social conscience, support the 'inclusive company'. Its chairman, Christopher Hasking, argued in 1994 as follows.

'The belief that Britain's economic prosperity should rely on companies that pay low wages and are not committed to improving the skills of staff is inappropriate for a developed western democracy. Most successful companies recognise this and, on their own initiative, pay decent wages, make proper social provisions for staff, do not discriminate and invest heavily in training.

'The problem is that, compared with other social democracies, Britain is very short of successful companies. Lacking skills and investment, the country cannot compete with its developed competitors, and it is impossible for low-skilled Britain to succeed against the low-cost developing world.

'So a sensible government would support the general aims of the Social Chapter and endorse the concept of the "inclusive company". It would restrain companies from exploiting staff and require them to contribute substantially towards the welfare of their staff, thereby promoting justice and reducing the state's social security burden. It would encourage co-operation with suppliers – many of them small companies – rather than condone the confrontation and exploitation that still prevails. And it would promote a greater link between companies and the communities in which they operate.'

Questions for discussion

1 *What do you see as being the main characteristics of the 'inclusive company'?*

2 *What do you see as being the main characteristics of the 'flexible firm'?*
3 *Are the two compatible?*
4 *What role should (a) the government and (b) the business community play in trying to create social justice?*

Planning for labour flexibility

There are a number of approaches to creating more flexibility in the use of human resources in an organisation. These include:

- new forms of employment contract
- introducing more flexible working times
- changing approaches to skills (e.g. multi-skilling)
- greater use of contract workers and part-timers
- more flexible reward systems.

New forms of employment contract

An employee's contract of employment sets out what he or she will be expected to do within the organisation. Reference can be made to this contract to check that a job is being performed in the expected manner.

A number of contracts are now being drawn up to allow flexibility. Employees may be expected to perform a variety of tasks which may alter from time to time. For example, a catch-all phrase is often written into a contract of employment that the employee is 'accountable for the performance within the capability of the job holder of such other duties as are required to achieve the overall purpose of the job'.

Flexible contracts may be for only a relatively short period of time (for example, two years) rather than the employee having a 'permanent' contract. The *Times Educational Supplement* reported in 1994 that 51 500 teachers in England and Wales were on fixed-term contracts, but many of these were limited to one year, while others were for less than a term's work. This figure accounted for 8.6 per cent of the teaching force compared with 4.6 per cent in 1983. The principal cause of this huge growth is the local management of schools, whereby schools have been given the responsibility for managing their own budgets. Headteachers and governors, worried by the prospect of not being able to balance their books if pupil numbers fall, are hedging their bets and creating what they consider to be an easily disposable category of teacher.

Flexible working times

Many organisations operate a **flexitime system**. There are 'core hours' when all or most employees are expected to be at work. Around this core there are flexible hours which employees can fit to meet their own requirements. This is particularly helpful to employees with other commitments. Employees have to meet a set target for the number of hours worked but experience short-term flexibility.

An advantage to the employer is that 'lateness' is eliminated because the employee works a full number of hours. Since employees are able to organise their own outside activities, such as appointments, during flexible hours they tend to take fewer days off. Greater freedom gives greater job satisfaction which may lead to increases in productivity.

Multi-skilling

A significant feature of the British industrial scene were demarcation disputes – arguments over 'who should do what'. The trade unions, in particular, insisted that only members of a relevant union could be asked to do certain tasks, such as mend a broken machine. This led to a great waste of time and other resources.

Multi-skilling involves training employees to do a range of tasks in the workplace. A machine operator can be trained in the art of performing routine maintenance work and repairs. This can be a great motivator because it gives a job variety as well as opportunities for higher pay as a result of the new skills and responsibilities. It means that a plant can be continuously productive, more competitive, and therefore possibly better able to provide good wages and conditions (because the demand for labour is derived from the demand for the final product).

Case Study
Multi-skilling in action

In the Japanese Toyota and Nissan car plants in the UK, the managements have agreed single-union deals. Only one union operates in each plant, and operators are flexible and able to do a number of different tasks. When Nissan started its car plant in Sunderland there were only three job classifications, whereas in the past some British car plants have had as many as 500 classifications.

Questions for discussion

1 *Why do managers prefer to have multi-skilled workers in a narrow range of job classifications?*
2 *Why might employees prefer such a scheme?*
3 *Why might some employees and trade unions oppose multi-skilling?*
4 *What are the benefits and drawbacks for the economy of allowing these schemes to operate?*

Use of contract workers and part-timers

As we have seen, organisations in both the public and private sectors are increasingly using contract workers and part-timers to carry out non-core functions.

Flexible reward systems

When an organisation does well it is better able to reward employees. Rewards can therefore be linked to productivity and other measures of performance. A common method is a salary range scheme. A 'rate for the job' is set against a mid-point of a salary range (e.g. in a salary range of £20 000–£25 000 the mid-point would be £22 500). An employee who equalled the rate for the job would receive £22 500. One who exceeded the rate by 10 per cent would receive £24 750, and so on. Features of a flexible payment system include:

- rewarding employees who develop extra skills
- linking pay to competence and performance
- increasing the proportion of pay that is tied to performance
- allowing employees greater choice of rewards.

Teamworking

Teamworking is discussed in depth on pages 254–61, but we introduce it here as a part of the discussion of management styles. It is an essential aspect of business life. The producer of a good or service relies on the quality of supplies bought in, and employees on a production line rely on the quality of inputs arriving from other workers. Interdependence is ever-present in business life.

> *A team is a small group who have developed to the stage where they are able to perform effectively, each member adopting a role necessary to work with others, using complementary skills.*

Teamworking becomes more significant when operating processes and/or technology require considerable interaction between people who may be carrying out different functions, but who share a common purpose. As organisations become flatter by stripping out layers of management and supervision, it becomes increasingly important to have successful teamwork.

Teamworking is particularly important during periods of crisis or rapid change. Practice in teamwork and co-operation with others towards a common goal will help you to develop insights into processes such as conflict and consensus. It will also help you to develop a view on how best you fit into the teamwork approach.

The Japanese style of teamwork can also be viewed as a variant of management style. This approach places a high degree of ownership of production processes in the hands of a work-team. Individuals are selected and trained to work as a team member. These individuals are then expected to work in a flexible way within their work roles and to accept considerable responsibility. The work-teams are expected to work hard and to perform to tight schedules, requiring considerable commitment to work, to the group and to the organisation. Individuals are thus accountable to working groups for their performance in the workplace. Understandably there is a debate as to whether such forms of teamwork involve greater 'work humanisation' or 'work intensification'.

Empowerment

The term **empowerment** in an organisational context is used to mean the increased participation by employees in their organisation. Empowerment is regarded in management theory as a means of encouraging initiative and entrepreneurialism in organisation members. In particular it may have an important part to play in helping women to rise above the invisible barriers that keep them in low-status roles within organisations.

Rosabeth Moss Kanter, in her widely acclaimed book *Men and Women of the Corporation*, argued that corporations needed to make fundamental changes to improve the quality of working life, and to create equal opportunities for all groups, as well as to enable all members of an organisation to use their talents to the benefit of the corporation. This would involve opening up management positions to individuals by promotion from a wide range of more junior positions, by changing systems such as appraisal and career development plans. Intermediate jobs might need to be created as a stepping stone to senior management. All this would involve developing empowerment strategies – such as autonomous work-groups, with decentralised authority and flatter hierarchies.

Empowering others in an organisation involves giving them the responsibility to use their talents and express themselves. Rosabeth Moss Kanter argues forcibly that:

> *'By empowering others, a leader does not decrease his power; instead, he may increase it – especially if the whole organisation performs better.'*

In her book *Giants Learn to Dance*, she outlined seven essential skills for modern managers. These were:

- the ability to operate without the hierarchy 'crutch'
- knowing how to compete in a way that enhances cooperation

- operating to the highest ethical standards
- developing humility
- being able to gain satisfaction from results and a willingness to stake your own rewards on them
- being multi-faceted, working across functions to find synergies
- developing a process focus on how things are done.

She outlined a 'post-entrepreneurial' model corporation in which project ideas should be allowed to come bubbling up from below. These ideas should be allowed to appear through the relationships programmes, and channels which form the middle of the organisation (see Figure 10.20). Top management is there to establish the values and goals of the organisation.

Figure 10.20 A post-entrepreneurial corporation

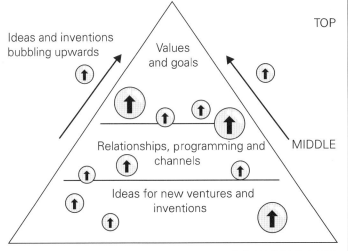

Part 2 Individual and interpersonal behaviour

In this part of the chapter we will be looking at some of the key factors which influence individual behaviour and relationships between individuals and groups. We start by exploring some aspects of motivation theory.

Motivation theory

Motivation is what causes people to act or do something in a particular way. By understanding why people behave in the ways they do, managers can improve the design of jobs, rewards and the working environment to match more closely the economic, social and personal needs of employees.

We all have different motives for the things we do. For example, some people strive for achievement, status and power while others are more concerned with money. Our personality, our expectations and our social background strongly influence the way we act. Managers must understand the needs of employees.

Maslow's hierarchy of needs

There has been extensive research into motivation and the behaviour of people at work. One of the most widely quoted theories is that of **Abraham Maslow** which provided an insight into people's needs.

Maslow's study of human behaviour led him to devise a hierarchy of needs, with basic needs at the bottom and higher needs at the top (see Figure 10.21). He claimed that people seek to satisfy a low level of need before moving on to a higher need.

Figure 10.21 Maslow's hierarchy of human needs

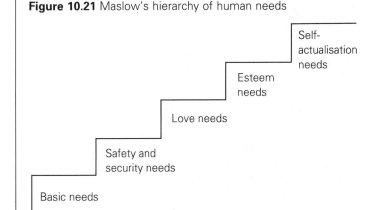

Physiological needs are basic. Food, shelter and clothing are required to meet the needs of the body and for physical survival. This basic level of need will be typically met at work by the exchange of labour for a wage packet or salary and by the physical conditions of the working environment.

Safety and security needs involve protection from danger and the provision of a predictable and orderly work space. Security of employment, and pension and sick-pay schemes are also relevant here.

Love needs are concerned with the individual's need for love and affection. This involves relationships and a feeling of belonging. At the place of work these needs can be satisfied by the companionship of fellow workers, working in a group or team, and company social activities.

Esteem needs are based on an individual's desire for self-respect and the respect of others. Employees have a need to be recognised as individuals, to have a job title or some form of status or prestige, and to have their efforts noticed.

Self-actualisation needs are concerned with personal development and individual creativity to achieve one's full potential. In order to meet these needs at work, individuals should be provided with the opportunity to use their creative talents and abilities fully.

Maslow felt that as an employee moves up the hierarchy he or she becomes more 'complete', someone who enjoys work and feels a direct involvement in it. However, the theory has its critics who question the realism of a hierarchy where needs are structured in such an ordered way. Maslow has also been criticised for producing a theory which only reflects middle-class values in American society.

Hard and soft approaches to human resource management

J. Storey, in his book *New Perspectives on Human Resource Management*, makes an important distinction between 'hard' and 'soft' approaches to people management.

The *hard approach* stresses the 'quantitative, calculative and business strategic aspects of managing the head count resource in as "natural" a way as for any other economic factor'. Such an approach concentrates on using the human resource in the most cost-effective way to maximise outputs relative to inputs. Emphasis is placed on encouraging employees to see their interests as being tied up with the interests of the organisation. Recruitment and development policies will be concerned with taking on and developing those employees who best fit in with the organisation's culture.

In contrast, a *soft approach* focuses on leadership, communication and particularly motivation. It recognises the qualitative difference between people and other resources. People have feelings and they react to a range of personal, interpersonal and other environmental variables. A soft approach therefore emphasises involving employees in the management of work – for example by the creation of self-managing teams – and is concerned to build commitment to the organisation by informing employees about the organisation's values and mission. The soft approach recognises that there will be differences in perceptions between members of an organisation – there will be a plurality of values and needs. The soft approach sets out to build a framework which takes on board these differences, and involves participants in sharing points of view and decision-making.

Understanding actions

Some people argue that the human-resource management approach has been 'talked up'. The reality is often that people in organisations are treated simply as working resources. Perhaps individuals are seen as potential sources of output which are best managed through systems and structures. Human resources are inputs that are fed into a system. A well-managed system is then made up of structures set out to obtain the maximum return on inputs.

There are many criticisms of such a systems approach. For example, David Silverman (*The Theory of Organisations*) argued that it fails to consider that it is the members of organisations who interpret what they understand to be their environment, who create meanings and definitions of what they experience, and then go on to regulate and adapt their working environment.

Silverman outlined an action frame of reference in which organisations are seen as the outcomes of interactions between motivated people who pursue their own goals and set out to resolve what they perceive to be problems. Individuals are *actors* within the work and other settings. They interact with other actors to whom they ascribe more or less significance. Individuals have personal needs within this setting. These needs may conflict with the aims of the organisation and help to change organisational activity.

Studies of organisational activities and approaches to managing people need to be aware of fundamentally different approaches. There are those who prefer to look at organisational performance in terms of procedures, structures and mechanisms, whilst others see the importance of delving into aspects of personality, interpersonal relationships, and psychological needs and drives.

Factors affecting motivation

Motivation is concerned with having an incentive to do something – the strength and direction of behaviour. A well-motivated person will have clear goals and the drive to take actions required to achieve those goals. In this sense motivation can be seen as stemming from two sources (see Figure 10.22).

Figure 10.22 Sources of motivation

- *Needs* are vested in the individual (or group).
- *Goals* rest in the environment which the individual (or group) moves towards (or away from).

In its simplest form, motivation can be said to arise from the recognition of an unfulfilled need. The goal is the direction through which that need can be met. Clearly an important factor determining motivation will be the perception of how likely an individual is to be successful in meeting a particular goal, as well as on previous experience.

We can thus present a simple model of the stages involved in the motivation process:

- *Step 1* – An arousal of the person concerned.
- *Step 2* – Goal-seeking behaviour.
- *Step 3* – Goal attainment.
- *Step 4* – Reduction of the arousal state (or fresh arousal to meet new goals).

So, motives arise out of needs. A psychological need is a state of tension within an individual which forms the basis for striving for a particular kind of goal. The psychological need therefore provides the motive power. **Normative needs** are conceptions of what a person ought to be like – they are based on the expectations which society places on an individual. They are normative in the sense that they represent a standard against which accomplishment may be measured. For example, in some communities, when people get to a certain age they may be expected to marry and have children; in many organisations it is expected that people will turn up to work at a given time; and so on.

As individuals develop, their needs may become more extensive and more complex. The young child that is closely supervised by parents may acquire strong dependency needs, so that for example it needs to hold hands when crossing the road. As children become more

confident these dependency needs may diminish so that help-seeking behaviour becomes less and less.

Common sense informs us that individuals have widely different needs, and thus motivations. Many psychologists have produced different lists of needs (Maslow's is but one example).

Case Study
Murray's classification of needs

The following list of human needs was drawn up in 1938 by H. A. Murray, and published in *Explorations in Personality*. Which of these needs do you see as being the most important motivating forces *to you*?

Abasement: To surrender. To comply and accept punishment. To apologise, confess, atone. Self-depreciation. Masochism.

Achievement: To overcome obstacles. To exercise power. To strive to do something difficult as well and as quickly as possible.

Acquisition: To gain possessions and property. To grasp, snatch, or steal things. To bargain or gamble. To work for money or goods.

Affiliation: To form friendships and associations. To greet, join and live with others. To love. To join groups.

Aggression: To assault or injure. To belittle, harm, blame, accuse, or maliciously ridicule a person. To punish severely. Sadism.

Autonomy: To resist influence or coercion. To defy an authority or seek freedom in a new place. To strive for independence.

Blame avoidance: To avoid blame, ostracism, or punishment by inhibiting asocial or unconventional impulses. To be well behaved and obey the law.

Counteraction: Proudly to refuse admission of defeat by restriving and retaliating. To select the hardest tasks. To defend one's honour in action.

Cognisance: To explore. To ask questions. To satisfy curiosity. To look, listen, inspect. To read and seek knowledge.

Construction: To organise and build.

Deference: To admire and willingly follow a superior. To cooperate with a leader. To serve gladly.

Defendance: To defend oneself against blame or belittlement. To justify one's actions. To offer extenuations, explanations and excuses. To resist 'probing'.

Dominance: To influence or control others. To persuade, prohibit, dictate. To lead and direct. To restrain. To organise the behaviour of a group.

Exhibition: To attract attention to one's person. To excite, amuse, shock, stir, thrill others. Self-dramatisation.

Exposition: To point and demonstrate. To relate facts. To give information, explain, interpret, lecture.

Harm avoidance: To avoid pain, physical injury, illness and death. To escape from a dangerous situation. To take precautionary measures.

Infavoidance: To avoid failure, shame, humiliation, ridicule. To refrain from attempting to do something that is beyond one's power. To conceal a disfigurement.

Nurturance: To nourish, aid, or protect the helpless. To express sympathy. To 'mother' a child.

Order: To arrange, organise, put away objects. To be tidy and clean. To be scrupulously precise.

Play: To relax, amuse oneself, seek diversion and entertainment. To 'have fun', to play games. To laugh, joke and be merry. To avoid serious tension.

Rejection: To snub, ignore, or exclude. To remain aloof and indifferent. To be discriminating.

Retention: To retain possession of things. To refuse to give or lend. To hoard. To be frugal, economical and miserly.

Sentience: To seek and enjoy sensuous impressions.

Sex: To form and further an erotic relationship. To have sexual intercourse.

Succorance: To seek aid, protection, or sympathy. To cry for help. To plead for mercy. To adhere to an affectionate nurturant parent. To be dependent.

Superiority: This need is considered to be a composite of achievement and dominance.

Understanding: To analyse experience, to abstract, to discriminate among concepts, to define relations, to synthesise ideas.

Clearly individual drives are determined by complex sets of needs. Human resource management requires an appreciation of these needs.

In setting out classifications of needs, researchers have generally indicated that there is a basic set of needs (e.g. for food, air, activity and rest). These needs lead to corresponding drives (e.g. hunger must be fed). Some of the needs are acquired within cultural contexts (e.g. the 'need' for achievement within capitalist societies). Stability in the patterns of rewards and in the goals presented in a cultural environment help to create the drive to meet these needs (e.g. the profit motive).

Individual differences

Individuals differ in many ways which influence all sorts of things, such as work performance, how they mix with others, their willingness to take risks and so on. Many of these differences are possible to observe or measure,

although the validity and accuracy of these measures is open to question.

Physical differences

Individuals differ by being tall or short, fat or thin, etc. Sensory capacities (sight, hearing, touch and smell) may also be important in the work situation. Motor or mechanical skills may also be needed – such as hand/eye coordination on a moving production line and in many other lines of work. Physical aptitudes may be closely tied in with other abilities such as cognitive and affective ones.

Differences in intelligence and aptitude

There has been a continual debate about the relative importance of 'nature' and 'nurture' in determining **intelligence** – that is, to what extent is intelligence determined genetically and to what extent is it nurtured by environmental factors such as parental support, access to educational play facilities, travel, and quality of schooling? There seems to be evidence that supports both views.

Intelligence has a number of ingredients. It is usually associated with the ability to solve mathematical and other problems, with the ability to sort out shapes, and hence with a person's **aptitude** to be successful in specified tasks. There are a number of ways of measuring intelligence and aptitude. Organisations may use tests which purport to measure intelligence and aptitude when they feel that these tests are helpful in selecting employees for posts requiring particular qualities. The variety of recognised mental abilities is illustrated by the list below.

■ *Verbal comprehension* – Verbal reasoning tests may include rearranging sentences, fitting in missing words, etc. Such tests have traditionally been used for selection purposes.
■ *Word fluency* – Tests in this category might include solving anagrams, identifying rhyming words, etc.
■ *Number* – Tests usually include mental and written arithmetic calculations, to be completed within a time limit.
■ *Space* – Tests involve arranging shapes into sequences and identifying relationships between shapes.
■ *Associative memory* – This often involves memorising by rote associated words.
■ *Perceptual speed* – Tests in this category involve rapid visualisation of similarities and differences in figures, shapes and text.
■ *Induction or general reasoning* – This may be tested by working out a rule in a series of numbers, or other tests involving identifying patterns and rules.

Intelligence and aptitude inevitably influence the ways in which individuals tackle tasks. Gordon Pask, in his book *An Approach to Cybernetics*, has drawn an interesting distinction in the way individuals approach learning tasks – he distinguishes between 'holists' (those who tackle the whole problem) and 'serialists':

> 'An individual student may be good at "seeing things as parts of a whole" or, conversely, he may have a special aptitude for "stringing sub-problems into sequences", which (on resolution) lead to the solution of a large problem.'

In other words, some students like to take a broad look at a new area of study, including information which they do not yet need, before they begin to see an overall picture. Others prefer to work steadily through a relatively narrow sequence and the broad picture emerges in the course of time. It can be quite irritating for a serialist to have to listen to a lecture given by a holist, and vice versa!

Another distinction that is often drawn is between **convergent** and **divergent** thinkers. Convergent thinkers prefer tasks where solutions are clear-cut – there may be one obvious best way of solving a problem. The convergent thinker hones in on the problem and works systematically towards its solution. In contrast the divergent thinker sees many different ways of tackling a problem. Divergent thinkers thrive on uncertainty which encourages them to be creative; they can conjure up all sorts of alternatives and different views on going about something.

Edward de Bono has also stressed the importance of **lateral thinking**. Lateral thinking is a way of solving problems by employing unorthodox and apparently illogical means. The lateral thinker is prepared to take risks and would be an invaluable member of a team which required creativity, flair and offbeat solutions to problems.

Different jobs have different requirements and it is important to be able to test an individual's ability to do a particular task. For example, secretaries may be tested on speed and accuracy, including spelling and use of grammar. Capability and competence are likely to develop with education, training and experience. Today the divide between vocational and academic work is increasingly becoming blurred. The emphasis is perhaps moving away from learning a body of knowledge for its own sake towards learning that can be applied in practical contexts. NVQs, for example, are concerned with developing applicable work-based competences, while GNVQs are concerned with developing more broad-based general competences which effectively prepare individuals for the changing world of work.

Differences in personality

Personality is widely regarded as a key factor in determining how successful an individual will be in working with others in an organisation.

> *Personality can be defined as the sum total of all the behavioural and mental characteristics by means of which an individual is recognised as being unique. Personality gives individuals a distinctive social character.*

Huczynski and Buchanan, in their book *Organisational Behaviour*, argue that if the concept of personality is to be helpful in understanding human behaviour then it is necessary to accept two propositions:

- Human behaviour has stable and enduring characteristics. When we examine the way individuals behave over a period of time we are able to identify regularities in the 'ways we think and in what we do that can be identified and studied'.
- The distinctive properties of an individual's personality can be measured and compared with others.

Huczynski and Buchanan warn us about the dangers of **stereotyping** in assessing personality. We are all 'informal' personality theorists. However, research indicates that many are poor judges of other people's personalities. In social interactions we tend *not* to draw on all aspects of personality. We usually meet someone in a specific role relationship (e.g. tutor/lecturer, seller/buyer, doctor/patient). We tend to assess personality in terms of this role relationship. The teacher may appear to be confident and informed when working with a group of students, and the students may generalise that the tutor is 'always like that'. However, the students' initial view might be challenged if they were to encounter the teacher in other life-roles – wandering around lost in an airport terminal, or standing helplessly by the side of a motor vehicle after an engine failure. Generally speaking, however, we tend to meet people in organisations when they are performing specific roles. As a result we have only a limited insight into their personality.

As with intelligence, there is considerable debate as to whether your personality is inherited or determined by your environment.

The learning process

Learning is a complex process. There are many views as to what factors are likely to lead to successful learning. Perhaps the most important single factor is to make sure that new learning builds on the previous knowledge and understanding of the learner.

The rule is 'find out what the learner already knows and then teach him or her accordingly'. The learner should then be exposed to fresh knowledge, skills, ideas etc. which build on this prior knowledge.

The secret of effective training and development is to provide just enough extra learning each time to stretch the learner a little bit further. Starting from what the learner already knows, in order to make him or her feel comfortable, introduce new skills and ideas. Trying to stretch the learner too far and too fast may be counter-productive.

The learning cycle

Kolb's learning cycle is a useful starting point for examining the learning process (see Figure 10.23).

Figure 10.23 Kolb's learning cycle

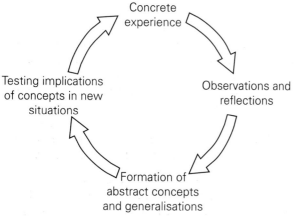

For example, a concrete experience for a college lecturer may be that he always arrives late for lectures in the first few weeks of term. His observations indicate that there is a lot of traffic on the road at the time he is going to the college. He begins to develop theories (concepts and generalisations) that it is the time he is setting out to work that is causing the difficulties because so many others are on the road at the same time. Perhaps he would benefit from setting off a quarter of an hour earlier? The next day he tests out the implications of his new theory by starting out fifteen minutes earlier, and lo and behold, he arrives well in advance of his lecture. His concrete experience is now that he arrives with plenty of time to prepare for his lecture. He feels more calm and relaxed. He reflects that this is a desirable state of affairs.

Learning can start from any point of the cycle, but according to Kolb it must involve all four points:

- Concrete experience is about responding to what happens, to events and direct experiences.
- Reflective observation involves having the ability to reflect on these concrete experiences, taking into account a number of views and perspectives.

- Forming abstract concepts involves integrating experiences and reflections into theories.
- Testing out implications involves putting theories into practice through experimentation.

Learning styles

Honey and Mumford, in their book *Using Your Learning Style*, argued that people have various learning styles (see Figure 10.24). They have a preference for a particular learning style although this can vary over time.

- Some people are *activitist*. They respond immediately to concrete experiences without spending too much time on the reflection process. They may be seen as being impulsive and action-orientated.
- *Reflectors* want to spend a considerable time reflecting on the implications of concrete experiences. They also want to spend time on observation and mulling over their reflections. They will be less action-orientated.
- *Theorists* want to take things a step further. They are concerned with creating ideas and generalisations based on their reflections. They will try to order and construct new theories. Again, they will not be action-orientated.
- *Pragmatists* are concerned with putting new theories into practice. They will want to test out the implications of new ideas and to see how they work. They thus have an action-orientation.

Figure 10.24 Learning styles

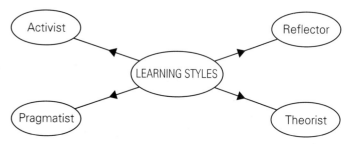

None of these learning styles is necessarily better than the others. They are different. However, from the trainer's or educator's point of view it is important to bear in mind that people have different preferred learning styles. This helps to explain why in a particular lecture or seminar some of the students will be actively interested in what is being said while others may appear to be bored.

Task

1 Answer the following questions which will help you to assess your own preferred learning style.
   a When you are faced by new experiences how do you respond?

b Do you prefer to sit and take notes and think about the implications of what you are told? Or do you prefer to engage in the experience of learning, for example by discussion, interaction, direct experience, and so on?

c Do you like to develop new theories based on your current observations of things that happen around you?

d Do you like to experiment with new ideas, in order to arrive at new approaches?

2 What can you now say about your preferred learning style?

3 Do you agree that different individuals have preferred learning styles?

Important factors in the learning process

A distinction is often made between surface and deep learning. **Surface learning** involves the acquiring of facts and information for short-term purposes (e.g. passing a test). Surface learning can only be applied in a specific context. **Deep learning** involves real steps forward in understanding and the development of skills. Deep learning can then be applied in a range of contexts.

Deep learning is most likely to exist when:

- the learner is motivated and can see the benefit of learning
- the learner enjoys the experience for its own sake
- there are clear objectives and targets to work towards
- the learner is given feedback on progress made
- learning is an active process in which the learner is involved in 'doing' rather than just 'listening'
- teaching and training techniques are related to the needs of the individual
- a variety of teaching methods are employed to maintain interest
- time is allowed to enable the learner to absorb the facts/opinions (the 'learning curve' takes place over time)
- reinforcement is provided for appropriate results.

What drives individuals?

Individuals have different drives depending on their personality, and the social and cultural environment in which they were brought up. **David McClelland** carried out a number of studies of what drives people on and acts

as a spur to motivation. He identified four main drives (see Figure 10.25).

Figure 10.25 McClelland's four main drives

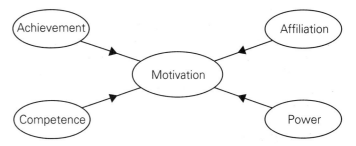

People from similar backgrounds may share the same drives because of the way they have been socialised.

Achievement motivation

This is a drive that individuals may have to pursue and achieve certain goals. By achieving these goals it becomes possible to climb the ladder of success. Accomplishment becomes important in its own right. Within an organisation, individuals with a strong achievement drive work hard and believe that they should and will receive personal credit for their efforts. As managers, people with this type of drive will expect employees to have the same achievement-orientated goals and values as themselves.

Some writers associate the Japanese idea of *kaizen* (continuous improvement) and the American work ethic with this achievement drive. Clearly this drive becomes difficult to accommodate in hard times – for example in periods of economic decline.

Affiliation motivation

This drive is to affiliate with other people on a social basis. Affiliation-driven individuals respond best when they are complimented on their favourable attitudes and cooperation. It is sometimes argued that girls have a stronger affiliation drive than boys (i.e. being part of a friendship group and empathising with friends is an important female drive). Affiliation-motivated employees and managers seek to surround themselves with friends. However, managers with a strong affiliation drive may find it more difficult to make hard decisions.

Competence motivation

This is a drive to be good or competent at something. Performing a job or task well is seen as being a reward in its own right. Competence-motivated employees will seek to master tasks and skills, and strive for solutions to problems. Employees and managers with a competence motivation will generally perform their work duties well.

It has been suggested that a simplistic comparison between a competence-motivated individual and an achievement-motivated one is that the former will ask 'How well can I perform the task?' whereas the latter will ask 'How much can I do?'

Power motivation

People with this motivation want to influence others and to change situations. They want to be in control of people and events. This may involve taking risks in order to achieve a position of power – and of course power can be used well or badly.

Power-motivated individuals often make effective managers but they may not always be popular. They are most likely to be successful if they seek power for the benefit of the organisation. When power is sought purely for personal reasons, they are unlikely to be successful because of the number of enemies they make.

Motivation and performance

The link between motivation and performance in the workplace is a positive one – the more motivated an employee, the better his or her performance is likely to be. Furthermore, the better their performance the more motivated they are likely to become. The link is therefore in both directions.

However, we also need to take account of two further factors:

■ the ability of an individual to do the job
■ the effects of too much motivation.

If someone does not have the ability they will not succeed, and therefore motivation will evaporate. This more complex set of relationships is illustrated in Figure 10.26, where there is a positive correlation between ability, performance, motivation and job satisfaction.

Figure 10.26 Positive motivating correlations

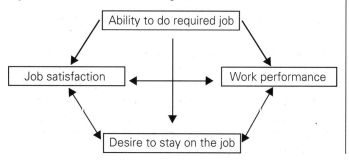

We should also bear in mind that high performance rates have the potential to increase stress. Inevitably, if individuals are exposed to excessive pressures they will not be able to cope.

Motivation models

Michael Armstrong, in his book *Personnel Management*, identifies four models of motivation which he terms:

■ the rational-man model
■ the human-relations model
■ the self-actualisation model
■ the complex model.

The rational-man model
This model assumes that an employee responds to rewards and sanctions in the workplace as a means of improving performance (see Figure 10.27). Financial rewards encourage effort while punishments also push employees into working harder. However, such a model has only a limited appreciation of the complex nature of human needs.

Figure 10.27 The rational-man model

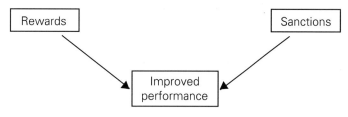

The human-relations model
This approach argues that humans are complex creatures who require recognition, personal fulfilment and satisfaction of social needs if they are to have the job satisfaction that will turn them into high performers (see Figure 10.28).

Figure 10.28 The human-relations model

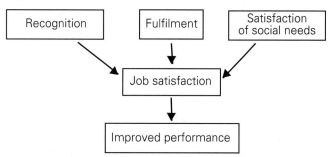

The self-actualising model
This model draws on the work of Herzberg, Maslow and McGregor. The broad approach is that intrinsic

motivating factors are more significant than extrinsic ones. If people are to be motivated in the long term they need to have their higher-level needs met (see Figure 10.29). Self-fulfilment is the key to real motivation, not just extrinsic factors such as rewards and sanctions.

Figure 10.29 The self-actualising model

```
┌─────────────────────────┐
│   Self-actualisation    │
│  through doing work     │
│  which is rewarding     │
│    in its own right:    │
│  through recognition,   │
│ variety, responsibility,│
│   personal and group    │
│     achievements        │
└─────────────────────────┘
            │
            ▼
┌─────────────────────────┐
│    Job satisfaction     │
└─────────────────────────┘
            │
            ▼
┌─────────────────────────┐
│  Improved performance   │
└─────────────────────────┘
```

The complex motivational model

Michael Armstrong argues that we need to develop a more complex understanding of motivation because human beings have a range of needs and expectations, because people work in widely differing situations, and because these situations are subject to continual change.

Armstrong argues that there are two main factors determining the effort a person puts into a job (see Figure 10.30):

- the value of the rewards to the individual, insofar as they are likely to satisfy his or her needs
- the expectation that the effort put in will lead to the desired reward.

However, effort is not sufficient. As well as effort there are two other factors that influence motivation:

- ability – which depends on intelligence, manual skills, know-how, etc.
- role perception – the individual's feelings about his or her job.

If the individual has the same perception of the job as does the organisation, then this will reap maximum returns. However, if there is not a match between the individual's perception of the job and the organisations perception, then this will lead to lower performance.

Figure 10.30 The complex motivational model

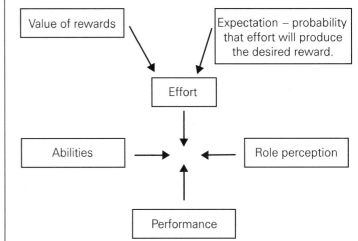

Motivation techniques

Michael Armstrong identified three basic approaches that have been adopted by motivation experts:

- *The carrot and stick approach* – This is the 'rewards' and 'sanctions' approach in which monetary rewards play a major part.
- *Motivation through the work itself* – Fulfilling work, as we have seen, can be motivation in itself for certain individuals.
- *The one-minute manager system* – This involves managers setting goals which subordinates can meet and giving them positive feedback when they do something right and negative feedback when they do something wrong.

The range of motivational techniques includes:

1 Money as a reward or incentive
2 Clearly spelling out work requirements
3 Developing commitment from employees
4 Motivating through the work itself
5 Rewarding and recognising achievement
6 Exercising leadership
7 Building up teamwork
8 Training and developing people
9 Eliminating negative aspects of the work.

Non-monetary techniques of motivation

Job enrichment involves giving employees an increase in responsibility and/or recognition. The aim of job enrichment is to make employees feel that their contribution has been upgraded so that it is more highly appreciated. Ways of doing this vary from an employee being given a new title, to an extension of the perks associated with a particular job.

Job enlargement involves giving employees a greater range of responsibilities. An employee who feels that a job is going 'stale', and as a result is losing interest in it, may feel rejuvenated when asked to take on additional tasks. For example, an employee who has been used to handling routine mail and answering telephone calls may gain fresh motivation if she takes on the additional responsibility of meeting clients and taking them out to dinner as part of the public relations function.

Employee participation in decision-making can be a great motivator. The flattened organisational structure in which decisions can be made at all levels of an organisation helps employees to feel important and valued for their contribution to the decision-making process. Effective employee participation goes beyond the factory floor suggestion-box.

Quality circles (QCs) are particularly important motivators. Although QCs are a fairly recent arrival on the British industrial scene, they are widespread today (see page 261).

Part 3 Teams and groups

Task

Think about the groups that you belong to.
1 What are the essential characteristics of these groups?
2 To what extent would you say that these groups operate as teams?
3 Is there a difference between a group and a team?

Most people would recognise the following as being features of a **group**:

- *A common aim or purpose* – for example, the aim of a student group may be to enjoy and pass a course with other students while having good social relationships.
- *A means of communication* – for example, a way of greeting other group members.
- *A set of rules which are known to group members* – for example, a way of working together to meet assignment deadlines.
- *A form of sanction for breaking group rules* – perhaps giving 'the cold shoulder' to students who do not work collaboratively to meet agreed deadlines.
- *A way by which individuals can achieve goals within the group, for them to continue membership* – for example, friendship between members who help each other with course tasks.
- *A way for group members to identify themselves as belonging* – this could be a name or uniform, and a set meeting place in college which group members share.

One definition of a **team** that differentiates it from an ordinary group might be:
> *A team is a group which has developed to the stage where it is able to perform effectively as a group, each member adopting the role necessary to work with others, using complementary skills.*

Examples of good teamwork features include:

- loyalty to the group
- accepted ways of behaving
- good time management
- high levels of communication
- freedom to express opinions and feelings
- complementary skills and roles.

Can you think of any other features to add to this list?

Group working

Many business decisions are made by groups, and managers spend a large proportion of their time working directly or indirectly as members of teams. Whenever a group is required to make a decision, there will be three strands involved in moving from the start of the decision-making process to the finish, the final decision. These strands are illustrated in Figure 10.31.

Figure 10.31 The decision-making process

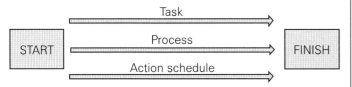

What is a task?

The **task** is the content of the work. For example, the task of a management meeting may be to decide on the location of a new factory; the task of an interview may be to select the best candidate to take up a particular post. Thus the task is the conversion of information and opinions from members into decisions or recommendations. In general terms, this covers what has to be done and why. Most groups give a lot of attention to the task.

What is the action schedule?

The **action schedule** is concerned with how a group is organised to do a given task. The schedule will cover such questions as who will fill the necessary roles, how progress will be checked and monitored, how it will be ensured that the group will keep to the time schedules. It will also deal with the procedures of decision-making. Most groups will give some attention to the action schedule. For example, an action schedule for a meeting might set down when the meeting will take place, who will attend, who will run the meeting, how decisions would be voted on and other procedural matters.

What is the process?

The **process** is the interaction that takes place between members of a group. It is about how people work together, their relationships and the feelings created by their behaviour within the group. It involves interpersonal skills such as listening to others and helping others to join in a discussion. It involves expressions of feelings and giving and receiving of feedback. In general it covers who does what and when. *Many groups pay little attention to the process.*

These three threads of group-working are all important in group decision-making. It will be obvious that a group that concentrates on its action schedule and its process entirely may have a wonderful time but is unlikely to achieve the task. It will not be long before morale will suffer and the group will disintegrate. In contrast, concentration purely on the task is likely to lead to

arguments about how things should be organised, and inattention to group members' thoughts and feelings will lead to mishandled resources and to misunderstandings.

Factors affecting group effectiveness

A number of important factors influence the effectiveness of a group, including its size, the flow of communication within the group and the style of management.

The size of the group

There are a number of reasons why it is easier to make decisions within small groups (i.e. five or six people) than in larger groups.

The larger the number of people drawn into the decision-making process, the more difficult it is to involve everyone, the more difficult it is to get everyone to agree, and the higher the level of dissatisfaction with the way the group operates. Individuals find it more difficult to identify with the group, and sub-groups start to form. In order to prevent a group from becoming fragmented, it is likely that a leader will need to take centralised control over decision-making as the size of the group grows.

Despite the disadvantages of large groups, there are also a number of clear advantages. A large group can call on a greater pool of skills, energy and resources. A further benefit is that, if members of an organisation feel that they are involved in the decision-making process, they may be more willing to implement policies.

Communication within the group

The main factors influencing the flow of communication within a group are its formal organisation, its informal organisation, and the means of communication employed. There are four basic types of communication network (see Figure 10.32).

The **wheel** and **chain networks** rely on a centralisation of the flow of information. Effective decision-making thus depends to a great extent on those in key central positions and on the quality of the communication channels to them. These centralised forms have the following characteristics:

- They are highly effective at making and carrying out straightforward, well-structured, predictable activities.
- Levels of satisfaction for group members are relatively low compared with those for members of less centralised groups.
- The centralised form helps to strengthen the leadership position in such groups.
- A stable structure rapidly emerges in the group.
- The group becomes dependent on those with greatest access to relevant information.

Figure 10.32 Types of communication network

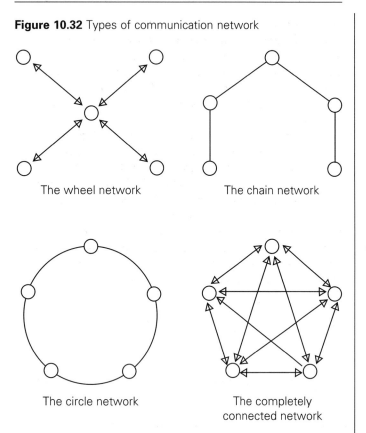

The wheel network

The chain network

The circle network

The completely connected network

In terms of our previous analysis, such a group structure lends itself to short-term operating control decisions.

In contrast, the **circle network** and the **completely connected network** lend themselves to a more open, decentralised form of decision-making. Members of these groups are mutually interdependent, and share the decision-making process. The group is not so dependent on key individuals, and levels of satisfaction are usually greater. Disadvantages are that, because responsibility is shared, there may not be an effective mechanism for pushing decisions through. There may be a lot of *talk* about action without the mechanism required to *create* action. Open networks may be more appropriate for periodic control and strategic decisions, where high-quality decisions need a substantial amount of discussion and shared analysis and evaluation. However, long-term and major policy decisions will also require leadership, perhaps in the form of a prominent individual who is able to say 'the buck stops here'.

Style of management
Earlier we looked at the way in which the style of management influences the effectiveness of decision-making when we explored trait, style and contingency theories (see pages 231–7).

Group decision-making

Generally speaking, the quality of decision-making in a group is likely to be higher because of the quantity and quality of data that can be drawn on. In any group situation individuals will take on formal or informal roles. In a formal situation, group meetings may involve officials such as a chairperson, a time-keeper and a secretary. In informal situations, group members frequently take parts – for example, one person may try to force a decision on the group, another will oppose any new ideas, a third will act as a peace-maker, and so on.

It has been suggested that the optimum group size is five people, because:

- the odd number will prevent an impasse
- a group that size is sufficiently large to avoid mistakes resulting from insufficient information, or the power of an individual with an entrenched view
- the group is small enough to involve everyone.

Gilligan, Neale and Murray, in their book *Business Decision Making*, identified the following features that should lead to effective group performance:

- The structure of the group and the status of group members should be stable and well formed.
- The group should be large enough to fulfil the tasks, but not so large as to encourage the formation of sub-groups.
- The group members should have the appropriate skills for the task.
- The atmosphere should be informal and relaxed.
- Objectives should be understood and accepted by group members.
- Discussion should be encouraged and members should be willing to listen to each other.
- Decisions should be reached by consensus.
- The leader of the group should not dominate, nor should there be evidence of a struggle for power.
- The group should operate with mild or moderate levels of stress.
- Disagreements should not be overridden; instead, the reasons for disagreements should be examined and an attempt made to resolve them.
- The allocation of tasks to members should be clear and accepted.
- The group should act in a cohesive way.

Teamworking

Organisations ought to consist of people working cooperatively together. Tom Peters, in his recent book

Crazy Times Call for Crazy Organisations, argues that a key component of managing people in organisations is to have trust in them:

> '*All this fancy management stuff boils down to the folk who actually do the work – the ad copywriters, movie cameramen, nurses, technicians, teachers and hotel keepers. . . . Hierarchies are collapsing. We are asking the average Mike or Mary to take on extraordinary responsibilities.*'

Teamworking is particularly important when operating processes or technology necessitate 'cellular' working, with work-teams from across an organisation *working on particular projects*. It is also important when there is considerable interaction between people carrying out different functions with a common purpose. The fast-moving, 'wired-up' organisation in a rapidly changing business environment must have good teamwork to channel resources in order to respond to new threats and opportunities.

The management team in an organisation needs to learn to share responsibility across the organisation. As organisations become flatter there is an increasing need for good teamwork. Managers will have larger spans of control, but work will be delegated to work-teams with responsibility for what they are doing.

The term 'organisational architecture' refers to managers' more general views about their organisations and how they are structured. It focuses particularly on how traditional departments and more informal project teams can fit together, and on the role of work-teams.

Team processes

Creating a team requires attention to two concepts:

- making sure that the task is carried out effectively (e.g. establishing a task, gathering and collecting information and evidence, analysing information, evaluation and decision-making)
- the maintenance function – ensuring that the team operates cohesively, possibly through encouragement, compromise, standard setting etc.

Attention needs to be given to combining these two elements. This may be the function of the leader, or of the group as a whole. Individual members of a team need to be aware of how their contributions add to or detract from the cohesiveness of the group.

Davis and Newstrom, in their book *Human Behaviour at Work*, use the following illustration to highlight the importance of teamwork:

> *My supervisxr txld me that teamwxrk depends xn the perfxrmance of every single persxn xn the team. I ignxred*

> *that idea until my supervisxr shxwed me hxw the xffice typewriter performs when just xne single key is xut of xrder. All the xther keys xn xur typewriter wxrk just fine except xne, but that xne destrxys the effectiveness of the typewriter. Nxw I knxw that even thxugh I am xnly xne persxn, I am needed if the team is tx wxrk as a successful team shxuld.*

In working together a team builds up an **ideology** which helps to determine the way in which group members think and act, as well as the satisfaction they get from being a member of the organisation. If the team ideology is strong and team members identify closely with the group, it will become increasingly cohesive. **Group norms** will establish what is or is not acceptable behaviour. Team members will want to be associated with the team and to be seen to be part of it, so the team builds up its own distinctiveness and culture.

Stages of team development

Tuckman and Jensen have produced a diagram that is useful in showing how small groups can be most effective (see Figure 10.33).

Figure 10.33 Stages of small group development

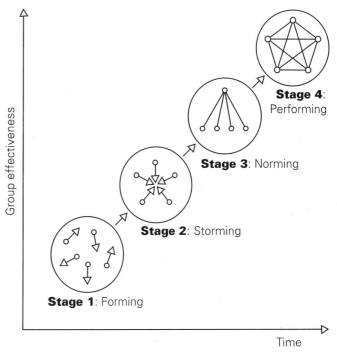

- *Stage 1: Forming* – A number of individuals come together. They are simply that – a loose collection with no clear sense of purpose.
- *Stage 2: Storming* – The group begins to exchange ideas, but there is as yet little structure to the group, and there are no clear plans to take the group forward.

■ *Stage 3: Norming* – The group begins to share ideas. Perhaps a leadership pattern begins to emerge, and the group starts to conform to a given set of ideas. Decisions begin to be formulated.

■ *Stage 4: Performing* – A clear organised pattern is established, based on mutual respect, the sharing of ideas and the drawing out of plans and proposals from all members of the team. Every member of the group is therefore able to make the best possible contribution to the group process.

Norming and performing?

A number of issues are worth considering in relation to the cycle outlined. First, when there is no appointed leader, the early stages of group formation may be dominated by individuals or small cliques of individuals, who are determined to dominate and pull the group towards their way of thinking. Quieter members of the group may not be heard at this stage.

Secondly, when the group focuses solely on the *task*, activities will probably be carried out more quickly in the short term, but lack of concern for the needs and development of the group will tend to reduce effectiveness over the longer period. Social relationships within the group may be poor so that no clear team spirit is created.

Thirdly, if the group focuses on *process* this may lead to stronger social relationships, but if the task is not carried out these relationships may quickly erode in the face of frustrations. People will want to see tasks completed if they are to achieve the reward of 'a job well done'.

Fourthly, if a group is at the *performing* stage, future development may not be easy, but changes will continue to occur. The group may begin to splinter or break up. Some members may move off into fresh fields of endeavour.

Finally, a group with established bonds and group numbers may not be ready to incorporate new members. This group may also be reluctant to accept new managers – particularly those with fresh ideas.

Case Study
The power of the team

In an important book written by D. McGregor, *The Human Side of Enterprise*, the author set out the following as being the main features of a well-functioning creative team. Think of a team that you belong to. How many of the following attributes can you apply to your team?

a The atmosphere tends to be informal, comfortable and relaxed.

b There is a lot of discussion in which everyone participates initially, but it remains pertinent to the task of the group.

c The task or objective of the team is well understood and accepted by the members. There will have been free discussion of the objective at some point, until it was presented in such a way that the members of the team could commit themselves to it.

d Team members listen to each other. They are not afraid of feeling foolish in each other's eyes. Every idea is given a hearing.

e Disagreements occur without being suppressed or overridden by group action. The team seeks to resolve these disagreements.

f Most decisions are reached by consensus with only the minimum of formal voting. The team seeks general agreement.

g Criticism is frequent, frank and relatively comfortable without personal attacks.

h People can freely express their feelings and ideas both about how the group operates and about ideas.

i When action is taken, clear assignments are made and accepted.

j The leader does not dominate nor do team members defer to the leader and there is little evidence of a struggle for power.

Team composition

The effectiveness of a team depends on the mix of the abilities of its members. If every team member wants to be the leader it is unlikely that decisions will be made or carried out. Successful teams require a range of appropriate personalities and qualities. Over the years a number of researchers have looked at the mix that makes for an effective group. For example, Robert Belbin, working in the early 1980s, identified the following eight roles required in an effective group (of course, it is possible that some individuals may be able to fill more than one role):

■ The chairperson – someone who heads the group and coordinates efforts.

■ The shaper – a would-be chairperson who drives the team towards finishing the task successfully.

■ The plant – someone with plenty of ideas who may be rather shy and quiet; the plant creates ideas and proposals.

■ The monitor evaluator – someone who is able to analyse and evaluate progress and acts as a quality-control check.

- The resource investigator – a person who is sociable and outgoing, bringing new contacts, ideas and developments to the team, but others will need to work on the resource investigator's ideas to make them work.
- The company worker – an administrator rather than a leader, someone who is good at ensuring that tasks are carried out, but is unlikely to be a creator or leader.
- The team worker – a person who works for the team and helps to keep it together, supporting others and encouraging and bringing the members of the team together.
- The finisher – who plays an important part in getting the task finished well, as he or she makes sure that the good intentions of the others are translated into a good end-result.

Clearly these characteristics can combine to produce a good team. Some people are good at fulfilling a particular role all the time, while others may take on more than one role. Individuals may take on different roles in different contexts, depending on how familiar they are with a particular task. For example, the teamworker in the accounts department may not have the skill or experience to play the same role in the works' football team.

One danger of a team working together for any length of time is that it can lose its powers of self-criticism. When a tightly knit group brings individuals' thinking into line with the group's thinking, this is often referred to as 'groupthink'. The views of dominant individuals can begin to hold sway in such a group, even when those views may have no real substance or value. This situation can come about when a team has become removed from the acid test of reality. To avoid 'groupthink' it may be necessary to change the composition of the team from time to time. Alternatively, individual team members can act as devil's advocate to test out all new ideas.

Team-building strategies

Since good teamwork is a key feature of a successful organisation, it is important to study team-building strategies. Teamwork is most likely to be successful when it operates in a supportive environment, and senior managers must create this atmosphere. The culture of an organisation should therefore be one that supports cooperation, trust and compatability.

Individuals should have the skills and abilities which enable them to perform specific roles within the team framework. It will also be important for members to recognise the roles of other members of the team.

From an organisation's point of view, effective team-building involves:

- knowing what you want the team to achieve
- deciding how you are going to help the team achieve the chosen objectives
- knowing what you expect of each member of the team
- encouraging participation in agreeing and setting objectives and targets
- making sure that there is free communication within the group so that information is readily available.

Case Study
Carter's pop

Carter's is a well-established producer of various types of fizzy drinks in the Midlands. For many years it was owned by one family and until recently it was run on a patriarchal basis. The organisation therefore had a traditional, formal hierarchical structure with clearly stated objectives and specifications of tasks, and defined relationships of authority and responsibility. Every job was defined, and there was a tradition of people within families working for the company from one generation to the next.

In 1992 the family that owned Carter's finally sold the business to Hero, a Swiss-owned food and drinks manufacturer. The Hero group is now trying to bring in new methods of management and organisation, more in line with its European style. It has adopted a flatter management structure with fewer bosses and greater emphasis on team-work. Hero hopes that this will result in better communication and cooperation between all levels of employees, which would encourage multi-tasking and improved productivity.

Questions for discussion

1 *What difficulties are the management likely to have in introducing team-working at Carter's?*
2 *What should the management attempt to find out before introducing a process of team-building?*
3 *How can management go about building new team-working processes at Carter's?*

Using specialist team-builders

When organisations need to go through a process of team-building they can either use internal experts or bring in an outside consultant.

When a consultant is used, the heart of team-building may be a series of off-site problem-solving sessions. These sessions will involve a 'family group' of employees, such as a manager and those who work with him or her, or a quality circle group. Sometimes, where there are clear task relationships within an organisation, it may be helpful to bring together members of interacting departments.

Before the team-building sessions take place the consultant may ask these people to fill in questionnaires which highlight problems that exist in working

Figure 10.34 A format for team-building

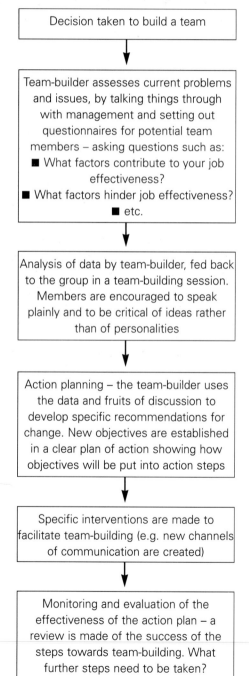

relationships and practices. These can then be discussed in the team-building sessions.

The 'team expert' helps group members to agree on an agenda, encouraging them to be open and direct. This sets the tone for effective group interactions, where there is constructive criticism and issues are 'laid on the table'. The team-building sessions may adopt the format shown in Figure 10.34.

Selecting the team

Team selection involves the matching of people with the roles within the team. Those charged with operating the 'hiring programme' need to have a complete set of job descriptions and specifications for all team posts, so that they can assess the human qualities required. Selectors need to find out enough about potential team members' background, training, personality, aptitudes, skills and interests so that they can choose the right people (see Figure 10.35).

Many factors affect the decision whether a particular employee should be chosen, in addition to their ability to do the job. Miller and Form, in their book *Industrial Sociology*, proposed a rating scale method. For example, to evaluate the *social skills* required, they stressed seven factors:

- the scope of social contacts
- the status range of contacts
- social demands of the job
- social leadership qualities
- skill intensity
- social participation
- personal responsibility for others.

Figure 10.35 Features to look for in selecting a high-performance team

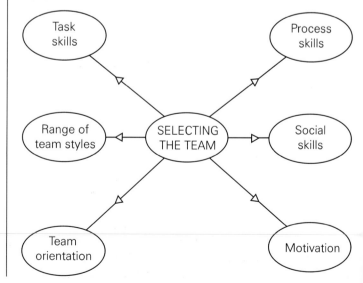

The implication is that an introvert who finds it difficult to make social contacts may not be the best person to select for a high-performance team that will meet over a considerable period of time.

Features of participatory management

Human-resource orientated organisations that stress the importance of team-working are clearly well down the path towards **participatory management**. This style of management exists when an organisation adopts a significant number of programmes aimed at the empowerment of employees.

Consultative management involves managers encouraging employees to think about issues, share their expertise and to contribute their own ideas to the decision-making process. Employees are encouraged to come up with their own suggestions for improvements in the workplace.

An organisation can attempt to motivate employees by developing special groups called '**quality circles**' (QCs). Quality circles are typically small groups of seven or eight people who meet on a regular basis to identify, investigate, analyse and resolve quality-related matters or other work-related issues. Members tend to be from the same work area. Quality circles have been particularly effective in Japanese industry.

The Japanese use the term *kaizen* to describe a process of continuous improvement in all areas of production. *Kaizen* will usually lead to productivity gains which, as time progresses, far outstrip conventional methods of improvement (see Figure 10.36).

Figure 10.36 *Kaizen* tends to lead to other forms of improvement

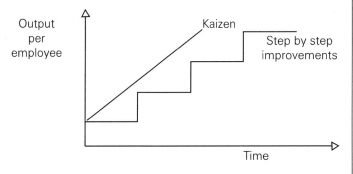

Teams of employees are formed into quality circles and meet regularly to consider ways of improving working practices and individual and group performance. The suggestions they make are then built into changing work practices. The working team jointly own the changes that are made and thus feel directly involved in the process.

Self-managing teams are groups that have a large degree of responsibility for their own decision-making. They exist as cells within a larger organisation and are sometimes called 'autonomous work groups' or 'sociotechnical teams'. The performance of a self-managing team is supported by a team leader whose purpose is to help the group obtain resources, provide coaching and guidance, and provide information links with other members of the team. The team leader will also play a key role in team-building. It is interesting to find today that in many schools and colleges team leaders are replacing departmental heads.

Task

As part of your coursework, try to build a team for a specific purpose. Keep a written record of how successful the team-building process has been.

First of all you will need to assess the readiness of the potential team. This will involve consideration of the following:

- Are the group members willing to devote their energies to developing team relationships and competence?
- Do they have time available for team-building?
- Apart from time, what other resources are required?
- Do the potential team members have a basic understanding of interpersonal skills, and are they able to put these into practice?
- Does the team's task require close team-working?
- Do any members of the group have previous experience of team-building?

Part 4 **Performance at work**

'You have got to have energy to work with us and you have got to have a sense of curiosity, but what I particularly like is to find people who are bright enough to want more, who can see that there are ways of getting more within the company, who can learn and grow and be somebody, who take all the information and education we give them and run with it and challenge the management. We have always believed in widening the windows of opportunity for everyone who works for us, whether they are making paper in Nepal or packing in the Littlehampton warehouse. Self-empowerment is the aim.' (from *Body and Soul* by Anita Roddick, founder of Body Shop)

The term **learning organisations** has been applied to those that are able, regularly and without drama, to look at the assumptions on which they are based in order to consider how they can best adapt and change. These organisations are 'in touch' with themselves and the environment in which they operate. They recognise the need to learn and adapt as an ongoing process. This contrasts with 'non-learning organisations' which become locked in a set of assumptions and patterns that determine the way they operate. Today, learning organisations take the process of learning to heart. They recognise the need to develop their people and the importance of life-long learning.

Coaching skills

Coaching is an informal and continuous process. It involves one person working with another so that skills, abilities and other qualities are improved. Coaching usually involves someone with 'more' expertise supporting someone with 'less' expertise.

Managers and supervisors have an important coaching role. A great deal can be gained by sitting down with someone else at work to discuss their performance on specific assignments or for a recent period of time. Coaching does not usually cost a lot of money and can reap tremendous benefits, for individuals and the whole work-group.

A good coach does not criticise the personality of the person being coached; he or she should concentrate on the work and the job.

The ingredients of coaching

There are five essential ingredients:

- Coaching should be part of the natural relationship between a manager and subordinates. It is an ongoing part of this relationship which helps to improve its quality.
- The coach observes his or her subordinates going about their everyday work and gives them advice and support where appropriate. When this becomes a natural state of affairs the subordinate will actively ask for coaching tips.
- The coach will seek to gain the confidence and trust of subordinates. It is only when subordinates have this confidence and trust that they will be able to benefit fully from coaching.
- Feedback given by the coach will be in the form of ideas and suggestions based on the manager's own experiences. This advice will be given on a give-and-take basis.
- Coaching advice should be given to encourage the long-term development of the individual receiving the coaching. It should not be seen purely as a short-term measure to achieve compliance within a given job role.

'Self-discovery'

Although coaching is informal and continuous, it should take place according to a plan that is agreed between a coach and a particular subordinate. The plan will set out when meetings are to take place and what will be discussed (e.g. issues for personal development).

Professor Kotter, in his book *The Leadership Factor*, argues that a manager should not always try to provide definite answers to the development issues that subordinates want to raise. It is better for the manager simply to suggest options or alternatives, so that the subordinate will actually make the choice for himself or herself. This is the process of 'self-discovery' whereby the subordinate is able to make personal choices which are supported by the learner receiving guidance from the coach.

Christopher Orpen, in his book *Behaviour in Organisations*, outlined a number of characteristics which subordinates see as being the features of a good coach. This is a manager who:

- . . . treats me as a person in my own right, uniquely different from other employees with whom he or she deals at work;
- . . . sets a good example, is an appropriate person on whom to model oneself;

- ... encourages and supports me, especially when things are obviously not going well;
- ... praises me when I do well, but still lets me know when I do poorly, in a straightforward and understanding manner;
- ... supports me to his or her superiors, wherever it is appropriate to do so;
- ... performs his or her own job conscientiously and competently, and enjoys a high reputation throughout the organisation as a result;
- ... does not try to pull rank on me, does not make me aware that he or she holds a higher position than me and should be listened to for that reason;
- ... keeps me fully informed about everything I need to know to perform well, including aspects of the organisation not immediately related to my current job;
- ... takes 'time out' from his or her normal duties and tasks regularly to coach me in my job, without forcing him or herself on me or requiring me always to do things his or her way;
- ... never underestimates what I am capable of doing, leads me forward and upward, often stretching me to perform even better than I thought I could.

Orpen produced a number of tips for coaching (see Figure 10.37) which can be summarised as follows.

Figure 10.37 Orpen's ingredients of successful coaching

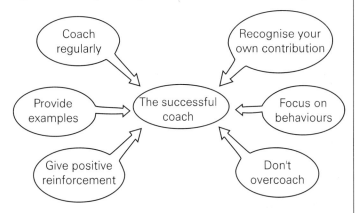

- Coach on a regular (not annual) basis.
- Recognise your contribution as the manager. As a manager you may be part of the problem for individuals working with you. You need to recognise this and jointly consider with subordinates ways of improving the work situation.
- Provide alternative examples when coaching. It is not enough to come up with verbal suggestions as to how improvements can be made. Wherever possible provide concrete examples (e.g. by modelling some appropriate actions through your own behaviour). When subordinates try out new ways of operating, give them feedback on how you think they are doing.

- Focus on behaviours, not attributes. It is much easier to change the behaviour of individuals than their personality traits and attributes. The coach therefore should be focusing on encouraging the way in which subordinates carry out particular actions rather than their underlying personality.
- Use positive reinforcement whenever possible. Wherever possible give rewards and positive feedback.
- Don't coach too closely. There is a danger of overcoaching. Individuals need to learn from their own mistakes if they are to become independent learners. You cannot be breathing down their necks all the time.

Training and development

Training and development are essential for individuals working for organisations.

Training is intended to ensure that as quickly as possible people can reach an acceptable level of performance in their jobs. It sets out to fill the gap between what someone can do and what they should be able to do. Training therefore builds up skills and knowledge to increase the competence of people in the workplace.

A common definition of **development** is 'the modification of behaviour through experience'. Development operates at all levels in an organisation from the new apprentice to the managing director. Development sets out to enable individuals to do better in their existing jobs.

The importance of education and training

Education and training are of benefit to individuals, organisations and the economy. It is imperative for individuals and organisations to engage in these processes if the UK is to remain competitive, if businesses are to flourish, and if individuals are to find rewarding jobs (see Figure 10.38).

Attitudes to vocational learning

In the autumn of 1993 the Department of Employment commissioned a **survey** of 1400 people in the UK to find out their attitudes to vocational learning, and how these attitudes linked with the learning actually undertaken.

The vast majority of the people in the survey agreed that learning was a good thing. Vocational learning was on the increase – nearly 50 per cent of the people interviewed had done some learning in the three years prior to the

Figure 10.38 A cycle of improvement

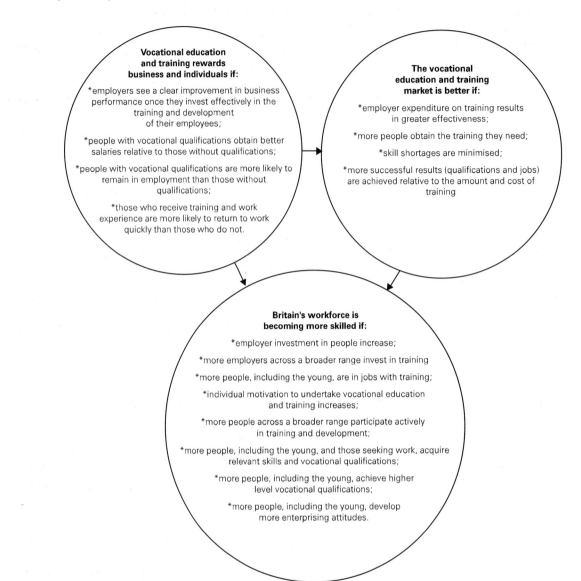

Vocational education and training rewards business and individuals if:

*employers see a clear improvement in business performance once they invest effectively in the training and development of their employees;

*people with vocational qualifications obtain better salaries relative to those without qualifications;

*people with vocational qualifications are more likely to remain in employment than those without qualifications;

*those who receive training and work experience are more likely to return to work quickly than those who do not.

The vocational education and training market is better if:

*employer expenditure on training results in greater effectiveness;

*more people obtain the training they need;

*skill shortages are minimised;

*more successful results (qualifications and jobs) are achieved relative to the amount and cost of training

Britain's workforce is becoming more skilled if:

*employer investment in people increase;

*more employers across a broader range invest in training

*more people, including the young, are in jobs with training;

*individual motivation to undertake vocational education and training increases;

*more people across a broader range participate actively in training and development;

*more people, including the young, and those seeking work, acquire relevant skills and vocational qualifications;

*more people, including the young, achieve higher level vocational qualifications;

*more people, including the young, develop more enterprising attitudes.

interview. One in five were doing some learning at the time. However, half had done no work-related learning in the past three years, and half did not anticipate doing any in the foreseeable future.

The survey found that some groups of people were much less likely to undertake vocational learning, but differences in their attitudes to learning was only one factor. Their age, gender, whether they were working, and if so what level of job they did, were all equally important factors. Their previous experience of learning was one of the most crucial factors.

The portrait of the likely learner was male, childless, in full-time non-manual work and having left education with a qualification. Conversely, a middle-aged woman with domestic responsibilities, having left education with no qualifications, was the least likely learner.

Most learning was funded or arranged by employers. They also had a big impact on the learning being done. Employers had suggested about half of all vocational learning done by those in work. Employees in jobs with formal assessment and career development were much more likely to be learners. Two-thirds of learners said that they had meetings to discuss their career and/or future learning, compared with less than half the non-learners. They were much more likely than non-learners to agree that their employer encouraged them to develop their knowledge about their job and ways in which it could be done better.

Five out of six people reported starting learning whilst in work. Workplace learning was most common. Just under a third of learning took place mainly at work, with a total of a quarter at educational institutions.

The main reason for starting learning varied greatly between those in work and those not in work. For almost half of those not in work, the main reason was to get a job. Those in work were more divided in their reasons for learning – the most common single reason was to make work more satisfying, whilst nearly a third were seeking other job-related advantages, including a change in the type of work done, promotion and updating of skills.

Attitudes of learners and non-learners differed. Non-learners were more likely to have left school at the first opportunity. Learners were much more likely to have achieved an 'academic' qualification than non-learners. Learners emphasised the nature of the work done more, whilst non-learners emphasised a job's terms and conditions.

Most people, whether recent learners or not, agreed that there were benefits to learning, both in terms of personal satisfaction and improved job prospects. There was no difference between learners and non-learners in how likely they were to see learning leading to better job prospects.

The importance of life-long learning

Learning is not something we do only at college or university. We all need to continue learning throughout life:

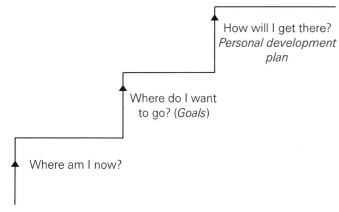

- from what we do at work
- from what we do in the home
- from what we do in our spare time.

Each of the above learning experiences is like a journey, and it is best if we know where we want to get to. Having a sense of direction enables us to

choose the best route, and the steps we need to take along the learning journey.

The first step is to look at where one is now, to do a review of present achievements and experience. The second step is to decide where one wants to get to – the learning goals. The third step is to plan how one is going to achieve these goals – this is a **development plan**.

Task

Set out a personal learning plan using the following headings.

Where am I now?
Educational record and achievements:
Work record and achievements:

A list of my chief qualities (e.g. perseverance, hard-working, a good mixer):
A list of my main weaknesses (e.g. poor time-keeping, lack of clear objectives):

Where do I want to be?
My main goals over the next year:
My main goals over the next ten years:

How will I get there?
Some specific targets for the next six months:
(These targets should be things that you can clearly achieve, and wherever possible it should be possible to measure improvements or success in terms of these targets.)

Evidence I will need to show that the targets have been met:
Precise steps I will need to take to meet the targets:

Who will help you to check that these targets have been met? What will you do when these targets have been met?

National standards in education and training

Recent years have seen a major overhaul of national standards for qualifications. A lot of the pressure for these changes came from employers and from those involved in working in education and training.

One reason for this overhaul was the wide variety of qualifications previously on offer, which made it difficult for employers and others to compare and assess the qualifications achieved. The old jungle of qualifications meant that nobody knew what they were buying, rather as if a street market attempted to operate with three or four different systems of weights and measures.

The **National Council for Vocational Qualifications** rationalised the range of qualifications on offer. They must now conform to certain standards, and qualifications are pitched at various levels.

One of the main thrusts of the rationalisation of qualifications was to provide a 'parity of esteem' of vocational and academic qualifications which are 'at the same level'.

National Vocational Qualifications

A **National Vocational Qualification** (NVQ) is a statement of competence clearly relevant to work, that is intended to facilitate entry into – or progression in – employment, further education and training. It is issued by a recognised body to an individual. The statement of competence should incorporate specified standards – the ability to perform a range of work-related activities, and skills, knowledge and understanding which underpin such performance in employment.

NVQs do not indicate simply that a person possesses the required skills and knowledge for an occupation. They also state that a person can apply those skills and knowledge in the workplace to the standards demanded by employers – in other words, that the holder of an NVQ is occupationally competent.

There are five levels currently recognised:

■ *Level 1* – Competence in the performance of work activities which are, in the main, routine and predictable, or provide a broad foundation for progression to a higher level.
■ *Level 2* – Competence in a broader and more demanding range of work activities, involving greater individual responsibility and autonomy than at level 1.
■ *Level 3* – Competence in skill areas that involve performance of a broad range of work activities, including many that are complex and non-routine. In some areas, supervisory competence may be a requirement at this level.
■ *Level 4* – Competence in the performance of complex, technical, specialised and professional work activities, including those involving design, planning and problem-solving, with a significant degree of personal accountability. In many areas supervision or management will be a requirement at this level.
■ *Level 5* – Competence which involves the application of a significant range of fundamental principles and complex techniques across a wide and often unpredictable variety of contexts. Personal accountability and autonomy feature strongly and often significant responsibility for the work of others and for the allocation of substantial resources.

General National Vocational Qualifications

NVQs prepare people for specific jobs. **GNVQ**s are designed to provide students with preparation for a broad range of employment opportunities. The emphasis is on creating flexible skills in an individual, combined with specific subject knowledge of an area like business, hospitality, information technology, or distribution.

A student is provided with the knowledge, skills and attitudes that are required in a variety of business occupations. The world of work is changing rapidly, and no longer can a person expect to have the same type of job throughout all his or her life. People need to develop flexibility so that they can quickly adapt to ever-changing demands in the workplace. New technologies and new products rapidly put out of date previous technologies and products. All people, whatever their age or previous experience, need to be able to adapt. This involves developing a good understanding of business principles and ideas. It also involves developing skills such as the ability to communicate effectively, to use information technology, and to have a sound grasp of working with numbers to make calculations.

A GNVQ course is a preparation for work and/or for further education and training. For example, a GNVQ Advanced qualification is recognised as being the equivalent of two traditional A-levels. Most universities recognise the GNVQ Advanced to be an appropriate qualification for entry to relevant university courses. It tells employers and universities that a student can work well with others and express ideas with confidence, has a good understanding of a relevant subject area, can use information technology to a good standard, will listen to others, make informed decisions, and many other things.

Employers and training

In 1994 the Policy Studies Institute carried out a **survey** of 600 employers. This indicated that 95 per cent of employers provided training for at least some of their employees. Typically employees were more likely to be given training the higher up they were in an organisation – 70–80 per cent of employers said that managerial, professional and technician staff were 'likely' to receive training, but only 30 per cent would provide training for unskilled manual workers (see Figure 10.39).

Figure 10.39 Training by occupation (1994)

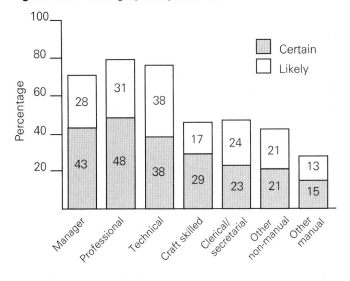

Much of this training activity was aimed solely at providing skills required for the current job. Vital though this is, not everyone would agree that it is enough to constitute life-long learning. 'The crux for lifetime learning is not whether employers train, but whether they provide continuous and progressive training for employees,' says the report of the survey. The report argues that a closer examination of this pattern of training, and the reasons behind it, is necessary if life-long learning is to be encouraged. It defines three types of training:

- job-specific training
- training for promotion
- other.

These definitions were based on what the employer saw as the main aim of the training: to improve performance in tasks in the employee's current job (job-specific training); to enable the employee to be promoted (training for promotion); and training for some other reason.

Training for many employees, particularly those in lower level occupations, was often restricted to job-specific training. Managers, professionals, technical and associate professionals were much more likely to receive training for promotion and were also more likely to receive other training. Indeed, nearly half the employers who provided other training restricted it to certain occupations, mainly managerial and other professional staff.

Although around 80 per cent of employers gave skilled craft and clerical employees job-related training, fewer than 40 per cent gave them promotion-linked training.

The report suggested that employers who are committed to life-long learning should extend training to groups who are currently neglected.

Training was more likely to be provided by larger than by smaller organisations. Public sector organisations were more likely to provide training than private sector ones, and employees were more likely to receive training in the service sector than in manufacturing.

Identifying training needs

The Policy Studies Institute survey discovered that the companies generally used one of four ways to identify training needs. These were:

- joint assessment – involving discussions between each employee and their manager (or supervisor)
- managerial identification – managers identifying training needs with little employee input
- employee identification – employees identifying their needs with little managerial input
- standardised training for the job provided automatically.

There were variations between employers of different sizes. Larger employers used more methods and were more likely to use methods involving input from employees. Service sector organisations used more methods and more often allowed employee input. Nearly all public service organisations allowed employees to identify their needs, whilst the proportion in the distribution, hotels and retail industries was much lower. Production organisations were slightly more inclined than service organisations to use managerial identification of training needs.

Managerial identification of training needs

Job and skills analysis

A useful starting point for identifying training needs is a **job analysis**. This is a description of the tasks that need to be carried out to perform a specific job. From the job analysis it is possible to outline a **training specification**:

- *Skills* – manual, social, intellectual, perceptual skills required to do a particular job.
- *Knowledge* – what the worker needs to know to do the job well.
- *Attitudes* – what attitudes the employee will need to do the job well.

Every job consists of a series of tasks, and these need to be analysed for training purposes.

Performance appraisal

Performance appraisal involves identifying what an employee is currently doing and comparing this with what he or she is expected to do. It is a good starting point to improving performance. A manager or supervisor and the employee should sit down to agree on:

- the overall purpose of the job
- the tasks that need to be carried out to achieve this purpose
- targets and standards for each task
- when these targets and standards will be reviewed, in order to explore the possibility of setting new targets and standards.

If the employee is not meeting the required targets and standards, this will need to be reviewed at an appraisal meeting. The performance appraisal programme should identify an individual's training needs. From an organisational point of view, the appraisal programme should identify the overall training requirements.

Individual training plans

Individual training plans can help to motivate employees and ensure that the training which has been identified is given. Individual training plans are most common in large organisations – in 1994, 91 per cent of organisations with 500 or more employees had such plans, compared with 25 per cent of organisations with only 10–20 employees.

Training methods

On-the-job training

This is perhaps the most common form of training, in which the employee becomes more knowledgeable and skilled through working with and alongside others. Clearly such training requires much planning to be effective. The responsibility for training should rest with a departmental supervisor. The trainee will require a 'mentor' who takes responsibility for day-to-day training, and the mentor will need instruction in giving the training.

The training may involve the mentor in demonstrating tasks that need to be performed, and then coaching the trainee through similar processes. On-the-job training is most successful when tasks can be quickly learnt and in one-to-one situations.

This type of training has the advantage of permitting the trainee to learn in the real environment of the job. The trainee experiences the work first-hand and gets a good feel for it.

One disadvantage of on-the-job training is that the trainee may acquire too narrow a view and be unable to generalise the skills. For example, a trainee teacher in a particular type of school may focus on skills and knowledge that are appropriate only in one or a limited number of schools. The trainee may come to copy the style of teaching of the mentor rather than using the style most appropriate in other circumstances. For this reason, on-the-job training should be complemented by off-the-job training. The fact that on-the-job training is cheap may prove to be a false economy – in the longer term, organisations need people with flexible skills rather than those who can operate in only one context.

Vestibule training

This is training that takes place for semi-skilled clerical and production jobs. It involves one skilled instructor training a number of employees at the same time. The trainees are provided with materials, equipment and so on similar to those they will actually use in the workplace. These simulate the work process. However, the emphasis is on learning rather than production. Vestibule training is used to train secretaries, bank clerks, machine operators, quality control inspectors, etc.

Classroom training

There are many types of training that can take place in the classroom. **Lectures**, for example, are a way of getting over a lot of information to a large audience. Wherever possible, interactive methods should be used to encourage audience participation.

Seminars are organised meetings involving delegates. The leader of the seminar will seek to move trainees towards certain learning outcomes.

Case studies are another useful learning tool. The case study is based on a real or fictional case. The learners are invited to tackle problems and issues in the case which replicate real work challenges. Often the tasks will be open-ended.

Role-plays involve trainees acting out assigned roles. There are no scripts or rehearsals. The players are provided with a description of a situation and, after being given time to plan their action, act the parts spontaneously. Role-playing is a form of learning by doing and is particularly good for developing interpersonal skills.

Programmed learning is a device whereby the learner works through a particular learning package at an individual pace. It may be paper-based (e.g. a manual or book) or may be computer- or television-based. The learner works through a sequence of instructions and is able to check answers on a regular basis. Such a form of training is cheap and easy to run and can focus on specific learning outcomes. However, it lacks the essential ingredient of human contact. Computer-assisted learning is becoming cheaper and more widely used, particularly with the development of computer books which can be stored on CD–ROM.

Simulations and games replicate real activities and situations. The 'player' or 'players' participate in a simulated activity and learn in an experiential way. Today there is an increasing trend towards 'virtual reality' simulations in which a player steps inside and interacts with an apparently real world. Mistakes can be made in the virtual world without great risk, or loss of resources and even human lives. Applications include learning to carry out a medical operation, learning to fly an aeroplane, etc.

Learner-controlled instruction is a method of training which gives learners considerable choice in deciding on the pace at which they learn and the sequence of the learning steps using a variety of media and instructions.

National Education and Training Targets

The **NETT**s are part of the recognition of a need for a wider learning society in which training and development become the order of the day. They set out eight specific targets for achievement in education and training for young people, working adults and employers. The *foundation* learning targets aim to raise attainment at school and at the start of working life. The *lifetime* targets set the benchmarks for improving investment in people by employers and by people themselves.

Figure 10.40 National Education and Training Targets

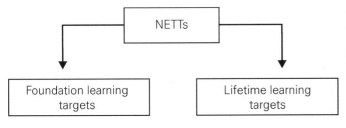

Foundation learning targets
- By 1997, 80 per cent of young people to reach NVQ level 2 or its equivalent.
- Training and education to NVQ level 3 to be available to all young people who can benefit from it.
- By 2000, 50 per cent of young people to reach NVQ level 3 or its equivalent.
- Education and training provision to develop self-reliance, flexibility and breadth.

Lifetime learning targets
- By 1996, all employees to take part in training or development activities.
- By 1996, 50 per cent of the workforce to aim for NVQs or units towards them.
- By 2000, 50 per cent of the workforce qualified to at least NVQ level 3 or its equivalent.
- By 1996, 50 per cent of medium to larger organisations to be 'Investors in People'. Organisations will be able to use the Investors in People badge if they can show an ongoing commitment to development of the human resource through training and development.

INVESTORS IN PEOPLE

In 1995 these targets were revised to make them clearer and achievable. The revised targets include:

For foundation learning:

- 85 per cent of young people to achieve five GCSEs at grades A–C, an Intermediate GNVQ and NVQ2, or vocational equivalent.
- 60–70 per cent of young people to achieve two GCE A-levels, an Advanced GNVQ and NVQ3 or vocational equivalent.

For lifetime learning:

- 60–70 per cent of the work force to achieve at least two GCE A-levels, an Advanced GNVQ and NVQ3, or vocational equivalent.

These targets clearly set the framework for training and development within organisations.

The Skill Needs in Britain survey in 1994 revealed that a substantial minority of employers (20 per cent) had a training facility within their organisation and that 17 per cent had full-time staff at the location to design and teach courses. Employers in the distribution and consumer services and the finance and business services sectors were the best provided for in-house training.

Counselling

Individuals at work often need to be interviewed and counselled. **Stress**, in particular, is frequently cited as a cause of concern at work. Stress is the general term applied to the pressures that people feel in life. Conditions causing stress are termed 'stressors'. The signs and symptoms of stress include anxiety, irritability, high blood pressure, rashes, ulcers and heart disease.

Almost any type of job situation can lead to stress, and of course individuals respond to stressors in different ways. Causes of stress include the amount of work that is expected of an individual, relationships with supervisors and colleagues, and the relationship between work and the home. Frustration, too, can be a cause of stress, where motivation is being blocked to prevent one from reaching a desired goal.

Counselling an individual in the workplace involves being a supportive listener. Someone who has a problem needs to talk through their difficulties. This means finding out exactly what the problem is, and helping the individual to work through to a solution. The best solution is usually the one the person suggests himself or herself.

A counselling protocol

- Listen with sympathy and intelligence. Encourage the person to get to the heart of the real issue or difficulty. Use phrases like 'Tell me a bit more', 'What do you see the real problem to be?', 'How do you see the way forward?', 'Who needs to take the next step?'.
- Move to a situation where the problem is clearly stated, so that both you and the interviewee have an agreement about what the real problem is. Make it clear that the problem can be solved.
- Focus on the problem rather than emotions. Don't let a wave of emotion distract you from the real issues. This involves considerable listening skills.
- Clarify issues by reflecting back to the interviewee your understanding of what he or she is saying.

- Go through the facts without being judgemental or making personal comments. Don't get involved in futile discussions about personalities or matters of opinion.
- Focus the discussion from time to time by summarising key issues and statements.
- Try to handle the interview in a pre-defined pattern, but be flexible enough to alter this if necessary.
- Conclude the interview by summarising the main points that have been made and getting the interviewee's agreement.
- Identify the next steps for the person you have been counselling, and if appropriate arrange a further appointment.

Discipline

Every organisation will from time to time have to deal with disciplinary issues, which may range from poor time-keeping and unsatisfactory work to gross misconduct. Generally speaking there will need to be graded levels of response to cases of indiscipline. For example, for persistent bad time-keeping it will be necessary to establish a series of warnings – somewhat like a football referee's use of yellow and red cards.

Employees should be made aware of the consequences – including possible dismissal – of breaking codes and rules, and be given a clear indication of the types of conduct that will lead to punishment.

Key ingredients of a disciplinary procedure
- It should be in writing and specify to whom it applies.
- It should show the disciplinary actions that can be taken, and specify who will be responsible for carrying out the actions.
- It should specify that individuals will be informed of the charge of indiscipline and given an opportunity to put their side of the story.
- It should allow for representation by a trade union official or chosen representative.

- It should ensure that disciplinary action is not carried out until a case has been thoroughly investigated, and there should be the right of appeal.
- No employee should be dismissed for a first offence, except for gross misconduct.

Figure 10.41 shows a typical pattern of warnings leading to discipline. Each warning should set out the nature of

Figure 10.41 A simple disciplinary procedure

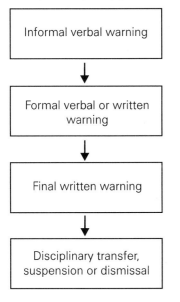

the offence, and the next likely step in the disciplinary procedure.

Gross misconduct

Summary dismissal (i.e. dismissal without notice) can occur within the law only if the employee does something that cancels the contract of employment. Examples of such actions might include: dishonesty, assault on the employer, damaging the employer's property, refusal to obey a reasonable and lawful instruction, revealing trade secrets to competitors, or revealing the employer's business records to others. Ideally the disciplinary procedure should specify what will be regarded as gross misconduct.

Appraisal

Most large organisations have well-established procedures for collecting and recording information to be used in personnel evaluation. These are called **appraisal schemes** and they are normally implemented by the personnel function. They are used mainly for white-collar staff, managers and technical staff, although large modern organisations may have an organisation-wide policy for appraisal.

The appraisal scheme usually requires individual post-holders to collect and record, in a set way, the impressions they have gained of each subordinate in their charge.

Use of an appraisal scheme enables an organisation to make the best use of the human resource by locating areas of strengths and weaknesses in job performance, perhaps identifying training and other employee needs. It also enables an individual to record his or her perceptions of the organisation and to contribute to outlining a career path.

The organisation should make time available for well-organised and structured appraisal interviews. The appraisor will need to be trained in the appraisal process. The appraisor and the appraisee may use a structured form containing such questions as:

- What were your most important objectives/ achievements during the last year?
- What were/are your major problems?
- What do you consider to be your main objectives during the coming year?
- In your present post, how do you feel you could improve your current contribution to the work-team?
- What action might be taken to bring about this improvement?

The structuring of the questions gives the appraisee an opportunity to talk about his or her aspirations and to set targets. If these are listened to carefully, individuals may gain the essential motivation that is required in an effective team. The person being appraised will feel that the company at least knows what his or her hopes and plans are.

The person who conducts the interview will in many cases be one organisational level removed from the person being appraised. This may help to prevent any workplace antagonisms or mistrust from creeping into the process.

Prior to the interview, the appraisee will fill in an appraisal form and send a copy to the appraisor. The two parties then conduct the appraisal interview using the form as the basis for discussion. Both parties sign the document to confirm that they are in agreement regarding the objectives, recommendations and actions to be taken.

When an organisation operates clear company-wide objectives (i.e. management by objectives), then precise and quantifiable targets may be required for each individual. A skilled appraisor would do many of the following:

- Agree on feasible objectives and targets with the appraisee.
- Emphasise targets and goals rather than criticise performance.
- Evaluate previous performance by reference to specific cases and examples rather than generalities.
- Make a point of taking an individual's criticism of the organisation seriously rather than trying to 'sweep it under the carpet'.
- Focus the interview on real job behaviour and performance.

Effective appraisal should lead to the development and motivation of the human resource. An effective performance management system will enable the organisation to monitor how well individuals are performing in their work roles, which will provide the sort of information to enable decisions to be made about coaching, training, development and rewards.

Further reading

- *Leadership in Organisations*, 3rd edition, by Gary Yukl. Prentice Hall, 1994.
- *Personnel Management*, 3rd edition, by G. A. Cole. DPP, 1993.
- *Organizational Psychology*, 3rd edition, by Edgar Schein. Prentice Hall, 1988.
- *Personnel Management – A New Approach*, 2nd edition, by Derek Torrington. Prentice Hall, 1991.
- *Organizational Behaviour*, 2nd edition, by David Cherrington. Allyn & Bacon, 1993.
- *The Financial Times on Management* by Christopher Lorenz and Nicholas Leslie. Pitman, 1992.
- *Modern Business Administration*, 6th edition, by Robert Appleby. Pitman, 1994.
- *Understanding Business and Finance*, 2nd edition, by Jill Hussey. DPP, 1994.
- *The Leadership Factor* by J. Kotter. The Free Press, 1990.
- *In Search of Management* by Tony Watson. Routledge, 1994.

11 Managing activities

On completion of this chapter students should be able to:

■ use techniques of work planning and organisation

■ identify the importance of management information and communications in the effective management of activities

■ coordinate human, physical and financial resources in carrying out activities

■ identify major constraints on effective management of activities

■ review effectiveness of self and others and improve the way activities and tasks are organised.

Part 1 Work planning and organisation

This chapter starts by introducing the concept of planning. Section 9 of the book explores planning in more depth.

Planning the use of resources is essential for all organisations. The key resources have traditionally been referred to as the five Ms – **manpower**, **machinery**, **materials**, **money** and **management**. However, increasingly, managers are also focusing on two other resources, namely **time** and **information** (see Figure 11.1).

Figure 11.1 The seven key ingredients of management

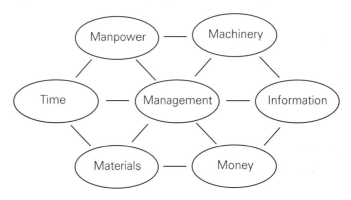

Once an organisation has identified clear objectives, the concern of planning is to set out how they can be achieved. Planning is about:

■ allocating resources to meet the objectives
■ setting out ways of evaluating performance against chosen targets
■ assessing the performance of the organisation (or parts of it) or of the plan, against the objectives (see Figure 11.2).

Planning means taking decisions today about what is to be done tomorrow. Planning also helps to bring objectives out into the open.

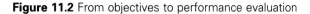

Figure 11.2 From objectives to performance evaluation

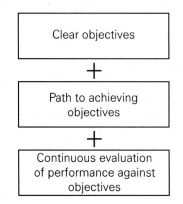

Clear objectives

+

Path to achieving
objectives

+

Continuous evaluation
of performance against
objectives

There is a saying: 'If you don't know where you are going then any road will take you there.' The point is that, without clear planning, you may achieve something but it is unlikely to amount to much. If objectives are clear then individuals and departments have definite guidelines and it is possible for them all to work in a coordinated way.

Planning also makes it possible for management to evaluate performance. Without evaluation there is ultimately no control. Of course, plans are unlikely to be met in every detail. However, they establish guidelines against which performance can be checked and if necessary modified.

Planning and control

Control is the *measurement* and *correction* of performance, and planning and controlling should go hand in glove. Indeed many writers on management theory argue that the two cannot be separated. They can be seen as the twin blades of a pair of scissors (see Figure 11.3).

Without objectives and a plan, control will not be possible because performance has to be compared with some established criteria. Responsibility for control rests with all managers and supervisors who are charged with putting plans into practice.

Figure 11.3 Without the two blades the scissors will not work

The control process

Control processes are broadly the same for a wide range of organisational activities. All involve, for example, ensuring product quality, organising office procedures, the administration of financial activities, and so on. There are three main steps in the control process:

- establishing standards
- measuring performance against the standards
- correcting variations.

Setting standards

Control processes can only be established in the context of the plans that have been drawn up. Standards should be established by clarifying **performance criteria**. These need to be set out in an understandable and precise way. Comparison of actual performance against the performance criteria will enable managers to ascertain how successful an operation is. For example, if a production manager's plan is to produce 100 units per hour with no breakages, and the plant produces only 90 units with a 50 per cent breakage rate, then something is clearly wrong and remedial action needs to be taken.

There are many different kinds of standards. For example, **verifiable goals** are a clear type of standard. An example of a verifiable goal would be for a group of workers to install a new machine by a given date, using a given number of hours of installation time. It could easily be verified whether this standard had been met. It becomes more difficult to measure the achievement of standards when goals are not so clear-cut – that is, where there are **non-verifiable goals**. Today the trend is increasingly to use performance indicators so that goals can be verified.

Measurement of performance

Ideally, the measurement of performance against standards should be forward-looking. In other words, managers and supervisors should try to *anticipate* deviations from standards. However, if deviations cannot be anticipated then they should be identified as quickly as possible.

For some activities it is relatively easy to measure performance against a standard. If it is easy to measure what people are contributing to a particular task, then it should also be easy to appraise performance against a standard. This is possible for routine tasks. However, there are many activities where this is not easy – for example, when people are engaged in non-routine activities or are producing one-off work. How, for example, would you identify a standard for a unique task that has never been done before? When work is of an intellectual nature then it will be less easy to establish a standard – how would you establish a standard for a creative director in a film production team, or for a lecturer who has a riveting yet slightly off-beat style of working with students?

The further removed a job is from the routine, the more difficult it will be to establish a standard of performance. Perhaps it is best, then, to resort to general performance indicators as a baseline and to recognise that some key aspects of performance may not be measurable.

Task

Suggest how easy or difficult it would be to establish a standard of performance for the following activities:

a designing and making a royal wedding dress
b assembly-line procedures in the mass production of chocolates
c playing as an international rugby fly-half, or as a football goalkeeper
d making routine repairs on a production line
e day-to-day bookkeeping tasks
f compiling of a set of final accounts
g working at the checkout of a supermarket
h activities of a nurse working in the casualty department of a hospital.

Correction of deviations

A deviation occurs when performance does not meet the standard. If managers have accurately set out the performance expected of resources (personnel, machines, money, etc.) then they will be able to see where under-performance occurs. They can then revise the plans, alter activities or change job descriptions as necessary.

Deviations can be corrected by one or more of the following actions:

- redrawing the plans
- modifying the goals
- reassigning or clarifying duties
- instituting better leadership
- using additional staff and/or other resources
- improving training.

Work planning methods

Gantt charts

Gantt charts are named after Henry Gantt, a management scientist who lived during the early years of this century. They are bar charts which compare actual progress with forecast progress. They can be used as a visual tool to indicate whether performances are on schedule. See Figure 11.4, which is based on the following table:

Month	Forecast	Actual	Percentage
1	300	240	80
2	350	350	100
3	400	440	110

Figure 11.4 A Gantt chart

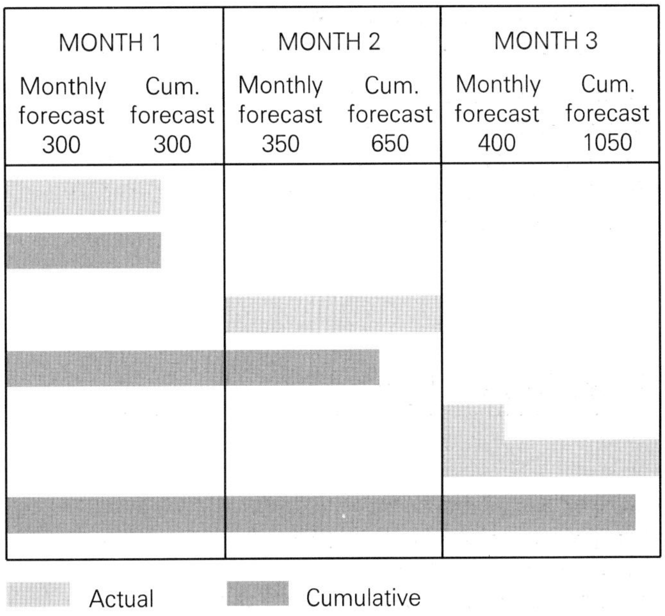

Milestone budgeting

It can be helpful to break projects down into discrete segments to simplify the planning and control process. Times and costs can be assigned to each segment. **Milestone budgeting** therefore makes it possible for a manager to divide a complex project into a number of simpler parts and to maintain control over each of the parts.

Network analysis

Network analysis is an extension of milestone budgeting. When coordinating a project, it is essential to map out the sequence of events that must be carried out.

Activities need to be performed in a planned sequence – for instance, in building a house the walls are normally assembled before the roof is put on; the layers of a sponge cake are made before the icing is put on, etc. These events can be linked in diagrammatic form as in Figure 11.5, where before B can be started, A must be completed.

Figure 11.5 Serial events in network analysis

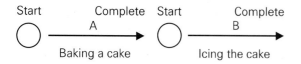

Some activities do not have to take place in sequence; they can be carried out simultaneously. For example, the icing could be prepared at the same time as the cake is being baked. This is illustrated in Figure 11.6, which shows that before you bake the cake and/or prepare the icing, you need to mix the ingredients for each – but the later stages of production can be carried out simultaneously.

Figure 11.6 Simultaneous activities in network analysis

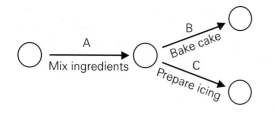

Network analysis can be used to map out programmes of activities in a way that creates the most effective planning.

Task

The organisation for which work is trying to design a network of activities for a new administrative procedure. You have been asked to map out programmes of activities in such a way as to create the most effective planning. Set out a network diagram to indicate the performance of the following activities:

Activity	Relation to other activities
A	Must be done first
B	Can be started only when A is finished
C	Can be started only when A is finished
D	Requires completion of B
E	Requires completion of C and D
F	Completes project and must await completion of all other activities.

A further important ingredient in constructing a network is *time*, which is a crucial element in project planning. Time needs to be incorporated into the diagram (see Figure 11.7).

Figure 11.7 Introducing time to a network analysis

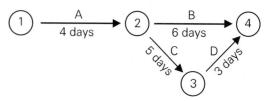

It now becomes easy to calculate the minimum time required to carry out a particular project. Those activities that take the longest to complete in moving from one stage to the next in a project are described as 'critical' activities. The **critical path** of a project is the path that these activities follow. It is essential that the activities are done well and that they are given priority if the project is not to fall behind. This too can be illustrated by a simple diagram (see Figure 11.8).

Figure 11.8 Establishing priorities in network analysis

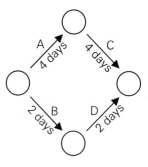

Activities A and B can be carried out simultaneously, as can C and D. However, activities A and C are the critical activities in that, if they fall behind in their execution, the whole project will suffer.

Program Evaluation and Review Technique (PERT)

PERT was first developed by the Special Projects Office of the US navy and was used successfully in the development of the Polaris Weapon System in the late 1950s. Thereafter it became particularly popular as a management technique in the 1960s and 1970s. Today the principles of PERT are still widely used under different names (e.g. process re-engineering).

PERT uses time–event network analysis. For example, Figure 11.9 might represent the major milestones of progress in the development and assembly of a passenger airline. Some of the steps might be as follows:

Figure 11.9 Planning aircraft assembly

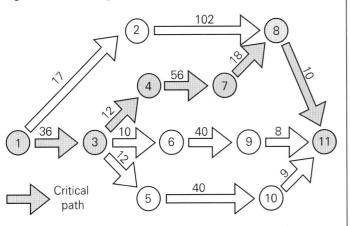

1 Decision that project will go ahead
2 Set out to procure engines for aircraft
3 Complete plans and specification for aircraft
4 Complete drawings of main body of aircraft
5 Award contract for tail section
6 Award contract for construction of wings
7 Finish manufacture of main body of plane, including internal fittings
8 Complete assembly of engine
9 Receive wings from sub-contractor
10 Receive tail from sub-contractor
11 Assemble various components of aircraft and deliver to airline

In this example only one time is shown for each of the activities. In the original PERT programmes three separate times were shown:

■ *The optimistic time* – the best-case scenario, the time that will be taken if everything goes to plan.

■ *The most likely time* – the project engineer's 'realistic' estimate of what is most likely to happen.

■ *The pessimistic time* – a worst-cast scenario, the time that will be taken if each set of activities falls behind schedule.

The Channel Tunnel project exemplifies a complex project that fell behind time schedules. When this happens, costs mount and mount. An organisation needs to be able to budget for this sort of occurrence if it is to avoid bankruptcy.

Case Study
Producing wine in the Laoshan Mountains

In the early 1980s, foreign investment in China was at an early stage but there were a number of people who saw the opportunities.

Michael Parry, a British accountant turned wine-producer, saw the opportunity of producing wine in China. At that time none of the existing Chinese wines was very good by international standards.

Mr Parry chose the Laoshan foothills to set up, and in 1984 he signed a joint-venture contract with the state Qindao winery, taking a 40 per cent stake in the Huadong Winery. The next year he brought from France 42 000 cuttings of 15 types of grape vines to see if they would take root. The imported grape varieties were introduced to the local peasants and long-term supply contracts agreed.

The first Chinese managers who were employed had had experience only of working in bureaucratic state enterprises. At first there was a lot of difficulty in introducing new methods. In the end Mr Parry had to invest nearly £750,000 in the business but by 1988 production had reached 60 000 cases a year.

However, in 1989 there was a slump in sales. The Tiananmen Square massacre led to a collapse of tourism in China which hit sales. The business went into receivership and in 1990 was bought by the British company Allied Domecq. It set about turning Huadong wine into an established brand with a worldwide distribution network and technical back-up. In 1993, production reached capacity at 100 000 cases. Post-tax profits reached £100 000. About 15 per cent of the company's sales were exports – the wines can be found in Chinese restaurants in Britain, the Netherlands, France and the USA.

Questions for discussion

1 *Why is it important to engage in project planning when setting out with such a venture?*
2 *What would be the key events in planning a network of activities for the Chinese wines venture?*
3 *Which events would be most critical to the success of the venture?*
4 *Would Mr Parry have benefited from taking into account a pessimistic time line in his project planning?*
5 *How would an organisation like Allied Domecq benefit from network analysis for its new China venture?*

Critical path analysis

As we have already seen, the critical path is the sequence of key activities that determine the time needed to complete a project.

Task

Think of any activity that you or an organisation have to carry out. Then:

a List all the tasks that need to be carried out, how long each will take and in what order they need to be done. (Are there some tasks that have to be finished before others can be begun, and if so which are they?).

b Draw a network to show the links between each task, representing each with a circle, identifying it with a letter or number and connecting the circles using arrows to show the order in which the tasks must take place pointing from left to right. The circles are the **nodes**, i.e. points in time when one or more activities finishes or starts.

A 'network' is a series of activities and nodes showing the sequence of activities and the time scale involved. We can break down each of the circles into three components – the top half of the circle gives the number of the activity and the bottom half can be used to show the earliest and latest times for finishing the activity.

Figure 11.10 An example of critical path analysis

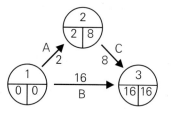

For example, in the set of activities shown in Figure 11.10, the earliest time to complete activity C is 16 days. This is because although activities A and C can be completed in 10 days, it takes 16 days to complete activity B and so the earliest time to arrive at node 3 is 16 days.

The latest time to finish an activity is calculated by working backwards from the end of a project.

Figure 11.11 shows the number of days required to finish a project with 12 nodes in it. Latest times are calculated by working backwards from right to left across the diagram. (Note that the two activities drawn in dotted lines are 'dummy activities', ones which do not use up time or resources.)

The pathway that is the most urgent – the one where, if tasks are held up, the whole project will be pushed behind schedule – is known as the critical path, which can be highlighted using a thicker line or colour to indicate it. In Figure 11.11 the critical path is B to E to F to H to J to N to P. The critical path will be the one for which both the earliest and latest times are equal at each and all of the networked nodes. In other words, every activity will need to start and finish on time or delay will take place.

Task

Return to the previous task and complete a critical path analysis of the activity you chose. Highlight the critical pathway.

Planning and control will involve putting the emphasis on activities along the critical path to ensure the success of a project. If performance of these activities falls below standards then extra resources will need to be channelled into them immediately or new techniques and plans devised to put the process back on course.

Activities which did not lie on the critical path will not be so urgent (which is not the same as saying that they are not 'critical' in the ordinary sense). The term **total float** is applied to the period by which a non-critical activity

Figure 11.11 A 12-node critical path

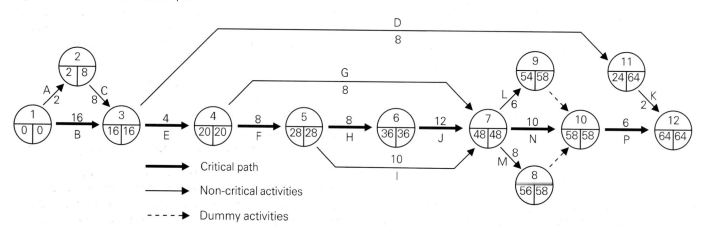

can if necessary be extended without increasing the total project time. Clearly, an activity should not extend beyond its total float time.

Advantages and disadvantages of network analysis

Network (and so also critical path) analysis offers a number of key benefits:

- It forces managers to plan properly.
- Planning has to work down the line from managers to subordinates. Each person involved in the plan will need to take a responsibility for part of the sequence.
- Emphasis is placed on the critical path.
- There can be forward-thinking control because time plans are made in advance of activities taking place. It is possible to measure performance against pre-determined standards.
- Because the network of activities is broken down into discrete sections, it becomes possible for managers to target their reports and recommendations to the correct point in the organisation.

However, network analysis does have some weaknesses:

- It is inappropriate when activities cannot be clearly identified and broken down into discrete sections.
- It is inappropriate for routine mass production operations (although it could be used in the first instance to make plans for such operations).
- Its prime focus is on time rather than on costs. Costs are extremely important in planning any project – ignore them at your peril. For example, a weakness of central planning in the former Soviet Union was that resources were wasted in trying to meet time deadlines *at any cost*.
- Although it forces people to plan, it will not do the planning for you!

Work method study

Method study is concerned with analysing an activity into its constituent parts and working out from this the best way of carrying it out. There is an assumption that there is a 'best way'. The early work in this field was carried out by the 'scientific management' school, of which **Frederick Taylor** was a leading proponent. He was employed at the turn of the century by the Bethlehem Steel Company, and he sought to find the most scientifically effective method of organising work.

Case Study
Shovelling bulky materials

The Bethlehem Steel Company required men to shovel large quantities of materials in a yard which was nearly two miles long. The men had their own shovels which they used to shift different types of materials.

There were considerable differences in the weights of materials. For example, Taylor found that a shovel-load of 'rice coal' weighed 3.5lb while a shovel-load of iron ore weighed 38lb. So, asked Taylor, what is a proper shovel-load? They cannot both be right. Under scientific management the answer to this question is not a matter of anyone's opinion; it is a question for accurate scientific investigation.

Taylor's research concluded that 21.5lb of any material was the optimum shovel-load. He then convinced the company to buy special shovels and the men were carefully trained to use the most efficient physical movements with these shovels. Exact targets were set for the volume of materials moved and payment was dependent on performance.

This led to impressive results. Before Taylor arrived the company employed 500 men at a handling cost of 7–8 cents per ton. After Taylor's methods were introduced, only 140 men were needed at a cost of 3–4 cents per ton, and wages rose by 60 per cent.

Questions for discussion

1 *What are the benefits of Taylorism?*
2 *What types of job task could 'scientific management' be applied to?*
3 *What types of job task would be inappropriate for 'scientific management'?*
4 *What might employees' attitudes be towards 'scientific management'?*

Today, Organisation and Methods (O&M) – commonly called **work-study** – has developed as a science to help managers use their labour forces more effectively. Its primary concern is to analyse efficiency in order to maximise the use of resources. By looking at ways in which activities are carried out using human and material resources, O&M tries to ensure that the techniques create the maximum possible benefits for the organisation. Its objectives are:

- to reduce costs by establishing the most cost-effective way of doing a job
- to standardise such methods
- to establish a time pattern
- to install such methods as standard working practices.

Work-study, therefore, entails a study not only of methods, but also of measurement in order to achieve higher productivity. Method-study examines both existing and proposed methods of undertaking a job, in order to determine how to do the job more easily, and therefore increase output. The steps are shown in Figure 11.12.

Figure 11.12 Stages in work-study

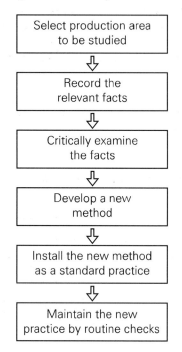

Figure 11.13 Stages in time-study

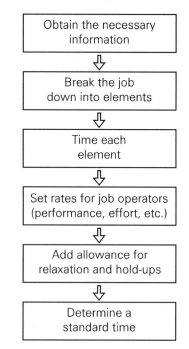

Time-study

Time-study (or 'work measurement') is the establishment of techniques to time activities so that they can be carried out with a defined level of performance – for example, to improve worker motivation, to create incentives and to improve future performance. The steps are shown in Figure 11.13.

In analysing an operation, the time-study engineer will sub-divide it into work elements and seek to find the most efficient way to carry out the work. In some cases this may lead to significant alterations in the way that work tasks are designed.

Once the most efficient method has been developed in theory, a small sample of qualified workers will be timed with a stopwatch while they carry out the prescribed procedures. A separate record is kept for each element of the work.

Because workers operate at different rates, the engineer will build in a margin for slower and faster workers (this will be a percentage figure). The process of adjusting the observed time by a percentage to give a normal or base time is called **levelling** or **performance rating**. For example, if in the initial test the engineer noted that an operator spent 20 minutes on a particular element, and

rated the experienced operator to be working at 20 per cent above 'normal', the 'normal' time for that element would be 24 minutes (i.e. 20 × 120 per cent).

Tasks

1 An engineer times a skilled worker carrying out a work element at 30 minutes. He/she assesses that the worker is operating at 50 per cent above the normal. What 'normal' time would the engineer ascribe to that element?

2 An engineer times a skilled worker carrying out an element at 12 minutes. He/she assesses that the worker is operating at 10 per cent above the normal. What would be the 'normal' time?

On top of the total of the times for individual elements are added allowances for unavoidable delays and rest periods. The final figure thus obtained is the **standard time** for the operation. Time-study experts claim that they can achieve an accuracy of plus or minus 5 per cent of the 'true' standard time.

Standard data

When the same operations have been observed and timed frequently using a stopwatch, it becomes obvious that there are regular patterns and uniform patterns for individual work elements. By systematically recording and tabulating the results of these operations, the time-study engineer can begin to create standard data. The engineer can then observe a particular job looking at such things as work layout, fixtures, etc. By knowing what elements make up the work, the engineer is able to choose the standard times corresponding to the work elements by using tables of ready-prepared standard data.

Predetermined elemental times

Predetermined elemental times are extremely sophisticated standard data. Over the years a lot of effort has gone into identifying and analysing basic units of work. For example, Lillian and Frank Gilbreth studied so-called 'Therbligs', which are basic finger, hand, arm and body motions (also commonly called 'basic divisions of accomplishments'). These are extremely short elements of work which are used time and time again in many occupations to move objects, hold them, grasp them, reach them, assemble them, etc. Standard time values have been established and tabulated for many types of Therbligs by studying a large sample of operations using a motion camera and a timing device. Motion engineers can thus be employed to identify best ways of carrying out operations based on a vast array of evidence from previous experience.

Operational management systems

Managing activities successfully depends on creating an effective **system** for production and operations management. This is as true for a service as for a manufacturing organisation, and many of the principles that apply to organising office workers are of equal value when related to manufacturing operatives.

In an operating system, inputs are transformed through processes to produce outputs. Inputs include labour, capital, management, the needs of consumers, information technology and many other things. These inputs are converted into final outputs. Transforming the inputs incorporates planning, operating and controlling the system (see Figure 11.14).

Figure 11.14 Processes turn inputs into outputs

INPUTS	PROCESSES	OUTPUTS
Capital	Including	Finished products
Labour	planning	
Needs of consumers	operating	
Information	and controlling	
Management	the system	
etc.		

Systems thinking is based on the idea that it is more helpful to look at groups of interrelated components than at the components themselves. Systems operate within boundaries, but these boundaries are not physical. Most organisations and parts of organisations are **open systems** in that they are influenced by their operating environment. The boundaries of a system are known as its **interfaces** because they coincide with the boundaries of other systems.

It is important to get a picture of the operations management system of an organisation. This is illustrated in Figure 11.15.

Figure 11.15 Operations management system

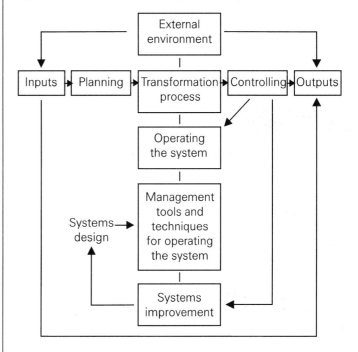

Katz and Kahn, in their book *Management*, set out five types of sub-systems which exist within organisations:

- *Supportive sub-systems* procure the inputs and dispose of the outputs of the technical sub-system (see below). In a business organisation they might be purchasing and sales.
- *Maintenance sub-systems* provide stability within an organisation. They provide the rules, the roles and the rewards. In a business organisation they might include health and safety rules and payments procedures.
- *Technical or productive sub-systems* are concerned with producing the product offered to the market.
- *Adaptive sub-systems* ensure that the organisation adapts to new circumstances. In a business organisation they might be research and development, and training arrangements.

■ *Managerial sub-systems* are concerned with planning, coordinating and controlling.

Features of plant and equipment

The design of plant and the positioning of equipment in an organisation should enable it to function efficiently. Although the design of the layout is a work-study issue, it needs to involve specialist engineers who take account of factors such as the structure of the plant, the availability of power points, maintenance requirements, and so on. Plant layout tends to be based on one of the following models.

Product (or line) layout
Plant is laid out according to the requirements of the product in a line of production. The semi-finished product 'flows' from one machine or stage to another. Control is straightforward because paperwork, materials handling and inspection procedures are minimised (see Figure 11.16).

Figure 11.16 Product layout

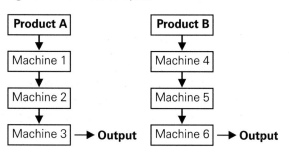

Product layout is just as applicable to services as to manufacturing. It applies to a sequence of activities in an advertising campaign, or stages in processing an insurance claim by a large insurance company.

Function (or process) layout
All operations of the same type are performed in the same area (see Figure 11.17). For example, spot welding may be in one location, riveting in another and stapling in

Figure 11.17 Process layout

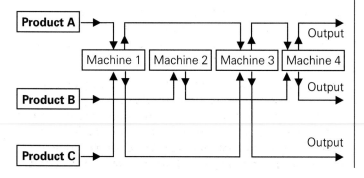

another (or retail banking in one area, mortgages in another, international banking in another, etc.). There may be a typing pool and/or a centralised print service. Although these systems are flexible, pre-production planning must ensure that machines are neither overloaded nor idle.

Layout by fixed position
Operations are performed with the materials or part-finished goods returning to a fixed position after each process (see Figure 11.18).

Figure 11.18 Fixed position layout

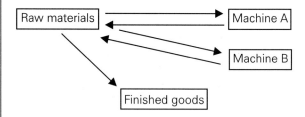

Whatever production layout is used, the aim must be to maximise the flexibility and ease of coordination so that process time and costs are minimised.

Plant performance, maintenance and safety

The justification for expenditure on new equipment is that it contributes towards the quality of goods and services being provided. Before equipment is bought, the general effects on the organisation have to be evaluated, and standard capital appraisal techniques have to be applied to see if such changes will be worthwhile.

Maintenance of plant and equipment is essential for the efficient provision of goods and services. If the size of the organisation warrants it, a separate maintenance department will be able to call on the services of specialists such as computer experts, electricians and joiners. The maintenance function should work to a plan to ensure that all equipment is checked and serviced in turn. The effectiveness of a maintenance programme can be judged on the basis of freedom from emergencies.

The process

In looking at the production process, we have to distinguish between goods and services. The important distinction between the two at operations level is that a service cannot be stored, as production and consumption take place at the same time. Many services, however, do come with a physical element; for example, when you open a bank account you are kept informed of your bank balance by means of statements.

There are five main types of process:

- job
- batch
- flow
- continuous
- just-in-time.

The operation of each type will depend on the nature of the work and the conditions necessary for working, and on the stage of an organisation's development. Many organisations start with job production, and as they develop and become larger move to batch production and finish up with flow or continuous production.

It is, however, rare to find any organisation where only one type of production is carried out. Certain items tend to be produced individually under job production conditions, others in batches and others in flow or continuous production. A major managerial decision is selecting the most appropriate method of production to meet the requirements of an organisation and the environment in which it operates.

Case Study
Engineering a change of clothes

Clothes design and manufacture is set to become more like engineering in the near future.

Engineers specifying a grade of steel or a type of plastic know exactly how it will behave during manufacture and afterwards. But clothes designers choosing silk or wool have only their previous experience to tell them how the material will make up, and how the finished garment will drape.

New developments from the Centre for Objective Measurement Technology at Bradford University will mean that it becomes possible to put together a standard 'fingerprint' of a fabric, including properties such as tensile and compressive strength, and then relate this to how it is processed. The fingerprint will give manufacturers a precise guide to a fabric's 'sewability' and allow clothing factories to become more automated.

Until now there has been no standardised objective measurement system to tell manufacturers how materials such as wool, cotton or silk will respond to processing or sewing into garments. Even artificial fibres vary from batch to batch, slowing down production as workers adapt, and requiring machinists to have a high level of experience and knowledge of each fabric in order to avoid puckered seams and other sewing damage.

A new intelligent sewing machine has been developed, which alters its stitching rate in response to fabric characteristics in the same way that a robot can be programmed to change the number of welds in different grades of steel. With intelligent sewing, the fabric is cut and its properties tested by on-line measuring systems that can predict likely sewing problems, and suggest how to avoid them. The system automatically sets the speed and thread tension of the sewing machines. The quality of finished seams is assessed automatically, and information about faults is fed back to the measuring system.

The machines have human operators but they do not need as much experience as in the past. This will cut costs while allowing UK manufacturers to respond to changing fashions. It will also make it economic to have shorter runs and many different fabrics and colours.

In the future, as in other branches of engineering, clothing designers will be able to work with computer-aided design and manufacturing systems, feeding finished designs direct to the production system.

Questions for discussion

1 What are the implications of the changes in textile technology outlined above on the organisation of production in textiles and textile design?
2 What will be the impact on (a) employment in, and (b) the competitiveness of, the UK textile industry?
3 What do you consider to be the main issues concerning the management of activities that will result from these changes?

Job production

Job – or 'make complete' – **production** is the manufacture of single individual items by either one operative or a team of operatives. Ships and bridges are built in this way, as are wedding cakes. It is possible for a number of identical units to be produced in parallel under job production – for example, several ships of the same type. Smaller jobs can also be seen as a form of job production – for example, writing this book, hand-knitting a sweater, rewiring a house. Job production is unique in that the project is considered to be a single operation which requires the complete attention of the operative before he or she passes on to attend to another job.

Job production has various attractions. Firstly, there is a unique product which exactly matches the requirements of the customer, often from as early as the design stage. It will therefore tend to be specific to a customer's order and not in anticipation of a sale. For example, someone doing a **customised** spray job on a motorcycle will first discuss with the customer the sort of design he or she would like. A detailed sketch will then be produced on a piece of paper. Once the sketch has been approved, the back of the sketch will be traced on to the relevant piece of the motorbike. The background work will be sprayed on with an airbrush before the fine detail is added. Finally, the finished work is handed over to the customer.

Secondly, as job production is concentrated on a specific unit, supervision and inspection of work are relatively simple.

Thirdly, specifications for the work can change during the course of production, depending on the customer's inspection, to meet his or her changing needs. For example, when a printing firm is asked to produce a catalogue for a grocery chain, it is extremely simple to change the prices of the goods described in the catalogue.

Fourthly, working on a single unit job, coping with a variety of tasks and being part of a small team striving towards the same aim provides employees with a greater sense of purpose.

There are, however, a few problems with job production:

- Employees, plant and machinery need to be versatile in order to adjust to a range of relatively specialised tasks associated with the same job. Trying to provide the right type of tools, equipment and labour to cope with such a range of specialised operations may be expensive.
- Because job production is unique, costing is based on uncertain predictions of future costs and not on the experience of past events. For example, the Channel Tunnel project cost between twice and three times as much as originally forecast.
- Unit costs tend to be high because of the 'setting-up' activities for each job, and there may be fewer economies from bulk purchasing.

Batch production

The term **batch** refers to a specific group of components which go through a production process together. As one batch finishes, the next one starts. For example, on Monday machine A may produce a type-1 engine part, on Tuesday a type-2 engine part, on Wednesday a type-3 engine part, and so on. All these engine parts will then go forward to the final assembly of different categories of engines.

Batches are processed continually through each machine before moving on to the next operation. This method is sometimes referred to as 'intermittent' production because different types of job are held as **work-in-progress** between the various stages of production.

We can identify various benefits of batch production:

- It is particularly suitable for a wide range of nearly similar goods which can use the same machinery on different settings. It therefore economises on the machinery needed and reduces the need for a flexible workforce.
- An organisation can respond quickly to customer orders by moving **buffer stocks** (or work-in-progress or partly completed goods) through the final production stages.
- Economies of scale are possible in techniques of production, bulk purchasing and areas of organisation.
- Costing of products is rather more predictable than for job production.

However, there are drawbacks associated with batch production:

- There can be considerable organisational difficulties. For example, sequencing batches from one job to another to avoid building up excessive or idle stocks of work-in-progress is difficult in terms of routing and scheduling.
- There is a time lag between the initial investment in materials and its eventual transfer into cash on the sale of a product.
- The time spent by staff on paperwork, stock control and effective plant utilisation can be lengthy.
- Part of a batch has to be held waiting until the rest is completed before moving on to another stage.

Flow production

Batch production is described as 'intermittent' because it is characterised by irregularity. If this aspect of batch production disappeared, it would then become **flow production**. Flow production is therefore a continuous process of parts passing on from one stage to another until completion. Units are worked on in each operation and then passed straight on to the next work stage without waiting for the batch to be completed. To make sure that the production line can work smoothly, each operation must be of equal length and there should be no movements or 'leakages' from the line (e.g. hold-ups to work-in-progress).

For flow production to be successful, there must be continuity of demand. If the demand varies there will be overstocking of finished goods or periodic shortages. Apart from minor differences, all flow products need to be standardised as flow lines cannot deal with variations in the product.

Achieving a smooth flow of production requires careful pre-production planning to ensure that materials are purchased and delivered on time, that sufficient labour is employed, that inspection procedures fit in with the process, and that all operations can be completed in their allotted times.

For example, assume that a production level of 800 units an hour is required and that there are three stages in the process, requiring the use of machines of type A for stage 1, which can each process 200 units an hour, machines of type B for stage 2, which can each process 100 units an hour, and machines of type C for stage 3, which can each process 400 units an hour. Figure 11.19 shows how a balanced flow can be achieved.

Figure 11.19 Flow production

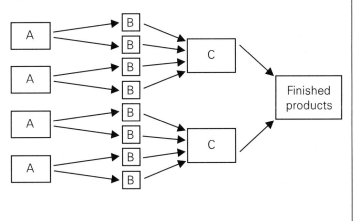

Task

Consider the traffic situation within your local town or city. Try to identify roads or traffic areas that are processed by batch, and those that are processed by flow. What factors influence the ways in which traffic is processed? How could the situation be improved?

We can identify various benefits of flow production:

- Labour costs tend to be reduced as comprehensive planning and investment will generate economies in both the type and the number of those employed.
- Deviations in the line can be identified quickly.
- As there is no rest between operations, work-in-progress levels can be kept low.
- The need for storage space is minimal as there is no waiting period between processes.
- The physical handling of items may be reduced.
- Investments in raw materials are more quickly converted into sales.
- As material and line requirements are easy to access, weaknesses are highlighted and control is more effective.

There are, however, a number of problems:

- It is sometimes difficult to balance the output of one stage with the input of another, and operations may function at different speeds.
- Providing a workforce with diverse skills to cater for circumstances such as cover for absence may be difficult and expensive, and regular absences can have far-reaching effects.
- Parts and raw materials need to arrive on time.
- One machine breaking down brings the whole operation to a halt. Maintenance must be preventative to ensure that emergencies do not cause the flow to stop.
- If demand falters, overstocking may occur.

Continuous production

Continuous process production is similar to mass production. However, instead of producing large numbers of individual items the product is produced in bulk. This system is suitable for producing basic materials such as refining oil or making plastics and chemicals and the process is dependent on the use of automated machines. Relatively few workers will be involved. They will be responsible for checking, monitoring, controlling and servicing the equipment rather than working directly with the materials.

Continuous process work is often rather uninteresting for the operatives. For example, in a modern brewery just a few people will be engaged in sitting in front of a huge computerised control panel with lights, dials and a screen. However, these employees will need to be vigilant because the leak of materials from a storage tank could cause millions of pounds worth of damage. Process workers may need to be selected carefully on the basis of their personal qualities.

Just-in-time production

Just-in-time (JIT) systems are frequently associated with the success of Japanese production in the 1970s and 1980s. Schönberger, in his book *Japanese Manufacturing Techniques*, described JIT in the following way:

> *'The JIT idea is very simple; produce and deliver finished goods just in time to be sold, sub-assemblies just in time to be assembled into finished goods, fabricated parts just in time to go into the sub-assemblies, and purchased materials just in time to be transformed into fabricated parts.'*

Such a system is therefore geared to ensuring that a plant has just enough resources, human and material, to meet its current production and distribution requirements. There are no stocks kept in reserve to protect against delivery problems. In mass production plants this will require a constant flow of deliveries of raw materials and components. The same principle will apply to labour. Employees have to be highly versatile and flexible. There is no reserve stock of labour, so if people are absent others will need to take their place. The requirement is therefore for labour to be multi-skilled and machinery to be multi-purpose.

We can identify a number of advantages of just-in-time manufacture:

- It is highly flexible, and this develops flexible attitudes within an organisation. People feel that they can solve problems for themselves.
- The system requires much lower levels of stocks.
- There is a continuous flow of new stocks into the organisation.
- Employees and other resources are respectively multi-skilled and multi-purpose.
- Costs are minimised.
- There is a continuous emphasis on improvement.

Just-in-time manufacture has some disadvantages:

- It depends on a continuous supply of new components, raw materials, etc. If for any reason these are not forthcoming, the plant will grind to a standstill.
- The system depends on flexible attitudes and flexible practices. If these are not forthcoming, then it is easy for employees to sabotage management plans.
- Because an organisation purchases ingredients and raw materials from outside suppliers, it is at the mercy of the quality-control and inspection standards of its suppliers.

Simplification, standardisation and specialisation

Production variety is inevitable within all organisations. While variety is often desirable, increases in variety may well add to organisational problems. For example, an increase in the number of component types will require more space in the stores. Control of variety is essential in reducing storage space, the number of production runs, types of machines and production aids, and in making production control easier (see Figure 11.20).

As firms move towards specialisation, opportunities increase to employ **mass-production** methods. This is the production of goods on a large scale. It usually follows that the greater the volume of mass production, the greater the benefits of economies of scale as the firm moves towards its lowest possible unit cost. It is often assumed that mass production may have a detrimental effect on quality. However, this is rarely the case. With mass production, quality will be more uniform and will depend not on the scale of production but on the skill of managers.

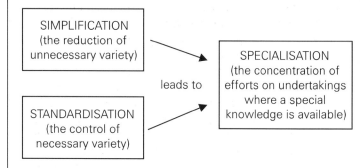

Figure 11.20 Simplification, standardisation and specialisation

The importance of the working team

Much of the above analysis of the process has focused on managing activities from the viewpoint that people at work are just another resource to be combined with other resources. We have already seen in the previous chapter on managing people that this should not be the case.

The early researchers of the 'scientific management' school wanted to improve techniques at work through time-and-motion study, mass production and other ways to produce more, more quickly, and more accurately. When and if all systems are run by robots this will be the best way to proceed. However, we have not yet reached this state of affairs.

The Tavistock Institute has emphasised the importance of the **socio-technical system**. The formula below stresses the importance of key relationships in this system:

$$E_o = E_m \times E_h$$

where E_o is the efficiency of output, E_m is the efficiency of the machine, and E_h is the efficiency of the operators (humans).

A well-designed machine today will operate at a very high level of efficiency. Robots and computer control add to the efficiency, so that a value for E_m could be, say, 90 per cent (or 0.9). Efficiency falls when such machines need to be cleaned, maintained, set up, etc.

However, when we look at the efficiency of people at work we see a lot of variation. We all know of people who do not enjoy their work and are frequently absent. Others can be absent through illness for long periods. The overall efficiency of operators could be as low as 30 per cent ($E_h = 0.3$). In this case the formula provides us with a measure of efficiency of:

$$E_o = 0.9 \times 0.3 = 0.27 \ (27 \text{ per cent}).$$

Clearly in such a situation there is much more scope to improve the human side of the equation than the technical side.

One of the factors leading to employee alienation and low work satisfaction is the nature of the production process. Mass production and the way it is organised can lead to unhappiness as people are physically removed from each other on the production line. The implication is that an employer may benefit from changing the layout of work so that people operate more closely together. Figure 11.21, for example, contrasts a functional layout with one in which people are grouped together to meet their social needs. In many work situations people can chat and work at the same time (e.g. on the production line in a chocolate factory). People who chat together may enjoy their work and be far more productive than people who are silent and bored. The emphasis should therefore be on developing a socio-technical approach to work which meets the needs of employees. Management must weigh up the costs and benefits of functional mass-production layouts compared with layouts that are sympathetic to human needs.

Figure 11.21 The functional layout in **a** is replaced by grouping for social needs in **b** and **c**

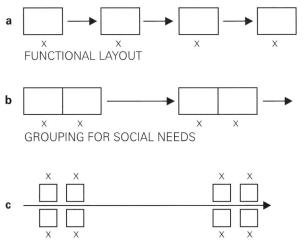

The flow of work from one operation to another is known as **procedure** (or work flow, method or system). Unfortunately, the human side of work flow in organisations is often ignored. Work flow is sometimes seen as a technical engineering factor rather than a technical and human engineering factor. In most cases it is possible to redesign work flow into teamwork activities by means of layout and integrated job assignments.

Case Study
Socio-technical experiments at Volvo

One of the most frequently quoted examples of developing a teamwork approach was that of Volvo in the 1970s at its Kalmar vehicle assembly plant in Sweden. The development of the plant cost about 10 per cent more than for a conventional car plant, but it was estimated that the payoff would come in increased employee motivation – and hence in productivity.

The factory was designed to produce 60 000 cars a year using teams of between 15 and 25 workers responsible for major production activities such as assembling electrical systems, car brakes, and so on. Each of the teams had its own work area and was given considerable operational freedom. The team members decided who would do what and the speed of the work line.

The plant did not have an assembly line. A team first collected a part-finished car from a storage zone and returned it there when they had completed their task on it. Teams were responsible for ordering their own supplies, equipment and stocks.

The process was very effective. Productivity levels and employee satisfaction were high, enabling Volvo to be particularly successful in the 1970s and 1980s. In the 1980s Volvo continued to use these practices in many of its other factories using smaller teams of workers. However, in the 1990s technological systems in car manufacture have moved towards increased capital intensity and the 'Japanisation' of car manufacture. Increasingly, work is carried out by factory robots and the human input has become less and less. Volvo has been squeezed in a highly competitive market. Some of the early practices at Volvo are no longer appropriate in an industry which is highly automated.

Questions for discussion

1 *What are the major benefits of the socio-technical experiments at Volvo?*
2 *Why would productivity rise in such a system?*
3 *Why might the increased spread of automation make human relations approaches less applicable in car manufacture?*
4 *For what other activities would the Volvo methods be appropriate?*

Creating more flexibility

John Dupuy, in his book *Flexible Jobs – the Key to Manufacturing Productivity*, has argued that one of the major causes of quality and productivity weaknesses in European and US manufacturers has been over-specialisation. A large US manufacturing plant may have 50–100 job classifications, compared with one or two classifications in Japan. 'Taylorism' may have reduced employees' responsibility so that they fail to identify with the products they produce:

> *'Craftsmanship has died, not so much because of social change or workers' attitudes, but because of the way manufacturing has been organised.'*

This has also led to problems in the relationship between management and workers, because the latter cannot identify with the organisation's goals and objectives, nor with organisational cultures.

Appropriate responses all involve giving people pride in what they produce. Activities that need different skills can be grouped together to provide an extended job range. A good example is **cellular manufacturing**, where several different types of machines are put at the disposal of one worker in a 'cell'. The company and the employee benefit – the company needs less labour, working capital is reduced because of faster throughput times, employees gain more job satisfaction with more variety and responsibility and less boredom.

Workers can be more involved in support activities such as machine maintenance and inspections, work-area housekeeping and quality discussions. 'Teams' can take over responsibility for a range of jobs where multi-skilling is encouraged. Job expansion often results in more work being done with fewer people. If a team of workers takes responsibility for quality control then there is no need for a separate quality-control team.

Control of production

A number of related functions are involved in the control of production.

Firstly, it is necessary to ensure that materials and parts are available in the right place at the right time. Delays and bottlenecks should be avoided. Computerised control systems have made it possible to ensure effective just-in-time procedures today (see above).

Secondly, there must be planning and monitoring of the whole production process. This involves keeping track on work flows, deadlines, and completion times.

Thirdly, there has to be maintenance to ensure that all machinery and equipment is in good working order and reliable.

Fourthly, there must be quality control to ensure that products meet appropriate standards. Figure 11.22 illustrates how the elements of production may be organised.

Figure 11.22 Organising elements of production

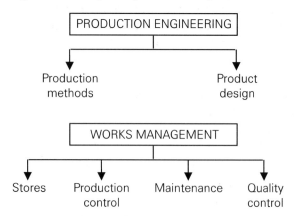

Production planning and control

All organisations should make plans that are designed to fulfil business objectives. These plans will depend on (a) the level of operation and (b) the time period. Much of production planning and control will be concerned with the organisation's hopes for the future and will need to be carefully coordinated with marketing policy, for example in areas such as product life-cycles. For the immediate future, however, production planning and control will look at questions like these in order to achieve the best use of existing resources:

- How do we meet this order?
- How close is the job to completion?
- Can it be completed on time?
- Do we need to use more of a particular resource?

Programming is concerned essentially with timetabling all the resources used by the production department. Production managers set dates for the delivery of resources and part-finished products and allocate production services accordingly. Delivery timetables will generate further timetables in areas such as purchasing, stock control and quality control.

Purchasing

Procuring materials is a key management function for any type of business. The importance of its role can be appreciated when one takes into account that an average manufacturing company spends about half of its income on supplies for raw materials and services.

The purchasing department aims to provide the organisation with a steady flow of materials and services while at the same time ensuring continuity of supplies. It aims to obtain the best value for money. **Value analysis** often makes it possible for considerable savings to be made, though a particular danger is that quality could be sacrificed to cost considerations. A successful purchasing department will keep costs down, produce a fast stock turnover, reduce obsolescence, ensure continuity of supplies, and reduce lead time (the interval between the realisation of a need and its ultimate fulfilment upon delivery).

We have looked at just-in-time (JIT) which relates purchasing decisions and stock levels to current production needs. It involves working with the lowest possible stock levels, while making sure that materials are always available when required, that they are of good quality, and that they are fit for the purpose intended.

Intelligent systems have recently been developed for the purchasing function. These systems can analyse a problem (e.g. decide on economic ordering levels), explain a process (e.g. through documentation), and make a choice from a selection of suppliers.

Stock control

In an ideal world in which businesses knew demand well in advance and suppliers always met delivery dates, there would be no problem with deciding stock levels. In practice, however, demand varies and suppliers are often late with deliveries, so stocks act as a protection against unpredictable events. Organisations hold stocks in a variety of forms:

- as raw materials
- as work-in-progress
- as finished goods
- as consumables
- as plant and machinery spares.

The aim of any stock control system is to provide stocks that cater for uncertainties but are at minimum levels, thereby ensuring that costs are kept low. Figure 11.23 illustrates the dangers of having the 'wrong' stock levels.

Buffer stocks can be built up as a preventative measure against running out owing to unexpected variations in demand. A minimum level should be set below which stocks should not fall, and this level will depend on the lead time between placing an order and its receipt.

Figure 11.24 illustrates an ideal situation in which stocks never fall below the set minimum level or go above the set maximum level. Stocks are replenished just at the point at which the minimum stock level is about to be breached. (It is worth noting that, in the example, should the replacement stock not arrive on time, the firm will at least be protected by the buffer stock.)

In reality, delivery times, re-order quantities and rates of usage will vary, and a continuous or a periodic review system will monitor and control the levels. At regular intervals stock is counted and recorded accurately so that

Figure 11.23 Implications of 'wrong' stock levels

Problems of low stocks	Problems of high stocks
■ It may be difficult to satisfy customer demands.	■ There is an increased risk of a stocked item becoming obsolete and therefore unusable.
■ It can lead to a loss of business.	■ The risk of stock losses is increased (e.g. through theft or damage)
■ It can lead to a loss of goodwill.	■ The costs of storage are too high.
■ Ordering needs to be frequent and so handling costs are higher.	■ Stocks can tie up a company's working capital.

Figure 11.24 Managing stock levels

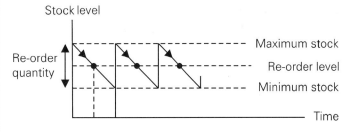

trading results can be calculated. The physical counting of stock can be time-consuming, and it is inevitable that inaccuracies will creep in. However, information technology is reducing the need for physical counting of stock.

Control and feedback

At the start of this chapter we looked at planning and control as being two blades of a pair of scissors. Management control is a **feedback** system which applies to all elements of managerial activity. Managers measure actual performance, compare this against standards and identify and explain deviations. To make the necessary corrections they need to develop a programme of corrective action and put this into action to achieve the desired performance (see Figure 11.25).

However, managers should not rely simply on making alterations after deviations have occurred. They need to be 'wise before the event'. So, in addition to feedback control they need **feedforward** control.

Feedforward systems monitor the inputs into a process in order to establish if these inputs are as planned. If they

Figure 11.25 Feedback control

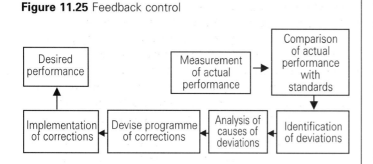

are not, then the inputs (or the process) can be changed in order to meet the required standards. The difference between feedforward and feedback is that, in the former case process monitoring is at the input side of the system so that corrections can be made *before* the system's output is affected (see Figure 11.26).

Figure 11.26 Feedforward and feedback

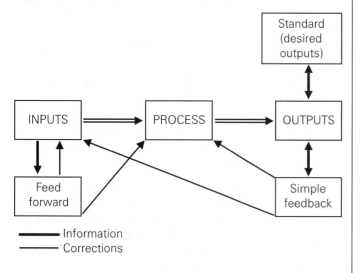

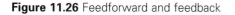

The use of forecasting

A method of future-directed control commonly used involves **forecasting** using the very latest information. For example, some supermarket chains decide on the next day's ideal level of staffing on the basis of the present day's sales figures. In some organisations, cash-flow forecasting is used to assess how much cash will be available in the near future.

Every organisation will have useful internal sources of data (e.g management accounts and budgetary information) that can help in preparing forecasts. These forecasts include costing and sales figures for individual products, breakdown of overheads, sales results for staff, performance data for operating units, etc. Reports are frequently prepared showing the potential of different projects, options for development and the time periods concerned.

The departments of an organisation will keep regular records of attendance, expenses, sales, etc. which provide the raw data for statistical projections. Informally, information can be collected from conversations with other people in the same line of business, and suppliers may indicate possible future price changes. Forecasts and information about the business environment will usually be collected from external sources such *Labour Market Quarterly Review* and Central Statistical Office (CSO) publications.

Setting standards

Managers have to set and adjust standards of performance, for employees, for capital equipment, for quality control, for timekeeping, for stocks, and for a thousand and one other important aspects of business life.

- *Physical standards* are non-monetary measurements which relate to the quantities of items made, number of hours worked, tolerances of materials used, quality of fabrics, etc.
- *Cost standards* are monetary measures of the costs of various activities (e.g. direct and indirect cost per unit, resource costs).
- *Capital standards* are monetary measures which relate to the capital invested in a business (e.g. the return on capital employed – ROCE).
- *Revenue standards* are monetary measures of sales, or revenue per employee.
- *Programme standards* relate to particular programmes that have been put into practice (e.g. for the research and development of a new product, or for reduction of the number of accidents in the workplace).
- *Intangible standards* are for those situations when it is not possible to measure performance in monetary or physical terms. This occurs when performance indicators are difficult to create because activities are new, because research has not been carried out into creating standards, or because the nature of the activity is so subjective that it is difficult to measure (e.g. activities involving interpersonal relationships). Increasingly, standards are being set for all sorts of activities using tangible means (e.g. the performance of schools and teachers, doctors and hospitals).
- *Performance standards* set the goals of an organisation. Clearly, if an organisation works towards defined goals then it is possible to check on whether standards are being met.

The importance of quality

Those of us who enjoy listening to music would undoubtedly prefer to listen using the best available system, but such a system might be outside our personal budget. When we purchase a good we may be aware that better models of the item exist, but we are prepared to forfeit **quality** in the interest of saving money or not exceeding our budget. Clearly, quality, reliability and cost should be seen as interrelated and often competing threads of production and consumption decisions.

Quality relates to the individual characteristics of each product or service that enable it to satisfy consumers. The basic objective of any control system is to satisfy the consumer as cheaply as possible with a product that can be delivered on time. Although quality control was seen in the past as a form of *inspection* at the *end* of a production process, today it is seen as a system that tries to coordinate groups in an organisation to improve products in a cost-effective way (see Figure 11.27).

Figure 11.27 The essence of quality control

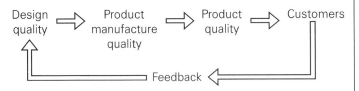

- *Design quality* is the degree to which features within a design satisfy consumers.
- *Product manufacture quality* is the success of a manufacturing process in matching design specifications.
- *Product quality* is the degree to which the finished good or service satisfies the wishes of customers.

There are five essential stages in the quality process:

- identifying the quality required by customers
- planning to achieve that quality by, for example, selection of the right materials, prevention of errors, and the training of operators
- monitoring the manufacturing process to ensure that plans are carried out
- correcting any problems such as excessive scrap
- providing long-term planning.

In recent years, many organisations have adopted a much broader approach to quality under the guise of **quality assurance**. With this approach, deliveries are expected to be of an appropriate quality and the operations of the organisation providing the good or service are designed in such a way as to ensure that the quality is achieved. The idea behind this approach is to make sure that an organisation gets the quality **right first time** and thus avoids problems arising from failure.

BS 5750 was developed by the British Standards Institution to provide a framework within which organisations can be certified as having comprehensive quality management. Quality circles (i.e. groups of workers at the workplace) are set up to identify problems and try to present solutions to quality issues. Another modern idea is the **zero-defects** approach, which aims to get workers to develop a commitment to flawless working. All such approaches are designed to eliminate problems and thereby ensure that quality is achieved.

Some organisations interpret 'quality' more broadly and talk about 'total quality management' or the 'total product'. Quality is then considered not only in the finished product but also in all other areas of the organisation – so that quality becomes everybody's business, from the most junior staff to the most senior member of the management team. In this way an organisation develops a framework enabling quality to be achieved at all levels, thus creating a genuine competitive edge over rivals.

Case Study
The development of 'Quality Man'!

There was a time when we thought of Japanese goods as being shoddy or cheap imitations of British goods. How things have changed! Today, the Japanese approach towards quality has overwhelmed us. Japanese manufacturing has moved from a position of low competence to one of supremacy.

The first success in this battle for markets has been on the basis of Japanese quality. Having achieved quality, Japanese manufacturers are today working on a new area and redefining their rules of engagement on the basis of flexibility and customer response. In this new war, quality will be a basic, manufacturing skill.

In order to understand how the Japanese have achieved quality we need to look at the seven ages of factory man. The following typology has been adapted from an article by David Pearson, Chief Executive, the Strathclyde Institute, in the October 1991 issue of *Director* (by kind permission of Director Publications).

The best and most capable of British producers tend to exist towards the top the following evolutionary scale. However, many still lie around the middle and some are in the early stages of development:

- *Stage 1 – Fordian Man.* This organisation is characterised by long flow lines, lengthy change time and large batch sizes. The Fordian man provides low variety, lacks flexibility and has high direct labour and inventory costs.
- *Stage 2 – Automation Man.* Organisations become obsessed with automation, mainly directed at reducing

direct labour costs, and the weaknesses at this stage concern a change of focus away from manufacturing issues and on to systems issues instead, poor labour relations, high capital and white-collar investment levels, and often poor product quality.

- *Stage 3 – Low Inventory Man.* In this stage managers begin to understand that equipment and people should be driven by market demand; but, at the same time, there is a growing recognition of the importance of developing employees. The negative tendency at this stage is to reduce market flexibility and limit the number of suppliers.
- *Stage 4 – Balanced Man.* This stage focuses on chasing and eliminating bottlenecks and results in higher throughput operations; but the negative consequences of this include high levels of capital investment.
- *Stage 5 – Integrated Man.* This stage is heralded by the understanding that marketing, R & D and production functions are all part of the same company rather than deadly warring enemies, and so they share information and systems. The growing strengths in this stage include better customer delivery and service, higher quality products and more choice, while the weaknesses include a growing dependency on expert systems.
- *Stage 6 – Low Overhead Man.* In this factory IT is used as a primary vehicle in the displacement of administrative and middle management jobs. The strengths of this stage include improving product cost structures and margins, a clearer vision of the strategic role of IT and shorter decision and information structures. Its weakness is that it becomes a much flatter, stress-laden organisation with a heavy dependency on expensive 'knowledge' workers.
- *Stage 7 – Quality Man.* This stage is characterised by organisations producing quality goods and services in the marketplace, where faults are measured in one or two parts per million; so quality, service to the customer and internal communication are excellent. Its weaknesses are the belief that quality is the ultimate business goal, a cost structure that becomes inflexible, and an inability to make production compromises.

Questions for discussion

1 *Why should businesses aim for the Quality Man end of this evolutionary scale?*
2 *What are the advantages and drawbacks to an organisation from putting the emphasis on quality?*
3 *Why might organisations in the UK lose out if they fail to concentrate on quality?*
4 *How do (a) employees, (b) managers and (c) customers benefit from an emphasis on quality?*

Efficiency and effectiveness

An important distinction has to be made between an *efficient* and an *effective* organisation.

Efficiency

For some organisations it is imperative to be able to compete on the basis of cost competitiveness, so the emphasis will be on **cost minimisation**. Costs are kept to a minimum when resources are used efficiently.

The key question will be how well those resources have been used, regardless of the purpose for which they are used. An efficient organisation might adopt measures of efficiency such as profitability, or output per employee, or machines being used to full capacity, and so on. Since all inputs used by an organisation are costly, they must be used in such a way that waste is kept to a minimum. When everything possible has been done to minimise costs, we can say that the firm is operating at its technically most efficient point.

A manager focusing on efficiency would argue that efficiency occurs:

- when for *labour* the percentage of time spent idle is minimised
- when for *materials* the percentage of waste or scrap is minimised
- when for *machinery*, output per machine-hour is maximised, so that machines are used to their full potential.

Business efficiency will stem from the best possible mix of manpower, machines, materials, money and managers (see Figure 11.28).

Figure 11.28 Measures of maximum efficiency

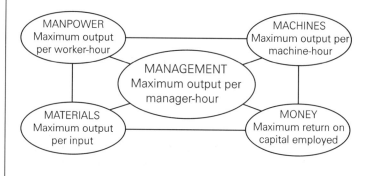

Effectiveness

An **effective** organisation, by contrast, may be concerned to show that it is better than competitors – for example by developing and sustaining unique products. An organisation that stresses effectiveness may concentrate on quality rather than quantity. The effective organisation will seek to channel resources into those aspects of activities that emphasise its edge over competitors.

Effectiveness implies the achievement of objectives. Organisations and their sub-systems may be working towards the achievement of a multitude of objectives in a variety of different categories – long-range/short-range, strategic/operational, general/specific. Clearly, for an organisation to be effective it must be able to express its objectives in an easily understandable way.

Johnson and Scholes, in their book *Exploring Corporate Strategy*, argued that the effectiveness of an organisation can be critically influenced by the ability to get all parts of the organisation's value chain working in harmony. They set out a number of measures of effectiveness, including:

■ *Use of people* – People need to be used in such a way as to meet the real objectives of the organisation.
■ *Use of capital* – An organisation should use capital in such a way as to serve the real needs of the organisation.
■ *Use of marketing and distribution resources* – Marketing and distribution resources should be used in such a way as to meet the best needs of the organisation.
■ *Use of research knowledge* – Research knowledge should be used in such a way as to meet the needs of the organisation most effectively.
■ *Use of production systems* – The use of a production system needs to be geared towards the basis on which the organisation competes.
■ *Exploitation of intangible assets* – These include image, brand name, or market information.

The organisation that is both efficient and effective will use its resources efficiently to meet organisational objectives effectively.

Changing and amending plans

Many of the plans and decisions that are made by organisations involve uncertainty. In a complex dynamic business world, change is ever-present. For this reason it is helpful to develop an **open-systems** approach to decision-making and planning.

An open-systems approach dispenses with the notion that the effects of decisions can be worked out precisely, and instead works on the premise that, at best, information is imperfect. An open-systems model therefore places more emphasis on feedback, learning and adaptation, together with their effects on ends and means. Plans are adjusted to changing circumstances and to changing perceptions of the meaning of available information.

Figure 11.29 illustrates one way in which an open-systems model might operate. The first stage involves the identification of objectives to be pursued. These will rarely be clear-cut and therefore will be subject to review. Thus, it can be seen that setting objectives involves setting out courses of action that will be appropriate to the organisation, and setting out measures for assessing their attainment.

Figure 11.29 Adjusting plans

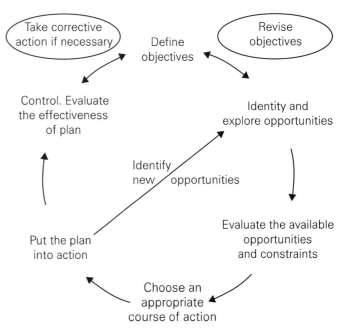

The second stage is to outline some of the possible courses of action and to evaluate them. The next stage involves comparing the likely results of alternative courses of action with the desired level of performance. At this stage the performance objectives have already been established. The organisation should now be asking questions such as: 'If we do X, how close will we be to achieving our target?'

Provided there is a match, the decision makers can then choose the most effective of the alternative courses of action that have been identified given the initial objectives. If an organisation's objective is to achieve some measure of guaranteed success, it might choose a course of action that avoids risk. Alternatively, it might be prepared to take a risk if the objective is to gamble on high returns.

If the chosen course of action does not look likely to meet the required objectives, planners should either reduce the target objectives to manageable proportions, or seek alternative courses of action to meet targets.

Once the plan is in operation, new opportunities may be identified. For example, when the early space programme had been implemented, researchers immediately became aware of new opportunities such as the Space Shuttle.

The results of plans will need to be clearly appraised and evaluated to improve the planning process. Corrective action can be taken where necessary. The key to successful planning is to build in effective control systems so that plans can be monitored and adjusted on an on-going basis. Some plans can be easily altered; some have built into them the possibility of future changes; and others involve action which is difficult to reverse. Wherever possible, flexibility should be built into the planning process.

Part 2 **Communications**

Clear communications are essential when managing activities. This part of the chapter therefore focuses on the importance of management information and communications.

Giving orders and instructions

Communication is the passing on of ideas and information. In business it is essential to have good clear channels of communication. The contact may be between people, organisations or places and can be in a number of forms – including speech, writing, data communication, actions and gestures. As communication probably takes up the largest proportion of managers' and administrators' time, the building and developing of communication skills must be viewed as a vital managerial requirement.

Case Study
Creating the 'hybrid manager'

One feature of the business world in recent years has been the development by managers of broad-based skills outside their traditional areas of expertise. The British Computer Society, among others, recently called for information technology (IT) professionals to spend time and effort extending their business skills in other areas. They referred to people able to do this as 'hybrid managers'. In making this pronouncement they have recognised that, although the role of a technical specialist is necessary, managers of the future must have a greater diversity of skills. These skills can be divided into five groups:

a Information management skills involve a broad understanding of information as a strategic resource and the ability to use information to develop decision-making needs.

b Financial skills are essential for any senior manager, and the use of such skills plays an effective part in reducing risk and maximising the ability to achieve objectives.

c Marketing skills are another key area and involve being able to contribute to satisfying customer needs and developing business strategies.

d General management skills involve problem-solving, decision-making, motivation and delegation.

e Last, but not least, hybrid managers must have good communication skills.

Hybrid managers must be able to communicate effectively in both spoken and written forms and should not try to blame other people for their lack of understanding. They should be good listeners and should seek to influence not through domination and authority, but through intelligence and reasoning. Communication is also the crux of human relations, and if hybrid managers want to develop effective and creative interdisciplinary teams, they will need to be the best communicators.

Questions for discussion

1 *What is a hybrid manager?*
2 *Why do more organisations need hybrid managers?*
3 *What are the advantages to an individual of being a hybrid manager?*
4 *Explain why good communication skills would improve a manager's ability to deal with day-to-day human relations problems.*
5 *Why would communication skills be important in developing an effective interdisciplinary team?*

Direction

Direction involves making sure that decisions are put into practice so that an organisation moves towards achieving its clear goals. Individuals within a particular work section need to be directed towards achieving specific targets.

Good communications will be an essential ingredient of direction. When misunderstandings arise, the organisation will almost certainly fall short of achieving its objectives.

Task

Which of the following attributes would you regard as essential for someone to be effective in directing specific activities in an organisation?

a the ability to make decisions
b sufficient technical knowledge of activities to understand them and how they relate to meeting organisational objectives
c communication skills and understanding of communication techniques
d leadership skills to get subordinates to act in the required way
e authority to ensure that instructions are carried out.

Successful communication

Effective communication requires not only the development of basic skills of speaking, listening, reading, writing and use of information technology, but also an awareness and an understanding of the subject, the audience and the environment.

For communication to be successful, not only must information be transmitted, it must also be fully received and understood. Listening and reading skills are therefore just as important as speaking and writing skills.

The passage of information can be seen as a flow from the transmitter (the sender) to the receiver (see Figure 11.30).

Figure 11.30 Information flow

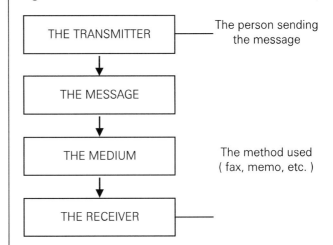

Communication problems are known collectively as **noise** and may lead to a message not being communicated adequately. Problems can arise for a number of reasons:

■ The language may not be properly understood. This can occur if the language is too technical or if the receiver comes from a different background from the sender.
■ The receiver may not want to listen to the content of the message. In this situation the message has to be redesigned to appeal to the receiver.
■ The sender may be using a poor channel of communication. Effective communication will be hampered if the means of passing the message is poor.
■ There may be too many steps in the message. If there are, or if it is just too complicated, it may not be properly understood.
■ The message may be set out badly or be ambiguous.
■ The environment may generate interference from other activities, particularly if the message is long or complicated and requires concentration by the receiver.
■ Cultural differences may influence how the message is interpreted.

What other barriers to communication would you add to the above?

A problem for managers is that people often try to keep information to themselves. Perhaps they are not sure about the accuracy of the information they hold, or they may be embarrassed about the information (e.g. that they have been sexually harrassed). Keeping the information to themselves may also give them power (e.g. understanding how an important process works). Alternatively, they may not be aware of how important the information could be to the organisation (e.g. how another company runs).

The objectives of communication

Possible objectives of communication are illustrated in Figure 11.31.

Figure 11.31 Objectives of communication

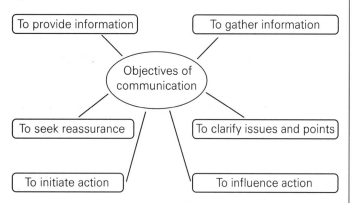

A communication will be successful only when it achieves the intended result. This effectiveness depends on the choice of destination, the clarity of the message, the choice of communication medium, and finally the right method of delivery.

The choice of destination

To be resource-efficient, there is no point in sending a message to every member of the organisation if it really only concerns a few individuals. Effective communication therefore involves a prior decision about who needs to receive the message.

Members of an organisation should not be overburdened with communications. If there are too many messages, people may stop reading them. This could mean that they miss the most important messages.

The clarity of the message

Messages should be clear and direct, with no possibility of misinterpretation. This involves careful consideration of the language used, which requires a keen sense of the *audience* as well as care in the way that words are put together.

Sometimes it will be necessary to repeat a message or to phrase it in more than one way. An effective lecturer, for example, will attempt to explain a task in a simple and clear way, but on noticing that students are unsure about the message will rephrase it until the students understand.

The choice of communication method

The main **media** of communication used in organisations are written (or printed), spoken, visual and/or electronic. In practice there is considerable overlap. We now examine each of these forms of communication.

Internal written communications

Written (and printed) communications are used to convey information and ideas to others within an organisation. They may also be used to confirm important verbal messages.

Memos
One of the most frequently used forms of internal communication is the memorandum (see Figure 11.32). The word derives from the Latin *memorare*, which means 'a thing to be remembered'. Today, 'memos' have a wider business use than just being a memory aid – they are used to communicate information, instructions and enquiries and are the internal equivalent of a letter. However, because they are internal, there are one or two minor differences. An organisation's name does not normally appear on a memo for internal use, and it is not necessary to have a salutation or a complimentary close. Memos should be kept as short as possible and should ideally deal with only one matter. They will frequently be distributed to more than one person. Many organisations provide their employees with pads of headed message forms.

The style of a memo may vary considerably. Instructions from senior management will probably be written in relatively impersonal language, whereas a quickly scribbled message to a close colleague may be written in a more chatty style. It is generally necessary to be more cautious when writing memos 'up' the ladder rather than 'down'. It is important to take account of people's sensitivities and of the position you hold.

Figure 11.32 Example of a memorandum

MEMO

To: All Staff
From: FA
Date: 25.6.96

Safety Reports

Please refer to the section on Safety Procedures on page 6 of the Staff Handbook and to my letter on filling out safety reports.
Reports are to be handed in to Section Managers by 3.7.96.

Task

What weaknesses can you identify in the following memo which has been sent by a sales representative to his sales manager?

MEMO

To: Jane Clarke
From: Mr Alan Davis

There are a number of issues which I want to bring to your attention.

1. The sales area that I am covering is too large. The South East of England is fair enough but not including London as well.

2. Expenses for trips are being paid too late. My last trip took three months before I received payments.

3. Did you say that we were to meet next Friday to discuss my appraisal?

4. Please could you have a word with the accountant to ask for some more financial data to be sent to our department.

5. Look forward to hearing from you.

ALAN.

Reports

A report is a written communication from someone who has collected and studied some facts or issues, sent to a person who has asked for the report for a particular purpose. The report will often form the basis for a

decision that needs to be taken. The following are examples of situations when a report would be appropriate:

- to supply information for legal purposes, perhaps as a result of an accident or incident
- to supply information to be presented to shareholders
- to present the results of some research and to recommend a form of action
- to assess the possibility of a change of policy.

A well-written report will be concise and not contain anything the reader does not need to know. It should be clear and arranged logically.

Reports may be informal or formal (set out according to a particular pattern). Informal reports, which could be written on a report form or as a memo, will consist of:

- title
- introduction
- body of report (complete with findings)
- recommendations
- action required.

A more usual structure for a long formal report will be:

- title page (name of organisation, name and post of writer, subject)
- table of contents/index
- terms of reference (explaining the research for the report)
- procedure (how the task was completed)
- findings
- conclusion (summary of findings)
- recommendations
- signature of writer and date.

In preparing a report, it will be necessary to consider aspects such as language style, circulation list, presentation of cover and binding, and confidentiality.

Agendas and minutes

An agenda is a formal outline of the issues to be discussed at a meeting. It consists of a number of headings, and must contain the date, time and place of the meeting. Ideally an agenda should be sent in advance to all those invited to the meeting so that they have an opportunity to prepare their contributions.

Minutes are a written record of what was discussed at a meeting, and who was there. In an organisation, minutes of meetings that involve a wider audience are often placed on a noticeboard or sent to key people to inform them of decisions that have taken place. Minutes must be presented in a clear and unambiguous way, and they require concise sentence construction.

Notices and house publications

Notices are another common form of written communication within an organisation. They can be placed in prominent positions and used to publicise any changes in policy, dates to be remembered, events taking place, functions, etc. House magazines, journals and company newspapers can also be a useful way to communicate policies, information, events and activities to employees. They are a particularly useful form of internal communication in large organisations.

External written communications

Business letters

Business letters are still the most widely used form of external communication. They provide a written record and can be used to send almost any type of information. A well-written letter conveys a favourable impression of an organisation. Business letters are usually typed or printed on headed A4 or A5 paper. A fully blocked layout is the most common form of display.

Letters should be written in a logical sequence and in a style that lacks ambiguity. They should be concise and yet not leave out any relevant information. A typical business letter will contain the following features:

- heading or letterhead
- reference, enabling the letter to be filed and traced later
- date
- address of the recipient
- salutation ('Dear . . .')
- subject heading
- body of the letter
- complimentary close ('Yours faithfully/sincerely . . .')

There is a convention about the pairings of salutation and complimentary close. 'Dear Sir/Madam' should be paired with 'Yours faithfully' and 'Dear Mr/Mrs X' should be paired with 'Yours sincerely'.

Fax and e-mail

A form of printed external communication that has undergone massive expansion over recent years is the facsimile or 'fax'. A fax machine sends information electronically over a telephone line.

Another alternative to writing letters is to use electronic mail. The 'mail-box' is a computer terminal linked to the telephone network; it can put messages into the system and store messages that have been sent through the system. A message can be sent to several mail-boxes at once, so the system can also be used for internal memos in a company with several branches. The message will be stored in a terminal's memory until the mail-box is 'opened'. There are now a number of subscriber-based electronic mail services such as Telecom Gold. To use such a system, a subscriber sends a message using the telephone line. The advantage over ordinary mail is speed.

Verbal communication

Verbal communication involves the transmission of information by word of mouth, either directly or on the telephone. Much of the time it involves face-to-face exchanges for the purpose of relaying messages, providing advice, personal discussion, analysis, giving instructions and guidance, etc.

Face-to-face contact creates a less formal relationship, enables communicators to get to know each other and allows for instantaneous feedback. The main disadvantage of face-to-face contact, however, is that it can be a time-consuming exercise which usually provides no permanent record of the discussion. It can also lack precision and create misunderstandings.

Effective body language is a key part of effective communication. The important thing is to take an open and honest posture when dealing with other people.

- Do not stand over people and talk down to them (unless, of course, the *aim* is to play the dominant leader).

- Do not make agressive gestures such as pointing your finger in a menacing way or raising your arm.

■ Also be wary of crossing your arms. This is a very defensive position which tends to indicate that you are uncomfortable in a position and are trying to defend yourself.

■ Do not hang your head in a submissive way. This again tends to show weakness.

■ Try to look alert, and nod your head in agreement when listening. Look interested and lean forward into a discussion rather than back and away from it. *If you adopt a confident posture you will feel more confident.* The important point is that you are playing a role – the more you play the role the more natural a part of your organisational life the role will become.

■ The use of eye contact is very important. Try to look someone honestly in the eye (without staring). There is nothing quite so disconcerting as someone who keeps looking away or jerking his or her head.

Verbal communication is important in meetings, which are held to deal with many issues and areas of concern. They provide an opportunity for staff to pool their experiences and knowledge.

Case Study
The skiver's guide to meetings

As a manager you will find that you spend more time in meetings than in any other activity. You will probably spend more time in meetings than at home. Here are some tips (many of them are 'tongue-in-cheek') on successfully minimising the amount of time you spend in meetings.

a The first essential is to make sure that you are absolutely first class in your job. This makes you indispensable. People will also know that you are too busy to attend their meetings.

b Make sure that the important decisions you make are clearly communicated. You can do this by sending memos and reports to the right people. Also briefly

buttonhole people in corridors, when they have a free moment, over lunch, etc. Make your points clearly and follow up with short written notes. (Send copies to everyone concerned including those at the top end of the organisation.)

c Try to minimise your time in large formal meetings. These will be dominated by people who enjoy making their voices heard, those that don't know what they are doing, and nit-pickers.

d Always arrive late for meetings. In this way you can make sure that you are sitting as far from the chairperson as possible. This makes it easier to leave early.

e As you enter the meeting room, shout a comment to an imaginary person in the corridor to give the impression that you have just come from another important meeting.

f Smile at other members of the meeting.

g Stay at the meeting for a short while. Make sure that you are marked in as being present. At the earliest possible point make a comment – preferably one that will be minuted but will not lead to endless discussion – and after about 20 minutes get up from your chair and mouth an unintelligible comment to the chair about rushing off to another meeting.

h Skim through the minutes of the meeting when they are published to pick out any important points. This will not take long (rarely more than five minutes).

Questions for discussion

1 *Does the above represent a skiver's charter or does it contain elements of good sense?*
2 *How would you rewrite the above advice?*

Visual communication

There can be no doubt that visual communication is often the most effective way of getting a message across. If people can see what is expected of them, how a process works, etc. they are most likely to remember it. Increasingly, visual communication techniques are being used within organisations – examples are the use of sophisticated overhead projectors, television, and multi-media.

For example, modern companies frequently make presentations at their annual general meetings, showing video features of the year's performance. This may be complemented by slide presentations using computer-generated graphics, with charts, tables and key pieces of written information often supported by music.

Increasingly, similar processes are being used for training and development within organisations. CD–ROM and CD–I have revolutionised communication within organisations, as has the development of 'virtual reality', whereby individuals feel that they are experiencing a real world of visual and other sensations.

Information technology (IT)

A number of factors have contributed to the importance of information technology in modern organisational life.

- The scale of many large organisations makes it impossible for every individual to meet face-to-face.
- Many organisations are geographically spread out, but require communication links between interrelated plants and offices.
- Modern business decision-making frequently requires up-to-date information drawn from a variety of business functions. For example, the marketing department may need sales figures from sales, costings from accounts, etc.
- Competition between firms is fierce. It is almost impossible for a company to find a market area that is not extremely competitive.
- The rate of change of industrial development has increased. Firms must therefore be quicker in responding to factors such as technological change, market forces and better competition.

Case Study
Technology in hospitals

For diagnosis and treatment, medicine uses some of the most technologically advanced machines. However, until recently the management of a hospital has often relied on low-tech systems such as the storing of patient records using handwritten notes. It is possible that with the development of IT systems hospitals could save millions of pounds.

For example. Ealing Hospital is investing in information systems as part of a package of re-engineering the organisation.

With 24 000 in-patients and 115 000 out-patients a year, the hospital finds it difficult to predict spending on nurses, doctors and drugs. The hospital is therefore shifting responsibility for allocating budgets from administrators to doctors in the hope that information about the consequences of their decisions will help doctors make wiser choices.

The hospital has moved into a variety of new IT applications. The first task was an improved patient administration system (PAS) which schedules appointments, manages waiting lists and keeps track of patient records. Today, most records are still typed into the PAS from documents that accumulate during the patients' visits to the hospital. Gradually, as different parts of the hospital are linked into the PAS, it is changing from an administrative archive to an up-to-the-minute information source.

Two of the first additions to the basic PAS were a system to track patients through emergency care, and a system to report back the results of tests in the pathology laboratory. Both immediately helped to reduce some of the most wasteful and error-prone work in the hospital – the constant typing and re-typing of the patient's name and medical details by different departments.

The pathology system also provided a more direct saving of doctors' time. Sending test results to the doctors' computer terminals as soon as they are complete has cut by over a quarter the time doctors and nurses spend on the telephone to the pathology department.

In 1995 more details are being added to computer records to provide a detailed management information system. Instead of scribbling orders for treatment on to a clipboard as they move through the wards, doctors will be asked to type them into a PC. Not only will this speed the communication of orders by gathering information in one easily accessible electronic place; it should also help junior doctors to find out about their patients at the start of a shift, and consultants to gather information on patients scattered across several wards.

The doctors' new managerial responsibilities bring medical benefits. Computers capture huge amounts of information about what treatments have been given. This information is being made available to doctors trying to fulfil their new managerial responsibilities to monitor quality and allocate budgets for treatment.

Questions for discussion

1 *What are the most important benefits for a hospital from developing IT systems for communicating information?*
2 *What factors will determine whether the benefits of using such a communication system outweigh the initial costs of installation?*

Most people today use some form of information technology when at work. In order to be able to do so, they may have had to develop:

- general skills in the use of IT for a range of applications
- specialist skills in the use of software and systems.

General IT skills are useful for all employees who come across information technology and its application in their working environment. Managers use IT as an aid for decision-making. Technicians, maintenance and craft workers need to deal with IT components in plants, machinery and vehicles. Clerical workers have to be familiar with a variety of word-processing, spreadsheet, database and similar applications. Professionals (accountants, architects, etc.) now use specialist IT applications to improve the efficiency of their work.

Specialist users of IT make up about 1 per cent of the working population. These people are in the IT professions. This is one of the fastest-growing job sectors in the country.

Modern information systems in large organisations

Every organisation must have some means of storing, processing and communicating information. In its simplest form the system will consist of filing cabinets, in-trays, out-trays and a telephone. Today, however, to have an information system that works effectively, it is necessary to organise all the required data in such a way that it can be readily recorded, stored, processed, retrieved and communicated by a variety of users.

An information system (see Chapter 9) converts raw data into either a finished report or an input for a further stage in the information processing cycle. The dominant form of information processing in modern organisations is computer-based. A computer system alone is not an information system; it is simply a tool that can improve the effectiveness of an information system.

The right mode of delivery

The way in which a message is delivered has an important impact on how it is received. A well-constructed, hard-hitting presentation will have more effect than a sloppy, badly prepared one. A memo labelled 'For the urgent attention of' will clearly be given precedence over a note dropped in to someone's in-tray.

The importance of listening

Listening is one of the most important managerial skills. Keith Davis, in his book *Human Behaviour at Work*, suggests ten steps to improving listening:

1 stop talking
2 put the talker at ease
3 show the talker that you want to listen
4 remove distractions
5 empathise with the talker
6 be patient
7 hold your temper
8 go easy on arguments and criticism
9 ask questions, and
10 Stop talking!

Briefing individuals and teams

When briefing individuals and teams it is important to bear in mind the guidelines outlined above. An effective briefing will be one that focuses on clear objectives.

The briefing should be presented in an appropriate language using appropriate means of communication. This involves having a sense of audience. Briefings need to take place in an atmosphere where there are no distractions, preferably in a room specially allocated to the purpose.

It is important to establish an agenda or framework for the briefing. The person running the briefing session should start with a clear introduction, such as:

'Today I want to brief you on . . .'
'There are a number of key elements we will need to look at. These are:. . . . I would like you to pay particular attention to these points.'
'I would like you to take notes on . . .'
'If you have any questions you will be able to ask me at . . .'
'We have X minutes for this briefing so I want you all to listen very carefully.'

Participation

Participation happens when people contribute ideas towards the solution of problems affecting the organisation and their jobs.

Individual participation should take place in an atmosphere of trust and respect. It will occur in a wide variety of settings and will involve managers asking individual subordinates to contribute ideas to decision-making and planning (e.g. in an informal chat or formal meeting in the office).

The manager who likes to delegate ground-level decision-making to subordinates is effectively encouraging them to participate in an on-going way. Encouraging individual participation is likely to be a good motivator but will not generate as many ideas as group participation.

Participation of groups of employees can take place at any level in an organisation. Subordinates can be invited as groups to participate in decision-making processes. At one level this may involve a group discussion of a decision which has already been made by a manager. At another level it will provide opportunities to group members to contribute to the decision-making process.

The term **democratic management** is sometimes used to describe a situation in which the manager acts as a chairperson outlining a problem to a group of employees. They are then invited to come up with the 'best' solution to the problem.

Ways to increase participation

There are a number of formal approaches to creating more participation.

Committees

Committees are groups of people who come together regularly to participate in decision-making. Professor H. Koontz, in his book, set out the following guidelines for more effective communication in committees:

- *Authority* – The committee's authority needs to be made clear so that members know whether their responsibility is to make a decision, a recommendation, or just to give the chair some insights into the problems under discussion.
- *Size* – The larger the group the more complex the interrelationships will be. As a general rule, a committee should be large enough to promote deliberation and include the breadth of experience required for the job, but not so large as to waste time or encourage indecision. Research into small groups shows that *five* may be an ideal number when the five members possess adequate skills and knowledge.
- *Membership* – The members of the committee must be representative of the interests they are intended to serve. They must also possess the required authority, and be able to perform well in the group. They should have good communication skills.
- *Subject matter* – Committee work should be limited to subject matter that can be handled in group discussion. An agenda and relevant information should be circulated well before a meeting.
- *Chairperson* – A person should be chosen who will be able to avoid the waste and the drawbacks inherent in the committee system by planning the meeting, preparing the agenda, seeing that the results of research are available to members ahead of time, formulating definite proposals for discussion or action, and conducting the meeting efficiently.
- *Minutes* – Effective communication involves circulating minutes and checking conclusions. To avoid disagreements about what has been said, it can be helpful to circulate minutes in draft form for correction or modification before the final copy is approved by the chairperson.
- *Cost-effectiveness* – The costs of operating the committee can only be deemed to be worthwhile if the results outweigh the costs. Results will be measured in terms of decisions made, activities put into practice, increased prestige and motivation of the committee members, etc.

Quality circles

Quality circles are an important way of increasing participation in organisational activities. A quality circle is a study-group of volunteers (5–15 people) who meet regularly to work on a variety of operational and employee problems at work. The quality circle will be made up of ordinary working employees and their immediate supervisors and managers. One supervisor or manager will usually operate as the circle's leader.

Quality circles do not deal with theoretical problems. They are concerned with putting ideas into action. This involves in-depth analysis, proposals for action, and presentations to management on what could be or ought to be done.

There are four main components of a quality circle framework (see Figure 11.33). The *steering committee*, staffed by senior managers, will make general policy and set up the framework and resources for the circles to operate. The facilitator is there to support the process in each of the circles as well as to provide an operational framework and guidance if required. The circles' leaders will often be the unit supervisors and they will stimulate discussion within their circle without dominating it. Leaders need to be familiar with problem-solving techniques and group dynamics.

Figure 11.33 Components of a quality circle framework

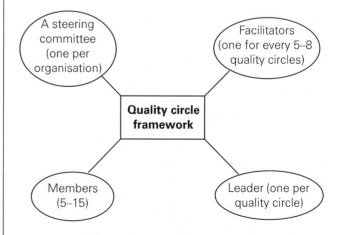

The circles will meet during company time, perhaps for one hour a week. Problem-solving techniques employed will include:

- brainstorming
- graphs showing the frequency of problems

- randomised sampling of product units produced
- cause-and-effect diagrams.

Suggestion plans

A suggestion plan is a formal system to enable employees to make creative suggestions to the organisation, often for a financial reward. Employees can simply write down ideas and put them in a collection box.

Joint consultative committees

A **joint consultative committee** is a way of bringing employees and managers together in the workplace to share decision-making. Such a committee meets formally and sometimes (but not always) involves union representatives. Some unions, however, see joint consultative committees as a means of weakening the influence of their union.

It is essential to disseminate the information coming out of joint consultative committees around the organisation. Minutes should be posted on notice boards.

Works councils

Works councils are particularly important in a number of European Union countries, including Germany and Sweden. The Social Chapter of the Maastricht Treaty emphasises worker participation as a way forward for obtaining agreement about work objectives. Works councils are there to put forward employee interests.

Briefing the team

The section above on participation makes it clear that a key function of management today is to work with teams of people. There is a lot of skill involved.

The Industrial Society defines a team briefing as being:
> '*A system of communication operated by line management. Its objective is to ensure that all employees know and understand what they and others in the company are doing and why. It is a management information system. It is based on the leader and his/her team getting together in a group for half an hour on a regular basis to talk about things that are relevant to their work.*'

Team briefings often take place on a cascade basis, working downwards from teams at the top of an organisation to ground-level teams. They make it possible to create planned and formalised face-to-face communications on a regular basis. Michael Armstrong, in *A Handbook of Human Resource Management*, identifies the following features of the process.

Organisation of teams for briefing

- Cover all levels in an organisation.
- Have the fewest possible steps between the top and the bottom.
- Have between 4 and 18 people in each group.
- Have the teams run by the immediate leader of each group at each level.

Subjects

- Policies – explanations of new or changed policies.
- Plans – as they affect the organisation as a whole and the immediate group.
- Progress – how the organisation and the group are getting on, what the latter needs to do to improve.
- People – new appointments, points about personnel matters (pay, security, procedures).

Timing and duration

- Ideally, a minimum of once a month for those in charge of others and once every two months for every individual in the organisation – but meetings should take place only if there is something to say.
- Duration not longer than 20–30 minutes.

Part 3 **Coordinating activities**

This part of the chapter focuses on what is involved in coordinating human, physical and financial activities. Some people regard coordination to be the essence of management because it has as its purpose the creation of harmony between individual efforts towards achieving goals. The central goal of a manager should be to reconcile differences in approach, timing, effort or interest (see Figure 11.34).

Figure 11.34 Reconciling goals

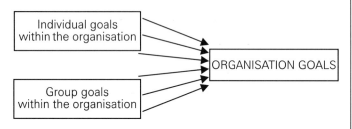

Clearly, then, a major part of coordination will be to establish clear goals and objectives. These should be communicated clearly to all parts of the organisation. Plans and policies need to be put into effect to ensure that these goals are met. Resources and activities should be channelled into the achievement of these goals (see Figure 11.35).

Figure 11.35 The coordination process in an effective organisation

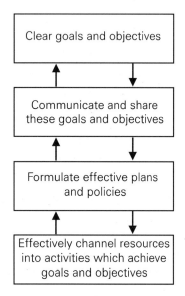

Peter Drucker, in his book *Management by Objectives*, recommended that managers should seek to maintain efficiency and effectiveness by agreeing *specific objectives* for their departments, units or teams. These objectives then need to be coordinated, so that the resources for the whole organisation focus on corporate objectives.

Case Study
Coordinating objectives

This study illustrates the way in which an overall organisational objective can be subdivided into sub-objectives.

Fizzy Pop Ltd is a manufacturer of soft drinks. Motivated by a general improvement in economic conditions, the managing director would like to see an annual increase in sales of 100 000. As a result, the following targets for sales have been agreed within the organisation following company-wide, area, and district sales meetings.

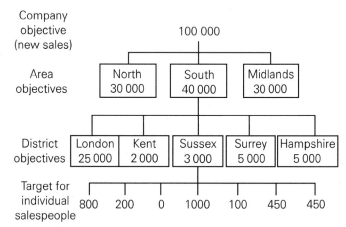

Questions for discussion

1 *What factors would influence the establishment of the organisational objectives for Fizzy Pop?*
2 *Why is it important to involve areas, districts and branches in establishing objectives?*
3 *What factors are likely to determine whether the objectives are achieved?*
4 *Why is it important to develop a coordinated plan?*

In the process of working towards objectives, many decisions will have to be taken. There are two main types of decision:

■ *Strategic decisions* establish the long-term broad objectives for the organisation. Strategic decision-making is usually the responsibility of senior management and will affect the whole organisation.
■ *Tactical decisions* are more routine and short-term. These are normally taken by junior and middle managers.

Developing a coordinated strategic plan

Planning is studied in detail in Section 9. However, it is necessary to point out here some of the aspects of a manager's role in coordinating strategic planning.

Effective managers, when creating a strategic plan, involve staff in such a way that each is committed to implementing the ideas. Every member of the organisation has to share a commitment to the strategy if it is going to work in a coordinated way.

Ralph Brody, in his book *Effectively Managing Human Service Organisations*, set out the following summary of steps in developing a strategic planning process:

- Determine why you want to develop a plan for your organisation's future. What benefits do you see from embarking on this process? Do the benefits outweigh the costs?
- Ensure the organisation's leadership is committed to the process.
- Form a strategic planning group.
- Analyse your situation, including strengths, weaknesses, opportunities and threats.
- Develop a vision of what the organisation would be like in 3–5 years.
- Prepare (or revise) a tentative mission statement, which may be altered later in the strategic planning process.
- Identify, after considerable input, the most critical issues facing the organisation.
- Prepare action plans containing goals for up to five years, implementation activities for the first year, and the names of those accountable for the follow-through.
- Draft a plan that is reviewed by the planning group, staff, board and selected persons outside the organisation.
- Implement the plan with the intent of making changes as circumstances change.
- Update the plan annually and, at least every five years, conduct another in-depth analysis.

Organisational objectives result from a clear corporate strategy. Commitment to these objectives stems from the participation of all stakeholders (see Figure 11.36).

Senior managers bear the responsibility for communicating to all parts of an organisation the basis on which strategic plans have been created. Appropriate programmes of activities can then be developed. The basis on which plans are created must include the key assumption about the environment in which plans will have to operate. Unless this is done, a number of sub-plans will be created by individual departments based

Figure 11.36 Strategic planning for effectiveness

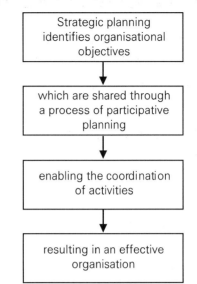

on personal assumptions and choices. This will almost certainly lead to a collection of uncoordinated efforts.

Coordinated action plans

Action plans are central to organisational activity. They apply to tactical or operational programmes that take place throughout the organisation. They, too, must be founded on desired objectives (see Figure 11.37).

Figure 11.37 Action plans

When setting out action plans, managers should include:

- the area to be addressed
- who is involved
- specific objectives to be achieved
- the action steps which need to be taken to achieve these objectives
- what evidence will be used to show that objectives have been achieved
- who will review progress towards the achievement of objectives
- when the review will take place.

If every manager understands the organisation's strategy, they will be able to review the recommendations of staff advisers and line subordinates to make sure that they are consistent. A useful idea would be for major decisions to be reviewed by a committee that included a staff specialist, a subordinate's superior, and the superior's superior.

The structure of the organisation should be such that particular managers or supervisors are given responsibility for the accomplishment of particular goals and for implementing appropriate actions.

Types of objectives

Objectives represent aims to be achieved that are:

■ relevant
■ attainable
■ measurable
■ time-limited.

A number of different types of objectives can be employed, depending on the overall goals of an organisation.

Impact objectives set out the outcomes to be achieved as a result of a programme of activities. This is the return which is expected from the organisation's use of resources. The following features should be built into impact objectives:

■ An action verb should be used to describe a change in condition; e.g. 'build', 'promote', 'increase', etc.
■ only *one* specific result should be set out for each objective.
■ Objective statements need to be realistic.

Task

Which of the following are the best written objectives for different types of organisations?

a Hospital – To raise the number of patients treated over each of the next three years.
b School – To increase the number of pupils awarded five or more GCSE A–C grades by 5 per cent in the coming year.
c Business – To improve profitability figures.
d Cinema – To increase the number of customers by 10 per cent in the coming year and to increase the number of seats in the cinema.
e Bookshop – To educate the general public to take more of an interest in serious fiction.

Write three alternative objectives for each of these organisations.

Activity objectives set out an organisation's proposed level of activities, for example:

■ to conduct three market surveys
■ to serve 10 per cent more customers
■ to install 200 fitted kitchens.

Operational objectives set out the intent to improve an organisation's general operation and its ability to fulfil its purpose. Examples would include:

■ to reduce staff absenteeism by 10 per cent per year
■ to increase the number of sponsors by 5 per cent
■ to obtain a government grant of £50 000 by the end of the tax year.

Process objectives are usually concerned with the interaction of people within the organisation. Examples include:

■ to develop community support for a new venture
■ to sponsor a conference
■ to develop a new method of interpersonal communication within the organisation.

Product objectives are intended to produce a particular outcome which is targeted at benefiting a specific group of people. They are designed to support impact or activity objectives. Examples are:

■ to provide a media campaign on substance abuse
■ to establish a consumer complaints procedure.

Generally speaking, most attention is usually given to impact objectives. However, many organisations will need to consider all five types of objectives, depending on their goals. Of course, there are many objectives which are very difficult to quantify.

Targets must be attainable. If they are set too high then people will become frustrated, and this can lead to a fall in effort and motivation. If a charity sets out to raise £1 million and succeeds only in collecting £50 000 in the first year, supporters may become dispirited, even though £50 000 is a considerable achievement.

Resource provision

Objectives can be viewed as targets to be achieved by the sub-sections of an organisation. Once objectives have been agreed, the necessary resources must be made available. These resources will include sufficient staff, space and equipment, together with skills and knowledge.

A plan is made up of a number of activities. Each activity contributes to the overall activity. Each activity requires a basket of resources, and these need to be specified (see Figure 11.38).

Figure 11.38 The detail of planning activities

```
          ORGANISATIONAL OBJECTIVES
                      ⇩
              Operational activities
  A  B  C  D  E  F  G  H  I  J  K  L
```

Activity A – responsibility of team X				
Resources required	Week 1	Week 2	Week 3	Week 4
Finance				
Machinery				
Raw materials				
Labour hours				
Other resources				

Forecasting

Forecasting future resource requirements is a key aspect of coordination. Accurate forecasting reduces uncertainty and increases confidence in the way that resources are used. *It is important to remember that resources used for any activity are being taken away from other activities.* However, forecasting is not easy, as trends can alter and shocks do occur.

The 'budget' represents the financial requirements for particular activities and should cover all resources used. Tolerance levels will need to be established for accepted levels of deviation from forecasts.

Coordinated control

Control, as we saw on page 274, is the comparison of actual results with expectation *and the taking of corrective action*. Standards are established and actual results are compared with these. Any differences are known as 'variances'. If a variance occurs it will need to be reported back to the originator of the standard, who may want corrective action to be taken.

IT systems and coordination

It is apparent that the coordination of activities may be an extremely complex process in anything other than a small organisation. The only way it can be achieved is to create a master strategic plan and then create a number of sub-plans and activities. Responsibility for activities needs to be delegated to discrete teams and individuals.

Information technology systems have been devised which facilitate the coordination function of managers. Capabilities for instantaneous access to and updating of records have opened up new possibilities for the planning, forecasting and organising of activities.

Introducing an information system may require considerable changes in the flow of information into an organisation, to ensure that the information gets to the right employees, in the form they require, at the right time. To maximise the benefits to be derived from introducing an information system, it may be necessary to make structural changes. This may imply creating a flatter structure, moving away from a highly functional hierarchy or a bureaucratic structure towards multi-disciplinary teams. Many business writers call this sort of organisation a **transformed business**.

In a transformed business, people involved in particular processes are given more freedom to make decisions and have more information at their fingertips. The business processes are handled by teams of people from different functions working together to achieve the aims of the organisation. Groups working together in a team share information, and computer terminals of different specialists are linked so that information is available to all. The great benefit is that teamwork is more enriching and satisfying. Work flows are also simplified, as a job stays with a team instead of passing from department to department. Teams have greater responsibility for their own destiny and this increases their overall business awareness. The whole process of coordination is simplified as teams work collaboratively with a given basket of resources.

Part 4 Constraints on managing activities

This part of the chapter looks at some of the main constraints which managers face when overseeing activities, including:

- the need to meet deadlines
- regulatory controls
- scarcity of and internal competition for resources
- external changes.

The need to meet deadlines

When we looked at critical path analysis (see pages 277–9) we came across one of the major constraints in organising business activity – time. Every activity must take place within a reasonable time scale because 'time costs money'. Project and activity planning involves devising a sequence for activities, and targets which need to be met within each time period.

Time, like any other resource, needs to be allocated in a well organised way. Time management experts often point out that successful managers are able to handle numerous and different activities by devoting themselves to one activity at a time. This means that they will focus on particular activities in a determined and persistent way rather than dividing their time over a range of activities. Deciding what to concentrate on requires the establishment of **priorities**.

ABC analysis

One way of allocating time to make sure that tasks are completed within their deadlines is called 'ABC analysis' (see Figure 11.39), which is a value analysis on the use of time.

- *A activities* are those that are ranked as being very important. They can be effectively carried out only by the person involved or by a team working with that person. They cannot be delegated.
- *B activities* are important, but can be delegated.
- *C activities* are less important, but usually represent the lion's share of the work (routine tasks, paperwork, telephone calls, etc.).

Managers who are determined to meet deadlines will focus their efforts on the most important A tasks. They will seek to complete one or two A tasks per day, earmark a further two to three B tasks, and set some time for C tasks. ABC analysis is thus a personalised

Figure 11.39 ABC value analysis of the use of time

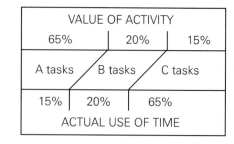

VALUE OF ACTIVITY		
65%	20%	15%
A tasks	B tasks	C tasks
15%	20%	65%
ACTUAL USE OF TIME		

form of critical path analysis. Like critical path analysis it focuses on making sure that essential tasks are given priority.

Meeting the deadline

In organisational life there are grave dangers associated with just meeting a deadline. This is sometimes called 'brinkmanship' because a person just saves a situation at the brink of a disaster. It is a far better practice to develop a time plan for a project (see Figure 11.40).

Figure 11.40 Planning to meet deadlines

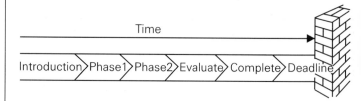

If activities are planned to just meet deadlines, they may take a bit longer than expected and be finished late, with all sorts of possible implications. Of course, the Japanese idea of just-in-time involves just meeting deadlines. However, JIT requires very high quality standards with very low tolerance levels. Such a system is effective in cutting down on waste, stocks, etc. because it is a highly efficient system. Organisations that do not operate to such high quality standards need to build in a bit of surplus time prior to the deadline date.

Time-planners

A number of management specialists recommend the use of time-planners as an aid to meeting deadlines. A time-planner may be a ring-binder with loose-leaf pages (like a Filofax). It is an appointment calendar, notebook, planning tool, address book, memory aid, telephone directory, reference work, etc. all rolled into one. Time-planners enable the user to put dates and times in writing, providing an overall picture of all agreements, plans and projects. Increasingly, time-planners are electronic and many managers today will have a notebook computer which integrates all the elements of a time-planner.

Regulatory controls

One important aspect of government is the regulation of certain types of activities in the public interest. The term 'regulation' means a legal requirement applying to a particular industry or to industry in general. For example, there are regulations relating to health and safety at work, to equal opportunities, to the number of hours that can be worked, and so on.

Regulatory controls are a major constraint on the management of organisational activities. Managers must be keenly aware of what is and is not allowed. They need to know any special regulations relating to their activities.

Regulations have been used to stop monopolies from using their power to exploit consumers. Some industries, such as gas and water supply, have a natural monopoly because it would not make sense to have two sets of gas and water pipelines. The government accepts that there are single suppliers of gas and water, but it regulates the activities of companies operating in these industries, in particular by constraining the prices that can be charged.

It is not only the government that regulates activities in markets. Producers also join together to form groups known as 'cartels' which can limit the freedom of trade within a particular market.

Case Study
The Environmental Protection Act 1990

This Act created two new systems for regulation of industrial pollution in the UK.

Integrated Pollution Control (IPC) applies to more than 5000 existing industrial processes with the largest pollution potential, and regulates all their releases to land, water and air. It is enforced by an Inspectorate of Pollution.

The second system covers 27 000 complex processes but controls only their emissions to the air.

Under both systems, operators have to employ the 'best available techniques not entailing excessive cost' to minimise releases of the most polluting substances, and to 'render harmless' all releases from their processes. IPC extends the types of control previously applied only to air pollution to all wastes – gases, solids and liquids – generated by organisations.

The new Inspectorate will ensure that the least environmentally damaging solution overall – the best practicable environmental option, or BPEO – is chosen to deal with these.

Questions for discussion

1 *Which industries is the Environmental Protection Act most likely to affect?*
2 *What types of activity in these industries will be most affected?*
3 *What will managers need to do to make sure that they are complying with the Act?*
4 *How is the Act likely to affect the planning and control of activities?*
5 *How is the Act likely to affect the coordination of activities?*

The European Union and business activities

The UK is a signatory to European Union treaties which bind organisations to comply with certain regulations relating to competition and trade. In addition, the EU has introduced directives aimed at protecting consumers. The following are some examples:

- *Misleading Advertising Directive* – This was adopted in 1984 and aims to protect businesses and the general public against the effects of misleading advertisements.
- *Product Liability Directive* – Introduced in 1985, this makes manufacturers and importers strictly liable for injuries caused by defective products.
- *Doorstep Selling Directive* – Introduced in 1985, this brought in a seven-day cooling-off period for certain sales contracts concluded at the consumer's home or place of work.
- *Consumer Credit Directive* – Introduced in 1987, this protects consumers who enter into credit agreements.
- *Toy Safety Directive* – Introduced in 1988, this harmonises toy safety standards.
- *Price Indication Directive* – Introduced in 1988, this requires the selling prices, and in some cases unit prices, of food and non-food products to be displayed.
- *Package Travel Directive* – Introduced in 1990, this establishes minimum standards of consumer protection for package travel and package holidays and tours.

The availability of resources

A basic fact of business life is that resources are limited. When an organisation has choices of activities, there are a number of ways of choosing one activity rather than another (see Figure 11.41).

Firstly, it can look at the past as a way of predicting the future. How successful have particular activities been? However, in a dynamic business environment the past is not always an accurate guide to the future.

Secondly, it can make projections of the likely future returns on particular activities. These returns need to be measured in terms of their contributions to organisational objectives. For example, suppose that an organisation seeks to maximise profits. If activity A will lead to good sales but limited profits, and activity B will lead to limited sales but large profits, the likelihood is that the organisation will plough its available resources into activity B. Projections of the future success of activities may involve market research.

Thirdly, the organisation can adopt a process of *experimentation* – try one activity and see how successful it is. If the activity is not successful it can try an alternative. However, this way of proceeding is rather 'hit and miss'. An organisation is only likely to adopt this approach when it does not have the time or resources to plough into research and analysis.

Figure 11.41 Ways of allocating scarce resources among activities

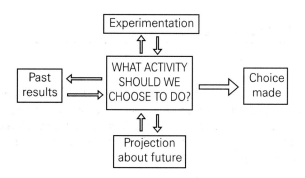

The best way forward is almost always detailed research and analysis yielding clear forecasts.

Analysis

Decision-tree analysis is a useful way of deciding how to allocate scarce resources. An example is shown in Figure 11.42.

Figure 11.42 Decision-tree analysis

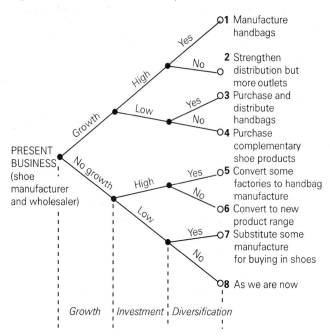

The decision-tree approach sets out to *rank* the options and progressively eliminate the weaker ones. To do this an organisation must work out a few key criteria that are required in future developments – for example, growth, investment and/or diversification. In Figure 11.42 we can see that if growth is an important business objective, then options 1–4 will be ranked more highly than 5–8. At the second step, if another important criteria is low investment, then options 3 and 4 would be ranked above 1 and 2. In a decision-tree analysis, options are identified and ranked at the same time. Clearly such a process lends itself to the use of a computer program as an aid to decision-making.

A problem with decision trees is that they tend to be simplistic. At each stage you need to be able to rank and quantify options. If you put the wrong numbers in at any point, the whole exercise becomes distorted. Decision trees are most effective when alternatives can be given clear numerical values. Be wary about using them when making decisions that cannot easily be quantified.

Risk analysis is a technique that enables decision makers to calculate the size of the risk they are considering taking. It is a mathematical model based on the probability of various outcomes. A number of variables are built into an on-going risk analysis so that it is possible to calculate the probability of success or failure. However, this method suffers from the same weaknesses as decision-tree analysis.

Regression analysis can be used to record the 'values' of a continuing series of activities, often in the form of a graph. The technique is therefore useful for looking at past trends, present trends and likely future trends once forecasts have been developed. Regression analysis is concerned with identifying the mathematical equations of these graphs so that future events can be predicted. It requires fairly sophisticated mathematical skills.

Linear programming is another mathematical technique which uses algebra to solve simple problems graphically. Linear programming is possible where there is an unchanging relationship between variables. Fairly complex problems can be solved using a computer.

Linear programming is particularly useful where there are a number of scarce resources each of which can be used for income-generating activities. It will seek to discover the best mixture of uses and resources. Linear programming is possible when:

- the problem can be stated in numbers
- factors in the problem have linear relationships
- there is at least one restriction on the factors involved (e.g. machinery can work for only so many hours a week, there are only X number of employee-hours available, etc.).

Case Study
Regulation and alternative use of scarce resources

The following is an extract from an article in *Shell UK Review 1993*, in which the company argued that legislators in the pursuit of their need to protect the environment should adopt a more systematic approach to policy-making.

'Much environmental regulation is too often prescriptive – defining in detail what should be done, rather than letting individual companies exercise initiative in achieving a specified environmental improvement. This kills experimentation and innovation, which are essential for progress. As far as possible, legislation should set boundaries and goals which companies can achieve in their own ways in pursuit of competitive advantage.

Good businesses approach environmental management in the same systematic way as they manage anything else. They start with measurement, risk-assessment and analysis – balancing the costs and advantages of any action and deciding on priorities; it is impossible to do everything at once. Only then can they invest in an integrated programme of action, gaining and learning from experience . . .

New processes and equipment to deal with pollution are rapidly emerging. But we should not expect the process to be trouble free – some will not work; others will work less well than alternatives; some may create other environmental problems. Time must be allowed for proper development and testing before large-scale investment . . .

'We have to choose how much of our limited resources to devote to cleaning up the legacy of the past, and how much to invest for the future. Hazardous sites of course must be cleaned up, but the costs are immense. Where contamination is stable and non-hazardous it can wait for better solutions to be developed.

'As always, it is a question of priorities and degree. Achieving the final stages of anything – removing, say, every last drop of a substance – can be disproportionately expensive. It may be better to go only so far, and to devote the saved resources instead to more effective, and urgent, improvements.'

Questions for discussion

1 *What constraints on the activities of Shell UK are highlighted in the extract?*
2 *How should managers at Shell UK respond to environmental regulation of their activities?*
3 *Identify the resource-use issues highlighted in the article.*
4 *Why are organisations like Shell UK not able to solve all of their problems?*
5 *What solutions is the company putting forward?*
6 *To what extent is management concerned with coming up with the best possible solution to insoluble problems?*

External changes

In this text we have continually stressed the importance of the external environment and its influence on business activities. Changes in the political, economic, social and technical environment can and frequently do constrain business activities.

For example, when the government is influenced by green issues it will raise taxes on some types of fuels more than on others. With the prospect of peaceful conditions developing in Northern Ireland as a result of political initiatives, the EU and US authorities made large sums of investment capital available, making the province an increasingly desirable location site for activities.

On the economic front, the cyclical pattern of booms and slumps acts as a boost to, and a constraint on, business activities. Changes in interest rates strongly influence investment decisions by business organisations.

Social constraints on business activities are numerous. For example, fashion determines the life-cycle of many products in the textile and fashion industry.

Technical changes mean that production processes can be revolutionised while others become outmoded. Suddenly, an organisation can find that one of its traditional activities is no longer viable.

So today's manager faces an environment of constant, rapid, radical change – a state of 'permanent white water' that approaches chaos. Managers therefore need to be continually alert to changes in the operating environment. They need to understand the complex web of relationships between variables in this environment, and how they are likely to change. Given the complexities of organisations and the environments in which they operate, it is essential for management to be shared between teams of people. The objectives and activities of each organisation are closely interrelated and cannot be neatly partitioned between managers – partial analysis of situations is not sufficient. Managers need to see themselves as generalists as well as specialists, and cultivate a broad understanding of the operating environment. Managers need to be able to lift their sights above the nuts and bolts of day-to-day managerial activity towards the wider horizon of change and potential chaos around them. Today, external changes can be so revolutionary as to wipe out whole areas of business within weeks – for example, as a result of new trading alliances, new computerised technology, or the arrival of new competitors.

Part 5 **Review and monitoring**

Another important aspect of managing activities is to review the effectiveness of yourself and others and to seek to improve the ways in which activities and tasks are organised. This part of the chapter looks at a number of key aspects of this, namely: value analysis, systems analysis, performance standards and indicators, and the impact of technology.

Ernest Archer studied over 2000 managers, executives and supervisors, as well as the research of major writers on organisations. As part of his conclusion he produced a decision-making framework which highlighted the decision maker's need to monitor the environment in which decisions are made. This means obtaining feedback on any deviations from expected, acceptable, pre-planned or normal states. First, it is essential that managers have a clear idea of how things 'ought' to be. The other eight stages involve the following tasks:

- Define the decision or problem to be tackled and clearly state the boundaries.
- Specify the objectives of the decision. What do you expect to achieve? What are the constraints?
- Diagnose the problem or situation and analyse its causes.
- Develop a range of alternative solutions and courses of action.
- Establish criteria for weighing up alternatives.
- Appraise the alternative solutions or courses of action.
- Choose the best solution.
- Implement the best solution or course of action.

Value analysis

The aim of **value analysis** is to check that organisational activities are giving best value for money, particularly in relation to satisfying customers as economically as possible. Value analysis involves examining all the elements of organisational activity in order to eliminate any unnecessary or wasteful expenditure.

For example, if designers were left free to operate without cost control guidelines, they could undoubtedly produce components of a higher quality than those required for a specific task. This would be costly, would fail to satisfy the manufacturer's objectives, and would not be regarded as value for money by the purchaser.

Value analysis therefore forces the organisation to look at its activities in terms of 'fitness for purpose'. A value-analysis team will be made up of experienced personnel with the specialist knowledge to be able to contribute to cost-cutting operations (or more specifically, maximising the benefits from efficient use of resources). In a manufacturing plant such a team might consist of:

- a designer – for knowledge of the product
- a member of the sales team – for knowledge of the market
- a production engineer – for knowledge of the production processes
- a member of the work-study team – for experience of efficient working procedures
- an accountant – for knowledge of cost analysis
- a buyer – for knowledge of sources of supply.

The value chain

Michael Porter, in his book *Competitive Advantage – Creating and Sustaining Superior Performance*, identifies a series of activities that need to be done well if a business is to develop a competitive advantage. The value chain is concerned with organising and linking these key activities (see Figure 11.43). The end-user or consumer looks at value in terms of what a business is offering in relation to competitive offers. The value chain is therefore concerned with making sure that a company organises activities to offer the best end-product.

Figure 11.43 The importance of value activities

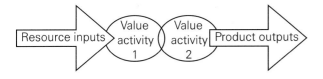

The linkages between activities are what give a business an edge. Many of these linkages will be with other businesses and organisations, such as suppliers and distributors.

Michael Porter identifies a number of *primary* and *support* activities which lead to profitability (the 'end margin' – see Figure 11.44).

There are five main **primary activities**:

- *Inbound logistics* – These activities deal with receiving, storing and distributing the inputs to the product. For example, in a food-processing company this would involve bringing in supplies of vegetables, meat, etc. It would concern activities such as transporting the materials from farms and other suppliers, handling the raw materials and keeping a check on stock.
- *Operations* – These transform raw materials into a final product. In a food-processing operation this would

Figure 11.44 The value chain

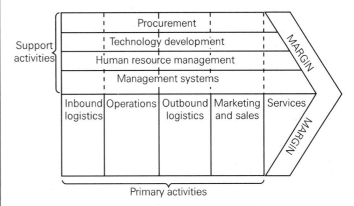

include mixing and blending ingredients, cooking foods and packing and labelling them.
- *Outbound logistics* – These activities relate to the storing and distributing of products to customers. Processed foods must be transported to and stored in warehouses before being delivered to shops and supermarkets.
- *Marketing and sales* – These activities make consumers aware of products and make it easy for them to purchase goods and services. Market research sets out to find out what types of processed food consumers want; advertising makes consumers aware of products, etc.
- *Services* – These activities are concerned with improving and keeping up the value of a product; for example, in the case of electrical goods, installing equipment, repairing it and providing spare parts.

Each of these primary activities is linked to four **support activities**:

- *Procurement* – This is the process involved in acquiring the various resource inputs, including setting up systems to make orders or make contacts. It will take place in many parts of the organisation.
- *Technology development* – All value activities involve technology even if it is just 'know-how'. Technological development may be directly involved with the product (e.g. research and development) or with the development of new processes; it may even be concerned with the development of raw materials.
- *Human resource management* – This is concerned with a whole range of activities to do with looking after people who work within an organisation and those with whom the organisation comes into contact.
- *Management systems* – A wide range of management activities, such as planning and financial control, are needed to support primary activities in many different ways.

An understanding of the value chain provides an excellent overview of ways of maintaining and improving business performance. Every organisation needs to concentrate on making the best use of its resources to provide value to consumers. Therefore it needs to examine and improve all of its primary and support activities, and the linkages between them. Many of these value activities and linkages occur inside the organisation (internal), many others take place outside (external). Organisations need to give equal emphasis to both.

Systems analysis

We have already looked at the systems approach in some depth on pages 281–2. **Systems analysis** can be used both as a means of analysing management problems and as a way of dealing with rapidly changing situations.

While the way in which an activity is organised, how long it takes and other aspects may change frequently, the decision-making process itself may remain relatively constant – for example, the skills required to make decisions, the experience required, the information needed, and so on.

Gerald Cohen, in his book *The New Right*, identifies the following steps in a systems approach to organising.

- Analyse the decision-making process to find out what decisions are required.
- Decide on the information needed to make the decisions.
- Determine the sources of the information.
- Group the decision-making management roles in a way which takes into account the economies that can be made from rational information flows. Decisions should be made at the point in an organisation where the bulk of the information is available. This saves on the cost of unnecessarily transmitting the information.
- Modify the structure of the organisation to group together the skills for decision-making. Some staff who have all the necessary information will not have the ability to evaluate it and make an effective decision. Others may not have the experience to weigh up the pros and cons of different courses of action. Therefore responsibility needs to be transferred to the point at which the right quality of decision can be made. Cost needs to be balanced against quality.
- Modify the structure of the organisation to take account of risks and side-effects. Any decision that has a major impact on a number of sub-systems should be taken jointly or at a level at which the effect on these sub-systems is allowed for.

Once a systems analysis approach has been implemented it lends itself very readily to the design and organisation of new projects. Also, because the approach focuses on inputs and outputs it is very outward-looking and quickly recognises changes in the external environment. A weakness of the approach is that it requires well-trained systems analysts to operate it, rather than lending itself to the untrained manager.

Open systems planning

In a changing business environment, **open systems planning** (OSP) helps organisations to analyse the environmental demands and expectations placed on them and plan to meet these successfully. The key features of OSP are as follows.

Firstly, defining the present situation is done by looking at the expectations and interactions between the organisation and its environment. Managers should identify key groups in the organisation's environment and ask the questions:

- How do we interact with them?
- What do we expect of each other?
- How do we affect their results and how do they affect our results?

Secondly, it is necessary to predict, realistically, the future environmental situation, and to ask the question: 'If no intervention for change takes place, what is the likely future situation?'

Thirdly, the ideal future situation should be defined. Assuming that managers and planners can take actions to influence the future situation, what would they like to create that is feasible?

- What would the situation be like if the people with whom we interact do so effectively with us?
- What would their ideal expectations be of us? What would be our ideal expectations of them?

Finally, action planning is used to identify specific action steps which will help to create the ideal future situation. These steps would include:

- changing the influences and functions of some external groups so that interactions improve
- changing operational activities in order to interact more effectively
- changing relationships and dealing with outside groups by collaboratively redefining expectations, purposes and workloads.

Clearly such a framework for change consists of being *proactive* in order to create positive improvements. It involves a recognition of your environment, and a recognition that you can make positive steps to influence relationships and expectations in your environment, and hence modify the environment itself.

Performance standards and indicators

We have already looked at performance standards and indicators in some detail on pages 279–81. A results-orientated approach compares achievements with agreed standards of performance for each activity or task. If results are not 'up to standard', then whoever is responsible for that activity will need to assess, with a line manager or quality circle, why the discrepancy has occurred. There are many possible reasons why performance can fall short of the standard (e.g. bottlenecks, delays, absenteeism). The quicker the cause of a problem is located, the easier it will be to rectify.

David Hanna, in his book *Designing Organisations for High Performance*, argues that high performers identify core operating principles:

'These operating principles are actually statements of core values and desired norms – the desired elements of culture. These principles become a code of ethics that spell out how the new operation will really operate. By consciously examining these core values and their relevance to the business situation, an organisation can do much to position itself for high performance. These statements, when managed effectively, become a new corporate conscience, inviting employees to behave in new ways to support the newly stated purpose or mission. Once people recognise these values are real, they progress even faster toward the desired cultural attributes.'

Case Study
Communication on all fronts

The following extract is taken from *Body and Soul*, the autobiography of Anita Roddick (founder of the Body Shop).

'After education, nothing has been more important to the Body Shop's success than our ability to communicate – with our staff at all levels, our customers, the community, the media and the world. I took the view that it did not matter a hoot how much I knew and cared about what the Body Shop stood for and about its role in the community and in society at large if I was unable to communicate my views to other people.

'How we communicate is gob-smacking. We use every available medium to preach, teach, inspire and stimulate, and in everything we do – whether it is a simple leaflet or a full-length video – our single-minded passion shines through. One of my favourite quotations is from the seventeenth-century French philosopher Descartes: "The passions are the only advocates which always persuade. The simplest man

with passion will be more persuasive that the most eloquent without."

'Wherever you go in the Body Shop organisation, throughout all our offices and warehouses you will see informational displays, statements of our philosophy, charts, illustrations, words and images, all designed to propagate our core beliefs and raise the consciousness of our staff.'

Questions for discussion

1 *Why is it important to convey the values of an organisation to staff?*
2 *How does an understanding of core values enhance performance?*
3 *What is the relationship between performance and clear objectives?*
4 *To what extent could the Body Shop be said to be operating with an effective open systems model?*

Appraising managers as managers

Koontz and Weirich, in an article entitled 'Measuring managers: a double-barrelled approach', set out 73 questions which could be explored in assessing the performance of managers. Each of these relate to the manager's ability to manage. In the area of *planning*, the questions relate to whether the manager:

■ sets out for the departmental unit both short-term and long-term goals in verifiable forms that are related in a positive way to those of superiors and of the company
■ checks plans periodically to see whether they are consistent with current expectations.

In the area of *organisation skills* the questions relate to whether the manager:

■ delegates authority to subordinates on the basis of the results expected of them
■ refrains from making decisions in that area once authority has been delegated
■ regularly teachs subordinates, or otherwise makes sure that they understand the nature of line and staff relationships.

Other areas covered were *staffing*, *leading* and *controlling*.

The impact of technology

A modern business system can be seen as consisting of three major sub-systems which impact directly on the management of activities.

The *management* sub-system is concerned with all the people and activities involved in planning, controlling and decision-making. The *operations* sub-system is concerned with all the activities, material flows and people directly involved with performing the primary function of the organisation (e.g. manufacturing operations).

The *information* sub-system is made up of the people, machines, ideas and activities that are concerned with gathering and processing data in order to meet the formal requirements of an organisation for information. It may include the way in which information is collected, stored, handled, exchanged and utilised for accounting purposes, monitoring stocks, or a range of other interrelated functions. *It is this information sub-system that has become particularly important in enhancing the effectiveness of the management function today.*

Activities can now be designed so that they are almost self-running with a high level of inbuilt technology. New systems can operate with very low tolerance levels and automatic control mechanisms. Such systems create instantaneous information about their current performance, and this information can be processed by computer.

Expert systems (ESs) are the first commercial spinoffs from research into 'artificial intelligence'. ESs are computer programs that embody some of the knowledge of human experts, knowledge that even those experts have until now found difficult to formulate and communicate. An ES has two distinct elements, a 'knowledge base' and an 'inference engine'.

The 'knowledge base' consists of all knowledge that it is humanly possible to collect on a particular subject. The area of knowledge an ES covers may be narrow, but an expert system aspires to quite comprehensive knowledge in that area. Because an expert system uses knowledge gathered from many different human experts, it will be more knowledgeable than any single human being.

The 'inference engine' is simply a collection of the rules that manipulate the knowledge in the ES. For example, one of the rules might be: 'If runny nose, then cold or excessive stimulation or allergy', – where 'runny nose', 'cold', 'excessive stimulation' and 'allergy' are all terms that need to be in the knowledge base.

ESs are different from ordinary computer programs in that they can work out new rules for their own guidance on the basis of existing knowledge and the inference engine. They are just one example of the way in which new technology is developing. It does not take too much imagination to see the potential for ESs in management decision-making and for the review and monitoring of activities in organisations. Expert systems may be able to come up with solutions to management problems in a cost-effective way.

Further reading

- *Business Studies*, 2nd edition, by David Needham and Robert Dransfield. Stanley Thornes, 1994.
- *Supervisory Management*, 6th edition, by P. W. Betts. Pitman, 1993.
- *Self Managing Work Teams* by Graham Wilson. Pitman, 1994.
- *Operation Strategy Text and Cases* by David Garvin. Prentice Hall, 1992.
- *Contemporary Business Communication* by L. Boone, D. Kurtz and J. Block. Prentice Hall, 1994.
- *Operations Management – Decision Making in the Operations Function*, 4th edition, by Roger Schroeder. McGraw-Hill, 1993.

5

Organisational structures and processes

12 Identifying structures

On completion of this chapter students will be able to:

■ identify and describe different organisational structures

■ evaluate the appropriateness of these organisational structures

■ participate in the design of different structures to meet identified needs.

There are many possible definitions of what makes an organisation. Here is a typical definition:

An organisation is a system, having an established structure and conscious planning, in which people work and deal with one another in a coordinated and cooperative manner for the accomplishment of recognised goals.

Task

What do you see as being the key words in the suggested definition? Set out a list of the key words and explain what you think they mean.

In their highly acclaimed book *Organising and Organisations* (1993), Sims, Fineman, and Gabriel argue that most definitions leave it unclear as to which human associations should be thought of as organisations. For example, it is easy to decide that armies and universities are organisations – but what about football crowds, tribes, theatre audiences, etc? These authors therefore propose a set of criteria which they feel would be useful to define the 'general space' occupied by organisations. Their criteria are as follows.

■ Organisations are associations of several people, who are aware of being members, and who are generally willing to cooperate.
■ They are mainly long-term and survive changes of personnel.
■ They profess some objectives which they pursue in a methodical, no-nonsense manner.
■ They involve a certain division of labour, with different people assigned to different tasks. This may amount to a hierarchy, a matrix or some other structure.
■ They involve a certain degree of formality and impersonality.

Organisational features

Most organisations have the following features.

A unique name
This can range from the St John Ambulance Brigade to the Monster Raving Loony Party.

Objectives
These identify the direction in which an organisation is seeking to move. By setting out a list of objectives, an organisation can check how successful it is in moving in the right direction.

Rules and regulations
Some of these will be written down. Other, informal, codes of practice are not written down but are recognised and responded to. Some rules are imposed externally by laws; every college, for example, has a set of rules governing safety on the premises.

Patterns and structures
Organisations, not surprisingly, are organised – they have set ways of doing things. In the army, for example, there is a clear structure comprising a hierarchy according to rank. Other organisations are more democratic, with many decision-makers with similar status.

Posts and offices
People within an organisation have varied responsibilities. A football club, for example, may have a manager, a trainer, a coach, a ticket seller, ground staff, etc.

Chain of command
In the majority of organisations there is a chain of command, set out in official and unofficial codes.

Power
Members of an organisation have varying levels of power vested in them. These powers may be set out in a written contract. For example, in a sports team the manager may select the team; the trainer may choose the training

programme; the physiotherapist may set out a schedule for treating injuries; and so on.

Records
Organisations need to have systematic and well-organised records.

Classifying organisations by their objectives

Business organisations

Business organisations take various forms, ranging from small one-owner businesses to multinational corporations. Some are concerned with making goods, and so we call these **industrial** organisations. Some are concerned with buying and selling, so we call these **commercial** organisations. Some are concerned with banking and insurance, so we call these **financial** organisations. Figure 12.1 outlines the features of a business organisation.

Figure 12.1 A business (or economic) organisation

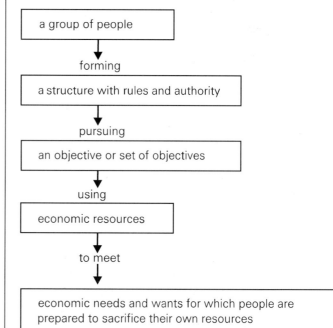

```
         a group of people

             forming

   a structure with rules and authority

             pursuing

     an objective or set of objectives

              using

         economic resources

             to meet

  economic needs and wants for which people are
  prepared to sacrifice their own resources
```

Government organisations

There are **government organisations** operating at both a local and a national level. Accountable to representatives elected by citizens, they are involved in running the country or sectors of it. Examples are the Department for Education and the county councils.

Public corporations

Public corporations are owned by the state on behalf of all the people. An example is the British Broadcasting Corporation. They set out to produce goods and services to serve the people of the country.

Quangos

'Quango' stands for 'quasi-autonomous non-governmental organisation'. A quango is an unelected public body run by a board of directors to manage a particular initiative. For example, local TECs (Training and Enterprise Councils) are responsible for providing training opportunities and schemes on behalf of local employers.

Economic interest groups

Economic interest groups are organisations representing groups of people with a shared interest. Examples are the Consumers Association (representing consumers), the Confederation of British Industry (employers) and the Trades Union Congress (trade unionists). Each trade union is an economic interest group, given special status in law.

Legal and political organisations

There are a number of **legal organisations** responsible for administering and supervising the legal process – for example, the courts. Many groups of people form themselves into **political organisations** (e.g. the Conservative Party). Others are probably less organised, such as a pressure group campaigning on an issue like the destruction of the countryside.

Charities

Charitable organisations like Oxfam and Help the Aged have a special status in law. In the past, charities were set up to provide for the poor, the helpless and the homeless. Nowadays many organisations have adopted charitable status in order to gain tax and other advantages (e.g. some public schools).

Mutual-help organisations

Some organisations have been set up so that members can help each other, rather than to make a profit. **Cooperatives** are a good example – any surpluses may be shared among the members. Some labour organisations work on this basis, members clubbing together to provide support for the sick and needy.

International and multinational organisations

Many organisations now have a membership in several nations, at either a government or private level. Examples are the Red Cross/Red Crescent and the European Union. Business organisations may have tentacles in many countries (e.g. IBM, Marks & Spencer, Shell, Laura Ashley).

Task

Classify the following organisations into the foregoing types (of course some organisations will fit into more than one class):

The Social Democrats	A local hospital trust
A grant-maintained school	The National Union of Mineworkers
Railtrack	The Department for Education
Mencap	The Office of Fair Trading
Midland Bank	Greenpeace
The High Court	The European Parliament
A women's refuge	The Inland Revenue
A partnership of solicitors	The Co-operative Retail Society

The development of organisational theory

The way in which organisations have been run has changed over the years and continues to change. Organisations that fail to change to meet new circumstances tend to suffer.

The early days of organising factories on scientific principles were a major influence on organisational theory.

Case Study
Factory organisation

The following is an extract from an influential article by Tom Burns in *New Society* on 31 January 1963.

'The industrial system was simply the factory system as developed by Arkwright: the term "factory" meaning "the combined operation of many work people, adult and young, in tending with assiduous skill a system of productive machines continuously impelled by a central power". It is the constant aim and tendency of every improvement in machinery to supersede human labour altogether.

'Factory organisation stayed for three generations at the point at which Arkwright had left it. Marx's account contains the same essentials: a collection of machines in a building all driven by one prime mover, and, preferably, of the same type and engaged on the same process. Attending the machines were men and women who themselves were attended by "feeders", most of them children, who fetched and carried away the materials. There was also a superior but numerically unimportant class of maintenance and repair workers. All of these worked under a master, with perhaps a chief workman or foreman. The primitive social technology of the factory system still confined it, even by the 1850s, largely to the mass production of textiles.'

Questions for discussion

1 *Why could the system described above be characterised as 'primitive social technology'?*
2 *What sorts of social relations would this system depend on?*
3 *Why would such a system not be appropriate in a modern economy?*

In time the organisation of industrial technology did change. In particular there was a huge growth in the numbers of administrative officials and managers in organisations. For example, in British manufacturing industry the proportion of administrative employees increased from under 9 per cent in 1907 to 20 per cent by 1948.

Organisational structures were transformed to include whole new layers, including training officers, inspectors, accountants, sales managers, cashiers, publicity managers, etc. People in these new posts acquired as part of their organisational personality a loyalty to the employer.

Scientific management

Scientific management was associated with developing 'scientific methods' of organising work. Its theory was closely associated with the work of **F. W. Taylor** (1856–1915). Scientific management was concerned with finding the most efficient ways of organising activities in the workplace. Managers were solely responsible for setting work schedules and tasks, and the workers performed these tasks. Scientific management was widely adopted in factories as a way of increasing production and profits.

Administrative management

This was a top-down view of how to run an organisation. Some of the key components of administrative theory were:

- A clear chain of command has to be established from the top to the bottom of a structure. Authority is then vested in those higher up the organisation. Each employee should have only one direct boss who passes down commands.
- Managers are responsible for functional areas, including responsibility for particular people.
- The organisation is based on the division of labour, and functional specialisation.
- Orders pass along and down the chain of command.
- Each official is responsible for about five or six subordinates.
- Jobs are designed to meet the needs of the organisation. Individuals are then recruited in order to fit the job requirements.

Bureaucratic structures

Max Weber (1846–1920) set out a model of how a bureaucratic organisation might operate, and this has served as a starting point for the study of organisational society ever since.

Weber's model was developed at a time when large organisations were becoming increasingly important in industrial society. He argued that bureaucracies are the most functionally effective form of organisation, although at times they operate in an 'inhuman way'.

Weber saw bureaucracies as representing the application of rational thought to practical problems in large industrial combines, in the civil service and in other important organisations such as schools, churches and government departments. His model of bureaucracy specified several typical characteristics (see Figure 12.2):

- A set of official positions for the purpose of carrying out given organisational tasks, to be governed by a set of rules and procedures.
- A hierarchical structure of official posts.
- Management based on office procedures, files, documents and 'office staff'.
- The appointment of trained officials to take on roles within the bureaucracy.

Today, various forms of bureaucracy are important ways of running political and economic systems in advanced industrial societies. Bureaucracy may be the most rational form of social organisation and it dominates the structure of many business organisations.

Advantages of bureaucratic organisations

The bureaucratic division of labour, combined with new technologies, has made possible massive increases in the production of goods and services.

A street scene in Max Weber's day

Figure 12.2 A bureaucratic structure

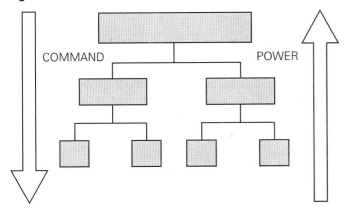

Secondly, a bureaucracy usually helps to create a predictable pattern for work cycles. People know what they are supposed to do, how they are supposed to do it and the extent of their responsibility. Production targets can be set, and plans established to meet them.

Thirdly, a bureaucracy is often seen as being a 'fair' way of doing things. Officials are appointed on the basis of their qualifications, and the organisation deals with individuals and groups with which it comes into contact on the basis of predetermined rules and procedures.

Provided that officials stick to the rules, there should be no possibility of giving preferential treatment.

Criticisms of bureaucratic organisations

Bureaucracies are sometimes accused of being slow-moving, unimaginative organisations because of the way they stick to rules and procedures. Decisions may be arrived at slowly because they have to be processed through the 'right channels'.

Secondly, within a bureaucracy it is all too easy to lose sight of the principal objectives. Instead of bureaucrats focusing on the aims and purposes of the organisation, they can become wrapped up in procedures and paperwork. The end result can be the loss of business and profits. In the extreme case, bureaucratic procedures confirm the old adage: 'The operation was a success, but the patient died'.

Thirdly, bureaucracies are sometimes seen to be inhuman structures which fail to account for the fact that many of their internal and external relationships are between people. This can have a depersonalising effect, concentrating on relationships that are remote and anonymous rather than on face-to-face contacts.

Systems views of organisations

Systems theory is a helpful way of thinking about organisational structures. *A system is a complex whole made from a set of interconnecting parts or things.* A system processes **inputs** to produce **outputs**, and this can be illustrated by drawing three 'black boxes' as in Figure 12.3.

Figure 12.3 The simplest representation of a system

In reality, organisational structures are made up of many inputs, processes and outputs.

Boundaries

A production system operates within defined boundaries. It is usually fairly obvious when production is taking place, and the inputs flow through this system.

Some of the resources used will be **current resources** – for example the ingredients and energy required to make a production run of biscuits. What actually goes into the production process will be **filtered**, which means that there will be barriers that select what is to be used in producing a good or service. For example, a quality-control arrangement of some kind would ensure that pieces of metal would be removed from the biscuit line.

Current resources come together with elements such as machinery (e.g. a production line) and buildings. The resources flow from one element to another across links between the elements. For example, in biscuit manufacture ingredients flow through a mixing element, through rollers, along dryers, and so on.

At the end of the production line there are output filters. Some outputs will be filtered into different lines, as when making different types of chocolate bars. Some outputs may be sub-standard and will flow into the reject line, or waste channel.

The inputs are often known as 'primary inputs' and 'secondary inputs'. The primary inputs are the settings (control parameters) that control the operations of the system – for example the speed of the line, the temperature, the quality standards, the hours worked. The secondary inputs are the current resources.

Closed and open systems

In an **open system** the output does not affect the input. In contrast, in a **closed system** the output *will* directly affect the input.

If a system is to work automatically, **feedback** is needed. Imagine being blindfolded and then being told to walk along the edge of a cliff; it would be difficult, because your eyes and other senses normally provide constant feedback, enabling corrective action to be taken as needed. An electric heater without any form of feedback is said to be an open-ended control system; such a heater, once turned on, stays on even if the room is too hot. If a heat sensor (thermostat) is added to provide feedback about the room's temperature, it can be made to turn the heater off when the set temperature is reached, and on again when the room cools down (see Figure 12.4).

Figure 12.4 A closed system

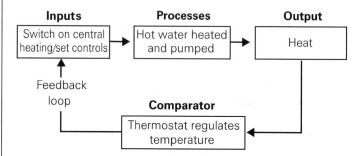

Organisational theorists treat organisations as systems. They examine the relationships between the elements of the organisation, and the interactions with other systems in the organisational environment. Human organisations are, on the whole, open systems which interact with elements in the wider environment. For example a business interacts with customers, suppliers, the government, pressure groups etc. It is affected by social, economic, and other changes.

Organisations are in a perpetual state of change so that there is a dynamic or moving equilibrium. People in organisations seek to ensure it survives, and often this involves moving the organisation 'on' to a new state of balance. Feedback of information is used to enable the organisation to adjust and modify.

Organisations are usually made up of several sub-systems, and changes in one sub-system are extremely likely to have an impact on other sub-systems. If one department changes the way it operates this may quickly affect the running of other departments. However, systems theory stresses the importance of looking at the organisation as a whole – the holistic approach. The synergy and interactions between the various sub-systems are more important than the individual components.

Organisation charts

In a very small organisation you are unlikely to find a formal structure. For example, in a one-person business the entrepreneur carries out most of the various business functions personally.

As a small firm grows a formal organisational structure starts to develop based on functional specialisms. The firm may then be divided up into hierarchical functional divisions.

Every organisational structure can be charted to show the departments, how they link together, and the principal lines of authority. This gives a snapshot view of how the organisation is made up. It shows lines of decision-making and levels of responsibility. Looking at a chart may expose any weaknesses in an organisation.

Organisation charts do have some potential drawbacks. For example, people lower down the chart may shirk the responsibilities they have by saying 'That's not my job, its hers!' Secondly, such charts show only the formal structure of the organisation but miss out the highly significant informal links that usually exist, and which help to keep the organisation running efficiently.

Formal and informal structures

The formal structure of an organisation is based on employees' official roles. If you asked the headteacher of a school or a hospital administrator to draw an organisation chart they would almost certainly set down the formal structure based on official definitions of what everyone *should* be doing. For example, the headteacher might present the chart shown in Figure 12.5.

Figure 12.5 The formal structure of a school

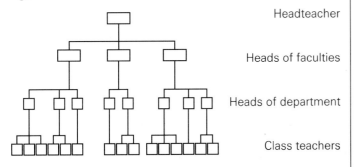

Headteacher

Heads of faculties

Heads of department

Class teachers

However, concentration on formal structure may disguise what really happens. For example, in the school it may be that the head of the science faculty is frequently away, so that many of the managerial decisions in science are made by one or two of the heads of department. In the school

there may be a number of teachers who regularly play golf together, and these teachers (whatever their ranks) could possibly be the major determinants of curriculum policy. In other words, decisions are made not only in staff meetings but also on the golf links. At the same time a number of teachers will be university graduates, and these may have a major say when it comes to making academic decisions about the curriculum (see Figure 12.6).

Figure 12.6 'Hidden' influences in an organisational structure

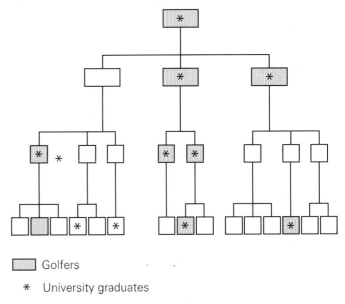

▨ Golfers

* University graduates

Managers, to be effective, should always be aware of these informal links. A lot of power may be vested in the informal, which is why people like secretaries and quite junior administrators can have a tremendous influence in an organisational structure.

Case Study
The office mafia

At Midtown Secondary School the senior management team is made up of a headteacher, two deputy headteachers and three senior teachers. This group meets once a fortnight to discuss developments and policies. There is no set agenda – items to be discussed are usually decided by the headteacher and one of the deputies.

Other members of staff are consulted once a week at a 20-minute meeting before the school day starts on a Monday. The briefing involves the headteacher introducing policy issues and allowing staff to present feedback to the senior management team who group together to give out announcements.

A number of major decisions about the school are made by the school governors. The headteacher and senior deputy are part of the board of governors.

The head and deputies rely heavily on the secretarial staff for day-to-day administration. These office staff deal with all incoming phone calls as well as all routine correspondence. They also handle the day-to-day accounts of the school and are responsible for the disbursement of money for staff expenditures. Because the head and deputies do little teaching, they spend a lot of the day in the school office where they mix with office staff. This means that particularly close relationships have built up between senior teachers and secretarial staff.

Questions for discussion

1 *Which groups within Midtown school are most likely to be involved in major decision-making processes about policy?*
2 *Is the informal structure of the school likely to be much different from the formal structure?*
3 *Which groups may feel that they are not playing an appropriate part in the decision-making process?*
4 *What suggestions do you have for improving the management of this school?*

Levels within the organisation

When drawing up an organisation chart it is usual to distinguish levels of individuals or posts which have roughly equal amounts of responsibility. For example, at the top level there may be the managing director, under whom are the middle managers (e.g. those responsible for marketing and production). Operatives tend to be at the lower levels (see Figure 12.7).

Figure 12.7 Formal levels in an organisation

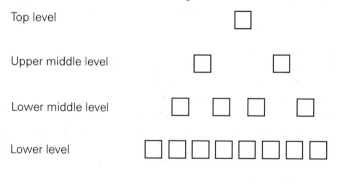

Top level

Upper middle level

Lower middle level

Lower level

Span of control

The **span of control** of an individual is the number of people he or she manages or supervises directly.

Figure 12.8 illustrates an organisation with a *narrow* span of control. No one member of this organisation is directly responsible for more than two subordinates.

Figure 12.8 A narrow span of control

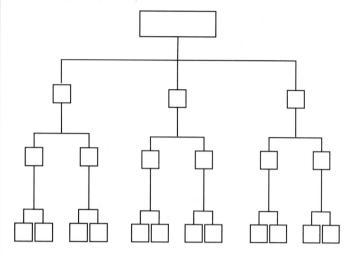

There is a limit to the number of people who can be supervised effectively by one person, depending on the type of work involved. Choosing the best span of control means striking a balance between control and trust. A narrow span of control enables close supervision and fast communications. However, there can be disadvantages. For example, there may be too many levels of management, and because the organisation is 'tall' it may be costly to run. Also, supervisors might tend to get too involved in their subordinates' detailed work.

Wider spans require much higher degrees of trust in subordinate staff, whilst needing fewer managers and allowing a hierarchy with fewer levels. Typically, spans are widest where the work of subordinates is routine and repetitive, or where subordinates are experienced, competent and fully trained.

Case Study
Exodus 18: 17–25

When Moses' father-in-law noticed that he was spending too much time organising the Exodus of the Israelites he gave the following advice:

'The thing thou doest is not good. Thou wilt surely wear away, both thou and this people that is with thee; for this thing is too heavy for thee; thou art not able to perform it thyself alone. Hearken now unto my voice, I will give thee counsel. . . . Thou shalt provide out of the people able men . . . and place such over them, to be rulers of thousands, and rulers of hundreds, rulers of fifties, and rulers of tens. And let them judge the people at all seasons; and it shall be, that every great matter they shall bring unto thee, but every small matter they shall judge; so shall it be easier for thyself, and they shall bear the burden with thee. If thou shalt do this thing, and God commands thee so, then thou shalt be able to endure, and all this people shall also go to their place in peace.'

Questions for discussion

1 *How sound do you think this advice was?*
2 *In what types of situation can this theory be applied?*
3 *Are there situations where this theory would be inappropriate?*

It is very difficult to specify an exact figure for the most effective number of people to be within a span of control. Generally speaking, the higher up an organisation an individual is the fewer people he or she should have in their direct span of control. The exact number will depend on factors that affect the time requirements of managing and the difficulty of management.

Harold Koontz has compiled a table which gives us some important considerations to bear in mind when deciding on the span of management (see Figure 12.9).

Organisational architecture

The term **organisational architecture** refers to managers' more general views about their organisations and how they are structured. It focuses particularly on how traditional departments and more informal project teams can fit together, and on the role of **work-teams**.

Today a lot of emphasis is placed on work-teams. The idea is that a business can be looked on as a series of projects carried out by small groups of people with **complementary skills**. This is a continuation of the movement away from the 'tall' or bureaucratic structure of organisations, which divides a business into clearly defined functions such as finance and marketing. In many organisations today there is a move towards flattening the organisational architecture (see Figure 12.10).

Figure 12.10 A flat organisational structure

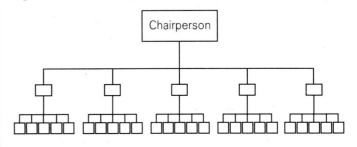

Tall organisations suffer from all of the problems of bureaucracy. Giving independence to work-teams in flatter organisations unleashes the creativity and flexibility which are required in a dynamic business world. Information technology provides instant access to information for all members of the modern work-team.

Line and staff organisation

Line organisation

Line organisation is the typical structure of a hierarchy. There are direct communication links between superiors and subordinates. Each member of the organisation has a

Figure 12.9 Factors influencing the span of management

Narrow span	Wide spans
Great deal of time spent with subordinates because:	Little time spent with subordinates because:
■ No or little training	■ Thorough training
■ Inadequate or unclear authority delegation	■ Clear delegation to undertake well-defined tasks
■ Unclear plans for non-repetitive operations	■ Well-defined plans for repetitive operations
■ Non-verifiable objectives and standards	■ Verifiable objectives used as standards
■ Fast changes in external and internal environments	■ Slow changes in external and internal environments
■ Use of poor or inappropriate communication techniques, including vague instructions	■ Use of appropriate techniques such as proper organisation structure, written and oral communication
■ Ineffective interaction of superior and subordinate	■ Effective interaction between superior and subordinate
■ Ineffective meetings	■ Effective meetings
■ Incompetent and untrained manager	■ Competent and trained manager
■ Complex task	■ Simple task
■ Greater number of specialists at lower and middle levels	■ Number of specialists at upper levels (top managers concerned with external environment)

clear understanding of the chain of command within the organisation and to whom he or she is responsible. This type of structure can be very effective because of its clarity – there are set rules and procedures which can be referred to. Figure 12.11 illustrates the way in which communication flows downwards.

Figure 12.11 The flow of communication in line organisation

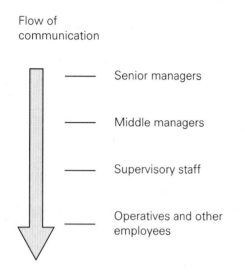

Line management is typically used to organise a firm's central activities such as the making and selling of products. In these areas there is a clear hierarchical framework. Larger organisations tend to have more rigid and bureaucratic structures than smaller ones. Although agreed and clear procedures are necessary, it is also important to have a degree of flexibility. Formal structures frequently undergo informal changes in the course of time as new situations arise.

Staff organisation

Staff organisation primarily serves the various line departments. Typical staff areas include personnel, corporate affairs, data processing, and office administration.

Staff departments typically cut across an organisation to provide a range of specialist services and consultancy skills. For example, any line department of a company might require specialist legal help from time to time, might want to have data processed or might need help with recruiting new staff. Figure 12.12 illustrates the way in which various staff areas can be made available to all line departments within an organisation.

Figure 12.12 Combining line and staff organisation

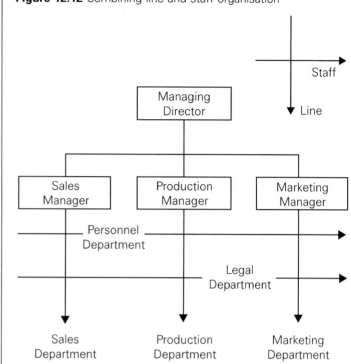

A staff department might itself be organised as a hierarchy. For example, the personnel department could have several tiers below the personnel manager.

Combined line and staff organisation

Most medium and large businesses combine elements of line and staff organisation. There are a number of advantages to having this blend:

- The line departments are able to concentrate on their central roles of marketing, making, selling etc. while being complemented by specialist service departments.
- Line managers need to familiarise themselves only with information related to their core activities.
- Staff groupings can be called in to provide specialist information and advice in a number of key areas.

However, there are also a number of potential disadvantages of combining the two areas. One major disadvantage is that it can lead to confusion because there is less clarity over departmental responsibility and lines of authority. **Unity of command** is often thought to be the mark of an effective organisation. Where there is more than one centre of responsibility confusion can arise because one section can blame another for failure to carry out work effectively or for a breakdown in communication. Where department managers compete with one another to secure high-status work, or where they try to avoid less prestigious work, problems can occur.

Another potential disadvantage arises from the fact that line managers often rise to a particular position through many years of dedicated hard work (this is particularly true in production departments), whereas many staff managers are recruited with a university background. In this situation some line managers may resent a staff manager's rapid rise to managerial status. Equally, some staff managers may regard themselves as superior to those who have 'worked their way up'. These clashes can be detrimental to the smooth running of an organisation.

In addition, some line managers may resent having to listen to the opinions of staff managers with *priorities* that are different from their own. For example, a corporate affairs or personnel manager might try to push a company into employing more youth trainees in order to project a certain image within the community; whereas a production manager may be more concerned with having a more experienced workforce.

In order to overcome these and other difficulties, it is essential for an organisation to devise a clear strategy to coordinate staff and line groupings. This strategy will involve setting out the goals of the company and then deciding on the responsibilities of line and staff groupings. The responsibilities need to be set out in a clear statement of policy. Some large companies even have an 'organisation and methods' department with the responsibility for clarifying such issues.

The superstructure of organisations

The superstructure of an organisation is the way in which employees are grouped into various departments or sections.

Grouping by function

This is probably the most common way of grouping employees. Functional organisation means that the organisation is divided into broad sectors, each with its own particular specialism or function (see Figure 12.13).

There are a number of clear advantages to organising on a functional basis:

■ If groups of specialists are given control over specific work areas, this prevents wasteful duplication within an organisation. Invoices can be processed in one department, new orders won by another and payments collected by a third. Provided clear guidelines are laid down as to who does what, the organisation's members will be clear about their responsibilities.

Figure 12.13 Grouping by function

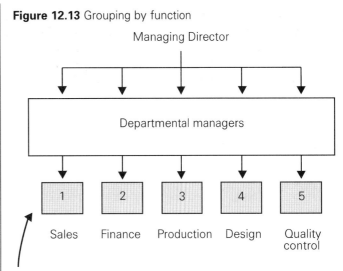

Functional Departments

■ Specialists are able to work in a pool of like-minded people.
■ Because each part of the organisation is pursuing its primary function, it will contribute to the overall well-being of the total system.

There are potential disadvantages:

■ Narrow specialisation may restrict an individual's or department's ability to develop a global view of the whole organisation.
■ Individuals cannot move easily between departments.
■ Rivalry can develop between departments, which may then try to block one anothers' initiatives. Departments may pull in opposite directions – in some organisations you can hear complaints such as 'This company is run by a bunch of accountants!' and 'Not enough attention is being paid to selling!'
■ As an organisation becomes larger, communication channels may become slower or distorted, particularly between upper and lower levels.

Grouping by product

When a large organisation produces a range of products, it may find it convenient to create a structure based on product lines. A firm in the publishing industry can have a newspaper division, a magazine and periodicals division and a books division. Each division then contains a mixture of all the specialist ingredients required to enable it to work independently. Pirelli, one of the world's leading tyre manufacturers, is divided into two divisions – for tyres and cables.

A great advantage of this form of structure is that divisions can concentrate on their own market area. It also becomes possible to assess the profitability and effectiveness of each sector. At the same time it is still possible to share expertise between divisions and to share services such as a combined transport fleet.

By isolating the various parts of a business organisation, it becomes possible to cut out loss-making divisions and to amalgamate divisions by merging them with similar divisions in other companies (see Figure 12.14). It also becomes possible to generate competition within a company and to allow greater scope to create an internal promotion ladder.

Figure 12.14 Making business decisions according to divisional profits

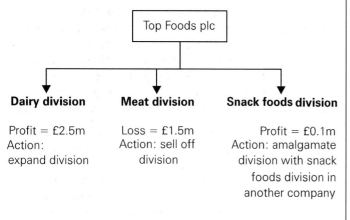

Top Foods plc

Dairy division	**Meat division**	**Snack foods division**
Profit = £2.5m	Loss = £1.5m	Profit = £0.1m
Action: expand division	Action: sell off division	Action: amalgamate division with snack foods division in another company

Grouping by process

When the manufacture of a product requires a series of processes, separate departments can be set up to perform each process. To take the example of a publishing company, within each of the divisions there may be departments responsible for carrying out stages of production – editing the copy, page layout and design, printing, etc. (see Figure 12.15).

Figure 12.15 Grouping by process in a publishing company

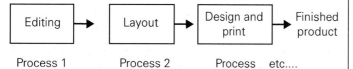

Editing → Layout → Design and print → Finished product

Process 1   Process 2   Process   etc....

There are a number of clear advantages to organising on a process basis:

■ It is possible to set up teams of like-minded specialists (e.g. designers).
■ It becomes easy to identify points in the production process at which things are going well or badly.
■ It is easy to introduce new technology at a given stage of production and to familiarise the appropriate staff with new skills and working practices.

There are potential disadvantages:

■ Process production works effectively only if there is a steady flow from one stage to another. If one process gets out of step by producing too much or too little, problems occur as stocks pile up or run out. This situation might arise if, say, one group of process workers goes on strike or has a high absenteeism level.
■ Sections of employees may become *too* specialist and fail to communicate effectively with other sections.
■ It may become difficult to transfer employees from one process to another if there are too rigid divisions between processes. Employees might prefer to stick with their existing work-group and continue to use the skills they have.

Grouping by geographical area

Large organisations tend to have branches spread throughout the country and sometimes overseas. Multiple retailing companies are a good example. Marks & Spencer has a shop on virtually every High Street in the United Kingdom and several overseas.

In this case, groups of shops are organised into regional divisions which have local supervision of such things as training of staff and distribution policy. Figure 12.16 illustrates a retailing organisation with five domestic divisions and two overseas divisions.

Figure 12.16 Grouping by geographical area

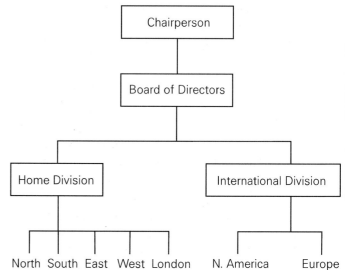

Chairperson

Board of Directors

Home Division — International Division

North South East West London   N. America   Europe

There are a number of clear advantages to organising on a geographical basis:

■ Setting up distinct regional divisions makes it possible to respond quickly to local needs, issues and problems. The organisation thus become more sensitive to customers, employees and other groups. At the same time, it might be possible to cut through a lot of red tape if the regional groups are allowed to make their own decisions.

■ Setting up national and regional divisions makes it possible to tailor the operations to local differences like language, laws and customs. Local knowledge is best gained by hiring local specialists.

■ National governments often look more kindly on multinational divisions that have a local head office.

There are potential disadvantages:

■ Having too many regional divisions can lead to wasteful duplication of facilities and roles. Too few divisions can lead to lack of coordination, gaps in communication and breakdowns.

■ Having an extensive regional structure requires the creation of a series of management positions. It is not always easy to recruit personnel of the required calibre to fill these positions.

■ Regional headquarters might take on a life of their own and start pulling in the opposite direction to central policy makers.

■ Although the local divisions will frequently have the best understanding of the situation 'on the ground', they might find themselves at loggerheads with central officials many thousands of miles away.

Grouping by type of customer

Some organisations set up different structures to deal with groups of customers. In a department store, the restaurant operates in a different way and has different procedures from that of the department selling underwear. The furniture department needs to set out a process of documentation and to make arrangements for delivery to customers, which clearly contrasts with purchasing procedures for toys.

Banks have a counter for foreign currency transactions and a department dealing with first-time accounts, as well as regular departments for dealing with private and business customers.

Many businesses have different procedures for dealing with large and small customers. Separate departments may handle these accounts, using different types of paperwork, offering different rates of discount and treating customers in different ways.

The advantages of running an organisation in this way are:

■ Different types of customer can be dealt with by separate departments.

■ Customers will be more inclined to deal with a business that has departments concerned with their particular needs.

■ It is easier to check on the performance of individual products.

There are potential disadvantages:

■ Divisions may compete with one another for the use of company resources.

■ The structure may be costly to set up and will be cost-effective only if there is sufficient demand.

■ More administration and accounting services will be required.

Project forms of organisation

Today, **project management** is used widely in organisations. A project team is responsible for managing a particular project. Companies that make and sell goods employ product managers who pilot particular products from the initial development stage through to final production and sales. The product manager is there to plan, coordinate, initiate, persuade, and hurry things up.

The product manager seeks to synchronise and maximise effort across the various departments of an organisation. An organisation that operates purely on functional lines can soon run into bottlenecks and confusion between the various departments, but a project manager can ensure that there is coordinated planning across the organisation to bring resources and people together correctly. The project manager is there solely to coordinate the activities.

Case Study
Project planning at Northern Foods

This study outlines some of the steps involved in bringing out a new recipe dish – Minced Beef Hotpot – at Northern Foods.

The first stage was to allocate a project manager to be responsible for the development of the dish.

Next, *concept development* started with the retailer (Marks & Spencer) drawing up a brief for the new product, which was passed to the manufacturer. At Northern Foods the development chefs then created the new recipe in a small kitchen. Samples were prepared by the chefs for trials.

Process development was the next step when both retailer and manufacturer were happy with the product. Food technologists were responsible for designing and implementing the process needed to recreate the original in the factory and to launch it into the marketplace. Making Minced Beef Hotpot for four people in a kitchen using a couple of saucepans and roasting dish in the oven is easy; but how do you make it in a factory on a large scale, maintaining strict standards of hygiene and retaining the home-cooked taste?

Factory layout had to be considered. The factory was divided into two sections which separated the raw and the cooked/processed foods. In the low-risk area, raw materials were to be stored and prepared, with raw ingredients loaded into cooking vessels at the barrier. In the high-risk area the cooked foods were to be packaged and prepared for despatch. Here, very strict safety and hygiene rules were to operate.

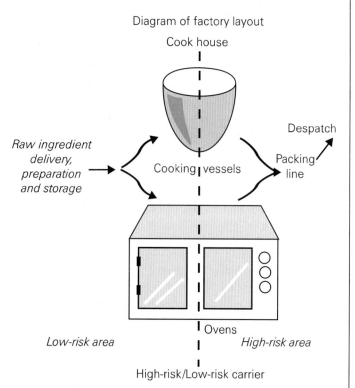

Diagram of factory layout

Next came *factory trials*. A specification was written for the new product which included the recipe, the suppliers of the ingredients, the processing and packing methods. The purpose of the first trial was to collect as much information as possible on the method, ease of processing, labour and time taken. Further trials were continued until the product was ready to launch.

However, before the product was finally ready for launch there were other key stages, including quality assurance checks, preparing the packaging, choosing the best heating instructions for consumers, etc.

At the *launch* the production process was monitored by development technologists. The retailer was present to observe the launch and approve the first packs off the line.

Questions for discussion

1 *Why does the development of a new recipe dish require a project manager?*

2 *Who would have been involved in the project team?*

3 *Who was responsible for checking that the team worked to schedule, and hurried up working arrangements as and when required?*

Matrix structure

An organisation need not necessarily have a single pattern of organisation. Many large businesses combine two or more patterns in a **matrix structure** – for example, they might combine functional and geographical lines of command.

In a matrix structure any member of the organisation may belong to two or more groups (see Figure 12.17). In the illustration, groups of employees are organised into product development teams (e.g. Minced Beef Hotpot, Cannelloni, etc.) as well as by functions (e.g. marketing or sales). In the example a particular group of workers, say production section A, will be accountable to both the project manager for Minced Beef Hotpot and the production manager. Each member of the organisation (below managerial level) is thus accountable to two or more managers. Marketing, sales and other key functional managers will have a global responsibility for their functions within the organisation, while divisional managers have responsibility for these functions on a divisional basis.

Figure 12.17 Example of part of a matrix structure

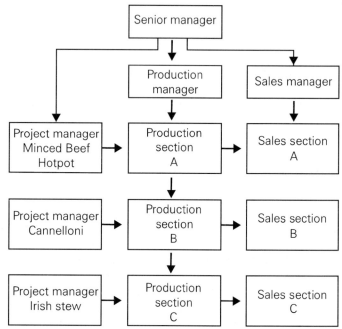

Each divisional manager will be responsible for a specific project. In order to carry out this project, he or she will be able to call on the full range of departments to collaborate in achieving project targets. Projects may be based on products, types of customer, geographical area or any other specific criteria. Inevitably a matrix structure can be complicated and it needs to be clearly laid out.

There are a number of advantages to be gained from implementing a matrix structure:

- A matrix makes it possible to run an organisation so as to focus on a number of aims at the same time – for example, servicing different types of customers, servicing different regions, producing different types of products.
- A matrix gives an organisation extra flexibility to respond to new situations where there is an increase in demand for its resources.
- The system makes it possible to draw groups from specific departments in the required numbers.
- There can be cross-fertilisation of ideas across departments rather than having departments working in isolation.

There are potential disadvantages:

- A complex matrix structure may be difficult to understand, and employees can lose sight of the major organisational aims.
- This system will often require extra administrative resources, costly in terms of time and money.
- Because a matrix establishes more than one chain of command, this can lead to power struggles, contradictory orders and general confusion.

Matrix and project organisation are becoming increasingly important because of the rapidly changing environment in which organisations operate. These structures support quick responses to changes. Also, with organisations setting clear targets and criteria to work towards, a project manager and team may be the best way to achieve the targets. The project manager can be given direct line authority over all the activities necessary to complete major end results.

Strategic business units (SBUs)

The **strategic business unit** is an extension of the project management principle. An SBU is a distinct little business acting as part of a larger business unit. The SBU acts as if it is independent. This makes it possible for work-teams in an organisation to concentrate on ensuring that particular products are given priority. A large modern company may produce hundreds of different product lines. The only way to ensure that each is given priority is to give a group of people 'ownership' and responsibility for its development. The SBU must then meet given performance targets and is accountable to the senior management of the larger organisation.

Deciding on an organisational structure

We have seen that each of the various approaches to running organisations has particular advantages and disadvantages. How can the best structure be chosen?

Obviously the size of the business is highly relevant – it is only worth having a project team if a project is large enough, it is only worth having a geographical structure if geographical markets are large enough, and so on.

The technology employed is important. Where different technologies are employed it is almost inevitable that there will be functional separation. Product divisions may be best if the technological differences apply to services.

The nature of the market is important. Where the market is differentiated it may be best to organise around different types of consumers. If the market is homogeneous, other structures may be better.

The number and variety of skills is another factor. If only a limited number of skills are to be used, wide spans of control are possible and roles can be clearly defined. If many skills are required then it may be better to use team-working.

Task

Are there any other factors that you would bear in mind when deciding how to run an organisation effectively?

Features of a successful organisation

A combination of the following ingredients will be a platform on which an organisation can build its success.

- *Unity of purpose* – All parts of the organisation should work towards a common aim. If parts work in different directions, this can be a source of confusion and is bad for the morale of employees.
- *Effective leadership* – Positions of authority and responsibility should be given only to those who are capable of being effective. Decisions can only be implemented if those in authority have the confidence and determination to see that they are carried out.
- *Flexibility* – An organisation should not be too rigid. It should be capable of altering course quickly if things do not go right, and adapt to changing circumstances.
- *Operational efficiency* – The operations must be studied and the results of this analysis used to ensure that things are done in the best possible way. At one level

this involves looking closely at each operation to see that time is not wasted, that costs are kept down and that work is done accurately. In addition, the functioning of the whole organisation needs to be studied at a global level. It is important that the various parts of the organisation work together smoothly and in the same direction (this is called 'overall efficiency').

■ *Good communications* – Each member of the organisation should understand clearly his or her rights and obligations. Lines of authority need to be clearly defined.

The size/technology/structure issue

In recent years there has been considerable debate about the relationship between an organisation's size, the technology it uses, and its most appropriate structure.

The size/structure issue is supposed to hinge on the tendency that, as organisations increase in size, they benefit from increasing specialisation and differentiation. This leads to an increasing number of sub-units which are grouped into functional and other categories.

As an organisation becomes more complex it requires more coordination and control, leading to structural changes, such as standardisation of rules and formal procedures. There is increased decentralisation, so that decisions can be made at lower levels, and more levels are created in the hierarchy. This leads to the growth of administrative, professional and clerical grades within the organisation. Personal supervision is replaced by more impersonal rules and regulations.

In the 1980s and 90s, larger organisations have tended to 'downsize', becoming leaner and fitter. The tendency has been to strip out layers of administrative control to create more autonomous units. Clearly, there is a relationship between structure and size, but this is likely to vary considerably between industries and to be influenced by the technology employed.

The origin of the view that there is a close relationship between technology and structure is often taken to be **Joan Woodward**'s study of manufacturing firms in south-east Essex between the 1950s and 60s. Woodward identified three different types of technical complexity in the firms that she studied:

■ *Unit or small-batch production* is for products that are made individually, for job production, for batches produced within a single week, etc.
■ *Large-batch and mass production* is for batches requiring over a week to produce, and for assembly lines.
■ *Process production* is for long or continuous standardised runs, repetitive procedures for chemicals, gas, etc.

Woodward felt that technical complexity increases as one moves from unit towards process production. For instance, in process production one is able to exert far more control and achieve far more predictable standardised results. Woodward drew out a number of class relationships between technology and organisational structure:

■ As technical complexity increases so too does the span of control of the chief executive, the number of managers, the ratio of managers to employees, the proportion of administrative employees, etc.
■ There is an inverse (U-shaped) relationship between technical complexity and the span of control of first-line supervisors and styles of management. In mass production the span of control is larger and employs formal mechanistic styles of management. At the two ends of the spectrum, unit production and process production, there is a smaller span of control and organic management styles.
■ Within the three technology categories, the most successful firms are those in which there is the closest fit between organisation and technology (e.g. a mass production firm employing mechanistic formal styles).
■ There is little or no relationship between size of the firm (numbers employed) and technical complexity and organisational characteristics.

Figure 12.18 Woodward's relationship between span of control and technology

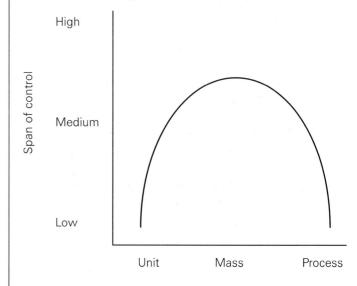

More recent work has thrown doubts on the validity of Woodward's findings. In particular, detailed research by the **Aston group** (which has been backed up by many other studies) set out to produce a more appropriate definition of technology (see *Organisational Theory* by John Jackson and Cyril Morgan). The Aston group focused on '**operations technology**' – that is, the equipping and sequencing of activities in the work flow.

All organisations can be said to have an operations technology.

The Aston group identified a measure which they called **work-flow integration**. Clearly this is determined by the extent to which work-flow processes are interdependent, automated, measurable and adaptable for other purposes. Measures of work-flow integration can be applied to any organisation. Using this measure the Aston group found that technology is moderately related to the following basic dimensions of organisational structure:

- the structuring of activities
- the concentration of authority
- line control of work flow
- a supportive component.

Most importantly they reported that factors other than technology were more influential in creating variations in structure. *They therefore strongly downgraded the importance of technology in determining organisational structure.*

The debate over the importance of technology in determining structure continues to sway back and forth, but the whole issue is clouded by the difficulty of defining 'technology' adequately. Indeed, it is often difficult to separate 'technology' from 'the organisation', particularly now that information and process technologies have come to dominate production.

There can be no doubt that today new technologies make it possible to change the ways in which organisations are structured. Project teams, for example, are able to share information and have instant access to data generated thousands of miles away. Computers are able to simplify the administrative process so that many of the middle layers of an organisation can be stripped away. The net result is that organisations are able to contract in size. Smaller organisations can become more personal, particularly where the emphasis is on team-work.

Clearly, the types of technology that can be employed vary from industry to industry. However, many modern technologies such as 'number-crunching' facilities and administrative procedures using IT have a pervasive effect.

Part 2 Structural factors influencing success or failure

Defining structure

The structure of an organisation can be defined in a number of ways. For example:

- Structure is 'those aspects of the pattern of behaviour in the organisation that are relatively stable and that change only slowly' (March and Simon).
- Structure is 'the relatively enduring allocation of work roles and administrative mechanisms that creates a pattern of interrelated work activities and allows the organisation to conduct, coordinate and control its work activities' (Child).

Both of these definitions refer to relative stability and enduring relationships. It is important to remember that modern organisations require considerable flexibility in their organisational patterns.

The Aston group, which studied 46 firms in the Birmingham area in the late 1960s, identified the following structural dimensions of organisations:

- *Specialisation* – the division of labour within the organisation, the distribution of official duties among a number of positions.
- *Standardisation* – procedures that are continually repeated and are acknowledged as part of standardised activities of an organisation.
- *Formalisation* – the extent to which rules, procedures, instructions, and communications are written down.
- *Centralisation* – where is the decision-making located in the organisation (who is the last person that would need to sanction or approve a particular decision)?
- *Traditionalism* – the extent to which there is a customary way of doing things (often this will not be written down).
- *Configuration* – the shape of the role structure of the organisation.

Configuration and reconfiguration

The **configuration** of an organisation is an important determinant of its success or failure. The configuration is the equivalent of a very detailed organisation chart.

- The *height* of the organisation is determined by the number of job levels from the chief executive to the most junior operative.
- The *width* is measured across the organisation (e.g. the number of people reporting to superiors at each level).

Cliff Bowman, in his book *Management in Practice*, identifies some of the major issues involved in the *reconfiguration* of organisations as they grow. In a relatively small organisation it may be easy to develop a simple top-down structure to deal with work tasks and problems as they arise. As the organisation grows, tasks become more complex and it is essential to avoid developing very messy structures for dealing with these problems. Problems often arise as to who is responsible for what, and who should make particular types of decision. Figure 12.19 depicts this diagrammatically. Structure 2 is clearly very messy and disorganised.

Figure 12.19 Development of a messy structure

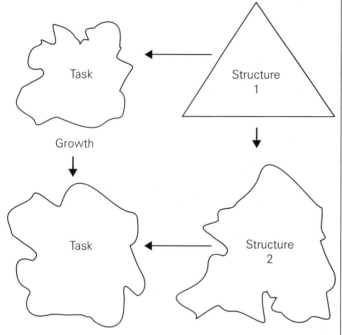

Clearly as organisations take on more work and expand into new areas they will require an upgraded level of organisation. This is particularly true today as organisations operate in a dynamic environment, with:

■ unpredictable shifts in demand
■ unexpected changes in sources of supply
■ continual customer demands for creativity or novelty
■ rapid technological changes.

The form of a very simple small organisation may be sketched as shown in Figure 12.20(a). The same organisation, as it becomes more complex, will increasingly become dependent on what **Henry Mintzberg** referred to as the **technostructure** – specialist staff who are responsible for quality standards and the ordering of materials. There will also be the need for new support staff who are concerned with providing a range of services like building maintenance, canteen facilities, public relations, and cleaning services. The organisation thus reconfigures to be more complex, as depicted in Figure 12.20(b).

Figure 12.20 (a) A simple form; (b) a reconfigured form

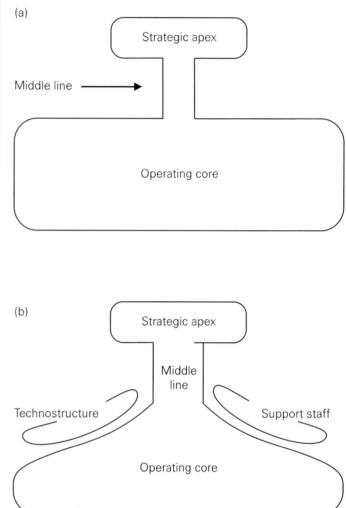

Developing an effective and efficient organisation depends on getting the right blend of roles. Clearly there is a lot of scope for tension. For example, middle line managers may feel that the technostructure takes some decision-making powers away from them. Unless there is effective cooperation between these two areas there may be a great loss of potential. At the same time, support staff may feel that they are not really a part of the decision-making process at all, and this may lead to lack of motivation. It is possible that support managers may begin to develop their own goals and objectives which contrast with the strategic goals. Clearly the well-managed organisation will be one in which decision-making is related closely to organisational objectives.

Case Study
Effective reconfiguration

Thomas Vollmann and Mark Brazas of IMD Lausanne suggest that organisational reconfiguration can be used as a tool to cope with radical changes in markets and technologies. Their idea is that a small, dedicated project team, often competing with other teams, can deal better with new emerging niche markets or new technologies than can an existing sub-unit within a company, even though the latter has been good at doing traditional work within the organisation.

However, care must be taken that the new 'start-up' entrepreneurial activity is integrated into the overall organisation in the dimensions where integration is important – where synergies are available. Preserving the project team's creativity, independence and freedom to try new, unconventional approaches, while keeping it integrated in the overall organisational framework, can be a delicate task in project management, which must address these issues:

- mission and goals
- resource allocation criteria
- performance measurement criteria
- decision-making responsibilities
- career path management.

Questions for discussion

1 *What advantages are there to be gained from reconfiguring an organisation by developing new project teams rather than giving new work to existing units?*
2 *Why might an existing unit not be a good place to locate new work and projects?*
3 *When an organisation creates new project teams, what factors will determine how effective these are in developing the organisational structure?*
4 *Why might it be difficult to balance unconventional new approaches with present approaches?*
5 *Why must project management address the issues of missions and goals, resource allocation criteria, performance measurement criteria, decision-making responsibilities and career path management in this instance?*

Symptoms of efficiency and deficiency

In judging whether an organisation is efficient or not, a number of contextual factors must be considered, including:

- the environment in which it operates (e.g. dynamic or static).
- the cultural background against which it is placed (e.g. different national and regional cultures)
- its internal culture (e.g. is it based on enterprise and initiative or on routine procedures?)
- the technology it employs.

Kenyon Greene, in his book *The Adaptive Organisation*, has written that 'the concept of organisation and environment is one of the most critical to modern management'. Maintaining a fit between an organisation and its external and internal environments is crucial. Greene identifies the external environments as comprising:

- the natural
- the technological
- the human resources
- the political
- the social or socio-economic
- the market.

In the internal environment the most significant components are:

- productivity
- motivational dynamics (more job satisfaction)
- value and attitude change
- new organisational goals
- effects of new technologies
- uses and misuses of power.

Case Study
In search of excellence

In 1982, Peters and Waterman (in their book *In Search of Excellence*) set out eight characteristics of 'excellent' innovative US companies. These were:

a *A bias towards action.* These organisations have a 'can do' and 'let's try' approach. People within these firms are enterprising. Managers get out of their offices and keep in touch informally with what is happening throughout the organisation. At Hewlett Packard this is referred to as MBWA ('management by wandering about').
b *Keeping close to the customer.* These US companies have an obsession with the customer. They are market-led and are concerned to find out the real needs and wants of customers.
c *Autonomy and entrepreneurship.* Innovative companies foster many leaders and innovators at all levels of the organisation.
d *Productivity through people.* 'Excellent companies' treat

the ordinary members of their organisations as the basic source of quality and productivity gains. Such organisations are opposed to an 'us and them' approach.

e *Hands-on, value driven.* Those at the top of such an organisation need to work hard to maintain the values of the company in a very public hands-on way. Senior managers are renowned for getting involved in the actual processes (design, selling etc.), thus publicly demonstrating their commitment to high standards.

f *'Stick to the knitting'.* These companies don't move into areas they know nothing about; they concentrate on what they can do best, and move on one manageable step at a time.

g *Simple form, lean staff.* 'Excellent' firms have a simple clear structure, with only the necessary number of people being employed in each function.

h *Simultaneous loose–tight properties.* These companies are both centralised and decentralised. Independent decision-making tends to be pushed down to the divisions, to the product development team and to the shop-floor. However, some key aspects of the organisation are controlled from the centre; e.g. quality, reliability, action, regular communication and quick feedback.

Questions for discussion

1 *Which of the above features of 'excellent' organisations are related to organisational structure?*

2 *Try to sum up in a brief statement of about 100 words Peters and Waterman's conclusions about aspects of efficient organisation.*

3 *In 1993, Peters and Waterman revealed that a number of the organisations that had shown excellence in 1982 had fallen behind. What environmental factors may have contributed to this loss of excellence?*

Kenyon Greene asserted that a major deficiency of many organisations is that they wait until a crisis descends upon them before responding. What organisations should do is anticipate crises and have a pre-plannned response. They should:

- sense and measure the present state within the internal environment
- provide alternative future configurations of the organisation based on forecasting and judgement
- sense and measure the present state within the external environment
- provide alternative future configurations of the relevant external environments
- provide an adaptable, dynamic model of on-going interrelationships between the organisation and the environment

- assess present and future goals, and ways of resolving conflicts between goals
- provide a cluster of flexible plans for change
- provide and develop a cluster of flexible actions which enable the organisation to move forward in a change environment.

The key is to develop self-organising/self-adaptive systems – literally 'the learning organisation'. Organisational structures need to be flexible and managers need to look to future changes. Unfortunately managers often place a low value on events, resources, people and situations that are at one remove in time and space, and place more value on the here-and-now. They also place too much reliance on things over which they have little control. Poor communication, disagreements and personality clashes can lead to low motivation and poor organisational performance.

Structures need to foster creative thinking and the ability to see possibilities that no-one has seen before. If managers expect people to be innovative, and give their permission for it, innovation is most likely to happen. However, this will occur only if the organisation is configured in such a way that decision-making is spread across the organisation, with informal structures and open communications. Managers need to trust employees and reward systems linked to innovation and success. Importantly, employees should know that if they fail then they can learn from their mistakes. An entrepreneurial organisation will invest heavily in management development and training. There should also be a toleration of mavericks because they often make things work and come up with unexpected solutions.

It is not too difficult to spot the symptoms of an *inefficient organisation*. There will be a lack of clarity about who is to make the decisions and too many levels in the chain of command. There will be duplication of the same tasks in different segments of the organisation, and poor use of resources and time. There will also be an unwillingness to adapt to new circumstances or new problems.

Manifest and latent functions

Writers sometimes draw a distinction between the **manifest** and **latent** functions of an organisation. The manifest functions are what appear on the surface to be the obvious functions of the organisation or its activities. The manifest function of a hierarchical structure might be to ensure that there is a clear chain of command and that some member of the organisation has overarching responsibility for decision-making. In contrast, latent functions are not obvious or explicit. For example, a latent function of a hierarchical organisation may be to exert a dominant top-down power culture within the organisation.

The manifest function of holding a meeting may be to convey information to those who attend, but the latent function may be to make it clear to staff who is in charge!

It is important that both the manifest and the latent functions should coincide with organisational objectives. This is not always the case. Sometimes the manifest functions coincide with organisational goals whereas the reality is that there is a potential for organisational goals to be subverted by the latent functioning of parts of the organisation. For example, a project team set up to develop new ideas may become an elite group which works just for its own ends. Again, the manifest function of having a clear pattern of control may be to assist decision-making, whereas the latent functioning may be that the organisation becomes bogged down in red tape.

Symptoms of inappropriate organisational structure

John Jackson and Cyril Morgan, in their book *Organisational Theory*, have identified the following symptoms of inadaptability in organisational structure:

■ Organisational decision-makers may not be able to anticipate problems before they occur. There may be a tendency in the organisation to wait until problems occur and then react to them because the organisation simply does not have enough information to develop contingency plans.

■ Decision-makers may err in trying to predict trends in their decision environment. Without proper coordination across divisions, the organisation may lose control over the relationship between its internal functioning and its environment.

■ The organisation may not be able to get information for decision-making.

■ The organisation, having identified a problem *vis-à-vis* its environment, may simply not be able to take corrective action quickly enough.

Symptoms of a poor fit between structure and environment may also reveal themselves in role conflicts and ambiguity. Clearly then there will be a need to tackle basic design issues for organisational structures.

These symptoms are the kind of things managers should be aware of as indicators of dysfunctional organisation design.

Synergy and design choice

When an organisation is based on multi-business lines (e.g. a conglomerate producing a variety of different products) then it may make sense to divide it up into a series of separate business divisions each perhaps based on a product line. However, for a single-business enterprise the emphasis needs to be to *create that structure which most effectively coordinates the specialised activities of an essentially integrated business unit*. If effective integration takes place then the business will benefit from **synergy**.

> *SYNERGY occurs when the sum of the parts working together is greater than the individual parts working on their own.*

A well-organised business structure will create synergy. For example, substantial advantages can be gained from coordinating activities such as finance, research and development, technology etc. Important decisions to be made include:

■ What activities should be pooled at corporate level?

■ How will interaction among divisions be developed and enhanced?

■ How will the management control system support these developments?

Galbraith and Nathanson, in their book *Strategy Implementation*, set out alternatives in a continuum ranging from high inter-division autonomy to high interdivision synergy (see Figure 12.21).

Figure 12.21 Galbraith and Nathanson's design alternatives.

	Continuum	
	Autonomy	**Synergy**
■ Corporate staffing level	Few	Many
■ Policies encouraging inter-division transactions	Weak	Strong
■ Performance control	Divisional only	Multiple

Corporate staffing level

At the synergy end of the continuum there will be a large number of staff working together collaboratively. They learn from one another, bouncing ideas and providing more knowledgeable insights based on shared understandings. However, this reduces the autonomy of individual divisions to make decisions, which may be stifling and slow down the decision-making process.

Inter-divisional transactions

Inter-divisional transactions at the autonomy end of the continuum result from a perceived need being identified by a divisional manager. The divisional manager then instigates the transaction. The weakness of this system is that transactions are unlikely to be made which weaken the profitability of the individual division concerned. This may weaken the overall operation of the business. At the synergy end of the continuum the emphasis would be on organising transactions to serve the needs of the whole business.

Control system

The arguments here are similar. At the synergy end of the continuum the control system is designed to meet the overall needs of the organisation, contrasted with divisional needs at the autonomy end of the continuum.

Part 3 Designing organisations

Starting from objectives

Organisation theory is concerned with identifying ways in which organisations are or should be structured in order to best meet the needs and aspirations of various stakeholders. In terms of management, the purpose of organisation is to work out and then make clear to all concerned what responsibilities are being delegated to which positions.

Much of the early work on organisational theory was put together by managers who were simply passing on their practical experiences. Their writings should therefore be seen as a combination of management and organisational theory. We have already seen that F. W. Taylor and the 'scientific management' school saw employees as being little more than machines. Henri Fayol described the formal organisation in terms of responsibility and authority linking the layers of employees within an organisational hierarchy. Max Weber focused on the importance of manifest rules and procedures, to which officials need to be seen to adhere. These early theories had a profound impact on the way in which large organisations were structured.

However, as we have already suggested in this chapter, tall hierarchical organisations based on bureaucratic lines may today no longer be appropriate in many fields of activity. Now, one of the most common methods of designing an organisation is to focus on objectives. For example, a typical proposal is:

1 Identify objectives.
2 Identify the major work necessary to meet those objectives.
3 Start at the bottom and organise the end activities first.
4 Decide what management positions are needed to manage the end activities and the intermediate management positions.
5 Group the related work and positions together in terms of desired results.
6 Make sure that the groupings form balanced packages with appropriate organisational status.
7 Establish an appropriate number of subordinates for each manager.

Clearly such an approach is logical and methodical, but designers rarely get the opportunity to build an organisation from scratch. The task is more usually one of restructuring an existing organisation. Restructuring enables an organisation to refocus on its objectives and to accommodate changes that have taken place in its environment. (It also has the latent function of enabling managers to appear active and thus enhance their position.) Redesigning an organisation follows the steps shown in Figure 12.22.

Figure 12.22 Steps in reorganising

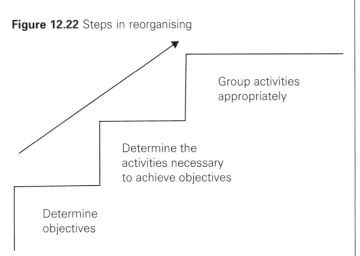

Litterer, in his book *The Analysis of Organisations*, proposed a means/ends chain which gives a clear picture of how an organisation can be organised to meet particular end objectives (see Figure 12.23).

The diagram depicts a situation in which key goals are set out. Then for each level of activity a means to the desired end is established. Clearly such an organisational structure is based on effectiveness.

Such a model is not built perfectly overnight. It develops out of practice, analysis of practice, and ongoing

Figure 12.23 Relating means to ends

evaluation, which requires a keen understanding of corporate strategy and of effective communication.

An important ingredient in the success of the organisation will be job design. Blocks of work will need to be identified and allocated to specific individuals who are organised into particular sections. These blocks of work will be identified as meeting the objectives of the organisation.

However, jobs should not be designed solely to meet the bare needs of the organisation. Consideration should also be given to the people who perform those jobs. *Job enrichment* involves giving an employee an increase in responsibility or recognition so that he or she feels that the contribution made is more highly appreciated. Ways of doing this vary from an employee being given a new title, to an extension of the perks associated with a particular job.

Job enlargement involves giving an employee a wider range of responsibilities. An employee who feels that a job is going 'stale' and as a result is losing interest in it may feel rejuvenated when asked to take on additional tasks.

Other aspects of organisational design

Earlier in this chapter we saw that a variety of organisational structures are available to the organisational designer. The structure chosen will depend on many contextual factors. In some cases it may be desirable to structure the organisation to cope with the sequencing of activities, and in other cases it may be important to group together a number of interrelated functions in a project team. Clearly, a key consideration should be to provide a structure that helps to coordinate interdependent activities.

In the course of time it may be necessary to change the structure to meet the changing reality of the organisational environment.

Case Study
Restructuring at IBM

Throughout the 1980s and early 90s, IBM was cited as one of the world's excellent companies with its large profits in the computer and communications market. Suddenly the situation changed as the world was flooded with new competing products. 'Big Blue', as International Business Machines is known, recorded the world's largest ever trading loss. IBM became an urgent case for restructuring and downsizing.

One of the first major changes introduced by the new Chief Executive, Lou Gerstner, was to reorganise the 70 000 strong sales force.

The new plan superimposes a sales force organised according to the industry of IBM clients on the firm's traditional geographic and product hierarchy. Instead of selling, say, mainframes in Italy, reps are now assigned to 14 global teams – one for banking clients, one for the travel industry, one for multinational oil companies, etc. Each team provides customers with information-processing systems tailored to their industry.

The new sales teams, with pay based on customer satisfaction, bypass country managers and instead report to 14 industry managers located around the world. For tax, employment and cultural reasons, IBM will continue to handle certain operations locally, like manufacturing, maintenance and repairs. The new structure is a matrix one.

Multinational clients had complained that it was impossible to deal with IBM as a single entity. Each country subsidiary set its own prices and wrote its own contracts, and sales people for different IBM products and services failed to provide coherent systems solutions. Nor were customers getting the benefits of IBM's global reach.

The industry teams, which include thousands of newly recruited business consultants, are also better positioned – between the customer and the technology – to influence the design of new systems. IBM has in the past come up with exciting new products, but its hierarchical structure often meant that years were wasted before these solutions were applied. This was a problem in North America – a market with only one country manager. It was even more a problem in Europe – a market with many separate country managers. In Europe country managers had acquired considerable powers.

Reorganising along client lines has been difficult in Europe because the existing divisions were run by nationals. Clients found it easier to wring special discounts and service packages from IBM local sales people.

In 1993 IBM saw its turnover drop by 13 per cent and the business lost a record $1.7 billion. However, things are beginning to look up. The company is shedding a lot of labour (10 000 employees in Europe in 1994) and carrying out other cost-cutting exercises.

Questions for discussion

1 *Identify some of the structural weaknesses in IBM that necessitated changes.*

2 *What should IBM have done to identify changes in its business environment?*
3 *Identify the structural changes that have taken place in the organisation of IBM's sales activities.*
4 *What problems might IBM face in pushing through its restructuring programme?*
5 *Identify any problems or weaknesses in the new arrangements.*
6 *What do you think will be the main benefits to IBM from its restructuring?*

Centralisation and decentralisation

Centralisation means keeping major responsibilities in an organisation within sections or units of the central headquarters. **Decentralisation** describes a situation in which many specific responsibilities have been delegated to branches. Delegation is the process of assigning responsibilities and decentralisation is the end result (see Figure 12.24).

Figure 12.24 The difference between centralisation and decentralisation

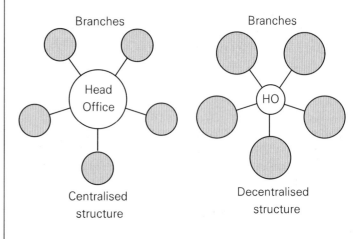

Organisations may choose to centralise certain key functions such as strategic planning and accounts, and purchasing in a retailing organisation. Other functions – such as recruitment – may be decentralised (i.e. left up to branches or departments).

While many firms are geographically centralised with major decisions being taken at the head office, others are organisationally centralised with decision-making being in the hands of a small group or section of management. When a centralised firm decides to push out new areas of decision-making to its middle or lower managers, or to its branches, then it is engaging in decentralisation.

Case Study
Centralisation/decentralisation at Shell UK

For any company, but particularly one with a wide geographical spread and a huge range of product types, decentralisation of one kind or another is essential. Most decisions, especially tactical ones, cannot be taken effectively at the centre, which may be miles or continents away, because they have to be taken quickly, on the spot, by people who know all the circumstances. There is often no time for a referral back to central office, even if it has a complete understanding of that particular problem.

One way of encouraging decentralisation that involves changing the structure of the company is to 'flatten' the organisational hierarchy by removing one or more of its layers, so that each divisional head reports directly to the Managing Director rather than to other directors who themselves report to the top person.

Another way is to create separate profit centres – sections of the overall business that are given the responsibility and resources (and guidance where necessary) to operate as if they were independent. For instance, Shell's bitumen business is now run by Shell Bitumen UK, a separate profit centre within Shell Oil UK. Emstar Ltd is responsible for Shell's energy management business in the UK, and Synthetic Chemicals Ltd, a subsidiary of Shell Chemicals UK, specialises in fine chemicals. Strategic decisions, with long-term implications for all parts of the company, are still taken centrally. Even so, many different people will be required to contribute to them, simply because the amount of input needed when a major decision has to be made can be immense.

Of course all decisions, at whatever level, are made in the context of the company's specific business objectives. These are determined by central management, but have to be in line with the general directions, capacities and culture of the company.

Questions for discussion

1 *Why does Shell need to make some decisions centrally?*
2 *Why is it important for Shell to decentralise some of its decision-making?*
3 *How might Shell benefit from such decentralisation?*
4 *What criteria should be used to decide whether decisions must be made at the centre? Will these criteria change in the course of time?*

Reasons for decentralisation

Not all situations can be understood in depth by the small number of people at the top of an organisation. The information may be very complex, varied and specialised, and it may be difficult to transfer information accurately from the edges to the top of an organisation.

Secondly, as in the Shell case study, decentralisation allows a swift response to local needs and conditions.

Thirdly, decentralisation can encourage employee motivation. Giving local staff more responsibilities is likely to result in their feeling involved in the organisational decision-making process.

Fourthly, an organisation that is strongly centralised needs to be highly regimented with little scope for individual initiative. This is what characterised eastern bloc centrally planned economies prior to *perestroika*. There is inflexibility and the need for constant supervision of subordinates.

Vertical and horizontal decentralisation

Vertical decentralisation exists when decision-making authority is pushed down through the layers of the organisation so that several layers of management and supervisory workers are allowed to make decisions. *Horizontal* decentralisation occurs when decision-making authority is pushed sideways across an organisation, perhaps by giving powers to the technocracy as well as to middle management.

Structural integration and business functions

There is no 'ideal' level of decentralisation for organisations. However, the goal should be to create the most efficient pattern of allocation of resources and to enable all problems to be given concentrated effort.

When dealing with complex and sophisticated tasks in a changing business environment it is often necessary to engage a range of experts in decision-making. This suggests a decentralised form of decision-making.

Tom Burns, in his book *Industrial Man: Selected Readings*, has described organic systems as those that are adapted to unstable conditions, when new and unfamiliar problems and requirements continually arise which cannot be broken down and distributed among specialist roles within a hierarchy. In this situation jobs lose much of their formal definition and the definitive and enduring demarcation of functions becomes impossible.

Responsibilities and functions, and even methods and powers, have to be redefined constantly. Each individual has to do his or her job with a knowledge of the overall purpose and circumstances of the organisation.

Interaction runs laterally as much as vertically, and communication between people of different ranks tends to resemble lateral rather than vertical command.

The trend today is towards flexible organisations, with teams of people coming together from various functional areas to work collaboratively on projects and in problem-solving activities. What is needed is a structure that allows the forming and reforming of expert groups, yet maintains the integrity of existing groups within the organisation. This structure will be more fluid then a matrix one. We look at this in more depth in the following chapter.

Further reading

- *Business Advanced* by Dave Needham and Robert Dransfield. Heinemann Educational, 1995.
- *Business Management* by Robert Erskine. Prentice Hall, 1991.
- *Management Appreciation* by Helen Harding. Pitman, 1987.
- *Management Theory and Practice*, 4th edition, by G. A. Cole. DPP, 1993.
- *Introduction to Management* by Richard Pettinger. Macmillan, 1994.
- *A Passion for Excellence* by T. Peters and N. Austin. Warner Books, 1990.

13 Changing structures

On completion of this chapter students will be able to:

- identify different organisational environments

- analyse the relationships between various structures and an organisation's performance and development

- participate in the management of organisational change.

The interface

An organisation is traditionally defined as a group of people with a common purpose. According to this view, the organisation is a distinct entity separate from its environment. A **boundary** can be drawn between the organisation and its environment. The task of the organisation is to maintain an adaptive equilibrium with its environment. The need for change occurs first outside the boundary and the organisation adapts accordingly. Taking this conventional view, the organisation can be identified as all or some of the following:

- *a physical place* – for example a department store in town such as Heelas in Reading
- *a particular group of people* – all the people who work for Heelas
- *a set of goals with systems* – Heelas as a profit-orientated organisation, which shares profits with employees, and with buying and selling systems designed to achieve certain goals
- *structures, procedures, informal behaviours and cultures for achieving goals* – at Heelas, a system in which employees are held to be 'partners' in the organisation, an emphasis on service and politeness, an ethos of looking after staff, etc.

The **environment** in which an organisation operates is all or some of the following:

- *a physical place* – for example the centre of Reading
- *a set of conditions* – for example a competitive retailing market involving organised buying and selling conditions and trading rules
- *a collection of individuals and other groups* – suppliers, customers, local council officials, VAT inspectors, competing organisations, etc.

Ralph Stacey, in his book *The Chaos Frontier*, suggests that the above is a too simplified view of the organisational environment. He argues that the

Figure 13.1 The traditional view of an organisation in its environment

environment is more than the physical places and groups of people around it. He says that what we should focus on are the *actions and perceptions* of an organisation. The only relevant environment is made up of those external factors *which create potential for action*. Thus, to continue our example, the relevant environment for Heelas in Reading is made up of those people who directly influence its actions and perceptions – the carpet dealers who supply carpets, the retailers in Reading it competes with, etc. According to Stacey:

> *'The environment of organisation A is really that set of its own actions and perceptions which are prompted or required by the environment, if organisation A is to survive and prosper. And that set of actions is unbounded, to all intents and purposes infinite [because there are so many potential actions and perceptions]'*

All the time, organisation A carries out a variety of its own actions which impact on the environment. Stacey argues that we should think of these actions 'as being organisation A itself'. An example of an action taken by A which impacts on the environment is a polluting process, or advertising that impacts on people's perceptions. The range of actions organisation A can take will be finite:

> *'So, organisation A itself is that set of its own actions and perceptions to which the environment has to adapt, and organisation A's environment is that set of its own actions and perceptions that it undertakes to adapt to its environment.'*

This broader view of the organisation and its environment is very helpful because it alerts us to the importance of the **interface** and the way in which the organisational boundary is constantly an interface between actions and perceptions. The relationship is thus a highly dynamic one (see Figure 13.2).

Static and dynamic environments

Open systems theorists are concerned with the relationship between a system and its environment. A large number of such theorists point to the interaction between the internal and external environments of an organisation in determining actions, change and growth. A lot of emphasis is placed on the external environment and the way in which it impacts on organisational activity.

Figure 13.2 Dynamic interaction between an organisation and its environment

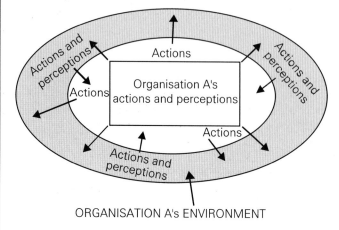

ORGANISATION A's ENVIRONMENT

Using case studies, Emery and Trist outlined 'typology of organisational environments', which are seen as being the causes for organisations being created within the environment. They devised a continuum from 'static' (or 'routine') to 'dynamic' (or 'turbulent') environments, and specified four major types, which we look at below.

A dynamic environment acts as a major constraint on the goals that can be set by the organisation and on the achievement of these goals (see Figure 13.3). Clearly this is because there is so much change going on and because the nature and pace of the change is unpredictable.

Figure 13.3 Environment and goal-setting

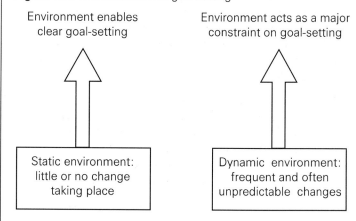

Type one – placid/random

The organisation cannot predict this environment but can act independently of it. In this environment organisations can exist as single, small units. This is the simplest form of environment. It represents the state of pure competition which is recognised in economics – there are a lot of small producers, each producing a very small part of the overall market.

Type two – placid/clustered

This is still a very quiet, slowly moving environment. Organisations survive by planning and predicting changes in the environment. Organisations are larger and more hierarchical than in type one.

Type three – disturbed/reactive

In this situation the organisation in question will need to consider a number of similar organisations (i.e. competitors). The existence and actions of these other organisations make it more difficult to predict the environment. Flexibility will be important if the organisation is to survive and this encourages decentralisation. In business this situation may exist when there are a relatively small number of competing firms.

Type four – turbulent field

This is a highly complex situation with a rapidly changing environment resulting from:

- interconnections between organisations
- greater interdependence between society and economic organisations
- increased use of research and development to meet competition.

Making sense of static conditions

In static conditions an organisation is faced with an environment which is relatively easy to understand and where changes are few. Johnson and Scholes, in their book *Exploring Corporate Strategy*, suggest that raw material suppliers and some mass manufacturing companies may perhaps be in this type of environment. Technical processes are straightforward, competition and markets may remain the same over time, and there may be few producers.

However, when one searches for examples of static conditions it is increasingly difficult to find them in modern economies. At one time we could have quoted funeral directors, solicitors and opticians as being good examples. However, these areas have been exposed to considerable changes and growing competition in recent years.

Task

From your own experience and reading, try to identify organisations that continue to operate in relatively static conditions.

In static conditions it is possible to analyse the past in order to forecast the future. In situations of low complexity it might also be possible to identify predictors of environmental influences – for example, where the sales of a particular product are closely related to real disposable income, or where the demand for a product is dependent on the growth in population in a specific region.

Making sense of dynamic conditions

In dynamic conditions it becomes difficult if not impossible for organisations to use the past in order to forecast the future. This may be the case when organisations operate in highly volatile international markets, where there are sudden and unpredictable leaps forward in technology, rapidly changing consumer preferences etc.

In these conditions the interpretation of events may be based on inspiration rather than cold and calculated analysis. Managers need to employ a range of techniques in order to minimise uncertainty. For example, they may use decision-tree analysis (see Chapter 11), or scenario planning where they predict a number of possible future scenarios before selecting the most likely. Increasingly managers are using computer forecasting and expert systems to juggle a multitude of variables. In such situations managers need to be generalists who have a broad feel for a host of environmental factors, including an understanding of politics, economics, technology, social, cultural and other issues and trends.

Making sense of complex conditions

Many organisations operate in highly complex environments. A multinational organisation is faced by complexity because of its diversity and because of the complexity that exists in each of its markets. The changeable nature of trading relations adds to this complexity.

One way of dealing with complexity is to allow separate units and divisions to focus on specific tasks, issues and problems – through decentralisation. Where organisations require vast quantities of information, sophisticated information management systems will be required to facilitate decision-making and analysis. Models may be developed to provide an outline of environmental conditions which can be used to predict likely changes.

In looking at the organisational environment, Johnson and Scholes draw together the following suggestions:

- If the organisation's environment is fairly static and simple, a detailed analysis of past environmental influences is a very simple and sensible procedure.

- The more the environment becomes dynamic, the more a focus on the future is essential – perhaps through some exercise such as scenario building.
- The more complex the environment becomes, in terms of information processing, the more it may be necessary to move towards more sophisticated techniques such as model-building and simulation.

Case Study
Changes in the telecommunications industry

From 1995 the world's largest telecommunications company, AT&T, is allowed to offer telephone services in the UK. The Department of Trade and Industry awarded the company a full public telecommunications operator's licence in 1994, allowing it to compete head-on with BT and Mercury.

The awarding of the licence came only weeks after Mercury, BT's biggest rival, announced 2500 job losses and a refocusing on its strongest market segments. Mercury's decision was viewed by some as a serious setback to competition in the UK telephone market.

The American AT&T's decision to enter the UK market is an indicator that competition is, in fact, increasing rather than decreasing, with US companies taking the lead. Several large US cable companies have plans to move into the UK telephone market.

In 1994 AT&T had 60 per cent of the long-distance telephone market in the USA. It planned to start offering services to UK businesses in August 1995, followed rapidly by a public telephone service.

AT&T has spelt out that it does not want to become embroiled in a price war, but rather wants to differentiate in terms of quality and service. The company is unlikely to build its own network because of the amount of available capacity on existing networks owned by BT, Mercury and other companies.

AT&T regards the UK as a vitally important market. The top three destinations for telephone traffic leaving the USA are Canada, Britain and Mexico.

Questions for discussion

1 *Using the information given, as well as personal knowledge, state what sort of environment British Telecom is operating in.*
2 *How is this environment likely to impact on the actions that are open to BT, in responding to competition?*
3 *How is the nature of the environment in which BT operates likely to impact on its ability to define and meet clear goals?*
4 *How are the actions of BT likely to influence its environment?*
5 *What do you see as being the major changes which will take place once AT&T and other US telephone companies start to compete in UK markets?*

Influence of technological change on stability

Today more than ever we are seeing an acceleration in the complexity of the technologies used by organisations for different purposes and processes. Johnson and Scholes have argued that the more sophisticated the technology employed by an organisation, the more elaborate the organisational structure will need to be. The reasons for saying this are as follows.

- A good deal of responsibility must be passed to the specialists concerned with the technology – the technocrats. This requires new relationships with management teams as well as with the operational core. In turn this may require the development of project teams, work groups, etc.
- The development of technology may lead to increased centralisation or decentralisation. For example, the use of bar-code scanning in retailing enables far more control from a centralised head office. Conversely, information technology may support decentralisation when independent project teams are able to draw on centralised services such as central data banks to their own ends, to make their own decisions.
- The extent to which an organisation needs to be innovative affects the extent to which experts drawn from disciplines across the organisation are pulled together, often for short periods of time for project work.

The **technological imperative** is that, frequently, work needs to be reorganised and organisation charts redrawn to cope with new technological requirements. In particular, the widespread use of IT and automated practices has meant that modern work requires fewer operatives and more complex machinery. It is far easier for managers to check on operational performance using information systems. This means that structures will regularly be altered to meet the needs of the time. Today's restructuring process may be outmoded tomorrow. Interrelationships between departments and groups of workers will alter when they work with new technologies.

New technology develops both within an organisation and in the organisational environment. The faster the rate of change of technology, the greater the number of changes that will need to be made within the organisational structure.

The contingency view

We have seen that there is no single best way to set up an organisation. Organisations operate within a wide variety of environments and these frequently change. A **contingency view** means that there is no 'one best way' to organise – it all depends on the situation.

At the end of the day, organisational designers have to say 'Today's structure depends on x, y and z factors. This may be the case tomorrow but we are not sure. It all depends on . . .'.

Part 2 Performance related to structure

Chapter 12 outlined a variety of different organisational structures. Here we analyse the relationship between structure and an organisation's performance and development.

Matching environment and structure

Jackson and Morgan have compared the structural features of an organisation with features of the environment using a contingency adaptation approach coupled with the dimension of complexity (Figure 13.4). Jackson and Morgan suggest the following analysis:

- In *Environment 1*, successful organisation will be mechanistic with bureaucratic structures. Companies will use standardised work processes as the means of control. These organisations cope well in a stable environment with few changes.
- In *Environment 2*, there will be some decentralisation and the use of standardised skills rather than processes. This will enable successful organisations to cope with moderately low uncertainty and a large number of environmental variables.
- In *Environment 3*, organic if centralised structures will be required. Usually there will be a need for close personal control to deal with increasing change.
- In *Environment 4*, there will be high uncertainty and a complex set of variables. This requires organic decentralised control coupled with close relationships between managers and specialists for control and results.

The range of structures

Peter Drucker, in his book *The New Realities*, has argued that in designing the building blocks of an organisation it is necessary to answer four questions. These should be kept in mind as we discuss a range of structures in the following paragraphs. His four questions are:

- What should be the units of organisation?
- What components should join together, and what components should be kept apart?
- What are the best size and shape for different components?
- What are the results needed from an organisation's structure?

Figure 13.4 Environmental/structural matching

	Simple knowledge environment	**Complex knowledge environment**
Placid environmental characteristics	1. MECHANISTIC ■ Little uncertainty ■ Little change ■ Standard work processes for control ■ Bureaucratic organisation *Examples:* Breweries Metal-box manufacture	2. MECHANISTIC ■ Moderately low uncertainty ■ Little change but a large number of variables in the environment ■ Standard work skill for control ■ Decentralised bureaucratic form *Examples:* Food products General hospitals
Turbulent environmental characteristics	3. ORGANIC ■ Moderately high uncertainty ■ Small number of variables but a lot of change ■ Tight personal control ■ Centralised organisation form *Examples:* Fast-food businesses Entrepreneurial firms	4. ORGANIC ■ High uncertainty ■ Large number of variables and a lot of change ■ Mutual adjustment for control ■ Decentralised organisation form *Examples:* Telecommunications High-technology firms

Bureaucratic structures

In modern times the 'dead hand' of bureaucracy has been subjected to criticisms on many fronts, not least in the eastern European bloc where sectors of the old state ministries have been dismantled. However, bureaucracy has a way of creeping back into large organisations that are based on posts and offices. It seems beyond dispute that bureaucracies rarely meet the needs of their many publics – those who control them, those who work in them, those who are clients or customers, etc. The criticisms can be summarised as follows:

■ They are rigid and not able to change.
■ They have an over-reliance on rules and regulations, rather than common sense, compassion and enterprise.
■ They encourage employees to become officious and status-conscious.

Case Study
The failure of bureaucratic organisation

While doing research for his highly acclaimed book *In Search of Management* (Routledge, 1994), Tony Watson worked as a participant observer at ZTC Ryland. As a result of his experiences he was able to identify some of the

ways in which organisations (and individuals who work for them) can become trapped in a series of little boxes, and the 'segmented thinking' which can become part of the culture of such structures. He illustrates the frustrations that managers can feel by quoting a number of examples, including the following:

' ''A lot of people have a very blinkered view. Take, for instance, finance. They have got a very strict set of rules which they apply and these don't always reflect the reality of (a) being in business and (b) customer requirements. And so you get all sorts of constraints put on you. Let me give you an example. In my budget two years ago I was going to spend half a million pounds on postage to send parcels out to customers, and this was based on the volume we knew we had to do multiplied by the cost of each package; good junior school sort of stuff. The accountants said 'You've got to cut your budget and Ted Meadows says that figure is too high.' My response was 'I don't care what Ted Meadows says, that is the figure and I stand by it.' They came back: 'But he still says it's too high.' 'OK then,' I said, 'cut it in half. It will make no difference.' And when it came back it was a quarter of a million pounds; it had been cut in half. Now he's got his objectives, he had to cut the budget and he saw this big chunk of money. And because he doesn't understand what happens, he just arbitrarily cuts it.''*

' ''So what did you do?'' I asked.

' "Nothing. I remained dignified, saying that this sort of thing is so stupid I am not prepared to discuss it. I went over budget by a quarter of a million pounds. This illustrates that somebody who is a financial whiz, no doubt, is so focused on getting a bottom line right that he is not prepared to find out what he is doing. You know. 'Cut this out, cut that, three less heads'; it's quite arbitrary." '

Questions for discussion

1 *What weaknesses of bureaucratic organisation are highlighted by this example?*
2 *Why might bureaucracies be likely to suffer from such weaknesses?*
3 *How might organisations seek to overcome the problems caused by 'segmented thinking'?*
4 *Can bureaucracies continue to survive in turbulent and complex organisational environments?*

Functional structures

A functional structure is based on the primary tasks that have to be performed by the organisation, such as production, marketing, finance etc. in a manufacturing company. These structures are commonplace and are typically found in organisations with a narrow product range. Businesses with a large product range will often be broken up into divisions, but each division is likely to have functional areas.

The advantages are that there are clear definitions of responsibilities, the control process is simpler to organise, specialist managers are employed, and the chief executive can be kept in touch with functional operations.

However, obvious weaknesses are that senior managers can begin to over-concentrate on routine operational activities and miss the important strategic decision-making process. There may be poor co-operation between functional areas. The organisation may also be poor at adapting to changing environmental conditions such as the development of new competition and technologies, because it is so wrapped up in operational activity.

Divisional structures

A divisional structure is one where the organisation is divided up into units which have responsibility for particular markets, product areas, services etc.

Multi-divisional organisations became particularly popular in the 1960s and 70s when many companies diversified into a range of products. At the time it was fashionable to spread your tentacles into a broad range of products.

Today the trend has been reversed, as organisations focus on their core lines.

Divisions are able to specialise and focus on their own particular problems and needs. Each division is able to develop targets and objectives which can be measured. A large organisation is able to acquire and divest itself of divisions depending on their performance and contribution to the whole organisation. Senior managers in the organisation are able to focus on strategy while divisional managers focus on operational activity.

Divisional structures have weaknesses. Tensions may arise between the centre of the organisation and its divisions. A number of divisional barons may develop each pulling in a different direction and fighting for resources and favours. This can lead to competition and conflict between divisions. Some divisions may grow too large as they focus on their own aggrandisement. The divisional organisation may be costly to run because it misses out on some economies of integrated activity. Finally, it may become difficult to coordinate the various divisions. The experience of the 1980s was that many organisations had spread their tentacles too broadly and had developed a soft underbelly of inefficiency.

Mechanistic and organic structures

Burns and Stalker, in their classic study of the electronics industry in the late 1950s and early 60s, stated the following:

'Industry organised according to principles of bureaucracy – by now traditional – is no longer able to accommodate the new elements of industrial life in the affluent second half of the twentieth century. These new demands are made by large-scale research and development and by industry's new relationship with its markets. Both demand a much greater flexibility in internal organisation, much higher levels of commitment to the commercial aims of the company from all its members, and an even higher proportion of administrators, controllers and monitors to operatives.'

Burns and Stalker drew a basic distinction between **mechanistic** and **organic** forms of organisation. The *mechanistic* form is represented by bureaucracy and is capable of being successful in a static environment. In contrast, *organic structures* are less rule-bound, have a less rigid division of labour, are less hierarchical and are more open to the influence of informal relationships within the organisation. There is greater emphasis on team-work and communication, and decision-making can be done literally across a network. Teams can share power and responsibility. Figure 13.5 contrasts lines of communication and command in mechanistic and organic forms of organisation.

Figure 13.5 Mechanistic and organic organisational structures

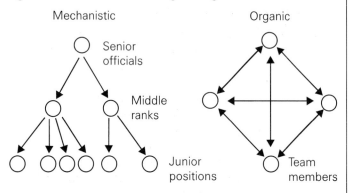

Organic structures are most likely to occur in groups where there is a need to share common expertise and skills. Such a network may be found among high-level technicians or research workers in the oil and chemical industries. Alternatively, it may be found in an advertising agency, where one person's skill might be drawing, another's design and layout, a third producing slogans and captions, and a fourth finding the best media for getting across a campaign. In such a system, members of an organisation are more likely to feel that their individual needs are being met – there is more of an opportunity for them to make an original contribution to decision-making and to feel that they are helping to shape organisational behaviour.

Organic approaches have also been successfully employed in manufacturing, particularly using the 'quality circle' approach. For example, today there are over 13 million Japanese participating in Quality Control Circles (QCCs), particularly in areas of production, related to science and engineering. QCCs arrived in this country in the 1980s mainly in manufacturing. Today QCCs are increasingly used in the service sector (e.g. in banks, universities and the civil service).

The process of organic team building is very important in a number of Japanese companies operating in the UK. The tractor manufacturer Komatsu aims to create a group spirit in its workforce at its greenfield site in Newcastle. The company has tried to keep terms and conditions the same for all employees. Everyone wears the same uniform, exercises in the morning, and starts and finishes at the same time and is entitled to the same sick pay and pension schemes. The aim behind this is to create a feeling of commonality and commitment. Groups of workers are organised in quality circles, with joint responsibility for identifying problems and coming up with solutions.

Although mechanistic (bureaucratic) and organic systems are in some ways in competition with each other, they may appear side-by-side in different parts of the same organisation. Mechanistic systems are often best suited to the pursuit of clear goals in stable conditions, such as producing a standard product for a market in which

demand is constant. Organic systems are most effective where conditions of demand, competition, production and other factors cannot be readily predicted.

Matrix structures

As we saw on page 332, the effect of matrix organisation is to separate a number of organisational activities into projects. At the same time the traditional structure (e.g. a functional hierarchy) determines the regular work for employees and patterns of interrelationships. Employees are assigned to a particular project, but when the project is completed the employees can fit back into their normal work pattern/roles. Of course, with a matrix structure an employee can be working on several projects at the same time.

It is important that each project be carefully managed by a project manager whose job it is to direct work towards the completion of the project. A project manager needs to be able to interact with a variety of people and to keep progress on schedule. The project manager will need to be able to motivate, communicate, develop challenging tasks and negotiate.

Developing a matrix structure is likely to be a major breakthrough for an organisation. At first it may seem a bit confusing to individuals who are not used to flexible working. People will be required to perform multiple roles, and sometimes they may be frustrated about the ambiguity of their roles ('How can I be expected to do my job well when you keep pulling me out to do . . .?'). The functional line manager may resent losing staff for a time. Another problem is that the condition *projectivitis* sets in – project team members become so obsessed with the project that unhealthy rivalries begin to develop between individuals and groups.

The main advantage of the matrix is that it enables individuals and teams to focus on specific projects, drawing together diverse skills. It also adds to the motivation of employees by broadening their experience of working life while giving them considerable responsibility. It fosters flexibility among employees and is generally an empowering process. Team members are then able to contribute more effectively to ongoing team projects.

Case Study
Developing CD–ROMs

Angela Jones works in the marketing and sales department of a publishing company. The marketing manager is Peter Davis.

Recently the company has decided to channel a lot of funds into the development of CD–ROM products. It will use current authors to develop computer books and simulations. The company has developed a link with a major software development agency who will write the programs for the new products.

Angela has been assigned as project manager to develop two CD–ROMs which will be sold internationally. One is an illustrated English dictionary, the other an illustrated world atlas. Angela is allowed to call on the expertise of the geography editor and the English editor within the publishing company. She will also need specialist support from the accounts and production departments. From time to time she will need to use specialist outside consultants.

Questions for discussion

1 *Do you think that appointing a project manager is a good way of developing the new CD–ROM products?*
2 *What qualities will Angela need to be an effective project manager?*
3 *What difficulties do you think Angela is likely to meet in developing these two projects to fruition?*
4 *What steps should Angela take to organise her project? Set out a flow chart, outlining the steps and highlighting those that may involve the most difficulty.*

Stages of organisational development and growth

Today it is widely recognised that organisations do not go through simple stages of development. There are so many internal and external influences that patterns of development are immensely complex.

A mathematical model can be used to study the problems likely to be faced by an organisation or any other organism going through a growth period. One possible mode of growth is **linear** (i.e. in a straight line). This might apply to an organisation faced by a fairly static market in which problems are easy to resolve without restructuring becoming necessary. Alternatively, an organisation may be faced by a period of **exponential growth**. Then, in each succeeding time period, the size of the organisational 'problem' increases by a constant percentage of the whole (see Figure 13.6). In each successive time period the difficulties are increased enormously. However, there may be a definite limit to the growth.

Figure 13.6 Types of growth

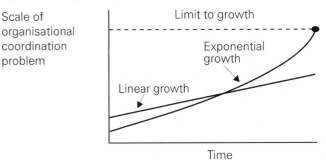

Although the presentation above is theoretical and mathematical, there is a very clear warning that as organisational problems grow they may become unmanageable.

In the 1970s L. E. Greiner, in his book *Evolution and Revolution as Organisations Grow*, set out five aspects of organisational growth:

- As the *size* of an organisation increases, problems of coordination and communication arise, particularly in a tall or dispersed organisation.
- The *older* an organisation is, the more deeply set will be the attitudes that exist within it, making it less flexible and difficult to change.
- In *evolutionary periods* there is little change in the management of the organisation, and reorganisation is gradual.
- In *revolutionary periods* there may be new management and new ideas. Substantial changes may need to be made because of the increase in size of the organisation or a radical alteration in its activities and environment.
- In a *rapidly growing industry* a business organisation may be forced to make changes. However, if the organisation is profitable it may be able to continue with existing practices.

According to Greiner, each evolutionary period is characterised by a dominant management style, and each revolutionary period by a dominant management problem.

Phases of growth

There are five phases of growth (see Figure 13.7). Each has a calm evolutionary period leading to a management crisis in which there is considerable confusion and conflict within the organisation. The period of crisis is the 'revolution'. Understanding the nature of the revolution requires a clear knowledge of the organisation's history and development.

Figure 13.7 Greiner's phases of growth

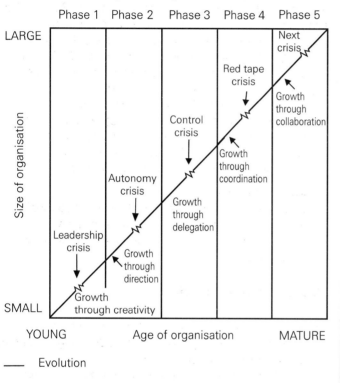

—— Evolution

Ν⁺ Revolution

The crises which occur during the growth of the organisation are as follows.

Crisis of leadership

In the early days of a small organisation there are likely to be close relationships between the owners and employees. Informal communication channels can be successful and stakeholders in the organisation will be committed to its success. As the organisation grows, new members join who are perhaps not as committed, forcing the owners into playing more of a managerial role with which they may not be comfortable. A crisis of leadership leads to the appointment of a professional manager.

Crisis of autonomy

As the organisation continues to grow it spreads and becomes more complex. Ground level supervisors will be more knowledgeable in specialist areas than managers. The supervisors will want to have more of a say in decision-making which lies within their competence. The crisis of autonomy will lead to a spreading of powers to those in junior management and supervisory posts.

Crisis of control

As the organisation devolves responsibilities lower down the hierarchy, senior managers begin to feel and to acknowledge that they are losing control of operations and over the interrelated functioning of the organisation. The crisis of control leads to the development of organisation-wide control systems.

Crisis of red tape

The organisation may start to become too large and bureaucratic, as a result of the complex coordination system. Confusion begins to develop between line and staff management and people are not clear about their responsibilities. There has to be collaboration involving more flexible management processes.

When Greiner was writing in the 1970s this pattern of growth and crises was fairly typical. It may be less so today as many organisations are developed by entrepreneurs with management training who are able to avoid some of the crises by building forward-looking organisations. However, you have only to read the newspapers and to study organisations in your own locality to discover many falling into the trap of crisis after crisis.

Centralisation and decentralisation

Chandler, in his historical study of business firms *Dupont and the Making of the Modern Corporation*, found that those operating in limited product markets using simple operations were fairly centralised and had functional structures. As such organisations moved into larger, more varied market conditions, they tended to develop complex control procedures. The businesses then moved towards increased vertical integration (i.e. taking over organisations operating at different stages of production, such as a wine bottling plant taking over a vineyard). This gave rise to a need for more specialisation to look after the flow of products from one vertical stage to another, which in turn led to a requirement for improved centralised service activities. For businesses that then moved into product diversification, the next step would be into a divisional structure. This was typical of a large percentage of UK businesses in the 1970s and 80s, resulting in increased decentralisation, specialisation of divisions and overall integration of organisations.

In recent years this decentralisation has become widespread in UK industry in manufacturing, services and in the public sector. Increasingly, organisations are split up into separate 'accountabilities'.

Case Study
A time of change at the BBC

John Birt took over as Director General of the British Broadcasting Corporation in January 1993. He immediately promised to create an effective BBC which would clear away red tape, territorialism and confusion.

The BBC's television services had overspent by £38 million in 1992. Birt said that a priority was to appoint a new finance director. Key structural changes would include:

- streamlining the operation to focus on aims and objectives, policy and performance
- the separation of programme production from commissioning and scheduling in television and radio, and the buying-in of programmes from a range of sources
- the creation of separate resources, engineering and service departments to run the production side.

So began the process of contracting out, reducing staff numbers, increasing productivity and rationalising studios and properties.

Birt prepared an all-embracing plan to take the BBC into a new world. Change was to be seen to be as important a part of the BBC's culture as was the aim to inform, educate and entertain. The architecture was created to monitor the progress, or lack of it, on a range of objectives. The emphasis that Birt wanted to establish was that programmes are the supreme objective, but only if the price and purpose are right.

The BBC has only recently begun to move from a culture of 'We know best; we are the best; we'll make it all ourselves; our size is our strength; what happens outside is their business.' Under Birt, the corporation is coming to realise that it has much to learn from competitors and that size can be a weakness. In a document called *Extending Choice*, the new management team at the BBC set out an agenda of distinctiveness, value-for-money and accountability. The first two of these are widely accepted; the concern comes over accountability.

The BBC has been criticised for seeming to show a lack of interest in what the public wants and requires. For example, some have complained that it has been too highbrow, concentrating on a minority upmarket taste. Also, competitors resent the BBC being (as they see it) unfairly subsidised by the government.

Birt has set the standard he would like to see for the BBC. He wants it to be the 'best managed public institution in the UK'. This was essential for the BBC to receive its new charter (which it was granted in 1994). The BBC receives substantial sums from the licence fees that the public pay for television viewing.

The new management regime has not been without its critics. For example, broadcaster Mark Tully openly criticised the corporation in late 1993. He claimed that an iron structure had been set in place in news and current affairs programming to restrict producers' freedom, and to ensure that they conform to what is known as 'Birtism'. He attacked the new 'internal-market' accounting methods which put a greater premium on bureaucracy than on creativity. Under this scheme, one part of the BBC must buy services from another at the full cost of the service (e.g. for using library services). Tully said:

> 'Accountants can easily argue that the whole management structure was too expensive, but it was that structure which preserved the independence of the various parts of the BBC and prevented the emergence of over-powerful director generals.'

He went on to argue:

> 'A broadcasting organisation which depends so much on individual human talent needs to have some flexibility, perhaps even an element of chaos, to allow for experimentation and eccentrics.'

Questions for discussion

1 *Where (if at all) does Birt's BBC seem to fit into Greiner's phases of growth? Is the BBC going through a revolutionary or evolutionary period?*
2 *Why is Birt trying to create an internal market at the BBC?*
3 *What advantages are there to be derived from breaking the BBC down into accountable sections?*
4 *What new developments and conditions are required if Birt's changes are to be effective?*
5 *What are the major stumbling blocks facing the BBC in its attempt to change practices and structure?*
6 *What do you think is meant by an 'effective' BBC?*
7 *What type of culture is Birt trying to establish at the BBC?*
8 *What new objectives is Birt trying to establish?*
9 *What is meant by creating an 'architecture . . . to monitor the progress . . . on a range of objectives'?*
10 *What factors are likely to determine whether the BBC is successful in making changes?*

The entrepreneurial organisation

In recent years, considerable emphasis has been placed on the **entrepreneurial organisation** as an alternative to the traditional organisations. Organisations today, faced by a turbulent environment of increasing competition, the widescale use of information technology, an emphasis on meeting consumers' needs, rapidly changing technologies, and many other factors, need to be innovative and enterprising.

The classic picture of the entrepreneur is that of one individual running a small business. However, recent American studies have shown that the companies demonstrating the biggest growth, and therefore in many ways the most entrepreneurial, were those that could be defined as medium-sized – those with turnovers between $25 million and $1 billion.

Common sense might suggest that the largest companies with the greatest resources should be the most innovative. However, bureaucratic practices can hold such organisations back. Stable markets can spell the death of entrepreneurship. The key to being competitive and entrepreneurial in today's harsh environment is to be big, but unbureaucratic. This has been termed **intrapreneurship**.

The challenge for large organisations is to devise ways of becoming intrapreneurial. Enterprise arises through *innovation*, particularly in developing new products and through process innovation – i.e. finding improvements to existing systems to improve quality, reduce costs, and so on. Opportunities for process innovation lie in new approaches such as 'just-in-time', quality-controlled production systems, etc. Some people suggest that it is better to leave the development of new products to new organisations. The implication for a large organisation is that new product development should be given to a new project team or structure which has considerable independence from the central organisation.

Innovative organisations need innovative people, and they need to create the structure within which these innovators can flourish. Innovators have the ability to think creatively, to see new opportunities arising from existing solutions, and the ability to put into practice new ideas. Many of the most effective organisations put extensive resources into making sure that they attract, recruit and retain the right people to foster an intrapreneurial culture. Innovative people may well be highly committed, slightly 'off-beat' people who would not fit in readily with a hierarchical structure.

The new entrepreneurial organisations therefore need to make sure that they encourage innovation and creativity

and that they create a culture of 'expectation' that innovation will be the normal, natural way of life of individuals within the organisation. The organisational structure must allow or encourage the following features.

- Innovation is encouraged and rewarded frequently.
- There is free access to information within the organisation. Employees have the ability to tap into information from any part of the organisation using advanced IT.
- Individuals are encouraged to talk to each other and to share experiences.
- Individuals are encouraged to look outside the organisation, to attend courses, and to meet freely with other experts in the field.
- The organisation is relatively flat and highly adaptable to a changing environment.
- There is a strong emphasis on the internal and external consumer and on servicing their needs.
- Managers have had experience in innovation so that they know what it feels like, enabling them to encourage others. Managers need to 'champion' innovation, helping the innovators to push through their ideas.

Expansion, consolidation and contraction

More research has been carried out into the relationship between the administrative component of an organisation and its size than into most other factors. It is commonly concluded that the fewer resources devoted to administration relative to direct production activities, then the more efficient the organisation should be. As a firm grows and benefits from economies of scale, the ratio of administrative costs to total costs should fall.

However, this argument may be a poor one. It assumes that administrators always detract from productivity, whereas in fact they may increase the total productivity of the organisation by introducing better control mechanisms, more efficient procedures etc.

Early research tended to indicate that as organisations expand they require a larger *proportion* of administrators in order to coordinate and integrate activities.

More recent studies indicate that they do indeed employ more administrators, but these comprise a smaller proportion of the total numbers employed – examples are seen in hospitals, schools and manufacturing organisations. Common sense and a number of empirical studies support the view that as organisations expand and become more complex, more administration is required.

However, they also benefit from economies of scale, leading to a decline in the proportion of administrative to other employees.

Organisations do need to be careful not to create unnecessary administrative work. Some managers will be happy to create unnecessary new posts simply to enlarge their own department – demanding new secretarial staff, supervisors etc. to push paper round the organisation.

Downsizing

During the 1980s many organisations engaged in **downsizing**, having found that they had grown too much. Decline in a market or crisis in a firm reduces the requirement for labour.

Major structural forces may affect whole industries, as happened in the 1980s. Factors leading to a reduction in demand for labour in manufacturing industry included the following:

- *Natural productivity growth* – Sales output per hour of labour input grew as a result of technological improvements in processes, product designs, and component materials. This affected mainly direct labour and indirect labour activities that supported manufacturing.
- *Information push-down* – Advances in information technology and information management transformed decision-making, management structures and the way in which work is done. Information push-down has tremendous potential to reduce the number of

administrators required as they are replaced by systems.

Natural productivity growth is particularly common in high-tech industries. Each year there can be improvements in the way manufacturing is organised, requiring dynamic restructuring. With each leap forward more can be produced with fewer people, unless there is a massive expansion in sales and other activities to compensate for the time savings.

Information push-down means that management layers can be eliminated. As Peter Drucker puts it in his book *The New Realities*:

> 'It turns out that whole layers of management neither make decisions nor lead . . . the need for service staffs – that is, for people without operating responsibilities who advise, counsel, or coordinate – shrinks drastically. Today's typical organisation, in which knowledge tends to be concentrated in service staffs . . . will likely be labeled a phase, an attempt to infuse knowledge from the top rather than obtain information from below.'

Throughout the world, companies are already delayering, reducing headquarters staff, managers and administrators, and pushing decision-making and information lower down in the hierarchy.

Case Study
Downsizing at Shell UK

In the decade prior to 1992, numbers employed by Shell UK were reduced from more than 20 000 to about 11 000 through a combination of natural wastage, redeployment and early retirement. However, after 1992 the company had no option but to look for ways to reduce the workforce still further. Restructuring took place across the company's entire operations.

Following a strategy review, around 800 jobs disappeared in Downstream Oil, including 500 at the Stanlow manufacturing complex. The split between employees being made redundant and those opting for voluntary severance was roughly 50–50. At Shell Haven, around 100 job reductions were targeted across all departments, to be implemented by the end of 1994. Other reductions were made elsewhere.

A large organisation like Shell could not just discard people at will, so it set up an outplacement service in 1992. This involves helping some people who have spent all their lives working for Shell. The role of outplacement is to help employees progress from the 'protected' environment of Shell to that of a more turbulent world outside, where they need to take charge of their own future.

Advice and support come in stages. The first step, 'pick-up' counselling, is brought into effect immediately after a line manager has broken the news of potential redundancy, to allow an employee to offload the natural feeling of shock, anger or despair.

The next stage is life-planning – exploring the question of 'Where to now?' The employee is encouraged to take a holistic view: the type of work that would be of interest and how it would fit with the rest of their lifestyle. Self-assessment plays a key part, allowing the individual to recognise his or her own strengths and build on them.

Next comes financial planning. For those used to the monthly arrival of a salary cheque and the expectation of a pension, such advice is invaluable.

The final stage of the outplacement process is action – getting down to finding a new position, using every possible avenue: recruitment consultancies, cold-calling, answering advertisements and personal networking.

Questions for discussion

1 *Why have large organisations like Shell been forced into restructuring in the 1990s?*
2 *What would be the consequences of failure to restructure?*
3 *What new developments have enabled mature organisations like Shell to restructure?*
4 *What is outplacement? Who does it benefit and how?*
5 *How might the concept of outplacement benefit Shell employees who continue to work for the organisation?*

When an organisation contracts there is always a good reason. For example, Shell UK suffered seriously in its retailing operation when faced by strong competition from supermarkets selling petrol as a 'loss leader'. As a result Shell cut back on the number of its service stations, as well as headquarters staff supporting the retailing function. At the same time, advances in information technology made it possible to reduce administrative operations and to use computer-based control systems to a greater extent. Generally, as organisations contract they are able to shed operational staff and administrative staff, and to strip out layers of management.

All organisations should try to create the best possible size and structure relative to the environment. This is called **rightsizing**. Downsizing, however, is often a knee-jerk reaction aimed at cutting direct costs. An effective organisation will always be adjusting its structure to create an optimum fit between business operations and the operating environment.

The influence of new technology

Technology does not develop in a continuous and steady stream. New ideas and methods come so fast that it is difficult for organisations to anticipate solutions to difficulties and problems that will be created. In the world of work this requires new organisational structures, new reward systems, and many other changes required to absorb new technology.

Changing power relations

'Power is the medium through which conflicts of interest are ultimately resolved. Power influences who gets what, when and how' (G. Morgan, *Images of Organisation*).

Within an organisation, power is usually dispersed among a variety of individuals and interest groups, who are thus able to influence decision-making processes. However, there is not a 'level playing-field' and so a number of key individuals and groups have far more influence and power than others.

Why do we need to have power relations within organisational life? Clearly, it is important that decisions be made if there is to be order rather than chaos. Without a mechanism to enable decisions to be made we would encourage chaos. Organisations therefore need to be managed. This management can take place in a top-down way or it can be organised by having democratic management processes, but it needs to exist.

In the course of time, power relations will change within organisations as they go through periods of evolution and revolution. Change agents will be required to create and determine the direction of change.

Power exists in a number of good and bad forms. For example:

■ You have power if you can force other people to do something they otherwise would not do – for example, meet to discuss quality issues.
■ You have power if you can manage a situation so that there is no open discussion of things which might damage you. If subordinates have a number of concerns about the way activities are being carried out, you have power if you can suppress discussion of these issues.
■ You have power if you can influence someone's decision of what is in their best interests – for example, if you can persuade a group of employees that they should take a reduction in pay in order to secure the long-term interests of the organisation.

Sources of power

Power may come from having control over resources, having a particular position, having particular expertise, being admired and valued, etc. Clearly in a hierarchical organisation those higher up will have better positions, more access to resources, and so on. In a more democratic structure, individuals will have more power because of the contributions they can make to the organisation by virtue of their expertise or personality.

Methods of using power

In a bureaucracy those higher up in the organisation are able to exert their power by rewards and sanctions and by controlling access to resources and information. In contrast, team-work approaches require a sharing of ideas, information and resources, and democratic approaches such as shared canteens, work areas, and other aspects of informality.

The way in which power is perceived determines its effectiveness. The prisoner who has little respect for the jailer may force the jailer to resort to brutality and the withdrawal of favours as the only means of exerting power. In contrast, the timid person who treats the holder of power with undue respect makes himself even more powerless.

Strategic contingency theory

Power relationships exist between individuals, groups and units within an organisational structure. There is also a power interface between an organisation and elements of its environment.

Strategic contingency theory asserts that the power of a unit within an organisation depends on the number of strategic contingencies determined by that unit. A strategic contingency is the unit's ability to cope with uncertainty. Each unit is not easily replaceable.

A unit that is able to deal with a variety of uncertainties is going to be very important to the running of the organisation – it will be indispensable and thus powerful. For example:

- An office administrator is often at the interface between an organisation and its many publics. The administrator may handle initial incoming calls and decide how to route particular issues and problems, and thereby build up unique sets of information about how the organisation operates. This can give considerable power.
- The maintenance department in a factory may be the only one that can deal with a variety of faults and breakdowns across the plant. This can give considerable power.

In planning an organisation it may therefore be sensible to limit the volume of strategic contingencies within the responsibility of particular individuals and groups. Team-working can help groups of people to free themselves from the powers of service functions within the organisation. Multi-skilling can free people from the 'expert power' of specialists, and so on.

Chaos theory and organisations

Since the 1970s a revolution has been occurring in parts of the scientific community. Instead of studying rigid scientific laws, some scientists began to study 'irregularities' or 'non-linearities' in nature, and once they began to look for these they turned out to be everywhere and important. Science had discovered what it came to call 'chaos'.

One of the key concepts in chaos theory is that tiny changes in input can result in overwhelming differences in output, a phenomenon described as 'sensitive dependence on initial conditions'. In the study of the weather this is known as 'the butterfly effect', because it is supposed that a butterfly flapping its wings over Beijing can, in theory, cause a storm over New York a week later.

In business theory there has been a similar shift in emphasis from order to potential chaos. We need to go no further than the titles of popular management books to appreciate this emphasis:

- 1947 – F. W. Taylor, *Scientific Management*
- 1979 – H. Mintzberg, *The Structuring of Organisations*
- 1988 – T. Peters, *Thriving on Chaos*
- 1992 – T. Peters, *Liberation Management – Necessary Disorganisation for the Nanosecond Nineties*.

Increasingly, the emphasis in business theory is on preparing for turbulence rather than for static conditions.

As Brian Goodwin, professor of biology at the Open University, put it:

'The edge of chaos is a good place to be in a constantly changing world because from there you can always explore the patterns of order that are available . . . What you do not want to do is get stuck in one particular state of order.'

Clearly the emphasis for the modern organisation should be on thriving on chaos. This requires forward-thinking and adaptive structures.

Tom Peters, who has been at the leading edge of applying chaos theory to organisational structure, made the following points in his 500th newspaper column in 1994.

- Organisations should not be overly frightened of failure. The blunders that sometimes accompany a leap into the unknown may be needed to thrive in these turbulent times.
- Developments such as continuous improvement, re-engineering, total quality, empowerment and customer service are only a prelude to the Age of Innovation based on perpetual revolution and re-invention.
- Organisations need to be wary of building core strengths and then staying with them regardless of changing market conditions. In turbulent times they may need to quickly get rid of core values and strengths in order to move on to the new areas.
- The existing structure of an organisation tends to determine its strategy, which may not be the best option.
- Design is important if new developments are going to be given a competitive edge. In the modern marketplace there are too many similar products. When Renault launched the Twingo it was doing so knowing that 40 per cent of potential consumers actively disliked it. However, 10 per cent were said to love it. The company went ahead and produced its distinctive product. It was a success.
- Too many organisations are dull and conservative. In chaotic times you need bubbling and challenging organisations.

Chaos theory is also concerned with how patterns change over time. Organisations exist in a turbulent world and so need to be able to live with chaos. Organisations and their environments are tightly coupled, so that changes within and without may have profound influences which are unpredictable.

An organisation will set up control systems which influence its own ongoing activities through a feedback loop. The influence of the feedback is often unpredictable because of the complexity of organisational activity. Business structures by their very nature can lead to disorder as well as order.

Business life today is therefore characterised by open-ended change resulting from internal systems as well as shocks and change in the external environment. Managers should understand that there are no simple sets of prescriptions and rules to help them cope with the open-ended changes. They need to develop new models for dealing with chaotic situations. They need to be aware that the traditional managerial model of setting objectives, planning and monitoring the feedback may not be adequate in a dynamic field of operation – they may have to be planning and controlling as things unfold.

Figure 13.8 The conventional feedback loop is interrupted by chaotic conditions

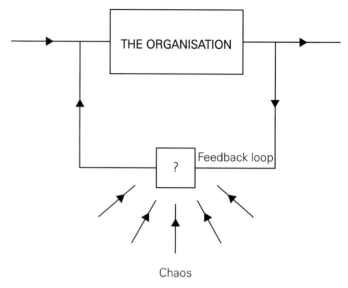

New trends

Transformational change is the only approach likely to be successful for organisations today. It is the approach that is concerned with thriving on chaos and introducing the Age of Innovation. New systems, techniques and designs will be required. Organisational structures need to be flexible and adaptive.

Flexible structures

An entrepreneurial organisation does not simply analyse the past in order to predict the future; it looks for opportunities to use all resources more effectively. An organisation with an entrepreneurial culture will actively seek change and be quick to respond. It will be 'market-led' and prepared to take risks. For all this to be possible the organisation must have a flexible structure that can be adjusted rapidly to meet changing circumstances. Kenyon Greene has used the term 'adaptive organisation'. He argues:

> *'The highest-level property of the adaptive organisation is the ability to change purposely the structure, function and behaviour of the organisation in keeping with experience and with the actual and dynamic demands imposed by the environment – that is, the highest-level property is the ability to learn. Top-level learning is itself a function of structure, including the degree to which learning ability is distributed throughout the various levels and parts of the organisation.'*

Greene argues that the adaptive organisation should have a modular structure. At each level there should be functionally overlapping units, so that breakdown or malfunction of any one unit does not create a crisis. Each unit should be semi-autonomous and built on a culture of local problem-solving, decision-making and control. This *decentralisation* and *empowerment* creates both a flexible and a resilient organisation.

Clearly these types of organisation – whether we call them flexible, adaptive or whatever – need employees who are highly motivated, capable of making decisions and solving problems, determined, and keen to accept new challenges. Is it realistic to expect that such individuals will be available to meet the needs of modern organisations?

Teleworking

Today more and more people are working from home, perhaps visiting their organisational base one day a week. **Teleworking** involves working from home with the tools of information technology – mainly a network of personal computers and databases, backed up by fax or other transmission systems.

Information technology is changing the nature of office work. Many tasks do not need to be carried out in centralised offices. Groups of specialists are still able to work as a team even when they are separated by large distances. Employers can tap into their workforce in any part of the country. This may create more employment for skilled women and men with young families, and for others for whom commuting is an inconvenience.

In the central office of Rank Xerox, employees work from their own homes using computer equipment linked to a company network. These 'independent' employees are free to work for organisations other than Rank Xerox.

Franchising

Franchising can be seen as an alternative way of creating a flexible organisation. A franchise operation is made up of many 'independent' units working for themselves under the trade name of an umbrella organisation. Franchising is growing rapidly in the UK.

A franchise system operates on the basis that an entrepreneur (known as the **franchisor**) has developed a particular product, such as fast food, ice-cream, cosmetics or the unblocking of drains. The franchisor sells the *right to trade under the recognised business name* to other individuals – who are called **franchisees**. A franchisee will have the sole right to trade under that name in a particular locality. Examples include Thorntons, Pizza Hut, Body Shop, Kleeneze, and Dayvilles (American ice-cream). Once an agreement has been made, the franchisee will normally make an initial payment to the franchisor and in return will receive help and advice in setting up the business. The franchisor will often supply

equipment and stocks of materials. For example, in the fast-food business cooking equipment might be supplied, with menus, recipes, packaging and clothing.

Once the new business is up and running, it is up to the franchisee to make a success of it. However, the element of risk is reduced because the business will have been proven to be a success elsewhere and expert help and assistance is provided.

Major *advantages* for the franchisor are that it does not have to risk its own capital, and it takes a regular share from the profits of the franchised outlets. The main *disadvantages* for the franchisee are that, while it owns the business, it may feel restricted by having to buy stocks from the franchisor, and it may be difficult to agree on changing the recommended methods.

Franchising is just one alternative to the traditional growth pattern of organisations which characterised the 1970s. Franchising illustrates the opportunities of:

- decentralisation
- enterprise at grass-roots level
- leaner, flexible, flatter organisations.

Such organisations are far more adaptable and flexible. They can adapt quickly to changes in local conditions, and franchisees are highly motivated because they experience the fruits of their own endeavours.

Part 3 **Managing change**

This part of the chapter explores some of the key aspects of organisational change and methods of managing change.

Greiner's model (see Figure 13.7) indicates that an organisation is likely to be faced with periods of both evolution and revolution. From time to time the organisation will need to go through a period of immense upheaval. In an environment of 'chaos' it is important for management to prepare organisations for the future. If flexibility is accepted as the norm then individuals will be prepared for change. If, on the other hand, structures are based on set patterns and procedures, then individuals will find it difficult to adjust.

When preparing an organisation for change there are a number of important considerations:

- *To what extent will the change interfere with an established socio-technical system?* In particular, how will it affect employees, their relationships, their expectations, 'hopes and dreams' etc. People who have worked for an organisation for any length of time will have built relationships and patterns of working with one another. They will have established set ways of doing things. They will have planned out their futures with the organisation. To suddenly alter the structure and method of working can destroy motivation. Some employees may even seek to sabotage new plans and structures to make them unworkable.
- *What is the organisation's history of change?* A previous record of successfully managed change will dispose individuals to accept new methods. If previous attempts have been bungled there will be difficulties in 'selling' change to employees.
- *What are the expectations about the change process?* Individuals will have varying expectations. Some may see change as being a threat. For example, they may hold the view that restructuring will lead to job losses. In a hierarchical structure individuals at the bottom of the organisational pyramid may not expect to be consulted – they will be used to decisions being handed down. In a more democratic structure individuals expect to be consulted and will be dissatisfied if they are ignored in discussions about the change process.
- *What are the power structures within the organisation?* Power is located at a number of points in an organisation, and there are both formal and informal sources of power. Often power – and thus the ability to resist change – is vested in particular groups and individuals who have acquired the ability to command resources, and the smooth movement of work flow.

They may have built up informal alliances with other groups in the organisation.

First and foremost it is necessary to *identify whether change needs to take place*. In a changing environment an organisation needs to evaluate its existing patterns and structures constantly in order to identify strengths and weaknesses. It is also highly likely that organisational planners will be identifying fresh areas for change as a result of internal and environmental audits.

A fairly common procedure is for managers to carry out an **organisational diagnosis**. Employees are asked to complete a detailed questionnaire like that shown in Figure 13.9. Clearly, if a number of staff make negative statements then there is a prima facie case for organisational redesign and change.

Figure 13.9 Part of an organisational diagnosis questionnaire

Please answer the following questions by ranking the statements:

1 = agree strongly
2 = agree
3 = neutral
4 = disagree
5 = disagree strongly

	1	2	3	4	5
1 I understand the objectives of the organisation	☐	☐	☐	☐	☐
2 Work is well organised	☐	☐	☐	☐	☐
3 My supervisor listens to my views	☐	☐	☐	☐	☐

Managing organisational change

A number of steps need to be carried out in preparing for organisational change. These are set out in Figure 13.10.

1 *Identify the change required.* This can be done through a diagnostic approach. The organisation will need to communicate the nature of the change to all concerned, so at this stage it is important to be able to prepare a clear, concise statement of what is required.

2 *Set out the strengths and weaknesses of the organisation.* A key question is whether the organisation is ready for change. Clearly there will be existing strengths (e.g. departments that will benefit from the change and who may have already had similar experience of making changes). It is important to show how the change fits with existing practices as well as identifying necessary

Figure 13.10 Preparing for change

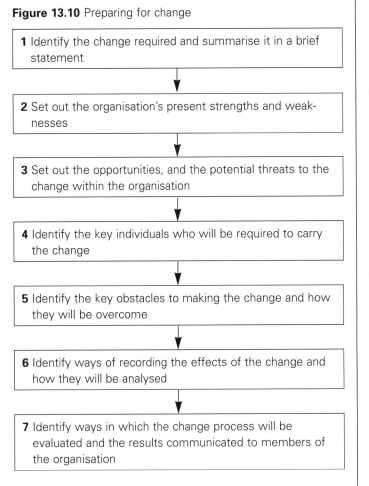

1 Identify the change required and summarise it in a brief statement

2 Set out the organisation's present strengths and weaknesses

3 Set out the opportunities, and the potential threats to the change within the organisation

4 Identify the key individuals who will be required to carry the change

5 Identify the key obstacles to making the change and how they will be overcome

6 Identify ways of recording the effects of the change and how they will be analysed

7 Identify ways in which the change process will be evaluated and the results communicated to members of the organisation

improvements. Where weaknesses are identified, then resources and time may need to be put into these areas to make sure that the change works.

3 *Environmental analysis.* Alterations to the organisational environment are likely to have played a major part in necessitating the change. These need to be identified so that people within the organisation do not perceive the change as being purely a management whim. Changes in the environment provide opportunities to be grasped. Threats should be highlighted as real dangers to the organisation and its employees.

4 *Key individuals.* It is essential to win support from those with most power in the organisation, in particular paying close attention to formal and informal power structures. The more people who can be made to take 'ownership' of structural changes the better. The benefits of change should be emphasised. Illustrate ways in which new structures and systems use existing knowledge and practice. Minimise the surprises, by consulting with and involving as many people as possible in the organisation.

5 *Identify the obstacles.* In particular it is necessary to explore the concerns of individuals and groups. Time spent building up trust and support, and explaining the

positive benefits, is not wasted. Clear objectives and a timetable should be communicated to all those involved. People can be prepared for change by encouraging training courses and development programmes.

6 *Ways of recording the changes.* Methods should be identified at the outset rather than waiting until the change is in place.

7 *Evaluation.* It is imperative to evaluate the results in order to show how successful the change has been. At first people may not be convinced that the change was worthwhile, so concrete evidence is helpful. The results could be communicated in a newsletter or in meetings.

Sources of innovation

Innovation is producing new solutions to new problems or providing new and better solutions to old problems.

Sometimes innovation comes in small incremental steps, paying great attention to detail. March and Simon, in their book *Organisations*, argue that most innovation within an organisation comes from borrowing ideas from the environment, by imitating what other organisations were already doing, or by bringing in people from outside with new ideas (perhaps borrowed from elsewhere).

However, it is easy to kill innovation within an organisation by stifling enterprise and individuality. Organisational structures enable innovation if they encourage it. In their book *In Search of Excellence*, Peters and Waterman argue for:

'. . . giving everyone in the organisation the space to innovate, at least a little bit. Answering the phones and otherwise behaving with common courtesy towards customers. Making things that work. Listening to customers and asking them for their ideas. Then acting upon them. Wandering around: with customers, with your people, suppliers. Paying attention to pride, trust, enthusiasm – and passion and love.'

Peters and Waterman criticised American businesses for losing a focus on 'product or people' and developing an 'overreliance on analysis from corporate ivory towers'. This leads to over-caution, inflexibility and an inability to innovate through experimentation – 'paralysis-induced-by-analysis'.

What is required is a recognition that innovation needs to be freed within an organisational structure by empowering innovators. For example, a self-managing team (SMT) is a work-group that operates without a visible manager and takes on responsibility for planning, organising, directing and monitoring jobs within the team as well as the administrative functions that support them. Management is shared across the team.

SMTs have tremendous potential to respond to change. Team members are taught to 'self-correct' – that is, to identify problems and to react to them quickly. SMTs can replace layers of management by doing jobs themselves. They encourage innovation because team members are encouraged to put forward their ideas openly in order to enhance work.

Control systems

Control is one of the main functions of management, and information systems provide data which can be analysed for control purposes. For example, financial analysis can be used to measure variations from financial plans.

Anthony, in his book *Management Control Systems*, suggests that control needs to take place at three levels:

- the strategic level
- the management level
- the operational level.

Each of these levels is important. Strategy control is concerned with organisational goals and purposes. Management controls are concerned with implementing procedures within the organisation. Operational controls are concerned with routine activities.

Control may best be achieved if the organisation is broken down into **responsibility centres**. This involves identifying sections with responsibility for particular activities and performance targets. For example, control over the income coming into the organisation is partly met by establishing sales targets for the sales department. Control over labour and other production costs comes from creating a detailed budget for expenditures on factors of production by the production department. Control over quality comes from creating visual and other standards which must be met by all departments involved in production. Organisations should employ a variety of different types of control mechanisms which are appropriate and give accurate measurements of 'what should be measured' so that control can be exerted.

Systems of control are particularly important in complex organisations to ensure effective integration of structures, processes and activities.

Organisations try to establish control procedures so that there is a **control loop** which sets out to ensure that the system responds positively to any shortfalls or deficiencies in performance (see Figure 13.11).

Figure 13.11 A feedback (control) loop

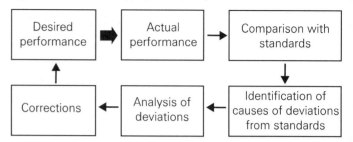

For example, most large organisations establish performance standards for employee work activities. Performance is monitored and assessed against standards, leading to the provision of feedback, rewards and sanctions. Performance appraisal is a good example of such a control mechanism.

However, while such controls can be effective in the short term they may be of little use for the control of open-ended situations in a change environment. Then, what managers are trying to work with may be ambiguous and unclear. A small open-ended change may have dramatic consequences for the organisation. Ralph Stacey, in his book *The Chaos Frontier*, argues:

'It is dangerous to confine the discovery of open-ended change to the top levels of the management hierarchy because small beginnings are more likely to be noticed first by those lower down in the hierarchy at the front line of the business. The detection of open-ended changes and the initial selection of those to be pursued therefore have to rely upon the spontaneous initiative and intuition of individuals anywhere and everywhere in the organisation.'

Stacey goes on to assert that organisations need a diversity of empowered people working for them – people with different perspectives – rather than a uniform monolithic 'company type' who would be more appropriate in a closed-system controlled organisation.

Driving and restraining forces

Before implementing organisational change it is important to carry out what is called a **force field analysis** to ascertain the relative strengths of the driving and restraining forces for change.

For example, in Figure 13.12 there is a rough representation of a force field analysis which is concerned with the introduction of an appraisal scheme in an organisation.

Figure 13.12 Force field analysis of the introduction of an appraisal system

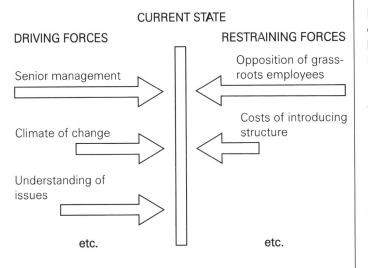

CURRENT STATE

DRIVING FORCES — RESTRAINING FORCES

Senior management

Opposition of grass-roots employees

Climate of change

Costs of introducing structure

Understanding of issues

etc.   etc.

- The arrows going from left to right represent the driving forces.
- The arrows going from right to left represent restraining forces.
- The length of an arrow represents the intensity of the driving or restraining force.

Clearly a strong driving force for change rests in power relations in an organisation. Driving through new procedures and practices will depend on securing the approval of those with most power. However, this may considerably underestimate the strength of resistance at grass-roots level. If commitment is required for the change to be successful, it may be better to use participative approaches – bringing in people from across the organisation.

Changes in organisations are strongly influenced by the magnitude, direction, and/or number of factors that encourage and support change (driving forces) and those that discourage change (restraining forces). Equilibrium exists when driving forces are balanced by restraining forces, and change takes place when this balance is upset. Kurt Lewin termed this 'unfreezing'. 'Moving' takes place when the strength of driving forces is greater than those of the restraining forces. The organisation will then 'refreeze' when balance returns.

Creating change therefore involves 'unfreezing' existing relationships. This is not always easy to do in an organisation that is stuck in its ways. Today, management theory and forward-thinking managers try to create a situation where people within an organisation have a 'mind set' which favours change – a state of perpetual 'movement'.

Case Study
Boehringer Ingelheim

Boehringer Ingelheim is a private German pharmaceutical company with its UK operation based at Bracknell. It is having to face up to increased competition within the industry and on an international scale. The company is responding in the mid-1990s by seeking to get employees more involved in the company. Empowerment is a major feature of organisational change.

Staff at Bracknell have attended presentations designed to spread the word about a performance project to improve efficiency, and a 'vision and leadership' programme with an ambitious aim of challenging the philosophy of a company that has been controlled by one family for more than a century.

Some employees found it difficult to adjust to a new openness and the idea of challenging the way things were done. However, in just a few months there were positive results.

For example, in the mailroom a second daily delivery between the company's sites has been reinstated. It had been dropped to save money, but it was actually costing more money because urgent packages that just missed the single delivery were being sent by more expensive means. This was so obvious, yet management had to be told about it.

Questions for discussion

1 *What factors are likely to act as driving forces and what as resisting forces in introducing the sort of empowerment process outlined above?*
2 *Why might the organisation benefit from 'unfreezing'?*
3 *Should the organisation 'refreeze' after a period of time?*
4 *Why might modern organisations benefit from continual change?*
5 *What sort of climate needs to be established for programmes of change to be successful?*

Creating ongoing change

We have seen that there are many ways of organising and reorganising organisations. The concept of **organisation development** has been popular for a long time as a means of continually adjusting an organisation to counteract deficiencies. The processes involved follow closely those outlined earlier in this chapter. Figure 13.13 highlights these and adds the dimension of control to that of the management of change.

Figure 13.13 Creating ongoing change

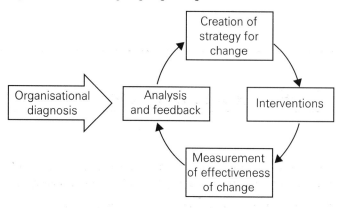

Organisational diagnosis becomes an ongoing part of development. Analysis of the results of the diagnosis provides the raw materials for a change strategy. Changes are made. The impact of change is measured and evaluated to provide ongoing feedback for fresh change.

Of course, in complex organisations operating in a turbulent environment it may not be possible to operate in this way because of the speed of changes. Adaptable and flexible structures have to be developed which respond quickly to the changing environment. Indeed, it is difficult to outline what these organisational structures should look like. The structure will depend on changes within the organisation and in the environment. All we can say is that these organisations should be made up of intelligent and adaptable people with a propensity to innovate.

Technology and change

Technology will always be a driving force for change. Technological developments mean that products are made in different ways, necessitating process re-engineering. Overnight the skills of swathes of employees from a particular functional area become outmoded.

At the same time, information technology enables an organisation to be organised more effectively, forcing structural changes. Automation of manual, white collar and managerial tasks using IT has had a profound effect on many aspects of organisational activity. For example, IT networks make it far easier to integrate activities through project teams and through information sharing. Communications technology means that it is no longer necessary for people to travel to meetings – videoconferencing, the use of fax, and other electronic media permit instant communication between people who are thousands of miles apart. There is far more control over errors, misdirection etc. than ever before. Organisations do not require so many people working for them when automated equipment can quickly replace standardised operations that were carried out by people.

It is impossible to overstate the importance of these and many other technological changes in transforming the way that businesses are organised. Businesses today can be much more flexible learning organisations. They need to be, because increasingly they are operating in complex dynamic environments.

Further reading

- *Management and Organisational Behaviour*, 3rd edition, by Laurie Mullins. Pitman, 1993.
- *Organizational Behaviour*, 2nd edition, by David Cherrington. Allyn & Bacon, 1993.
- *Essentials of Organisational Behaviour*, 4th edition, by Stephen Robbins. Prentice Hall, 1993.
- *Entrepreneurship and Economic Change* by M. Binks and P. Vale. McGraw-Hill, 1990.
- *Management* by Peter Drucker. McGraw-Hill, 1990.

14 Communicating in organisations

On completion of this chapter students should be able to:

- evaluate the effectiveness of different communication systems

- identify and evaluate relationships between organisation type and communication system

- examine and evaluate the impact and implications of technology on communication and administrative systems

- communicate through formal and informal organisation channels, using a variety of appropriate media

- make recommendations for improved organisational communications.

Models of communication

As we saw on page 295, communication is the process of conceiving, sending, receiving and interpreting messages.

Within an organisation there will be a variety of communications. Internal communications will be between various members and parts of the organisation, e.g. directors, managers, shareholders, employees, etc. Messages will flow vertically between the various levels of an organisation and horizontally across a particular level.

At the organisational boundary, communication will take place between the organisation and its environment, e.g. with suppliers, customers, competitors, etc.

It is essential that information, ideas and instructions are communicated clearly. The recipients of information needs to understand what they should do or what they are being told. The Chinese philosopher Confucius said: 'If language is not correct, then what is said is not what is meant; if what is said is not what is meant, then what ought to be done remains undone.'

Communication skills are particularly important today. Individuals rarely work in isolation; they work as part of an integrated team. When you give instructions to other people you should try to check that their understanding is the same as yours, perhaps by asking them to 'say back' to you what you have said.

Another aspect of communication is the need to avoid secrecy. Wherever possible, modern organisational structures should encourage openness so that people know what is happening within the organisation. The more knowledgeable they are, the better the decisions that they can make.

Blau and Scott's model

Blau and Scott suggest that communication has three main ingredients.

- **Error correction**, i.e. pointing out mistakes to other people so that they can put them right.

- **Social support**, i.e. providing approval to other people which makes them feel better and supports their successes.
- **Competition**, which relates to communications that pit individuals and groups against each other, e.g. by displaying prominently on a company noticeboard the operating results of various departments.

Vertical communication often takes a top-down route in each of the ingredients outlined above. However, considerable gains can be made by superiors who are prepared to listen to what their subordinates say. It is possible, however, that if there is too free a flow of communication up and down an organisation this may lead to problems of coordination.

Lateral communication supports cooperation within an organisation, can lead to better decisions, encourage self-confidence and reduce stress. However, it is important for lateral communication to be a two-way process between individuals and groups or it may create informal patterns of dependency, status, etc. Clearly, the more communication there is in an organisation the better. However, it needs to be effectively channelled or it may lead to poor coordination and the creation of dysfunctional power relations.

Drucker's model

In his book, *Management*, Peter Drucker set out four fundamentals of communications (see Figure 14.1).

Figure 14.1 Drucker's four fundamentals of communications

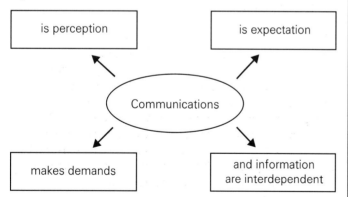

1 **Communications is perception**. Drucker poses a riddle common to the Buddhist, Muslim and Jewish religions: 'Is there a sound in the forest if a tree crashes down and no one is around to hear it?' The correct answer is 'no' because there is no sound unless there is someone there to perceive the sound waves. The emphasis in communication therefore should be on the recipient of a message rather than the sender. Good communication occurs when perception of the message matches the message. Messages need to be framed in such a way that they match the experience of the recipient.

2 **Communication is expectation**. People who receive messages expect to hear certain things. They are in tune with what they expect. They may well misunderstand or fail to hear the unexpected. The human being resists attempts to 'change its mind'. Before communicating, therefore, we need to know what the recipient expects to see and hear. If the message we want to send is different from the recipient's expectations, we will need to prepare the recipient, i.e. gradually awaken him or her to new ideas so that new messages will come to be expected.

3 **Communications makes demands**. The receipt of any communication is not easy – it demands effort and concentration on the part of the recipient. Therefore, it is important wherever possible to motivate recipients, by presenting them with communications which fit with their 'aspirations, purposes and values'.

4 **Communications and information are interdependent**. Communication and information are not the same thing. 'Communication is perception; information is logic.' Information is impersonal and the more it can be freed from human values and emotions, the more informative it becomes. Today, we have the means through computers and information technology to create vast quantities of information. We are experiencing the information revolution. More than ever we need effective communications in organisations to take advantage of this revolution.

The inadequacy of downward communication

Drucker points out that for far too long organisations have focused on trying to communicate downwards: trying to get across what *we* want to say. However, this will be futile unless recipients are prepared to receive the message. This does not mean that managers and others should not bother with clear and concise communication skills. What it does mean is that it is necessary to find out more about the listener and what he or she is able and willing to hear. There is no point in having 'the information superhighway' at your fingertips unless you can communicate effectively.

Drucker argues that we need to start thinking about communicating upwards: 'Upward communication must be focused on something that is common to recipient and sender.' Communication must be informed by the values, beliefs and aspirations of the recipient. Drucker argues that management by objectives can be a useful starting point. The subordinate should be asked to identify the major contributions that he or she can make to the organisation, i.e. what subordinates should do and be accountable for. Although this may not tally with what the superior expects, it at least enables the subordinate to focus on key issues, such as effective use of resources and accountabilities. This builds effective communication from the bottom up.

Increasingly, organisations are working in this way. Self-managing teams and quality circles are being given greater responsibility for defining their own work roles and accountabilities. Delegation of budgets and local management in schools and hospitals place ever more emphasis on the account holder, e.g. allowing a doctor in a hospital trust to make the statement: 'This is what I tell you I can do'. Drucker states:

> *'A performance appraisal based on what a person can do and has done well, is a foundation for communications . . . There can be no communication if it is conceived as going from the "I" to the "Thou". Communication works only from one member of "us" to another. Communication in organisation is not a means of organisation. It is a mode of organisation.'*

Figure 14.2 Drucker's emphasis on communications within the organisation

Communication in organisation is not a means of organisation. It is a mode of organisation

Case Study
Body Shop communications

The following extract is taken from Anita Roddick's autobiography, *Body and Soul*.

'We bombard our staff with information about everything from dirty tricks in the cosmetics industry to the breakdown of communism in the USSR. Every shop has a fax machine, and our communications network includes bulletins which go out to all the staff to keep them up to date with new ideas, new developments, and new products. In addition we have a multi-lingual monthly video magazine, *Talking Shop* . . .

'We communicate with our customers via leaflets and posters and information boards in the shops, and they can communicate with us through the suggestion boxes to be found in every shop. We don't just pay lip service to their views – six members of staff work full time cataloguing their suggestions and replying to them. In addition, we hold regular forums, when we open up a shop from six till nine in the evening and invite customers to come and tell us what they like, what they don't like, and what products they would like to see added to the range. It has always been Body Shop policy to find out what customers want by simply asking them, a concept thought to be eccentric in the retail trade.'

Questions for discussion

1 *To what extent does the model provided by the Body Shop fit with Drucker's view of communication from the bottom upwards?*
2 *How does the model provided by the Body Shop show a recognition of the importance of 'perception' and 'expectations'?*
3 *How is the Body Shop likely to benefit from the way in which it communicates?*

Formal and informal models of communication

We have seen that information can flow in an organisation in a variety of directions: upwards, downwards, sideways, even diagonally (e.g. between different levels in different functions). The more communication there is, the greater will be the complexity of coordinating communication flows. In addition to formal communications there will also be a variety of informal communications. It is not only in the board meeting, the industrial relations committee and in day-to-day instructions in organisations that communication takes place.

It also takes place through informal contacts, such as discussions in the staff canteen, informal telephone conversations, etc. It is through these informal channels that relationships within the organisation – and consequently actions – may truly be shaped. For example, standard procedure may be for decisions to be made downwards in a hierarchy. However, informally, lower-level operatives may outline the way an activity should be carried out in an informal discussion with the supervisor.

In any organisation many of the operating and middle-management decisions are made by informal communications between people. The purpose of formal communication channels may simply be to rubber stamp procedures and decisions which have been agreed on informally.

Formal communication

In large organisations formal communication systems will be in place, e.g. regular meetings, conferences, and so on, but even so informal relationships will be very important. After an informal discussion, a superior may request that ideas are 'put down on paper' so that they can be formally approved at the next meeting.

The advantages of formal communications are:

■ They provide records and evidence of decisions that have been made.
■ They are part of the accepted command and control structure of the organisation.
■ They are based on accepted definitions of power within the organisation.

The disadvantages are:

■ They take time to be put into action.
■ More importantly, they tend to fit the top-down model so that they may not be 'heard' by the recipient.
■ Formal communications may be lost across an organisation.

Informal communication

Informal communication may more closely meet the needs of a flexible organisation, because communications can be made as and when required. If informal communication is part of accepted practice, then individuals will not be afraid to contribute to discussion and decision-making. Informal communication is spontaneous, and thus responds to new situations both within the internal organisation and to the wider environment. Informal communication can be used to identify bottom-up concerns and perceptions.

Informal communication also has its disadvantages.

■ It may conflict with formal communication systems, as when two individuals agree to an informal procedure which has been forbidden by company policy.
■ It may lead to communication overload within an organisation, so that coordination becomes ineffective.
■ It may act as a threat to existing power relations within the company. A superior may feel that his or her decisions are being undermined by informal agreements.

■ It may lead to unfounded rumours which spread like wildfire through an organisation.
■ It may lead to deliberate or inadvertent bias in the information given by those who use these channels.

The effective organisation will need to create a good balance between formal and informal communications. The greater the recognition given to informal communication the better, so that it may be channelled in an appropriate direction.

Communication channels and networks

A communication channel is the path through which messages are sent from a source to a destination. Most communication is two-way, e.g. a conversation between two people (see Figure 14.3).

Figure 14.3 Communication channels: a two-way flow

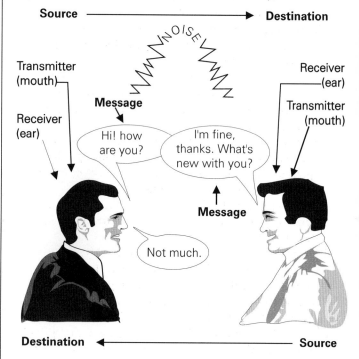

An organisation represents a complex pattern of communication channels. It is not difficult to see why such a network is so complex. Figure 14.4 contrasts the number of stages in the communication process between two and between seven individuals. Since each stage of communication may involve complex channels, it is hardly surprising that communication can rapidly translate into chaos.

Figure 14.4 Increased complexity in communication with larger numbers.

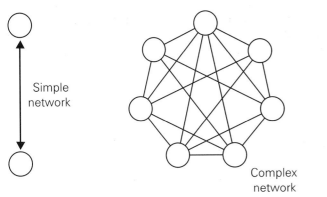

Simple network

Complex network

There are a number of problems that can arise along a communication channel.

- Confusion may arise as to the source of a message, e.g. buyers often associate a poor advertisement with the wrong product.
- An inappropriate message may be sent out from the source, e.g. when the source does not clearly understand the issues involved.
- The message may become amplified in transmission, e.g. an order for 500 blankets is amplified into an order for 500 000 blankets.
- There may be a variety of different sources of noise which confuse the message, e.g. the message may be poorly expressed, or the recipient may concentrate on the wrong parts of the message.
- The message may become distorted in transmission, e.g. a member of the organisation may change the emphasis of the message as a deliberate act of sabotage to make someone else look foolish.
- The message may be delayed in transmission, e.g. because it is not given priority, it may arrive too late for an important meeting.
- The message may be wrongly interpreted by the receiver. When President Kennedy told the people of Berlin, 'Ich bin ein Berliner' – meaning 'I am a Berliner' (showing that he stood shoulder to shoulder with the people of Berlin) – he jumbled up his use of German. What he actually said was 'I am a dumpling'. This turn of phrase had less impact in the perceptions of the people of Berlin than he had intended.

Formal and informal channels of communications in organisations

A distinction may be made between the formal and informal communication channels that exist within an organisation.

Formal communication channels are deliberately set up by management. These would include written information, such as reports, memos, etc. which are regularly prepared and presented for formal presentations such as conferences and meetings. These communications are routinely collected as part of the organisation's procedures, and such procedures are officially sanctioned by the organisation. Formal channels include written, spoken, visual, electronic and any other form of communication channel which is officially recognised by the organisation. Most organisations will use a variety of formal channels.

Informal channels will be made up largely of 'off the cuff' communications which often cut across existing structures and patterns in an organisation. Informal channels have the potential to be destructive to the official organisation, but they can also be unofficial ways of making the organisation more effective. They can provide a dynamic ingredient in static situations. Part of the art of management should be to identify why informal communications are taking place. By identifying the strengths of existing informal communications, it may be possible to build them into re-engineered communication systems.

An over-reliance on unofficial channels usually indicates that official channels are perceived to be inadequate.

Top-down communication

Top-down communication was often standard practice in large, traditional organisations. The advantage of this method is that major decisions are made by managers, who create the systems they want to see implemented. Multi-layered hierarchies are then able to push decisions downwards through formalised communication structures. However, a major weakness of top-down communication is that it creates layers of people whose perceptions may vary. The view of the manager, the supervisor and the operative will be conditioned by their working environment. Messages will become confused and distorted.

A large bureaucracy may have poor channels for upward communication, so that suggestions from the base of the organisation may only move one or two levels up the hierarchy before being lost. This may be particularly true when supervisors have a vested interest in blocking messages which place them in a poor light.

Departmentation and segmentation of an organisation may mean that communication only works effectively within that department or segment. Walls may be built between the parts of an organisation, reducing overall efficiency.

As organisations become larger, 'mandarins' (senior managers) may build up larger spans of control in order to enhance their own powers. When this occurs it can become increasingly difficult for superiors to communicate effectively with subordinates, because they are not able to spend enough time on individual communications.

All of the above difficulties are accentuated by information overload, a common problem in the large organisation. There may be too many channels of communication and simply too much information for employees to take in.

Solutions

Prescribed and clear communication channels
One solution is for the organisation to have clearly defined, well publicised channels of communication. The organisation will have set routines and pathways of communication. This may work in an organisation where work can be carried out according to standard patterns. It may, however, be inappropriate for a dynamic, adaptive organisation. On page 255 we examined the nature of the 'wheel' and 'chain' networks of communication. For these networks to be effective, they depend on the qualities and abilities of those in key positions in the organisation and on the quality of the communication channels available to them.

Democratic networks and channels
On page 256 we also looked at the circle and completely connected networks as alternatives to centralised communications. Today many firms are becoming increasingly flexible and are developing less centralised communication networks. Headquarters of organisations are becoming smaller as electronic data-handling reduces the need for staff and more decisions are pushed outwards to branches and local offices. The all-channel network (see Figure 14.5), whereby every member of an organisation can communicate freely in a democratic way, encourages the ready exchange of ideas and information. It will accept informal contacts between members of an organisation. When employees in an organisation know many other employees they will be able to talk freely to each other and to share insights. For example, at Shell UK, management training involves trainees working for six months in a range of departments across the company. This enables them to develop general skills, a wide variety of knowledge about the various functions of the organisation and a range of informal contacts. It provides a sound foundation for all-channel networks of communication.

Wherever possible the organisation should build up the frameworks for a multi-level, free flow of communications. This involves providing opportunities

Figure 14.5 The all-channel network

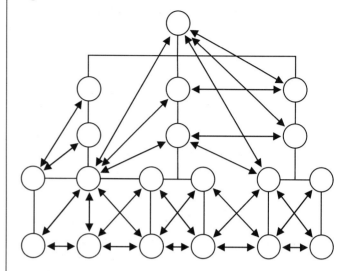

for as many people as possible to contribute to decision making and discussion. The quality circle is one such idea. It enables people who are directly involved in particular activities and decisions to contribute ideas in all appropriate situations.

Information technology
An information system is any system that provides information for activities carried out within an organisation. A management information system is one that provides such information for managers. However, it is increasingly common for a large number of people in organisations to have managerial responsibilities. Information technology solutions are therefore employed to provide effective communication systems serving all members of an organisation. Information comprises data that have been processed so that they are useful to the recipient.

Information systems

An information system will be made up of the following:

1 **Computer hardware.** This is the equipment, such as terminals and keyboards, that is used to gather, enter and store data and then to process data into usable information.
2 **Computer software** provides the programmes that are used to operate the hardware and to produce information.
3 **Data stored in databases.** The data stored will depend on the information needs of the organisation.
4 **People** who operate and use the information system.
5 **Procedures.** These are the rules, instructions and methods for operating the information system.

Today, organisations increasingly seek recruits with IT capabilities or the willingness to develop these capabilities.

Systems analysis

Before introducing computers to a communications and information system, it is necessary to carry out a **systems analysis** to investigate the ways in which the information system can be of use. Nowadays the emphasis is usually on providing solutions that meet the needs of the organisation rather than buying commercially produced business packages.

Systems development is a procedure used to design and develop an information system. The systems analyst looks at an organisational system as a coordinated whole and examines the ways in which the parts of the organisation fit together and support each other. The systems analyst then attempts to integrate within the organisation and its needs a multi-level, cross-functional and timely flow of information. The information system will then (it is hoped) serve the needs of both the management sub-system and the operating sub-system.

An example of a modern computer-based information system is that operated by the commercial banks to handle customer information. A business or private customer may have several accounts with a bank: a current account, savings account, mortgage account, and loan account. Using a customer information system, it is possible to cross-reference such accounts easily so that the bank can quickly call up statements of a customer's activities, even though the customer may be dealing with several departments of the bank. Such information makes it possible for a bank to develop a more detailed picture of its customers, to provide a better service, to supply up-to-date information and to market new services to existing customers.

Case Study
Using information technology for internal communication of data at Lloyds Bank

In the UK alone, Lloyds has more than six million account holders across the complete range of personal and business banking services, generating an ever-increasing volume of transactions. Each transaction has to be accounted for, and there is constant competitive pressure to ensure that the bank remains more efficient than its competitors. The bank has therefore made a major investment in information technology (IT) as a means of increasing efficiency. It uses IT in three main areas:

- customer accounting

- business services
- internal communications and management information.

Here we focus on the latter. With more than 2,000 branches in the UK, the volume of internal communications is enormous. To speed the transfer of information between branches and computer centres, the bank has its own data communication networks. There is a large, high-speed network in the UK and international links with continental Europe and the USA.

With information technology the bank is revolutionising how it provides services through its branches. By means of a computerised central database of information accessible in the branches, customers are given a service tailored to their needs.

Office automation technology provides facilities such as electronic diaries and mail, and word processing. These are designed to reduce the amount of paperwork on employees' desks by storing information in a convenient and easily accessible manner.

Questions for discussion

1 *Why does a large bank like Lloyds require an effective IT-based communication system?*
2 *What types of communication would be made using this system?*
3 *How can users of the system convert data into information? Give an example.*
4 *How can such a system prevent information overload?*
5 *Why is it important to allow free access of communications using this system, rather than having top-down controls over communications and information?*
6 *What kind of information might not be included in such a system?*

Designing an information system

Systems design involves the preparation and planning of an information system by drawings, sketches and plans. It is concerned with deciding how a system should be developed. The form of design depends on a number of factors.

1 **The resources available to an organisation**. The five basic resources of any organisation are machines, materials, money, methods and people. There would be no point in designing an expensive information system for a company that had little money to spare.
2 **The information requirements of users**. Systems design clearly needs to be coupled with an

understanding of who needs what information, and in what form.

3 **The user's ability to make use of the information provided** and to operate the system. The designer needs to make the system as user friendly as possible. This involves keeping jargon and technical language to a minimum. Other features that can be built into a system include speed of communication, to reduce waiting time.

4 **The requirements for the system.** The designer needs to understand what is expected of the system, in regard to

a cost
b performance
c reliability
d flexibility
e expected life-cycle.

5 **The use to which data operations will be put.** A number of important operations can be carried out on data.

a *Capturing data* involves recording data generated by an event or occurrence, e.g. from invoices, sales slips, meters, counters.

b *Verifying the data* ensures that data have been recorded accurately, e.g. checking that an instrument is working correctly, or cross-checking recording procedures.

c *Classifying data* entails putting different types of data into appropriate sections, e.g. the sales of a company could be classified according to the different departments that make the sales.

d *Sorting data* involves placing data elements into a specified order, e.g. an inventory file could be sorted by money value, or by code number.

e *Summarising data* can be used to aggregate data, e.g. by totalling various figures, such as sales, or by drawing up balancing figures for a balance sheet. Alternatively, it could be used to present data logically in a common form, e.g. by producing a list of all employees that were working the night shift on a particular date.

f *Calculating using data*, involves computing various figures in a mathematical way, e.g. adding, subtracting, dividing. Wages of employees can be calculated by multiplying hours worked by the wage rate and then subtracting necessary deductions.

g *Storing data* involves transferring data to the appropriate medium, e.g. floppy disk, microfilm, etc.

h *Retrieving data* involves calling up information from the place of storage.

i *Reproducing data* is the process of transferring the same data from one medium to another. At a simple level, this could involve photocopying material or commanding a computer to copy it, or calling up data from one screen to another, as with stock exchange dealing.

j *Communicating* enables the transfer of data from one place to another. This can take place at any stage of the data-processing cycle. The ultimate aim of information processing is to provide information for the final consumer.

Systems analysis reveals the order in which the above operations need to be carried out in particular activities. This information will be needed in systems design. The designer will then use a number of tools, such as flow charts and decision tables, to help produce the best possible design for the information system.

Systems evaluation

The systems designer will suggest alternative plans for implementation. Some of these will be set out as imperatives, i.e. features of design that must be adhered to, whatever the final system. The designer will also suggest a number of desirable features, which are optional.

It will then be necessary to find suppliers who are able to provide suitable computer equipment to meet the design needs. This might involve finding equipment that has the 'best fit' with the desired system in terms of cost, reliability, ease of maintenance, etc. Other considerations will be the potential to extend a system in the event of future growth, and the overall level of support from the supplier, e.g. in the form of training. These and other factors will need to be weighed up before a final decision is made.

Case Study
The development of global communication links at Ford

In the early 1990s, the Ford Motor Company spent nearly $100 million creating a massive database which can be accessed from any of 17 000 terminals worldwide, with a maximum response time of four seconds.

The system, called Worldwide Engineering Release System (WERS), links Ford's hundreds of sites across the world to a database which holds engineering information about parts for all cars produced by the company – Thunderbirds, Mustangs, Escorts and many more. Ford believed that this system would give the company at least a two-year lead over rivals. Of course, by the mid-1990s most large motor manufacturers were employing similar systems.

WERS was set up to replace six separate systems which were difficult to link up. The new system links 20 000 engineers and designers working for Ford in Europe, the USA, South America, Australia and the UK.

The advantage of having centralised information which is accessible worldwide is that manufacture can be switched to available capacity, and designers need not be in the same factory, site or even country as the engineers or assemblers.

The system is capable of handling 500 000 queries daily. One of the key requirements of the design was speed, which is why the system has been built to respond to queries within four seconds.

Questions for discussion

1 *Who will benefit from Ford's new Worldwide Engineering Release System? How will they benefit?*
2 *In what ways will the new system help to make Ford more competitive?*
3 *What types of internal communication system or model can be supported by such a system?*
4 *Why might grass-roots employees appreciate working with this communication system?*
5 *Why is it important to an organisation like Ford to use such a high-powered communication system?*
6 *How can such a system support decentralisation and empowerment within the organisation?*

Dysfunctions of information technology

Although information technology has great potential to liberate employees from routine tasks and to provide them with new skills and powers, it can also have a number of dysfunctional effects. The computer in the workplace may limit employees' freedom of movement and stifle informal communication which formerly took place through conversation.

Technology in itself is not a liberating force; it depends on the way in which the application of technology is managed. An employee placed in front of a computer screen carrying out routine operations may feel alienated and powerless.

K. Weick has identified five deficiencies of working with computers, which can lead to a chaotic understanding of the world.

1 **Action deficiencies**. The operator works with symbols on a screen, which are representations of the real world. The operator is thus divorced from real-world sights, sounds and actions.
2 **Comparison deficiencies**. The operator has to rely on one uncontradicted source of information – his or her computer terminal. Operators cannot move around, looking at things from different angles and perspectives.
3 **Affiliation deficiencies**. Working with a screen discourages the operator from sharing ideas and discussions with other people.
4 **Deliberation deficiencies**. On the screen it is hard to separate what is important from what is unimportant.
5 **Consolidation deficiencies**. Material on the screen does not look like work in progress. It presents a static picture rather than an ongoing workflow that needs to be built on and worked at.

These considerations are highly important. More and more people are engaged in activities involving the use of IT communications systems. These systems have tremendous potential to integrate work and to enhance fruitful interdependence in organisations. Increasingly, new systems are being developed which enable integration of software applications.

A major breakthrough in modern computing came with the development of graphical user interfaces (GUIs or 'gooies'). GUIs are designed to make technology easier to understand and use, and in so doing they have changed the face of computers. A GUI presents the user with a series of small pictures called *icons* which represent the various options available.

A mouse is used to move an arrow around the screen and select the appropriate icon for the desired action. At the press of a key, the screen then redraws itself to show the next set of options. If the user has selected word processing, for example, the screen will change to provide a second series of options, and each option chosen will lead to a further set of options.

Window systems go one stage further, giving the same type of graphical interface, but allowing the user to carry out several tasks simultaneously. For example, the user could be writing a document in the word-processing window while carrying out some other function at the same time in another window.

Today's book and laptop computers are light and easy to transport, and can easily be linked to vast communications networks. Hardware manufacturers such as Apple, IBM and Motorola are developing combined integrated projects so that all of the major software packages can be used on their hardware.

There is no shortage of hardware and software designed to facilitate effective communication. However, the effectiveness of communications within an organisation depends on its own communication systems. The way in which an organisation is constructed determines its effectiveness (see Figure 14.6). A company may have the best available resources, but unless it has an effective structure its communication system may fail.

Figure 14.6 Constructing an organisation's communications system

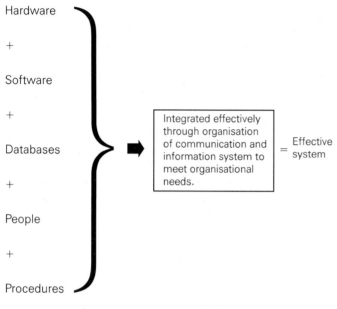

Criteria of efficiency/deficiency in communications

Bavelas and Leavitt's study of different channels of communication indicated that the 'star-shape' channel, radiating around a central individual, is effective for simple tasks. However, the central individual will suffer from overload once communications reach a given level of complexity.

All-channel communication, where everyone can communicate with everyone else, is slow, but is the most effective for technical tasks.

It is possible to identify a number of requirements or criteria for effective communication networks.

- Messages must reach all of the individuals required.
- Both senders and recipients need to share an understanding of what is being communicated, and to be able to act upon it.
- Channel sizes should be adequate. For example, a database which forms part of an organisations networked communication system needs to be able to handle all of the enquiries that are made of it at any one time – imagine how frustrated customers would be

if, on asking the bank for a balance on their current accounts, they were told that the system could not be entered because it was being over-used. If the channel size is not large enough, then organisations will need to introduce an organised queuing system. However, if communication channels are frequently overloaded, there is a strong case for redesign of the communication system. For example, if supervisors and managers do not have enough time to read suggestions coming through an organised suggestion box, they may be losing out on valuable information from the grass roots. There is a strong argument for building in time for managers to meet employees or to have time set aside for reading suggestions.

An effective communication system should be economic. There should be no unnecessary waste, such as people attending meetings and conferences when they have nothing to gain from them, or brochures and leaflets which are not read. Clearly, in designing a communication system the organisation needs to find out the requirements of its users. It should then build the system to serve these needs. Important questions to consider include:

- How do people want to be consulted?
- When do they want to be consulted?
- What media do they respond to most readily?

The communication system should be technically efficient, and employees need to know how to use the system. Training enables them to do a wide range of tasks more effectively.

A communication system needs to be reliable, i.e. it should perform its intended function without constant checks or alterations. One cause of malfunction is the 'gaps' which frequently occur when someone is not sending on a message, or has not been trained to communicate clearly. Gaps may also occur when people leave a post or are often absent from the workplace. Careful planning in the design and delivery of communication systems is essential, and there should be a procedure for reviewing them regularly to check that they are working effectively. 'Blocks' can occur in the communications system either through information overload or through deliberate sabotage. From time to time new channels will need to be devised.

Symptoms of poor communications include:

- **management failure**, where decisions are being made late and with a poor sense of direction. Indications of this may be increasing waste, disagreement and lack of coordination
- **human failure**, when individuals and groups working within the organisation show increasing signs of alienation and disenchantment, as well as making more

mistakes. Indications of this include increasing numbers of disputes and disagreements, rising tempers, high levels of absenteeism, etc.

■ **resource waste**, where firms fail to use their resources adequately. Sales orders may not be met and there will be rising stocks and inventories, overstaffing, etc. Clearly, such an organisation is losing touch with its environment and with its capacity to coordinate activities.

The relationship between organisation type and communication systems

The type of organisation strongly influences the type of communication system in use. In a large, static organisation, there may be many formalised channels of communication, such as in a traditional manufacturing company or in a government department with set routines. In more dynamic environments, such as research organisations, and in new firms operating in highly competitive situations, it may be more common to have all-channel networks.

Bureaucracies are based on highly formalised patterns of communication, which are predominantly top-down. More organic structures are typified by a much more flexible pattern of communications.

In the past, larger organisations have tended towards elaborate formalised communication systems which were built up and modified over a period of time. However, more recently, as these organisations have reduced staffing levels, they have introduced flexible networks supported by information technology. For example, Shell UK carried out a restructuring programme in the 1990s aimed at improving communications, including workshops and communications training activities. A major objective has been to encourage employees to identify improvements in their own work areas which can be pushed through using their own initiative. A flatter approach to organisational design has been introduced, making communications quicker and easier. The emphasis has been on teamwork and cutting layers of complexity out of the organisation.

The culture of an organisation will have an important influence on communications. Friendly, open organisations will encourage participation. Others, more steeped in a tradition of 'us and them', are likely to focus on formal communication channels. The typical downward form of communication in such organisations

will consist of instructions and orders, and management-organised training and advice.

The type of communications involved will depend on the organisation's stage of development. Initially, an organisation may use informal personal relationships. As it expands, it may then develop formalised communication channels in a functional/divisional structure. As the organisation is usually faced by a fluid environment, it may again need to adapt more flexible forms of communication. A network structure is likely to develop for control, authority and communication and there may be an increasing emphasis on lateral communications. Communication will increasingly consist of information and advice, rather than in commands and instructions.

Typical activities will be the formation of discussion groups to discuss data and problems, the use of the quality circle jointly to identify and tackle work issues, and an increased emphasis on conferences and meetings with colleagues and customers.

The importance of control

It is important to develop controls for communication systems. At a simple level, when discussing issues or problems with a colleague at work, it is helpful to find out how much they have understood of what you have said. Figure 14.7 illustrates this simple communication-process model. If you find that people do not understand what you are saying, then you will have to alter the way in which you communicate your message.

Figure 14.7 A simple communication-process model

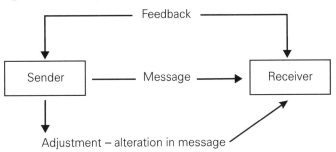

The same principle applies to any form of communication used within an organisation. Control mechanisms can, for example, find out how effective memos or notices are, so that appropriate alterations to methods and procedures may be made. Controls should enable an organisation to make continuing adjustments to its communication system in order to meet organisational goals and objectives. For example, if a firm sets standards for message recognition, and these standards are not met, communication systems will need to be altered. The standards set form the basis for control.

Further reading

- *Communication Skills: A Thematic Approach* by D. Pepperell. Stanley Thornes, 1988.

- *People in Business* by C. E. Stafford. Cambridge University Press, 1991.
- *Computers and Information Systems in Business* by L. Gremillion and P. Pyburn. McGraw-Hill, 1988.
- *Management* by Peter Drucker. McGraw-Hill, 1990.

15 Identifying and changing organisational culture

On completion of this chapter students should be able to:

- identify organisational cultures, rules and norms

- identify and analyse the factors which influence changing organisational cultures, rules and norms

- identify and evaluate the relationships between organisational cultures, structures and performance

- influence and adapt to organisational change.

Organisational culture

The formal and informal cultures of organisations

The culture of an organisation is an amalgam of the organisation's past achievements, present ambitions, recruitment criteria, attitudes to staff, customers and the outside world – and the attitudes of the outside world towards the organisation. It is an extremely powerful force. A simple definition of organisational culture is 'the way we do things around here'.

However, the culture of an organisation is not easy to identify. Talk to any managing director and he or she will have a fairly clear picture of 'the way we do things around here', perhaps based on perceptions or relationships, and the attitudes, values, rules and norms in the organisation. When you contrast this view with someone else's in the organisation, however, you may be presented with a different view. Identifying a culture from inside an organisation may be difficult because employees are so wrapped up in organisational activities and their own sets of relationships. Identifying a culture from outside an organisation may be equally problematic because it will be difficult to disentangle the web of relationships and activities that take place within the organisation. Pinning down cultures is, in practice, always an elusive task.

Before reading further, refer back to the introduction to organisational cultures on pages 222–3. There it was stated that

> 'Culture gives an organisation a sense of identity – "who we are", "what we stand for", "what we do". It determines the way in which, through the organisation's legends, rituals, beliefs, meanings, values, norms and language, "things are done around here".'

The formal culture

The formal culture of an organisation is represented in official definitions of culture which can usually be found in the literature provided by the company, e.g. the annual report, and in statements made by officials within the organisation. *The formal culture of an organisation is that which is formally recognised as representing the 'party line' on culture within the organisation.*

The official culture underpins the way in which the objectives of the organisation are viewed. Statements about objectives provide a good guide to the formal culture. The **mission statement** usually gives a guide as to the beliefs of the organisation, e.g. its attitude to employee participation, responsibility for the environment and wider community, and so on. A third guide to identifying culture is the assumptions that are made within the organisation. These are the things that are taken for granted by members of an organisation: for example that they can discuss things freely with each other; that they expect to work hard, to enjoy their work and to be well rewarded. These assumptions are a natural part of organisational life. They are often difficult to pin down, simply because they are so deeply embedded in people's day-to-day expectations.

Views about objectives, beliefs and assumptions all contribute to an organisational culture which create norms of behaviour and attitudes to customers, staff and suppliers.

Case Study
Saatchi and Saatchi

In January 1995 Maurice Saatchi resigned from the advertising agency of Saatchi and Saatchi. He had built up the agency with his brother Charles. It became the world's most famous advertising agency, numbering among its clients the Conservative Party and British Airways. It created some highly memorable campaigns (e.g. 'Labour isn't working' – a poster campaign showing long unemployment queues which helped to bring down the Labour Party in 1979).

During the 1990s Maurice Saatchi increasingly lost control of the agency as new managers moved in. Finally, he resigned, making the statement that the agency had been taken over by people 'who cared little for advertising, clients or the views of staff'.

Questions for discussion

1 *What do you think is the 'culture' of an organisation?*
2 *Why might cultures change over time?*
3 *To what extent does the case study indicate that the 'culture' of an organisation is determined by the perceptions of those involved in the organisation?*

The creation of the formal culture can be seen as an attempt by those with most power in an organisation to

influence the culture of that organisation. Organisations take a particular view of themselves which is expressed in advertising, e.g. 'Your caring sharing Co-op'.

Task

Can you identify aspects of formal culture in the advertising slogans that organisations use to promote their image?

Organisations also make statements about themselves and their values which are intended to raise the morale of staff, e.g. in a company newspaper. This inspirational view of what an organisation is (or should be) gives a fair idea of formal definitions of culture.

Those responsible for managing an organisation will try to create a culture within an organisation. Clearly, the creation of this internal cultural environment is very important and should be designed to match the objectives of the organisation and the external environment. There are many ways of creating and changing this environment (see pages 346–9). Some managers will try to create loose, informal relationships, while others will try to tie things down to highly prescribed relationships and ways of operating. For example, when in the 1970s Sir Robert Moffat took over the Port Talbot steel works in Wales, which employed 13 500 people, it had a reputation for poor labour relations and had become a manager's 'graveyard'. Moffat's solution to problems was to create a book two inches thick, which named and described every job there was in the plant. The creation of such unambiguous definitions of working practice was a revolution in the steel industry, which was then characterised by many different unions, each negotiating separate deals for different groups of employees. Moffat, therefore, set out to create clear working arrangements and relationships in the organisation in a highly formalised structure. Whether or not we agree with this process, it is clear that such an alteration of relationships would have a profound impact on the culture of the organisation.

The informal culture

The way in which culture actually operates may be different from the official definitions. *The informal culture of an organisation is that which is embedded in the real interactions and perceptions within an organisation, i.e. culture in action.*

Some writers draw a distinction between the formal stated culture, which they call **corporate culture** and the informal culture in action, which they call **organisational culture** (see Figure 15.1).

Figure 15.1 The difference between formal and informal cultures

Corporate culture	Organisational culture
Formal	Informal
Explicit	Explicit and implicit
Based on management rhetoric	Based on culture in action
Based on wishful thinking	Based on 'reality'

Edgar Schein, in *Organisational Culture and Leadership*, defined organisational culture as:

'the deeper level of basic assumptions and beliefs that are shared by members of an organisation, that operate unconsciously and define in a basic "taken for granted" fashion an organisation's view of itself and its environment'.

Although organisational culture is difficult to identify and measure, we all know that it is there. Those people who have moved from one organisation operating in a similar framework to another will be aware that wide differences can occur for a variety of reasons, e.g. the history and development of the organisation, the personalities concerned, the organisation of work processes, etc.

Formality/informality

An alternative way of differentiating between formal and informal cultures is according to the level of formality in the organisation. For example, a formal culture may exist in a hierarchical, bureaucratic organisation based on set patterns and procedures, e.g. in the traditional civil service. An informal culture would be based on much looser informal arrangements, such as in a loose, flexible, modern organisation.

Positive and negative cultures

A positive culture is one that is based on objectives, values, and assumptions which match with those of its stakeholders. It is this fit between the way in which the organisation functions and operates and the individuals and groups that make up the organisation that creates the positive culture.

Anita Roddick, founder of the Body Shop, reflecting on the company's success, recently commented in *Body and Soul*:

'When people talk about the Body Shop they talk about our philosophy, our campaigning, our social and educational policies and the way we have managed to humanise business practices.

What everyone wants to know – and no one seems to be able to work out – is if there is a direct link between the company's values and its success. When people ask us how we do it, I tell them it is easy.

- *First, you have to have fun.*
- *Second, you have to put love where your labour is.*
- *Third, you have to go in the opposite direction to everyone else . . .*

Running in the opposite direction and breaking the rules has always been part of the culture of the Body Shop. I get a real buzz from doing things differently from everyone else. It was breaking all the rules of retailing, for example, to use our windows not to promote a product but an issue we feel strongly about.'

For the culture of the Body Shop to be positive, it is essential that values and assumptions such as those outlined above match with both the actual practice in the organisation and the values of employees, consumers, suppliers, etc. The evidence strongly indicates that the success of the Body Shop in recent times has resulted from the creation of this positive culture. Unfortunately, there are also many recent examples of organisations with negative cultures which have led to poor performance. For example, a report produced on the London Ambulance Service in January 1995 identified a culture of conflict. The report stated:

'The service suffers from a conflicting culture, some staff seeing themselves as part of a hierarchical emergency service like the fire or police, others as part of an informal caring service. Crews and controls do not understand each other's problems, generating both a "blame culture" and, "dangerously", a lack of respect among crews for instructions of control staff.'

The report stemmed from the tragic death of a young girl. Her parents had made five separate calls to the ambulance service for emergency treatment. The ambulance took nearly an hour to arrive. The report also outlined a wide range of inefficiencies within the organisation.

The above case highlights the example of a negative culture in which there is lack of understanding between the various people in an organisation, a clash of values and misinterpretation of objectives.

Backward-facing and forward-looking cultures

One important aspect of organisational culture is the emphasis on tradition. Some organisations are heavily influenced by previous practice, legends and ways of doing things. Other organisations are innovative and entrepreneurial, with little respect for previous patterns or methods, e.g. Anita Roddick's statement above that 'running in the opposite direction and breaking the rules has always been part of the culture of the Body Shop'.

A company with a backward-facing culture is likely to be:

- product or procedure led
- controlled by traditional managers who have worked their way up through the organisation
- conservative in attitude
- resistant to change
- inward looking
- a risk avoider.

Such organisations are becoming fewer in a modern, dynamic, business environment.

In contrast, entrepreneurial organisations are likely to be:

- market led
- inclined to trust the human resource to make decisions at ground level
- keen to introduce talented managers who will bring in bright new ideas
- seeking change
- keenly aware of changes in the external environment, with the capacity to choose appropriate strategic options to make a response
- prepared to take risks.

Case Study
The Virgin Group

The Virgin Group entered the financial services sector in 1995. It has created a 50/50 venture with the Norwich Union called Virgin Direct. This will sell a range of personal financial services, such as life pensions, investment and personal equity plans.

At the same time the organisation has introduced Virgin Cola which is retailed through independent shops. The market share of Virgin Cola quickly took a 15 per cent share of the cola market by early 1995. Virgin is also planning to market Virgin Vodka nationwide by setting up a separate vodka company with William Grant, the manufacturer of Glenfiddich malt whisky.

Virgin feels that it can create value products which meet the needs of consumers. While these ventures are expected to be Virgin's last big sweep into an entirely new area for some time, the group will continue to launch new ventures within its existing core businesses – the airline, retail, communications and trading. The aim of trading,

which includes the latest joint ventures in drinks and financial services, is to expand the brand where it can add value and help market products.

Virgin research has indicated that people associate the Virgin name with innovation, competitive prices and quality of product.

Questions for discussion

1 *What is your perception of the culture of the Virgin Group?*
2 *What are the advantages of being associated with this particular type of culture?*
3 *What sorts of relationships would you expect to operate at Virgin, e.g. with employees, researchers, customers, etc?*
4 *How can management at Virgin seek to promote this culture?*

Autocratic and democratic cultures

Power relations within an organisation have a profound impact on culture. The old-fashioned autocracy based on the founder/leader of an organisation is still around, but is far less prevalent. The autocratic structure tends to be based on the top-down approach to decision–making and the dominant values will be those of a single person. For example, former prime minister Margaret Thatcher was often associated with autocratic views and, therefore, the way in which her cabinets operated was vastly different from those of her successor, the more democratic John Major. The advantages of autocracies is that they are based on clear powers and chains of command. However, they will be inappropriate in situations where flexibility is required. Autocracies are likely to be characterised by strong traditions, beliefs and norms of behaviour. Autocracies do not suit individuals who are creative and like to work to flexible patterns.

Democratic cultures will develop in situations where decisions need to be made at grass-roots level and where empowerment is important to the organisation's success. Organisations such as Mars and many Japanese companies in Britain are organised on more democratic lines. The culture of 'working together' manifests itself in shared washroom and canteen facilities, coupled with the operation of 'quality circles'.

This contrasts with some traditional British companies where the management has its own car-parking facilities close to the building entrance, its own executive suite and restaurant. The managers wear suits. Office staff enter by one entrance to the organisation and start work later than manual operatives, who have to clock in at an earlier time. Office staff may receive a monthly salary paid directly into their bank account, while manual staff receive a weekly pay packet. Of course, some of these stereotypes are disappearing, e.g. the distinction between 'white collar' office staff and 'blue-overalled' maintenance staff. However, these distinctions are still in evidence on the railways, airlines, and even in universities and colleges. Even when these distinctions have been disguised, there often continues to be a 'them and us' attitude, resulting from the reality of interpersonal relationships.

Profit-driven/social responsibility cultures

Another important feature in organisational culture stems from differences in key organisational objectives. A clear distinction exists between those organisations that set out with the profit objective uppermost and those driving towards social responsibility.

In a profit-driven organisation the emphasis will be very much on revenue maximisation and cost minimisation. Individuals will be rewarded according to how effectively they manage particular sets of resources. This emphasis, for example, is illustrated by the comment of John Baker, the Chief Executive of the newly privatised National Power, quoted in The *Independent* in 1990:

> *'The job is not about shouldering national responsibilities but about meeting contracts, improving profitability, seeking out opportunities but exploiting them only if it pays to do so. Our task will not be to keep the lights on whatever the costs. It will probably pay us to ensure we never overstress our plant.'*

The emphasis on profit has a clear impact on values within the organisation. Performance is related to individual accountabilities. Individuals flourish within an organisation according to their success in meeting performance standards. The assumptions that people take to heart are based on these values.

By contrast, in organisations geared towards social responsibility, the emphasis will be on the environment, the wider community, quality relationships within the organisation, etc. Individuals will be highly valued when their contribution most clearly reflects these values. Organisations traditionally associated with social responsibility include schools, hospitals, care centres for the elderly and environmental protection agencies. It is not surprising that individuals working within these organisations are not comfortable with the cultural shift that has emphasised the importance of profit in recent years. The media of the mid-1990s is full of examples of groups of public-service workers who have felt demoralised by cultural changes in their sector, e.g. teachers, nurses, prison officers, and social workers.

Public image

The public image of an organisation is an important ingredient of its culture.

Image is an amalgam of an individual's personal experience of a company or product, plus whatever he or she has read or heard from other sources. Advertising can help create or reshape an image, but personal experience and the comments of other users are far more potent.

Shell is an example of an organisation with a first-class public image. It is a prominent brand name in the market, with an image that has been gradually built up over many years. Maintaining a desired image is always hard work, and nowhere more so than at the customer interface. Shell service stations, for instance, serve hundreds of thousands of customers every day. Each of these encounters can consolidate or weaken the image – depending on the personality and expertise of the people involved. Staff selection and training are crucial, as well as making sure that employees display the type of values that the organisation would like to see reflected. This can only come about by creating the right opportunities to ensure that employees enjoy working for their organisation. The name of the game is **empowerment** and **trust**.

Shell holds special courses for everyone involved with service stations – licencees, managers, cashiers, console operators, forecourt staff, cleaners – to make sure that the basic 'service' responsibilities, such as safety, cleanliness and product availability, are properly understood, as well as the need for the 'human touch' – a friendly smile and a cheerful 'hello'.

Tribal features

The concept of **tribal features** has been applied by some business writers to the impact of organisational culture on groups and individuals. (A tribe is a social division of people based on common descent, territory and culture.) They argue that people will increasingly take on the shared values of a particular organisational culture (see Figure 15.2). They will begin to develop the same assumptions and values. They may start to dress alike and to use the same sort of language. They will begin to think in similar patterns and feel more comfortable with someone from their own tribe. They may be quite hostile to the attitudes and values of people from other tribes. For example, a television programme recently featured a documentary about groups of managers who were asked to work collaboratively on a project. Some of the managers were from profit-oriented private industries, while others worked for the voluntary sector and charities. There was an immediate clash between the way the two

Figure 15.2 'Tribal' differences

groups wanted to operate. The private-sector individuals wanted to establish targets and plans, while the voluntary-sector managers wanted to spend time finding out more about the other managers on the team and arriving at common agreement. There was a clash between those who wanted to move on with the task, and those who favoured moving on with the process. The managers quickly divided into two distinct social groups.

There is no doubt that an organisation can quickly socialise individuals into the norms and patterns of behaviour of the tribe. Socialised individuals will then be likely to perpetuate the legends and the norms of the tribe. They may become defensive towards outsiders. Studies have shown that new police officers, teachers and soldiers may take quite a long time to be accepted as part of the tribe. In order to win acceptance, they will need to develop the values and take on board the assumptions of the tribe. Particularly influential will be the tribal chiefs

(high-status individuals). Failure to socialise will lead to individuals becoming outcasts, who will then either leave the organisation of their own free will, or play a minor role in tribal affairs.

Rules and codes of behaviour

Some of the most important rules in an organisation are unwritten, i.e. group norms. **Norms** are generally agreed, informal rules which guide a group member's behaviour. Often group members may not realise the full impact of these norms because they become assumptions which are 'taken for granted'. These norms may relate to such matters as working extra hard when a deadline needs to be met, contributing to the farewell present of colleagues, keeping the office tidy, etc. Many of the norms of an organisation will contribute to the success of the organisation.

- **Prescriptive norms** set out behaviour that should be carried out, e.g. being polite to customers, recycling envelopes within the organisation, etc.
- **Proscriptive norms** set out behaviour that should not be carried out, e.g. sitting in the head of department's chair, smoking in the office, etc.

Working groups will establish prescriptive and proscriptive norms which become deeply embedded in the culture of the organisation.

Norms develop:

- over a period of time. They become **institutionalised norms** within a particular organisation, e.g. calling a senior manager Mrs Smith, rather than Molly.
- because they carry over from previous practice and situations, e.g. when a doctor changes from one group practice to another, he or she will continue the professional conduct of allowing routine patients only 10 minutes of time.
- though explicit statements from other group members – 'That's the way we do it around here!'
- because of a critical event in the group's history. A particular event determines the way things are handled in future, e.g. a member of a Premier League football team makes an 'off-the-cuff' comment to the media which is widely misreported. The club's players, therefore, agree that in future they will not talk to the media.

Normative pressures are very important in organisational life. In an entrepreneurial organisation there may be a strong emphasis on hard work and commitment. This value rubs off on all group members. By contrast, in a non-entrepreneurial organisation the norm may be that everyone goes home at 5 pm and does not think about the organisation again until they arrive at work the next day.

Norms will both reflect the formal culture of an organisation and informal relationships between people. Whatever organisation you work for you will quickly get a feel for norms of behaviour by the reactions you get from fellow employees to your own actions.

More formalised rules and codes of behaviour are also an important part of the cultural framework. Rules and regulations will often be set down in formal rule books. A **code of behaviour** is a conventionalised set of principles or rules. Many rules will have corresponding sanctions if they are not complied with. 'Abiding by the rules' is regarded as essential in many organisations. However, in other organisations rules will not be clear-cut and there will be considerable scope for interpretation.

Subcultures

A subculture is a culture within a culture. For example, in a departmentalised organisation there may be different subcultures according to departmental divisions (see Figure 15.3).

Figure 15.3 Departmental subcultures

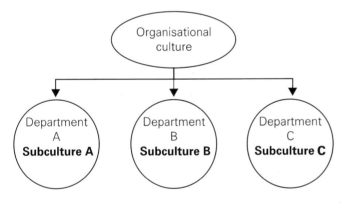

Members of a particular subculture will share a common set of values, expectations, beliefs and assumptions which will differ from those of other subcultural groups. They may dress differently, speak differently, act differently, and tend to associate primarily with people in their own grouping.

The existence of subcultures is not necessarily a bad thing. Within an organisation it may be important to have different groupings of people, e.g. researchers with a research-driven culture, accountants with a finance-driven culture, marketers with a sales culture. It may be important for certain groupings to be more risk oriented, more people oriented, more flamboyant or conventional, etc. The important thing is that these cultural groupings are all working towards the same organisational objectives.

Winning teams

Highly successful organisations are likely to be based on the 'winning team' principle. They will have highly integrated teams of people who share the same values and aspirations (see Figure 15.4). There will be a strong bond between team members, which leads to powerful group norms.

Figure 15.4 Manchester United 1994: a famous example of a winning team

The factors which lead to the cohesiveness of such a team include:

1 the severity of the initiation into the group. Research tends to indicate that the harder it is to get into a team, the more committed successful individuals will be to that team. Individuals will be prepared to make 'sacrifices' to get into the team, e.g. by training and hard work. Once they have achieved team membership they will want all their efforts to be worthwhile and will strive to maintain the success of the team. Their motivation will drive towards the successful achievement of team objectives.

2 the existence of external threats or competition. Rivalry and threat are both strong driving forces. When individuals can identify a common enemy, they will work closely to defeat this enemy. For example, during both world wars all social classes in Britain worked together as never before. Everyone perceived themselves to be threatened by a common enemy. They were prepared to forget their divisions and cooperate. Of course, once the threat disappears, the old rivalries and divisions may come to the surface again. Members of a business organisation will be prepared to work hard together to defeat 'the opposition'. People who have been to school and

university together may become bitter rivals when they work for competing companies, or opposing political parties.

The team spirit tends to increase the longer the team is together, and tends to be stronger in smaller rather than larger teams.

Another important ingredient of success is the achievement of success, as in the adage 'nothing succeeds like success'. The winning team may continue as the winning team for a long time because of cultural expectations that arise within the team. In cricket we talk about the great West Indian cricket teams of the 1970s and 1980s, and in football we recall the 'Busby Babes' and Don Revie's Leeds, etc. These teams were successful with a relatively small playing personnel over a number of years. They were the great winning teams which rallied around success. Business organisations can learn a lot from the 'winning team approach'.

Winning departments

Winning departments within an organisation will be those departments which share the features of winning teams. 'Everyone' may want to work in that department so that it is difficult to get into. The department may see itself as being in competition with other departments, i.e. to stay at the top. It may experience relatively low turnover of personnel and may be relatively small in size (if not, it may be arranged in subsections). Importantly, the department will have a history of success. All of these factors will serve to create the values and norms of success. Success becomes the tradition of the winning department. It is noticeable that most if not all winning departments are characterised by a leader or group of leaders with exceptional, winning qualities.

Power and influence

We have already looked at power and influence in some depth on pages 233–6. A widely used definition of power is: *the capacity to change the behaviour or attitudes of another in a desired manner.*

Power can reside in individuals and in groups. More significantly, it can be vested in organisational cultures. A group of team members may have the power to change the behaviour of a member of the team by putting normative pressure on him or her. A group of subordinates may have the power to negate the decision of a superior by ignoring the superior's ruling on a particular matter.

Power is vested in individuals when:

■ they are able to confer rewards on others – **reward power**

■ they are able to punish others – **coercive power**
■ they are recognised to have legitimate authority – **legitimate power**
■ they are liked by others – **referent power**
■ they have a particular skill or ability – **expert power**.

This means that most of the time tutors have considerable power over their students because:

■ they mark students' work (**rewards**)
■ they can fail students (**coercion**)
■ the students accept their authority as tutors (**legitimation**)
■ the students think they are OK (**referentialism!**)
■ the students think they know what they are talking about (**expertise**).

However, it is not difficult to see that a tutor could quickly lose this power.

Different individuals have varying power bases within an organisation. These power relationships are important in determining the relationships between individuals, and thus the organisational culture. High-status, powerful individuals are in a position to influence most strongly the culture of the organisation. However, power within an organisation is often vested in the most unexpected places, e.g. with the caretaker who holds the keys to the building and is in charge of it for most of the hours of the day and night. It is important, therefore, to explore the informal power relationships within an organisation, as well as more formal structures.

Research has highlighted two major sources of power for groups or departments within an organisation.

Control over critical resources

Some groups and departments within an organisation have most control over the critical resources, i.e. the resources on which other departments depend. The most commonly quoted example is the hold of the finance department over the purse strings. Without money, other departments are highly restricted. For example, a common complaint of football managers is that they cannot win matches without buying 'match-winning players'. Control over critical resources is thus a key determinant of organisational power. Those with power are most able to determine culture, e.g. the accountant may be able to impose in some measure a finance-driven, profit-oriented culture on an organisation.

Power through dependence

In a similar way, groupings in a company hold power if other groups' actions are contingent on what the specific group does. For example, if we consider critical-path analysis, the departments which perform activities that lie along the critical path have considerable power. The success of the whole operation depends on their meeting targets on time.

In different industries, strategic contingencies will be vested in different departments. For example, in food processing, which involves the development of new products, they may lie in research and sales.

Groupings within an organisation can increase their power (or reduce their lack of power) by reducing their dependence on other groups. Clearly, departments which control strategic contingencies have the ability to be most influential within the organisation and, therefore, to contribute to organisational culture in a major way.

The influence of key individuals and departments within an organisation will be important in shaping culture. However, they cannot determine culture because culture cannot be forced on individuals and groups. Values cannot be forced on unwilling recipients.

Tasks and working practices

The culture of an organisation will filter down to all aspects of organisational behaviour. In an organisation like Marks & Spencer, which prides itself on its consumer orientation, this culture will affect all operational activities, e.g. the way staff deal with customers, the care given to the packaging and display of products, and allowing customers to return unsuitable goods.

As the culture of an organisation changes in the course of time, it will adopt different working practices. For example, under pressure from environmentalists, McDonald's has phased out the polystyrene containers that used to litter city streets; Tesco is promoting recycling; Guinness is supporting the protection of elephants in Kenya; and Sainsbury's is funding dolphin protection patrols in south China.

The importance of culture, therefore, is that it is all-pervasive and manifests itself in all of an organisation's tasks and working practices – 'the way things are done around here'.

Task

Identify some of the tasks and working practices of three organisations known to you which reflect the cultures of these organisations.

Cooperation and competition

It seems inevitable that both competition and cooperation will be typical features of any organisation. The question is whether it is possible to achieve a balance between the two forces.

Some people believe competition to be a natural drive, and an inherent feature, of human nature. For example, the current Conservative government favours competition and in 1994 ensured that 'competitive games' featured in the compulsory curriculum for PE in schools.

There are other thinkers who argue that competition is an anti-social force and that we should instead concentrate on cooperation. They argue that it is only through cooperation that there will be a sustainable future for people on earth. For a number of years, several Labour-controlled local education authorities have encouraged 'cooperative games' and 'cooperative sports' in schools.

Every organisation is faced by a competitive and changing environment. It would seem to be necessary for an organisation to compete to be successful. At the same time, it may need to cooperate with other organisations in joint ventures. The implication for the culture of an organisation is that unless competitiveness becomes part of the culture the organisation may expose a 'soft underbelly' and die.

However, within the organisation the emphasis must be, in many ways, on cooperation. Individuals, groups, departments, and divisions are mutually interdependent. They need to cooperate in order to meet common objectives. A culture of cooperation is, therefore, essential, but there should also be some scope for competitiveness within the organisation. Organisational plannners need to decide on the boundaries of acceptable competition within the organisation. For example, individuals and groups may be encouraged to enhance their own performance and earning potential provided that this does not hold back others within the organisation and makes the most effective contribution to organisational objectives.

Whatever organisation you work for, you will need to learn about the predominant culture and subcultures. You will need to explore the functioning of this culture, i.e. to what extent it contributes to the achievement of stated objectives. You will also need to get a feel for how you fit into the predominant culture and whether it is something you can be comfortable with.

Factors influencing organisational culture

The culture of an organisation will develop over time. A number of factors influence this culture:

■ history
■ ownership
■ size
■ technology
■ goals and objectives
■ the external cultural environment
■ organisational ethics
■ product ethics
■ business practice
■ trading policies.

The history and ownership of the organisation

The history of an organisation has an important influence on its culture. In the early days the organisation will take root, and a dominant culture will be put in place. In time this culture will alter as new people and new ideas enter the organisation, as new relationships are formed, and as the external environment changes. In studying cultures it is important to research their history by talking to people who have been involved at various stages of development and by looking through the paperwork and documents associated with each particular stage, e.g. advertisements, company policy documents, brochures, and annual reports.

When we look at the early history of organisations and the way in which they operated during this time, we often find that they were heavily influenced by the values of their founders. Much of this vision may be deeply embedded in current culture.

When Anita Roddick set up the Body Shop in 1976 she operated from a single shop in Brighton. She could never have dreamed of the ensuing success of the organisation. She says:

'The Body Shop style developed out of a Second World War mentality (shortages, utility goods, rationing) imposed by sheer necessity and the simple fact that I had no money. But I had a very clear image in my mind of the kind of style I wanted to create: I wanted it to look a bit like a country store in a spaghetti western.

'It is curious, looking back on it, how necessity accorded with philosophy. Even if I had had unlimited funds, for example, I would never have wasted money on expensive packaging – the garbage of conventional cosmetics ... The cheapest containers I could find were the plastic bottles used by hospitals to collect urine samples, but I

could not afford to buy enough. I thought I would get round the problem by offering to refill empty containers or to fill customers' own bottles. In this way we started recycling and reusing materials long before it became ecologically fashionable, but again it was born out of economic necessity rather than a concern for the environment.'

These early principles and ideas have gone on to shape the predominant culture of the Body Shop, which is identified today as an environmentally conscious company, with a deep-felt concern for important moral and ethical issues. It is likely that these values will continue to be a core ingredient of Body Shop values. Figure 15.5 shows the importance of core values.

Figure 15.5 The importance of the core values of the founders of an organisation

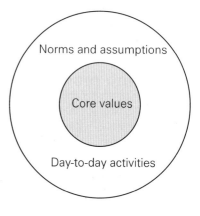

In the course of the history of an organisation, however, changes can take place in culture. For example, Boots the chemist is now also a retailer of wines and spirits. It is inconceivable that the founder Jesse Boot, who was a teetotaller, would have allowed such a development. Many of the early industrialists in this country came from Quaker families, e.g. Huntley and Palmer, and Rowntree. Originally, these companies placed a very strong emphasis on social values and paternalistic employment practices. Today, many of their organisations have become part of much larger groupings owned by shareholders, including major international financial institutions. This has often led to an increase in the emphasis on profits and a decline in the emphasis on social conscience.

Case Study
Changes in the retail cooperatives

Nowadays, people tend to think of the Co-op as just another supermarket chain. This is not the case. Co-ops place far greater emphasis on serving the community. The first co-op was set up by a group of weavers in Toad Lane in Rochdale in 1844. At that time, these workers were being paid low wages partly made up of tokens, which could only be exchanged in the company shop where prices were high. Twenty-eight weavers, known as the Rochdale Pioneers, pooled money to buy foodstuffs at wholesale prices, which they then sold cheaply to members. Profits were shared among members in the form of a dividend depending on how much each had bought. Since then, co-ops have spread and there are many retail co-ops in Britain.

To become a shareholder in a co-op you need only buy a £1 share and this entitles you to vote at meetings to choose the president and other officers of the local co-op society.

In the latter part of the nineteenth century the co-ops flourished and societies sprang up all over Britain. It was the co-ops that introduced the first supermarkets. However, the profit-oriented multiples like Tesco and Sainsbury's proved to be too competitive for the co-ops, which were organised into too many small societies and did not really benefit from bulk buying. Many of the senior officials in co-ops were people who had worked their way up through the ranks or who had won support in elections in their local areas, rather than professional managers. These inexperienced managers were generally not as efficient as those managing the new multiples, or as cut-throat. They also clung to their social conscience.

During the 1970s and 1980s the co-ops increasingly lost market share. They came to be associated with a rather dowdy image and downmarket products. The co-ops have continued to suffer with the development of hypermarkets.

To fight back, small societies have merged together, closing hundreds of small shops and branches. During the 1980s the Co-op began to build its own Leo hypermarkets. It increasingly employed specialist managers with good qualifications and retailing experience. It began to develop a new, slicker image. Co-ops still continue to be located in many traditional working-class areas as well as having high street stores, which are often indistinguishable from those of other retailers. The Co-op has had to project a similar image to that of most other retailers – hi-tech checkouts, wide variety, clean and bright shops, and value for money. The Co-op continues to serve the local community, e.g. by sponsoring community projects and by offering customers a square deal. However, it has undoubtedly changed over the years.

Questions for discussion

1 *Compare and contrast your image of today's Co-op with the perceptions of your parents and grandparents. What are the major changes that you can identify?*

2 *To what extent has the 'culture' of the Co-op been shaped by its history?*
3 *To what extent does the Co-op retain elements of its early culture?*
4 *Why has the culture of the Co-op changed over the years? Have these changes been inevitable?*

The size of the organisation and its technology

The size of an organisation is likely to have a major effect on the culture. The larger an organisation becomes the more difficult it is to run it on informal, personal lines. Increasingly, the organisation will need to employ professional managers with a range of organisational theories. As organisations expand, new divisions and departments are created, leading to new structural forms. For example, a small school may have a single staffroom and a relatively small number of subject departments. As the school increases in size, it may develop a number of faculties made up of departments. Each faculty may then have its own staffroom and resource base. In the small school there may be a unifying culture, but as the school separates into faculties, faculty subcultures start to develop. The same type of development is common across a range of growing organisations, e.g. hospitals, businesses, and any army regiments.

Because larger organisations are run by professional managers, they tend to try to put into practice the conventional wisdom of the day relating to organisational structure. For example, in the early 1900s managers in manufacturing organisations and offices might have tried to create a functional bureaucracy, or an organisation based on scientific lines. More recently, managers have been trying to rearrange the organisational architecture, and new organisational forms have sprung up, such as the hollow organisation, the networked organisation, the learning organisation, the modular corporation, the virtual organisation, the horizontal organisation, and many more.

The technology of the organisation will also influence its culture. Often there will be a close relationship between technology and size. For example, as organisations expand, they are able to utilise economies of scale using highly mechanised and automated production systems. In organisations in which people spend most of their time working with large machines, they may have little contact with other employees. In contrast, in people-intensive organisations there will be much human contact.

Perhaps we can contrast a 'machine-centred culture' with a 'people-centred culture'. The nature of the work performed inevitably influences employees' perceptions of the work situations and values in the workplace.

At one end of the spectrum is the job that involves endless repetition of a simple and tedious operation, where there are only a few seconds in which to perform the task before it has to be repeated. Employees get little sense of achievement from producing a very small part of an end product which they may never see. There may be very little time for conversation with workmates because of noise and the urgency to perform the next operation. In such an organisation employees may see themselves as being rather insignificant and relatively worthless.

At the other extreme, there are jobs involving personal involvement and individual contributions to the techniques of production. These jobs may require high levels of training and expertise and give employees prestige, as well as providing meaning in their working life. The culture in such an organisation may be rich in terms of shared values and aspirations.

Dorothy Wedderburn and Rosemary Crompton investigated work attitudes in a large chemical plant, which they called 'Seagrass', in northeast England. They found that 'different attitudes and behaviour within the work situation could be manifested by different groups of workers largely in response to the differences in the prevailing technologies and control systems'. For example, the process workers in the plant (which was mainly automated) found their jobs interesting, and felt that they had enough scope to try out their own ideas and sufficient freedom to organise their own work tasks. In contrast, workers in the machine shop felt that their work was boring and gave them little freedom to organise their own work tasks.

Attitudes produced by the job situation tended to be reflected in attitudes to supervisors: workers who found their jobs interesting and enjoyable tended to have a favourable view of their supervisors, while employees who found work boring tended to resent supervision.

Today, many employees work with information technology systems which give them access to information on demand. This development has the potential of empowering people to make decisions and to be more independent. Of course, this is not always the case. For example, there are still many secretarial employees who spend all day tapping other people's work into a word processor.

Goals and objectives

Goals and objectives are an important determinant of culture. In an effective organisation the culture will match with the objectives. A look at the aims and objectives of an organisation gives us an initial feel for the formal culture of that organisation.

For example, in an analysis of 208 1993–4 primary school brochures, Ian Copeland found that primary schools emphasised a number of aims (see Figure 15.6). The survey covered the independent sector as well as county-controlled and church schools, in six local education authorities. 'Maximisation of personal development' was the aim that more than half the schools declared to be their top priority.

Clearly, these stated aims will filter down into the life of the school, although it is important to bear in mind that rhetoric will often fade at the implementation stage. The aims established by the governors of a school may be quite different from the perceived aims of other participants in school life.

Tasks

1 What are the stated aims and objectives of the college or university where you are studying? Perhaps you could informally interview the principal of the college to find out whether these stated aims meet with his or her perceptions.
2 What are the views of other stakeholders and participants in university or college life? What is the relationship between their aims and objectives and its culture?

Different types of organisation will have different aims and objectives. The aims and objectives of charities, for example, will often be quite different from those of profit-maximising organisations. These goals and objectives help to create the cultural frameworks which shape behaviours within the organisation. Petrock's *Non-profit Making Strategies* has identified a number of major cultural frameworks of organisations (see Figure 15.7) which influence the ways in which staff are expected to function.

■ Bureaucratic frameworks are conservative, traditional and hierarchical. Employees are expected to follow the rules and go through the 'right channels'. The organisation and individuals within it tend to follow 'risk avoidance' strategies. Employees have the security of knowing how business will be conducted and do not have to take the responsibility of making unpredictable decisions. Clients will be confident that they will be treated consistently.
■ Entrepreneurial frameworks allow employees to take risks and to be innovators. Empowerment and experimentation are key themes. However, the organisation may become poorly focused, resulting in confusion.

Figure 15.6 Primary schools' expressed aims, 1993–4

Aims	County	Voluntary aided	Junior county	Infant county	% All
Personal development	52	60	50	36	48
Prepare for adult economic and civic life	25	27	36	4	21
Courtesy and consideration	13	20	19	33	22
Secure, happy school environment	18	23	19	24	21
Respect for environment	7	10	3	2	5
Good partnership with parents	7	2	3	16	8
Equal opportunities	15	13	25	9	15
Christian ethic/ moral values	6	47	12	6	13

(Source: *The Times Educational Supplement*, January 1995)

Figure 15.7 Types of cultural framework

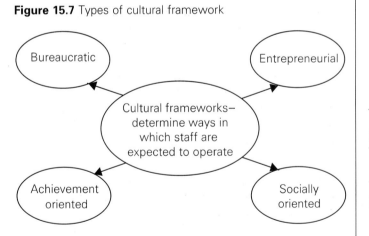

- Achievement-oriented frameworks encourage employees to set high standards and to achieve these standards. This brings a lot of satisfaction when they are successful. However, the danger is that there may be an emphasis on setting unachievable goals, and employees may be pushed too hard so that a 'sweatshop culture' develops.
- Socially-oriented frameworks emphasise the importance of relationships. Employees feel a strong

sense of support and caring among themselves, e.g. in a school or hospital. However, if the organisation is poorly focused this can lead to confused and inappropriate decision-making and poor use of resources.

Case Study
The National Trust

The National Trust was incorporated in 1907 by an Act of Parliament which set out its aims as follows:

'The National Trust shall be established for the purposes of promoting the permanent preservation for the benefit of the nation of lands and tenements (including buildings) of beauty or historic interest and as regards lands for the preservation (so far as practicable) of their natural aspect, features and animal and plant life.'

The Trust is administered by staff based at head offices in London, Gloucestershire and Wiltshire, and at sixteen regional offices. Policy is determined by the Council – half of which is elected by members, half nominated by institutions with related interests.

The National Trust has many stakeholders, often with conflicting views of how the organisation should be run. These many and varied interests include the needs of farming, public access, sport and recreation, nature conservation, archaeology and industrial archaeology. Decisions need constantly to be made as to where the emphasis of management should lie, e.g. when to favour the farm tenant, when nature conservation or archaeology is of paramount importance, when a young plantation needs protection or where public access can be improved.

Questions for discussion

1 *Why might an organisation, such as the National Trust, which has a wide variety of stakeholders, find it difficult to translate its aims into clear policies?*
2 *What factors are most likely to influence the predominant culture of an organisation like the National Trust?*

The external cultural environment

Organisational culture will develop out of the organisation's relationship with its external environment. The relationship between culture and environment is a two-way process (see Figure 15.8).

Figure 15.8 Culture/environment interface

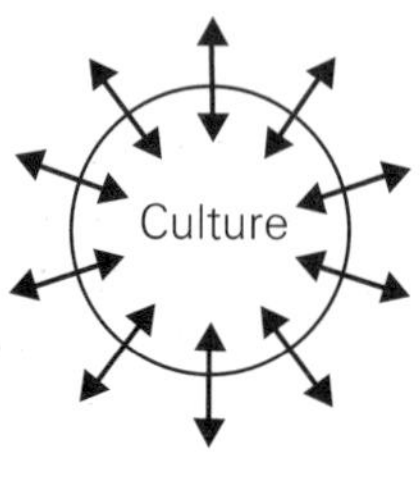

Environment

Culture

Schein argues in *Organisational Culture and Leadership* that 'the environment initially influences the formation of the culture, but once culture is present in the sense of shared assumptions, those shared assumptions, in turn, influence what will be perceived and defined as the environment'. For example, an organisation operating in an environment of rapidly changing technologies may feel that it needs to be at the cutting edge of technological development. By increasing the stakes in such development, it will make a contribution to perceptions within the industry that technology should be the driving force for competitiveness. The technological environment

and the organisational culture of technology-driven development thus reinforce each other.

Similarly, organisations which have employees operating in overseas markets may find that these employees feed back into the organisation new cultural dimensions and styles. For example, the British manager who spends some time working for an American division may bring back new approaches, such as greater informality with subordinates and even a new style of dress. These new approaches may influence the traditions, norms, and assumptions of the organisation. If a number of British managers start to bring in new ideas from abroad, this may lead to changes in business relationships in the UK.

Differences in national and regional cultures often play an important part in 'the way we do things around here'. For example, Randlesome and Butler suggest that German business people are considered highly sensitive to infringement of their personal space. Open-plan offices are the exception and executives like to protect themselves behind solid, closed doors. This contrasts with Japanese practice, where the open-plan office is common. Open-plan structures enhance teamwork approaches. However, a person's position in the Japanese hierarchy is subtly announced through the positioning of furniture.

When looking at national cultures we need to avoid stereotyping. However, important differences do occur, and this leads a number of organisations to employ foreign nationals as partners in joint ventures when trading and doing business in their country.

Organisational ethics – product ethics, business practice and trading policies

The ethics of an organisation are important in determining 'the right way to do things around here'. For example, at the end of 1992 the Co-operative Bank announced its strategy of only taking deposits from, and offering financial services to, organisations that were not involved in controversial activities, including factory farming, blood sports, production of animal fur, the manufacture of tobacco and political repression. The bank believes that it is necessary to take up a stance in order to show the public that it is an ethical banker. It does not hide the fact that its ethical stance is likely to bring in new custom.

The ethics of an organisation will pervade all forms of organisational activity, e.g. whether 'white lies' are tolerated in business dealings, whether corners are cut in consumer safety, etc.

In his book, *Effectively Managing Human Service Organisations*, Ralph Brody sets out some of the central values that ethical organisations can work with. These provide some useful indicators as to day-to-day business practice. They include:

- job ownership
- the primacy of the consumer
- work quality.

Job ownership as a central value

Job ownership involves creating within the organisational culture a profound commitment to jobs. This can be done by fostering a climate 'that furthers job ownership by instilling in staff a sense of higher purpose, emotional bonding, trust, stakeholder involvement, and pride in their work'.

- A sense of higher purpose is achieved when staff believe in the significance of their work. This is illustrated by the story of a traveller who encountered three builders constructing a wall. In response to the question 'What are you doing?', the builders answered in turn, 'I am laying bricks', 'I am building a wall', 'I am building a cathedral'. It is this latter sense of purpose that needs to be fostered.
- A sense of emotional bonding is created when staff deeply care for each other and have a powerful sense of togetherness.
- A sense of trust is difficult to define. However, staff know when it exists and when it is absent.
- A sense of stakeholder involvement is very important at every level. Staff not only feel that they must set out to achieve common goals, but that they are empowered to do so: 'Management, supervisors, service staff, clients, support staff, and board members – each participate in the overall purpose of the organisation.'
- A sense of pride in one's work means that all staff do the best they can. They set out with the motto, 'Quality is our most important product'.

Primacy of consumers as a central value

Today, emphasis on the consumer is a key aspect of most activities in a large number of organisations. Meeting and, where possible, exceeding customer expectations is an important value in the business world.

In the service field there are many different types of needs to be met and it is not always easy to identify the customer – is it the direct consumer, the trustees, volunteers, fund donors, sources of referrals, elected officials or one of a number of other individuals and groups with a stake in decision-making? Service organisations are there chiefly to serve their clients' needs.

Work quality as a central value

The effectiveness of any organisation is determined by the quality of its work. Therefore, it is important to deliver quality products and services. There are two key dimensions to this:

- Product and service outcomes need to meet the needs of customers and other stakeholders.
- The *process* dimension of quality output involves the way in which staff interact with clients and customers. It is not enough to be technically competent; it is also necessary to be socially competent, i.e. by showing care and commitment – whether it be to the hospital patient or the customer in a shop or bank.

The concept of 'business ethics' is nowadays taken very seriously by many organisations. Ethics are moral principles or rules of conduct that are generally accepted in a society. An ethic is, therefore, a guide as to what should be done or what should not be done.

Ethical organisations are concerned to develop principled business and trading practices based on a value-driven mission. Such an organisation is likely to build up a strong trust-based culture, because it is concerned for its customers, its staff, the quality of its products and its processes, and its responsibility to the community.

Today's consumers are more concerned than ever about what an organisation stands for, who it trades with, what it does, whether it is an equal opportunities employer, its record on safety, and how it behaves in the community as a whole. When the consumer magazine *Which?* carried out a survey in the mid-1990s it found that 63 per cent of those who responded were concerned about the activities of companies they might invest in. Increasingly, we find shareholders asking pertinent questions about the ethics of organisations at company meetings. Public confidence in companies falls when they are shown to be morally unsound. Employees, too, generally do not want their company to act in an unethical way. Many people prefer not to work for such an organisation, or will sabotage its efforts wherever possible.

Product ethics are a key part of the ethical equation. The following issues are among those that need to be considered:

- What is included in the product? Does it contain, for example, natural products, or synthetic ingredients with harmful effects?
- How are the inputs obtained? For example, are they sourced from fair trading relationships, or by exploitation of trading partners?

■ How safe and acceptable are the outputs? Are they sound products or are they potentially dangerous?

These and many other questions are very important. Employees are strongly aware of bad practice, and their attitudes will often be antagonistic. The culture of an unethical organisation is likely to be characterised by back-stabbing, disenchantment, lies and deceit.

Case Study
The 'Yorkshire Terriers'

The legal firm Dibb Lupton Broomhead (DLB) has been referred to in legal circles as 'The Yorkshire Terriers'. At the beginning of 1995 the firm published advice in the *Independent on Sunday* that employers should sack workers suffering from stress.

The firm's advice was sent out following a landmark legal judgement in favour of John Walker, a former social worker who claimed £200 000 damages after suffering a nervous breakdown because his workload was too heavy. The firm recommended: 'Even if dismissal is unfair, the maximum compensation is usually £17 500, a far cry from the £200 000 Mr Walker is claiming from his former employers.' The suggestion was that dismissal is the cost-effective solution.

The *Independent on Sunday* reported that DLB had developed a reputation as the Rottweiler of the legal profession. The firm grew in under ten years from humble origins in Leeds to the ninth largest in Britain. Its 21 partners are expecting payouts in 1995 of on average £250 000 each.

A profile of the business in the magazine *Legal Business* in 1994 told of DLB's hard work and high rewards. Successful partners were paid well, while unsuccessful ones were fired. Clients benefited from a £1m entertaining budget that included helicopter rides to the races and day trips on Concorde. The cover of *Legal Business* showed a photograph of some DLB partners with a warning – 'These men will eat you for breakfast'.

Questions for discussion

1 *How would you describe the culture of DLB?*
2 *Why do you think the firm had developed this culture?*
3 *What would be the benefits for the firm of having this culture? What would be the drawbacks?*
4 *What would be the benefits and drawbacks of the culture to clients?*
5 *What would be the benefits and drawbacks of the culture to individual partners?*

The idea of organisations working in and for the community is not new. Many of the great entrepreneurs of the past, such as William Hesketh Lever, took action to support their ethical beliefs. Marks & Spencer today contributes to a programme which it claims touches all areas of the community. It includes contributions to: 'health and care', with involvement in projects for elderly people, mentally ill and disabled people, abused people; to hospitals and to Childline; to 'arts and heritage'; and to 'community services, education and training'.

Health and safety have come to the forefront of company policies over recent years. Accidents at a chemical plant or an incidence of pollution in the North Sea can permanently tarnish an organisation's image, both internally and externally.

At the same time, organisations have become increasingly aware of the adverse effects their products can have on the health and safety of consumers. A recent report attacked standards in the food industry and called for the government to fund better research and training for environmental health officers, and to legislate against farmers who produced infected stock. Food scares such as the salmonella-in-eggs scandal, listeria and 'mad cow disease' shocked consumers and led to sudden short-term changes in demand.

The list of ethical decisions facing industry is almost endless: buying cheap imports produced by 'sweated labour' overseas, Sunday trading, dumping of goods on foreign markets, investment in areas of high unemployment, contributions to political parties, encouragement of trade unions, treatment of employees, pension schemes, and so on.

No organisation, faced by all these pressures, will be able to please all parties all of the time. However, by becoming good corporate citizens and being socially responsible for their actions, organisations can generate considerable goodwill and develop a useful competitive advantage in the long run. By developing a culture based on sound ethics, it will motivate its people, its clients and customers and the community at large. The organisation with an ethical culture will produce ethical products and employ ethical business and trading practices.

Influencing and adapting organisational culture

The culture of an organisation can change owing to either unplanned or planned interventions in the range of factors that influence its culture. Changes in the external environment, e.g. an intensification in competition or a change in technology, will feed into changes in the internal culture. The personnel who make up an organisation may also change. This will be particularly significant when the new people are 'high up' in the organisation and thus have the power to make influential changes.

Features of the culture itself are likely to determine the nature and extent of the change process. For example, some writers have contrasted change-oriented (morphogenetic) cultures with stability-oriented (homeostatic) cultures. In a **morphogenetic** culture, change will be regarded as a desirable process in its own right. In contrast, in **homeostatic** cultures change may be seen as a threat which needs to be avoided.

Significantly, there may be a deliberate decision to change the culture of an organisation. This will involve trying to shift the norms and assumptions of the organisation in new directions. Managerial styles will be a vital factor in determining how and why such changes are implemented.

Managerial styles

Authority and hierarchy/responsibility and freedom

We have all met people who continually talk about the poor style of management of somebody at work. In particular, complaints are made about overbearing managers who think that they know all the right answers and blame other people when things go wrong.

Muczyk and Reimann have identified two important dimensions to managerial leadership.

- The first dimension is the extent to which managers allow subordinates to make decisions, i.e. the **autocratic–democratic dimension**.
- The second dimension is the extent to which managers direct the work of subordinates and tell them how to get on with their jobs i.e. the **permissive–directive dimension**.

The directive autocrat, for example, does not permit much individual initiative within the organisation. This may lead to frustration and time-serving attitudes, where employees do a day's work, but their hearts and minds are not in it. In contrast, the permissive democrat allows people to carry out their jobs in the way they see fit and to participate in decision-making structures.

However, these styles can be altered:

1 by individuals altering their style of managing. This may be because they suddenly 'see the light'; because they are gradually forced to do so by changing circumstances; because they are retrained to change their style; or because they are threatened that unless they change their style they will lose their jobs.

2 by introducing new managers with different styles. Typically, when organisations want a culture shift, they employ new managers to 'ring the changes'. Existing managers may be so set in their ways that they find it difficult to change, and it will also be difficult to change people's perceptions about these managers. For example, prisoners would find it difficult to believe that the harsh prison governor has suddenly become a firm believer in prisoners' welfare and their participation in decision-making.

We have seen throughout this book that a major change in organisations has been a shift away from hierarchical structures, with clearly defined authority patterns, towards greater responsibility and freedom. Changing organisational cultures has involved a wide range of changes, such as employing different types of managers, employing more flexible employees who are better able to make decisions for themselves, changing decision-making structures, etc.

However, it is important to remember that the direction of change has not all been one way. For example, in education the 1960s and 1970s were characterised by a number of new types of schools such as Summerhill and Holland Park in London, which were based on more democracy in the organisation. During the 1980s and 1990s, with the backlash against 'permissive' education, a number of institutions have moved towards less-democratic structures with more emphasis on direction, autocracy, and discipline.

The culture of a large organisation such as a school can be turned around by appointing a new 'inspirational' leader with the ability to generate a 'transformed culture'. For example, Garth Hill Secondary School in Berkshire in the 1980s and Garibaldi School in Nottinghamshire in the 1990s are widely quoted examples of schools that were transformed by visionary headteachers. In both situations the new headteacher moved into a school which had dwindling pupil numbers, poor levels of examination performance and low morale. The new heads focused values in the school on raising the self-esteem of pupils and of staff. Each emphasised the importance of new resources so that the school could become, for example, a beacon of excellence in information technology and vocationally related courses. The private sector was encouraged to become involved in providing resources for the schools. The visual character of the schools was transformed, e.g. by creating professional suites of computer and conference rooms, focusing on the visual impact of internal decoration, etc. Within two to three years the culture of these schools was transformed, leading to the increased motivation of staff, pupils, parents and other stakeholders.

However, it is not always easy to transform organisational culture in this way. There are many recent examples where such a cultural transformation has failed, often because the management vision has not filtered down to staff, as in the following case study.

Case Study
Wilmorton College, Derby

Wilmorton College in Derby is an example of a college which has built up an excellent reputation in recent years for the quality of its teaching and the professionalism of its lecturing staff. However, during the 1990s major problems surfaced at managerial level, and an official inquiry was held to ascertain the causes.

The report of the inquiry, published in December 1994, painted a picture of managerial ineptitude in the college in the period leading to the departure of the principal Andrew Stromberg in July 1994.

Relations with the 200 teaching staff deteriorated, with strikes and 'an explosion of discontent' as Mr Stromberg tried to push through a restructuring plan in a way that was considered 'confrontational and conspiratorial', and which disrupted teaching. According to the report, stress levels were so high that 'the mental state of some of the staff giving evidence to the inquiry was distressing'.

The inquiry found inadequate financial control, failure to observe procedure 'and a determination of the governing body to stifle any questioning of executive decision-making'. It concluded that although there was no fraud, 'these are the conditions in which fraud and malpractice can flourish, and no public body should allow them to develop'.

The report stated that governors 'failed the basic test of acting in the public interest' and 'failed to curb the impetuosity of the principal' in a 'lamentable catalogue of incompetence'. It pointed to the last few months in which no governors' meeting had a quorum and members were brought in unconstitutionally. Governors who objected to decisions were removed. The treatment of one, who was a staff member and union leader, 'offended the rules of natural justice'. He was deemed to be unfit to serve by the meeting, without being given the opportunity to defend himself. A number of people were appointed to carry out duties which were beyond their competence, and the management committee broke a wide range of procedural rules. There was also a suggestion of unlawful payments of allowances to governors.

The general implication of the report was that although Mr Stromberg was a 'visionary' with new ideas as to how to make the college entrepreneurial, he failed to communicate and share his vision with the majority of people who worked within the college. By breaking a number of rules and regulations, the management committee at Wilmorton became alienated from the staff, who became increasingly disenchanted, to the detriment of the organisation. Instead of creating an entrepreneurial forward-moving culture, the principal created a culture of alienation based on a 'them and us' approach in which lecturers who remained working at the college began to wonder what the objectives of the college were.

In particular, Mr Stromberg was associated with three disastrous building projects costing over £500 000: converting a city-centre nightclub into an adult learning centre, and opening a restaurant and a commercial gymnasium. A former professional footballer was hired (without advertising the job) to run the gym. The gym only took in a very small income and was unlikely to break even.

The restaurant was run on an 'open-ended budget', which eventually ran to £170 000. Mr Stromberg failed to disclose that the nightclub had been reported to need a new roof, to be damp, 'in extremely poor' condition, and more expensive to renovate than the cost of a new building. The report of the inquiry declared: 'The building remains a wasting capital asset with little chance of any immediate use . . . put bluntly, the process was a shambles from beginning to end.'

Questions for discussion

1 *What sort of culture do you think that Mr Stromberg was trying to create at Wilmorton College?*
2 *What deficiencies would you identify in his approach?*
3 *What difficulties/obstacles do you think stood in his way to making the desired cultural changes?*
4 *How do you think he should have gone about making the changes that he proposed? Perhaps you might argue that he should not have tried to make these changes, or made them in a modified form.*

It is not easy to make the right managerial interventions when attempting to adjust culture. The sensitive leader must try to foster a climate for change based on trust and sound judgement. The leader who wants change must make sure that he or she is able to convince people of the necessity for and best direction for that change. The case study of Wilmorton Collge illustrates the fairly common example of a visionary leader who has been unable to share a vision.

Group needs/task needs/individual needs

Research in the USA has established a contrast between person-oriented and production-oriented leaders. In particular, emphasis is placed on two dimensions of leadership: **consideration** and **initiating structure**.

Managers who rank high on the **initiating structure** dimension are concerned mainly with production tasks and getting jobs completed. They want to see patterns for organising work, they lay down rules and directions for subordinates, etc. Other leaders do not score highly in this dimension.

Managers who rank high on the **consideration** dimension are concerned mainly with personal relationships and being liked by subordinates. They will help subordinates, do them favours, be concerned with their welfare, etc.

Research indicates that in some measure these dimensions are independent, so that a manager can have concern both for production and for people. The team-management approach which this implies can be highly successful (see Figure 15.9). A number of effective leaders combine these two elements to create a successful culture emphasising both task and process. Perhaps the most effective sports managers, public-service managers, and private-sector managers are able to blend successfully these two dimensions. Can you think of examples?

Figure 15.9 Dimensions of management behaviour

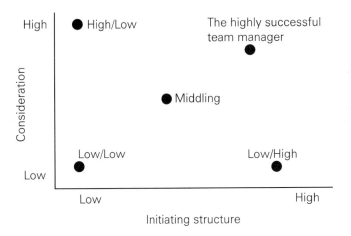

Within organisations, and in subgroups in organisations, there will be individuals who are particularly adept at helping people to focus on the task in hand. These people are said to have a **task-oriented** focus. Other people will be good at helping the process along, i.e. in supporting others. These people are said to have a **process-** (or **relations-oriented**) focus.

Organisational cultures will often be characterised by an emphasis on task focus or relations focus. For example, production departments and organisations are sometimes characterised as being primarily concerned with questions such as 'When will we get the task completed?', 'Where will the bottlenecks occur?', 'How can we speed up production?' In contrast, a relations-oriented culture will focus on 'How can we help individuals to be fulfilled?', 'How can we facilitate the interaction of team members?', 'How can we look after individual welfare?'

Influencing and adapting culture, therefore, might be concerned with shifting predominant attitudes in an organisation from, for example, task orientation towards relations orientation. Clearly, this may involve a considerable shake-up in existing values, requiring extensive restructuring and the training of management and staff to cope with a new climate.

Making changes

We have already seen that the process of change involves three steps, as shown in Figure 15.10.

Figure 15.10 The process of change

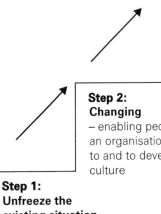

Step 3: Refreezing – creating a sense of permanence to the new cultural form so that it becomes the accepted predominant culture

Step 2: Changing – enabling people within an organisation to adapt to and to develop a new culture

Step 1: Unfreeze the existing situation – involves enabling participants in a given culture to recognise the need to change the culture

The model in Figure 15.11 helps us to understand the considerations which determine whether change is worthwhile. Before making a change there has to be a genuine groundswell of opinion in favour of change. The individual/organisation has to decide whether it can cope with an appropriate new culture and whether it has the know-how and experience to put into effect a well-structured plan for change. Clearly, when these factors pull together there is a strong synergistic thrust towards change.

Figure 15.11 Deciding whether it is worth changing the culture

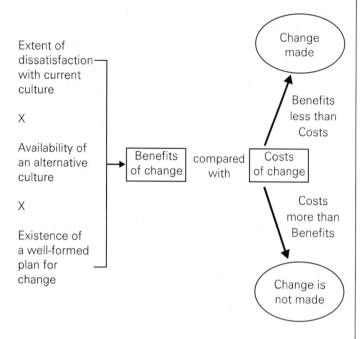

Barriers to change

In implementing change, however, an individual/organisation has to calculate the major barriers standing in the way, and to develop strategies for counteracting this resistance.

We can look at these barriers to change on an organisational and an individual basis.

Organisational barriers

These include:

1 **Structural inertia**. The culture of an organisation will be frozen at a particular moment in time. The organisation will be organised in such a way as to maintain existing relationships and ways of going about things. It will take considerable force to break down these existing patterns. Change threatens the logic of the 'way things are currently done'. Clearly, the best chance of altering this logic is if there is considerable disquiet about existing patterns.

2 The **existing power structure**. It is highly likely that organisational change will involve changing the balance of power. This will be resisted by those whose power is most threatened. In many cases, organisational change involves the removal or redeployment of people in senior positions in the organisation.

3 **Resistance from work groups**. Over time the work group in an organisation becomes a powerful force based on formal and informal relationships between people. Work groups develop subcultures and values.

These can become very resistant structures which may be difficult to budge.

4 The **failure of previous change initiatives**. If the organisation has previously experienced unsuccessful change initiatives, then individuals and groups may become resistant to change. They may treat the prospect of further change with disdain.

Individual barriers

In addition, there may be a number of important individual barriers to change. Individuals in the organisation may resist change for a number of reasons, which are important to them – their reservations should not be treated lightly. They include:

1 **Fears about the impact of the change on individuals and families.** For example, if the changes lead to restructuring and downsizing, then redundancy and unemployment will be inevitable. In addition, there will be the fear of downgrading and loss of status.

2 **Fears about having to increase commitment to the organisation.** There may be a worry that extra hours and involvement will be required by the changes.

3 **Fear of the unknown.** When people do not know what to expect, they may be reluctant to trade an old culture for a new one. Also, if they have a distorted view of what the change will entail (resulting, perhaps, from media reports about similar changes elsewhere) they will be resistant to change.

4 **Tradition and set ways.** People who have been working in a particular way will often have the view: 'We like what we are doing around here'. They will thus be resistant to changing their ways.

5 **Loyalty to existing relationships**. People within an organisation build up a loyalty to managers, to workmates, and the working team. People who have built up these relationships will not want to see them destroyed by new ways of working.

6 **Failure to accept or recognise the need for change**. Often people will not see that there is a need for change. If things appear to be running smoothly, they will see little point in changing. However, the task of strategic management is to look beyond the 'here and now' and to anticipate needs in the near future.

Overcoming these barriers to change requires careful planning and attention to detail. Change needs to be introduced in a sensitive way.

Case Study
Highlighting a lack of shared values at BCL Cellophane

A shrinking market and growing competition prompted BCL Cellophane in Bridgwater to review its culture. Cellophane manufacture is a complex chemical process, but it is a very traditional business.

In the late 1980s BCL Cellophane had a conventional approach to management. It was very much a top-down blame culture. As the company moved towards the 1990s, it recognised that unless it changed it would go out of business.

The major problems stemmed not from marketing and distribution, but from inadequacies in its manufacturing. Management set out to improve teamwork by breaking down the mistrust between management and workers and creating a common approach to problem solving. It invited the Coverdale Organisation to initiate a training programme to tackle the problems under its business results scheme. The scheme involved linking payment for the training with the improvements in performance it produced.

The training approach was geared to developing teamwork by concentrating on techniques to explore the effect of particular behaviour on working in teams. It also set out ways of tackling problems, planning ahead and seeing plans through.

The programme began with an initial diagnosis of the company's problems. Specific, measurable project aims were set. These were then translated into precise targets, down to individual shift level. A monitoring process was set up to log and measure progress.

The factory management identified the objective of reducing factory waste from 17.45 per cent to 15 per cent in March of the first year. This was translated into specific objectives at each level. The attempt was to create a permanent change in culture and attitudes, and in the way in which the organisation was run.

The market in which Cellophane operated was a very tough one, declining at the rate of 12 per cent per year. There were a number of key producers, all competing for the remaining market.

Research indicated that BCL Cellophane was suffering because there were no shared values and very little contact between sales staff and the shop floor. Coverdale took the unprecedented step of training people from various disciplines together. The shopfloor began to see that sales people were human and had problems, too. A major breakthrough came when people's behavioural patterns and attitudes started to change.

Changes were also made in the internal structure of the organisation. Training started at the top with the resetting of precise goals. The management structure was flattened. Previously, there had been eight or nine levels of management.

Management increasingly realised that productivity depended on sharing responsibility for production with the workforce: if it could not trust its workforce, it would be unlikely to succeed. Shared training helped to create shared methods.

A mark of the success of the project was the way that a major programme of redundancy at the plant was handled, only a year into the scheme. Forty per cent of the workforce had to be made redundant, yet production had to be pushed even higher. Efforts were made to do this as quickly as possible and without disruption, and the company found alternative jobs for all who wanted them. At the same time, the drive to increase production continued and output was raised from 25 to 35 tonnes per employee per year. In the new atmosphere, people were seeking change instead of resisting it.

Questions for discussion

1 *Why did BCL Cellophane need to change its culture in the late 1980s?*
2 *How was the culture changed?*
3 *What was the effect of these changes?*
4 *Why and how might have employees resisted these changes?*
5 *Why do you think that employees were prepared to accept changes?*
6 *What lessons can be learnt from the case study about managing the change process?*

Reactions to change

People within an organisation can respond to change in three main ways:

- They may **accept** the necessity of change and comply with the change process. Indeed, they may be quite thankful for the change. For example, people who have been labouring for a number of years in an oppressive organisation will welcome the 'new broom' approach that aims to introduce fresh, 'enlightened' ideas. Achieving acceptance for cultural change is perhaps the most important part of the process. Some of the methods of paving the way for such acceptance are outlined on pages 400–403.
- **Resistance** is a common reaction to change. This will take all sorts of subtle and unsubtle forms. For example, it may lead to personal antagonism, e.g. the cool atmosphere facing the new principal or senior management team. Employees may be slow in carrying out instructions or will deliberately misinterpret them in order to make new changes unworkable. Resistance may take the form of maintaining the old culture in an informal way in order to circumvent the new culture.

- A more extreme form of resistance is **open conflict**. This may take the form of acrimonious flare-ups at staff meetings, deliberate sabotage and wilful destruction of the representations of the new culture. For example, a new organisational logo representing the 'new way of doing things around here' may be turned upside down, damaged or defaced. Those with power in the previous organisational structure may declare open warfare on the newcomers. Conflict is highly destructive and will only begin to be resolved when the usurpers gain the upper hand or when the old guard gains a decisive hold on its territory. Where cultural change brings open conflict, it is often tempting to draw comparisons with the behaviour of groups of apes and other primates, such as the staking out of territory and the ritual beating of chests.

Preparing for cultural change

It is very important that the ground is prepared for the change process. This involves carrying out an audit to find out whether the organisation is ready for change, identifying possible supporting forces for it, and estimating the strength of the resisting forces.

It is essential to identify clearly the supporting forces so that they can be maximised. Who is likely to be in favour of change, and what factors are most likely to encourage them to support it? How much power and influence do they have in the organisation? The key is to find ways of building on the strengths presented by supporting forces and on the potential of internal and external forces for change. In particular, the emphasis needs to be on winning the support of senior management and showing key stakeholders the benefits of change. At the same time, restraining forces and their powers need to be minimised.

The change process should be timed and planned to move the organisation towards an effective culture, as outlined in the progression shown in Figure 15.12. The

Figure 15.12 The organisational learning curve

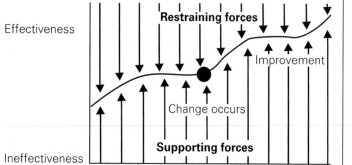

movement towards the effective organisational culture is sometimes referred to as the **learning curve**.

Force-field analysis (see pages 364–5) is the term used to describe the process of identifying the constraining and supporting forces and their relative strengths.

Building the support for change

Building the support for change can only be successful if the groundwork is properly carried out. This includes:

- Identifying the main issues that concern people about proposed changes. Weaknesses in their reasons for opposing change can then be pointed out. The convert is often the best supporter of new ideas. If people know that their reservations are understood, they are more likely to respect the new views and ideas.
- Clarifying the reasons for and the need for change. The reasons should be set out in organisational terms rather than simply as someone's pet idea. If people perceive that the rationale for change is personal egotism or aggrandisement, then they are likely to oppose it. The reasons need to be stated in clear, impersonal terms.
- Avoiding, wherever possible, threatening existing group relationships (unless, of course, they represent the need for change). If change can be built on existing networks and relationships, then whole groups may agree to shift towards a new culture.
- Creating expectations that change will be for the better. The best way of doing this is by being able to identify tangible improvements. When expectations are translated into actual behaviours, then change is most likely to occur. People will not 'buy into' outlandish theories unless they can see the practical implications of change.
- Encouraging participation, which is a powerful influence on change. When members of an organisation share in the change process, they will be able to claim ownership of it. Change should not be forced upon people; they should be encouraged to implement the changes themselves.
- Making people within the organisation aware of how they will benefit personally. It is important to identify the rewards, incentives and long-term benefits of the change, and confirm that current benefits, such as pension schemes, are being protected.
- Maintaining effective communications, essential in building support for change. Everyone should be aware of the changes in advance. They need to know who will be affected and how they will be affected. Preparation for charge may include awareness raising, training and development programmes.
- Involving the key stakeholders in the process. For example, Japanese companies starting up in the UK

have appreciated the importance of involving unions in developing organisational cultures. It is important that organised groups of stakeholders are consulted and share joint responsibility for the change. Without this understanding, there is the potential for tension and conflict.

Case Study
Changing organisational culture at Shell's Stanlow plant

When Dominic Boot took charge of Shell's Stanlow complex in Cheshire in 1990, he inherited a plant in a state of turbulence. The Mersey oil spill in 1989 and the fatal chemicals plant explosion in 1990 cast a long shadow over the site. In these two years the manufacturing plant hardly made a profit.

Widespread change was required if the plant was to achieve environmental and operational targets and to become cost-competitive.

The lack of reliability had generated a loss of confidence in the workers at Stanlow and this was coupled with a blame culture. Mr Boot moved to Stanlow from The Hague, where he had played a leading part in developing the environmental policy for the Shell Group's manufacturing operations. He spent the first two months at Stanlow simply walking about collecting information and listening to people's views. Stanlow is Shell's fifth biggest refinery, as well as being a chemicals manufacturing plant.

Mr Boot is quoted in *Shell Review* as noticing two things: *'Shop-floor staff had a feeling that failure was inevitable, which meant that they were ignoring their strengths and achievements; meanwhile management were active in shaping new visions for the future on the social and technological front. Everywhere there seemed to be a disconnection from reality, and also from each other, with no one focusing on day-to-day problems. Whereas there were kernels of good in the visionary ideas, they were not connected to the immediate problems. It was important to tone down the roseate vision of the future and to start looking at how to deal with the everyday things, rather than building castles in the air. We also had to stop blaming poor design, poor maintenance or operational practices for our failures. Rather than automatically say, when something goes wrong, "How can we fix it?", we should be asking, "How did it fail and how can we improve it?"'*

To take this positive approach required building a team spirit and overcoming a 'psychological firefighting' attitude. Rather than looking at how it could prevent a crisis,

Stanlow had been operating on a 'scramble' situation – when a crisis happened, it was all hands to the pump – a reactive approach, rather than a proactive one. Repair rather than prevention was the doctrine. This way of running things at Stanlow needed to be changed.

Improving reliability at the plant involved building people's confidence. Manufacturing reliability went hand in hand with cleaning up the environment, and this involved changing perceptions. Mr Boot remarked: 'There was this perception that the oil industry had to be dirty, that unless you had dirty boots and fingernails, you were not doing a proper job. This didn't apply everywhere. A refinery could be clean.'

He set up an environmental seminar, involving people in manufacturing work at Stanlow as well as local authorities, industry, schools and the neighbouring community.

Stanlow then introduced environmental standards – a shared responsibility for everyone involved. Operational and environmental targets were set for individual production units, making each person accountable. In doing so, Mr Boot was looking for results and to bring back a sense of pride at Stanlow.

Examples of success were soon apparent:

- In 1993 reductions in flare loss saved the refinery £3000 a day.
- In 1994 the amount of oil in effluent water fell to a quarter of the 1991 level.
- In 1993–4 the number of smoking incidents was cut drastically, while unscheduled shutdowns and equipment failures, which drained away £58 million in 1990, cost barely more than £4 million.

The success of these changes was communicated to staff, creating an on-going culture that was now seeking positive change.

Questions for discussion

1 *Why do you think cultural change was required at the Stanlow plant?*
2 *What deficiencies can you identify in the system that Dominic Boot took over?*
3 *What positive steps did Mr Boot take to manage the change process?*
4 *Identify the things that Mr Boot did well.*
5 *What signs can you identify that the changes are being managed effectively?*

Quality circles

The case study highlights the way in which people in an organisation can be made to feel part of a change process.

It is understandable that, given the previous record of the plant, there would be a groundswell of opinion in favour of making changes. Dominic Boot helped to generate an atmosphere of trust by walking around and talking to people, rather than by forcing change upon them. Clearly, the more people involved in the change process, the better the chances of success. We have already identified the quality circle (see page 261) as a major force for successful organisational change. The advantage of quality circles is that employees are given an on-going opportunity to suggest ideas and to participate in a process of continuous cultural improvement.

Monitoring change – review and feedback

In planning for change it is essential to devise ways of measuring its effects and its success. Developing mechanisms for reviewing change should not be an afterthought. Figure 15.13 provides a framework for monitoring change.

Figure 15.13 A framework for reviewing and modifying the change process

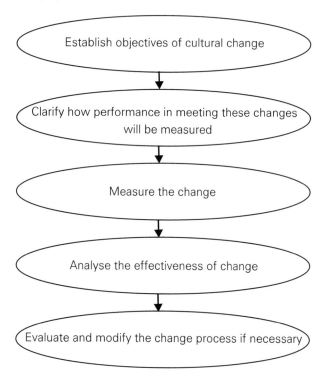

Establish objectives of cultural change

Clarify how performance in meeting these changes will be measured

Measure the change

Analyse the effectiveness of change

Evaluate and modify the change process if necessary

Communication strategies

Effective communication strategies are a key part of managing cultural change. If individuals and groups are to share a clear cultural vision, then they need to have shared understandings. One of the biggest hurdles occurs if messages are confused. A leader, or group, wanting to

implement change will need to think about how best to communicate values and visions. This will involve considering:

- who needs to know (everyone who will be affected)
- when they should be told (as soon as possible)
- how will they be told (they should be part of a participative process, so they will help to shape the vision)
- the best means of communication (whatever works best in the organisation, e.g. through quality circle discussions, team briefings, or company newsletters)
- a method of checking that the message is being received (this will work best if the recipients are given the opportunity to restate the message in their own terms).

Anyone who is concerned with cultural change will need to focus attention on clear communications and maintaining effective communications channels.

Mission statement and charter approaches to cultural development

A clear, shared mission statement (see pages 634–6) provides an important step towards creating a shared vision of a desired culture. The mission statement can be seen as having a focusing effect, drawing together objectives and enabling people to stretch themselves beyond their present capabilities. It helps groups within an organisation to develop new levels of shared commitment.

It is important that people are able to visualise new levels of commitment. For example, when Dominic Boot took charge of Shell's Stanlow plant, he set out a number of principles which all staff could work towards. These were:

- reliability
- safety
- costs
- people
- the environment.

A new image, the Penta Q (see Figure 15.14), is now displayed at various points around the Stanlow complex which serves to remind people of these shared principles.

Many organisations spell out shared values in the form of a written charter which sets out their commitment to quality and to their stakeholders. Today, many organisations have charters which show their commitment to their many publics, e.g. a patient's charter in the National Health Service and employees' charters in many large public companies. The charters set out a commitment to standards of excellence – which we can regard as indicators of cultural excellence.

Figure 15.14 Shared principles – the Penta Q badge of Stanlow

Further reading

- *Management and Organisational Behaviour*, 3rd edition, by Laurie J. Mullins. Pitman, 1993.
- *Introduction to Organisational Behaviour*, 4th edition, by Richard M. Steers, HarperCollins, 1991.
- *Introduction to Management* by Claudia Rawlins. HarperCollins, 1992.
- *Organizational Cultures: Types and Transformations* by Dianna Pheysey, Routledge, 1992.
- *Essentials of Organizational Behaviour*, 4th edition, by Stephen P. Robbins. Prentice Hall, 1993.

Financial accounting framework

16 Financial reporting requirements

On completion of this chapter students will be able to:

- identify and explain the factors influencing the reporting process

- examine the needs of different user groups

- evaluate and illustrate the requirements of regulatory bodies.

Information needs

The activities of businesses affect a wide range of individuals and organisations, each with their own particular areas of concern and each with their own demands for information. To satisfy these needs the government and other regulatory bodies impose reporting requirements on businesses. In addition, many businesses choose to provide further information voluntarily. Much of the information demanded is of a financial nature and so it falls on the business's financial reporting function to fulfil these regulatory and social responsibilities.

Owners

Business owners can be either sole traders, partners or shareholders in limited companies. The interests and priorities of these groups are varied. For example, owners of unincorporated businesses (sole traders and partnerships) are more likely to be involved in the daily management of the business and so their interests may be more akin to those of an employee. It is also true that these small business owners will rely less on a formal reporting system to know how well the business is doing. However, the concerns of company shareholders detailed below are universal to all business owners, even if they do possess informal information channels.

- *Profitability* – efficient use of resources to provide the desired financial return.
- *Liquidity* – ability to generate cash to ensure continued trading and to make dividend payments.
- *State of financial affairs* – nature of the business's assets and liabilities.
- *Financial risk* – nature and value of prior charge capital (e.g. preference shares and loans).
- *Future prospects* – an evaluation of future market and financial conditions.
- *Market risk* – knowing what business the company is in, allowing owners and potential owners to judge the stability of the company's performance in the face of changing market conditions.

The following businesses, for example, have experienced significant changes in market conditions:

GEC with the end of the cold war
London Rubber Company with the advent of AIDs
Clearing banks and third world lending
Financial institutions with significant holdings of
    London office space
IBM and the ascendancy of the PC.

Task

Identify five more companies that have experienced significant market changes. Of what value was it for shareholders to know the business their company was engaged in?

Investors

Of major concern to business investors is the ability of the firm to pay interest and make repayments of the loans forwarded. Many of the information needs of owners apply also to investors. In particular, the generation of cash and the relationship of outstanding company liabilities to marketable assets will be of interest.

Management

The role of management is to plan, make decisions, coordinate and control business activities. The financial accounting system is an integral part of the management information system that facilitates the fulfilment of these responsibilities. The information required tends to be concerned with the very recent past supplemented with projections for the future.

Suppliers

Before dedicating resources to a customer, a supplier will want to be sure that the customer's business is financially secure. The supplier will have the same concerns as investors to ensure that debts are paid, and promptly.

Credit sales oil the wheels of trade but are increasingly seen as exploitation by the strong of the small and weak. Small businesses often crash not because of lack of profits but because of the lack of cash, aggravated by customers not paying on time. Businesses must now report how long it takes to pay their suppliers.

Customers

Like suppliers, customers will be interested in the stability of their trading partners. Many businesses conduct a

financial investigation into the affairs of new credit customers. The need for reliable and up-to-date information is particularly acute where the supply of goods or services is of strategic importance to the buying business. In the car industry there is significant investment in time and money to appraise the financial standing of potential component manufacturers. Production halted as a result of a bankrupt supplier could cost millions of pounds in lost production.

However, large profits being earned by suppliers can also cause concern. Suspicion that they are being exploited is another reason customers demand financial information. Monopolies, especially those recently returned to the private sector, have their accounts critically appraised by consumer groups and industry watchdogs. For businesses with large market shares it is a difficult task to satisfy shareholders with high financial returns and to placate other parties who are intent on finding evidence of monopoly exploitation.

Case Study
Regulating utilities

The following is an extract from *The Economist* of 10 September 1994:

'Next Thursday, worried cabinet ministers are due to begin a review of utility regulation in Britain. And no wonder they are vexed. Britain has had a decade to get used to privatised utilities, yet rows over the prices they charge have blown up throughout the summer. The first came in May, after the government proposed to allow competition in the supply of gas to homes. That would end the single national price, which hides a subsidy to some customers (such as those who live far from gas fields, in the south west) from others. In the long run most consumers would gain, as competition forced prices down, but some would face higher prices. That prospect prompted howls of protest. Then, in July, consumer groups damned new caps on water and sewerage prices as too lenient; in August they attacked cuts in electricity prices as too modest.

'More woes lie ahead. Railway privatisation will doubtless bring even louder moans about the level of fares and the punctuality of trains. And before 1998, when competition is due to start in the supply of electricity to small customers, the power industry is certain to suffer from a row similar to that now dogging gas.'

Questions for discussion

1 *What changes in information needs have been experienced by privatised businesses?*

2 *Consider the change in interest groups and the type of information they demand.*

Employees

Employees are concerned about the security of their jobs and opportunities for personal gain. The following will be of interest to employees:

- security of markets and market share
- plans for organisational change and strategic direction
- financial solvency to pay their wages
- evidence of being exploited and so an opportunity to press for a greater remuneration package.

Government agencies

The government requires information concerning businesses to:

- assess and collect tax (the Inland Revenue is principally interested in payments to employees and sub-contractors and in the level of business profits; Customs and Excise monitors the value of sales and purchases that attract VAT)
- compile statistics on business activity that can help it plan economic and industrial policy.

The general public

Other individuals and organisations may be indirectly affected by a business and hence desire some information. In particular a business may affect:

- employment opportunities
- economic activity in the area – which in turn has a knock-on effect for other businesses for supplies and services demanded
- environmental impact – whether in terms of local conditions (road noise, water pollution etc.) or of a more general nature (use of scarce natural resources).

Figure 16.1 Information pressures

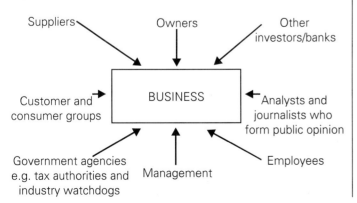

The need for regulation

The different stakeholders have different information needs but they all have the same concerns about the fullness and quality of information they receive. Of particular concern is **comparability**. Users wish to compare the financial results of a business with its past results to establish **trends,** and with results of similar businesses to monitor **performance**. Without any guiding framework for the preparer of accounting information, there would be no consistency between financial statements and hence they would be of little use.

Case Study
Money for nothing

The following article appeared in The Economist in December 1993.

British company bosses are in mourning. New rules proposed on December 16th will, if adopted, kill off one of their best-loved scams: acquisition accounting. Shareholders, however, are delighted that Britain's Accounting Standards Board wants to act decisively, if belatedly, to close a much-abused loophole.

The device works like this. First, acquire a company. Next, think of all sorts of costs that might be incurred when integrating this new firm into your old one. These can include sacking employees of either company in order to rationalise duplicated activities; closing retail outlets; painting the new firm's vans with your corporate logo; and so on. Then, call these expenses 'acquisition' costs, and add them to the liabilities of the company you have bought.

What that does is lower the value of the acquired firm's assets, so increasing the gap between what you paid for it and what accountants say it is worth. That difference is called 'goodwill'. In Britain (unlike almost every other country), the acquiring firm writes off goodwill immediately against its reserves, rather than subtracting it gradually from its profits as Americans do. What have you done? You have spent a fortune improving your new acquisition and maybe your old firm, too; that, with luck, will lead to higher future profits. None of this spending reduces your profits. Lovely.

During the 1980s British firms went on an acquisition binge. One reason – admittedly among many – was this much-used accounting trick. Indeed, having used it to boost profits once, some firms were locked into buying again, just to keep profits rising. Coloroll, a home-furnishings firm that grew rapidly in the 1980s through a string of acquisitions and then collapsed, provides a vivid example of the pros and cons of this approach.

Under the new rules, only those costs that the acquired firm 'would have incurred anyway' can be set against its assets, before consolidating its accounts with those of the new owner. That leaves some room for debate, but not much. If British companies buy fewer firms in the 1990s, you will know one reason why.

Questions for discussion

1 *Why did shareholders applaud the introduction of regulations that appear to reduce profits?*
2 *Why was it necessary to continue the 'acquisition binge' to keep profits rising?*
3 *How could the practices described in this article undermine the efficient working of a market economy?*

It is more difficult for a business to deceive interested parties if there are rules laid down concerning how accounts must be prepared and presented. For the user of financial statements it is important that the assumptions made when preparing the accounts are known. If they use the same conventions this facilitates comparisons and meaningful conclusions – hence the need for accounting regulations.

Illustration
Julie Covy set up in business as 'Teksi' to provide a taxi service in her local town. She bought a car for £12 000 and in its first year the business achieved takings of £20 000, with vehicle expenses of £4500. How much profit has the business made? Without some guiding principles answers may vary from a profit of £15 500 to one of £3500.

Regulatory influences

Regulations influencing financial reporting originate primarily from two sources:

- *legislation* in the form of the **Companies Act 1985** as modified by the **Companies Act 1989**
- *statements of best accountancy practice* issued by the **Accounting Standards Board**.

Legal requirements

The Companies Act 1985 lays down requirements concerning:

- the content of accounts
- accounting principles
- valuation rules.

The regulations, and particularly the Companies Acts, relate primarily to financial statements prepared for limited companies. However, members of the main accountancy bodies are under an obligation to use **best accounting practice** in the preparation of all accounts intended to give a **'true and fair'** view of a business's trading performance and financial position. In practice this means that all business accounts are prepared according to generally accepted accounting concepts and valuation rules.

Outwardly, however, the accounts for unincorporated and incorporated bodies do look significantly different as the content rules of the companies acts have been drafted with the responsibility structure of *limited companies* in mind. The requirement for directors to report on their stewardship of company resources is the overriding emphasis of the **disclosure rules**. The following information is required within 10 months of the end of an accounting period (normally one year) for a private limited company, and within seven months for a public limited company:

- **Balance sheet**.
- **Profit-and-loss account**.
- **Cash flow statement**.
- **'Notes to the accounts'** that describe the company's accounting policies and provide an analysis of certain items contained in the financial reports.
- **Auditor's report** that confirms that the financial reports are consistent with the company's accounting records and that they do provide a true and fair view of its trading performance and state of financial affairs.
- The **directors' report** that provides details of non-financial aspects of the business, such as principal activities and employee policies, in addition to certain explanations of the financial statements. The directors' review of past performance and opinion concerning future developments can be particularly valuable for those not involved with the day-to-day running of the business.

This information is filed with the Registrar of Companies and is available for public inspection. Failure to conform to these reporting requirements leads to financial penalties for the company and the risk of criminal prosecution for the company's directors, resulting in a fine and possible disqualification from being a director.

Task

Obtain the annual reports of two companies, one from a business that you perceive to be doing well and another from a company that may be experiencing difficult trading conditions. What information does the directors' report provide:

a *to substantiate your opinions*
b *concerning future developments that would be of particular interest to the business's stakeholders?*

Content of published accounts

The law prescribes certain information that must be disclosed in the accounts of a limited company and the manner in which it must be presented. Although more than one format is specified, it is usual for most students

Figure 16.2 Profit and loss account: format 1

£000s

	Note	Year X2	Year X1	Guidance
1 Turnover	1	5 000	4 500	
2 Cost of sales	2	(2 000)	(1 900)	
3 Gross profit or loss		3 000	2 600	Item 1 minus item 2
4 Distribution costs	2	(1 000)	(900)	Less
5 Administration expenses	2	(500)	(400)	Less
6 Other operating income		500	400	Add
7 Income from shares in group companies		100	100	Add
8 Income from shares in related companies		50	20	Add
9 Income from other fixed asset investments		50	0	Add
10 Other interest receivable and similar income	4	50	30	Add
11 Amounts written off from investments		(100)	(10)	Less
12 Interest payable and similar charges		(500)	(400)	Less
13 Tax on profit or loss on ordinary activities		(650)	(500)	Less
14 Profit or loss on ordinary activities after taxation		1 000	940	Item 3 add/less items 4–13
15 Extraordinary income		100	0	Add
16 Extraordinary charges		(50)	0	Less
17 Extraordinary profit or loss		50	0	Add or less
18 Tax on extraordinary profit or loss		(20)	0	Add or less
19 Other taxes not shown under the above items		(10)	(10)	Less
20 Profit or loss for the financial year		1 070	930	Item 14 add/less items 15 to 19

Notes:
1   Although the standard format does specify some profit sub-totals, the accounts should be prepared with additional sub-totals to facilitate clear presentation. For example, it would be normal practice to insert a sub-total after item 6 to give a clear indication of profit from operating activities only.

2   The line numbers need not be disclosed although items should appear in the order listed. Items 1 to 20 not disclosed on the face of the profit-and-loss account should be disclosed in 'Notes to the accounts'.

3   The current period's figures should be compared with the previous period's.

4   Items with a nil value for both years need not be detailed.

to be become familiar with 'Format 1' for both the profit and loss account and the balance sheet (see Figures 16.2 and 16.3).

Problems of stewardship

In recognising that the owners of many companies are divorced from the management of the business, the following information is required by the Companies Acts to ensure transparency in the directors' stewardship of the business:

■ directors' emoluments and benefits
■ transactions in which the directors have a personal interest.

Social issues

To provide information on some social issues, the directors' report that accompanies the financial statements is required to give details concerning:

■ worker participation
■ the employment of disabled workers
■ donations to charitable and political organisations.

Business size

Many of the reporting needs for businesses are the same irrespective of the size of the company. However, there has been a realisation that to require the same reporting

Figure 16.3 Balance sheet: format 1

	19X2 £	19X2 £	19X1 £	19X1 £
A Called-up share capital not paid[1]				
B Fixed assets				
I Intangible assets				
II Tangible assets				
III Investments				
C Current assets				
I Stocks				
II Debtors				
III Investments				
IV Cash at bank and in hand				
D Prepayments and accrued income[2]				
E Creditors: Amounts falling due within one year				
F Net current assets (liabilities)				
G Total assets less current liabilities				
H Creditors: Amounts falling due after more than one year				
I Provisions for liabilities and charges				
J Accruals and deferred income[3]				
K Capital and reserves				
I Called-up share capital				
II Share premium account				
III Revaluation reserve				
IV Other reserves				
V Profit and loss account				

Notes:

1 Called-up share capital not paid may be disclosed as a sub-heading of debtors.
2 Prepayments and accrued income may be disclosed as a sub-heading of debtors.
3 Accruals and deferred income may be disclosed as a sub-heading of creditors, either within one year or after more than one year as appropriate.
4 The letters and numbers for each line do not have to be shown.
5 The current period's figures should be compared with the previous period's.
6 Items with nil values for both years need not be disclosed.

requirements for all companies would be disproportionately burdensome for small companies. Hence small and medium-sized companies, as defined by the Companies Acts, are relieved of some of the reporting provisions. The public should not be too disadvantaged by these concessions and those who have a particular interest, for example banks providing finance, can insist on additional financial reports as necessary to fulfil their information needs.

A business is classified as being either small or medium-sized if it can satisfy two of the three criteria used to measure company size:

	Small – no more than	Medium – no more than
Sales	£2 800 000	£11 200 000
Balance sheet total net assets	£1 400 000	£5 600 000
Number of employees	50	250

Small companies need only file with the Registrar of Companies an abbreviated balance sheet and a special auditor's report. Medium-sized companies need only file an abbreviated profit-and-loss account but must provide a full balance sheet, a special auditor's report and a directors' report. There is a requirement for all companies to provide a full set of accounts to the members of the company if requested.

Valuation

Accounts may be prepared according to one of two valuation conventions:

- **historical cost** – the value placed on an item or transaction at the time it arose
- **alternative cost** – a valuation based on current cost having made an adjustment for the changing value of money.

Most accounts are prepared on the historical cost basis, although many companies do take the opportunity to include a more up-to-date valuation of land and buildings to give the users of the accounts better information concerning the value of the business. The basis for valuation should be disclosed as an accounting policy of the business.

Accounting standards

The preparation of accounts is also subject to the influence of accounting guidelines issued by the Accounting Standards Board (ASB). The ASB reports to the Financial Reporting Council (FRC) which oversees the accounting standards process. Its members are appointed by the Governor of the Bank of England, Secretary of State for Trade and Industry and various interested organisations, including the users and preparers of company accounts.

The ASB took over the work of the previous standard-setting regime called the Accounting Standards Committee (ASC), which was composed largely of accountants – the actual preparers of accounts. It was considered that a more independent standard-setting process was needed.

The ASB issues accounting standards in the form of **Financial Reporting Statements** (FRSs) and final draft versions as a sign of intention in the form of **Financial Reporting Exposure Drafts** (FREDs) (see Figure 16.4). The accounting standards produced by the extinct ASC are called *Statements of Standard Accounting Practice* (SSAPs) and previous drafts were called *Exposure Drafts* (EDs).

Figure 16.4 The accounting standard setting process

The Accounting Standards Board identifies an area of accounting practice which it considers requires guidelines to ensure appropriate and consistent treatment.

Consultation
There is a consultative period during which the ASB invites comments from individuals and organisations that are interested in the subject area under review. Interested parties represent both preparers and users of financial statements.

Financial Reporting Exposure Draft (FRED)
The ASB issues a FRED which is a new standard in draft form. At this stage accountants are expected to be aware of this indication of best practice even though it is not yet accepted as a full accounting standard.

Financial Reporting Standard (FRS)
The ASB produces a Financial Reporting Standard having taken into account further submissions made as a result of the FRED. The ASB is authorised to issue accounting standards, unlike its predecessor the Accounting Standards Committee that had to submit the accounting standard to the professional accounting bodies.

Accounting standards indicate current best accounting practice and are to be applied to all financial statements intended to give a 'true and fair' view of the financial affairs of a business and of its performance for a particular accounting period. There is an obligation on the part of members of the main professional accounting bodies to comply with accounting standards in cases where they either prepare accounts or are required to **audit** them. Non-compliance should be disclosed in the notes to the accounts, or failing this, in the auditors' report. However, they are not so prescriptive that they should be applied in cases where they are thought likely to confuse a true and fair view. In addition, it is not necessary to comply with accounting standards for items that are not of a significant or material value.

For the time being the ASB has accepted many of the accounting guidelines issued by the previous ASC and the list of current accounting standards is detailed here:

FRS 1	Cash Flow Statements
FRS 2	Accounting for Subsidiary Undertakings
FRS 3	Reporting Financial Performance
FRS 4	Capital Instruments
FRS 5	Reporting the Substance of Transactions
FRS 6	Acquisitions and Mergers
FRS 7	Fair Values in Acquisition Accounting
SSAP 1	Accounting for the Results of Associated Companies
SSAP 2	Disclosure of Accounting Policies
SSAP 3	Earnings per Share (amended by FRS 3)
SSAP 4	The Accounting Treatment of Government Grants
SSAP 5	Accounting for Value Added Tax
SSAP 8	The Treatment of Taxation under the Imputation System in the Accounts of Companies
SSAP 9	Stocks and Long-term Contracts
SSAP 12	Accounting for Depreciation
SSAP 13	Accounting for Research and Development
SSAP 15	Accounting for Deferred Taxation
SSAP 17	Accounting for Post Balance Sheets Events
SSAP 18	Accounting for Contingencies
SSAP 19	Accounting for Investment Properties
SSAP 20	Foreign Currency Translation
SSAP 21	Accounting for Leases and Hire Purchase Agreements
SSAP 22	Accounting for Goodwill
SSAP 24	Accounting for Pension Costs
SSAP 25	Segmental Reporting

Some of the accounting standards are quite specialised and relate only to a proportion of companies whereas others affect most companies. All companies that use fixed assets and maintain a stock of materials will be affected by SSAP 9 and SSAP 12. It is the responsibility of the preparer of accounts to be aware of the accounting standards and to apply their recommendations where appropriate.

The requirements of a number of the accounting standards will be referred to later in this chapter, and SSAP 12 and FRS 1 are outlined in Chapter 18.

Urgent Issues Task Force (UITF) Statements

Reporting to the ASB, the Urgent Issues Task Force considers current issues which the ASB deems require some guidance before an accounting standard can be issued or amended to address the problem. The UITF also issues 'Abstracts' for areas of reporting that are covered by legislation or accounting standard but where some controversy or confusion has arisen when they have been applied to specific cases. Its pronouncements, therefore, tend to be focused on issues of a specialised nature.

Accounting principles

The Companies Act 1985 specifies certain basic concepts that should be applied when preparing a set of financial reports. In addition, SSAP 2 gives guidance on the application of these fundamental accounting concepts, identifying the possibility that there may be a range of acceptable accounting methods on which a business can base its specific accounting policies.

The matching or accruals concept

Financial statements are necessarily prepared for a defined period of time. Apart from varying periods at the start or termination of a business, they are always prepared for periods of one year if for publication; and often on a monthly basis for internal use within the business. For the profit-and-loss account to report accurately what has happened in the period, it is important to identify:

- the actual value of work supplied to customers
- the value of resources consumed while making these supplies.

Many business transactions do not result in a simultaneous receipt or payment of cash, so accounts cannot be prepared reliably from records of cash transactions alone. Common problems at the end of an accounting period include:

- Credit sales to customers remain unpaid.
- Work has been started for a customer and costs have been incurred, but payment cannot be requested until the work is complete.
- Materials have been purchased for stock to satisfy future sales orders.
- Materials have been purchased on credit and not been paid for.
- Equipment purchased in the current year will continue to give good service in the future.
- Equipment purchased in a previous year has given good service but is not worth as much at the end of the year as at the beginning.

Much of the work of those who prepare accounts is to overcome these problems so that the financial statements are meaningful.

The going-concern concept

When a business buys assets, whether for use in the business or for resale, it is usually on the basis that they will provide a future benefit in excess of their cost. If we take the case of stock for resale, SSAP 9 states that it should be valued in the balance sheet at the lower of (a) its cost or (b) its net realisable value (market value less costs of selling) under *normal market conditions*. The accounts are prepared on the assumption that the business will continue in operation for the foreseeable future – the 'going-concern' principle. If the business had to stop trading and its assets liquidated, then the market value of fixed assets and stock under these conditions may be significantly less than normal. If the business cannot be assumed to be a going concern then the assets would have to be valued at 'net realisable values' under distress conditions (e.g. auction values for bankrupt stock). Confirmation that the going-concern concept can legitimately be applied is an important reassurance that users of accounts need.

Consistency

Items of a similar nature should be accounted for on a consistent basis from one period to the next. For example, if it has been accounting policy to depreciate (i.e. spread the cost) of motor vehicles over four years, then it would be inconsistent to depreciate over six years in the next accounting period. This is important so that the reported performance of one period can be properly compared with another.

Prudence

Financial statements should be prepared on a prudent basis. Gains should only be recognised when they are reasonably certain and losses should be provided for as soon as they are identified as a possibility. The **prudence concept** prevails over the **accruals concept** if the two conflict.

Other accounting concepts

Materiality
Strict adherence to accounting conventions need not be followed where items are not so significant as to affect the user's understanding of the business's performance and financial state of affairs. Take, for example, the classification of research and development expenditure.

According to SSAP 13, development expenditure can be deferred and treated as an intangible asset in the balance sheet only if certain rules are satisfied to demonstrate that the expenditure will give future benefits, such as a commercially viable new product. If a business with a sales turnover of £1 million incurs £50 000 development expenditure, then the treatment of the expenditure is a material issue and so should be accounted for in strict accordance with the accounting standard. However, if GEC with turnover in excess of £9 billion was to incorrectly defer £1 million of development expenditure then that would not be considered material to the understanding of the performance of the business. The materiality of an individual item will depend on the size of the business.

Separate valuation of similar items
For each classification of assets and liabilities in the balance sheet, the balance of each should be the sum of all the component items separately valued. Taking stock as an example, each item should be valued at the lower of cost or net realisable value. If a particular item is likely to result in a loss on sale, then this should be recognised in the accounts immediately and cannot be offset against unrealised profits on other items. Although this concept is not mentioned in SSAP 2 it is a requirement of the Companies Act 1985 and is generally accepted as good practice.

Accounting bases

Accounting bases are generally accepted methods of applying the accounting concepts to practical situations. Different bases have evolved in response to the needs of a diverse range of business activities.

Example – Depreciation
There are various methods of spreading the cost of a fixed asset over the years that are to benefit from its use. One method simply spreads the cost evenly over the years involved. So for a machine that costs £4000 and which is to be used for four years before being scrapped, the depreciation charge is £1000 per annum. Another method is to estimate how many hours it will be used each year and spread the cost in direct proportion to this. Hence if the same machine's life is estimated to be 10 000 hours and it is used for 1500 hours in its first year, the first year's depreciation charge is £4000 × 1500/10 000 = £600. Each method may be acceptable provided it is appropriate to the circumstances and is applied consistently.

Accounting policies

Accounting policies are the specific accounting bases adopted as being the most appropriate to the business's circumstances. There is a requirement that these accounting policies are disclosed in a note to the accounts.

Case Study
Body Shop's principal accounting policies

Accounting policies for the year ended 28 February 1994

The financial statements have been prepared under the historical cost convention and in accordance with applicable accounting standards.

Goodwill

Goodwill arising on the acquisition of a subsidiary or business is the difference between the consideration paid and the fair value of the assets and liabilities acquired. Goodwill is written off immediately to reserves.

Valuation of investments

Investments held as fixed assets are stated at cost less any provision for permanent diminution in value.

Depreciation

Depreciation is provided to write off the cost, less estimated residual values, of all tangible fixed assets, except freehold land, over their expected useful lives. It is calculated using the following rates:

- freehold buildings – over 50 years
- leasehold property – over the period of the respective leases
- plant and equipment – over 3 to 10 years.

Stocks

Stocks are valued at the lower of cost and net realisable value. Cost is calculated as follows:

- raw materials – cost of purchase on first-in/first-out basis
- work in progress and finished goods – cost of raw materials and labour together with attributable overheads
- net realisable value – estimated selling price less further costs to completion and disposal.

Research and development

R&D expenditure is charged to the profit-and-loss account in the year in which it is incurred.

Turnover

Turnover represents the total amount receivable in the ordinary course of business for goods sold and services provided. It excludes sales between companies in the Group, discounts given, VAT and other sales taxes.

Questions for discussion

1 *Suggest alternative policies for each item in the list.*
2 *What would be the effect on the accounts if your suggested alternatives were adopted?*
3 *How valuable is Body Shop's statement of accounting policies?*

Information to aid the interpretation of financial reports

Earlier in the chapter it was stated that the nature of a business affects the perceived opportunities and risks that the company affords its investors. An analysis of business activity is required by law and in the accounting standards.

The Companies Act 1985 laid down a legal requirement to provide financial information concerning the composition of **turnover** and **profit**. Where the company provides more than one product or service the accounts should disclose the amount of turnover and profit before tax attributable to each class of business. In addition, where the company operates in more than one geographical market – either individual countries or groups of countries – then an analysis of turnover for each market should be provided.

Since the introduction of a legal requirement to analyse turnover and profits, the accounting standards regime has added to this with a more comprehensive analysis.

SSAP 25 – Segmental Reporting

This standard, issued in 1990, requires certain information to be analysed by geographical area and by business class. The information in question is:

- turnover
- profit or loss before taxation (and usually before interest)
- net assets (usually excluding interest-bearing assets and liabilities)

The geographical analysis should be on the basis of where the supply is made from, but if materially different should also be analysed by area being supplied. Figure 16.5 shows an example of segment analysis.

Figure 16.5 Segment analysis in the accounts of Grand Metropolitan for the year ending 30 September 1993

	Turnover £m	Profit £m	Net assets £m
Class of business			
Continuing operations			
Food	3066	227	2131
Drinks	3418	561	1778
Retailing	1153	170	1751
	7637	958	5660
Discontinued operations			
Food	26	1	0
Retailing	457	76	658
	483	77	658
	8120	1035	6318
Geographical area			
UK and Ireland	1343	245	1312
Continental Europe	1550	137	630
USA	4499	576	4058
Rest of North America	214	26	151
Africa and Middle East	182	15	31
Rest of World	332	36	136
	8120	1035	6318

The categories used to analyse the business activities are a matter of judgement for the company to decide. The overriding factor is to ensure that the user of the accounts is able to appreciate fully the implications of a number of major influences on each segment:

- rates of return on investment
- past growth and potential for future development
- the degree of risk.

The geographical analysis should be categorised with the following considerations:

- the economic climate
- the stability and nature of the political regimes
- foreign exchange control regulations which might affect the company's ability to pay returns on investments
- foreign currency exchange rate fluctuations.

In analysing the class of business the following factors should be considered for each segment:

- the nature of the supply of goods or services
- the organisation of the company's activities

- the markets served and the channels of distribution used.

FRS 3 – Reporting Financial Performance

FRS 3 was introduced to help the users of accounts understand a company's underlying performance by requiring greater information concerning the composition of reported profit figures.

Before the issue of FRS 3, it had become normal practice to distinguish between profits relating to **normal trading activities** and those of an **extraordinary** nature. Extraordinary items were excluded from important comparisons of profit and accounting **ratios**. Problems arose in the subjective judgement of what was extraordinary. It was widely accepted that companies would try to classify as extraordinary any large item that adversely affected results. In addition, the existing reporting formats provided little information to help users of accounts understand the impact of restructuring due to the acquisition and disposal of businesses. In these cases it was difficult to make meaningful comparisons with previous results that potentially related to different types of businesses.

FRS 3 requires the profit-and-loss account to distinguish between operations that are continuing and those that have been discontinued by the accounting year end. The standard also defines certain terms and explains how they should be accounted for:

- *Ordinary activities* – Any activities related to the company's business. These include the effects of changes in the company's environment such as political, regulatory, economic and geographical influences. Items are considered ordinary even if they are infrequent or unusual in nature.
- *Exceptional items* – Material items, whilst falling within ordinary activities, that are exceptional in terms of size or incidence. Certain exceptional items are to be disclosed on the face of the profit-and-loss account. These include the costs of fundamental restructuring of the business and profit or loss on the sale of a business operation or the sale of fixed assets.
- *Extraordinary items* – Material items that possess a high degree of abnormality and fall outside of ordinary activities. These are considered very rare.

Compliance with accounting standards

Like the pronouncements of the Accounting Standards Committee, the accounting standards accepted and issued by the ASB are not enforced directly by the law. However, a number of mechanisms exist to exert sufficient pressure for preparers of accounts to comply.

Figure 16.6 Analysis of operating profit in the accounts of Dixons Group for the year ending 30 April 1994

	Continuing £m	Discontinued £m	Net assets £m
Turnover	1578.3	343.1	1921.4
Costs of sales			
base	(1400.2)	(338.8)	(1739.0)
exceptional	(20.0)		(20.0)
Gross profit	158.1	4.3	162.4
Distribution costs	(30.0)	(5.1)	(35.1)
Administration expenses			
base	(66.6)	(12.4)	(79.0)
exceptional	(4.5)		(4.5)
Other operating income	0.3		0.3
Operating profit	57.3	(13.2)	44.1

In a note to the accounts, Dixons identified the nature of its excep-tional items. 'UK Retail exceptional charges comprise provisions of £20.0 million for store closure costs and £4.5 million for the rationalisation of the Group's administrative offices.'

Although there is no legal requirement to comply with accounting standards, the Companies Act 1989 does require public and large private companies to state whether their accounts have been prepared in accordance with them.

Non-compliance with an accounting standard must be highlighted and an explanation given.

The Financial Reporting Panel which, like the ASB, reports to the Financial Reporting Council, has the task of examining company accounts. Where the panel decides that non-compliance with accounting standards has undermined a 'true and fair view' of a company's activities, then it will encourage revision of the accounts, and if necessary take court action to compel compliance.

The role of auditors

The accounts of a limited company must be audited by a firm of independent accountants who are **registered auditors**. The auditors are asked to verify the accuracy of financial records and to ensure that the accounts are consistent with these records. The accounting treatment and disclosure of all material items should be confirmed as being in accordance with relevant legislation and as complying with accounting standards where appropriate. The overriding responsibility of auditors is to confirm that the accounts provide a 'true and fair view' of the valuation of assets and liabilities as at the date of the accounts and of the profit or loss up to that date (usually one year). To fulfil this responsibility, the auditors may actually encourage or concur with a departure from an accounting standard if this facilitates a true and fair view of the financial aspects of the company.

Of particular interest to the auditors will be to verify that it is appropriate to apply the going-concern principle for the valuation of assets and liabilities. If assets have to be disposed of as a result of cessation of business, then appropriate (often lower) market values should be used in preparing the accounts. Hence some of the audit will be devoted to the company's future outlook.

Auditors may have difficulty confirming that the financial reports do give a true and fair view, in which case they may issue a 'qualified' audit report. Reasons for a qualified audit report fall into two main categories:

- There might be **uncertainty**. The accounting records may be inadequate for them to carry out a full audit of financial transactions, or there may be uncertainty concerning the outcome of a known situation (e.g. a law suit or the applicability of the going-concern concept). For example, in Figure 16.8 the auditors' report for Tiphook plc in relation to their financial reports dated 30 April 1994, although not actually qualifying the accounts, does illustrate a number of uncertainties that could lead to a qualified audit report if considered important enough to undermine the going-concern concept.

- There might be **disagreement**. The accounting records may not be factual or the financial reports may not be in accordance with the accounting records. The non-compliance with relevant legislation and accounting standards may also be cause for disagreement.

For interested parties, the reluctance of the auditors to state that the accounts provide a 'true and fair view' seriously undermines their value.

An effective audit of a company's accounts does not come cheap, and is paid by the shareholders out of their profits. The audit at Sainsbury's cost £500 000 in 1994, on turnover of £10.5 billion and an operating profit of £0.8 billion.

Stock Exchange requirements

Public limited companies listed on the London International Stock Exchange are required to disclose additional information in accordance with its 'Yellow Book'. One requirement is to issue an *interim* financial report of performance, including details of turnover,

Figure 16.7 An unqualified audit report

AUDITORS' REPORT
TO THE SHAREHOLDERS OF
J SAINSBURY plc

We have audited the financial statements on pages 39 to 56 which have been prepared under the accounting policies set out on page 39.

Respective responsibilities of Directors and Auditors
As described above the Company's Directors are responsible for the preparation of financial statements. It is our responsibility to form an independent opinion, based on our audit, on those financial statements and to report our opinion to you.

Basis of opinion
We conducted our audit in accordance with Auditing Standards issued by the Auditing Practices Board. An audit includes examination, on a test basis, of evidence relevant to the amounts and disclosures in the financial statements. It also includes an assessment of the significant estimates and judgements made by the Directors in the preparation of the financial statements, and of whether the accounting policies are appropriate to the Company's circumstances, consistently applied and adequately disclosed.

We planned and performed our audit so as to obtain all the information and explanations which we considered necessary in order to provide us with sufficient evidence to give reasonable assurance that the financial statements are free from material misstatement, whether caused by fraud or other irregularity or error. In forming our opinion we also evaluated the overall adequacy of the presentation of information in the financial statements.

Opinion
In our opinion the financial statements give a true and fair view of the state of affairs of the Company and the Group as at 12 March 1994 and of the profit for the 52 weeks then ended and have been properly prepared in accordance with the Companies Act 1985.

CLARK WHITEHILL
Chartered Accountants and Registered Auditor
London, 10 May 1994

Figure 16.8 Extract from a qualified audit report for Tiphock plc

Fundamental uncertainties

The financial statements have been prepared on a going-concern basis which assumes that the Company and the Group will continue in operational existence for the foreseeable future having adequate funds to meet their obligations as they fall due. The validity of this assumption depends on the satisfactory resolution of the following matters:

1. the continued support of the Group's principal bankers;
2. the necessary resolution in relation to the Group's borrowings being passed by shareholders at the forthcoming Annual General Meeting;
3. the availability of finance to fund the capital expenditure programme;
4. ... the cessation of operating losses and a return to profitability.

Overload

The burden of providing so much information led to representations by business organisations to government. The government responded with a review of reporting requirements with special emphasis on the obligations of small businesses on whom regulations are a disproportionate burden. One consequence was the abolition of the small company audit. Companies with turnover of less than £90 000 need not have their accounts audited. Turnover of between £90 000 and £350 000 requires the company to have an independent accountant's report to confirm the accounts have been prepared in accordance with the Companies Acts. Only companies with turnover of over £350 000 need have a full audit. However, the benefit of these changes is probably not great as third-party investors continue to request fully audited accounts to safeguard their interests.

The tendency towards more onerous and complicated disclosure requirements is shown by the size of accounting standards issued by the ASB. SSAP 2 contains just five pages of advice, whereas the more recent Financial Reporting Standards sometimes have 100 pages or more!

With no regulations, users would have little confidence in accounting information. However, regulators and the accounting profession need to consider the relative costs and benefits of their rule-making, or UK industry will be at a real competitive disadvantage whilst it labours to fulfil reporting obligations.

profit and shareholder dividends. Although this is not required by law and it is not an audited statement, the provision of information on a more regular basis is considered important for those who trade on the stock exchange.

Sole traders and partnerships

No requirement exists for sole traders and partnerships (unincorporated businesses) to file accounts for public scrutiny, nor is there any legislation concerning what information the owners of the business should receive. Most businesses in this category are small, and so the owners of the business are sufficiently involved in its running to be well informed. Larger partnerships may include in their partnership agreement some form of reporting requirement to keep all partners – including silent ones – informed, even if only on an annual basis. However, where accounts have been prepared by a member of one of the main accountancy bodies, a responsibility is placed on the accountant to observe the requirements of accounting standards as endorsed by the Accounting Standards Board.

Government departments, particularly those concerned with taxation, will require financial statements in sufficient detail to allow the computation of tax according to tax regulations. For income tax purposes a profit-and-loss statement is required with reasonable detail concerning the analysis of costs to verify their eligibility for tax purposes. Details are also required concerning expenditure for fixed assets, as a proportion of these can be deducted from gross income in the form of 'capital allowances' before tax rates are applied.

Customs and excise require all transactions subject to value-added tax to be properly documented and recorded, with the VAT element separately recorded in a VAT account.

Although there are no requirements to disclose financial information other than to tax authorities, there are significant pressures on reporting accountants to present a true and fair view of an unincorporated business's financial state of affairs when preparing accounts.

Financial information for managers

Financial accounts for use inside the business should be prepared on a regular basis to provide management with up-to-date information concerning financial performance. These are often called **management accounts**. The emphasis is on helping management to plan, make decisions and control the business functions, so their design will depend very much on the specific needs of the particular business. It is possible to identify some common features:

- *Reporting period* – They are often prepared monthly, with figures for the month and year to date.
- *Timeliness* – They are usually prepared to strict timetables so that management receive timely information, often within one week of the period end.
- *Detail* – Analysis of sales and costs is usually far more detailed than accounts for publication, including a breakdown by department.
- *Format* – The format of management accounts is not prescribed by law so an emphasis will be placed on clear presentation, with a structure relevant to the activities of the business. Different versions of the management accounts may be issued depending on the specific area and level of responsibility of the recipient manager.
- *Comparisons* – Actual performance is compared with the budget and possibly with the same period of the previous year.
- *Forecasts* – Accounts may include a revised forecast of results up to the year end.
- *Performance measures* – Financial and non-financial *ratios* may be included.

The accounting system is designed with the requirements of both management and the regulatory bodies in mind. Because of management's need for greater detail in most businesses, the system is designed around internal needs, and modifications for external reporting requirements tend to be added afterwards.

Stakeholder accounting

In an attempt to address the bias in financial reporting towards the business owners, a new form of financial report has been developed to provide a clearer picture of how the wealth generated by a business is shared between the various stakeholders. This alternative performance report is called a **value-added statement**. It identifies 'value added' as the difference between the value of sales charged to customers and the cost of goods and services purchased from other businesses. The value added is then shown as being shared between employees, the government and those who provided capital. Amounts retained in the business, although legally belonging to the shareholders, are presented as an investment in the future of the company to ensure continuity and growth for everyone's benefit. Figure 16.9 shows an example.

Figure 16.9 A pictorial value-added statement

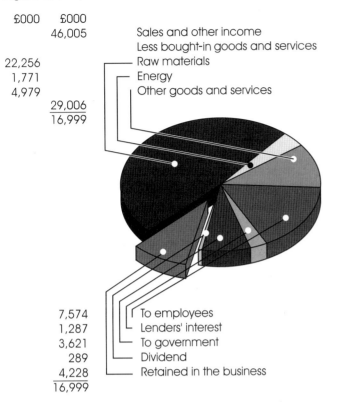

£000	£000	
	46,005	Sales and other income
		Less bought-in goods and services
22,256		Raw materials
1,771		Energy
4,979		Other goods and services
	29,006	
	16,999	

7,574	To employees
1,287	Lenders' interest
3,621	To government
289	Dividend
4,228	Retained in the business
16,999	

(Source: *Management Accounting*, November 1994)

Task

Examine the value-added statement in Figure 16.9 and discuss its benefits compared with the normal presentation of performance in the profit-and-loss account.

Summary

The need for financial reporting stems from the demand for information by the various stakeholder groups. The needs of external groups, including business owners who may be remote from the day-to-day activities of the business, have been largely satisfied with a regulatory framework originating from two sources. The requirements of the Companies Acts directly relate to limited companies, but where issues of good accountancy practice are concerned they are also applied in the preparation of accounts for unincorporated businesses. Accounting standards issued by the Accounting Standards Board are enforced on the preparers of accounts with the encouragement of the 1989 Companies Act and by the accountancy profession.

Once accounts are prepared and audited they are issued to company members and filed with the Registrar of Companies, where they are available for public inspection. Financial information for internal use is provided in the form of management accounts, having regard to the business's activities and its organisational structure.

Recent regulations have concentrated on information concerning the nature of business activities and the financial effect of business reorganisations. For other stakeholders, innovations in social accounting include environmental reporting and value-added statements.

Further reading

- *Accounting Standards*, 4th edition, by J. Blake. Pitman, 1994.
- *Foundations of Business Accounting* by Roy Dodge. Chapman & Hall, 1993.
- *Finance for Non-Financial Managers – An Active-Learning Approach* by A. H. Millichamp. DPP, 1992.
- *Accounting for Non-Accounting Students*, 3rd edition, by John Dyson. Pitman, 1994.
- *Finance and Accounting*, 3rd edition, by Richard Giles and John Capel. Macmillan, 1994.
- *An Introduction to Financial Accounting* by Colin Rickwood and Andrew Thomas. McGraw-Hill, 1992.
- *Accounting in the Business Environment* by John Watts. Pitman, 1993.
- *The Meaning of Company Accounts*, 5th edition, by Walter Reid and D. R. Myddelton. Gower, 1992.
- *The Students Newsletter*, Chartered Association of Certified Accountants, monthly.

17 Recording financial information

On completion of this chapter students will be able to:

■ identify and investigate the systems needed to record financial transactions

■ examine the roles of different components within the accounting system

■ apply the appropriate concepts and conventions to the recording of transactions.

Financial transactions are recorded for a number of reasons: to satisfy the reporting requirements identified in Chapter 16; to enable payments to be made for resources (whether they be goods and services from other businesses or the wages of employees); and to ensure the receipt of monies for sales to customers.

The Companies Acts require the accounting records to be sufficient to describe transactions in some detail. The records should be adequate to disclose the financial position of the company at any time. In particular, the records should:

■ analyse the receipts and payments of cash
■ record the assets and liabilities of the business
■ show details of period-end stock-takes, and for businesses not in the retail sector, details of individual buyers and sellers.

The precise form of accounting records is not prescribed by law. This makes sense as the financial transactions and recording requirements of different businesses are so diverse. However, although accounting systems differ, they tend to conform to certain accounting conventions.

Accounting equations

For accounting purposes we have to accept the business as an entity separate from its owners, whether this is legally the case or not. The accounts have to recognise that the business is in possession of certain assets even if they legally belong to the business owners, as in the case of sole traders and partnerships.

Business assets originate from one of two sources:

■ business owners – the value of assets provided by the owners of the business is called **capital**
■ suppliers and investors who have provided assets without receiving payment – these amounts owed are called **liabilities**.

It follows, therefore, that the value of assets in a business equals the sum of resources provided by the owners and the amounts owed to suppliers and investors. This logic underpins the accounting equation, which is:

$$\text{Assets} = \text{Capital} + \text{Liabilities}$$

By rearranging the accounting equation we can say that:

$$\text{Capital} = \text{Assets} - \text{Liabilities}$$

i.e. capital is represented by the 'net worth' of the business.

The double-entry system

Most accounting systems used by businesses operate on the basis of the **double-entry** concept. Every transaction has two aspects to it. Let us examine some transactions for a fictional furniture shop.

The Hardwood Shop buys for £500 cash a table that it intends to sell to a customer.

- The shop has gained an asset in the form of a table.
- The shop has also reduced its cash balance by £500.

The Hardwood Shop buys a set of chairs for £400 on credit from Timberworld Ltd.

- It has gained an asset in the form of a set of chairs.
- The shop now owes Timberworld £400.

The Hardwood Shop settles its debt with Timberworld by paying the £400 owed.

- The debt is extinguished.
- The shop's cash balance is reduced by £400.

At the end of these transactions the Hardwood Shop has increased its stock of items for resale by one table and one set of chairs. Its cash balance is reduced by £900. Assuming that the Hardwood Shop has purchased wisely (having regard to its potential to sell on to its customers the furniture for not less than £900) it cannot be asserted that the shop is any worse off after the purchases. In fact the best indication we have of the value of the furniture purchased is that it is worth £900. So a decrease in cash is exactly matched by an increase in furniture.

Recognising the dual aspect of every transaction is an important concept that underpins business accounting systems.

Illustration of the dual aspect concept

Carol Harvey set up in business with £3000 selling children's clothing on a market stall.

Transaction 1
Carol pays the money into a business bank account.

| ASSETS | | LIABILITIES & CAPITAL | |
Detail	Amount	Detail	Amount
Detail	3 000	Capital–Harvey	3 000

Dual aspect

| Assets increase | Bank balance of £3000 |
| Capital increases | Net worth belonging to C. Harvey £3000 |

Transaction 2
Carol now purchases on credit terms £2000 of clothing from Charles Gray. Note: Items purchased for subsequent resale are classified as the asset *stock*. The debt to the supplier is a liability.

| ASSETS | | LIABILITIES & CAPITAL | |
Detail	Amount	Detail	Amount
Bank	3000	Capital–Harvey	3000
Stock	2000	Charles Gray	2000
	5000		5000

Dual aspect

| Assets increase | Stock increases by £2000 |
| Liabilities increase | Charles Gray is owed £2000 |

Transaction 3
Carol sells on credit a sweat shirt to her sister Joyce at cost price. Although Carol has not received payment, her sister will pay eventually so the debt is treated as an asset.

| ASSETS | | LIABILITIES & CAPITAL | |
Detail	Amount	Detail	Amount
Bank	3000	Capital–Harvey	3000
Stock	1990	Charles Gray	2000
Joyce	10		
	5000		5000

Dual aspect

| Assets increase | Joyce will pay in the future £10 |
| Assets decrease | Stock depleted by £10 |

Transaction 4

Carol pays Charles Gray the £2000 she owes him.

ASSETS		LIABILITIES & CAPITAL	
Detail	Amount	Detail	Amount
Bank	1000	Capital – Harvey	3000
Stock	1990		
Joyce	10		
	3000		3000

Dual aspect

Assets decrease	Bank is depleted by £2000
Liabilities decrease	The debt with Charles Gray is deleted

Transaction 5

Carol receives cash from Joyce.

ASSETS		LIABILITIES & CAPITAL	
Detail	Amount	Detail	Amount
Bank	1010	Capital – Harvey	3000
Stock	1990		
	3000		3000

Dual aspect

Assets increase	Bank increases by £10
Assets decrease	Joyce will not pay Carol again

These statements prepared for Carol Harvey giving details of her assets and liabilities are examples of **balance sheets**. They are called balance sheets simply because they are a set of balances that make up the business's net worth at a point in time.

Apart from the initial capital paid into the business, we have only considered transactions that have not led to a change in the capital balance. Remember that capital is the difference between the assets and the liabilities tied up in the business. Transactions so far have involved:

Transactions	One aspect	Second aspect
2	Assets increased £2000	Liabilities increased £2000
3	Assets increased £10	Assets decreased £10
4	Assets decreased £2000	Liabilities decreased £2000
5	Assets increase £10	Assets decrease £10

The net effect of each transaction on the net worth of the business is nil. Now let us examine the case where Carol *does* enter into a transaction where she receives more for something than she paid for it.

Transaction 6

Carol sells for £1100 cash stock that cost her £800.

ASSETS		LIABILITIES & CAPITAL	
Detail	Amount	Detail	Amount
Bank	2110	Capital – Harvey	3300
Stock	1190		
	3300		3300

Dual aspect

Assets increase	Bank goes up by £1100
Assets decrease	Stock goes down by £800
Capital increases	Owner's net worth has increased by £300

This last transaction gives us an insight into the ways in which owner's capital can change. Capital changes because:

- the owner(s) invests more money in the business
- the owner(s) takes money out of the business
- the business makes a profit which increases the net worth of the business.

Task

Jo Green finished February 199X with the assets, liabilities and capital shown in the following balance sheet:

Assets	£	Liabilities and Capital	£
Van	10 000	Capital	20 000
Stock	5 000	Creditors	2 000
Debtors	1 000		
	6 000		
Cash	22 000		22 000

You are required to identify the dual aspect of each of the following transactions and to prepare a new balance sheet after each.

1 *Stock costing £2000 is sold for cash.*
2 *Debtors pay their debt of £1000.*
3 *Stock costing £1500 is bought on credit.*
4 *Jo pays £2000 for past supplies received on credit.*
5 *Jo sells on credit stock costing £500 for £1000.*

We have now examined the basic framework for an accounting system, but it is not practicable to record business transactions in this way because:

- It would be too time-consuming to prepare a statement of assets, liabilities and capital after every transaction.
- The statement provides us with information only at a point in time – it does not tell us what happened during a particular period, such as volume of business activity and how profitable it was.
- Details of past business transactions are hard to access for audit and enquiry purposes.

The ledger account

To avoid the need to prepare a balance sheet after every transaction, a system of bookkeeping has evolved that enables us to record just the dual aspect of every transaction. The system is called double-entry bookkeeping. We start with a ledger book with pages similar in format to that at the base of this page.

Every classification of asset, liability, capital and transaction is known as an **account** and has its own section of the ledger, perhaps running into many pages.

At this stage it is important to familiarise yourself with important accounting terms. Some are everyday words, *but you should understand the special significance placed on them by bookkeepers and accountants.*

- **Sales** – relate to revenues received or receivable from customers in the normal course of trading. They may include the provision of goods or services, and if part of the usual terms of business, also commission earned in the capacity of an agent. They exclude income from activity that is not part of the formal business, for example the sale of a fixed asset or bank interest. Sales are recorded net of trade discounts given to customers.
- **Purchases** – relate to the acquisition of goods intended for resale to the business's customers. They *include* raw materials used to make goods for sale. They *exclude* the buying of fixed assets or items consumed in the business as an overhead. Purchases are recorded net of trade discounts.
- **Returns in** – relate to goods returned by the customer, having been originally recognised as sales.

- **Returns out** – relate to goods originally recognised as purchases but have been subsequently returned by the business to the supplier.
- **Carriage in** – the cost of bringing goods into the business.
- **Carriage out** – the cost of delivering goods to customers.
- **Discount received** – discounts given by suppliers for paying promptly (e.g. 3 per cent discount for paying within 7 days). These are *settlement* discounts that should not be confused with *trade* discounts given as a percentage off list prices.
- **Discounts allowed** – discounts given by the business to customers for paying promptly.
- **Stock** – the term used to describe those materials and goods purchased for resale but currently remaining unsold.
- **Expenses or overheads** – purchases of goods or services that are consumed within a short time period. Examples include electricity, stationery, repairs to equipment, wages and rent. Various small items (say under £100) such as staplers and hand tools that are considered too small to record as a fixed asset are also treated as an expense.
- **Debtor** – a customer who owes the business for a supply of goods or services.
- **Creditor** – a supplier who supplied the business on credit terms and remains unpaid.

To provide greater information concerning how the net worth of a business changes, ledger accounts are opened for each type of transaction. Some types of transactions may be analysed further – for example the business may wish to monitor the product analysis of sales, and so separate sales accounts would be used for each product.

Debit and credit

The terms **debit** and **credit** are used to describe the effect a transaction has on a particular ledger account. It is not adequate to say 'plus' this account and 'minus' that because the dual aspect of a transaction has to be

Ledger							
				Name		Bank	
				Number		6 000	
Date	Narrative	Ref.	Value £	Date	Narrative	Ref.	Value £
	Carol Harvey		3 000		Creditor		2 000
	Joyce		10				
	Sales		1 100		balance c/f		2 110
			4 110				4 110
	Balance b/f		2 110				

recognised within the framework of the accounting equation. An increase in assets is *not* the same as a decrease in liabilities, so to avoid confusion the terms debit and credit are used.

Debits and credits affect ledger account balances in different ways depending on the type of account:

	Debit	**Credit**
Asset	an increase	a decrease
Liability	a decrease	an increase
Capital	a decrease	an increase
Expense	an increase	a decrease
Sales revenue	a decrease	an increase

It can seem confusing trying to remember which account should be debited and which credited. *You may find it easier if you consider the effect of each transaction on the bank account.* Assets are debits so money in the bank is a debit. If we add money to the bank account we must *debit* the bank ledger account. If we take money out of the account we must *credit* it.

Of course not all transactions involve the bank account, but it may help us to think as if they do. If the business sells an item on credit what are the entries? A clue can be found by considering the similar position of selling for cash. In this case the bank will increase so we would debit bank and the other entry must be to credit sales. So selling on credit must also result in sales being credited and the other entry must be a debit. Someone who now owes us money is an asset and so we debit a debtor account in their name (e.g. Joyce Harvey in the previous illustration).

It is normal convention that the left-hand side of the ledger account is used to record the debit entry of a transaction and the right-hand side records the credit entry.

Example of double-entry bookkeeping

The following transactions were made by Rodney Enterprises during January 199X:

5/1/9X	Rodney paid into his business's bank account	19 000
6/1/9X	Purchased a motor van for cash	8 000
7/1/9X	Purchased stock on credit from Apex	6 500
8/1/9X	Sold stock for cash	5 000
9/1/9X	Sold stock on credit to Booker & Co.	2 000

Before making the entries in the respective ledger accounts it would be useful at this stage to prepare a

journal of the entries we intend to make. *This can provide a valuable record of transactions for later reference* (see Figure 17.1).

Figure 17.1 The journal

Journal		
Narrative	Debit £	Credit £
Bank	19 000	
Capital – Rodney		19 000
Rodney paying in business capital		
Motor van	8 000	
Bank		8 000
Purchase of van		
Purchases	6 500	
Apex		6 500
Purchased stock on credit from Apex		
Bank	5 000	
Sales		5 000
Cash sales		
Booker & Co.	2 000	
Sales		2 000
Credit sales to Booker & Co.		

Take note of the *format* of the journal. It is normal practice to enter the debit entry first and to slightly inset the credit entry. Always provide a narrative after each transaction to be posted.

The ledger accounts are shown in detail on the next page.

The ledger of Rodney Enterprises

Bank account							
Date	**Narrative**	**Ref.**	**Value £**	**Date**	**Narrative**	**Ref.**	**Value £**
5/1/9X	Rodney		19 000	6/1/9X	Motor		8 000
8/1/9X	Sales		5 000				

Motor account							
Date	**Narrative**	**Ref.**	**Value £**	**Date**	**Narrative**	**Ref.**	**Value £**
6/1/9X	Bank		8 000				

Purchases account							
Date	**Narrative**	**Ref.**	**Value £**	**Date**	**Narrative**	**Ref.**	**Value £**
7/1/9X	Apex		6 500				

Apex account							
Date	**Narrative**	**Ref.**	**Value £**	**Date**	**Narrative**	**Ref.**	**Value £**
				7/1/9X	Purchases		6 500

Booker & Co. account							
Date	**Narrative**	**Ref.**	**Value £**	**Date**	**Narrative**	**Ref.**	**Value £**
9/1/9X	Sales		2 000				

Sales account							
Date	**Narrative**	**Ref.**	**Value £**	**Date**	**Narrative**	**Ref.**	**Value £**
				8/1/9X	Bank		5 000
				9/1/9X	Booker & Co.		2 000

Task

The following transactions relate to a new business set up by Josey Trash:

		£
5/4/9X	Josey paid into her business's bank account	2 500
6/4/9X	Purchased shop fittings	1 000
7/4/9X	Purchased stock on credit from Trash	1 200
8/4/9X	Sold stock for cash	500
9/4/9X	Paid rent with cash	200
10/4/9X	Sold stock to Sean Bean on credit	100
11/4/9X	Paid Trash	1 200
12/4/9X	Sold goods for cash	300

1 Prepare *ledger accounts* for bank, shop fittings, purchases, sales, rent, capital – Josey, Trash and Sean Bean.
2 Prepare a *journal* for the above transactions.
3 Post the transactions to the appropriate ledger accounts.

The administrative process of buying and selling

The process commences with the decision to acquire the goods or services of another business. A **purchase order** will be completed detailing what is required together with any other pertinent information such as place of delivery and date required. In larger businesses it is likely that the firm has a specialist purchasing department that has responsibility for placing all orders with other firms. In that case the individual will send a **purchase requisition** detailing what is required and by when to the purchasing department, who will then identify the most appropriate supplier and issue a purchase order accordingly.

On receipt of the *purchase order*, the selling firm may transfer the details of the order on to a **sales order**. The purpose of this is to ensure that all information they require has been provided, and once input into the firm's information system it will provide the basic information for subsequent stages in the sales accounting process. The goods will be delivered together with a form called an **advice note** (or **delivery note**) which the customer will have to sign to confirm that a supply has been made. In the case of the provision of a service, such as maintenance of equipment, the engineer will require the customer to sign a **work completed form**. On receipt of goods, it is usual practice for the department receiving the goods (in large organisations, a dedicated goods-received department) to make out a **goods-received note** (GRN), with copies sent to whoever wanted the goods in the first place, the purchase department, and the purchase ledger section of the accounts department.

The selling firm is now in possession of two documents signed by the customer: a request for a supply of goods and services (purchase order), and confirmation that the order has been satisfied (advice note). The selling firm can now issue a document stating the amount payable for the supply. This is called an **invoice**. In the hands of the seller it is a **sales invoice**, in the hands of the buyer it will be called a **purchase invoice**. The sales invoice will be recorded on the **debtor ledger** where it will remain outstanding against the customer until payment is received.

The buying firm should now be in possession of three documents relevant to the transaction: a purchase order, a GRN and a purchase invoice. If all three documents agree, the purchase invoice can be recorded on the **creditor ledger** as a verified debt to the supplier.

The buyer should make payment before the end of the agreed credit period, which is typically 30 days after delivery – although other terms may have been agreed, including a discount for prompt payment. When payment is made the buying firm will remove the invoice from the purchase ledger and the supplier will remove the same document from its sales ledger.

The process is now complete! Figure 17.2 shows a summary.

The precise procedures and documents used will depend on the business, but this example illustrates common principles.

The administrative process of buying and selling seems unnecessarily complex, but it must be remembered that the following factors are common to many commercial transactions:

- The premises of firms doing business may be geographically remote from one another – perhaps even on the other side of the world.
- The number of transactions can be vast.
- It would be insecure for cash to be carried around by delivery drivers.
- The administrative procedures required to control cash receipts and payments would also be very onerous.

It is little wonder that inter-business trade is often based on credit. The paperwork system is its downside.

Important documents for the purchasing activity

Purchase order

The **purchase order** is a request from buyer to seller to provide certain goods or services. It can be in the form of

Figure 17.2 Paperwork flow in the buying and selling process

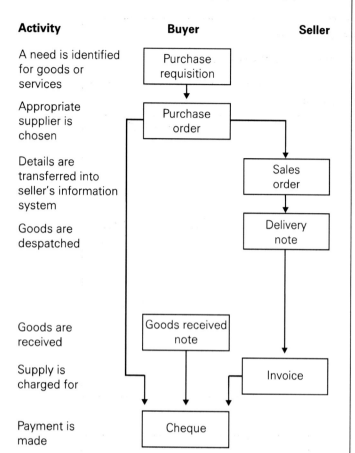

- Once delivery has been made, an invoice is sent by the supplier to the customer – it is in effect a request for payment.
- Before paying, the buyer's accounts department checks the invoice details against the purchase order and the GRN to ensure prices, quantities and other details are correct.
- Depending on the type of purchase and the organisation's administration procedures, the invoice may need authorising by a departmental manager before payment is made – for example, a rent bill that has no corresponding purchase order or GRN.
- The invoice will include value-added tax if the supply is of a taxable nature and has been made by a VAT registered business.

Books of prime entry

Since the number of transactions a business enters into is potentially very large, most businesses would find posting a double entry for every transaction to be too onerous. In fact it would probably clutter the ledger accounts so much that trying to analyse them would become very difficult. It is normal practice, therefore, for transactions to be summarised for an accounting period before being posted to the ledger accounts. These summary records are called *books of prime entry* and are really just a place where the transactions of buying, selling and payment, as described above, are listed and analysed.

Sales journal (or sales day book)

The **sales journal** is a listing of all the sales invoices prepared in respect of credit sales (see Figure 17.5).

The sales journal in Figure 17.5 is analysed to provide information concerning the make-up of sales. As a minimum, the information required for each transaction includes the invoice number, the customer's name, the total value for each transaction and the amount of VAT included where appropriate. In addition, a computerised system is almost certain to include a **customer account number field**.

When items are returned by customers they are called **returns inwards**. There are two methods by which these transactions can be recorded. We could just consider them as *negative sales* and deduct them in the sales journal. Alternatively it may be more convenient, and provide valuable information concerning sales returns, if we record them in a separate **returns inwards journal**. The layout of the journal would be similar to the above sales journal.

a pre-printed form, a letter, a verbal request or an electronic message between two businesses' computerised information systems. The traditional purchase order form highlights the information conveyed whatever method is used (see Figure 17.3).

- The purchase order must be signed by a duly authorised individual (e.g. the purchasing manager).
- The purchasing organisation will make a number of copies of the purchase order. One may be sent to the Goods Inwards Department to ensure goods received are in accordance with the order. Another usually goes to the accounts department to check the supplier's invoice when it arrives.
- Before sending the goods on credit, the supplying organisation will check the creditworthiness of the customer. They will retain the order in case of any query over what has been supplied.

Invoice

An invoice is a document issued by a seller to a buyer detailing goods and services supplied and the amount of money due (see Figure 17.4).

Figure 17.3 A typical purchase order form

CARSON ENGINEERING LTD

St Francis Road, Kettering, Northants. Tel 01536 000000

PURCHASE ORDER

To: Gerards Supplies,
Rockingham Road,
Kettering

Order no: P10256

Quantity	Ref.	Description	Price	Value
100	X1056	T assembly	0.575	57.50

Deliver to: the above address
Delivery required by: 29 May 199X

Authorised by: Kate Rawlings   Date: 25/5/9X

Figure 17.4 A typical invoice

GERARDS SUPPLIES

Rockingham Road, Kettering, Northants. Tel 01536 000000

SALES INVOICE

To: Carson Engineering,
St Francis Road,
Kettering

Invoice no: 20565
Your purchase order: P10256
Date: 31 May 199X
VAT registration number: 480 5621 21

Quantity	Ref.	Description	Unit Price	Total
100	X1056	T assembly	0.575	57.50

Sub-total	57.50
VAT @ 17.5%	10.06
Total value	67.56

Terms: Net 30 days from invoice date. E&OE

Figure 17.5 An extract from a sales day book

Sales Day Book							May 9X
Quantity	Invoice number	Customer	Total amount	VAT	Spades	Forks	Wheel-barrows
25/5/9X	30123	Grayston	235.00	35.00	200.00		
25/5/9X	30124	Viking	1 175.00	175.00	200.00		800.00
25/5/9X	30125	Apollo	587.50	87.50	100.00	400.00	
	Month total		15 333.75	2 283.75	5 400.00	3 250.00	4 400.00

Purchases journal (or purchases day book)

The purchases journal is a listing of all the purchase invoices received in a period (see Figure 17.6).

The purchases journal in Figure 17.6 is analysed to provide information concerning the make-up of purchases. The minimum information required in the purchase journal for each transaction is a reference number (either the supplier's invoice number or some internally generated number), the name of the supplier, the total value for each transaction and the amount of VAT included where appropriate.

When items are returned to the supplier they are called **returns outwards**. As with sales returns we have two methods by which these transactions can be recorded. We could consider them as *negative purchases* and deduct them in the purchase journal, or we could record them in a separate **returns outwards journal**. The layout of the journal would be similar to the above purchases journal.

Cash book

The **cash book** is a record of bank receipts and payments. The book should analyse the transactions in some way. In the illustration in Figure 17.7, the analysis

Figure 17.6 Extract from a monthly purchase day book

Purchase Day Book							May 9X
Date	Reference number	Supplier	Total amount	VAT	Raw materials	Components	Sub-contracting
25/5/9X	100233	Canning	470.00	70.00	400.0		
25/5/9X	100234	Jason's	235.00	35.00			200.00
25/5/9X	100235	Visuality	117.50	17.50		100.00	
	Month total		5 228.75	778.75	900.00	1 150.00	2 400.00

Figure 17.7 A typical cash book

Cash Book										
Date	Receipts Narrative	Ref.	Code	Value £	Date	Payments Narrative	Ref.	Code	Value £	
22/5/9X	Bal. b/f			20 560.00						
24/5/9X	J Jones	10023	6010	2 275.00	24/5/9X	BT	3061	3017	1 750.00	
25/5/9X	Casey	10024	6010	150.00	24/5/9X	Wages	3062	3002	15 250.00	
					25/5/9X	Daley	3063	7010	1 210.00	
					31/5/9X	Bal. c/f			4 775.00	
				22 985.00					22 985.00	
1/6/9X	Bal. b/f			4 775.00						

is by code number (more on this later). Alternatively columns could be utilised as shown later for petty cash.

As with the other books of prime entry, every transaction should be adequately referenced to enable the source document to be located. The reference may relate to an internal document such as a cheque requisition form or to the identifying numbers on paying-in slips and cheques.

The format of this cash book is the same as that of a ledger account. The important feature to note is the balancing off at the end of an accounting period. In the example in Figure 17.7, the total of cash at the beginning of the period and the receipts made during the period are in excess of the period's payments. It follows that the difference between the two must be the balance of cash left at the end of the period. This is inserted at the end of the payments and both sides of the cash book can be balanced off to the same column totals. The final cash balance at 31 May 199X carried forward (c/f) becomes the brought-forward (b/f) balance at 1 June 199X.

It is not essential to format the cash book like a ledger account. An alternative method would be to simply list receipts and payments in a similar way as used with the purchases and sales journals.

Another variation in format may be seen where a business experiences significant cash transactions in addition to those at the bank. The cash book will have an additional column for both the receipts and payments with each column headed 'cash'. The cash book will thus also be used to record cash transactions as well as bank transactions. Transfers between cash-on-hand and the bank will be recorded as a payment out of one and a receipt into the other.

Petty cash

Petty cash is the term used to describe the cash 'float' held in many offices to cover small payments that can be more conveniently made in cash. The petty cash book is a record of amounts paid out from the petty cash float. It

has a columnar analysis of the payments made (see Figure 17.8).

Most businesses operate an 'imprest' petty cash system. The person responsible for custody of the petty cash is given a fixed 'float'. Periodically the petty cash float is replenished to its original level by drawing out of the bank an equal amount of cash to that expended. In the above illustration, £57.20 has been paid out during the period 22/5/9X to 31/5/9X. On 31/5/9X a cheque for £57.20 is drawn on the bank to bring the petty cash back up to its authorised level of £100.00. The petty cash book is balanced off as illustrated.

Components of the accounting system

Large organisations may have thousands of customers and suppliers, while some of those that deal with the general public – such as the utility companies and the banks – have millions of customers. The impracticality of any one individual (or indeed any one department) recording both sides of every transaction means that in practice most businesses have separated the recording of individual creditor and debtor accounts from the double-entry system. In the double-entry system, all entries in respect of debtors are totalled and either debited or credited to a **debtor ledger control account**. The same treatment applies to creditors with postings to a **creditor ledger control account**. The accounting system therefore comprises personal ledgers, bank/cash ledgers, and the nominal (or general) ledger.

Personal ledgers

- Purchase ledger (creditor's ledger) – with separate accounts for debts incurred with individual suppliers as a result of supplies obtained on credit.
- Sales ledger (debtor's ledger) – with separate accounts for amounts owing by individual customers as a result of making sales on credit.

Figure 17.8 A petty cash book

Petty Cash Book								May 9X
Paid in	Date	Narrative	Reference	Total amount	VAT	Cleaning	Motor expenses	Sundries
100.00	22/5/9X	Balance b/f						
	24/5/9X	Floor cleaner	326	4.70	0.70	4.00		
	26/5/9X	Window cleaner	327	18.50		18.50		
	29/5/9X	Petrol	328	23.50	3.50		20.00	
	30/5/9X	Tea and milk	329	10.50				10.50
		Total paid		57.20	4.20	22.50	20.00	10.50
57.20	31/5/9X	Bank						
	31/5/9X	Balance c/f		100.00				
157.20				157.20				
100.00	1/6/9X	Balance b/f						

These personal ledgers have been separated from the main double-entry system in most businesses and they provide a memorandum record of individual debtors and creditors. The balance on each ledger should be reflected by the same balance on the nominal ledger's corresponding control account.

Bank and cash ledgers

The cash book and petty cash book provide detailed information concerning cash transactions and for most businesses are used primarily as books of prime entry only, despite some holding running account balances like the one illustrated earlier.

Nominal ledger (or general ledger)

The nominal ledger is the double-entry system. It consists of accounts for all the assets, liabilities, capital and transactions of the business – including control accounts for debtors, creditors and bank. As the dual aspect of every transaction is recorded within the nominal ledger, the ledger 'balances' in the sense that total debits equal total credits.

Illustration

Taking the purchases journal detailed earlier as an example, the accounting entries would be as illustrated in Figure 17.9.

Note that the double entry is completed in the nominal

account. The purchase ledger is only concerned with analysing the total posted to the creditors ledger control account. The same approach is adopted when posting cash paid to creditors.

- Debit the purchase ledger control account (and the individual creditor accounts in the purchase ledger)
- Credit the bank control account.

It follows that, at any point in time, the balance on the purchase ledger control account should equal the total of the purchase ledger accounts.

The sales ledger (or debtors ledger)

The sales ledger has several features (see Figure 17.10):

- The ledger is analysed into individual customers.
- To facilitate easy access to records, particularly in a computerised system, each customer is assigned a customer account number (e.g. Perkins Engines may be given an alphanumeric code PER005).
- Sales invoices to the customer are recorded with: date, invoice number and value.
- Cash receipts are matched against the invoices to which they relate.
- A running balance is maintained of invoices outstanding on the ledger.

On a computerised system, payments made to the business are matched against invoices outstanding and a

Figure 17.9 How a transaction reaches the nominal ledger

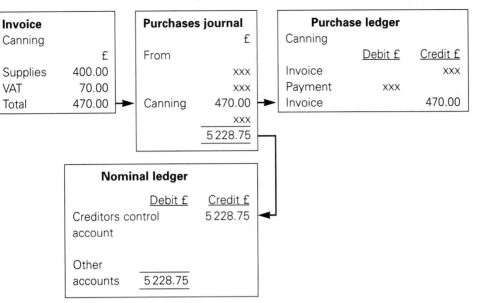

In the nominal ledger

	Debit £	Credit £
VAT	778.75	
Purchases – raw materials	900.00	
Purchases – components	1 150.00	
Sub-contracting	2 400.00	
Creditors control account		5 228.75

In the purchase ledger

	Debit £	Credit £
Canning		470.00
Jason's		235.00
Visuality		117.50
Other suppliers (all listed individually)		4 406.25
Total		5 228.75

program routine will remove these records from the ledger at the month end. A copy of the ledger account is often sent to the customer once a month as a reminder of the amounts outstanding. This copy is called a *customer statement.*

Task

1 *For the credit sales transactions listed at the top of the next page, prepare an analysed sales journal.*
2 *Prepare the individual sales ledger accounts and post the transactions to them. Balance off the ledger accounts.*

Ledger account balances 1/6/9X

Account name	£
Jenkins & Co	560
A Duxbury	45
P Tutty	250

Date	Name	Supply of:	Invoice no	Value £
1/6/9X	Jenkins & Co.	Computer software	3256	400.00
4/6/9X	P Tutty	Stationery	3257	50.00
7/6/9X	Duxbury Ltd	Computer software	3258	250.00
10/6/9X	P Tutty	Textbooks	3259	120.00
13/6/9X	Jenkins & Co.	Textbooks	3260	170.00
16/6/9X	P Tutty	Stationery	3261	10.00
19/6/9X	Duxbury Ltd	Textbooks	3262	65.00
22/6/9X	P Tutty	Textbooks	3263	75.00
25/6/9X	Duxbury Ltd	Computer software	3264	180.00
28/6/9X	Jenkins & Co.	Stationery	3265	35.00

Figure 17.10 Illustration of a sales ledger record

GERARDS SUPPLIES

Debtor name: Carson Engineering

Account Number: CA102

Address: St Francis Road, Kettering

Date	Transaction type	Reference	Customer reference	Amount	Account balance
30/4/9X	Invoice	20150	P10215	235.00	292.50
21/5/9X	Payment	456		−57.50	235.00
31/5/9X	Invoice	20565	P10256	67.56	302.56

Purchase ledger (or creditors ledger)

The purchase ledger holds similar information for suppliers as the sales ledger does for customers. A computerised system will provide a facility to generate printed remittance advices and cheques for invoices selected for payment. In a fully automated system payment will be triggered once an invoice date satisfies the payment terms held on file for that supplier. For example, if in the illustration in Figure 17.11 Gerards Supplies is on 30-day terms, then payment for invoice number 20150 will be actioned around the end of May 199X without any operator input.

Payments made to the supplier are matched against invoices outstanding. These invoice details will be removed from the ledger at the month end.

Nominal ledger

Features of the nominal ledger are:

■ Each ledger account is assigned an account code.

■ The dual aspect of every transaction is recognised within the ledger.

Code list

How the nominal ledger is classified is of interest to many people in an organisation, and not just accounts staff. Managers are often held responsible for a particular type of expenditure or for expenditure that relates to a particular 'cost centre' (department or section of the business's organisational structure). Other staff place orders with outside suppliers and they may be required to code the supply to a particular nominal code. To ensure all staff are coding transactions correctly and consistently, it is standard practice for the financial accountant to issue a code list. This list provides the basic structure for the accounts system and is designed to suit business reporting needs having regard to business activities and organisational structure.

Typical features include income and expenditure codes that are common across the business, with function or location codes which enable transactions to be analysed

Figure 17.11 Illustration of a purchase ledger record

CARSON ENGINEERING					
Creditor name: Gerards Supplies				Account Number: GER01	
Creditor Address: Rockingham Road, Kettering, Northants					
Date	Transaction type	Reference	Supplier reference	Amount	Account balance
30/4/9X	Invoice	P10215	20150	−235.00	−292.50
15/5/9X	Payment	3025		57.50	−235.00
31/5/9X	Invoice	P10256	20565	−67.56	−302.56

by department (alternatively called profit centres or cost centres). Figure 17.12 shows an example.

In this example, the full nominal code is obtained by adding the cost centre code to the expenditure code. Hence an invoice for stationery for the sales office would be coded 306124.

Codes can be analysed in a number of ways. The total of all codes beginning with 301 measures the business's total wages bill. The total of all codes with 122 as the last three digits indicates the cost of running the sales team operating in the east. Analysing all the transactions by the last three digits enables a printout to be issued each month to every cost-centre manager, comparing actual sales and expenditure with budget. As codes are added to the list, financial transactions can be analysed in greater detail, but if the coding structure is too complex it becomes unwieldy and time-consuming to use.

The trial balance

The totals of all account balances are listed to form the 'trial balance'. The trial balance has a column for the debit balances and a column for the credit balances. It is prepared after the ledger accounts have been 'balanced off'. We should therefore find that the trial balance does balance – i.e. total debit equals total credits, as the double-entry system generates a debit and a credit posting for every transaction. If the trial balance does not balance, one of the following errors may have occurred:

- Only one side of a transaction has been posted (e.g. a debit but no credit).
- The two sides of a transaction have been posted with different values.
- There is an arithmetic error, either in the actual ledger account or in the preparation of the trial balance.

The trial balance is the source of much of the information required to prepare financial reports and an example is provided at the start of Chapter 18.

Figure 17.12 Extract from a code list – sales department only

Expenditure code	Description	Cost centre code	Description
301	Wages and salaries	120	Sales – North
302	Motor vehicle expenses	121	Sales – South
303	Subsistence	122	Sales – East
304	Entertainment	123	Sales – West
305	Training	124	Sales office
306	Stationery		
307	Meetings		
308	Sundries		

Accounting periods

The **financial year** is often divided into monthly periods. At the end of these interim accounting periods, accounts are balanced off. Balances are carried forward (c/f) at the end of one period and brought forward (b/f) in the next.

At the end of each financial year, it is necessary to balance off the transaction accounts so that there is no balance brought forward at the start of the new financial year. The following transaction accounts are transferred by journal to the trading account: sales, returns in, opening stock, purchases, returns out and carriage in. In addition, sundry income accounts and the expenses accounts (e.g. electricity and rent) are transferred to the profit-and-loss account (see Chapter 18 for an example).

Balances on accounts in respect of assets, liabilities and capital are carried forward at the end of the year. These accounts represent items that are of a continuing value to the business.

Accounting for stock

Many small businesses do not maintain a system to record stock as it is used. The accounting system in its basic form has just two accounts concerned with stocks. One account is used to record purchases during the period and is updated from the purchase journal. The other account contains the stock valuation at a point of time. The stock account balance does not change unless it is adjusted by a journal at the time of a subsequent stock valuation. For example, Denning & Co. started the year with stock of £12 900 and finished with stock valued at £19 250. The completed ledger account for the year will look like this:

Ledger – Stock							
Date	Narrative	Ref.	Value £	Date	Narrative	Ref.	Value £
1/1/9X	Balance b/f		12 900	1/1/9X	Trading account		12 900
31/12/9X	Trading account		19 250	31/12/9X	Balance c/f		19 250
			32 150				32 150

Task

Balance off the ledger accounts *stock* and *purchases* at 31 March 199Y by preparing a journal and posting the entries in the ledger accounts. Note that stock was valued at £8100 on 31.3.9Y.

Ledger – Stock							
Date	Narrative	Ref.	Value £	Date	Narrative	Ref.	Value £
1/4/9X	Balance b/f		5 500				

Ledger – Purchases							
Date	Narrative	Ref.	Value £	Date	Narrative	Ref.	Value £
30/6/9X	Purchase journal		12 650				
30/9/9X	Purchase journal		15 630				
31/12/9X	Purchase journal		18 320				
31/3/9Y	Purchase journal		9 960				

Outline of the system

Let us summarise the system so far (see Figure 17.13). Financial transactions are evidenced by invoices, credit notes, cheques and counterfoils etc. Transactions are categorised and recorded in an appropriate journal or one of the cash books. The details on the purchases and sales journals are entered line by line into the purchase and sales ledgers.

In many double-entry accounting systems the purchase ledger, sales ledger and cash books are replaced by **control accounts**. Control accounts are part of the nominal ledger and mirror the movements on the other ledgers by recording all transactions but in total form only. This allows further breakdown for the responsibility of the various ledgers.

The trial balance is constructed after the books of prime entry have been used to update the relevant ledger accounts. Identification of each nominal account in a manual accounting system will be either by account name or a code number. In a computerised accounting system the main identification key will be an account code.

Task

Westfield Supplies Ltd has experienced the transactions detailed on the next page during the month of January 199X. Study the information and complete the three exercises listed at the end.

Figure 17.13 Overview of the accounting system

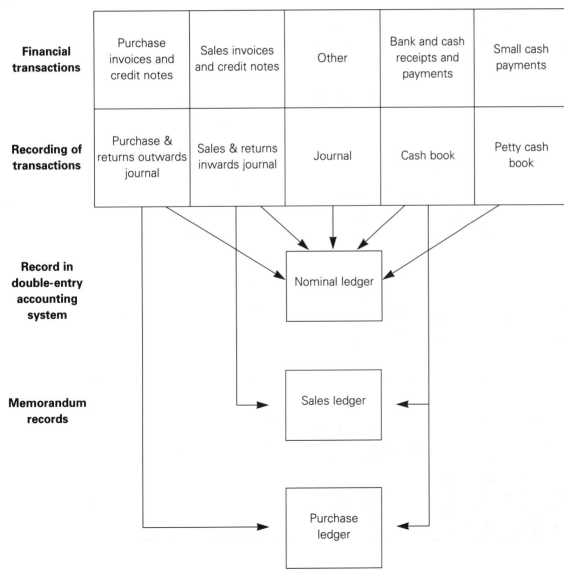

Financial transactions	Purchase invoices and credit notes	Sales invoices and credit notes	Other	Bank and cash receipts and payments	Small cash payments
Recording of transactions	Purchase & returns outwards journal	Sales & returns inwards journal	Journal	Cash book	Petty cash book

		£
1/1/9X	Purchased goods for resale from Wells Engineering on credit	1 200
2/1/9X	Paid rent by cheque	3 000
3/1/9X	Components sold on credit to John Bryant	3 500
4/1/9X	Purchased goods for resale from Jason Robards on credit	4 200
5/1/9X	Purchased goods for resale from Corniche Manufacturing on credit	400
8/1/9X	Assemblies sold on credit to Desborough Workshops Ltd	5 400
9/1/9X	Components sold on credit to John Bryant	1 600
10/1/9X	Paid for stationery by cheque	900
11/1/9X	Purchased on credit some office chairs from Phipps & Drew	650
12/1/9X	Purchased goods for resale by cheque	100
15/1/9X	Assemblies sold on credit to Desborough Workshops Ltd	2 400
16/1/9X	Components sold goods on credit to Willis Bros.	950
17/1/9X	Received cash from John Bryant	2 500
18/1/9X	Components sold on credit to John Bryant	200
19/1/9X	Received cash from Desborough Workshops Ltd	1 600
22/1/9X	Paid Wells Engineering by cheque	2 300
23/1/9X	Assemblies sold on credit to Desborough Workshops Ltd	1 700
24/1/9X	Paid Wells Engineering	1 200
25/1/9X	Paid Corniche Manufacturing	400
26/1/9X	Components sold goods on credit to Willis Bros.	800
29/1/9X	Paid wages	6 000
30/1/9X	Received cash from Willis Bros.	950
31/1/9X	Assemblies sold on credit to John Bryant	750

■ The accounting year runs from 1 October to 30 September.

■ The accounting records had the following balances brought forward on 1 January 199X, being the balances carried forward at 31 December 199W.

Sales ledger		Debit £	Credit £
	John Bryant	2 500	
	Desborough Workshops Ltd	1 600	

Purchase ledger		Debit £	Credit £
	Wells Engineering		2 300
	Corniche Manufacturing		400

Nominal ledger		Debit £	Credit £
	Office furniture	11 000	
	Bank control account	10 100	
	Debtors control account	4 100	
	Creditors control account		2 700
	Stationery	200	
	Wages	11 650	
	Sales		89 600
	Purchases	40 800	
	Other accounts	14 450	
	Total of nominal accounts	92 300	92 300

1 *Enter the month's transactions on to the appropriate book of prime entry and provide an analysis of transactions consistent with the nominal ledger structure.*
2 *Make appropriate postings to the sales ledger, purchase ledger and nominal ledger.*
3 *Ensure that the total of the personal ledgers do reconcile to the corresponding nominal control account.*

Stock records

Stock is a resource that flows in and out of the business, but so far we have only attempted to record receipts of stock with the maintenance of a stock purchases account. Because no record of stock issues has been made, the only way to ascertain the value of stock at a point in time has been by undertaking a stock-take. A stock-take requires all stock items to be counted and valued on the basis of how much they cost the business. Many small businesses do operate on this basis, but while it requires the minimum of paperwork and is simple, it has shortcomings:

- In larger stores it is difficult to monitor individual stock balances and the risk of running out of stock is increased.
- The cost of materials used cannot be reported to management without a full count and valuation of all the stock in the stores.
- There are no records of stock issues and hence it is difficult to ascertain economic yet adequate levels of individual stock items.
- There is no information concerning the purpose of the stock issues. This raises a number of questions. Was the stock used for bona fide purposes? Has the customer been charged correctly? How much material did each job require?

To overcome these problems many businesses operate a stock control system that records stock as it is received and issued. With this information it is possible to update an individual item's recorded stock balance every time there is a stock movement. If the information is used in this way the system is called a **perpetual inventory system**.

Task

Casey & Co. operates a perpetual inventory system to control stocks of automotive parts. This means it maintains a book of prime entry for stock issues in addition to that for stock purchases. This enables the bookkeeper to prepare monthly accounts that reflect accurately the stock balance without the need for a stock-take every month. To provide a running stock balance, all stock movements are posted to a single stock account (making redundant the purchases account that we have used so far). From the following information prepare a nominal ledger account for stock at 30 June 199X, showing clearly the current stock balance:

	£
Purchase journal	38 100
Returns out journal	3 500
Stock issues	29 300
Stock balance 1 June 199X	17 700

Documentation required by a stock control system

Stores receipt note

Documentation required to record the receipt of stock into stores may be in the form of a special **stores receipt note**. However, for many organisations the goods-received note (GRN), duly signed by a storeman, is evidence enough of goods being received into stores. Where this is the case, a copy of the GRN has to accompany the goods from the Goods Received Department to the stores. The signed GRN is then forwarded to the Inventory Control Section where it is used to update stock records.

Stores issue note (or materials requisition note)

The **stores issue note** (see Figure 17.14) is required to ensure that:

- the issue of stock is properly authorised
- the job or customer concerned is properly charged
- there is a source document for updating the stock records.

In a manufacturing firm the number of different materials required to perform a particular activity may be large. However, they will almost certainly have been specified precisely at the time of product design. This information is recorded on a **bill of materials** that is simply a list of stock materials necessary for the task. To minimise duplication of records, this bill of materials is often used as the stock issue documentation. Another major advantage of the bill of materials is that forward planning of stock requirements is made a lot easier. Production personnel can notify inventory control of the products they will be manufacturing in the future without the need to specify all the individual material requirements. This procedure has been facilitated by computerisation throughout the production function, with integration of production planning and inventory control systems.

Figure 17.14 A sample stores issue note

Stores Issue Note			No. 12345
Quantity	Reference	Job or sales order number	Stock record updated
95	P125X	300125	
Issued to:		Storeman:	
Authorised by:		Date:	

Stock (or stores) record card

Stock record cards contain full information concerning each stock item. Basic information includes: a description, the unit of measure (e.g. kilograms or packets of 100), a stock reference, the location in the stores (e.g. row number and bin number), the desired stock levels (minimum and maximum), the re-order stock level and quantity. There will also be transaction details for both receipts and issues of stock: date, reference, quantity, and price. An example of a stores record card is to be found in the exercise later in this chapter.

Stock valuation

Prices rarely remain stable, and over time stock items will be purchased at different prices depending on underlying inflation and prevailing market conditions. The problem arises of how we should deal with this in the stock records. For example, two consignments for the same item of stock are received, one for 10 items at £10 each and the other for 10 items at £11 each. If 15 items are issued from stores what are the accounting implications? We need to know for external reporting purposes:

■ how much to charge the trading profit and loss account for materials used
■ how to value the closing stock in the balance sheet.

In addition we also want to use the most appropriate method to provide relevant information for decision-making purposes.

Several methods have been devised to deal with the problem. There is no 'right' method but the Companies Acts and accounting standards require the balance sheet valuation to be based on historical cost (i.e. what the materials cost the business) or net realisable value if this is lower (market value less selling expenses).

■ *First-in-first-out (FIFO)* – The oldest stock is assumed to be issued first and the purchase price of these items

is used to cost stores issues. The most recently purchased stock (often at higher prices) is assumed to be remaining in stores. It is based on what the business paid for the stock and so satisfies legal requirements.
■ *Last-in-first-out (LIFO)* – The latest stock received is costed out first. This method is based on historical cost but is not favoured by the tax authorities as it lowers reported profits.
■ *Average cost* – An average cost for each stock item is calculated every time there is a receipt of stock. The calculation is on a weighted average basis.
■ *Standard cost* – A target price is set for all stock items at the start of a year and this is used to record all stock receipts and issues. Stock records are easier to maintain but this method requires the differences between the actual cost and the standard cost to be accounted for (material cost variances).

To operate a LIFO or average-cost system requires a perpetual stock control system to keep track of all the transactions and make the necessary calculations. It is possible to conform to the FIFO method without a stock system by working back and valuing the closing stock using the last prices paid.

Task

A shop stocks winter coats that sell at £55 each. The shop takes in weekly deliveries. There were 10 coats in stock at the beginning of week 1 that had cost £29 each. Then the deliveries were as follows:

Week no.	Coats bought		Number of coats sold
	Number	Cost each	
1	20	30	15
2	30	33	33
3	40	29	35
4	30	35	39

Stock cards appear below for weeks 1 and 2 using FIFO, LIFO and weighted average cost. You are to complete the records for weeks 3 and 4.

Stores record card – FIFO

Week	Receipts					Issues			Balance		
	GRN no.	Quantity	Unit price	Amount	Stores req	Quantity	Unit price	Amount	Quantity	Unit price	Amount
1	b/f								10	29	290
1		20	30	600					10	29	890
									20	30	
1						10	29	290	15	30	450
						5	30	150			
2		30	33	990					15	30	1440
									30	33	
2						15	30	450	12	33	396
						18	33	594			

Stores record card – LIFO

Week	GRN no.	Quantity	Unit price	Amount	Stores req	Quantity	Unit price	Amount	Quantity	Unit price	Amount
	Receipts				**Issues**				**Balance**		
1	b/f								10	29	290
1		20	30	600					10	29	890
									20	30	
1						15	30	450	10	29	440
									5	30	
2		30	33	990					10	29	1430
									5	30	
									30	33	
2						30	33	990	10	29	350
						3	30	90	2	30	

Stores record card – weighted average cost

Week	Receipts				Issues				Balance		
	GRN no.	Quantity	Unit price	Amount	Stores req	Quantity	Unit price	Amount	Quantity	Unit price	Amount
1	b/f								10	29	290
1		20	30	600					30	29.67	890
1						15	29.67	445	15	29.67	445
2		30	33	990					45	31.89	1435
2						33	31.89	1052.3	12	31.89	382.7

Exercises

1 *Identify which valuation method provides the highest stock valuation under conditions of (i) rising prices and (ii) falling prices.*

2 *Research the method of stock valuation used by two different businesses. Comment on the possible reasons for their choice of method.*

Physical stock-take

Whether a stock system is in operation or not, it is important that stock balances are physically verified at least once during an accounting year. Where no stock records are maintained, it is necessary for a stock-take at the accounting year end. However, if an effective and accurate perpetual inventory system is in operation, the stock record card will be a true reflection of the actual stock in the stores. The firm's accountants may then have confidence in using the stock record cards for valuing

stock at year ends, without the need for a full stock-take. In these circumstances the stock-take of items can be carried out on a continuous basis throughout the year without disrupting normal business activities.

Accounting concepts and the accounting records

For financial reports to conform to the accounting concepts stipulated in the Companies Act 1985 and Statements of Standard Accounting Practice 2, various adjustments are made to the information taken from the accounting records. These adjustments are described in detail in Chapter 18. It is important that the base information from which they are prepared has also been recorded with these provisions in mind. We shall consider each of the main accounting concepts in turn and examine how the accounting system described conforms to these requirements.

Matching (accrual)

The records should reflect an accurate matching of revenues with cost incurred. This principle is observed in a number of recording practices. For example, where costs have been incurred to satisfy a credit sale, we recognise a sale even though the customer has not yet paid by recording sales in the nominal ledger from the sales journal, not from the later entries of cash receipts in the cash book. The same principle is applied to the recording of purchases with the use of the purchases journal. Similarly, the accounting of stock usage based on stock issues rather than when it is purchased is another example of the matching concept in practice.

Prudence

At all times the accounting records should be maintained with a conservative perspective of the business's financial position. The sale of goods or services to a customer is recorded in the accounts only when the supply has been made, not when a sales order is received. In this way a gain is not recorded until it is certain to be realised. Likewise stock is valued at the lower of cost or net realisable value. No assumption is made that a profit will be made, but a loss will be recognised immediately if it is considered likely.

Consistency

Similar items should be accounted for on a consistent basis. Clearly the information obtained from the records would be meaningless if there is no consistent basis on which transactions are recorded and classified. Taking a relatively minor case as an example, if it is the practice to code postage to the account 'postage and stationery', useful analysis of expenditure levels will be lost if half way through the year postage is coded to a 'sundry expense account'.

Going concern

Unless the situation warrants contrary treatment, the accounting records assume that the going-concern concept applies. The valuation of assets, in particular, is on the assumption that normal trading conditions will continue and that the economic benefits assumed at the time of the asset's acquisition will persist. This applies to the accounting for fixed assets (more details in Chapter 18), and in the valuation of stocks. If trading conditions deteriorated to the point that the business's future viability was in doubt, stock would have to be valued at the net realisable value under distress sale conditions.

Accounting with computers

In most businesses the accounting function was the first department to use computers. The large volumes of similar transactions are well suited to being computerised. In addition to the efficiency of data handling, computerised systems have facilitated the use of the vast bank of data for management reporting purposes. Reports that would otherwise be very time-consuming to prepare include:

- individual job costs
- individual department costs
- comparison of actual spend with budget
- real-time reporting of stock levels
- age analysis of debtors.

For medium to large businesses the accounting software may be bespoke or adapted to cater for the unique requirements of the business. These systems usually run on mainframe or minicomputers. Smaller businesses can now utilise, at low cost, a standardised package written for microcomputers, such as from Sage or Pegasus.

The **databases** stored on magnetic disk for each accounting module are generally classified into two types of file:

- *Master file* – information that identifies the data subject and is common for all transactions (e.g. name and address).
- *Transaction file* – information concerning each transaction (e.g. date and number of units sold).

Both types of information are accessed by the same data key – i.e. an account number for customers, suppliers and nominal accounts, a payroll reference for employees, and a product number for stock items (see Figure 17.15).

Reports from the accounting system may have been designed at the time the software was written, although many accounting packages now allow users to specify their own report formats.

Computers can output information in a number of different forms:

- paper printout
- computer screen, enabling the user to make enquires of the databases where a hard copy is not required
- computer file, for later printing or for use on other programs such as spreadsheets
- microfilm or microfiche – the contents of a computer file are photographically transferred to a physical but compact medium
- communication networks allow the above outputs at remote locations.

Figure 17.15 Computer applications for accounting

Applications	Master file details	Transactions	Output
Sales ledger accounting	Details of customers: account number name address credit limit	Sales invoices Cash received	Invoices for customers Sales journal Cash receipts list Analysis of sales by: customer sales area product etc. Aged debtor analysis
Purchase ledger accounting	Details of suppliers: account number name address	Purchase invoices Cheque payments	Purchase journal Cheques and remittance advices Analysis of purchases by supplier Aged creditor analysis
Stock control	Details of stock: reference number description supplier unit of measure desired levels	Quantity and value: receipts issues allocations for future known commitments	Stock movement enquiries Stock valuation lists Reorder lists Stock-take lists
Payroll	Payroll number Name Address Pay – period, amount Tax code Bank details	Hours worked Wages paid Tax and national insurance deducted	Payslip Bank transfer details Payroll summary, analysed by department End of year details – P60 Termination – P45
Job costing	Job number Name Description Details as appropriate	Labour allocations Stores issues Direct purchases Overhead absorbed Sales on completion	Job cost reports
Nominal ledger	Account code Name Report code	Purchases Sales Payroll Stock movements Cash transactions Journals	Account enquiries Trial balance Financial reports

The same information can be accessed and reported on in different ways to satisfy the specific needs of the situation. The information stored with respect to sales ledger accounting should satisfy the needs shown in Figure 17.16.

The output from one accounting module is often in digital form ready for inputting to another module without the need to re-enter data manually (see Figure 17.17).

Advantages of computerised accounts

- Computers are fast. Data input is often faster than manual systems with custom designed data entry screens.
- Data entry screens can be used by staff with no knowledge of double-entry bookkeeping.
- Data can be validated on input, which ensures valid codes, correct double entry of transactions and reduces transposition errors.

Figure 17.16 Sales ledger accounting

Information need	How it can be satisfied
The financial controller wants to know how much cash is likely to be collected next month	The debtor accounts are read one at a time to estimate the amount of cash to be received from each depending on age of debt and settlement terms
The credit controller wishes to identify debts that are overdue	An aged debtor listing with every unpaid invoice analysed into age bands (e.g. 0–30 days, 31–60 days etc.)
A credit control clerk wishes to send one of three letters of varying severity to all debtors who are overdue in paying	Create three files of customers depending on the age of their oldest debt outstanding. Using the files created, the mail merge facility on a wordprocessor is operated to address a standard letter to each customer
The sales manager wishes to know the sales turnover of a particular customer during the last year	An account enquiry will report the sales value processes for the period requested
The management accountant wishes to report to management on a regular basis the product analysis of sales	Each supply is coded in accordance with nominal ledger codes for each product group

Figure 17.17 Typical data links

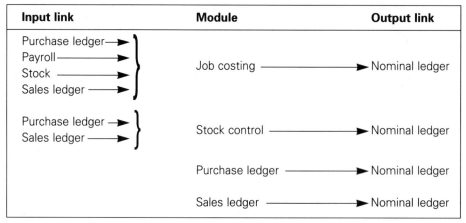

There is accurate retrieval of information and performance of calculations.

- Data can be stored in database files, allowing it to be accessed for more than one use.
- This is a powerful capability for sorting and analysing data.
- The humdrum of report preparation is vastly speeded up, thus saving on accountant's time. The actual design and content of the reports is facilitated by report templates that can often be specified and altered by the user without the aid of a computer expert. Reports can be professionally presented without the need for typist time and type checking, previously the bane of an accountant's life.

Disadvantages of computerised accounts

- Some systems, especially those that are old and used on mainframe computers, can be inflexible in use. Changes to database fields and report design may require a computer programmer.
- Staff require training.
- The systems can be initially expensive on hardware, software and implementation.
- They can pose a security risk if not properly controlled with password access and data backup procedures.

Case Study
Marks and Spencer plc

The following is reproduced from the M&S Annual Report in 1994. It appeared under the heading 'A fresh approach to information systems'.

Every time a customer makes a purchase, the Marks & Spencer till does a lot more than produce a receipt. The information is used by a highly sophisticated computer system that whirs away efficiently behind the scenes. During the past ten years in which a £350 million investment in IT has been made, M&S has seen benefits in both profits and customer service.

One of the most tangible benefits to customers is that food shelves do not sell out early on a Saturday as they used to and a wider range of goods are available on a Monday. The electronic point-of-sale tills feed information about exactly what has been sold in each store at the end of each day's business; information that the computer system uses to work out what will be allocated to each store at the food depot that night for delivery the next day. Printed picking notes instruct the warehouse team, for example, how many trays of Chicken Kiev to pick that night for delivery to the Marble Arch branch the next morning. Up to 500 suppliers deliver food to central depots, but it is transported in fewer than five lorries a day per store.

Among the benefits for clothing, IT developments mean that stores are no longer sent garments in fixed size ratios, but instead receive deliveries that respond to their individual requirements. Each time a purchase is made, the tills feed information to M&S central computers which calculate what stock is needed. This information is then fed into suppliers' computers where it is used to organise the following day's or week's deliveries. When a new season's line goes into stores in a variety of colours, IT allows sales to be monitored during the first few days and production of faster selling colours and sizes to be stepped up. A supplier using advanced piece-dyeing techniques that enable pre-knitted garments to be dyed after they have been made, can accept an order, for example, for more blue jumpers and dye the pre-knitted garments accordingly within 48 hours ready for delivery to the distribution centre and store.

Questions for discussion

1 *Describe a manual system and its documentation that would be adequate to control the stock stored at a M&S central depot and the procedures necessary for stock movements to branches.*
2 *Make a list of benefits that M&S enjoy from the use of IT in its stock order processing system.*
3 *Make a list of the costs incurred with the computerised system.*
4 *What are the security implications of this system?*
5 *How integral is the management of information at M&S to the company's overall business strategy?*
6 *Describe how you envisage the information generated by the stock system at M&S is utilised by their accounts function.*

Spreadsheets

Spreadsheets are used extensively in accounts departments to augment the basic accounting system, especially for analysis work and flexible reporting. This trend has accelerated with the introduction of accounting packages that can save data in spreadsheet format. Data files created in this way can then be accessed and used by a compatible spreadsheet package, such as Lotus 1–2–3 or Microsoft's Excel. The advantage for users is that they can manipulate data using software that:

- they may already be familiar with
- does not require programming knowledge
- is flexible in use
- facilitates good presentation of reports
- allows the combination of information from a number of different sources.

Once designed, the basic spreadsheet format can be used time and again for similar problems. Some accounting routines are particularly suited to spreadsheet application.

A simple matrix

It is quite common to meet a matrix of numbers that requires simple row and column totals (see Figure 17.18). A special 'sum( )' command at the end of each column and row does away with the need for manual calculations that are laborious even when using a calculator. Another advantage over preparing reports by hand is that typing is not needed for high-quality presentation, which has the risk of introducing errors.

Large volumes of simple calculations

Tasks involving large volumes of repetitious calculations are ideal for spreadsheets. An example is updating a price list where there may be hundreds or thousands of products to have their price changed by the same percentage (see Figure 17.19). Once the calculation has been performed for one product, it is a simple task to copy the routine for all products.

Figure 17.18 Example of a report that is often included in a set of internal accounts

STAFF NUMBERS					
Function	North	South	East	West	Totals
Area managers	1	1	1	1	4
Sales managers	2	3	1	2	8
Sales representatives	25	39	12	21	97
Support staff	9	11	3	5	28
Engineering manager	2	2	1	2	7
Engineers	16	18	6	14	54
Totals	55	74	24	45	198

Figure 17.19 Example of a repetitious task

	A	B	C	D
1	Product	Price	Inflate by	New Price
2	12357X	10.50	5%	11.53
3	1248A	1.25	5%	1.31

In the example shown the formula input into cell D2 is +B2*C2, i.e. multiply B2 by C2. The basic formula is copied down the D column for all the product lines. The price list can then be printed with only the new prices shown.

Creating and using a database

The spreadsheet is a powerful tool for **statistical analysis** of a mass of data. The data can be input manually or retrieved by the accounting system. The spreadsheet could output:

- a summary of the whole set of data (see Figure 17.20)
- an **exception report** for those items that satisfy some condition (e.g. all customers with a Barnsley address)

- a graphical presentation of the data (e.g. analysis of employees by age group in pie chart form).

The database may be thousands of lines long, but each of the following tasks could be done quickly:

- Identify those items with usage of less than four times the current stock balance.
- Identify all items with unit price over £10.00.
- Calculate totals for each category of stock based on the first letter of the product code.

Complex calculations performed with some regularity

A complex calculation such as discounting cash flows for project appraisal uses the spreadsheet's ability to solve formulas. Again use is being made of the spreadsheet's capability for accuracy and time saving.

Financial modelling

For the accountant responsible for financial budgeting, the spreadsheet's ability to mirror the quantitative relationships between business activities and financial transactions is of great value.

Figure 17.20 Statistical analysis of data from the stock accounting module

Product no.	Description	Current balance (units)	Current balance (£)	Annual usage (units)	Annual usage (£)
P125	Red	42	231	140	770
P126	Orange	187	420	980	2 205
P127	Cyan	23	782	46	1 564

Example of a budget for a car repair shop

The activity in a certain garage repair shop is measured in man-hours. Customers are charged at £30 per hour. Departmental capacity is measured and limited by the number of man-hours available. Each worker can provide 1606 direct hours per year at a cost of £8 an hour. In the long run, the number of workers is variable. Departmental overheads are fixed at £150 000. Using this information we can prepare a departmental budget to calculate the annual gross profit (see Figure 17.21).

Once constructed, the model can easily recalculate gross profit with different values input for varying assumptions regarding hours sold, selling price and costs.

When constructing a spreadsheet model the overriding rule is be methodical and design your spreadsheet to allow flexibility for possible future changes. In particular, use separate sections of the spreadsheet for input of data, workings and final reports. In the example, note that no values have been input by the user in the workings and output sections of the spreadsheet. Advantages of this approach are:

- It ensures that all assumptions are clearly evident from reading the input section alone.
- The spreadsheet is totally flexible and allows assumptions to be changed on a 'what if' basis.
- It ensures that all users of the spreadsheet know where data is to be input and that important formulas are not overwritten.

In larger spreadsheets it is also good practice to arrange the different sections diagonally across the spreadsheet. For example, the input section may be in the cell range A1 to E50, the workings section in G60 to K100 and the output section K110 to O200. In this way column widths can be set according to the requirements of each section. In addition, if there is a need to insert or delete columns as the design of the spreadsheet progresses, these changes can be made in the knowledge that other sections will not be adversely affected in terms of lost data or presentation.

The widespread use of spreadsheets within accounts departments testifies to their usefulness. Accounting staff used to compile schedules painstakingly using analysis sheets and adding machines. For most those days have gone and many would be lost without a PC on their desk.

Figure 17.21 Example

	A	B	Input into column B by the user using Microsoft Excel
1	INPUT SECTION		
2	Hours to be charged	20 000	20 000
3	Selling price/hour	£30.00	30
4	Direct hours worked/year/person	1 606	1606
5	Wages per direct labour hour	£8	8
6	Overheads	£150 000	150 000
7	WORKINGS		
8	Man-years required	12.5	+b2/b4
9	Number of workers employed	13	ceiling(b8,1)
10	OUTPUT		
11	Sales revenue	£600 000	+b2*b3
12	Costs:		
13	Wages	£166 400	+b9*b4*b5
14	Overheads	£150 000	+b6
15	Total costs	£316 400	+b13+b14
16	Gross profit	£283 600	+b11–b15
17	Gross profit to sales	47.3%	+b16/b11

Summary

This chapter has examined the basic financial recording systems. The design of an accounting system will be dependent on the data to be processed and the reporting needs of the business. The recording system may have to be capable of processing thousands or millions of transactions. For practical purposes these transactions are classified by type and recorded in books of prime entry. These may be manual books or computer files and comprise listings for sales, purchases and cash transactions. An additional prime book may also be maintained for stock issues. The totals recorded in each book are periodically posted to the nominal ledger. Personal ledgers for customers and suppliers are maintained to control receipts and payments for transactions on credit.

The nominal code system can be used to provide management with appropriate analysis of transactions and can aid accountability with reporting by cost centre. Whether the recording system is based on manual ledgers or on a computer system, both forms could be augmented by other tools such as spreadsheets. The form and systems for recording should suit the requirements of the business having regard to the relative costs and benefits of each.

Further reading

- *Foundations of Business Accounting* by Roy Dodge. Chapman & Hall, 1993.
- *Business Accounting*, 6th edition, by Frank Wood. Pitman, 1993.
- *Principles of Accounting*, 9th edition, by E. F. Castle and N. P. Owens, revised by G. Whitehead. Pitman, 1994.
- *Financial Accounting*, 2nd edition, by A. R. Jennings. DPP, 1993.
- *Book-keeping – A Guide for Beginners* (Volume 1: Books to Trial Balance; Volume 2: Final Accounts) by M. J. Maloney. Stanley Thornes, 1988.
- *Accounting in the Business Environment* by John Watts. Pitman 1993.
- *Accounting and Finance – a Firm Foundation*, 3rd edition, by Alan Pizzey. Cassell, 1990.
- *Foundation Accounting* by A. H. Millichimp. DPP, 1992.

18 Preparing financial reports

On completion of this chapter students will be able to:

■ identify and illustrate the structure of the main financial statements

■ identify and explain the differing requirements of a range of organisations

■ prepare financial statements from given data, incorporating appropriate adjustments.

Introduction to financial reporting

Much of the work of an accounts department is concerned with the *recording* of transactions, but it is by the quality of information it *outputs* that management, owners and other interested parties often judge its performance. Like other information this should be relevant, timely, accurate and well presented. Financial reporting tends to focus on three principal types of financial statement, each being modified where necessary for the range of quite disparate businesses that form the private sector:

■ the profit and loss account
■ the balance sheet
■ the cash flow statement.

Competence at preparing financial reports comes through practice, and so this chapter concentrates on developing skills through problem-solving.

Computerised systems

The features and main advantages of computerised accounting systems were discussed in Chapter 17. The features most pertinent to the preparation of accounts are high speed, accuracy, excellent presentation and flexibility in use.

A standard **template** of each report is constructed with the capability to specify which nominal accounts make up a particular figure in the report. There may be a dozen different sales accounts for each of the products sold by a business, but one report may want a consolidated sales figure, while another report concerned with individual product analysis can use each account balance individually. The ability to specify numerous reports with different levels of detail and different areas of focus makes computer-produced financial reports a valuable and flexible means for providing management information.

The financial reporting system consists primarily of two components:

■ a **computer file** of nominal account balances (a trial balance in digital form)

■ a **report generator** that allows the user to request standard reports and to design new reports as required.

The trial balance

A large amount of the information required for preparing financial statements comes from the **trial balance**, which is a listing of nominal account balances described in Chapter 17. Figure 18.1 shows an example. The information contained in the trial balance is of two types:

■ that which relates to balances at the accounting period end (i.e. assets, liabilities and capital)
■ running totals of transactions that have occurred during the year.

Each type of information forms the basis for two of the main financial statements:

■ the balance sheet
■ the trading and profit-and-loss account.

For the preparation of financial reports, additional information will usually be required in **notes** accompanying the trial balance. In particular, where the trial balance has not been updated with prime data concerning stock usage, the minimum information necessary is a period-end stock valuation. The stock-take for Denning & Co. at 31 May 199X valued stock at £10 000.

From the trial balance for Denning & Co. we can identify the **assets employed in the business**:

	£	
Equipment	15 000	
Stock	10 000	(end-of-period balance)
Debtors	10 000	
Bank and cash	3 000	
Total	38 000	

We can do the same for **liabilities**:

Trade creditors	6 000
Total net assets	32 000

Applying the accounting equation 'capital = assets – liabilities', we know that the owner's capital invested in the business at 31 May 199X is £32 000 (£38 000 less £6000).

This is interesting information but does not provide us with a full picture of what happened during the period year to 1/5/9X. From the trial balance we know that at the beginning of the accounting period the owner's capital was £8000; how did it increase by £24 000? The answer is that the business added to the owner's net worth by making a **profit** during the period.

Trading and profit-and-loss account

A profit is made by a business if it charges its customers more than the cost of resources it consumed during the period. Most of the cost items in the case of Denning would appear to be quite straightforward. The exception is the amount of stock used. It is important to match the cost of stock actually sold to the amounts charged to customers. The calculation of stock used is:

Figure 18.1 Illustration of a trial balance

Trial balance – Denning & Co.				31 May 199X
Code	**Account name**	**Debit £**		**Credit £**
1000	Sales			120 000
2000	Purchases	70 000		
3000	Wages	20 000		
3001	Rent	5 000		
3002	Electricity	3 000		
4000	Equipment	15 000		
5000	Stock at 1 June 199W	8 000		
6000	Debtors	10 000		
7000	Bank and cash	3 000		
8000	Trade creditors			6 000
9000	Capital (b/f) 1/6/9W			8 000
	Totals	**134 000**		**134 000**

	£
Stock at the beginning of the period	8 000
Add stock purchased during the period	70 000
Total amount available for use	78 000
Less stock at the end of the period	10 000
Therefore the value of stock sold is	68 000

Not all of the information required to prepare a set of accounts is contained in the trial balance. It is usual to be provided with further information and we will consider the nature and purpose of this later in the chapter. However, at this stage it is important to note that the stock account at the end of a period will not have been updated with the current stock balance. All purchases of stock during the period will have been debited to the purchases account. Therefore, before we can proceed we need the closing stock figure. This can be obtained by conducting a stock-take at the period end.

We can now calculate Denning's profit for the period using a **trading and profit-and-loss account** (see Figure 18.2). Its name arises because we are combining two ledger accounts:

- the trading account – which identifies gross profit by deducting the cost of stock sold from sales revenue.
- the profit-and-loss account – which identifies net profit by deducting expenses from gross profit.

Figure 18.2 Denning's trading and profit-and-loss account for the year ended 31 May 199X

	£	£
Sales		120 000
Opening stock	8 000	
Purchases	70 000	
	78 000	
Less closing stock	10 000	
Cost of sales		68 000
Gross profit		52 000
Less expenses:		
Wages	20 000	
Rent	5 000	
Electricity	3 000	28 000
		24 000

Bookkeeping

It is possible to do just as we have done in the case of Denning & Co. and produce financial statements without involving ourselves further with the double-entry accounting system. However, in practice there is a need to *balance off* accounts that accumulate transaction totals (sales and costs) for one period before the system can start recording the next period's transactions. Both the trading account and the profit-and-loss account are 'accounts' in the sense that they form part of the double-entry system. The account balances that we use in constructing the trading and profit-and-loss account need to be transferred to them. The process is documented on what is called a **journal**. A journal is used for all entries in the double-entry system that do not originate from a prime document (see Figure 18.3).

A further journal is required to change the value of stock from its 1 June 199W value to that at 31 May 199X. Remember we added opening stock to purchases and then deducted closing stock, so we should expect two entries to be posted (see Figure 18.4).

Although not strictly necessary we could extract a further trial balance having posted these journals (see Figure 18.5).

A final journal will be prepared before a new accounting period commences, to transfer the balances on the trading and profit-and-loss account to the capital account. The capital account will have a final balance when carried forward on 31 May 199X of £32 000.

From the above it should be evident that the only balances remaining after the transfer to the (trading and profit-and-loss account are those accounts that are presented on the **balance sheet** (see Figure 18.6). *The balance sheet derives its name from the fact that it is composed of these remaining balances, rather than the coincidental fact that both sides of the balance sheet do in fact balance because of the double-entry principle.*

Accounts presentation and definition of terms

It will be useful at this stage to identify and define some of the terms you will come across when constructing a set of accounts for a *sole trader*.

Figure 18.7 shows a **pro forma** for a trading and profit-and-loss account for a sole trader, and Figure 18.8 shows a pro forma for a balance sheet – both assumed to be dated 31 December 199X.

It should be noted in Figure 18.7 that 'carriage in' is added to purchases in the trading account whereas 'carriage out' is treated as an expense. This is because gross profit is a measure of how much a customer has been charged in excess of the cost of bringing the goods into existence. In the case of a manufacturing business this cost is the cost of manufacture, for a trading business buying goods solely for resale it is the cost of procuring those goods. Carriage in is part of the cost of procuring materials and is therefore to be included in unit stock valuations at the end of accounting periods. Some

Figure 18.3 Denning's journal sheet 456

Journal Sheet			
Accounting period: May 199X			Number: 456
	Code	Debit £	Credit £
Sales	1000	120 000	
Trading account	9001		120 000
Trading account	9001	70 000	
Purchases	2000		70 000
Profit-and-loss account	9002	20 000	
Wages	3000		20 000
Profit-and-loss account	9002	5 000	
Rent	3001		5 000
Profit-and-loss account	9002	3 000	
Electricity	3002		3 000
Close down accounts to trading and profit-and-loss a/c's			

Figure 18.4 Denning's journal sheet 457

Journal Sheet			
Accounting period: May 199X			Number: 457
	Code	Debit £	Credit £
Trading account	9001	8 000	
Stock	5000		8 000
Clear stock account to trading account			
Stock	5000	10 000	
Trading account	9001		10 000
Stock balance at 31 May 199X			

suppliers include this item in their list prices, others may charge separately. Neither approach should undermine our attempt to treat costs of a similar nature on a consistent basis. Carriage out is a distribution expense just like advertising. As such it is not practicable (nor indeed admissible by UK accounting regulations) to include this cost as part of stock values. Hence if it is to be written off in the period to which it relates it should be treated as an expense in the profit-and-loss account.

Definitions of new terms

- *Capital brought forward* – The total investment of the owner in the business at the end of the previous accounting period, being the amount of funds invested plus or minus the accumulated profits, losses and drawings made since the business commenced.
- *Drawings* – The amount of funds withdrawn by the owner, either in cash or in kind, during the accounting period.
- *Capital carried forward* – Capital brought forward adjusted for the period's changes in capital: plus profits, less losses, less drawings.

The trading account

The following exercises test your understanding of the nature of stock accounting, introduced in Chapter 17. This is extremely important for the preparation of trading accounts.

Figure 18.5 Revised trial balance for Denning & Co.

	Trial Balance		31 May 199X	
Code	Account name		Debit £	Credit £
4000	Equipment		15 000	
5000	Stock		10 000	
6000	Debtors		10 000	
7000	Bank and cash		3 000	
8000	Trade creditors			6 000
9000	Capital b/f 1/6/9W			8 000
9001	Trading account			52 000
9002	Profit-and-loss account		28 000	
	Total		66 000	66 000

Figure 18.6 Denning's balance sheet

	Balance Sheet	31 May 199X
	£	£
Fixed assets:		
Equipment		15 000
Current assets:		
Stocks	10 000	
	10 000	
	3 000	
	23 000	
Current liabilities:		
Trade creditors	6 000	
Net current assets		17 000
		32 000
Financed by:		
Capital brought forward		8 000
Profit for the year		24 000
Capital carried forward		32 000

Figure 18.7 Pro forma for a trading and profit-and-loss account

	£	£	£
Sales			30 000
Less returns in			500
			29 500
Opening stock		6 000	
Purchases	18 200		
Add carriage in	400		
Less returns out	(600)	18 000	
		24 000	
Less closing stock		7 000	
Cost of sales			17 000
Gross profit			12 500
Discount received			200
			12 700
Less expenses			
Wages		1 500	
Depreciation – buildings		500	
Depreciation – plant		1 000	
Carriage out		500	
Discount allowed		200	
Rent		1 500	
Advertising		500	
Stationery, telephone and post		1 000	
Motor running expenses		1 000	7 700
Net profit			5 000

Figure 18.8 Pro forma for a balance sheet

	£	£	£
	Cost	Depreciation	
Fixed assets			
Land and buildings	20 000	5 000	15 000
Plant and machinery	10 000	5 000	5 000
	30 000	10 000	20 000
Current assets			
Stocks		7 000	
Debtors		2 000	
Bank and cash on hand		500	
		9 500	
Current liabilities			
Trade creditors	2 000		
VAT	500	2 500	
Net current assets			7 000
Total assets less current liabilities			27 000
Long term liabilities			
Bank loan			(7 000)
			20 000
Capital brought forward			17 000
Profit for the period		5 000	
Drawings		(2 000)	3 000
Capital carried forward			20 000

Tasks

1 Prepare a simple trading account for Brampton Electronics using the information below for the year ended 31 December 199X. A stock-take on 31 December valued stock at £34 802.

Account balances at 31 December 199X

Account	Debit £	Credit £
Stock	24 800	
Purchases	110,987	
Sales		200 985

2 Prepare a trading account for Higham Plumbing Supplies using the information below for the year ended 31 December 199X. A stock-take on 31 December valued stock at £49 827.

Account balances at 31 December 199X

Account	Debit £	Credit £
Stock 1/1/9X	45 980	
Purchases	298 630	
Carriage in	970	
Carriage out	25 300	
Returns in	12 647	
Returns out		2 300
Sales		506 100

3 Prepare a trading account for Delaney Supplies Ltd using the information below for the year ended 31 December 199X. A stock-take on 31 December valued stock at £25 384.

Account balances at 31 December 199X

Account	Debit £	Credit £
Stock 1/1/9X	22 645	
Purchases	198 560	
Carriage in	987	
Carriage out	2 350	
Returns in	602	
Returns out		300
Sales		387 410

Revision questions

1 'The trading and profit-and-loss accounts are part of the double-entry system but the balance sheet is not.' Explain this statement.

2 The stock figure included in the trial balance is the opening stock valuation. Why is the closing stock valuation not included?

3 What do the following terms mean and how are these transactions used when preparing financial statements? Returns in, returns out, carriage in, carriage out.

4 Which ledger accounts and books of prime entry are maintained to update the trading account?

Preparing accounts from the trial balance

When preparing a set of accounts it is possible to take figures from the trial balance and insert them into the financial statement without understanding the true nature of the balances. However, difficulty may be experienced and it is best to grasp the fundamental principles before progressing further. You may come across some items that are difficult to place without knowing these basic rules. To revise our study of the double-entry system in Chapter 17:

	Debit	Credit
Transaction	A cost in the trading and profit-and-loss account	Income in the trading and profit-and-loss account
Item of continuing value	An asset in the balance sheet	Capital or a liability in the balance sheet

Here are some common problems because descriptions are not always informative:

Description	Treatment
Bank balance	How do you know whether it is money in the bank or an overdrawn balance? A debit indicates an asset so it is money in the bank, a credit shows an overdraft.
Returns	Are they returns in or out? A debit indicates returns in as they represent a net off of sales.
Discounts	Are they discounts received or discounts allowed? Discount allowed is a cost, so will be represented by a debit balance.

General approach to preparing a set of accounts

■ With account headings it is important to be methodical and tidy in your work. Every accounting statement requires an appropriate heading, including the name of the business, the title of the accounting statement (e.g. trading and profit-and-loss account or balance sheet), and the date. A trading and profit-and-loss account is measuring the transactions *during a particular period* (e.g. for the year ended 31 December 1996). A balance sheet is stating the financial position *at a point in time* so should be given a specific date (e.g. as at 31 December 1996).

■ Use different columns, if necessary, to help the reader of the accounts appreciate the composition of totals and sub-totals. Figures in columns to the right generally represent totals of figures inset to the left.

■ You should indicate the denomination and currency being used in the accounts. Initially you may be concerned only with round pounds (£) but you should be aware that many of the large companies report in round millions of pounds (£m)! Accounts are meaningless without this information.

■ It is a good idea, at least at first, to go through the trial balance identifying each item as relating either to the trading and profit-and-loss account or to the balance sheet. Then as you use an item in an accounting statement, tick it off on the trial balance.

■ Assets are presented on the balance sheet in order from the least liquid (fixed assets) to cash (highly liquid). Hence debtors are presented before cash but after stocks.

■ If the balance sheet 'balances' (i.e. the capital side equals assets net of liabilities), then this is a good indication that you have included all items on the trial balance. However, this test will not indicate whether the adjustments that we will come across later are accurate, or that you used each item correctly (i.e. in the right financial report or presented in the correct manner).

Example of a set of accounts from a trial balance

Josephine Murphy has recorded the financial transactions for her business for the year ended 31 December 199X. She has asked us to prepare her trading, profit-and-loss account and balance sheet from the information given in the trial balance in Figure 18.9. Stock at 31 December 199X was valued at £8900. The answer is given in Figure 18.10.

Figure 18.9 J. Murphy's trial balance

	Debit £	Credit £
Bank	1 010	
Debtors	5 550	
Creditors		5 650
Sales		66 580
Stock 1/1/9X	6 800	
Purchases	32 560	
Rent	5 500	
Wages	11 500	
Drawings	12 500	
Electricity	650	
Capital		12 510
Motor vehicle at cost	6 500	
Carriage in	810	
Parcel delivery to customers	320	
Motor expenses	640	
Cash discount	400	
	84 740	84 740

Task

Now have a go yourself at drawing up accounts from a trial balance. Jason Reynolds has recorded the financial transactions for his business for the year ended 31 December 199X. He has asked you to prepare his trading and profit-and-loss account and balance sheet from the information in the trial balance below. Stock at 31 December 199X was valued at £19 600.

Trial balance	Debit £	Credit £
Bank		2 300
Debtors and creditors	36 100	23 560
Returns in	5 650	
Sales and purchases	89 500	140 680
Stock 1/1/9X	16 900	
Carriage out	2 560	
Land and buildings	64 000	
Wages	21 500	
Drawings	15 500	
Electricity	1 165	
Capital		100 745
Motor vehicle at cost	11 500	
Carriage in	810	
Returns out		250
Motor expenses	2 650	
Cash discounts	500	800
	268 335	268 335

Figure 18.10 J. Murphy's accounts

Josephine Murphy
Trading and profit-and-loss account
for year ended 31 December 199X

	£	£	£
Sales			66 580
Opening stock		6 800	
Purchases	32 560		
Carriage in	810	33 370	
		40 170	
Closing stock		8 900	
Cost of sales			31 270
Gross profit			35 310
Less expenses			
Cash discount		400	
Rent		5 500	
Wages		11 500	
Electricity		650	
Motor expenses		640	
Delivery		320	19 010
Net profit			16 300

Josephine Murphy
Balance sheet
as at 31 December 199X

	£	£
Fixed assets		
Motor vehicles		6 500
Current assets		
Stocks	8 900	
Debtors	5 550	
Bank	1 010	
	15 460	
Current liabilities		
Creditors	5 650	
		9 810
		16 310
Financed by		
Capital b/f at 1 January 199X		12 510
Profit	16 300	
Less Drawings	12 500	3 800
Capital c/f at 31 December 199X		16 310

Adjustments to the trial balance

Chapter 16 stressed that it is necessary to comply with the Companies Acts and accounting standards to ensure that meaningful information is conveyed by financial reports. The unadjusted trial balance is not necessarily in a form that complies with these regulatory requirements. Let us remind ourselves where the trial balance originates from. It is a listing of account balances that have been derived from the accounting transactions of the business. These accounting transactions are evidenced in the first place by invoices and by bank and cash documentation. These records do not necessarily reflect the services to customers and the cost of resources used.

We shall consider four types of adjustments to the trial balance to ensure we correctly match costs with revenues as required by SSAP 2:

- **Accruals** – Some costs have not been reflected in the accounting records, such as electricity consumed during the current charging quarter.
- **Prepayments** – Payment for goods or services has been made in advance of their consumption, such as rent paid for future months.
- **Depreciation** – Assets have been purchased that will give economic benefit in future periods. We need a mechanism for charging each accounting period with a fair share of the cost of assets used.
- **Bad and doubtful debts** – It is unfortunate but a fact of business life that some products sold on credit will never be paid for. This cost should be spread over the periods that gave rise to the loss rather than charge it to the period when the debt is eventually 'written off' as irrecoverable.

Accruals

An expense accrual is made in recognition that the accounting records currently understate the cost of resources consumed. The *dual aspect* of the adjustment is that we must also recognise that suppliers are owed more than the personal ledgers indicate.

The adjustment is made by transferring *more* to the profit-and-loss account than is necessary to balance off the expense account concerned. As a result of this process we create a *credit balance* on the expense account after the transfer to the profit-and-loss account. *This balance has to be incorporated in the balance sheet as a current liability with the title 'accrual'.*

Where a number of accruals have been made it is acceptable to consolidate them as one figure on the balance sheet. However, make sure you provide workings to show the balances that make up the total figure.

Tasks

1 John Late started trading on 1 January 199X and he is now at the end of his first year of trading. However, certain expenses he has incurred have not yet been invoiced by his suppliers. His unadjusted trial balance as at 31 December 199X was shown below.

	Debit £	Credit £
Sales		35 100
Purchases	25 980	
Electricity	1 200	
Telephone	900	
Motor expenses	2 350	
Motor vehicle at cost	8 150	
Bank and cash on hand	2 505	
Trade debtors and creditors	1 300	1 150
Capital		6 135
	42 385	42 385

- Stock at 31 December 199X was valued at £5600.
- *Electricity charges* for the first three quarters of 199X up to 30 September 199X were £500, £400 and £300 respectively. Usage for the final quarter to 31 December 199X is estimated to be £500.
- *Telephone charges* for the first three quarters of 199X up to September 199X were £350, £300 and £250 respectively. Usage for the final quarter to 31 December 199X is estimated to be £250.
- At the year end, a *repair bill* had not been received for work completed just before the Christmas holiday. The invoice when received would be for £150.

Your tasks are:

a Prepare and balance off the ledger account for each expense, *having made the necessary adjustment for costs to be accrued*.
b Prepare for John Late the trading, profit-and-loss account and balance sheet for the period ending 31 December 199X.

To give you a start, the answer for the electricity charges is shown below.

After the accrual adjustment the charge for electricity in the profit-and-loss account will now be £1700. The cost accrual of £500 will be included with similar adjustments for telephone and motor expenses under current liabilities in the balance sheet. Now complete the remainder of the exercise yourself.

2 John Late has now reached the end of his second year of trading. Various expenses remain unpaid at the end of 199Y. His unadjusted trial balance as at 31 December 199Y is shown below.

	Debit £	Credit £
Sales		46 500
Stock at 1/1/9Y	5 600	
Purchases	23 450	
Electricity	1 160	
Telephone	800	
Motor expenses	2 950	
Motor vehicle at cost	8 150	
Bank and cash on hand	3 100	
Trade debtors and creditors	1 500	2 160
Capital		15 505
Drawings	17 455	
	64 165	64 165

- Stock at 31 December 199Y was valued at £7140.
- Quarterly *electricity charges* paid during the year were £475, £525, £350 and £310. Usage for the final quarter to 31 December 199Y remains unpaid and is estimated to be £550.
- *Telephone charges* paid during the year were £275, £265, £250 and £260. Usage for the final quarter to 31 December 199Y remains unpaid and is estimated to be £270.
- *Motor expenses* paid during the year amounted to £3100. At the year end the monthly petrol bill had not

Ledger – Electricity									
Debit					**Credit**				
Date	Narrative	Ref.	Value £		Date	Narrative	Ref.	Value £	
	Bank		500		31/12/9X	Profit and loss		1 700	
	Bank		400						
	Bank		300						
31/12/9X	Balance c/f		500						
			1 700					1 700	
					1/1/9Y	Balance b/f		500	

Ledger – Electricity								
Debit Date	Narrative	Ref.	Value £	**Credit** Date	Narrative	Ref.	Value £
	Bank		475	1/1/9Y	Balance b/f		500
	Bank		525	31/12/9Y	Profit and loss		1 710
	Bank		350				
	Bank		310				
31/12/9X	Balance c/f		550				____
			2 210				2 210
				1/1/9Z	Balance b/f		550

been received. The charge outstanding is estimated to be about £110.

Your tasks are:

a Prepare and balance off the ledger accounts for electricity, telephone and motor expenses, having made the necessary adjustment for costs to be accrued.

b Prepare for John Late the trading, profit-and-loss account and balance sheet for the period ending 31 December 199Y.

With this problem it is important to recognise the *accruals brought forward*. Some of the actual expenditure in 199Y relates to costs accrued for in 199X.

To give you a start, the answer for the electricity charges is shown above.

It is inevitable that allowances for expense accruals are not always accurate. If accruals prove to be inaccurate the accounts are not subsequently restated with the new information – over or under accrual of cost is absorbed in the next accounting period. In the case of John Late's electricity at the end of 199X, £500 was accrued and £475 subsequently billed. The expenditure in 199Y will be reported at £25 less than would otherwise have been the case. Now complete the remainder of the exercise.

Prepayments

A **prepayment adjustment** is made in recognition that the accounting records currently overstate the cost of certain resources consumed. The *dual aspect* of this situation is to also recognise that we have an asset in having paid in advance for the resources to be consumed in a subsequent period.

The adjustment is made by transferring *less* to the profit-and-loss account than is necessary to balance off the expense account concerned. As a result of this process

we create a *debit balance* on the expense account after transferring to the profit-and-loss account. *This balance is incorporated in the balance sheet as a current asset with the title 'prepayment'.*

Where a number of prepayments have been made it is acceptable to consolidate them as one figure on the balance sheet. However, make sure you provide workings to show the balances that make up the total figure.

Tasks

1 Kate Early has reached the end of her first year of trading. Various expenses relating to the next financial year have been prepaid at the end of 199X. Her unadjusted trial balance as at 31 December 199X was as shown below.

	Debit £	Credit £
Sales		28 410
Purchases	16 850	
Stationery	425	
Rent	2 500	
Rates	1 250	
Computer maintenance	450	
Computer at cost	1 500	
Bank and cash on hand		200
Trade debtors and creditors	1 800	500
Capital		1 665
Drawings	6 000	
	30 775	30 775

■ Stock at 31 December 199X was valued at £1140.
■ *Stationery.* On 31 December 199X, Kate had in her cupboard £150 of unused stationery.
■ *Rent.* Kate signed a five-year lease at £2000 per annum payable a quarter in advance.
■ *Rates.* Kate pays business rates of £1000 per annum.

Ledger – Stationery							
Debit Date	Narrative	Ref.	Value £	**Credit** Date	Narrative	Ref.	Value £
	Bank		425	31/12/9X	Profit and loss		275
				31/12/9X	Balance c/f		<u>150</u>
			<u>425</u>				<u>425</u>
1/1/9Y	Balance b/f		150				

She has paid for the full year 1 April 199X to 31 March 199Y.

- *Computer maintenance.* When Kate purchased her computer on 1 January 199X she also signed a three-year maintenance contract entailing a one-off payment of £450.

Your tasks are:

a Prepare and balance off Kate's expense accounts, with an adjustment for prepaid amounts.

b Prepare for Kate Early her trading and profit-and-loss account for the year ended 31 December 199X and a balance sheet at that date.

To give you a start, the answer for stationery is shown above.

The trial balance figure of £425 has been split into two parts. Expenditure amounting to £150 has been deferred and carried over to 199Y as a prepayment. The charge to the profit-and-loss account has been correspondingly reduced. The balance on the stationery account should be shown in the balance sheet as a prepayment under current assets. Now complete the remainder of the exercise yourself.

2 Imagine that Kate Early has reached the end of her second year of trading. Various expenses relating to the next financial year have been prepaid at the end of 199Y. (Remember certain payments were also made during 199X in respect of 199Y.) Her unadjusted trial balance as at 31 December 199Y was as shown below.

	Debit £	Credit £
Sales		39 625
Stock at 1 January 199Y	1 140	
Purchases	24 850	
Stationery	600	
Rent	2 500	
Rates	1 350	
Computer maintenance	300	
Computer at cost	1 500	
Bank and cash on hand	2 650	
Trade debtors and creditors	2 575	900
Capital		4 940
Drawings	8 000	
	45 465	45 465

- Stock at 31 December 199Y was valued at £3540.
- *Stationery.* On the 31 December 199Y, Kate had in her cupboard £125 of unused stationery, after paying £450 for stationery during the year.
- *Rent.* Kate is continuing to pay one quarter in advance on her £2000 per annum property lease.
- *Rates.* Kate's business rates for 199Y/199Z have increased to £1100 per annum. She has paid for the full year 1 April 199Y to 31 March 199Z.
- *Computer maintenance.* There remains one year to run on her three-year maintenance contract that had entailed a one-off payment of £450.

Your tasks are:

a Prepare and balance off Kate's expense accounts, *with adjustments for expenses prepaid.*

b Prepare for Kate Early her trading and profit-and-loss account for the year ended 31 December 199Y and a balance sheet at that date.

To give you a start, the answer for stationery is shown on the next page.

Ledger – Stationery									
Debit Date	Narrative	Ref.	Value £	**Credit** Date	Narrative	Ref.	Value £
1/1/9Y	Balance b/f		150	31/12/9X	Profit and loss		475
	Bank		450	31/12/9X	Balance c/f		125
			600				600
1/1/9Y	Balance b/f		125				

Complete the remainder of the exercise yourself.

Depreciation

The item **depreciation** arises through the need to satisfy the *accrual concept for fixed assets*. Fixed assets are items that will be used in a business for more than one accounting period. Depreciation is the mechanism used to spread the asset's cost over the periods that will benefit from its use. A formal definition of terms is provided in SSAP 12, Accounting for Depreciation.

■ *Depreciation* is the measure of the wearing out, consumption or other reduction in the useful economic life of a fixed asset, whether arising from use, effluxion of time or obsolescence through technological or market changes.
■ *The useful economic life* of an asset is the period over which the present owner will derive economic benefits from its use.
■ *Residual value* is the realisable value of the asset at the end of its useful economic life, based on prices prevailing at the date of acquisition or revaluation, where this has taken place. Realisation costs should be deducted in arriving at the residual value.
■ *The net book value* is the cost of the asset not yet depreciated and charged to the profit-and-loss account. It is calculated from:

Net book value =
Original cost − accumulated depreciation to date

The accounting standard does not prescribe a set method for calculating depreciation, nor does it set specific asset lives. It is accepted that the calculation is best done in the light of the relevant circumstances.

Whatever the depreciation method, the depreciation is charged as an *expense* to the profit-and-loss account, and the *asset's value* in the balance sheet is reduced. The journal entries are:

■ Debit depreciation charge account.
■ Credit provision for depreciation account.

On transferring the balances to the profit-and-loss account, the entries are:

■ Debit profit-and-loss account.
■ Credit depreciation charge account.

Methods of calculating depreciation

There are two methods for calculating depreciation that you should be familiar with.

In the **straight-line method**, the estimated depletion in the asset's value is spread evenly over its estimated economic life:

$$\text{Depreciation charge per year} = \frac{\text{Cost} - \text{Residual value}}{\text{Estimated life in years}}$$

For example, a motor vehicle costing £10 500 with an estimated life of three years and a residual value of £1 500 would be depreciated as follows:

$$\text{Depreciation per year} = \frac{£10\,500 - £1\,500}{3}$$
$$= £3000 \text{ per year}$$

Note: The straight-line method may be referred to in terms of the asset's estimated life or as a certain percentage of cost. For example, 'depreciate the asset evenly over 10 years' means the same as 'depreciate at 10% on cost'.

The **reducing-balance method** does not depreciate the asset evenly over its estimated life. It assumes that the asset provides better service in its early years with either reduced effectiveness or increased maintenance costs in subsequent years. It is calculated by applying *a percentage rate to the asset's net book value at the beginning of the year*.

Depreciation per year =
Net book value at start of the period × Depreciation rate

In examination questions the rate of depreciation will be given to you. However, if you should wish to calculate the required rate of depreciation to depreciate an asset over a given number of years (N), the formula is:

$$\text{Rate} = 1 - \left[\sqrt[N]{\frac{\text{Residual value}}{\text{Original cost}}} \right] \times 100\%$$

Illustration using the two depreciation methods

Two companies both depreciate the £10 500 original cost of a new motor vehicle over three years. However, Flat Ltd uses the straight-line method with a residual value of £1500, and Express Ltd uses the reducing-balance method using a rate of 48 per cent. What will be the annual depreciation charge for each company over the three years? What will be the net book value of each car?

Using the straight-line method the answer is:

	Year 1 £	Year 2 £	Year 3 £
Annual depreciation charge	3 000	3 000	3 000
Original cost	10 500	10 500	10 500
Accumulated depreciation	3 000	6 000	9 000
Net book value	7 500	4 500	1 500

Using the reducing-balance method the answer is:

	Year 1 £	Year 2 £	Year 3 £
Annual depreciation charge	5 040	2 621	1 363
Original cost	10 500	10 500	10 500
Accumulated depreciation	5 040	7 661	9 024
Net book value	5 460	2 839	1 476

The final net book value of the two cars is similar. However, using the reducing-balance method results in high charges to the profit-and-loss account in the first year.

Classification of capital expenditure

The correct classification of expenditure is important. Revenue expenditure incorrectly capitalised and recorded as a fixed asset would be in breach of fundamental accounting principles. Deferring costs incorrectly to the balance sheet would not be prudent and would also not allow the matching of costs with revenues.

Generally, all expenditure related to the acquisition and installation of a fixed asset can be included as being part of the cost of the asset. Hence delivery charges, legal fees and installation expenses can be included. Expenditure that increases the economic value of a fixed asset is also capital expenditure. This includes accessories for machines and building alterations.

Specifically excluded is that expenditure required to improve the condition of existing fixed assets such as repair and redecoration costs. However, expenditure incurred to improve the condition of newly acquired assets can be treated as capital expenditure.

Tasks

Zip operate a courier service from Northampton, delivering parcels and small consignments of goods in the locality and further afield using the nearby motorway network. You have been asked to account for their fixed asset transactions that have occurred during the accounting year ended 31 December 1995. The following items of expenditure have been extracted as possible fixed asset transactions by one of the partners, John Pierce.

Date	Description	£
1/4/95	Second-hand Ford Van	6 000
	Service plan for six months	200
	Delivery	100
		6 300
1/7/95	Building work at the leasehold premises	
	Redecoration to outside of building	500
	Remove partition wall to enlarge the reception area	750
	Replace electrical wiring in the garage area	500
		1 750
1/10/95	Computer for the office:	
	Processor, visual display and keyboard	800
	Software	300
	One year's maintenance contract	100
	20 computer disks	15
		1 215

Zip uses the following depreciation policies:

- Building work is depreciated over the remaining life of the lease that is due to expire on 31 December 1999. No residual value is assumed.
- All motor vehicles are one year old when purchased and are depreciated straight-line over three years. Residual value of £100 is assumed.

- Computer equipment and software are depreciated at 50 per cent based on net book values.
- Assets owned for part of a year are depreciated on a pro-rata basis.

Disposal of assets:

- On 31 March 1997 the computer and software were sold for a total of £300 when John Pierce purchased a new system.
- On 30 September 1997 the Ford Van was sold for £1500.

Your tasks are:

1 Classify each item of expenditure as either capital or revenue.
2 Calculate the total capital cost for each fixed asset item.
3 Provide possible explanations for the depreciation policies adopted.

4 Calculate the annual depreciation charge for each asset.
5 Calculate the pro-rata charge for the year of purchase and if appropriate the year of disposal.
6 Prepare ledger accounts for 1995, 1996 and 1997 to record, in respect of each asset: cost, depreciation charge each year, accumulated provision for depreciation and profit or loss on disposal.

To give you a start, here is the answer for the motor vehicle.

$$\text{Depreciation of the motor vehicle for a full year} = \frac{6100 - 100}{3} = £2000$$

Depreciation charge in 1995 is £2000 × 9/12 = £1500
Depreciation charge in 1997 is £2000 × 9/12 = £1500

Ledger accounts for the motor vehicle are shown below.

Ledger – Motor/cost

Debit Date	Narrative	Ref.	Value £	**Credit** Date	Narrative	Ref.	Value £
1/4/95	Bank		6100	31/12/95	C/F		6100
1/1/96	B/F		6100	31/12/96	C/F		6100
1/1/97	B/F		6100	30/9/97	Disposal		6100

Ledger – Motor/accumulated depreciation

Debit Date	Narrative	Ref.	Value £	**Credit** Date	Narrative	Ref.	Value £
31/12/95	C/F		1500	31/12/95	Depreciation		1500
31/12/96	C/F		3500	1/1/96	B/F		1500
				31/12/96	Depreciation		2000
			3500				3500
30/9/97	Disposal account		5000	1/1/97	B/F		3500
				30/9/97	Depreciation		1500
			5000				5000

Ledger – Motor/depreciation								
Debit Date	Narrative	Ref.	Value £	**Credit** Date	Narrative	Ref.	Value £
30/12/97	Acc. depreciation		1 500	31/12/95	Profit and loss		1 500
30/12/96	Acc. depreciation		2 000	31/12/96	Profit and loss		2 000
30/9/97	Acc. depreciation		1 500	31/12/97	Profit and loss		1 500

Ledger – Motor/disposal account								
Debit Date	Narrative	Ref.	Value £	**Credit** Date	Narrative	Ref.	Value £
30/9/97	Costs		6 100	30/9/97	Acc. depreciation		5 000
31/12/97	Profit and loss		400	30/9/97	Bank		1 500
			6 500				6 500

When the motor vehicle is disposed of, the balances on the asset cost and accumulated depreciation account are transferred to an asset disposal account. Sale proceeds are also posted to the disposal account. The balance arising as a result of a difference between the sale proceeds and the asset's net book value represents either a profit or a loss on disposal. In this example, a profit of £400 was made on disposal. A profit is deducted from expenses in the profit-and-loss account (a loss would be added to expenses).

Now prepare the records for the building work and computer equipment.

Depreciation and final accounts

Final accounts with depreciation of fixed assets will have the following features:

- The trial balance will include an accumulated depreciation account. This account will not have been updated with the current year's depreciation charge unless a depreciation charge account is also listed as a debit balance. The method for calculating depreciation will be detailed in the notes below the trial balance.
- The current period's charge for depreciation should be included with the other expenses in the profit-and-loss account.

- The updated accumulated depreciation provision should be disclosed as shown in the pro forma balance sheet illustrated earlier (see Figure 18.8).

Tasks

1 *Straight-line exercise.* The following trial balance has been extracted from the books of John Royston.

	Debit £	Credit £
Motor	9 800	
Furniture	5 900	
Motor – accumulated depreciation		2 400
Furniture – accumulated depreciation		1 180
Sales and purchases	43 200	68 000
Stock at 1/1/9X	4 800	
Motor running expenses	1 500	
Rent	1 000	
Bank	3 500	
Creditors		100
Capital		4 020
Drawings	6 000	
	75 700	75 700

- Stock at 31 December 199X was valued at £5400.
- The motor vehicle is depreciated over four years with an estimated residual value of £200. Furniture is depreciated by 10 per cent on cost each year.

Prepare for John Royston his trading and profit-and-loss account and balance sheet for the year ended 31 December 199X.

2 *Reducing-balance exercise.* The following trial balance has been extracted from the books of Joan Reaney.

	Debit £	Credit £
Sales and purchases	38 900	95 450
Computer	2 200	
Computer depreciation		1 100
Factory plant	19 500	
Factory plant depreciation		7 020
Rent	10 000	
Power	3 250	
Wages	15 400	
Capital		13 070
Drawings	7 500	
Debtors and creditors	18 600	7 260
Stock 1/1/9X	12 800	
Bank		4 250
	128 150	128 150

- Stock at 31 December 199X was valued at £8260.
- The computer is depreciated at 50 per cent reducing-balance basis. Factory plant is depreciated at 20 per cent of brought-forward net book value.

Prepare for Joan Reaney her trading and profit-and-loss account and balance sheet for the year ended 31 December 199X.

3 *Asset purchases exercise.* The following trial balance has been extracted from the books of Jason O'Connor.

	Debit £	Credit £
Sales and purchases	56 890	112 450
Equipment	23 000	
Equipment depreciation		12 850
Motor	25 900	
Motor depreciation		5 250
Rent	5 000	
Power	2 500	
Wages	12 500	
Capital		33 480
Drawings	9 000	
Debtors and creditors	14 250	3 650
Stock 1/1/9X	11 740	
Bank	6 900	
	167 680	167 680

- Stock at 31 December 199X was valued at £8260.
- Depreciation is calculated straight-line from the month of purchase assuming no residual values. Equipment is depreciated over 10 years and motor vehicles over four years.
- On 1 April 199X, Jason had purchased a piece of equipment for £3000 and on 1 October 199X a new motor vehicle for £9200.

Prepare for Jason O'Connor his trading and profit-and-loss account and balance sheet for the year ended 31 December 199X.

4 *Asset disposals exercise.* The following trial balance has been extracted from the books of Josephine O'Dell.

	Debit £	Credit £
Sales and purchases	90 600	190 650
Land	30 000	
Buildings – cost/depreciation	60 000	9 000
Equipment – cost/depreciation	25 600	5 200
Motor – cost/depreciation	11 260	4 500
Wages	25 680	
Capital		44 400
Drawings	12 000	
Debtors and creditors	18 290	14 630
Stock 1/1/9X	7 340	
Suspense account		600
Bank		11 790
	280 770	280 770

- Stock at 31 December 199X was valued at £6050.
- Depreciation is calculated on a straight-line basis from the month of purchase. Depreciation rates based on cost are: buildings 4 per cent, equipment 10 per cent and motor vehicles 25 per cent.
- On 30 June 199X, Josephine sold an item of equipment for £500 that had cost £2500 exactly six years previously. On 30 September she sold another item of equipment for £100 that had cost £800 five years six months previously. None of the asset accounts have been updated with these transactions and the sales proceeds have been credited to a suspense account.

Prepare for Josephine O'Dell her trading and profit-and-loss account and balance sheet for the year ended 31 December 199X.

Bad and doubtful debts

We have already identified that sales for most businesses are on a credit basis. It is an unfortunate fact that there is always the risk of the customer defaulting. It may be found that a customer:

- wilfully flouts the terms of trade

- questions the ability of our business to substantiate its claim in court
- has insufficient cash to settle the debt on time
- has been declared bankrupt.

In all cases the business has to consider the cost of pursuing payment and the likelihood of eventual success. There will come a time when the debt has to be considered unrecoverable and at that point we need to reflect this in the accounting records. Let us consider what has happened to the debt so far.

At the time of satisfying the sales order the customer's account will have been debited with the invoice value. The *dual aspect* of the transaction will have been to credit sales. Until we recognise that the debt is bad, the profit-and-loss account will show a profit from this sale.

When a debt is considered bad the bookkeeping entries are:

- Credit the customer's account.
- Debit the bad debt account.

The reason we do not debit the sales account is because of the need to assign responsibility for the cost of the debt. If we reduced sales, the proportion of gross profit to sales would change which undermines controls for pricing policy and the purchasing of stock. Once a sale has been made it is the responsibility of the credit control section of the finance department to chase payment. Accountability is strengthened by giving the credit control section a right of veto before a credit sale is made – especially for credit checking new customers and where existing customers have infringed settlement terms. Having identified bad debts as an administration responsibility, they should be written off as an expense in the profit-and-loss account.

The problem of waiting until a debt is proven to be non-recoverable is that it may distort the performance of accounting periods. The debt may be retained on the customer's account in the hope that it might be collected in the future. When the debt is eventually written off it may be in a different accounting period from the time of sale. It is a task of the person who prepares financial reports to make an adjustment to account for this timing discrepancy. However, when assessing the recoverability of debts, although it may be possible to identify some old debts that are irrecoverable, it is often difficult and time-consuming to assess the recoverability of all debts. In such circumstances it is usual practice, on the basis of past experience, to consider a proportion of debts outstanding as non-paying.

This allowance for future bad-debt write-offs is called a **provision for bad and doubtful debts**. The provision is created with the journal entries:

- Debit bad debts account.
- Credit provision for bad and doubtful debts.

Although the provision has a credit balance, it is included under current assets in the balance sheet as it relates specifically to debtors. Here is an example:

Current assets:		£
Stocks		4000
Debtors	2000	
Provision for bad debts @ 5%	(100)	1900
Prepayments		100
Cash at bank and on hand		100
		6100

The provision remains *unchanged* as a balance from one year to the next unless further adjustments are made via the bad-debts account. Using the figures above, if in the next year debtors increase to £2400 and the provision is to be kept at 5 per cent of debtors, then the provision will have to be increased by £20 (debit bad-debts account, credit bad-and-doubtful-debts provision). Conversely, if debtors fall, then a proportion of the provision is released (debit provision, credit bad-debts account).

Tasks

1 *Bad-debt provision exercise.* Martin Spicer extracted the following balances from his books on 31 December 199X.

	Debit £	Credit £
Bank	5 600	
Debtors	29 800	
Provision for bad debts		2 000

- Stocks were valued at £19 100.
- He estimates that bad debts are 5 per cent of debtors.

Your tasks are:

a Prepare the journal entry required to effect the change to the bad-debt provision.
b Prepare the current-assets section of Martin's balance sheet at 31 December 199X.

2 *Bad-debt provision exercise.* Marion Spencer extracted the following balances from her books on 31 December 199X.

	Debit £	Credit £
Bank	1 600	
Debtors	80 100	
Provision for bad debts		4 100

- Stocks were valued at £9300.
- She considers it very unlikely one debt for £400 will be paid. In addition, 3 per cent of the remainder should also be covered by the provision.

Your tasks are:

a Prepare the journal entry required to effect the change to the bad-debt provision.

b Prepare the current-assets section of Martin's balance sheet at 31 December 199X.

3 *Bad-debts and final accounts exercise.* The following trial balance has been extracted from the books of Jennifer Hardy.

	Debit £	Credit £
Sales and purchases	36 000	78 600
Bad debts	250	
Provision for doubtful debts		800
Stock at 1/1/9X	3 000	
Rent	3 250	
Bank	12 450	
Debtors/Creditors	28 950	14 650
Capital		4 850
Drawings	15 000	
	98 900	98 900

- Stock at 31 December 199X was valued at £5400.
- Provision for bad debts should be stated at 4 per cent of debtors.

Your task is to prepare for Jennifer Hardy her trading and profit-and-loss account and balance sheet for the year ended 31 December 199X.

Accounts with all four adjustments

You should now be ready to attempt the preparation of accounts with all four adjustments required.

Tasks

1 Christine Boyes has provided you with the following trial balance for her accounting year ended 31 January 199Y.

	Debit £	Credit £
Sales		224 580
Purchases	101 250	
Stationery	1 270	
Rent	5 000	
Electricity	2 600	
Computer maintenance	500	
Computer at cost	6 000	
Computer depreciation		4 000
Motor cost	25 900	
Motor depreciation		10 800
Land and buildings (£20 000 and £40 000 respectively)	60 000	
Buildings depreciation		5 000
Bank and cash on hand	8 910	
Returns	500	350
Carriage in	200	
Carriage out	1 890	
Bad debts	540	
Doubtful debt provision		1 250
Opening stock 1/2/9X	30 580	
Motor expenses	5 065	
Disposal account		200
Wages and salaries	42 180	
Telephone	2 500	
Trade debtors and creditors	38 650	18 400
Loan from Jason Boyes		20 000
Capital		59 455
Drawings	10 500	
	344 035	344 035

- Stock at 31 January 199Y was valued at £24 570.
- Land and buildings costs are £20 000 and £40 000 respectively.
- Depreciation policy: buildings 4 per cent on cost, motor 25 per cent on cost and computers 50 per cent reducing balance. Depreciation is charged from the month of purchase to the month of disposal.
- A motor vehicle was purchased on 1 June 199X for £9000.
- A computer with original cost of £2000 was sold on 31 July 199X for £200 having been used in the business since 1 February 199V. The asset accounts have not been updated with the disposal.
- The provision for doubtful debts should represent 4 per cent of debtors.
- The rent agreement for a small office was for £4000 per annum.
- The following costs are to be accrued as due: telephone £300, electricity £400.
- An invoice from Christine's solicitor for £1054 is expected shortly in respect of legal work during the year.

Your task is to prepare for Christine Boyes her trading and profit-and-loss account and balance sheet for the year ended 31 January 199Y.

2 Satya Mistri has provided you with the following trial balance for his accounting year ended 30 June 199Y.

	Debit £	Credit £
Plant and machinery	95 500	38 420
Motor vehicles	38 500	12 980
Debtors	40 800	
Creditors		29 600
Stock as at 1 July 199X	25 710	
Sales		202 450
Purchases	96 400	
Returns in	400	
Carriage out	780	
Electricity	2 960	
Motor expenses	7 694	
Stationery, postage and telephone	8 630	
Wages	31 350	
Rent	10 000	
Capital		73 674
Drawings	19 750	
Suspense account		2 200
Provision for doubtful debts		650
Bank overdraft		3 500
Bank loan		15 000
	378 474	378 474

- Stock at 30 June 199Y was valued at £29 580.
- The bank loan is repayable in three years' time.
- Depreciation policy: plant and machinery over 10 years, motor vehicles over four years. Depreciation is charged from the month of purchase to the month of disposal, with no residual values assumed.
- A motor vehicle was purchased on 1 January 199Y for £10 000.
- Plant and machinery with an original cost of £7000 was sold on 31 March 199Y, having been used for five years. The proceeds have been posted to a suspense account although no other entries have been made for this transaction.
- The provision for doubtful debts should represent 2 per cent of debtors.
- The balance for rent is for the period 1 July 199X to 30 September 199Y.
- The following costs are to be accrued as due: telephone £400, electricity £490.

Your task is to prepare for Satya Mistri his trading and profit-and-loss account and balance sheet for the year ended 30 June 199Y.

Accounts for incorporated businesses

Accounts for limited companies are prepared on a similar basis as those for a sole trader. However, you should be familiar with a number of new terms and slight variations in the layout of the financial statements:

- *Share capital* – The capital of an incorporated business is represented by a number of shares at a certain nominal value (e.g. 2500 shares of a nominal value £0.50).
- *Authorised share capital* – This indicates the maximum number of shares that can be issued as specified in the company's memorandum of association. The amount of authorised share capital is disclosed for memorandum purposes only and is not an actual nominal account balance.
- *Issued and fully paid share capital* – This is the number of shares actually issued and paid for by the shareholders. The shares are stated at their nominal value even if the shareholder paid a higher market price for them. This is the amount of share capital recorded in the accounts and in the capital section of the balance sheet.
- *Class of share* – The accounts will have to disclose the class of shares that the share capital is composed of (i.e. ordinary or preference shares), distinguishing between classes that carry different rights.
- *Share premium account* – The difference between the share issue price and the nominal value of a share is credited to the share premium account. It is disclosed immediately below the issued and paid share capital in the balance sheet.
- *Profit-and-loss account* – The balance in the profit-and-loss account represents the accumulated retained earnings of the company.
- *Directors' salaries* – Salaries paid to sole traders and partners are treated as appropriations of profit. The salaries paid to company directors, even though they may also be major shareholders, are treated as an expense in the profit-and-loss account.
- *Appropriation account* – The appropriation account is disclosed at the foot of the profit-and-loss account and shows how the profit earned in the year has been used. Common appropriations include: taxation, payment of dividends and transfers to other reserves.
- *Corporation tax* – The company pays tax to the Inland Revenue based on the level of profits earned. This is treated as an appropriation of profit as noted above. The current year's tax will not have been paid at the date of the accounts and so should be provided for as a current liability.
- *Dividends* – The profits returned to shareholders are called dividends. At the date of the accounts some of

those dividends may have been paid (interim dividend) and some the directors propose to pay (final dividend) pending ratification by the members in general meeting. Proposed dividend is a current liability in the balance sheet.

- *Debentures* – Debentures are long-term loan stock issued under the company's common seal. They often carry a fixed rate of interest with a specified date of redemption. If the company is listed on the stock exchange, then the debentures can be bought and sold very much like shares.

Some of these characteristics increase the number of adjustments that have to be made after the trial balance has been struck. In particular, it will be common to come across items that require an accrual at the year end because they have not yet been paid. These may include proposed dividend, debenture interest and taxation. You will know whether debenture interest requires accruing if the debit balance in the trial balance for interest paid is less than the debenture value at the stated rate of interest.

Example

The following trial balance has been extracted from the books of Stewart Ladds Ltd.

	£	£
Purchases	442 150	
Sales		896 320
Staff wages and salaries	180 400	
Rent	50 000	
Motor expenses	18 730	
Post, stationery and telephone	21 760	
Directors' salaries	65 000	
Dividends paid	16 000	
Share capital		100 000
Profit-and-loss account		65 760
Motor vehicles	65 120	
Furniture fixtures and fittings	110 900	
Motor vehicle depreciation		30 690
Furniture fixtures and fittings depreciation		40 180
Debtors	38 780	
Creditors		25 971
Stock at 1/1/9X	160 100	
Bank	40 980	
Debentures @ 10% interest		50 000
Provision for doubtful debts		999
	1 209 920	1 209 920

- The company has an authorised share capital of 300 000 ordinary shares of 50p each.

- Stock at 31 December 199X was valued at £140 900.
- Corporation tax for the year has been computed as £24 970.
- The directors are to propose the payment of a final dividend of 10p a share.
- Provision for doubtful debts is to be restated at 5 per cent of debtors.
- Depreciation policy requires depreciation to be calculated on a straight-line basis, 25 per cent for motor vehicles and 10 per cent for furniture, fixtures and fittings.
- Telephone charges of £800 are to be accrued as due.

We are to prepare for Stewart Ladds Ltd a trading and profit-and-loss account for the year ended 31 December 199X and a balance sheet at the same date. The answer is given in Figure 18.11.

Figure 18.11 Accounts of Stewart Ladds Ltd

Stewart Ladds Ltd
Trading and profit-and-loss account
for year ended 31 December 199X

	£	£
Sales		896 320
Opening stock	160 100	
Purchases	442 150	
	602 250	
Less closing stock	140 900	
Cost of sales		461 350
Gross profit		434 970
Less expenses		
Rent	50 000	
Wages	180 400	
Motor expenses	18 730	
Post	22 560	
Directors' salaries	65 000	
Depreciation–motor	16 280	
Depreciation–FFF	11 090	
Bad debts	940	365 000
Profit before interest		69 970
Interest		5 000
Profit before tax		64 970
Tax		24 970
Profit after tax		40 000
Dividends paid	16 000	
proposed	20 000	36 000
Retained profit for the year		4 000
Retained profit at 1 January 199X		65 760
Retained profit at 31 December 199X		69 760

Stewart Ladds Ltd Balance sheet as at 31 December 199X			
	Cost £	**Depreciation** £	**NBV** £
Fixed assets			
Furniture fixtures and fittings	110 900	51 270	59 630
Motor vehicles	65 120	46 970	18 150
	176 020	98 240	77 780
Current assets			
Stocks		140 900	
Debtors	38 780		
Bad and doubtful debt provision	1 939	36 841	
Bank		40 980	
		218 721	
Current liabilities			
Creditors	25 971		
Accruals	800		
Tax	24 970		
Interest	5 000		
Dividend	20 000	76 741	
Net current assets			141 980
Total assets less current liabilities			219 760
Long-term liabilities			
Debentures			50 000
			169 760
Issued and full paid			
Share capital			100 000
Profit and loss account			69 760
			169 760

Task

The following trial balance has been extracted from the books of Simmons & Co. Ltd.

	£	£
Debenture interest	250	
Creditors		1 250
Stock at 1/1/9X	8 250	
Bank	900	
Debentures @ 10% interest		5 000
Staff wages and salaries	10 420	
Electricity	730	
Rent	2 000	
Motor expenses	2 690	
Post, stationery and telephone	1 630	
Directors' salaries	18 360	
Dividends paid	2 000	
Purchases	27 810	
Sales		71 840
Share capital		10 000
Profit-and-loss account		1 250
Motor vehicles	15 800	
Furniture fixtures and fittings	8 400	
Motor vehicle depreciation		3 000
Furniture fixtures and fittings depreciation		6 900
	99 240	99 240

- The company has an authorised share capital of 50 000 ordinary shares of £1 each.
- Stock at 31 December 199X was valued at £11 500.
- Corporation tax for the year has been computed as £1440.
- At the company's annual general meeting the directors are to propose the payment of a final dividend of 8p a share.
- Depreciation policy requires depreciation to be calculated on a straight-line basis, 25 per cent for motor vehicles and 10 per cent for furniture, fixtures and fittings.
- Charges in respect of telephone £400 and electricity £320 are to be accrued as due.

Your task is to prepare for Simmons a trading and profit-and-loss account for the year ended 31 December 199X and a balance sheet at the same date.

Financial reports and business activity

The nature of a business influences the format of its financial statements. The main categories of business for accounting purposes are:

- trading, including retail
- manufacturing
- service.

Trading businesses

Trading businesses comprise the wholesale and retail sectors of industry. All of the businesses we have been preparing accounts for so far have been trading businesses (i.e. they buy goods for resale). They have not been concerned with the manufacture of goods and do not work on the goods to increase their value. As we have seen, the main financial statements comprise the trading account, the profit-and-loss account and the balance sheet.

Manufacturing businesses

Manufacturing businesses make changes to the materials they purchase. This may involve radical changes to the nature of the material, say from iron ore to stainless steel at British Steel. On the other hand the manufacturing process may lead only to cosmetic changes, such as painting or grinding. Finished goods from one business may be the raw materials for another – steel from British Steel could be the raw material from which car panels are made. Whatever the process there will generally be three categories of stock at any point in time:

- raw materials – the goods purchased by the business
- work in progress (WIP) – goods which has been partly manufactured
- finished goods – goods which have been fully manufactured.

Just as movement in the level of stock for a trading company means that it is not adequate to deduct purchases from sales to arrive at gross profit, we cannot ignore the movement in the value of WIP and raw materials when calculating the profit of a manufacturing business.

A manufacturing business therefore prepares a manufacturing account in addition to the trading and profit-and-loss account. This is required to account for different categories of stock and to provide information on the production process. The production process involves the business in the following costs:

- **Direct costs** – All costs that can be directly and easily attributable to specific products are classed as direct costs. Direct costs vary with the level of production. There may be other costs, such as electricity to power the production process that also vary with production; but because they are difficult to allocate accurately to work done, they are treated as factory overheads. The total of all direct costs is called **prime cost**.

- **Direct materials** – Direct materials are the raw materials purchased from suppliers. To calculate the amount of stock used we use a similar calculation as applied to stock in the trading account:

		£
	Opening stock of raw materials	22 500
Add	Purchases of raw materials	157 500
		180 000
Less	Closing stock of raw materials	25 000
=	Direct materials	155 000

- **Direct labour** – Employees whose work can be directly attributed to clearly identifiable products are called direct workers. The amount of their wages that is related to productive time is called direct wages or direct labour.

- **Direct expenses** – Expenses that can be attributed to particular products are called direct expenses. They include work sub-contracted out, such as specialist machining, and royalties paid to use a product or production process that has been patented.

- **Factory overheads** – All costs associated with the production process which cannot be attributed to specific products are classified as factory overheads. These include apportionments of general business expenses such as site rent and rates, in addition to more specific factory-related items such as production supervision that may not be attributable to specific products.

Total production cost is prime cost plus factory overhead.

The cost of manufactured finished goods is transferred to the trading account after an adjustment has been made for changes in the value of work in progress. This adjustment is made because the trading account is concerned only with finished goods ready for sale. An example is shown in Figure 18.12.

The balance sheet of a manufacturing business will be similar to that of a trading business. The only exception will be the analysis of stocks under current assets. For Johnson Pressings Ltd the section current assets will be:

Current assets:	£
Raw materials	25 000
Work in progress	42 000
Finished goods	75 000
Debtors	90 000
Bank and cash	18 000
Total	250 000

Figure 18.12 A manufacturing, trading and profit-and-loss account

Johnson Pressings Ltd
Manufacturing, trading and profit-and-loss account
for year ended 31 December 199X

	£	£
Opening stock of raw materials	22 500	
Add purchases of raw materials	157 500	
	180 000	
Less closing stock of raw materials	25 000	
Direct materials		155 000
Direct labour		135 000
Direct expenses		28 000
Prime cost		318 000
Factory overheads		
Management and supervision	56 000	
Indirect wages	65 000	
Rent	50 000	
Power	35 000	
Depreciation of equipment	34 000	240 000
Total production cost		558 000
Add: Opening WIP		34 000
Less: Closing WIP		42 000
Production cost of completed units		
transferred to the trading account		550 000
Sales		910 000
Opening stock of finished goods	65 000	
Add: Production cost transfer	550 000	
	615 000	
Less: Closing stock of finished goods	75 000	540 000
Gross profit		370 000
Less expenses		
Administration costs	155 000	
Selling and distribution costs	115 000	270 000
Net profit		100 000

Tasks

1 Neeson Joinery, a sole trader and manufacturer of kitchen and bedroom furniture, have asked you to prepare a manufacturing, trading and profit-and-loss account for the year to 31 December 199X together with a balance sheet at that date. The trial balance for the year to 31 December 199X was as shown.

	Debit £	Credit £
Purchases/sales	210 200	635 140
Direct wages	147 540	
Overheads	187 500	
Raw materials at 1/1/9X	4 650	
WIP at 1/1/9X	12 980	
Finished goods at 1/1/9X	21 870	
Debtors/creditors	16 420	11 320
Bank	25 680	
Plant and machinery – cost/depreciation	64 630	28 610
Motor vehicles – cost/depreciation	32 900	16 300
Capital at 1/1/9X		58 000
Drawings	25 000	
	749 370	749 370

- Stocks at 31 December 199X were valued at: raw materials £7850, WIP £13 410 and finished goods £28 340.
- Depreciation has already been charged and is included in overheads.
- Overhead costs are to be apportioned 50 per cent to the factory, 30 per cent to distribution and 20 per cent to administration.

2 Brampton Tools Ltd manufactures machine tools for the automotive industry. You have been asked to prepare manufacturing, trading and profit-and-loss accounts for the year to 31 December 199X together with a balance sheet at that date. The trial balance for the year to 31 December 199X was as shown on the next page.

	Debit £	Credit £
Purchase of raw materials	825 500	
Raw material stock at 1/1/9X	240 980	
Work in progress at 1/1/9X	195 650	
Finished goods stock at 1/1/9X	85 210	
Carriage in	3 650	
Motor vehicle expenses	16 940	
Direct wages	650 830	
Indirect wages	186 420	
Salaries	298 320	
Electricity	60 100	
Consumable materials (oil, rag etc.)	23 654	
Repairs and maintenance of equipment	94 600	
Rates	79 000	
Stationery	25 423	
Salespersons' travel and subsistence	62 489	
Land	350 000	
Buildings – cost	950 000	
Equipment – cost	843 200	
Motor vehicles – cost	296 700	
Buildings – depreciation		160 250
Equipment – depreciation		356 000
Motor vehicles – depreciation		124 980
Sales		2 801 236
Debtors/creditors	230 850	56 810
Bank		5 630
Provision for bad debts		4 500
Share capital – 650 000 shares @ £1		650 000
Motor vehicle disposal account		200
Profit-and-loss account		1 359 910
	5 519 516	5 519 516

- Stock balances at 31/12/9X were: finished goods stock £65 237, WIP £258 115, raw materials £210 790.
- The company directors have proposed a final dividend of 15p per share.
- Corporation tax of £124 300 is to be provided for.
- The following accruals are to be made: electricity £5900, motor expenses £560.
- Bad debts provision is to be adjusted to 2 per cent of debtors.
- Rates account includes an annual payment of £64 000 to 31/3/9Y.
- Fixed assets purchased on 1/10/9X: motor vehicles £9600, equipment £28 800.
- The sale of a distribution van on 30/6/9X, purchased exactly three years earlier for £7200, resulted in proceeds of £2000.
- Depreciation is to be provided from the month of purchase to the month of disposal at the following rates: buildings 2 per cent pa on cost, equipment 10 per cent pa on cost, motor vehicles 25 per cent pa on cost (no

assets were in the last year of their estimated useful lives).
- Costs are to be apportioned to the company's departments on the following bases:

	Factory	Distribution	Administration
Motor vehicle costs	20%	60%	20%
Electricity	80%	10%	10%
Buildings	60%	20%	20%
Equipment	75%	5%	20%
Salaries	30%	30%	40%

Service businesses

Service businesses include professional firms (such as lawyers and accountants), office cleaning, property maintenance and staff agencies. What tends to differentiate these businesses from others is the fact they do not provide tangible goods to any great extent, perhaps only using consumable materials such as cleaning materials, stationery etc. Hence there is no need for a trading account, only a profit-and-loss account and balance sheet. An example is shown in Figure 18.13.

Figure 18.13 Profit-and-loss account for service business

Higson Office Cleaning Profit-and-loss account For the year ended 31 December 1995		
	£	£
Sales		150 000
Less expenses:		
Salaries and wages	90 000	
Office costs	10 000	
Travel	20 000	120 000
Net profit		30 000

There are some businesses generally classified as being part of the service sector that do utilise stocks to a significant degree. A business involved in landscape gardening may stock plants and trees that constitute a large proportion of the costs of running the business. Garages use car parts that can form a significant value of the work done. Trading accounts would be appropriate in these circumstances.

It is therefore difficult to generalise about the most appropriate format of accounts because of the diversity of activities. In particular, the holding and use of significant stocks will determine whether a trading account is necessary.

Tasks

1 *Non-trading sole trader exercise.* The following trial balance at 31 December 199X has been extracted from the books of Starbright Cleaning Services, an office cleaning firm.

	£	£
Stationery/post	120	
Wages	26 580	
Motor vehicle – cost and depreciation	8 800	4 400
Equipment – cost and depreciation	3 300	900
Sales		46 600
Debtors	5 900	
Bank	2 420	
Drawings	14 870	
Capital at 1/1/9X		11 360
Telephone	590	
Cleaning materials	680	
	63 260	63 260

- Depreciation is calculated straight-line over four years for the motor vehicle and straight-line over three years for the equipment.
- Accruals are to be made in respect of the following costs: telephone £100 and wages of £230.

Your task is to prepare for Starbright Cleaning Services the profit-and-loss account for the year ended 31 December 199X and a balance sheet at that date.

2 *Non-trading limited company exercise.* The following trial balance at 31 December 199X has been extracted from the books of Innovative Solutions Ltd, a firm of management consultants.

	£	£
Rent	10 000	
Electricity	2 380	
Stationery/post	3 600	
Salaries – directors and staff	124 600	
Furniture fixtures and fittings – cost and depreciation	15 400	6 400
Equipment – cost and depreciation	9 200	4 600
Consultancy fees		200 800
Commissions		19 330
Debtors/creditors	30 950	600
Bank	28 640	
Dividends paid	40 000	
Share capital		20 000
Profit-and-loss account		13 040
	264 770	264 770

- Authorised share capital consists of 30 000 £1 ordinary shares.
- Corporation tax of £17 000 is to be provided for.
- Depreciation is calculated on the reducing-balance basis: 50 per cent for equipment and 20 per cent for furniture, fixtures and fittings.
- Accruals are to be made for the following costs: electricity £200, telephone £300, and staff bonuses of £3250.

Your task is to prepare for Innovative Solutions Ltd the profit-and-loss account for the year ended 31 December 199X and a balance sheet at that date.

Cash flow statement

The **cash flow statement** is the third primary financial statement, and it complements the profit-and-loss account and balance sheet. A cash flow statement is required by Financial Reporting Standard 1 for all companies not classified as 'small' by the Companies Acts. The cash flow statement provides valuable information concerning how financial resources flow through a company during an accounting period. It redresses a weakness of the balance sheet that only provides details of financial resources at a point in time. Essentially the statement is concerned with identifying where cash came from and went to during the accounting period.

If we look at two balance sheets from the same business (see Figure 18.14) we can explain the movement in cash in terms of what has happened to the other balances.

Figure 18.14 Balance sheets from two consecutive years

	199Y (£000s)	199X (£000s)	Change (£000s)
Fixed assets	150	125	+25
Current assets			
Stocks	25	22	+3
Debtors	30	35	–5
Cash	5	15	–10
	60	72	
Current liabilities	20	25	–5
Net current assets	40	47	
Total net assets	190	172	
Capital and reserves			
Share capital	110	100	+10
Profit-and-loss account	80	72	+8
	190	172	

Item	(£000s)	Explanation
Retained profit for the year	+8	The difference between the two P & L account balances
Increase in stocks	−3	An increase in stocks uses cash
Decrease in debtors	+5	A decrease in debtors indicates that customers paid more than the current period's sales that were included in the profit figure above
Decrease in creditors	−5	More cash was paid to suppliers than the period's purchases
Purchase of fixed assets	−25	An outflow of cash
Share issue	+10	An inflow of cash
Decrease in cash	−10	This reconciles with the balance sheet changes, 15 down to 5

We can now construct a simple cash flow statement as shown below.

Unfortunately most business accounts are not this simple. Some of the balance sheet items may be affected by more than one type of transaction. Let us examine possible reasons for item changes.

Fixed assets in the balance sheet will be stated net of the following movements:

- Acquisition of new assets – an outflow of cash.
- Less net book value of disposals – not a cash flow.
- Less depreciation – not a cash flow.

Share capital and loan stock will be stated net of the following movements:

- Raising new finance – issues of shares and debentures and taking out new loans.
- Less repayment of finance – redemption of shares and debentures and the repayment of loans.

Retained profit includes a number of items that are not necessarily cash flows:

- Profits and losses on the sale of fixed assets and investments. These will have been calculated by deducting asset book values that may not have been paid for in the current period.
- Depreciation will have been charged and this is a book entry only.
- Dividends proposed and tax provided for will not have been paid.
- Transfers from the profit-and-loss account to other reserves are book entries only.

As the profit-and-loss account balance changes for such a disparate number of reasons, not all cash-related, it is generally accepted that the account changes should be analysed. In particular, there is a need to provide greater insight into the ability of the business to generate cash from operating activities. The cash flow statement required by FRS 1 has the following outline format:

- *Cash inflow (outflow) from operating activities* – The operating cash flow is usually derived by adjusting operating profit for non-cash items, such as depreciation, and by changes in working capital (see the reconciliation for the example below).
- *Net cash inflow (outflow) from returns on investments and servicing of finance* – Investment returns include dividends and interest received. Servicing of finance includes dividends paid to the company's shareholders and interest paid on debentures, loans and finance leases.
- *Taxation* – Corporation tax on profits actually paid in the period.
- *Investing activities* – These relate primarily to the net cash flow of the acquisition and disposal of fixed assets.
- *Net cash inflow (outflow) before financing* – Sub-total of all the above cash flows.
- *Financing* – Cash inflows include share and debenture issues and new loans taken out. These are stated net of loan repayments and redemption of existing shares and debentures.
- *Increase (decrease) in cash* – The total of the above cash flows will equal the change in cash (on hand and at the bank) and cash equivalents (investments that were within three months of maturity when acquired).

Example of a cash flow statement

The balance sheet and other information concerning Divest Ltd for the year ended 31 December 199Y are provided below and in Figure 18.15. We are required to prepare a cash flow statement consistent with the requirements of FRS 1.

Extract from the profit-and-loss account 199Y

	(£000s)
Operating profit	40
Interest receivable	5
Interest payable	(30)
Profit before tax	15
Taxation	(10)
Profit after tax	5
Dividend	(125)
Retained profit for the year	(120)

Figure 18.15 Balance sheets for Divest Ltd

Divest Limited Balance sheet for the year ended 31 December 199Y	199Y (£000s)	199X (£000s)
Fixed assets		
Leasehold property	400	500
Equipment	200	300
	600	800
Current assets		
Stocks	200	250
Debtors	120	140
Bank	50	10
	370	400
Current liabilities		
Creditors	50	110
Proposed dividends	100	40
Taxation	10	20
	160	170
Net current assets	210	230
Total assets less current liabilities	810	1 030
Long term liabilities – debentures @ 12%	200	300
Net assets	610	730
Capital and reserves		
Ordinary share capital – £1 shares	500	500
Profit-and-loss account	110	230
	610	730

- Depreciation is charged on the reducing-balance basis: leasehold property 2 per cent and equipment 20 per cent.
- Proceeds from fixed asset disposals amounted to £150 000. Depreciation is charged for fully in the year of disposal.
- During 199Y the proposed dividend and tax relating to 199X were paid. In addition, an interim dividend of 5p a share was also paid.
- Debentures with nominal value of £100 000 were redeemed on 30 June 199Y at par value.

The answer can be worked as follows:

- Leasehold property: the property will have been depreciated by £500 000 × 2% = £10 000, so the net book value of property disposed of is £90 000 (£100 000– £10 000).
- Equipment: the equipment will have been depreciated by £300 000 × 20% = £60 000, therefore the net book value of property disposed of is £40 000 (£100 000–£60 000).
- Sale proceeds are £150 000, hence we know that included

in the year's profit is £20 000 for profit on sale of fixed assets (£150 000–£90 000–£40 000).
- As there are no balance sheet entries for interest payable or interest receivable we know that the profit and loss figures were those actually received and paid.
- Dividends paid comprise those in current liabilities last year plus this year's interim dividends. The current year's proposed dividends are not a cash flow.
- Tax paid relates to last year's profits and included as a £20 000 current liability in 199X.
- The only change in finance was the redemption of debentures, £100 000.

Our next task is to calculate operating cash. The following is a reconciliation of operating cash flows to operating profit:

	(£000s)
Operating profit	40
Add depreciation charged – lease	10
– equipment	60
Less profit on sale of fixed assets	(20)
Add decrease in stocks	50
Add decrease in debtors	20
Less decrease in creditors	(60)
Operating cash	100

We now have enough information to construct the cash flow statement, which is shown in Figure 18.16.

Figure 18.16 The cash flow statement for Divest Ltd

Divest Limited Cash flow statement for the year ended 31 December 199Y	(£000s)	(£000s)
Net cash inflow from operating activities		100
Returns on investments and servicing of finance:		
Interest received	5	
Interest paid	(30)	
Dividends paid (25+40)	(65)	(90)
Taxation		(20)
Investing activities:		
Disposal of fixed assets		150
Net cash inflow before financing		140
Financing activities:		
Redemption of debentures		(100)
Increase in cash		40

You should now verify that the cash flow reconciles to the change in cash and cash equivalents ('cash in bank') in the balance sheets in Figure 18.15.

It is evident from the cash flow that the providers of finance are withdrawing most of the profits earned in the period and that the reduction in debt was only achieved by reducing the asset base of the business. The implications for future performance can only be assessed with the aid of additional information, perhaps in this case with an explanation in the directors' report.

Task

The balance sheet and other information concerning Liquidity Ltd for the year ended 31 December 199Y are provided below. You are required to prepare a cash flow statement consistent with the requirements of FRS 1.

Liquidity Ltd
Balance sheet
for the year ended 31 December 199Y

	199Y (£000s)	199X (£000s)
Fixed assets		
Plant	320	300
Motor	160	150
	480	450
Current assets		
Stocks	120	100
Debtors	140	150
Bank	0	50
	260	300
Current liabilities		
Creditors	45	50
Bank overdraft	15	0
Proposed dividends	25	30
Taxation	25	30
	110	110
Net current assets	150	190
Total assets less current liabilities	630	640
Long term liabilities – debentures @ 10%	(50)	(100)
Net assets	580	540
Capital and reserves		
Ordinary share capital	300	300
Profit-and-loss account	280	240
	580	540

Extract from the profit-and-loss account

	199Y (£000s)
Operating profit	100
Interest paid	(10)
Profit before tax	90
Taxation	(25)
Profit after tax	65
Dividend – proposed	(25)
Retained profit for the year	40

- Depreciation is charged as a percentage of net book values: plant at 10 per cent and motor vehicles at 20 per cent. Depreciation is not charged in the year of purchase.
- During 199Y, the proposed dividend and tax relating to 199X were paid.
- Debentures with nominal value of £50 000 were redeemed on 31 December 199Y at par value.

Although the cash flow statement is a requirement for companies, it can provide valuable information for all types of businesses. There is no reason why a cash flow in modified form cannot also be prepared for sole traders and partnerships.

Summary

We have examined how three principal financial reports, the profit-and-loss, balance sheet and cash flow statement are prepared. In addition we have considered how they are adjusted to satisfy generally accepted accounting principles and modifications to format to adapt them to different business activities and business forms.

When preparing financial reports we must always be aware that they are only of value if they are comprehensible to the user and satisfy the need for information that is relevant to the situation. For reports to be used by persons external to the business we must comply with accounting standards and legislation. For internal reports where we are not constrained by regulation, the accountant must identify the specific needs of management.

Further reading

- *Corporate Reports – Their Interpretation and Use in Business* by Peter Walton and Michael Bond. Stanley Thornes, 1986.
- *Finance and Accounting*, 3rd edition, by R. S. Giles and J. W. Capel. Macmillan, 1994.
- *Students' Newsletter* from the Chartered Association of Certified Accountants, issued monthly.
- *Students' Guide to Accounting and Financial Reporting Standards 1994/95* by Geoff Black. DPP, 1994/5.
- *Workbook of Accounting Standards*, 2nd edition, by Alan Sangster. Pitman, 1993.
- *Accounts Demystified – How to Understand and Use Company Accounts* by Anthony Rice. Pitman, 1993.
- *Business Accounting I*, 6th edition, by Frank Wood. Pitman, 1993.
- *Accounting in the Business Evironment* by John Watts. Pitman, 1993.
- *Accounting and Finance – a Firm Foundation* by Alan Pizzey. Cassell, 1990.

Marketing

19 Customers and behaviour

On completion of this chapter students should be able to:

■ identify and evaluate criteria used to segment markets

■ identify approaches used to understand buyer behaviour and evaluate their contribution to marketing practice

■ identify and evaluate the relationship between brand loyalty and company image.

Segmentation

Not all customers are the same. They do not all have the same tastes or want the same things. It is possible to divide the customer population into discrete **segments**, a process we can liken to dividing an orange into segments. For example, Levi makes jeans, but the jeans market is split into a number of segments all catered for by Levi. One way of segmenting this market is by sex, another way is by type of jeans – loose-fit, regular-fit, stone-washed, pre-washed, etc. (see Figure 19.1).

Figure 19.1 Two ways of dividing up (segmenting) the jeans market

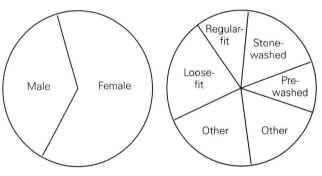

Segmentation can be defined as the strategy whereby a firm partitions the market into sub-markets (segments) which will respond in similar ways to marketing inputs.

Tom Cannon, in his book *Basic Marketing: Principles and Practice*, supports this view when he defines market segmentation as the 'subdividing of a market into distinct and increasingly homogeneous sub-groups of customers, where any group can conceivably be selected as a target market to be met with a distinct marketing mix'. The two points he makes are:

■ segments or parts of the market are more homogeneous (similar) than the market as a whole
■ each of these parts of the market can be reached with a specific **marketing mix**.

Segmentation enables an organisation to develop a marketing mix which satisfies the requirements of different *groups* of customers. This can be contrasted with **market aggregation** or **undifferentiated marketing** where a single marketing mix is developed for the whole market (hence 'mass marketing'). Today, because of the increasing trend towards market segmentation, it is very difficult to think of a product that is not differentiated in some way. For example, there are many different types of flour and sugar. Even Saxo table salt, which used to sell to virtually everybody in this country, has been differentiated, and there are more products for health-conscious consumers.

Reasons for market segmentation

Market segmentation enables an organisation to *identify marketing opportunities*. By understanding different parts of the market as well as the market as a whole, it may be easier to identify opportunities. Segmentation may, therefore, help the organisation to pursue four types of product and market opportunities. These are:

- *Market penetration* – to increase the value/volume of sales in current markets
- *Product development* – which offers a wider product range to existing markets by catering more closely for the needs of different segments
- *Market development* – to develop existing products in segments identified in new markets
- *Diversification opportunities* – involving entry into new markets with new products.

Market segmentation enables the organisation to *maximise the efficiency* of its marketing efforts by using a different marketing mix for each market segment. Undifferentiated marketing is sometimes said to be like firing a blunderbuss to pepper the whole marketplace, whereas segmentation is like firing a rifle instead (see Figure 19.2). By hitting the target – customers – more efficiently, without wasting ammunition, marketing activities become more efficient and this helps to improve profitability.

Figure 19.2 Marketing by blunderbuss or by rifle

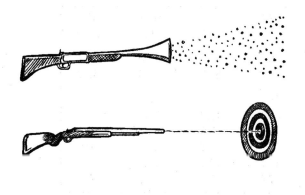

Another reason for market segmentation is that it helps an organisation to develop a better understanding of **customer needs and requirements**. By doing this it can make fine adjustments to the marketing mix in each segment, and this allows it to respond even more closely to any changes which may need to take place. This may enable some organisations to dominate certain market segments and gain **competitive advantages**.

In some circumstances, particularly for services, *specialists can be used for each of the market segments*. Banks, for example, may have small-business advisors, corporate advisors and personal financial advisors, each with different knowledge and different roles.

Segmentation allows *resources* to be used more efficiently. For example, the efficiency of activities is likely to improve when they are concentrated on those sectors most likely to respond to such activities. This facilitates budgeting and financial analysis which can then take into account activities from each segment. This in turn helps aid the process of planning, which helps customer needs to be planned for with greater precision.

Three stages of market segmentation

There are generally accepted to be three phases in the market segmentation process (see Figure 19.3).

Figure 19.3 Three phases of the market segmentation process

- *Segmentation* – As we have seen, there are a number of different bases for segmentation which may depend on a number of variables – such as types of customers and markets.
- *Targeting* – When segments in a market have been identified, targeting takes place. This may involve aiming at a single segment with a single product, or offering a single product to the whole market, or offering a number of products to a number of segments.
- *Positioning* – The positioning process now begins. This involves using the marketing mix (in a way which takes into account the thoughts and perceptions of consumers) to position the product in a particular place in a segment relative to other products and brands.

Case Study
Repositioning Lean Cuisine

The Findus Lean Cuisine range was repositioned in a bid to revive falling shares against rivals Weight Watchers and Healthy Options. Lean Cuisine, once the market leader, had a 32 per cent value share compared with Weight Watchers' 42.5 per cent and Healthy Options' 25.6 per cent. The repositioning process involved the development of new packaging design, extending the Lean Cuisine brand, lower food prices and a £3 million though-the-line push to reposition the brand away from calorie-counted meals to low-fat, tasty and nutritional food.

The change of strategy followed a difficult time for Lean Cuisine, which was hit hard by its main rivals, Heinz and Birds Eye Walls. Findus felt that, by pricing products too highly, it had lost market share. Their aim was to reposition their product more competitively on price and put more emphasis on the quality of recipes and nutritional value.

Findus recognised that one problem arose from packaging, which emphasised the number of calories in their meals. The feeling was that this tended to put consumers off, on the assumption that 'low calorie' meals meant 'reduced taste'. New packaging continued to emphasise that the meal was low in fat and provided calorie information, but better photography and appetising descriptions helped to reinforce the image of a tasty and nutritious meal.

According to their account director at Light & Coley, the brief was to give the brand a healthy repositioning. Other brands had built up their market share by keeping their prices 20p on average lower than Lean Cuisine. Price reductions were therefore central to the new strategy. Despite the competition, the segment for 'light meals' has increasing importance for all competitors and has experienced a 47 per cent growth since 1987.

Questions for discussion

1 *What do you know about the market for frozen meals?*
2 *Which segments does Findus target?*
3 *Explain how and why Findus decided to reposition its Lean Cuisine range.*
4 *What other strategies could Findus have adopted?*

Choosing a basis for market segmentation

Demographic segmentation

Demographic factors, which can be measured with relative precision, have helped many organisations to define a base on which to segment their market. Because demographic variables can be closely related to customer needs and purchasing behaviour, this helps producers to target their products more effectively. Demographic segmentation may involve dividing the population into discrete segments – for example by age for clothes retailing, by sex for the sale of cosmetics, by family size for different sized packages of breakfast cereals, or in many other ways.

Task

Study Figure 19.4 which shows projected population figures for the UK. Comment on how these demographic changes

Figure 19.4 Projected population figures

Projected population figures		1992 (base)	1995	2000	2010	2020
Home population	millions	58.0	58.6	59.6	61.1	62.1
	index	100.0	101.0	102.8	105.4	107.0
Sex distribution	males %	48.9	49.0	49.3	49.6	49.7
	females %	51.1	51.0	50.7	50.4	50.3
Age distribution	0–14 %	19.3	19.5	19.5	18.1	17.2
	15–29 %	22.0	20.6	18.9	19.1	18.5
	30–44 %	21.1	21.6	22.6	19.9	18.1
	45–59 %	16.9	17.8	18.5	20.2	20.9
	60–74 %	13.7	13.5	13.0	14.9	16.6
	75+ %	7.0	7.0	7.5	7.8	8.7

might affect the way in which the UK *life assurance industry* targets its customers.

Segmentation by age is widely applied. A good example is the way in which banks and building societies develop products for students, young children, elderly customers, etc. Many products are also segmented by gender – clothing, alcohol, cosmetics and cars are segmented in such a way. Marketers may also segment according to ethnic background, particularly for clothes, food and music. Levels of education can be a segmentation variable – some products clearly require a higher level of intellectual ability (for example, it would expected that professional people with a higher level of educational attainment would be more likely to buy broadsheet newspapers than tabloids).

Socio-economic segmentation

Income, occupation and social class are fundamental determinants of the pattern of segmentation adopted within a market. Income in particular is a useful way of dividing a market as it directly affects people's purchases.

Expenditure and consumption patterns can be broken up according to the 'social class' of the consumer through **socio-economic grouping**. Assigning people to classes according to income is called **social stratification**. Each class has a pattern of behaviour which serves to reinforce its purchasing and consumption patterns. Socio-economic groups classify people according to their similarity of income, occupation and education. One of the best known classifications used to divide people in the UK is shown in Figure 19.5.

This form of socio-economic grouping provides a reliable picture of the relationship between occupation and income. Members of a group will give similar priorities to their needs. For example, we would expect As and Bs to spend more of their income on private education, private health care and antiques than the other socio-economic groupings.

Lifestyle segmentation

Lifestyle is another demographically based variable, but one which groups individuals according to how they spend their time – which has links with family, income, occupation, culture and education. It deals with people and not the product and attempts to relate lifestyle patterns to purchasing behaviour.

Figure 19.5 Socio-economic groupings

Socio-economic group	Social class	Type of occupation	Examples
A	Upper/upper-middle class	Higher managerial, administrative, professional	Surgeon, director of a large company
B	Middle class	Intermediate managerial, professional, administrative	Bank manager, headteacher, surveyor
C1	Lower middle class	Supervisory, junior managerial or administrative, clerical	Bank clerk, nurse, teacher estate agent
C2	Skilled working class	Skilled manual workers	Joiner, welder, foreman
D	Working class	Semi-skilled and	Driver, postman, porter
E	Those at lowest level of subsistence	Low-paid/unemployed	Casual workers, state pensioners, unemployed

Over recent years, organisations have paid increasing attention to the lifestyles of consumers. A lifestyle is a behaviour pattern adopted by a particular sub-section of a community. By understanding such a lifestyle producers can develop products and target them at this group. For example, someone 'upwardly mobile' and ambitious will be seeking an affluent lifestyle and a higher material standard of living. The British Yuppy is reputed to be a young (24–35), well-educated and upwardly mobile professional. Affluence comes from working hard in particular areas (e.g. high finance) and money is spent on expensive clothes, cars and homes in high-status districts. Agencies frequently advise their clients on how to design and position new products to appeal to groups with similar lifestyle patterns.

Psychographics is one way used to measure lifestyle. There are some problems with this as lifestyle is difficult to measure, and not all consumer needs are related to lifestyle. It may also be difficult to reach customers with a particular lifestyle. However, lifestyle analysis does provide another useful basis on which to divide a market.

Sagacity lifestyle grouping, for example, works on the principle that people have different behavioural patterns and aspirations as they go through life. Four main stages of the life-cycle are thus defined, further sub-divided according to income and occupation groups (white-collar or blue-collar occupation) (see Figure 19.6).

The life-cycle stages are defined as follows:

- *Dependent* – mainly under-24s, living at home or full-time students
- *Pre-family* – under-35s, who have established their own household but have no children.
- *Family* – parents, under 65, with one or more children in the household.
- *Late* – includes all adults whose children have left home, or who are over 35 and childless.

The *occupation groups* are:

- *White* – head of household in the ABC1 occupation group.
- *Blue* – head of household in the C2DE occupation group.

Another simple way of generalising about lifestyle identifies four categories:

- *Upwardly mobile and ambitious* – seeking a more affluent lifestyle and a higher material standard of living. This type of consumer would be looking for new ways of making money and be prepared to adopt new products.
- *Traditional and sociable* – conformation to group norms and patterns of behaviour provide reassurance. Patterns of purchase and consumption would be conformist.
- *Security and status seeking* – lifestyle emphasises status, income and security. Well-known brands which help to emphasise status and security are purchased.
- *Hedonistic preference* – lifestyle emphasises enjoyment now with the immediate satisfaction of needs. Little thought is given to the future.

Geographic segmentation

Geographic segmentation assumes that consumers in different regions may be affected by climate, natural factors, population density, different levels of income, etc. By dividing markets into regions it is possible to recognise and cater for the needs of customers in the regions. For example, certain countries are assumed to have common characteristics which influence buying attitudes. In international marketing it makes sense to analyse particular market segments in terms of such characteristics as population, income per head, trade

Figure 19.6 Sagacity life-cycle groupings

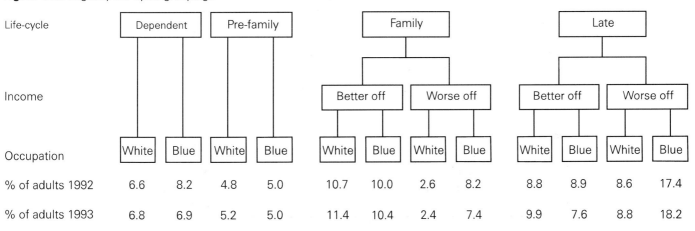

Life-cycle	Dependent		Pre-family		Family				Late			
Income					Better off		Worse off		Better off		Worse off	
Occupation	White	Blue	White	Blue	White	Blue	White	Blue	White	Blue	White	Blue
% of adults 1992	6.6	8.2	4.8	5.0	10.7	10.0	2.6	8.2	8.8	8.9	8.6	17.4
% of adults 1993	6.8	6.9	5.2	5.0	11.4	10.4	2.4	7.4	9.9	7.6	8.8	18.2

Figure 19.7 The markets of western Europe in 1992 (source: OECD)

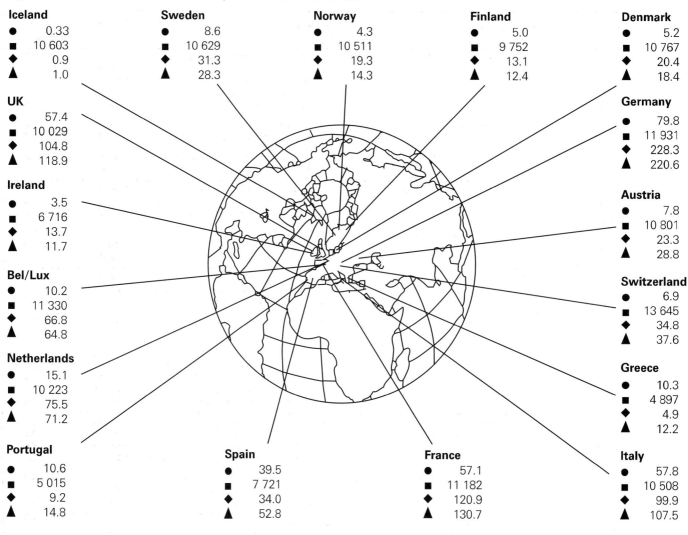

Iceland
- ● 0.33
- ■ 10 603
- ◆ 0.9
- ▲ 1.0

Sweden
- ● 8.6
- ■ 10 629
- ◆ 31.3
- ▲ 28.3

Norway
- ● 4.3
- ■ 10 511
- ◆ 19.3
- ▲ 14.3

Finland
- ● 5.0
- ■ 9 752
- ◆ 13.1
- ▲ 12.4

Denmark
- ● 5.2
- ■ 10 767
- ◆ 20.4
- ▲ 18.4

UK
- ● 57.4
- ■ 10 029
- ◆ 104.8
- ▲ 118.9

Germany
- ● 79.8
- ■ 11 931
- ◆ 228.3
- ▲ 220.6

Ireland
- ● 3.5
- ■ 6 716
- ◆ 13.7
- ▲ 11.7

Austria
- ● 7.8
- ■ 10 801
- ◆ 23.3
- ▲ 28.8

Bel/Lux
- ● 10.2
- ■ 11 330
- ◆ 66.8
- ▲ 64.8

Switzerland
- ● 6.9
- ■ 13 645
- ◆ 34.8
- ▲ 37.6

Netherlands
- ● 15.1
- ■ 10 223
- ◆ 75.5
- ▲ 71.2

Greece
- ● 10.3
- ■ 4 897
- ◆ 4.9
- ▲ 12.2

Portugal
- ● 10.6
- ■ 5 015
- ◆ 9.2
- ▲ 14.8

Spain
- ● 39.5
- ■ 7 721
- ◆ 34.0
- ▲ 52.8

France
- ● 57.1
- ■ 11 182
- ◆ 120.9
- ▲ 130.7

Italy
- ● 57.8
- ■ 10 508
- ◆ 99.9
- ▲ 107.5

Key
- ● Population (millions)
- ■ GDP per capita (£s)
- ◆ Exports total (£ billion)
- ▲ Imports total

carried out by the country, as well as tastes, and the nature of competition in the market.

Figure 19.7 gives some useful indicators for businesses looking at the markets of western European countries.

Geo-demographic segmentation

The newest methods of segmentation combine geographic and demographic segmentation principles. These are based on the belief that households in a particular locality exhibit similar purchasing behaviour. The best known of the **geo-demographic methods** is that provided by

ACORN, which stands for A Classification Of Residential Neighbourhoods (see Figure 19.8).

Behaviouristic segmentation

This looks at **consumer behaviour patterns** – frequent/ infrequent purchase, loyalty to a product, etc. For example, one segment of the market may always purchase your product while another is made up of people who frequently switch brands. An experienced drinker may stick with Guinness, while an inexperienced one may try out a range of beers and stouts.

Figure 19.8 An ACORN profile of Great Britain

ACORN categories	ACORN groups	ACORN types	Number	Percentage of total
A THRIVING	1 Wealthy Achievers, Suburban Areas	1.1 Wealthy suburbs, large detached houses	1 442 502	2.5
		1.2 Villages with wealthy commuters	1 797 707	3.1
		1.3 Mature affluent home owning areas	1 528 768	2.7
		1.4 Affluent suburbs, older families	2 097 330	3.7
		1.5 Mature, well-off suburbs	1 691 487	3.0
	2 Affluent Greys, Rural Communities	2.6 Agricultural villages, home based workers	913 933	1.6
		2.7 Holiday retreats, older people, home based workers	397,028	0.7
	3 Prosperous Pensioners, Retirement Areas	2.8 Home owning areas, well-off older residents	798 595	1.4
		3.9 Private flats, elderly people	538 478	0.9
B EXPANDING	4 Affluent Executives, Family Areas	4.10 Affluent working families with mortgages	1 209 200	2.1
		4.11 Affluent working couples with mortgages, new homes	727 725	1.3
		4.12 Transient workforces, living at their place of work	199 689	0.4
	5 Well-Off Workers, Family Areas	5.13 Home owning family areas	1 473 807	2.6
		5.14 Home owning family areas, older children	1 708 143	3.0
		5.15 Families with mortgages, younger children	1 265 830	2.2
C RISING	6 Affluent Urbanites, Town & City Areas	6.16 Well-off town & city areas	615 061	1.1
		6.17 Flats & mortgages, singles & young working couples	425 844	0.8
		6.18 Furnished flats & bedsits, younger single people	253 342	0.4
	7 Prosperous Professionals, Metropolitan Areas	7.19 Apartments, young professional singles & couples	644 936	1.1
		7.20 Gentrified multi-ethnic areas	545 485	1.0
	8 Better-Off Executives, Inner City Areas	8.21 Prosperous enclaves, highly qualified executives	419 968	0.7
		8.22 Academic centres, students & young professionals	374 489	0.7
		8.23 Affluent city centre areas, tenements & flats	252 981	0.4
		8.24 Partially gentrified multi-ethnic areas	399 302	0.7
		8.25 Converted flats & bedsits, single people	498 993	0.9
D SETTLING	9 Comfortable Middle Agers, Mature Home Owning Areas	9.26 Mature established home owning areas	1 874 129	3.3
		9.27 Rural areas, mixed occupations	1 962 700	3.4
		9.28 Established home owning areas	2 275 878	4.0
		9.29 Home owning areas, council tenants, retired people	1 504 114	2.6
	10 Skilled Workers, Home Owning Areas	10.30 Established home owning areas, skilled workers	2 568 946	4.5
		10.31 Home owners in older properties, younger workers	1 737 110	3.1
		10.32 Home owning areas with skilled workers	1 768 020	3.1
E ASPIRING	11 New Home Owners, Mature Communities	11.33 Council areas, some new home owners	2 160 798	3.8
		11.34 Mature home owning areas, skilled workers	1 753 391	3.1
		11.35 Low rise estates, older workers, new home owners	1 608 442	2.8
	12 White-Collar Workers, Better-Off Multi-Ethnic Areas	12.36 Home owning multi-ethnic areas, young families	633 900	1.1
		12.37 Multi-occupied town centres, mixed occupations	1 037 306	1.8
		12.38 Multi-ethnic areas, white collar workers	602 606	1.1
F STRIVING	13 Older People, Less Prosperous Areas	11.39 Home owners, small council flats, single pensioners	1 083 493	1.9
		13.40 Council areas, older people, health problems	969 253	1.7
	14 Council Estate Residents, Better-Off Homes	14.41 Better-off council areas, new home owners	1 368 305	2.4
		14.42 Council areas, young families, some new home owners	1 711 087	3.0
		14.43 Council areas, young families, many lone parents	894 221	1.6
		14.44 Multi-occupied terraces, multi-ethnic areas	483 733	0.9
		14.45 Low rise council housing, less well-off families	1 002 866	1.8
		14.46 Council areas, residents with health problems	1 097 833	1.9
	15 Council Estate Residents, High Unemployment	15.47 Estates with high unemployment	631 135	1.1
		15.48 Council flats, elderly people, health problems	382 915	0.7
		15.49 Council flats, very high unemployment, singles	495 479	0.9
	16 Council Estate Residents, Greatest Hardship	16.50 Council areas, high unemployment, lone parents	1 055 713	1.9
		16.51 Council flats, greatest hardship, many lone parents	516 253	0.9
	17 People in Multi-Ethnic, Low-Income Areas	17.52 Multi-ethnic, large families, overcrowding	358 707	0.6
		17.53 Multi-ethnic, severe unemployment, lone parents	553 009	1.0
		17.54 Multi-ethnic, high unemployment, overcrowding	297 252	0.5
	Unclassified		280 967	0.5
	TOTAL		56 870 164	100.0

Segmentation by use

Usage rate is an important factor to consider when segmenting a market. A small number of consumers may be responsible for the bulk of the purchases of a particular product. Certain products may also be used in a variety of ways. For example, software packages may have various uses for businesses in different industries. The software company then has to base its segmentation on the type of use to which the product is put.

Segmentation by type of organisation

Different organisations require different products. By understanding how organisations differ it may be possible to concentrate on one or more types of organisation. The **Standard Industrial Classification** (SIC) is the government's official way of classifying organisations and dividing markets, and this is frequently used as a basis for segmentation (see Figure 19.9).

Benefit segmentation

Benefit segmentation involves dividing a market in terms of the benefits that customers seek. In other words, the form of segmentation will roughly follow customer needs and requirements. For example, a car buyer may seek space and comfort. These benefits may be provided by a luxurious model or an estate car. Similarly, the market for drinkers may be segmented to provide benefits for customers who wish to purchase low-alcohol products or products with a high-alcohol content. Benefit segmentation will depend on whether benefits can be easily identified. Having identified these benefits they must be capable of being divided into recognisable segments.

Segmentation according to customer size

As organisations and individuals differ so widely, it may be possible to divide a market according to the **size of customer**. The needs of smaller customers and larger customers may be quite different. For example, larger customers may be offered a range of additional services as well as discounts.

Single and multivariable segmentation

It is important that the appropriate basis is used for segmentation. However, given the number and range of bases, it is possible to develop the segmentation process on either a single or multivariable basis.

Using a *single* base involves segmentation by using just one variable – for example, dividing a market geographically or according to age. Though this is fairly

Figure 19.9 Standard Industrial Classification groupings

DIVISION 0 – AGRICULTURE, FORESTRY AND FISHING
Farming and horticulture
Forestry
Commercial sea and inland fishing

DIVISION 1 – ENERGY AND WATER SUPPLY INDUSTRIES
Coal-mining and manufacture of solid fuels
Extraction of mineral oil and natural gas
Production and distribution of electricity, gas and other forms of energy

DIVISION 2 – EXTRACTION OF MINERALS AND ORES, MANUFACTURE OF METALS, MINERAL PRODUCTS AND CHEMICALS
Metal manufacture
Extraction of stone, clay, sand and gravel
Manufacture of non-metallic mineral products
Chemical industry (includes paints, varnishes and inks, pharmaceutical products, some perfumes, etc.)

DIVISION 3 – METAL GOODS, ENGINEERING AND VEHICLE INDUSTRIES
Foundries
Mechanical engineering
Electrical and electronic engineering
Manufacture of motor vehicles and parts
Instrument engineering

DIVISION 4 – OTHER MANUFACTURING INDUSTRIES
Food, drink and tobacco manufacturing industries
Textile industry
Manufacture of leather and leather goods
Timber and wooden furniture industries
Manufacture of paper and paper products, printing and printing products
Processing of rubber and plastics

DIVISION 5 – CONSTRUCTION
Construction and repairs
Demolition work
Civil engineering

DIVISION 6 – DISTRIBUTION, HOTELS AND CATERING, REPAIRS
Wholesale distribution
Retail distribution
Hotel and catering (restaurants, cafes and other eating places, public houses and hotel trade)
Repair of consumer goods and vehicles

DIVISION 7 – TRANSPORT AND COMMUNICATION
Railways and other inland transport
Air and sea transport
Support services to transport
Postal services and telecommunications

DIVISION 8 – BANKING, FINANCE, INSURANCE, BUSINESS SERVICES AND LEASING
Banking and finance
Insurance
Business services
Renting of movables
Owning and dealing in real estate

DIVISION 9 – OTHER SERVICES
Public administration, national defence and social security
Sanitary services
Education
Medical and other health services, veterinary services
Other services provided to the general public
Recreational services and other cultural services
Personal services (laundries, hairdressing and beauty parlours)
Domestic services
Diplomatic representation, international organisations, allied armed forces

easy and straightforward, it has only limited value because it lacks precision.

On the other hand, **multivariable segmentation** uses more than one basis to divide a market. This helps to target customer segments with greater precision. In Figure 19.10 the market is segmented according to three variables – socio-economic grouping, usage and region (for the sake of this example, we have identified only three). In the box highlighted you would find Bs from the South who are heavy users. As different bases for segmentation are added to this process, a larger number of segments results and this helps an organisation to target specific segments with a more appropriate marketing mix.

Figure 19.10 Example of multivariable segmentation

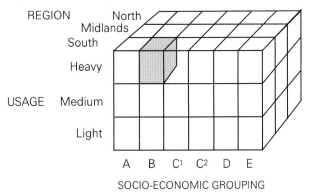

REGION
North
Midlands
South
Heavy
USAGE Medium
Light

A B C¹ C² D E
SOCIO-ECONOMIC GROUPING

Targeting

Segmentation helps an organisation to understand the market and break it up into segments which match customer needs and requirements. The next step is to identify one or more segments which has a need that can be met by the organisation. This process is known as **targeting**.

Concentration strategy

This involves targeting a single segment with a single product. The organisation's resources are thus concentrated on a very small part of the overall market (see Figure 19.11).

Figure 19.11 Concentrating on one segment

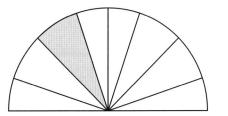

This is sometimes called **niche marketing**. For example, Porsche targets a very exclusive segment of the market for cars. The main benefit of this targeting strategy is that it allows for a high degree of *specialisation* and the development of a marketing mix focused specifically on

the needs of a distinctive group of customers. Another benefit is that it allows a small organisation to compete with a large organisation in an identified segment. One problem is that if product sales in that segment decline, this lack of diversification may affect the performance of the organisation.

Mass marketing strategy

If a single product is targeted at the whole market, this is known as **mass** or **undifferentiated marketing** (see Figure 19.12).

Figure 19.12 Mass-marketing strategy

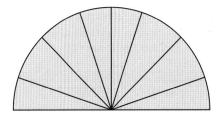

Probably the most famous example of a mass-marketing strategy was that for the Model T Ford. The great benefit of mass marketing is the economy of scale offered by mass production techniques. However, as this approach focuses on customer similarities rather than differences, today there are few examples in the private sector where mass marketing takes place.

Selective marketing

Selective marketing involves the use of a differentiated approach which targets a number of products at a number of segments in the market by tailoring a separate marketing mix for each segment (see Figure 19.13).

Figure 19.13 Tailoring a separate marketing mix for each segment

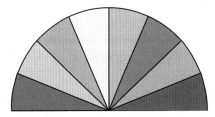

A good example of selective marketing is the market for cars, where the larger manufacturers target products at a whole range of segments – the Vauxhall Corsa, Tigra, Astra, Cavalier, Calibra, Omega, Frontera etc. . . . .

Positioning

Even though parts of the market may have been divided into segments, within each segment buyers will not all have identical needs. **Positioning** takes into account the thoughts and perceptions of customers, to place a product relative to other products and brands. The position is, therefore, how the product is perceived in the minds of customers. Targeted customers will then create an image of the product which helps them to think about how it stands out against competitors.

Positioning a product involves identifying the key variables considered to be important for customers. These are then used to develop and highlight the product's image. For example, price is a key variable for groceries, quality for furniture and taste for wine. Market research is therefore important in order to understand a customer's motivations for product purchase.

For example, product development for the Vauxhall Frontera involved a series of focus groups where the needs of potential customers were identified through discussion. These covered both the 'rational' and the 'emotional' reasons for purchase. The 'rational' reasons included being able to drive in confidence in adverse conditions, for off-road leisure pursuits, good driving visibility, safety, space, fuel economy and being able to park and drive easily around towns and cities. The 'emotional' reasons included the activity image, fun, off-road appearance, versatility, high-quality exterior styling, prestige of ownership and superiority. By understanding these benefits Vauxhall was then able to determine and develop the best market position for the product.

One visual tool used by marketers to develop a picture of customer perceptions is **perceptual mapping** (see Figure 19.14). This can be used to help to show how a customer views brands and their attributes. Positioning may involve introducing a product into a position where it competes head-on with other products in that position. Alternatively, it may involve moving into a position where there is a gap in the map, where consumers do not perceive products with similar attributes.

Repositioning involves moving the product away from its current market position. For example, a repositioning may take the product to another part of the market which helps to emphasise attributes and strengths over those of its nearest competitors.

So, what are the stages in the positioning plan? Having segmented the market and targeted the appropriate segments, an organisation must:

- find out about the perceptions of targeted customers
- develop a product which caters for such needs

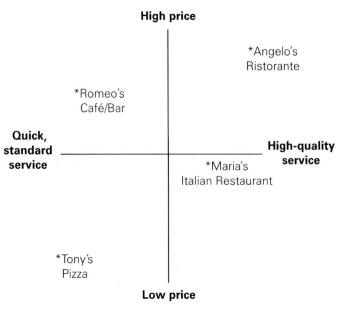

Figure 19.14 An example of perceptual mapping for the positioning of a number of Italian food outlets in the same town

- use customers' perceptions and image to identify the market position
- use marketing mix to develop attributes and image at the chosen market position
- communicate attributes and image to customers.

Buyer behaviour

The process of buying a good or service is not quite as simple as it might seem. People or organisations rarely go to their supplier without first thinking carefully about what they want. Wherever there is a choice, decisions have to be made and such decisions may be influenced by complex motives which reflect on consumer characteristics and personality. This analysis of the decision-making process is known as **buyer behaviour** and the need to understand such behaviour is a crucial issue in marketing.

Case Study
The 'north/south' divide!

The two lists below, compiled by Nielsen, show consumer choices of brands in the two parts of the island of Ireland. The surprise is that they are clearly so different. Only eight of the top 20 most popular brands in Northern Ireland figure

	Republic of Ireland	Northern Ireland
1	Lyons Tea	Coca-Cola
2	Coca-Cola	Ariel
3	7-Up	Flora
4	Pampers	Daz
5	Dairygold	Persil
6	Tayto (crisps)	Kellogg's Cornflakes
7	Yoplait (yoghurt)	Andrex
8	Kellogg's Cornflakes	Pampers
9	Barrys Tea	Pepsi-Cola
10	Persil	Nambarrie (tea)
11	Ariel	KitKat
12	Club (soft drinks)	Heinz Baked Beans
13	Maxwell House	Golden Wonder Crisps
14	Flora	Nescafé
15	Lucozade	Tayto (crisps)
16	Petit Filou	Müller (yoghurt)
17	KitKat	McKinney's Sugar
18	TK (soft drinks)	Punjana (tea)
19	Bold	Golden Cow Easi Spread
20	Knorr (packaged soup)	Kleenex Toilet Tissue

in the top 20 of the Republic and, of those, only Coca-Cola and Kellogg's Cornflakes occupy roughly the same position.

Ariel, Flora, Persil and KitKat are all higher in the Northern Ireland list while Pampers and Tayto crisps are lower. The two countries prefer different soft drinks and different brands of coffee. In Northern Ireland they like Nescafé and in the Republic they prefer Maxwell House. The question is, why are these differences so pronounced?

We know that the island is divided. The populace of Northern Ireland is mainly Protestant and pro-British while the Republic is independent and overwhelmingly Roman Catholic. We also know that there are political divisions, underlined by 25 years of political crisis. But are these divisions responsible for different choices of groceries?

The island has been divided for seven decades, and over this period we have seen the development of the consumer age. Even the oldest brands on the list were relatively new in 1920. As the 'two Irelands' have developed, differences have become greater. There are, for example, different supermarket chains in the Republic, and different television advertisements on different channels. Partition coincided with the arrival of radio. Since then they have seen mass production, pop music, commercialisation, motorways and the development of modern society as we know it. Quite naturally, many of the everyday things that everybody takes for granted have developed separately north and south of the border. Inevitably, as a result, choices in the kitchen have been affected. To the north they like Müller yoghurt, while to the south they like Yoplait and Petit Filou. The north likes Flora while the south prefers Dairygold.

Though the countries have many similarities, such as support for the rugby union side, the drinking of Guinness or Jameson's whiskeys and the watching of Coronation Street, the differences are probably more striking. Many would argue that were there to be an all-Ireland television channel many of these differences would soon erode. However, others view these differences as a more deep-rooted reflection of the development of two cultures.

Questions for discussion

1 *Try to explain why you think the list of leading brands varies so widely between the Republic of Ireland and Northern Ireland.*
2 *How, if at all, might an understanding of the differences in buyer behaviour help organisations to improve the performance of their brands?*

Features of buyer behaviour

Consumers want to make purchases in order to satisfy their needs and wants both today and for the future. We all regularly make decisions about our purchases. Sometimes these decisions are made quickly, while in other circumstances we may spend a lot of time weighing up the alternatives. These alternatives can be broken into three different categories:

- *Routine response behaviour* – This describes what happens when we frequently buy items of low value that require very little thought. For example, we might go into the newsagent to buy *The Times* every weekday morning.
- *Limited decision-making* – Some thought might be necessary if an unfamiliar brand comes to the market. For example, if a new chocolate brand is launched in competition to a well-known brand, the consumer might try to find out more information before making a purchase.
- *Extensive decision-making* – Some products are durables purchased less frequently. The buyer will need to think about the benefits of different products and will require further information.

Nearly all purchases involve an element of **risk**. Whenever we make a purchase we hope to obtain something that provides us with value for money as well as a certain degree of satisfaction. However, this does not always happen. For example, if goods are flawed or faulty they will not live up to our expectations or provide us with the satisfaction we require. The supplier can reduce this risk factor by providing reliable goods which persist in providing high levels of satisfaction. This helps to create **customer loyalty**. Customer loyalty will:

- create a customer base which provides regular income and turnover

- mean that customers will support their supplier when faced with new competitors and products
- provide goodwill which will help to develop and strengthen the supplier's market position.

The opposite to customer loyalty is **customer dissatisfaction**. Too much customer dissatisfaction will reduce customer loyalty and this may harm on organisation's image.

Impulse-buying contrasts directly with many patterns of behaviour. Impulse-buying occurs when we get a powerful urge to buy something immediately, and it may involve strong or irrational emotions. For some consumers impulse-buying may be regular behaviour. Marketers often try to encourage impulse-buying – for example, when placing confectionery close to supermarket checkouts.

Models of consumer purchase behaviour

Marketers need to understand the buying behaviour of their customers. Models of purchase behaviour help us to understand the various stages in the buying process as well as all of the influences which interact on the motive to purchase. By understanding this buying process, marketers can develop a strategy that recognises and takes into account the different buying responses.

Kotler and Armstrong, in developing their stimulus–response model of consumer behaviour in *Principles of Marketing*, refer to the consumer's mind before, during and after a purchase as the buyer's 'black box'. It is called this because it is sometimes very difficult to find out what goes on in this black box! Marketing stimuli in the form of the marketing mix, as well as other stimuli which may be economic, technological, cultural and political, influence buyer behaviour. In the black box the decision-making process takes place – and the response will be a decision about product, brand, dealer, and the timing or size of the purchase (see Figure 19.15).

Another frequently used model of the consumer buying process recognises five distinct stages. These are:

- problem or opportunity recognition
- information search
- evaluation of alternatives
- purchase decision and act
- post-purchase evaluation.

We will look at this model of purchase behaviour in some detail. As can be seen, a lot takes place before the purchase decision and act are made. Consumers will not

Figure 19.15 Stimulus–response model of consumer behaviour

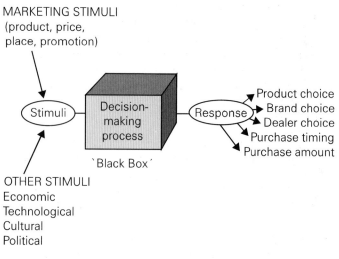

always go through each of these stages. If consumers are exhibiting routine response behaviour, making impulse purchases or only using limited information, they may omit several stages. It is also important to notice that there are three main areas of influence in this model of consumer purchase behaviour, and these are broken into three distinct areas: personal, psychological and social.

Figure 19.16 An integrated model of the consumer decision process

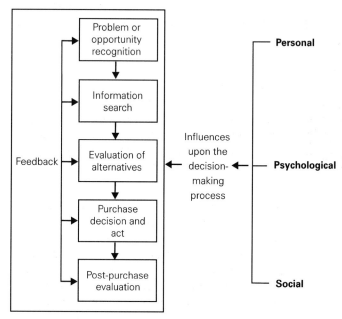

Problem or opportunity recognition
This first stage starts when the consumer becomes aware that there is a discrepancy between their existing

or actual state of affairs and a desired state of affairs. For example, as your car begins to run out of petrol the gauge informs you of your current state of affairs, and you realise the need to refill as soon as possible – you therefore make a decision. Once the problem has been recognised you do something about it. Replenishment is probably the most common type of opportunity recognition, when consumers may not be aware of a problem.

Another form may occur when a consumer sees something new on the market which provides desirable benefits, about which they may require limited information. Problem recognition may also stem from dissatisfaction with a current product or brand. Changing financial status may affect problem recognition. For example, extra income may help consumers to purchase items that they might not otherwise have considered. The speed of recognition is another influencing factor. Some consumers are quicker than others in recognising a desired state of affairs.

Information search

After recognising the problem or opportunity, the second stage for the consumers is to gather information which will help them to achieve the desired state of affairs. For example, as your petrol tank empties you may think about the whereabouts of a suitable filling station, as well as the price of petrol and the quality of service at that station.

The search for information may be internal or external. An **internal search** for information will involve using the buyer's memory for information about products that may help to provide the desired state of affairs. This may include previous experiences, memories of promotions and other communications, and exposure to other forms of marketing. An **external search** involves finding information additional to that provided by the memory. Other sources of information may include family and friends, shop displays, catalogues, brochures, leaflets, consumer publications, package labelling and demonstrations.

In most instances consumers solve problems through internal research. Information kept in the mind will simply be used to help with the decision-making process. Finding external information may require considerable time and effort, and one of the dangers of providing too much information is that of overloading the consumer with contradictory facts and figures. The number of brands a consumer considers is known as the **evoked set**. In some instances the consumer already knows the evoked set, while in others the external research process is used to reveal the brands. Even then a consumer may not know all the brands. **Repetition** may be used by

advertisers to increase the size of a consumer's evoked set. Evidence shows that consumers are more likely to be influenced by repetition when making a low-involvement purchase with little thought required.

Evaluation of alternatives

The buyer now has to evaluate the alternatives included in the evoked set created by the information search process. Some evaluation may take place at the same time as the search process as the consumer accepts or rejects the information received. However, if this does not happen simultaneously, the consumer will then develop a series of **evaluative criteria** to help with the selection. These criteria will be the features or benefits the consumer wishes to consider when making a choice from the alternatives. For example, when buying a car the consumer may consider safety, price, reputation, reliability, performance, etc.

The consumer will make comparisons of the features of the products in the evoked set. The criteria for evaluation may include *objective* elements, such as an independent road test from a magazine, and/or may include *subjective* criteria such as a consumer's perception of the image generated by the product. Consumers may attach a different level of importance to each criterion so that some may be weighted more than others.

Marketers may try to influence consumers in their evaluation process by framing the alternatives – that is, by stressing the characteristics that appeal to the criteria identified by consumers – and this may help many consumers with recall.

Purchase decision and act

At the end of the research and evaluation process, the consumer will make a purchase decision and carry out the act of purchase. By this time the consumer will have evaluated each item in the evoked set according to personal evaluative criteria until only one passes the test.

One important decision for the consumer is the location of the outlet for the purchase. The choice of seller will probably occur after product selection. Influences such as credit facilities, delivery, after-sales service may influence such selection.

Post-purchase evaluation

The act of purchase creates either satisfaction, which removes the difference between the actual and desired state of affairs, or creates dissatisfaction which may still leave a discrepancy. Shortly after a purchase, particularly for expensive products, consumers may experience **cognitive dissonance**. If consumers are not sure that they have made the right decision they may feel guilty or worried that they have made the wrong decision. In response to cognitive dissonance they may even decide to return the product or change it for an alternative. Some consumers attempt to reduce dissonance by finding information which provides them with reassurance about their purchase. Marketers can help in reducing dissonance by providing supporting information.

While the five stages in the decision-making process are taking place, they are affected by the three broad external influences shown in Figure 19.16.

Personal factors

One important personal factor is our set of **demographic characteristics**, which include age, sex, race and stage in our family life-cycle. As we saw earlier these can be used as a basis for market segmentation.

Demographic factors may influence family purchasing decisions or form the basis for marketers to target specific groups of consumers with a range of benefits. For example, in the summer of 1994 Honda launched the Honda Civic Bali – the personal profile of the targeted consumer was: young (21–45), female, independent, stylish, interested in travel and looking for value for money.

Situational factors are another type of personal influence. These are the conditions that exist when a customer has to make a purchase. For example, a queue may deter a customer from entering a shop, bad weather or the prospect of shortages may cause consumers to 'stock up', or uncertainty may cause them to delay making large purchases (i.e. lack of 'feel-good' factor). Time is another situational factor – if a consumer is in a rush, for example, he or she may not process information thoroughly.

The level of involvement is an important personal factor. How much interest and attention should a consumer spend searching for each product? The whole consumer buying process will depend on the consumer's willingness to be involved with purchasing decisions. Low-involvement buyers engage in limited decision-making, and may evaluate a product after they have bought it. With high-involvement buyers, extensive decision-making involves time and effort before a choice is made.

Psychological factors

Psychological factors operate within consumers and are responsible for determining their behaviour patterns. Though psychological factors operate internally, they may be influenced by social factors (see later).

The starting point in the consumer's purchasing decision is a felt need. This reflects the difference between the actual and desired state of affairs. **Motives** are a form of

inner energy which drive a person towards the satisfaction of a felt need. The individual is thus drawn to take action to satisfy a need, in order to reach a condition of equilibrium. Motives, therefore, are situated between individual needs and a form of action. In doing so they:

- activate behaviour (when we are hungry this need motivates us to take action)
- are directional in that they determine a particular type of action
- reduce tension in order to create the equilibrium condition.

Perhaps the best known theory of individual motivation is that of **Abraham Maslow**. He suggested that, although it is difficult to analyse individual needs, it is possible to develop a hierarchical picture that can be split into five broad categories. These are described in Chapter 10. Maslow asserted that a satisfied need will no longer act as a **motivator**. Once basic needs have been met, the individual will move further up the scale of needs. The implications of Maslow's theory are easy to perceive, as different products and services are related to different needs. For example, life assurance is rooted in a desire for safety, a BMW car is related to esteem needs, etc. There are, however, a number of problems associated with this theory.

- It is noticeable that in western societies there are far more products related to self-fulfilment needs than in less developed countries. Higher needs therefore do not exist in many individuals from these countries.
- It is likely that some individuals may be working towards needs at more than one level at the same time.
- The theory does not take into consideration that some people with the same motives adopt different behaviour patterns.
- The model assumes that once lower needs have been satisfied individuals will try to satisfy higher needs. In real life this may not always happen. In real life it is conceivable that someone may satisfy their self-fulfilment needs before developing their self-esteem needs.

The behaviour of individuals is also determined by their **perceptions**. Perception is the process by which an individual selects, organises and interprets inputs in order to develop a more meaningful view of reality. These inputs may be received through the five senses of sight, hearing, touch, smell and taste. Different people may perceive inputs in different ways and some may perceive the same inputs in different ways at different times!

Selectivity limits our perceptions and we ignore many of the stimuli from our environment. There are three steps in the perception process:

- *Step 1 – Receiving information.* We do not have the ability to take into account all the information inputs in our environment. Studies show that on average we perceive more than 500 advertisements daily, but only a few of them ever break though our 'perceptual screen'. *Selective exposure* is the process by which individuals select inputs to be exposed to their awareness. *Selective distortion* occurs where an individual distorts information to make it more compatible with his or her own views. *Selective retention* enables an individual to remember information inputs which support beliefs and forget inputs that do not.

■ *Step 2 – Organise and integrate information.* New information needs to be organised and integrated with the information that is already stored in the memory.

■ *Step 3 – The perceptual process.* The individual will then try to create *meaning* from the information inputs. This might be based on the fact that the information seems familiar or that it appeals to a hidden part of the individual's identity.

Marketers will try to make their message stand out so that it catches the consumer's attention. The psychological concept of **closure** helps to make a message stand out. Closure refers to how an individual creates a complete picture from fragments of a picture – advertisements that help consumers to do this may break through perceptual screens.

Individuals have self-perceptions or **self-images**. The 'self' is an individual's perception of himself or herself. Within this 'self' there are various ways to maintain and enhance this image. The individual will make choices – of car, music, clothing, places to shop – which fit his or her perception of 'self'. By discovering how customers wish themselves to be perceived in terms of an image, organisations can design, promote and retail goods that are consistent with those sought by prospective purchasers.

A consumer's **ability and knowledge** will influence his or her decision to make a purchase. We all have different skills and abilities. For example, when purchasing a computer a well-informed consumer may comprehend the mound of literature with the accompanying software packages. Another buyer may have problems understanding this information and require help. Similarly we all have different levels of knowledge; an individual's ability to search for, recall and use knowledge may influence the purchasing situation.

Consumers also have **attitudes and beliefs**. Attitudes are feelings that either favour or do not favour a purchase. We all have different feelings about politics, music, books and television programmes. Attitudes may change through widespread experience or interaction with others. Beliefs, on the other hand, are the specific thoughts of individuals. For example, an individual may believe that Rover cars are better than those of Ford. This belief may be based upon fact, opinion or even blind faith. Marketers are interested in attitudes and beliefs because they help them to understand the feelings of customers towards products, brand images and services. Only by understanding these is it possible to develop an effective strategy which seeks to improve consumer attitudes and beliefs.

There are three related components of an attitude (see Figure 19.17):

■ the *cognitive* component referring to the consumer's information or knowledge about a product or concept

■ the *affective* component dealing with the feelings or emotional reactions

■ the *behavioural* component, which may cause the consumer to act in a particular way.

All three components of an attitude exist in a stable relationship and help to form an overall attitude.

Figure 19.17 The components of attitudes

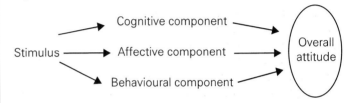

Consumer attitudes are generally very difficult to change. The marketer can either attempt to change attitudes or can find out consumer attitudes and then make the product consistent with them.

Marketers frequently try to monitor attitudes. One way of doing this is through an attitude scale. This may consist of a series of key words or phrases that refer to a product. By analysing the intensity of response it may be possible to determine where consumers have strong positive or negative attitudes.

Another important area of interest for the marketer is the need to understand **personality**. Personality includes all of the behavioural and individual traits which can be uniquely identified with customers. These may include aggression, dogmatism, assertiveness, competitiveness, etc. It is possible to find a relationship between these characteristics and buying behaviour. If any customers have similar personalities, it may be possible to divide up the market on the basis of such stereotypes. For example, various models of cars, records and fashion products all reflect the personality traits of customers. Think of products you use which reflect your own personality.

Case Study
Targeting students

There are a million students in the UK who, as a group, are considered difficult to target. The main problem is that student behaviour is influenced by rapidly changing fashions. Students also lead a relatively insular life which centres on their particular social habits and their work. However, as students have an estimated spending power of £4 billion a year, many companies are trying to target these consumers of tomorrow.

One such company is Beatwax. It began by organising university promotions for record companies and this quickly expanded into video and film production. As other companies became aware of the student market, the Beatwax client base broadened.

In recent years there has been a 20 per cent rise in enrolment in universities and colleges of higher education. The market for students is growing faster than at any other time. Chris Ward, who set up Beatwax, is keen to dispel the notion that students have little money:

> 'With student loans, they have as much money to spend as they ever did. They are just further in debt when they leave higher education. But it doesn't stop them spending money on the clichéd things that students have always spent money on – drink, music, cigarettes and convenience foods.'

One of Beatwax's most recent campaigns was for the tea producer Twinings. It has distributed 20 000 herbal tea sachets around universities and colleges in the expectation that, if students try the product and like it, they will buy it on a regular basis and continue to do so after graduation. Golden Wonder has also run a promotional campaign for its Pots of the World brand – which is a more exotic version of that staple student fare, Pot Noodles.

Beatwax targets students on their home territory, not through television programmes or newspapers but through university or student publications. Such publications are read by 86 per cent of students. Beatwax also has access to campus radio stations and poster sites, and there are growing opportunities to use video. As campaigns are directed solely at students they can be more daring and often use outrageous humour.

Questions for discussion

1 *Using specific product examples based on your own experiences, comment on the psychological factors which seem to influence the purchasing behaviour of students.*
2 *How might such consumer behaviour change after students leave higher education?*

Social factors

Social factors are the forces which *other people* exert on our buying behaviour. They include:

- culture and sub-cultures
- role and status
- group and reference group influences
- family influences
- social class.

Culture encompasses standard patterns of behaviour and plays an important role in shaping our purchasing patterns. It stems from the traditions, beliefs and values of the community in which we live. It can be defined as 'the complex of values, ideas, attitudes, and other meaningful symbols that serve humans to communicate, interpret, and evaluate as members of society'. For example, although alcohol is an ingrained feature of western life, it is forbidden in Muslim communities. Culture is handed down from one generation to another and provides each society with a unique series of values.

The symbols of culture may be *tangible* products such as forms of housing, tools and clothing, or *intangible* concepts such as values, attitudes, beliefs and laws. Culture will have an important influence on the lives of everybody within each community, and so will determine their consumer buying needs. For example, tastes for different types of alcoholic drinks differ widely not just in various parts of the world but also in different regions in the UK.

Culture will determine how, why, when and for whom products are purchased. It is not a static concept and cultures are continually changing over time. For example, in recent years we have seen greater concern for environmentally friendly products, increased emphasis on health and fitness, as well as increased dependence on convenience products. Marketers must constantly monitor cultural changes in order to adapt their marketing activities, because strategies that are successful for one culture may not be successful for another.

Though a nation might be characterised by one culture, there may be a series of **sub-cultures** existing within it. A sub-culture is a sub-group with its own distinctive behaviour. Within the UK, sub-cultures are based on race, religion, age, rural versus suburban, etc. Sub-cultures are important for organisations who wish to target their brands to those who share the values of that particular sub-culture. These groups may in themselves be important market segments for marketers.

Status is the relative position that any individual member has in a group, whether the group be formal or informal. We all have a certain status in any situation. **Roles** are what other members of each group expect from people with a certain status. For example, teachers have a certain status within society and we would expect certain roles to be fulfilled by teachers. Where status and roles can be recognised, it may be appropriate to target products at such individuals.

An individual's buying behaviour may be influenced by many groups. Although we generally like to view ourselves as individuals, it is very likely that many of our purchasing decisions are based on the groups to which we belong. A group becomes a **reference group** when it influences a person's attitudes, values and behaviour. We may all belong to a series of reference groups such as professional groups, families, cricket teams, church, etc. A reference group may serve an individual by being a source of information and comparisons. Advice, word-of-mouth help, common values may all influence purchasing behaviour. Consumers tend to keep their purchasing behaviour in line with members of their reference group.

People are affected in different ways by reference groups. How strongly an individual is influenced will depend on his or her level of involvement within the group and susceptibility to its influence. Marketers may use reference group influence in their promotions. Within each small group there are **opinion leaders**. These individuals may adopt products before other members of the group and then serve as an information source for others. Opinion leaders can play a crucial role in interpersonal communications within groups.

Of all the groups to which we belong, our **family** probably exerts the most influence on our buying behaviour. Many of us will be members of two families during our lifetime – the family into which we are born (*the family of orientation*) and the family into which we marry (*the family of marriage and procreation*). The role that we have within a family directly affects our purchasing decisions. There is an almost infinite variety of family roles, and these constantly change. H. L. Davis and B. P. Rigaux point to four distinct family patterns (see Figure 19.18). These are:

■ autonomic, where an equal number of decisions are made by husband and wife
■ husband-dominant
■ wife-dominant
■ syncratic, where decisions are made jointly by both partners.

A number of factors have affected family roles over recent years – the growing number of working women, the impact of two wage-earners, the increasing number of single-parent families, etc. Marketers need to be aware of these changes and their consequences for buyer behaviour.

Social class represents a ranking of people into 'higher' or 'lower' positions. A class may also be called 'open' because people have the freedom either to move into it or out of it. Within different societies the criteria for determining social classes vary widely.

Within each social class people tend towards similar patterns of behaviour. For example, social class may

Figure 19.18 Husband/wife roles in family purchasing

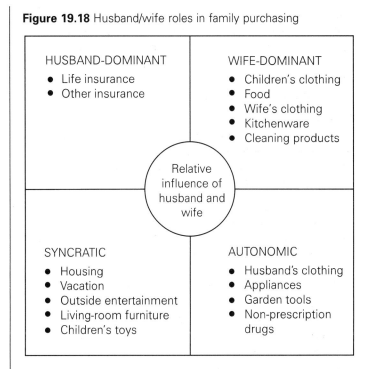

determine housing, cars, type of occupation etc. Social class is a major determinant of consumer behaviour and, as we saw earlier in this chapter, socio-economic grouping may be used as a basis for segmentation.

Loyalty and image

In the exchange process, a crucial element in fostering **loyalty** is brand strategy. **Branding** is of importance for both buyers and sellers.

For buyers, branding reduces the random nature of product selection. It helps them to identify more easily products that may satisfy their needs, and enables them to reduce time spent on evaluating alternatives. A brand also represents certain qualities and characteristics which they may use to develop a clearer picture of what the product offers. **Brand loyalty** is the long-standing decision to make repeat purchases of a product or service. As buyers become loyal to a particular brand they help to stabilise the brand and reduce the risks involved in the organisation's activities. It is possible for organisations to charge consumers a slightly higher price when they have developed brand loyalty. This is known as a **premium**. For example, Domestos, Fairy Liquid and Dettol are all well-known products with a range of brand strengths for which consumers do not mind paying a little bit more.

It is also important to consider the roles that brands play. For example, a young woman going to a party might wear a particular branded item because she feels it will help her to be better accepted in that social situation. In this way the branded garment is reducing risk. She may also wear an expensive watch in order to communicate a message. For a group, brand loyalty may be important because it represents the way they interact with the brand, and for the marketer it is important to understand this interaction.

Sellers also benefit from brand loyalty. It plays an important part in the decision to purchase a product and encourages repeat purchasing. New products which carry a brand are more likely to be successful because consumers are already familiar with that brand name. Branding also simplifies the process of promotion – if one product from the range is promoted, the repeated exposure to the market of the brand name may help to develop other products.

There are many threats to brand loyalty. With an increasing number of well-differentiated products competing with each other in today's marketplace, manufacturers cannot rely on brand loyalty for their successes. An organisation must use internal audit procedures to determine what its distinctive brand qualities are and to what extent these qualities will help to determine a brand's potential for success. One way of doing this is by using a weighted approach to calculating a brand's strengths (see Figure 19.19).

Scaling techniques are another way of evaluating and quantifying the various qualities a brand might possess to get a better understanding of its profile. The two most common scaling techniques are Likert scales and semantic differential scales.

Likert scales quantify a respondent's reaction to a series of factors. For example, the question might be asked: 'What do you think of our new product?' In response the respondent ticks one of the following:

Very good	Good	Satisfactory	Poor	Very poor
☐	☐	☐	☐	☐

Each response may be scored so that the final score from the survey respresents the score for the new product. This rating can then be compared with the scores achieved by other products. This technique, used with groups of consumers either from different areas or from different socio-economic backgrounds, will help to form a basis for segmentation.

A **semantic differential scale** (see Figure 19.20) presents respondents with a range of attitudes. (This is sometimes known as an 'attitude battery'.) It measures the feelings of respondents about a number of statements, key words or phrases. For example, the interviewer might ask a respondent: 'What groups of people would consider buying these brands of decaffeinated coffee?' The semantic list would then be given to the respondent to fill out. The closer to the left-hand side of the scale, the more the respondent agrees with that statement, word or phrase; and similarly the closer to the right-hand side the more he or she agrees with that statement, word or phrase.

Perceptual mapping, which is discussed on page 494 (see Figure 19.14), can also be used for brand mapping. Computers can further develop this technique using multidimensional scaling.

Fostering brand loyalty to develop usage

As we saw earlier in this chapter, usage rate may provide an important basis for segmentation. By looking at the volume purchased by different users, as well as their frequency of purchase, it is possible to develop a useful knowledge of various parts of the market.

One approach is to divide a market into users and non-users. Non-users can then be further divided into potential users and non-potential users. Actual users can be grouped as light, medium or heavy (see Figure 19.21).

Figure 19.19 Scoring brand strengths

Success factors	Scoring criteria High 10	Med 5	Low 1	Weight (W)	Brand score (S)	Weighted score (W × S)
Quality	X			0.4	10	4.00
Innovation		X		0.25	5	1.25
Service		X		0.2	5	1.00
Advertisements			X	0.15	1	0.15
					21	6.40

Figure 19.20 Example of mapping brands using semantic differential scales

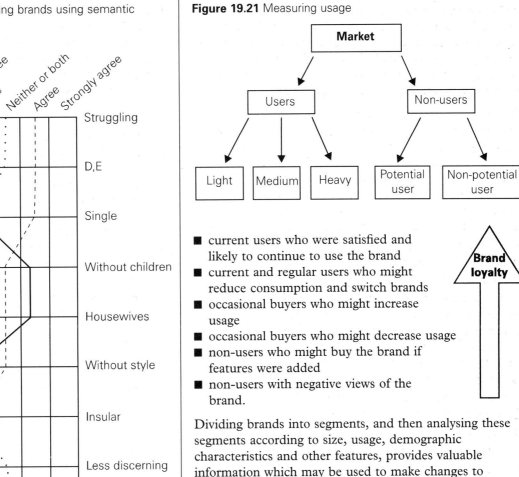

Profile Brand A ——— Profile Brand B - - - Profile Brand C · · ·

Figure 19.21 Measuring usage

- current users who were satisfied and likely to continue to use the brand
- current and regular users who might reduce consumption and switch brands
- occasional buyers who might increase usage
- occasional buyers who might decrease usage
- non-users who might buy the brand if features were added
- non-users with negative views of the brand.

Dividing brands into segments, and then analysing these segments according to size, usage, demographic characteristics and other features, provides valuable information which may be used to make changes to the product and help with the development of brand strategy.

Another study of brand loyalty was undertaken by the *Chicago Tribune*. This was in areas which covered soap, scouring cleanser, coffee, canned peas, margarine, orange concentrate and headache tablets. It showed conclusively that brand loyalty does exist within individual product groups. However, it also showed that those customers who are the most loyal to brands are not always heavy users. Another study (by W. J. Tucker) also looked into consumer choice of brands by giving 42 women brands that were previously unknown to them. By the end of twelve trials, half the respondents reached the criteria set for brand loyalty. It is possible to conclude that, even if there is no difference between brands, some consumers will still exhibit brand loyalty. It should, therefore, not be regarded as trivial by marketers.

There is, however, always the latent problem of cognitive dissonance, where the level of dissatisfaction between the actual and desired state of affairs may affect brand loyalty and reduce the likelihood of repeat purchases. Group behaviour and group cohesiveness may also change over time and it is important to monitor trends to assess how they affect brand purchasing behaviour.

Analysing markets in terms of brand preferences and usage is important because it may be possible to convert light users into medium users and medium users into heavy users. It also helps an organisation to target the potential users. A study by Target Group Index revealed that, while nearly all housewives bought baked beans, only about one-third could be considered to be heavy users. In other markets, too, the survey found that heavy users accounted for around one-third.

In some markets it is possible to consider brand loyalty as a basis for market segmentation. If each individual brand is then analysed further, it may be possible to understand more closely the motives of each of the users. For example, one analysis of a brand frequently purchased in the USA revealed:

Organisational buying behaviour

Organisational buying behaviour refers to the behaviour of producers, resellers, and central and local government institutions. It tends to be more complex than the consumer decision process, for several reasons:

- Organisational buying decisions may involve many different people who exert some form of influence.
- Decisions may take longer because of tendering procedures, or because of the need to consult a committee or convene a meeting of interested parties.
- Organisations buy products designed to meet the requirements of the organisation as a whole.
- Buying may involve a complex product, including technical support and advice from staff, training, installation, special procedures and specifications.
- Organisational buyers are influenced by both rational needs (cost, quality, reliability etc.) and emotional needs (status, fear, recognition etc.).
- Organisations may employ buying experts.

Howard and O'Shaughnessy, identify three types of buying behaviour:

- *Routinised buying behaviour* – This occurs where products are bought frequently. Purchases are habitual and the buyer has known preferences.
- *Limited problem-solving* – This category relates to new or unfamiliar products from suppliers who are known and where the product is in a familiar class of products.
- *Extensive problem-solving* – Purchases in this category are unfamiliar products from unfamiliar suppliers. In this area considerable information is required to meet a range of criteria which would determine approval of the purchase.

The **buying centre** refers to the group of people within an organisation involved in a purchasing decision. It may also be called the **Decision-Making Unit (DMU)**. Members of the DMU will have one or more of the following roles:

- *Users* are members of the organisation who will actually use the product (for example, a technician who needs a new set of tools)
- *Influencers* are technical personnel who set out the specifications for purchasing a product and may evaluate the products of competitors. Their expertise provides them with power within the organisation.
- *Deciders* make the ultimate buying decision about the product and the supplier. For most decisions buyers

will be the deciders but, if a large expenditure is involved, the decider may be a senior manager.

- *Buyers* select suppliers and negotiate the terms of the sale.
- *Gatekeepers* have the crucial role of controlling the flow of information to persons throughout the buying centre. They may be office staff or technical personnel.

Throughout this process it is possible that one person may have multiple roles. This will depend on the size, structure and various components within the buying centre.

As with consumers, organisations will engage in a buying decision process which starts with the recognition of a need (see Figure 19.22). This recognition may come from either within or outside the organisation. To take a simple example, an *internal* need would determine that more stationery is required. If a competitor is using better technology, this – as an *external* factor – may influence the purchase of technology. Next, product specifications are developed to determine how to solve the need, and searching begins for products and suppliers. As possible products and suppliers are identified they are evaluated, and the product which meets all the criteria is then ordered. Finally, the product and supplier performance

Figure 19.22 The organisational buying process

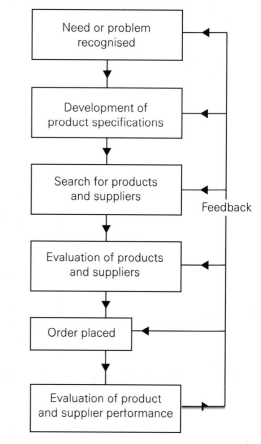

- Need or problem recognised
- Development of product specifications
- Search for products and suppliers
- Evaluation of products and suppliers
- Order placed
- Evaluation of product and supplier performance

Feedback

are evaluated by making a comparision with the original specifications.

If only one supplier is identified this is known as **sole sourcing**. Though this has been discouraged in the past, today with better communications it can lead to better prices, terms and buying arrangements.

As the buying process takes place a number of factors can influence the decisions taken. These are sometimes divided into four distinct categories: environmental, organisational, interpersonal, and individual.

Environmental considerations involve 'uncontrollable' forces in the business environment – such as politics, legal influences, regulations, actions of pressure groups, changes in the economy, the actions of competitors and technological change. Any one of these forces may generate uncertainty about specific types of purchases.

Organisational influences are factors within the organisation which might influence the buying process – for example, changes in the nature, size and functioning of the decision-making unit, new purchasing procedures or different buying objectives.

Interpersonal factors reflect the relationships between individuals involved in the DMU – for example, where the power lies and who uses the power. When selling to organisational markets it is important to assess where the power lies.

Individual factors are the personal characteristics of all the members of the DMU. For example, what is their age, sex, technical expertise, personality and position in the organisation? These factors can affect individual styles used

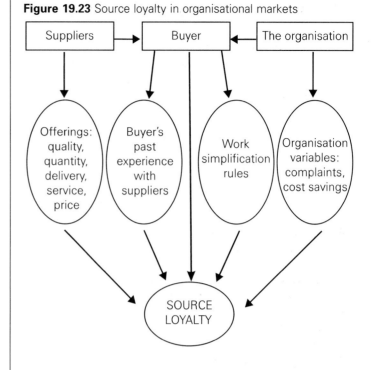

Figure 19.23 Source loyalty in organisational markets

for the negotiation process, and it may be useful to know how these might affect the decision to make a purchase.

Models of organisational buying behaviour

A number of different models have been devised to explain the process. For example, a model developed by Wind expresses **source loyalty** within organisational markets (see Figure 19.23).

Figure 19.24 The decision process model of industrial purchase behaviour

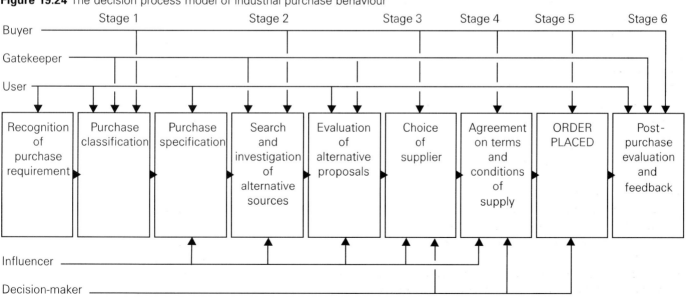

Wind's theory looks at the offerings provided by the supplier in terms of quantity, quality, delivery, service and price and shows how this helps to build up a relationship between the buyer and the supplier. The organisation will be concerned about a number of organisational variables, such as complaints and cost savings, and may try to simplify the buying process by relying on the same supplier until good reasons exist not to do so.

Another model of organisational buying behaviour looks at the decisions taken at each step in the buying process. It assumes that the buyer will go through six sequential steps and that various members of the decision-making unit will be involved in these stages (see Figure 19.24).

- *Stage 1* – A problem has been recognised. The user will determine the purchase requirement and classify this for the buyer.
- *Stage 2* – The precise nature of the purchase is determined.
- *Stage 3* – Alternative proposals are evaluated. The role of the influencer is important for this stage.
- *Stage 4* – This involves locating sources, determining conditions and reaching agreement. The decision maker will make the decision.

- *Stage 5* – After terms have been agreed the order is placed.
- *Stage 6* – Product evaluation takes place to ensure that the product meets specifications.

Further reading

- *Behavioural Studies for Marketing and Business* by Frank Spooner. Stanley Thornes, 1992.
- *Meeting Customer Needs* by Ian Smith. Butterworth–Heinemann, 1994.
- *Marketing – A Behavioural Analysis*, 2nd edition, by Peter Chisnall McGraw–Hill, 1985.
- *The Marketing Pocketbook*. The Advertising Association/ NTC Publications Ltd, published annually.
- *Principles of Marketing* by Geoffrey Randall. Routledge, 1993.
- *Advances in Consumer Marketing* by Mark Jenkins. Kogan Page, 1994.

20 Product policy

On completion of this chapter students should be able to:

- plan and carry out a product audit

- identify and evaluate different approaches for the management of product development

- identify and evaluate different product-branding strategies.

Product audit

Case Study
The Mini

If you were asked to name the most famous cars of all time, you might think of the VW Beetle, Model T Ford, Citroen 2CV, E-type Jaguar and other famous names, many of which helped to develop the modern motor car. The Mini sits comfortably among such revered names. It was in August 1959 that the British Motor Corporation (BMC) launched the first Mini. It came in two types – the Austin Seven and the Morris Mini-Minor – and sold for £496.19s.2d. It was designed by Alec Issigonis and was instantly a remarkable hit, noted for its size, handling and interior space.

Though the Mini has been declared by some as the best car ever built, it has never been the most profitable. BMC did not know, until it was told by Ford, that the company was making the car at a loss – it did not have the cost-analysis systems used by American companies.

Figure 20.1 One of the first Minis

Reproduced by kind permission of BMIHT/Rover Group

In recent years most of the demand for the Mini has come from abroad. The French adore it; in Japan it has become a cult car, and the Japanese simply cannot get enough of them. Since 1959, though the design is little changed, the engine has been cleaned up to meet modern environmental standards.

Today, however, a big question mark hangs over the future of the Mini. Though production has passed 5.3 million cars, the official line from Rover, the current manufacturer of the car and a part of BMW, is that the company will continue to build the car while demand is there, but senior sources at the company do not expect it to see its fortieth birthday.

According to Professor Garel Rees at Cardiff Business School, the Mini was only reprieved in the 1980s because the Metro, which was designed to replace it, failed to live up to expectations, so there was spare capacity at the Longbridge plant in Birmingham. He believes that Rover can keep making the Mini as long as it does not get in the way of another car.

According to Rob Golding, who has written a book about the Mini, Rover is wrestling with the dilemma of what to do with the car. The options may include scrapping it, subcontracting its manufacture, or setting up a joint venture with an assembler. Though the Mini is still popular and the 'heart says keep the Mini going', its fate will depend on a hard business decision. However, the Mini does keep a toehold for Rover in the 'micro' segment of the car market and, with increasing traffic congestion, this segment may grow rapidly over the next few years.

Questions for discussion

1 *Describe broadly the features and benefits of the Mini.*
2 *The Mini created a completely different product concept, which surpassed expectations, yet at the time, was a competitive response to the Bubble car! Why do you think that the Mini has been so successful?*
3 *Has the concept of the Mini really been fully exploited? Is the Mini, the icon of the 'swinging 60s', set to die? What future, if any, do you think the Mini has?*

At the heart of a transaction or an exchange is the product. The product provides a range of physical or functional characteristics, many of which we might like and some of which we might not like, which accompany the good or service being offered. For example, if we want to buy a newspaper in the morning, we might wish to go to a local newspaper shop. The shop may or may not be conveniently located on the way to work or college. There may be many parking spaces outside the shop. The shop itself may be well laid out; there may be an opportunity to buy other products at the same time and you may be dealt with courteously and attentively. Not only are we being provided with the opportunity to buy the **tangible good** on sale, we may also be well catered for with an **intangible service**.

On the surface there are often clear tangible benefits – things you can touch and see. Tangible features of a product include:

- shape
- colour
- size
- design
- packaging
- taste.

The intangible features may not be quite so obvious. These include the reputation of the business (e.g. 'You can be sure of Shell') or the corporate or brand image (e.g. the Shell logo). There are extra features to be considered such as:

- after-sales service
- availability of spare parts
- customer-care policy
- guarantees.

A product is made up of a range of features which serve to meet the customer's requirements. For example, a customer buying a new car may not just want a family saloon – additional requirements could include:

- a blue car
- four doors
- a well-known name
- a long guarantee
- credit facilities
- after-sales free servicing
- low petrol consumption
- a proven safety record.

In fact, results of a survey of 1720 car drivers carried out early in 1994 (the annual Lex survey) revealed that while 41 per cent of respondents were interested mainly in security and 37 per cent in safety, only 6 per cent were mostly interested in the top speed and 14 per cent in acceleration. Environmental concerns featured prominently, with 27 per cent of respondents expressing this as their main interest. The survey pointed out that environmental worries are not yet sufficiently strong to induce people to switch from car travel to other modes of transport, but could nevertheless influence the type of car that people would prefer to buy. The Lex survey thus indicated that the days are long gone when motorists sought principally speed and acceleration in choosing a car. The motorists indicated that they would like the following improvements in their next car:

Security	41%
Safety	37%
Fuel efficiency	32%
Driver comfort	16%
Reliability	15%

Acceleration	14%
Ease of driving	11%
Styling of car	10%
Top speed	6%

By understanding the complex series of motives which motorists may have when purchasing a car, marketers can develop products which more closely satisfy such needs.

A product, therefore, may be more broadly described as *a series of tangible and intangible benefits and features designed for the use and enjoyment of customers in order to satisfy their needs.*

The important part of this definition is that customers are not just buying an item or receiving a service or solution to a problem, though these are important. A product, as we shall see, is more than this.

Product concept

Have you ever thought about why you buy products? At a simple level you may buy a coat to keep you warm or a newspaper to read. However, as we have seen, consumer buying behaviour is a complex process. We all have a range of different motives for making our buying decisions. For example, think about the sort of clothes you wear and then contrast them with the sort of clothes you would definitely not want to wear! A product, for many of us, is something which fits with our perception or self-image (see Figure 20.2). Products are not just purchased to meet a single need; the ownership and use of a product involves a whole range of factors that make up the **product concept**.

For example, it may appear that a couple choose to holiday in the West Indies because they are attracted by the sand, sun and surf. However, when questioned further, it may come to light that they are more concerned with the 'image' which they present – friends, associates and 'significant others' will become aware that they are able to afford to holiday in the West Indies. Holidaying in the West Indies is associated with a particular lifestyle. In the public imagination it may represent being rich and able to afford exotic things.

The purchaser of an expensive modern car will probably be interested in the quality and reliability of the vehicle. He or she may be attracted by the 'state of the art' technology and many of the other features of the car. However, a significant part of the product concept may also involve the ingredient of showing the world that 'they have arrived'.

Product dimensions

Products comprise a number of important dimensions. These include:

Figure 20.2 A product may reflect our self-image

- generic dimensions
- sensual dimensions
- extended dimensions.

Generic dimensions are the key benefits of a particular product which relate to its function. Shoe polish cleans shoes. Freezers store frozen food. Deckchairs provide a comfortable seat on a sunny day. Hairdressers cut and style hair.

The **sensual dimensions** of a product are those that have an effect on the senses – design, colour, taste, smell and texture. A ring doughnut has a shape, appearance, texture, taste and smell all of its own. The sensual benefits of a product are frequently highlighted by advertisers. This is clearly a case when advertising food and drinks, e.g. 'smooth and creamy', 'the amber nectar'.

The **extended dimensions** of a product include a wide range of additional benefits. Examples are servicing arrangements, credit facilities, guarantees and maintenance contracts.

Another interpretation of a product and its various elements of provision appears in Kotler and Armstrong's *Principles of Marketing* (5th edition). They also perceive three different levels of a product which can be used for planning purposes (see Figure 20.3).

Figure 20.3 The three levels of a product

Figure 20.3 The three levels of a product

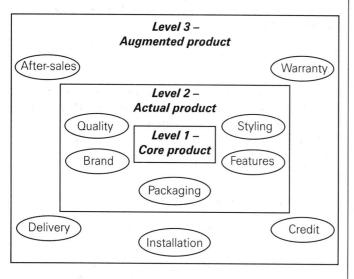

Level 1 – The core product

This consists of the benefits customers are provided with when they purchase and use a good or service. For example, the core benefits of purchasing a car would relate to how it works.

Level 2 – The actual product

This consists of five elements, including the brand, quality, styling, features and packaging. Again, with the car, these would relate to the benefits associated with owning that brand, the elements of design, as well as performance and capabilities beyond the normal function.

Level 3 – The augmented product

A number of support issues, which are important to the customer, help to take the product and the benefits that it offers one stage further. For example, for a car this may be after-sales service and extended warranty conditions, as well as free delivery and the provision of acceptable credit facilities. These elements in a product may be key features in developing its competitive advantage.

The importance of the audit

Product development requires planning and this may depend upon the extent to which the product mix variables currently match marketing objectives. An audit involves a thorough evaluation of the products offered by the organisation and can help marketers to focus not only on the positive elements of performance, but also on where the organisation is going wrong.

For example, an internal audit of a product mix may involve listing products, evaluating their types and classifications and then examining their performance over a period of time in order to identify trends. It will be important to examine various market segments and the relationships between them. Useful ratios are the net profit made per product and per region, the net profit as a percentage of sales and the market share per region and country. Important elements may be cash flow and risk (see page 516) and helpful tools of analysis may be the product life-cycle (see page 512) and the Boston matrix (see page 515).

The audit will help the organisation to identify which products should be phased out, which should be modified and which new products will enter the portfolio and at what time. It should set out objectives for volume of sales, turnover and profits and establish how each of the products within the organisation will be supported by staff.

Product classification

All products fall into two broad categories: consumer products and industrial/organisational products. Whereas consumer products are used by the final consumer to satisfy their personal needs, industrial goods are bought to satisfy the industrial objectives of the organisation, which will usually be the production of other goods or services.

Consumer products

Consumer goods can be further classified into convenience goods, shopping goods, speciality goods and unsought goods (see Figure 20.4).

Figure 20.4 Types of consumer good

Convenience goods

These are usually frequent purchases of generally low-value consumable items. For example, milk, margarine, soap and newspapers. They generally fall into three different types:

- **staples**, such as bread and potatoes, which must be frequently replenished
- **impulse items** purchased on the spur of the moment or out of habit
- **emergency items**, prompted by unexpected needs.

Convenience goods are sold through retail outlets where goods are made available in the most convenient form possible. For example, a recent trend has been for petrol service stations to sell newspapers, coal, coffee, sandwiches and other consumables. Promotion for convenience goods tends not to be at the retail level, but by the manufacturer who develops acceptance of the brand and attempts to stimulate demand for it.

Shopping goods

Consumers choose their shopping goods more carefully. These may include items which are expected to last longer than convenience goods, and may include items of furniture, clothing, jewellery and electrical appliances. They are purchased after the consumer has made comparisons between competing goods in terms of price, quality, credit facilities and availability. The purchaser of shopping goods will have some information about the goods before the shopping trip and will collect more while shopping. With shopping goods, stock turnover is lower and the retail margin is likely to be higher. Personal selling in the place of purchase may be important, as would be the relationship between manufacturer and retailer who might work jointly with the promotion.

Speciality goods

These goods may have unique qualities which buyers might wish to possess. Buyers will usually prize the qualities of a speciality good, plan the purchase and know precisely what they want. For example, buyers may be prepared to travel many miles to attend a new season's launch at a fashion house. These goods tend to have a high price, a reputable brand and are only available at a few retail outlets, e.g. a Ferrari F40.

Unsought goods

Consumers may well not think about buying these, e.g. life assurance, funeral expenses insurance, or notebook computers, unless prompted to do so. Personal selling activity may be required to make the consumer aware of the benefits of these products.

Classifying consumer goods into the above four categories helps the marketer to understand how consumers behave when purchasing each type of good, and this enables them to take account of consumer behaviour when developing marketing strategies. There are, however, two problems associated with this.

- Although most products fit neatly into a category, some may not. For example, is a Jaguar car a shopping product or a speciality product, and is an electrical plug a convenience product or an unsought product?
- Consumers have different priorities and behaviour patterns, so it is very difficult to generalise about products on the basis of consumer behaviour.

When looking at these classifications and relating them to purchases we can only consider the behaviour of the majority of buyers.

Industrial products

Whereas consumer goods are classified according to consumer behavioural patterns, industrial goods may be classified according to type of product. These are installations, raw materials, accessory equipment, component parts and materials, and industrial supplies (see Figure 20.5).

Figure 20.5 Types of industrial good

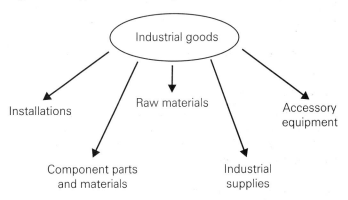

Installations

These types of purchases include any major material or equipment which is long-lived. It might include land, cranes, railway locomotives and plant and machinery. These usually cost huge sums of money and are a major purchase for the organisation. This sort of equipment is often customised and may involve a series of engineers and sales staff working together to design the product to meet the specific needs of each installation. For this reason, sales staff usually require a technical background and products are generally marketed on a single seller/manufacturer-to-user basis.

Raw materials

These are natural products used in one or several processes to become part of the finished goods. They include minerals such as copper, iron ore and coal as well as chemicals and agricultural products. Such products are usually graded and standardised. Prices are often determined by central markets.

Accessory equipment

This includes more short-lived items of equipment, which do not form part of the finished product but may be used either directly or indirectly to help produce it. For example, it may comprise small items of machinery, office equipment, workshop tools or computer software. These are routine purchases and do not involve the vast sums of expenditure necessary for installations.

Component parts and materials

These are used to become part of the final product. They are either finished parts in themselves, which are then ready for assembly, or are products which need further processing before assembly. Underneath the bonnet of a car, there are many different component parts such as spark plugs, air filter and battery. Component parts should be regularly and continuously supplied to a specified quality so that production is not slowed or halted.

Industrial supplies

Industrial supplies are the convenience goods of the industrial market. They help operational activities to take place, but do not become part of the final product. They may include:

- **maintenance** equipment, such as light bulbs, cleaning equipment, paint and toilet rolls
- **repair** items, such as screws, fittings, nails and repair equipment.
- **operating supplies**, such as oils, heating fuel and office stationery.

Collectively, these are often referred to as MRO items. Industrial supplies are regular purchases and may be bought from a number of suppliers. There is frequently price competition.

The product life-cycle

Central to the planning process will be decisions about the portfolio of products on offer. Answers will be needed to questions such as:

- When shall we launch product A?
- What would we realistically expect the performance of each of our products to be?
- Which products will require support?
- Which products would we expect to do well/badly?

To find the answers, an organisation will use a series of tools to aid the planning process. One such tool will be the **product life-cycle**.

The classic life-cycle

Markets are in a constant state of change. Over a period of time tastes and fashions will alter and the technology used to produce goods and services will move on. As a result, there will always be demand for new products, and old products will become redundant.

The product life-cycle is a useful mechanism for planning changes in marketing activities. **It recognises that products have a finite market life and charts this through various phases.** The sales performance of any product introduced to a market will rise from nothing, reach a peak and then, at some stage, start to decline. The life-cycle can be further broken down into distinct phases, as shown in Figure 20.6.

Figure 20.6 The classic life-cycle

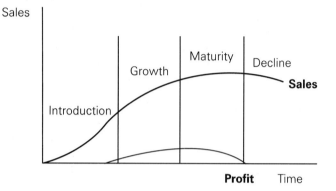

- **The introductory phase.** During this period it is necessary to create demand. Growth is slow and volume is low because of limited awareness of the product's existence.
- **The growth phase.** Sales rise more quickly. It is during this phase that the profit per unit sold usually reaches a maximum. Towards the end of the phase, competitors enter the market, which reduces the rate of growth.
- **Maturity.** In this period most of the potential customers have been reached. However, there will still be plenty of scope for repeat purchases. Competition from sellers in the market becomes stronger and new firms enter the market.
- **Decline.** The product becomes 'old' and sales start to fall. Perhaps a new or improved product will have entered the market.

The concept of the product life-cycle is perhaps best understood when related to real products and current developments.

Case Study
Making a Jag in the USA?

Though buying Jaguar for $2.5 billion in 1989 was an important strategic acquisition for Ford, the move has caused the company many problems. Sales of the British-made luxury cars have plummeted to around 27 000 per year, a figure which barely topped the number sold only to USA in 1989. As a result, profits turned into losses measured in hundreds of millions.

To counter this decline, a redesigned version of the XJ6 was launched in autumn 1994 in order to revive sales. Privately, however, managers at Ford concede that Jaguar's full recovery is some years away.

This recovery awaits the development of an exciting new mid-sized saloon aimed at a broader market than its predecessors. This still secret Jaguar is named the DEW99 and has taken the place of the X200, a model which Ford killed on the drawing board because it would have been too expensive to mass produce. With the help of the Americans, designers at Jaguar's plant in Coventry are trying to develop a car which will compete with the Mercedes E class and the BMW 5-series.

The benefit of the link with Ford for the new Jaguar is that it will be able to use parts from Ford's other luxury models so that, when the new Jaguar comes on the market at the end of 1997 or early 1998, though it will look like a Jaguar and sound like a Jaguar with the unique V8 engine, it will include parts from other models, such as the Ford five-speed automatic transmission.

The hope is that the new Jaguar will sell like a Ford and push Jaguar's sales up to 100 000 by the late 1990s. Such success, however, brings other problems. High-volume sales would mean expensive alterations to the Jaguar factory in Coventry – will the next move be to build the new Jaguar at Ford's Lincoln plant in Wixom, Michigan or in Ohio?

Questions for discussion

1 *Comment upon Jaguar's product dimensions as well as the three levels of product.*
2 *Given the position of the XJ6 in its product life-cycle, how has Ford attempted to boost its flagging fortunes? What aspects of the marketing mix do you think needed adjustment?*
3 *What factors might have affected the length of the product life-cycle for the XJ6?*
4 *To what extent, if at all, has Jaguar relied too much upon the success of one type of product?*
5 *Comment upon the proposals for the DEW99. In your view, will such changes provide Jaguar with a better future?*

Injecting life into the product life-cycle

The life-cycle of a product may last for a few months or for hundreds of years. To prolong the life-cycle of a brand or a product, an organisation may inject new life

into the growth period by readjusting the ingredients of the marketing mix (see Figure 20.7).

Figure 20.7 Injecting new life into a product

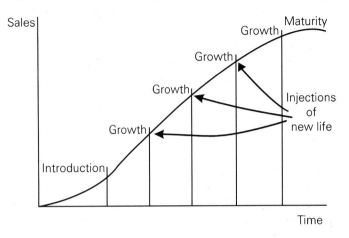

A readjustment of the marketing mix might involve one or several of the following activities.

■ Change or modify the product, to keep up with or ahead of the competition. For example, in 1992 Mars took the unprecedented step of slightly altering the ingredients of the Mars Bar, as well as changing its shape. In 1990 Rowntree introduced the 'Blue Smartie' to improve Smarties' competitiveness against M & Ms, and in 1992 it brought out the 'Gruesome Greens'.

■ Alter distribution patterns, to provide a more suitable place for consumers to make a purchase. For example, Next started catalogue (mail order) trading in 1989.

■ Change prices to reflect competitive activities. For example, the price of home computers was slashed in the mid-1990s as an increasing number of similar products became available.

■ Run a promotional campaign. For example, the Guinness campaigns have helped to extend the life of a well-established product.

Alternative product life-cycles

To a large extent the classic life-cycle of a product is a gross simplification. There are, in fact, many alternative explanations which help to illustrate the life-cycles of products. In *Economie d'Enterprise*, J. L. Cordon and J. P. Raybaud identified a series of different life-cycles as shown in Figure 20.8.

a *Apprentissage long* (**long introductory period**). For example, some novels are available in bookshops for a long period before the public starts to buy them in significant numbers.

Figure 20.8 A series of possible life-cycles

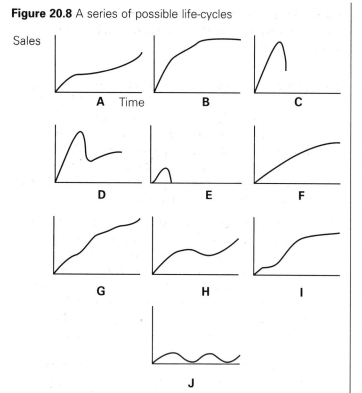

i *Introduction manquée* (**false start**). Sometimes the launch and introductory phase of a product fail to catch the public imagination. Seven-Up was launched with six different names before 'Seven-Up' took off.

j *Mode* (**fashion**). Some products have booms and slumps in sales according to fashion or season. The sales of swimwear and fireworks are examples.

Task

Try to identify one other product to match each of the life-cycle alternatives suggested by Cordon and Raybaud.

Consumers and the life-cycle

Looking at the life-cycle from the consumer angle provides important insights into changes in a market and their influences upon strategies. For example, in the introductory phase of the life-cycle, consumers who are 'early adopters' try products. As the product moves into growth, more consumers become adopters. As the life-cycle of the product moves on, competition intensifies. The number of competitors operating in the market increases as it nears maturity. Organisations fight to retain their market share and this might lead to product diversification and price cutting. Consumers become more selective about their purchases. During maturity, suppliers depend on repeat purchases. Usage falls during decline (see Figure 20.9).

Figure 20.9 The consumer and the product life-cycle

Stage	Users/buyers
Development	Few trial or early adopters
Growth	Growing number of adopters
Shakeout	Growing selectivity of purchase
Maturity	Saturation of users, repeat purchase reliance
Decline	Fall in usage

Product portfolios

Businesses selling a single product are always likely to be vulnerable to variations in the marketplace. By spreading investments across a **range of products**, an organisation reduces its risks.

Most companies produce a range of products, each of which has a life-cycle. By using life-cycles, companies can

b *Pas d'apprentissage* (**virtually no introductory period**). Some new 'wonder drugs' become stars straight away.

c *Feu de paille* (**'straw on fire'**). These are products that rise quickly in popularity and are 'burnt out' in a very short period. This is the case with some children's toys, such as trolls. Some pop groups are 'one-hit wonders'.

d *Feu de paille avec marché résiduel* (**'straw on fire' but with a reasonable residual market**). Some products boom quickly but in decline still leave a sizeable market. Though the skateboard craze came and went, skateboards are still available in the shops. There is usually scope for some of the more efficient firms to stay in the market.

e *Echec* (**flop**). Many new products flop. An often-quoted example is Clive Sinclair's C5 road vehicle (a type of motorised tricycle).

f *Cycle long* (**long cycle**). Many products continue to go from strength to strength, such as potato crisps and chocolate bars.

g *Relances successives* (**periodic rejuvenations**). Many products are frequently injected with new life.

h *Nouveau départ* (**relaunch**). Some products need to be relaunched to bring them out of decline. To do this a product may need to be redesigned or have its image substantially altered. For example, the Babycham drink has recently been relaunched because of declining sales over a number of years.

plan when to introduce new lines as old products go into decline. The collection of products produced by a company is known as **portfolio**.

In Figure 20.10, T_1 represents a point in time. At that point Product 1 is in decline, Product 2 is in maturity, Product 3 is in growth and Product 4 has recently been introduced. This helps to avoid serious fluctuations in overall profit level and ensures that the most profitable products provide support for those which have not yet become quite so profitable. Figure 20.11 indicates how the portfolio can be managed to develop profitable growth.

Figure 20.10 A product portfolio

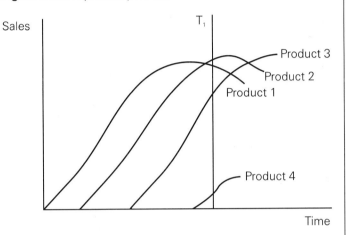

Figure 20.11 Developing new products and the impact on profits

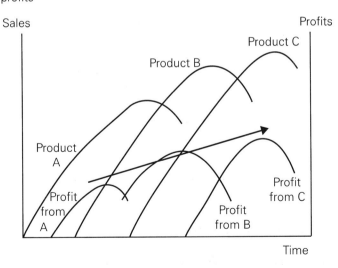

Any organisation does well to bear in mind the simple principle known as **Pareto's rule**. This suggests that 20 per cent of time and effort put in tends to produce 80 per cent of the results. An extension of this idea is that 20 per cent of customers can account for 80 per cent of a firm's

sales. This is a useful 'rule' to remember when trying to work out which products are the real breadwinners in a particular situation.

Boston market-share/market-growth matrix

In Chapter 4, when looking at the competitive process, we looked at the Boston Consultancy Group's matrix, which can also be used for portfolio analysis. The unique feature of this matrix is its ability to plot market share (high and low) against market growth potential (high and low). It then labels four quadrants as:

- **Dogs** – low market share and low growth, operating with cost disadvantage with few opportunities.
- **Question marks/Problem children** – low market share in fast-growing markets. These have poor profit margins and high demands for cash.
- **Prospects/Stars** – products competing rapidly in high-growing markets. These are the new market leaders which require large investment to develop growth.
- **Yielders/Cash cows** – high market share in markets which are no longer expanding. These are usually highly profitable products.

The Boston matrix helps to analyse the portfolio in terms of:

- cash flow
- market share in relation to competition
- market growth rate
- identification of market opportunities
- developing a balanced portfolio.

Profit Impact on Marketing Strategies (PIMS)

Another theory which helps us to understand the importance of factors affecting products and their profitability was developed in the USA and called the Profit Impact of Marketing Strategies (PIMS). In Chapter 3 we looked at how this study highlighted the relationship between market share and profitability. The survey carried out by PIMS looked at product successes and failures and identified that organisations with products which had a large market share were simply more likely to be profitable.

Another feature of the PIMS survey was that it identified the importance of the relationship between the **quality** of goods and services and those of competitors, which enabled them to gain market share and thus be more profitable. With high-quality products organisations can demand higher prices which help them to become more profitable. This fosters customer loyalty, and repeat purchases help to build market share. Promotional and other marketing activities are rarely an adequate substitute for product quality.

Economic and risk analysis

With any product portfolio economic and risk analysis must be part of the on-going process of research and development. This analysis may be based on future estimations of costs and revenues.

Cash flows

A large quantity of information related to outputs, prices, costs, taxes and royalties to be paid will need to be collected and assessed. When this information is available for reliable estimates to be made, the net cash flow over a period can be calculated. This is the total amount of cash coming into the company, based on expected volumes of product sales after allowing for product expenditure.

At this stage the most uncertain assumption often relates to the product price. Some companies do not try to forecast the future price, but assume a price which is prudent and realistic and test the economic viability of a new product against that price.

One example of a business' net cash flow over more than 10 years is illustrated in Figure 20.12. For the first years the cash flow is *negative* while the project is being investigated and there is expenditure on research and development (R&D), plant, materials, etc. Then the cash flow becomes *positive* after the product has been launched.

Figure 20.12 Forecasted cash flows

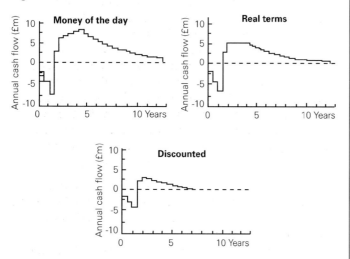

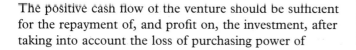

The positive cash flow of the venture should be sufficient for the repayment of, and profit on, the investment, after taking into account the loss of purchasing power of

money as a result of *inflation*. The cash flow must therefore produce a sufficient return in terms of the *money of the day* to offset this loss of purchasing power. To take account of likely future inflation, a **real-terms cash flow** – expressed in terms of money with a constant value – is calculated from the cash flow in terms of money of the day (see Figure 20.12).

The likely **return on the investment**, taking into account the risks inherent in the venture (and hence its economic acceptability) is examined by calculating a **discounted cash flow**. The risks are many and varied, and include technical and commercial risks, and the risks of significant increases in technical costs, among other external factors (e.g. a change in tax structures).

It is extremely difficult to anticipate such possibilities in detail and, consequently, some companies prefer to test the economic acceptability of a project at a discount rate appropriate to an assumed level of risk. Such a discount rate is called the **project screening rate** and is usually in the range 5–20 per cent. A company is not completely free to choose what it feels to be an appropriate rate; it must compete with others in the market.

Figure 20.13 Cumulative cash flow

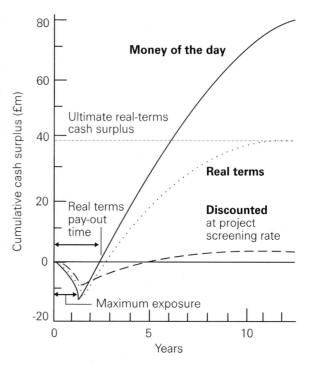

A useful way of understanding the future economic performance of a project is to examine the **cumulative cash flow**. This is the progressive sum of the annual cash flows. Figure 20.13 provides an example. From this a number of important measures of the **economic acceptability** of the venture are immediately apparent, such as the 'pay-out time', the 'maximum exposure' and the 'ultimate cash surplus'. The economic acceptability can now be judged according to the project's ability to meet the requirement that the cumulative cash surplus, discounted at the project screening rate, is positive and sufficient to justify the risks taken.

It is helpful to relate the time it takes to recover the investment in a project to the life-cycle of the project. In Figure 20.14, for example, there will be a continuous drain on resources until the launch. The investment can then be recovered through revenue from sales until the point at which the investment is finally recovered (in Figure 20.14 this takes place during the growth stage).

Figure 20.14 The investment recovery process during the product life-cycle

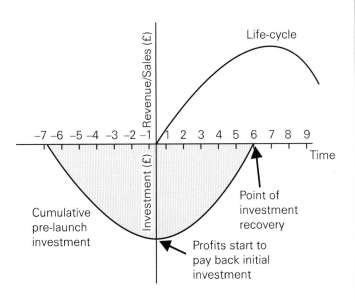

Forecasting product success

Earlier in the chapter we looked at the life-cycle of a product based on consumer demand. However, it is also important to look at *restrictions imposed from the production side*. We can illustrate this by looking at the exploration of oil fields.

Interest in exploring an area for oil may be triggered by a geologist's curiosity, a news item or by an invitation from a government to bid for exploration rights. Before this can be developed further, a realistic assessment must be made of:

■ the probability of finding economic oil fields
■ the contract terms that might be applicable
■ economic aspects, such as production and transportation costs.

These assessments are made to establish whether an exploration programme is justified, i.e. whether anticipated benefits exceed expected costs.

An initial estimate of the resources contained in a prospective area can be expressed in the form of an **expectation curve** (see Figure 20.15). Expectation curves highlight the uncertainty associated with exploration (or any other form of production), particularly at an early stage.

Figure 20.15 Expectation curves

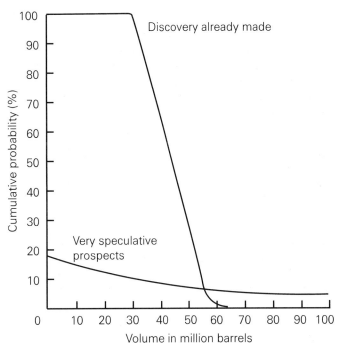

Based on an analysis of the geological information, expectation curves show the probabilities of finding reserves of a certain magnitude in the area. In a well-defined area, with a history of discoveries, for example, there may be a high degree of certainty about the current reserves, but little chance of finding major additions. A speculative venture in a little-known area, on the other hand, means that the chances of finding any hydrocarbons may be low, but there is an outside chance of making a very large discovery (e.g. the discoveries of oil in the mid-1990s off the Falkland Islands).

As with all new major products developed by a large company, several steps of evaluation take place before the final go-ahead is given. The activities involved in an exploration programme are aimed at defining the geological structures as accurately as possible (see Figure 20.16). A preliminary investigation identifies whether there is a possibility of discovering oil. On the basis of this information, contracts are signed with the landowners to provide the basis for the right to develop the field. A

Figure 20.16 A typical exploration programme

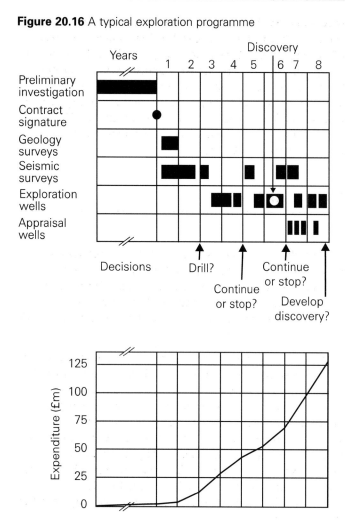

geological survey is then carried out, and periodic seismic studies take place throughout the development stage. Exploration wells are drilled to locate a point of extraction. Only after this has been done is it possible to determine whether oil and gas is present and whether the geological assumptions are valid. A cycle of further surveys and appraisal wells is undertaken to reduce the geological uncertainties and to provide an increasingly accurate estimate of oil and gas reserves.

Information obtained from these activities is used in planning the field development. With each cycle the costs of the exploration programme increase significantly. An efficient exploration is, therefore, one which obtains the maximum information with the minimum effort.

Range strategy

An important element in developing a product line is to analyse whether extending the brand is possible. A **line extension** is the further development of one or more brands in order to make them appeal to different market segments which are in some way related to the original product line. This can provide a useful way of expanding a product, building upon past achievements and improving both sales and profitability with minimum risk and effort. For example, Reckitt and Colman revived the Dettol brand with a series of line extensions which included foambath, soap, Dettox cleanser, antiseptic wipes, etc. to cater for more specific consumer requirements in the marketplace. By doing this, the company increased the size of the brand so that line extensions accounted for more than 50 per cent of the brand size.

Line extensions may be used to revive a brand, build upon past achievements, use extra capacity and even to limit the actions of competitors.

There are three elements to range strategy which may include:

- **width** – how many product lines a range contains
- **depth** – the average number of items within each line
- **consistency** – how the different products in the range relate to each other with regard to their use, requirements and distribution.

Packaging

An important part of any product is its packaging. A package involves the development of some form of container or wrapper for the product. The package may influence consumers and affect their desire to make a purchase. For example, think about the various types of packaging for confectionery products: the tube is a fundamental part of the Smarties brand and is a core strength; boxed chocolates rely heavily upon presenting the products in a way which reflects the sense of occasion on which they might be consumed, as well as the consumer's lifestyle.

However, packaging must be viewed as more than just a cosmetic cover for a product. For example, it may be used to protect the product – as with fresh foods – so that the product can serve its purpose. In some instances packaging has also been developed to prevent tampering, as with baby foods. Packaging may also be designed to help consumers to use and/or store the product more easily. Some types of packaging might also be reusable or recyclable.

Case Study
Lyons Tetley packaging evaluation system

Lyons Tetley uses 16 key criteria on its packaging design. The company points out that these criteria do not apply to every product sector and that they are not all independent of each other. For example, the first two seem to present a paradox, such as how to fit into a sector yet stand out from the competition.

The 16 criteria are:

1 **Relevance** – Does the design fit the product sector? Are the colours right for the sector?
2 **Saliency** – Does the design stand out?
3 **Eye appeal** – Is it pleasing to the eye?
4 **Information hierarchy** – Are the correct legal requirements satisfied?
5 **Range identification** – Does the product fit the whole of the product range?
6 **Convenience** – Is the package convenient for opening, handling, storage, etc.
7 **Environmental awareness** – Does it satisfy, or take advantage, of current environmental demands?
8 **Positioning** – Is it attractive to the type of consumer it is aimed at?
9 **Cost effectiveness** – Does the package cost, plus the cost of the product, make the total product price competitive yet also provide an acceptable profit?
10 **Provenance** – Does the design express the history or geography of the product?
11 **Authenticity** – Is it the 'Real Thing'?
12 **Differentiation** – Is it like other products or competitors?
13 **Quality** – Does the design express the quality of the product?
14 **Currency** – Is the design up to date? Does it reflect nostalgia?
15 **Internationalism** – Does the design translate abroad?
16 **Protection** – Does the pack protect the product, keep its quality over its prescribed life as well as during transportation and handling?

Questions for discussion

1 *What are the benefits of such criteria and how might these be used?*
2 *Identify a product package and then comment upon how well it meets the above criteria. Compare findings.*

There are a number of major considerations to take into account when designing packaging, e.g. cost. It might be possible to develop a truly innovative package which is both useful and attractive for consumers, but will they be willing to bear the cost? Packaging should be easily distinguishable and help the consumer to differentiate the product from its competitors. It should also be used to build upon the core strengths of the brand.

Packaging may be chosen to attract attention. Size, colours, shapes, designs, verbal and non-verbal symbols may all be used to communicate various features of the product. Packaging must also be able to meet the needs of the sellers, i.e. it must be transportable and capable of being handled without damage. More recently, concern has been expressed about the environmental impact of some forms of packaging, particularly non-biodegradable packaging. Some manufacturers, for example, of liquid detergents, have responded with cardboard refills to reduce the use of plastic.

New products

The product life-cycle and the Boston matrix help to show that products do not last forever. Consumer preferences are constantly changing and it is important for an organisation to be continually involved in developments and innovations designed to meet the needs of tomorrow's customers.

In any well-run company, research and development have strictly commercial functions – to further the company's business objectives by creating better products, to improve operational processes and to provide expert advice to the rest of the company and to customers. However, some research is not expected to pay for itself within a foreseeable time span. Large companies may allocate as much as one-tenth of their research budget to **blue-sky** investigations which may lead to the development of new products and a possible payoff in the distant future.

A new product may be one which:

- replaces an old product
- opens up a new market
- broadens an existing market.

It may involve a major innovation or simply a line extension reflecting a change in range strategy. It is often said that only about 10 per cent of newly launched products are really 'new'. In fact, it is possible to turn old products into new products by finding a different market for them and by packaging them in a different way.

Product development may be *proactive* or *reactive*. Proactive development involves taking the lead in a market with the launch of innovative new products which are completely different to those of competitors. For example, Mercedes used airbags in their cars several years before other car manufacturers. Reactive developments follow innovations made by others to a market. Developing a reactive approach to marketing new products can reduce the risk factor involved with being the first into a market.

Structure of new-product development

It is important to develop within an organisation a structure which encourages new-product development. Such developments may be carried out by committees, departments, project managers and venture teams. For example, a committee may be set up which includes representatives of management, and of other areas such as finance, marketing, and production, as well as research. This team, however, may only be concerned with approving plans rather than itself developing the products. Venture teams, on the other hand, comprise a similar group of specialists, but with each member undertaking a particular responsibility and working within the task group to develop the new product.

Within an organisation anyone who is working on a project or is affected either up or down the line by this work is considered to be an internal customer. If there is no internal customer for work from any area of the organisation, then the research project is unlikely to fit into the developmental process.

Case Study
Wall's Tangle Twister

Many product advances are made possible by breakthroughs in production techniques. Twenty years ago, lollies were little more than tapered blocks of ice on a stick. The technology – pouring juice into a rigid metal mould – restricted a company like Wall's to simplicity. Then the lolly embraced rubber technology: by casting ice in a flexible rubber mould, the lollies could be shaped more intricately because the mould could be peeled off.

More recently, the Tangle Twister hit the High Street freezers. This was made possible by an ingenious invention from Wall's design engineers. They came up with a nozzle that could make a lolly by twisting together three separate flavours of ice. The innovation represented a quantum leap in lolly technology.

Such ideas are dependent on the combination of research and development, production engineering, investment funds, investment in people and the key edge of information technology.

Questions for discussion

1 *What is meant by 'technology', and how does new technology provide for the development of new products?*
2 *Comment upon the impact of new technologies on the life-cycle of products.*

3 *To what extent does the case study emphasise the integrated elements required to bring new technologies to the fore?*

Stages in the new-product development process

There are a number of distinct stages in new-product development. These are:

- Step 1 – ideas
- Step 2 – screening of ideas
- Step 3 – marketing analysis
- Step 4 – product development
- Step 5 – testing
- Step 6 – launch and commercialisation.

As products go through each stage, crucial decisions have to be made about whether to go forward with the project or to abandon it. There is, therefore, a mortality rate through the product development process (see Figure 20.17).

Figure 20.17 Fall out from product development stages

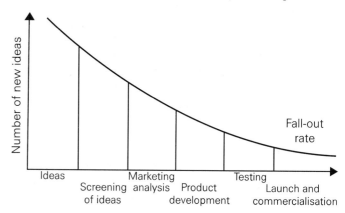

Ideas

New products start from ideas. Such ideas may be completely new and unrelated to past experiences or may simply be an on-going development from an existing product. It may help if an organisation encourages ideas from within. Sources of ideas may be:

- **Research and development**. Product research and development goes hand in hand with market research and development. Considerable research is required between these areas, and processes need to be standardised.
- **Brainstorming sessions**. These involve a number of people in a relaxed environment. A leader introduces key words and concepts in order to encourage participants to contribute ideas.

- **Suggestions box**. Financial incentives may be used to encourage people from all over the organisation to offer their ideas.
- **Sales force**. As the sales force works in the marketplace, it is close to customers and in a strong position to understand their needs and requirements. Ideas from the sales force may be particularly useful.
- **Forced relationships**. One or more products may be 'joined' or forced together to form a single product. For example, shampoo and conditioner or a radio and cassette player.
- **Competitors**. If competitors seem to be doing well, it may be possible to use their ideas to develop the organisation's own success.

Screening of ideas

Once ideas have been generated, the next step is to screen for the most likely ideas and reject the rest. It is important to identify ideas which are likely to match the organisation's objectives. Considerations at this stage may include:

- whether the product matches the organisation's capabilities, particularly in terms of technology and ease of manufacture. Value engineering may also be necessary: by assessing costs of manufacture, the potential profitability of a product may be identified.
- how well the product fits in with other products in the organisation's portfolio and to what extent the product would help to build upon the organisation's strengths.
- an assessment of the unique elements of the idea so that any competitive advantages it may provide can be identified.
- testing of the concept before any financial investment takes place. In the early stages, this may be undertaken by finding out how potential customers react to the idea.
- the likely demand for the product.

Marketing analysis

Once the ideas have been screened, marketing analysis begins. This involves a thorough analysis of the product's potential market as well as the product's place within that market.

Marketing analysis attempts to provide more detailed information about the commercial aspects of the project and may involve both primary and secondary research. For example, it may help to answer the following questions:

- How will consumers react to the product?
- What is the likely size of the market?
- Will the market sustain its size?
- What is the likely competition?
- How should the product be packaged?
- What sort of promotion should accompany the product?
- In what ways should the product be made available to customers?
- What advantages will the product have over the competition?
- What price will the market bear and what pricing strategies should be adopted?
- What additional features should be developed?

This type of research helps to identify the market volume (number of units which could be sold) as well as market value (value of expected sales). It may also help to identify the market potential by focusing upon the purchasing power within the market as well as the external factors which could influence the performance of the product within the market, such as competitive controls, taxation, inflation.

Product development

If the idea has survived the test of marketing analysis, it is time to translate the idea into a product. Marketing information is used to develop a suitable design. Design is simply the art of making things of the quality that people want and/or packaging them or presenting them in an attractive way. The layout of a bookshop, for example, has to be designed – customers must be able to find quickly what they want. In this case, the right use and allocation of space is vital to ensure profitability; as is the concept of a service. Many retail shops have been investing heavily in technology so as to benefit from point-of-sale data capture.

A company might be reluctant to change an earlier design, particularly if it provides status (e.g. the radiator grille on a BMW car). Conversely, small ('cosmetic') changes may be made to products to bring them up to date, e.g. in 1993 Shell updated its logo to create a more 'modern' feel.

Once a design is completed, the product researchers build a prototype, which will be as close as possible to the finished product. It is important at this stage to ensure that the product can be manufactured efficiently. This process may involve many revisions and refinements. It is also necessary to consider **built-in obsolescence**, e.g. fashion clothes are designed for just a season, and cars only last for a few years before repairs are necessary. Manufacturers are able to sustain long-term demand by limiting life-spans of products. The opinion of some is that this leads to a huge waste of resources, but others see it as boosting demand, employment and output in the economy.

Product development also includes an assessment of the packaging (see page 518) required as well as the process of branding (see below).

Testing

Testing is a vital stage in the development process, which may provide valuable information that could be used to fine tune the product and minimise many of the risks of the venture.

A **test market** involves testing the product in a consumer market which is thought to be typical of the whole market. By putting the product into the marketplace, even on a small scale, it is possible to assess consumer reaction to the product and also to monitor its performance. Test marketing is normally carried out in a television region. Testing the market enables an evaluation to be made of the full market size and this helps the organisation to make vital decisions about production. Alternatively, if performance in the test market is unsatisfactory, it may be possible to find out where the problems lie and adjust elements in the marketing mix in such a way as to make the product more acceptable for users.

For industrial marketing, where organisations are likely to have fewer customers, test marketing may not be feasible. In these circumstances, more rigorous product testing, as well as a series of trials, may ensure that the product meets the standards required for the market.

Launch and commercialisation

The launch is the most spectacular day in the life of a product (a launch may roll from TV region to TV region, however, and spread over a period of time). It is the time when a product is finally revealed to the critical scrutiny of the customer in the marketplace. In recent years, the launching of products has become an art. At one time there was considerable secrecy associated with the launch. Today, a common marketing technique is to provide sneak glimpses, and to 'leak' information to whet the appetite of the market.

The major part of the advertising budget on a new product will normally be spent in the pre-launch and launch period to create maximum impact. Promotional pricing, trial offers and free gifts are also effective ploys.

The launch should either make potential customers widely aware of the new product or make them want to find out more about the product. While new product development is an important activity for companies, it is one that has a high degree of risk associated with it; a number of the new products that are launched every year either fail to be accepted by the market or do not meet the financial criteria expected of them.

The success of a launch and the development of a product for full-scale commercialisation will depend upon how well marketing programmes and systems have been developed. Production facilities have to be developed and the sales force and other marketing intermediaries have to be trained so that customers can be provided with detailed information about the product. Many factors may lead to a product's failure, such as technical faults or poor timing of the launch. In contrast, the ability to satisfy customer needs and provide a positive approach to innovation in the market, combined with efficient organisation, may ensure a product's success.

Product branding

As consumers, we identify products in a variety of different ways. A brand image comprises a range of features which identify the products of a particular organisation, e.g. a name, sign, term, symbol or other creative element.

Why is branding important and what are the benefits for both consumers and producers? The reputation of a brand might encourage the consumer to buy its newly launched product without fully considering the competing products. Branding is, in itself, a form of product differentiation which communicates quickly and effectively a great deal of information about a product range. For example, the brand name Levi's instantly conjures up an image of the qualities we may associate with jeans.

Task

What characteristics and qualities do you associate with the following brands:

- British Telecom
- McVitie's
- Heinz
- Crosse & Blackwell
- Knorr?

A brand may not be identified by words alone. For example, a brand of tea bags may be recognised by a picture of its 'Tea Folk', and a make of toilet tissue by the sight of a Labrador puppy. A trade mark provides legal protection of the brand for its owner, covering design, brand name and abbreviations. This type of protection may also be extended to cover colours and shapes.

Branding provides consumers with an assurance that they are purchasing a product they like and can rely upon, and this reduces the importance of price competition. Branding also helps to foster loyalty, which involves long-standing decisions by consumers to repeat the purchase of products. This provides the producer with a stable market, and enables popular or 'premium' brands to be sold at higher prices than their competitors.

For the producer, branding will lead to wider acceptability of products by both wholesalers and retailers, and this may reduce any difficulties in personal selling and give the manufacturer more control over distribution. It may also make it easier for the manufacturer to obtain display space in a large store. Branding provides unique selling propositions (USPs) which help to differentiate the product from its competitors and, therefore, make it an essential item for retailers to stock.

There are three different types of brands.

- **Manufacturer brands**. These associate the producer with the product. Where this happens the producer may be involved with promotion, distribution and, to some extent, the pricing of the product. For example, HP sauce, PG Tips and Wall's sausages.
- **Own-label brands**. These brands are owned by the resellers who may also be the wholesalers or retailers. Manufacturers are, therefore, not associated with the products. Own-label brands include famous names such as St Michael (Marks & Spencer) and George (Asda). Most competition over recent years has been focused on own-label brands competing with manufacturer brands.
- **Generic brands**. These brands only show the product category and will not include the company name or any identifying terms. An example is bin liners. Though these brands have been sold at vastly reduced prices, today they only account for a small proportion of retail turnover.

Branding strategies

Organisations have to think carefully before introducing any form of brand strategy. For example, products may be difficult to brand because of their homogeneous nature, such as coal, milk, nails or staples. It is also important to understand *how* consumers differentiate between brands, as well as other competitive features of a market. There are three types of branding strategy.

- **Multi-branding or individual branding**. This is a strategy of naming each product from an organisation differently, even though it might cater for similar consumer tastes. For example, both Lever Brothers and Procter & Gamble use individual branding for washing detergents, so when we think of Tide, Bold, Dreft and Daz, we do not automatically associate them with the same company. The benefit of this is that a brand with a bad name will not reflect on the company as a whole. It also enables a business to try to increase market share by introducing more than one brand at the same time.
- **Family branding**. This uses the power of the family name to brand products. For example, Vauxhall, Kraft and John West have wide product portfolios and the use of the brand name may help to develop consumer confidence.
- **Brand extensions**. This involves extending a product line to take advantage of a brand which is already well known, e.g. the use of confectionery names such as Mars and Opal Fruits to develop ice-cream products.

Organisations tend to use a combination of branding strategies. For example, Persil is one of many individual Lever Brothers' brands. It also has its own 'family' of detergent products and has been extended into the manufacture of washing-up liquids.

Brand image

The creation of a brand image which matches customer needs more closely than competing products is a function of **product positioning**.

Every person has a self-image which relates to his or her qualities, activities and lifestyle. This personal image is built up through interpersonal contacts and the ways in which others are perceived to respond to the individual. It consists of:

- actual self-concept – what the individual perceives himself or herself to be like
- ideal self-concept – what the individual would prefer to be like
- expected self-concept – how the individual would like to be perceived in the future.

Self-image influences individuals in their choice of brands and products because when they make a purchase they try to do so in a way which fits into their perception of 'self'. When consumers make purchases, they attempt to match brand image with self-image. The brand, the retail outlet from which it is purchased, and its promotion will all, therefore, have a symbolic value for the consumer. A brand image attempts to fulfil consumer needs. For example, Osgood, an American researcher, carried out a survey of car owners in Texas. The survey showed that a high degree of congruence existed between the perceptions car owners had of themselves and of their cars.

When marketers launch products, it is critical that they understand how their customers wish to be perceived in terms of image. The product position is the customer's concept of the attributes of a product relative to the various attributes of competing brands. For example, when Rover repositioned its brands upmarket, doing so helped the company to develop a brand image that reflected more closely the criteria which many customers view as important when purchasing a motor car. In *Exploring Corporate Strategy*, Johnson and Scholes, when considering public-sector post-privatisation strategies, pointed out that 'establishing a clear positioning strategy is the most important single issue for organisations'.

One technique used by marketers to find out how their products are perceived by consumers is that of **perceptual mapping**. A grid is drawn which shows key features and benefits. The perceptions which respondents have are then plotted.

For example, there are four hairdressing salons in Midtown. Angelo's is the top-of-the-range salon charging high prices and giving high-quality service in luxurious premises. Belinda's charges a reasonably high price, but offers a more basic service. Maria's places some emphasis on service, but charges a relatively low price. Tony's, at the bottom end of the range, charges a low price for a quick turnover (see Figure 20.18).

The perceptual map can be used to help identify where consumer needs are not being met. For example, there is no low price, high-quality hairdressing service in Midtown. Repositioning would enable an organisation to change its image to meet such needs. The map also helps organisations to identify how brands are perceived and assess their products' strengths and weaknesses in relation to those of competitors.

Organisations can adopt a variety of positioning strategies. These may include:

- **Positioning in relation to a target market.** A business may position in relation to a specific market segment. For example, Lucozade used to be a drink for the sick and the elderly; it was repositioned as a drink for the young and sporty.
- **Positioning by product and class.** Some products are positioned at the top of the market, such as a

Figure 20.18 Perceptual map for hairdressing businesses

BMW. The other end of the car market includes, for example, the Fiat.

- **Positioning in relation to competitors.** Some products position themselves directly in relation to their competitors, such as Coca-Cola and Pepsi-Cola, which openly compete with each other for customer loyalty.

Further reading

- *Marketing: A Global Perspective* by Harold Chee and Rod Harris. Pitman, 1993.
- *Marketing*, 5th edition, by Michael J. Baker. Macmillan, 1991.
- *Marketing Principles and Practice* by Dennis Adcock, Caroline Ross and Roy Bradfield. Pitman, 1993.
- *Positioning: The Battle For Your Mind* by Al Ries and Jack Trout. McGraw-Hill, 1986.
- *Business Marketing* by Andrew C. Cross, Peter M. Banting, Lindsay N. Meredith and I. David Ford. Houghton Mifflin, 1993.
- *Successful Product Management* by Stephen Morse. Kogan Page, 1994.
- *Basic Marketing Principles and Practice*, 3rd edition, by Tom Cannon. Cassell, 1992.

21 Pricing policy

On completion of this chapter students should be able to:

- analyse the relationships between types of costs and sales

- identify and describe different pricing strategies and evaluate their applications

- examine the ways in which organisations respond to price competition.

The meaning of price

Imagine being one of those who applied to buy the Jaguar XJ220. The **price** was a mere £415 000 (£55 000 of which was tax!). At the time of its launch it was rated not just as the ultimate status symbol but also as a good short-term investment. Only 280 were built so, in order to allocate sales among the 1400 who applied to buy the car, a ballot was held. Two years after the launch, however, the street value of the car was just £180 000. For a variety of reasons owners claimed disappointment with the product and some refused to pay staged instalments, claiming that it was not the 'ultimate' Jaguar they were promised. Some unhappy buyers settled out of court. Jaguar expected to make £98 million from sales of the car, but instead *losses* were estimated in tens of millions of pounds.

Without going into the technical and economic reasons for what went wrong, we can consider what expectations were created by the price tag of £415 000 – for Jaguar, for the prospective owners of the XJ220, as well as for the government.

For buyers, the price generated a series of expectations based on the value which they hoped would provide them with an element of satisfaction or utility. In this instance, after taking delivery of the car, they would have been able to decide whether the satisfaction they gained from it was worth the price they paid. For Jaguar the price related directly to profitability – the company expected to make a profit of £98 million but is now looking at a loss. And we must not forget the government – if all had gone well the government would have collected £15.4 million in taxation.

The Oxford English Dictionary defines price as the *sum or consideration or sacrifice for which a thing may be bought or attained*. However, producing a watertight definition of price which gives a clear indication of its importance in the marketing mix is like trying to define the length of a piece of string. In some situations, a particular definition will be appropriate, in others it will not.

A major problem stems from the fact that 'price' has different meanings for different groups of people:

Is this worth £415 000?

- For *buyers*, price helps them to measure the value placed on the exchange. This value will relate to how they perceive the transaction and the satisfaction or utility they expect to gain from it. They will undoubtedly want to consider whether the transaction was worth the price paid and the buying power sacrificed. This is because the amount paid will involve sacrificing the next-best alternative that could be bought (sometimes known as **opportunity cost**). Price will also have a psychological impact on customers which may influence their perceptions.

- For *sellers*, price is a key element in the marketing mix which, in the short term, may be used to stimulate demand or to respond to the actions of competitors. Price also generates revenue and may be a vital selling point. Getting the price 'right' is an important tactical decision because it is a key factor influencing revenue and profit:

  (Price × Quantity sold) − Total costs = Profits

  Price may be a major determinant of both the quantity sold and total costs (because of the quantity sold).

- For the *government*, the price of products will determine the levels of taxation collected. Prices will also be an influence upon the general retail price index – and hence votes!

Case Study
A competitive price for Le Shuttle?

The prices charged by Eurotunnel and its competitors are closely related to each other because they offer a similar product – that is, a short journey between France and the United Kingdom. In early 1994 the prices of standard fares between Dover and Calais were as shown in the table following.

	Winter off-peak	Summer off-peak	Summer peak weekend
Le Shuttle (car and unlimited passengers)	£220	£280	£310
Stena Sealink (car and up to 5 passengers)	£126	£220	£320
P&O (car and up to 8 passengers)	£139	£139–221	£289–320
Hoverspeed	£142	£297	£338

Eurotunnel is hoping to capture 50 per cent of the cross-channel market by 1996. Indeed, it needs to capture such a high share of the market if it is to pay back the money it has borrowed for massive construction costs.

Eurotunnel in effect offers a 'no frills attached' product at a competitive price. The price it charges will be considerably more than competitors in the winter when it hopes that the prospect of faster journeys will capture the custom of many motorists. It is essential for Eurotunnel to be seen to be the quicker service. The journey time is 35 minutes, the same as for the hovercraft, but 40 minutes quicker than the ferry. However, ferries require cars to arrive at least 20 minutes before the ferry departs, and with 10 minutes extra to disembark the time taken in a crossing is more like 105 minutes from motorway to motorway, compared with an hour by tunnel.

A number of national newspapers have summed up the advantages and disadvantages of the two methods in the following way:

	Le Shuttle	Car ferry
Winter price	Substantially more expensive	Relatively cheap
Summer price	A little bit more expensive	Relatively cheap
Time taken	About one hour	Nearer two hours
Comfort	Own car seat	Passenger lounges
Sea view	None	Yes
Frequency	Up to 4 per hour	Every 90 minutes
Reliability	Weatherproof	Uncomfortable in bad seas
Booked trips	No	Yes
Restaurants	No	Yes
Shopping	No	Yes

Of course these advantages and disadvantages will vary. Passengers may find that they are faced with unforeseen delays when using either service. Travelling in your own car has the advantage (if you see it that way) that you do not have to mix with other people. But then again, some passengers may prefer to travel in a well-equipped boat with plenty of recreational activities, opportunities to make purchases, and a sea view.

As a new venture, Eurotunnel is reluctant to get involved in a *price war* with its rivals. This could have disadvantages for all involved. Instead Eurotunnel will focus on some of the major *non-price advantages*, such as missing unpleasant weather conditions and a no-booking system. Eurotunnel wants its service to be seen as a kind of rolling motorway linking Britain and France.

Eurotunnel has moved into a very profitable market in which the rival ferry companies have been making healthy profits. It seems likely that profit margins will be cut back and that some cross-channel operators will link together. Sealink and P&O are hoping that the Office of Fair Trading will allow them to provide a combined service offering two sailings per hour.

Questions for discussion

1 *What factors do you think are most likely to give Le Shuttle a competitive advantage?*
2 *What factors are most likely to give it a competitive disadvantage?*
3 *Why did it set its prices at the levels shown early in 1994?*
4 *Why did Eurotunnel not want to start a price war with its rivals?*
5 *What has subsequently happened to the pricing strategy of Eurotunnel, and the pricing strategy of its rivals? Explain the changes that have occurred. What are likely to be the effects of these changes?*

Approaches to pricing decisions

Selecting the right price is one of the most critical decisions to be taken in the marketing mix. If Eurotunnel had set its price too high or too low then Le Shuttle may have become an expensive failure.

The importance of price within the marketing mix varies from one market to another and between different segments in the same market. In low-cost, non-fashion markets, price can be critical – for example, in the sale of white emulsion and gloss paint for decorating. In such markets competitors engage in **price competition**. Their

activities will emphasise price as a major competitive issue and will attempt to use it as a basis for matching or beating the activities of competitors. On the other hand, in other markets such as markets for fashion clothing, price can be one of the least relevant competitive factors – competitors will engage in **non-price competition** which focuses on areas of the marketing mix other than price. Sales are increased through other means which help to emphasise each product's unique features.

Certain products are designed to suit a particular price segment (e.g. economy, family cars) while others perform a specific function regardless of cost (e.g. sports cars). For consumers with limited budgets price is a key purchasing criterion, while for others 'money is no object'.

A number of situations can be identified in which pricing decisions have to be made. The most important of these are:

■ *when a price needs to be set for the first time* – This can happen when a new product is launched on the market, when new outlets are used, when new contracts are made, or when businesses move into new international markets.
■ *when it becomes necessary to make a change in the pricing structure* – This may be because of the development of competition (e.g. European Union competitors selling in the UK after the creation of a single market), or a movement along the product life-cycle, or a change in demand or cost conditions. For example, the product life-cycle reflects the development of a product over time; this may help an organisation to adjust the marketing mix to reflect changes at each stage. A product may be launched at a high price in the introductory phase because of slow sales growth and high unit expenditures. During later stages, such as growth and maturity, prices may be allowed to fall, particularly as competitors enter the market.

It should be remembered that *price is only one element in the marketing mix* and any change in price should match changes to other parts of the mix. Also, any changes in the mix should be geared at providing the direction which enables the organisation to achieve its corporate objectives. Before selecting an appropriate price, an organisation will therefore need to consider and match *objectives*, with *strategies* and *techniques* (see Figure 21.1).

There are a whole host of influences on the pricing decision. Some of these may be internal while others will be external to the organisation. **Internal influences** on price may include:

■ the objectives of the organisation
■ the pattern of costs
■ existing prices of similar and other products produced by the company

- existing ideas about price-setting in the organisation
- the organisation's knowledge of the market
- pressures or feedback from salespeople and other members of the organisation
- levels of research and development and the pace of new product development.

External influences on price may include:

- the strength and behaviour of competitors
- the attitudes and influences of other groups involved in the chain of production and distribution (e.g. what size margin do distributors want, and how much power do they have?)
- pressure from suppliers of raw materials and components used in the product
- elasticity of demand for the product
- motivations of customers
- existing and anticipated government policies
- general conditions in different markets.

Because there are so many variables involved, and because information available at any one time is liable to be imperfect, it will be necessary to select certain 'critical' factors to help make pricing decisions.

Figure 21.1 An example of matching techniques and strategies with objectives

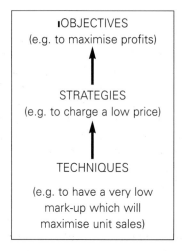

Pricing objectives

The starting point in pricing is to be clear about the **pricing objectives**. These are the goals which the organisation wishes to achieve through its pricing efforts. Some possible objectives are as follows.

Profit maximisation

A key assumption of many business theories is that **profit maximisation** is the most important pricing target. While it is true that unless businesses can make profits in the long run their futures will remain uncertain, studies of actual business behaviour reveal that profit targets tend to be at realistic or satisfactory levels rather than at simple short-term maximised levels.

Price competition

A **competitive price** is one that gives a competitive edge in the marketplace. It is not necessarily one that is lower than that of a rival because other elements of the marketing mix add to the competitive edge. For example, it is possible for the manufacturer of Gillette razor blades to argue that they are better quality than those of rivals, giving scope to charge a higher yet more competitive price than those applying to other blades (see Figure 21.2).

Figure 21.2 The combination of higher price and other benefits can lead to a competitive advantage

A further element of competitive pricing is that it *deters new entrants* to a particular market. Large firms with some degree of monopoly power may be inclined to keep prices relatively low in order to secure long-term market dominance. From time to time in business you will hear the owner of a small company say: 'Of course we would like to diversify into producing *x* but we simply couldn't compete with the prices offered by the big fish.'

Yield on investment

A profit-related pricing objective may aim for a specific **return on an investment**. This involves a degree of uncertainty because it may be difficult to predict prices and costs. Any money that is allocated to a particular use also bears an opportunity cost. Could this money be spent in a better way? What are the alternatives that are sacrificed? Investors usually have expectations of what they regard to be an appropriate return on their investment. The need to provide a specific yield may be an important factor in determining pricing decisions. Investors will quickly make their feelings known to managers if they feel that the wrong pricing decisions are made.

Sales maximisation

Generating a lot of sales implies that an organisation can produce on a larger scale. High sales may also give a good **profile in a particular market**. Sometimes organisations (or parts of organisations) set out to generate high sales figures because it makes them look good. The sales manager who sells a lot will need to lead a large sales team, thus enhancing his or her own position and salary and bonus. Connected to this may be the requirement to price to increase *market share* or to obtain *brand leadership* – a product may be launched at a low price in order to develop a high share of a developing market. It is, however, important to realise that, although market share may be increasing, unit sales may be falling in a market declining in size.

Satisficing

H. A. Simon put forward the view that businesses might want to **satisfice** – that is, to achieve given targets for market share and profits from sales which may not maximise sales but would instead inflate boardroom egos. This can arise when the managers of an organisation are clearly different from the owners. If the managers can set price at a level which provides sufficient profits to keep the shareholders satisfied, then a proportion of the profits can be diverted to provide more perks for managers and larger departments.

Satisficing policies are most likely to be associated with industries where there is only a limited degree of competition. Satisficing objectives are fairly common in many organisations ranging from schools to oil companies. Managers will readily produce long lists of achievements which do not always relate to the profit margin or bottom line.

Survival

Survival may be another pricing objective. If an organisation feels that it is losing market share, or if it needs to respond quickly and with flexibility to some competitive activity in the marketplace which could affects its future, pricing may simply be designed to ensure survival, even if losses are made in the short term.

Product quality

For an organisation that has a reputation for its **high-quality products**, pricing may reflect higher production and other costs which have been borne in the various processes that help to ensure the customer is totally satisfied with the quality of the product.

Other objectives

There are many other possible objectives in establishing price. For example, an organisation may set price simply to maintain market share or to create price stability.

In setting the objectives outlined above, it is essential to remember that groups other than customers may be affected by price changes. Other groups to be considered include:

- *competitors*, who may choose to match price cuts or not to match price increases
- *distributors*, who may insist on high margins and thus resist price-cutting
- *employees*, who may ask for wage increases (wages are often one of the most important component costs)
- *government bodies*, who may withold contracts, certificates or grants
- *shareholders*, who may seek higher dividends.

The pricing process

Pricing objectives help to focus the organisation's pricing policies and decisions. They may also relate to the time period over which prices are set. The next stage is to establish an appropriate strategy (see Figure 21.3). Three broad strategies can be considered: 'high-price', 'market-price' and 'low-price'. Before going on to examine each of these in turn, it will be helpful to look at the relationship between price and sales.

The demand curve

A demand curve shows the quantity of a product that consumers will be willing to buy at different prices. Common sense seems to tell us that more of a product will be bought at a cheaper price than at a higher price. For example, market research on the number of adults who would use weekly a new swimming pool produced these results for different prices:

£4	100	75p	1200
£3	150	50p	1400
£2	250	40p	1500
£1	800	30p	1600

The demand for a product is commonly shown graphically, as in Figure 21.4, which plots the demand curve for the swimming pool.

Figure 21.3 Stages in the pricing process

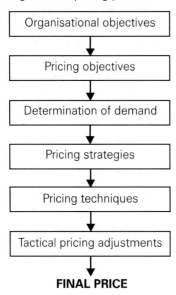

```
Organisational objectives
        ↓
Pricing objectives
        ↓
Determination of demand
        ↓
Pricing strategies
        ↓
Pricing techniques
        ↓
Tactical pricing adjustments
        ↓
   FINAL PRICE
```

Figure 21.4 The demand curve of a swimming pool

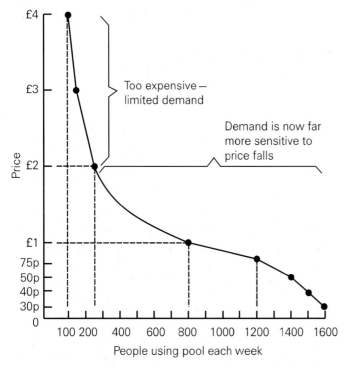

An individual demand curve can be likened to a snapshot taken at a particular moment in time showing how much of a product would be bought at different prices. At that moment in time, price is seen to be the only variable that can be altered which will influence the quantity purchased.

Most demand curves drawn from real situations have a shape which is more of a squiggle than a straight line. However, the common factor of nearly all demand curves

is that they slope down to the right, indicating that – assuming conditions of demand remain the same – more units will be bought at a lower price than at a higher price. Therefore, in this chapter we will simplify demand curves into straight lines.

Most businesses need to consider carefully the effect of increasing their sales. If they want to sell only a small number of items (e.g. designer jeans) in the marketplace, they will probably be able to do so at a high price. However, if they want to sell a lot of items then they will only be able to do so at a relatively lower price (see Figure 21.5).

Figure 21.5 A 'trade-off' between price and quantity demanded

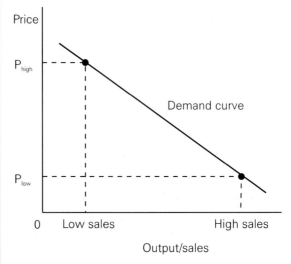

It is, however, possible to increase sales or keep sales constant without lowering price. This can be done by raising the **demand** for the product. An increase in demand leads to a shift in the demand curve to the right, as in Figure 21.6.

Figure 21.6 A shift to the right in the demand curve

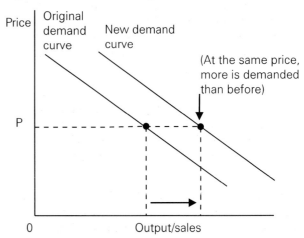

Factors which might cause an increase in the demand for a product include:

- an increase in the number of people (population) available in the market
- a change in tastes in favour of this product
- an increase in the price of competing products
- an increase in the incomes of people making up the market.

The demand curve for most products is continuously shifting as a result of pressures such as changes in tastes and fashion. Most businesses can influence and shape these external factors by a careful use of the marketing mix – for example, by changing the product's advertising, and by sales promotion, as well as adjustments in price.

Low-price strategy

A **low-price strategy** should be considered when consumers respond very positively to any small downward changes in price. In technical terms we can measure this response by calculating the **price elasticity of demand**. This is a measure of changes in quantities purchased as a response to price changes:

Price elasticity

$$PED = \frac{\text{Percentage change in quantity demanded of product A}}{\text{Percentage change in price of product A}}$$

Demand is said to be 'elastic' if the change in quantity demanded is of a greater *proportion* than the change in price that initiated it. For example, if the price of a particular brand of washing powder is lowered by 10 per cent and there is an increase in sales of 20 per cent, then the demand for the product is said to be elastic because the change in price leads to a more than proportionate response in quantity demanded. In this case the price elasticity of demand is 20 per cent divided by 10 per cent, which is 2.0.

The key consideration in lowering price is to *increase revenue*. If the percentage increase in quantity demanded is proportionately higher than the percentage change in price that triggered the rise in demand, then revenue will increase. Products with an elasticity value greater than 1.0 are said to have *elastic demand*.

However, it must be remembered that elastic demand does not always mean that an organisation will benefit from price reductions. If an organisation in a price-sensitive market lowers its price, then there will be a strong chance that other competing organisations will follow suit.

Another consideration is *cost*. If a firm lowers the price of a product, and sells more, it will usually have to pay out more in expenses and other costs ('the cost of sales').

A low-price strategy is important when it is easy for consumers to compare competitors' prices. For example, brands of washing powder sit side-by-side on the shelves of a supermarket, so there is a strong incentive to charge a low price. This is also true when the product cannot be classed as a *necessity*. Necessities tend to have low price elasticities of demand compared with luxury items. It is therefore possible to charge a relatively higher price for necessities in the knowledge that the consumer 'needs' to buy the product. When the product is in plentiful supply, however, it would be a mistake to charge a high price, because the product is readily available from competitors.

In the situations outlined above, in which price cuts may lead to large increases in turnover, then a low-price strategy may well strengthen an organisation's position – for example, when selling to supermarket customers. Price in these situations plays a crucial role in the marketing mix.

Market-price strategy

There are situations where one or more of the following conditions apply:

- products are bought frequently
- competitive products are highly similar
- a few large companies dominate supply in a specific industry.

In any of these situations, firms could quickly lose all their business if they set prices above the competition. Conversely, if they lower prices their competitors may be forced to follow. Firms tend to set prices at market-price level and the role of price is therefore *neutral*.

One model which helps us to understand this type of pricing was produced by P. Sweezy. This is known as the **kinked demand curve** theory (see Figure 21.7). With this theory it is argued that price remains the same even if, as shown, marginal costs rise from MC_1 to MC_2. Though competitors will follow a price decrease none will follow a price increase. They will assume that price is elastic for a price rise but is inelastic for a price fall. The kinked demand curve therefore leads to a form of neutral or going-rate pricing at which an average market price is established.

High-price strategy

A high-price strategy can be either a long-term or a short-term policy. A long-term policy will mean that the firm seeks to sell a high-quality product to a select market. This is true of international car sales where Jaguars, Rolls Royces and Lamborghinis are sold at exclusive prices. High prices are an essential feature of up-market

Figure 21.7 The kinked demand curve

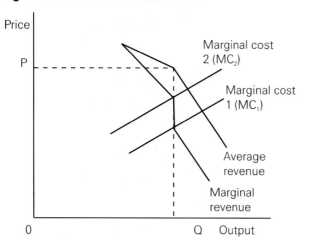

products – it is essential to maintain an exclusive *image*, and for this to be reflected in the price.

A short-term policy is based on advantages gained by a patented product, a heavy investment in new equipment, research, or by some other form of *barrier to entry* to a market by competitors.

Pricing techniques

How are prices set in practice? A number of factors largely determine the pricing techniques used. These are:

■ cost
■ demand
■ competition
■ the time period.

In some instances practical pricing may involve elements from more than one of these determinants.

Cost-based pricing

The quantity of product sold (the sales volume) is a critical factor in the success of any kind of business. The reason is that every business has to pay two different kinds of costs associated with generating sales: fixed costs and variable costs.

Fixed costs are so called because they remain the same no matter how many units of product are sold. For instance, a shop has to pay the same rent, rates, heating and lighting, wages, insurance and much else no matter how large or small its sales are in a particular month. The same applies to a factory or any other kind of business.

Variable costs are those that vary according to the number of units sold. For instance, if a shop sells

confectionery, the more confectionery sold to customers, the more has to be bought from the wholesaler. If a factory makes furniture, the more furniture sold the more wood and other materials have to be bought from the supplier. In other words, *these costs vary directly with the number of units that are sold.*

At the risk of further adding to the complexity of this process, it may be useful to mention **semi-variable costs** at this stage. These comprise an element of fixed and variable cost. For example, electricity bills consist of a standing charge as well as a charge for usage. The standing charge is fixed and the unit charge may vary with production levels but not in the same way as variable-only costs. Another feature of costs is that in the long-run all costs are likely to become more variable in nature. For example, as a business develops and expands its capacity there will be a crucial threshold where fixed costs may suddenly have to rise by a significant amount. These are known as **stepped costs**.

All organisations, no matter what their activities or the extent to which they influence pricing, will have to cover costs either through sales or from other sources of funding. Costs are, therefore, clearly likely to be an important determinant of pricing techniques and, if setting or planning prices for the longer term, it may be necessary to look not just at fixed and variable costs but also more closely at the influence of semi-variable and stepped costs.

The relationship between volume and costs

The difference between the *variable costs* of each unit of product and the price paid by the customer is called the **margin**. So, clearly, the ratio of variable costs to the margin remains the same no matter how many units are sold.

However, the ratio of *fixed costs* to the margin changes with the number of units sold. For instance, if your fixed costs are £1000 a year and you sell 100 units, then each unit has to 'carry' £10 of fixed costs. If the margin is £20, then the fixed costs represent 50 per cent of the margin. If, on the other hand, you sell 500 units, then each unit has to carry only £2 of fixed costs – which is 10 per cent of the margin.

Let us use the example of a service station to illustrate the nature of costs:

■ Fixed costs at the service station include staffing, insurance, heat/light, security and office costs.
■ Variable costs are the price paid by the service station to the refinery for bulk supplies of petrol, diesel and lubricants; plus items such as stationery and sales promotion.

Figure 21.8 shows typical values for the total fixed and variable costs of a service station. Both lists have been greatly simplified for the sake of clarity.

Figure 21.8 Typical costs for a petrol service station

Fixed costs (£000)		Variable costs (pence per litre)	
Staff	35.0	Fuel	30.00
Insurance	2.0	Bank charges	0.30
Heat/light/power	5.5	Sales promotion and advertising	0.15
Security	1.5		
Local business tax	6.0	Postage and stationery	0.03
Maintenance and repair	2.0		
Office	6.5		
Depreciation	3.5		
Totals	**62.0**		**30.48**

To recover total fixed costs of £62 000, a service station selling half a million litres a year must add 12.4p per litre (£62 000 divided by 500 000) to the variable cost. A similar-sized but more successful service station selling three million litres a year would have to add only 2.06p per litre. In other words, the *minimum price per litre* (before profit) that the lower-volume station must charge its customers is 42.88p (30.48 + 12.4); whereas the higher-volume station can cover all its costs, both fixed and variable, by charging 32.54p (30.48 + 2.06). The higher-volume station can afford to charge less per litre, and still make a bigger margin – to be used for further investment and distribution to shareholders.

We can illustrate this point graphically by using an example related to the three pie charts in Figure 21.9. Assume:

- each unit of sales has a retail price of £1.00
- variable costs per unit are 60p in each case
- fixed costs are £50 000 a year in each case
- each of the three retail outlets has the same fixed costs (rents, local business taxes, staff, depreciation, etc.)

The pie charts show how the per-unit ratio between fixed costs and variable costs changes with the number of units sold. The more units sold, the lower the *proportion* of the unit price taken by fixed costs.

- Each unit sold by retail outlet no. 1 must carry 60p variable costs and 33p fixed costs, leaving a margin of 7p.
- Each unit sold by retail outlet no. 2 must carry 60p variable costs and 25p fixed costs, leaving a margin of 15p.

Figure 21.9 Cost and margins per unit sold

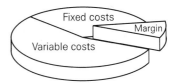

Retail outlet no. 1 sells 150 000 units a year

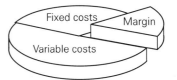

Retail outlet no. 2 sells 200 000 units a year

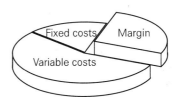

Retail outlet no. 3 sells 500 000 units a year

- Each unit sold by retail outlet no. 3 must carry 60p variable costs and 10p fixed costs, leaving a margin of 30p.

Retail outlet no. 3 therefore makes the most efficient use of its fixed costs. As a result it will have the financial resources to invest in improved premises and equipment, and thus improve its own efficiency, the quality of its service to customers and its profitability.

There are two generally accepted pricing techniques based on the use of costs. These are cost-plus pricing and contribution pricing.

Cost-plus pricing

Any study of how firms price products in the real world invariably reveals a very high proportion of small businesses using no other basis than a **mark-up** on the cost of providing the product or service concerned. Information about costs is usually easier to piece together than information about other variables such as likely revenue. Firms will often therefore simply add a margin to the **unit cost**.

The unit cost is the average cost of each item produced. If a firm produces 800 units at a total cost of £24 000, the unit cost will be £30.

The process of cost-plus pricing can best be illustrated in relation to large firms where *economies of scale* can be spread over a considerable range of output. For a large firm, unit costs will fall rapidly at first as the overheads are spread over a larger output. Unit cost then becomes relatively stable over a considerable quantity of output. It is therefore a relatively simple calculation to add a fixed margin (e.g. 20 per cent) to the unit cost. The firm is able to select an output to produce and to set a price that will be 20 per cent higher than the unit cost of production (see Figure 21.10).

Figure 21.10 Select a target output 0Q and then add 20 per cent to the unit cost to get price

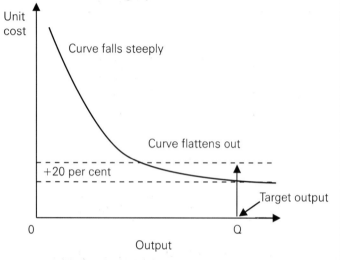

Cost-plus pricing is very popular. One survey showed that 59 per cent of large and small companies in the UK use the cost-plus method on all products, and 33 per cent use it on some products (while only 3 per cent use contribution pricing – described later – on all products and only 13 per cent use contribution pricing on some products). There are, however, many dangers generally associated with cost-plus pricing:

- If the price is set too high, sales may fall short of expectations; and if the price is set too low, then potential revenue is sacrificed.
- Cost-plus pricing indicates a *production-orientated* approach to the market. Emphasis on costs leads to tunnel vision that looks inwards at the company's product rather than outwards to the customers' perception of the product.
- This type of pricing does not identify a profit goal nor does it look at market share, both of which should have some influence on price.
- It is considered to be inflexible in that it does not take into account changing circumstances within the market. In particular it generally disregards the actions of competitors.
- It also ignores price elasticity of demand which would provide a clear indication of the effect of any price increase or decrease on revenue.

Task

The Victoria Hotel is a medium-sized provincial hotel, appealing mainly to the business traveller. It has 60 rooms, charged at a flat rate throughout the week of £40 a night excluding breakfast. Room utilisation has been 60 per cent during 199x. You are helping the manager review the hotel's financial results for the year to 31 December 199x, set out in income/expenditure chart Figure 21.11 at the top of the next page.

Drinks are priced with a 200 per cent mark-up on cost, and food is priced at a 200 per cent mark-up in the bar and 300 per cent in the restaurant. The property costs and the 'other' costs are considered fixed but casual workers are a variable cost.

1 The manager is concerned that the information is not presented in a format that allows her to determine the relative profitability of each area of the business. You are to rearrange the data with all costs allocated to the three profit centres: rooms, restaurant, and public bar.
   a Reallocate the costs for food and drinks.
   b Apportion the property costs on the basis of floor area.
   c Apportion the cost of the kitchen to the restaurant and bar in proportion to food cost.
   d Apportion management costs to the profit centres in proportion to total sales.
2 What does the new format convey regarding the profitability of each profit centre?
3 If one of the profit centres makes a loss, should that area of the business be closed down? Support your views with figures.
4 Comment upon (a) the benefits and (b) the problems associated with this approach to pricing.

Contribution pricing

It can be argued that a more marketing-orientated approach to pricing, which takes into account the cost–volume relationship, is **contribution pricing**. This involves separating out the different products that make up a company's portfolio, in order to charge individual prices appropriate to each product's share in total costs.

We have already identified two broad categories of costs: variable (direct) costs vary directly with the quantity of output produced or sold; fixed (indirect costs) have to be paid, irrespective of the level of output or sales. When an organisation produces a range of individual items or products, or sells products in a variety of markets, it is easy to determine direct costs, but not indirect costs. For example, in a food processing plant producing 100 different recipe dishes, it is easy to work out how much

Figure 21.11 Income/expeniture chart

Floor area (m^2)	Rooms and reception (1500)	Restaurant (250)	Bar (250)	Kitchen (125)	Management and administration (125)	Total (2250)
Income	£	£	£	£	£	£
Room let	438 000					438 000
Food		160 000	37 500			197 500
Drinks		66 000	159 000			225 000
Totals	438 000	226 000	196 500			860 500
Expenditure						
Wages – permanent	60 000	15 000	15 000	37 500	63 000	190 500
Wages – casual	27 000	40 000	34 000			101 000
Food				52 500		52 500
Drinks			75 000			75 000
Rent and property-related					270 000	270 000
Other	35 000	5 000	5 000	5 250	51 075	101 325
Totals	122 000	60 000	129 000	95 250	384 075	790 325
PROFITS	316 000	166 000	67 500	−95 250	−384 075	70 175

goes on each line in terms of raw materials, wages, input and other direct costs. However, the same process cannot be applied to indirect costs – the salary of the managing director, the business rates paid on the factory building, and so on.

> **Contribution** is the sum remaining after the direct costs of producing individual products have been subtracted from revenues.
>
> **Unit contribution** is the selling price minus the direct cost.

When the contributions of all the individual products that a firm produces have been added together they should more than cover the firm's indirect costs.

There are strong arguments in favour of contribution pricing because of the way it separates out the individual products and analyses them *in terms of their ability to cover direct costs which can be attributed to them*. A new product may be brought 'on stream' because it can be shown that it will cover its direct costs and make a contribution to covering the company's total indirect costs.

In contrast, if we were to analyse individual products in terms of the relationship between their total revenue and total costs, calculations might show a loss. For example, if two products used the same distribution facilities, it would not make sense to expect both products to cover their own distribution costs individually. Contribution

pricing enables a more rational analysis of individual products. Prices can then be set in relation to each product's own direct costs (see Figure 21.12).

Figure 21.12 Calculating profits using contributions

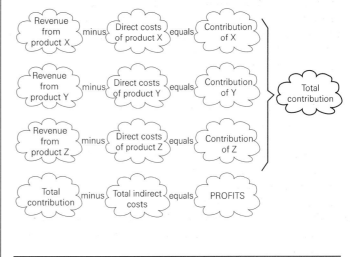

Task

Look again at the earlier task on hotel pricing. The manager is concerned that the hotel rooms are considerably under-utilised during weekends using the current pricing techniques. Market research has shown that although the hotel's catering is highly rated at £15 for a restaurant meal and £5 for breakfast, its location out of town has deterred would-be customers at weekends. The manager believes that if the rooms were priced low enough they could develop an appealing package of food with a one-night stopover at the hotel. Advise the manager on the benefits of a contribution approach to costing. How effective would this approach be in meeting the criticisms of the cost-plus approach to pricing?

By manufacturing and selling enough units to produce a total contribution in excess of fixed overheads, a business will make a profit.

One way of showing visually how this type of pricing works, and also how pricing adjustments might affect profitability, is through **break-even analysis**. The *break-even point* is the unique point at which an organisation makes no profit and no loss (point B in Figure 21.13). If sales are beyond the break-even point profits are made, and if they are below the break-even point losses are made. To calculate the break-even point:

- Calculate the unit contribution (identify a selling price and then deduct variable costs).
- Divide the fixed costs by the unit contribution. The sales value can be calculated by multiplying the units to break-even by the selling price.

In Figure 21.13, the line A shows sales based on predictions of turnover, line C shows total costs (fixed and variable), and line D shows fixed costs. E is the margin of safety – the difference between a selected level of output and the break-even point at B.

Figure 21.13 A single break-even chart

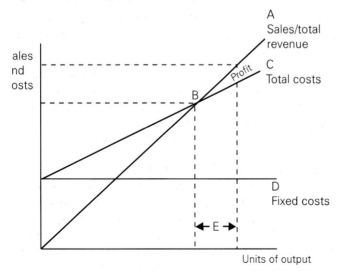

A break-even chart is a simple visual tool which enables a manager to anticipate the effects of changes in pricing,

production and sales on the profitability of a business and is of much greater use to the marketer than the full-cost approach. It is particularly useful for relating prices of goods and services to demand for them and then analysing their effect on overall profitability. It emphasises the importance of earning revenue to make profits and may help those who are unused to interpreting accounting information.

Case Study
The airline business

Competition in the air-travel business is fierce – witness the price competition between carriers on transatlantic flights.

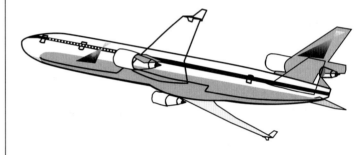

One such airline is Richard Branson's Virgin Atlantic. This operates on only the busiest international routes, where it can fill most of its planes' seats. It is the only way a small airline can compete with the likes of British Airways.

Although Virgin is competitive on price, Branson knows his firm cannot compete on this alone. Bigger airlines benefit from economies of scale. So Virgin attempts to provide a better service for a lower fare than its rivals.

Virgin launched a new service in 1992 called Mid Class for the full price of an economy ticket. By reducing the number of Economy Class cabins, there are fewer seats on a plane, but Branson thinks Virgin gains in two ways:

- by filling a greater proportion of seats as flights rarely operate at full capacity
- by encouraging more early bookings and less need for last-minute price discounting.

The rationale behind the move was that customers who are prepared to pay the full price of an economy ticket would prefer to travel with Virgin if they got better service for their money.

The following are some illustrative costs and revenues for a full-capacity return flight operation to North America:

	£
Depreciation of plane	25 000
Fuel	27 000
Flight crew costs	3 000
Cabin crew costs	6 000
Food	4 000
Selling costs and administration	10 000
Landing fees	15 000
Maintenance	10 000
	100 000

Total costs are identical for Mid Class and Economy Class.

A plane with large Economy Class can carry 375 passengers with an average revenue per passenger of £350.

A plane with Mid Class can carry 325 passengers with an average revenue per passenger of £425.

Questions for discussion

1 *Analyse and then comment on the fixed costs and variable costs in this operation.*
2 *Identify the break-even point for a standard economy class plane and a plane with the new Mid Class (draw a break-even chart for each level of service and identify the break-even point for each).*
3 *If 80 per cent of seats were filled, how much profit would each type of service make?*
4 *Some airlines sell tickets at £100 each. How can last-minute price discounting make sense?*
5 *Evaluate Richard Branson's decision to introduce Mid Class.*

Although contribution pricing is market-based and takes into account the cost–volume relationship, this approach to pricing has certain limitations. It can be argued that, in reality, fixed costs are likely to change at different levels of activity and that a stepped approach to fixed costs would provide a better representation. It also reduces business activity to an equation – how to generate enough contribution to cover fixed costs and provide a surplus for profit. Variable costs and sales are also unlikely to be linear – discounts, special contracts, and overtime payments mean that the total cost line should really be a curve. This type of pricing is dependent on the accuracy of forecasts made about costs and revenues. Sudden changes in the market or in the prices of raw materials would affect forecasts.

Demand-oriented pricing

Market research is essential to establish and monitor consumers' perceptions of price. **Demand-oriented**
pricing involves reacting to the intensity of demand for a product, so that high demand leads to high prices and weak demand to low prices, even though unit costs are similar.

When a firm can split up the market in which it operates into different segments, it can carry out a policy of **price discrimination**. This involves selling at high prices in a section of the market where demand is intense (where demand is *inelastic*), and at relatively low prices where demand is *elastic* – where there is a more than proportionate response in quantity demanded as a result of a fall in price (see Figure 21.14). Price discrimination may be carried out in a number of situations.

Figure 21.14 Price discrimination

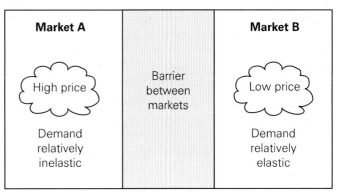

Customer-oriented discrimination

Some customers may have an intense demand for a product while others may have only a weak demand. Discrimination would involve selling the same type of product to the first type of customer at a high price and to the second at a lower price. However, you can only do this if you can physically divide up your market so that the customer with the intense demand cannot get hold of the lower-priced item.

It is common practice to introduce some products at a higher price and then later to reduce the price. For example, many books are initially sold in hardback at a high price. When that segment of customers has been satisfied the cheaper paperback is produced.

Product-oriented discrimination

Slight modifications can be made to a product to allow high- and low-price strategies. For example, many car models have additional extras (the two- or four-door version, with or without sunroof, etc.). Customers have the choice of the cheaper or more expensive version. In a similar way, you can purchase cheaper or expensive versions of the same sewing machine, depending on whether you are prepared to pay for the additional facilities associated with the expensive version.

Time-oriented discrimination

Sellers are able to discriminate when demand varies by season or time of day. In high season, a product can be sold at a high price. At other times, prices will need to be reduced. This applies to a wide range of items from fashion clothes to river cruises. Some products experience varying intensities of demand during the course of a single day – for example, telephone calls are charged at a higher rate during 'peak' hours.

Situation-oriented discrimination

This applies to houses – the same type of house may sell for one price in the centre of a town and for another price in a quiet suburban area. House prices also vary widely from one region to another. Cinema and theatre seats may be priced according to their proximity to the screen or the stage. Although production costs are similar, demand varies with the situation.

Perceived value-for-money

In general, customers have views about what constitutes **value-for-money**. If prices are too high, customers might not consider that they are getting value for money. If prices are too low, they will begin to question the quality of a product.

From the consumers' point of view, therefore, value-for-money is a key ingredient when weighing up prices. Research carried out by the magazine *Marketing* in the early 1990s on over 800 shoppers confirmed this view. It was possible to argue that superior value in a shop will overcome disadvantages in location, to some degree. Customers will beat a longer path to a superior outlet. In the survey, reasons given for choosing where to shop varied by region, with southerners giving more weight to 'quality' in the value equation. Northerners rated their reasons like this:

1 Prices/value-for-money
2 Nearest to home
3 Variety of goods
4 Convenient/handy
5 Know layout

Southerners' ratings were slightly different:

1 Prices/value-for-money
2 Easy parking
3 Convenient/handy
4 Good-quality products
5 Know layout

Low-prices/value-for-money was thus the outstanding reason for the choice of store. Other questions in the research confirmed that consumers carefully weighed prices versus quality, in reaching a value judgement. Only

a minority bought on price alone: 9 per cent 'always checked and chose the cheapest', and 13 per cent always bought things on special offer even if they were not needed on that occasion. By monitoring customer perceptions of price, a seller realises that the appropriate price band for a sale is, in fact, fairly limited (see Figure 21.15).

Figure 21.15 Customer perception of price

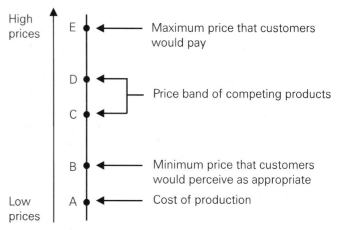

Assume that a product costs £A to produce. The business cannot sell the product for less than £B without its quality being questioned ('How can it be sold for such a low price? Is there something wrong with it?'). Competing products are selling for prices between £C and £D, and the maximum chargeable price would be £E. Then, if the product is 'nothing special' in terms of customer perception, the price should be pitched between £B and £D. However, if the product is really exciting, and captures the imagination of consumers, it can be pitched anywhere between £C and £E.

Psychological pricing encourages the process of pricing which emphasises the emotional element of customer perceptions. For example, odd-pricing at £99.99 assumes that consumers will be more prepared to pay that price than £100. Many products, too, are priced artificially high on the basis of their prestige.

Competition-oriented pricing

The nature and extent of competition is a very important influence on price. If a product is faced by direct competition, then it will compete against other very similar products in the marketplace. This will constrain pricing decisions so that price setting will need to be kept closely in line with rivals' actions. In contrast, when a product is faced with indirect competition (i.e. competition with products in different segments of the market), there will be more scope to vary price. This opens up the possibility for a number of strategies. For example, a firm might choose a high-price strategy to give a product a 'quality' feel. In contrast, it might charge a low price so that consumers see the product as a 'bargain'.

Markets are sometimes classified according to the level of competition that applies. An extreme level of competition is termed **perfect competition** (it exists in theory rather than practice). The other extreme is **monopoly**, where a single firm dominates a market. In the real world, most markets lie between these extremes and involve some level of *imperfection*. If a perfect market could exist there would be no limitations to new firms entering the market, and buyers would know exactly what was on offer and would incur no costs in buying from one seller rather than another. Products would be almost identical. In a monopoly situation, only one firm exists and barriers prevent new firms from entering the market (e.g. a very high cost of setting up, the existence of patent and copyright restrictions, and other barriers). The seller has considerable powers to control the market.

In imperfect markets with monopolistic competition, there may be few or many sellers. Products are usually **differentiated** and consumers do not have perfect information about the differences between products. In the real world, businesses do strive to give themselves the protection of monopolistic powers. They seek to reduce competition, and they seek to make their products seem 'better' than those offered by their rivals. Monopolistic power enables firms to push up prices and hence make larger profits. However, larger profits should not always be viewed as a cost to consumers, because profits can be ploughed into research and development, into advanced technology and the production of large outputs at lower average costs.

The level of competition is a key determinant of price. Where there are many close competitors, there is little or no scope to charge a price which is above the market price. In a situation where there is no competition, the seller can often charge a relatively high price. However, the seller cannot charge more than the consumer is prepared to pay. At the end of the day consumers can spend their income on alternative products. Between these two extremes, we find hundreds of different markets. In some the consumer has most power, in others it is the seller.

The time period

Most of the strategies discussed so far relate to the medium or long term. In the short term, pricing can be used as an incisive tool to influence selling targets and develop marketing objectives. Typical short-term attack-

based policies include skimming pricing, penetration pricing, destroyer pricing, and promotional pricing.

Skimming pricing

At the launch of a new product, there will frequently be little competition in the market, so that demand for the product may be somewhat inelastic. Consumers will have little knowledge of the product. **Skimming** involves setting a reasonably high initial price in order to yield high initial returns from those consumers willing to buy the new product. Once the first group of customers has been satisfied, the seller can then lower the price in order to make sales to new groups of customers. This process can be continued until a larger section of the total market has been catered for. By operating in this way the business removes the risk of underpricing the product.

The name 'skimming' comes from the process of skimming the cream from the top of milk (see Figure 21.16).

Figure 21.16 Skimming

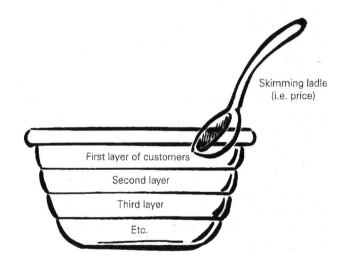

Penetration pricing

Whilst skimming may be an appropriate policy when a seller is not sure of the elasticity of demand for the product, **penetration pricing** is appropriate when the seller knows that demand is likely to be elastic. A low price is therefore required to attract consumers to the product. Penetration pricing is normally associated with the launch of a new product for which the market needs to be penetrated (see Figure 21.17). Because price starts low, the product may initially make a loss until consumer awareness is increased.

A typical example would be that of a new breakfast cereal or a product being launched in a new overseas market.

Initially it would be launched with a relatively low price, coupled with discounts and special offers. As the product rapidly penetrates the market, sales and profitability increases. Prices can then creep upwards.

Figure 21.17 Environment appropriate for penetration pricing

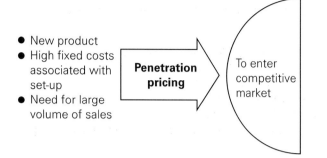

Penetration pricing is particularly appropriate for products where economies of scale can be employed to produce large volumes at lower unit costs. Products which are produced on a large scale are initially burdened by high fixed costs for research, development and purchases of plant and equipment. It is important to spread these fixed costs quickly over a large volume of output. Penetration pricing is also common when there is a strong possibility of competition from rival products.

Destroyer pricing

A policy of **destroyer pricing** can be used to undermine the sales of rivals or to warn potential rivals not to enter a particular market. Destroyer pricing involves reducing the price of an existing product or selling a new product at an artificially low price in order to destroy competitors' sales (see Figure 21.18). For example, when in late 1993 the new Costco stores entered the UK market, British supermarkets in the localities of Costco stores slashed their prices to loss-making levels in an attempt to beat off the new American rivals.

This type of policy is based on long-term considerations and is likely to lead to short-term losses. The policy is most likely to be successful when the company that initiates it has lower costs than its competitors or potential rivals. However, it cannot be sustained in the long term because it will erode the profit base required to initiate reseach and development projects.

Promotional pricing

Prices can be lowered from time to time to promote a product. **Promotional pricing** can be used to inject fresh life into an existing product or to create interest in a new product. Promotional pricing can be employed to increase the rate at which a product turns over. This can

Figure 21.18 Destroyer pricing

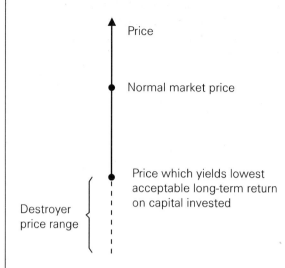

be used to reduce levels of stock or to increase the rate of activity of a business.

A form of promotional pricing is the use of **loss-leaders**. Supermarkets frequently use loss-leaders to boost sales. A loss-leader is a good which is sold at little or no profit or even at a loss. Only a small number of the items sold by supermarkets are loss-leaders. The aim of selling in this way is to give the impression that all items in the shop are cheap – a shopper seeing that cornflakes are 10p cheaper in one supermarket may falsely expect all prices to be cheaper in that store. Another use of loss-leaders is to attract new customers, who will then spend on other, profitable items.

Case Study
Identifying different pricing strategies

Three examples of pricing are outlined below. Read each short case and then consider the questions for discussion.

Making violins
The sounds of a violin float from an upstairs window. This is Neasden, the man with the violin is Jed Murphy and he has just finished making it. He has been making violins for nine years and before that he was a freelance musician. Setting up his business enabled him to combine his training in science and woodwork with his musical skills. . . . The violin begins life as a log. The back, sides and neck are made from maple and the front from spruce. The work is slow and painstaking. It requires great skill and dedication. A violin can take four weeks to make, and a cello five. The price for a violin is a mere £3000.

Getting rid of a discount culture

John Hoerner, the chief executive of the Burton Group, recently stated that the high street retailer's stores – which include Burtons, Dorothy Perkins and Top Shop/ Top Man – were trying to move away from the discount culture that has affected their performance. The group has thus significantly reduced the level of markdowns and has been selling more items at full price. This, however, has been combined with more competitive opening price points, better merchandise and more attractive stores. . . . Though the group has been hampered by past discount-led pricing strategies, they believe that customers are starting to change their attitudes to such pricing techniques.

Euro Disney

Euro Disney does not rule out further price cuts to pull in more visitors after disappointing attendances. The company chairman revealed that the public's perception, particularly among the local population, was that the resort was over-priced in spite of 13 per cent cuts in hotel charges. . . . While the management will not be cutting prices merely to pull in large numbers of visitors, there is an argument to provide temporary reductions to help to correct public perceptions.

Questions for discussion

1 *What factors might have influenced price decisions in each case?*

2 *Comment briefly on the nature of the different pricing strategies.*

Responses

When setting prices, managers and others rarely enjoy complete freedom to make decisions. There are often just too many factors to be considered, and within the organisation itself there can be groups with differing pricing expectations. For example, a production manager may want to see low prices to increase volume, an accountant may want products to provide positive cash flows to improve financial stability, marketers may wish to see higher prices for some products so that profits can be used to support other brands, while sales staff may wish to see a more competitive approach to pricing which would make the products easier to sell.

In pursuing corporate objectives, one of the major elements in pricing is to establish a market position which provides an element of supremacy over that of competitors. Where price competition exists, an organisation actively uses price as a key feature in order to establish some form of leadership over competitors. When such competition becomes a price war, price then becomes the most important element in the marketing mix.

To be able to compete effectively on price an organisation should:

- be a low-cost producer (for example, if a number of organisations compete on price, the lowest-cost producer will have the best margin)
- be able to change price quickly to respond to the actions of competitors
- stress the competitive nature of price in its marketing mix
- constantly monitor the actions of competitors.

Wherever price reductions are considered, it is important to assess their impact on profitability. The hope will be that in reducing price the drop in price and the subsequent effect on profit per unit will be offset by an increase in sales. Price-cutting can be damaging to all concerned. For example, after the 'broadsheet battle' where some broadsheet newspapers competed by cutting prices, The *Daily Telegraph* warned shareholders that it may take up to five years for profits to recover levels achieved before the cuts in cover prices. Price-cutting may also affect other elements in the product such as new developments, customer services and other customer benefits. Though price-cutting may add to market share, it has to be seriously considered whether this objective is more costly than it is worth.

With *non-price competition*, sellers focus on other aspects of the marketing mix instead of price. These might include product features, promotion, packaging, brand and line developments, service, credit facilities, etc. For example, when Reckitt & Colman revamped the Dettol range during the 1980s and early 1990s, the company emphasised the brand heritage and tried to develop a famous brand in a way which would improve its convenience of use for consumers. In doing so it was trying to increase the profitability of the brand and use the reassurance which had already been created within the market. Dettol was a premium brand and such non-price developments built on customer loyalty.

The benefits of non-price competition are:

- Customers are unlikely to be attracted to low-price competitors.
- Brand qualities will distinguish it from competitors.
- Customers will feel a high degree of loyalty to brands irrespective of price (price is not the most important reason for this loyalty).

- The superiority created by heritage and reputation will make the brand worth the price paid.

To compete on non-price factors, marketers must emphasise the superiority of non-price features in the minds of buyers. Though theoretically such organisations are not competing on the basis of price, price is still an important ingredient of the marketing mix. For example, prices of such products will probably be slightly higher than those of rivals.

Finally, it is worth noting that prices must not be set apart from wider considerations such as legal, economic, political and ethical factors which might, in some way, influence pricing decisions.

Further reading

- *Competitive Marketing – A Strategic Approach*, 2nd edition, by John O'Shaughnessy. Routledge, 1989.
- *Discovering Marketing – An Active Learning Approach* by D. Stokes. DPP, 1994.
- *Marketing Warfare* by Al Ries and Jack Trout. McGraw-Hill, 1986.
- *Marketing – A Resource Book* by Andy Hutchins. Pitman, 1995.
- *Pricing: Concepts and Methods for Effective Marketing*, 2nd edition, by Andre Gabor. Gower, 1988.
- *Principles of Marketing* by Geoffrey Randall. Routledge, 1994.

22 Distribution policy

On completion of this chapter students should be able to:

■ identify intermediaries and examine their role

■ analyse factors influencing the selection of channel intermediaries

■ analyse the scope, key areas and goals of a physical distribution system.

What is distribution?

Distribution (or **place** in the four Ps of the marketing mix) is the process of making goods or services available for those who want to buy them. It includes:

■ the process of moving goods and services to the places where they are wanted
■ the channels through which the products are made available.

Distribution may involve a single step, or any number of steps. For example, local bakers may make the bread and then supply it direct to their customers. In contrast, a furniture store may supply chairs and tables that have been manufactured in Scandinavia, have passed through a number of hands and been stored two or three times before arriving at their final destination.

A number of key decisions influence distribution. Managers try to ensure that goods are moved efficiently to meet customer needs in a timely manner. They will also be concerned to choose the best channel of distribution so that efficiency and sales opportunities can be maximised. Such decisions should never be underrated. Organisations such as Avon and Reader's Digest, and many more, have built and developed their successes on their ability to use this element of the marketing mix to reach customers and satisfy their needs.

The **channel of distribution** is the system through which goods are transferred from producer to end-user. It consists of one or more individuals and organisations who help to make products and services available for end-users. Every organisation must constantly appraise its existing channels and, from time to time, they will need to be reorganised.

Intermediaries

Manufacturers may lack the financial resources to carry out expensive direct-marketing operations. The expense of direct marketing often requires that several similar or complementary products are promoted at the same time, to spread the cost between the products. By contracting out the process of distribution, manufacturers can concentrate on their core functions.

According to S. Dibb, L. Simkin, W. Pride and O. C. Ferrell, a marketing intermediary 'links producers to other middlemen or to ultimate users of products'. The intermediary is also a specialist. When a company sells its products in this way, it benefits from the specialist's expertise in a wide range of areas, such as packaging, pricing and where to sell. The author of a book may be able to produce a very good product but will lack the time, know-how, contacts and money required to publish the book and promote it to booksellers.

Using intermediaries

Intermediaries facilitate and simplify the exchange process by **reducing the number of marketplace contacts and transactions**. For example, in Figure 22.1, without an intermediary (A), 16 transactions take place; with an intermediary (B), only eight transactions take place. So,

Figure 22.1 Using an intermediary to improve efficiency

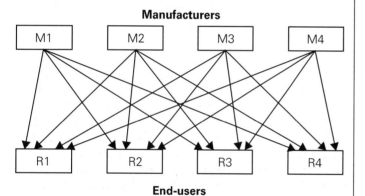

A Without an intermediary

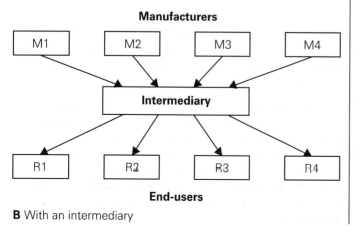

B With an intermediary

instead of 16 journeys to make, requiring 16 sets of paperwork, only eight are needed. (This is a simplification, as in the real world, thousands of transactions would be involved.)

The intermediary has, therefore, reduced the number of journeys, reducing fuel and other costs. It will also have cut down upon paperwork, have lower sales force costs and make savings in areas such as invoicing and administration.

Another benefit of using an intermediary is **lower storage costs**. The producer does not need to store so much stock, as the intermediary will take on the responsibility of holding the supplies necessary to meet any changes in end-user demand.

One important function of the intermediary is that of **sorting**. This involves developing a package which provides an assortment of benefits for the consumer. For example, an intermediary may stock computer desks, disks, hardware, software and other information technology (IT) supplies. A single producer is unlikely to manufacture all of these and may also be unhappy about supplying small quantities to individual customers. The intermediary:

- collects stock items from a large number of manufacturers
- divides stock into the proportions required by individual customers
- in certain circumstances, puts stock items together to provide an assortment (i.e. computers available with a range of software packages)
- distributes each assortment to individual customers.

In this way intermediaries are breaking bulk by taking goods in large quantities from manufacturers and then sorting them into smaller quantities which are much more suitable for the next distribution stage.

By virtue of their position in the distribution chain, intermediaries are much closer to customers and end-users than manufacturers. This means that they will have a better idea of customer needs and priorities in the market. For example, they may know which goods are selling well and how they have been received. With this in mind, they may advise customers on what to buy as well as manufacturers on what to make.

Distribution through intermediaries facilitates **standardisation**. For example, intermediaries often grade goods into different types. Standardisation of procedures may also take place in terms of prices, payment terms and delivery schedules.

By undertaking these activities, intermediaries help to **lower the costs** of handling and administration, **improve sales** with specialist knowledge and advice of routes into markets, and also provide a **range of services**, such as credit, personal selling and sales promotion, for customers who are either end-users or in the next phase of distribution.

Channel alternatives

There are many different types of distribution channel, and these usually depend upon the product and the market. For example, selling cosmetics may involve a sales force using a catalogue and visiting individual customers, as Avon does. Alternatively, it might be more appropriate to establish franchises in high-street department stores. It is important for marketers to analyse channels in order to identify those which reach the market in the most appropriate way.

When looking at how to develop a marketing channel, it is important to establish the major **objectives**. It is also necessary to explore any **constraints** in achieving these objectives and examine possible alternatives. The alternatives then need to be evaluated before a decision can be made as to how to plan the channels (see Figure 22.2).

Figure 22.2 Planning channels

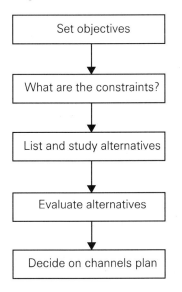

The distribution channel is the route to the customers. In defining the objectives it is necessary to consider:

- the customers' needs
- the nature of the competition
- the nature of other services (intermediaries) involved.

If the overriding objective is to supply customers the day after a product has been manufactured, for the lowest price on the market, it is necessary to discover the quickest and most effective channels with the fewest

delays, and learn how rivals are operating and what they are offering.

Some alternative distribution channels are shown in Figure 22.3. Using a **zero-level channel** without intermediaries, and selling directly from producer to consumer or industrial user is more usually called **direct marketing**, e.g. a factory shop selling direct to the public. Catalogues, mailshots and direct-mail advertisements help to facilitate this type of channel.

Figure 22.3 Some alternative channels of distribution

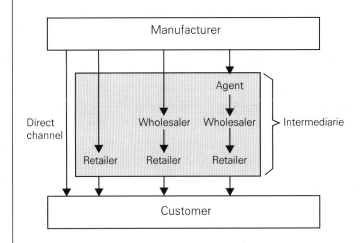

Direct marketing has become increasingly popular in the UK, with an average annual rise of about 15 per cent. It enables producers to target specific markets and also provides a measurable response to marketing activities. In business-to-business industrial markets, direct marketing is particularly important. Major purchases, such as installations, machinery and equipment, are usually arranged between producer and user. Direct marketing does have weaknesses, as it can be an expensive way of contacting customers. Similarly, if customers are bombarded by poorly targeted direct mail, such an approach can lose its value.

In consumer markets, a **single-level channel**, using one intermediary, is becoming more widespread. Large retail chains tend to buy directly from manufacturers, rather than from wholesalers.

Two-level channels are still common in consumer markets, since many small retailers are not sufficiently large and do not have the purchasing power to buy directly from manufacturers, so they tend to use the traditional channel of distribution (see Figure 22.4). Wholesalers buy in bulk and are then served by a small sales force. They act as a link between the manufacturer and the retailer.

Figure 22.4 The traditional channel of distribution

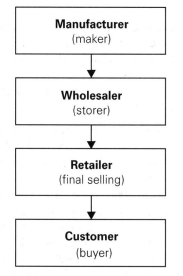

The main criteria used in evaluating channels are:

- economic performance
- control
- adaptability.

In evaluating the **economic performance** of alternative routes, costs must be weighed against revenues in order to make profit calculations. **Control** is also a major consideration because customers often blame the producer for problems in distribution. A distribution channel should also be capable of **adapting** to changing circumstances.

A business operating a single plant and selling in several scattered markets can choose to distribute directly from the plant or through a range of localised intermediaries. On the other hand, a firm with several plants and several markets must weigh up a range of distribution channels. Does it use the same distribution channels for all its products, or does it set up specialist routes?

The choice of distribution channel may have a marked effect upon other areas of the marketing mix, such as price, promotion or product. For example, if it is decided to distribute through a chain of readily accessible discount stores, this will have implications for the public perception of the product.

Some manufacturers require tight distribution schedules. Nowhere is this more true than in the distribution of fresh food, and this limits the number of intermediaries that can be involved in the distribution process. It is important for any organisation, however, to analyse what is involved in each of the stages of distribution and to minimise the number of stages. Would it be possible to market products directly to customers, or is it better to concentrate on the core functions and allow others to sell goods on to final users?

Types of intermediaries

Wholesalers

These stock a range of goods from competing manufacturers to sell on to other organisations such as retailers. Most wholesalers take the title to the goods and so assume many of the risks associated with ownership. They may provide a range of services for their customers, including the breaking of bulk, packing and labelling, storage, technical advice, training, promotion and delivery.

Some wholesalers handle a wide range of general merchandise, but the majority specialise in particular lines, e.g. tobacco, steel. Many outlets are small and operate within a limited geographical area. In contrast, a number (particularly in the grocery trade) are large and have regional and even national distribution capabilities.

The largest single unit in the British wholesale trade is the Co-operative Wholesale Society (CWS). The CWS also manufactures many own-brand lines, owns interests overseas, such as tea estates in India, and maintains a shipping and transport fleet.

The past 20 years have seen the growth in size and importance of cash-and-carry warehouses, and voluntary groups, in wholesaling. Most small retailers buy a large proportion of their stock from a **cash-and-carry** warehouse (see Figure 22.5). Retailers are responsible for transporting the selected goods from the wholesale warehouse to their premises, and they are able to buy the goods at a 'trade discount'. The inside of a cash-and-carry warehouse is

Figure 22.5 Examples of cash-and-carry organisations

	Depots	Approx. av. sq. ft.
Booker Cash & Carry	162	40 000
Today's Supergroup	95	30 000
Landmark Cash & Carry	83	50 000
Nurdin & Peacock Trade & Business Warehouses	46	86 000
Sterling Supergroup	43	15–16 000
Makro Self-Service Wholesalers (SHV Holdings NV)	25	145 000
Mojo (Argyll)	18	20 000
Bestway	14	100 000
Batleys of Yorkshire	13	100 000
Hancock	10	17 000
M6 (Nurdin & Peacock)	10	78 550
Watson & Philip Trademarkets	8	50 000

similar to that of a large supermarket, except that goods are packed in bulk and the buildings are sparsely decorated.

Some wholesalers have been set up by **voluntary groups**. A voluntary group is made up largely of small retailers (see Figure 22.6) who have agreed to buy most of their stock from the group wholesaler. For example, the retailers might be contracted to purchase at least 70 per cent of their supplies from the group wholesaler. The group wholesaler buys goods in bulk from manufacturers at discounted prices. The voluntary group movement was a reaction to the growth in power and influence of chains of supermarkets which were undercutting the small corner shop from the mid-1960s. Some well-known shops operate under the voluntary group system – Late Shop, Happy Shopper, VG, Spar, Mace and Wavyline.

Figure 22.6 Voluntary groups

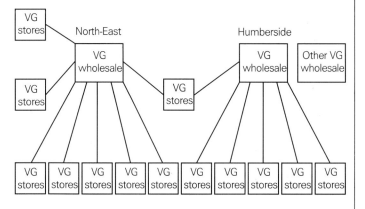

With the increasing trend towards globalisation as well as the single market, inevitably there has been a move towards larger wholesale units capable of marketing products internationally. Though this increases specialisation, from which customers benefit, it could well pose a threat to agents and brokers.

Agents and brokers

These differ from wholesalers in that they do not purchase the manufacturer's goods and take title, but instead, earn a commission on the sales they make. In doing this, they assist in the transfer of goods between the producer and the end-user.

An agent differs from a broker by working permanently on behalf of either a seller or a buyer. A broker only works temporarily on behalf of a business and normally transacts between a number of different sellers and buyers. Though agents and brokers perform few intermediary functions, they may have considerable specialist knowledge of a given type of market.

Retailers

The French word *retailler* means 'to cut again'. We have already seen that the wholesaler breaks down bulk supplies from the manufacturer. The retailer then cuts the bulk again to sell individual items to consumers. To categorise the many different types of retailer you need to consider the following:

1 **Ownership.** Who owns the retail unit? Is it independently owned by a sole trader? Is it owned by a large multiple with shareholders? Is it a cooperative or a franchised outlet?
2 **Range of merchandise.** Does the retail outlet specialise in a range of goods or does it have a spread of interests? Examples of specialist outlets include ice-cream parlours, furniture stores and fast-food outlets. Woolworths is an example of a more general outlet. Harrods at one time claimed to sell everything from 'a pin to an elephant'.
3 **Pricing policy.** Some retail outlets concentrate on the bottom of the price range. They offer discounts and low prices, buying in bulk and selling large quantities. The early policy of Jack Cohen, founder of Tesco, was 'pile them high, sell them cheap'. In contrast, other retail outlets aim for an upmarket price image. This is true of exclusive fashion shops, clothing and jewellery stores. Here, the mark-up may be several hundred per cent for many items.
4 **Location.** Low-price stores frequently choose locations where business rates and other site costs are minimised. In contrast, large multiples and department stores need a town-centre location, or a site near a major road. Small 'corner' shops need a healthy volume of local custom for their livelihood – their strength is in offering local convenience.
5 **Size.** Many variety stores are now over 50 000 sq. ft, but superstores and hypermarkets have areas from 25 000 to 100 000 sq. ft.

Case Study
Costco: will it work?

In December 1993 the first grocery warehouse club in the UK – Costco – opened its doors to the public in Thurrock, Essex. It has 35 tills, employs 350 staff and has 749 parking spaces. Dubbed 'the silent enemy', warehouse clubs are believed to be the lowest-cost form of retail distribution in existence.

Only members may shop in warehouse clubs, for which they pay an annual subscription. In the USA, the home of these clubs, they cover anything from 100 000 to 250 000 sq. ft. They operate inexpensively. No advertising takes place and goods are displayed in cut cases. The range is 3500 to 4500 lines, which compares with the 16 000 usually found in a supermarket. The motto for warehouse clubs in the USA has been 'stack it high and watch it fly'.

In Britain many feel that the mere existence of Costco will help to push down prices. The company has used no promotional support and believes that much of its notoriety is due to other supermarkets trying to stop its planning application in Thurrock.

On the day the Thurrock Costco opened, 6000 members, each paying a fee of £17–£22, had already joined. The Costco philosophy is clear – use low prices to pull in those with an eye for a bargain and with deep pockets, and then try to get them to buy on impulse.

Questions for discussion

1 *Given that Costco has many trade customers, would you describe it as a wholesaler or a retailer?*
2 *Comment upon the advantages and disadvantages of the Costco formula of retailing. Could the Costco approach spread to other areas of retailing?*

Independent retailers

Independent retailers, according to the Census of Distribution, are retail organisations with fewer than ten branches. The average number is one or two branches. The market share and number of independent retailers have been declining over recent years, particularly in food.

Many small shops in the UK are owned by one person whose business interests are confined to a single shop. These retailers often set up in business by putting their life savings into starting the shop. They then buy stock by borrowing money from the bank and paying it back when they have sold the goods. There are, of course, advantages and disadvantages to being a small operator (see Figure 22.7).

The number of independent retailers has declined throughout the last part of the twentieth century (see Figure 22.8). Joining a voluntary group (as described earlier in this chapter) has proved to be the best route to survival for many independent shop owners. Niche operations have also provided opportunities, eg. for independent stores selling vegetarian food.

Multiple chains

Multiple chains are organised by joint-stock companies, with a high degree of control being exercised by

Figure 22.7 Advantages and disadvantages of small retail outlets

Advantages	Disadvantages
Personal relationship with customers	Price competition from multiples who are aided by buying economies and scale of operations
Convenient for shoppers, providing a local 'round the corner' service	Owner needs to be a 'Jack of all trades', frequently lacking specialist retailing lacking specialist retailing knowledge
Can buy in stock to meet personal requirements of customers	Lack of capital to expand or improve business
Can work longer hours	Located away from high-volume sales areas
Low overheads, low site costs	Growth of use of cars has led to one-stop shopping in large shopping centres
Benefits from joining voluntary group	
Can offer personal credit facilities to shoppers	
Can arrange home deliveries	

Figure 22.8 The British retail grocery trade

	Number of shops		Shares of all commodity turnover (%)	
	1971	1992	1971	1992
Cooperatives	7 745	2 481	13.2	10.4
Multiples	10 973	4 577	44.3	77.8
Independents	86 565	32 662	42.5	11.8
All grocers	105 283	39 720	100.0	100.0

professional managers. The Census of Distribution defines a multiple store as one having more than ten branches. Some multiples are classified as specialist stores, concentrating on a narrow range of items such as clothing and off-licences (see Figure 22.9). Others are variety chains like Marks & Spencer and Boots.

Some of the main features of a multiple are:

■ centralised buying (in bulk at a discount)
■ concentration on fast-moving lines; usually selling products which are brand leaders or own-store labels
■ merchandise is widely known, often through national advertising
■ located in 'busy' shopping areas, clustered together with other well-known multiples (usually in city streets and shopping centres)
■ prices are usually relatively low; volume sales are made

Figure 22.9 Some specialist wholesalers

Off-licences	Approx. number of branches
Thresher	1 600
Victoria Wine	1 515
Greenall Cellars	477
Unwins	291
Oddbins	186
Davisons	76
Fullers	61
Majestic Wine Warehouses	48
Co-op	16

- shops project a strong corporate (unified) image – easily recognised shop signs, distinctive colours and logos and uniform store fittings
- centralisation of many key functions, e.g. accounting, advertising, recruitment, public relations and operating policies.

Supermarkets

A supermarket is defined as a store with at least 200 sq. m. (about 2000 sq. ft) of selling area, using mostly self-service methods and having at least three checkout points. The layout of a store is designed to speed customer flow and reduce time spent shopping.

Supermarkets are a feature of shopping in the 1990s. New and larger supermarkets continue to be developed in most areas of population growth.

Supermarkets have thrived with the development of brand names, the increasing number of working women with less time for shopping, and consumer preferences for easy shopping at low prices. They have high turnovers at a low mark up – by maximising sales, they are able to spread their operating costs over a large output in order to minimise unit costs.

In recent years supermarkets have been able to meet consumer demands for green and organic products by using their considerable buying power to influence producers. Because the supermarket business is highly competitive, it is also responsive to consumer preference changes.

Hypermarkets

Hypermarkets are simply large supermarkets. They have a massive selling area and offer a very wide range of household goods at discount prices. As well as food and clothing, they stock lines as diverse as DIY equipment, motoring accessories, cosmetics, children's toys and hardware. They aim to provide a cheap alternative for all the basic shopping needs of an average household. They may also contain restaurant facilities and stock consumer durables, such as televisions, at a discount. They are usually located on the outskirts of towns where land is cheaper.

Department stores

The definition of a department store, according to the Census of Distribution, is a store with a large number of departments and employing more than 25 people. Department stores are to be found on 'prime sites' in most towns and cities. They provide a very wide range of services so that customers can do all of their shopping under one roof. The store generally provides a high standard of service and comfort. Each department within the store has its own manager and staff.

A department store might charge slightly higher prices for quality goods. However, while department stores generally have an upmarket image, they can also use the advantage of bulk buying and large scale to offer discount prices on many items. Department stores continue to be a force in the marketplace with their reputation for quality and service, and the added service of offering credit accounts. They include many famous names such as Harrods, Debenhams, Binns, John Lewis Partnership and Owen Owen. In the last decade they have moved increasingly towards customer self-selection. They have also operated a policy of 'leasing' shopping space to other retail names with a compatible image – this makes for better use of space and is an added attraction for customers.

Discount stores

Discount stores, such as Argos and Comet, concentrate on selling large quantities of consumer durables at discount prices. The aim of these stores is to produce a high level of total profit by means of a very high turnover of stock. As the name implies, they attract custom by the discounts they offer. In recent years, these stores have moved away from the original warehouse-like service, and have increasingly begun to offer credit facilities.

Discount stores tend to be located at edge-of-town positions. They are well-stocked and offer a wide choice. Examples are discount toy sellers and discount pet-food sellers.

Cooperative retail societies

Today, there are fewer than 30 cooperative retail societies operating in various parts of the UK. There used to be several hundred, but over the years many of the smaller societies have joined together. The co-ops have always tried to do more than just run a shopping business. They set out to serve the local community in a variety of ways. For example, a co-op might support a local education service for members, subsidise health care and other social activities, or finance cooperative theatre ventures and recreational facilities. See Chapter 15 for more information on co-ops.

Mail-order companies

Mail-order firms sell goods either through agents or by members of the public ordering from a free catalogue. A mail-order agent receives a commission of about 10 per cent of the sales made. Some firms have their own delivery service, while others use the Post Office or other carriers. Many goods sold by mail order are paid for on credit terms.

Mail-order companies bypass intermediaries and so have the opportunity to sell goods at competitive prices. They are also able to use computerised methods for handling orders and stocks and sell from large warehouses situated in locations where rates are cheap and communication links are efficient.

Franchises

In the USA, one-third of all retail sales are made through firms operating under the franchise system. It is a method of selling that is becoming increasingly popular in the UK.

A franchise is a permission to market a product in a specified area. The person taking out the franchise puts up a sum of money as capital and is issued with equipment by the franchising company to sell or manufacture the product in which the franchise company deals. The firm that sells the franchise is called the **franchisor** and a person taking out a franchise is called the **franchisee**. The franchisee has the sole right of operating in a particular area. Franchising is particularly common in 'fast foods', e.g. McDonald's and Spud-U-Like. The advantages of franchising are outlined in Figure 22.10.

Distributors or dealers

Another way for a manufacturer to sell goods to the consumer is by using **distributors** or **dealers**. These enter into a contract to buy manufacturers' goods to sell to customers. Their function is similar to wholesalers and retailers, except that they will normally offer only a limited product range based upon the products of a single supplier. These products may be backed up by specialist services and facilities such as credit and after-sales servicing.

Figure 22.10 Advantages of the franchising system

Advantages to the franchisee	Advantages to the franchisor
Trades under a well-known name	Franchisor does not risk own capital
Has a local monopoly	Supplies equipment and training courses, which are tax-deductible
Works for himself or herself, and receives most of the profits	Takes a percentage of profits
Is supplied with equipment	Has people working indirectly for the organisation who will work long hours because they are also working for themselves
Receives training	

Direct selling

The most commonly quoted examples of direct selling are mail order and direct-response advertising, but these more often than not involve some form of intermediary. Mail-order firms usually buy the commodities they sell through the catalogues in bulk from manufacturers. Direct-response advertisers – such as firms that advertise in newspapers, in leaflets delivered through letterboxes and in television advertisements giving the name and address of the firm – are often simply wholesalers who buy in bulk from manufacturers. It is, therefore, probably more accurate to say that direct selling means simplifying the chain of distribution by bypassing the retailer.

Manufacturers can themselves bypass middle operators by owning retail units. Examples of this are breweries that own public houses, oil companies with their own petrol stations and textile manufacturers with their own factory shops.

Television selling

Television selling is already big business in the USA, Australia and other countries and has recently been introduced in the UK. In the USA, the Homes Shopping Network is a 24-hour viewing business, which became a huge success story in the late 1980s. The typical format is for each product to have a four-minute slot, during which time viewers can phone in on one of 200 free lines, order an item and pay by quoting their credit card number. The products sold are mainly brand names, and they are presented in an entertaining and informative way.

Channel selection

Choosing between different distribution channels in order to develop distribution strategies involves crucial decisions for many organisations. Very few distribution channels are the same and, as we have seen, it is important to evaluate them according to three important criteria: economic performance, control and adaptability.

Intensive distribution

This involves securing as many outlets as possible so that access to the market and availability for customers is maximised. It is effectively saturation coverage of the market, so that consumers have the best opportunity to purchase the product with the minimum of effort. This type of distribution is particularly suitable for convenience and impulse purchases such as videos, soft drinks and household consumer goods. Manufacturers want the goods to be made available in as many different outlets as possible. For example, the local supermarket may sell videos.

With intensive distribution, mass coverage of the market and low unit prices usually make wholesaling necessary.

Selective distribution

Selective distribution involves choosing only a limited number of retailers to stock a particular product. This enables the organisation to protect its image and to create better relationships with retailers so it can exercise more control over the distribution process. This may lead to cooperative advertising, where the manufacturer pays a proportion of the retailer's advertising expenditure in return for having the product prominently displayed. The manufacturer may also provide a range of other services for the retailer such as training and point-of-sale materials.

Exclusive distribution

In some circumstances, producers may grant exclusive rights to retailers to sell their products in a particular area. This is an extreme form of selective distribution. It is not an appropriate strategy for convenience products, but is often used when there is only a limited market available. For example, Porsche dealers have to be able to provide services which closely match the qualities of the product they are selling. Though some market coverage may be lost by the exclusivity of such an agreement, the image and prestige of the product is maintained. With this type of distribution, producers and retailers cooperate in many areas of marketing.

Case Study
The importance of dealer relations

Vauxhall does not sell its cars directly to the private motorist. They are distributed and sold through a network of dealers in over 600 franchised units.

Before their appointment for a five-year period, dealers are closely vetted. Vauxhall ascertains not only whether a dealership can meet the company's standards, but also whether it can provide the recommended levels of customer care.

Vauxhall dealerships are provided with a standardised corporate identity so that they are instantly recognisable to customers. Interior design and decor are intended to create a welcoming environment which facilitate and complement car display.

As car sales are seasonal, dealers' targets are variable during the year. Each dealer is expected to achieve an annual sales figure and the size of dealerships varies widely. Dealers are provided with training and support by Vauxhall, designed to help them maintain the required levels of customer care. Such programmes may cover almost every aspect of dealership business, ranging from finance and accounting to sales and vehicle servicing right through to senior management. All dealership personnel are required to participate in a number of training programmes.

To support dealers in their sales efforts, Vauxhall provides point-of-sale materials, as well as a full range of literature. Promotion also takes place in national and local advertising media.

Outdoor events, agricultural shows, sporting events and fetes provide good opportunities to show products to the public. Vauxhall makes available to its dealers a range of show materials, e.g. mobile hospitality units, all designed to emphasise the nature of the product and its identity. The annual Motor Show attracts much attention and helps to develop corporate identity.

Questions for discussion

1 *Would you describe Vauxhall's distribution strategy as intensive, selective or exclusive?*
2 *What are the advantages of using a dealer network?*
3 *What other, if any, forms of distribution are suitable for the selling of cars?*
4 *Discuss the criteria Vauxhall would need to see satisfied before granting a new franchise.*

Other factors affecting channel selection

Having decided upon the appropriate distribution channel, a number of issues may influence the eventual selection of channel members.

- The image of the product and how this image may be projected by the chosen distributor.
- The size, nature and quality of the sales force of the channel member. The intermediary may only have a

small sales force or the sales force may not have the high level of knowledge required for dealers, particularly with goods which have a high degree of complexity.

- The ability and expertise to provide after-sales servicing.
- The financial standing of the intermediary. Distributors buy a large number of goods on credit and so their reputation, creditworthiness and ability to pay debts promptly will be considered.
- The need for intermediaries to carry specialist equipment, such as that for car servicing.
- The strategy of competitors – manufacturers can use distribution techniques which compete with those of other organisations in the same market.
- The location of channel members in areas which have the highest concentration of customers.

Channel patterns

Channel members may combine a range of activities or pass them on to other members. Most distribution channels are formed by formal agreement, which allows producers and their intermediaries to develop strategies that provide mutual benefits.

Vertical channel integration occurs when two or more stages in the channel are combined under one management, e.g. if a wholesaler owns a number of retail outlets and also performs retailing functions. **Total vertical integration** involves owning all distribution activities from the producer to the buyer. Oil companies may extract oil, distribute it to refineries by pipeline and then use their fleet to distribute the final product to their service stations.

Where integration takes place in marketing channels so that a single channel member manages all channel activities, this is known as a **vertical marketing system (VMS)**. The great benefits of this are increased efficiency and cost savings. **Corporate VMS** combines all channel stages under one ownership, as with the oil company above. **Administered VMS** involves independent channel members setting up an administrative system to coordinate the functioning of the channel. Under a **contractual VMS** organisational agreements between channel members are formalised through contractual relationships. Agreements then outline the rights of each channel member.

Where institutions at the same level of operations combine – a wholesale may combine operations with another wholesaler or a number of garage chains may merge – this is known as **horizontal channel integration**. It is possible for organisations to merge both horizontally and vertically.

Within the distribution channel there are certain conventions and behaviour patterns. As organisations are working with each other, there are certain expectations from each channel member. Retailers expect wholesalers to deliver goods on time and, in return, wholesalers expect prompt payment.

It may be important for some organisations to exert **channel leadership**. The controlling or dominant member of the channel is known as the **channel captain**. Such leadership reflects the member's power within the marketing channel. There are five non-economic and two economic sources of power within the marketing channel (see Figure 22.11).

Figure 22.11 Sources of power to achieve channel leadership

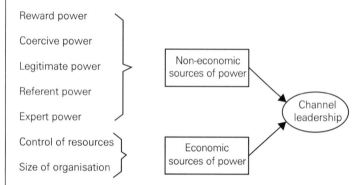

If a channel member offers a reward to other channel members, then this is **reward power**, e.g. granting a franchise or dealership to another member. Franchisors may exert considerable power over franchisees. **Coercive power** involves the threat of economic punishment of another member. **Legitimate power** reflects the powers provided by contractual relationships. **Referent power** occurs where channel members agree to emulate and follow the channel leader. **Expert power** occurs where the channel captain provides and uses expertise for other channel members, e.g. assistance with promotions based upon marketing expertise. The **size and level of operations of the channel leader** also influence other channel members, e.g. smaller members of the channel may depend on the channel leader for most or all of their business.

Channel leadership may take place at any stage in the channel. For example, BMW, as a manufacturer, is the channel captain for its distributors. Retailers, such as Marks & Spencer, may be powerful channel captains. Wholesalers may also be channel leaders; they may be of considerable importance for independent retailers.

Channel cooperation occurs where channel members work together to achieve individual and channel goals. Channel cooperation assumes that, in working together, members consider themselves to be part of a unified system so that individual members do not make decisions which disadvantage others. By working together to satisfy the needs of a market, each member's actions help other members to achieve objectives.

Though it is assumed that all distribution channel members are working together to achieve similar goals and objectives, disagreements may occur from time to time between channel members. For example, a franchisee may be unhappy with the decisions and actions of a franchisor. This is known as **channel conflict**. Conflict between two or more retailers or wholesalers at the same level is known as **horizontal conflict** and where conflict occurs between channel members at different levels, this is **vertical conflict**.

Conflict may arise for a variety of reasons. Each organisation has a role to play in the distribution process and the conflict might arise if other organisations are not undertaking their role effectively. For example, retailers may become concerned if wholesalers are not maintaining quality or making prompt deliveries. The solution to channel conflict is cooperation. This may involve the setting of realistic performance targets and instituting channel coordination procedures which provide direction and control. It often falls to the channel captain to provide the leadership required to ensure the cooperation of all parties.

Case Study
A 'systemised retailer'

Iceland PLC considers itself to be a systemised retailer. Such systems enable it to respond quickly to changing customer tastes or competitive tactics.

The company makes extensive use of information technology to run the business. EPOS systems have been in use since the mid-1980s. Their flexibility and information flow have been enhanced by a new generation of Iceland-developed software. Raw data generated by EPOS is analysed by Iceland's executive information system, one of the most advanced tools in retailing. The system automatically flags exceptions to predicted performance, so that problems can be tackled immediately. It also allows users to analyse turnover by store and product enabling the sales mix to be adjusted at every outlet. It provides instant feedback on the success of product launches and promotions.

Using its updated three-year database on product and store performance, Iceland can predict demand with considerable accuracy, enabling it to provide suppliers with longer-term indications of requirements, rather than just placing orders on a weekly cycle. This helps Iceland to minimise stock in

the system and allow those involved to take advantage of 'just in time' deliveries.

At Iceland's automated warehouse in Deeside, sophisticated scanning systems minimise labour inputs at both depot and store. Throughout Iceland the use of new technology helps to reduce costs and ensure maximum efficiency.

Questions for discussion

1 *At what stage(s) is Iceland in the distribution process?*
2 *How important is it to develop a distribution system which enables organisations to respond to changes in consumer tastes and competitive trends?*
3 *What is meant by:*
   a *EPOS*
   b *information flows*
   c *flexibility*
   d *weekly cycle*
   e *raw data*
   f *scanning systems?*

Physical distribution

Physical distribution includes all the activities involved in moving products, both inwards to manufacturer or outwards towards customers. **Physical distribution management** (**PDM**) describes the role of managers in developing, administering and operating systems to control the movement of raw materials and finished goods.

Physical distribution management is an important part of the marketing mix. It helps an organisation to meet customers' needs profitably and efficiently. In doing so, it enables manufacturers to provide goods for customers at the right time, in the right place and in the condition required. It may also reduce the *lead time* – between when a customer makes an order and when that order is delivered.

There are many different aspects to physical distribution, most of which are integrated and should be designed to work together as a whole. For example, if a book that you wanted was not available at your local bookshop, what processes would be put into operation if you placed an order? They would probably be along the lines of Figure 22.12. Think of all the different stages that take place to ensure that the need of the customer ordering the book is met. First, the customer uses a bookshop – he or she knows where to go to obtain the book. The bookshop then uses some form of **communication system** to

Figure 22.12 The processes or ordering a book

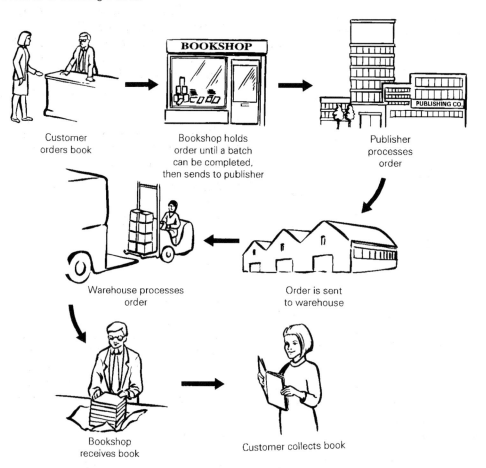

Customer
orders book

Bookshop holds
order until a batch
can be completed,
then sends to publisher

Publisher
processes
order

Warehouse processes
order

Order is sent
to warehouse

Bookshop
receives book

Customer collects book

inform the publisher of this need. The publisher processes the order, again using some form of communication system or **information technology**. Copies of the book are stored in a **warehouse** where stocks are held and inventories monitored. The book is then **transported** to the bookshop to be picked up by the customer.

Costs are an important element in each stage of the distribution process. The stages are interdependent, so if one breaks down or causes a delay, the customer's need is not met as well as it should be. For physical distribution to work, therefore, each of the stages must work effectively.

Trading off costs against service

The physical distribution system balances the need for customer service against the need to minimise costs. Maximising customer service potential may entail a large amount of stock and warehousing space, a considerable number of distribution staff and rapid transport. However, minimising costs implies the reverse – minimum stock, limited storage space, a skeleton staff and cheap transport. Designing a physical distribution

system, therefore, involves trading off costs against service, or inputs against outputs (see Figure 22.13).

Inputs include all the distribution costs – freight costs plus inventory costs plus warehousing costs plus other service costs. It is important to take a detailed look at these costs and to assess how they can be controlled to minimise waste. It is essential to know the distribution cost of every product dealt with. This involves a detailed analysis of how much labour time, transport time and other factors are spent on each product.

Outputs can primarily be measured in terms of the value of services to customers. Distribution can give a clear competitive benefit in meeting customer needs, e.g. a quick, prompt and efficient service. Every business must decide whether it is going to give a distribution service that is better than, the same as or worse than those of its competitors. Weaknesses in distribution will clearly need to be compensated for by strengths in other areas of the marketing mix.

The system chosen depends largely on the scale of the operations and the size of the market. If an organisation operates from a single plant, it may try to locate in a

Figure 22.13 Balancing inputs against outputs

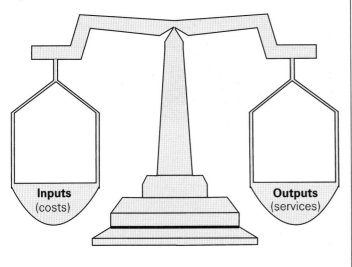

central market position or it may choose the spot with the best transport and communication links. For example, a business handling mail from customers overseas may choose to locate near an airport.

A business that wishes to maximise customer service will have the highest **inventory costs**, because it needs to hold stock to meet all foreseeable requirements. There are three types of stock inventory costs:

- **Carrying costs**. These include costs of storage, materials handling, insurance and losses from spoilage.
- **Replenismnent costs**. These relate to the purchase of goods, as well as handling charges.
- **Stock-out costs**. These include sales lost when the demand for goods exceeds supply, as well as the costs of back orders.

The major inventory decisions are when to order and how much to order. The danger of keeping too little in stock is **stock outs** (shortages) and this may mean losing custom because of dissatisfaction with the quality of service. In contrast, too much stock adds to the cost and wastage through goods becoming soiled or out of date.

Quite clearly, distribution is a key area of marketing. It should be seen as a very important part of meeting customer needs and requirements. Responsibility for physical distribution is often shared between the sales manager, inventory control manager and transport manager. It is imperative, however, that these functions are centrally coordinated through the marketing function.

Transport

Transport is a key component in physical distribution. Choosing the best possible transport system involves weighing up a number of components. For example, what forms of transport should be used? Can these forms of transport be integrated? What are the best possible routes? Does a company use its own fleet or outside carriers? How does a business maximise safety? How does it minimise costs? How does it make sure that the products arrive on time and in the best possible condition?

There are six main types of transport for moving goods, each of which has its own distinctive advantages and disadvantages. These are:

- railways
- roads
- inland waterways
- air
- pipelines
- sea.

Railways

Railways carry heavy and bulky freight over land for long distances, particularly between major cities. However, rail is not always appropriate for reaching out-of-the-way destinations and is costly for guaranteed speedy deliveries. It is frequently used for coal, grain, cars and iron.

Roads

These provide the most flexible form of transport with door-to-door delivery. Motor transport is fast over short and sometimes long distances, and some companies run their own fleet relatively cheaply. However, road travel is subject to traffic delays and breakdowns and drivers are limited by law to working only so many hours in a day.

Inland waterways

Inland waterways are the cheapest way of transporting heavy, low-value goods which are non-perishable, e.g. coal, grain, and sand. Few markets are, however, accessible by water and other forms of transport are normally required to move goods to the destination. Droughts, floods and bad weather conditions may affect this type of transport.

Air

This is the fastest way of transporting goods between countries, as long as the ultimate destination is reasonably accessible. It is particularly suitable for urgent, relatively light and expensive loads. Though it only accounts for a small amount of commercial transport, air transport is growing.

Pipelines

Pipelines are expensive to construct, cheap to run, but expensive to repair. Most carry petroleum products or chemicals. These move products slowly and at very low cost.

Sea

Sea transport is a cheap way of carrying high-volume, bulky loads between countries. It is generally slow, lacks flexibility and may be affected by weather conditions.

Containers

Containerisation of loads has made possible the integration of these different forms of transport. Routes and services have been simplified to cut out wasteful duplication. Special types of vehicles have been designed to carry special loads. Direct motorway connections between cities have proved to be of major importance in determining location decisions, as have fast intercity rail services and air links.

Choosing the most appropriate transport

Different methods of transport may prove to be more or less cost-effective in different situations depending on the cost of transport relative to the type of good being transported, the price of the good or the speed with which it is needed. Heavy bulky items may be sent by road, rail or sea depending on the distances involved. Urgent items such as first-class post or important medical supplies may be sent by air. What are the criteria for selecting the mode of transport?

1 **Cost**. It is important to compare the costs of transport with the benefits each mode provides. For example, sending goods by sea instead of air may be cheaper but may also be slower and less reliable.
2 **Time**. Transit time affects the quality of service the supplier can provide.
3 **Accessibility**. It may be difficult to move goods door to door using certain transport modes.
4 **Reliability**. It is important to choose a mode of transport which provides a consistent service, delivering goods on time and in acceptable condition.
5 **Traceability**. The ease with which goods can be found in transit may be an important factor.
6 **Capability**. The ability of the transport mode to ship goods in certain conditions, e.g. frozen goods or liquids and gases, should be considered.

Case Study
Reducing transport costs at Shell

Greater cost effectiveness is a worthwhile target. Over the last few years Shell Transport has reduced the cost of transporting oil products by £2 per tonne (a 20 per cent reduction).

The increased efficiency is based on:

- the UK's improved road system
- larger, more efficient road tankers
- making deliveries outside the rush hour
- better planning systems (to translate hundreds of thousands of orders a year into sensible delivery schedules)
- better information systems (details of backlogs of orders to be delivered and other information, e.g. every order from the distribution terminals is now available on the personal computer of everyone who needs the information)
- more efficient handling of customer orders and payments
- investment in depots
- use of contracts
- use of salaried drivers
- maintenance of safety at all times
- working closely with refineries.

Questions for discussion

1 *Which of the benefits outlined above are (a) internal economies of scale (i.e. economies resulting from the expansion of Shell Transport itself) and (b) external economies (resulting from growth outside Shell)?*
2 *What other factors may have influenced Shell's extensive use of road transport?*
3 *What future developments might affect distribution costs of petrol? Explain what the effects would be.*

Other types of channel flow

As we have seen, physical distribution is about getting the product or service to the customer. Of course, several other channel flows take place at the same time. For example, the **title of ownership** of goods will need to go to the purchaser, and this may be in the form of a receipt or invoice. On the other hand **payment** will flow from the purchaser to the seller (see Figure 22.14).

Information also needs to flow both ways between the buyer and the seller. The seller must make clear what the terms of the offer are and the buyer needs to specify his or her requirements. To start this off, the seller **promotes** the product to the buyer (see Figure 22.14).

Figure 22.14 Other types of channel flow

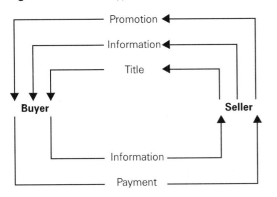

Nowadays, it is common practice for producers to **integrate** these flows. For example, promotional materials for other products may accompany the invoice, receipt or delivery of one product.

Physical distribution accounts for around one-third of all marketing costs and has a significant effect upon customer satisfaction. Physical distribution systems must be constantly adapted to ensure speed, reliability and quality of service. The main aim of managing physical distribution is to keep costs under control while improving customer service. This sometimes undervalued area of the marketing mix should be constantly evaluated to ensure that the organisation uses it to gain competitive advantage.

Further reading

- *Strategic Marketing Channel Management* by Donald Bowersox and Bixby Cooper. McGraw-Hill, 1992.
- *Strategic Purchasing and Supply Chain Management* by Malcolm Saunders. Pitman, 1994.
- *Beyond Partnership: Strategies for Innovation and Lean Supply Relationships* by Richard Lamming. Prentice Hall, 1993.
- *Distribution Resource Planning*, 2nd edition, by Andre Martin. Pitman, 1993.
- *Transport and Logistics* by Don Benson and Geoffrey Whitehead. Woodhead Faulkner, 1994.
- *Effective Pipeline Management* by David Farmer and Rien Ploos von Amstel. Gower, 1991.
- *Logistics of a Distribution System*, 2nd edition, by Peter and Nigel Attwood. Gower, 1992.
- *Physical Distribution Systems* by Alan McKinnon. Routledge, 1988.

23 Communication policy

On completion of this chapter students should be able to:

■ analyse the role of the sales force and its relationship with other elements in the communication mix

■ identify and evaluate the use of various forms of non-personal selling in markets

■ examine the structure, organisation and methods used in advertising operations

■ identify and analyse the key decisions in deciding a communication mix.

The role of the sales force

Every day of your life you are involved in some form of **personal selling activity**. It might be persuading a friend to accompany you to a sports event or a relative to buy something for you. What you are doing is using a relationship to sell your ideas to someone else. Personal selling involves interaction between individuals or groups of individuals, in contrast to other *non-personal* areas of the **promotional mix** such as advertising, public relations and sales promotions.

Personal selling involves persuasive communication between a seller and a buyer which is designed to convince the customer to purchase the product on offer through an exchange process. The objective of personal selling is therefore to make a sale, and it is the culmination of all the marketing activities that have taken place beforehand. It involves matching a customer's requirements with the goods or services on offer. The better the match, the more lasting the relationship between the seller and the buyer.

The role of personal selling will vary from business to business. It can be one of the most expensive areas of the promotional mix. Though the cost of salaries, commissions, hotel and travel expenses may be high, the great benefit of personal selling is that it is a two-way process of personal communication which allows an organisation to obtain first-hand information about its customers. This personal communication element can be very important as the final sale might come as a result of protracted negotiations.

Personal selling is important in both consumer and organisational markets. However, in consumer goods markets advertising often helps the process and is often the driving force which *pulls* a product through the distribution network. In organisational markets, on the other hand, personal selling may have to work harder to *push* the product through to the market (see Figure 23.1).

The main benefit of personal selling is the ability to communicate with and focus on customers individually and with precision. For example, if you go into a travel

Figure 23.1 The push/pull effect

agency and ask for details about a holiday, the sales assistant may explain and point out the features of various packages as well as any discounts or promotions they might offer. All of the other areas of the promotional mix are targeted at *groups* of people.

Though we may all have mental stereotypes of the typical salesperson, selling involves special skills. Whereas there is a tendency to downgrade the role of the salesperson in the UK, in many countries (Germany, for example) sales staff require a high degree of technical competence and are generally accepted to be part of the corporate elite. Salespeople are key intermediaries who present information to customers and then provide **feedback** on customer needs.

Many organisations spend more on personal selling than on any other area of the promotional mix, and within organisations large numbers of individuals may find that personal selling forms part of their role. Personal selling may involve individuals developing special skills and using them in many different operational situations. To do so sales staff need to know their products and be well trained in selling techniques.

So, what sort of tasks do sales staff undertake? McMurray and Arnold identify seven different selling tasks which those involved in sales might have to undertake:

■ *Product delivery* – As part of their role they may have to deliver the product personally. For example, though the prime function of a milkman is to deliver your milk, he may wish to develop his 'round' by selling other complementary products.
■ *Inside order-taking* – Many sales staff rarely leave their organisation to sell. In large stores they may work on counters. They may sell over the telephone or work in some form of showroom.
■ *Outside order-taking* – This involves geographically based sales staff visiting prospective or existing customers in order to make a sale. It may involve regular calls to existing customers as well as identifying new customers.
■ *Goodwill building* – As part of their role, sales staff may assist customers with installing products, post-sales advice, help with displays, etc.
■ *Technical representation* – Sales staff may be required to have good technical knowledge to help customers to gain the most benefit from their purchases. They may also be required to help install or use products (for example, sales-based project engineers).

■ *Creative selling of tangibles* – This involves selling tangible goods, from make-up to computer systems.
■ *Creative selling of intangibles* – This involves selling services such as banking and advertising, often when customers may not have a perceived need.

Though selling activities and techniques will vary from one person to another, and will also depend on their role within the organisation, there is a commonly used *mnemonic* known as the **five Ps** which describes personal selling and the sequence of events it creates (see Figure 23.2).

Figure 23.2 The five Ps of selling

■ **Preparation** – Sales staff should be adequately trained and familiar with the product, customers, competition and the market.
■ **Prospecting** – This involves identifying customers or *prospects* before selling takes place.
■ **Pre-approach** – It is important to learn about the customer before the approach.
■ **Presentation** – This involves using active selling skills.
■ **Post-sale support** – Following up sales helps to create repeat business.

Preparation

Selling in a highly competitive world means that preparation has never been so important. Though it has been said that sales people are born and not made, skills, knowledge and training can improve everybody's performance. Training is designed to build on a person's selling skills and to use their personal abilities and understanding to follow the psychological stages of the sales process. Product knowledge is vital as it allows feedback from the prospect's questions about the product's technical specifications, benefits and functions.

Comprehensive records on customers should be kept and updated after each visit. Keeping sales records enables the salesperson to respond exactly to each customer's individual needs. Knowledge of competitors and their products enables the seller to respond to queries about the relative merits and demerits of products. Good preparation improves the chances of closing a sale.

Prospecting

Identifying customers is a traditional role fulfilled by a salesperson. **Prospects** must be located before any selling can begin. Though sales staff will already have a list of customers or accounts, a salesperson may have to carry out **cold-calling**. This involves visiting or telephoning an organisation that the business has not previously had any dealings with. Cold-calling by sales representatives has unpredictable results and can be demoralising if there is a poor reception.

An alternative to cold-calling might be the use of telephone **canvassers**, whose job it is to find potential customers and then pass on the details to sales representatives. Sometimes it is possible to use independent **agents** to find customers. Working on a commission-only basis, agents may reduce the need for an organisation to employ as many sales representatives, particularly if there are a large number of low-value accounts. Insurance, for example, is sold by agents.

Many organisations use **direct-mail** techniques to stimulate enquiries for sales staff to follow up. A good mailshot will make it clear what is on offer and help to initiate the selling procedure.

A growing type of selling approach is the use of the telephone. **Telemarketing** is often regarded as a fairly cost-effective alternative to cold-calling in person.

Pre-approach

It is necessary to learn about a potential customer before the meeting. Pre-approach may involve finding out about the past history of transactions, if any, by researching records; and finding out who salespeople are dealing with and whether they have achieved access to a decision maker, as well as ascertaining general needs and aspirations.

Presentation

The presentation stage is based on a strategy known as AIDA:

A A customer's *attention* is captured and he or she is made *aware* of the product.

I The *impact* made by the presentation stimulates the customer's *interest*.

D The customer is persuaded that he or she is *deprived* by not having the product, and this helps to stimulate a *desire* for it.

A *Action* involves the purchase of the product.

Probing is quite important in the early stage of the presentation, in order to find out the prospect's needs and where his or her priorities might lie. The salesperson can then try to match the product or service with the prospect's requirements. This may involve elaborating on the product's advantages, concentrating on aspects such as savings in costs, design ingredients, performance specifications, after-sales service, etc.

During the presentation, the salesperson must constantly evaluate whether the product is appropriate to the needs of the prospect. It is unethical to sell something that is not needed – although this may often happen! The larger and more complex the order, the more complex the negotiations over the conditions of supply. Sometimes sales aids such as product demonstrations, samples and literature will help the process.

The prospect may have a variety of objections to the purchase. These objections might be genuine, or a result of a misunderstanding. There might also be a reluctance to make a commitment at this stage. Logical, well-presented arguments and incentives may overcome such objections.

Timing is crucial to **closing** the sale. A salesperson must look for **buying signals** which indicate that the prospect is close to a decision and almost ready to put a signature on an order form and discuss the contractual arrangements.

Post-sale support

This stage involves following up the sale. Promises that might have been made during the negotiations will have to be met. If the salesperson guarantees delivery by a certain date, that date must be held. Contacting customers to see if they are happy with the product will encourage repeat buying and improve the supplier's reputation for concern for its customers.

Sales staff may also have a number of other related functions. Communication, for example, is an important role. Sales staff operate as an **information link** between suppliers and their customers. As a result, personal selling involves a boundary role – being at the boundary of a supplying organisation and also in direct and close contact with customers. The role is often not only one of selling but also one of interpreting the activities and policies of each organisation to the other (see Figure 23.3). As a result, a considerable amount of administration may also accompany the selling role.

Figure 23.3 The information link between customers and suppliers

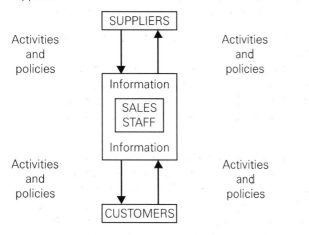

Personal selling enables organisations to be close to their customers and, as a result of the information link, they can react more quickly to changes in the marketplace. However, it is important not to think about selling as an isolated area of the promotional mix. Selling activity should be supported with advertisements to help prepare the ground for selling and to help pull products through markets. It may also be helped by promotions and public relations activities. The sales function should be integrated with other areas of promotional activity.

Deployment

The size, nature and deployment of the sales force will be determined by many factors. Often large and widespread markets can only be supplied by a massive salesforce whereas small concentrated markets tend to make personal selling cost-effective. Given its costs, an organisation also has to consider the *need* for personal selling. No matter what other sales techniques are used in some markets, if customers become used to personal selling they will tend to expect close contact with a representative from their suppliers. In these circumstances, particularly if a competitor uses personal selling, it can become very difficult to do anything but become locked into the use of personal selling techniques.

Many organisations are dependent on their sales force for generating much of their income. Given the important role of sales staff in creating this revenue, the effective development and management of the sales force is necessary. There are a number of crucial issues, including:

- the size of the sales force
- its recruitment
- the setting of objectives

- training and remuneration
- sales force organisation/allocation
- management and motivation
- performance evaluation.

In the early stages of development it is important to determine **the size of the sales force**. The decision is important because its size is a crucial determinant of sales generated and profits made. Given that markets are constantly changing, the sales-force size may have to be adjusted periodically to reflect its potential to generate profits. Though it may seem easy to cut the size of the sales force, thus reducing costs by increasing the size of territories, this may have a knock-on effect on the motivation of other members of the sales staff and the organisation may find it difficult to respond to potential opportunities when better market conditions emerge.

Recruiting the right type of sales staff is another important issue. Every organisation is different. They operate in different types of market and may have different types of customer to whom they may wish to convey a particular type of image. Sales staff may also need considerable technical expertise. Recruitment should therefore be aimed at attracting the best applicants by choosing those with specifically identified characteristics and requirements for each post. Some typical characteristics of salespeople are:

- energy
- desire for status
- competitive nature
- empathy
- self-confidence
- industriousness
- perseverance
- determination to succeed.

The first stage in the recruitment process is to identify a series of traits and characteristics, such as those above, in order to generate a well-thought-out *job description*. Having developed this it will then be possible to identify specific requirements for each post.

Recruitment may take place from many sources. For example, the first source may be from those within the organisation who know the business well. Other sources may include employment agencies, recruits leaving education, applicants who read advertisements in the press, etc.

Having recruited sales personnel, the next step is to set their **sales objectives**. These objectives are effectively 'performance criteria' in that they provide sales staff with guidelines on targets as to what they are expected to achieve in the future. They also serve the purpose of helping with the evaluation of sales-force performance. Objectives will be provided specifically for each salesperson as well as for the sales force as a whole. For example, each salesperson may be evaluated by average order size, number of calls made and efficiency at generating orders from calls. The sales force as a whole may be assessed on the value of sales generated, unit volume of sales, market share or profit generated by sales.

Training sales staff can be an expensive process. Some organisations put newcomers through formal in-house training programmes and also require them to attend courses at educational institutions, while others may adopt a more informal approach based on learning while doing the job itself (i.e. on-the-job training). The training programme may aim at new staff, experienced staff or even both, and focus on three different areas:

- the organisation
- the products
- methods of selling.

An organisation must develop a **remuneration** package designed to attract, retain and motivate sales staff. This plan should provide managers with good control over sales staff but also provide individuals with a series of incentives. There are normally three different remuneration systems:

- *Salary only* – Sales staff are paid a specific sum for the job over each time period. This provides maximum security, particularly for those in the smaller income-generating sales territories, and is easy to administer. The problem is that there is no incentive for extra sales made.
- *Commission only* – Remuneration is determined solely by the sales generated. Commission may be on a single percentage or a sliding scale involving different percentages at different levels of sales. This will act as a considerable incentive to effort but may encourage staff to look for short-term accounts rather than build long-term business. If the level of sales fluctuates this may cause considerable uncertainty. It may also lead to disputes between staff over sales territories.
- *Salary plus commission* – With this package, sales staff are paid a fixed salary plus commission. This method will attempt to achieve a balance between having security and the provision of incentives. It will encourage staff to be part of the organisation and to look for new sales leads.

Organising and allocating the sales force

The sales force has to be organised and allocated in a way which maximises its effort and brings in optimum returns. Three clear-cut factors influence the size, shape and deployment of staff into sales territories.

The first factor is the **sales potential** of each territory. It is important that sales territories have similar sales potentials. The danger is that if one territory has larger sales potential than another, the extra effort made in the territory with the larger potential will be offset by a reduction in work in another territory with less potential.

The second factor is the **workload** required in each sales territory. It would be wrong to give a salesperson a territory which was beyond his or her capability. The geographic spread of the territory is important because those in the larger territories may have to travel much longer distances to generate similar levels of sales.

Thirdly, the **shape and size** of the territory may be an important factor in determining the ease with which sales staff can reach customers while at the same time minimising selling costs. An important aspect of this is *call-planning*. Given the various characteristics of the sales territory, it should be possible to work out how many calls sales staff can make each day. The ideal territory is one in which staff do not spend too much time travelling but have a good call rate.

Having identified and considered the above factors, there are then a number of methods of allocating the sales force:

- *By area* – With this method a sales representative concentrates on a specific geographical area. For example, the area may range in size from London to Africa or the Far East. The great benefit of allocating by this method is that staff develop good local knowledge of specific conditions and requirements in different countries and parts of countries.
- *By product* – If a company manufactures many goods, a sales representative may be given specific responsibility for either one or a range of products. For example, where technical specifications are complex, a salesperson may specialise in one type of high-tech product. With great product knowledge, sales staff can respond to detailed enquiries with a certain level of authority. However, overall travelling expenses may be higher and a single customer may have to deal with more than one sales representative from the same company.
- *By customer* – It is possible to specialise in specific types of customer. A computer manufacturer may have sales staff specialising in selling to schools, retail businesses and different types of product manufacturers. The great benefit of this form of allocation is that sales staff learn a lot about the motives and requirements of specific types of buyer.
- *By type of market* – It is possible to allocate sales staff by breaking down the market into segments – for example, male and female markets, business and consumer markets. Again, as with division by customer, this method enables staff to get to know about the specific needs of particular groups of

customers. The problems are likely to be travelling costs and the blurred distinctions between one type of market and another.

■ *By type of customer service* – Different types of customer may require different types of service. For example, a wholesaler will give a different service to a multiple from that provided for a small retailer.

Most organisations use one or more of the above methods for allocating sales territories. Over recent years, **key-account holding** has emerged as another major factor influencing allocation, further developing the customer-orientated approach. A key account is a single major customer to whom a significant proportion of overall sales are made. Dealing with such customers requires special skills and extra investment.

Managing the sales force

Managing the sales force requires a good understanding of many of the selling situations and problems staff are likely to face. A major objective is to minimise non-selling time and so maximise selling time. Another objective may be to reduce selling costs, such as those for travel and accommodation.

It is important for sales staff actively to pursue organisational policies such as increasing market share and improving profitability, but at the same time they must achieve a balance between the development of new accounts and providing a range of services for existing customers. Another vital role is that of extracting information from the market. Sales managers will expect their staff to provide call reports which give detailed feedback from customers, and to provide work schedules which show where they expect to be.

It is always important to *motivate* sales staff. One of the main problems is that when sales staff leave an organisation they may take valuable customer accounts with them. Sales managers can provide a range of incentives such as job security, power and authority, as well as a range of financial benefits. Sales contests which promote special items as well as other incentive programmes can be useful motivators. On the other hand some organisations use 'negative' schemes which provide for a range of financial penalties if sales targets are not met.

Performance evaluation takes place largely by comparing sales achieved with individual sales objectives, and by considering the number of visits, profitability units and accounts generated by individual sales staff. Qualitative *feedback from customers* also provides information on areas such as customer service, organisational skills, knowledge of product, attitude, appearance, relationship building and individual customer satisfaction.

When a sales force is working well this can lead to improved customer retention and loyalty, new customers attracted through recommendations, improved morale and increased productivity. It may also lead to lower advertising and promotional costs because the selling process becomes an effective source of new business.

Performance evaluation is an important control mechanism. At the end of the evaluation process it may be necessary to make crucial decisions about individual members of the selling force as well as other areas such as performance targets, training or forms of motivation.

Though personal selling is traditionally one of the most expensive forms of promotion, it is usually extremely important for organisational and reseller markets. Over recent years better communication methods, made possible by the use of mobile technologies, have assisted with the traditional problem of sales-force management, to enable selling activities to become better focused.

Non-personal selling

Whereas personal selling involves the making of sales by individuals and emphasises the importance of 'salemanship', non-personal selling involves using the **media** as a form of controllable communication.

The media plan

The characteristics of various media will commend them to creative areas such as sound, vision and script. The success of any promotional campaign depends on using creative skills effectively and making the correct choice of media.

The **media plan** identifies the media to be used and the dates and times when the promotional messages will be seen. The success of the plan will be determined by how many people view or hear the message. Media selection will therefore depend on the target audience (i.e. the number of potential customers the promotional campaign is intended to reach), as well as the number of times the message is transmitted. These are known as **coverage** and **frequency**.

The first stage in using media involves developing an understanding of the media habits of the targeted audience. For example, television stations provide information about demographic distribution, communications, size and nature of companies, spending patterns, leisure activities and incomes of their viewers.

Advertisers will also want to have reliable information about the size of audience for each type of medium so that they know how many people they are able to reach. Various organisations carry out research into media use – examples are: *for television*, the Broadcasting Audience Research Board (BARB) (see Figure 23.4); *for independent radio*, the Joint Industry Council for Radio Audience Research (JICRAR); and *for major newspapers and magazines*, the National Readership Survey.

Figure 23.4 Millions viewing each of the four terrestrial channels in February 1995

BBC 1		ITV	
1 EastEnders (Thu)	16.45	1 Coronation Street (Mon)	18.84
2 EastEnders (Tue)	16.14	2 Coronation Street (Fri)	17.84
3 Casualty	15.06	3 Coronation Street (Wed)	17.67
4 National Lottery Live	14.71	4 Home Alone	15.18
5 Antiques Roadshow	13.44	5 Peak Practice	14.22
6 EastEnders (Mon)	12.27	6 International Gladiators	13.29
7 News and Weather		7 The Bill (Fri)	13.11
(Sun 18.05)	11.96	8 Blind Date	12.66
8 Animal Hospital	11.08	9 Emmerdale (Tue)	11.92
9 Noel's House Party	11.00	10 Barrymore	11.89
10 Neighbours			
(Tue 17.37)	10.87		
BBC 2		**C4**	
1 The X Files	6.38	1 Brookside (Tue)	7.22
2 Bottom	6.09	2 Brookside (Mon)	6.83
3 Horizon	5.28	3 Brookside (Wed)	6.51
4 Jeremy Clarkson's		4 Brookside (Thu)	6.15
Motoring World	5.25	5 Brookside (Fri)	5.93
5 Geoff Hamilton's		6 Cutting Edge (Mon)	5.88
Cottage Gardens	5.23	7 ER	5.09
6 Food And Drink	4.79	8 Countdown (Tue)	4.59
7 Star Trek: The		9 Countdown (Wed)	4.26
Next Generation	3.79	10 Countdown (Thu)	4.21
8 Steptoe And Son	3.56		
9 The World At War	3.40		
10 Randall & Hopkirk			
(Deceased)	3.22		

Where programmes appear in omnibus or repeat editions, ratings for the highest single showing only have been included. Source: BARB

The ideal media choice will be one which reaches the largest number of potential customers at lowest cost. The advertiser must, therefore, distinguish between those media which are affordable and those which are not. An important factor is **cost-effectiveness**.

For an advert to be cost-effective, it must not only have good coverage but its frequency must produce the required impact on the targeted audience. The **threshold concept** illustrates that unless advertising for a particular brand reaches a certain level, it will be wasted. An advertisement's effectiveness will therefore relate to advertising expenditure – the number of times people are exposed to a message will help to determine whether they remember it.

Media coverage helps to create preferences for a product or service which can translate into a purchasing decision. It might also encourage existing customers to purchase more and reinforce consumers' feelings that they have made the right decision. It will allow organisations to develop a strategy for a brand and take a range of actions, perhaps in response to those of competitors, so that market share and other objectives can be achieved.

Case Study
Women's monthly magazines

Look at Figure 23.5, which lists of some of the women's monthly magazines on the next page, and then consider the discussion questions which follow.

Questions for discussion

1 *Comment on the advertising rates for the various types of magazine.*
2 *How could an advertiser justify paying such rates?*
3 *Using examples, by referring to different parts of various product markets, explain why monthly magazines could be a cost-effective form of advertising.*
4 *What other considerations might influence advertisers to make decisions about the promotion of their products in these magazines?*

In developing the media plan a number of other factors may influence media choice. If a competitor is using a particular medium, then an organisation may feel it necessary to follow the strategy of that competitor. The nature of the product is another influence – some products may be more suited to colour press supplements while others are geared to the needs of customers who read technical journals.

Types of media

Printed materials
Printed materials make up by far the largest group of media in the UK. The group includes all newspapers and magazines, both local and national, as well as trade press, periodicals and professional journals. There are about 9000 regular publications in the UK which can be used by the advertiser. They allow the advertiser to send a message to several million people through the press or to target magazines of special interest from railways to snooker. They also allow the advertiser to communicate

Figure 23.5 Women's monthly magazines

	Circulation (000s)	Women's readership (000s)	(%)	Page rate (£) Mono	4-colour
Prima	665	2 343	10	9 135	15 225
Good Housekeeping	457	2 175	9	7 990	9 400
Family Circle	346	1 925	8	6 050	9 800
Woman & Home	395	1 889	8	4 680	8 000
Cosmopolitan	477	1 837	8	8 420	9 900
Vogue	179	1 494	6	8 200	10 250
Ideal Home	250	1 447	6	5 082	7 432
BBC Good Food	427	1 362	6	–	11 064
Homes & Gardens	175	1 360	6	3 943	6 282
Essentials	410	1 272	5	4 900	7 700
Clothes Show Magazine	173	1 220	5	–	4 106
She	257	1 079	5	4 850	5 700
House & Garden	141	981	4	4 490	7 180
Elle	202	905	4	4 400	5 900
Marie Claire	314	902	4	4 400	6 450
Needlecraft	90	882	4	1 201	1 725
Mother & Baby	114	833	4	2 476	3 974
Country Living	182	791	3	3 995	4 700
House Beautiful	308	724	3	4 250	5 000
'19'	197	707	3	3 215	5 340
Living	170	699	3	3 030	4 850
Looks	227	687	3	4 500	6 100
Practical Parenting	130	647	3	2 700	4 800
New Woman	269	614	3	4 200	5 600
Woman's Journal	151	568	2	3 270	4 940
Company Magazine	250	549	2	4 340	5 100
Options	156	542	2	–	5 500
Annabel	56	540	2	1 418	2 150
BBC Good Health	–	534	2	2 100	2 800
Hairflair	48	504	2	850	1 500
Country Homes & Interiors	106	483	2	1 960	3 115
Home & Country	85	438	2	1 281	2 037

with people in a certain trade or profession as well as those in a particular region.

The printed media allow for accurate targeting and positioning. Types of customers can be identified by analysing readership profiles (see Figure 23.6). Long or complex messages can be sent and, as the message is durable, it may be read repeatedly. If an advertisement appears in a prestige publication it may take on the prestige of that particular publication. Colour quality is today offered in an increasing number of newspapers and magazines; tear-off reply coupons which follow up advertisements are also popular.

Advertisements in the printed media are sometimes criticised for having a poor impact. There are many competing messages which the reader is not forced to read and some publications have a short time-span. Printed advertisements have static rather than dynamic qualities.

Broadcast media
Broadcast media include commercial television and commercial radio. Television is the most powerful medium – it reaches 98 per cent of households and viewing figures can exceed 20 million. TV advertisements are usually of a high creative quality, helped by both sound and colour. Messages are dynamic as they have voice, images, movement and colour, and can be repeated over and over again. The main disadvantage of such an expensive medium is that it is sometimes difficult to target a broadcast to a particular group of consumers.

Figure 23.6 Readership profiles of national dailies, 1994

	Tabloid/ broad- sheet	Circula- tion	Adult readership		Adult readership profiles						
					Sex		Age			Class	
					Men	Women	15/34	35/54	55+	ABC1	C2DE
		(000s)	(000s)	(%)	(%)	(%)	(%)	(%)	(%)	(%)	(%)
Population profile					48	52	36	32	32	48	52
The Sun	T	4 071	9 920	22	55	45	44	31	24	30	71
Daily Mirror	T	2 493	7 148	16	54	46	35	32	33	32	69
Daily Mail	T	1 794	4 456	10	50	50	28	34	37	65	35
Daily Express	T	1 367	3 482	8	52	48	27	32	41	60	41
The Daily Telegraph	B	1 008	2 617	6	55	45	23	34	44	84	16
Daily Star	T	747	2 201	5	65	35	51	32	17	25	74
Daily Record (Scotland)	T	737	1 925	4	53	47	40	35	25	32	68
Today	T	587	1 777	4	55	45	40	38	22	44	56
The Times	B	485	1 314	3	59	41	35	38	27	87	14
The Guardian	B	403	1 344	3	55	45	39	39	21	84	17
Financial Times	B	297	739	2	72	28	37	45	19	89	11
The Independent	B	281	1 055	3	62	38	45	38	16	85	15

Recent developments in television have seen franchise changes and the emergence of Carlton, GMTV and others companies. There have also been some mergers between television franchisees such as Yorkshire and Tyne-Tees, and some advertisers believe that this reduction in competition will inevitably lead to higher advertising rates. Direct broadcasting by satellite has been available since 1989 when Sky started using the Astra satellite, and this is reaching an increasing number of households. Though cable TV penetration in the UK is relatively low, it is developing.

There are more than 120 independent local radio (ILR) stations in the UK (including 12 in London), as well as several independent national radio (INR) stations (including Classic FM and Virgin). Local radio stations can be geared to many different types of audiences. Radio is a good way of communicating a sense of urgency and action. Advertisement costs are low in comparison with those of TV. One of the problems of radio, however, is that for many it is just a background medium.

Outdoor media
Outdoor media include fixed posters and hoardings, advertising on buses, taxis, underground trains and other forms of transport, as well as neon signs and electronic screens. This is particularly useful for providing frequency and supporting the images created through the broadcast media.

If an outdoor medium is well sited, its impact may be considerable. Posters can be in colour and there is a wide choice of locations and sites with little competition from other advertising matter. In fact many posters become a

sole attraction where people have little to do except look at the advert or fellow passengers.

Audience research figures for poster sites are available from a number of bodies. For example, the Outdoor Site Classification and Audience Research (OSCAR) assesses the audience of the 120 000 roadside panels and provides demographic information based on those likely to see the panels so that coverage and frequency can be assessed from each investment.

Outdoor media suffer from the intrusion of noise and clutter from the immediate environment. Advertisements may become part of the scenery and go unnoticed. Outdoor posters are always subject to damage from vandalism and graffiti, and many people today feel that hoardings intrude in the environment.

Direct mail
Direct mail is personally addressed advertising sent through the post. Every month every British household receives on average six and a half direct mail items. By using direct mail an organisation may establish a direct relationship with its customers. The advertiser supplies promotional literature to encourage sales and then tries to cater for the customers' perceived needs.

It often also includes **direct selling**, which does not involve a long distribution chain. It is recognised as the most rapidly increasing form of promotion because it allows an advertiser to reach a narrowly identified target audience.

The ability of direct mail to target precise segments in a market makes it cost-effective, as it eliminates the supply of mailshots to those unlikely to buy. Geodemographic and lifestyle systems such as PIN, ACORN and MOSAIC help the direct-mailer to identify types of consumer according to where they live and the lifestyles they follow. The majority of mailshots are read and organisations often use sales promotions such as offers and competitions to encourage a response.

If a good impression is made on a consumer, direct mail can offer an organisation the opportunity to send a long message and some detailed copy. Organisations such as the Automobile Association, Reader's Digest, Consumers Association and the National Geographic Magazine are well established in using direct mail techniques. It is the easiest form of promotion to measure as it is possible to calculate the number of mailshots sent out, the cost of the campaign, the response rate and the number of sales made. For example, Royal Mail offers its 'Mailsort' services for volume mailings. By presorting mail before handing it over, users can be provided with discounts on postage costs. Royal Mail points out that direct mail is the most selective form of promotional message reaching people in their households, and that it has a high impact in comparison with other advertising messages.

Cinema

Though **cinema** has declined in relative importance as an advertising medium, it tends to be popular with the young and is a good way of targeting a specific type of audience. A cinema has a captive audience, and the physical size and loud volume of advertisements makes them almost impossible to ignore. The quality of sound and vision helps the audience to recall cinema commercials better than those on television. Cinema audiences fluctuate widely and are dependent on the popularity of the films being shown. Commercials tend to be shown once during a programme and are not reinforced unless the recipient is a regular cinema attender.

Sales promotion

Sales promotion describes a category of techniques which are used to encourage customers to make a purchase. These activities are effectively *short-term* and may be used to increase sales, to respond to competitive activities, to help with the task of personal selling, or simply as an alternative to advertising. The Institute of Sales Promotion defines sales promotion as follows:

Sales promotion is the function of marketing which seeks to achieve given objectives by the adding of intrinsic, tangible value to a product or service.

Sales promotions might include point-of-sale materials, competitions, demonstrations and exhibitions. The essential feature of a sales promotion is that it is a short-term inducement to encourage customers to react quickly, whereas advertising is usually a more long-term communication process involving the building and developing of a brand.

As you walk down a high street or through a shopping mall, you will see many different examples of sales promotions. Such promotions may serve many different purposes. For example, *competitions*, *vouchers* and *trading stamps* may be designed to build customer loyalty and perhaps increase the volume purchased by existing customers. *Product sampling* is a strategy which is often used to introduce new products into the marketplace. *Clearance sales* of overstocked goods will increase sales during seasons when business would otherwise be slack. Many sales promotions are undertaken in response to the activities of competitors to ensure that an organisation remains competitive. Nearly all oil companies and petrol retailers offer competing promotional activities which change from time to time.

Sales promotions can have a more direct influence on sales than other promotional methods such as advertising. They enable the manufacturer to have a direct influence on the actions of the customer and, in some cases, encourage retailers to stock brands. Sales promotions may also help products in decline by injecting new life, encourage impulse buying, arouse interest in new products, or simply persuade customers to switch brands.

It is frequently argued that sales promotions are at their most effective when used together with other promotional techniques such as advertising. For example, in Figure 23.7(a) sales promotions alone sharply increase sales with each successive promotion. Figure 23.7(b) illustrates what is known as the **ratchet effect**. In this instance advertising slowly builds sales and then the impact of sales promotions sharply increases sales on the back of

Figure 23.7 Sales promotion alone (a), and in (b) sales promotion with advertising

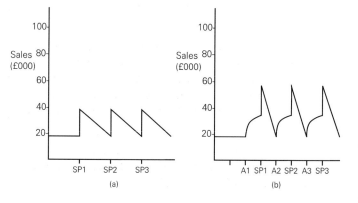

the advertising. This effect has been identified in many types of consumer goods and service markets.

Sales promotions can be divided into two broad areas:

- those designed to enhance the sales of a product to the trade
- those which assist the trade in promoting and selling products to the final consumer.

Selling into the pipeline is the expression often used to describe promotions which move products from the manufacturer into the distribution system. **Selling out of the pipeline** describes promotions which trigger the end-user to make a purchase (see Figure 23.8).

Figure 23.8 Promotions into and out of the pipeline

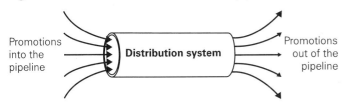

Promotions into the pipeline

These are techniques used to sell more stocks into the distribution system and are addressed directly at the distributors. *Dealer loaders* are among the inducements used to attract orders. They might include a 'free case' with so many cases bought – for example, thirteen for the price of twelve is known as a 'baker's dozen'. *Dealer competitions* might be linked to sales, with attractive prizes for the most successful dealer. *Promotional gifts* such as bottles of spirits, clocks, watches or diaries sometimes influence the choice of goods dealers stock.

Point-of-sale (POS) materials such as special displays, posters and racks can be offered against volume orders or offered on loan for a period. Some organisations might offer the use of a video recorder together with a promotional cassette for customers to play. *Publishing of dealers' names* in advertisements, sales literature or catalogues always encourages the support of particular dealers.

Extended credit often encourages dealers to stock goods, particularly if they sell and receive payment for the product before they have to pay suppliers. *Sale-or-return* can be used to encourage a dealer to stock an untried product and helps to remove the danger of being left with unsold stock.

Staff training is often provided for the dealer if the product involves detailed explanations, demonstrations or dealer servicing, as is the case with cars.

Promotions out of the pipeline

These assist the trade in promoting and selling products to the end-users. Manufacturers tend to be responsible for the bulk of sales promotions, though recently retailers have started to become more involved. Sales promotions to the end-user require a careful creative approach, as repeated use, or a tasteless promotion, might damage a brand.

Sample or trial packs are either given to customers or sold to them at low prices to encourage them to try the product, in the hope that this will stimulate them to make a full purchase. *Bonus packs* offer customers more of the product for the same price, giving greater value for money – beer and lager cans often offer extra beer for the same price. *Coupon offers* in the form of 'money off' are distributed door-to-door, or appear as part of an advertisement or on a pack.

Price reductions are always popular with consumers. They can, however, prove expensive for manufacturers and retailers, as many of those who buy the product might be regular users who would have been prepared to pay the full price. *Premium offers* may offer an extra product for the same inclusive price.

Competitions may interest consumers, particularly if there is an attractive prize. Scratch cards, free draws and bingo cards are popular. *Trading stamps* or *vouchers to collect* have largely disappeared from the retailing scene but are still popular at petrol stations. A certain quantity of stamps or vouchers is given every time a purchase is made, and these can be redeemed later for goods or services. This helps to reinforce brand loyalty.

Charity promotions can be popular with young customers, who collect box tops or coupons and send them to the manufacturer, who then makes a donation to a charity.

Demonstrations at the point of sale, which involve giving away samples or demonstrating a product, often generate considerable interest. These tend to be expensive, however, and are often not considered to be cost-effective.

Point-of-sale displays are designed to push products to consumers from the location where they are sold. An effective point-of-sale display attracts customers' attention and encourages them to approach and inspect the product before making a decision to buy.

Merchandising is the physical process of stocking goods so that they are in the right place at the right time, making it easy for customers to walk around a store, select the goods they require and take them away. It provides a competitive advantage to the retailer by supplying products at the right eye-level and at a location relative to height. Look at the sweet and crisp displays in your local supermarket. It also involves providing access for the physically handicapped, the placing of own brands next to manufacturer brands so that prices can be compared, and the siting of impulse items near to the cash registers.

Case Study
Wooing customers with music and literature

Sindy has been relaunched as a fresh-faced streetwise fashion doll, but that alone is not enough to hit back at the market share of Barbie! What can a girl do? The answer is to give youngsters something to put in their cassette players. For a short period of time all customers buying Sindy at Woolworths were provided with a two-song cassette featuring Kylie Minogue or Rozella. The deal provided hefty point-of sale support and combined Woolworth's strengths in toys and music.

The great benefit of using music for sales promotions is that choice is highly subjective and it can be manipulated to fine-tune a marketing strategy. For example, the romance of the Gold Blend couple was published in a paperback called *Love Over Gold* and this was then followed up with a promotional album of smoochy hits for St Valentine's Day.

Research with Shredded Wheat revealed that many core loyal users around the age of 55–65 had interests which included gardening and walking. As past promotions had been geared towards gardening, the summer promotion was for a book themed on country walks, produced by AA Publishing. The Shredded Wheat logo was carried on the cover. The purpose of the offer was to encourage and reward loyalty from existing users and also to build upon and enhance brand values. Consumers had to collect ten tokens from packs and then pay 50p postage.

Questions for discussion

1 *How is it possible to target certain types of customers with sales promotions using music and books?*
2 *Comment on your own experiences of promotions which use literature or music.*
3 *Given that promotions are a short-term technique, is it possible for them to provide longer-term benefits?*

The effects of individual sales promotions vary widely. Though most promotions such as free samples will clearly lead to an immediate increase in sales, on the whole sales promotions are a short-term measure and have little effect on brand loyalty over a longer period. For the manufacturers of staple goods such as washing-up liquid and bleach, sales promotions will not affect total market size which will be relatively fixed – though they will encourage buyers to move away from competing brands. Probably the greatest overall benefit of sales promotions is their ability to inject life into a brand in a way that is completely different from, but often just as effective as, a big advertising spend.

Public relations

Public relations or **publicity** encompasses all of the actions of and communications from an organisation. The forces in an organisation's external environment are capable of affecting it in a variety of ways. The forces may be social, economic, political, local or environmental and could be represented by a variety of groups such as customers, shareholders, employees and special-interest groups, and by public opinion. Reacting to such elements in a way that will build a positive image is very important.

The purpose of public relations (PR) is therefore to provide an external environment for an organisation in which it is popular and can prosper. Building good-will in such a way will require sound organisational performance and behaviour and the communication of such actions and attitudes to its many publics. Lord Mancroft once defined PR quite wryly as *'The art of arranging the truth so that people like you.'*

The direct selling of goods and services is not an objective of public relations. Whereas advertising is about relatively short-term objectives, public relations is long-term; it works by sending free messages to various groups through the activities the organisation undertakes in order to improve its reputation and maintain or develop its positive image. For example, PR may help an organisation to improve its visibility and create a series of perceptions such as that it is innovative, progressive, popular, dynamic or caring.

According to Frank Jefkins, in his book *First Marketing*, PR involves a transfer process which helps to convert the negative feelings of an organisation's many publics into positive ones (see Figure 23.9).

For a public relations programme to be effective it should be sustained and systematic. To develop the programme, good relationships with the media are important. Public relations may be particularly important if there is a sudden splurge of bad publicity such as an accident,

Figure 23.9 The PR transfer process

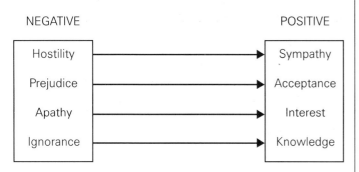

dishonesty, loss of jobs or any other negative event. For example, the massive increases in the pay of chief executives of newly privatised industries did little to improve public perceptions of those organisations. The danger is that such events can do considerable damage in the short term to reputations that have been steadily developed over many years.

Public relations can be developed as a strategic device to provide an organisation with a competitive advantage. By identifying the unfavourable attitudes of interest groups and their influence over the external environment, an organisation can develop a **PR strategy** to create better perceptions by reducing the negative effects and building on more positive profiles and imagery. One framework for a practical public relations programme is the six-point model shown in Figure 23.10.

Figure 23.10 Framework for a PR programme

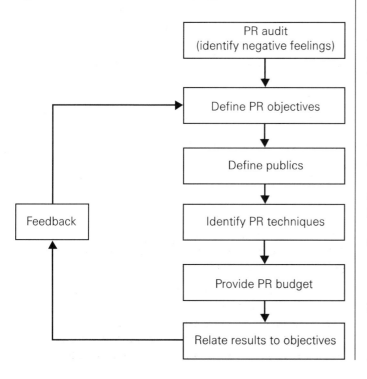

Case Study
Where advertising may be bad PR

Marketing ethical drugs is a complicated business and pharmaceutical companies have had to develop sophisticated ways of communicating their messages to decision makers. These decision makers often include non-medical administrators, health service managers, medical advisors, pharmaceutical advisors, GPs and many other groups.

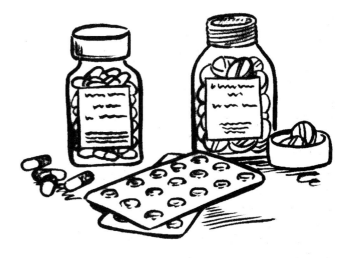

PR strategies targeted at various groups are now an effective way of developing trust and 'building bridges' with customers. PR helps to create awareness of problems, often long-term issues, so that confidence and knowledge are developed before drugs become available. PR is seen as a long-term process which prepares the market. PR events in this industry are also unique. They may include sponsoring conferences or organising satellite links between experts so that key opinions may be used to educate and to debate the issues. These filter through to buyers.

Kingston Business School recently placed PR as the third most important element of the marketing mix for pharmaceutical products. One reason for this is growing cynicism about advertising. The argument is that advertising itself is bad PR for many audiences, whereas PR activities are targeted, more constructive and provide the pharmaceutical companies with greater credibility.

Questions for discussion

1 *How does PR meet many of the criticisms levelled at advertising?*
2 *What sort of PR activities would be suitable for individuals and organisations to use in the pharmaceutical industry?*

Types of public relations activities

Charitable donations and *community relations* are good for an organisation's image, often provide a lot of good publicity and also help to promote and provide for a good cause.

Hospitality at top sporting events is a popular method used by organisations to develop their customer relations. For example, there are opportunities to entertain customers at events such as the FA Cup Final, the Wimbledon Championships and the Grand National.

Press releases covering events affecting the organisation – such as news stories, export achievements, policy changes, technical developments and anything that enhances the organisation's image – are a useful form of public relations. *Press conferences* are used to cover newsworthy events which are of general interest to a variety of media.

Visits and *open days* are a popular method of inviting various people to improve their understanding of what an organisation stands for. The Sellafield Visitors Centre, for example, claims to provide a 'window in on the nuclear world' and has become a top tourist attraction in the North West of England.

Sponsorship of sporting and cultural events is viewed as a useful opportunity to associate an image with a particular type of function. Examples are the NatWest Trophy, the FA Carling Premiership and the Embassy World Snooker Championship.

Corporate videotapes have become increasingly popular over recent years as a method of providing a variety of interested parties with information about company activities.

Minor product changes are also good public relations activities. For example, the British Union for the Abolition of Vivisection (BUAV) continually attacks organisations which use animals in the testing of cosmetic, toiletry and household products. Body Shop's reputation has been developed and enhanced by the ways in which it responds to the views of outside bodies in its eco-virtuous approach to bodycare products.

Magazines, *publicity literature* and *education services*, in both the private and public sectors, provide strong informed links between organisations and their various publics. For example, most organisations will send out magazines and brochures in response to enquiries in order to indicate what their functions, beliefs and activities are.

Other PR activities have included clubs, appearances on TV, awards, competitions, hot air balloons as well as anything which serves to maintain interest in and support for an organisation's activities.

So, is all publicity good publicity? There are many dangers within the PR process. Not all press releases may reach the media and some may be changed or altered in a way which affects the message. Marketers may not be able to control the timing of the communication and this may also backfire on the organisation – for example, announcing a major sponsorship deal at a time of reduced profitability. The PR process may also put an organisation in view of its various publics and these may set them up for a range of criticisms. For example, if a chemical company informs the world about the safety of its processes and then an accident occurs, the public relations process will be viewed as shallow; in fact many might believe that PR has been seen as more important than safety. Similarly an organisation might promote itself as a good employer and then announce a number of redundancies. It must always be remembered that PR activities may backfire and that the PR process is a twin-edged sword.

Advertising

Advertising is a method of communicating with groups in the marketplace in order to achieve certain objectives and results. **Advertisements** are messages sent though the media which are intended to inform or influence the people who receive them. According to the American Marketing Association, advertising is '*any paid form of non-personal presentation and promotion of ideas, goods or services by an identifiable sponsor*'.

Advertising messages may be sent through a variety of media forms, such as TV, radio and the press (see Figure 23.11). Promotional materials supplied with a product, promotional events or company brochures are not generally regarded as advertising.

There are a range of advertising objectives. These may include:

- to assist with selling
- to increase sales
- to create awareness of new products and developments to existing products
- to provide information about a product
- to create and build an image for a product
- to encourage desire to own the product
- to generate enquiries
- to change views or attitudes (e.g. government advertisements about the effects of smoking).

At all stages in the advertising process it is important to assess how effectively advertisements have contributed to

Figure 23.11 The top 20 advertisers, 1993

Rank	Advertiser	Advertising expenditure			
		Total (£000)	TV (%)	Radio (%)	Press (%)
1	Procter & Gamble	94851	96.8	0.1	3.1
2	Lever Brothers (Unilever)	67425	94.2	..	5.8
3	Kellogg Company of GB	60166	98.7	0.1	1.2
4	Ford Motor Company	56941	64.5	2.3	33.2
5	British Telecommunications	56419	61.7	1.8	36.4
6	Vauxhall (General Motors)	43035	40.5	2.2	57.2
7	Procter & Gamble (Health & Beauty)	39400	90.9	1.0	8.1
8	Rover Group (BMW)	39013	51.7	1.2	47.1
9	Dixons Stores	37749	8.3	3.5	88.2
10	Elida Gibbs (Unilever)	36851	91.3	..	8.7
11	Renault (UK)	36012	49.5	2.8	47.7
12	Birds Eye Wall's (Unilever)	35953	83.8	0.1	16.1
13	Peugeot Talbot	35643	33.5	0.5	66.0
14	Mars Confectionery	32322	95.9	0.8	3.3
15	VAG (UK)	30910	21.9	0.5	77.7
16	Citröen (UK)	29683	43.0	0.5	56.4
17	Nissan (GB)	29658	38.9	0.9	60.1
18	Gallaher Tobacco (American brands)	29264	..	0.2	99.8
19	Pedigree Petfoods (Mars)	28550	98.7	..	1.3
20	Brooke Bond Foods (Unilever)	27420	96.0	..	4.0

the communication process. In order to measure the link between advertising and its objectives, the **DAGMAR model** has become a standard part of advertising practice. This stands for: **Defining Advertising Goals for Measured Advertising Results**. In other words, before any advertising campaign is started an organisation must define its communication objectives so that achievements can be measured both during and after the campaign.

There are a number of different types of advertising:

- *Informative advertising* provides information which may increase awareness.
- *Persuasive advertising* uses a variety of methods designed to encourage consumers to desire the product.
- *Reminding advertising* for a well known product simply reminds consumers about the product.
- *Reinforcement advertising* tries to assure product adopters that they have made the right choice.
- *Pioneer advertising* provides information in the introductory phase of the product life-cycle.
- *Competitive advertising* points out the differential advantages of the brand over competing products.
- *Defensive advertising* lessens the damage caused by the promotional campaign of a direct competitor.

Advertising agencies and the media

The starting point for an **advertising campaign** is to produce an advertising plan. This will involve allocating a budget to a range of activities designed to meet advertising objectives. There are seven steps in an advertising campaign. These are:

- Identify the target market.
- Define advertising objectives.
- Decide on and create the advertising message.
- Allocate the budget.
- Develop the media plan.
- Execute the campaign.
- Evaluate the effectiveness of the campaign.

To plan a campaign an advertiser will consult an **advertising agency**. Such an agency is a link between the advertiser and the consumer. The role of the advertising agency is to create, develop, plan and implement an advertising campaign for its client. The extent to which an agency does so will vary according to its type. Some agencies offer all kinds of services, while others specialise in creative work. Such agencies offer skilled expertise which can be shared with clients.

One advantage of using an agency is that it would not be economic for the majority of advertisers to employ a full-time team. Agencies also offer the media an economic way of selling airtime and space, because they can deal with a small number of agencies rather than with thousands of individual advertisers.

The team of experts in an advertising agency services clients, who are known as **accounts**. An account executive supervises the work for a particular client and, together with the account director, works to meet the client's objectives. To achieve this they lead an account group comprising representatives from each of the main departments contributing to the campaign (see Figure 23.12).

Figure 23.12 Composition of an account group

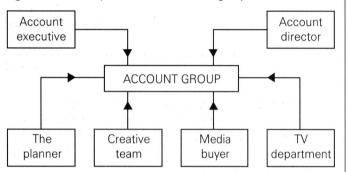

The account executive has to understand the needs of the client in the context of its operations and its industry, and interpret these to the agency. He or she will also have to present the agency's proposals to the client. The job requires diplomacy in order to keep all the interested parties happy.

The planner assists the account executive, maintains the performance of activities and uses specialist market research to assess the reactions of the public. From such analysis the planner can decide on a strategy for a campaign and also test adverts to see how the public responds.

The creative team may consist of an art director who will create and develop rough drawings or illustrations called *visuals* and a copywriter who produces the words known as *copy* for an advertisement. They will also commission further *artwork* for the adverts.

The media buyer buys 'space' in newspapers and/or magazines or 'time' on TV or radio. The media buyer works with a media planner to decide the type of media to carry particular advertisements.

The TV department will, where necessary, commission the production of a commercial, organise the shoot and edit and supply the finished advert.

Having agreed on the objective of the campaign, the agency will then work out some ideas. These are discussed with the client. The agency then provides ideas

in the form of *storyboards* which show roughly what the commercials/advertisements will look like. The roughs will be tested on a target audience and the campaign will then be carefully planned. The client will need to approve the ideas. Production then begins on the final advertisement. A production company is signed up to make the TV commercial and the media department books suitable slots in television time as well as space in newspapers and magazines. A *test launch* may be used to assess consumer reaction to the campaign. Researchers follow up the campaign by finding out how the public responds, and this information is fed back to the client.

Case Study
The annual Cannes advertising festival

Every year the creative, arty inhabitants of the world's adland descend upon Cannes for the annual advertising festival. Many people outside the industry think that this is an occasion for high frivolity, champagne swigged by the magnum, and for commercials which few understand to be declared as pure genius. Perhaps there is something in this view. However, the festival is also a reliable test of advertising effectiveness and provides useful feedback on the effectiveness of media activities.

In a talk at a recent festival, Donald Gunn, of the Chicago-based agency Leo Burnett, attempted to answer the question 'Do award-winning commercials sell?' For years many have felt that a lot of adverts were created to impress other members of the advertising industry rather than to impress consumers. Mr Gunn took 200 of the most-lauded advertisements from around the world in order to answer this question and checked whether or not they helped to improve market share and build brand awareness. The result was that 80 per cent were successful by at least one of these measures.

Donald Gunn cited a number of examples. A series of amusing ads for the New York lottery turned a 10 per cent decline in sales one year into a 12 per cent gain the following year. The rather large, rowdy person advertising Tango in the UK helped to double brand awareness. The Levi advertisement for Europe has had stunning results.

Questions for discussion

1 *Compare and contrast two advertisements of your choice. Comment on: (a) the media used, (b) the effectiveness of artwork and copy, (c) the benefits gained for the advertisers, and (d) your feelings about the effectiveness of each.*

2 *Why are some advertisements more effective than others?*

The success of the relationship between the advertiser and its agency depends largely on trust and confidence. It is important at the outset that the advertiser establishes what type of services the agency will provide, the remuneration it will receive and the legal implications of the relationship. For example, how easy is it for an advertiser to ditch an agency and move elsewhere? Four often tricky areas are the following:

- *Copyright* – This normally belongs to the agency or to the freelance professionals used to produce the materials.
- *Exclusivity* – The advertiser would probably not wish the agency to act on behalf of competitors for the duration of the relationship.
- *Confidentiality* – Information of a sensitive business nature supplied by the advertiser should be kept confidential.
- *Indemnity* – The advertiser may be legally liable if an advertisement created by an agency infringes a third party's trademark.

Agency remuneration

The controllable methods of promotion are often categorised as **above-the-line** or **below-the-line** (see Figure 23.13). While changes in the law have now extinguished the origins of the system, the terms are still often used. 'Above-the-line' refers to media such as TV, radio and press, for which commission is paid to the advertising agency. 'Below-the-line' comprises all media and promotional techniques for which fees are paid in preference to commissions – these might include exhibitions, sales literature and direct mail.

Agencies have in the past been paid by commission. The agency would book space for the advertiser, who would then be charged by the media, who would pay a commission to the agency. However, over recent years agencies have become more involved in below-the-line promotional activities and have therefore billed their clients for activities. Many agencies today charge a straight fee for their services and then reimburse any commissions from the media to their clients.

The advertising budget

The **advertising budget** is the amount of money allocated for advertising purposes over a period of time. It is sometimes difficult to determine the level of the budget, but it should, ideally, be large enough to satisfy advertising objectives and to convey the required message

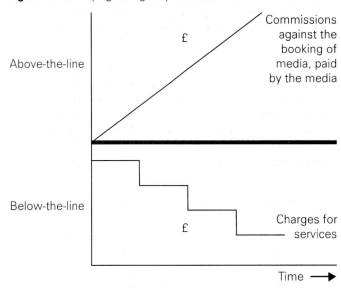

Figure 23.13 Paying for agency services

to target audiences. One factor determining the advertising budget will be the type of industry in which the organisation operates. Clearly, budgets in consumer goods industries will be large in comparison with budgets for industrial goods.

Three techniques are used to determine the advertising budget.

The objective-and-task approach
Having stated the objectives of the advertising campaign, advertisers then list the tasks required to meet such objectives. When the cost of each of these tasks is carefully calculated, the tasks are totalled. The total cost is then the amount of the advertising budget. The problem with this method is that it is sometimes difficult to determine the cost of achieving individual objectives.

The percentage-of-sales approach
With this method the advertising budget is linked to sales. The budget then becomes a percentage of:

- last period sales
- projected sales
- past and projected profits.

The percentage is determined by sales growth and what the industry spends on advertising. The problem with this method of budget-setting is that sales revenue creates the budget rather than the other way round.

The competition-matching approach
With this method of budget-setting, an organisation will set its budget in relation to the budget allocated by competitors. For example, it may simply allocate the

same percentage of sales for advertising purposes as competitors.

The communication mix

The key element in promotion is the effective use of the **communication process**. The process of communication involves sending *messages* to customers through various channels or media in order to create *awareness* and *understanding* of why they might wish to buy or think more favourably about goods, services or organisations.

Organisations are the **senders** in the communication process and consumers are the **receivers**. A sender will put information in a form that a receiver can understand. This might involve using oral, visual, verbal or written messages to transmit ideas. This process is called **encoding**. The sender will also choose a particular **medium** to use to send the message to the receiver (television, radio, newspapers). The consumer interprets the message through a process of **decoding**. If the consumer interprets the message as required, it should have the impact the seller wished for (see Figure 23.14).

Figure 23.14 The communication process

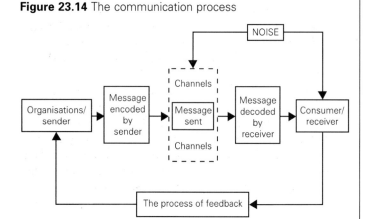

Though the message from promotional activities flows through to the receiver, there is no guarantee that the receiver will either receive the full message or understand it. This is because the process may be subject to some form of interference which affects the flow of information. This is known as **noise** and may lead to the downfall of the message. It will take the form of any barrier which acts as an impediment to the smooth flow of information and may include linguistic and cultural differences between the sender and the receiver. Noise in the competing environment may affect communication so that the meaning of the message is lost. For example, nearly all promotional activities compete with similar

activities from other organisations. One leaflet put through your door may be lost amongst a sea of direct mail from other organisations.

Another example of 'noise' is the remote controller of a video recorder: a survey in the UK showed that, whereas 43 per cent of people watch adverts at the time of watching a programme, if they record a programme 90 per cent 'zap' through the adverts using their remote controller.

To improve the chances of a message getting through, it may be necessary to repeat the message several times rather than rely on one transmission. It might also be necessary to use a variety of channels of communication media to counteract any noise in one particular channel.

Feedback from the receiver to the sender enables the organisation to monitor its performance and satisfy itself that the messages are getting through and are having the desired effect.

A number of factors will determine the **effectiveness** of the process of communication. Personal factors such as linguistic, cultural and educational differences are bound to cause problems with encoding and decoding messages. Advertisers and their copywriters have to develop messages and express ideas so that their target market can understand them. Group factors or influences may also affect a message. Feelings about a particular product such as a motor car and its quality or lack of it may be reinforced by group opinions. Message factors will also determine effective communication within the communication mix. The strength, duration and frequency of the message will be important as well as the type of media channel chosen.

Evaluating the effectiveness of the communication mix

The promotional mix requires high levels of expenditure and it is, therefore, crucial that organisations try to analyse how effective their investment in such expenditure has been. The main problem is that markets and various influences are complex and the actions by competitors or the influences within the external environment may dampen the effect of promotional expenditure and make precise analysis difficult.

The effectiveness of promotional activities should be evaluated before, during and after a campaign. Evaluation carried out before a campaign is usually known as a **pre-test**. It is used to discover and centre on customer perceptions. Such information may be useful for developing the direction of the campaign. Pre-tests may also be used to test the promotional messages themselves. One method of doing this is through a **focus group** which may judge the effectiveness of promotional materials.

One model which looks at the effectiveness of advertising involves five distinct stages:

- *Exposure* – This is measured in terms of coverage (the number of customers reached) and frequency (the number of times promotions have been screened).
- *Awareness* – This is how potential consumers have been made aware of the product and its features during the campaign. Recall or recognition tests may be used to measure awareness.
- *Attitudes* – The effectiveness of the campaign may be monitored in terms of how well it has changed consumer attitudes in favour of particular brands or product features.
- *Sales* – This is an important objective and it would be expected for promotional activities to affect sales. However, as with all of the other activities in the business environment, this can be difficult to measure.
- *Profits* – Again this relates to an important objective but, as with sales, it may be influenced by other factors. It is important, however, that such a campaign earns a sufficient contribution to cover its costs.

Evaluation of effectiveness *after* a campaign is known as a **post-campaign test**. It is important to match at this stage the outcome of the promotional activities with the objectives identified at the beginning of the campaign. It may be possible to measure the effectiveness of the campaign in terms of sales, changed perceptions, repositioning strategies, market share, etc. Many post-tests involve evaluating some form of recognition or recall.

For example, a **recognition test** would involve asking respondents if they recognised an advertisement. The interviewer might then ask supplementary questions about parts of the promotion. Recognition tests may be *aided* or *unaided*. With aided tests respondents are shown a number of product names and brands to help with recall. With unaided or spontaneous tests, subjects are not provided with any clues when asked to identify an advertisement. The results in Figure 23.15 were obtained by asking people the question '*Thinking back over the past week, which commercials can you remember seeing or hearing?*'

Use of the communication mix

The quality of promotional resources used in the communication mix will determine the effectiveness of the promotion campaign. If the promotion budget is small the nature of promotions and activities used will be completely different from those which would be used if the budget were larger. For example, if trying to appeal to a large market segment, an organisation will require a larger budget and more ingredients in the promotional mix.

The organisation's objectives will also determine the types of promotional activities used. For example, an objective to create, inform and educate consumers would be expected to involve extensive use of personal selling.

The characteristics of each market segment will also dictate the ingredients to be included in the promotional mix. If dealing with a small, highly specialised market segment, promotional activities would be expected to emphasise the nature of the product and a sophisticated mailshot backed up with personal selling might be the most appropriate way to reach such customers. The reason for choosing such a method would be *cost-effectiveness*. In relation to the number of customers, promotional activities are highly targeted and, therefore, produce the best response per customer. In contrast, promotions which reach millions of customers by using advertisements and sales promotions can also be justified given the size of the markets, the sales generated and the low cost of advertising *per person in that market*.

Figure 23.15 Spontaneous recall (Source: *Marketing*)

	Brand	Agency/Media buyer	Weeks in chart
1	Daz (unspecified)	*Leo Burnett/P&G in-house*	41
2	Persil	*JWT/Initiative*	39
3	Ford	*Ogilvy & Mather*	43
4	Coke/Coca-Cola	*HK McCann*	19
5	Ariel/Ariel Automatic	*Saatchi & Saatchi/P&G in-house*	41
6	Renault (unspecified)	*Publicis/Optimedia*	18
7	Tango	*Howell Henry Chaldecott Lury*	22
8	Andrex	*JWT*	37
9	Nescafé	*McCann-Erickson*	28
10	PG Tips	*BMP DDB Needham/Initiative*	21

Other influences in the promotional mix may include:

- *The type of market* – In industrial markets, mixes will involve more personal selling, whereas in consumer markets, greater emphasis will be on advertising.
- *The phase of the product life-cycle* – In the early stages awareness may be emphasised through advertising, while in the latter phases sales may be stimulated through sales promotions.
- *The intensity of market coverage* – If a product is marketed through intensive distribution, it might require more advertising (e.g. consumer goods). If a product is exclusively distributed, as for luxury goods, then more personal selling would be required.
- *Cost of promotional methods* – Given the high cost of some promotional methods, it is important to look at the various types of media available to maximise the return from an investment.
- *Ability to target a market with specific promotions* – It may not be possible to target a market effectively using some promotional methods. For example, how might an accountant target customers through the media? There may be very few cost-effective methods of doing so.

Further reading

- *Admap*. NTC Publications, published monthly.
- *Promotional Practice*. DPP, published annually.
- *Effective Sales Management*, 2nd edition, by John Strafford and Colin Grant. Butterworth–Heinemann, 1993.
- *The Effective Advertiser* by Tom Brannan. Butterworth–Heinemann, 1993.
- *Selling – Management and Practice*, 4th edition, by Peter Allen. Pitman, 1993.
- *Advertising*, 3rd edition, by Frank Jefkins. Pitman, 1994.
- *The Discourse of Advertising* by Guy Cook. Routledge, 1992.
- *Public Relations in Practice: A Casebook* by Danny Moss. Routledge, 1990.
- *How to Produce Successful Advertising* by David Farbey. Kogan Page, 1994.
- *Increase Your Sales the Tock Way* by Alfred Tock. Gower 1990.

8

Personnel management in the organisation

24 Personnel policy and function

On completion of this chapter students should be able to:

■ distinguish between different theoretical and practical approaches to the management of human resources

■ recognise the changing national and international context within which personnel management operates

■ evaluate the different ways in which organisations determine and plan for human resource needs.

Part 1 **Personnel policy**

The personnel management debate

The place of personnel management in organisations has changed dramatically over recent years. It is to be hoped that the old-fashioned view which saw personnel as a separate function with responsibility for 'hiring and firing' is fading into the mists of time. This chapter sets out the possibility of viewing personnel as a human resource concern which works across the organisation in a strategic way.

Chapter 10 introduced some of the old **scientific management** approaches to organisation. **Fordism** can be seen as representing the classic example of mass production in a hierarchical system. Employees were regarded as important components of the work machine. In the early part of this century the Ford company filled an important gap in the consumer market by creating at the same time a high demand for cheap cars coupled with a plentiful supply of them. Ford factories in America were able to capitalise on the supply of cheap labour in the form of immigrants desperate for work.

Case Study
Fordism today?

Today Fordism is still evident in areas such as fast-food retailing, where the emphasis is on using Fordist systems of control, and automated machines that de-skill work and control work flow (Ford described these as 'farm machines'). Ford's machines were simple to operate, even by an unskilled operator coming straight from farm work. In today's burger bars, similar machines and systems are very much in evidence.

Buzzers instruct operatives when to stir the sauce or take the fries out of the fryer. The till is simply a panel of product buttons which, when pressed, price the items, add up the sale, and can show how much change to give.

Computers give a breakdown of hourly/daily/weekly sales of products, while the customers are like cattle herded to the sales till or drive-in booth.

In keeping with modern work practices, approximately 80 per cent of employees in fast-food restaurants work part-time, with flexible contracts which permit their hours to be changed on the day.

Questions for discussion

1 *To what extent do the practices in modern burger bars continue to reflect a Fordist vision?*
2 *From your own experience of burger bars, comment on the extent to which employees are part of the machinery of production.*
3 *Why is the fast-food industry able to operate using the personnel practices that it does?*
4 *Why are people prepared to work in the fast-food industry?*

The scientific managers focused on the 'bottom line' and were concerned with 'structuring the structure' of the organisation so as to create profit and productivity. The emphasis was very much on inputting the 'Five Ms' of money, materials, men, machines and methods into an organisation that was based on 'sound' scientific principles (see Figure 24.1).

Figure 24.1 An organisation based on scientific principles

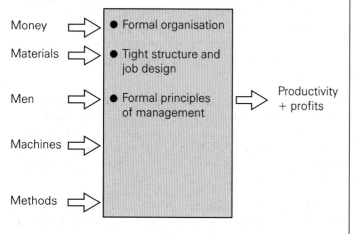

In contrast, a human relations approach is concerned both with profitability and with social relations and outcomes in the organisation. Social organisation and business organisation are therefore seen as intertwining themes (see Figure 24.2).

There is an increasing shift in many organisations towards human resources. No longer is human resources management (HRM) seen as being solely the responsibility of the human resources (or personnel)

department. Today this role is increasingly being seen as one for all managers. Managers across the organisation are being given responsibilities for selecting, motivating, developing and evaluating employees.

Perhaps more importantly, the emphasis has shifted from seeing employees as costs to seeing them as assets. There is an increasing recognition that employees are the most important resource in the organisation, particularly in creating a competitive edge.

Figure 24.2 An increased emphasis on the human side of organisation

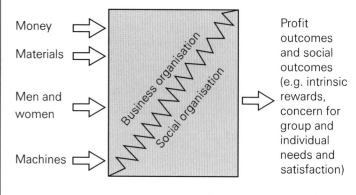

Task

The following diagrams represent responses of a group of people involved in working for a service organisation when presented with the terms 'scientific management' and 'human relations'. Try out the same activity with a group of students who are familiar with these two terms. Write the terms in circles on a piece of flip-chart paper and see what responses they come up with.

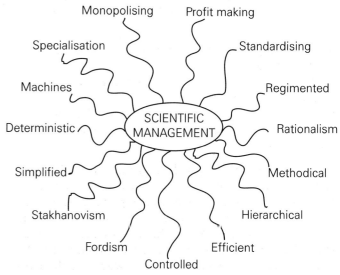

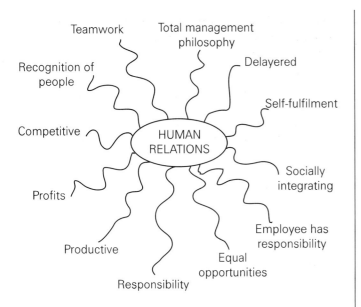

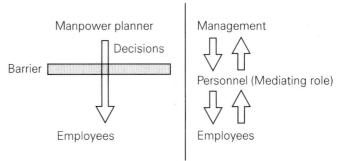

and feelings and who are able to express their views. Personnel managers need to be able to understand the needs, wants, aspirations and views of the people in the organisation. So while personnel is a management function it is also concerned with the people at work. Personnel therefore is a mediating force between 'the management' and 'the employees'. Instead of personnel being seen as distinct and above the ground-level worker, it provides this important mediating role (see Figure 24.4).

Figure 24.4 The mediating role of personnel management

Figure 24.3 contrasts two positions: emphasis on human resources as a key to competitive edge, and human resources as a necessary cost.

Figure 24.3 Different views of people at work.

HR as key to competitive edge	HR as a necessary cost
■ HR as a role for all managers	■ HR as a specialist function
■ Employees seen as assets	■ Employees seen as costs
■ Employees seen as most important resource	■ Employees seen as just one type of resource

In a well-received book on people at work, *Personnel Management* by Derek Torrington and Laura Hall, the authors set out to make a distinction between 'personnel' and 'human resource management'. In their early comments they suggest a number of reasons why some people have wanted to change to the term 'human resources':

■ for a change or facelift for a new era of personal relationships
■ because the terms 'manpower' and 'manpower planning' are sexist
■ because personnel managers hope that adopting the new term may increase their status in the organisation.

They then follow this up by looking at some of the more substantive differences. They see 'personnel' as being a work force-centred discipline. The importance here is that the people who work for the organisation are the starting point for personnel work. The human resource is in many ways a less flexible resource than money, materials and machines because it concerns people, who have thoughts

Traditionally, personnel is associated with the 'employment procession' of recruitment: selection – induction – training – transfers – termination of employment. However, in a modern business organisation personnel is also responsible for 'appraisal', which is a key part of monitoring and helping an employee to develop a clear career path and for the administration of disciplinary procedures; for workplace bargaining with unions; developing and supervising payment systems for employees; supervising health and safety; equal opportunities; and many other areas related to employment.

Because the personnel manager works at the interface between management and employees, he or she may spend more time working with ground-level workers than with senior managers. The personnel manager is therefore likely to take on board many of the cultural assumptions and values of ordinary people at work.

The distinction that Torrington and Hall make between personnel management and human resource management can be simplified as in Figure 24.5.

Some commentators argue that the difference between personnel management and human resource management is really just a matter of words. You could argue with equal force that a particular organisation has a personnel or a human resource focus. However, perhaps the important distinction is at a strategic level. Strategy is concerned with clearly identifying the core values of an organisation, and the direction in which the organisation wants to move.

Figure 24.5 Contrasting personnel and human resource management

Personnel management	Human resource management
■ People have a right to proper treatment as human beings at work	■ Management of human resources is like any other form of resource management
■ People will only be effective if their job-related personal needs are met	■ Human resource management should be shared by people across the organisation rather than being split up artificially into work for specialists
■ Interventions are required by personnel to ensure that job-related personal needs are attended to	
■ Because other line managers do not see themselves as people specialists they may neglect personnel work – necessitating the specialist personnel input	■ People have a right to proper treatment as human beings at work
	■ Efficient management with a focus on human needs is required across the organisation
	■ Human resource managers are needed to support other managers in their human resource work and to make sure that the organisation is directed at a strategic level to human resource management
	■ At the same time, human resource managers are concerned with making sure that there are enough people working in the right places, at the right time

The human resources approach is concerned that all managers should recognise the importance of the human resource rather than leaving it to the personnel manager. The emphasis should be that 'we are all human resource managers now' just as we are all 'marketers'. The business manager today needs to be a specialist in a field but also a competent generalist. A key part of this 'generalism' is a focus on human resource management and concern for working relationships. Effective human resource strategies often lower costs of production, improve product development, and enhance marketing and other activities. Employees can create a competitive advantage for an organisation through innovation, creativity, flexibility, improved performance, superior customer care, etc. Importantly, people can provide a distinctive product or service quality which cannot be matched even by the most sophisticated machines. People are more prepared to shop in department stores with friendly, knowledgeable staff, to eat in restaurants where they receive personal attention, and so on. The organisation needs to cherish and support the people who

give it this distinctive edge. Human resource management therefore plays a key strategic role in the same way that marketing or finance does.

We can thus look at HRM as a strategic function. The tools and tactics of HRM are then concerned with particular activities such as recruitment, development, equal opportunities policy, etc.

Figure 24.6 HRM as a strategic function

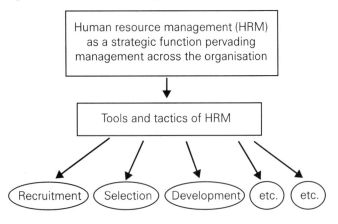

Policy frameworks for HRM

Effective human resource management will be based on plans and policies. These plans and policies should reflect organisational objectives and plans. We have already suggested that human resource objectives should be a key determinant of organisational objectives (see Figure 24.7).

Clearly, different organisations will have different objectives depending on a range of factors such as: whether they are in the public or private sector, whether they are public service or profit-making organisations, whether they are large or small, whether the organisational culture is entrepreneurial or conservative, etc.

There are two main ways of viewing the term **policy**. On the one hand it can be seen as an expression of broad intentions to achieve specific objectives. In this sense it refers to the theory which underpins the methods we use to arrive at objectives. For example, an organisation may have a policy to recruit the most able graduates available in the labour market. It is then a matter of putting this policy into practice.

Another way of looking at policy is to view it as meaning the 'right and proper' way of achieving objectives. An organisation may therefore have a policy of ensuring that all employees 'are treated with utmost respect', or 'of

Figure 24.7 Human resource policies based on key roots

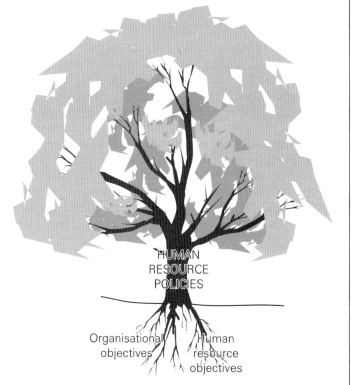

ensuring equal opportunities for all members of the organisation'. Policy-making will usually incorporate these two elements; that is:

- the technical element concerned with how objectives will be met
- the moral (ethical) element concerned with commitment to principles and values.

Policy frameworks are essential in effective personnel policy-making. Personnel policy will usually have the following four features:

- It will clarify and establish commitment to particular objectives by setting out the technical and ethical outlines for achieving these objectives. These outlines will set out the theory which underpins practical actions.
- It will be set out in a written statement of policy. Wherever possible, policies should be codified in a written form as well as being part of a shared understanding within the organisation.
- It will act as a guide to behaviour and actions rather than a hard-and-fast detailed outline of everything that should be done.
- It will set out standards for action and behaviour which will be as broad as possible in order to provide an operating framework.

A simple but useful way of looking at policy is to regard it as *a public commitment to a way of acting in the future*.

Personnel policy will therefore consist of a number of interrelated policies concerned with employment in an organisation.

Policy guidelines thus provide all members of an organisation with a clear focus as to how they should operate and how things should be done in the personnel field. This provides a standard against which actions can be measured and judged.

The emphasis is on *the future*. When a new policy is introduced an organisation should not be concerned with measuring previous actions against this policy. Instead it should be concerned with the implementation of the policy *now and tomorrow*.

Human resource management emphasises the strategic approach to using people effectively. Johnson and Scholes, in their book *Exploring Corporate Strategy*, emphasise the importance of people in the strategic equation when they state that organisational planning needs to be concerned with 'the aspirations, expectations, attitudes and personal philosophies which people hold'. Organisational strategy will therefore need to take account of what people want organisations to do in order to create the policy frameworks for putting strategic plans into action. We can highlight four main areas of personnel policy.

The guiding principles

The mission statements of many organisations today include important comments about visions of the place of human resources; for example:

- 'to cater for the social and work needs of all members of the organisation'
- 'to secure the optimum personal development of company members'.

It will then be necessary to convert mission statements into policies which establish guiding principles for an organisation. These guiding principles will be concerned with 'teamwork', 'empowerment', 'equal opportunity', 'personal development', and so on.

Employee recruitment and development

Organisations should set out clear policies concerned with recruitment and the development of their people. Policies may cover the selection process, and the types of people required by the organisation. Other policies will be concerned with the career progression and development of people within the organisation, including appraisal.

Industrial relations

Industrial relations policies will be concerned with the recognition of trade unions and employee rights, with bargaining, consultation, profit-sharing, and so on.

Terms and conditions

Increasingly, organisations are developing policies to deal with the terms and conditions of people at work. Traditionally these areas were covered by legislation and through collective bargaining, but policy statements are now being produced to cover these areas, including working conditions, differential rates of pay, pension provisions, holiday entitlements, and so on.

The problem with policies

Care needs to be taken not to create a 'dead hand' of policy-making. For example, in recent years with the development of a professional managerial class in schools and colleges, we have seen the creation of mountains of policies. There is considerable evidence that the creation of these policies is wasteful in resources and can have a negative effect on teacher motivation.

Dennis Kravetz, in his book *The Human Resources Revolution*, points out some of the stultifying effects of policy-making. He reports that some company policy manuals are the size of dictionaries. He cites the case of one company, which has a conference room full of floor-to-ceiling files of policies, rules, grievance hearings and arbitration cases. Almost inevitably the cultural tone in the organisation is based on 'going by the book' and on confrontation. Kravetz argues that with the move to human relations there will be less emphasis on going by the book, as people need to develop the independence to work freely without being tied down by regulation. As workers become more professional they will need to be allowed to exercise more personal discretion. He illustrates the stupidity of creating prescriptive rules by citing the example of a company where the rule is that everyone takes lunch between 12 noon and 1 pm. This means that everyone in the company abandons their work between these hours, including senior managers.

Case Study
Health and safety and equal-opportunities policy

Over 500 people die each year at work and several hundred thousand lose time through injury or illness. Most of these problems could be prevented if people were trained effectively to do the jobs required.

It is compulsory for an organisation that employs more than five people to have a health and safety policy. The work force should be able to understand and implement it when needed. Most organisations now operate an equal-opportunities policy as it is illegal to specify age,

race or gender when advertising vacancies. The policy should set out to eliminate bias, prejudice and stereotyping. If these are practised within an organisation they can lead to poor work performance and low morale.

Sainsbury's policy on equal opportunity is a good example. It states:

> 'Our policy is designed to ensure that no employee receives less favourable treatment on the grounds of sex, race, colour, ethnic origin, religion, disability or marital status.'

It is these types of policy that allow the organisation to reach the maximum potential of the work force. Effective personnel policies can translate into higher productivity, and then into lower cost per unit. The net effect is to create greater competitive advantage.

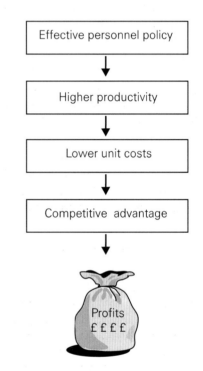

Questions for discussion

1 *How can equal-opportunities and health and safety policies be seen as (a) costs and (b) benefits to organisations? Where is the net balance likely to lie?*
2 *Why must organisations that employ more than five people have health and safety policies?*
3 *Look at the Sainsbury equal-opportunities policy statement. Give examples of ways in which this would translate into practical actions.*
4 *Describe what you consider to be the five most important ingredients of a specific personnel policy.*

Control within personnel practices

The implementation of personnel policies requires some form of control to ensure that policy is being put into practice. This will require the exercise of authority to try to make sure that personnel practices are carried out in line with policy.

In some organisations this involves managers creating systems, plans, rules and codes of conduct which govern practice – for example, health and safety regulations, reporting procedures for accidents, training plans. Managers in these circumstances take on the responsibility for steering personnel practice.

In other organisations there is a greater emphasis on self-management and regulation. A good example of this is the 'quality circle' approach in which employees are considered to be part of a team and not simply as subordinates. The responsibility for control is more on self-regulation, so that equal-opportunities practice would be something that the team worked at together, health and safety would be a shared concern, and much of the policy-making could be generated within the quality circle.

Another type of control consists of monitoring and modifying policy and practice on an on-going basis. Once a policy has been set out, it will be necessary to monitor the extent to which it is being adhered to in practical action.

Difficulties may arise in some circumstances:

■ Managers and others responsible for implementing a plan might forget to put it into effect. For example, the organisation may have a policy of recording all accidents, however minor. Some managers may feel that they are too busy to do this, leading to a distortion in the records. If this policy is important then it will be necessary to make sure that practice complies with policy.
■ The implementation of the policy may be a lot more difficult than expected. For example, an organisation may ask employees to report all cases of sexual harassment in line with a new policy. However, problems may occur if the person to whom the harassment has to be reported is instrumental in harassing others. If this problem is addressed immediately then the policy may be successful. If the issue is ignored the policy may prove to be a 'white elephant'.

Quantitative techniques are frequently used to monitor the effectiveness of policies. Examples are statistical recording of sexual and racial harassment, and ethnic

monitoring of recruitment policies. However, it is also important to use **qualitative assessment techniques**, such as in-depth interviews of specific individuals to find out what their views are of sexual harassment policies. Some of the most effective personnel managers are those who 'manage by walking about', talking to people in the workplace.

Monitoring actual practice is thus a highly important way of checking that theory is being put into practice. The ring-binders of personnel policies that lie on the personnel manager's desk are of little use unless they are put into effect. Personnel policies should be regularly reviewed to ensure that they are working, and to assess whether they need to be changed or adapted to new circumstances. Often the people who create policies are reluctant to change them because they feel slighted at the failure of a 'pet idea', but this is short-sighted. Ideas are of little worth unless they work in practice, and personnel managers are usually judged on their 'performance in action' rather than their 'performance in theory'.

The control process in personnel practice should look something like Figure 24.8. Monitoring of practice enables remedial action to be taken.

Figure 24.8 Control in personnel

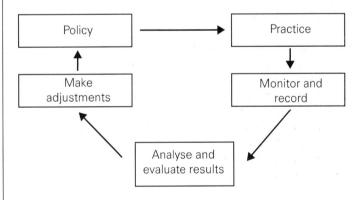

Some organisations will create their control procedures in a top-down way. Many will try to create organisational effectiveness through trust. More than ever, organisations need to get commitment from employees rather than simply compliance. For example, total-quality management requires that employees actively engage in finding and correcting defects at their source, taking initiative and working towards improvement. Companies wanting a competitive edge through extra customer service need employees who go the extra distance to deliver the service. At the same time, speed-based production strategies demand interdependence, communication, trust, high motivation, discipline and attention to detail.

Centralisation and decentralisation of personnel tasks

In some companies employing as many as 100 workers, you will find a lone personnel manager working himself or herself to the bone. In contrast, in some larger modern organisations you will find personnel departments comprising a range of specialists housed in an extensive suite of offices. Until the late 1980s it was common to find specialised personnel departments in large organisations. Today we have seen that HRM is becoming more of a strategic function which is powered by specialists prompting other managers to take on human resource responsibilities.

Organisations tend to swing between centralisation and decentralisation. The fashion in recent years in the UK has been away from centralisation of personnel functions. Decentralisation is the process of devolving planning and control. The decentralised unit or team will be responsible for most of its activities. There are several advantages of decentralisation:

- The decentralised unit is closer to the customer. If human resource activities are carried out across an organisation, then the customer will be the recipient of human resource services (i.e. individual employees).
- Decentralised units can become more focused and are able to concentrate on core objectives.
- Decentralised units are able to respond quickly to problems on the ground. The manager responsible for appraising subordinates will quickly get a measure of aspirations and frustrations.
- Decentralisation enables all team members to contribute to human resource planning and decision-making.
- Decentralised units are able to create their own identity, which reflects the needs of individual members and the context in which the unit operates.
- Decentralisation can lead to greater individual and team satisfaction because individuals are able to contribute more to decision-making processes.

The choice between centralisation and decentralisation relates in practice to larger organisations. In some organisations the personnel function will play a major role in recruitment, selection and training. For example, in a retailing organisation with a high turnover of staff, who will all require some level of training, it will be essential to have a number of personnel officers with generalist roles for organising personnel functions at shop level, as well as training officers. Typically these officers will be spread geographically depending on shop sites.

Decentralisation will be the logical organisational structure in such a situation.

However, it is likely that at the head office of a large retail company there will be a personnel manager (or director), and a training and development manager with overall responsibility for personnel matters, training and development within the organisation. The head office may also have a human resource planner responsible for planning the recruitment for the organisation on a national level – this person would also identify labour market and product market trends. In addition, a senior recruitment and selection manager may be responsible for planning systems for recruitment and selection and organising all new recruitment campaigns when new retail or wholesale stores are opened up (see Figure 24.9).

Figure 24.9 Example of human resource management in a large retail organisation

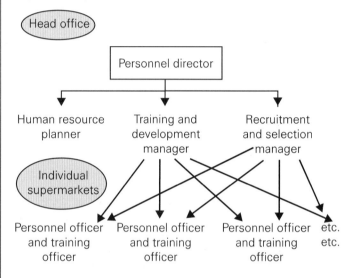

We can see in such a picture that there is a combination of centralisation and decentralisation. Wherever possible, personnel matters and decisions are handled on the ground. However, at the same time there is a need for a centralised core which focuses on strategic issues.

As a general rule, organisations will stick with a centralised form of organisation for personnel when it is a critical function which needs to establish a common pattern for operations – for example, in a single business such as an independent manufacturing plant that is not part of a larger group. However, many local businesses are parts of larger organisations. Marks & Spencer and Laura Ashley, for example, operate in America and France, thus necessitating an increasing decentralisation of the personnel function. Where organisations operate on a divisional basis then it becomes inevitable that the personnel function is decentralised, although key functions will still be performed at head office.

In large organisational units the personnel function will often be quite large and will incorporate a number of specialist roles (see Figure 24.10).

Figure 24.10 Specialist roles in personnel management

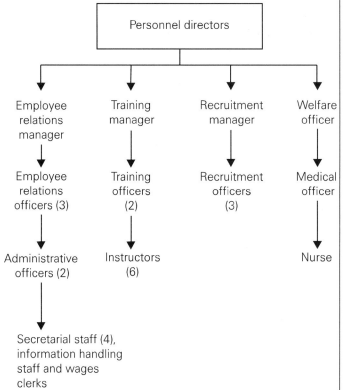

The structure outlined might represent that in a large food processing plant. The employee relations department will be staffed by specialists dealing with industrial relations matters such as negotiation, collective bargaining, employee motivation and interpersonal relationships. The training department will play a major role in the induction and development of new staff. The recruitment department will be responsible for the recruitment and selection process. The welfare and medical department will take responsibility for looking at the highly sensitive area of personal hygiene, and the medical welfare of employees. The organisation outlined above will have made a substantial commitment to the human resource in recognition of the high value-added contribution made by people in the workplace.

Peter Drucker, in his book *The Coming of the New Organisation*, argues that the organisation of the 1990s will be information-based and similar to an orchestra or hospital in the way that it operates, rather than the traditional command and control organisation. A key element of this change is the new emphasis on teams and teamwork. These teams will normally be made up of members from different specialisations. Team-working needs to be built into organisation. Emphasis on the

self-managing team suggests the possibility of decentralising key aspects of human resource management to empowered units within the overall organisation.

Decentralisation is not just about splitting up personnel into smaller divisional personnel units. More importantly it is concerned with spreading the human resource message to self-managing teams and units within the overall organisation. It is about increasingly asking managers and employees to see themselves as having a role in human resource management rather than leaving it to the 'experts'.

Areas covered by HRM planning

There are a number of stages involved in human resource management planning. These can be shown in a simplified form as in Figure 24.11.

Figure 24.11 Important elements of human resource planning

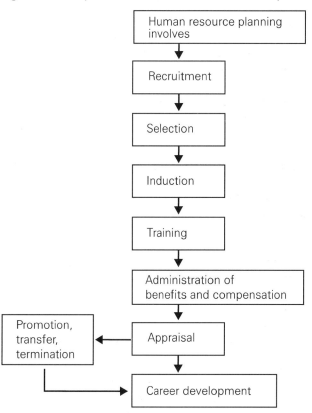

Recruitment

The purpose of **recruitment** is to buy in and retain the best available human resources to meet the organisation's needs. It is therefore important to be clear about:

- what a job entails
- what qualities are required to do the job
- what incentives are required to attract and motivate the right employee.

A number of stages can be used to describe and set out the nature of particular jobs, including job analysis, job description, job specification, and recruitment profiles.

Job analysis

This is the process of examining jobs in order to identify the key requirements of each. Job analysis can be conducted by direct observation of employees at work, by information obtained from interviewing job-holders, or by referring to documents such as training manuals. Information can be gleaned directly from the person carrying out a task and his or her supervisory staff. Three different stages of job analysis can be identified:

- *Task analysis* involves the study of a particular task which is aimed at achieving a particular objective or end-product. For example, a particular employee may have the task of ensuring that all the assemblers in an electronics factory are supplied with a steady flow of components.
- *Activity analysis* is the study of the elements involved in a given task. For example, one of the activities involved in circulating components in the electronics factory may be taking them down from the shelves in the stock room. Activities can be subdivided into *physical* (e.g. lifting, sorting) and *mental* (exercising judgement).
- *Skills analysis* is the study of the ability needed to carry out a given task effectively. A wide range of skills may be identified, such as the ability to work in groups, to work independently, to perform manual operations, to make calculations, to communicate, to follow written instructions, and many more.

Job description

This will set out how a particular employee is to fit into the organisation. It will therefore need to set out:

- the title of the job
- to whom the employee is responsible
- for whom the employee is responsible
- a simple description of the role and duties of the employee within the organisation.

Job specification

This goes beyond a mere description; in addition it highlights the mental and physical attributes required of the job-holder. For example, a job specification for a trainee manager's post in a retail store included the following:

'Managers at all levels are expected to show responsibility. The company is looking for people who are tough and talented. They should have a flair for business, know how to sell, and to work in a team.'

Job analysis, description and specification can all provide useful information to a business in addition to serving as recruitment instruments. Another use is for staff appraisal, which is a means of monitoring staff performance and is a feature of promotion in modern companies. In some companies, employees and their immediate line managers discuss personal goals and targets for the coming time period (e.g. the next six months); the appraisal will then involve a review of employees' performance during the previous six months and the setting of new targets. Job details can serve as a useful basis for establishing dialogue and targets. Job descriptions can be used as reference points for arbitrating in disputes as to 'who does what' in a business. Job analysis can serve as a useful tool for establishing performance standards.

Recruitment profiles

The person responsible for interviewing and recruiting is not always the person with a specialist knowledge of the job in question. For example, the personnel department may be given the responsibility for recruiting staff for all of the functional areas within a company. Personnel will therefore ask for a **recruitment profile** giving the nature of the skills required, the type of person sought and a description of the job. The job requisition (recruitment profile) will therefore provide the specialist knowledge required to enable personnel to recruit the appropriate individuals. Recruitment profiles are also used to give advertising agencies and specialist recruitment companies more information.

Selection

Selection involves procedures to identify the most appropriate candidate to fill each post. An effective selection procedure will therefore take into consideration the following:

- keeping the costs of selection down
- making sure that the required skills and qualities have been specified, and developing a process for identifying them in candidates
- making sure that the candidate selected will want the job, and will stay with the company.

Keeping the costs of selection down will involve factors such as holding the interviews in a location that is accessible to the interviewing panel and to those being interviewed; ensuring that the interviewing panel has available to it all the necessary documentation, such as application forms, that should be studied before the interviews take place; and that a short-list is made up of suitable candidates, so that the interviews do not have to take place a second time, with new job advertisements being placed.

The skills required should have been identified through the process of job analysis, description and specification. It is important then to devise ways of testing whether candidates meet these requirements. One way of doing this is to study applicants' application forms and to interview the most suitable people. Some employers go further and give applicants aptitude tests, putting them through a number of 'real life' situations to see how they cope with given business situations.

Yes, this person seems to have the aptitude to work in our consumer complaints department!

To gauge whether applicants will stay with the organisation, it is important to ask them about their future intentions, and to familiarise them with the working environment into which they will be placed. There is no point in attracting a first-class candidate only to find that he or she does not like the working environment.

It is important to monitor the job selection process continually to see how effective it is. Ratios can be a useful method of appraising a selection process. These may include:

Number of interviews : number of offers made.

The most effective ratios would involve the minimisation of interviews relative to offers made to fill the post as required:

Number starting work : number of suitable employees.

If a high number of workers who are offered employment prove to be unsuitable or turn down a job offer, there is clearly something wrong with the interviewing procedure.

Induction and training

These are another major area of personnel work. New workers in a firm are usually given an **induction programme** in which they meet other workers and are shown the skills they must learn. Generally the first few days at work will simply involve observation, with an experienced employee showing the 'new hand' the ropes. Many large firms have detailed **training** schemes which are conducted on an 'in-house' basis – this is particularly true of larger public companies such as banks and insurance companies. In conjunction with this, staff may be encouraged to attend college courses to learn new skills and get new qualifications. Training thus takes place both through:

- *on-the-job training* – learning through experience at work
- *off-the-job training* – learning through attending courses.

Administration

The administration of benefits and compensation is another part of the HRM responsibility. Human resource managers play a key part in the creation of a strategy, plans, policies and procedures to ensure that the salary structure and benefits package is appropriate to attract, recruit and retain employees. Decisions made in this area will be crucial. Developing a competitive strategy involves attracting and keeping the best available people.

At an operational level the personnel department will be responsible for the payment of wages and salaries. Employees will contribute to a variety of benefit schemes, both organised by the company and private ones. In many companies the administration of contributions (e.g. by deductions from wages and salaries) will be a routine administrative task. Personnel officers will be responsible for accounting for sickness, accident benefits and company pension schemes. Compensation will need to be awarded to organisation members who have suffered a loss through invalidity, work-related sickness, etc.

Appraisal

Appraisal is an essential part of human resource development. Appraisal schemes should be designed to provide a basis for regular discussions on objectives, achievements, development needs, and future career development. Appraisal should identify areas where the appraisee has performed well and areas in which improvements can be made. There may be discussion of the appraisee's readiness for promotion. A summary will be provided of any development needs and a record of any development provided during the year.

Promotion, transfer and termination

Developing procedures to move human resources to different positions of responsibility and to widen their experience through transfers, as well as termination of employment, will be an important area of human resource work.

Promotion within a firm depends on acquiring qualifications to do a more advanced job. In banking, for instance, staff are expected to pass banking examinations. At the same time a candidate for promotion must show a flair for the job. It is the responsibility of the training department within an organisation to make sure that staff with the right skills are coming up through the firm or being recruited from outside.

The personnel department has a responsibility for negotiating the smooth transfer of employees between departments. This may be necessary if employees are not able to 'get on', or if it is felt necessary to give an employee a 'change'.

Termination of employment may be the result of resignation, retirement, dismissal or redundancy. When employees retire after a long period of service to an organisation, they will appreciate some form of recognition for their service. Companies such as the John Lewis Partnership keep in contact with retired employees, and arrange regular reunions. At John Lewis, personnel staff will often attend the funerals of people who have worked for the company for many years, even though the funeral may be twenty or thirty years after the person retired.

The procedure for dismissal of employees must follow strict guidelines. On the other hand, redundancy occurs when a business or firm closes down, when part of a business closes down, or when particular types of workers are no longer required. It is the job that becomes redundant rather than the person.

Career development

One view of employee development is that it should focus on organisational needs. The purpose of development is to further the organisation. The alternative view is that individuals have a right to further their potential and the organisation should enable them to do so. When people see that the organisation is committed to their individual

needs, then they in turn will be committed to the organisation. It is a two way process.

The above outline of important activities which lie within the responsibility of personnel management make it obvious why it is important to have clear missions and objectives on which to base operational activities.

Corporate objectives and HRM

In their book *Personnel Management*, Torrington and Hall make the proposition that:

> *'Personnel management is a series of activities which, first, enables working people and their employing organisations to agree about the objectives and nature of their working relationships and, secondly, ensures the agreement is fulfilled.'*

The important point being made in this proposal is that at a strategic level it is essential to create a human resource strategy which is an integral part of corporate policy. It is then necessary to translate objectives into practical actions:

> *'Only by satisfying the needs of the individual employee will the employer obtain the commitment to organisational objectives that is needed for organisational success, and only by contributing to organisational success will employees be able to satisfy their personal employment needs.'*

A number of specialists in the field argue that HRM only exists in practice when there is an integrated system of policies and practices for managing the human resource (e.g. for recruitment, selection, bargaining, employee development) which are at the same time integrated with the wider business strategy. This is the strategic view of human resource management. When we look at the implementation of HRM in practice, we can see that organisations use a variety of approaches. At one end of the continuum there are organisations that are genuinely working towards strategic HRM, where human resource considerations are a central part of organisational policy-making. At the other end of the continuum there are organisations that may use the term HRM but in reality operate a firefighting approach in which personnel activities respond to problems and difficulties in the workplace (see Figure 24.12).

Figure 24.12 The HRM continuum

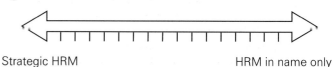

Strategic HRM   HRM in name only

At the strategic end of the continuum there are two varieties of HRM, the hard and the soft approaches. The *hard approach* recognises people as the key organisational resource but with an 'instrumental approach' – it is seen that if you treat people well they will provide better results for you. The mission of the organisation includes an important emphasis on the human resource but the overall intention is to maximise other organisational returns such as profits and sales. This is a business-orientated approach to strategic management.

A *softer approach* also recognises people as a key organisational resource, but the emphasis is on nurturing and developing people because they are people. The qualitative difference from harder approaches is that the softer approach emphasises humanity. Believers in the soft approach would also argue that this will lead to higher business returns.

The strategic approaches to human resource management enable positive and planned steps in the right direction. In a dynamic business environment, human resource managers need to stop focusing on short-term firefighting, and to focus on long-term strategic planning.

The reality, however, is that in many organisations personnel planning and policy-making plays second fiddle to other organisational planning. Personnel is frequently seen as a servicing function that responds to company objectives over which it has little influence. In the worst-case situation, a number of personnel managers are simply firefighters, responding to many and varied issues and problems as and when they arise. These four positions are illustrated in Figure 24.13.

Moving towards a strategic HRM approach

Increasingly, organisations are seeking to develop a strategic approach which integrates human resource management. Clearly, this involves a shift from past practice but it is one that becomes important as people are recognised as the premium resource of organisations and as intelligence and flexibility give organisations a competitive edge.

John Storey, in *Management of Human Resources*, identifies five types of managed change processes which can move an organisation towards HRM.

- *Type 1* – This is the top-down approach where management recognises the need for a strategic approach and sets out to impose HRM solutions on an organisation. There is a clear vision from above, and a carefully planned approach to the management of change. However, if the vision is not communicated

Figure 24.13 The HRM continuum expanded

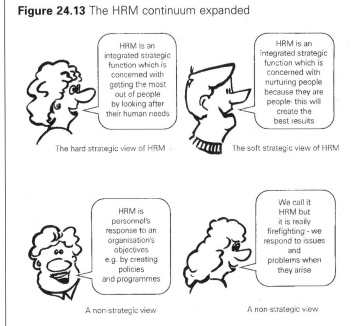

The hard strategic view of HRM

The soft strategic view of HRM

A non-strategic view

A non-strategic view

clearly, it may be ignored or rejected, so that at grass-roots there is no commitment to the new approach.

- *Type 2* – This is the top-down piecemeal approach. Rather than creating an integrated view of HRM, new initiatives are developed in the organisation in a piecemeal way. This may be the chosen way of operating for managers who take the view 'We'll try this first, see how it works, and then bring in the next bit!'. Unfortunately this creates contrasting practices within an organisation and may lead to a lack of commitment to change. Too many people will point out contradictions in policies and practices.
- *Type 3* – This is where various groups in an organisation will bargain over piecemeal changes. It has the advantage of greater participation, but it is riddled with the disadvantages of the piecemeal approach.
- *Type 4* – Called systemic-jointism, this involves transforming the whole system to incorporate the HRM approach. It has the advantage of being a participative process based on shared understandings of change. This should lead to wholesale commitment to the new HRM approach. Unfortunately, in the real world this approach has rarely been used.
- *Type 5* is a mixture of the other four types.

Part 2 National and international labour markets

Labour is bought and sold in the marketplace. Employers demand labour and employees supply labour. The price of labour (the wage rate) depends on the relative strengths of supply and demand. If there is a high supply of unskilled labour, for example, then wages for this labour are likely to be relatively low. Similarly, when there is scarce supply of skilled labour, then wages for that are likely to be relatively high.

Supply and demand

The supply of labour

The **supply of labour** depends, first, on the total population of the country. Factors such as birth and death rates, and the ease of migration into and out of the country, alter the total population and hence the total supply of labour.

Secondly, the size of the working population depends on the age structure of the population. In Britain the working population is regarded as all people between the ages of 16 and 65 who are available for work.

Thirdly, the supply of labour depends on the working population's preference for leisure. Generally speaking, as people become more affluent they prefer to substitute leisure for work.

When considering the supply of labour one should also take into account skills and training. A highly skilled and trained work force is clearly more valuable than a poor-quality one.

Figure 24.14 Slump and boom

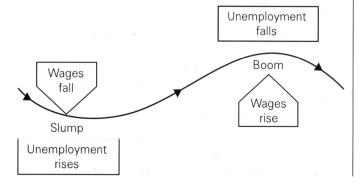

The demand for labour

The **demand for labour** is secondary or derived, in that its level changes with the demand for goods and services. In a period of boom the demand for labour will increase, whereas in a period of slump the demand for labour will fall. It follows that the total wage bill will increase in a boom and fall in a slump. **Unemployment** will fall in a boom and rise in a slump (see Figure 24.14).

Illustrating the market for labour

Figure 24.15(a) shows the supply (S) and demand (D) lines for labour. A rise in the demand for labour (Figure 24.15(b)) will lead to an increase in the number of people employed, and to a rise in the wage rate. A fall in the demand for labour (Figure 24.15(c)) will lead to more unemployment and a fall in the wage rate.

Particular labour markets and immobility

In the real world (i.e. the real economy) there is not just one labour market but many. There is the market for computer programmers, the market for fashion designers, the market for teachers, and so on. There are also regional labour markets: the market for computer programmers in central Scotland, the market for computer programmers in the north-east of England, and so on. Wage rates in each of these markets depend on demand and supply conditions.

Of course, there is overlap between these markets. If the wage rate of computer programmers in Scotland doubled, then programmers might move from the north-east of England to work in Scotland. If the wage rate of fashion designers doubled, then a teacher might retrain to become a fashion designer. However, there is always considerable immobility between different labour markets. **Regional immobility** exists when people are not prepared to move from one region of a country to another. **Occupational immobility** exists when people in one occupation are not prepared to retrain to do another job.

Factors limiting the supply of labour

In an ideal world there would be an abundant supply of labour possessing all the skills and capabilities required by employers. In the real world the supply of labour is

Figure 24.15 The dynamic market for labour

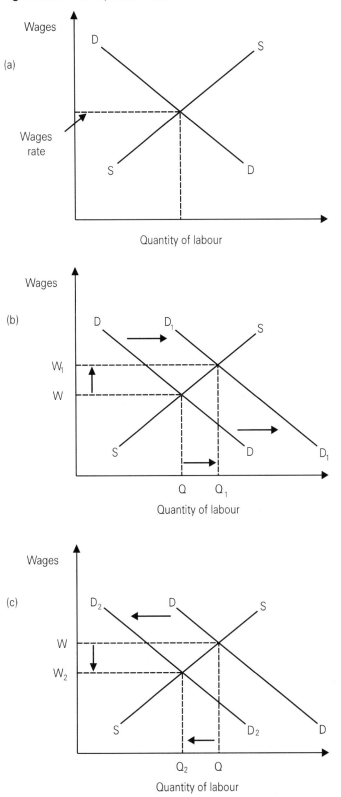

limited in many important markets. Some natural skills are rare. Other skills can be developed through study, practice and training. For example, as a degree-level student you are acquiring skills and knowledge that will make you an effective employee, and the harder you work the more skilled you will become. The more employees who are trained and educated to higher levels, the more skilled will be the work force.

It is therefore essential that the education and training system of a country develops people to meet the requirements of the modern labour market.

Factors that tend to restrict the supply of labour therefore include:

- the natural skills of the population
- limitations of the education system
- the non-availability of training opportunities
- the unwillingness of employers and employees to take advantage of training opportunities
- restrictions on importing skills from other countries and regions
- limitations resulting from trade unions and other groups controlling the supply of labour.

If labour becomes more productive, this has the effect of moving the supply curve of labour to the right (Figure 24.16(a)). A given quantity of labour can now produce more output. The technical term for this is an **increase in productivity**. When restrictions are placed on the supply of labour, this will have the effect of increasing the price of labour (Figure 24.16(b)).

For example, when trade unions and professional bodies insist on long apprenticeships and periods of training, this reduces the possible supply of labour. Those already trained can benefit from the generally higher wages.

Factors influencing the demand for labour

We have already seen that the total (aggregate) demand for labour in an economy will contract during a slump and rise during a boom. In a period of slump many people will be dismissed because there is no work for them to do, and there will therefore be a surplus of skilled labour.

During a boom period, however, more and more workers will be in employment. Moreover, they will be in a strong position to gain pay increases because employers have to compete for labour. In a period of boom, unemployment will be falling and there will be a shortage of skilled labour in many occupations.

Many large organisations today operate in both national and international labour markets. Increasingly there is mobility between these markets. For example, now that

Figure 24.16 The effects of changes in supply

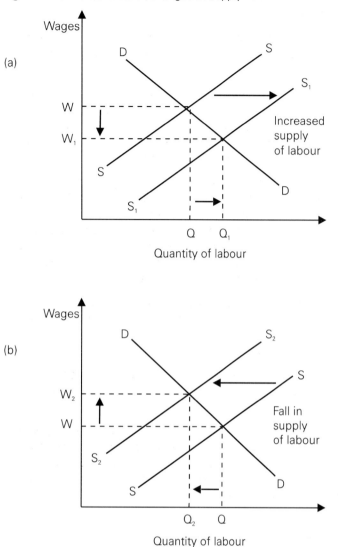

Quantity of labour

jobs. Indeed, the so-called 'brain drain' for engineers and scientists is no new phenomenon. However, we are increasingly seeing the international recruitment of business managers, and 'top people's salaries' are having to reflect earnings in the international labour market.

Another important aspect of the international labour market is variations in wages between countries. Increasingly, UK-based companies are transferring manufacturing operations to the Pacific Rim where wages are lower and there is often an abundance of skills. Countries like India have a plentiful supply of information technology specialists. This means that airlines and travel operators, for example, can transfer their booking arrangements to offices in India. In recent times migration around the world has increased. Visit any major airport today and you will see groups of Thai, Filipino, Mexican and other groups moving from one job location to another. Organisations now need to consider the world labour market as having an influence on business decision-making.

Acquiring human resources

An important part of the work of the human resource department is planning. In simple terms we can reduce this down to three main elements (Figure 24.17):

■ assessment of the present supply of labour
■ assessment of the future needs for labour
■ development of a programme to meet future needs.

Figure 24.17 HR planning

An assessment of present supply will start out by examining how many people are required to perform each of the tasks needed to meet specific organisational objectives. This is not easy because the achievement of objectives usually depends on a number of integrated tasks and activities. For example, you can only have checkout staff in a supermarket if they are being supported by others who are putting goods on the shelves.

The organisation will often need to carry out a **skills inventory** to work out the quality of its employees (i.e. their potential to produce outputs).

qualifications and training standards in the European Union have been recognised on a union-wide basis, it is possible for qualified employees of one country to take up jobs in another.

A recent pattern is for skilled Europeans to move between EU member states. This often happens when employees are working for an EU-wide organisation which moves them around between locations (e.g. in oil companies like Shell). It is not unusual for senior managers in large companies to have had experience in working in several countries. We are beginning to see the development of a European labour market. Jobs for graduates, for example, are often advertised simultaneously in several countries. Of course language skills are always a boon.

We are also seeing the development of a world labour market. This is particularly the case for highly paid skilled

The next stage is to project the number of employees who are required to meet the on-going objectives of the organisation in both the short term and the long term. For example, a supermarket chain which is opening new stores must calculate how many people will be required (car park attendants, checkout operators, warehouse staff, lorry drivers, managers, etc.). Changes in the economic environment have an important effect on these projections. Some supermarkets are highly responsive to upturns and downturns in the economy and consumer spending, changing the number of staff employed tomorrow depending on today's sales figures.

Once human resource planners have identified employment requirements, they must develop a programme setting out specific actions required to attract, hire, train, or promote the people required to meet organisational objectives.

Case Study
Recruitment for a new Tesco store

When Tesco opens a new store the organisation requires a detailed analysis of the available supply of labour in a particular area and ways of attracting appropriate people. When Tesco opened its store in Dover, for example, the recruitment schedule for 500 staff started 12 months in advance.

Staff managers and store managers were recruited from existing Tesco staff at other locations, and then initial research was carried out in the Dover area. Tesco hired an advertising agency to support the campaign. The agency outlined potential competitors for staff in Dover. Salaries in the area were noted, along with the available transport, housing and Job Centres. Research was carried out into the type of people likely to work in the store and the numbers unemployed in the area.

```
RECRUITMENT SCHEDULE
Countdown 12 months before store opens:

1 Recruit senior management.
2 Initial research into area.
3 Advertising agency researches media and area.
4 Advertising agency presents campaign package.
5 Recruitment centre opens.
6 Advertisements for supervisory staff appear.
7 Advertisements for general staff go out.
8 Store opens.
```

The advertising agency researched the local media, including daily and weekly newspapers and local radio.

Tesco uses the local rather than the national press for recruitment.

After about three weeks of collecting the necessary data, the agency put together a package for Tesco which included a suggested budget.

Tesco always sets up a recruitment office either in offices above the local shopping centre or at the local Job Centre. In Dover a terraced house in the middle of town was used. The recruitment centre was kitted out in red with colour posters and red arrows so that it stood out.

The budget for the recruitment campaign was set at about £35 000 and slightly less than that was spent. Out of 470 staff, only 30 vacancies were left after the initial recruitment drive. The first advertisement did not specify job vacancies but invited people to go along to the centre. In this way, Tesco attracted about 200 applicants before even opening the recruitment centre.

The adverts that were placed in local newspapers were simple and direct. Tesco's personnel department felt that the benefits and salary offered were the key ingredients in attracting staff.

Supervisory and skilled vacancies were advertised 19 weeks before the store opened and general vacancies were advertised 13 weeks before.

Tesco's Dover campaign received a good response, but if it had not the agency would have been able to drawn on ideas in the original package. A contingency plan would have been put into effect immediately, perhaps with radio commercials or leaflet drops.

Questions for discussion

1 *Why was it important to research the labour market before carrying out the recruitment drive?*
2 *Why was it important to establish recruitment needs before carrying out the recruitment drive?*
3 *Describe the different techniques used to attract managerial, supervisory and general staff. Why do you think different techniques were used in each case?*
4 *Why was it important for the recruitment drive to be successful first time?*
5 *What is a contingency plan?*

Flexibility in the labour market

Since about 1980 there have been two major trends in the labour market:

- the increasing number of women employees
- the growth of part-time work.

Several explanations can be put forward to account for the increase in female employment – the growth of part-time jobs, the fact that women put off starting a family until their middle to late twenties, as well as economic necessity. Evidence shows that families headed by a male breadwinner are outnumbered 3 to 1 by homes where both partners work. Women's earnings are making an important contribution to prevent family incomes from falling below the poverty line.

Furthermore, the trend towards greater female employment is likely to be encouraged by the final abolition of Wages Councils in 1993. These fixed statutory minimum wages for two million people of whom 80 per cent were women.

Additionally the 1990s have seen a change in the structure of the UK's population – an ageing population (with its average age rising). The likely effect is a decline in the number of young people with a rise in the age of the working population. According to one report, by the year 2001 there will be 2.7 million fewer people aged between 15 and 19 but 2.9 million more aged between 30 and 59.

Women re-entering after raising a family are likely to replace the missing young from the work force – the so-called 'women returners'. Indeed, this indicates a shortage of young entrants and a need to search out alternative sources of labour.

Businesses could increase the number of older workers on their payroll. Redundant workers and those who have taken earlier retirement are likely to be willing to provide part-time work and the increasing flexibility which employers are seeking.

Organisations are now operating more in a climate of competition. Businesses have had to become more responsive in terms of price, quality and the range of goods and services produced. They have also introduced increased flexibility in the use of their resources. **Labour market flexibility** has been recognised by employers and the government for some time. For example, a 1985 White Paper (*Employment: The Challenge for the Nation*) included references to flexible hours, job sharing, home working and self-employment.

Several definitions of flexibility are to be found. These cover flexibility in the pattern and organisation of work and a broad range of practices. For example, **numerical** flexibility refers to the ability of firms to adjust the numbers of workers or the number of hours worked in line with changes in the level of demand for their goods and services. Typically this refers to the use of part-time,

temporary, and sub-contracted workers. **Temporal** (or working-time) **flexibility**, on the other hand, can be seen as a particular form of numerical flexibility, relating to changes in the number and timing of hours worked from day to day or week to week, for example through flexitime or annual-hours contracts.

In the 1990s the vast majority of the UK's largest organisations have been restructured, leading to job losses at all levels. This applies in both the private and public sectors. Temporary employment is used to supplement existing employees in the concept of the flexible firm. This distinguishes between the **core workers** (full-time), **peripheral workers** (part-time or temporary) and **external workers** who are not employees of the firm itself.

We can see this process occurring on a regular basis. For example, in the television industry the government now requires that 25 per cent of BBC and ITV output must be sourced from external programme-makers. Instead of the change being from full-time to part-time staff, the change is to an increase in the numbers of peripheral workers used. Producers buy-in contract services for their productions, such as set construction, catering, transportation, or programme research. There are also more employees with short-term or part-time contracts and fewer people working full time.

The 'permanent temp' has become a feature of the flexible work force. The use of stand-ins or locums among medics and chemists has been commonplace for many years, while 'temping' is common with secretarial staff. It is now reckoned that there are few industries or professions that do not use permanent temps. The old concept of a 35–40 hour week and a 50-year career are gone forever as a way of life. New thinking, aided by information technology, is beginning to alter not only the way we work, but where we work, and when.

Organisations must now take a more strategic view of employment policy in the labour market. This will involve developing planning both for the supply side and the demand side. On the supply side, measures are needed to recruit and retain multi-skilled, capable employees, and to develop and train employees to a high level. The **learning organisation** is one that is able to cope with flexibility. It is able to:

- identify and understand the competencies it will require in its employees
- operate a human resources culture which encourages personal development, and the mentoring and coaching of organisational members, so creating the competencies it requires on an ongoing basis
- provide incentives and rewards for individual growth and achievement.

On the demand side, organisations must ensure that they anticipate their future needs and are able to recruit and retain the right kind of human resources in a competitive and changing environment.

Employment legislation and European influences

UK employment legislation is wide-ranging and covers the rights and obligations of employees in the workplace. This section looks at this subject under the headings contracts of employment, health and safety, and equal opportunities.

Contracts of employment

When a new worker is taken on, he or she must be given a written contract of employment within 13 weeks of starting the job. Under the Contract of Employment Act, the written contract must include the title of the job, the date when the job starts, the hours of work, the rate and method of pay, holiday arrangements, the period of notice of termination that must be given, pension scheme arrangements, rights concerning trade union membership, and the organisation's discipline rules.

The personnel manager will agree on a date with the employee for work to start, and the contract of employment becomes binding from this date. The period of notice that an employee must be given when being dismissed is stated in the contract, which is a legal document.

Over the years, an elaborate system for the dismissal of staff has developed as a result of cases that have come before industrial tribunals or other courts. The heart of the matter lies in the difference between what is termed 'fair dismissal' and what the court regards as 'unfair dismissal'.

Fair dismissal can take place when grounds can be shown such as:

- wilful destruction of company property
- sexual or racial harassment
- continuous bad timekeeping
- a negative attitude at work
- inability to do the job
- sleeping on the job.

In some cases (e.g. bad timekeeping) employees would normally receive written warnings and suspensions before dismissal. **Unfair dismissal** would almost certainly be deemed to have occurred in any of the following circumstances:

- *Pregnancy* – An employee can be sacked only if she is unable to do her job properly as a result of being pregnant (e.g. stacking shelves).
- *Race* – A worker cannot be sacked on grounds of race.
- *Homosexuality* – A homosexual should not be sacked unless it can be proved that his or her standard of work is affected.
- *Union membership* – An employer cannot sack a worker for belonging to a trade union.
- *Criminal record* – If an employer does not find out about an employee's criminal record until some time after employment starts, the employer cannot sack the worker on these grounds unless it was a very relevant crime (e.g. a cashier who has a record of stealing the petty cash).

Health and safety

The personnel department will also normally be involved with health and safety at work. There are thousands of pages of legal regulations covering this aspect of employment. Some firms go so far as to employ a specialist health and safety officer.

The Health and Safety at Work Act 1974

This Act covers all persons at work except domestic servants in private households. Sets of regulations under the Act deal with different kinds of work in various places. All those receiving training or work experience in the workplace are covered by the Act.

The Act establishes a responsibility of both employers and employees to provide safe conditions at work. Employers or employees who do not abide by the rules can be punished in a court of law. The employer's duty is to ensure, as far as is reasonably practicable, 'the health, safety, and welfare at work of all employees'. This general responsibility includes:

- the provision and maintenance of plant and systems of work
- arrangements for use, handling, storage and transport of articles and substances
- maintenance of the place of work and access to and egress from it
- the working environment.

It includes the duty to provide:

- adequate welfare facilities
- necessary information, instruction, training and supervision.

Also, the employer must consult with union safety representatives if there are any. A notice containing the requirements of the Act must be displayed.

An example of an area covered by the Act is the use of protective guards on machines such as food-slicing machines and industrial presses. Accidents can occur if the guards are faulty or if they are removed. The Act lays down training standards for workers in potentially hazardous occupations. Generally the workplace must be designed in such a way as to minimise the risk of accidents.

An employer must prepare a written statement of policy with respect to the health and safety at work of employees, and show it to an inspector if required. An employer must show similar responsibilities to non-employees, such as visitors in a school or college party, who need to be given information and instruction about health and safety requirements.

The employee's duty is to take reasonable care to ensure both his or her own safety and the safety of others who may be affected by what he or she does or does not do.

The Act is backed up by a **Health and Safety Executive** which includes representatives of employers, employees and local authorities. Health and safety **inspectors** are appointed with responsibility for making sure that the law is being observed.

There are also laws and codes applying to specific industries. For example, there are laws relating to miners, workers in the explosives industry and in textiles. Many industries also set their own additional safety regulations. A firm's personnel officer will normally attend conferences and refresher courses on safety as a regular feature of his or her duties.

The Factories Act 1961

Until it is fully replaced by regulations under the Health and Safety at Work Act, the Factories Act remains important. It covers most businesses that use mechanical machinery and therefore includes a wide range of premises including garages, printing works, building sites and engineering works. A factory is defined as a place where people are employed in manual labour (work done mainly by hand) in any process for, or incidental to, the making, repairing, altering, cleaning, adapting for sale or demolition of any article. The following are some stipulations of the Factories Act:

- Adequate toilet and washing facilities must be provided.
- The inside of buildings must be properly heated and ventilated.
- Floors must not have slippery surfaces.
- Machinery such as presses must have fenced screens to prevent serious injury.

- Fire escapes must be provided and kept in good order. Fire doors should not be locked or obstructed.

The Offices, Shops and Railway Premises Act 1963

Most of this Act's provisions are similar to those covered by the Factories Act. This one is applied in office and shop conditions. The following are examples of requirements:

- Temperatures must not fall below 16 degrees centigrade in places where people work for any length of time.
- There must be adequate supplies of fresh or purified air.
- Toilet and washing facilities must be adequate for the number of employees and kept in a clean state. There must be running hot and cold water with soap and clean towels.
- Suitable lighting must be provided wherever people walk or work.
- The minimum amount of space for each person is 12 square metres of floor space.

Reporting of Injuries, Diseases and Dangerous Occurrences Regulations 1985

Injuries that result from accidents at work where an employee is incapacitated for three or more days *must be reported to the authorities within seven days*. Injuries involving fatalities must be notified immediately by the most practical means (e.g. by phone). Listed diseases must also be reported.

Control of Substances Hazardous to Health Regulations 1988

Employers must carry out an assessment of work tasks that are likely to create risks for the health and safety of employees. Following on from the assessment, decisions need to be made on how to prevent or limit risks of exposure to such substances. Workers dealing with dangerous substances should be given appropriate information and training. Measures taken to meet the regulations need to be continually monitored. Substances covered by the Act are all those potentially harmful to health, whether in solid or liquid form or in the form of a gas or vapour.

Noise at Work Regulations 1989

Employers have an obligation to reduce the risk of hearing damage to employees to the lowest practical level. The employer has an obligation to make sure that, when the sound reaches or exceeds a set level, ear protectors are worn.

Other regulations

Other regulations cover the use of electricity in the workplace, the provision of first-aid facilities, fire precautions, and other important areas.

Enforcement of the laws and regulations is principally by the Health and Safety Executive backed up by local authority inspections. Inspectors have substantial powers, including the right to enter premises, to obtain information and to take possession of articles and substances. Offending organisations can be taken to court to face substantial fines as well as prison sentences.

Negligence at common law

An employee can claim for damages arising from an employer's negligence if the employer fails 'to abide by the duty of care to the employee so that the employee suffers injury or damage to health'. The employer has a duty of reasonable care for the safety of employees, and this responsibility extends to when he or she sends employees to the premises of third parties. Negligence occurs when there is a breach in the duty of care which applies to:

- safe premises
- a safe system of work
- safe plant, equipment and tools
- safe fellow workers.

The European dimension of health and safety

Health and safety is also an important part of the Single European Act, which lays emphasis on providing safe working conditions in all member states. The emphasis is on harmonising working conditions.

In addition, new **directives** have been established about the technical requirements and safety standards for specific products. A manufacturer needs to show that products are produced to European standards. This should involve:

- a manufacturer's declaration backed up by test results
- a certificate of standard from an independent body
- the provision of test results by the independent body.

The directives include such areas as gas appliances, personal protective equipment, machinery safety including mobile machinery and lifting equipment, and many others.

Equal opportunities

Businesses have a legal obligation to provide **equal opportunities at work**. In addition, many enlightened employers provide their own codes of conduct which go beyond the bare essentials of statutory obligations. For example, Littlewoods has produced its own code of practice – *Littlewoods Equal Opportunities Code of Practice* is a 21-page booklet covering policy on the company's recruitment and advertising; selection processes; training; career development; job satisfaction; terms and conditions; part-time employment; responsibilities of managers and supervisors; ethnic minorities and religious beliefs; and employees with domestic responsibilities. It states that no job applicant or employee should receive less favourable treatment on grounds of gender, marital status, social class, colour, race, ethnic origin, creed or disability, or be disadvantaged by conditions or requirements that cannot be shown to be relevant to performance. The company's aspirations, at least so far as employees are concerned, are backed up by an equal-opportunities internal appeals procedure to be 'invoked in cases of alleged sexual or racial harassment'. Where this process fails to resolve a problem, the employee can then use the company's formal grievance procedure.

Women at work

The Equal Pay Act 1970 aimed to eliminate discrimination on grounds of sex in relation to pay, overtime, piecework rates and holiday entitlements. The Act gave all female employees the right to treatment equal to that given to male employees in the same employment who are doing the same or 'broadly similar' work. This Act was amended in 1984 to include equal pay for work of equal value.

The Sex Discrimination Act 1975 made sex discrimination unlawful in employment training and related matters. This Act was updated in 1986 to remove restrictions on women's hours of work which had prevented them from taking on manufacturing jobs involving shift or night work.

The main problems for women as a group have been low pay and a concentration in low-paid occupations. Economic expansion in the UK from the 1950s onwards has created more and more jobs for women. There has been a growth particularly in the proportion of married women at work, so that over half now have employment. Women do over 80 per cent of all part-time jobs, which are especially low paid.

The 1984 amendment to the Equal Pay Act, which allows for job evaluation to see whether work is of equal value, is regarded as an important change, as is the 1994 ruling by the European Court that part-time workers are entitled to the same pension and other rights as full-time employees.

The effect of passing the Equal Pay Act and the Sex Discrimination Act was to raise women's pay to 75 per cent of men's; however, by 1984 it had fallen back to 59 per cent of men's earnings in non-manual work and to 61.5 per cent in manual work.

Ethnic minorities at work

The Race Relations Act 1976 makes it unlawful to discriminate against a person, directly or indirectly, in the field of employment.

Direct discrimination consists of treating a person, on racial grounds, less favourably than others are or would be treated in the same or similar circumstances. Segregating a person from others on racial grounds, for example, constitutes less favourable treatment.

Indirect discrimination consists of imposing a requirement or condition which, although applied equally to persons of all racial groups, is such that a considerably smaller proportion of a particular racial group can comply with it, and which cannot be shown to be justifiable on other than racial grounds. Examples are:

- a rule about clothing or uniforms which disproportionately disadvantages a racial group (e.g. Sikhs) and cannot be justified
- requirements of higher language standards than are needed for safe and effective performance of the job.

The **Commission for Racial Equality** has produced a code of practice for the elimination of racial discrimination and the promotion of equality of opportunity in employment. This code aims to give practical guidance which will help employers, trade unions, employment agencies and employees to understand not only the provisions of the Race Relations Act and its implications, but also how best they can implement policies to eliminate racial discrimination and to enhance equality of opportunity. The code covers a variety of areas including recruitment, training and appraisal.

Ethnic minorities tend to be concentrated in a range of relatively low-paid occupations compared with the national average – such as health, catering and cleaning.

European social policy

The **Treaty of Rome** enshrines the principles that member countries will:

- ensure that every citizen enjoys the freedom to take a job or set up in business anywhere in the union

- establish minimum standards for health and safety at work
- ensure equal treatment for men and women in employment.

At the Maastricht conference, many governments wanted to expand the range of social policy covered by the EU laws. The UK government would not agree to the acceptance of new laws that would increase regulation of the labour market. The UK therefore opted out of the **Social Chapter**.

The treaty's Social Chapter gives legal force to the social charter signed by eleven EC leaders in December 1989. This gave the European Commission powers to develop social legislation without facing a national veto. For the first time, ministers from the eleven countries are able to agree, on the basis of *qualified majority voting*, directives on:

- health and safety
- working conditions
- information and consultation of workers
- sex equality in treatment at work and in applying for jobs.

If they are *unanimous*, the eleven can agree to directives on:

- social security and social protection of workers
- protection of workers where the employment contract is terminated
- representation and collective defence of the interests of workers and employers
- conditions of employment for third-country nationals living in the community.

Before the Maastricht Treaty was signed, the only area of employment law enforceable by qualified majority voting was health and safety. The reforms therefore involve a big increase in community powers.

The Social Chapter from which Britain has opted out includes the following rights:

- to work and to fair remuneration for work carried out
- to the improvement of living and working conditions
- to social protection, particularly for those excluded from the labour market (including migrant workers)
- to education and training throughout life
- to freedom of association and negotiation (the right to trade union membership and to participate in free collective bargaining)
- to freedom of movement in the community, equal treatment between community workers, and recognition of professional qualifications

■ to information, consultation and participation of workers in their enterprises

■ to health, particularly in the field of prevention and health care

■ to protection of health and safety at work

■ to protection of children and young people (notably a minimum working age and the protection against physical and moral dangers), the elderly (including pension rights and minimum incomes) and the disabled

■ to consumer protection, including the right to information and to protection from environmental risks.

Of course, most of these principles are enshrined in existing UK law. However, the UK government did not want to be bound by regulations on such things as minimum wages. The fear was that having workplace legislation dictated by directives from Brussels would reduce the ability of the UK to create competitive labour market conditions that would enable us to sell our products in competitive world markets.

Part 3 The role of the personnel function

A systems approach to human resource management provides us with a useful model. It enables us to look at the effects of taking actions in one part of the system on other parts of the system – for example, the impact of raising standards for selection on on-going training and development. We have already looked at some of the components of the human resources system – recruitment, selection, induction, training, development, etc.

Adding a longitudinal dimension

Cynthia and Mark Legnick-Hall, in their book *Interactive Human Resource Management and Strategic Planning*, have argued that in order to understand the interactive nature of HRM we need to add a longitudinal dimension to the systems approach. They identify five main stages of this longitudinal relationship which relate both to the organisation and to the individuals employed (see Figure 24.18).

Figure 24.18 Five stages of the longitudinal relationship

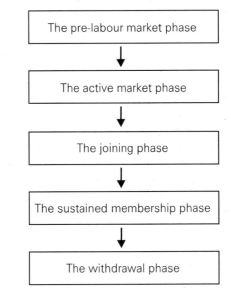

The pre-labour market phase

This occurs prior to an individual taking up a post and prior to the organisation taking on workers. For the individual it is a period of learning about types of work and work roles, developing basic work skills, and acquiring values which will be of help in the workplace (e.g. time-keeping, hard work, standards).

For the employing organisation it is a period of examining the product and labour markets in order to develop human resource strategies. As strategies are refined they can be translated into plans and forecasts.

The active market phase

For the individual this is the period between starting a job search and obtaining a position. For the organisation it is the period in which it concentrates on recruitment, selections, and placements. It is also the period in which reward systems are set out as well as terms and conditions of work.

The joining phase

For the individual these are the early days in the workplace. It is during this period that the employee finds out whether expectations are to be met. For the organisation it is the period in which the induction of new employees is carried out. It is important to ensure that the expectations of inductees are met or there will be a high turnover of labour.

The sustained membership phase

This is the main part of working life of an individual. During this period the employee learns to fit in with the life of the organisation by taking on the norms and expectations which are part and parcel of working life. The organisation needs to create the culture which encourages people to stay. It will be necessary to provide training, development and reward packages to fulfil individual employees. Appraisal, job enrichment and job enlargement will be important at this stage.

The withdrawal phase

This is the period during which employees and organisations disengage. Retirement planning is important for both employees and the organisation so that a smooth transition can be made.

Combining the systems and the longitudinal approaches to human resource management provides us with important insights into the complexity of the decision-making process. It gives an invaluable basis on which to get a clearer understanding of the role of the personnel function.

The personnel function within the management team

It is not easy to identify with clarity the role of the personnel function within an organisation because it has such a wide variety of activities. Personnel work involves:

- a *strategic and policy-making role*, concerned with the development of the human resource mission
- a *welfare role*, concerned with looking after people and their needs
- a *supporting role*, concerned with helping line managers to develop their human resource work
- a *bargaining and negotiating role*, concerned with acting as an intermediary between different groups and interests
- an *administrative role*, concerned with the payment of wages, the supervision and implementation of health and safety codes and laws
- an *educational and development role*, concerned with the education and training of employees and in supporting their career development.

These activities and many more demand considerable skills on the part of personnel specialists. The diverse strands pull a personnel manager in many different directions. Not least is the ambiguity between the personnel specialist's welfare role for employees, coupled with concern for the welfare of the organisation. This tension will be particularly obvious, for example, when the organisation needs to order redundancies or to restructure its operations.

In his important book *The Management of Human Resources*, John Storey highlights different ways in which the personnel function contributed to management teams in 15 organisations at the start of the 1990s. Storey collected evidence both from personnel managers and from line managers with whom they interacted. He identified four main types of practitioner in personnel work (see Figure 24.19).

Figure 24.19 Storey's four categories

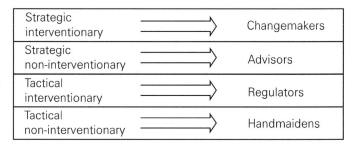

- *Handmaidens* are personnel managers who play a subservient role to line managers they serve. Their role is relatively uncoordinated and lacking in clarity.
- *Regulators* play a more 'hands on' role which is based on setting out, putting into practice and monitoring the observance of 'employment rules' (which range from personnel procedure manuals to joint agreements with trade unions). Regulators can be seen as 'managers of discontent' concerned to develop temporary tactical

truces with organised labour rather than creating an overall strategy for effective human relations.

- *Advisors* are personnel managers who are familiar with current developments in their organisation but leave the running of day-to-day affairs to line and general manager colleagues. This involves a 'hands off' approach unless asked for help.
- *Changemakers* are concerned to place human relations management on a new footing. They try to create an effective working environment which fosters employee commitment. It is this group which sets out to create the human relations environment which fosters 'the new world of work' involving empowerment, team work, concern for the individual and the organisation.

A look at the way in which the personnel function operates in practice reveals a wide variation on these four themes. However, they do provide a useful model for exploring the personnel function.

Support and line staff

Storey's discussion of types of personnel specialist provides a useful starting point for examining how personnel management fits into an organisational structure. We have already seen that an emphasis on HRM means that all managers and supervisors in an organisation should take on human resource management responsibilities. However, when we look at how organisations actually operate in the real world we need to examine how they are structured to meet their objectives.

The chain of command in most organisations is established through line management. Line management establishes responsibilities, powers, channels of decision-making etc. For example, in the production department the 'line' might be production manager–production controller–supervisor–operators. However, a feature of most modern organisations is that there is an additional element of staff management. Staff managers are there to provide support *across* the organisation. They are involved in the creation of plans and procedures which they recommend to provide as the basis for organisation-wide policy and activities such as recruitment procedures.

In modern organisations there are many different types of staff, two of which are highlighted below. However, there is considerable overlap between these types.

Advisory staff can be used to support and aid decision-making by line managers. For example, personnel managers and officers can advise managers on recruitment, training, employment law, and a host of other policies and activities. Personnel staff may perform these roles as handmaidens and advisors.

Personnel workers are often quoted as being the typical example of *service staff* in an organisation. Personnel workers may perform many services for departments and divisions, for example in keeping employee records, and identifying and screening potential new recruits. They may also be involved in the interviewing and selection process, as well as in a training capacity. Personnel will be responsible for the organisation of welfare programmes, the induction of new employees, workplace bargaining and many other activities. Personnel may operate as the changemakers concerned with developing new ways of working and interacting within organisations. They may act as regulators who create and maintain employment rules. Alternatively, they may play a less interventionist tactical role in a subservient capacity to line managers.

The growing importance of line managers in human relations

John Storey's research of 15 major employing organisations in the private and public sectors, published in 1992, indicates that line managers are taking increasing responsibility for HRM at ground level. He puts forward the argument that, as organisations de-layer, and particularly as they cut back headquarters staff, responsibilities become devolved to cost and profit centres at lower levels within the organisation. For example, in the 1980s Lucas Industries split up into 130 separate businesses, and managers in these business units took on increasing responsibility for the management of an array of resources. This meant that 'line managers have come to the fore . . . not only as the crucial delivery mechanism for new approaches in human relations . . . but more assertively, as themselves the designers and drivers of new ways'.

Storey's research indicates that in a large proportion of major companies the development of an HRM approach in management is a reality. Line managers are taking on an increasing role in 'directly briefing employees, the whole raft of measures involving "managerial leadership"; the shift towards more individualised forms of pay; of more appraisal; of devolved management accountability; and of deproceduralising . . .'.

However, it is important to bear in mind that such changes will be truly effective only when there is a commitment to HRM as a strategic mission of the organisation. At the same time it is clear that, in many if not most smaller companies, personnel continues to play a staff role in supporting line managers in recruiting, selection, etc. The place of the personnel function in an organisation will depend on a wide range of contextual factors, such as:

- whether the organisation is a traditional or relatively new one
- the personalities involved
- the type of organisation (people-intensive or capital-intensive)
- the availability of people, and competition for people in the locality of the organisation.

Storey argues that senior managements in many large companies now consider human resources at a strategic level. He quotes the example of an interview he had with the director of Ford of Europe, in which it was stated:

'Every month the Executive Committee of Ford of Europe moves, in the afternoon, from the boardroom to a more relaxed atmosphere to discuss the ''people'' issues of involvement, appraisal, employee relations, etc. . . . In total it adds up to a very considerable proportion of the board's time.'

Case Study
Problems of flatter structures

During the late 1980s and early 90s it became fashionable for organisations to move towards de-layered 'flatter' structures. However, research by Roffey Park Management Institute suggests that 90 per cent of a survey of 200 managers saw little benefit from this development. Instead, it can create lower morale and a lessening of career opportunities.

The aim of the exercise is to create self-managing teams and to make the communication process easier by stripping out surplus layers. However, on the human resource side the impact can be negative as individuals begin to lose sight of career progression. Instead of seeing a future in the organisation, they seek to move from one organisation to another for improvement.

Researchers at Roffey Park Management Institute argue that career management needs to be handled carefully. Individuals want to identify their own goals and objectives and to identify ways of increasing satisfaction. Human resource management will need to help individuals to create a fulfilling vision through recruitment, personal development plans and lateral moves. Ways of introducing development opportunities must be identified to enhance employee loyalty.

Questions for discussion

1 *Why might the de-layering of organisations lead to a reduction in career opportunities?*
2 *How can this lead to a reduction in employee motivation?*

3 *What policies and procedures can be introduced by those responsible for human resource management to counteract these negative views and to retain motivation?*
4 *Should the responsibility for creating employee commitment be with human resource generalists (e.g. line managers) or with human resource specialists (e.g. personnel managers)?*

Approaches to HRM planning

The achievement of organisational objectives stems from the effective use of people. Long-range planning for the human resource is a complex process and will be successful only when the personnel team is regarded as an important part of the management team.

In exploring human resources planning activities, it is useful to follow the line taken by Torrington and Hall in contrasting 'soft' and 'hard' approaches.

Soft approaches

'Soft' human resources planning involves (see Figure 24.20):

- setting out where the organisation wants to be in the future
- identifying where the organisation is at the moment
- analysing environmental influences and trends
- establishing plans to take the organisation forward.

The vision of where the organisation wants to go should be derived from the mission statement, which should have a clear human resource focus. For example, an organisation that emphasises the importance of innovation and flexibility will want to nurture flexible and imaginative people. The nurturing of these people will be based on care for individual training and development, on career and reward structures and on many other factors.

Before identifying the direction an organisation wants to move in, it is essential to identify where it is coming from. This will highlight the changes that need to be introduced, the sizes of the changes, the resources required, the processes to be employed, and so on. An analysis of current resources is required in order to be able to forecast future needs.

Human resource specialists must work from the heart of an organisation in order to manage cultural change and to help reshape the organisation. For example, if they wanted to create a 'virtual organisation' in which flexible

Figure 24.20 Moving forward

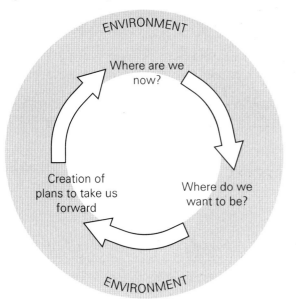

Figure 24.21 Matching demand and supply at the right price

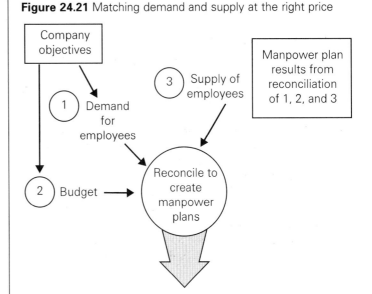

teams were brought together for specific purposes, they could achieve this only by transforming interpersonal relationships in the workplace and by altering existing perceptions and attitudes. Human resource planning therefore involves careful collection of data about formal and informal systems and organisational cultures. This data needs to be analysed carefully and translated into plans covering organisation structure, recruitment, planning etc.

Hard approaches

'Hard' human resource planning involves more traditional activities, such as looking at whether the organisation has enough people for the tasks to be done.

Every organisation must know how many employees it will need to take on in the short, medium and long term, and the availability of appropriate people and how they can be recruited. It must also assess their training and development needs. The manpower plan must match the objectives of the organisation which are established in its corporate plan (see Figure 24.21).

The key to solving the manpower equation is to ensure that the organisation's demand for labour is met by available supply at the right price (i.e. within the budget available). Many internal and external factors need to be considered. Internal factors include:

- plans to introduce new machinery and equipment
- the availability of finance
- expected labour turnover and absenteeism
- wage rates in comparable firms and industries.

External factors include:

- national and local population trends
- government policies on labour market issues (e.g. maximum numbers of hours that can be worked by individuals, health and safety regulations)
- the expansion or contraction of rival firms, and other firms competing for the same supply of labour.

Factors in HRM planning

Analysing current resources and forecasting future needs involves a number of major considerations, which can be examined under the following headings:

- the economic climate
- skills analysis
- skills availability
- demographic trends
- government incentives.

The economic climate

The economic climate will determine whether there is a boom or recession in the demand for goods and services, and so will influence the demand for labour in the market. Figure 24.22 sets out some of these relationships.

Generally speaking, firms will be reluctant to take on more workers in recessionary times, though of course this will depend on the sector of the market in which the firm is operating.

In the mid-1990s organisations are operating in a climate of increased unemployment world-wide. The UK's

Figure 24.22 Economic conditions and the demand for and supply of labour

Economic conditions	Demand for products	Demand and supply of labour
Upturn in economic activity	Increase in demand for products	Start of increase in demand for labour, but there may be a surplus supply from a previous recession
Continued boom in economic activity	High demand for products, imports sucked in	Continued increase in demand for labour, shortages in supply increasingly obvious, leading to wage rises
Start in downturn of economic activity	Small fall in demand for products	Demand for labour stops rising, still shortages in supply for specific skills and in some areas
Continued downturn of economic activity	Fall in demand for products	Fall in demand for labour, rising unemployment increases supply of labour, falling wages

unemployment rate was 9 per cent at the start of 1995, and a depressing number of forecasts indicate that unemployment of well over 2 million people is not just a temporary phenomenon, but one likely to be with us throughout the 1990s.

It was during the 1970s that the familiar scenery of people's working lives began to show visible changes. The large employment organisations which had been day-time homes for so many all their lives began to decline. The tradition of a man going out to work to support a family at home became a statistical rarity, and by the end of that decade only 14 per cent of households fitted the stereotype. 'Long term unemployment', 'youth unemployment' and 'redundancy' became familiar terms and have been attached to all social groups. 'Work'

started to mean things other than the conventional full-time job. Second and third careers, moonlighting and the black economy became part of our language, together with 'the chip'.

However, while there continues to be a pool of unemployed people, they do not necessarily have the particular types of skills and abilities required, in the right place and at the right time. For multi-skilled, talented, hard-working core workers there are plenty of opportunities in dynamic organisations. These employees are at a premium and when the economy is booming can attract large salaries and rewards packages. Organisations, however, need to consider ways of retaining these employees at times when the labour market is depressed as well as when it is booming.

Case Study
Employing labour in the Cambridge Triangle

One of the most booming employment areas in the 1980s and the early 1990s has been the Cambridge Triangle. In particular this area is renowned for 'intelligence-based' organisations, often in the microelectronics, information technology and telecommunications areas.

In the late 1980s and early 90s there were recessionary trends in the UK economy. Many companies in the Cambridge Triangle shook out labour in 1991–92. These organisations began to develop flexible structures with a core labour force. The emphasis was on sub-contracting non-essential functions.

However, when the economy began to move into recovery in 1994, organisations started to compete for contracted services. Suddenly organisations found that they were not able to buy in the services on which they had previously relied. Once again they had to start expanding their core work forces. In addition they had to offer packages which would maintain the loyalty of all their employees.

Questions for discussion

1 *How have changes in economic conditions affected employment practice for hi-tech firms in the Cambridge Triangle?*
2 *What are the problems associated with sub-contracting non-essential functions and services?*
3 *What are the implications for developing an effective human resources planning framework?*

Skills analysis

An organisation will need to assess its present supply of skills and to identify the sorts of skills required and how these can be acquired.

A starting point, therefore, is to carry out a **skills inventory** which may take the form of a written record of the numbers of existing employees possessing various skills. The analysis may be of employee numbers by job categories. There may be breakdowns by sex and age, as well as of employees leaving the company, preferably classified according to the reason for leaving. The skills analysis will produce useful information showing, for example, the age profile of employees. This sort of information will reveal likely future shortfalls in employee numbers caused by retirements. The skills analysis will also indicate the number of employees who have recently received training and those requiring training.

The next step will be to estimate the implications of the skills analysis. The organisation will look at its future intentions and map out the types of skills – and hence people – it will need. *Job analysis* will be a key element of this planning process. HRM planners need to know in detail what tasks will have to be performed in the future, and the personal and social characteristics of the work. Job analysis enables management to secure the best possible people to secure its on-going objectives. It permits the organisation to identify the qualities required by its future employees, whether they be existing employees who receive training for future roles or new employees brought into the organisation.

George Thomason, in *A Textbook of Personnel Management*, describes how personnel departments are using ever-more sophisticated data to identify skills needs. An example is 'workload data', which is useful for measuring the amount of work that employees will be expected to carry out. The best sources of this data are indicators, such as the forecasted level of demand for the product the employees will produce. A more traditional way of measuring workload is by using a performance indicator for a standard unit of manpower – for example, 'a trained operator working at a standard pace in standard conditions will produce x units'.

However, historical data are more likely to be available to the personnel department relating to stocks and flows of manpower – the output created by a given stock of manpower in the past in a given time period. On the basis of this data, calculations can be made as to how much given numbers of employees can produce in the future under a number of conditions. This will then show how many employees (of this type) will be required to meet the organisation's objectives.

Skills availability

Having identified the skills *required* by an organisation, it is necessary to study the skills *available* to meet those needs. The skills will either be available within the organisation, or will need to come from the available external supply. Both internal and external recruits may require training and development to bring skills up to the required level (see Figure 24.23).

Figure 24.23 Skills available to meet skills requirements

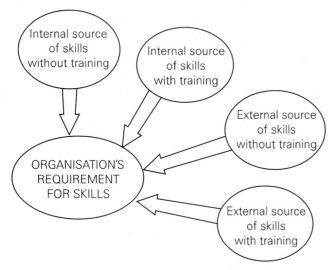

It may be possible to develop new skills by promoting internal candidates and by using training and development programmes, or alternatively the organisation may need to recruit new people. For example, suppose that an organisation has identified that it needs to develop the training function, requiring the appointment of training officers at each of its plants. It should go through the following processes:

- Define the role of 'training officer' within the organisation's strategy.
- Identify the skills and experience required by training officers.
- Assess what skills could reasonably be expected from internal and external recruitment.
- Identify an appropriate course of training for the new officers.
- Identify how many training officers would be required, over what period.

- Estimate the natural loss of such officers, for example by promotion or moves to other organisations (this could be calculated from the experiences of other firms).
- Put together a plan for recruitment, training, etc. of new training officers over a period of time. Allocate a budget for this purpose.

Labour market statistics

The production of local and national labour market statistics is becoming increasingly sophisticated. Employment trends are published regularly by government departments. Two examples, from the Department of Employment, are *Quarterly Labour Force Survey* and *Employment Gazette*. The Confederation of British Industry (CBI) produces its *Quarterly Industrial Trends Survey*. These surveys and others provide a wealth of useful, detailed information. In addition, the *Labour Market Quarterly Reports* (available from the Department of Employment, Skills and Enterprise Network, Room W801, Moorfoot, Sheffield S1 4PQ) give wonderful summaries of nearly all of the relevant information at a general level.

Task

The information shown in Figure 24.24 is taken from the *Labour Market Quarterly Report* for May 1994. Study the chart and identify the main trends. Comment on how these trends could be of use to manpower planners.

Many employers are also keenly interested in information which is provided on a local basis principally by Training and Enterprise Councils (TECs) and by local offices of the Department of Employment. These employers carry out their manpower planning in a local context. It is far more important for them to know about the supply and demand for labour in their own 'neck of the woods' than on a national or international level. Regional information (see Figure 24.25) and more localised information is therefore highly important.

Further useful sources of information about the demand and supply of labour are other employers, employer's associations, local job centres, and of course local and national newspapers.

Demographic trends

More people are available for work in Britain than ever before. At the beginning of 1990 the work force in employment stood at nearly 26 million, and more and

Figure 24.24 The British work force (in thousands, seasonally adjusted)

		Employees in employment				Self-employ-ment	HM forces	Work-related govt. training*	Workforce in employment	Change on previous quarter
		Manu-facturing	Services	Other	TOTAL					
1990	Q1	5 049	15 483	1 790	22 322	3 449	306	423	**26 501**	2
	Q2	5 014	15 557	1 782	22 353	3 461	303	410	**26 528**	27
	Q3	4 963	15 591	1 764	22 318	3 422	303	397	**26 440**	−88
	Q4	4 868	15 565	1 741	22 174	3 383	300	402	**26 259**	−181
1991	Q1	4 734	15 465	1 706	21 904	3 345	298	390	**25 937**	−322
	Q2	4 614	15 395	1 668	21 677	3 306	297	333	**25 613**	−324
	Q3	4 534	15 406	1 629	21 569	3 260	297	318	**25 445**	−169
	Q4	4 503	15 348	1 616	21 467	3 213	295	336	**25 311**	−134
1992	Q1	4 445	15 392	1 581	21 428	3 166	293	345	**25 233**	−78
	Q2	4 419	15 343	1 545	21 307	3 120	290	307	**25 023**	−210
	Q3	4 326	15 178	1 512	21 016	3 152	284	297	**24 749**	−274
	Q4	4 267	15 238	1 476	20 981	3 092	280	337	**24 689**	−60
1993	Q1	4 270	15 220	1 460	20 951	3 040	275	336	**24 601**	−88
	Q2	4 270	15 254	1 421	20 945	3 092	271	296	**24 603**	2
	Q3	4 257	15 394	1 380	21 031	3 126	267	288	**24 712**	109
	Q4	4 253	15 375	1 351	20 978	3 158	258	311	**24 705**	−6

*The figures for self-employment and work-related government training are not seasonally adjusted

Figure 24.25 Employees in employment in Britain, (in thousands, *not* seasonally adjusted)

	December 1993	Change from December 1992
South East including Greater London	6 899	−34
East Anglia	783	+4
South West	1 679	+22
West Midlands	1 975	+2
East Midlands	1 508	+1
Yorks and Humberside	1 828	−3
North West	2 307	−12
North	1 089	+5
Wales	957	+7
Scotland	1 975	−1
Britain total	21 001	−9

more jobs need to be created to absorb this potential labour force.

Figure 24.26 The British labour force projected up to the year 2000

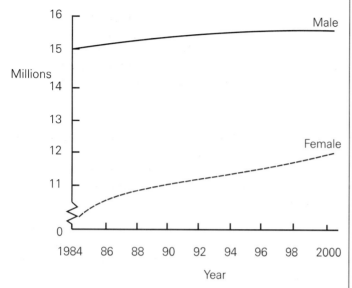

However, as was demonstrated all too painfully in the recession of the early 1990s, when a downturn comes in the economy then parts of the work force are 'shaken out'. In the 1980s and 90s successive Conservative government employment ministers have taken measures to increase flexibility in labour markets. This has made it increasingly easy for employers to shake out surplus employees.

Demographics are highly important to manpower planners. Generally speaking, older employees are thought to be more reliable while younger employees are thought to be more flexible and versatile. Female employees are seen as being more amenable to working part-time than are male employees. Manpower planners will therefore want to look at forecasts of future changes in the numbers of males/females, employees in different age groupings, as well as regional demographics. Demographic forecasts are usually quite reliable.

Case Study
Jobs, careers and training at McDonald's

The policy at McDonald's is to employ local people, and to train and develop them to their best potential.

McDonald's have two levels of recruitment opportunity: crew members or trainee managers. Crew members are paid hourly, which offers the benefit of part-time work with hours to suit each individual's requirements. The company

recruits graduates and non-graduates as trainee managers, but it believes firmly in also promoting from within. All crew members are provided with the opportunity to advance to management positions within the company, provided they show the necessary enthusiasm, hard work and loyalty.

Within the UK, McDonald's currently employs over 27 500 people. McDonald's has its own training centre where all levels of management staff are trained in the company's operations and procedures. All staff undergo continuous training and the company's internal training programme is recognised by the HCTC (Hotel and Catering Industry Training Company).

Two initiatives currently being offered by McDonald's are:

- the 'Seniors' programme, which is a recruitment scheme for older workers
- an education scheme which involves the award of scholarships to students undertaking a recognised business studies course, and awards to employees which can be used for either tuition or books.

Questions for discussion

1 Why is it McDonald's policy to employ local people?
2 What are the implications of this policy for manpower planning?
3 What factors will McDonald's need to consider to ensure that it is able to recruit enough people with the right skills?
4 What schemes does the case study identify for the development of McDonald's employees? How are these schemes likely to improve organisational performance?
5 What qualities are crew members likely to require if they are to move to managerial positions?
6 Why do you think McDonald's introduced a 'Seniors' programme?
7 Explain how McDonald's might benefit from its education scheme.

Government incentives

The government provides **incentives** to organisations to employ and train people, and clearly where these incentives are available they will have important implications for human resource planning. Government incentives reduce the cost of recruiting and employing people and act as a **subsidy** to human resource development.

Assistance may be given to create new jobs or to protect existing ones. However, to receive assistance an organisation needs to show that the scheme would not go ahead without the grant. Grants are given on the basis of the minimum amount required to get a project off the ground.

Regional assistance from the government falls into three categories:

- development of structurally backward areas
- development of rural areas
- conversion of regions of industrial decline.

It is also possible for firms to qualify for regional assistance from the European Union.

Today firms can benefit from employment and training packages supervised by the Department of Employment, Training Agency, and local Training and Enterprise Councils. Government incentives act as an important stimulant in that they reduce the cost of employing people.

Financial implications: budgets and costs

One of the main purposes of any form of planning is to allocate resources as effectively as possible. Given organisational objectives and the organisation's demand for labour, and the internal and external supply of labour, it will be necessary to allocate the human resource budget in order to maximise effectiveness.

The budget will be expressed in quantitative terms to attain objectives which are, as a general rule, also expressed in quantitative terms. Human resource planners have to plan how to make best use of budgets which are allocated to them for a given time period, so they have to establish priorities.

Usually the starting point will be to look at the existing and previous budgets to see the traditional pattern of expenditures. It will then be necessary to identify the major spending priorities for the coming period and to establish key headings. Spreadsheet packages are important tools for budgetary planning because they enable the user to try out a range of 'What if . . .?' alternatives.

The size of a human resource budget will probably depend on the priority given to human resources in the organisation. The budget is likely to be larger in organisations that are people-intensive – where human resource management is recognised as a distinct organisational activity – than in smaller organisations where these conditions do not apply.

Where a personnel department is responsible for recruitment, selection, training etc. as a functional responsibility, a budget will be allocated directly to that department. However, when line managers take on a variety of human resource tasks then part of the budget will be allocated to line managers.

When a personnel department introduces its own cost centres these should be consistent with the cost allocation and reporting systems which exist as part of the organisation's financial systems. The personnel department should not introduce an independent cost-coding system.

Effective human resource management can be a costly business. This is inevitable in 'intelligent organisations' in which people are the prime resource. In the past, human resource management was often seen as an undesirable cost of business activity. Today there is more emphasis on the benefits and an appreciation of the considerable strategic advantage that can be gained from effective people-centred organisations. However, any form of manpower planning will need to focus on using budget allocations in the best possible way to ensure the most appropriate supply of employees, and to retain and develop that work force within the organisation.

Further reading

- *A Handbook of Personnel Management Practice*, 4th edition, by Michael Armstrong. Kogan Page, 1993.
- *Investing in People – Towards Corporate Capability* by Peter Critten. Butterworth–Heinemann, 1993.
- *Management and Organisational Behaviour*, 3rd edition, by Laurie Mullins. Pitman, 1993.
- *Managing People* by Rosemary Thomson. Butterworth–Heinemann, 1993.
- *Human Resources Management – An Experiential Approach* by John Bernardin and Joyce Russell. McGraw–Hill, 1992.

Payroll Systems
HRIS Systems
↓
Integration

25 Administrative systems and evaluation

On completion of this chapter students should be able to:

- participate in the process of designing and using administrative and information systems which support the personnel function

- evaluate ways in which the personnel function can contribute to the development of the individual employee.

Part 1 Personnel administrative and information systems

The personnel function has an important administrative role within an organisation. In complex organisations it will require intricate information systems to manage a large flow of work and to maintain and update records. Examples of the sort of work that have to be carried out in an administrative capacity include:

- maintenance of **employee records**
- organisation and maintenance of **payment systems**
- **pension** administration and record-keeping
- production of records related to **disciplinary procedures** and disciplinary cases, etc.

Computers now play an invaluable part in personnel work. **Databases** give instant access to employee records, and provide users with other information. For example, although health and safety legislation runs to thousands of pages, computerised versions enable search facilities to identify relevant pieces of legislation in just a few seconds. **Spreadsheets** enable manpower planning budgets to be created and altered rapidly. Processing of documents such as formal letters to staff can be carried out quickly through **word-processing** facilities. These and a range of other **software** applications serve to make the workload of the personnel function more manageable.

Today, personnel managers want personnel information systems that will enable them to keep a track of employees as they progress through employment with the organisation, from the initial application and selection procedures, through training, development activities, accidents at work, sickness, pensions contributions, right through to retirement. All aspects of administration and employee progression should be incorporated in this information system.

Jennifer Rowley, in an article in *Business Studies* magazine, defined a management information system (MIS) as any system that provides information for the management activities carried out within an organisation. She then went on to make the point that today the term 'management information system' is reserved almost exclusively for computerised systems that 'consist of hardware and software which accept data and store, process and retrieve information'. Clearly, management information systems will be most effective if they meet the needs of organisations and managements in the specific contexts in which they operate.

Management information systems should be able to convert raw data into useful information. Too often in the past, computer programs were created which purported to support managers, but which were of little use in the specific situations in which managers were operating. Today there is more emphasis on providing solutions for specific organisational needs.

Information systems, then, should support the key activities of managers and meet their information needs for planning, organising, staffing, communicating, and using information appropriately. This chapter examines how a personnel information system (PIS) can help a manager to perform these activities more effectively.

Why use computers?

Most if not all practitioners in the human resource field now recognise the need for a computer-based personnel information system (CPIS). Michael Gallagher, in his book *Computers and Human Resource Management*, argues that four main factors have contributed to the growing recognition of the importance of a CPIS:

■ Today the emphasis is no longer on employment for life in organisations but on increased productivity, freezes on recruitment and flexible working practices.

Because the human resource is the most important in the organisation, we need to have as much information about it as possible in order to inform manpower and personnel policies.

■ The increasing burden of legislation and the need to generate statistics for government departments and other agencies requires higher-level data management capabilities.

■ The rapid development of computer technology means that desktop computers have the potential to handle huge quantities of information, and process this information rapidly.

■ There is now a ready availability of computer-based systems tailored to the needs of a personnel department.

The hardware and software used by the personnel function will need to be geared towards the specific needs of human resource managers operating in a particular context. Computers come with a comprehensive basic program, but human resource specialists will need to buy additional, more specialised programs, depending on how they intend using the machines. At the most basic level, a program will be needed which stores and manipulates data for payroll purposes (such as employee name, date of birth, date of joining the organisation, current salary scale and point, national insurance number and classification, starting and finishing point of contract, increment dates). Such programs are readily available.

In medium-sized and large organisations, much of the work connected with wages is done by computer. This involves the calculation of wages, the printing of wage slips and the production of payment instructions to a bank. Data relating to the time an employee works are picked up by computer from magnetic tape or other means, producing a continuous recording of wages. Computers are able to handle a lot of work quickly and accurately.

One danger of using a computer to calculate and record wages is the risk of losing information if something should happen to the wages program or disk. Therefore, it is prudent to keep at least two 'backup' copies of a disk which are updated at least once each day.

Today 'wired organisations' go far beyond the payroll system in the computerisation of their personnel function. An important contribution to this change has been the increasing sophistication of easy-to-use desktop computers. Computers used vary from the full-sized desk console with monitor, printer and feed, to slim, laptop (portable) machines with built-in screens. The latter have huge potential for carrying information around from site to site in a large organisation. A **modem** puts the machine 'on line' to a world of information technology. It also gives the computer the potential to use **electronic mail**, and an ability to communicate with other computer users.

Applications on desktop systems can be used for a wide variety of personnel activities, such as using a database to record interview statistics (e.g. for ethnic monitoring purposes), to record and analyse injury and sickness statistics, etc. Spreadsheets can be used to model changes in national insurance contributions on the overall wage bill (perhaps in anticipation of the government's budget), and for many other 'What if . . .?' activities.

Computerised personnel information systems

The development of a computer-based personnel program nowadays often involves a program designer or systems analyst working with an organisation to provide a tailored solution. Programs can be designed for organisations working in a particular industry or market sector.

Michael Gallagher defines a CPIS as 'a computer-based information system which is designed to support the operational, managerial and decision-making functions of the personnel division in an organisation'. A CPIS can support management at a number of levels of decision-making (see Figure 25.1).

At senior management level the CPIS should support strategic decision-making which involves the human resource, and thus it will inevitably be concerned with corporate policy-making. At a strategic level it is important to have information about likely changes in the future demand and supply of labour – for example, will there continue to be a ready supply of external labour to recruit? What is the current age profile of employees working for the organisation? Will shortages in key areas arise in the future? At a strategic level, too, it will be necessary to work out the future problems which may occur for recruitment, development, remuneration of staff etc. It will be important to analyse the current strengths and weaknesses of the employing organisation and the potential opportunities and threats (i.e. a SWOT analysis).

At a strategic level the organisation will be concerned with establishing its potential to maintain a competitive edge in human resourcing – for example, will its projected training and development investments keep it ahead of the field? If it increases the training and development budget, what will be the implications for future cost structures?

At middle management level the CPIS should provide managers with programs which support their work. They will want administration systems that enable them to record employee absences, changes in wage bills resulting from altering hours worked, monitoring the numbers of people working for the organisation with registered disabilities, etc. They will also want control systems – such as one whereby, if an employee's absence goes beyond a certain period, a letter is automatically sent to his or her home enquiring about the absence.

Middle managers will also want to use an information system that enables them to generate visual reports identifying human resource trends, and to do 'What if . . .?' projections (e.g. if we changed over from full-time workers to employing part-timers on a particular shift, what would be the implications?).

At an operational level, information systems are of tremendous use in carrying out routine activities – such as

Figure 25.1 CPISs at different levels of management

Level	Information use	Examples
Senior-management strategic level	Creation of strategic plans for organisational and human resource purposes	Manpower planning, forecasting human resource requirements, identifying changes in the human resources environment, and their possible implications
Middle-management planning and decision-making	Tactical and day-to-day human resource planning and decision-making	Creation of reports for human resource planning, development of control systems, creation of systems and programmes for routine work
Operational level	Use of IT for routine operations such as wages processing, looking at employee records, etc.	Wage payments, processing, recording of absences

the actual recording of wage payments, the recording of accidents, the sending out of notices, and the production of training materials.

Case Study
Transformed businesses

Many business writers use the term 'transformed business'. Such an organisation is run according to business processes rather than functional specialisms. The business processes are handled by teams of people from different functions, working together to achieve the main aim of the process.

In a transformed business, people involved in particular processes are given more freedom to make decisions and have more information at their fingertips by virtue of information technology. Instead of having to get permission from their line manager, they are allowed to make important decisions. Senior managers then become more

concerned with external matters than with running the internal system.

Organisations based on business processes put a high premium on information and on sharing IT facilities. IT has a very important role to play. Groups working together in a team will need to share information, and computer terminals of different specialists are linked so that information is available to all.

One major benefit is a cost reduction as a result of simplifying the work flow. A job stays with one individual or team instead of passing in batches from specialist to specialist. The team is given the authority to make decisions, as well as the information and tools needed.

Another benefit is the improved responsiveness to customers' needs. Front-line staff are given powers to act rather than pass problems up to line managers.

Improved job satisfaction can be a result. Staff can share customer satisfaction with a job well done. They are more challenged and more fulfilled. The staff are part of a learning, adapting organisation focused on the customers' requirements.

Questions for discussion

1 In a 'transformed organisation', who will be responsible for strategic human resource decisions?
2 Who will be responsible for tactical human resource decisions?
3 Who will be responsible for operational human resource decisions?
4 To what extent is information technology an essential ingredient of the transformed business?

The nature of an effective CPIS

The nature of an effective CPIS will depend on the organisation in question. A lot will depend on the size of budget available – the more money there is to spend, the better the opportunity to buy an effective system tailored to the actual needs. Of course, there is no point in buying a new system which is no better than the one currently being used. The structure of the organisation (centralised or decentralised, tall or flat) will influence the choice of system, as will the nature of the business (people-intensive or capital-intensive, manufacturing or services).

Michael Gallagher has set out the following as being key parts of any good CPIS:

■ *Personnel records* – These are records of individual employees, showing salaries and allowances, grades, dates of starting, age, etc.

- *Training records* – These show employees' qualifications, skills and experience, the sorts of courses they have been on, recent developments, etc.
- *Absence records.*
- *Pension records.*
- *Recruitment records* – These include details of all vacancies and applicants for posts.
- *Industrial relations data* – This should be kept in a meaningful way to support on-going negotiations on, for example, wages and conditions.
- *Manpower planning data* – This should enable human resource planners to identify past, present and future changes in the demand for and supply of labour from both internal and external sources.
- *Establishment* – This is the establishment of budgets within the personnel function, such as budgets of expected numbers required to fill particular posts, and actual numbers in order to identify actual and potential shortfalls.

Criteria for evaluating a CPIS

In the past most personnel information systems were paper-based. Files were kept on individual employees, as were records of job specifications, job advertisements and so on. This was a long and laborious process which depended on effective filing systems, and having long-serving company members who knew where all the records were kept and the procedures for processing information. Calculations and projections were done by manual methods, or by using calculators. Today, modern computers can quickly generate spreadsheets, and huge quantities of data can be accessed from computer databases to be instantly converted into charts and diagrams.

In evaluating the effectiveness of a computer-based personnel information system, an organisation needs to look at the extent to which it meets its needs.

- To what extent do the benefits of using the system outweigh the costs? How much time and money is saved by using the system? What extra things does the computer enable us to do which enhance our competitive edge? For example, if we want to consider increasing output by 5 per cent, will the system enable us to project the cost implications for increasing manpower? Will it enable us to examine alternative ways of using the labour force more productively? *The key to cost-effectiveness is in finding or designing a system that meets the specific needs of an organisation.*
- To what extent will the system provide our managers with more and better information? *The better the information, the better the decisions that can be made.*
- To what extent will the system enable users to be more proactive? Will users have access to accurate key

information to enable them to make informed contributions to strategic and middle-management decision-making, including manpower planning? *Having access to details about the supply and demand for labour, about training, labour turnover, etc. will enhance the credibility of the human resource function and its ability to inform strategic and tactical planning.*
- To what extent does the system enhance the creative use of information? *Forecasting, projections and modelling, for example, enable much more versatile and useful ways of using information for human resource purposes.*

In effect, a good system will enable human resource managers to make responses which are significant, intelligent, speedy, versatile, wide-ranging, up-to-date and authoritative.

It is essential that hardware and software match real needs. An expert in this field, Michael Gallagher argues that the system should have a number of basic requirements, as follows:

- It must be an on-line system.
- Confidentiality of data must be safeguarded.
- The emphasis should be on screens (not paper).
- The design of the system must maximise flexibility.
- It must be user-friendly.
- It should have an effective report generator/query language.
- Data must be easily accessible (e.g. through keys such as 'personnel number' and 'employee name').
- Information must be displayed in a way that is easy to understand.

Systems for personnel selection

Recruitment and selection is an area of personnel work that lends itself readily to systematic procedures.

Most organisations will regularly need to fill vacancies as staff turns over. Most of the steps involved are fairly routine – job analysis and specification, advertising the post, handling of correspondence from applicants, checking of applicants' capabilities and attributes against job criteria, sending out correspondence to applicants, organising interview times and locations, selecting applicants, including details of successful applicants in company records, etc. Two things immediately become obvious:

- Recruitment and selection can be simplified in a number of routine personnel administrative procedures.
- Most of these procedures can be computerised.

Figure 25.2 sets out the employer's schedule when selecting people for a job.

Figure 25.2 Job selection – the employer's schedule.

1. The need to recruit an extra member of staff is identified

2. A new job description is set out, or an existing one is updated

3. The job specification is reviewed and revised

4. Advertisements are designed and placed in appropriate media

5. Job details and application forms are sent to applicants

6. Applications are sorted out and a shortlist drawn up

7. Interview invitations are sent to shortlisted applicants

8. Interviews take place (and an oral job offer may be made)

9. Referees are invited to comment

10. If the references are satisfactory, a written job offer is sent

11. The offer is accepted

12. A written contract of employment is signed

A computer file can be set up for each candidate in competition for a particular job. Information can then be retrieved quickly by using key criteria, such as previous experience, qualifications above NVQ level 3, etc. A search of all candidates' records can then reveal those that meet the selection criteria.

Storing records in a computerised database speeds up administrative procedures enormously. For example, by keeping records of names and addresses of applicants, standard letters can be sent by a mail-merge process to all applicants, or to selected applicants.

Computerised records are also very useful for management purposes. For example, it is easy to discover the number of applicants for a particular post, the numbers meeting the selection criteria, who has been called for interview, the number of internal candidates, and so on.

Systems for training and assessment

Training and development are an important part of the personnel information system. An organisation can gain a competitive edge by having a better trained and developed work force than that of rivals. While ensuring that employees have access to new training and development opportunities, it is essential to keep up-to-date records of past training, the types of courses being run in and outside the organisation, and the budget set aside for training purposes. In addition it is important to keep a record of on-going appraisals and assessments of employees.

Records of employees' training and development will enable an organisation to decide which members of staff are in need of specific training, and to know quickly who holds particular qualifications that would enable them to perform a particular duty.

It may be useful to keep a record of employees' ratings of particular courses in case the organisation thinks of using that course in future. Also, records of particular courses which are on offer in-house and through external trainers may help the organisation to match employees' needs with training opportunities.

Statistical information and data analysis

The interpretation of statistical information is a key part of personnel work. Human resource managers manipulate vast quantities of people-related information and need to have this in advance of decision-making. This is particularly important if human resource management is to play a strategic rather than a firefighting role.

One of the main benefits provided by computers comes in the form of the manipulation of statistical information. For example, imagine that an organisation has agreed to pay a weekly bonus if plant absenteeism falls below 12 per cent, on the following scale:

Rate of absenteeism (%)	Bonus
11–12	£0.50
10–11	£1.35
9–10	£2.25
8–9	£3.40
7–8	£4.25
6–7	£5.10
5–6	£6.00

Clearly it would be essential to keep on top of the implications of this decision. For example, in the course of time the age and salary structure of employees working in the organisation might change, and the organisation might declare redundancies or take on extra staff. These developments could have implications for its bonus decision. This example illustrates the importance of statistical monitoring of such things as time lost through illness and other reasons for absence, changes in pay structures, budgeted use of manpower, etc.

Modelling is an important ingredient of human resource planning. A model is a form of simulation enabling us to ask 'What if . . .?' questions. For example, in pay bargaining we can model the possibilities presented by different wages and conditions offered to employees.

Transactions processing systems (TPSs) are important for the routine operation of the CPIS. Transactions are events which take place in an organisation. A TPS provides important information involving the following operations:

- *classifying data* – such as new applicants for a job according to their level of qualifications
- *calculating* – for example, calculating the number of hours lost due to sickness in a particular week
- *sorting* – arranging data into a sequence, such as listing employees according to the length of time since they last went on a training course
- *summarisations* – reducing large amounts of information into a briefer form, such as a summary of the most important trends in absences
- *storage* – of large quantities of personnel information for future use.

Legal requirements

Under the **Data Protection Act 1984**, organisations wishing to store personal information on a computer system must register with the government-appointed Data Protection Officer. They must indicate the type of data they are storing, and the use they make of it. Any individual has the right to request (on payment of a small fee) details of any information held about them by any

firm, and to
computerise
the scope of
use them mu

In terms of
information

- obtained
- held for s
  the peopl
- not disclo
  which it i
- in approp
  excessive
- accurate a
- kept only
- available
  individual
- kept in a secure place.

Clearly these are important considerations to bear in mind in the collection and disclosure of data, in its registration, and in the way personal data and records are kept. Employees should understand why particular pieces of information are being recorded (e.g. for ethnic monitoring purposes).

Records should not be kept or stored in such a way that unauthorised people can gain access. This is a particular problem for computerised personnel information systems which may be networked and have the potential to be 'hacked' into. Considerable discretion should be exercised in deciding what and what not to include in a CPIS. Certain 'sensitive' information – such as medical records and records of disciplinary actions – may best be kept on separate paper-based records in a locked filing cabinet.

The personnel fun
the development
Through this
will in turn
employe
The

...tion can make a major contribution to
...of individuals and groups of employees.
...process of development, the organisation
...benefit from more motivated, more effective
...es.

...nature of the work that an employee is expected to
...arry out will play a major part in determining whether he
or she joins an organisation, is committed to working for
it, and stays with it. In recent years many organisations
have moved away from the segmentation of work roles
towards job enlargement and job enrichment. This has
often been coupled with the development of the
'autonomous working group' which sets out to give more
freedom and independence to people at work.

Skill levels: the broad picture

Organisations' human resource activities need to be seen
within the context of the organisational environment. It is
therefore helpful to look at the existing level of skills in
the UK.

The trend towards an increased demand for higher-level,
better, broader and more flexible skills in the future is
clear:

- The number of highly skilled jobs is rising at the
  expense of lower-skilled ones.
- Higher skills are being demanded within most jobs.
- Skill requirements for many jobs are broadening,
  demanding greater flexibility among workers.

The qualification level of the UK work force is improving,
but the nation still lags well behind a number of our
major competitors such as Germany and Japan.

The nature of skills needed by different businesses varies
widely and continually changes. The Skills and Enterprise
Network suggests that when looking at skills it is helpful
to use a three-way classification (see Figure 25.3).

Core skills are very general skills that are needed in
almost any job. They include basic literacy and
numeracy, the ability to work well with others, and often
a basic capability to use information technology.

Vocational skills are needed in particular occupations or
groups of occupations, but are less useful outside these
areas. While these skills are less general than core skills,

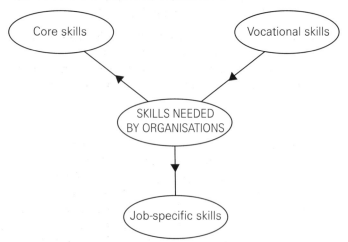

Figure 25.3 Skills needed by organisations

they are nonetheless highly transferable between jobs in a
given field. A simple example is the ability to use a
particular computer package.

Job-specific skills are those whose usefulness is limited
to a much narrower range of employment. Often these
are forms of knowledge rather than skills as traditionally
defined, and could be specific to individual firms. An
example could be the ability to set out and write a letter
in the company style.

In the past, assumptions were made that general
education was responsible for providing the core skills
and a foundation for the other skills; vocational skills
were the responsibility of employers and the education
and training system; and job-specific skills were the
responsibility of individual employers. Today these
assumptions are breaking down. For example, General
National Vocational Qualifications set out to develop core
skills, vocational skills *and* contribute to general
education.

Areas of increased skill demand

If the UK is to regain a competitive edge it must develop
the skill levels of employees. Clearly these skill
developments will need to be in response to increased
skill demands. Three areas of increased demand can be
identified:

- occupational trends
- higher skill needs
- broadening work demands.

Occupational trends

For many years the occupational mix of employment in
the UK has been moving towards higher-level
occupations, and away from manual (particularly
lower-skilled) jobs. This trend is highlighted in Figure

25.4, which is based on information provided by the Institute for Employment Research in 1994.

Overall, new jobs are most likely to arise in skill-intensive knowledge-based occupations, in services and manufacturing. An increase in higher-level qualifications and skills will be needed to match occupational changes.

Higher skill needs

In 1994, according to the Skill Needs in Britain survey, nearly two-thirds of employers reported that the skills needed by the average employee were rising. Larger organisations and service sector establishments in particular noted this trend. Increases in skill needs were particularly strongly associated with the use of computerised or automated equipment. Three-quarters of users of such equipment had seen skill levels in their jobs increasing. The role of 'monitoring skills' in jobs has increased, reflecting the change in many jobs from manual dexterity to responsibility for automated integrated equipment or processes. The use of 'social skills', especially communication skills, workplace social relations and customer contact, was also positively linked to increased skill levels in jobs.

Broadening work demands

An increasingly wide range of general work skills are demanded in many jobs. Job enlargement and job enrichment have brought about an increasing need for multiple skills. Much of this change is the result of new technology and restructuring of the work force. Job enlargement can largely be seen as taking on a larger number of roles at a similar level of the production process. Job enrichment is associated with the managing of tasks at different levels.

Education and training both have key roles to play in achieving the necessary skill levels. The education and training sector needs not only to supply the wide range of core skills, but also has a role in developing the broad vocational skills needed for increased flexibility within broad types of job. The NVQ approach has the capacity to help with skills specification and to aid job definition.

Case Study
Utilisation of skills

To utilise skills effectively, employers need to specify accurately a range of skill requirements – technical, personal, and behavioural – and recruit or develop employees to meet this specification. Where employers fail to do this accurately, employees may be under-utilised.

There is some evidence in the UK that there is a poor match between general entry level qualifications and early utilisation. This is most obvious in research in the information technology labour market, where some observers have noted a 'creeping graduatisation' of technical-level jobs.

A series of studies by the National Institute of Economic and Social Research in the 1980s showed that the UK had a deficient supply of skills at the intermediate level and a lack of breadth at craft level in a number of occupations and activities.

Because of the skills shortage at intermediate levels,

Figure 25.4 Projected change in employment by occupation in the UK, 1993–2001

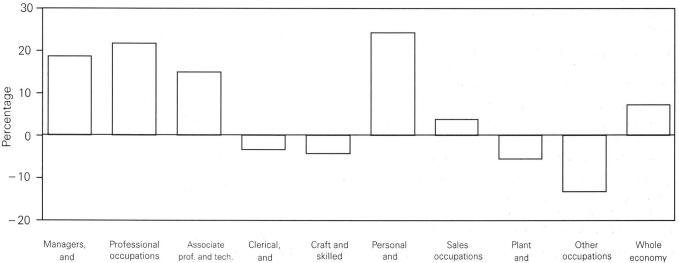

graduates were being dragged down to cover the deficiencies. The net effect is that people are operating below their potential skill levels.

Questions for discussion

1 *What deficiencies in skills utilisation are outlined in the above case?*
2 *What do you think would be the likely cause of this mismatch in skills utilisation?*
3 *What are the implications for inefficiency at organisational and national levels?*
4 *What suggestions would you put forward to secure a better match between skills and jobs?*

Skills audit

At a national level it is essential to identify the skills that will be required in the future and to audit existing skill levels. Such an audit makes it possible to identify training needs to be met at a macroeconomic level.

In exactly the same way it is essential for individual organisations to forecast the skills they will require in the future and to plan ways of providing these.

An organisation can recruit externally, but often it makes far more sense to develop skills within. Development programmes should be aimed at ensuring career progression and development for existing employees.

Problems with the supply of skilled labour can have a damaging effect on efficiency and competitiveness. A survey carried out by the Department of Employment in 1994 showed that a significant percentage of workplaces had skill shortages that were having an effect on reducing output. Employers were taking a number of measures to counteract this difficulty, including:

- increasing the range of jobs carried out by current employees
- increasing the productivity of current employees
- increasing training and changing the organisational structure of the workplace.

In this way, organisations need to be proactive in auditing skills and taking steps to ensure that appropriate skills are provided.

Employers can support the development of employees by offering sufficient education and training to meet the requirements of a modern workforce. A number of major companies, such as Rover, have in-house training schemes which encourage employees to engage in a lifelong learning process. Many other organisations are developing programmes for employees to work towards progressively higher NVQ levels.

Training and Enterprise Councils (TECs) and **Independent Training Organisations** (ITOs) have a key role in supporting organisations by:

- raising employers' awareness of the importance of anticipating future skill needs, developing a systematic strategy for meeting them, and if possible becoming an 'Investor in People' (see Chapter 10)
- liaising between employers and educational institutions at all levels to ensure that education and training provision generates the skills required for the future.

Benefits to organisations – a summary

There are a number of clear benefits to an organisation of carrying out a skills audit and evaluation:

- The organisation is able to develop a clear picture of the existing facets of its human resource.
- It is able to project future requirements.
- It is then able to bridge the gap between existing capability and required ability.
- It is able to develop an effective human resource strategy for the on-going motivation and development of its human resource.
- It is able to budget for training and development programmes.
- A clear understanding of human resource needs enables it to develop a competitive advantage in every aspect of organisational performance.
- The organisation is able to identify the key people required to meet current organisational objectives.

Skills audit and evaluation is central to organisational objectives. It is the basis for having the right people in the right place at the right time, with the right level of motivation. This is the on-going challenge for development and training.

Identifying training needs

Stephen Robbins, in his book *Personnel – The Management of Human Resources*, suggested that from the organisation's point of view four questions need to be answered:

- What are the goals of the organisation?
- What tasks need to be completed to achieve these goals?
- What behaviours are necessary for each job-holder to complete his or her tasks?

- What deficiencies do job-holders display in the knowledge, skills or attitudes required to perform the necessary behaviours?

This is a helpful model because it creates a direct connection between training for knowledge, skills and attitudes, and the achievement of organisational objectives (see Figure 25.5).

Figure 25.5 Plugging the training gap.

Successful achievement of
organisational objectives

Creation of appropriate knowledge,
skills and attitudes

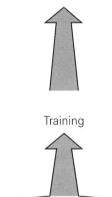

Training

Identification of deficiencies in
knowledge, skills and attitudes

In order to identify deficiencies in knowledge, skills and attitudes, it is necessary to look for indications of deficient performance. Examples are customer complaints, poor-quality reject levels, accidents, poor attendance, etc. The training manager or individual responsible for training will need to identify ways of plugging the training gap.

- *Knowledge development* is concerned with developing what the learner already knows about the task in hand. A trainee teacher has to improve subject knowledge, a trainee electrician has to be able to put together an electrical circuit and to be aware of which materials act as good and bad conductors of electricity.
- *Skills development* is concerned with the acquisition of abilities acquired by training. The trainee teacher will need to develop clear communication and voice

control, the electrician will need to develop the art of bending and twisting wires.
- *Attitude development* is concerned with influencing the way in which a person behaves towards something – for example, developing a caring and concerned attitude in a new teacher or a safety-first attitude in an electrician.

Training at an organisational level

It is essential to maintain a competitive advantage. An organisation must therefore continually be assessing current states of employee development in order to identify ways of adding value to the human resource. Whenever the organisation changes its objectives it must identify the training needs to take it forward, especially when it introduces new technologies or processes. Changes in the law or in consumer attitudes may push or pull the organisation towards new training initiatives, on health and safety at work, on consumer service, etc.

Training at a departmental level

Training needs will be identified by reviews of current performance against expected development. If the department has a poor record on accidents or attendance there may be a training need. When the department is asked to take on new responsibilities, then training will be required – for example when school departments take on the responsibility for the mentoring of new teachers.

Training at a job level

Training needs will be identified by indicators such as accidents and poor performance in the workplace. Job enhancement and job enrichment mean taking on wider and often new responsibilities which will require training and preparation.

Training at an individual level

Appraisal interviews are an important way of identifying next steps which can be taken to carry an individual forward. Assessment-centre ratings can identify strengths and weaknesses of individuals.

Case Study
Employee training and development

The following is an extract from the Employee's Handbook of a food-processing company.

'The company has a development and training programme for employees. For those with potential who wish to progress, opportunities exist for widening their experience and for promotion.

'The most important person in this company is your immediate boss. As well as giving you everyday instruction which will enable us to manage our business, he/she will be able to help you in many of the problems that arise in the course of your employment.

'In your first six months there will be opportunities during appraisal interviews with your supervisor to review your performance, and to identify any training and development needs. The training needs of all employees are constantly reviewed. Together with your supervisor, line leader and a number of designated instructors, we will teach you the skills you require. As important, you will be taught the safe way to work.

'The company encourages you to continue with education programmes in your spare time. If you want to take up a spare-time course of study, discuss it with the Personnel Manager who will help and advise in choosing the course. Under certain conditions, the company will refund your tuition and examination fees.

Questions for discussion

1 *Why do you think this company emphasises the importance of training?*
2 *Who will be the prime beneficiaries of the training process?*
3 *Should training be seen as a cost or a benefit?*
4 *Why do you think the handbook says 'The most important person in this company is your immediate boss'? What does this tell you about the company organisation? Do you think that the most important person should be seen to be an employee's immediate boss?*
5 *Give examples of the company's involvement in (a) on-the-job training, and (b) off-the-job training.*
6 *How does the company benefit from reviewing the training needs of its employees? Does the handbook give you the impression that the training needs of all employees are given equal weighting?*

Organisational approaches to identifying training needs

It is often argued that the emphasis an organisation places on training is the acid test of its commitment to human resources development. The organisation which fails to train staff will become highly reliant on external sources of labour supply. Survey after survey in recent years has, however, identified the UK's poor performance on the training front. There is much room for improvement in education and training in the workplace.

Many employees in the key intermediate grades have no more than basic qualifications. Only 50 per cent have A-levels or a vocational equivalent. Of course, those without such qualifications can pick up skills 'on the job' – but they may be slower to adapt, which reduces the competitive edge of an organisation.

Effective management is essential for business success, and for developing the potential of employees. However, a substantial minority of the UK's managers (almost 40 per cent) do not have qualifications at A-level equivalent or above.

In late 1994, the National Advisory Council for Education and Training Targets suggested new targets for Lifetime Learning. These are discussed on pages 269–70.

A number of writers argue that because training and development are expensive activities they should be appraised carefully by organisations in investment terms. Organisations can, for example, make a choice between investing heavily in the development of a large number of employees or focusing most of the investment on a smaller number of targeted employees. Organisations must consider the return they expect to make on individuals and their training and development. It would be pointless to invest in individuals whose return on investment would be zero.

Organisations therefore need to weigh up the risks and the returns of a particular development activity. The returns would include improved job performance and productivity sustained beyond the payback period on the investment.

The risks involved would be that:

- the employee might not stay with the organisation up to the payback time
- the employee might not benefit from the training owing to lack of ability
- training may prove to be inappropriate so that it does not transfer into performance
- employees will not be sufficiently motivated to make use of the training.

Cummings and Schwab, in their book *Performance in Organisations*, developed a model for assessing human resource investment decisions. Their model describes three types of training and development programmes:

Figure 25.6 Application of Cummings and Schwab's model

Programme	Performance and potential of individuals
DAP	Individuals who have performed well in the past, have made good use of training and development, and have a lot of potential for the future
MAP	Individuals who have performed well in the past, have made good use of training and development, but have little potential for future on-going development (e.g. someone close to retirement)
RAP	Individuals who have shown little interest in training and development and have little potential for future development

- A Developmental Action Programme (DAP) is based on a high level of investment. This will involve extensive participation by subordinates in decision-making and an extensive development programme to increase the promotability of the trainee.
- A Maintenance Action Programme (MAP) implies a more modest investment. It involves less intensive training and is designed to combat skill obsolescence rather than to create promotability.
- A Remedial Action Programme (RAP) is a low-level (minimal) investment scheme. Training and development focuses simply on setting performance targets coupled with feedback on performance. If the employee fails to improve, the cost to the organisation has been insignificant.

In this model, an organisation will choose an appropriate type of human resource investment in individuals depending on previous performance and potential. Figure 25.6 illustrates the types of programme that would be justified for different individuals.

Methods of managing learning and self-development

The management of learning and self-development should be seen as a mutually beneficial process for organisations and the individuals who will be involved. It should be a carefully planned process.

The **competence-based approach** to learning has become particularly popular in the UK in recent years

and lies at the heart of National Vocational Qualifications (NVQs) and General National Vocational Qualifications (GNVQs). The process involves identifying the competences require to carry out specific activities and improving employees' competence through education and training coupled with practical activities. The main stages are as follows:

- Identify and describe the competences needed to carry out a task successfully. These competences are identified by a Lead Body which is responsible for setting out standards in a particular industry.
- Set out clear and understandable performance criteria which can be explained to trainees so that they know exactly what they have to do to show competence.
- Create means of assessing whether competence has been achieved to a set standard.
- Trainees should then experiment with the use of a competence to show that they are acquiring capability in its use. For example, trainee hairdressers will experiment with mixing hair dyes.
- Trainees should then practice the competence (e.g. by mixing hair dyes and applying it to a model's hair).
- Once the trainee has acquired consistency through practice, he or she should apply the competence in a real job situation.

Trainees who successfully complete **units of competence** can accumulate **credits** towards a vocational qualification in a particular job area. The competence model provides a useful way of meeting skills requirements by providing clear objectives (performance criteria).

Training and development cannot be forced on employees. It is essential for managers to create a commitment to learning and personal development. This is best achieved when organisations stress the value they place on development.

When employees fail to meet standards this should be discussed at appraisal meetings. It is likely that the organisation will be able to provide opportunities through training and development for individuals to enhance their performance potential. From the organisation's point of view, an important aspect of appraisal will be to identify learning and development requirements for all employees. Strategies related to the management of change will need to be employed to build a commitment.

Types of learning and training opportunities

Today, learning and training opportunities for employees are many and varied.

In-house schemes

In-house training schemes are still very popular, particularly in large organisations. The advantage of having your own training facility is that it can be tailored specifically to your own needs. It is also possible to evaluate the effectiveness of such training and to modify it to changing circumstances. The style and method of training will reflect the culture of the organisation and reinforce its values. However, in a dynamic business environment there are benefits to exposing employees to different perceptions that can come only from outside the organisation. Internal trainers may have only a limited range of skills, so increasingly organisations are contracting out training functions to agencies.

Outside consultants

Consultants have expertise which they can apply to specific organisational needs. They need not be a drain on resources because they are employed only for specific contracts, and their services can quickly be dropped if their input proves to be fruitless. A variety of consultants can be employed to cover many different training needs. However, a disadvantage is that the use of outsiders can offend existing organisation members, who may feel 'I could have done that for half the price!'. In addition it may limit the development of members of the organisation who could perhaps have benefited from being given responsibility for that particular aspect of training.

Management colleges

There are a number of management colleges in various parts of the country. Organisation members can benefit from working together with other learners from a variety of similar (and dissimilar) organisations who are attending courses to develop particular knowledge skills and attitudes. Visiting a management college can be a welcome career break in itself and may stimulate employees who can bring new ideas back into the organisation. Qualifications such as degrees and diplomas also serve to increase the motivation and self-esteem of learners. However, not all the courses on offer are appropriate – some are too theoretical and divorced from the everyday reality of organisational life. Some may also have a style and approach which clashes with the culture of the particular organisation that is paying for the course.

Courses are also put on by training organisations in many parts of the country. For example, the Industrial Society offers short, highly professional courses.

Distance learning

Distance learning involves following a course at a distance from the teacher or trainer, usually by correspondence or some other means. The media of teaching and learning are increasingly sophisticated today, and include videos, audio-cassettes, on-line computer terminals and CD–ROM. The learner is able to pursue the course at an individual pace. This is a cost-effective means of training because much of the learning can be done at home.

The lack of human contact is a disadvantage for some, who need a stimulus and motivating force. The learner is left largely to his or her own initiative to make progress, although tutoring is possible through letter and report writing, telephone calls, electronic mail, etc.

Open learning

The Open University has been particularly successful in pioneering open learning in this country. The Open University and Open College in partnership with the BBC have established a way of providing courses up to degree standard for many people who previously would have missed out on such education. Learners study through books, notes, television programmes, audio-cassettes, and other means. Course members then attend intensive summer schools, and meetings with course tutors and other students. They are able to choose units which relate to their specific needs. The Open University makes sure that the units are written in a way that is accessible to a wide audience.

Organisations may find that the courses are focused more on individual needs than on organisational needs. They are concerned more with education and personal development than with job-specific training.

Computer-assisted learning

Computer-assisted learning is a growth area. Learning programmes are based on individuals following a course with the aid of computers, books, manuals, CD–ROM, etc. The programmes are interactive – the learner is faced with a menu of options based on information that has been pre-programmed into the computer, and given feedback on particular decisions made. The learner is then able to ask for further information. Hence, simulations enable learners to experience an activity or situation 'for real', without having to worry about the implications of making mistakes.

'Virtual reality' is increasingly being used in training. The learner is able to experience a simulated scenario which feels as if it is real. 'Interactive video' is another popular form of training and learning.

Secondment

Secondment involves placing someone with another organisation for a period. The aim is to broaden experience, so that the individual can bring back skills as well as contacts to the organisation. Employees can be seconded to other divisions within a large organisation, with the same aim.

Mentoring and coaching

Mentoring and coaching involves a more experienced member of an organisation pairing up with a less experienced member for guidance and training purposes (see page 262).

Designing training and development programmes

In designing training and development programmes it is essential to start by looking at the objectives of training – what is to be achieved at the end of the period. In the well-managed organisation training objectives will be part of corporate strategy which feeds back into the organisational goals and missions.

The design of training and development programmes will also depend on an understanding of the employees who are to benefit. This involves looking at their previous learning experiences. Learning opportunities need to be designed in such a way that trainees will derive maximum possible benefit from them. For example, there would be little point in giving formal lectures to individuals with only short concentration spans who would benefit more from an active approach to learning. Training courses need to be designed so that they move trainees on in steady steps and cater for a variety of abilities and aptitudes. Training and development should be seen as an on-going process.

Review, appraisal and reward processes

Appraisal is more traditionally associated with managerial development. However, this traditional perspective is changing so that today more and more employees within organisations are involved in appraisal.

There are many different types of appraisal system. **Qualitative appraisal** may take the form of a relatively unstructured interview in which the appraiser develops a

report on the performance of the appraisee. Alternatively, a **quantitative appraisal** may be employed in which the appraiser ranks performance along a scale – excellent, good, adequate, inadequate, etc.

The appraisee will be seen at regular time intervals, and will be given feedback on job performance. The assessment of individuals will normally be against some specified performance standards, often related to a job description. At a review meeting it is possible to establish individual objectives and targets for the subsequent time period. Individual development plans can then be created which set out how employees will work towards targets. The review meeting will also include an assessment of performance over the previous period against targets. This assessment will often be linked to rewards (e.g. an individual who has met or exceeded targets will be entitled to performance-related pay). The process is illustrated in Figure 25.7.

Figure 25.7 The review, rewards, appraisal process

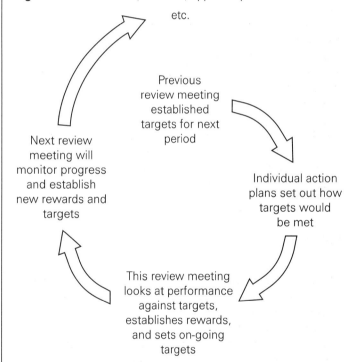

etc.

Previous review meeting established targets for next period

Individual action plans set out how targets would be met

This review meeting looks at performance against targets, establishes rewards, and sets on-going targets

Next review meeting will monitor progress and establish new rewards and targets

Appraisal also provides an excellent framework for designing training and development programmes. The review will act as a basis for establishing ways of improving performance. Learning and development goals will therefore be an integral part of this process.

Clearly, learning and development must be tied in with the reward system of the organisation, so that employees see them as both worthwhile in their own right and valued by the organisation. Appraisal should be seen by the organisation as an excellent vehicle for creating programmes for employee development.

Further reading

- *Managing People and Technological Change* by John Bailey. Pitman, 1993.

- *The Human Resource – Managing People at Work in the 1990s* by Roland Pearson. McGraw–Hill, 1991.
- *Communication, Technology and the Development of People* by Bernard Woods. Routledge, 1992.
- *Behaviour in Organisations*, 5th edition, by Jerald Greenberg and Robert Baron. Prentice Hall, 1995.

9

Planning and making decisions

26 The planning framework

O n completion of this chapter students should be able to:

- examine the process of organisational planning

- analyse the relationship between corporate, functional and individual objectives

- evaluate objectives of different business functions within the overall organisational plan.

Defining the planning framework

In his book, *In Search of Management*, Tony Watson argues that in the past managers were trained to identify the managerial role by remembering the mnemonic POSDCORB:

- Planning
- Organising
- Staffing
- Directing
- Coordinating
- Reporting
- Budgeting.

He explains that more recent research gives a different picture of management and he quotes the summary Rosemary Stewart gives (in *Managing Today* and *Tomorrow*) of her research:

> 'The picture that emerges . . . is of someone who lives in a whirl of activity, in which attention must be switched every few minutes from one subject, problem, and person to another; of an uncertain world where relevant information includes gossip and speculation.'

Management work varies widely from one manager to another depending on the type of organisation, the people he or she works with, the nature of the work, time constraints and many other factors. From Rosemary Stewart's perspective, management work becomes less clear cut and perhaps more 'disorganised'. Tony Watson sets out to synthesise these disparate views based on his own experience of management work. He suggests that we:

> 'recognise that management as a function does indeed have the various sub-functions of planning, coordinating, commanding and the rest. Yet we should equally recognise that the activities which bring about these functions do not fulfil them in as obvious or as direct a way as people once thought. Because of . . . [factors such as widespread ambiguity, the existence within organisations of a variety of often conflicting interests and purposes, etc.] planning, coordinating, "commanding" and the rest can only be done in what amounts to "feeling the way in the dark". And this involves the incremental processes of incessant

negotiating, guessing, manipulating, and speculating which researchers observe as central to managerial behaviour.'

Watson, therefore, suggests using caution when making assumptions about the ease with which managers can manage. Management planning is often an imprecise art, struggling to achieve clarity and purpose in a changeable and sometimes hostile environment.

Planning is concerned with developing a hierarchy of plans which can be translated into actions. It involves defining organisational objectives and setting out routes to meet these objectives. Planning also makes it possible to evaluate and control performance against clear performance standards. Without evaluation there is no control.

Figure 26.1 shows the relationship between activities and objectives. With a clear planning framework based on specific objectives, it becomes possible to direct many, if not all, operational activities towards meeting organisational objectives. However, in a dynamic business world based on turbulence, this is easier said than done. Nonetheless, developing a clear planning framework should be an important aim of any organisation.

Figure 26.1 Providing direction through planning

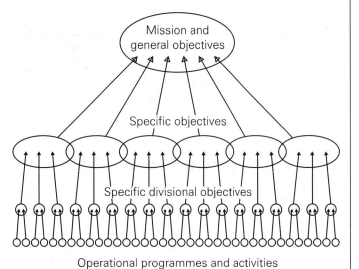

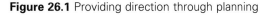

Operational programmes and activities

The hierarchy of plans

Organisational planning takes place at a number of levels (see Figure 26.2). It is particularly important that managers are aware of these different levels and that top-level planning provides clear direction for lower-level planning.

Figure 26.2 A hierarchy of plans

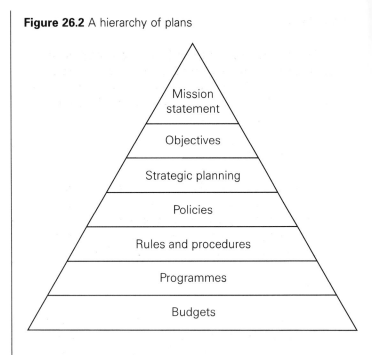

An important starting point is to establish the purpose or mission of the organisation. Objectives and goals can then be formulated which direct the organisation and its activities towards the achievement of its mission. Strategies can be formulated at a high level in the organisation, setting out key aspects of direction and focus. Once strategies are in place, policies can be established to put into practice strategic decisions. At a lower level it is essential for the organisation to plan procedures and rules which outline day-to-day operations as well as programmes for putting activities into action. An important part of operating activities will be working towards budgetary plans.

From mission to ground-level operational activities

In this section we look at how the vision or mission of an organisation can be translated into a variety of individual activities which all pull towards the achievement of that mission.

Imagine that a new manager of an English football team makes a public statement: 'Over the next three years we are going to become the team that all other teams want to emulate. We shall go on to head the Premier League and win European honours, as well as playing the most attractive football in England.' This manager is building up a big vision. However, the vision will not materialise unless it can be translated into all the activities the club engages in, including training, youth development, sponsorship projects, ticket sales, and supporter involvement. Effective planning, therefore, involves creating a framework of plans from top to bottom.

Objectives

Objectives should provide the reference point upon which all decisions about the future of an organisation can be made. Corporate objectives are made for the company as a whole and sub-sets of objectives are created for each sub-section of the organisation.

Strategic planning

As we shall see on pages 658–9, strategy is concerned with basic directions, broad intentions and the general approach to business planning. Strategy is often formulated at higher levels in organisations and maps out the general objectives for organisational activity.

Policies

Policies are general statements which guide thinking and action in decision-making. They define an area within which a decision is made and ensure that the decision contributes to the meeting of an objective. For example, a large organisation will have policies on equal opportunities, health and safety at work, dealing with customers, etc.

Increasingly, organisations set out their policies in writing. For example, all schools have written policies covering assessment, sexual harrassment at work and many other areas. Policies are forward thinking. They clarify ways in which people should operate and act. People at work can then simply follow the guidelines of the policy rather than having to analyse a situation every time it appears. For example, if there is a clear equal opportunities policy, then the human resources department will be able to set up interviews as part of selection procedure according to policy guidelines.

Rules and procedures

Rules and procedures set out a required method of handling particular activities. For example, the following is part of the customer care procedure at the Body Shop:
> *'SMILE DAMMIT SMILE*
> *Never treat customers as enemies,*
> *approach them as potential friends.*
>
> *Think of customers as guests,*
> *make them laugh.*
>
> *Acknowledge their presence within 30 seconds:*
> *smile, make eye contact, say hello.*
>
> *Talk to them within the first 3 minutes.*
> *Offer product advice where appropriate.*
> *Smile. Always thank customers and invite them back . . .*

> *TREAT CUSTOMERS AS YOU'D LIKE TO BE TREATED.'*

Rules must be followed and allow no discretion for interpretation; procedures set out more flexible guidelines.

Programmes

A programme is a set of policies, procedures, rules and tasks which make up a particular course of action, e.g. a road-building programme, a youth development programme, etc. Programmes may be on a very large scale, such as a school development programme, or on a small scale, e.g. a programme introduced by a single supervisor to increase the skills of a group of workers through a training programme.

All programmes require the coordination and timing of a network of activities. They are usually part of a network of overlapping programmes. Planning programmes is important because it is concerned with an organisation's day-to-day activity. Planning a programme may involve tools such as critical path analysis (see page 278). One of its key aspects is planning for provision of resources, such as staff, space and equipment.

Budgets

Money is always one of the key resources required for any series of programmes. A budget sets out the financial requirements for the plan. The financial operating budget is often called the **profit plan**. It is expressed in numbers, e.g. units of money, units of product, labour hours, machine hours, etc.

Corporate objectives and mission statements

Many organisations in the UK have adopted vision and mission statements. Most public companies include a mission statement in their annual report, and aspects of this statement frequently appear in advertisements.

A **vision** is a mental image of how things might be. It sets out to crystallise organisational aims in a clear picture based on 'excellence'. The vision should be inspiring and challenging. It may be created by the leader of an organisation or may result from a process of joint 'visioning' by members of the organisation.

It is important that a vision is achievable and meaningful. For example, a second-hand car dealer who had a reputation for selling poor quality vehicles would find it difficult to make convincing a vision of 'being the best quality car business in the country'. Vision usually relates to quality, caring values, service to customers, concern for community values, etc.

A **mission statement** is a generalised form of objective which sets out the overriding purpose of the organisation. For example, in 1962 the American President John Kennedy set out a mission for the space agency NASA to 'land a man on the moon and return him safely to earth' before the decade was over. NASA succeeded in both of these aims.

The mission statement of the Automobile Association (AA) focuses on people and service. It aims to 'make AA membership truly irresistible' and 'to be the UK's leading and most successful motoring and personal assistance organisation'. The key to the AA's success is, therefore, the extent to which it manages to achieve its mission.

In its mission statement Pedigree Petfoods, the leading producers of pet food in the UK, says:

> 'We work constantly towards identifying and satisfying consumer needs. It is the activity from which all else springs. We never forget that we cannot influence millions of consumer choices until we have convinced first one, then a second and a third consumer that our product is worthy of purchase. Our success is based on thorough research of the wide range of needs for pet animals and their owners. The knowledge which we gain is translated into a range of quality products which satisfy these needs better than any of our competitors.'

Clearly, then, Pedigree Petfoods describes itself as a market-driven organisation.

Today, it is fashionable for large organisations to place copies of their mission statement in prominent locations in the workplace so that employees are constantly reminded of it. Very often, part of the mission relates to creating quality working relationships.

Sometimes organisations adopt aggressive mission statements in competitive markets. For example, Japanese motor cycle manufacturer Honda's 'We will crush, squash, slaughter Yamaha' (one of its major rivals). This proved to be effective.

Corporate objectives are those set out for the whole organisation. They are often expressed in financial terms which are fomulated by senior managers, e.g. desired profit levels, sales targets, rates of growth. These corporate objectives are designed to meet the expectations of shareholders and other key stakeholders.

Corporate objectives are typically created using a top-down approach. The board of directors of a business, for example, identifies corporate objectives for a forthcoming financial period. Company-wide objectives are then broken down into divisional objectives, etc.

Figure 26.3 A hierarchy of objectives

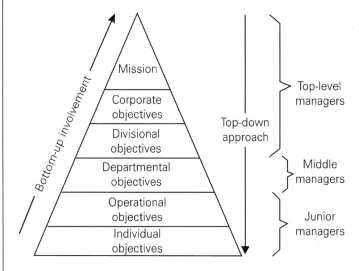

Within an organisation there is a hierarchy of objectives. (see Figure 26.3). Working down the organisation, objectives become more specific, e.g. when they relate to particular operational activities.

Strategic objectives are translated into more specific overall objectives, covering key result areas for the organisation. Peter Drucker, for example, identifies the following key result areas in *The Practice of Management*:

- market standing
- innovation
- productivity
- physical and financial resources
- profitability
- manager performance and development
- employee performance and attitude
- public responsibility.

Specific objectives that could be drawn from some of the key result areas might include:

- to become the market leader by next year (market standing)
- to increase output per head by 5 per cent within two years (productivity).

These objectives then need to be translated down to the lowest level of operational activity. For example, senior managers establish divisional objectives, and divisional managers then translate these into departmental and functional objectives.

Case Study
Company founder with a mission

In 1986 Anita Roddick, founder of the Body Shop, wrote in *Body and Soul*:

'What is our mission statement? It's easy – we will be the most honest cosmetic company around. How will we do it? That's easy too – we will go diametrically in the opposite direction to the cosmetic industry.'

More recently, she has written:

'We have evolved a simple credo. It goes like this: you can run a business differently from the way most businesses are run; you can share your prosperity with your employees and empower them without being in fear of them; you can rewrite the book in terms of how a company interacts with the community; you can rewrite the book on Third World trade and global responsibility and on the role of educating the company, customers and shareholders; finally, you can do all this and still play the game according to the City, still raise money, delight the institutions and give shareholders a wondrous return on their investment.'

Questions for discussion

1 *How would you go about converting the mission and credo of the Body Shop into generalised objectives?*
2 *How might these generalised objectives work down into specific objectives for operational activities in individual shops?*

Generalised objectives at corporate level feed down into 'unit objectives', e.g. individual schools under local education authority supervision, departments within a department store, etc. These objectives tend to be of an operational nature, that is, they are concerned with translating overarching objectives into practical and measurable steps.

Each tier of objectives needs to:

■ contribute to the attainment of corporate objectives
■ be attainable
■ be unambiguous
■ be measurable, wherever possible.

Many people argue that objectives must be measurable, so that their success, or otherwise, may be identified. Johnson and Scholes, however, disagree. They argue in *Exploring Corporate Strategy* that 'open' statements of objectives can be just as helpful as 'closed' ones. They believe that open objectives can play a crucial role in focusing strategy. They quote the example of open-ended mission statements. Statements such as 'to be a leader in technology' are not easily measurable, but they concentrate thinking within an organisation.

However, Johnson and Scholes agree that closed objectives are essential in many planning situations and are particularly important where there is no scope for getting things wrong.

Criteria for setting objectives

Organisations need to consider a number of criteria when setting objectives.

1 Objectives should be set out as clearly as possible. Managers and their subordinates need to be aware of what they are aiming to achieve. Vague aims such as 'to increase efficiency', 'to be more successful', or 'to reduce levels of delinquency' have a limited effect. At the same time, objectives should not be drawn so tightly that there is little room for applying alternative, equally successful solutions.
2 Wherever possible, objectives should be quantified. In many cases it is possible to identify appropriate measures, such as the time to complete a project, reduction in the level of waste in a particular activity, desired market share, unit costs, return on investment, etc. In setting out an objective it may be helpful to ask:

■ What is it?
■ When is it expected to be completed?
■ Where will it be achieved?
■ Who will be involved?

Clear and precise objectives should be evolved in the early days of planning, so that control mechanisms can then be established to ensure plans are being achieved.

Task

Look at the planning process in your local college or place of study. What are the general and specific objectives of these plans? (Examples might be student recruitment figures, expansion of building projects, development of library facilities, student attendance rates, pass rates on particular courses, etc.)

a How are these objectives created?
b How is the achievement of objectives monitored?
c What control mechanisms are in place to ensure that objectives are met?

---

3 Objectives should be broken down into those which are considered essential and those which are desirable at a particular level. If critical objectives are not met, then the organisation will fail to meet its key objectives, so priority needs to be given to them. For example, an organisation which is committed to maintaining staff levels may regard the objective of raising its market share by 5 per cent as essential.

Other objectives may be seen as being desirable. For example, an organisation that considers a 5 per cent increase in market share to be essential may also have as a desired objective increasing the number of major clients by 5 per cent. However, it is not vital to achieve this if the increased number of purchases by smaller clients enables the organisation to maintain staff levels.

4 Objectives should be set out in statements that are easy to communicate and to understand.

5 Groups of objectives need to be compatible so that there is no inconsistency between actions performed to achieve these objectives.

6 Objectives should be capable of adjustment. In a dynamic operating environment it is important to be flexible, particularly when it is found that inappropriate objectives have been set. For example, if performance standards have been set too high, then this can be demotivating and counterproductive.

7 Wherever possible, assessment procedures need to be put into place to check that objectives have been met. The collection of evidence should be economical and easy. For example, at an operational level there is no point in setting up a performance appraisal system that is expensive and time consuming. The purpose of setting clear objectives is to enable the organisation to use resources effectively. The assessment process is shown in Figure 26.4.

Figure 26.4 Assessing achievement of objectives

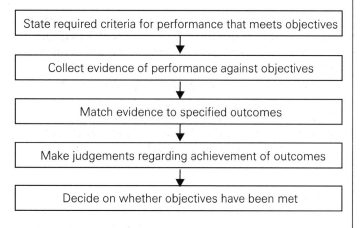

Personal objectives

The following checklist may be useful in establishing criteria for a set of objectives for a particular job.

1 Do the objectives cover the main features of the job?

2 Is the list of objectives too long? Perhaps some objectives can be combined.

3 Are the objectives verifiable?

4 Do the objectives indicate:

    a quantity

    b quality

    c cost

    d time?

5 Are the objectives reasonable?

6 Are the objectives in order of priority?

7 Does the set of objectives include objectives for improvement and self-development?

8 Are the objectives coordinated with other job and activity objectives across the organisation?

9 Have the objectives been effectively communicated?

10 Do the short-term objectives fit with longer-term ones?

11 Are the objectives clear and precise?

12 Do the objectives allow for feedback and alteration?

13 Are there enough resources available to support achievement of the objectives?

14 Does the job holder have sufficient power and authority to achieve the objectives?

15 Are objectives established through a process of consultation and agreement?

16 Are subordinates able to carry out work delegated to them as a result of these objectives?

Understanding business functions

We have seen that planning takes place at a number of levels within the organisation. So far we have focused on the creation of missions and objectives. We look next at how strategies are worked into operational activities through the decision-making process.

First, we outline the major business functions within the organisation. These functions often provide the units around which plans are created, although it is important to understand the interrelationship between plans across the organisation.

1 Marketing

The marketing department is responsible for identifying, anticipating and satisfying customer requirements profitably. Marketing and sales are sometimes combined in a single department, but there is an important distinction between the two. Marketing is concerned with influencing the company to produce what the customer wants; selling tries to get the customer to want what the company is offering. The marketing department, then, is concerned primarily with investigating consumers' needs and wants. This involves carrying out market research to find out who comprises a particular market, what they want, where they want it and at what price. In a manufacturing company there is very close cooperation between the marketing and production departments so that the wishes of consumers can be closely tied in with product development.

2 Sales

The sales department is responsible for generating orders for a good or service. The size of this department varies considerably, as does the way in which it operates. Some companies employ a large sales force covering different regions. Sales representatives visit businesses and other customers in order to secure orders for products. Other firms sell their product by means of advertising or other publicity and employ only a small sales force. The sales manager works from a central office-based location. Sales team meetings are called from time to time to discuss strategy and to analyse performance.

3 Publicity

Publicity is closely allied to sales and marketing. The publicity department is responsible for a number of areas which may include advertising, promotions and public relations.

4 Distribution

Distribution departments are generally responsible for control over warehousing and despatch as well as transport. The distribution manager is responsible for ensuring that the company employs the most cost-effective and reliable distribution channels.

5 Customer relations

The goodwill of customers can be maintained only by an effective policy of customer care. The customer relations department is concerned with handling customer complaints and feeding back suggestions and problems to other functional areas.

6 Human resources

Human resource management (HRM) emphasises the importance of developing strategies and plans designed to support the organisation's most important resource – its people. Human resource management is concerned with emphasising the extent to which employees have an active role in most of the decision-making that takes place in the organisation. It is concerned with linking the planning of 'people' activities and relationships with corporate objectives. The mission statement of most modern organisations emphasises the importance of creating a quality environment coupled with opportunities for development of people at work. Objectives for human resource management then need to be translated into more specific objectives and the organisation of operational activities.

Human resource management is concerned with increasingly involving people in decision-making in the organisation and motivating them through this involvement. Teamwork and quality circles are typical features of human resource management. The notion of personnel has been replaced by that of human resources. However, HRM functions within an organisation are still responsible for:

- recruiting, training, developing and deploying the people in a business
- ensuring that terms and conditions of employment are appropriate, competitive and properly administered
- an employee relations policy.

7 Labour relations

Some companies employ specialists in the labour relations field. These officers are responsible for industrial relations and the monitoring of employees' perceptions of working conditions.

8 Health and safety

Every organisation must pay close attention to health and safety regulations and laws. Large companies frequently employ an in-house advisory service on health matters. A wide range of guidance notes and pamphlets relating to clinical matters, such as diabetes, hypertension and alcoholism, is available from this department. Organisations also produce guidelines on safety performance and on the identification and correction of every unsafe act and condition before they lead to an accident.

9 Production

The production manager is responsible for making sure that raw materials are provided and made into finished goods effectively. He or she must make sure that work is carried out smoothly, and must supervise procedures for making work more efficient and more enjoyable.

In a manufacturing company the production function may be split into five main sub-functions (see Figure 26.5).

10 Production and planning

Production and planning set standards and targets for each section of the production process. The quantity and quality of products coming off a production line are closely monitored.

Figure 26.5 The sub-functions of production

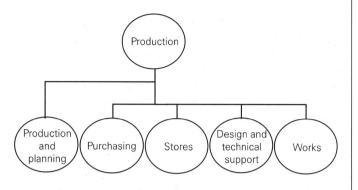

11 Purchasing

The purchasing department is responsible for providing the materials, components and equipment required to keep the production process running smoothly.

12 Stores

The stores department is responsible for stocking all the necessary tools, spares, raw materials and equipment required to service the manufacturing process.

13 Design and technical support

The design and technical support department researches new products or modifications to existing ones; estimates costs of producing different quantities and using different methods; designs and tests new product processes and product types; and develops prototypes through to the final product. It may also be responsible for arranging work-study programmes and making suggestions as to how working practices could be improved.

14 Works

The works department is concerned with the actual manufacture of a product. This encompasses the maintenance of a production line and the carrying out of other necessary repairs. The department may also have responsibility for quality control and inspection.

15 Finance and accounts

Finance and accounts has been left until last here, although many people would choose to place finance first when looking at business functions.

Constructing a marketing plan

A broad look at the process of marketing planning helps explain the process of functional planning.

Marketing and financial objectives are brought together in a total marketing plan. The financial objectives of an organisation are usually tied up with the strategic objectives, which may, for example, be described in terms of profit making and growth. A company may seek to maximise long-term revenues for shareholders by clearly identifying a target market and giving priority to satisfying the market with a quality product.

Developing an effective marketing plan, therefore, involves investigating buyer expectations in order to make decisions about product, price, place and promotion. If the plan is effective, then not only will consumers be satisfied, but so other strategic objectives of the company will be achieved, such as meeting particular financial targets (see Figure 26.6).

Figure 26.6 Developing a marketing plan

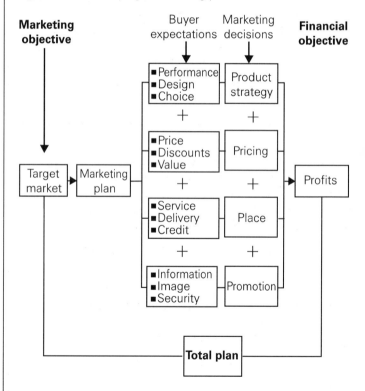

Tactical marketing planning

A marketing plan for an organisation must be grounded in strategic considerations. However, it is also essential to plan carefully the tools and tactics of marketing.

The various units involved in marketing (and indeed in all other areas of an organisation) are continually developing their action plans. These plans need to be realistic; neither too ambitious nor constraining. The main tasks are to decide on priorities and on how control mechanisms and evaluatory tools can be developed. Figure 26.7 offers an example of how to prepare an action plan.

Figure 26.7 Developing a tactical action plan

| Decide on the areas to be audited (e.g. current performance, external environmental factors, use of resources) |
| Create a list of priorities |
| Think about them in terms of urgency, need, desirability, size and scope (possible links between them) |
| Select and sequence priorities for action |
| Produce a draft plan as a basis for discussion |
| Consult and canvass advice and views on the draft plan |
| Produce a market action plan for the relevant area |

The marketing plan of a large organisation is made up of a number of plans from each of the subgroups within the marketing department. It builds on the vision created by the mission statement and other ingredients of the marketing strategy of the organisation.

The key ingredients of tactical marketing planning are:

■ assessing current performance using quantitative methods such as ratios, and qualitative analysis
■ clarifying objectives
■ establishing ways of implementing plans.

The marketing plan also includes plans for:

■ product mix
■ pricing
■ distribution
■ promotion
■ market research
■ sales
■ advertising.

The product mix plan

An internal audit of the current product mix involves listing the products and examining their performance over a period of years in order to identify trends. It is important to examine market segments and the relationships between them. Useful ratios are the net profit made per product and per region, the net profit as a percentage of sales and the market share per region and country.

The product mix plan helps the organisation to identify which products should be phased out, which should be modified and which new products will enter the portfolio and at what time. It sets out objectives for volume of sales, turnover and profits. It establishes how each of the products will be supported within the company, e.g. by sales staff. Product objectives are also concerned with the type of packaging used.

The product mix plan sets out the contribution and/or volume objectives for individual products, market segments and customer groups.

The pricing plan

Pricing is important for any company. A starting point will be to evaluate the quality of pricing decisions that have been taken in the past and the effects of competitors' pricing policies.

The business may wish to explore the price elasticity in the various markets which it serves. The pricing plan sets out the principles that cover pricing and discounting of products. Lower prices do not always mean more or better business; it may be better to build a sound long-term business than to price in order to attract short-term or specific orders. If in doubt, it usually makes sense to price high as the price can always be reduced or special offers introduced. If a business prices low, it will find it difficult to put up the price in the short-term and may find itself out of business. The pricing plan should answer questions such as 'Do we need big volume turnover and can we manage it?' and 'Do we need to aim for lower volume with a bigger margin?'.

The physical distribution plan

Effective channels of communication can give an organisation a critical competitive edge. Where physical distribution costs are high, it is important to use the most effective channels, to control stock efficiently and to minimise breakages and delays. The physical distribution plan needs to be integrated with other key areas of the marketing mix. A useful ratio to compare distribution performance over a number of years is:

$$\text{Distribution effectiveness ratio} = \frac{\text{Distribution costs}}{\text{Sales}}$$

As part of an on-going distribution analysis, an organisation may introduce new objectives such as the development of a new channel, adding or bypassing distributors, identifying ways of improving distributors' performance, etc.

The promotional plan

In many large companies, promotions are tied to the life-cycle of a product. Promotional activity is required at its launch and periodically to inject new life into the product. Promotion is also closely tied to seasonal fluctuations and other short-term influences on demand. Advertising is a key ingredient of the promotional plan, but it is only a very small part of promotion. Advertising on its own seldom, if ever, succeeds.

A satisfied customer is the best form of promotion and planning has much in common with market research, in that the aim is to be consumer led.

The market research plan

Market research planning is particularly important where the nature and market of products are constantly changing. The market research plan covers three main areas:

■ gathering of market data
■ constantly checking on performance in the marketplace
■ continuously monitoring the performance of competitors.

The sales plan

Many organisations also have a separate sales plan. This sets out targets and intended activities in areas such as customer service and sales penetration. Specific plans are likely to be formulated for given groups of customers and specific accounts. The plan should also set out how the sales force is to be recruited and trained. A useful ratio for assessing sales performance is:

$$\text{Selling performance} = \frac{\text{Selling costs}}{\text{Sales}}$$

A business may wish to assess the expenses of selling activities as a percentage of sales:

■ per market
■ per product
■ per order
■ per salesperson.

The advertising plan

Large organisations may have advertising plans which are separate from other promotional plans. However, the two clearly need to complement each other. The advertising plan contains details of which media are to be used, how to allocate the sales and advertising budget, the type of audience to be reached, procedures for tracking the success of campaigns and other features.

Objectives of advertising (and promotion) include:

■ awareness of levels (how many people know about our product?)
■ image objectives (how can we improve and monitor perceptions of the image of our brands/company?)
■ technique objectives (whether to use displays, demonstrations, leaflets).

A ratio that may be used to assess advertising performance is:

$$\text{Advertising performance ratio} = \frac{\text{Advertising costs}}{\text{Sales}}$$

Marketing action plan

All of the planning activities outlined above should be set out in an action plan that indicates objectives and priorities, resources to be used, timetable, checkpoints and controls.

The various aspects of marketing tactical planning have been described in detail in order to highlight some of the information that needs to be included in any form of functional planning.

Planning provides a framework for functional activities. The use of ratios and performance targets gives an organisation direction and performance criteria against which it can measure the effectiveness of its plans. It also facilitates the important process of control.

Human resource planning

Planning for human resources is one of the most important, yet most frequently neglected, areas of planning. Human resource planning can only be effective if personnel are regarded as a key factor in management. The human resource director and other personnel managers should play a key part in corporate planning. At the same time, all managers have a responsibility for human resource issues and these should be considered as a main ingredient of most, if not all, decision-making.

The prime aim of human resource management is to plan for future labour and staff needs. This involves employing the right people, at the right time, with the right skills. The two main objectives driving effective human relations management are:

- to forecast likely future demand for labour and the future supply of labour in order to estimate the gap between demand and supply
- to analyse and improve the present use of the existing resource. A human relations approach recognises people as the most vital resource and tries to create genuine job satisfaction. Managers need to integrate all aspects of their sub-plans so that they pull in the same direction. For example, one of the objectives of training will be to upgrade existing skills. However, training will also impact on other aspects of human resource policy, e.g. recruitment and redeployment. It is essential to look at each aspect of policy as part of an integrated whole.

Human resource planning needs to be considered in the same way as investment in products, i.e. strategically.

One of the key parts of planning for human resources is to create a working organisational structure. In designing a structure it is necessary to differentiate tasks into work packages and jobs linked to supervisory and management control.

Management and staff planning is necessary to identify the types of structures and relationships in the organisation as well as, for example, numbers of employees. Human resource planning needs, therefore, to be based on statistics and forecasts. Staff planning needs to be based around corporate planning, e.g. if old products are to be phased out and new ones introduced, then it may be necessary to develop plans for training, retraining, redundancies, recruitment, selection, etc. Important areas for the creation of plans include:

- recruitment and selection
- pay and conditions
- working relationships and motivation
- training and development
- industrial relations.

Case Study
Bass Brewers' mission statement

Bass PLC is a producer of beer and soft drinks (Bass Brewers Ltd and Britvic Soft Drinks). It is also a retailer providing a leisure service (Bass Taverns, Bass Leisure and Holiday Inn Worldwide).

The mission statement of the brewing arm is:

'1 Our primary objective is to establish an increasingly pre-eminent position in the UK beer market. We also intend to attain a leading position in overseas markets where opportunities to add value have been identified.

'2 We will achieve these objectives by the following means:

- We will own an unrivalled range of brands.
- We will provide our customers with quality, value and service second to none.
- We will be highly cost competitive.
- We will attract, develop and motivate a team of people of outstanding quality who will share in the success they generate.
- We will create an entrepreneurial culture in a company which anticipates, responds to and shapes changes in the market.

'3 In pursuing these objectives we will achieve superior financial performance and attractive returns for shareholders.'

Questions for discussion

1 What priority does Bass Brewers' mission give to the human resource?
2 Why do you think that an organisation like Bass Brewers places emphasis on human resource development?
3 How do you think that the statements about human resource development at Bass will be translated into specific objectives and actions in its 'people at work' area?
4 What kinds of working relationships does the mission statement set out to foster?
5 What methods of motivating employees would you expect to see in place?

Case Study
Personnel activity at Bass Brewers

A personnel manager for Bass Brewers Ltd may deal daily with a wide and varied range of issues. Some of these are covered below.

The Personnel Department aims to provide an effective service for Bass employees. A *Bass Personnel Procedure Manual* has been produced to further this aim. The manual is constantly updated and staff in the Personnel Department consult it to ensure that they are handling situations fairly and appropriately.

Bass personnel managers are responsible for a variety of human resource matters, including the recruitment and selection of new employees, from job advertisement to an appointment. Bass invests a great deal of time and money in its employees, and so at an interview it is important that as much information can be obtained from the potential recruit as possible to ensure that he or she will be suitable for the job. Information required includes whether the candidates are teamworkers or have leadership qualities, their hobbies and sports (whether they play competitive sports), their time-keeping, etc. References are taken up, and tests are carried out on personality and aptitude.

Disciplinary action is also the responsibility of personnel managers. This is carried out in formal stages:

a If an employee commits a misdemeanour, he or she is given a verbal warning by the manager.

b If the situation does not improve the employee is warned again, this time in writing.

c If the offence is still being committed, there is a final written warning.

d The final step is suspension or dismissal.
   However, the employee may appeal against the disciplinary procedure at every stage. This is part of the procedural agreement with the trade unions.

Formal meetings are conducted regularly with various unions at Bass Brewers. The main aim from a personnel viewpoint is to sort out potential problems.

Questions for discussion

1 *How does the personnel work at Bass Brewers tally with the mission statement?*

2 *Why is it important for an organisation like Bass to ensure that its corporate objectives filter down to operational planning?*

A human relations approach to planning for people at work ensures that an organisation is flexible in a turbulent business environment. Team-working enables employees to become directly involved in business decision-making. They are then able to identify with the organisation's targets and objectives, and are far more likely to create a quality product. If employees know what the quality objective is and by what criteria completed work is to be assessed, they will be able to make a much more effective contribution to corporate objectives.

Production planning and control

Much of production planning and control is concerned with the company's plans for the future and needs to be carefully coordinated with marketing policy, e.g. product life-cycles. In the short term, production planning and control looks at immediate issues such as:

- How do we fulfil this order?
- How close is the job to completion?
- Can it be completed on time?
- Do we need to use more labour?

In order to cope, the department has to organise itself in such a way as to gain the most from its materials, labour and plant. The production controller has one of the most difficult jobs in any organisation. He or she needs to understand fully the organisation of production processes and costing and administrative procedures, and needs to use complex mathematical techniques to solve problems.

The production programme

Programming involves timetabling the vast resources used by the production department. Much of its success depends on the abilities of the production planning and control department, whose staff set dates and timetables for the delivery of finished products and allocate production services accordingly. Delivery timetables generate further timetables in areas such as purchasing, stock control and quality control.

Financial planning

The emphasis on finance found in every organisation stems from the profit objective. Many writers argue that the profit objective is the primary objective of all organisations, except those that operate as charities and similar concerns. An organisation that concentrates on **primary profit targets** is able to establish a clear pattern of objectives, all directed towards the bottom line. For example, Figure 26.8 shows that at every level in the organisation the primary objective is profit. This is a simple model which gives clear direction.

However, it is frequently criticised. People who are finance-oriented, such as accountants, generally see things in terms of the bottom line and figures. It is argued that they fail to take account of those strategies and processes that actually create the profits, e.g. marketing and human resource management.

The implication is that the profit objective on its own is not sufficient. Policy making should involve as many decision makers as possible from across the organisation.

Before outlining the nature of the financial planning function in the organisation, we explore some of the issues relating to profit maximisation and other financial objectives.

Figure 26.8 Company objectives and unit objectives

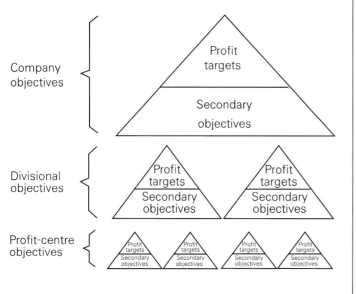

Company objectives

Divisional objectives

Profit-centre objectives

Profit maximisation

In the long run firms need to make a profit. People, as a rule, will only invest in a business if they are satisfied with the return they receive. This suggests that profitability is a major business objective, although not necessarily the only one. The principle of profit maximisation is illustrated in Figure 26.9. A business has calculated the total cost of producing different outputs of a product and the total revenues that would result. Profit maximisation involves calculating the output that will achieve greatest total profit (i.e. the point Q on the profit-maximising output axis at which the difference between total revenue and total cost is greatest).

However, in the real world this process is far more complex than simply drawing a diagram – it involves a thorough programme of research, taking into account costings for different levels of outputs, the effects of

Figure 26.9 Profit maximisation

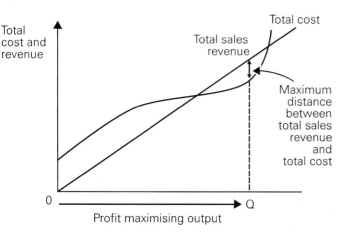

charging different prices, calculations of potential sales and many other factors.

If profit is measured simply in money terms, then it would seem logical to assume that in the long term the rational business will seek to maximise the difference between its total revenue and its total cost. Accountants, for example, claim to be able to weigh up quickly the success of a business in terms of the financial profit.

Market leadership

Many firms seek to be market leaders. They may want to sell more products than all rival brands combined, or simply to sell more than the next best-selling brand. The most reliable indicator of market share is relative to other brands, i.e. the ratio of a company's market share to that of its largest competitor:

$$\text{Relative market share} = \frac{\text{Market share of the company}}{\text{Market share of nearest competitor}}$$

A well-known study (by the Boston Consultancy Group) argued, on the basis of statistical information, that a ratio of 2:1 would give a 20 per cent cost advantage (i.e. a company would be able to operate with costs 20 per cent lower than its nearest rival). If a company dominates the market it can produce on a larger scale than its competitors. Profits can then be ploughed back into research, advertising and further expansion to maintain market leadership.

Maximisation of sales

In some large companies the salaries earned by managers may depend on the size of the business. Thus, their objective may be to make the business as large as possible. Controlling a large business concern might also give individuals satisfaction derived from the power at their command. Increased sales might also mean reduced sales for competitors, which in the long term can be seen as being consistent with a policy of profit maximisation.

In a college or school, a headteacher's or principal's salary will increase when the number of students goes over a certain threshold. This is of particular significance as most senior managers are relatively close to retirement age, and their pensions are determined by their final few years' salary. Such managers would have a major incentive to increase the number of students in their colleges.

Growth

Firms can benefit from growth. A firm that grows quickly will find it easy to attract investors and will be able to produce on a larger scale. However, one of the biggest mistakes that business people make in the early days is that of overtrading – there might not be enough cash to pay bills in the short term, managing a large staff can be difficult, and so on.

Operating in a wide range of markets

Operating in several markets makes it possible to spread the risk. If one market fails, another may support the loss. However, opening into new markets also exposes a business to fresh risks. It may be better to operate in a small number of well-known markets than to expose the business to new risks.

'Management by objectives'

In *The Practice of Management* (1954) Peter Drucker outlined the concept of **Management by Objectives (MbO)**, in which managers set out specific objectives for each area of business performance, including the work and progress of subordinates, and set attainable targets at each level of the organisation, agreed by consultation. These objectives need to be coordinated with the strategic objectives of the whole organisation.

Peter Drucker wanted to find out how best to manage a business to make sure that profits are made and that the enterprise is successful over time. He felt that business objectives help management to explain, predict and control activities. The business should establish a number of objectives in a small number of general statements. These statements can then be tested in the light of business experience, and it becomes possible to predict performance. The soundness of decisions can be examined while they are being made, rather than by looking back on what has happened. Performance in the future can be improved in the light of previous and current experience.

Figure 26.10 shows that specific objectives can act as a standard to measure performance. If objectives are not met, they may need to be readjusted or processes and activities altered. Alternatively, if they are met, new and higher objectives can be set.

Such objectives force the business to plan its aims in detail and to work out ways of achieving them. Management is the job of organising resources to achieve satisfactory performance.

Drucker listed eight areas in which performance objectives need to be set out:

- market standing
- innovation
- productivity
- physical and financial resources
- profitability
- manager performance and development
- worker performance and attitude
- public responsibility.

Figure 26.10 Using objectives as a standard

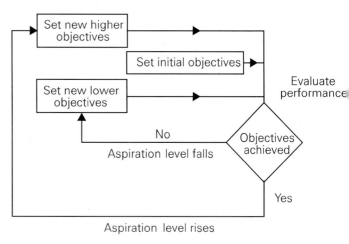

Managers need to have information which enables them to measure their own performance and the performance of their organisation.

How high a priority is profit making?

We have seen that there are a number of prime objectives for business organisations. Some of these are easily measurable in money terms. How much importance should we give to pure profit making? Some thinkers argue that 'the business of business is business!' (Milton Friedman). Profitability is the chief spur to business activity.

However, in an important study carried out by Shipley in 1981 (*Journal of Industrial Economics*), the author concluded that only 15.9 per cent of a sample of 728 UK firms could be regarded as 'true' profit maximisers. His conclusion was reached by cross-tabulating replies to the two questions shown in Figure 26.11. Shipley considered as true maximisers only those firms that claimed both to maximise profits and to regard profits to be of overriding importance. Of course, a number of criticisms can be levelled at any form of statistical analysis of motivations. However, there would appear to be a clear case for arguing that profit is only part of a set of business objectives.

The profit objective may be expressed in a number of ways. For example, directors may be concerned with return on investment (ROI). This figure looks at the return made on assets invested in the organisation. A second ingredient is the rate of profit growth, e.g. annual

Figure 26.11 Responses from a sample of 728 firms

	% of all respondents
1 Does your firm try to achieve:	
a maximum profits?	47.7
b satisfactory profits?	52.3
2 Compared with your firm's other leading objectives, is the achievement of a profit target regarded as being:	
a of little importance?	2.1
b fairly important?	12.9
c very important?	58.9
d of overriding importance?	26.1
Those responding both 1a and 2d	15.9

(Source: Adapted from Shipley, *Journal of Industrial Economics*, 1981)

growth of after-tax profits of 7 per cent. Establishing these objectives may be done in a number of ways, such as by looking at what is 'normal' in the industry, or previous years' figures. A third element, which is a popular one, is growth in earnings per share. Clearly, shareholders are a major stakeholder in the organisation and this is an objective which they can relate to. Of course, a danger of focusing on earnings per share is that the company may begin to borrow more money in order to maintain earnings per share.

Once the organisation has established corporate objectives in financial terms, then these objectives need to be segmented into divisional objectives and profit-centre objectives. The expected rate of return from each division may well depend on the amount of risk taken and on market conditions. Large conglomerate organisations will often try to divest (get rid of) divisions that are not meeting profit targets. Finally, divisions (or other major segments) of an organisation need to set profit-centre targets for each sub-section within their domain. Clearly, different profit targets need to be set depending on the nature of the activities considered. Centres that create clear profit lines, e.g. particular types of food in a food factory, can be given clear targets. However, some activities cannot be treated as profit centres, such as community affairs departments.

Finance and accounts

The chief accountant is responsible for supervising the accounts department. The accounts section must keep a detailed record of all money paid in and out, and must present the final balance sheet, source and use of funds, the profit and loss account and other financial records at regular intervals. Modern accounts are stored on

computer files, and accounting procedures are greatly simplified by the use of computers. Within the accounts department there are two main sub-divisions.

Financial accounting department

The financial accounting department is responsible for keeping records of financial events as they occur. Accounts need to be kept of all money paid to or by a company, and records must be kept of all debtor and creditor transactions. The payment of wages also requires calculations involving deductions for national insurance, pensions and other factors. As well as keeping day-to-day records, the financial accounting department is also responsible for producing periodic records such as the annual accounts and interim figures for discussion at meetings of directors.

Management accounting department

The management accounting department has the responsibility for nudging the company in certain directions as a result of its analysis of figures. Management accountants break down figures in order to extract information about a company's present performance and the sorts of improvements that can be made in the future. Using systems of budgetary control, they set targets for achievement and limits for spending on the various parts of the business.

Within the accounts department, other sub-functions might include a cashier's department and a wages department. The cashier's department is concerned with handling all cash transactions as well as cheques and other payments through bank accounts. These records are kept in a cash book or on a computerised system.

The wages department is responsible for supervising the payroll and calculating and paying wages. The data for these calculations are generated by the works department or other departments responsible for recording the amount of work carried out by employees.

Administration

We should not underestimate the role of administration in organisational planning. Many large firms have a central office or administration department, which might handle the filing of materials and the company's mail, word-processing and data-handling facilities. The modern office is increasingly using computers and information technology.

In many organisations each department has its own clerical and support staff. However, it is common practice to have an office services manager or administration officer with the responsibility for coordinating office services and offering expert advice to departmental managers.

Information and computing

In a modern company a large proportion of the staff work directly with, or have access to, computer terminals. Information technology refers to the large and developing body of technologies and techniques by which information is obtained, processed and disseminated. The term, therefore, embraces computing, telecommunications and office development. These three areas, which were initially distinct, are now seen as having more and more in common. They are progressively merging, while at the same time expanding to play an ever-greater part in business activity.

The role of the information and computing function is to promote effective exploitation of IT in a company and to provide the guidance, support and coordination necessary to achieve this objective.

Public-sector accountability and objectives

In looking at planning we must not ignore the importance of the public sector, which is still responsible for many planning decisions in the UK. For example, the public sector plays a major part in decisions made about the construction of new roads, and local authority approval needs to be obtained for any house-building projects.

In industry there are three major elements of public-sector involvement:

- direct state participation through public corporations, known as the nationalised industries, and other Crown corporations
- industries in which there is public-sector involvement together with private investment, e.g. the government held a 39 per cent share in British Petroleum from the Second World War until the late 1980s, when shares were sold to the public
- industries in which there is a public-sector involvement at local government level rather than at the level of national government.

Businesses that receive support from the government to establish new activities, such as research and development or product development in a particular field, make up a fourth group.

Public corporations

In the UK the government still owns a number of industries and businesses on behalf of the people. Most of these take the form of public corporations. In recent years, however, there has been a sustained period of privatisation of government enterprises.

Privatisation means the denationalisation of state-controlled industries. We are all familiar with privatisation such as the sale of the electricity boards, the water boards, British Telecom and British Gas. However, privatisation also includes the sale of council houses, the contracting out of local authority controlled services, such as street cleaning, and the introduction of private prisons.

A public corporation is set up by an Act of Parliament. Examples of public corporations are the Bank of England and the British Broadcasting Corporation (BBC).

Once a public corporation has been formed, the government appoints a chairperson to be responsible for the day-to-day running of the industry.

There are a number of reasons for setting up public corporations. These underpin the 'objectives' of such organisations:

1 **To avoid wasteful duplication.** Imagine the problems caused by having three electricity companies operating in one town.
2 **To set up and run services that might not be profitable**, e.g. a ferry service to some of the islands of Scotland, a postal service to remote villages, etc. Clearly, there is a community-interest objective in these cases.
3 **To gain the benefits of large-scale production**, i.e. using the nation's resources in a rational way.
4 **To protect employment, particularly in areas of high unemployment**. A government-run activity may continue where a private sector one would move out.
5 **To control industries that are important to the country**, e.g. central banking, and broadcasting.

When a public corporation is set up, an independent body is also formed to protect consumers' interests. Consumers can take their complaints to this body. The Post Office Users' National Council takes up complaints made by users of the Post Office about the late delivery of letters, for example. The government keeps the power to make major decisions about how public corporations should run, such as whether to close down large sections of the railway network. However, the chairperson and managers of the public corporation decide the day-to-day issues such as wages and, in the case of the BBC, programming. If the government tries to interfere in these areas, it leads to considerable public debate.

Whereas a limited company has to make an annual report to its shareholders, a public corporation must present its annual report to the appropriate government minister, who makes a verbal report to Parliament. At this time MPs have the opportunity to criticise or support the way in which the corporation is being run. A committee of MPs has the job of studying the running of each public corporation and of reporting on its operation. For example, there is a select committee acting as a watchdog

Figure 26.12 Influences on decision-making in a public corporation

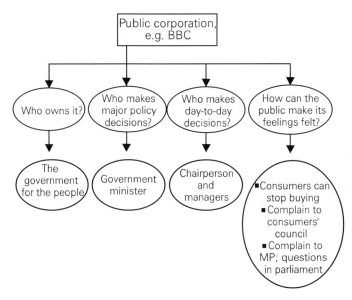

over the BBC. Figure 26.12 highlights some of the aspects of decision-making and control in a public corporation.

Other central government enterprises

In addition to public corporations, the other two major areas of government control over economic activity occur where an activity is run by:

- a government department
- a public company in which the government has a shareholding.

When an activity is run by a government department, a government minister has overall charge of the department. The department is staffed and run by civil servants, e.g. the Customs and Excise Department, which deals with the collection and supervision of some taxes.

The major criticisms of such a form of organisation from the business point of view are:

- Decisions are made slowly because there are many links in the chain of command, usually wrapped up in rules and regulations.
- The organisation may appear to be inefficient because of lack of competition.
- There is no external agency to protect the public's interest by checking on how the department is run. While in many cases there will be a mechanism for making complaints, it may be so complex as to be inaccessible to the ordinary person.

Local government enterprises

In the UK certain services in local areas are supervised by locally elected councils. These councils usually run some form of business organisations such as municipal car parks, leisure centres, bus services and public toilets. However, since the late 1980s, council activities too have been subjected to the policy of privatisation. Today, many activities such as road cleaning and refuse disposal are contracted out to those firms that put in the lowest tender for a particular job. Council officials simply monitor the effectiveness with which the work is done and may refuse to continue a contract if work fails to meet the required standards. Local councils receive money from two main sources: a grant given to them by central government and a local tax. Local councils often subsidise loss-making activities, such as local parks, which provide a benefit to the community.

Public-sector objectives

The above remarks indicate some of the difficulties of establishing planning objectives for public-sector organisations. Many public-sector activities involve only limited competition, so it is difficult to establish how efficient they are. How do we know if particular activities are taking too long and are wasting resources? What criteria are used for establishing targets when it is difficult to make comparisons (except with past performance)?

In 1948 the government set out the objective for nationalised industries – they were to meet the demand for their product at a reasonable price which would enable them to break even over a number of years. In the years that followed there was much criticism of the way in which the targets were set for public corporations. Under the break-even policy, for example, it was possible to charge some customers who could be supplied cheaply (such as gas users in cities) the same price as other customers who were far more expensive to supply (gas consumers in remote areas).

In 1961 the government set more precise financial targets for public corporations. Taking into account conditions in the market, the targets became the rate of return on the assets employed in a specific industry.

In 1967 even more stringent rules were set, whereby the cross-subsidisation of one group of consumers by another was to be avoided. New investment was expected to yield a rate of return similar to what the investment capital would earn in the private sector. It was recognised that some activities of public corporations (e.g. supplying to rural areas and engaging in activities which were not profitable) were of a social rather than a commercial nature (see Figure 26.13). These social contributions needed to be given a money value, and the government would provide a subsidy to meet these activities.

Figure 26.13 Social and commercial objectives of a public corporation

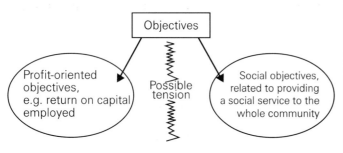

In 1979 the newly elected Conservative government embraced a policy of privatisation. The emphasis was on cutting out unprofitable operations in order to make these industries attractive to prospective shareholders. Over the years, this has meant cutting down loss-making operations such as some steel works, coal mines and shipyards.

A large number of nationalised industries were privatised during the 1980s including electricity, British Telecom, British Gas, British Steel, British Aerospace, British Airways, British Shipbuilders, the National Bus Company, the British Airports Authority, the National Freight Corporation and, more recently, British Rail and British Coal.

In the Acts of Parliament that have privatised industries, the government has set up regulatory bodies, such as OFTEL (for telecommunications) and OFGAS (for gas), with the responsibility of checking that the privatised industries keep to established rules governing prices, competition and the quality of service offered. Today's remaining nationalised industries are expected to meet financial targets and to show a real rate of return on assets that indicates resources are being used as effectively as if the capital were employed by the private sector.

Public-sector organisations, meanwhile, such as the National Health Service and the BBC, have been broken down into a number of independent sections. Each section (e.g. individual fundholding GPs and hospitals) is expected to manage its own budget and to use resources efficiently.

Case Study
The changing shape and style of management in the public sector

In recent years there has been a revolution in the accountability and objectives of public-sector organisations. Today, both of the major political parties tend, across a broad range of services, to place a great deal of emphasis on output and performance measures.

It is likely that providers will be penalised for failing to meet performance targets. From the prison service to English Heritage, social security to hospital trusts, administrators and fundholders routinely speak about 'customers' and 'markets'. Fundholders run and manage their own budgets and determine their own policies and decisions.

Since the early 1980s about two-thirds of central government's workforce has been hived off into 'Next Steps' executive agencies. At the same time, there have been massive privatisations.

There has also been a profound cultural change in the way organisations are run. Once, public-sector managers were frequently criticised for inefficiency, wastefulness and incompetence. This is rarely the case today. In schools, hospitals, prisons and many other areas of the public sector, business planning takes place in a detailed way. Public-sector managers are explicitly defining tasks, establishing who is responsible for carrying them out, measuring performance, establishing how much they will cost and controlling that cost.

As consumers of public services have become more aware of their rights, they have started to demand improved quality. The Conservative government introduced the Citizen's Charter, which places a demand on public-sector managers to meet given performance indicators in terms of the standard of service they provide to their customers. The Labour Party has proposed a quality commission to monitor performance in the public sector.

Before these changes, managers would have argued that because public services are often monopolistic, it would prove impossible to introduce effective performance measures equivalent to competition in the private sector. However, public-sector managers have devised a range of measures to check on progress over time (e.g. school exam results and attendance figures). The devolution of executive responsibility away from civil servants and to 'Next Steps' managers has meant that decisions are being made closer to the customer.

Responding to consumer preferences is not easy. Indeed, there are many segments of consumers making purchases from the public sector. For example, in the local post office, groups of consumers often have conflicting demands – professional people want speed, pensioners may want time to chat with the person behind the counter, parents with young children want accessibility, etc. Similarly, the absence of competition creates incentive problems – brightening up the local post office is unlikely to attract extra custom.

Similar difficulties are posed throughout the public sector. Who are the customers of the prison service? Is it the courts? The police? The public? The prisoners? However, these issues are now being tackled. Management devolution has changed the way things are seen and the way plans are made. Increasingly, progress is being made towards creating a new definition of public accountability.

Questions for discussion

1 *How are public-sector organisations accountable to the public?*
2 *What objectives do public-sector organisations concentrate on today?*
3 *How can a concentration on these objectives enable organisations to plan operations more effectively?*
4 *Who are the stakeholders in the public sector?*
5 *How are objectives determined for public-sector activities?*
6 *Why might different groups of stakeholders have different perceptions about what objectives should be?*
7 *Is it possible to reconcile these differences?*

Role of the owner/manager within small business planning

One of the main reasons for the failure of small businesses is lack of planning. Producing a business plan enables an entrepreneur to:

- minimise risks and potential problems
- avoid making potentially ruinous moves
- go ahead with a business venture having confidence that there is a direction to follow and clear plans
- study a framework of ideas which can be used to identify potential weaknesses and strengths.

Small business entrepreneurs need to have a clear direction so that they know:

- where the business is likely to go
- how it is going to get there
- what resources are required
- whether they are going to be able to meet objectives.

When starting to plan the entrepreneur should carry out an environmental analysis looking at a variety of influences on the business, e.g. the general state of the economy, and the existence of competition. Entrepreneurs will need to consider the quality of their ideas and whether they have the resources and ability to steer the business proposition through to success. The business plan enables owners to check and monitor the business. Planning, therefore, provides both structure and direction (see Figure 26.14).

Figure 26.14 Using planning to create a successful business

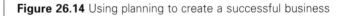
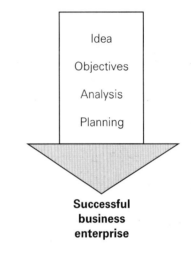

Idea

Objectives

Analysis

Planning

Successful business enterprise

Planning can also be used to provide guidance for the management of the business. Moreover, it can show others the direction the business is following. Support from people and organisations outside the business, such as lenders, will almost certainly be needed; they may supply the business with resources, including financial ones, but are unlikely to provide support for a business with no clear plans.

Business plans can be laid out according to a number of different formats and these depend largely upon the nature of the business proposition and the intended users of the plan. Each business plan will be tailored to a specific business project.

Business plan outline

The business

- Name of business
- Address and location

- History or background
- Brief description of activities
- Proposed date for trading or startup
- Legal identity – sole trader, partnership, company
- Objectives
- Professional advisors

Key personnel

- Name of directors and managers
- Background, experience, knowledge and expertise
- Relevant work and business experience
- Future personnel requirements
- Recruitment proposals

The nature of the business

- Description of product (including price)
- Patents, trademarks, copyrights, etc.
- Suppliers
- Proposed developments of product
- Market – size and potential
- Trends in the marketplace
- Needs of customers
- Benefits offered to customers
- Description of competitors' strengths and weaknesses
- Unique features of product compared with competition
- Projected turnover – three months, six months, one year, etc.
- Break-even analysis
- Production techniques
- Reasons why proposals are achievable

Marketing plan

- Marketing objectives
- Environment
- Market research
- Marketing methods – product, price, distribution (place), promotion

Future

- Strengths, weaknesses, opportunities and threats (SWOT)
- Socio-economic trends
- Technological trends
- Action plans
- Timetable of activities

Resources

- Premises, size and cost
- Machines
- Vehicles

- Equipment
- Overheads
- Materials
- Management salaries
- Labour costs

Financial analysis

- Startup capital
- Working capital
- Grants
- Own resources
- Loans
- Assets available as security
- Cash-flow forecast over three years
- Profit and loss forecast over three years
- Balance sheet

Other information

- Address of accountant
- Address of solicitor
- Insurance arrangements
- VAT registration
- Summary

The owner of a small business, once armed with a clear plan, will need to check performance periodically against objectives in order to modify or confirm objectives and performance standards.

Use and application of SWOT analysis

A SWOT analysis is a useful planning tool. It sets out to focus on the **strengths, weaknesses, opportunities** and **threats** facing a business at a given moment.

Carrying out a SWOT requires research and analysis of an organisation's current and potential future position. The SWOT is used to match an organisation's strengths and weaknesses with the external forces in the business environment.

The internal audit element of SWOT analysis is the organisation's strengths and weaknesses; opportunities and threats reflect influences external to the organisation in the business environment (see Figure 26.15).

Figure 26.15 The planning balance sheet

SWOT analysis	
Within the organisation	**In the environment**
Strengths +	Opportunities +
Weaknesses −	Threats −

A small business may have the following SWOT elements:

Strengths:
Good product
Good relationships with customers
Good management team
Weaknesses:
Few economies of scale
Liquidity problems
Little experience of other markets
Opportunities:
New markets
Changing tastes
Diversification
Threats:
Actions of competitors
Recession
New legislation

It is essential that an organisation is able to match its activities and potential to the environment in which it operates. An internal audit, therefore, looks at current strengths and weaknesses, e.g. in marketing, human resources, finance, management, organisational structure and integration of activities. The organisation then needs to focus on accentuating strengths and minimising weaknesses.

The external audit provides a detailed look at what is happening in the environment.

Economic factors to consider

- What is happening to interest rates?
- How are changes in interest rates likely to affect sales, revenues, costs, etc?
- What is happening to the rate of inflation?
- How will changes in price levels affect costs and revenues?
- Can price rises be passed on?
- What are the economic conditions in the markets in which the company is trading?
- Are they going through a period of boom/slump?
- What is the current level of unemployment?
- How does this affect demand for goods?
- Are new markets opening up for the company's products?
- Are disposable incomes rising or falling?

Legal and political factors to consider

- Will changes in the law affect the way the product is made or sold?
- Will changes in the law affect pricing, packaging, distribution, product guarantees, etc?
- What will be the effect of new taxes, subsidies, grants, etc?
- Will markets open up or close down as a result of new political alliances?

Population and social factors to consider

- Is the size of the population rising or falling?
- What is happening to the age and gender structure of the population?
- What social issues affect consumers (e.g. environmental issues, animal rights issues, equal opportunities issues)?

Technological factors to consider

- What new processes and techniques are being developed?
- How will they affect the product and the products of rivals?
- What is the impact of new technology on costs?

The development of a detailed SWOT analysis enables managers to understand the challenges and opportunities which are facing their organisation and products. The SWOT analysis introduces managers to a dynamic business environment and enables them to anticipate and embrace radical changes. The SWOT analysis is not a one-off process. It is a continual attempt to understand the business in its environment.

Gap analysis

Gap analysis is a useful planning tool. It is used to outline the gap between what a company's profits might be and what they are likely to be if it carries on operating as it is at the current time.

The gap provides a useful warning: 'If we don't do something to change the way we are working, we will start going backwards!' The starting point is to set out the desired profit target on a graph (see Figure 26.16 – for simplicity this is represented by a straight line). The profit target is set out over the next few years. The second stage is to draw a profit forecast based on the assumption that the organisation makes no changes in its range of operations. There are three main ways of making the projections for this line:

1 the sum of the profit targets for individual operating divisions (probably the simplest method)
2 a model of the organisation's profits given certain assumptions
3 total up the results of the operating plans of all managers.

Whichever method is chosen you will be able to draw a line showing the **expected profit**. Very often this line will move down, simply because by standing still in a competitive environment profits are likely to fall – divisional and line managers know this only too well.

Figure 26.16 Gap analysis

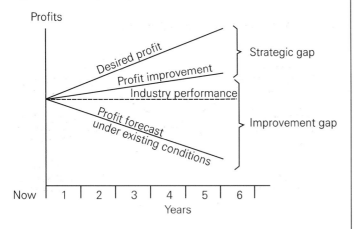

We can draw two more lines on the graph (Figure 26.16):

■ **The industry performance line** shows the return on an equivalent investment made within the industry in which the organisation is operating, e.g. by looking at figures for other companies. This will be easiest if there is a similar organisation operating in the same industry.
■ **The profit improvement line** shows the improvements that could be made to profits by altering strategies in the existing sectors of the company.

The **improvement gap** identifies the scope for improvement by altering strategies in the existing sectors of the company. The **strategic gap** shows the scope for improvement by invigorating the organisation, by implementing new strategies, including movement into new sectors and activities.

Gap analysis identifies the importance of continued transformation of an organisation in dynamic markets. It is often complicated and time consuming to prepare and requires detailed forecasts and information. It may require more than just financial information.

Gap analysis is also used in the public sector in a slightly different way, i.e. to assess whether likely future demands for a public service will lead to a gap in its provision, and to anticipate the size of this gap, e.g. in the provision of public transport or hospital beds. The profit target line might then represent a forecast of desired use of service. The profit forecast line would represent projected provision of service under existing planning conditions.

Suitability, acceptability and feasibility

All organisations need to know whether their plans and proposals are worth putting into practice. They, therefore, need to establish criteria to decide whether to go ahead with a plan or not.

There are three important techniques for evaluating options:

■ suitability
■ acceptability
■ feasibility.

Suitability

Suitability is concerned with whether plans and solutions fit the situation. For example, SWOT analysis provides a good view of the internal organisation and the external environment. The company would then need to look at whether plans and proposals provide a suitable use of resources in a given environment, for example, whether a plan:

■ fits with internal weaknesses or external threats facing an organisation
■ builds on an organisation's existing strengths and environmental opportunities
■ matches the organisation's stated objectives.

Acceptability

Acceptability is concerned with whether a plan will be acceptable to the organisation and to those with a significant interest in it. For example, is the level of risk acceptable and are shareholders and other stakeholders prepared to agree to the plans? They may have reservations based on what they consider to be ethical, fair and reasonable.

Feasibility

Feasibility is concerned with whether plans can work in practice and primarily whether the organisation has adequate resources to carry out particular plans, for example, whether:

■ the funds are available
■ the organisation will be able to sustain the required level of output
■ the organisation will be able to deal with the competition that it generates
■ it will be able to meet the required market share.

Planning cycles

The planning process is a cyclical process based on continual improvement.

We have seen that planning takes place at a number of levels. At each level, if organisations, divisions, operating units, and individuals have clear guidelines, then it will be possible for them to work in a coordinated way.

Planning also makes it possible for management to evaluate performance. Without evaluation, there is no control. Of course, plans are unlikely to be met in every detail. However, they establish guidelines against which performance can be checked and, if necessary, modified. A useful model is set out in Figure 26.17.

Figure 26.17 A cyclical model of planning

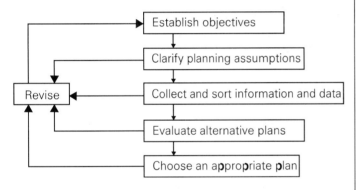

Another method of approaching planning involves (see Figure 2.18):

- **Diagnosis**. Where are we and why? This usually involves some form of audit of company performance, which will then be analysed.
- **Prognosis**. Where are we going? This involves looking at possible future scenarios in the light of present performance and trends.

- **Objectives**. Where do we want to go? What is important?
- **Strategy**. What is the best way of achieving objectives?
- **Tactics**. What specific actions will enable day-to-day targets to be met?
- **Control**. How far has the company progressed? A company will need to establish performance indicators against which it can measure its success.

Figure 26.18 An alternative planning model

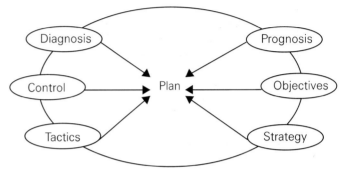

Further reading

- *Business Planning*, 2nd edition, by Bill Richardson and Roy Richardson. Pitman, 1992.
- *An Introduction to Business Planning* by Kevin Scholes and Mary Klemm. Macmillan, 1993.
- *Strategic Management* by G. A. Cole. DPP, 1994.
- *A Strategy of Change* by David C. Wilson. Routledge, 1993.
- *Concepts of Strategic Management Formulation and Implementation* by Lloyd L. Byars. HarperCollins, 1992.

27 Decision-making

On completion of this chapter students should be able to:

- examine and explain the process of decision-making by individuals in organisations

- identify and evaluate organisational factors which affect decision-making

- select and use decision-making techniques.

Decision-making within the planning process

Decision-making involves choosing a course of action from a series of alternatives. It lies at the heart of the planning process.

A plan does not exist until a decision has been made which involves the commitment of resources and the choice of a particular course of direction or action.

Decision-making is only one part of the process of planning. Reaching a decision may take a long time involving research, experimentation and/or reflection on previous experience. Some decisions may be arrived at instantly; others will take a while to formulate.

Types of decision-making

Most classifications of types of decision are based upon the predictability of decisions. For example, Herbert Simon, in *Models of Man*, made an important distinction between programmed and non-programmed decisions.

Programmed decisions are straightforward, repetitive and routine, so that they can be dealt with by a formal pattern, e.g. the reordering of stock by a company. **Non-programmed decisions** are novel, unstructured and consequential. There is no cut-and-dried method for handling situations which have not arisen before.

Simon thought that these two types of decisions were the two ends of a continuum, with all shades of grey lying in between. In *Business Decision Making*, Gilligan, Neale and Murray extend this analysis to identify three types of decisions that managers might encounter, depending on the degree of certainty or uncertainty associated with the outcome, the time period involved, the frequency with which decisions have to be made, the extent to which the subject is routine or non-routine and the implications of the decision for the organisation.

1 **Strategic decisions** are major decisions involving overall strategy. They often require a considerable exercise of judgement by the person responsible for making the decision, because, although such decisions require a considerable amount of analysis, important pieces of information will frequently be missing and so risk will be involved. Examples include the development of a new product, investment in new plant or the development of a new marketing strategy.

2 **Periodic control decisions** are made less frequently than short-term decisions (see below). They are concerned with monitoring how effectively an organisation is managing its resources. Such decisions might include the review of pricing strategies for certain products, the review of problems occurring in an on-going company budget, or the reappraisal of the way in which the sales force is being used. They are concerned with checking for and rectifying problems concerned with meeting company objectives.

3 **Short-term operating control decisions** are decisions that have to be frequently made and involve short-term predictable operations such as the ordering of new stock, the design of a production schedule or the preparation of a transport route for deliveries.

Figure 27.1 Types of decisions

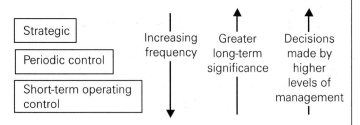

Levels of decision-making

The structure of the decision-making process should be based on the types of decision that need to be made. Routine decisions should, therefore, be dealt with by routine procedures, ensuring that time and money are not wasted unnecessarily on them. There would be no point, for example, in a senior manager spending large amounts of time on a routine task that could be done by someone with less experience. Similarly, decisions requiring in-depth analysis and thought will require careful consideration by someone with a breadth of experience.

Organisations therefore need to develop procedures for decision-making most suited to the nature of the

environment in which they are operating. Gilligan, Neale and Murray recommend, in broad terms:

'Short-term operating and periodic control decisions should be made by junior and middle management who are involved in the day-to-day administration of the organisation, and not by the company's senior management. The task of senior management is to concentrate upon non-routine, non-recurring, strategic decisions in which there is a high degree of uncertainty regarding the outcome and for which, as a consequence, a far greater element of judgement and creativity is required. In those organisations in which senior management does become embroiled in the day-to-day, straightforward operating decisions, the effectiveness and motivation of lower levels of management is likely to suffer, whilst at the same time, because of the preoccupation with short-term decisions, less time is available for long-term issues, with the result that the managerial focus switches from long-range strategic development of the company to short-range control. Thus, insofar as it is possible to generalise, the primary concern of senior management should be with strategic decisions, whilst short-term operational decisions should be left in the hands of operating management. Middle management then acts as the meeting point between the two, taking as its focus the periodic control decisions.'

Strategic decision-making

In recent years a strong emphasis has been given in business management to strategic decisions. Johnson and Scholes in *Exploring Corporate Strategy* identify the following characteristics of strategy:

■ Strategic decisions are likely to be concerned with the scope of an organisation's activities. For example, does the organisation concentrate on one segment of the chocolate market, or does it concentrate on a wide variety of sweets, confectionery, ice-creams, etc? The decision about the scope of an organisation's activities is vital, because it establishes the boundaries in which the organisation operates.

■ Strategy refers to the matching of the activities of an organisation to its environment. For example, does an organisation operate in a local, national or European market? Clearly, this decision is of key importance in deciding a range of other matters such as how the product is marketed or what finance is required. An organisation needs to weigh up the opportunities and threats presented by the environment in which it operates, e.g. the opportunity of increased sales or the threat of increased competition in a wider market.

■ Strategy is concerned with a matching of the organisation's activities to its resource capability. Clearly, the business needs to understand its resource limitations if it is to make the best use of opportunities. An organisation that fails to invest in new technology may rapidly fall behind because of a capital resource deficiency.

■ Strategic decisions, therefore, have major resource implications. Decisions need to be made to ensure that the organisation has the most appropriate resources to move forward. For example, in the late 1980s Mars moved into the ice-cream market in order to compensate for the fall in sales of chocolate bars in the summer months. This required a considerable research programme and investment in new capital equipment by the company.

■ Strategic decisions are likely to affect operational decisions. When Mars moved into the ice-cream market, it had to introduce a new training programme for employees, as well as making changes to sales and distribution methods.

■ The strategy of an organisation will be affected by the values and expectations of those who have power in the organisation. Those groupings of stakeholders that have most influence in the organisation will be able to shape the strategy according to their values and expectations. For example, an influential group of senior managers and directors may have a vision of their company expanding to dominate a market.

■ Strategic decisions are likely to affect the long-term direction of a company as they tend to involve thinking about where the organisation is going in the longer period.

■ Strategic decisions are usually complex. This complexity arises because such decisions usually involve a high degree of uncertainty. They are likely to require an integrated approach involving all elements of the organisation. They are also likely to require and involve major changes in the organisation.

It is little wonder, therefore, that so much emphasis is placed on strategic decision-making. Strategic management is a highly complex process requiring a range of information and the ability and foresight to consider many variables and possible scenarios in a dynamic business environment. It entails deciding on a strategy and planning how that strategy will be put into effect.

There are three main elements to strategic management (see Figure 27.2):

Figure 27.2 The tripartite strategy management process

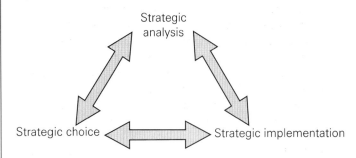

1 Strategic analysis is concerned with understanding the strategic position of an organisation. For example, what is the scope of operation? How can a company match its activities to its environment? How can activities be matched to resource capability?

2 Strategic choice involves:
  a Setting out a menu of strategic options
  b evaluating these options
  c selecting a strategy that is 'best' for the organisation.

3 Strategic implementation involves putting the chosen strategy into action.

Case Study
Competition in confectionery ice-cream

The market for confectionery ice-cream did not exist in 1989. By 1993 it was worth more than £150 million a year and is one of the fastest growing areas in Britain's £850 million ice-cream sector (1994).

Figure 27.3 Popular confectionery: the ice-cream bar

Created by Mars, which was first with its ice-cream bar in 1989, confectionery ice-cream enables chocolate companies to balance the seasonal fluctuations in their business – sales boom in winter, only to fall away in the summer.

However, Mars has been faced by strong competition. Nestlé took over Lyons Maid and quickly entered the market. At the same time, Wall's, part of the giant Unilever Group and producer of Magnum, Europe's best-selling ice-cream, teamed up with Cadbury's to produce ice-cream versions of its chocolate lines.

In the mid-1990s Mars is having difficulty in getting its Mars ice-cream bars into retail outlets. Wall's, which has more than 60 per cent of the impulse market (e.g. lollies bought from shops), and Nestlé's Lyons Maid (12 per cent) supply freezers free of charge to small retailers and corner shops on condition that they stock only their ice-cream in the cabinet. Not only do they supply freezers to shops; they also maintain and service them. The shop just has to pay the electricity bill.

Several experts have commented that if Mars had had access to freezers at an earlier date, it could have made its position impenetrable. Now it is just one of a number of competitors. Wall's has spent more than £20 million on freezer cabinets over the past ten years.

Mars offers a range of well-known brands including Mars, Bounty, Twix and Snickers in ice-cream form. Wall's has Cadbury's Dairy Milk, and Nestlé sells its Milky Bar, KitKat and Aero.

Mars is undoubtedly frustrated that it is unable to compete on equal terms in small shops.

Questions for discussion

1 *How would Mars' move into confectionery ice-cream have involved strategic decision-making?*
2 *How does the case study indicate that there were some weaknesses in Mars' strategic thinking which have prevented the company from dominating the market?*
3 *What relative weaknesses does the case study indicate in Mars' position compared with other competitors?*
4 *How have Wall's and Nestlé's moves into this market involved strategic decision-making?*
5 *What lessons can be learnt from the case study about strategic decision-making?*

Competitive strategy

In *Competitive Strategy* (1980), Michael Porter outlined five major strategic forces facing an organisation (see Figure 27.4). The ability of a company to make profits is determined by the way in which it deals with these forces.

Figure 27.4 Strategic forces and competitive strategy

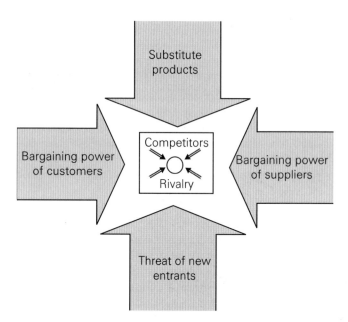

It is only natural that if a successful firm is making high profits, competitors will be enticed into its market segment. Predators naturally think 'There are nice profits to be made – let's have a slice of the action!' Competing firms as well as new entrants seek to increase their share of the market. Management must, therefore, plan a strategy to keep ahead of the threats.

Porter outlines four general strategies for ensuring that a company has a competitive advantage:

1 *Cost leadership* involves creating a very low cost base. Competitive advantage in the marketing mix can, therefore, be based on low prices and value for money.
2 *Differentiation strategy* is based on making a company's products different from those of its competitors. Providing the cost of creating the differentiation is less than the resulting increases in customer valuation of the product, the company will gain a competitive advantage.
3 *Focus strategy* based on cost leadership, where the organisation sets out to be the 'key player' in a particular market segment by relying on competitive advantage.

4 Focus strategy based on differentiation, where the organisation sets out to be the 'key player' in a particular market segment by basing its strength on differentiation.

Professor Kotter argues in *A Force for Change* that 'Strategy involves looking at the larger picture and developing major decisions for an organisation to move in. It is concerned with the Generalship of business.'

Case Study
Newcastle United

The success of Newcastle United in the mid-1990s has been cited as an example of effective strategic thinking.

Figure 27.5 On the ball with strategic thinking

When former footballer Kevin Keegan became manager of Newcastle United in February 1992, Newcastle was second from the bottom of the old Second Division with a debt of £6 million. At the time, he admitted that he wanted to be a football doctor who could cure a very sick patient.

Today, Kevin Keegan is three years into a 10-year contract. Together with the chairman of the club, Sir John Hall, he has built up Newcastle United, overtaking many other big football clubs that were considered superior to them – 'playing-wise, business-wise and revenue-wise'. Success has lifted Newcastle's turnover from £5 million a year to £20 million. The club is simply unable to satisfy demand for seats in its imposing £20 million stadium. Newcastle has developed an entertaining blend of tradition and innovation, which has brought much pride back to the people of the northeast of England.

As Newcastle battled its way up and out of the then Second Division, Keegan was determined that the club would never return to its former position. Getting Keegan on a lengthy contract has enabled the club to plan a long-term strategy. Their dream is to turn Newcastle United into an institution fit to rival Barcelona and AC Milan in a European super-league.

So how has Newcastle United achieved this success so quickly? Employing Kevin Keegan and buying good players is only part of the picture. At the heart of this success has been the formulation and development of a clear-cut strategy, targeted at a series of specific and attainable goals and objectives (such as to join the European elite), together with a series of practical actions taken to pursue this direction (new manager, players, ground, pursuing good results on the field of play, etc.).

Questions for discussion

1 *What is the vision that the success of Newcastle United has been based upon?*
2 a *Why is it important to convert this vision into a strategy?*
  b *What do you think are the ingredients of this strategy?*
3 *What sort of strategic decisions have been taken to put planning into action?*
4 *What external and internal factors might cause strategic planning at Newcastle United to be blown off course?*

The strategic process can be divided into two main areas:

- **ends** – setting the longer-term goals as well as the shorter-term objectives
- **means** – taking decisions and developing the ability to achieve them.

The process of strategic decision-making can also be shown as a management cycle (see Figure 27.6).

The importance of innovation for mature organisations

An important contribution to thinking about corporate strategy was that made by Igor Ansoff in his book of that name. Ansoff indicated that an organisation needs to identify its basic growth vectors, i.e. the directions in

Figure 27.6 The strategic management cycle

Figure 27.7 The strategic staircase of progress

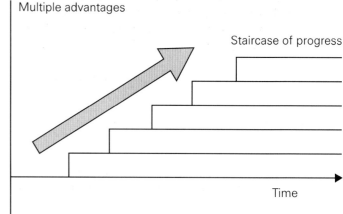

which it is seeking strategic growth, such as by product development diversification.

Organisations need constantly to ask themselves 'Where do we go from here?' Failure to ask this question can lead to an organisation's rapid decline, particularly one that has been in existence for a long time. Innovation should be a key part of the strategic development of mature organisations.

Innovation involves making a change to something in order to make it either different or new. According to Charles Baden-Fuller and John Stopford in *Rejuvenating the Mature Business*, organisations can challenge maturity and create value for all their stakeholders through strategic innovation. They point out the contrast between dynamic organisations and mature ones. For example, whereas managers in mature organisations perceive a stable environment, slow growth in demand and a need for only minor changes in technology, managers in dynamic businesses constantly look for new strategies ignored by the mature business. In 'mature organisations, features such as greater variety, higher quality or more speedy reaction are commonly seen as incompatible with low cost.'

The aim of strategic innovation is to develop a series of stages of innovation, each step of which builds on previous changes. This continuous staircase of innovation (see Figure 27.7) then provides multiple advantages and as Baden-Fuller and Stopford point out, 'When leaders have multiple advantages, the follower has little scope for profitable positions'.

Baden-Fuller and Stopford then relate strategic innovation to the world of economic and organisational change. They depict top management caught in the cogs

between the dynamic economics of the market (responding to customer preferences, competitive activities and new technologies) and the intransigence of the organisation (see Figure 27.8).

Figure 27.8 Outside factors represent relentless forces if the organisation fails to innovate

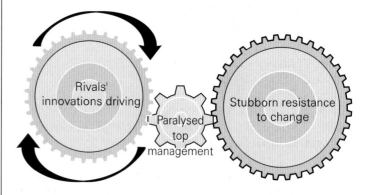

To achieve this strategic change, Baden-Fuller and Stopford point to the need for both radical and incremental moves (see Figure 27.9): 'Radical in the

Figure 27.9 The truly entrepreneurial organisation strategically innovating to drive change through the marketplace

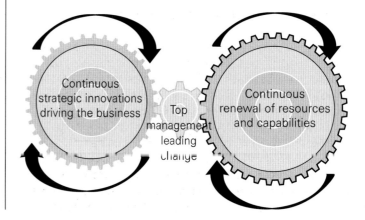

sense that beliefs are altered, structures are torn down, skills modified and new technology introduced. It is also incremental in the sense that for any organisation which has limited resources, change must be undertaken from within and in a way that does not take unnecessary risks.'

Case Study
The transformation of public utilities to private-sector concerns

In recent years we have seen the transformation of public utilities into private-sector concerns in many areas such as gas, water and electricity.

This provides an interesting case study of organisations having to adjust their strategies in order to cope with a changing external environment. The accountancy firm Arthur Andersen has developed a model for British and American organisations that have followed this pathway, including the water industry in Britain and railways and airlines in the USA. The model identifies five stages which are involved in the transformation. These are set out in 'Predictable Patterns: Navigating the Continuum from Protected Monopoly to Market Competition':

Stage 1: Equilibrium
Stage 2: Rumblings in the provinces
Stage 3: Identify crisis
Stage 4: Refocus
Stage 5: Dynamic competition

Stage 1: Equilibrium

This is the initial period in which companies are vertically integrated and have their strategy determined by regulatory policies. They cross-subsidise the markets in which they operate and set out to provide an equitable and universal service. Customers are passive because they do not understand their potential influence. Power within the organisation tends to be in the hands of technocrats, e.g. engineers, lawyers and accountants.

Stage 2: Rumblings in the provinces

A combination of changes in technology, the development of new market substitutes and/or changes in public policy lead to the emergence of competitors at the edge of the industry – typically in activities where profits are high, markets are attractive and it is relatively easy to compete on price. Managers initially try to ignore these changes. Managers who warn of potential competition are told that the advantages of economies of scale, barriers to entry, etc. will serve to keep out the competition. However, customers are becoming increasingly aware of alternatives. Once competition moves in at the edges, the existing structure quickly begins to change. Once high-margin customers have been attracted away, the burden of cross-subsidy becomes greater.

Stage 3: Identify crisis

Now the market is becoming increasingly attractive to the new competitors, who are beginning to take an increasing market share.

Faced with such losses, the previous state monopoly begins to appeal to the regulators. This fails, forcing them to resort to price-cutting strategies and extensive cost reductions. As the market becomes hotter, mergers may begin to occur and firms who have miscalculated will face bankruptcy. The culture of organisations begins to switch from the 'top-heavy bureaucracy' to the 'lean and mean entrepreneurial organisation'.

Hard-headed managers who are good at downsizing become more important in the business structure and lawyers continue to maintain their importance. Concern for returns on capital lead investors to seek more influence in the organisation. Employees feel unsettled by all the changes, particularly to work organisation. Customers increasingly begin to 'play the field'.

Stage 4: Refocus

Refocus occurs when the remaining players in the field begin to create more effective strategies to meet the new environment in which they operate. Companies begin increasingly to operate in distinct market segments and to unbundle their services. Organisations focus on their core strengths. They engage in horizontal growth, which is based on better meeting the needs of consumers. With the increasing emphasis on the customer, the marketing department begins to play a key role in the organisation. Marketing begins to dominate the strategic process as well as finance.

Stage 5: Dynamic competition

This is a point of equilibrium 'not because it is quiet but because it represents the full adjustment of the industry to a competitive marketplace'.

The success of the organisation depends on how it adapts to supply and demand. The resources and capabilities of the organisation need to be focused directly on meeting customer needs. This situation is exactly the same as that faced by organisations which have been brought up in a competitive environment in the private sector.

Questions for discussion

1 *Why and how will the strategy of an organisation in the public sector differ from one that operates in the private sector?*
2 *What are the main adjustments that are required in strategic thinking as an organisation moves from the public to the private sector?*
3 *Why is it essential for an organisation to refocus its strategy as it makes these changes?*
4 *Why does marketing strategy become so important as an organisation moves fully into the private sector?*

Functional and operation level decision-making

Decisions are not made just at the top of an organisation. Decision-making is an everyday process which is carried out at all levels.

Functional decision-making involves decisions made in personnel, marketing, finance, etc. Different decisions lie within the province of different people within the functional hierarchy.

Management decisions usually require levels of judgement. These decisions take place at all levels of management. There are two aspects of decision-making to be considered when looking at the level in the functional hierarchy at which these decisions are made:

1 The nature of the problem. Is it a clearly structured problem requiring set solutions? Or is it an unstructured problem requiring considerable thought and analysis? An unstructured problem can be tackled in a variety of ways, a number of which may be equally valid.

The general rule is: the more unstructured the problem, the more it lies in the province of senior management; the more structured the problem, the more likely it is to be located within the scope of operational decision-making (see Figure 27.10).

Figure 27.10 Nature of problem and locus of decision-making

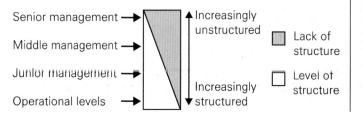

2 The nature of decision-making. We have already seen that some decisions are programmed, while others are non-programmed (page 657). Programmed decisions are increasingly likely to be taken by operational levels (see Figure 27.11).

Figure 27.11 Nature of decisions to be taken and locus of decision-making

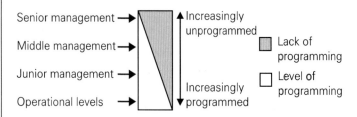

The above analysis is rather simplistic in that it primarily relates to organisations with functional hierarchies. In many modern organisations, decision-making is increasingly spread out within the organisation so that there are networks of empowered individuals. In such a situation, all members of an organisation make programmed and non-programmed decisions and deal with structured and unstructured problems (See Figure 27.12).

Figure 27.12 Locus of decision-making in an entrepreneurial democratic organisation

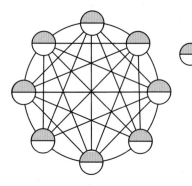

Decision makers taking programmed/ unprogrammed decisions involving structured/ unstructured problems

Information technology as a decision-making tool

Advanced computers are increasingly being used as decision-making tools, particularly for making programmed decisions. An expert system in a computer can be fed with huge quantities of data relevant to making particular decisions. The computer can then sift through the various options in order to suggest the most favourable one.

The advantages of using computers for programmed decisions are that:

- they are quick
- they are reliable
- they are accurate
- they have extremely large memories
- they can make objective decisions based on the best available evidence.

We look at the importance of computers in the decision-making process in more detail on pages 683–4.

Case Study
Using computers to make decisions in medicine

Today, computers are used to make many decisions concerning the use of resources in the health service. For example, fund-holding GPs use computers as a desktop aid to decide which drugs to prescribe to patients for particular illnesses. The GP can quickly compare the cost and applications of particular drugs.

Hospital managers use computer programmes to plan investment in new equipment, to schedule the inflow and outflow of patients into available hospital beds, etc.

It has also been suggested that expert systems can be used to decide on which patients should be given priority in treatment. The argument is that resources should be channelled where they will be most effective. If £100 000 could save 30 lives, then this might be better than spending the same money on trying to save patients who are almost certain to die. Using a computer model based on previous treatments and success rates, hospitals can make the best decisions for allocating scarce funds.

Questions for discussion

1 *What sorts of programmed decision might computers be useful for in health service decision-making?*
2 *What sorts of decision might computers be inappropriate for in health service decision-making?*
3 *Is it appropriate and reasonable to use computers to make decisions about which patients should be treated?*
4 *Is it ethical to consider cost-effectiveness when making decisions about whether to give life-saving treatment or not?*

An open-systems decisions model

Many of the decisions that need to be made by individuals within organisations involve uncertainty. In a complex, dynamic society change is ever-present. In such an environment it is helpful to develop an open-system approach to decision-making. A closed-system approach assumes that organisations have clearly defined and unambiguous goals.

An open-systems approach dispenses with the notion that the effects of decisions can readily be computed and calculated and works on the premise that at best information will be imperfect. An open-systems model places emphasis on feedback, learning and adaptation, together with the effects of these upon ends and means.

An open-systems approach can be used to show how the decision-making process may be made more flexible. The system can then adjust to changing circumstances and to changing perceptions and understandings of available information.

Figure 27.13 illustrates one way in which an open-systems model might operate.

Figure 27.13 The decision cycle

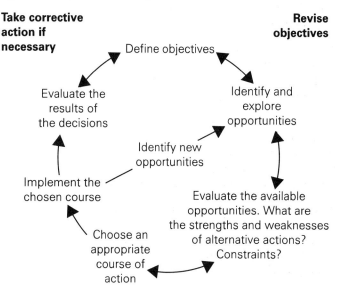

Stage 1: Define objectives

Objectives are rarely clear cut and this stage involves the identification of objectives to be pursued. These will be open to review. Setting objectives involves selecting courses of action that are appropriate to the organisation and establishing measures for assessing their attainment.

Stage 2: Identify and explore opportunities

The next stage is to identify as many opportunities for an organisation, division, department, operating unit, etc. as possible. Exploration involves identifying the potential impacts of these opportunities.

Stage 3: Evaluate opportunities and implications of taking a particular pathway/decision

Evaluation processes range from an inspired guess to a highly researched piece of analysis and assessment. Choosing a particular alternative in decision-making may be based on:

- previous experience. Organisations and managers have a collective experience of handling similar decisions and activities. However, they may need to be careful when the decision is based on new considerations or a changed organisational environment.
- experimentation, by trying out various alternatives to see which is likely to be the best, e.g. testing out alternative new products before deciding on the best choice.
- detailed research and analysis. This is perhaps the best way of making a decision. It requires a full understanding of the situation before making a calculated decision.

At this point, the organisation should be considering whether making a particular decision will help it to meet its objectives.

Stage 4: Choose the action

Provided that the decision maker can show a clear match between an action and objectives, he or she can then choose the most effective of the alternative courses of action. For example, if an organisation's objective is to achieve some measure of guaranteed success, it might choose a course of action that avoids risk. Alternatively, it might be prepared to take a risk if the objective is to achieve high returns.

If the chosen course of action does not look likely to meet the required objectives, the decision maker should either reduce the target goal to manageable proportions or seek alternative courses of action to meet the original target.

Stage 5: Implement the chosen course

Once the groundwork has been covered and all aspects of potential decisions have been discussed, a decision can be made. The effects of the decision should then be closely monitored. Putting the decision into practice may quickly lead to the identification of new opportunities. For example, once the USA had implemented its space programme, researchers immediately became aware of fresh opportunities such as the Space Shuttle. These possibilities help organisations to meet their objectives in new and different ways.

Stage 6: Evaluate the results of the decision

The results of the decision need to be clearly appraised and evaluated to improve the decision-making process. Corrective action can be taken if necessary.

The decision-making cycle is an on-going process. The open-ended nature of the process means that the quality of decisions should increase with time.

The open-systems approach highlights the importance of evaluation to decision-making. Results need continually to be fed back to decision makers so that they can reappraise decisions in the light of an increasing quantity and quality of information. Feedback can lead to adjustment. A simple illustration of how this can have beneficial effects is in the training of cricketers using computer programs that simulate their bowling action. Programs have been developed which play back to the bowlers a picture of their action in bowling a cricket ball. The cricketers are thereby provided with feedback on current performance, enabling them to take corrective action, to appraise existing technique and to develop an understanding of new possibilities.

The nine-phase decision-making process

Ernest Archer studied more than 2000 managers, executives and supervisors, as well as the research of major writers on organisations. In his book *Decisions, Decisions*, he produced a decision-making framework which highlighted the decision maker's need to monitor continually the environment in which decisions are made (see Figure 27.14).

The model necessitates obtaining feedback on any deviations from expected, acceptable, pre-planned or normal states.

1 **Monitor**. First, it is essential that managers have a clear idea of how things 'ought to be'.

The other eight stages involve the following tasks:

2 **Define** the decision or problem to be tackled and clearly state the boundaries.
3 **Specify** the objectives of the decision. What do you expect to achieve? What are the constraints?
4 **Diagnose** the problem or situation and analyse its cause.
5 **Develop** a range of alternative solutions and courses of action.
6 **Establish** criteria for weighing up alternatives.

Figure 27.14 Archer's model of decision-making

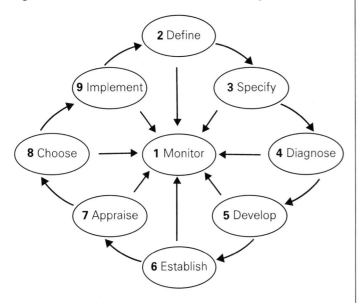

7 **Appraise** the alternative solutions or courses of action.
8 **Choose** the best solution.
9 **Implement** the best solution or course of action.

In the modern business environment there are many factors that encourage the growth of group decision-making. First, the modern business environment is so complicated that effective decision-making now requires groups of minds working together to tackle problems and think things through. Second, participative management has become increasingly fashionable in business circles. The encouragement of a wider number of people within an organisation to think of themselves as managers and to become involved in decision-making means that a greater range of expertise can be drawn upon. At one time, a large bank branch had just one person at the top – the manager – now there are several 'managers'.

For any company, and particularly for those with wide geographical spreads and a range of product types, decentralisation is essential. Most decisions, especially tactical ones, cannot be taken effectively at the centre, which may be miles – or continents – away; they have to be taken immediately, on the spot, by people who know all the circumstances.

Decision-making within a problem-solving sequence

Decision-making can be seen as a necessary response to problems and issues.

Strategic decisions are likely to involve the anticipation of problems and issues. Strategic decisions need to be made to keep ahead of problems.

At a managerial level, as we have seen, decisions involve both closed and open-ended problems. Many problems facing managers are not straightforward – there is no one best solution to the problem. Decision-making, therefore, needs to be based on experienced analysis and sound judgement. At an operational level, problems are often clear cut, so that simple programmed decisions can be made.

In simple situations it should be relatively easy to provide the best solution to a problem, which leads to the achievement of the end objective (see Figure 27.15).

Figure 27.15 Problem-solving

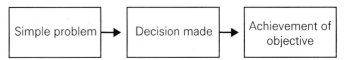

Problem-solving and decision-making can be seen as two elements of a single process. Good management is all about using managerial experience, instinct and flair to make the best possible decisions.

What is a problem?

Much has been written about the nature of a problem. Some writers see a problem as something which needs to be understood and solved. Others see a problem as existing when there is a discrepancy between the desired state of affairs and the actual state of affairs. The problem solver is, therefore, concerned with finding out 'what went wrong' and then 'putting it right'. Once the problem is solved, the number of problems becomes fewer.

In contrast, the incremental theory states that problems increase rather than become fewer. The actions taken in problem-solving are likely to create new problems. For this reason, the theory says, we should recognise our limited understanding and the complex relationship between variables. Problem-solving, therefore, should not aim to solve all problems, just the most important ones in a given situation.

In practical terms it is helpful for managers to concentrate on two aspects of problem-solving:

■ a 'what went wrong' approach which can be used when deviations from the norm or the expected occur
■ as a way of making choices between alternatives which affect the future (e.g. performance).

The literature is full of examples of problem-solving models which are based around identifying causes of problems, considering alternative solutions and then implementing decisions.

Andrew Leigh provides an excellent 'no nonsense' questions-based framework for decision-making in *Decisions, Decisions* (see Figure 27.16).

Figure 27.16 Andrew Leigh's question sequence

Steps in problem-solving

Step 1

Diagnose the problem fully and correctly. It is not easy to do this because problems are usually interconnected. There is a saying that a properly defined problem is half solved. It is essential, therefore, to spend considerable time trying to diagnose the real nature of a problem.

The first part of this process should be concerned with identifying the symptoms of difficulty in a situation, e.g. the symptoms of poor performance in the prison service in early 1995 were low levels of staff morale, lack of cooperation between prison staff and outside agencies and other issues. Clearly, there is likely to be a variety of possible causes of these symptoms. A mistake would be to jump to a quick solution to the symptom, e.g. raising wages of prison officers.

To get to the root causes of a particular problem, it is essential to collect and analyse information relating to that problem both within and outside an organisation, e.g. by interviewing people, charting the incidence of particular events, etc.

Step 2

Identify the constraints and decision criteria. It is essential that any decisions made can be put into effect. There is no point in suggesting a course of action which is not

feasible. The constraints to be considered vary widely, but may often include the size and sources of funds, the knowledge and skills of the people concerned and the support for a particular decision.

Managers must also decide on the standards against which the alternative choices can be measured, i.e. the decision criteria. For example, the criteria might include that the solution must:

- cost less than £100 000 to implement
- be put into effect within the next six months
- not divert the organisation from its core strengths.

Step 3

Identify alternatives. It is important to identify as many practicable solutions as possible. Too often, managers seek 'a solution', meaning the first acceptable solution. The more alternatives considered, the better the final decision is likely to be. However, if too much time is spent seeking alternatives, this can be costly and may lead to confusion (alternatives overload).

Step 4

Evaluate the alternatives. It is often helpful to put forward as many alternatives as possible and then to screen out those solutions which are unacceptable, not feasible, etc. Evaluation of alternatives involves weighing up the advantages and disadvantages of each solution.

Step 5

Choose the best solution from the range of alternatives.

Organisational factors affecting decision-making

Decision-making takes place within an organisational setting. The organisational setting has a profound influence on the decisions that can be and are made. For example, in an organisation that is tightly controlled from the top, there is little scope for decision-making lower down the hierarchy. The car manufacturer Henry Ford is the classic example of a leader who set out plans, policies and programmes from above, limiting the freedom of subordinates to make personal contributions.

Frequently, decisions are made by a political process involving the creation of coalitions between the various groups that have power within an organisation.

Policy conflicts

Organisations are made up of stakeholders with varying levels of influence and power within the organisation. While the objectives of the organisation reflect a general agreement between stakeholders, it is likely that policies which are generated within the organisation may clash with one another (see Figure 27.17).

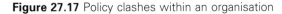

Figure 27.17 Policy clashes within an organisation

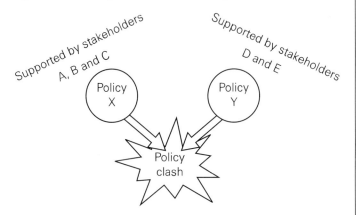

There are a number of reasons why this may occur:

1 differing interpretations of organisational objectives. For example, the local traffic-planning department devises a scheme to ration parking within the town centre by introducing a 'pay and display' scheme. The objectives of the scheme are improving fairness, reducing traffic congestion, raising revenue for the local council, etc. However, the way the local traffic wardens interpret the objectives is to give the owner of every car found in a 'pay and display area' without a valid parking ticket an immediate £20 fine. The problem with this scheme is that visitors to the town who are not aware that they are in a 'pay and display' area are being penalised alongside local residents. This creates considerable hostility in tourists, which embarrasses the traffic-planning department and local council. Clearly, there is a need to clarify the objectives and the way in which they are interpreted. In the short term, this might lead to conflict between the various departments: 'How do you expect us to be able to do our job when you don't make the objectives clear!'

2 deliberate misinterpretations of objectives. At any time it is possible for managers or other decision makers deliberately to misinterpret objectives, often to increase their own power and prestige. Individual managers may start to create their own policies which further the interests of their own department. Several different managers may adopt different policies which pull against each other. For example, in an organisation which tries to combine the mixed objectives of creating social welfare and making profits, e.g. a hospital trust or grant-maintained school, there will be some managers who favour one of these objectives and some who prefer the other.

3 changes in policy. Dynamic organisations frequently adjust their direction according to changes in circumstances. This leads to alterations in policy. Unless these changes are communicated to and agreed by all sections of an organisation, some people may continue working to old policy guidelines, while others are working to new guidelines. This may be as a result of deliberate sabotage or genuine lack of understanding. The solution lies in clearer communication and coordination.

4 internal politics. At any one time, segments of an organisation may be allied with particular stakeholders, e.g. employees, while other segments are allied with other stakeholders, e.g. shareholders. This may lead to a variety of formal and informal policy-making with a number of policies clashing.

5 bad management. Poor management may result in lack of focus and conflicting policies.

6 inevitable differences in policy. There is a certain inevitability in the way that policies may clash or work against each other. Policies designed to deal with particular problems and issues often create spin-off problems and issues that work against other policies. Trade-offs then need to be made. For example, the government that pursues policies designed to reduce inflation may create more unemployment, while the government that sets out policies to reduce unemployment may create more inflation; the government that tries to reduce both unemployment and inflation may find that these policies work against each other – so a trade-off will need to be made.

Case Study
Conservative government policy on standards in education

The Conservative government of the early to mid-1990s introduced performance standards for measuring the success of schools, the aim being to make it possible to compare the results of one school with another. Results of GCSEs and A levels were published annually in a league-table format alongside other indicators such as truancy rates. The policy was part of a drive to improve standards in education and to identify schools where performance was poor or falling. Inspectors of schools were then able to identify poor performers and suggest remedial action in these schools. Indeed, where schools were failing in a number of areas, it became possible to put a team of experienced teachers into the school to help to raise standards.

At the same time, all schools had to create a set of objectives and policies which governed their operation and activities. School governors became responsible for making sure that the school drew up plans and policies and that these policies were regularly reviewed. Clearly, the objectives of the school were determined by local circumstances and the nature of the school. In this way, the school was expected to establish objectives which reflected the wishes of major stakeholders, including parents, pupils and teachers. Every school is different, and while most schools shared similar objectives, there were qualitative differences in the nature of objectives, e.g. the emphasis on pastoral care, extra-curricular activities, attitudes to competition/cooperation, etc.

The problem of national league tables was that they only represented a narrow range of performance criteria, e.g. academic achievement or attendance at school. Moreover, they did not reflect the objectives of individual schools. It is as if all firms in the confectionery industry were to be judged on the number of packets of sweets they produced in a year (regardless of the type of sweets, the number in each packet, quality, etc).

Questions for discussion

1 *Why might government policy differ from policies made locally at school level?*
2 *How might this lead to a mismatch in the performance criteria which would be appropriate at government and school level?*
3 *Are national league tables of performance appropriate in such a situation? What are their strengths and weaknesses?*
4 *What alternatives would be more appropriate than national league tables?*
5 *How might government policy and school policy come into conflict?*
6 *What do you think would be the likely results of such a clash for:*
   a *the government*
   b *school governors*
   c *school managers*
   d *teachers*
   e *other stakeholders in the school?*

Policy conflict is likely to occur in organisations in which there are differences in perspective between members of the organisation. For example, in an organisation structured on functional lines, the marketing department is likely to think in terms of marketing, the accounts department to stress the importance of finance and numbers, the human resources department to emphasise people, etc. In an international company based on divisions, department heads are likely to think in a geographical way and to create regional policies. Resolution of conflict involves encouraging people to think organisationally, i.e. to work towards the organisation's objectives as the priority.

Values

Decision makers often make decisions on the basis of the values which they regard to be important. The term 'value' in this context refers to the subjective ranking of the importance or quality of a particular policy or action, e.g. it is better to carry out policies which are environmentally friendly or which treat people as individuals rather than as extensions of machinery.

It is not just decisions based on ethical issues which are based on values. All business decisions are based on implicit or explicit values.

Everyone in an organisation makes decisions on the basis of the values they hold. Decision makers frequently have differing perceptions about the existence and severity of problems, as well as the range of possible solutions. These perceptions will be shaped by previous experience of the problem and the solution, depth of knowledge, bias and relationships with others involved in the decision-making process. Past experience in job responsibilities has an important influence on attitudes and values. Bias and loyalty also plays a significant part in decision-making. For example, a prejudice against female managers may lead to veiled discrimination in the recruitment and selection process. Loyalty may mean that decisions are made on the basis of existing practices and friendships rather than on rational and logical thinking. Some managers may value profits above all else, while others value human relations and compassion. These values determine the decisions that are made, e.g. whether or not to provide a staff canteen or recreation facilities.

Case Study
A clash of values – profit orientation or 'the inclusive company'?

Within Europe in the mid-1990s there was a clash of thinking between those such as the free marketers in the Conservative Party who wanted to see a return to nineteenth-century free markets and those such as the Scandinavians and German Social Democrats who pressed the case for social justice based on providing minimum standards for all citizens.

The free marketers in Britain argued that barriers such as minimum wages and powerful trade unions prevented businesses from keeping down costs in order to be competitive in a highly competitive global economy. They claimed that the route to prosperity was to minimise the part played by the state and business in creating social justice.

The concept of the 'inclusive firm' is of a business that recognises its responsibilities to its staff, suppliers, customers and the community, as well as satisfying the needs of investors (see Figure 27.18) The Social Democrats argued that the vision of the inclusive firm shares the same principles as the EU Social Chapter, i.e. increasing job opportunities, improving hiring and working conditions, promoting dialogue between management and workers and encouraging investment in training.

Figure 27.18 Responsibilities of the 'inclusive firm'

Companies such as Northern Foods, which has always had a strong social conscience, supported the inclusive firm in both theory and practice. Christopher Hasking, Chairman of Northern Foods, commented in July 1994 in *The Independent*:

'The belief that Britain's economic prosperity should rely on companies that pay low wages and are not committed to improving the skills of staff is inappropriate for a developed Western democracy.

'Most successful companies recognise this and, on their own initiative, pay decent wages, make proper social provisions for staff, do not discriminate and invest heavily in training. The problem is that compared with other social democracies, Britain is very short of successful companies. Lacking in skills and investment, the country cannot compete with its developed competitors, and it is impossible for low-skilled Britain to succeed against the low-cost developing world. So a sensible government would support the general aims of the Social Chapter and endorse the concept of the "inclusive company". It would restrain companies from exploiting staff and require them to contribute substantially towards the welfare of their staff, thereby promoting justice and reducing the state's social security burden. It would encourage cooperation with suppliers – many of them small companies – rather than condone the confrontation and exploitation that still prevails. And it would promote a greater link between companies and the communities in which they operate.'

Questions for discussion

1 *What sorts of value would be predominant in the inclusive company?*
2 *How might these values clash with those of someone who had worked for a more conventional form of company?*
3 *How would the values of the inclusive company translate into specific policies?*
4 *What steps would be necessary in transforming a traditional organisation into an inclusive company?*

Miles and Snow, in *Organisational Strategy, Structure and Process*, drew a different type of distinction between prevalent values in an organisation. They distinguished between:

■ **defender organisations**, in which values are principally conservative and concerned with low-risk strategies in secure markets, and where decisions are based on tried and trusted methods
■ **prospector organisations**, in which values are based on innovation and breaking new ground.

Within the same environment the two types of organisation may operate in quite different ways.

Within the same organisation different divisions, departments, groups and individuals may operate with different value systems. It is often important to ensure that the personality types of individuals that are recruited match with those of the organisation's objectives, although there is a counterargument that organisations may benefit from having represented within them a variety of beliefs and values. For example, in an entrepreneurial organisation, it might be the cautious accountant who prevents financial disaster; in a conventional business, such as a veterinary partnership, the introduction of a younger partner with bright and interesting new ideas might prove invaluable, etc. An individual's values influence the way he or she approaches decision-making.

Studies of managers indicate that there are two main sets of values that influence decision-making:

■ the organisation's goals – profit maximisation, the inclusive company, etc.

- personal goals – job security, promotion, a high income, etc.

Different individuals give different weightings to the relative importance of these two sets of goals. Some managers are seen to be 'all for themselves', while others are viewed as 'company people'. However, it is often difficult to make a clear distinction – someone who appears to be 'a good company person' may, in fact, be a shrewd 'go-getter'.

Bargaining and trade-offs

Bargaining and trade-offs need to be made frequently in order to push through decisions. Within the organisation different groups and individuals give different priorities to particular plans and actions.

When it comes to making a choice as to the best way of solving a problem or making use of an opportunity, there will be different sets of values at stake. Successful managers use bargaining techniques to win support for their most-favoured decisions. Bargaining takes place at a number of levels within the organisation:

- **Top-down bargaining** may mean offering concessions if people further down the organisation are prepared to accept a particular decision, e.g. if employees meet a particular target before Christmas in order to fulfil an important order, they will be entitled to an extra day's holiday over the New Year.
- **Bottom-up bargaining** may involve granting certain concessions in return for authority to make a particular decision. For example, if senior management grants authorisation to purchase a particular machine, then the middle manager concerned will personally oversee the installation of the equipment.
- **Horizontal bargaining** involves making trade-offs and deals between segments, such as departments at the same level. For example, if personnel is supported in pushing through a decision to introduce new recruiting procedures, then it will support marketing in its request to extend the market-research budget.

Bargaining allows the exchange of offers, counteroffers and concessions, either formally or informally.

Perhaps the most significant determinant of bargaining strength is **relative power**. A powerful individual (e.g. one with considerable command over resources) is in a strong position to exert bargaining power.

In terms of bargaining power, it is often the person with most to gain who may be at a disadvantage.

Negotiating tactics also affect the strength of bargaining power. Effective tactics may involve trying to reduce the aspirations of the opposing negotiaters so that they are

prepared to accept a reduced bargain. Various techniques used include 'the big lie', when the negotiator is convinced that the opposing side has an alternative partner who can be brought into the bargain.

In negotiations, the size of the initial offer is also an important determinant of success in bargaining. Where one side sets its sights low, it is unlikely to achieve very much. The level of expectations of those involved in bargaining is very important. Those individuals and groups who have high hopes and expectations are likely to gain most.

Another factor of importance in bargaining is the way in which participants approach each other's position in the bargain. A win/win approach, where both sides will benefit, is the most likely to be successful and is likely to lead to long-standing relationships and alliances. Alternatively, a win/lose approach may lead to the loss of a friend when the party to the bargain becomes aware of this attitude or when the loss is incurred.

Personality issues

The personality of the decision maker is a prime factor in the way that decisions are approached. Decisions are usually made by people. Even when they are made by machines, the machines have first been programmed by people.

Decision-making requires a number of skills. Some decisions need a particular type of skill, such as the ability to follow a set pattern of rules, while others require a range of different skills, such as the ability to respond to novel and changing situations.

Some individuals may have the sorts of personality that are suited to analysing and evaluating various options, but are hopeless at implementing a decision; others may have the strength to implement decisions, but are ineffective at evaluating the results. Some people are cautious, while others are rash. Different decisions require different types of decision maker. Comments such as 'He can never make up his mind' or 'She comes up with ideas but never puts them into practice' are all criticisms of attitudes to decision-making. Some decisions require caution, while others required single-mindedness, and still others a combination of the two. The ability to make a decision and to put it into effect depends on intelligence and confidence. Individuals have varying abilities to cope with uncertainty, depending on, for example, status, which in turn depends on age, gender, education, social class, etc.

Perception

An individual's perception of a situation will also have a major influence on how decisions are made. Given the same set of stimuli, individuals select what they regard to be important. The way that each perceives a situation depends on his or her own previous experience and understanding. For example, when a Boeing-747 exploded in mid-air over the Scottish town of Lockerbie in December 1988, some of the residents at first thought that they were experiencing a major earthquake. This interpretation of events was due to the wide media coverage of a catastrophic earthquake in Armenia the previous week, which was still very much in the public imagination. Also, they had no other way of explaining the widespread devastation. Other residents of the town, who realised there had been an explosion in the sky, were immediately able to recognise that an aeroplane had crashed.

It has been suggested that there are four main ways in which perception influences the decision-making process:

1 Decision makers are sometimes influenced by factors of which they are not conscious at the time. For example, a personal manager interviewing a candidate for a job may take an instant like/dislike to him or her for no apparent reason.
2 When making abstract decisions, a decision maker might simply be influenced by emotional factors.
3 When it is not clear what the exact nature of the problem is, a decision may be made on the basis of influences that are really irrelevant to the given issue, e.g. a novice gambler selects a horse on the basis of the horse's name, rather than on the form card.
4 The comments and views of high-status individuals may be given more attention than those of low-status individuals. Status can be a key factor in influencing decision-making in group meetings.

Attitudes to risk

An individual's attitude to risk can have a bearing on decision-making. Preference theory is based on the idea that individuals have different attitudes to risk:

- Risk averters are only willing to take lower risks than those indicated by probabilities.
- Gamblers are willing to take higher risks than those indicated by probabilities.

Higher-level managers are more accustomed to taking large risks than are lower-level ones, and their decision areas tend to involve greater elements of risk. Most managers tend to be risk averters because failure will be seen as a threat to their own lifestyles and plans.

Research has indicated that people who are more intelligent are likely to study and analyse a situation in some depth before making a decision, whereas those with less intelligence are more inclined to 'hope for the best'

(Scodel *et al.*, 1959). Individuals who worry about failure are less likely to take big risks.

Decision takers and decision makers

Decision-making is an integral part of management. Being able to make effective decisions is a test of management expertise.

Henry Mintzberg identified four classes of decisions that managers make depending on the role they are playing. It is essentially this ability to make decisions that sets managers apart from the rest. The four roles that managers play are (see Figure 27.19):

- entrepreneur
- disturbance handler
- resource allocator
- negotiator.

Figure 27.19 The four roles of the manager

As entrepreneurs, managers make decisions about changing what is happening in an organisation. They may have both to introduce change and to take part in deciding what changes are to be made. In principle, they are acting voluntarily. For example, a sales manager might identify opportunities that would result from diversifying into new countries and new brands.

This is very different from the manager's role as disturbance handler, where decisions have to be made because of events that are beyond the manager's control, for example, when an overseas country in which a company sells its products suddenly raises import restrictions. The manager needs to have the skill to make an appropriate response to such a disturbance.

The resource allocation role of the manager is a key part of organisational management. Managers need to make decisions about how to allocate money, people, equipment, time and other resources. Mintzberg pointed out that in the resource allocation role the manager schedules time, programmes work and authorises actions.

In the negotiator's role the manager has to negotiate with others and, in the process, be able to make decisions about the commitment of organisational roles.

The relationship between a decision maker and a decision taker is an important one. Decisions are generated ('made') by managers and others within the organisation. They are then received ('taken') by other members of the organisation.

The skill of management involves making and communicating decisions so that they are taken in the spirit intended and are understood clearly. Receivers of decisions are far more disposed to accept them when:

- they have been consulted about the decision to be made
- they have been involved in the decision-making process
- they clearly understand the reasons behind the decision
- they fully understand the decision (i.e. it is communicated with precision) and its implications
- they accept the decision
- the decision puts them in a winning position
- they can present their views on the decision.

All members of organisations are both decision makers and decision takers. In a modern democratic organisation all members should be frequent decision makers. Individuals make better decision takers if they are empowered decision makers.

Roles and responsibilities

Decision-making is traditionally featured as solely a management role. Today, this is no longer the case. In a 'modern' organisation all members are seen as being decision makers. However, this places considerable responsibility on the individuals concerned.

Charles Ford, a researcher, studied eight executives over a number of years. He identified several personal characteristics which helped to make them effective decision makers. They are:

- self-confidence, self-assurance and impatience, which often led these decision makers to be abrupt and sometimes tactless with subordinates
- respect for opposition and conflict, but mainly on substantive issues
- a sense of security leading to unilateral decision-making
- an ability to focus on the relationship between problem, impact, and solution – these decision makers were able to ignore irrelevant material.

Clearly, the above analysis only relates to a particular type of decision maker, i.e. those who are able to snap their fingers and create instant one-person decisions. Other

types of decisions require a considerable amount of teamwork and cooperation. This may require the ability to work with others, to communicate clearly and to share ideas on an equal footing. In this situation, the teamworker with analytical and problem-solving skills is essential. There are many types of decisions and, therefore, many types of role to be played. The types of decision-making process depend on the structure of the organisation, whether tall, functional bureaucracies or lean, organic structures. Whichever the type of decision, there will be considerable responsibilities involved. The more these responsibilities can be shared, the easier it will be for individuals to take risks.

In making a particular decision a number of people may be involved, for example, the one who:

- identifies a problem (a troubleshooter)
- tries to identify the cause of the problem (a diagnoser)
- identifies alternative solutions to the problem (a researcher/analyst)
- selects the best solution to the problem (a decision maker)
- carries out the decision (a decision taker)
- looks at the impact of the chosen solution (a monitor/ evaluator).

In most cases groups will be involved rather than individuals, and several roles can be performed by the same group. However, a variety of skills is required and many responsibilities are involved in this complicated process.

Decision-making styles

We now look at different styles of decision-making. Research has shown that there are differences between people in their orientation to decision-making, which may be called 'style'. We look at this first and then consider differences between a quantitative and a qualitative approach, the top-down/bottom-up process, and the impact of organisational cultures on styles of decision-making.

A decision-style model

Different individuals approach problems in different ways. Some use a logical/analytical approach, and others employ more creative/entrepreneurial approaches. Rowe, Boulgaides and McGrath, in *Managerial Decision Making*, identified four styles:

1 **The directive style.** People who use this style are looking for simple solutions which they will then seek

to force through in a directive way. They do not spend much time on research or looking at alternatives. They want a 'quick fix' solution.

2 **The analytical style**. People with this style are prepared to live with complexity and ambiguity. They spend considerable time in collecting and analysing information. They enjoy problem-solving and want the best solution based on detailed analysis.

3 **The conceptual style**. This is a more socially oriented approach to solving problems than the previous two. A number of broad alternatives are considered and the emphasis is on solutions involving creativity and commitment.

4 **The behavioural style**. People who adopt this style are highly committed to the organisation and to creating positive relationships between people in the organisation. It is a people-oriented style and therefore involves people in the decision-making process through meetings, consultation, etc.

Individuals are unlikely to employ just one style. They may use a variety of styles for different types of decisions. However, they tend to have a favoured or predominant style. A problem arises when different members of an organisation or team have different styles; they are likely to clash because they approach problems in different ways.

Tests have been devised for finding out what a person's preferred style is. It may be inappropriate for people with similar styles to work together. Research has shown that senior executives often have a balance of the four styles, and can easily move from one style to another when appropriate.

Quantitative and qualitative styles

Different individuals will be disposed to using a quantitative or qualitative style. For example, the analytical decision maker may be inclined to use statistical information before arriving at a decision. In contrast, the directive decision maker may prefer to make an intuitive decision based on what feels right. This decision maker may not consciously weigh up the advantages and disadvantages of the alternatives, but simply make a decision based on hunches.

Indeed, research shows that top management often has to rely on intuitive judgement in decision-making simply because there are insufficient available data. Many of the most exciting decisions made by entrepreneurial organisations may be based on intuition rather than calculated analysis. However, it would be unwise to make all managerial decisions on the basis of intuition. Businesses operate in complex environments requiring sound judgement. The more that chance can be removed

from the equation, the more successful a businessperson is likely to be at decision-making.

Judgemental decisions are made on the basis of previous experience and/or knowledge. A manager acquires judgemental skills through both experience and study – relying on experience is not enough. Managers working in a particular organisation may view issues solely through the eyes of their department or organisation. To widen their knowledge they need to look at case studies, theories and practice from a broad range of organisations. Managers who say 'I have been working in industry for 30 years' as if that provides them with a wealth of experience may be deluding themselves. In fact, they may have been working in a very small office cut off from most of the recent developments and practices in industry. However, the manager who has only studied books may have had no practical experience of putting theory into practice. Sound judgement is perhaps based on a combination of practice, observation of others' practice, and theory. All of these require a process of reflection on the learning that has taken place if they are to bear fruit in 'quality judgement'.

Quantitative styles

Some managers prefer to rely on quantitative approaches when making decisions. Quantitative techniques are based on measuring alternatives in numerical terms, e.g. cost-benefit analysis (see page 680). Quantitative approaches are very helpful in that they enable decision makers to reduce alternatives to a common denominator in order to make an objective decision. For example, if a company wishes to maximise its return on a £10 000 investment over a three-year period, then it may choose project A in Figure 27.20:

Figure 27.20

Initial investment	Year 1 return	Year 2 return	Year 3 return
£10 000 (Project A)	£3 000	£5 000	£8 000
£10 000 (Project B)	£2 000	£3 000	£4 000
£10 000 (Project C)	£3 000	£4 000	£4 000

Many decisions cannot be reduced to such simple mathematical calculations. Often, decisions involve variables which cannot be quantified (except perhaps by highly dubious 'guestimates'). Those in favour of quantification argue however, that without clear quantities resources may not be used wisely because decisions are made through highly subjective qualitative procedures.

Qualitative styles

Qualitative factors are those that are difficult to measure in numbers, such as the quality of relationships between members of a team, the value to an individual of being given responsibility at work, or the satisfaction that somebody gets from working for an 'ethical organisation'.

There are literally millions of examples of apparently well-laid quantitative plans which have been proved to be nonsensical after an unexpected event such as an oil spillage or war; qualitative factors first need to be identified. Some may be quantifiable, but if they are not, then it is essential to find out as much as possible about these factors and to decide how important they are. Is it important for an organisation to be seen to be environmentally friendly, for example?

Managers then need to make a subjective evaluation of how much weight to give to qualitative factors in decision-making. Some people argue that if the ethics and principles that underpin a decision are right, then the numbers (i.e. the profits) will follow. Too much concentration on a numerical approach (getting the bottom line healthy in the short term) may have an adverse effect on profits in the longer term.

The emphasis, therefore, should be on striking the best possible balance between a quantitative and a qualitative approach.

Case Study
Concern over risk to nuclear-power stations

An aeroplane crash, such as the one at Lockerbie in 1988, could cause even greater devastation than the Chernobyl disaster if the wreckage hit a nuclear-power station, according to Dr Raymond Seymour, a scientific advisor to Somerset County Council. He disputes the official estimate of the chance of an aircraft directly hitting a nuclear-power station as being once every 2 million years. Dr Seymour, a radiation expert, stated that the risk is ten times higher.

Much of the wreckage of the Lockerbie Boeing-747 came down within ten miles of the BNFL reactor at Chapelcross. If the bomb had detonated about a minute earlier, the debris would have landed around the reactor. Dr Seymour said: 'The effect of such a disaster could be far worse than Chernobyl and the chances of it happening near any new nuclear-power stations are unacceptable.'

In his evidence, given on behalf of a consortium of 23 local authorities opposing the Hinkley C reactor in Somerset, he said that the main risk came from jets from the Royal Navy airbase at Yeovilton which fly to a practice bombing range in the Bristol Channel.

A spokesperson for the electricity generators argued that, even in the extremely unlikely event of an aircraft crashing into the power station, there was only a one in ten chance of this causing a big release of radioactivity and a one in two chance of this leading to meltdown.

Aircraft are not allowed within two miles horizontally of a nuclear-power station or within 2000 feet vertically.

Questions for discussion

1 *Why might quantitative techniques be useful in:*
   a *making siting decisions for nuclear reactors*
   b *calculating safety risks for nuclear reactors?*
2 *What do you think Dr Seymour meant by 'the chances of it happening near any new nuclear-power stations are unacceptable'?*
3 *Why might qualitative approaches be more important in making decisions about major safety issues?*
4 *Why do you think that Dr Seymour's calculations differ from the official estimates?*
5 *What criteria do you think should be applied to the siting of nuclear reactors? Explain your reasons. How many of these criteria can be measured using quantitative techniques?*

The top-down/bottom-up process

We have already contrasted top-down and bottom-up approaches to decision-making. A contrast can be made between organisations where directions are given from above and organisations which encourage participation, allowing ideas to bubble up from below (see Rosabeth Moss Kanter on page 244).

- An **autocratic directive leadership style** is one where the leader makes the decisions and then expects subordinates to carry them out in a specified way.
- An **autocratic permissive leadership style** is one where the leader makes the decisions but allows latitude for subordinates to carry out directions in their own way.
- A **directive democratic leadership style** is one where decisions are made participatively, but there is close supervision of the ways in which they are carried out.
- A **permissive democratic leadership style** is one where decisions are made participatively and individuals can interpret the ways in which they carry out activities.

The top-down style is likely to predominate in the early days of an organisation, when a single individual may hold considerable powers and a particular vision of the way the organisation should operate. He or she will want to stamp this vision on all decisions that are made.

On page 244 we argued that this approach is no longer appropriate in dynamic environments requiring empowered, motivated employees. We have suggested that organisations should be structured in such a way as to involve as many people as possible in the decision-making process. Genuine involvement creates genuine commitment. When an organisation recognises and respects the needs of its employees, it is more likely to survive and flourish.

The impact of culture

The culture of an organisation has a major effect on the style of decision-making. The strategies and policies which organisations employ are greatly influenced by the previous experience of managers and by the social and political processes which operate within the organisation.

An organisation which has been around for a long time and is set in its ways is likely to be characterised by highly formalised decision-making processes. Individuals will have built up traditional power bases in such an organisation. They will therefore have considerable control over the way in which decisions are being made. The television programme 'Yes, Minister' depicted the civil service as an example of an organisation with a hierarchical structure and set patterns of making decisions. The real power of political decision-making is vested in the government minister's Private Secretary, who has been in the institution for many years. The Private Secretary knows all the routines and established ways of tackling problems. The culture of the organisation constrains the ability of new and enthusiastic ministers to make sweeping and sudden changes.

The culture of an analytical-based organisation or department may be one which fosters a quantitative approach to problem-solving. For example, assessment procedures and quality-control departments proliferate in modern universities. Staff in these departments have an 'administrative' and 'quantitative' approach to their work. They demand information by prescribed dates and usually in terms of figures. The emphasis is on creating a body of analytical data which can be used for quality control and measurement. Unfortunately, the procedures involved are often impenetrable to outsiders.

Entrepreneurial organisations are characterised by a culture of continual change, e.g. an advertising agency, contemporary music company or radio station. Here the emphasis is on thinking up 'the next good idea' before the current one is out of date. Decisions are often made in an intuitive way by creative people who are encouraged to produce bright new ideas. Decisions can be made quickly and involve swift changes in direction.

Decision-making techniques

There are many different techniques employed in decision-making. Some of these were outlined on pages 275–81. One of the key considerations when making a particular decision is 'What is the expected/likely return?' This is an essential consideration in an organisation which is concerned to use its resources effectively. It is important to be able to show stakeholders, such as shareholders, that their capital is being put to optimum use. Two techniques for looking at returns are:

- investment appraisal
- cost-benefit analysis.

Investment appraisal techniques

An economic analysis of capital investment projects needs to take place regularly within an organisation. Profitability is the most important measure of the financial acceptability of decisions.

Investment involves the immediate risk of funds in the hope of securing returns later. There are often more investment proposals than the necessary finance to back them. It is therefore important to be able to compare projects in order to assess the degree of risk. A good decision provides a high return, while a poor decision may result in few benefits. Managers must try to make decisions that maximise returns and provide shareholders with the best possible investment.

Entrepreneurs use their creative and imaginative skills to look for investment opportunities. In the early stages they gather information in order to appraise alternatives. When decisions involve non-financial aspects, such as the image of a business, this can be difficult.

The decision-making process is concerned primarily with weighing up the benefits against the costs. Once the decision has been made, projects can be put into action and their results monitored.

The primary objective of any investment decision is to obtain a return on investment that is greater than the initial outlay of capital. Three important criteria determining that outlay will be:

- the sum invested
- returns on the sum invested
- the length of time the project is expected to last.

We now look at:

- accounting rate of return (ARR) method
- payback method
- discounted cash flow (DCF) – net present value
- discounted cash flow – internal rate of return.

1 Accounting rate of return method

This method is concerned simply with expressing profitability as an average rate of return (ARR) on an investment. It is generally regarded to be a quick and convenient guide for assessing the profitability of alternative projects. Profit is expressed as an average over the life of the project, and capital is considered to be the initial outlay or the capital invested.

It is calculated by dividing the average annual profit by the initial investment:

$$\text{ARR} = \frac{\text{Average annual profit}}{\text{Initial investment}} \times 100$$

For example, using this method it is possible to select one of the alternative projects shown in Figure 27.21.

Figure 27.21 Using the ARR method to make a comparison

	Project A £	Project B £
Initial cost	−10 000	−20 000
Year 1 cash receipts	+4 000	+9 000
Year 2 cash receipts	+5 000	+9 000
Year 3 cash receipts	+5 000	+12 000
Year 4 cash receipts	+4 000	+10 000
Total cash receipts	+18 000	+40 000
Profit over four years	+8 000	+20 000
Average annual profit	+2 000	+5 000
Initial investment	10 000	20 000
ARR	20%	25%

Project A provides an accounting rate of return of 20 per cent and project B an accounting rate of return of 25 per cent. Using this form of appraisal, project B would be the better form of investment.

The accounting rate of return method can be criticised for being based upon book values and therefore failing to take heed of changing price levels over time. It also fails to consider the timings of cash receipts. For example, a project that returns cash to the business quickly is helpful to the business, but this is ignored using this method.

2 Payback method

The purpose of this method is to establish how quickly the investment cost can be repaid. The shorter the

payback period, the better the project. Using this method, for example, it is possible to select one of the two investment possibilities, both costing £15 000, shown in Figure 27.22.

Figure 27.22 Comparing returns using the payback method

	Project A £	Project B £
Initial cost	−15 000	−15 000
Year 1 cash receipts	+3 000	+1 000
Year 2 cash receipts	+3 000	+3 000
Year 3 cash receipts	+4 000	+3 000
Year 4 cash receipts	+5 000	+3 000
Year 5 cash receipts	+3 000	+5 000

Project A repays the initial cost by the end of year 4, whereas project B does not repay until the end of year 5. Using the payback method, we would choose project A.

The essential feature of the payback form of capital appraisal is that it takes timing into consideration – the early return of funds could be of primary importance to firms with liquidity problems. For businesses where capital equipment is continually being changed, it can provide a rough guide to the extent of a risk. The main criticism of the payback method is that it does not take account of cash flows. For example, if two projects both pay back in three years, they are regarded to be of equal ranking. However, one may pay back far more in the first few years (making it more attractive to a business).

3 Discounted cash flow (net present value)

The discounted cash flow (DCF) method of appraising investment decisions leans heavily on the principal of opportunity cost. Before managers commit a company to an investment decision, the benefits of which will be reaped over a number of years, the real value of future returns needs to be assessed. Because the value of money alters with time, it is helpful to look at future flows in terms of their present value.

Interest payments compensate for:

- cost of time (not having the money now)
- cost of inflation (price rises erode the real value of money over time)
- risk of investment.

The interest rate gives a guide to the future value of investment. Alternatively, the current value of investment can be compared with what it was worth in the past. If an investor has £1000 in a bank account where it is earning 10 per cent interest, the balance will stand at £1100 at the end of the first year. By compounding this annually:

Figure 27.23 DCF tables from 1 per cent to 10 per cent over six years

	% rate of discount									
Future years	1	2	3	4	5	6	7	8	9	10
1	0.990	0.980	0.971	0.962	0.952	0.943	0.935	0.926	0.917	0.909
2	0.980	0.961	0.943	0.925	0.907	0.890	0.873	0.857	0.842	0.826
3	0.971	0.942	0.915	0.889	0.864	0.840	0.816	0.794	0.772	0.751
4	0.961	0.924	0.888	0.855	0.823	0.792	0.763	0.735	0.708	0.683
5	0.951	0.906	0.863	0.822	0.784	0.747	0.713	0.681	0.650	0.621
6	0.942	0.888	0.837	0.790	0.746	0.705	0.666	0.630	0.596	0.564

- at the end of year 2, it will be worth £1210 (£1100 + £110)
- at the end of year 3, it will be worth £1331 (£1210 + £121).

At the end of this time, the investor can say that £1331 was worth £1000 three years earlier.

This can be shown another way, i.e. what would £1000 now have been worth three years ago at a 10 per cent rate of interest?

$$\frac{£1000}{£1331} \times £1000 = £751.30$$

Two years ago?

$$\frac{£1000}{£1210} \times £1000 = £826.40$$

One year ago?

$$\frac{£1000}{£1100} \times £1000 = £909.10$$

Thus, assuming a constant rate of interest of 10 per cent, £1000 now was worth £751.30 three years ago, and will be worth £1331 in three years' time. The time element has been taken into account.

DCF tables are available relating rates of interest to a period of time in years (see Figure 27.23).

Looking at the net surplus returns for two projects that have an initial capital investment of £200 000 (see Figures 27.24 and 27.25), it is clear that project A is the project to opt for as, at today's value, returns will be higher. If net present value (NPV) comes out at less than the original investment, it is not worth considering the project.

The clear advantage of the net present value method is that it takes into account the time value of money and is also easy to calculate. The dangers of depending on it are that both interest rates and cash flows are subject to uncertainty.

Figure 27.24 Earnings from two projects

Earnings	Project A £	Project B £
Year 1	100 000	80 000
Year 2	110 000	100 000
Year 3	100 000	100 000
Year 4	80 000	100 000
Year 5	20 000	30 000
Total return	410 000	410 000

4 Discounted cash flow (internal rate of return)

This method aims to find out the average return on an investment throughout its lifespan. The internal rate of return is then compared with the criteria for the project to see if it is worthwhile. This method is therefore concerned with percentage returns on investment, and not with cash figures. Using the example given in Figure 27.26 and the discounts rates shown in Figure 27.23, we can try to find the internal rate of return by trial and error.

At 10 per cent it would be:

$$
\begin{array}{rl}
-20\,000 + & 8\,000 \times 0.909 = \quad 7\,272 \\
+ & 5\,000 \times 0.826 = \quad 4\,130 \\
+ & 5\,000 \times 0.751 = \quad 3\,755 \\
+ & 5\,000 \times 0.683 = \quad \underline{3\,415} \\
& \qquad\qquad\qquad\quad 18\,572 \\
-20\,000 + 18\,572 & \qquad\quad = \underline{-1\,428}
\end{array}
$$

The return is clearly not 10 per cent, and so we need to try a lower rate. At 6 per cent it would be:

$$
\begin{array}{rl}
-20\,000 + & 8\,000 \times 0.943 = \quad 7\,544 \\
+ & 5\,000 \times 0.890 = \quad 4\,450 \\
+ & 5\,000 \times 0.840 = \quad 4\,200 \\
+ & 5\,000 \times 0.792 = \quad \underline{3\,960} \\
& \qquad\qquad\qquad\quad 20\,154 \\
-20\,000 + 20\,154 & \qquad\quad = \underline{154}
\end{array}
$$

We have shown that the internal rate of return lies

Figure 27.25 Discounted cash flow at a rate of interest of 10 per cent

Earnings	Project A	Project A NPV*	Discount	Project B Earnings	NPV*
Year	£	£	factor	£	£
0		200 000			200 000
1	100 000	90 000	0.909	80 000	72 720
2	110 000	90 860	0.826	100 000	82 600
3	100 000	75 100	0.751	100 000	75 100
4	80 000	54 640	0.683	100 000	68 300
5	20 000	12 420	0.621	30 000	18 630
		£323 920			£317 350

*NPV: Net Present Value

Figure 27.26

Year	£
0	−20 000
1	+8 000
2	+5 000
3	+5 000
4	+5 000
	£23 000

between 6 and 10 per cent. To obtain the exact internal rate of return:

1 take the lower rate (6 per cent)
2 add it to the difference between the two interest rates (4 per cent) multiplied by the difference at the lower rate (154), divided by the total difference between the two rates (1582), i.e.

$$6 + \frac{(4 \times 154)}{1582} = 6.39\%$$

As long as the firm can borrow money at a rate lower than 6.39 per cent, it will find the project worthwhile. The internal rate of return expresses returns as a percentage of investment cost.

Cost-benefit analysis

Cost-benefit analysis is normally associated with the evaluation of large-scale, government-backed investment projects. The siting of an airport or the building of a new underground rail link are typical examples of projects for which cost benefit analysis would be used.

However, cost-benefit analysis is a much more widely applicable technique. It can, in fact, be used to weigh up

any policy decision, although it is not a magic solution to problem-solving.

Carrying out a cost-benefit analysis involves organising all the relevant information involved in a particular decision in such a way as to focus on the key issues and to concentrate on the real choices to be made. It is an attempt to put a money value on all the costs and benefits of a particular decision – including intangible factors. Although it is often very difficult to measure intangibles in money terms, this is not always the case. Johnson and Scholes give an example of the expected costs and benefits of a particular decision and the basis on which the intangibles can be identified (see Figure 27.27).

Figure 27.27 The benefits and costs incurred in constructing a new town-centre car park

Costs/benefits	Bases of quantification
Costs	
1 Acquiring site	Already owned, market value known
2 Construction costs	Tenders obtained
3 Loss of amenity (gardens)	Known usage of gardens and notional entry charge (if privately owned)
4 Increased transport costs	Known usage of gardens and private (car) travel
Benefits	
1 Revenue	Demand and price forecasts
1 Reduced congestion in streets	Incremental increase in consumer spending due to easier access

Source: G. Johnson and K. Scholes, *Exploring Corporate Strategy*

A local authority is considering whether to construct a new town-centre car park to be built on existing public gardens. The main costs and benefits are identified in Figure 27.27. Clearly, the basis on which costs and benefits are measured needs to be justified. Different people will have varying ideas about the values given. For example, if the town centre is felt by some people to be 'spoilt' by the creation of the car park, they may want to place a high value on the cost of losing the amenity (the garden).

The first task in preparing an analysis of, for example, building a new training centre for unemployed people, is to find out who would benefit and who would lose out by its construction. This would then need to be converted into measurements in money terms. One way of doing this is to ask the people who would benefit from the centre how much they would be prepared to pay to see the project carried out. A person who was going to lose out could be asked the minimum amount he or she would be prepared to accept as compensation for the project taking place. Then the gains and losses need to be added up. If the gains outweigh the losses, the project passes the test. Clearly, it would be necessary to eliminate from the research people who said 'I would not want the project to go ahead at any price!'.

Although cost-benefit analysis has a number of problems, when it comes to ascribing money values to costs and benefits, it does at least force decision makers to focus on the main issues and interest groups involved in the decision. Weights can then be attached to the costs and benefits identified.

Exploring the implications of decisions

Before taking a decision it is important to work through the effects and implications of that decision. This involves looking a number of steps ahead in order to work out the full impact of a decision. We consider four possible techniques used in planning ahead:

- estimating probability
- expected values
- decision trees
- scenario planning.

Estimating probability

Most (if not all) decisions involve a number of interacting variables. The impact of these variables is uncertain, but we can usually measure the probability (likelihood) of these variables having an effect. Suppose that there are five variables involved in a particular decision, for example when we are trying to estimate the cost of production of a product using five separate processes – A,

B, C, D, and E. We know that the estimates of process A have a 90 per cent chance of being accurate; process B, a 60 per cent chance; process C, a 90 per cent chance; process D, a 70 per cent chance; and process E, a 90 per cent chance. When we estimate the probability of the costing of the total project being accurate, we reach a figure of only 30.6 per cent:

$$90\% \times 60\% \times 90\% \times 70\% \times 90\% = 30.6\%.$$

It is very important to estimate probability because it provides a useful measure of the riskiness of a project. For example, if we know with 80 per cent accuracy what the revenues or costs of a project are likely to be, then this may enable us to go ahead with confidence. We may 'know' that if we achieve 80 per cent forecasting accuracy, we are certain to make a profit. However, with a probability of 30.6 per cent the situation may be far from clear. But probability should not govern actions. Enterprise thrives on risks, although different individuals, groups and institutions have different attitudes towards risk. For example, pension funds are likely to be very cautious about how they channel their funds because they cannot afford to make losses; alternatively, speculators and gamblers are more likely to take risks.

Expected values

Risk situations can be analysed by setting out probability distributions based on past frequencies so as to calculate the degree of risk involved in any situation. Information from past situations is used in order to predict the future. For example, if a particular fault occurs in a production line between five and seven times a month, it is likely to happen next month between five and seven times, all things being equal.

In making a particular decision, it is necessary to compare the decision alternatives. Each possible outcome, therefore, needs to be weighted by its probability of occurrence. The sum of these weighted figures represents the 'expected value' of a particular alternative.

Decision trees

A decision tree is a particular way of setting out a problem and decision-making alternatives. Examining the decision tree enables the manager to weigh up alternatives, compare the likely financial implications of each, adjust these figures according to their probability and then make a comparison. The decision tree is a helpful way of making sequential decisions because it sets out the steps involved in an easy-to-understand sequence.

Figure 27.28 shows how a manager in a textile factory has to make a decision between using plant to produce underwear only or nylon shirts only. Currently, the firm produces underwear only, but the manager believes the demand for nylon shirts is growing. There is the possibility of buying a new factory so as to produce both types of garment. (Decision points are shown in Figure 27.28 by square boxes.)

In analysing the decision tree the manager works backwards from the second decision point. At this point, the most desirable decision is to expand by buying the new factory and produce both types of garment. The expected payoff of £6 million is three times greater than the expected payoff of not expanding (£2 million) if there is a low demand for underwear at point A.

If the manager continues to work back along the tree to the first decision point, he or she can calculate the expected values for the possible alternatives of producing either underwear or nylon shirts. The expected value of producing only underwear is £13 million (0.7 × £16 million + 0.3 × £6 million). The expected value of producing only nylon shirts is £8.8 million.

The logical decision, given current expectations about events, is to expand to a new factory plant so that both lines can be produced. This leads to the greatest expected payoff.

Scenario planning

In planning for the future in an uncertain environment, it is important to outline a range of possible pictures of what might happen. The term **scenario planning** describes this projected view of the future.

The oil giant Shell was one of the first organisations to devise the scenario-planning approach in response to the oil crises of the 1970s.

Scenario planning involves outlining a series of potential scenarios of the future situation. For example:

■ Scenario 1 assumes present trends continue.
■ Scenario 2 assumes a sudden contraction, such as the halving of the quantity of oil available, while the demand for oil continues to rise at present rates.

It requires a detailed analysis of trends, forecasts and probabilities in order to generate alternative scenarios.

Figure 27.28 Deciding what to produce

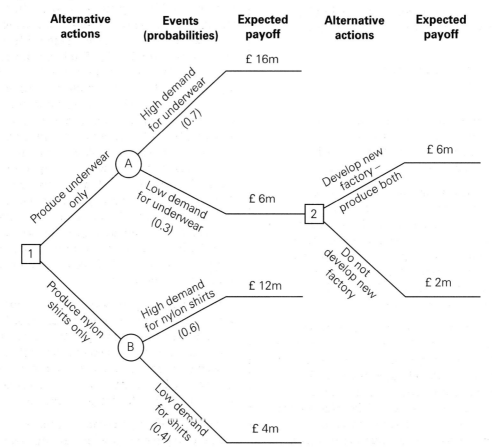

Planning can then be rehearsed for each of the scenarios. This is a form of contingency planning (see Chapter 28).

The cost and value of information

It is sometimes argued that an organisation can never have sufficient information available. However, we should regard this statement with caution. It is possible to have information overload. When this occurs the quality of decision-making may start to deteriorate. It is important that organisations have tools, techniques and people with the capability to handle information.

A further consideration is that information comes with a cost attached. Collecting and analysing information takes time. Not least of the costs involved is the opportunity cost. Time spent on information collection, sorting and analysis is taken away from other purposes. It is possible that people within the organisation spend so much time in collecting information that they can do little else. For example, this is a frequent criticism of organisations that introduce paper-based quality-control systems. People spend so much time collecting information and filling in bits of paper that they forget the real purpose of the organisation and of their own jobs. The result is that the organisation 'only looks good on paper'.

It is important also for information to be used quickly. Nowadays information can quickly become outdated.

Information technology as a decision-making tool

The American business author Peter Drucker sees the late twentieth century as the dawning of the age of the information-based organisation, the latest stage in the development of the modern business corporation.

At the beginning of the century management was separated from the ownership of a company, as shareholders handed over responsibility for its running to paid managers. This led to the growth of the command-and-control organisation made up of departments and divisions. Now we are entering a third period of change, with the development of the information-based organisation of knowledge specialists.

In this third phase, members of staff are freed from day-to-day administrative tasks by computers. Computers bring a large proportion of employees closer to the work of management; departmental hierarchies are broken down, creating a much flatter organisational structure with the opportunity to develop more skills. Networking of computer systems gives people access to many disciplines. When a company uses a number of personal computers, it is possible that some of the information on one of these may be useful to another user. Then, rather than continually swopping data on floppy disks, it is possible to connect the machines together using a local area network. This consists of a mixture of hardware and software which enables data to be transferred between the machines. Networking thus makes it possible for a range of experts to tap into each other's specialist skill areas while sitting at their own work stations. Such employees no longer need to work in the same building and may even be able to work quite easily from home. No longer is knowledge compartmentalised; instead, it becomes part of a pool of mutually shared information. Information technology saves time, cuts costs and makes companies more competitive.

However, we are still a long way from the widespread development of information-based organisations that are democratically structured. Rather than restructuring job design, many companies have tended to automate the existing organisational structure. Dramatic contrasts can be made between companies that have combined information technology with a more effective decision-making structure and those that have simply borrowed the new technology and retained the existing structure. This point is illustrated by the 'Management in the Nineties', a TV programme report, which included a telling comparison of two organisations in the pensions business, each of which was responsible for managing an investment portfolio of £15 million. It showed how a new-model business compared with an older style organisation. The traditionally run business is represented by the division of a bank, employing 108 professional staff and 36 support staff. The newcomer, Battery March, a Boston-based financial investment management firm, handles a comparable business, but with eighteen professional staff and seventeen support staff. From the outset, Battery March's founder operated on the principle that there was a better way of managing funds which would add value to the company's services. The operation was consciously organised to make best use of the creative contribution of analysts and professionals with a strong emphasis on teamwork. It was a vision that depended on information technology.

Buying and selling stock directly, computer to computer, takes care of some routine clerical work. Technology is also used extensively to monitor stock and fund changes, select best options, and so on, to enable staff to concentrate more on the creative aspects of the business. As a result, Battery March enjoys lower costs and a record of highly effective performance.

It is not just younger companies like Battery March that are exploring the possibilities for innovative organisation.

Rank Xerox, for example, has questioned the need for all white-collar workers to work in a central office. It is one of the trail-blazers in the use of networkers, i.e. home-based specialists and professional workers contracted to the company, but also working for other clients.

Computer simulations

Computer-based simulations are important aids to decision-making. A computer simulation involves feeding in a range of relevant data to a program in order to simulate a real situation. The program can then be used for training purposes or to assist with real decisions. Computers can be used to run programs working out probabilities and decision trees, investment appraisal techniques, scenario planning, etc.

Decision support systems

A decision support system (DSS) involves managers using computer systems on a daily basis to support their decision-making. The DSS can be thought of as an extension of the manager's mind, exploring the consequences of alternative decisions. Key features of a DSS are:

- a comprehensive data and model base
- a sophisticated software system for managing each decision
- a powerful command language to help decision makers interact with both data and models.

Figure 27.29 shows the components of a DSS.

Figure 27.29 A decision support system

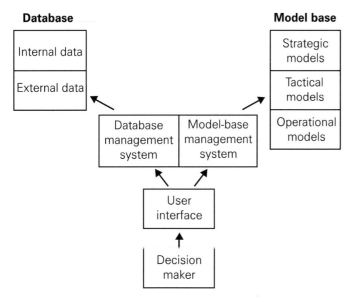

Limitations of techniques for decision-making

It is important to remember that the use of decision-making techniques is not a science. Techniques are helpful in that they provide information, but it is ultimately the decision maker – a human being – who makes the decision.

The person who works out the probabilities of winning a prize in the National Lottery in order to decide how much to invest in order to win may win nothing. Quantitative techniques and models are often flawed because they are based on past events, which may be of limited use in predicting the future. In an environment of chaos, traditional decision-making tools may only have limited applicability. When deciding on which types of techniques to employ, we need to consider how useful they will be in yielding appropriate information. If techniques enable us to make better decisions about the suitability, acceptability or feasibility of plans and actions, then we should employ them. However, the manager who spends days producing simulated models and scenarios may be completely divorced from the reality of day-to-day business activity.

Application of decision-making tools within the problem-solving sequence

In a problem-solving sequence the starting point is the identification of the problem, followed by the identification of alternative solutions and then the choice of a specific solution. The techniques employed are concerned with each of these stages in the cycle. For example, decision-tree analysis involves weighing up the implication of alternative decisions in order to compare the payoff. This leads back to the heart of the problem at each decision point. If the problem is not identified clearly at each point, then the analysis is wasted.

Cost-benefit analysis involves providing details of the costs and benefits of alternative decisions. Identifying the costs and benefits leads back to identifying and defining the problems around which the decision is to be based. A successful outcome depends on clear definitions of the problem.

Using decision-making techniques forces clarification of:

- the nature of the problem
- the alternatives to be considered
- the values that can be ascribed to alternative decisions.

Decision-making techniques, therefore, supply useful information. Even so, when it comes to the final decision, particularly at senior management level, a manager may often have to rely on intuition to decide what to do with that information.

Further reading

- *Exploring Corporate Strategy*, 3rd edition, by Gerry Johnson and Kevan Scholes. Prentice Hall, 1993.
- *Rejuvenating the Mature Business: The Competitive Challenge* by Charles Baden-Fuller and John Stopford. Routledge, 1992.
- *Strategic Investment Decision Making* by Richard Butler, Richard Pike, John Sharp and Les Davies. Routledge, 1993.
- *The Competitive Challenge: Strategies for Industrial Innovation and Renewal* by David J. Teece. HarperCollins, 1989.
- *Corporate Strategy and Financial Decisions* by Tony Grundy. Kogan Page, 1992.
- *The Challenge of Strategic Management* by David Faulkner and Gerry Johnson. Kogan Page, 1992.
- *The Strategy Concept and Process: A Pragmatic Approach* by Arnaldo C. Hax. Prentice Hall, 1991.
- *Business Decision-Making* by C. Gilligan, B. Neale and D. Murray. Philip Allan, 1990.

28 Contingency planning

On completion of this chapter students should be able to:

■ identify and evaluate how organisations plan for contingencies

■ compare and contrast pragmatic and planned approaches to contingencies

■ identify and evaluate alternative strategies for coping with risk

■ prepare and evaluate contingency plans.

Contingency planning

The dictionary provides us with a number of definitions of a **contingency**, including:

■ a possible but not very likely future event or condition
■ something dependent on a possible future event
■ a fact, event, etc. incidental to something else.

In late 1994, millions of people in the UK began to develop new contingency plans – they all started to plan what they might do if they won on the new National Lottery! Of course, their ability to realise these day-dreams was contingent on actually winning a lottery prize.

There are many ways in which we are contingency planners. Most of us think ahead, and set down the groundwork of contingency plans:

'What would I do if I lost my present job?'

'How will I change my route to work if and when a new bypass is built?'

'What new model of car will I buy if I receive a salary increase in May?'

Planning for contingencies is highly important both for individuals and for organisations. At all times, organisations are faced with a wide spectrum of possible scenarios concerning future developments in the external environment and in internal relationships. A multitude of variables are continually changing – for example, the prices of raw materials, consumers' demand for products, the actions of rivals. Planning for contingencies therefore involves imagining 'What if . . .?' situations.

Risk and uncertainty are everywhere in the business world. Managers do their best to make sure that their plans are well-prepared, but they can rarely hope to have certainty about the outcomes. They must estimate the *probability* of the likely success of chosen plans. In this way 'uncertainty' is converted into an estimation of 'risk'. Forward-looking plans can be created in a meaningful way only if they are related to the best-possible judgements based on reasonable assumptions about contingencies.

Most organisations have contingency funds to cater for unexpected costs. The government, too, has contingency funds to deal with unforeseen national disasters such as floods, storm damage, etc.

Case Study
The Japanese earthquake in 1995

On 17 January 1995 the most devastating earthquake to strike a Japanese city in 70 years left more than 4000 people dead. The quake, which measured 7.2 on the Richter scale, badly damaged the cities of Osaka, Kyoto and Kobe. Many of the buildings in these cities were destroyed by quake damage and the fires that followed.

The earthquake damaged or destroyed a number of major manufacturing plants in the area. Many of these supplied key components to other Japanese companies.

The Japanese economy is highly integrated. The prevailing philosophy is that of lean production and just-in-time manufacturing and supply. Often the contract to supply components for manufacturing (e.g. of motor cars) is given to one supplier. The impact on a number of Japanese industries away from the earthquake zone was immediate. Manufacturers were suddenly without supplies of essential components, forcing them to shut down production facilities.

Just-in-time manufacturing includes contingency planning. A company plans for unexpected events so that it always has just enough components and supplies, with a bit extra to cope with hold-ups and other problems. However, the extent of the earthquake damage in January 1995 was colossal. The effect has been to force Japanese organisations to rethink their contingency planning.

Questions for discussion

1 *What is a contingency and what is contingency planning?*
2 *How do Japanese manufacturing systems normally take account of contingencies?*
3 *Why did the earthquake in 1995 have such a dramatic impact on Japanese industry?*
4 *What suggestions can you make as to how Japanese organisations should in future take account of the possibility of earthquakes?*

Contingency planning is important at all levels of an organisation. At the *strategic level*, senior managers must make sure that the scope of an organisation's activities is appropriate and that it will continue to be appropriate in a changing environment. The management will have to weigh up a range of 'What if' issues, such as: 'What if rivals develop a new product?' and 'What if foreign companies enter the market?' Strategists need to work out what effects these contingencies will have on business performance and profits, and to devise a range of possible strategies. It will be necessary, for example, to look at the resource capability of the organisation, and the implications for resource planning and operational decision-making. It will be necessary, too, to look at how values and expectations within the organisation may need to be altered and how these alterations can be made.

During the 1970s and 80s, Shell UK developed **scenario planning** as a strategic process to determine a series of alternative ways of dealing with eventualities such as changes in exchange rates, the discovery of new oil fields, another war in the Middle East, the development of Pacific Rim economies, etc. By setting out a range of scenarios – a 'worst-case' scenario, an 'optimistic' scenario, etc. – it was possible to outline contingency plans to prepare for each.

The sheer uncertainty of the business environment today means that business thinking has sometimes to move beyond strategic planning. The rapidly changing scene often means that managers have to think faster than existing planning mechanisms allow. This does not mean that strategic planning has no place in the modern environment; rather it means that some decisions have to be made so quickly that they require fast on-the-ground decision-making.

At a *functional managerial level*, it is important for managers to anticipate events that might get in the way of existing plans. This involves imagining a series of scenarios and planning a suitable response. For example, imagine that you have applied for additional funding in your department for a research project requiring £100 000. You could set out a number of contingency plans:

Contingency plan 1
You receive 10 per cent less funding than expected. Instead of employing three full-time researchers you will employ two full-time and one part-time. Instead of the project lasting for two years it will last for 20 months.

Contingency plan 2
The funding plan is rejected. You will apply to alternative funding bodies, and will reapply for funds again next year. Immediate action will involve finding out why your research bid has been rejected.

Contingency plan 3
The funding plan is accepted. You will employ three full-time researchers and will run the research project for two years. At the same time you will apply for extra funding in order to extend the project into a second phase.

<table>
<tr><td>

Contingency plan *n*

. . . .
</td></tr>
</table>

The planner must try to imagine every possible contingency so that there are no unpleasant surprises. Of course, we do sometimes speak of 'unexpected contingencies', because things happen that cannot humanly be predicted at the functional managerial level.

Contingency planning is also very important at an *operational level*. For example, in planning stock levels it is usually wise to plan to have enough to meet demand levels beyond the forecast. In a supermarket, computerised stock control methods will ensure that there is always a safety margin of supplies available to meet sudden surges in buying. These levels will be worked out by statistical monitoring over a considerable length of time. Should stocks run below a certain level then there will be 'contingency arrangements' to make sure that fresh supplies can be brought in quickly, perhaps from a centralised warehouse using a 'contingency distribution' system. Should supplies from a contracted supplier fail to materialise, then there will need to be contingency plans in place to purchase from an alternative supplier.

Task

1 Imagine that you are a florist in the centre of town. Of your business, 90 per cent comes from the sale of flowers and potted plants. The flowers have a shelf-life of about four days, while the potted plants last up to a month or more. You buy most of your stock from one large nursery, but your supplier may decide to increase prices by 5p in the pound. He tells you that every other grower is likely to do the same because of rising costs throughout the industry. You have enough flowers in stock to last three days and enough potted plants for a month. You bought all your stock at the old price.

You now have a choice of alternative responses:

■ Option 1 – Continue selling your stock to customers at the old price and try to make savings elsewhere, perhaps by cutting down on staff and services.
■ Option 2 – Increase all your prices straight away, so that you can buy new stock at the increased price without difficulty.
■ Option 3 – Can you think of other alternatives?

Questions

a *To what extent will your action be contingent on your supplier's action?*

b *What would you do? Explain your answer.*

c *What could you do if your supplier, instead of increasing prices, reduced them? Would you reduce your prices straight away too?*

2 Imagine that you are the managing director of a company owning a chain of five petrol service stations. You have to buy all your petrol and lubricants from suppliers at the world price (set by the open market). Your stations each hold a week's supply of petrol (which costs you £20 000 per site, £100 000 in total) and a month's supply of lubricants (which costs you £1000 per site, £5000 in total).

Suddenly, the world price of petrol and lubricants increases by 10 per cent. As a result, your stock of petrol has increased in value by £10 000 and your lubricants by £500. However, these increases exactly equal the increased price you have to pay for new stock. You now have a number of alternatives:

■ Option 1 – Continue selling all your existing stock to customers at the old price and try to make savings elsewhere, perhaps by cutting down on staff.
■ Option 2 – Increase all prices straight away, so that you can buy new stock at the increased price without difficulty.
■ Option 3 – What alternatives can you think of?

Questions

a *To what extent will your decision be contingent on that of your suppliers?*

b *What would you do?*

c *What would you do if the world price of petrol and lubricants fell by 10 per cent? Would you reduce your prices straight away?*

Ad hoc *approaches to contingency planning*

The Latin term *ad hoc* means 'for a particular purpose only'. Contingency planning will frequently be required to deal with an unexpected situation that may be unique, and which may never arise again. In this situation planning will require considerable creativity and spontaneity. Setting out a contingency plan for one particular purpose requires *innovative thinking*.

However, managers can draw on their own previous experience of similar situations and events, or features of situations they have heard or read about. To a certain extent, effective management is *always* contingency management, in that theory and practice are combined to make decisions in a particular situation. *Ad hoc* (or pragmatic) contingency planning, therefore, is unlikely to be done 'in a vacuum' – rather, managers will draw on their bank of experience and theoretical knowledge to come up with a framework for dealing with particular types of situations and problems. This will involve:

- identifying the problem or situation
- analysing the nature of the problem
- identifying alternative ways of dealing with the problem
- deciding on a solution
- evaluating the decision or course of action.

In some situations this process of reasoning will need to take place very quickly. A fire chief faced with a burning building full of people will on the spot have to come up with a plan for the evacuation of a building with which he or she is unfamiliar. The situation is unique, but the planning process is familiar. The key to successful contingency planning, as with all planning, is to formulate a sequence of integrated steps. Planning will be unsuccessful if there is no link between steps, or if some steps contradict others.

Planned approaches

Ad hoc approaches are needed when there is a lack of clarity about all the alternative courses of action that can be taken, because the situation is novel and unique. In contrast, in a planned situation it is possible to work out the whole range of alternative scenarios, and to see the relationships between contingencies and results. Because the planner has far more information to hand, it is easier to plan.

The first step is to identify the possible contingencies – for example, the events that might get in the way of implementing the plan. It is then possible to devise a range of contingency plans to cater for each of these events. A particular form of contingency planning is termed **fail-safe analysis**, in which the planner covers all possibilities that could cause failure.

It is also necessary to identify factors that could endanger the plan. For example, is anyone likely to oppose the plan? Whose cooperation is required for the plan to be successful? What resources will be required? and so on. Also, what is the probability of the plan being successful? This probability will increase if all of the potential traps are identified in advance.

Strengths and weaknesses of alternative plans need to be weighed up through a process of detailed analysis and evaluation. Contingency planning should therefore be as detailed a process as any other form of planning. Sometimes it may need to be more detailed, because of the uncertainties involved. Forecasting will be an important ingredient of contingency planning.

Reviewing contingency plans

The monitoring and reviewing of contingency plans has to take account of uncertainties. Nevertheless, contingency plans must be based on organisational objectives, so it is important to check the extent to which objectives are being met.

The review process should be established at the same time as the plans are being prepared. This involves having a clear idea of the results expected from a particular plan, and how they will be measured and interpreted. In other words, contingency planning should not be a random process, it should be a detailed and determined approach to achieving results.

Coping with risk

There is an element of **risk** in an activity when the outcome cannot be predicted with any certainty, or when outcome is known but its full consequences are not. Individuals vary in their attitude to taking a risk, and we can identify three basic positions:

- The *risk-lover* is someone who enjoys a gamble, even when mathematical analysis shows that the odds are unfavourable.
- The *risk-neutral person* will gamble only if the odds on a gain are favourable. The person will not be concerned with the range of possible outcomes, only with the odds being in their favour.
- The *risk-averse person* will gamble only if the odds are strongly favourable.

Organisational activity is fraught with risk. For example, organisations use resources for particular purposes and there is always the chance that these could be used to better effect. There is always the chance that stakeholder objectives would be better met by alternative policies. *So, taking any decision or course of action involves the risk of missing out on a more appropriate choice.*

Risks are an ever-present part of planning, but planners try to minimise them by weighing them up and looking at the probabilities of different events occurring. There are a number of alternatives available for coping with risks, including:

- taking no action
- hedging
- obtaining more information
- selecting diverse courses of action
- detailed contingency planning.

Each of these alternatives needs to be considered in terms of the importance and urgency of the decision, and the time horizons.

Taking no action

One way of dealing with a risky situation is to take no action. Inaction typifies the cautious decision maker, or the one who believes that things are already being done in the best way possible. A monopolist may assume that, because it has no competition, it can go on producing in exactly the same way with no need for change. The same applies to a firm that has a tradition of being a market-leader.

It is surprising how often people and organisations assume that if they ignore a particular threat it will go away. This may be because they feel that the threat is only temporary and will recede – for example, the small shop-keeper who believes that customers may switch temporarily allegiance to the local hypermarket, but 'it will never last'.

Some people choose inaction because, although they acknowledge that a risk exists in the medium to long term, they believe that it can be ignored in the short term. A motorist may believe that if he parks his car on double yellow lines for five minutes then the traffic warden will not come, but the same motorist would not risk this action for a two-hour period. In other words, *the risk increases with time*.

The *importance of the risk* also needs to be considered. For example, a business may be far less concerned about losing a small customer than a major customer.

However, it is important to question the wisdom of taking no action to deal with a risk. It would be folly to jeopardise the future of the organisation.

Hedging

Hedging is a method of reducing risk. We can illustrate the process by reference to the market for copper.

Suppose that the current market price for copper for immediate delivery is £1000 per tonne. This is called the 'spot price'. If the copper is not needed for three months, an alternative to paying the spot price is to buy in the 'forward market'. This would involve paying, say, £1100 now for delivery of the tonne of copper in three months' time. In this way the purchaser hedges against the risk of the price of copper rising by say, £1500 over the period. Paying, today, £100 more than the spot price can be seen as an insurance premium. A risk-averse and a risk-neutral organisation is likely to hedge when planning for the

future in this way. The risk-lover may decide not to hedge, hoping that in three months' time the price of copper will be no more than £1000 on the spot market.

Hedging involves taking actions now to cushion oneself against future shocks. Forecasting will therefore be an important part of the hedger's toolkit. Accurate analysis of current and future trends reduces uncertainty and increases confidence in decision-making.

Insurance is an obvious example of taking a precaution to stave off future risks. A premium is paid, and in the event of an accident (i.e. a risk resulting in a loss) the insured person or company receives compensation from the central insurance pool. It is possible for an organisation to build in an element of 'insurance' into most plans. For example, by holding extra stocks it insures itself against a surge in demand, or by producing a variety of products it insures itself against one of them selling badly.

In choosing a plan, an organisation may decide on one that has the greatest element of insurance built into it, rather than one that yields the best results in terms of immediate profits, returns, etc. Organisations not prepared to take certain risks may choose a plan that is *sub-optimal* because this at least builds in an acceptable degree of safety. The acceptability of a plan will then be determined by the stakeholders' preference for risk. An organisation influenced by speculative investors will have a far higher propensity for risk-taking than one influenced by pension funds and other conservative institutions.

We can sum up by saying that hedging is important where decision makers do not have a preference for risk, when the risk increases over time, and when it is important to minimise the risk taken.

Case Study
Trading commodities

Trading is either 'spot' or 'term'. The latter means that a contract has been signed for goods to be delivered at a certain future date to a certain place, and often at a fixed price – this is the 'futures market'.

The table below shows futures prices per tonne for wheat and barley. Futures prices are lowest at harvest time and highest just before harvest – reflecting the costs of storage from the previous harvest.

	Wheat	Barley
March	110.30	102.10
May	111.90	105.00
September	106.50	103.55

On the same day, the futures prices for crude oil from the Brent Field were as follows ($ per barrel):

Spot	17.80
April	17.95
May	18.20
June	18.30
July	18.35

Questions for discussion

1 *What is the difference between a* futures price *and a* future price?
2 *Does buying futures eliminate all risk?*
3 *Why do organisation's hedge?*
4 *For what type of product would you expect today's futures prices to fall in successive months, and for what types of product would you expect them to rise?*
5 *What factors are likely to cause an increase in the futures price for oil?*
6 *A trader buys 1000 barrels of oil at $20 a barrel in March which he expects to sell in two months' time. Suppose the price of oil falls in the meantime to $18 a barrel. How can the trader hedge by selling 1000 barrels of May oil futures?*

Obtaining more information

Another way of dealing with risk is to obtain more information about alternative courses of action. The more informed you are the more reliable your decisions will be. The less informed you are the greater the probability of failure.

When decisions need to be made urgently there may not be sufficient time to collect enough information to make an 'unrisky' decision. The emphasis should therefore be on collecting as much information as possible and analysing and interpreting this in the time available. However, by implication, urgent decisions that are taken quickly are likely to be relatively risky ones.

The more important a decision, the more time should be spent on collecting good-quality information. Attention to detail is essential for successful projects. Anticipating potential outcomes increases the chances that plans will be carried out properly.

Selecting diverse courses of action

The importance of individual risks can be reduced by carrying out a variety of actions. For example, large organisations produce a diversity of products rather than a single product in order to spread the risks and benefit from the synergy of diversification. However, the more diverse the range of actions the greater the pressure exerted on existing resources – putting a range of alternatives into effect (or just planning them) is also a time-intensive process. Also, when decisions are urgent it may not be possible to employ a diverse range of actions.

Important actions need to be done well, so an organisation can reduce the likelihood of failure by comparing and contrasting a range of plans to minimise risks.

Detailed contingency planning

Contingency planning, as we have seen, is about making the unknowable as knowable as possible. Detailed contingency planning involves the use of a variety of techniques and tools. At a strategic level it involves the application of financial ratio projections, sensitivity analysis, decision matrices, simulation modelling and other means of assessing risks. Detailed contingency planning takes time because it requires a lot of research into, and analysis of, the organisation and its changing environment.

Making contingency plans

Routine organisational planning involves managers and others in setting out, in detail, ways of meeting objectives in an orderly manner. Contingency planning uses many of the same processes and procedures as other forms of planning. However, in addition it needs to take account of a variety of new factors. Managers sometimes say that action B is contingent on the results of action A, or that plan C is contingent on the successful completion of plan D, etc. Of course, many plans are also contingent on unpredictable factors which appear 'out of the blue'.

Thus, contingency planning is based necessarily on forecasts and projections that are uncertain. The relationships between planning variables are also uncertain. The process is a bit like trying to plan a network of activities, without knowing fully what each activity will entail, its outcome, or exactly how it will influence the following activity. *There has to be a flexible approach to meeting contingencies.* Consider the following comments from an English rugby player just before an important international match:

> *'Dynamism is more a state of mind. Previously we have, perhaps, been guilty of taking to the field stuck on playing to a single game-plan. What [the coach] is looking for is a rather more flexible strategy whereby should plan A fail, then we have the mental and physical capacity to change to plan B, and so on. . . . What this does require*

is an altogether greater contribution from all involved so that from 1 to 15 we all have a role to play, whether we are taking the ball up through the forwards, the backs or through a combination of both. If all 15 play these roles as expected then our decision makers are left free to use the complete armoury at their disposal.'

Identifying contingencies

In making plans we have to ask: 'How probable is it that a particular event will occur?' This probability can be assessed by guesswork, or by using statistics and mathematics. Guesswork depends on wisdom (from previous experience), hunch, and intuition.

The first step in identifying contingencies is to clarify those conditions which currently enable the organisation to operate as it does. These we call the 'primary conditions'. We need then to ascertain the 'secondary conditions' which enable the primary conditions to exist in the way they do at present. It may then be possible to imagine future conditions that could inhibit or enhance the secondary conditions (see Figure 28.1). Armed with the results of this analysis, it becomes easier to draw up contingency plans that respond to the events that work for or against the organisation.

Figure 28.1 Identifying contingencies

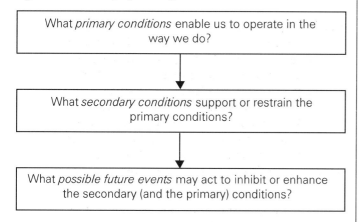

Consider an example of a business organisation importing raw materials. We could set out some important relationships in the manner shown in Figure 28.2.

In this case, the organisation would need to develop contingency plans – either to cement its relationships with country A, or to look for alternative sources of supply. The example also shows that contingency planning involves *thinking a number of steps ahead*. **Scenario planning** is a useful tool when preparing a series of alternative plans.

There are a number of ways in which contingencies can be identified, including the following:

- by using experience and/or research
- by forecasting and projecting
- by imagining a 'worst-case' scenario
- from intuition and/or guesswork
- by acknowledging rumours.

Figure 28.2 An example

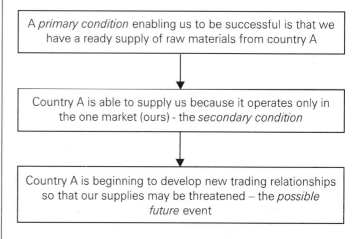

Experience and/or research

It may be possible to predict contingencies when a situation has been faced before. When planning and constructing buildings over geological fault lines, experts do not know when or where an earthquake will strike, but they can use their experience (and that of others), and research, to make assumptions about the possible size and intensity of future quakes. They could, of course, install expensive probes in the earth's core, or they could take the pragmatic approach and say: 'It may never happen, but just in case we will build to this very high standard.'

Forecasting and projecting

Forecasts and projections can be put together in many ways, including using computer-based and other models. A good example is a weather forecast, which nowadays may be the result of highly complex computer simulations based on present and, past conditions.

Demographers develop forecasts based on past birth and death rates, present birth and death rates, fertility rates and many other factors. Future projections of population can then be used, for example, to plan residential accommodation for elders, social services, pension provision etc. 'What if' scenarios can be used in developing plans for the future.

Unfortunately, in many areas of forecasting the 'What if' scenarios are not as predictable as for population changes. For example, a business dealing in international markets faces 'What if's related to exchange rates, the supply of raw materials, the intensity of demand for products, the strength of competition and many other factors.

Imagining a 'worst-case' scenario

This involves developing a picture of all the things that could go wrong. The emphasis is on coping with the worst possible adverse conditions. The process sounds pessimistic, but in fact it can be a very useful way of forcing people to think about what *could* go wrong, and to be prepared for it.

Intuition and/or guesswork

Intuition is always an important part of the repertoire of a successful manager. It enables the manager to identify possible contingencies and ways of dealing with them. Of course, many people would argue that intuition is simply experience coupled with business acumen and intelligence. Inspired guesswork, too, is often an important source of contingency planning.

Acknowledging rumours

Rumours can sometimes genuinely predict change within an organisation or in the wider business environment. Planners should take account of the possible implications of rumours rather than brushing them aside. For example, there may be a rumour that the organisation will lose a government contract. Remember the adage: 'There is no smoke without fire!'

Case Study
Game theory as a form of contingency planning

The Nobel Prize for Economics was awarded in 1994 to three men who had made important contributions to economics in the development of game theory. Game theory is a form of contingency planning which is concerned with trying to anticipate what your rivals will do in order to maximise your own game plan. It is all a matter of trying to answer questions like 'If we take this action what will they do?' and 'If we then respond by doing . . . what will their counter be?'

This approach is typical of that taken in many industries dominated by a few firms. When these firms cut prices, bring out new products, offer special terms to customers, build new plants, etc., what will their rivals do?

One of the winners of the Nobel Prize, John Nash, described an interesting way of working out how games will end up if players are not prepared either to commit themselves or to collude. This outcome is now commonly referred to as the 'Nash equilibrium'.

The diagram illustrates the Nash equilibrium. In this game plan there are imagined to be two firms in an industry. If they both choose to charge high prices they will each make a healthy profit of £3 million. If they both charge low prices

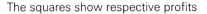

The squares show respective profits

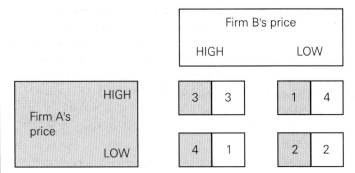

they will make only £2 million each. If one charges a high price and the other a low price, then the low-price firm will make £4 million and the high-price firm only £1 million.

The logical solution would be for both firms to charge a high price. However, because neither firm can trust the other, and because it does not want to be the loser in the situation, both firms will end up by charging low prices and making only £2 million profit.

Game theory can be applied to a whole range of aspects of organisational strategy – for example the range of products offered to the market, the type of business culture, prices charged, discounts and special offers, etc. The activities of each firm in the market are contingent on what the others are doing. Game theory has developed using a variety of mathematical techniques to explore ways in which firms can seek a competitive advantage. It illustrates for us the important interconnections that occur between firms in a dynamic market in which business plans made by firms are contingent on the actions and expected future actions of rivals.

Questions for discussion

1 *In the Nash equilibrium situation, why would the choice of action of firm A be dependent on the choice of action of firm B?*
2 *Why do not both players go for the optimum solution?*
3 *How can businesses in the real world discover and anticipate the actions of their rivals?*
4 *To what extent can the anticipation of rivals' actions be seen as an 'exact science'?*

Evaluation of the impact of contingencies

In January 1995, the United Nations organisation was concerned to develop contingency plans for refugees in camps in the Goma area of Zaire, arising from a civil war in Rwanda. One major cause of concern was volcanic activity in the area. Japanese scientists had identified increased seismic activity which could have heralded volcanic eruptions. If the explosions occurred, lava would have reached the camps in two days. It was therefore necessary to evaluate the likelihood of such a tragedy occurring – it was felt to be a fair possibility. The next step was to devise contingency plans to evacuate the refugees from the area as quickly as possible, should the need arise.

Risk analysis and other mathematical tools can be employed to estimate the likelihood of a risk turning into reality. Risk analysis sets out to outline, for every critical variable in a decision problem, a **probability distribution curve**. This involves finding out (on the basis of experience and from asking experts in the field) the probabilities of each variable. However, rather than arriving at a single 'best estimate' of probability it may be more appropriate to come up with a range of values of probabilities.

Contingency planning can then be employed to prepare solutions for a number of probabilities across the range – for example, the 'best-case' situation, the 'mid-range' situation', the 'worst-case' situation. Computer programs can be employed to produce sophisticated results.

We now look at some techniques that can be employed in analysing risks for strategic planning.

Financial ratios

Financial indicators can be interpreted as measures of the risks taken by an organisation. For example, the *gearing ratio* is the ratio of shareholders' capital to loan capital. An organisation places itself in an increasingly risky position if it has to borrow a rising proportion of its capital structure, so the gearing ratio is one useful indicator of risk exposure. The organisation must have a plan to cope with a situation in which it has an increasing borrowing requirement.

A forecast of *cash flow* is also important. An organisation that develops a weak cash-flow position exposes itself to bankruptcy. Contingency plans are needed to show how the liquid capital of the organisation can be increased in such a situation.

Sensitivity analysis

Sensitivity analysis is a very useful tool for carrying out 'What if . . .?' predictions. It enables the analyst to test the *extent* to which outcomes will be affected by the assumptions that have been made.

For example, if an organisation expects that its profit would increase by 10 per cent if sales revenue increased by 20 per cent, as a result of a 10 per cent increase in spending on advertising, it could calculate what would be likely to happen if, instead, the same increase in advertising led only to a 5 per cent increase in sales revenue. It might deduce that this could lead to a fall in profits.

Sensitivity analysis takes full advantage of computer spreadsheet applications. It is possible to feed into the spreadsheet a range of relationships between variables involved in particular planning decisions. The relationships between the variables represent the assumptions being made, which can be varied. The analysis can show the extent to which final outcomes (e.g. profit) are sensitive to alterations in the assumptions.

Decision trees

Decision trees set out a visual network showing how the choices that make up an overall decision can be broken down into smaller choices, each with its own probability. Using a decision tree, a manager can evaluate some of the important considerations involved in making a choice.

Decision trees are useful in contingency planning for the following reasons:

- They set out clearly the nature of a problem.
- They give a simple outline of the implications of particular choices.
- The decision can be tackled logically, step by step.
- An assessment is made at each step of the probability of likely results stemming from the decision point.
- Subjective factors relating to judgements and possible consequences are built in at each stage.

However, decision-tree analysis can be a time-consuming process and it may not be practicable when urgent action is required. Also, because in some situations it is highly subjective, it may be unrealistic and may come to be seen as a management 'toy' rather than a tool. Another problem is that, as one moves along a decision tree, the probabilities set out may prove to be increasingly unrealistic as one decision branch feeds into another. However, decision-tree analysis is a useful way of accounting for potential contingencies involved in an interrelated network of activities.

Modelling

Models can be used to encompass many of the techniques already described, as well as others, to provide an overall picture of the complex relationships which are likely to affect the future of an organisation. Sophisticated models can be set out for all sorts of purposes – for example, charting the future of the economy, outlining likely developments in the organisation's external environment, forecasting cash flows and profits. Much of the modelling that takes place involves complex computer programs, and is based on quantitative techniques.

Simulation can be used to identify key contingencies that lie ahead. Of course, models are only as reliable as the data employed, and the accuracy of the programmed relationships between variables.

Selection of a risk strategy

The **risk strategy** an organisation chooses will depend on the prevailing attitude towards risk in that organisation. For example, those with a sizeable research budget can choose to put their money into safe projects that are certain to yield a slow but steady return on investment; or they may choose 'blue sky' projects which stand to make very high returns if things work out well, or nothing at all if the project fails. The majority of organisations select a risk strategy that falls somewhere between these two extremes (see Figure 28.3).

Figure 28.3 The risk spectrum

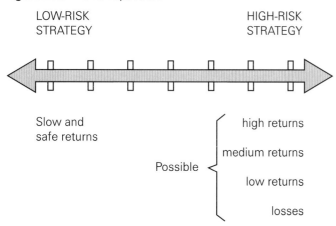

Many organisations will tend to go for the low-risk strategy, because members and stakeholders are naturally cautious. For example, banking is traditionally carried out on prudential lines. The shareholders of banks might rapidly lose confidence in the directors if they chose a high-risk strategy. Bankers tend to be cautious by nature – although because of the size and extent of their business the High Street banks are able to make large profits from 'slow and safe returns'.

Other organisations, in new and dynamic fields, may be prepared to take bigger risks. Virgin, for example, is often quoted as an example of an entrepreneurial organisation

that is prepared to take risks, in the entertainment and travel industries.

In the early 1990s, when Robert Horton took over as chairman of BP, he wanted to inject a lot of new life into the organisation. At the time BP's performance (and size) was a long way behind that of the market leader, Shell. Horton encouraged managers to adopt a more entrepreneurial approach and to develop a number of 'blue sky' drilling and exploration projects. Some of these projects were successful, creating massive returns for BP. Unfortunately, however, Horton lost favour with key stakeholders at BP because of his style of management.

Risk analysis is part and parcel of the development of a risk strategy, because it provides important information about probabilities. The acceptability of projects will depend on the organisation's perception of an acceptable risk. For example, in a prudent organisation stakeholders might have stipulated that projects can go ahead only if there is a greater than 7 in 10 chance of success. If risk analysis suggests that there is a 7.5 in 10 chance of a particular project succeeding, the project meets an important criterion of acceptability.

Scheduling and monitoring contingency activities

A contingency plan outlines major activities and specific tasks. As with any other form of plan, activities should be specified to be completed within a given time period. They should enable objectives to be met, result in identifiable outcomes, and involve a **sequence**.

Clearly, in many cases it will not be possible to lay down a definite sequence of activities because of the need to retain flexibility – and the need for a particular activity may never arise. However, the important point about a plan is that it contains a schedule to cater for contingencies. If plan B is contingent on event A happening, then it is important to have the resources available for plan B, and the sequence of steps for plan B clearly charted, before event A happens.

It will also be important to have contingency funds available to support scheduled activities in contingency plans. In particular, the resources available should cover the most 'resource-intensive' plan – otherwise the plan will be nothing more than wishful thinking. This is as true of the lifeboat rescue service, which needs to prepare for a variety of often unique contingencies, as it is for the old established traditional business operating in an apparently stable environment. An organisation that fails to develop a schedule for important contingency activities stands to be 'caught with its pants down'.

The operation of contingency plans also needs to be **monitored** against their objectives and targets. Clearly this may be a less precise art than with other forms of plans. However, performance needs to be checked on an on-going basis, so it is essential to clarify the objectives of the plans and the ways in which their performance will be monitored. Remedial action will have to be taken if performance falls short of standards.

Whenever alternative contingency plans have been developed, it will be necessary to have a means of deciding between them – a way of making an appropriate choice that is most likely to lead to the organisation's objectives.

Looking at the subject in this way, we can see that contingency planning should where possible be as detailed an operation as drawing up any other form of plan. No type of planning should be left to chance simply because it is based on probabilities rather than hard and fast data. In today's complex business environment, nearly all planning involves elements of contingency.

Further reading

- *The Essence of Change* by Liz Clarke. Prentice Hall, 1994.
- *Strategic Management and Organisational Dynamics* by Ralph Stacey. Pitman, 1993.
- *The Skills of Management*, 3rd edition, by David Rees. Routledge, 1991.
- *Successful Change Strategies – Learning from Chief Executives*, by Bernard Taylor. Director Books, 1994.

NAME INDEX

SUBJECT INDEX